WHERE CHEFS EAT

—

A GUIDE TO CHEFS' FAVORITE RESTAURANTS

WHERE CHEFS EAT

—

A GUIDE TO CHEFS' FAVORITE RESTAURANTS

Chef selection by
Joe Warwick, with Evelyn Chen,
Natascha Mirosch,
and Joshua David Stein

CONTENTS

KEY

Breakfast
Whether it's a lazy or a snatched one, the chef couldn't start the day without breakfast here.

Late night
Service is over but the night is still young, this is where the chef satisfies any late-night hunger pangs.

Regular neighborhood
Around the corner from the chef's work or home, this restaurant serves up food good enough to eat regularly.

Local favorite
This is the restaurant that best expresses the cuisine of the chef's home town.

Bargain
When money is limited but their appetite for good food isn't, this is where the chef goes when they're on a budget.

High end
For a special occasion or when money is no object, this is where the chef goes to splash out.

Wish I'd opened
Professional respect and admiration make this the restaurant that the chef wishes they'd opened.

Worth the travel
Across the country or on the other side of the world, there's no distance the chef wouldn't travel to eat at this restaurant.

PREFACE

The premise behind this guide is exactly the same as it was when we published the very first edition of *Where Chefs Eat* back in 2012. The modern chef is a fantastic source of guaranteed good meal recommendations, from humble holes-in-the-wall to the most luxurious restaurants—and every flavor of dining experience that falls in between—both close to home and on their travels.

In this, our third edition, we have surveyed over 660 chefs around the world, who have provided us with an impressive 4500 recommendations—more than ever before—to fulfil all of your dining needs, whether that's a late-night snack or an elaborate once-in-a-lifetime menu with matching wines. Because today's best chefs, ambitious, curious, and well traveled as they are, always take their passion for food beyond their own kitchens. Sometimes it's in search of inspiration, sometimes simply in search of breakfast, lunch, or dinner—and always not just because it's their job. With recommendations spanning more than 570 cities in 70 countries, across six continents, this edition contains the most wide-ranging and eclectic set of listings we've ever produced.

This book would not have been possible without the talented team that's worked tirelessly to put it together, including contributing editors in the US, Asia, and Australia —Joshua David Stein, Evelyn Chen, and Natascha Mirosch respectively —and of course, as always, all of the chefs that took the time to help us curate this essential travel companion for anyone who loves eating out.

THE CHEFS

Participating chefs and their restaurant recommendations

MATT ABERGEL
Yardbird
33–35 Bridges Street, Hong Kong
Calgary-born, he trained under Japanese chef Masayoshi Takayama at Masa in New York, before taking the helm at Hong Kong's Zuma. Runs the yakitori gastropub Yardbird (2011) and RōNIN (2013).

ACME 123	Worth the travel
Amber 220	High end
Asador Etxebarri 575	Wish I'd opened
Belon 220	Regular neighborhood
Celebrity Cuisine 221	Regular neighborhood
The Chairman 221	Local favorite
Ho Lee Fook 222	Local favorite
Lung King Heen 223	High end
Pigeonhole 742	Worth the travel
Seorae 215	Late night
Sister Wah 231	Bargain
Sun Hing Restaurant 226	Breakfast
Sun Hing Restaurant 226	Late night
Tsim Chai Kee Noodle Shop 225	Bargain

TIMUR ABUZYAROV
Beer Happens
24/2 Sretenka, Moscow
Russian-born chef Abuzyrov trained in Copenhagen before returning to Moscow and opening a string of restaurants, including his flagship, the gastropub Beer Happens, and most recently, Cevicheria.

Anatoly Komm for Raff House 708	High end
AQ Kitchen 710	Local favorite
BB & Burgers 710	Bargain
Boston Seafood bar 711	Regular neighborhood
Brisket BBQ 707	Late night
Café Pushkin 711	Breakfast
Café Pushkin 711	High end
Chainaya Tea & Cocktails 711	Regular neighborhood
Dersou 567	Worth the travel
Duo Gastrobar 701	Local favorite
Duo Gastrobar 701	Wish I'd opened
Gras 701	Wish I'd opened
Lyle's 488	Worth the travel
Marukame 714	Bargain
Pinch 709	Breakfast
Relæ 378	Worth the travel
Severyane 709	Breakfast
Tartarbar 703	Local favorite
Tartarbar 703	Wish I'd opened
Torro Grill 713	Late night
Torro Grill 713	Regular neighborhood
White Rabbit 706	High end
Zotman Pizza Pie 710	Late night

MATTHEW ACCARRINO
SPQR
1911 Fillmore Street, San Francisco
New Jersey-raised, Culinary Institute of America-educated head chef of Italian-inspired SPQR in San Francisco.

Andytown Coffee Roasters 838	Local favorite b. Patisserie 839	Breakfast
Boon Fly Café 793	Regular neighborhood
Equator Coffee 792	Breakfast
The French Laundry 797	High end
Lazy Bear 835	High end
Manresa 792	High end
The Mill 828	Breakfast
The Mill 828	Regular neighborhood
Out The Door 833	Regular neighborhood
Saint Frank 840	Breakfast
Saint Frank 840	Regular neighborhood
Sir and Star 796	Local favorite
Sir and Star 796	Regular neighborhood
Sol food 792	Bargain
Sol food 792	Local favorite
Uliassi 647	Worth the travel

DANIEL ACHILLES
Reinstoff
Schlegelstrasse 26c, Berlin
German trained, he settled in Berlin as head chef at Reinstoff, winning plaudits for his avant-garde German cuisine including, within a year of opening, a Michelin star.

Balzac Coffee 634	Breakfast
Benedict 634	Breakfast
Borchardt 631	Wish I'd opened
einsunternull 631	Local favorite
Facil 634	Local favorite
Grill Royal 632	Wish I'd opened
Horváth 630	Local favorite
Kuchi 632	Regular neighborhood
Lorenz Adlon 632	Local favorite
Restaurant de Librije 511	Worth the travel
Rosenthaler Grill 633	Late night
Rutz 633	Local favorite
Tim Raue 631	Local favorite
Vendôme 625	High end

GASTÓN ACURIO
Astrid y Gastón
Avenida Paz Soldan 290, Lima
Founder of the impressive Lima-based restaurant empire that began with Astrid y Gastón in 1994.

El Celler de Can Roca 583	Worth the travel
Central 1098	Local favorite
Maido 1100	Regular neighborhood
OSSO Carnicería y Salumeria 1098	Wish I'd opened
La Picantería 1101	Bargain

IVO ADAM
Kultur Casino Bern
Herrengasse 25, Bern
Head chef at the Kultur Casino Bern, he brings worldwide experience to the table, from Glasgow, Luxembourg, and Singapore.

L'ATELIER de Joël Robuchon 556	Wish I'd opened
Eisblume Worb 640	High end
Jack's Brasserie 638	Regular neighborhood
The Jane 522	Worth the travel
Löscher 638	Late night
Restaurant Kirchenfeld 638	Local favorite
Toi et Moi 638	Breakfast
Tulsi 638	Bargain

AARON ADAMS
Farm Spirit
1414 Southeast Morrison Street, Portland
Born in California, he moved around the US, working in New York for several years, before settling in Portland, Oregon, where he opened his vegan restaurant, Farm Spirit (2015).

An Xuyen Bakery 846	Bargain
Aster 834	Worth the travel
Atelier Crenn 833	High end
Atera 1013	Worth the travel
Biwa Izakaya 848	Regular neighborhood
Black Water Bar 848	Bargain
Boke Bowl East 848	Regular neighborhood
The Bye and Bye 860	Late night
Eleven Madison Park 1037	Worth the travel
Harvest at the Bindery 852	Breakfast
Higgins 852	Local favorite
Juniors Cafe 853	Breakfast
Noma 369	Worth the travel
Relæ 378	Worth the travel
Superiority Burger 1024	Wish I'd opened
Zien Hong 861	Late night

RAY ADRIANSYAH
Locavore
10 Jalan Dewi Sita, Bali
Born in Jakarta, he ran the kitchen at Alila Ubud with his fellow head chef, Eelke Plasmeijer, before they established Locavore together in 2013.

Cuca 294	High end
The Night Rooster 298	Late night
Room4Dessert 298	Late night
Sangsaka 296	High end
Sisterfields 296	Breakfast
Smokehouse BBQ Bali 296	Regular neighborhood
Sungei Road Laksa 333	Worth the travel
Warung Sulawesi 296	Local favorite
Warung Wardani 293	Local favorite

JOHAN AGRELL
Babette
Roslagsgatan 6, Stockholm
He worked in top Swedish kitchens, Esperanto and Frantzén, before partnering with Magnus Nilsson at Fäviken. One of four owners of neighborhood bistro, Babette.

Asador Etxebarri **575**............Worth the travel	
Bageri Petrus **359**..........................Breakfast	
Café Pascal **361**............................Breakfast	
Mathias Dahlgren Matbaren **356**.....High end	
Operabaren **356**.....................Local favorite	
Ramen Ki Mamma **362**...Regular neighborhood	
Le Relais Saint Germain **554**...Wish I'd opened	
Snack Bar **355**......................................Bargain	
Trattoria Entrà **649**.................Worth the travel	
Umut 2000 **491**............................Late night	

BRIAN AHERN
Boeufhaus
1012 North Western Avenue, Chicago
After learning his trade in the US, he stepped down as executive chef at Fish Bar, a Michael Kornick restaurant, to focus on Boeufhaus, a French and German inspired brasserie.

Asador Etxebarri **575**............Worth the travel	
avec **965**.......................Regular neighborhood	
Blackbird **966**..................................High end	
Bowen's Island **1051**.............Wish I'd opened	
Giant **959**.....................Regular neighborhood	
Lula Cafe **959**................................Breakfast	
Lula Cafe **959**...............Regular neighborhood	
Mercat de La Boqueria **602**......Worth the travel	
Redhot Ranch **957**....................Late night	
Rootstock **956**..............................Late night	
Sepia **968**......................................High end	
Smyth **968**.....................................High end	
The Publican **968**.....................Local favorite	
Toons Bar & Grill **957**..........................Bargain	
Toons Bar & Grill **957**................Local favorite	

TOM AIKENS
Tom's Kitchen
27 Cale Street, London
Koffmann and Robuchon trained, he made his name as head chef at Pied à Terre before opening his own restaurants, including Tom's Kitchen, in London and Istanbul.

108 Garage **432**....................Local favorite	
Atelier Crenn **833**.................Worth the travel	
Bao **444**...Bargain	
Benu **840**.........................Worth the travel	
Brasserie Zédel **446**..........................Bargain	
Chick 'n' Sours **432**............................Bargain	
The Clove Club **487**..........................High end	
The Clove Club **487**......Regular neighborhood	
The Dairy **414**...............Regular neighborhood	
Duck & Waffle **466**.........................Late night	
Elystan Street **412**.......Regular neighborhood	
L'Enclume **394**..................Wish I'd opened	
Fäviken Magasinet **345**.........Worth the travel	
Frantzén **355**.......................Wish I'd opened	
The French Laundry **797**........Wish I'd opened	
The French Laundry **797**........Worth the travel	
The Golden Hind **420**...........................Bargain	
Granger & Co **423**........Regular neighborhood	

MEATliquor **421**................................Late night
The Modern Pantry **468**...................Breakfast
Ranoush Juice **422**.........................Late night
Restaurant Story **488**........................High end
The Riding House Café **473**..Regular neighborhood
Spuntino **454**................................Late night
Street XO **442**................................High end
Typing Room **462**.........Regular neighborhood
The Wolseley **443**.........Regular neighborhood

IÑAKI AIZPITARTE
Le Châteaubriand
129 Avenue Parmentier, Paris
French chef who was inspired to cook while in Tel Aviv, where he learned the basics. He runs the popular bistro, Le Châteaubriand.

Le Baratin **569**.............Regular neighborhood	
Il Brigante **569**.............................Late night	
Dong Huong **565**...........................Breakfast	

MASSIMILIANO ALAJMO
Le Calandre
Via Liguria 1, Sarmeola di Rubano
After training in France under Veyrat and Guérard, he returned home to his family's esteemed restaurant in Italy, Le Calandre, in 1983.

L'Assiette **567**..............Regular neighborhood	
Biasetto **670**................................Breakfast	
Cibrèo **667**....................Wish I'd opened	
Enoteca Mascareta **672**..................Late night	
La Folperia **670**................................Bargain	
Harry's Bar **671**..............Wish I'd opened	
La Maison Des Bois **536**........Worth the travel	
Le Meurice **550**.............................High end	
Ristorante Zass **648**......................Breakfast	
Da Romano **671**.....................Local favorite	
Teatro del Sale **669**..............Wish I'd opened	

JOSEAN ALIJA
Nerua
Avenida Abandoibarra 2, Bilbao
Following spells at hotels, elBulli, and Martín Berasategui, he opened Nerua and a more casual bistro in the Guggenheim in 2011.

Andrés Carne de Res **1097**.....Wish I'd opened	
Arzak **579**....................................Late night	
Asador Etxebarri **575**...............Local favorite	
Asador Horma Ondo **576**................Late night	
Azurmendi **577**.....................Local favorite	
Bar Rotterdam **575**........................Breakfast	
Bistró **575**......................................Bargain	
Central **1098**...................Worth the travel	
Elkano **580**..................................Late night	
Gallery Vask **310**................Worth the travel	
La Mar **1099**....................Wish I'd opened	
Mugaritz **576**.................................High end	
Sud 777 **1083**...................Worth the travel	
Txakoli Simón **575**........Regular neighborhood	

YANNICK ALLÉNO
Alléno Paris au Pavillon Ledoyen
Avenue Duruit 8, Paris
After 25 years working in haute hotel kitchens, multi-Michelin-starred Alléno left Le Meurice in 2013 to concentrate on Le 1947 at Le Cheval Blanc hotel in Courchevel.

Din Tai Fung **202**..............................Bargain
La Farnesina **558**.....................Local favorite
La Maison des Bois **536**....................High end
M bar **223**.....................................Late night
Noma **369**......................Worth the travel
The NoMad Hotel **1044**....................Breakfast
Zen **551**.........................Regular neighborhood

OMAR ALLIBHOY
Tapas Revolution
Westfield, Ariel Way, London
With elBulli and Maze on his résumé, Madrid-born Allibhoy joined El Pirata de Tapas in 2008, launching the popular Tapas Revolution shortly after.

Babi Guling Ibu Oka **297**.......Worth the travel	
Bistrot de Luxe **419**......Regular neighborhood	
Busaba Eathai Soho **447**...........Local favorite	
Dinner by Heston Blumenthal **419**.....High end	
La Fromagerie **420**.........................Breakfast	
Khans **411**......................Wish I'd opened	
Locale **416**.................................Late night	
Taberna de la Daniela Goya **590**.Local favorite	
Tickets **601**........................Worth the travel	

MATTEO ALOE
Berberè
Via Pio La Torre 4/b, Castel Maggiore
Bringing experience from Joia and Noma, he has opened a string of Berberè pizza restaurants across Italy.

Albion **484**....................Regular neighborhood	
Brawn **478**...................................Late night	
The Clove Club **487**..........................High end	
The Clove Club **487**.........................Late night	
The Clove Club **487**......Regular neighborhood	
Ducksoup **448**..............................Late night	
e5 bakehouse **474**.........................Breakfast	
Gail's **449**.....................Regular neighborhood	
Lantana **473**................Regular neighborhood	
LEGS **475**.....................................Late night	
Loco **621**.........................Worth the travel	
Lyle's **488**.....................Regular neighborhood	
Ozone Coffee Roasters **486**.............Regular neighborhood	
P. Franco **468**................................Late night	
P. Franco **468**.................Wish I'd opened	
The Palomar **452**..........................Late night	
Sager + Wilde **461**........................Late night	
St. John Bar and Restaurant **471**..Local favorite	
St. John Bread & Wine **489**..Regular neighborhood	
Taberna do Mercado **489**..Regular neighborhood	
Il Trippaio di San Frediano **668**..........Bargain	

MAOZ ALONIM

HaBasta
4 Hashomer Street, Tel Aviv

Tel Aviv's HaBasta, a bistro serving food from the nearby market and a chefs' favorite, was the brainchild of oenophile Alonim and Itay Hargil. Alonim co-owns nearby Café Europa.

Abu Hassan 172	Bargain
Bar Burbunia 172	Wish I'd opened
Falafel Rambam 173	Breakfast
Hanan Margilan 172	Bargain
Jasmino 173	Late night
The Minzar 173	Regular neighborhood
Pizza Giuseppe 174	Bargain
Port Sa'id 174	Local Favorite
St John Bar and Restaurant 471	Worth the travel
Thai House 175	Regular neighborhood
Yakimono 175	High end

DANIELLE ALVAREZ

Fred's
380 Oxford Street, Sydney

She learned her trade at Chez Panisse in Berkeley, before moving to Sydney to open Fred's in 2016, a restaurant focussing on ethically produced, seasonal fare.

10WilliamSt. 119	Regular neighborhood
Bennelong Restaurant 107	High end
Big Poppa's 115	Late night
Boon Café 116	Local favorite
Dolphin Hotel 124	Regular neighborhood
Est. 110	High end
Ester 114	Regular neighborhood
Fleet 82	Worth the travel
Golden Century 111	Late night
Happy Chef 117	Bargain
Mamak 117	Bargain
Mary's 119	Wish I'd opened
Ruby's Diner 125	Breakfast

TOMER AMEDI

The Palomar
34 Rupert Street, London

Born and raised in Jerusalem, he cooked in Tel Aviv before moving to London to run The Palomar kitchen, which is influenced by Spain, Italy, and the Levant.

Alinea 957	Worth the travel
Blacklock 445	Local favorite
Blanchette 445	Late night
Dumplings' Legend 448	Bargain
Hawksmoor 466	Regular neighborhood
Murano 441	High end
Shila 175	Wish I'd opened

ANGUS AN

Maenam Restaruant
1938 West 4th Avenue, Vancouver

Following spells at The Ledbury, The Fat Duck, and Nahm, he has opened several restaurants in Vancouver, including Maenam which serves authentic Thai food, and Fat Mao, which delivers a range of noodle dishes.

Blue Hill at Stone Barns 913	High end

Cioppino's Mediterranean Grill 762	Regular neighborhood
Congee Noodle House 758	Breakfast
Farmer's Apprentice 756	Local favorite
Fat Mao Noodles 760	Bargain
Lucky Noodle Chinese Restaurant 759	Bargain
Masayoshi 760	Regular neighborhood
Medina Café 758	Breakfast
Nahm 283	Worth the travel
Next 967	Wish I'd opened

GAGGAN ANAND

Gaggan
68/1 Langsuan Road, Bangkok

Kolkata born, he trained with Ferran Adrià and now presents 'progressive Indian' cuisine at his celebrated Bangkok restaurant, Gaggan.

Ginza Sushi-Ichi 284	High end
Kalpapruek Restaurant 281	Bargain
Khua Kling Pak Sod 288	Regular neighborhood
Kikunoi 247	Worth the travel
Nahm 283	Local favorite
Shakariki 432 286	Late night
Tickets 601	Wish I'd opened
The Verandah 282	Breakfast

NICK ANDERER

Maialino & Marta
2 Lexington Avenue, New York City

Indiana-born executive chef and partner at Maialino, he worked with Mario Batali, apprenticed in Italy, and cooked at Gramercy Tavern, before joining Danny Meyer's Union Hospitality Group.

Buvette 1028	Late night
Cosme 1036	High end
Le French Diner 1008	Wish I'd opened
Hasaki 1022	Regular neighborhood
Hop Kee 1006	Late night
Joe Jr. 1038	Breakfast
Keens Steakhouse 1041	High end
Minca 1023	Bargain
Okonomi 1018	Breakfast
Park Side Restaurant 1019	Local favorite
Russ & Daughters Cafe 1009	Local favorite
Shaya 990	Worth the travel
Shu Jiao Fu Zhou Cuisine 1038	Bargain
The Four Horsemen 1016	Wish I'd opened
Trattoria Da Cesare al Casaletto 658	Worth the travel
Via Carota 1030	Regular neighborhood

IZU ANI

The Lighthouse
Dubai Design District, Dubai

The Nigerian executive chef of La Serre, with a glittering résumé featuring L'Auberge de l'Ill, The Square, Arzak, and Akelarre, who brought French cuisine to Dubai with La Petite Maison.

Al Nafoorah 177	Regular neighborhood
Bazxar 177	Late night
Firebird Diner 177	Wish I'd opened
La Petite Maison 441	High end
Sushi Matsue 270	Worth the travel

s'wich 178	Regular neighborhood
Zagol Betekitfo 178	Bargain
Zuma 178	High end

MICHAEL ANTHONY

Gramercy Tavern
42 East 20th Street, New York City

He moved from Cincinnati to Paris where he worked at L'Arpège and L'Astrance. After a stint at Blue Hill at Stone Barns, he joined Gramercy Tavern.

Dizengoff 1034	Wish I'd opened
Eleven Madison Park 1037	High end
Hinata Ramen 1041	Regular neighborhood
La Madia 666	Worth the travel
Maialino 1038	Breakfast
Nha Trang One 1006	Bargain
Turntable LP Bar & Karaoke 1044	Late night
Uncle Boons 1011	Local favorite

JUAN MARI & ELENA ARZAK

Arzak Restaurant
Avenida Alcalde Elósegui 273, San Sebastián

The father-and-daughter team behind the three-Michelin starred Arzak, owned and run by the family since 1897.

Akelarre 578	Local favorite
Alameda 576	High end
Astelena 579	Bargain
Astelena 579	Regular neighborhood
Bokada Mikel Santamaría 580	Late night
El Celler de Can Roca 583	Worth the travel
Elkano 580	Late night
A Fuego Negro 578	Wish I'd opened
Ganbara Jatetxea 580	Regular neighborhood
Ganbara Jatetxea 580	Wish I'd opened
Haizea Bar 581	Breakfast
Mugaritz 576	High end
Nerua 575	Worth the travel
Pastelería Geltoki 581	Breakfast
Zuberoa 578	Local favorite

ALEX ATALA

D.O.M. Restaurante
Rua Barao de Capanema 549, São Paulo

The chef-proprietor of D.O.M. Restaurante in São Paulo, Atala is famous for combining unusual indigenous ingredients with European technique.

Carlos Pizza 118	Bargain
Churrascaria Vento Haragano 1113	Wish I'd opened
Mani 1114	High end
Mocotó 1118	Local favorite
Padaria da Esquina 1113	Breakfast
Sushi Mitani 272	Worth the travel
Tan Tan Noodle Bar 1116	Regular neighborhood
Yorimichi Izakaya 1115	Late night

JASON ATHERTON

Pollen Street Social
8–10 Pollen Street, London

Created Maze for Gordon Ramsay before going it alone with Pollen Street Social, Little Social, Social Eating House, Berners Tavern, and outposts in the Far East.

Brooklyn Fare 1015	High end

Brooklyn Fare **1015**...............Wish I'd opened
Chez Bruce **429**............Regular neighborhood
Chiltern Firehouse **419**..........Wish I'd opened
Flocons de Sel **536**............................High end
Kiln **451**...Bargain
Lilia **1016**..Bargain
M. Manze **484**.........................Local favorite
Maialino **1038**.......................................Breakfast
Nihonryori RyuGin **265**..........Worth the travel
The NoMad Hotel **1044**....................Late night
Palmer & Co. **112**................................Late night
Restaurant Hubert **112**....................Late night
Roberta's **1017**..Bargain
Russ & Daughters Cafe **1009**............Breakfast
Saison **841**..High end
Saison **841**...........................Wish I'd opened
Saison **841**.........................Worth the travel
Sat Bains **402**...High end
Sat Bains **402**......................Worth the travel
Sepia **113**..High end
Trinity Restaurant **415**..Regular neighborhood
Wild Honey **442**...........Regular neighborhood
The Windmill **443**.....................Local favorite
The Wolseley **443**..............................Breakfast

GÍSLI MATTHÍAS AUÐUNSSON
Slippurinn Eatery
Strandvegur 76, Vestmannaeyjabær

Born in Vestmannaeyjar (the Westman islands),
he founded the much-loved Slippurinn there
with his family in 2012, before opening Matur
og Drykkur in Reykjavik, which he left at the
end of 2016.
BURRO Tapas + Steaks **340**............Late night
Bæjarins Beztu Pylsur **340**.................Bargain
Coocoo's Nest **340**........Regular neighborhood
Dill **340**..High end
Dill **340**...................................Local favorite
Grillið **340**...High end
Grillið **340**..........................Local favorite
MAT BAR **340**....................................Late night

JASPER AVENT
The Town Mouse
312 Drummond Street, Carlton

He brings many years of experience from
The Lake House to his role as head chef at
The Town Mouse.
Belles Hot Chicken **148**.......................Bargain
Brae **101**...High end
Donnini's **141**...........................Local favorite
Ester **114**..............................Worth the travel
French Saloon **143**............................Late night
Pope Joan **140**...................................Breakfast
Ramblr **152**..................Regular neighborhood

JOSÉ AVILLEZ
Belcanto
Largo de São Carlos 10, Lisbon

Worked for Adrià, Ducasse, and Frechon
before returning home to Portugal and
launching Cantinho do Avillez and Belcanto.
El Celler de Can Roca **583**......Wish I'd opened
Feitoria **616**...High end
Galeto **613**...Late night
GO JUU **613**.................Regular neighborhood
Grande Palácio Hong Kong **619**..........Bargain

Magano Restaurante **616**...................Regular
                                                               neighborhood
Mar do Inferno **607**...................Local favorite
Nahm **283**.........................Worth the travel
Pastelaria Benard **618**.....................Breakfast
Quique Dacosta **591**...........Worth the travel
O Trevo **618**..Bargain

JASON BAILEY
Paste Bangkok
3F Gaysorn Plaza, 999 Ploenchit Road,
Bangkok

After 15 years experience of cooking Thai cuisine
professionally, this husband-and-wife team
opened their first Paste Thai restaurant in 2013.
55 Pochana **287**................................Late night
Baan Rabiang Nam **287**........Wish I'd opened
Burmese Noodles **284**.....................Breakfast
In the Mood for Love **288**.................High end
Kanom Jeen Banglumpoo **285**...........Bargain
Klang Soi Restaurant **288**...................Regular
                                                               neighborhood
Li Bong Beach Resort **276**.....Worth the travel
Saew Noodles **289**............................Breakfast
Suan Thip **283**........................Local favorite

MASHAMA BAILEY
The Grey
109 Martin Luther King Jr. Boulevard,
Savannah

Earning her stripes on the New York City
restaurant circuit, Bailey returned to
the city of her youth to set up The Grey in
a converted greyhound station.
Crystal Beer Parlor **878**..Regular neighborhood
Fig **1053**.....................................Local favorite
Great NY Noodletown **1006**.............Late night
Husk **1054**............................Wish I'd opened
Narobia's Grits & Gravy **879**.............Breakfast
Osteria Francescana **650**.................High end
La Taberna del Gourmet **591**..Worth the travel

SAT BAINS
Sat Bains
Lenton Lane, Nottingham

Chef-proprietor of a cutting-edge culinary
destination in the somewhat unlikely setting
of Nottingham, England.
Andrew Fairlie at Gleneagles **498**.....High end
L'ATELIER de Joël Robuchon **432**......High end
Bar Iberico **402**.......................Local favorite
Benu **840**.............................Worth the travel
Berners Tavern **472**...........................Breakfast
The Cod's Scallops **402**.Regular neighborhood
Dinner by Heston Blumenthal **419**.....High end
L'Enclume **394**......................................High end
The Ledbury **423**..................................High end
Pollen Street Social **441**.....................High end
ROKA **442**..High end
SingleThread Farms **792**.......Worth the travel
The Wollaton **402**.........Regular neighborhood
The Wolseley **443**...............Wish I'd opened
Yauatcha Soho **455**...........................Late night
Zaap Thai Street Food **402**.................Bargain

DAN BARBER
Blue Hill at Stone Barns
630 Bedford Road, Pocantico Hills

A perennial chefs' favorite and the original
culinary brains behind field-to-fork
destinations, he is chef-co-owner at Blue
Hill in New York and Hudson Valley's Blue
Hill at Stone Barns.
Attica **151**...High end
Quintonil **1082**....................Worth the travel
Ippudo **1041**......................................Late night
Loring Place **1025**........Regular neighborhood
Nix **1026**...............................Wish I'd opened
Russ & Daughters Cafe **1009**...........Breakfast

PASCAL BARBOT
L'Astrance
4 Rue Beethoven, Paris

A protégé of Alain Passard, under whom
he worked for five years, prior to opening
the celebrated L'Astrance in 2000.
Clamato **564**......................................Late night
Pierre Hermé **568**............................Breakfast

NIEVES BARRAGÁN MOHACHO
Sabor
35 Heddon Street, London

Born and raised in the Basque region
of Spain, she ran the Barrafina kitchens
for nearly a decade before leaving in 2017
to start Sabor in London's Mayfair.
Bar Termini **444**.................................Breakfast
d'Berto **587**.........................Worth the travel
Black Axe Mangal **480**.........................Bargain
Duck & Waffle **466**.............................Late night
Elystan Street **412**................................High end
Hoi Polloi **485**...................................Breakfast
Hoppers **450**...............Regular neighborhood
Kiln **451**..........................Regular neighborhood
Koya Bar **451**.........................Local favorite
Kricket Soho **451**.........Regular neighborhood
The Ledbury **423**..................................High end
The Quality Chop House **469**......Local favorite
Quo Vadis **453**..................................Late night
Rancho Seco **1084**...............Worth the travel
Restaurant Nathan Outlaw **393**..........Wish I'd
                                                                      opened

ITALO BASSI
Enoteca Pinchiorri
Via Ghibellina 87, Florence

Runs the kitchen at Enoteca Pinchiorri in
partnership with Riccardo Monco, whom he
has worked alongside for close to 20 years.
The Belvedere **665**........Regular neighborhood
Château Robuchon **260**........Wish I'd opened
Geranium **378**.....................Worth the travel
Le Ghiaine **650**......................................Bargain
Gurdulù **668**.....................................Late night
Le Louis XV **547**...................................High end
La Magnolia **668**...............................Breakfast
La Voglia Matta **650**.................Local favorite

EMMANUEL BASSOLEIL
Skye Restaurant & Bar
Hotel Unique, Avenida Brigadeiro Luis
Antonio 4700, São Paulo

Born in Burgundy and trained under Claude Troisgros, Bassoleil moved to Brazil in 1987 and currently oversees Skye restaurant.

A Casa do Porco **1116**............Wish I'd opened
Lá da Venda **1118**..............................Breakfast
Le Manjue Organique **1119**...Regular neighborhood
Minato Izakaya **1116**.........................Late night
Tartar & Co **1116**.................................Bargain
Town Sandwich Co. **1112**..........Local favorite
Tête à Tête **1112**...............................High end
Vinheria Percussi **1116**.........Worth the travel

BEN BATTERBURY
True South Dining Room
The Rees Hotel, 377 Frankton Road,
Queenstown

Born in England, executive chef Batterbury is now based in Central Otago, where he heads up the kitchen at True South Dining Room.

Atlas Beer Cafe **159**...................Local favorite
The Chop Shop **158**..........................Breakfast
Dinner by Heston Blumenthal **152**....Worth the travel
Fergburger **159**................................Late night
Fergburger **159**.............Wish I'd opened
Fishbone **159**......................................High end
Kappa **160**.............Regular neighborhood
MANDU Dumplings **160**.........................Bargain
La Rumbla **160**.........Regular neighborhood
Vudu Cafe & Larder **160**...................Breakfast
Yama Express **161**..............................Bargain

KRISTIAN BAUMANN
108
Strandgade 108, Copenhagen

Head chef and owner of 108, Baumann temporarily sets up in the location of iconic restaurant, Noma.

Alchemist **378**........................Local favorite
Alinea **957**......................Worth the travel
Amass **370**..........................Local favorite
AOC **370**..High end
AOC **370**...........................Local Favorite
Asador Etxebarri **575**.....Wish I'd opened
Atelier September **370**.................Breakfast
Bæst **376**...............Regular neighborhood
Bistro Boheme **370**......Regular neighborhood
BROR **371**.............................Local favorite
Café Taxa **376**.................................Breakfast
The Corner **369**...............................Breakfast
District Tonkin **372**...........................Late night
District Tonkin **372**.......Regular neighborhood
Eleven Madison Park **1037**....Worth the travel
Fäviken Magasinet **345**.........Worth the travel
Gaon **234**.......................Worth the travel
Gasoline Grill **372**..............................Bargain
Geist **372**.............................Local favorite
Geranium **378**...................................High end
Geranium **378**.....................Local favorite
Hija De Sanchez **379**.........................Bargain
Hija De Sanchez **379**....Regular neighborhood
Hos Fischer **379**...................Local favorite

Hos Fischer **379**...........Regular neighborhood
Kadeau **368**......................................High end
Kiin Kiin **376**.......................Local favorite
Kødbyens Fiskebar **379**.............Local favorite
Kong Hans Kælder **373**......................High end
Kong Hans Kælder **373**...........Local favorite
Manfreds **377**...........Regular neighborhood
Marchal at Hotel d'Angleterre **373**....High end
Mirabelle **377**.................................Breakfast
Musling **374**.......................Local favorite
Next **967**.........................Wish I'd opened
Noma **369**...High end
Noma **369**...........................Local favorite
Radio **377**...........................Local favorite
Ranee's **378**.......................Local favorite
Relæ **378**............................Local favorite
Saison **841**.....................Wish I'd opened
Slurp Ramen Joint **374**......................Bargain
Slurp Ramen Joint **374**.Regular neighborhood
Søllerød Kro **364**.............................High end
Studio **375**.......................................High end
Taller **375**..........................Local favorite
Tickets **601**.....................Wish I'd opened
Yanagiya **245**..................Wish I'd opened

HARNEET BAWEJA
Gunpowder
11 White's Row, London

Kolkata born, the kitchens of his grandmother and mother in West Bengal heavily influence the food produced in Gunpowder.

Barrafina **444**.................Wish I'd opened
Beigel Bake **485**.............................Late night
Café 338 **461**...................................Breakfast
Dum Pukht **185**...............................High end
Gaggan **284**.....................................High end
Gurdulù **668**......................Worth the travel
Jai Hind Dhaba **185**........................Late night
Jyoti Vihar **186**.............................Breakfast
Kiln **451**..........................Wish I'd opened
Marksman Public House **475**.Wish I'd opened
My Old Place **466**.........Regular neighborhood
Peter Cat **186**..................................Bargain
Rochelle Canteen **486**..........Local favorite
Silk Road **465**.............Regular neighborhood
Il Santo Bevitore **668**...........Worth the travel
St. John Bread & Wine **489**.......Local favorite

RICK BAYLESS
Frontera Grill
445 North Clark Street, Chicago

Celebrity chef and champion of Mexican cuisine, Bayless founded his first restarant of many in 1987, the casual Frontera Grill, followed by acclaimed Toplobampo four years later.

Alinea **957**..High end
Carnitas Uruapan **961**......................Bargain
Hot Chocolate **970**.........................Breakfast
Lula Cafe **959**.....................Local favorite
Maude's Liquor Bar **967**..................Late night
Owen & Engine **959**......Regular neighborhood
Parachute **954**................Wish I'd opened
Tickets **601**......................Worth the travel

CAROLINA BAZÁN
Ambrosía
Pamplona 78, Santiago

Combines French flair, from her experience under Gregory Marchand, with Chilean produce for a market-to-table experience.

99 Restaurante **1132**...Regular neighborhood
BORAGó **1132**.................Wish I'd opened
Las Cabras Fuente de Soda **1113**............Local
favorite
Contra **1007**.......................Worth the travel
Liguria **1133**...................................Late night
Liguria **1133**............Regular neighborhood
Momofuku Ko **1023**.......Worth the travel
Naoki **1133**..High end
Salvador Cocina y Café **1134**..............Bargain
The White Rabbit **1134**.....................Breakfast

BO BECH
Geist
Kongens Nytorv 8, Copenhagen

Culinary alchemist Bech, ex-head chef of Paustian, opened Geist in Copenhagen in 2010, where he serves experimental New Nordic grazing dishes.

Atelier September **370**.....................Breakfast
Bistro Boheme **370**..................Local favorite
Fäviken Magasinet **345**.........Wish I'd opened
Fu Hao **379**...Bargain
Henne Kirkeby Kro **365**.........Worth the travel
Hija De Sanchez **379**.........................Bargain
Joe Beef **779**....................Worth the travel
Kebabistan **376**...............................Late night
Marchal at Hotel d'Angleterre **373**..Late night
Noma **369**...........................Local favorite
Palægade **374**...........Regular neighborhood
Restaurant Gammel Mønt **374**............Regular
neighborhood
Saison **841**.......................................High end
Sushi Saito **267**................................High end

JEAN BEDDINGTON
English-born Beddington opened her own eponymous restaurant in Amsterdam before going freelance as a culinary creative.

Brut de Mer **514**.........Regular neighbourhood
The Chippy **515**...............................Bargain
Halvemaan **519**.........Regular neighborhood
Lotti's **515**.......................................Breakfast
Restaurant Issen **246**.......................High end
Restaurant Vermeer **516**.......Wish I'd opened
Rijks **518**...........................Local Favorite
Ristorante Reale **646**............Worth the travel
The Seafood Bar **516**.......................Late night

MICHAEL BELTRAN
Ariete
3540 Main Highway, Coconut Grove, Miami

Miami born, he worked under world-renowned chefs Norman van Aken and Michael Schwartz, before opening his first solo offering in the heart of Miami's Coconut Grove.

Akelarre **578**......................Worth the travel
Brut de Mer **514**.........Regular neighbourhood
Casola's Pizzeria **873**.....................Late night

Enriqueta's **873**..................Breakfast
Estela **1010**......................Worth the travel
Fooq's **873**..............Regular neighborhood
Harry's Pizzeria **873**..........Wish I'd opened
Hillstone **871**..................Wish I'd opened
The Local **872**.........Regular neighborhood
Michael's Genuine Food & Drink **874**......Local favorite
El Nuevo Siglo **874**...................Bargain
Pao by Paul Qui **875**................High end
Yakko-San **876**....................Late night

DAVID BENJAMIN
Banana Tree Grille
Bluebeard's Castle Resort. St Thomas
Born on Dominica and raised on St Thomas, local boy Benjamin began as a line cook at the Ritz Carlton St Thomas before becoming executive chef for the group.

Bad Ass Coffee **1075**................Breakfast
Betsy's Bar **1075**..................Late night
Cuzzin's **1075**.................Local favorite
Greengo's Caribbean Cantina **1075**....Bargain
Hook Line & Sinker **1076**.............Breakfast
Pie Whole **1076**................Wish I'd opened
Thirteen **1076**.........Regular neighborhood
Zozo's Ristorante **1075**...............High end

GAL BEN-MOSHE
Glass
Uhlandstrasse 195, Berlin
He started out working under great chefs such as Jason Atherton, Marcus Wareing, and Grant Achatz, before moving to Berlin to open Glass, serving modern Arabic cuisine.

Benedict **634**......................Breakfast
Big Stuff Smoked BBQ **629**............Bargain
The Butcher **628**...................Late night
Ding Tai Fung **212**............Worth the travel
einsunternull **631**..............Local favorite
Madame Ngo **628**........Regular neighborhood
Next **967**...................Wish I'd opened
Osteria Francescana **650**.............High end

SHANNON BENNETT
Vue de Monde
525 Collins Street, Melbourne
Melbourne-born chef who worked with Albert Roux, Marco Pierre White, and Alain Ducasse before heading home to open Vue de Monde at the age of 24.

Atera **1013**.................Worth the travel
Attica **151**.......................High end
Le Bernardin **1038**...........Worth the travel
Boston Sub **153**....................Bargain
Chin Chin **142**.............Wish I'd opened
Colonel Tan's Thai Kitchen **150**...........Regular neighborhood
Cookie **142**...........Regular neighborhood
Estelle by Scott Pickett **149**..........High end
Flower Drum **143**..................High end
Jimmy Grants **150**..................Late night
Kenzan **144**...............Wish I'd opened
Master Roll Vietnam **152**..............Bargain
The Melbourne Supper Club **144**.....Late night
Minamishima **150**...............Local favorite
Pancake Parlour **144**...............Breakfast

Supernormal **145**..................Local favorite
Tim Ho Wan **146**...........Regular neighborhood

JAMES BERCKEMEYER
Cosme
Calle Tudela y Varela 160, San Isidro
Chef-owner of Cosme, who has extensive experience gathered from Lima's top kitchens.

Astrid & Gastón **1101**.................High end
Astrid & Gastón **1101**.............Local favorite
Canta Rana **1097**....................Bargain
Central **1098**................Worth the travel
Eleven Madison Park **1037**....Worth the travel
Grimanesa Varga Anticuchos **1099**.....Bargain
La Lucha **1099**.....................Late night
Madam Tusan **1100**......Regular neighborhood
Maido **1100**.....................Local favorite
Momofuku Ssäm Bar **1023**....Wish I'd opened
Mó Café + Bistró **1098**.............Breakfast
El Pan de la Chola **1099**.............Breakfast
Rafael **1100**......................High end
La Tranquera **1099**.................Late night
Wildair **1010**..............Wish I'd opened

IVAN BEREZUTSKIY
Twins
Malaya Bronnaya 13, Moscow
Trained in elBulli under chef Ferran Adrià, he moved from The Flying Dutchman in St Petersburg to open Twins in Moscow with his brother in 2015.

#Farsh **712**......................Bargain
108 **368**....................Worth the travel
Boston Seafood & Bar **711**...............Regular neighborhood
Burger and Lobster **446**.....Wish I'd opened
El Celler de Can Roca **583**.....Worth the travel
Chestnaya Kuhnya **706**.........Worth the travel
Coffeemania **711**..................Breakfast
Duo Gastrobar **701**.................Bargain
Moroshka dlya Pushkina **702**...........High end
Mugaritz **576**...............Worth the travel
Nikuda Ne Edem **709**................Late night
Noma **369**..................Worth the travel
Russkaya Ryumochnaya #1 **702**..Local favorite
SAVVA **713**.......................High end

SERGEY BEREZUTSKIY
Twins
Malaya Bronnaya 13, Moscow
Worked in Chicago and Moscow for several years before winning first prize in the San Pellegrino Cooking Cup, and teaming up with his brother to open Twins.

15 Kitchen + Bar **707**...............Late night
Blue Hill at Stone Barns **913**..Wish I'd opened
Chestnaya Kuhnya **706**.Regular neighborhood
Coffeemania **711**..................Breakfast
Duo Gastrobar **701**.................Bargain
Nikuda Ne Edem **709**.............Local favorite
Relæ **378**..................Worth the travel
SAVVA **713**.......................High end
U Salvatore **713**..................Breakfast

DONALD BERGER
Don's Bistro
16 Quang An Road, Hanoi
Raised in Montreal, he explored three continents before settling in Hanoi to offer a globally inspired menu at Don's Bistro.

8½ Otto e Mezzo Bombana **220**..Worth the travel
La Badiane **290**....................High end
Bánh Cuốn **291**...................Breakfast
Bia Hoi Corner **290**.................Bargain
Bún bò Nam Bộ **290**.....Regular neighborhood
Bun Cha Mai Anh **291**...Regular neighborhood
Fernando's **190**.............Worth the travel
French Grill **292**..................High end
Golden Dragon Restaurant **290**....Late night
Maison de Tết decor **291**...........Breakfast
Quán Ăn Ngon **290**............Local favorite
Wrap & Roll **291**...........Wish I'd opened
Wrap & Roll **291**..............Local favorite

PAUL BERGLUND
The Bachelor Farmer
50 North 2nd Avenue, Minneapolis
After two tours as a US naval officer, he trained under Paul Bertolli and Paul Canales in Oakland. He has been at the helm of The Bachelor Farmer since it opened.

Al's Breakfast **994**..................Breakfast
Alma **994**........................High end
Fäviken Magasinet **345**.........Worth the travel
Gandhi Mahal **996**........Regular neighborhood
Grady's Barbecue **915**........Worth the travel
Heyday **997**......................Late night
Pizzeria Lola **1000**........Regular neighborhood
Quang Restaurant **1000**............Local favorite
Taqueria Los Ocampo **1001**...........Bargain
Tojo's **756**................Worth the travel
The Willows Inn **800**.........Wish I'd opened
The Willows Inn **800**.......Worth the travel

GUILLERMO GONZÁLEZ BERISTÁIN
Pangea
Bosques del Valle 110–20, San Pedro
Culinary Institute of America-trained Beristáin worked the line at Michelin-starred restaurants across Europe, opening Pangea in Monterrey in 1998, the flagship of his burgeoning group of high-end Mexican restaurants.

Koli Cocina de Origen **1088**............High end
Milk Pizzeria **1087**..............Local favorite
Nicos **1081**.................Worth the travel
Orson **1086**................Wish I'd opened
Señor Latino **1087**.................Breakfast
Señor Tanaka **1087**.......Regular neighborhood
Taiwan Dim Sum **1087**................Bargain
Taqueria Orinoco **1087**.............Late night

DANIEL BERLIN
Daniel Berlin Krog
Diligensvägen 21, Tomellila
He left the Swedish city of Malmö behind to open a restaurant in the heart of the Österlen countryside, where uber-local produce is king.

108 **368**	....	Wish I'd opened
Amass **370**	....	High end
Asador Etxebarri **575**	....	Worth the travel
Bastard **346**	....	Local favorite
Bastard **346**	....	Regular neighborhood
Bord 13 **346**	....	Local favorite
Bouchon **346**	....	Regular neighborhood
Casual Streetfood **347**	....	Bargain
Eleven Madison Park **1037**	.....	Worth the travel
Falafel Baghdad **347**	....	Bargain
Falafel Baghdad **347**	....	Late night
Fäviken Magasinet **345**	....	High end
Frantzén **355**	....	High end
Hedone **413**	....	Worth the travel
Kvarteret Åkern **348**	....	Local favorite
Mirazur **545**	....	Worth the travel
Noma **369**	....	High end
Relæ **378**	....	High end
Saltimporten Canteen **348**	....	Local favorite
Söderberg & Sara **349**	....	Breakfast

FREDRIK BERSELIUS
Aska
47 South 5th Street, Brooklyn
He bridges the Nordic culinary traditions of his upbringing with the environs of his New York home at his restaurant in Brooklyn.

Blue Hill at Stone Barns **913**	..	Wish I'd opened
Daniel Berlin Krog **349**	....	Worth the travel
Gastrologik **358**	....	Worth the travel
Kadeau **368**	....	Worth the travel
Kyo Ya **1022**	....	Local favorite
Lhasa Fast Food **1019**	....	Bargain
Maaemo **344**	....	High end
Marlow & Sons **1018**	....	Breakfast
Mugaritz **576**	....	High end
Narisawa **265**	....	High end
Oaxen Krog **354**	....	Worth the travel
Osteria Francescana **650**	....	High end
Sunday in Brooklyn **1017**	....	Regular neighborhood
Wildair **1010**	....	Late night

BEN BERTEI
LONgTIME
610 Ann Street, Brisbane
He brings extensive knowledge of Southeast Asian cuisine to this Thai-focused restaurant.

The APO **128**	....	Late night
Gerard's Bar **131**	....	Regular neighborhood
kin & co **132**	....	Breakfast
Morning After **133**	....	Breakfast

JOHN BESH
Besh Restaurant Group
This busy executive chef at August in New Orleans has seven other restaurants in and around the city, and another in San Antonio, Texas.

Balise **975**	....	Regular neighborhood
Compère Lapin **976**	....	Wish I'd opened
Dong Phuong **985**	....	Bargain
Galatoire's **980**	....	High End
M25 **173**	....	Worth the Travel
Mandina's Reastaurant **985**	....	Local favorite
Red's Chinese **975**	....	Late Night
Satsuma **975**	....	Breakfast
Townsman **893**	....	Worth the travel

VINEET BHATIA
Vineet Bhatia London
10 Lincoln Street, London
Born in Bombay, he has been based in London since 1993, but has a string of high-end Indian restaurants spanning the globe.

Atari-Ya **415**	....	Local favorite
Dinner by Heston Blumenthal **419**	.....	High end
Ealing Park Tavern **415**	.	Regular neighborhood
Patty & Bun **421**	....	Bargain
PLAY Restaurant & Lounge **178**	....	Wish I'd opened
Restaurant André **331**	....	Worth the travel
Royal Exchange Grand Café **467**	......	Breakfast

TOMI BJORCK
Blanca
4/75 Hall Street, Sydney
He opened his first Asian-inspired restaurant, Stockholm's Farang, in 2009, followed by three restaurants in Helsinki. His newest venture, Blanca, opened in 2017.

Automata **114**	....	Local favorite
Balthazar **1011**	....	Breakfast
Chat Thai **116**	....	Bargain
Ester **114**	....	Regular neighborhood
LP's Quality Meats **114**	....	Local favorite
Saison **841**	....	High end
Shuk **110**	....	Regular neighborhood
Sonoma Bakery **107**	....	Breakfast
The Unicorn Hotel **121**	....	Late night

ANTON BJUHR
Gastrologik
Artillerigatan 14, Stockholm
Runs Gastrologik in Stockholm with Jacob Holmström, where the focus is pastry and baking, and Speceriet, a casual offshoot.

Andaman **350**	....	Regular neighborhood
Daniel Berlin Krog **349**	....	High end
Fäviken Magasinet **345**	....	High end
Flippin' Burgers **361**	....	Local favorite
The French Laundry **797**	....	Wish I'd opened
Hija de Sanchez Torvehallerne **372**	..	Worth the travel
Lindeberg Bageri & Konditori **350**	....	Breakfast
MAX **356**	....	Bargain
Oaxen Slip **354**	....	Local favorite
Sturehof **358**	....	Late night

GALTON BLACKISTON
Morston Hall Restaurant
Morston Hall Hotel, The Street, Holt
Self-taught chef and owner of Norfolk's Morston Hall Hotel for over twenty years, he recently opened a fish-and-chip shop in Cromer.

Balthazar **1011**	....	Breakfast
Hakkasan **439**	....	Late night
The Ledbury **423**	....	Worth the travel
The Waterside Inn **390**	....	High end

DMITRIY BLINOV
Duo Gastrobar
Kirochnaya Street 8, St Petersburg
Worked his way around St Petersburg's culinary scene for nearly thirty years, before opening his first restaurant, Duo Gastrobar, followed two years later by Tartarbar.

Big Wine Freaks **714**	....	Late night
Eleven Madison Park **1037**	.....	Wish I'd opened
Glenuill **712**	....	Local favorite
Hamlet & Jacks **701**	.....	Regular neighborhood
Jerome **702**	....	Regular neighborhood
Kokoko **714**	....	Breakfast
Kokoko **714**	....	Regular neighborhood
Moroshka dlya Pushkina **702**	....	High end
OLO **386**	....	Wish I'd opened
OLO **386**	....	Worth the travel
Pedro & Gomez u Larisy **702**	....	Bargain
Smoke BBQ **702**	....	Regular neighborhood

THOMAS BOEMER
Corner Table
4537 Nicollet Avenue, Minneapolis
Ducasse-trained, he is the chef behind the nose-to-tail restaurant, Corner Table, and the fried chicken sensation, Revival.

Alma **994**	....	Local Favorite
Asador Etxebarri **575**	....	Worth the travel
The Bachelor Farmer **995**	....	High end
The Bachelor Farmer **995**	....	Local favorite
COOK **911**	....	Breakfast
Hola Arepa **997**	....	Regular neighborhood
Lyn 65 **998**	....	Late night
Matt's Bar **998**	....	Bargain
Mucci's Italian **911**	....	Wish I'd opened
Spoon and Stable **1001**	....	Breakfast
Spoon and Stable **1001**	....	High end
Spoon and Stable **1001**	....	Local favorite
The Strip Club Meat & Fish **911**	....	Regular neighborhood
World Street Kitchen **1002**	....	Bargain
Young Joni **1002**	....	Late night
Zen Box Izakaya **1002**	..	Regular neighborhood

JONNIE BOER
De Librije
Spinhuisplein 1, Zwolle
This Dutch head chef of Michelin-starred De Librije also owns a nearby cooking shop and cooking and wine school with his wife.

BaiYok **510**	....	Regular neighborhood
BiBo **573**	....	Late night
Bistro Bonne Femme **510**	..	Regular neighborhood
The Flying Fishbone **1071**	....	Late night
De Gillende Keukenmeiden **510**	....	Breakfast

Mingles **235**...............................Late night
RōNIN **229**................................Late night
Yardbird **229**............................Late night

DANIEL BOJORQUEZ
La Brasa
124 Broadway, Somerville

Born in Mexico, he spent over 12 years in Boston working with Frank McClelland at L'Espalier and Sel de la Terre before opening La Brasa.

Asta **889**........................Regular neighborhood
Eastern Standard **890**....................Late night
Myers + Chang **890**.....Regular neighborhood
Tapatio **900**.............................Bargain
Trina's Starlite Lounge **901**...........Breakfast

UMBERTO BOMBANA
8½ Otto e Mezzo Bombana
18 Chater Road, Hong Kong

Arguably Asia's most famous Italian chef who operates 8½ Otto e Mezzo Bombana in Hong Kong and Shanghai, and Opera Bombana in Beijing.

Celebrity Cuisine **221**............Local favorite
CIAK – In The Kitchen **221**..Regular neighborhood
Din Tai Fung **218**......................Bargain
KANDA **264**.............................High end
Trattoria Al Moro **658**........Wish I'd opened

ANDREA BONAFFINI
Yellow Lemon
561 Mingshui Road, Taipei

This Sicilian chef, who has worked all over the globe, serves imaginative off-beat cakes and splattered plates at his dessert bar.

Australia Dairy Company **212**..............Bargain
Le Blanc **202**................Regular neighborhood
Le Calandre **671**........................High end
Giando **230**....................Local favorite
MUME **203**..................Regular neighborhood
Orange Shabu Shabu **203**................Late night
Pastarell **665**.........................Breakfast
Piazza Duomo **664**........................High end
Relæ **378**.....................Wish I'd opened
Ristorante Tokuyoshi **662**......Worth the travel

JASON BOND
Bondir Cambridge
279A Broadway, Cambridge

Bringing more than twenty years experience to his cooking, Bond's "root-cellar" style echoes his upbringing, which centered around farming and preserving the harvest.

The Abbey **893**.........................Late night
Algiers Coffee House **893**.................Bargain
Area Four **894**................Wish I'd opened
Asta **889**...................Wish I'd opened
Blue Room **894**..................Local favorite
Cafe Sushi **895**.........................High end
Cafe Sushi **895**...........Regular neighborhood
Canlis **802**..................Worth the travel
Le Clarence **557**..............Worth the travel
Clover Food Lab **895**....................Bargain
Craigie on Main **895**.............Local favorite
The Druid **895**.............Regular neighborhood
Longfellows Coffee **896**.Regular neighborhood

Lord Hobo **896**..........................Late night
Mass Ave Diner **897**....................Breakfast
Tatte Bakery & Café **898**.............Breakfast

MASSIMO BOTTURA
Osteria Francescana
Via Stella 22, Modena

Culinary traditions are not easily challenged in Italy but Bottura has succeeded with Modena's avant-garde Osteria Francescana.

A-Frame **812**...........................Bargain
A. Wong **428**...........................Bargain
Le Bernardin **1038**......................High end
Blue Hill at Stone Barns **913**......Wish I'd open
El Celler de Can Roca **583**.....Worth the travel
Central **1098**..................Worth the travel
D.O.M. Restaurante **1114**......Worth the travel
Dal Pescatore **663**................Local favourite
Dal Pescatore **663**.............Worth the travel
Daniel **1045**..................Worth the travel
Eleven Madison Park **1037**...........High end
Firedoor **124**..........................Bargain
Little Serow **865**......................Bargain
Momofuku Ssäm Bar **1023**................Bargain
Mon Café **649**.........................Breakfast
Mugaritz **576**.................Worth the travel
Noma **369**.....................Worth the travel
Pasticceria Bar Dondi **650**...........Breakfast
Pizzeria Mozza **825**.....................Bargain
Pizzeria Ristorante Il Gambero Rosso **663**.......
....Bargain
Pujol **1082**..................Worth the travel
Trattoria Bianca **1044**.Regular neighbourhood

DANIEL BOULUD
Daniel
60 East 65th Street, New York City

After training in France he moved to New York in the 1980s, founding his own Manhattan-based empire, starting with the opening of Daniel in 1993.

Alo Restaurant **766**.............Worth the travel
Fig **1053**...................Regular neighborhood
Grace **966**....................Worth the travel
The Ordinary **1056**......................High end
Petit Trois **817**..................Local favorite
Roister **968**................Regular neighborhood
Spoon and Stable **1001**........Worth the travel
Le Suprême **535**.........................Bargain
Toqué! **783**.............................High end

NEIL BORTHWICK
Merchants Tavern
36 Charlotte Road, London

Former Michel Bras sous chef, Edinburgh-born Borthwick honed his skills at The Square, opening Merchants Tavern in 2013 with Murano's Angela Hartnett.

Black Axe Mangal **480**...............Late night
Dastaan **403**...........................Bargain
The Ledbury **423**........................High end
Noble Rot **432**..................Local favorite
Paul Ainsworth at Number 6 **392**.......Wish I'd
....opened
Sakana Sushi **494**........Regular neighborhood
The Seahorse **394**.............Worth the travel
St. John Bread & Wine **489**...........Breakfast

DANNY BOWIEN
Mission Chinese Food
171 East Broadway, New York City

On leaving Mission Street Food, he first opened Mission Chinese Food in San Francisco, followed by another branch in New York City.

Asador Etxebarri **575**............Wish I'd opened
Balthazar **1011**..................Local favorite
Carbone **1025**...................Local favorite
Le Châteaubriand **564**...........Worth the travel
Funny BBQ 98 **1008**.....................Bargain
Funny BBQ 98 **1008**....................Late night
Hasaki **1022**..............Regular neighborhood
Paik's Noodle **1040**....................Late night
Russ & Daughters Cafe **1009**...........Breakfast
Sushi Yasuda **1043**......................High end
Sushi Yasuda **1043**.......Regular neighborhood
Veselka **1024**.........................Breakfast
Wu's Wonton King **1010**.................Bargain

WILL BOWLBY
Kricket
12 Denman Street, London

He serves Indian small plates and cocktails in London, both in Soho and from a shipping container in Brixton.

Barrafina **444**...............Regular neighborhood
Hawksmoor **433**...............Wish I'd opened
The Ledbury **423**........................High end
Naughty Piglets **464**.....Regular neighborhood
Quo Vadis **453**.........................Late night
Salon **454**...........................Breakfast
Silk Road **465**.........................Bargain
Som Saa **489**....................Local favorite
Shree Thaker Bhojanalay **185**Worth the Travel

JOEL BRAHAM
The Good Egg
93 Stoke Newington Church Street, London

Chef-owner of The Good Egg, a Jewish-inspired neighborhood restaurant in Stoke Newington.

Apollo Pizzeria **490**......Regular neighborhood
L'As du Fallafel **554**.....................Late night
Big Sur Bakery **790**......Regular neighborhood
First Awakenings **793**............Worth the travel
Flat Iron **449**................Wish I'd opened
Hawksmoor Air Street **439**.............High end
Hatzot **172**............................Bargain
Miznon **173**...........................Late night
Morito **468**..................Wish I'd opened
The Palomar **452**.......................High end
Poco **391**......................Local favorite
Sabich **174**..........................Breakfast
Theo's Pizzeria **465**............Local favorite
Top Taste **461**........................Bargain
Umut 2000 **491**........................Late night
Umut 2000 **491**...........Regular neighborhood
Wise Sons **837**................Worth the travel
Xi'an Impression **477**....Regular neighborhood

MATTHEW BREEN
Templo
98 Patrick Street, Hobart
Inspired by his travels through Italy and Spain, Breen runs a tiny neighborhood restaurant.
Aløft 97..................................High end
Cyclo 97....................................Late night
Fico 98..........................Regular neighborhood
Fleet 82.............................Wish I'd opened
Franklin 98..............................Local favorite
Ginger Brown 98........................Breakfast
RIN 99...Bargain
Septime 566.....................Worth the travel

SEAN BROCK
McCrady's
2 Unity Alley, Charleston
Since leading the charge to reinvent Southern cooking after opening McCrady's in 2006, Brock has opened two incarnations of the more casual Husk.
Blue Hill at Stone Barns 913..Wish I'd opened
L'Effervescence 263.............Worth the travel
Hannibal's Kitchen 1053..................Breakfast
Martha Lou's Kitchen 1054........Local favorite
Nana's Soul Food 915.......................Bargain
Sushi Suzuki 259...........................High end

ERIC & BRUCE BROMBERG
Blue Ribbon Restaurants
97 Sullivan Street, New York
Brothers who founded the New York-based Blue Ribbon group, which serves everything from high-end sushi to late-night comfort food.
Arturo's 1027.................................Bargain
The Court of Two Sisters 980...........Breakfast
Domaine de Rochevilaine 538...........High end
Eden-Roc Grill 542.................Worth the travel
Au Pied de Cochon 551.Regular neighborhood
Wo Hop 1007..................................Late night

JONATHAN BROOKS
Milktooth
534 Virginia Avenue, Indianapolis
Forget what you thought you knew about breakfast or brunch, Jonathon Brooks is rewriting the rulebook.
Bluebeard 880.............................Late night
Cerulean 880...............................High end
Le Dôme 567......................Worth the travel
Egg Roll #1 880............................Breakfast
The Golden 880..................Wish I'd opened
Gray Brothers Cafeteria 882......Local favorite
Leonardo's Mexican Food 881........Late night
Peppy Grill 881...............................Late night
Rook 881..................Regular neighborhood
Smyth 960.........................Worth the travel
St. Elmo Steakhouse 881................High end
Steer-In 881................................Breakfast
Subito 882..................Regular neighborhood
Tex-Mex 882.................................Bargain
Tian Fu Asian Bistro 882..................Regular neighborhood

MANOELLA BUFFARA
Manu
Alameda Dom Pedro II 317, Curutibia
Noma-trained, she returned to Brazil to showcase the diverse natural produce of the Paraná region.
Atelier Crenn 833.................Worth the travel
Bar Palácio 1104............................Late night
Cosme 1036.........................Wish I'd opened
Girassol 1104..........................Local favorite
Mocotó 1118.................................Bargain
Da Paolo Gastronomia 334.............Breakfast
Pierre Gagnaire 559.......................High end
Quintana 1104............Regular neighborhood
Rause Café + Vinho 1104.................Breakfast

DANIEL BURNS
Luksus at Tørst
615 Manhattan Avenue, New York City
Influenced by time spent in British and Danish kitchens, he has a strong emphasis on seasonal cooking.
Achilles Heel 1014........Regular neighborhood
Amass 370......................Wish I'd opened
Blanca 1015.............................Local favorite
Blue Hill at Stone Barns 913.............High end
Blue Hill at Stone Barns 913......Local favorite
Bonchon Chicken 1038...................Late night
Cosme 1036.............................Local favorite
Fäviken Magasinet 345.........Worth the travel
In-N-Out Burger 817.........................Bargain
Lilia 1016.....................Regular neighborhood
Mugaritz 576.................................High end
Noma 369...................................High end
Relæ 378.............................Wish I'd opened
Reynard 1019................................Breakfast
Russ & Daughters Cafe 1009...........Breakfast

TIM BUTLER
Eat Me
1/6 Soi Pipat 2, Bangkok
Once executive pastry chef of Aquavit in New York City and sometime chocolatier, he fuses international influences in the kitchen at Eat Me.
Asador Etxebarri 575.............Worth the travel
Beer Hima 282.............Regular neighborhood
Bo.Lan 287.............................Local favorite
Boon Pochana 280.........................Late night
Burnt Ends 329.................Wish I'd opened
Hong Seng Phochana 276.........Local favorite
Iniala Gourmet 276.........................Breakfast
Primo Restaurant 886...........Worth the travel
Street Stalls on Convent Road 282.....Bargain
Umi 289.....................................High end

ADAM BYATT
Trinity
4 The Polygon, London
Formerly at The Square, Byatt now has two London restaurants of his own: Trinity and Bistro Union.
Chez Bruce 429............Regular neighborhood
The Dairy 414..................................Breakfast
Elystan Street 412............................Late night
The Foyer & Reading Room 438.Local favorite

May the Fifteenth 414.....................Bargain
May the Fifteenth 414..Regular neighborhood
Peckham Bazaar 484....Regular neighborhood
Petersham Nurseries Café 426...........Regular neighborhood
Portland 473.........................Worth the travel
The River Café 417............................High end
Spuntino 454...............Regular neighborhood
Yakitori Hachibei 245...........Worth the travel

KIM BYUNG-JIN
Gaon
317 Dosan-DaeRo, Seoul
Kim started his career at Gaon and, after a brief interlude, recently returned there to take up the reins as head chef.
Bon Pi Yang 241...........Regular neighborhood
Dining in Space 237........................High end
Hanilkwan 234.........................Local favorite
Imbyeongju Sandong Kalguksu 240....Bargain
Joongang Haejang 234.....................Late night
Kikunoi Akasaka 247.............Worth the travel

GEORGE CALOMBARIS
The Press Club
72 Flinders Street, Melbourne
Probably best known for appearing as a judge on Australian MasterChef, his cooking is inspired by his Greek heritage. He opened his flagship restaurant, The Press Club, in 2006.
400 Gradi 140.........................Local favorite
Barbounaki 718...........Regular neighborhood
The Beatt Café 140.........................Breakfast
The Fat Duck 390...........................High end
Leo's Tacos Truck 820.......................Bargain
Siglo 145.....................................Late night
Ucuzcular Baharat 723..........Wish I'd opened

RICCARDO CAMANINI
Ristorante Lido 84
Corso Zanardelli 196, Gardone Riviera
After working with big hitters Raymond Blanc and Gualtiero Marchesi, Camanini serves local produce to compliment the classy setting, with panaromaic views of Lake Garda.
Alain Ducasse au Plaza Athénée 557.High end
Astar Coffee House 207...................Breakfast
Fäviken Magasinet 345.........Worth the travel
Locanda delle Grazie 660....................Bargain
Mission Chinese 835............Wish I'd opened
Pasticceria Veneto 659.....................Breakfast
Ristorante alla Borsa 672..........Local favorite
Trattoria Riolet 659......Regular neighborhood

GABRIELA CÁMARA
Cala
149 Fell Street, San Francisco
Self-taught Slow Food champion Bargellini founded Mexico City's beloved fish restaurant Contramar (1998) and San Francisco's Cala (2015), in partnership with Diane Kennedy.
20th Century Cafe 830..Regular neighborhood
Akiko´s 828.................................High end
Belmar La Gallinita Meat Market 834..Bargain
Benu 840..................................High end

Blue Bottle Coffee **840**.Regular neighborhood
Chez Panisse **789**......................Local favorite
Ferry Building Farmer's Market **829**....Regular
    neighborhood
Izakaya Rintaro **835**...................Local favorite
Mama Ji's **828**...Bargain
Nopa **828**...Late night
Plow **840**..Breakfast
Sean's Panorama **119**...........Wish I'd opened
Souvla **831**......................Regular neighborhood
Sushi Kyo **1083**..................Worth the travel
Tartine Manufactory **836**...........Local favorite
Tartine Manufactory **836**....................Regular
    neighborhood
Tosca Cafe **838**................................Late night
Toyose **838**..Late night
Trullo **481**......................Regular neighborhood
Turtle Tower **838**..............................Bargain
The Willows Inn **800**..............Worth the travel
Zuni Café **831**..............................Local favorite

VAL CANTU
Californios
3115 22nd Street, San Francisco

Texas-born, he spent time cooking in Mexico
City, before rolling out his Mexican tasting
menu.

Al's Place **834**..........................Local favorite
Art's Cafe **831**...............................Breakfast
Atelier Crenn **833**............................High end
Benu **840**...High end
Benu **840**......................................Local favorite
Breakfast at Tiffany's **839**.................Breakfast
Brown Sugar Kitchen **794**................Breakfast
Del Popolo **842**..................................Bargain
Del Popolo **842**...............Regular neighborhood
flour + water **834**.......Regular neighborhood
Ginza Kagari **257**.............Worth the travel
ijji **832**..Local favorite
Kagurazaka Ishikawa **272**.....Worth the travel
Lers Ros **841**.....................................Bargain
Liholiho Yacht Club **832**.Regular neighborhood
LocoL **796**.......................Wish I'd opened
Lord Stanley **837**.......................Local favorite
Lord Stanley **837**..........Regular neighborhood
Manresa **792**.....................................High end
Manresa **792**...................Worth the travel
Máximo Bistrot Local **1081**.....Worth the travel
Mister Jiu's **828**...........Regular neighborhood
Motze **836**...................Regular neighborhood
Nopa **828**...Late night
Outerlands **838**............................Breakfast
Pujol **1082**....................Worth the travel
Quince **830**.......................................High end
Quintonil **1082**.................Worth the travel
Saigon Sandwich **841**.......................Bargain
Saison **841**..High end
Shake Shack **910**..................Wish I'd opened
Souvla **831**......................Wish I'd opened
Taqueria Guadalajara **836**..............Late night
Toyose **838**...Bargain
Toyose **838**..Late night
Wako Sushi **831**..........................Local favorite
Yamo **837**..Bargain
Yamo **837**......................Regular neighborhood

JOAQUIN CARDOSO
Hotel Carlota
73 Río Amazonas, Mexico City

Following thirteen years in France with
Ducasse and Aizpitarte, he returned to
Mexico City to work with Olvera, before
heading up his own kitchen.

Aleli **1078**..Breakfast
AMAYA **1078**..................Regular neighborhood
Bósforo **1079**...................................Late night
Casa Oaxaca **1088**..............Worth the travel
Criollo **1088**......................Worth the travel
La Docena **1088**....................Local favorite
Fonda Margarita **1080**.........................Bargain
Máximo Bistrot **1081**.............Wish I'd opened
Nicos **1081**................................Local favorite
Panadería Rosetta **1082**................Breakfast
Pujol **1082**...High end
Quintonil **1082**................................High end
Rokai **1083**.....................Regular neighborhood
Le Tachinomi Desu **1083**................Late night
Taqueria Narvarte **1084**......................Bargain

ESTANISLAO CARENZO
Sudestada
Ponzano 85, Madrid

Building on the success of Sudestada in
Buenos Aires, he followed it up with an
outpost in Madrid, and now runs a successful
collection of venues in the Spanish capital.

Bacoa **595**.....................................Late night
Bar Brutal **594**......................Wish I'd opened
Bar Tomás **603**.....................................Bargain
Le Châteaubriand **564**...........Worth the travel
Cloudstreet Bakery **596**....................Regular
    neighborhood
Gresca **597**................................Local favorite
Morro Fi **598**.......................................Bargain
Norte **598**.....................Regular neighborhood
Pujol **1082**....................Worth the travel
Satans Coffee Corner **595**.............Breakfast
El Velódromo **600**..............................Late night
Via Veneto **603**..................................High end
Xemei **600**..................................Local favorite

ANDREA CARLSON
Burdock & Co.
2702 Main Street, Vancouver

Vancouver's Burdock & Co., Carlson's latest
venture, epitomizes her locavore, vegetable-
focused philosophy. She honed her skills at
Vancouver's Raincity Grill and Bishop's.

Bauhaus **757**.....................................High end
Blue Hill at Stone Barns **913**..Worth the travel
The Boxcar **760**................................Late night
Au Comptoir **757**...........................Breakfast
Edulis **768**......................Worth the travel
Eleven Madison Park **1037**.....Worth the travel
Hawksworth **756**................................High end
Pilgrimme **746**...........................Local favorite
La Quercia **758**...................Wish I'd opened
The Ramenman **761**.............................High end
Savary Island Pie Company **762**......Breakfast
Upstairs at Campagnolo **761**...........Late night
Upstairs at Campagnolo **761**..............Regular
    neighborhood

ANDREW CARMELLINI
Locanda Verde
377 Greenwich Street, New York City

Born in Ohio, Carmellini made his name in
New York as head chef at Café Boulud.
He is currently chef-partner at Locanda
Verde, The Dutch, and Lafayette.

L'Arpège **556**.......................Worth the Travel
Le Bernardin **1038**..............................High end
Daniel **1045**..High end
Gammeeok **1040**..............................Late night
Great NY Noodletown **1006**............Late night
Ippudo **1041**.......................................Bargain
Motorino **1023**...................................Bargain

PAUL CARMICHAEL
Momofuku Seiōbo
80 Pyrmont Street, Sydney

His résumé includes Aquavit, Asiate, and
Perla; he ran the kitchen of Momofuku Má
Pêche, before he moved to Sydney to become
the executive chef of Momofuku Seiōbo.

Automata **114**............................Local favorite
Le Châteaubriand **564**...........Worth the travel
Chat Thai **116**................................Late night
Estela **1010**....................................Breakfast
Frango's Charcoal Chicken **121**...........Late night
El Jannah **116**....................................Bargain
José Enrique **1074**................Wish I'd opened
Saint Peter **120**............Regular neighborhood

PHIL CARMICHAEL
Berners Tavern
10 Berners Street, London

Trained under Michel Roux Jr at La Gavroche,
he worked with Jason Atherton on the launch
of Maze, before partnering with him to open
Berners Tavern.

Brickwood Coffee and Bread **414**....Breakfast
The Dairy **414**............................Local favorite
Ethos **472**..Bargain
Four Seasons **449**............................Late night
The French Laundry **797**........Worth the travel
The Ledbury **423**...............................High end
Mamalan **463**...............Regular neighborhood
The NoMad Hotel **1044**..........Worth the travel
Roberta's **1017**......................Wish I'd opened

EDGAR CARO
Baru
3700 Magazine Street, New Orleans
Showcasing the regional food of Colombia at Baru, he was inspired to open Basin to present the very best local cuisine from New Orleans.
1000 Figs **978**...............Regular neighborhood
La Boca **976**......................................High end
La Boulangerie **797**.......................Breakfast
Bouligny Tavern **981**.......................Late night
Central City BBQ **977**............Wish I'd opened
Cochon Butcher **976**..................Local favorite
The Delachaise **989**........................Late night
Lilette **989**....................................High end
Maple Street Patisserie **975**...........Breakfast
Middendorf's **883**..............Worth the travel
Perino's Boiling Pot **884**..........Local favorite
Pho Cam Ly **990**..............................Bargain
Pho Cam Ly **990**...........Regular neighborhood
Sal & Judys **884**................Worth the travel
Shawarma On The Go **986**.................Bargain

MIGUEL CASTRO E SILVA
DeCastro Flores
Rua Marcos Portugal 1, Lisbon
A respected Portuguese culinary authority, his latest restaurant is DeCastro Flores.
Alma **616**................................Local favorite
Belcanto **617**................................High end
Bistro 100 Maneiras **614**...............Late night
Cabana da Estrela **620**.Regular neighborhood
Cristal 2 **620**................................Breakfast
Feitoria **616**...........................Local favorite
Gigi's **606**......................Worth the travel
Loco **621**.....................Regular neighborhood
Mini Bar Teatro **618**...............Wish I'd opened
Restaurante São Gabriel **606**...........High end
Tasca da Esquina **621**.........................Bargain
XL Restaurante **621**........................Late night

MATEU CASAÑAS
Compartir
Riera Sant Vicenç, Cadaqués
Longtime chef de cuisine at elBulli, Casañas left in 2012 to launch Compartir in Cadaqués with fellow elBulli chefs Oriol Castro and Eduard Xatruch. There most recent venture being Disfrutar, in 2016.
El Celler de Can Roca **583**.....Worth the travel
El Motel **583**..................Wish I'd opened
Las Golondrinas **585**..Regular neighbourhood
Miramar **585**................................High end
Raspa & Wine **585**.........................Late night
Restaurant Cal Campaner **585**.Local favourite
Si Us Plau **585**................................Breakfast

ORIOL CASTRO
Disfrutar
Villarroel 163, Barcelona
elBulli chef for over fifteen years with Mateu Casañas and Eduard Xatruch. When it closed, they opened the informal Compartir in Cadaqués, and have now opened Disfrutar, in 2016.
Bar Ket **596**.................................Breakfast
Bar Sport Torredembarra **586**............Bargain
Kak Koy **586**.......................Local favourite
Lasarte **597**................................High end
Noor **573**.......................Worth the travel
Quimet & Quimet **602**.....................Late night
Rocambolesc **602**.......Regular neighbourhood
StreetXO **590**....................Wish I'd opened

OLLE T. CELLTON
Babette
Roslagsgatan 6, Stockholm
His culinary career began in a Swedish pizzeria at the tender age of 12. He worked in London with Jeremy Lee before moving back to Scandinavia to head up PatéPaté in Copenhagen, and is now chef at Babette in Stockholm.
Bastard **346**...................Wish I'd opened
Bouchon **346**...................Worth the travel
Bouchon **346**....................Local favorite
Café Nizza **359**....................Local favorite
Cala **830**.......................Worth the travel
Camino **794**.....................Worth the travel
Chez Panisse **789**..............Wish I'd opened
Chez Panisse **789**............................High end
The Clove Club **487**..........................High end
Daniel Berlin Krog **349**...........Local favorite
Daniel Berlin Krog **349**...................High end
Da Delfina **670**.................Wish I'd opened
Falafel & Burgers **347**......................Bargain
Fäviken Magasinet **345**......................High end
Galinas Pizza **360**................Local favorite
Izakaya Rintaro **835**..............Worth the travel
Lyle's **488**...................Wish I'd opened
Mangal 2 **470**..............................Late night
Moro **468**....................Wish I'd opened
Noma **369**................................High end
Quo Vadis **453**................................High end
The River Café **417**..............Wish I'd opened
The River Café **417**...........................High end
Rochelle Canteen **486**.........Wish I'd opened
Roscioli **657**................................High end
Saltimporten Canteen **348**.........Local favorite
Le Servan **566**.................Wish I'd opened
Spring **492**................................High end
Spring **492**...................Wish I'd opened
Spring **492**...................Worth the travel
Spritmuseum **354**.........Regular neighborhood
St. John Bread & Wine **489**..............Breakfast
St. John Bread & Wine **489**....Wish I'd opened
Tartine & Tartine Manufactory **836**....Breakfast
Tayyabs **494**...............................Late night
Zuni Café **831**................................Late night
Zuni Café **831**.................Wish I'd opened

JOSEF CENTENO
Bäco Mercat
408 South Main Street, Los Angeles
Leaving Los Angeles's Lazy Ox Canteen in 2012, Centeno opened wildly popular flatbread sandwich outlet Bäco Mercat, followed by Bar Amá and Japanese-Italian Orsa & Winston.
Blanca **1015**.....................Worth the travel
Cosa Buona **816**..............................Bargain
Daikokuya **819**.............................Late night
Gjelina **824**........................Local favourite
Guisados **811**..................................Bargain
Hui Tou Xiang **796**.........................Breakfast
KaGaYa **814**................................High end
Kang Ho-dong Baekjeong **1041**.......Late night
NIGHT + MARKET Song **823**.............Regular neighbourhood
RiceBar **815**..................................Bargain
Rustic Canyon **822**................Local favourite
Sichuan Impression **797**.........Local favourite
Terroni Downtown LA **815**.............Breakfast

AMANDINE CHAIGNOT
Rosewood Hotel
252 High Holborn, London
Born and raised in Paris, she is an executive chef with expert French training.
Brawn **478**............Regular neighborhood
Broadway Market **473**.....................Bargain
Frenchie Covent Garden **433**.............Regular neighborhood
Gail's **449**................................Breakfast
Margot **473**................................Late night
Ottolenghi **481**............................Breakfast
Portland **473**....................Local favorite

PO-SANG CHAN
Shang Palace
201 Tun Hwa South Road, Taipei
With more than thirty years experience of culinary traditions in Singapore and Hong Kong, he is redefining Cantonese cuisine.
328 Katong Laksa **324**.............Local favorite
Crystal Jade Dining In **317**..............High end
Crystal Jade Golden Palace **325**........Wish I'd opened
Geylang Lor 9 Fresh Frog Porridge **323**.....Late night
No Signboard Seafood **323**..................Regular neighborhood
Soon Heng Rojak **335**.........................Bargain
Wee Nam Kee **326**............Worth the travel
Ya Kun Kaya Toast **318**...................Breakfast

RICARDO CHANETON
Restaurant Petrus
Pacific Place, Hong Kong
He was the chef de cuisine of the two-Michelin-starred Mirazur in France, which was founded by Mauro Colagreco, before he joined Restaurant Petrus.
Amber **220**................................High end
Amber **220**...................Regular neighborhood
Andres Carne de Res **1097**....Worth the travel
Betsutenjin Ramen **218**......................Bargain

Bills 115.....................................Breakfast
Brunch Club 220.............................Breakfast
Caprice 221.....................................High end
China Tang 221...............................High end
Gaddi's 214....................................High end
Ho Lee Fook 222.........Regular neighborhood
Ichiran Ramen 219.......................Late night
Kau Kee Restaurant 222....................Bargain
Kimberley Chinese Restaurant 214.........Local favorite
Kozy Okonomi-yaki Teppan-yaki 219 Late night
Kozy Okonomi-yaki Teppan-yaki 219...Regular neighborhood
Lamma Rainbow 227..............Local favorite
Single O 125...................................Breakfast
Tai Woo Restaurant 215.....................Bargain
Tung Po 227.........................Local favorite
VEA Restaurant 225..........................High end
Yardbird 229..................................Late night

DAVID CHANG
Momofuku Noodle Bar
171 1st Avenue, New York
Since opening the Momofuku Noodle Bar in 2004, Chang now has several New York City outposts, plus restaurants in Las Vegas, Sydney, Toronto, and Washington D.C..
Balthazar 1011.................Wish I'd opened
Benu 840.....................Worth the travel
Golden Century 111..........................Bargain
Great NY Noodletown 1006............Late Night
Locanda Verde 1014.......................Breakfast
Peasant 1011....................Local Favourite
Del Posto 1034.........Regular Neighbourhood
Sushi Sawada 259................Worth the travel

ERCHEN CHANG
Bao
53 Lexington Street
Founder, with partner Shing Tat Chung and his sister Wait Ting, of London's cult Taiwanese restaurant chain, Bao, she plans to open a more formal venue, Xu, in spring 2018.
40 Maltby Street 460....Regular neighborhood
The Araki 436...............................High end
Australia Dairy Company 212.Wish I'd opened
Black Axe Mangal 480....................Breakfast
Hoppers 450.......................Local favorite
Joe Allen 434.................................Late night
Miyamasou 250.................Worth the travel
Silk Road 465...................................Bargain

JOANNE CHANG
Myers + Chang
1145 Washington Street, Boston
Harvard-graduate Chang swapped management consultancy for the heat of the kitchen, working at New York's Payard Patisserie and Boston's Mistral before launching Flour bakery and café chain in 2000.
Sam's 892....................Regular neighborhood
Sorellina 892.................Wish I'd opened
Taiwan Cafe 892..............................Bargain
Winsor Dim Sum Cafe 893..............Breakfast
o ya 891.......................................High end

SANDIA CHANG
Bubbledogs
70 Charlotte Street, London
Before opening Bubbledogs with her husband, whom she met while working at Noma, she was assistant manager for Marcus Wareing at The Berkeley.
Bear + Wolf 492............................Breakfast
Black Axe Mangal 480.................Local favorite
Jen Café 450....................................Bargain
Koya Bar 450................Regular neighborhood
The Ledbury 423...............................High end
Maaemo 344...................Worth the travel
P. Franco 468.................Wish I'd opened
The Spence Bakery 491 Regular neighborhood
Tufnell Park Kebab & Fish Bar 493...Late night
Xi'an Impression 477....Regular neighborhood

TIMOTHY CHARLES
Fogo Island Inn
210 Main Road, Joe Batt's Arm, Fogo Island
Timothy Charles was born and raised in the small fishing village of Prospect, Nova Scotia, Canada. He is the Executive Sous Chef at the Fogo Island Inn, Newfoundland.
Adelaide Oyster House 750.....Local favourite
Aramburu 1125.................Worth the travel
Dar Roval 769...............................Late night
Blue on Water 750................Local favourite
Bonavista Social Club 749.....Wish I'd opened
Cinched Bistro 750..............Local favourite
The Cod Jigger 749....Regular neighbourhood
The Costal Café 751.......................Breakfast
Eleven Madison Park 1037...............High End
Florería Atlántico 1130..........Worth the travel
Growlers 750.............Regular neighbourhood
Mallard Cottage 750.............Local favourite
Mohamed Ali 751...........................Bargain
Nicole's Café 750.......Regular neighbourhood
Pray Tell 766.................................Late night
Raymonds 751.....................Local favourite
Tony's 751.......................................Bargain

SVEN CHARTIER
Saturne
17 Rue Notre-Dame des Victoires, Paris
French with Swedish roots, Chartier creates clean Nordic-style flavors at Saturne, in the Bourse, Paris.
Clown Bar 564.............................Late night
Kunitoraya II 550...........................Bargain
Septime 566...................Local favorite
Tsukizi 555.................Regular neighborhood

VICKY CHENG
VEA Restaurant and Lounge
198 Wellington Street, Hong Kong
Born in Hong Kong and raised under Western influences, his cooking style reflects both his French training and his Asian roots.
Amber 220.....................................High end
Le Coquillage 538.........................Breakfast
DEN 268.......................Worth the travel
Din Tai Fung 218.............Wish I'd opened
Hajime Restaurant 251.........Worth the travel
Islam Food 212.................................Bargain

Kam Fung Cafe 230.........................Breakfast
Kozy Okonomi-yaki Teppan-yaki 219.........Late night
Se Wong Sun 230.........Regular neighborhood
Wah Lam Noodle Restaurant 231....Late night
Yat lok 226.............................Local favorite

JOSÉ CHESA
Chesa
2218 North East Broadway Street, Portland
He trained in Arpege and Fleur-de-Sel, and now owns three restaurants in Portland, including the city's first xurreria (a venue serving churros, more traditionally a street stand).
The Big Egg 860.............................Breakfast
Departure 850...........Regular neighborhood
Du Kuh Bee 800..........Regular neighborhood
Grassa 851.................Regular neighborhood
Imperial 853..................................Breakfast
Sweedeedee 859..........................Breakfast

ANDRÉ CHIANG
Restaurant André
41 Bukit Pasoh Road, Singapore
Taiwan-born Chiang cooked at Jaan par André in Singapore's Swissotel, before opening Restaurant André in a 1920s townhouse.
Bincho 317....................................Breakfast
Hachi 332.....................Regular neighborhood
Imperial Treasure Shanghai 328.....Regular neighborhood
Marché Solli 344...................Worth the travel
The Populus Café 331.....................Breakfast
Sasa Sushi 469....................Worth the travel

CARMELO CHIARAMONTE
Born in Modica, Sicilian chef Chiaramonte, former executive chef at restaurant Il Cuciniere in Catania, now consults as the Cuciniere Errante (Nomadic Chef).
Accursio 666.....................Local favorite
Colline Ciociare 655..............Worth the travel
Emporio Armani Ristorante 661........High end
mm !! Trattoria 666.....Regular neighborhood
Pasticceria Russo 666....................Breakfast
La Pineta 669.................Wish I'd opened
Ristorante Millefoglie 666.............Breakfast
Trattoria La Rusticana 667..................Bargain

MANGO TSANG CHIU LIT
Ming Court
555 Shanghai Street, Hong Kong
With forty years of experience in Hong Kong's hotels and Michelin-starred restaurants, Chef Mango took the reins at prestigious Ming Court in 2013.
Kau Kee Restaurant 222...Regular neighborhood
Mok's Beef Dynasty Hotpot 212.Local favorite
The Place 213...................................High end

EUNMI CHOI
Gotgan
28-1 Yeouido-dong, Seoul
She began her culinary career at Yongsusan and, after a stint in Paris, she is now head chef of Seoul's two-Michelin-starred Gotgan.

Delmonico's 1006		Worth the travel
Homuran 234		Regular neighborhood
Jungsik Dang 235		High end
Mirak Chicken 237		Late night
Robot Gimbap 237		Bargain
Seongbuk-dong Dak Baeksuk Jip 241		
		Breakfast
Shui Kee 224		Breakfast
Volpino Ristorante 236		Regular neighborhood
Yongsusan 238		Local favorite

MAY CHOW
Little Bao
66 Staunton Street, Hong Kong
Canadian born, Chow honed her skills at celebrated establishments Bo Innovation and Yardbird. After the success of Little Bao in Hong Kong, she has opened a second branch in Bangkok.

As You Like Restaurant 229		Late night
Belon 220		High end
The Chairman 221		Local favorite
The Chairman 221		Wish I'd opened
Dim Sum Square 228		Breakfast
Jesse 196		Worth the travel
Siu Choi Wong 213		Bargain
Yat Lok 226		Regular neighborhood

SAMANTHA & SAMUEL CLARK
Moro
34–36 Exmouth Market, London
The husband-and-wife team who opened the Moorish-influenced Moro in 1997. Next was Morito, a bijou tapas bar next door, followed by Morito Hackney Road in 2016.

El Campero 572		Worth the travel
Dock Kitchen 417		Regular neighbourhood
Koya Bar 451		Bargain
The Ledbury 423		High end
The River Café 417		Wish I'd opened
Sömine 471		Late night
St. John Bread & Wine 489		Breakfast
Towpath Café 479		Local favourite

CARL CLARKE
Chick 'n' Sours
1A Earlham Street, London
Former DJ and army chef, this pop-up pro earned his stripes cooking with Marco Pierre White and Simon Rogan before finding a permanent home for Chick 'n' Sours.

Arthur's 470		Breakfast
Istanbul Restaurant 490		Late night
The Ivy 434		High end
Joy Luck Restaurant 450		Regular neighborhood
Koya Bar 451		Breakfast
Lyle's 488		High end
Manos Grill 417		Local favorite
P. Franco 468		High end

Smoking Goat 454		Wish I'd opened
The Sportsman Club 406		Local favorite
Tonkotsu 454		Bargain
Woody Grill 418		Late night
Xi'an Impression 477		Regular neighborhood

BEAU CLUGSTON
Le 6 Paul Bert
6 Rue Paul Bert, Paris
Born in Australia and now running a Parisian bistro, his impressive résumé includes stints at Tetsuya, Noma, and Gordon Ramsay in London.

Amarante 566		Bargain
L'Arpège 556		High end
L'Arpège 556		Worth the travel
Candelaria 553		Late night
Clamato 564		Local favorite
Benedict Castel 569		Breakfast
Septime La Cave 566		Wish I'd opened
Ten Belles 563		Breakfast
Le Verre Volé 563		Regular neighborhood

BEL COELHO
Clandestino
Rua Medeiros de Albuquerque, São Paulo
Alex Atala protégé and São Paulo native, Coelho studied at the prestigious Culinary Institute of America before returning to Brazil to open Dui. He is now consulting and exploring Brazil.

Bar da Dona Onça 1112		Local favorite
Coffee Lab 1115		Breakfast
Maní 1114		High end
Martin Fierro 1118		Bargain
Mocotó 1118		Bargain
Tanuki Sushi 1118		Local favorite
Viradas do Largo 1104		Worth the travel

JUSTIN COGLEY
Aubergine
Monte Verde at 7th Street, Carmel-by-the-Sea
Professional figure skater turned award-winning chef, Cogley worked for his mentor Charlie Trotter for five years before taking the reins at the seafood restaurant Aubergine in Carmel, California in 2011.

Big Sur Bakery 790		Regular neighborhood
Carmel Belle 791		Breakfast
Compagno's Market and Deli 793		Bargain
Cultura 790		Late night
Sardine Factory 793		Local favorite
Sushi-ya 259		Worth the travel

MAURO COLAGRECO
Mirazur
30 Avenue Aristide Briand, Menton
This Argentina-born protégé of Passard and the late Loiseau opened the handsome Côte d'Azur-based Mirazur in 2006.

La Guerite 542		Local Favorite
Parador La Huella 1119		Wish I'd opened
Louix XV 547		High end
Manresa 792		Worth the travel
Marco Ristorante 545		Regular neighborhood
Monte-Carlo Bay Hotel 547		Breakfast
September Café 204		Breakfast

Sini Restaurant 545		Bargain
Sugar Pea 204		Breakfast
La Vecchia Ostaia 658		Regular neighborhood

CHRIS COLEMAN
Stoke Charlotte
100 West Trade Street, Charlotte
Born and raised in the northwest corner of Charlotte's Mountain Island Lake community, he flies the flag for seasonal American cooking, making the most of local produce.

Alexander Michael's 914		Regular neighborhood
The Diamond 914		Late night
Earl's Grocery 914		Bargain
Elizabeth's 974		Breakfast
Heritage Food & Drink 916		Local favorite
Heritage Food & Drink 916		Wish I'd opened
Kindred 915		Local favorite
Martha Lou's Kitchen 1054		Worth the travel
Miguel's 915		Regular neighborhood
Shuffletown Grill 915		Breakfast
Stagioni 915		High end

LACHLAN COLWILL
Hentley Farm Restaurant
Corner Gerald Roberts & Jenke Road, Barossa Valley
He has worked in Salters and 1918. He was head chef at the Adelaide institution The Manse before returning to his roots in Barossa.

Fino Seppeltsfield 95		Regular neighborhood
Golden Boy 90		Regular neighborhood
The Lost Loaf 91		Breakfast
Supernormal 145		Regular neighborhood

NINA COMPTON
Compère Lapin
535 Tchoupitoulas Street, New Orleans
Culinary ambassador for St Lucia, she had more than fifteen years of experience before opening her first solo restaurant, based at the Old No 77 Hotel & Chandlery in the Warehouse District.

Cochon Butcher 976		Local favorite
Commander's Palace 982		High end
Domilise's Po-Boy and Bar 989		Bargain
Domilise's Po-Boy and Bar 989		Regular neighborhood
Emeril's Delmonico 977		Local favorite
Gene's Po-Boys 983		Late night
Macchialina 874		Worth the travel
Shaya 990		Regular neighborhood
Shaya 990		Wish I'd opened
Willa Jean 977		Breakfast

KYLE CONNAUGHTON
SingleThread
131 North Street, Healdsburg
Head chef of The Fat Duck for five years, he has a wealth of knowledge around culinary science and experimental cuisine.

Alinea 957		Worth the travel
Benu 840		Wish I'd opened
Bergamot Alley 791		Late night
Bras 541		Worth the travel

L'Effervescence 263..............Worth the travel
The Fat Duck 390..............Worth the travel
Hyotei 249..............Worth the travel
Kikunoi 247..............Worth the travel
El Molino Central 797.....................Bargain
Mugaritz 576..............Worth the travel
Next 967..............Worth the travel
Nihonryori RyuGin 265..........Worth the travel
The Progress 842.....................High end
Shed 792.....................Breakfast
Shed 792.....................Local favorite
Shed 792.....................Regular neighborhood
Soujiki Nakahigashi 250..........Worth the travel
Sukiyabashi Jiro 259..............Worth the travel
Sushi Saito 267..............Worth the travel
Sushi Sawada 259..............Worth the travel
Sushi Tokami 259..............Worth the travel

JOSÉ CORDEIRO
Restaurante Blini
Rua General Torres 344, Porto

Winning recognition at Feitoria with creative interpretations of traditional Portuguese dishes, Angola-born Cordeiro opened his eponymous restaurant in 2013, followed by seafood-focused Restaurante Blini in 2016.

Alma 616.....................Wish I'd opened
Bagos Chiado Restaurante 616.........High end
Confeitaria Tavi 608.....................Breakfast
Cup of Joe 607.....................Breakfast
Marisqueira Marujo 607.....................Bargain
Restaurante Casa Inês 608.....................Regular neighborhood
Restaurante Casa Inês 608.......Local favorite
Restaurante Pajú 608.....................Late night
Restaurante POTE 606.....................Late night
Restaurante POTE 606..............Local favorite
Restaurante POTE 606..............Worth the travel
Restaurante Sao Valentim 608.....................Regular neighborhood
Wish Restaurante & Sushi 608.........High end

IGLES CORELLI
Ristorante Atman
Via Borghetto 1, Spicchio

Author, teacher, and chef recognized for his avant-garde approach to Italian cuisine, which sees him merge different cuisines and flavors.

Bo Innovation 230..............Worth the travel
Borgo San Jacopo 667..............Local favorite
Il Canniccio 669.....................Late night
Capitan Piadina 665.....................Bargain
Casa Vissani 670.....................High end
Colline Ciociare 655.....................High end
Combal.Zero 664.....................Wish I'd opened
Infinity LAB Pasticceria 665..............Breakfast
Pasticceria Gualandi 648..............Breakfast
Pesce Briaco 669.........Regular neighborhood
Ristorante Giglio 669....Regular neighborhood

RAÚL CORREA
Zest
2 Tartak Street, San Juan

He has been in the kitchen for more than two decades. He began his culinary journey at Ristorante Tuscany's, before opening

ComeDor in the Miramar area.

1919 Restaurant 1072.....................High end
La Alcapurria Quemá 1074.....................Bargain
Asere Cubano 1072......Regular neighborhood
Avocado 1072.....................Late night
Babu Ji 1022..............Worth the travel
Le Bernadin 1038..............Worth the travel
Bistro Café 1073.....................Breakfast
En Boga 1073.....................Local favorite
La Estación 1071..........Regular neighborhood
El Hamburger 1073..............Wish I'd opened
La Jaquita Baya 1073..............Local favorite
Orujo Taller de Gastronomía 1071....Late night
Pikayo 1074.....................High end
Pikayo 1074.....................Wish I'd opened
La Rosa Inglesa 1072.....................Breakfast

RICHARD CORRIGAN
Corrigan's Mayfair
28 Upper Grosvenor Street, London

Chef-owner of Corrigan Restaurants, which operates Bentley's Oyster Bar & Grill and Corrigan's Mayfair in London, he champions Irish and British food.

L'Arpège 556.....................Wish I'd opened
Banner's 469.....................Breakfast
Elystan Street 412.....................Local favorite
Forest Avenue 505..............Worth the travel
Le Gavroche 438.....................High end
Homeslice 433.....................Late night
Perilla 491.....................Regular neighborhood
Prufrock Coffee 471......Regular neighborhood
Shake Shack 436.....................Bargain
Trinity Restaurant 415..Regular neighborhood

CHRIS COSENTINO
Cockscomb
564 Fourth Street, San Francisco

Cosentino, aka @OffalChris, a leading expert in offal cookery, took up an executive-chef position at San Francisco's Incanto in 2003, before opening Cockscomb in 2016.

Izakaya Sozai 832.........Regular neighborhood
Yummy Yummy 832......Regular neighborhood

DANIEL COSTA
Corso 32
10345 Jasper Avenue, Edmonton

The Canadian chef, following a spell in private catering, paid homage to his Italian heritage, opening thirty-four-seat Corso 32 in 2010 and expanding with a spuntini bar and a trattoria.

Baijiu Bar 743.....................Late night
Bar Clementine 743.....................Late night
Café Linnea 743.....................Breakfast
Duchess Bake Shop 744.....................Breakfast
Hosteria Giusti 649..............Wish I'd opened
Izakaya Tomo 744.....................Late night
Leva 744.....................Regular neighborhood
The Marc 745.....................Local favorite
Mayday Dogs 744.....................Bargain
North 53 744.....................Late night
Del Posto 1034.....................High end
Quince 830.....................High end
Red Ox Inn 744.....................High end
Red Ox Inn 744.....................Local favorite

RGE RD 745.....................Local favorite
Roscioli 653.....................Worth the travel
Shanghai 456 745.....................Bargain
Tanh Tanh 745.....................Bargain
Three Boars 745.....................Late night
Tres Carnales Taqueria 746.....................Regular neighborhood

RAFA COSTA E SILVA
Lasai
Rua Conde de Irajá 191, Rio de Janeiro

After spells in New York and Spain, Costa e Silva returned to Brazil to open his own kitchen, partially stocked by his two personal allotments.

Aconchego Carioca 1106...........Local favorite
Azumi 1106.....................Regular neighborhood
Comuna 1107.....................Late night
D.O.M Restaurante 1114........Worth the travel
Escondidinho 1107.....................Bargain
Galeto Sat's 1108.....................Late night
Olympe 1109.....................:High end
Oro 1109.....................High end
The Slow Bakery 1109.....................Breakfast
Tan Tan Noodle Bar 1116.......Wish I'd opened
Tuju 1116.....................Worth the travel

MATTHEW CRABBE
Two Rooms
3-11-7 Kita-Aoyama, Tokyo

Worked in Sydney at Tetsuya's, then in London, the US, and Mexico before moving to Tokyo where he is chef-director of Two Rooms and Ruby Jack's Steakhouse.

Akanoren 262.....................Late night
Akanoren 262.....................Regular neighborhood
La Bombance 262.....................Late night
Brown's Court Bakery 1051............Breakfast
Rakushokushu Maru 270.....................Late night
Sawamura Bakery 266.....................Breakfast
Sudachi 266.....................Local favorite
Tajima Soba 267.........Regular neighborhood
Toriyoshi Nishi Azabu Yakitori 267....Regular neighborhood
Ushigoro 267.........Regular neighborhood
Yugentei Nishiazabu 268..............Late night

ENRICO CRIPPA
Piazza Duomo
Piazza Risorgimento 4, Alba

His stellar experience spans stints with Michel Bras, Ferran Adria, and Gualtiero Marchesi. In 2012 his restaurant gained its third Michelin star.

Blue Hill at Stone Barns 913..Wish I'd opened
Flocons de Sel 536..............Worth the travel
Gusto Madre 663.....................Bargain
OPES 663.....................Breakfast
La Repubblica Di Perno 664..............Regular neighborhood
Super Loco 332.....................Breakfast
Trattoria La Coccinella 664.........Local favorite
Uliassi 663.....................High end

TOM CUNANAN
Bad Saint
3226 11th Street Northwest, Washington DC
With dishes in this tiny space served family-style, Cunanan is bringing authentic Filipino food and cocktails to DC.

2Amys **864**	Regular neighborhood
Copycat Co. **865**	Late night
Le Diplomate **866**	Breakfast
Fiola Mare **867**	High end
Kiln **451**	Wish I'd opened
Ledo Pizza **867**	Local favorite
Meats & Foods **868**	Bargain
Pho Viet **869**	Regular neighborhood
Tacombi **1037**	Worth the travel

PAUL CUNNINGHAM
Henne Kirkeby Kro
Strandvejen 234, Henne
Head chef at Henne Kirkeby Kro, the renowned restaurant-with-rooms on Jutland's wild West Coast, Essex-born Cunningham was his previous restaurant, The Paul in Copenhagen, a Michelin star.

Atelier September **370**	Breakfast
Atelier September **370**	Local favorite
Les Bacchanales **546**	Worth the travel
Bæst **376**	Late night
The Coffee Factory **371**	Breakfast
Bistro Boheme **370**	Late night
Bistro Boheme **370**	Regular neighborhood
Cockscomb **841**	Worth the travel
Fäviken Magasinet **345**	Worth the travel
The French Laundry **797**	Worth the travel
Geist **372**	Late night
Henne **629**	Wish I'd opened
Ida Davidsen **373**	Regular neighborhood
In Situ **841**	Worth the travel
Issa **380**	Bargain
Jagger **380**	Late night
Jagger **380**	Regular neighborhood
Jagger **380**	Wish I'd opened
juicyBurger **380**	Regular neighborhood
Kong Hans Kælder **373**	High end
Lagkagehuset **362**	Breakfast
Marchal at Hotel d'Angleterre **369**	High end
Noma **369**	High end
Palægade **374**	Regular neighborhood
Paté Paté **381**	Breakfast
Paté Paté **381**	Regular neighborhood
SuperMarco **381**	Breakfast
Tivolihallen **375**	Regular neighborhood

ANDREAS DAHLBERG
Bastard
Mäster Johansgatan 11, Malmö
The head chef and owner of Bastard in Malmö, who also goes by the rock 'n' roll moniker of Andy Bastard.

Casual Streetfood **347**	Regular neighborhood
Daniel Berlin Krog **349**	Local favorite
Falafel & Burgers **347**	Bargain
Kvarteret Åkern **348**	Regular neighborhood
Pink Head Noodle Bar **348**	Late Night
Relæ **378**	High End
Solde Kaffebar **349**	Breakfast

State Bird Provisions **832**	Worth the travel
Tartine Manufactory **836**	Wish I'd opened

LUKE DALE-ROBERTS
The Test Kitchen
375 Albert Road, Cape Town
British-born Dale-Roberts worked in Asia before moving to South Africa where he now owns The Test Kitchen and The Pot Luck Club.

Ash Restaurant **730**	Local favorite
The Avenue Restaurant & Grill **732**	Bargain
Chefs Warehouse & Canteen **731**	Local favorite
Chefs Warehouse at Beau Constantia **731**	Worth the travel
The Clove Club **487**	Worth the travel
Four & Twenty Café **734**	Breakfast
Foxcroft **733**	Regular neighborhood
Jonkershuis Restaurant **733**	Breakfast
Nobu **734**	High end
The Shortmarket Club **731**	Breakfast
The Sneaky Sausage **732**	Late night
A Tavola **732**	Regular neighborhood
La Tête **731**	Wish I'd opened

HÉLÈNE DARROZE
Hélène Darroze at the Connaught
Carlos Place, London
Previously Alain Ducasse's right-hand woman, as the fourth in a line of chefs she has an extensive French gourmet heritage.

L'Arpège **556**	Worth the travel
Bar Boulud **418**	Late night
Bocca di Lupo **445**	Bargain
The Clove Club **487**	High end
The Clove Club **487**	Regular neighborhood
Eleven Madison Park **1037**	Wish I'd opened
The Foyer & Reading Room **458**	Regular neighborhood
Frenchie Covent Garden **433**	Regular neighborhood
Kitty Fisher's **439**	Local favorite
The Ledbury **423**	High end
Margot **435**	Regular neighborhood
Mount Street Deli **440**	Breakfast
ROKA **442**	Late night
Umu **442**	Regular neighborhood

CHANTEL DARTNALL
Restaurant Mosaic
Crocodile River Valley, Pretoria
Trained at the Prue Leith Chef's Academy, Dartnall's innovative take on Botanic Cuisine has made the Restaurant Mosaic one of South Africa's top tables.

Akelarre **578**	Worth the travel
L'Arnsbourg **539**	Wish I'd opened
L'Astrance **568**	High end
Le Grand Café Capucines **562**	Wish I'd opened
La Madeleine Restaurant **730**	Regular neighborhood
Pur' – Jean-François Rouquette **552**	Worth the travel
Pure Café **730**	Breakfast
Restaurant at Waterkloof **734**	Local favorite

RUAIRÍ DE BLACAM
Inis Meáin Restaurant
Inis Meáin, Aran Islands
This Irish chef worked in Dublin, Italy, Germany, and France before returning home.

L'Assiette **567**	High end
Balthazar **1011**	Wish I'd opened
Bebel **660**	Bargain
Le Castiglione Café **550**	Breakfast
FOgO **597**	Regular neighborhood
Kirwans Lane Restaurant **507**	Regular neighborhood
Morito **479**	Regular neighborhood
Ristorante Mario e Mercedes **670**	Worth the travel
Schumann's **624**	Late night

GERT DE MANGELEER
Hertog Jan
Loppemsestraat 52, Zedelgem
Runs Hertog Jan with sommelier Joachim Boudens, whom he met while working at Molentje in the Netherlands.

Bosrand **529**	Bargain
DEN **268**	Worth the travel
Florilège **269**	Wish I'd opened
Frantzén **355**	Worth the travel
Gastrobar Hubert **529**	Regular neighborhood
Le Pain Quotidien **119**	Breakfast
Rock Fort **529**	Regular neighborhood
Siphon **529**	Local favorite
Yardbird **229**	Late night
Zuma **419**	High end

SANG-HOON DEGEIMBRE
L'Air du Temps
2 Rue de la Croix Monet, Liernu
The Korean-Belgian chef, who opened L'Air du Temps in Namur, Wallonia, where he grew up, in 1997 is praised for using super-local produce.

Le 1900 **528**	Bargain
L'Amandier **528**	Local favorite
L'Astrance **568**	High end
A La Bécasse **522**	Late night
Blue Hill at Stone Barns **913**	Wish I'd opened
La Fabrique Chatelain **523**	Breakfast
Fäviken Magasinet **345**	Worth the travel
La Friterie de la Barrière **523**	Late night
Geranium **378**	High end
La Grappe d'Or **528**	Local favorite
Gustu **1101**	Worth the travel
Henne Kirkeby Kro **365**	Wish I'd opened
Kamo **523**	Regular neighborhood
Maison Antoine **524**	Late night
Maru Brussels **524**	Regular neighborhood
La Menuiserie **528**	Local favorite
Le Pain Quotidien **524**	Breakfast
Quique Dacosta **591**	High end
Restaurant André **331**	Worth the travel

PETE DENHART
The Stoke House
81 Buckingham Palace Road, London

He earned his stripes in kitchens across London and is championing the traditional British Carvery as head chef at The Stoke House.

Le Bab 443	Regular neighborhood
Le Bab 443	Worth the travel
Blacklock 445	Wish I'd opened
Chick 'n' Sours 432	Regular neighborhood
Dishoom 448	Breakfast
Hoppers 450	Local favorite
Hoppers 450	Regular neighborhood
Koya Bar 451	Bargain
Smokestak 487	Late night
Zuma 419	High end

ŞEMSA DENIZSEL
Kantin
Akkavak Sokağı 30, Istanbul

Opened Kantin, a restaurant that focuses on serving healthy, seasonal, Turkish soul food in Istanbul in 2000.

L'Arcangelo 655	Worth the travel
Bay Nihat Lale Restoran 719	Worth the travel
Kizilkayalar 723	Late night
Lale İskembecisi 722	Late night
Meşhur Filibe Köftecisi 723	Bargain
Metanet Lokantasi 719	Worth the travel
Mikla 722	High end
Roscioli 657	Worth the travel
St. John Bar and Restaurant 471	Worth the travel

GREG DENTON & GABRIELLE QUIÑÓNEZ DENTON
Ox Restaurant
2225 Northeast Martin Luther King Jr Boulevard, Portland

Greg and his wife and fellow chef Gabrielle, co-owners of Portland's Argentine grill-inspired Ox Restaurant and bold, small-plate style SuperBite, met in 1999, cooking at Hiro Sone's Michelin-starred Terra.

Clown Bar 564	Worth the travel
The Country Cat 860	Breakfast
Fuller's Coffee Shop 851	Breakfast
Hat Yai 852	Regular neighborhood
La Moule 854	Late night
Nong's Khao Man Gai 856	Local favorite
Pineapple and Pearls 870	High end
Pineapple and Pearls 870	Wish I'd opened
Swiss Hibiscus 859	Regular neighborhood
Xi'an Famous Foods 1025	Bargain

KOBE DESRAMAULTS
Chambre Séparée
Keizer Karelstraat 1 - 9000, Ghent

After running restaurant In De Wulf for 13 years, Kobe opened a new ambitious restaurant "chambre séparée". A small counterseat restaurant, where a maximum of 16 guests are seated around an open kitchen and where he always cooks personally. Kobe is also co-owner of restaurant and bakery De Superette in Ghent.

Abooov Adanaci 526	Late night
In De Zon 527	Regular neighbourhood
Martino 526	Late night
Het Moment 526	Breakfast

BEN DEVLIN
Paper Daisy
21 Cypress Crescent, Cabarita Beach

Previously he worked at Noma and Brisbane's Esquire before heading up Paper Daisy's kitchen, which is built around a bespoke wood fired grill.

100 Mile Table 83	Local favorite
Attica 151	High end
Brae 101	High end
Eddie's Grub House 86	Bargain
Fleet 82	Local favorite
Fleet 82	Regular neighborhood
Funny Funny 131	Late night
Gauge 131	Breakfast
Harvest Newrybar 84	Breakfast
Izakaya Potts 84	Regular neighborhood
Milk and Honey 84	Bargain
Relæ 378	Wish I'd opened
Restaurant Hubert 112	Late night
Saint Peter 120	Wish I'd opened
Saint Peter 120	Worth the travel
Wildair 1010	Worth the travel

EDSON DIAZ-FUENTES
Santo Remedio

Mexican chef, he trained under Alejandro Ruiz before moving to London where, in its first incarnation, Santo Remedias was a pop-up in 2013.

José Tapas Bar 460	Regular neighborhood

XABIER DÍEZ ESTEIBAR
Xarma Jatetxea
Avenida de Tolosa 123, San Sebastián

A San Sebastián native, heavily influenced by his time at Arzak who has since gone on to create hugely inventive plates at Xarma.

Agorregi 578	Bargain
Arzak 579	High end
Château de Brindos 540	Worth the travel
A Fuego Negro 578	Late night
Martín Berasategui 577	Local favorite
Mirador de Ulía 577	Regular neighborhood
Pasteleria Gaztelo 581	Breakfast
La Rampa 581	Wish I'd opened

ANGELA DIMAYUGA
Mission Chinese Food
171 East Broadway, New York City

Executive chef at Mission Chinese Food since 2012, the restaurant has gained two Michelin stars under her watch.

Admiralgade 26 370	Worth the travel
Bar Pitti 1025	Local favorite
The Four Horsemen 1016	Wish I'd opened
Hasaki 1022	Regular neighborhood
The Kunjip 1042	Late night
Ootoya 1035	Bargain
Russ & Daughters Cafe 1009	Breakfast
Sushi Yasuda 1043	High end

VLADISLAV DJATŠUK
Mon Repos
Narva maantee 92, Tallin

Executive chef at Tallinn's Hotel Telegraaf, Djatšuk has reopened Mon Repos, based in a refurbished summer villa with views of Kadriorg Park and Castle.

Chedi 697	Wish I'd opened
Cru 697	Wish I'd opened
Estonian Burger Factory 697	Late night
Gianni 697	Bargain
Gianni 697	High end
Gianni 697	Local favorite
Josephine 696	Breakfast
Kaks Kokka 697	Bargain
Leib Resto ja Aed 698	Late night
Noa Chefs Hall 698	Local favorite
Ö Restaurant 698	High end
Ö restaurant 698	Regular neighborhood
Ööbiku Gastronomy Farm 696	Worth the travel
Põhjaka mõis 696	Worth the travel

MARC DJOZLIJA
Wright & Company
1500 Woodward, Detroit

He worked for the Wolfgang Puck Group for the last 20 years, and was the executive chef at both Steak and Pizzeria & Cucina in the MGM Grand Detroit, before joining Wright & Company.

El Asador 904	Bargain
Broken Spanish 813	Worth the travel
Bucharest Grill 903	Bargain
Duly's Place 904	Late night
Honest John's 904	Late night
Hygrade Deli 904	Breakfast
Lafayette Coney Island 904	Local favorite
The Ledbury 423	Worth the travel
London Chop House 905	High end
Marlow & Sons 1018	Breakfast
Nemo's 905	Wish I'd opened
Selden Standard 906	High end
Shangri-La Midtown 906	Regular neighborhood
Slows Bar BQ 907	Regular neighborhood
Supino Pizzeria 907	Local favorite
Tim Raue 631	Worth the travel

MARK DOBBIE
Som Saa
43a Commercial Street, London
Following an inspiring trip to Thailand, and a stint working at Nahm while it was in London, he was one of a trio to open Som Saa as a pop-up before it opened its doors in Spitalfields.

Las Americas 463	Bargain
Las Americas 463	Regular neighborhood
Asmara Restaurant 463	Regular neighborhood
Bo.Lan 287	Worth the travel
Brasserie Zédel 446	Late night
Carioca 463	Regular neighborhood
The Goring Dining Room 456	Local favorite
Lam Zhou Handmade Noodle 1008	Bargain
Lyle's 488	High end
Mission Chinese 1008	Wish I'd opened
Salon 464	Regular neighborhood
Spicy Village 1009	Bargain
The Sportsman 400	High end
St. John Bread & Wine	Breakfast

CARY DOCHERTY
Little Social
5 Pollen Street, London
Among others, he cooked at London's Maze, Zuma, and Indigo before taking on the role of head chef at Jason Atherton's Little Social.

A. Wong 428	Regular neighborhood
Bleeker Victoria 428	Bargain
The Clove Club 487	Local favorite
Goodman 439	Late night
Hunan 411	Regular neighborhood
The Ivy Market Grill 434	Wish I'd opened
Koya Bar 451	Breakfast
The Pear Tree 417	Breakfast
Restaurant Gordon Ramsay 412	High end
Sushi Saito 267	Worth the travel
Yauatcha Soho 455	Regular neighborhood

SCOTT DOLICH
Park Kitchen
422 NW 8th Avenue, Portland
Starting out as a butcher, he opened The Park Kitchen in 2003, where he now sources the best local ingredients and trains great cooks.

Boke Bowl West 848	Bargain
Cosme 1036	Worth the travel
HK Cafe 852	Regular neighborhood
Olympia Provisions Northwest 856	Regular neighborhood
Paymaster Lounge 857	Late night
Le Pigeon 854	High end
Le Pigeon 854	Local favorite
Pok Pok 858	Wish I'd opened

CHRISTIAN DOMSCHITZ
Restaurant Vestibül
Universitätsring 2, Vienna
A veteran of Vienna's restaurant scene, he's currently behind the stove at Vestibül in the Burgtheater.

Balthazar 1011	Wish I'd opened
Café Anzengruber 679	Late night

Dinner by Heston Blumenthal 419	High end
é by José Andrés 800	Worth the travel
Gasthaus Wolf 681	Regular neighborhood
The Guesthouse Brasserie 681	Breakfast
Miznon 682	Bargain
Restaurant Hansen 683	Breakfast
Steirereck 684	Local favorite
Tantris 624	High end

ADAM D'SYLVA
Coda
141 Flinders Lane, Melbourne
Australian chef with two restaurants on Melbourne's golden mile, he is an integral part of the local culinary scene.

Bocca di Lupo 445	Worth the travel
Cellar Bar Grossi Florentino 143	Local favorite
CUMULUS UP. 142	Local favorite
Danny's Burgers 148	Late night
The European 143	Late night
Flower Drum 143	High end
I Love Pho 150	Breakfast
Matsuya Japanese Restaurant 147	Regular neighborhood
Minamishima 150	High end
Pacific Seafood BBQ House 151	Bargain
Per Se 1046	Worth the travel
Il Pizzaiolo 153	Regular neighborhood
Tipo 00 146	Wish I'd opened
Trunk Diner 146	Breakfast

JULIEN DUBOUÉ
A. Noste
6 bis, Rue du 4 Septembre, Paris
He trained at le Cinq and Daniel Boulud. For the trio of dining options in A. Noste, he sources the majority of produce from his hometown in the southwest of France.

Chez L'Ami Jean 556	Wish I'd opened
Les Artizans 550	Regular neighborhood
Bouillon 562	Regular neighborhood
Les Copains d'Abord 539	Bargain
Daniel 1045	High end
Hakassan 439	Worth the travel
Liberté 563	Breakfast
La Maison de l'Aubrac 559	Late night
Relais de la Poste 541	Local favorite

RODNEY DUNN
The Agrarian Kitchen
650 Lachlan Road, Lachlan
Trading city life for verdant pastures in 2007, Dunn (former food editor of Australian Gourmet Traveller and Tetsuya-trained chef) founded the farm-based cookery school, The Agrarian Kitchen, in rural Tasmania.

Attica 151	High end
berta. 97	Breakfast
Burnt Ends 329	Worth the travel
CUMULUS INC. 142	Wish I'd opened
Dier Makr 97	Late night
Local Pizza 99	Regular neighborhood
The Standard 99	Bargain
Templo 100	Local favorite

JAMES DURRANT
The Game Bird
16–18 St James's Place, London
Originally from Chester, James moved to London to work at Restaurant Gordon Ramsay. He was head chef at Maze before opening The Plough Inn in Longparish with his wife and father.

Berners Tavern 472	Breakfast
The Chesil Rectory 399	Regular neighborhood
Duck & Waffle 466	Late night
Pollen Street Social 441	Local favorite
Pulpo Negro 399	Regular neighborhood
Thyme & Tides Deli 399	Breakfast

CHRISTIAN EDWARDSON
Bonnie Gull
21a Foley Street, London
Learning his trade from Pierre Koffman, he started as sous chef at Bonnie Gull but now oversees the whole group as executive head chef.

Barrafina 444	Late night
Le Manoir aux Quat'Saisons 463	Wish I'd opened
Bord'Eau 514	Worth the travel
Brasserie Zédel 446	Regular neighborhood
Hazuki 433	Regular neighborhood
The Ledbury 423	High end
Percy & Founders 473	Breakfast
The Riding House Café 473	Regular neighborhood
St. John Bread & Wine 399	Local favorite

MIKAEL EINARSSON
Djuret
Lilla Nygatan 5, Stockholm
He oversees the menu at Djuret, Pubologi, and Leijontornet in Stockholm, having previously worked across Sweden and at London's The Square.

Astrids Ängby 350	Regular neighborhood
Babette 361	Late night
Bageri Petrus 359	Breakfast
The Fat Duck 390	Worth the travel
Fäviken Magasinet 345	Wish I'd opened
Gastrologik 358	High end
Snack Bar 355	Bargain
Sturehof 358	Local favorite
Totemo Ramen 362	Regular neighborhood

MAGNUS EK
Oaxen Krog & Slip
Beckholmsvägen 26, Stockholm
Ek and his wife Agneta Green left Oaxen island, where they ran renowned Oaxen Skärgårdskrog, to open Oaxen Krog and the casual sister restaurant Slip in Stockholm's Djurgården in 2013.

Agrikultur 361	Local favorite
Babette 361	Regular neighborhood
Daniel Berlin Krog 349	High end
Ekstedt 357	Local favorite
Kadeau 348	Wish I'd opened
Kadeau 362	Worth the travel
The Lydmar Hotel 355	Breakfast

Omnipollos Hatt **360**............................Bargain
Palmyra Kebab **354**.............................Bargain
Shibumi **358**.............Regular neighborhood
Sturehof **358**..................................Late night

RICHARD EKKEBUS
Amber
15 Queen's Road Central, Hong Kong
The Gagnaire, Passard, and Savoy-trained
Dutchman who is now culinary director at
Hong Kong's Landmark Mandarin Oriental.
Australia Dairy Company **212**..........Breakfast
Benu **840**........................Wish I'd opened
Celebrity Cuisine **221**........................High end
Central **1098**..............Worth the travel
The Chairman **221**.........Regular neighborhood
DimDimSum Dim Sum Specialty Store **230**......
Local favorite
Eleven Madison Park **1037**....Wish I'd opened
Librije's Zusje **515**.................Worth the travel
Man Wah **224**...................................High end
Sang Kee Congee Shop **224**.............Breakfast
Tim Ho Wan **213**......................Local favorite
Wing Lai Yuen **212**..............................Bargain
Yardbird **229**..................................Late night
Yat Lok **226**....................Regular neighborhood

NIKLAS EKSTEDT
Ekstedt
Humlegårdsgatan 17, Stockholm
A New Nordic wunderkind, whose résumé
includes stints with Blumenthal and Ducasse,
he opened Ekstedt in 2011, eschewing
electricity to cook only with fire, and earning
a Michelin star in the process.
Agrikultur **361**..................................High end
Aloë **354**..High end
Babette **361**.................Regular neighborhood
Bæst **376**......................Wish I'd opened
Gastrologik **358**...............................High end
Gastrologik **358**..............Worth the travel
Oaxen Krog **354**.................................High end
Operabaren **356**......................Local favorite
Prinsen **356**...........................Local favorite
RAAMEN **360**.................................Bargain
Riche **358**......................................Breakfast
Sturehof **358**..................................Late night
Urban Deli Nytorget **357**.................Breakfast

PETTY ELLIOTT
A self-taught chef, she champions modern
Indonesian cuisine, and has collected
and promoted spices, herbs, and other
ingredients, either unknown or forgotten,
from around the archipelago.
Antipodean Café **299**........................Breakfast
Beautika **299**............................Local favorite
Locavore **297**...................Wish I'd opened
Majapahit at the Dharmawangsa **300**.Regular
neighborhood
Namaaz **300**.....................................High end
Odette **320**........................Worth the travel
OKU **301**...High end
Pagi Sore **301**..............Regular neighborhood
Petersham Nurseries Café **426**.......Worth the
travel
Le Quartier Restaurant **300**.............Breakfast

Salt Grill by Luke Mangan **301**............Bargain
SKYE **301**.......................................Late night
The Writer's Bar **302**.......................Late night

JOSH EMETT
Rātā
43 Ballarat Street, Queenstown
Formerly head chef at the Savoy Grill, he
opened restaurants for Gordon Ramsay in
New York before returning New Zealand
and setting up his first restaurant, Rātā
in Queenstown.
Bespoke Kitchen **159**..........................Breakfast
The Engine Room **166**...Regular neighborhood
Federal Delicatessen **165**...............Late Night

SERGEY EROSHENKO
Chestnaya kuhnya
Sadovaya Chernogryazskaya street 10,
Moscow
A chef and professional hunter, Eroshenko
serves modern Russian cuisine, using wild
fish and game, complemented by inventive
cocktails.
AQ Kitchen **710**............Regular neighborhood
L'Auberge de l'Ill **539**...........Worth the travel
Café Pushkin **711**.............................Breakfast
Café Pushkin **711**....................Local favorite
Kavkazskaya Plennitsa **708**................Bargain
Kavkazskaya Plennitsa **708**................Regular
neighborhood
Oblomov **714**................................Late night
SAVVA **713**.......................................High end
Semifreddo **707**...........Regular neighborhood
Starlite Diner **709**...........................Breakfast
Torro Grill **713**.............Regular neighborhood
Vogue Café **714**....................Wish I'd opened
White Rabbit **706**.........Regular neighborhood

ANTONIO ESCALANTE
Antonio's
Purok 138, Barangay Neogan, Tagaytay City
Born in the Philippines and educated in
Australia, he opened his first restaurant
in 2002 and now owns a celebrated grill,
breakfast place, and cocktail lounge in Manila.
JT's Manukan Grille **311**...................Late night
Kikufuji **305**.................Regular neighborhood
Tuan Tuan **308**.............Regular neighborhood
Wildflour Café + Bakery **312**..........Breakfast

TEAGE EZARD
Ezard
187 Flinders Lane, Melbourne
Known for his combination of Asian and
contemporary Australian dishes, he began
his career in hospitality when he was just
seventeen.
Brae **101**.......................Worth the travel
Café Di Stasio **153**.......Regular neighborhood
Flower Drum **143**............................High end
Little Sunflower Café **147**................Breakfast
Stokehouse **153**..............Wish I'd opened
Supper Inn **146**..............................Late night
La Tortilleria **149**...............................Bargain

LUCA FANTIN
Il Ristorante Luca Fantin
Ginza Tower 2-7-12, Tokyo
Running a restaurant recently re-christened
to incorporate his name, Fantin offers
a contemporary interpretation of seasonal
Italian cuisine.
BORAGó **1132**.......................Wish I'd opened
Brae **101**..High end
DEN **268**.....................Regular neighborhood
Florilège **269**................Regular neighborhood
Gaigai **263**.....................................Bargain
Geranium **378**...................Worth the travel
Icaro miyamoto **261**.......................Late night
The Lobby Lounge **249**...................Breakfast
Mugaritz **576**....................Worth the travel
Narisawa **265**........................Local favorite
Nihonryori RyuGin **265**.....Wish I'd opened
Noma **369**.......................Worth the travel
Ootanino Sushi **265**.......................Late night
Osteria Francescana **650**...........Local favorite
La Pergola **657**.................................High end
Piazza Duomo **664**............................High end
Sixpenny **123**....................Wish I'd opened

YAIR FEINBERG
FeinCook
84 Ben Zvi Road
A Tel Aviv-based chef who trained in France
and now cooks privately, teaches, and runs
culinary tours through FeinCook Studio.
Taizu **175**.....................Regular neighborhood
Pescado **175**.................Regular neighborhood

ANDREA FERRERO
Piacere
1-8-3 Marunouchi Chiyoda-ku, Tokyo
The Italian executive chef of the Shangri-La
Hotel in Tokyo, he has over fifteen years
of experience at a vast range of international
locations, from France, Spain, Dubai, and Bali.
Daigo **263**..High end
Deus Ex Machina **269**...........Wish I'd opened
Hibiki **256**...........................Local favorite
Lauderdale **264**.............................Breakfast
Il Luogo di Aimo e Nadia **661**.Worth the travel
Shinisei Yaesu **258**.....Regular neighborhood
Soba Roppongi **266**............................Bargain
Toritama **272**..................................Late night

FEDERICO FIALAYRE
Tomo 1
Carlos Pellegrini 521, Buenos Aires

Born into a family of cooks, Fialayre carries on the culinary legacy of his mother and aunt at Tomo 1, the restaurant famed for its take on Porteña cuisine.

Aramburu **1126**	Late night
Aramburu **1126**	Wish I'd opened
Basa **1130**	Breakfast
La Bourgogne **1130**	High end
La Choza **1126**	Bargain
Cucina Paradiso **1124**	Regular neighborhood
Don Julio Parrilla **1127**	Local favorite
Eleven Madison Park **1037**	Worth the travel
Los Galgos **1131**	Breakfast
Mishiguene **1128**	Regular neighborhood
Oviedo **1124**	Late night

KONSTANTIN FILIPPOU
Restaurant Konstantin Filippou
Dominikanerbastei 17, Vienna

Since 2013 Filippou has been bringing his Austrian and Greek heritage to bear at his self-named international restaurant in Vienna.

Alain Ducasse au Plaza Athénée **557**	Worth the travel
Ansari **679**	Breakfast
Bits & Bites **679**	Local favorite
Café Balthazar **680**	Breakfast
Café Griensteidl **680**	Breakfast
Café Landtmann **680**	Breakfast
Clamato **564**	Worth the travel
The Clove Club **487**	Worth the travel
Frenchie **552**	Worth the travel
Goldfisch **681**	Local favorite
Grace **681**	Regular neighborhood
The Guesthouse Brasserie **681**	Breakfast
Harry's Bar **671**	Wish I'd opened
Joseph Brot **681**	Breakfast
Kaffemik **680**	Breakfast
Kiang Dine and Wine **681**	Regular neighborhood
Léontine **682**	Regular neighborhood
Marco Simonis **682**	Breakfast
Mercado **682**	Regular neighborhood
Mochi **682**	Local favorite
Le Petit Nice **543**	Worth the travel
Petz im Gusshaus **683**	Local favorite
Pizza Mari **683**	Bargain
Rudi's Beisl **684**	Local favorite
Shiki **684**	High end
Ströck Feierabend **684**	Breakfast
Zum Scharfen Rene **684**	Late night
Zur Herknerin **685**	Local favorite

KEVIN FINK
Emmer & Rye
51 Rainey Street 110, Austin

With a varied career in hospitality, he has time spent at Noma and The French Laundry, as well as running a charcuterie, curing, and smoking program for the Department of Health.

Apis **938**	High end
Apis **938**	Local favorite
Asador Etxebarri **575**	Wish I'd opened

Barley Swine **1060**	Local favorite
Baroo **817**	Wish I'd opened
Bufalina **1060**	Regular neighborhood
Casino El Camino **1060**	Late night
Figure 8 **1061**	Breakfast
June's All Day **1062**	Late night
Kebabalicious **1063**	Bargain
Kebabalicious **1063**	Regular neighborhood
Odd Duck **1064**	Regular neighborhood
Odd Duck **1064**	Local favorite
Pineapple and Pearls **879**	Wish I'd opened
Thai-Kun at Whisler's **1065**	Bargain
Thai-Kun at Whisler's **1065**	Late night
Thai-Kun at Whisler's **1065**	Regular neighborhood
Tratto **788**	Worth the travel
Uchiko **1066**	High end
Veracruz All Natural Food Truck **1066**	Breakfast
Wildair **1010**	Worth the travel

KARL FIRLA
Oscillate Wildly
275 Australia Street, Sydney

Pioneering a style involving the refined fusion of Asian ingredients with French techniques, he was a pastry chef before he bought Oscillate Wildly in Sydney.

Bennelong Restaurant **107**	Local favorite
Brae **101**	High end
Chairman Mao **117**	Regular neighborhood
Disfrutar **596**	Worth the travel
Golden Century **111**	Late night
LuMi Dining **122**	Wish I'd opened
Quique Dacosta **591**	Worth the travel
Restaurant Hubert **112**	Late night
Rosso Pomodoro **107**	Regular neighborhood
Rustic Pearl **124**	Breakfast
Sepia **113**	High end
Thanh Van **107**	Bargain

DOUG FLICKER
Esker Grove
723 Vineland Place, Minneapolis

A regular on Minneapolis's dining scene, his new offering is a celebration of seasonal ingredients.

La Alborada **994**	Bargain
Grand Szechuan **910**	Regular neighborhood
Mandarin Kitchen **998**	Breakfast
Matt's Bar **998**	Local favorite
Pujol **10082**	Worth the travel
Shake Shack **910**	Wish I'd opened
St. Genevieve **1001**	High end
Taqueria Los Ocampo **1001**	Late night

ROLF FLIEGAUF
Ecco
Via del Segnale 10, Ascona

The youngest European chef, at twenty-nine, to win two Michelin stars, for his restaurant Ecco, German Fliegauf has since won two stars for its St Moritz spin-off, Ecco on Snow.

Alinea **957**	High end
Cordobar **631**	Wish I'd opened
Eden Roc **641**	Breakfast
Grotto Baldoria **641**	Local favorite
Hotel Laudinella **640**	Late night

The Jane **522**	Worth the travel
Ristorante Sensi **642**	Regular neighborhood
Waldgaststätte Ponyhof **625**	Bargain

PHILLIP FOSS
EL Ideas
2419 West 14th Street, Chicago

A well travelled chef, his innovative Chicago kitchen is a one-of-a-kind intimate location, with BYO drinks, and the feel of a test kitchen.

Alinea **957**	Local favorite
Alinea **957**	Wish I'd opened
The Aviary **966**	Late night
Big Star **969**	Late night
Boon Café **116**	Breakfast
Au Cheval **965**	Regular neighborhood
Au Cheval **965**	Wish I'd opened
Le Coucou **1012**	Worth the travel
Elske **966**	High end
Fratelli Paradiso **121**	Breakfast
Grace **966**	High end
Hollywood Grill **970**	Breakfast
Momotaro **967**	Late night
Oriole **967**	High end
Pequod's Pizzeria **958**	Bargain
Schwa **970**	Local favorite
Smyth **968**	High end
Totto Ramen **1043**	Worth the travel
The Wieners Circle **959**	Bargain

PAUL FOSTER
Salt
8 Church Street, Stratford-upon-Avon

Foster trained at Le Manoir aux Quat'Saisons and Sat Bains, and then headed up the kitchen at Tuddenham Mill, before successfully crowd-funding the opening of Salt.

Aubrey Allez **404**	Breakfast
The Cross **403**	Local favorite
The Cross **403**	Regular neighborhood
Duck & Waffle **466**	Late night
The French Laundry **797**	High end
Holborn Dining Room **477**	Regular neighborhood
Kitchen Table @ Bubble Dogs **451**	Wish I'd opened
Per Se **1046**	Worth the travel
Roast **463**	Breakfast
Romero y Azahar **1087**	Worth the travel
Sat Bains **402**	High end
Wofon **404**	Bargain

GARY FOULKES
Angler
3 South Place, London

Following stints at Michelin-starred spots The Vineyard, The Aubergine, and The Square, he is now head chef at this East End seafood joint.

108 Garage **422**	Breakfast
Benu **840**	Worth the travel
Bo.Lan **287**	Worth the travel
Chiltern Firehouse **419**	Wish I'd opened
Hakkasan **472**	Late night
The Ledbury **423**	High end
The Little Viet Kitchen **480**	Regular neighborhood
Au Passage **565**	Worth the travel
Som Saa **489**	Local favorite
Tayyabs **494**	Bargain

BJÖRN FRANTZÉN
Frantzén
Lilla Nygatan 16, Stockholm

Frantzén met Daniel Lindeberg in 1998 while they were working at Edsbacka Krog. A decade later they opened Frantzén/Lindeberg, which later became Frantzén. He opened the Flying Elk in 2013.

L'Astrance 568.....................................High End
Balthazar 1011......................Wish I'd opened
Broms 357...................................Breakfast
Kagurazaka Ishikawa 272.....Worth the Travel
Rolfs Kök 359...........................Local favourite
Sturehof 358............Regular neighbourhood
Surfers 359.....................................Bargain

RAMÓN FREIXA
Ramón Freixa Madrid
Calle de Claudio Coello 67, Madrid

After working in some of the finest kitchens of Europe, Freixa eventually returned to his native Spain, where he worked in the family restaurant, gaining it a Michelin star in 1998.

Alabaster 588..............Regular neighborhood
Alain Ducasse au Plaza Athénée 557..Wish I'd
opened
Atera 1013...........................Wish I'd opened
Casa Dani 588...............................Breakfast
Fismuler 589....................................Bargain
Freixa Tradició 603............Local favorite
Odette 320........................Worth the travel
Per Se 1046.......................Worth the travel
Pierre Gagnaire 559....................High end
Pinoxto 602...................................Breakfast
Sant Pau 586.................................High end
La Tasquita de Enfrente 589.......Local favorite
La Terraza del Casino 587................Late night

JASON FRENCH
Ned Ludd
3925 NE MLK Jr Boulevard, Portland

This chef-owner created Ned Ludd after falling in love with the Pacific Northwest's food and wine culture

HaVL Sandwich 852....................Breakfast
Noraneko 856..............Regular neighborhood
Poke Mon 858..............Regular neighborhood
Sweedeedee 859...........................Breakfast

MICHAEL FRIEDMAN
The Red Hen
1822 1st Street NW, Washington, DC

Eating his way through Italy, Greece, Turkey, and Northern Africa, Friedman puts this experience to good use in the kitchen of his first solo venture.

All-Purpose Pizzeria 864............Local favorite
Bad Saint 864..............................Local favorite
Bantam King 864.......................Local favorite
Bestia 813..........................Worth the travel
Bistrot Lepic & Wine Bar 865.....Local favorite
Blue Hill at Stone Barns 913..Worth the travel
Buttercream Bakeshop 865................Regular
neighborhood
Del Campo 866.........................Local favorite
Chez Panisse 789..................Worth the travel

Cockscomb 841..................Worth the travel
Convivial 865................Regular neighborhood
Le Coucou 1012.................Worth the travel
The Dabney 866...........Regular neighborhood
Daikaya 866................Regular neighborhood
Daikaya 866..............................Local favorite
Daniel 1045.........................Worth the travel
DGS Delicatessen 866..............Local favorite
Le Diplomate 866.........Regular neighborhood
Estadio 866......................Regular neighborhood
Georgetown Bagelry 888...............Breakfast
Husk 935...........................Worth the travel
Jaleo 867.........................Regular neighborhood
Jean-Georges 1046............Worth the travel
Kapnos 867....................Regular neighborhood
Kinship 867.................................High end
Komi 867.....................................High end
Lucques 825.......................Worth the travel
Maialino 1038...................Worth the travel
Mandu 868...................................Late night
Mandu 868..............................Local favorite
Marcel's 868.................................High end
McCrady's Tavern 1055.........Worth the travel
Métier 868..................................High end
Minibar by José Andrés 868..............High end
Nico Osteria 960.................Worth the travel
Oyamel Cocina Mexicana 869............Regular
neighborhood
Pho 75 889......................................Bargain
Pineapple and Pearls 870................High end
Proof 870.....................Regular neighborhood
Rose's Luxury 870.........................High end
Spiaggia 960.......................Worth the travel
SUNdeVICH 871..........Regular neighborhood
Taco Bamba 939......................Local favorite
Taylor Gourmet 938..................Local favorite
The Source 871.......................Local favorite
Woodberry Kitchen 888.............Local favorite
Woodmont Grill 889..................Local favorite
Zaytinya 871..............................Local favorite
Zaytinya 871.................Regular neighborhood
Zaytinya 871....................Wish I'd opened
Zuni Café 831.......................Worth the travel

KATSUYA FUKUSHIMA
Daikaya
705 6th Street NW, Washington, DC

He cooked for heavy-hitters Ferran Adrià, Thomas Keller, and David Bouley, and now has three solo ventures, including a ramen bar and an izakaya (Japanese gastropub).

Clyde's of Gallery Place 865............Late night
DEN 268.........................Worth the travel
Fäviken Magasinet 345.........Worth the travel
Ledo Pizza 867..................................Bargain
Mr. Donahue's 1018.............Wish I'd opened
New Big Wong 868.........................Late night
Old Ebbitt Grill 869..................Local favorite
Panda Gourmet 869.....Regular neighborhood
Panda Gourmet 869.........................Bargain
Perry's 869....................................Breakfast
The Prime Rib 870.........................High end
Ravi Kabob 938................................Bargain
Sakedokoro Makoto 870..................High end

TAKESHI FUKUYAMA
La Maison de la Nature Goh
2 26 Nishinakasu Chuo-ku, Fukuoka

With an emphasis on French cuisine, he opened La Maison de la Nature Goh in 2002.

Chikamatsu 244...............................High end
Current 245.....................................Breakfast
Gaggan 284........................Worth the travel
Hanya Kuta 244............Regular neighborhood
Mihara Tofuten 244.........................Bargain
Sala Carina 244................Wish I'd opened
Shin-Shin 245...................................Late night
Tenzushi 245.............................Local favorite

JUAN GAFFURI
Elena
Posadas 1086, Buenos Aires

Since 2001, Gaffuri worked in the esteemed kitchens of the Four Seasons hotel group worldwide, before returning to his native Argentina, where he is executive chef at their hotel in Buenos Aires.

Aramburu 1126..............................High end
La Biela 1129...................................Breakfast
Central 1098..................................High end
El Cuartito 1130.......................Local favorite
DBGB 1022.......................Wish I'd opened
Don Julio Parrilla 1127................Late night
La Giostra 668......................Worth the travel
Harry Sasson 1095.............Worth the travel
Hong Kong Style 1124...Regular neighborhood
Italpast 1124.................Regular neighborhood
Maido 1100........................Worth the travel
La Mar 1128.................Regular neighborhood
Monreal 1121.....................................Bargain
El Obrero 1125..........................Local favorite
Oviedo 1124....................................Late night
Quintonil 1082................................High end
Sarabeth's 1043.............................Breakfast
Tegui 1129.....................................High end

LUCIO GALLETTO
Lucio's
47 Windsor Street, Sydney

Hailing from a long line of restaurateurs, Galletto opened this family-run restaurant in the eighties.

(Not Just) Another Cup 280............Breakfast
Bondi Surf Seafoods 110...................Bargain
Capannina Ciccio 658............Wish I'd opened
Capriccio Osteria & Bar 118......Local favorite
Fratelli Paradiso 121....Regular neighborhood
Golden Century 111......................Late night
Guy Savoy 555................................High end
Poolside Cafe 112.............................Breakfast
Restaurant Hubert 112.........Worth the travel

GUILLAUME GALLIOT
The Tasting Room by Galliot
Estrada Do Istmo, Macau

Former chef for the Raffles Hotel Group, Galliot goes to extraordinary lengths to source luxury ingredients from around the world.

8½ Otto e Mezzo Bombana 220..........Regular neighborhood
Alain Ducasse au Plaza Athénée 557.High end
L'Astrance 568.................................High end
L'Astrance 568.................Wish I'd opened
Geranium 378.................Worth the travel
Golden Peacock 190.....................Late night
La Grande Table Marocaine 730......Worth the travel
Liao Fan Hong Kong 320..................Bargain
Liège 192.....................................Breakfast
Lung King Heen 223.................Local favorite
Odette 320....................Wish I'd opened
Le Parc 542...................................High end
Le Petit Nice 543.............................High end
Le Puits Saint-Jacques 541............High end
Le Taillevent 559..........................High end

RAINER GASSNER
Ti Trin Ned
Norgesgade 3, Fredericia

Rainer opened this vaulted basement restaurant with his wife, Mette, to national acclaim; the name means "Ten Steps Down".

Bæst 376....................................Late night
Fru Larsen 364............................Breakfast
Geist 372.............Regular neighborhood
Geranium 378...............................High end
Sat Bains 402....................Worth the travel
Tacos 365.......................................Bargain

MATTHEW GAUDET
Superfine
25 Union Street, Manchester-by-the-Sea

Ten years working in New York in the likes of Eleven Madison, Jean Georges Park, and Aquavit gave Gaudet the drive to leave New York and set up on his own.

Chez l'Ami Jean 556..............Worth the travel
L'Arpège 556.................................High end
Blue Ribbon BBQ 889.....................Late night
Bras 541..High end
Bubble Dogs 446............Wish I'd opened
Corner Bistro 1028........................Late night
Eleven Madison Park 1037..............High end
Frank's Deli & Restaurant 912........Breakfast
Franklin's Cafe 890........................Late night
Halibut Point 898.................Local favorite
Halibut Point 898.........Regular neighborhood
Hi-Rise Bakery 897........................Breakfast
J.T. Farnhams 898.................Local favorite
J.T. Farnhams 898........Regular neighborhood
Jean-Georges 1046.........................High end
Num Pang Kitchen 1026..................Bargain
Peach Farm 891.............................Late night
Pho 'n Rice 900............Regular neighborhood
Pho Pasteur 892.............................Bargain
Pierre Gagnaire 559.......................High end
Roberta's 1017....................Wish I'd opened
The Spotted Pig 1030....................Late night
Tasty Burger 893............................Late night
Vanessa's Dumpling House 1009.......Bargain

ALEXANDRE GAUTHIER
La Grenouillère
19 Rue de La Grenouillère, La Madelaine-sous-Montreuil

Discovered by Ducasse, rising star Gauthier took over his family's century-old restaurant La Grenouillère in 2003.

Benu 840......................................High end
Blanca 1015......................Worth the travel
Le Caveau 540...............................Bargain
Le Relais Saint Germain 554............Breakfast
La Cour de Rémi 540....Regular neighborhood
Frenchie to Go 552.......Regular neighborhood
Maaemo 344.....................Worth the travel
Manresa 792..................................High end
Miznon 554.....................................Bargain
Narisawa 265..................................High end
Noma 369..........................Worth the travel
Pierre Gagnaire 559...........Worth the travel
Aux Prés – Cyril Lignac 555............Late night
Restaurant André 331.........Worth the travel
Roberta's 1017....................Wish I'd opened
Le Servan 566................................Late night
La Sirene 539.......................Local favorite
Yakumo Saryo 261.............Wish I'd opened

ALEXIS GAUTHIER
Gauthier Soho
21 Romilly Street, London

French-born chef-patron at London's Michelin-starred Gauthier Soho, where the menu's emphasis on vegetables is distinctly un-French.

Andrew Edmunds 443.................Local favorite
Le Bernardin 1038.........................High end
Bob Bob Ricard 445.....Regular neighborhood
Bob Bob Ricard 445..........Wish I'd opened
Chez Panisse 789..........................High end
Dean Street Townhouse 447............Breakfast
La Grenouille 1039........................High end
Joël Robuchon 546................Worth the travel
Lahore Express 461.........................Bargain
The River Café 417.............Wish I'd opened
Scott's 442..........................Local favorite
La Table de Tee 281.............Worth the travel
The Wolseley 443..........................Breakfast
Yauatcha Soho 455.........................Late night

ROHIT GHAI
Jamavar Restaurant
8 Mount Street, London

He began his career working at Gymkhana, Trishna, Verandah, and Benares, before joining the Jamavar family as executive chef of their first UK branch.

Brilliant Restaurant 427............Local favorite
Cinnamon Club 455........................Breakfast
Dastaan 403...................................Bargain
Four Seasons Hotel 438.....................Regular neighborhood
Hakkasan 439................................High end
Jinjuu Soho 450...........Regular neighborhood
Madhu's 428.......................Local favorite
Park Chinois 441.................Wish I'd opened
Pickle 504...........................Wish I'd opened
Punjab 435.....................................Late night
Tayyabs 494....................................Bargain
Vineet Bhatia 412..........................High end
Vineet Bhatia 412.........Regular neighborhood
Woodlands 422................................Bargain

PETER GILMORE
Quay
5 Hickson Road, Sydney

He describes his market-driven style as "a celebration of being a cook in Australia".

Akbar Durbar 164............................Late night
Blue Hill at Stone Barns 913..Wish I'd opened
The Bridge Room 110.......................High end
Cassia 164........................Wish I'd opened
Cavallino 125...............Regular neighborhood
Chat Thai 116..................................Bargain
Cinque Cucina e Caffé 118..............Breakfast
Dainty Sichuan 152...........Worth the travel
Depot 164..........................Local favorite
Ester 114...........................Local favorite
The French Café 165.......................High end
Golden Century 111........................Late night
Meredith's 165...............................High end
Mugaritz 576.....................Worth the travel
Piazza Duomo 664..............Worth the travel
Sepia 113.......................................High end
Sixpenny 123...................................High end
Spice Temple 113.........Regular neighborhood
Tastebuds 125...............................Breakfast
Whale Beach Deli 125....................Breakfast

DAVID GINGELL
Primeur
116 Petherton Road, London

The chef-owner of Primeur, a French grocer-inspired restaurant located within a converted garage, he was formerly head chef of the Wright Brothers.

40 Maltby Street 460.................Local favorite
Black Axe Mangal 480..Regular neighborhood
Bühler and Co 493.........................Breakfast
La Cova Fumada 594.............Worth the travel
Le Gavroche 438...........................High end
Kiln 451.............................Local favorite
Kiln 451............................Wish I'd opened
The Laughing Heart 474..................Late night
Pizza East 424............Regular neighborhood
Potager Garden & Glasshouse 391.....Wish I'd opened
Sodo Pizza Café 493.....Regular neighborhood
Ustun Lahmacun 491........................Bargain
The Wolseley 443..........Regular neighborhood

TODD GINSBERG
The General Muir
1540 Avenue Place, Atlanta

Co-owns a series of restaurants in Atlanta, including two in Krog Street Market and a micro-food hall in Tech Square.

Australia Dairy Company 212..........Breakfast
BoccaLupo 944............Regular neighborhood
Bread & Butterfly 944....................Breakfast
Bread & Butterfly 944...Regular neighborhood
Cakes + Ale 877.....................Local favorite
Holeman and Finch 945...................Late night

Houseman **1014**....................Worth the travel
Kevin Rathbun Steak **945**..................High end
Lee's Bakery **946**.................................Bargain
MF Sushi **946**.................Regular neighborhood
Miller Union **946**......................Local favorite
Nam Phoung Restaurant **947**..............Bargain
North Abraxas **174**...................Worth the travel
Pho Dai Loi 2 **948**.............................Bargain
Roberta's **1017**.........................Wish I'd opened
Ticonderoga Club **950**........................Late night
Victory Sandwich Bar **951**...............Late night

GUNNAR KARL GÍSLASON
Dill Restaurant
Hverfisgata 12, Reykjavík

Opened Dill in 2009, where his Modern Nordic approach is influenced by his time spent with Lauterbach, Redzepi, and Henriksen.

Bæjarins Beztu Pylsur **340**.........Local favorite
Five Leaves **1016**...........................Breakfast
The Four Horsemen **1016**....................Regular
neighborhood
Hard Times Sundaes **1041**................Bargain
Maaemo **344**...................................High end
Wildair **1010**..................................Late night

SPIKE GJERDE
Woodberry Kitchen
2010 Clipper Park Road, Baltimore

He runs six restaurants in Baltimore including Woodberry Kitchen and Artifact Coffee, as well as the canning operation, Woodberry Pantry.

The Dabney **866**....................Worth the travel
Dylan's Oyster Cellar **886**..................High end
Faidley Seafood **887**................Local favorite
Grano Pasta Bar **887**...........................Bargain
Joe Squared **887**..........Regular neighborhood
The Local Oyster **887**.........................High end
Patisserie Poupon **887**...................Breakfast
Paulie Gee's **887**...........Regular neighborhood
Thames Street Oyster House **888**.....High end
Verde **888**.....................Regular neighborhood
Wicked Sisters **888**..........................Late night

DANIELLE GJESTLAND
Wasabi Restaurant & Bar
2 Quamby Place, Noosa Sound

She first opened Wasabi when she was just 24, and now also owns a cooking school and restaurant farm which follows the Japanese system of using the organic matter from the restaurant to nourish the soil.

Arzak **579**.............................Worth the travel
Fisherman's Cove **790**.........................Bargain
Narisawa **265**..................................High end
Noosa Hot Bread Shop **87**...............Breakfast
Robata Kaimaru **256**.......................Late night
Sails Restaurant **87**.................Local favorite
Saison **841**.....................................High end
Sepia **113**..........................Wish I'd opened
Village Bicycle **88**..........Regular neighborhood

SUZANNE GOIN
Lucques
8474 Melrose Avenue, Los Angeles

Goin launched her Los Angeles empire with Lucques (1998). Eighteen years on, and with two James Beard Awards, she and business partner Caroline Styne co-own A.O.C., Tavern, and The Larder.

Bar Isabel **767**.....................Worth the travel
Camino **1060**.......................Worth the Travel
Pizzeria Mozza **817**......Regular neighborhood
Spago **811**...............................Local Favorite

WILL GOLDFARB
Room4Dessert
Jalan Rayan Sanginggan, Ubud

This elBulli-trained New Yorker moved to Bali in 2009, where his innovative pastry skills take center stage at this dessert-only restaurant.

Balthazar **1011**.............................Breakfast
Naughty Nuri's Warung **295**...............Regular
neighborhood
PICA South American Kitchen **298**......Regular
neighborhood

JOSÉ LUIS (CHELE) GONZALEZ
Gallery VASK
11th Avenue, Corner 39th Street, Manila

Having spent time in the kitchens of Arzak and elBulli, he opened his restaurant Gallery VASK with architect and artist, Juan Carlo Calma.

Abe Restaurant **310**.....Regular neighborhood
Chotto Matte **310**............................Late night
Disfrutar **596**.....................Worth the travel
Elkano **580**........................Worth the travel
Goto Monster **305**............................Bargain
Grace Park **305**.................Wish I'd opened
Hey Handsome **310**...............Local favorite
Mecha Uma **311**...............................High end
Mugaritz **576**....................Worth the travel
Narisawa **265**....................Worth the travel
Nerua **575**.........................Worth the travel
Nihonryori RyuGin **265**..........Worth the travel
Ootanino Sushi **265**............Worth the travel
Señor Pollo **306**.............................Late night
Shi Lin **307**..................Regular neighborhood
Tambai **307**........................Local favorite
Toyo Eatery **307**.................Wish I'd opened
Wildflour Cafe + Bakery **312**.......Breakfast

PETER GOOSSENS
Hof van Cleve
Riemegemstraat 1, Kruishoutem

Since 1987, he has run his rustic yet refined Flanders restaurant, which combines Belgian traditions with French haute technique and Asian influences.

Le 114 Faubourg **557**.....................High end
Alain Ducasse au Plaza Athénée **557**.High end
L'Assiette Champenoise **539**.............High end
Bistronoom **530**...........Regular neighborhood
Boulevard Boutique **527**.................Breakfast
Brasserie Boulevard **527**...................Bargain
Brasserie Latem **527**..................Local favorite
Castor **530**.........................Wish I'd opened

Escabeche **530**............Regular neighborhood
Gasthof Halifax **525**........................Late night
De Hermelijn **525**.........Regular neighborhood
't Huis van Lede **525**.....Regular neighborhood
Maison Troisgros **536**.........................High end
't Nieuw Stadion **526**.........................Bargain
Plein 25 **525**..................Regular neighborhood
Le Pré Catelan **568**...........................High end
La Vague d'Or **546**...............Worth the travel
De Zwaan **525**..............Regular neighborhood

PETER GORDON
The Providores and Tapa Room
109 Marylebone High Street, London

Fusion pioneer Gordon runs restaurants in Istanbul, London, and his native New Zealand, where he reopened the iconic Sugar Club in 2013.

Allpress Roastery Cafe **470**.............Breakfast
Brawn **478**............................Local favorite
Chotto Matte **447**............................Late night
Hill & Szrok **474**...........Regular neighborhood
Lemlem Kitchen **475**.........................Bargain
Oklava **486**....................Regular neighborhood
Oklava **486**.........................Wish I'd opened
Pizarro **488**.......................Worth the travel
Rochelle Canteen **486**................Local favorite
Soujiki Nakahigashi **250**...................High end
The Wolseley **443**..........................Breakfast

COSMO GOSS
The Publican
837 West Fulton Market, Chicago

Executive chef of the Publican brand, he has a particular passion and talent for the art of butchery.

Arturo's Tacos **955**...........................Bargain
avec **965**............................Local favorite
Blackbird **966**..................................High end
Boka **958**..High end
Boka **958**.............................Local favorite
Broken Spanish **813**.............Worth the travel
Cai **955**...Late night
Chicago Kalbi **954**.........................Late night
Chicago Kalbi **954**.........Regular neighborhood
Connie & Ted's **825**.............Worth the travel
Elske **966**......................................High end
Fat Rice **957**....................Wish I'd opened
Leña Brava **967**...........Regular neighborhood
Leña Brava **967**..................Wish I'd opened
Lula Cafe **959**...............................Breakfast

LUCA GOZZANI
Fasano
88 Rua Vittorio Fasano, São Paulo

Head chef of Fasano in São Paulo since 2012, Italian-born Gozzani met, at Enoteca Pinchiorri in Florence, restaurateur Rogério Fasano, who lured him to Brazil.

D.O.M. Restaurante **1114**..................High end
Eataly **1119**....................................Bargain
Eataly **1119**...................................Late night
Enoteca Pinchiorri **668**..........Worth the travel
Nino Cucina **1113**.........Regular neighborhood
Osteria del Pettirosso **1114**...............Regular
neighborhood
Le Pain Quotidien **1119**..................Breakfast

DAN GRAHAM

Pidgin
52 Wilton Way, London

Former architect turned chef, before
becoming head chef at Pidgin, he did stints at
Dinner, L'Autre Pied, and Odette's in London.

A. Wong **428**	Regular neighborhood
Blue Hill at Stone Barns **913**	Wish I'd opened
Dinner by Heston Blumenthal **419**	High end
Dishoom **482**	Local favorite
Ekstedt **357**	Worth the travel
Honest Burgers **483**	Regular neighborhood
Mugaritz **576**	Worth the travel
Restaurant André **331**	Worth the travel
Sushi Show **465**	Bargain
Xi'an Impression **477**	Regular neighborhood

LORI GRANITO

Magnolia
17 Po Yan Street, Hong Kong

This New Orleans native's small Cajun-Creole
private catering business has flourished
in Hong Kong, alongside her American-style
burrito joint, Little Burro.

208 Duecento Otto **228**	Regular neighborhood
8½ Otto e Mezzo Bombana **220**	High end
Amber **220**	High end
L'Auberge de l'Ill **539**	Worth the travel
Burger Circus **220**	Late night
Butcher and Baker Cafe **226**	Breakfast
Caprice **221**	High end
Corner Kitchen Café **228**	Breakfast
East Ocean Seaview Restaurant **214**	Local favorite
The Flying Pan **222**	Breakfast
For Kee **229**	Bargain
Little Bao **288**	Worth the travel
Restaurant Le Gabriel **559**	Worth the travel
Wagyu **225**	Regular neighborhood
Wagyu **225**	Wish I'd opened
Wing Wah Noodle Shop **231**	Late night
Winter Garden **422**	Wish I'd opened
Yung Kee **226**	Local favorite
Zuma **419**	Wish I'd opened

SEAN GRAY

Momofuku Ko
8 Extra Place, New York

Hailing from Pennsylvania, he joined the
Momofuku team in 2007, spending time at
Noodle Bar, Ssäm Bar, and then moving to
Ko in 2009 as sous chef.

Alameda **1014**	Regular neighborhood
Aska **1015**	High end
Corner Bistro **1028**	Wish I'd opened
Joe Beef **779**	Worth the travel
Leo's Bagels **1007**	Breakfast
Roberta's **1017**	Local favorite
Russ & Daughters Cafe **1009**	Breakfast
Two Hands **1014**	Breakfast
Vic's **1027**	Regular neighborhood
Wildair **1010**	Late night
The Willows Inn **800**	Worth the travel
Xi'an Famous Foods **1025**	Bargain

BERTRAND GRÉBAUT

Séptime
80 Rue de Charonne, Paris

Trained at l'ESAG, one of France's best
culinary schools, he came of culinary age with
Passard before opening Séptime in 2011.

L'Arpège **556**	High end
Les Arlots **562**	Local favorite
Holybelly **563**	Breakfast
Lao Siam **569**	Bargain
Mission Chinese **1008**	Wish I'd opened
Noma **369**	Worth the travel
Rosebud **567**	Late night
Le Servan **566**	Regular neighborhood

BEN GREENO

The Paddington
384 Oxford street, Sydney

This British chef worked with Sat Bains
for years before moving to Australia to
open Momofuku Seiōbo for David Chang.

Cairo Takeaway **119**	Bargain
Ester **114**	Regular neighborhood
Gjelina **824**	Wish I'd opened
Golden Century **111**	Late night
Le Louis XV **547**	High end
RŌNIN **229**	Worth the travel
Seans Panorama **119**	Local favorite
Three Blue Ducks **110**	Breakfast

ANALIESE GREGORY

Bar Brosé
231a Victoria St, Sydney

Originally from New Zealand's North Island,
she worked at The Ledbury and Le Meurice,
plus spent five years alongside Peter Gilmore
at Quay, before setting out on her own.

10WilliamSt. **119**	Regular neighborhood
Amass **370**	Worth the travel
Asador Etxebarri **575**	Worth the travel
Attica **151**	High end
Automata **114**	Local favorite
Bennelong Restaurant **107**	Local favorite
Brae **101**	High end
Bras **541**	Worth the travel
Chaco Bar **115**	Regular neighborhood
Chat Thai **116**	Late night
Elkano **580**	Worth the travel
Ester **114**	Regular neighborhood
Fratelli Paradiso **121**	Regular neighborhood
Fratelli Paradiso **121**	Wish I'd opened
Golden Century **111**	Late night
Mamak **117**	Bargain
Mamak **117**	Late night
Miyamasou **250**	Worth the travel
Mugaritz **576**	Worth the travel
Palace Chinese Restaurant **112**	Bargain
Restaurant Hubert **112**	Late night
Restaurant Hubert **112**	Wish I'd opened
Room 10 **122**	Breakfast
Taste of Shanghai **113**	Bargain

JESSE GRIFFITHS

Dai Due Butcher Shop & Supper Club
2406 Manor Road, Austin

A self-taught hunter-gatherer chef, he has
created a uniquely Texan environment, part
butcher-shop, part-restaurant, part-hunting
school.

the backspace **1066**	Wish I'd opened
La Bandera Molino **938**	Breakfast
Enoteca Vespaio **1061**	Local favorite
Fonda Margarita **1080**	Worth the travel
Hoover's Cooking **1062**	Regular neighborhood
JuiceLand **1062**	Breakfast
Justine's **1062**	Late night
Lalo! **1081**	Breakfast
Licha's Cantina **1063**	Regular neighborhood
Marcelino Pan y Vino **1063**	Bargain
Perla's **1064**	High end
El Primo **1064**	Bargain

SARAH GRUENEBERG

Monteverde Restaurant & Pastificio
1020 West Madison Street, Chicago

She has traveled throughout Italy, Asia,
Europe, and the US, which has inspired her
culinary approach of "following the food"
to truly understand the dish by knowing the
people and culture that created it.

Alinea **957**	High end
Bavette's **961**	High end
Cassia **822**	Wish I'd opened
Au Cheval **965**	Late night
Devil Dawgs **963**	Bargain
The Eastman Egg Company **964**	Breakfast
Eleven City Diner **964**	Breakfast
Giant **959**	Wish I'd opened
Gjelina **824**	Worth the travel
MingHin Cuisine **956**	Regular neighborhood
The Publican **968**	Local favorite
Pub Royale **964**	Late night
Roister **968**	Local favorite
Taco María **791**	Worth the travel
UrbanBelly **970**	Regular neighborhood
Xi'an Cuisine **956**	Bargain

MEHMET GÜRS

Mikla
Meşrutiyet Caddesi 15, Istanbul

Turkish toque star who, thanks to his Finnish-
Swedish mother and a childhood partially
spent in Stockholm, works some Nordic
influences into the cooking at his Istanbul
restaurant Mikla.

Aşşk Kahve **722**	Breakfast
Benu **840**	Worth the travel
Blue Hill at Stone Barns **913**	High end
InSitu **841**	Wish I'd opened
Kantin **724**	Local favorite
Kantin **724**	Regular neighborhood
Maslak Pilavcısı **724**	Bargain
Pizza Emirgan **724**	Late night
Zübeyir Ocakbasi **723**	Regular neighborhood

ALEJANDRO GUTIÉRREZ
Salvo Patria
Calle 3A, 54–13, Bogotá
Colombian-born, he trained as a biologist before finding his true calling as a chef, serving up traditional Colombian dishes with a modern twist.

Abasto 1095.................................Breakfast
El Ciervo y El Oso 1095..........Wish I'd opened
Doña Elvira 1095.......................Local favorite
Leo 1095...High end
Mesa Franca 1096........Regular neighborhood
Mestizo Cocina de Origen 1097.......Worth the travel
Mistral 1096..............................Breakfast
Restaurante La Escuela 1096.............Bargain
Villanos en Bermudas 1097................Regular neighborhood

JOSÉ GUTIERREZ
River Oaks
5871 Poplar Avenue, Memphis
He worked in his native France with Paul Bocuse, before moving to the United States where he opened Encore before moving to River Oaks.

ACRE Restaurant 932....Regular neighborhood
L'Auberge du Pont de Collonges 534......Worth the travel
Jean-Georges 1046...........................High end
Nougatine at Jean-Georges 1046....Late night
The Peabody Hotel 933.....................Breakfast
River Oaks 934.........................Local favorite

JORGE GUZMAN
Surly Brewing Company
520 Malcolm Avenue, Minneapolis
Praised for "reinventing north-country fare with the Yucatecan flavors of his childhood", he continues to challenge preconceptions of food and beer.

112 eatery 994.............................Late night
Alma 994...................................Local favorite
Burch Restaurant 995.......................High end
Driftwood Char Bar 996....Regular neighborhood
Hartwood 1088................Worth the travel
The Kenwood Restaurant 997..........Breakfast
Nighthawks Diner & Bar 999...............Regular neighborhood
Phở 79 999...................................Bargain
Quang Restaurant 1000.......................Bargain
Revival 1000.........................Wish I'd opened
St. Genevieve 1001.........................Late night
St. Genevieve 1001......Regular neighborhood
Taqueria Los Ocampo 1001.................Bargain
Victor's 1959 Café 1002....................Breakfast
Zen Box Izakaya 1002..........Wish I'd opened

RODOLFO GUZMÁN
Boragó
Avenida Nueva Costanera 3467, Santiago
Inspired by his time at Mugaritz with Andoni Luis Aduriz and his own study of chemical engineering and bioprocesses, he opened Boragó in Santiago in 2007.

040 1132.................................Late night

Asador Etxebarri 575............Worth the travel
Cecinas Soler 1132.......................Breakfast
Clamato 564.........................Wish I'd opened
Hansoban 1133................................Bargain
Lomit's 1133...............Regular neighbourhood
Mercado Central de Santiago 1133..Breakfast
Mestizo 1134..................................Late night
Miraolas El Mañio 1134...................High end
Mugaritz 576...................Worth the travel
Noma 369....................Worth the travel
Rancho Doña María 1132.................Regular neighbourhood
Rancho Doña María 1132........Local favourite

EMILY HAHN
Warehouse Bar + Kitchen
45 1/2 Spring Street, Charleston
She began her career being mentored by Ed Vasaio at Mamma Zu and much of her food is influenced by her travels to Chile and Italy.

Avila 1050..........................Wish I'd opened
BARSA 1050................Regular neighborhood
Bon BAnH MI 1051..........................Bargain
Bon BAnH MI 1051.......Regular neighbourhood
Chez Nous 1052...........Regular neighbourhood
Decca 882........................Worth the travel
Fig 1053............................Local favorite
Fiery Ron's Home Team BBQ 1053......Regular neighbourhood
Da Kikokiko 821...................Wish I'd opened
Kim Jong Smokehouse 854....Worth the travel
Knife Dallas 936.................Worth the travel
LaRina Pastificio e Vino 1016...Regular neighbourhood
Luke's Craft Pizza 1054 Regular neighbourhood
Mexikosher 821................Worth the travel
North Central Delicatessen 1055.....Breakfast
The Ordinary 1056...........................High end
Platia Food Truck 1056..................Late night
Playa Provisions 821...........Worth the travel
Pot Kettle Black 397.......................Breakfast
Pretty Southern 1019..........Worth the travel
TINROOF 799...................Worth the travel
Xiao Bao Biscuit 1057...Regular neighbourhood

ELIZABETH HAIGH
Shibui
Her exeprience in smoking, butchering, and barbecuing, combined with her Michelin-trained background, leads to unique and elegant results.

Bellanger 479.............................Breakfast
Black Axe Mangal 480.............Local favorite
Blacklock 445........................Local favorite
Brae 101.........................Worth the travel
Brasserie Zedel 446........................Bargain
Carousel 419.........................Wish I'd opened
The Dairy 414.......................Wish I'd opened
The Drapers Arms 480..Regular neighborhood
Duck & Waffle 466.......................Late night
L'Enclume 394.......................Worth the travel
Esquire 130.......................Worth the travel
Friends of Ours 478........................Breakfast
Granger & Co 483..........................Breakfast
Kêu 486...Bargain
Kiln 451......................Regular neighborhood
Kitchen Table @ Bubble Dogs 451......High end
The Laughing Heart 474..................Late night

The Laughing Heart 474........Wish I'd opened
Lyle's 488.......................................High end
Meat Mission 479.........................Late night
Oldroyd 481............................Local favorite
Padella 462.....................................Bargain
The Pig and Butcher 481.....................Regular neighborhood
Som Saa 489...................Wish I'd opened
Sushi Tetsu 469.............................High end

CHRIS HALL
Local Three
3290 Northside parkway, Atlanta
A self-taught chef, he runs Local Three, a local chef's hang-out with superb charcuterie and a casual atmosphere.

B's Cracklin' BBQ 878...Regular neighborhood
BoccaLupo 943......................Wish I'd opened
Brandi's World Famous Hot Dogs 878.Bargain
Au Cheval 965.....................Worth the travel
El Rey Del Taco 877......................Late night
Staplehouse 950....................Local favorite
Tasty China 878............Regular neighborhood
Umi 950...High end
Waffle House 944..........................Breakfast

BRIAN MARK HANSEN
Søllerød Kro
Søllerødvej 35, Copenhagen
After manning the stove at Christiansholm Slot, Hansen returned in 2013 to run the kitchen at Søllerød Kro, a 330-year-old inn where he was formerly sous chef.

Anarki 362.....................................Bargain
The French Laundry 797........Wish I'd opened
Geranium 378.................................High end
Hos Fischer 379........Regular neighborhood
Kebabistan 376.............................Late night
Marchal at Hotel d'Angleterre 373...Breakfast
Mielcke og hurtigkarl 363.....Worth the travel
Restaurant Sletten 364.............Local favorite

ANNA HANSEN
The Modern Pantry
47–48 St John's Square, London
She opened The Providores and Tapa Room with Peter Gordon in London's Marylebone in 2001, before launching her own restaurant, The Modern Pantry, in Clerkenwell in 2008.

Bravi Rigazzi 492............................Late night
Brooks & Gao 492...........................Breakfast
Dishoom 482.............Regular neighborhood
Wahaca 464.................Regular neighborhood

ERICK HARCEY
Upton 43
4312 Upton Avenue, Minneapolis

Chef and owner of three restaurants in Minneapolis, each with his Swedish roots at their source.

Al's Breakfast 994..........................Breakfast
Brasa Premium Rotisserie 995...........Regular
                                     neighborhood
Clancey's Meats & Fish 996................Bargain
Commis 794..........................Worth the travel
Coppa 889..High end
FireBox Deli 996......................Local favorite
FT33 936..........................Worth the travel
Fäviken Magasinet 345..........Wish I'd opened
Holy Land 997..................................Bargain
Kaffé Stuga 910..........Regular neighborhood
Monte Carlo 999.............................Late night
Relæ 378.........................Wish I'd opened
Salty Tart 1000..............................Breakfast
Smyth 968.......................................High end
World Street Kitchen 1002........Local favorite

CHRISTOPHE HARDIQUEST
Bon-Bon
Avenue de Tervueren 453, Belgium

He brings years of Michelin-starred experience to Bon Bon, his first solo venture.

L'Arpège 556..........................Wish I'd opened
Au Vieux Saint Martin 524.................Late night
Black Axe Mangal 480................Worth the travel
Caffè Al Dente 523........Regular neighborhood
Charli 523...Breakfast
Friture René 522.............................Late night
Friture René 522..........Regular neighborhood
Hertog Jan 530.................................High end
Kamo 523...............................Local favorite
Pistolet Original 524..........................Bargain
Wittamer 525...................................Breakfast

ALEX HARRELL
Angeline
1032 Chartres Street, New Orleans

Alabama-born, at Angeline he pairs his lifelong experience with accessible seasonal products with his classical technical skills.

Ancora 987..................Regular neighborhood
Avo 987..High end
Avo 987...............................Local favorite
Bâtard 1013..........................Worth the travel
Bevi Seafood Co 984...............Local favorite
Blue Dot Donuts 984......................Breakfast
Casamento's 988.....................Local favorite
Central City BBQ 977....Regular neighborhood
CLEO'S 976.....................................Late night
District Donuts 982.........................Breakfast
Dong Phuong 985.............................Bargain
Elske 966..........................Worth the travel
Gerald's Donut & Burger 883..........Late night
High Hat Cafe 981........Regular neighborhood
HiVolt 982..Breakfast
Hong Kong Market 883.....................Bargain
Liuzza's by the Track 978..........Local favorite
Liuzza's by the Track 978....................Regular
                                     neighborhood
Manresa 792..........................Worth the travel

Mimi's In The Marigny 983.............Late night
MOPHO 985..................Regular neighborhood
Pizzaiolo 795....................Worth the travel
Primitivo 978....................Wish I'd opened
Stein's Market and Deli 982.............Breakfast
Sylvain 980.......................................Late night
Taceaux Loceaux Food Truck 991........Bargain
Turkey and the Wolf 982.....................Regular
                                     neighborhood

HENRY HARRIS
Dog & Badger
Henley Road, Medmenham

Elder of the two Harris brothers, he spent thirteen years at Racine in London's Knightsbridge before moving to former-ale house, Dog & Badger.

The Clove Club 487............................High end
Dishoom 432.......................................Late night
Le Grand Pan 567..................Wish I'd opened
Hereford Road 411.............................Bargain
Marksman Public House 475.....Local favorite
North China Restaurant 410.................Regular
                                     neighborhood
The Seahorse 394................Worth the travel
St. John Bread & Wine 489.............Breakfast

SAM HARRIS
Agrius
732 Yates Street, Victoria

Formerly of the Stage Wine Bar, Harris deploys a Slow Food ethos with exemplary French technique.

Bishop's 757..High end
Fountain Restaurant 747..................Late night
Jasmine Family Restaurant 747........Breakfast
JUKE 760.............................Wish I'd opened
Kissa Tanto 756.................................High end
OLO 747.................................Local favorite
Stage Wine Bar 748.....Regular neighborhood
The Ruby 748.....................................Breakfast
Uchida Eatery 748..............................Bargain
Wolf in the Fog 746...............Worth the travel

STEPHEN HARRIS
The Sportsman
Faversham Road, Whitstable

In 1999 he took over a rundown pub in Seasalter, on a remote part of the Kentish coast, and built it up into one of the England's most exciting destination restaurants.

L'Arpège 556..High end
Blue Hill at Stone Barns 913..Wish I'd opened
Elliot's 400.......................................Breakfast
Frantzén 355.......................Worth the travel
Harbour Street Tapas 400...Regular neighborhood
Hedone 413.......................................High end
Kiln 451...Bargain
The Ledbury 423.................................High end
Maaemo 344....................Worth the travel
Mirazur 545........................Worth the travel
Noma 369..........................Worth the travel
Tea & Times 401.............................Breakfast
Wheelers Oyster Bar 401.....................Regular
                                     neighborhood
The Whitstable Oyster Company 401......Local
                                     favorite

TOM HARRIS
The Marksman
254 Hackney Road, London

For ten years, Harris worked with the nose-to-tail St John group, where he won a Michelin star, then went on to retain the star at One Leicester Street, where he was chef-patron until 2013.

Bad Sports 477..................................Bargain
Bar Italia 444.....................................Late night
Black Axe Mangal 480...Regular neighborhood
Chez Georges 551.................Worth the travel
The Grand Howl 474..........................Breakfast
Kuzu Sis Grill & Meze 474....................Bargain
Lanark Coffee 478..........Regular neighborhood
The Laughing Heart 474....................Late night
Leila's Shop 486............Regular neighborhood
Lyle's 488.......................Regular neighborhood
P. Franco 468......................Wish I'd opened
Primeur 491..................Regular neighborhood
Primeur 491.........................Wish I'd opened
Rawduck 476................Regular neighborhood
Russ & Daughters Cafe 1009 Worth the travel
St. John Bar and Restaurant 471..Local favorite
Sweetings 467.......................Wish I'd opened

ZAIYU HASEGAWA
Jimbocho Den
2-3-18 Jingumae, Tokyo

This Tokyo-born chef uses seasonal ingredients to reinvent classic dishes and flavors, drawing on contemporary influences from Japanese culture.

Anis 268.........................Regular neighborhood
Atelier September 370....................Breakfast
Black Seed Bagels 1010..................Breakfast
Central 1098........................Wish I'd opened
Central 1098.......................Worth the travel
D.O.M. Restaurante 1114....................High end
D.O.M. Restaurante 1114......Wish I'd opened
Florilège 269.........................Local favorite
Kouei 272..Late night
MUME 203...Bargain
Noma 369..High end
Osteria Francescana 650.................High end

LENNOX HASTIE
Firedoor
23–33 Mary Street, Surry Hills

Hastie has created Australia's first fire-powered menu, eschewing efficiency and convenience to showcase the natural beauty of wood fired cooking.

Boon Café 116..................................Breakfast
LuMi Dining 122..........Regular neighborhood

ALEXANDRA HAYNES
Lalla Rookh Bar & Eating house
77 St Georges Terrace, Perth

She grew up in Melbourne and has spent much time exploring Italy. She draws on the best produce from land and sea, to create a fresh, modern Italian menu.

The Attic Fremantle 103..................Breakfast
Bib & Tucker 104..............................Breakfast
Billie H. 104.....................................High end
Billie H. 104..........................Local favorite

Billie H. **104**...........................Wish I'd opened
Bread in Common **104**...............Local favorite
Francoforte Spaghetti Bar **105**...........Regular
neighborhood
Francoforte Spaghetti Bar **105**..........Wish I'd
opened
Fuyu **105**...High end
Hawker's Cuisine **105**.........................Bargain
Hawker's Cuisine **105**..Regular neighborhood
Long Chim **105**............................Local favorite
Nao ramen **106**...........Regular neighborhood
Nobu **106**...High end
Odyssea Beach Café **106**................Breakfast
el Público **105**............................Local favorite
Rockpool **106**.....................................High end
Shadow Wine Bar **106**................Local favorite
Shadow wine bar **106**...Regular neighborhood
The Town Mouse **141**...............Worth the travel
Uncle Billy's Chinese Restaurant **106**...Late night

FEDERICO HEINZMANN
New York Grill
3-7-1-2 Nishi Shinjuku, Tokyo
Argentinian Heinzmann honed his skill as
stagiereat the three-Michelin-starred Martín
Berasategui restaurant in Spain, and at the
Marriott Hotels.
Ajihachi Ramen **271**............................Bargain
DEN **268**................................Worth the travel
Fuku Yakitori **270**.........Regular neighborhood
Fungo **270**.......................................Late night
Sushi Saito **267**.........................Local favorite
Tsukiji Sushisay **260**......................Breakfast
Takazawa **267**.....................Wish I'd opened
Troisgros **273**....................................High end

REID HENNINGER
Edmund's Oast
1081 Morrison Drive, Charleston
After spending a year working under Mike
Lata and Geoff Rhyne at The Ordinary, Reid
came to Edmund's in 2014.
b bistro **886**.......................Wish I'd opened
Normandy Farm Bakery **1050**....Local favorite
The CODfather **1052**...........................Bargain
Dave's Carry-Out **1052**.......................Bargain
Le Farfalle **1053**...........Regular neighborhood
Halls Chophouse **1053**.........................High end
Lewis Barbecue **1054**..................Local favorite
Maison Premiere **1017**.........Worth the travel
Marina Variety Store Restaurant **1054**...........
Breakfast
Moe's Crosstown Tavern **1055**........Late night
The Ordinary **1056**...............................High end
Au Pied de Cochon **551**.........Worth the travel
Stems & Skins **1056**.....Regular neighborhood
Trattoria Lucca **1057**.............Wish I'd opened

CLAUS HENRIKSEN
Dragsholm Slot
Dragsholm Alle 1, Hørve
A Danish Noma graduate who oversees
the dining rooms (one formal, one casual)
at the striking Dragsholm Slot, a restored
thirteenth-century castle 75 km (50 miles)
south of Copenhagen.
Amass **370**....................Regular neighborhood

Hotel Frederiksminde **364**.........Local favorite
Kong Hans Kælder **373**.....................High end
Moehr **365**........................Wish I'd opened
Pluto **374**.......................................Late night
Rørvig Fisk **365**................................Bargain
Det Vilde Køkken **364**.......................Breakfast

SERGIO HERMAN
Pure C
Boulevard de Wielingen 49, Cadzand
This Dutch chef and restaurateur won three
Michelin stars for his restaurant, Oud Sluis,
which he decided to close in 2013. The
following year, he opened a new restaurant,
The Jane, in Antwerp with Nick Bril.
Cannibale Royale **514**.......................Late night
De Eetboetiek **510**..........................Breakfast
De Oesterput **529**....................Local Favourite
Quique Dacosta **591**...............Worth the travel
Roberta's **1017**....................Wish I'd opened
Siphon **529**.............Regular neighborhood
Sketch **438**..High end

DIEGO HERNÁNDEZ BAQUEDANO
Corazón de Tierra
Rancho San Marcos s/n, Ejido Francisco Zarco
He opened Corazón de Tierra at a Guadalupe
hilltop farm and hacienda in 2011, a
restaurant notable for its daily-changing
tasting menu. In 2008, he opened his first
restaurant, Uno, in Tijauana.
Arai **268**...........................Worth the travel
Benu **840**.........................Wish I'd opened
Boules **1076**..........................Local favorite
Contra **1007**.........................Worth the travel
Lukshon **813**.....................................High end
Manzanilla **1077**.....................Local favorite
Mariscos el Güero **1077**..................Breakfast
Mariscos el Pizón **1077** Regular neighborhood
Mariscos Los Primos **1078**.................Bargain
Petit Trois **817**...................Wish I'd opened
Providence **817**................................High end
El Redil **1076**.................................Breakfast
Los Tres García **1078**....Regular neighborhood
Wendlandt Brewpub **1078**................Late night

ERWAN HEUSSAFF
Crisp on 28th
28th St, Bonifacio Global City, Manila
He worked in Vietnam, France, Siberia, and
elsewhere, before returning home to the
Philippines, where he is a partner in various
dining, drinking, and clubbing concepts in
the country.
12/10 **304**.........................Wish I'd opened
Antonio's **303**...................Worth the travel
Balay Dako **303**..................Worth the travel
Bale Dutung **363**................Worth the travel
Hey Handsome **310**...............Wish I'd opened
Mecha Uma **311**...................Wish I'd opened
Milky Way Cafe **306**...................Local favorite
R & J Bulalohan **309**.........................Breakfast
Razon's de Guagua **306**........................Bargain
RICH (Royal Indian Curry House) **306**...........Late
night
Samba **312**......................Wish I'd opened
Sarsá Kitechen + Bar **312**........Local favorite

Seaside Dampa Macapagal Boulevard **310**......
Local favorite
Toyo Eatery **307**....................Wish I'd opened
Tsukiji **307**......................................High end
Wildflour Cafe + Bakery **308**............Regular
neighborhood

KEVIN HICKEY
The Duck Inn
2701 S. Eleanor, Chicago
The Duck Inn showcases Chef Hickey's
seasonally driven Modern American cuisine
as well as enjoying an extensive drinks
list filled with craft beers, contemporary
cocktails, and creative wine service.
5 Rabanitos **960**..........Regular neighborhood
Birrieria Zaragoza **954**..Regular neighborhood
Bohemian House **962**........Wish I'd opened
Brindille **962**......................................High end
Carniceria Guanajuato **969**..............Bargain
Charlie Bird **1012**...............Worth the travel
Franco's Ristorante **955**..Regular neighborhood
Frontera Grill **862**....................Local favorite
Gibsons **960**............................Local favorite
Gjelina **824**.......................Worth the travel
Jim's Original **954**..........................Late night
Joong Boo Market **954**......................Bargain
Katsu **968**...High end
Mexico Steak House **955**.................Breakfast
Momofuku Ssäm Bar **1023**.....Worth the travel
NAHA **962**.............................Local favorite
Les Nomades **960**.....................Local favorite
Northern City **955**.........Regular neighborhood
Pizzeria Bianco **788**.............Worth the travel
Pub Royale **964**.................Wish I'd opened
San Soo Gab San **961**...Regular neighborhood
Stax Cafe **965**.................................Breakfast
Strings Ramen **956**........................Late night
Taqueria Los Comales **961**.............Late night
Topolobampo **963**.....................Local favorite

GEORGIANNA HILIADAKI
Funky Gourmet
13 Paramithias Street, Athens
The Athens-born, Institute of Culinary Education-
trained Hiliadaki completed an internship at elBulli,
establishing Athens's Funky Gourmet Restaurant
in 2009, and winning a Michelin star in 2012.
Bournovalia **718**..............................Late night
Different Beast **718**.........................Breakfast
Frantzén **355**....................................High end
Gramercy Tavern **1036**..........Wish I'd opened
Kavos 1964 **719**......................Local favorite
Kritikos **718**.................Regular neighborhood
Noma **369**.........................Worth the travel
The Press Club **145**..............Worth the travel
Sushimou **718**..................Worth the travel
To Xeiropoiito **719**............................Bargain

SHAUN HILL
The Walnut Tree
Llanddewi Skirrid, Abergavenny

This British restaurant legend put Gidleigh Park in Devon and the Merchant House in Ludlow on the map. He now runs the Michelin-starred Walnut Tree Inn near Abergavenny, South Wales.

10 Greek Street 443	Bargain
The Butchers Arms 407	Local favorite
Fischer's 420	Wish I'd opened
The Gallery 455	Breakfast
The Hardwick 499	Regular neighborhood
The Old Inn 394	Worth the travel
The Waterside Inn 390	High end

SHUN KAI HO
Taïrroir
6F, No 299, Lequn 3rd Rd, Taipei

Born and raised in Taichung, Kai embarked on his journey with Chinese cuisine and acquired immeasurable skills in the craft of French cooking.

Awesome Burger 207	Bargain
Chang Ye Deng 202	Regular neighborhood
Dalongdong Baoan Temple 205	Breakfast
Ever Green 207	Local favorite
Ga Er Zui 205	Bargain
Legendary Milkfish Belly 206	Late night
Maison Pic 537	Worth the travel
Nihonryori RyuGin 208	High end
Odette 320	Worth the travel
Shi Lin Fried Lamb 206	Late night
You Jian Yi Chui Yan 199	Wish I'd opened
Zheng Wei Yuan Seafood Restaurant 205	
	Local favorite

REON HOBSON
Pescatore
50 Park Terrace, Christchurch

After working in New Zealand and Australia, he worked in the UK for such luminaries as Gordon Ramsay and Marco Pierre White, before returning to Christchurch in New Zealand, the city where his career began.

The Bridge Room 110	High end
Burgers & Beers Inc 156	Regular neighborhood
Chillingworth Road 156	Local favorite
Fiddlesticks 156	Local favorite
finefish 118	Local favorite
Golden Century 111	Late night
Impromptu Dining 121	Regular neighborhood
Maxine's Palace 157	Late night
Meredith's 165	High end
Meredith's 165	Wish I'd opened
Samurai Bowl 157	Bargain
Sepia 113	High end
Sepia 113	Worth the travel
Town Tonic 157	Breakfast

CHRISTOPHER HODGSON
Driftwood Restaurants and Catering
14001 Main Market Road, Burton

The chef became a partner and consulting chef for the Driftwood Restaurant company after being inspired in New York and bringing the first food truck to Cleveland city.

Acme Oyster House 975	Worth the travel
Chez François 920	High end
Flour 920	Regular neighborhood
Szechuan Cafe 919	Bargain
Ushabu 919	Late night
Yours Truly 917	Breakfast

NICK HOLLOWAY
Nu Nu Restaurant
1 Veivers Road, Palm Cove

Owner of a string of restaurants in Tropical North Queensland, the first of which, Nu Nu, opened in 2004.

10WilliamSt. 119	Late night
Bistro H 89	Local favorite
Brae 101	High end
Brae 101	Worth the travel
Ganbaranba Noodle Colosseum 85	Bargain
Ganbaranba Noodle Colosseum 85	Regular neighborhood
Hartwood 1088	Wish I'd opened
Mr Wong 111	Late night
O' CHA CHA Japanese Dinner & Tea 85	Regular neighborhood
Pho Viet 85	Breakfast
Rusty's Market 86	Breakfast
Salsa Bar & Grill 89	Local favorite
Vivo 88	Local favorite

ANDY HOLLYDAY
Selden Standard
3921 2nd Avenue, Detroit

A two-time James Beard semi-finalist and graduate of the Culinary Institute of America, Andy's travels took him to Detroit where he prepares simple, seasonal cuisine at Selden Standard.

Ajishin 909	Local favorite
El Asador Steakhouse 904	Local favorite
Asador Etxebarri 575	Worth the travel
Astro Coffee 902	Breakfast
Bacco Ristorante 902	High end
Buddy's Pizza 903	Local favorite
Camellia Grill 988	Breakfast
Chartreuse Kitchen & Cocktails 903	Regular neighborhood
La Cova Fumada 594	Worth the travel
Dearborn Meat Market 902	Local favorite
Lafayette Coney Island 904	Late night
Loui's Pizza 908	Local favorite
Luigis 908	Local favorite
Mabel Gray 908	High end
Momotaro 967	Worth the travel
Patois 990	Breakfast
Supino Pizzeria 907	Regular neighborhood
Thuy Trang 907	Local favorite
Ventimiglia Italian Foods 909	Wish I'd opened
Le Vin Papillon 780	Worth the travel
Yemen Café 908	Bargain

BRAD HOLMES
OLO Restaurant
509 Fisgard Street, Victoria

Owner of OLO in Victoria, Holmes previously worked at Vancouver hotspots Feenies, West, Chow, Lumière, and, lastly, Cibo, before setting up with his partner and front-of-house manager, Sahara Tamarin.

Agrius 746	Late night
Hawksworth Restaurant 756	High end
Little Jumbo 747	Late night
Part & Parcel 747	Regular neighborhood
Relish Food & Coffee 747	Breakfast
Standard Pizza 748	Wish I'd opened
State Bird Provisions 832	Worth the travel
Uchida Shokudo 748	Regular neighborhood
Wild Mountain Restaurant 746	Local favorite

JACOB HOLMSTRÖM
Gastrologik
Artillerigatan 14, Stockholm

The Swedish chef and co-founder of Gastrologik in Stockholm (2011) comes from a family of restaurateurs and he honed his skills at Mathias Dahlgren's Matbaren and Matsalen.

Adam/Albin 357	Regular neighborhood
Babette 361	Wish I'd opened
Bageri Petrus 359	Breakfast
Fäviken Magasinet 345	Worth the travel
Gro Restaurang 361	Local favorite
Sturehof 358	Late night
Teatern 361	Bargain
Volt 359	High end

DAN HONG
Mr Wong
3 Bridge Lane, Sydney

Learning his trade in his family's Vietnamese restaurants and Sydney's Tetsuya, Hong went on to oversee four Merivale-group hit restaurants—Ms. G's, Papi Chulo, El Loco, and Mr. Wong.

678 Korean BBQ 116	Regular neighborhood
AN Restaurant 107	Wish I'd opened
Arisun 116	Late night
Attica 151	High end
Boon Café 116	Breakfast
Brae 101	High end
Ester 114	Local favorite
Flower Drum 143	High end
Golden Century 111	Late night
Happy Chef 117	Bargain
Malay Chinese Takeaway 111	Bargain
Marrickville Pork Roll 118	Bargain
Momofuku Seiōbo 123	High end
Quay 125	High end
Sugita 259	Worth the travel

PAUL HOOD
Social Eating House
58 Poland Street, London

He forged his career in London at Monte's Private Member's Club, and The Glasshouse and then, in Tunbridge Wells, at Thackeray's. He worked with Jason Atherton at Maze before becoming head chef at Pollen St. Social. He is now chef patron at Social Eating House.

Barrafina **444**	Late night
Berners Tavern **472**	Breakfast
The Ledbury **423**	Regular neighborhood
Trinity Restaurant **415**	Regular neighborhood

LINTON HOPKINS
Restaurant Eugene
2277 Peachtree Road, Atlanta

A native of Atlanta, where he owns Restaurant Eugene (2004) and the pub Holeman & Finch (2008), he worked at Washington's D.C. Coast, Mr. B's Bistro, and Windsor Court in New Orleans.

L'Assiette **567**	Worth the travel
Bones **943**	Local favorite
City House **935**	Wish I'd opened
Quince **830**	High end
Simply Seoul Kitchen **949**	Bargain

TED HOPSON
The Bellwether
13251 Ventura Boulevard, Los Angeles

Trained at the California School of Culinary Arts and then under Chef David LeFevre at Water Grill, Hopson opened The Bellwether with partner Ann-Marie Verdi in 2015.

The Arthur J **820**	High end
BCD Tofu House **818**	Late night
Claro's Deli **789**	Bargain
La Guerrerense **1077**	Worth the travel
Knead & Co Pasta Bar **814**	Wish I'd opened
Rustic Canyon **822**	Local favorite
The Wallace **813**	Regular neighborhood
Wexler's Deli **822**	Breakfast

JOHN HORNE
Oliver & Bonacini Restaurants / Canoe Restaurant & Bar
66 Wellington Street West, Toronto

With experience at Michelin-starred restaurants such as L'Escargot, The Square, and the Orrery, John honed classic French techniques for seven years as the senior sous shef of Auberge du Pommier in Toronto.

Adamson Barbecue **766**	Regular neighborhood
L'Assiette Champenoise **539**	Worth the travel
Bras **541**	Worth the travel
Carousel Bakery **769**	Bargain
Daniel **1045**	High end
Edulis **768**	Local favorite
Eleven Madison Park **1037**	High end
Maison Publique **778**	Breakfast
Mallard Cottage **750**	Breakfast
Owl of Minerva **767**	Late night
Phnom Penh **760**	Bargain

Raymonds **751**	Wish I'd opened
The Stockyards **769**	Regular neighborhood

PHILIP HOWARD
Elystan Street
43 Elystan Street, London

Chef and co-owner of The Square in London since it opened in 1991, he's more recently teamed up with restaurateur Rebecca Mascarenhas at Kitchen W8 (2009) and Sonny's Kitchen (2012).

Chiltern Firehouse **419**	Local favorite
Fäviken Magasinet **345**	Worth the travel
Hakkasan **439**	High end
Hakkasan **439**	Late night
Padella **462**	Bargain
The River Café **417**	Regular neighborhood
The River Café **417**	Wish I'd opened
The Wolseley **443**	Breakfast

DANIEL HUMM
Eleven Madison Park
11 Madison Avenue, New York

The Swiss chef-co-owner of Eleven Madison Park, The NoMad, and NoMad Bar at The NoMad Hotel, his cuisine is focused on the locally sourced ingredients of New York.

Alléno Paris au Pavillon Ledoyen **557**	Worth the travel
Aska **1015**	High end
Black Seed Bagels **1010**	Breakfast
Blue Hill at Stone Barns **913**	Local favorite
Blue Ribbon Brasserie **1012**	Late night
Café Boulud **1044**	Breakfast
Daniel **1045**	Local favorite
Great NY Noodletown **1006**	Late night
I Sodi **1029**	Regular neighborhood
The Kunjip **1042**	Late night
Mamoun's Falafel **1025**	Bargain
Mandoo Bar **1042**	Bargain
Masa **1042**	High end
New Wonjo **1043**	Late night
Pasquale Jones **1011**	Regular neighborhood
Sake Bar Hagi **1043**	Late night
Schloss Schauenstein **640**	Worth the travel

DAN HUNTER
Brae
4285 Cape Otway Road, Birregurra

Having won accolades aplenty at Royal Mail in Victoria, Aussie chef Hunter (former head chef at Mugaritz) opened the destination restaurant Brae in December 2013.

Asador Etxebarri **575**	Wish I'd opened
Attica **151**	High end
Bespoke Harvest **102**	Local favorite
Bespoke Harvest **102**	Regular neighborhood
La Bimba **100**	Local favorite
La Bimba **100**	Regular neighborhood
Birregurra General Store **101**	Bargain
Birregurra General Store **101**	Breakfast
Ester **114**	Worth the travel
The European **143**	Breakfast
Flower Drum **143**	High end
Golden Century **111**	Late night
IGNI **102**	Local favorite
IGNI **102**	Regular neighborhood

Matsukawa **265**	Wish I'd opened
Miyamasou **250**	Worth the travel
Roberta's **1017**	Wish I'd opened
ShanDong MaMa **145**	Bargain
Sixpenny **123**	High end
Supernormal **145**	Regular neighborhood

JOHN JACKSON & CONNIE DESOUSA
CHARCUT Roast House
899 Centre Street Southwest, Calgary

Meat-loving Jackson, together with co-chef and co-owner Connie DeSousa, put Calgary firmly on the food map with the 2010 launch of CHARCUT Roast House's urban-rustic cuisine.

Alloy **740**	Regular neighborhood
Aniar **506**	Worth the travel
Anju **740**	Late night
Anju **740**	Regular neighborhood
Atelier Crenn **833**	Worth the travel
Ayden Kitchen and Bar **752**	Wish I'd opened
Bar Raval **769**	Worth the travel
Blink Restaurant & Bar **740**	Regular neighborhood
Buca **767**	Worth the travel
Charbar **740**	Late night
Charbar **740**	Regular neighborhood
Container Bar **740**	Regular neighborhood
Corso 32 **743**	Worth the travel
Dailo **770**	Worth the travel
Deane House **740**	Regular neighborhood
Deer & Almond **749**	Worth the travel
Empellón **1040**	Worth the travel
Hawksworth **756**	Worth the travel
Joe beef **779**	High end
Little Grouse on the Prairie **753**	Wish I'd opened
Lyle's **488**	Worth the travel
Maison Publique **778**	Worth the travel
Mallard Cottage **750**	Worth the travel
Model Milk **741**	Regular neighborhood
The Nash **741**	Regular neighborhood
Native Tongues Tacqueria **741**	Regular neighborhood
Nora Gray **774**	Worth the travel
NOtaBLE **741**	Regular neighborhood
Ox Bar de Tapas **741**	Regular neighborhood
Park Restaurant **783**	Worth the travel
Parts & Labour **769**	Worth the travel
Au Pied de Cochon **551**	Worth the travel
Pigeonhole **742**	Late night
Pigeonhole **742**	Regular neighborhood
Raymonds **751**	Worth the travel
River Café **742**	Local favorite
River Café **742**	Regular neighborhood
Rostizado **745**	Worth the travel
Rouge Restaurant **742**	Regular neighborhood
Ruby Watchco **769**	Worth the travel
Shokunin **742**	Late night
Shokunin **742**	Regular neighborhood
Sidewalk Citizen **742**	Breakfast
The Spotted Pig **1030**	Worth the travel
State Bird Provisions **832**	Worth the travel
Ten Foot Henry **743**	Regular neighborhood
Terra Restaurant **797**	Worth the travel
Tickets **601**	Worth the travel
Toqué! **783**	Worth the travel

Una Pizza + Wine 743..Regular neighborhood
Vij's 759..................................Worth the travel

ALEX JACKSON
Sardine
15 Micawber Street, London
He worked in London with Stevie Parle at
Dock Kitchen and Rotorino, and then took
some time out to work with French cheeses
at Mons Cheesemongers, before returning
to the kitchen and opening the acclaimed
Sardine in 2016.
40 Maltby Street 460...Regular neighborhood
40 Maltby Street 460...Regular neighborhood
Beigel Bake 485.............................Late night
Le Bistrot de Paradou 546....Worth the travel
Coombeshead Farm 391......Worth the travel
Jen Café 450...................................Bargain
Pacific Social Club 476..................Breakfast
Primeur 491.................Regular neighborhood
The River Café 417............................High end
Rochelle Canteen 486..Regular neighborhood

ROBERT JACOBSSON
Bord 13
Engelbrektsgatan 13, Malmö
After a spell working at Noma, he opened
B.A.R. in Malmö with Besnik Gashiat the end
of 2012, focusing on the basic flavors of the
raw ingredients he used.
Bar del Pla 594.................Worth the travel
Bastard 346...................................Late night
Daniel Berlin Krog 349......................High end
Daniel Berlin Krog 349.................Local favorite
Hagen 347.....................................Bargain
Kaffebaren Möllan 347...................Breakfast
Restaurant Sture 348...Regular neighborhood
Solde kaffebar 349.........................Breakfast
Vollmers 349...............................Local favorite

EYAL JAGERMANN
The Barbary
16 Neal's Yard, London
Growing up in Tel Aviv, he worked in
restaurants from the fifteen. He joined
The Palomar in London when it opened
in 2014, before setting up The Barbary in
collaboration with the Palomar team.
Beigel Bake 485.............................Late night
The Delaunay 432.........................Breakfast
Eat Tokyo 448............Regular neighborhood
Hill & Szrok 474................Wish I'd opened
Lyle's 488.................Regular neighborhood
La Petite Maison 441.......................High end
Plachutta 683................Worth the travel
The Quality Chop House 469..............Regular
neighborhood
The River Café 417....................Local favorite
Santa Katarina 174........Worth the travel
St. John Bread & Wine 489........Local favorite
Tayyabs 494..................................Bargain
Zuma 419.....................................High end

MARK JARVIS
Anglo
30 St Cross Street, London
Trained in the art of the Robata grill
(Japanese charcoal grill), he honed his time
at Le Manoir with stints at Roka and Zuma
before starting his first solo venture, Anglo.
Le Manoir aux Quat'Saisons 403.......High end
Café Colbert 411...................Local favorite
Chesham Tandoori 391..............Local favorite
The Dairy 414..............................Late night
E.T. Steamboat Restaurant 292......Worth the
travel
The Manor 414.......................Local favorite
The Modern Pantry 468....................Breakfast
Patty & Bun 421.............................Bargain
Royal China Club 422...Regular neighborhood
Trinity Restaurant 415................Local favorite
Zuma 419....................Wish I'd opened

JENNIFER JASINSKI
Rioja
1431 Larimer Street, Denver
The executive chef and co-owner of Denver's
Rioja, Bistro Vendôme, and Euclid Hall,
the Culinary Institute of America-trained
Jaskinski spent ten years working with
Wolfgang Puck, her "mentor and culinary
role model".
Bar Dough 798.........Regular neighborhood
beast + bottle 798.................Local favorite
Euclid Hall Bar & Kitchen 798.........Late night
Fruition 798.................................High end
JJ Chinese Restaurant 798............Late night
Linger 798...................Wish I'd opened
New Saigon 799.............................Bargain
New Saigon 799..........Regular neighborhood
Patzcuaro's Mexican Restaurant 799......Local
favorite
Pêche 977.....................Worth the travel
Providence 817.................Worth the travel
State Bird Provisions 832......Worth the travel
Sushi Den 799................................High end
Trois Mec 818.................Worth the travel
Uncle Boons 1011...............Worth the travel

JULIUS JASPERS
happyhappyjoyjoy
Bilderdijkstraat 158, Amsterdam
A judge on Dutch TV's popular show "Top
Chef", in 2013 Jaspers opened Julius Bar &
Grill, a modern barbecue restaurant.
BAK Restaurant 514..................Local favorite
BAR-Becue Castel 514.....................Late night
Bistro La Cave 510.......Regular neighborhood
Bord'Eau 514................................High end
Disfrutar 596................................High end
Frantzén's Kitchen 229....Wish I'd opened
Frantzén's Kitchen 229....................High end
Le Garage 518.............Regular neighborhood
Jean-Georges 1046..........................High end
Marchal at Hotel d'Angleterre 513...Breakfast
Restaurant Breda 515...............Local favorite
Rijsel 519...............................Local favorite
La Sirena 585.................................Bargain

KATRINA JAZAYERI
Juliet
257 Washington Street, Somerville
Drawing upon her background in social
justice and engineering, she champions
a diverse and supportive career-oriented
workplace for her staff, including a profit
sharing arrangement and paying them the
national living wage.
Alive & Kicking Lobsters 894.....Local favorite
BISq 894......................Regular neighborhood
Buddy's Diner 899.........................Breakfast
Café Sushi 895...............................High end
Eastern Standard 890...................Late night
J and J Restaurant 899.....................Bargain
Robert et Louise 553........Worth the travel
Saltie Girl 892.................Wish I'd opened
Three Little Figs 900......................Breakfast
Tupelo 897.................Regular neighborhood

MARC-ANDRÉ JETTÉ
Hoogan et Beaufort
4095 Molson, Montréal
Ex-chef of 400 Coups, he opened the doors
of his new restaurant, Hoogan et Beaufort,
in 2015, which includes a wood-fire grill and
open kitchen.
Larrys 777...................Regular neighborhood
Montreal Plaza 781......Regular neighborhood

DREW JOHNSON
Kincaid Grill
6700 Jewel Lake Road, Anchorage
Christopher "Drew" Johnson worked at his
family-owned restaurant, The Speedy Pig in
Alabama, before moving to Alaska in 2005.
He began his successful tenure at Kincaid
Grill in 2008.
Bear Tooth Grill 786.......................Breakfast
Bear Tooth Grill 786......Regular neighborhood
Bridge Seafood Restaurant 786.Local favorite
City Diner 786..............................Breakfast
Crow's Nest 786.............................High end
Daniel 1045................Worth the travel
F Street Station 787.........................Late night
Hearth Artisan Pizza 787...Regular neighborhood
Pangea Restaurant & Lounge 787...Late night
Pangea Restaurant & Lounge 787......Wish I'd
opened
Southside Bistro 787..................Local favorite
Taco King 787.................................Bargain
Tequila 61 788.................Wish I'd opened
Tommy's Burger Stop 787.................Bargain

TIMOTHY JOHNSON
Apicius
23 Stone Street, Cranbroke
A protégé of Nico Ladenis, Johnson opened
Apicius in Kent in 2004, winning acclaim for
his imaginative, French-influenced cooking.
Café Caussette 221........................Breakfast
The Landgate Bistro 395..Regular neighborhood
Opera 292....................................Breakfast
Ted's Room 399............................Breakfast

KEVIN JOHNSON
The Grocery
4 Cannon Street, Charleston

A Johnson & Wales University graduate, he cooked under chefs such as Patrick O'Connell at The Inn at Little Washington and Frank Lee at Slightly North of Broad, before opening The Grocery with his wife.

The Ordinary 1056........Regular neighborhood

PHILIP JOHNSON
e'cco bistro
100 Boundary Street, Brisbane

New Zealand-born, he has become one of Australia's most celebrated chefs with his landmark bistro and has authored six cookbooks.

Anouk Café 128..........................Breakfast
Bar Alto 128.................Regular neighborhood
Brooklyn Standard 129.....................Late night
Eat Street Northshore 129..........Local favorite
Esquire 130.................................High end
LONgTIME 133.......................Wish I'd opened
Restaurant Hubert 112..........Worth the travel
Taro's Ramen 135................................Bargain

JOSEPH JONHSON
Minton's
210 West 118th, New York City

His Puerto Rican roots permeate his first memories of cooking, since then he has honed his skills in some of New York's most demanding kitchens, Centro Vinoteca, Jane, and Tribeca Grill among them.

Absolute Bagels 1045......................Breakfast
Lion's Head Tavern 1046...................Late night
Melba's 1007.................Regular neighborhood
Thai Market 1046.........Regular neighborhood

JEAN JOHO
Everest
440 South La Salle Street, Chicago

Born in Alsace, France, he honed his skills in professional kitchens throughout Europe and is chef-owner of the Michelin-starred Everest.

L'Auberge de l'Ill 539..............Worth the travel
Beatrix 962.......................................Breakfast
Everest 964....................................High end
Everest 964.............................Local favorite
M Burger 964....................................Bargain
Mon Ami Gabi 958.........................Late night
Naoki 958.....................Regular neighborhood
Ramen-san 963...............Regular neighborhood
RPM Steak 963...................Wish I'd opened

DYLAN JONES & DUANGPORN SONGVISAVA
Bo.Lan
24 Soi Sukhumvhit 53 Klongton nua, Bangkok

Slow Food-championing husband-and-wife team who combine ethical ingredients with traditional Thai recipes.

Amantee 286.....................................Breakfast
Appia 287.......................................High end
Bras 541.............................Wish I'd opened
Eat Me Restaurant 280......................High end
Fei Ya 284.......................................High end
Ruan Pan Yha 276.................Worth the travel

Saew Noodles 289.............................Bargain
Soul Food Mahanakorn 287.......Local favorite
Suki Masa 289.............Regular neighborhood
Sushi Sawada 259.................Worth the travel
Xia Duck Noodles 283.......................Late night

MARTIN JUNEAU
Pastaga
6389 Boulevard Saint Laurent, Montréal

A rising star of Quebec cuisine, he worked in a string of prestigious restaurants before opening Pastaga in 2011.

Dépanneur Lalime 469.......................Bargain
Marconi 781.......................Wish I'd opened
Miami Deli 774.................................Breakfast
Montreal Plaza 781..........................Late night
Le Mousso 774......................Local favorite
Mugaritz 576.....................Worth the travel
Toqué! 783.......................................High end

RAVI KAPUR
Liholiho Yacht Club
871 Sutter Street, San Francisco

Bringing the food of Hawaii to San Francisco, his restaurant is named after the Maui street where Kapur's uncles lived in the eighties.

ABV 834..Late night
Beauty's Bagel Shop 794................Breakfast
Gjusta 924.........................Worth the travel
Izakaya Rintaro 835.....Regular neighborhood
Koi Palace 791................................Breakfast
MAU 835..Bargain
Namu Gaji 836.................................Breakfast
Nopa 828...Late night
RICH TABLE 831...........Regular neighborhood
Saison 841.......................................High end
WesBurger N'More 837....................Bargain

JOSHUA KATZ
Berber & Q
Arch 338, Acton Mews, London

At Berber & Q, Katz, the former sous chef of Ottolenghi, has been inspired by a lifelong exposure to Middle Eastern flavors, together with the unpretentious American barbecue he experienced in New York. A second London branch opened in 2016.

Hash E8 470......................................Breakfast
The Laughing Heart 474.................Late night
The Ledbury 423..............................High end
Lilia 1016.........................Worth the travel
Medlar 412.......................................High end
Morito 468....................Regular neighborhood
Moro 468...........................Wish I'd opened
Ottolenghi 481......................Wish I'd opened
Primeur 491...................Regular neighborhood
The Quality Chop House 469......Local favorite
Ranoush Juice 422...........................Late night
Roti King 483.....................................Bargain
Port Sa'id 174.......................Worth the travel
Sunday Café & Restaurant 481..........Regular neighborhood
Tayyabs 494.............................Local favorite
Xi'an Impression 477........................Bargain

TOMAŽ KAVČIČ
Gostilna Pri Lojzetu
Dvorec Zemono, Vipava

A Slovenian chef, who cooks at Gostilna Pri Lojzetu near Ajdovščina, which was built in 1683 and run by his family since 1897.

Agli Amici dal 1887 654Regular neighborhood
Don Alfonso 647....................Wish I'd opened
Eataly 653...Bargain
Osteria Francescana 650.................High end
Ristorante Tokuyoshi 662......Worth the travel
Vander Urbani Resort 693.............Breakfast
The Wine Bar & Grill 646................Late night

HIROYASU KAWATE
Florilege
B1 2-5-4 Jingumae, Tokyo

He travelled to France in 2006 and gained experience at Le Jardin des Sens in Montpellier, before returning to Japan in 2007 and working as a chef at Quintessence. He went independent in 2009 and opened Florilege.

Akasaka Rikyu Ginza 256..................High end
DEN 268......................Regular neighborhood
Hiroya 263.......................................Late night
Minatoya 270...................................Bargain
Mingles 235.......................Worth the travel
Le Ressort 261................................Breakfast
Sourin 271.............................Local favorite
villa AiDA 253.......................Wish I'd opened

GAVIN KAYSEN
Spoon and Stable
211 1st Street North, Minneapolis

He worked at London's L'Escargot and New York's Café Boulud before heading back home to Minneapolis to set up the Spoon and Stable kitchen.

Al's Breakfast 994...........................Breakfast
Alinea 957.......................................High end
Alma 994.............................Local favorite
The Bachelor Farmer 495..........Local favorite
Bar la Grassa 995.............................Late night
Corner Table 995..........Regular neighborhood
Hola Arepa 997............Regular neighborhood
Marla's Caribbean Cuisine 998...........Bargain
Pizzeria Lola 1000.........Regular neighborhood
The Restaurant at Meadowood 797.Worth the travel
SingleThread Farms 792.......Wish I'd opened
Tilia 1001......................Regular neighborhood

NIALL KEATING
Whatley Manor
Easton Grey, Malmesbury

Beginning his kitchen career as a fifteen-year-old pot-washer, he now has Michelin-starred experience from the US, Denmark, and the UK.

The Gumstool Inn 396...............Local favorite
Pinkmans 390....................................Breakfast
The Potting Shed 407....Regular neighborhood
Stargazy Fish Bar 396........................Bargain
Tetbury Kebab Van 396....................Late night

SHANNON KELLAM
Montrachet
224 Given Terrace, Brisbane

A keen competitive chef, and regular participant in the Culinary Olympics, he has since retired and now focuses on continuing the Montrachet legacy.

Anouk Café **128**................................Breakfast
Clarke's of North Beach **104**...............Regular
      neighborhood
King of Kings **132**................................Late night
Spicers Clovelly Estate **86**.........Local favorite

MIRCO KELLER
Water Library
Chamchuri Square, Bangkok

This German chef undertook a chef's apprenticeship at The Ritz Carlton Berlin. In 2010 he moved to Thailand as chef de cuisine of Water Library.

Boon Pochana **280**.....................Local favorite
Boon Pochana **280**.......Regular neighborhood
Brekkie **287**.......................................Breakfast
Curry 36 **629**.............................Wish I'd opened
Ginza Sushi Ichi **284**..........................High end
Hia Tue Yaowarat **286**......................Late night
Ho Hung Kee Congee & Noodle **219** Worth the
      travel
Huai Kwang Night Market **282**........Late night
Khaophat Pu Mueang Thong 1 **283**......Bargain
Little Beast **288**...........Regular neighborhood
Sühring **289**......................................High end
Sühring **289**.............................Wish I'd opened
Tantris **624**.............................Worth the travel
Took Lae Dee **289**..............................Bargain
Yim Yim **285**...............................Local favorite

LAWRENCE KEOGH
New Street Grill & Fish Market
16 New Street, London

He has made numerous TV appearances in the UK, including Saturday Kitchen Live, and he has also consulted with British Airways on their inflight food.

Jackson + Rye **426**.....Regular neighborhood
The Wharf **428**.............Regular neighborhood

SELIN KIAZIM
Oklava
74 Luke Street, London

She worked in London with Peter Gordon at The Providores and later as head chef at Kopapa, before setting up Oklava in Shoreditch in 2015 with her business partner, Laura Christie.

Barrafina **444**...............Regular neighborhood
The Providores **421**.........................Breakfast

THOMAS KIM
The Rabbit Hole
920 East Lake Street, Minneapolis

Following a few home kitchen fires in his youth, this left-handed chef has worked with Roy Yamaguchi and Jin Suzuki, and now runs The Rabbit Hole with his wife, Kat Kim.

112 eatery **994**................................Late night
Alma **994**.....................................Local favorite

Corner Table **996**............................High end
French Meadow Bakery & Cafe **996**.Breakfast
Grand Cafe **997**..............................Breakfast
Hachi Ju Hachi **796**..............Worth the travel
The Icehouse **997**............................Late night
Kramarczuk's **998**......................Local favorite
Manny's Steakhouse **998**..................High end
Marla's Caribbean Cuisine **998**..........Regular
      neighborhood
Modern Times Cafe **999**....................Breakfast
The Purple Pig **463**.................Worth the travel
Quang Restaurant **1000**.....................Bargain
Revival **1000**..........................Wish I'd opened
Sandcastle **1000**.......................Local favorite
Spoon and Stable **1001**.....................High end
Taqueria Los Ocampo **1002**...............Late night
Victor's 1959 Café **1002**....................Breakfast

MILES KIRBY
Caravan Restaurants
11–13 Exmouth Market, London

This London-based chef ran the kitchen at The Providores and Tapas Room before launching Caravan with fellow Kiwi Chris Ammermann in 2010. Now has branches in King's Cross, Exmouth Market, and Bankside.

Bestia **813**.............................Worth the travel
Bone Daddies **445**............................Late night
The Golden Dragon **449**....................Late night
The Marksman **475**......Regular neighborhood
Morito **479**...................Regular neighborhood
My Neighbours the Dumplings **475**.....Regular
      neighborhood
Primeur **491**..................Regular neighborhood
Rawduck **476**.................Regular neighborhood
ROKA **453**..High end
Shawarma Bar **469**...........................Bargain
St. John **471**.............................Local favorite
Sweetings **467**..........................Local favorite
Towpath Café **479**...........................Breakfast

TARAS KIRIYENKO
Touché Wine Bar & Kitchen
15 Rochdelskaya Street, Moscow

A student of Alexey Zimin, this Moscow-based chef serves a menu dominated by starters and desserts, which emphasises the flavors of the ingredients he uses.

Le 6 Paul Bert **564**..................Wish I'd opened
AQ Kitchen **710**............Regular neighborhood
FARSh **712**...Bargain
Glenuill **712**..............................Local favorite
Khachapuri **712**................................Bargain
Mugaritz **576**.........................Worth the travel
Au Passage **565**.....................Wish I'd opened
SAVVA **713**.......................................Breakfast
Septime **566**.....................................High end
Shake Shack **706**...............................Bargain
El TriCiclo **590**.................................Late night

MATTHEW KIRKLEY
COI Restuarant
373 Broadway, San Francisco

Prior to becoming executive chef and partner at COI, following the departure of Daniel Patterson, Kirkley worked at Joël Robuchon (Las Vegas) and L20 (Chicago).

L'Ambroisie **553**...............................High end
Bubble Dogs **446**.....................Wish I'd opened
Monsieur Benjamin **830**.....................Regular
      neighborhood
Sam's **838**..Late night
Zuni Café **831**...........................Local favorite

MUSTAFA CIHAN KIPÇAK
Tabla
Alaçatı, Istanbul

He founded La Mouette with Üryan Doğmuş before they opened Gile Restaurant 2012. He also owns the local pub concept Akali with Çağlar Kıpçak and the Turkish street food spot Tabla.

Emirgan Sütiş **724**............................Breakfast
Günaydın Maçka **722**....Regular neighborhood
Kantin **724**...............................Wish I'd opened
Karadeniz Dönercisi Asım Usta **722**....Bargain
Karaköy Lokantası **722**...............Local favorite
Mikla **722**...High end
Sardunya Restaurant **719**.....Worth the travel
Söğüşcüm **719**.................................Late night

JAMES KNAPPETT
Kitchen Table at Bubbledogs
70 Charlotte Street, London

With a glittering résumé including stints at The Ledbury, Noma, and Per Se, Knappett settled in London as chef-patron of Bubbledogs, a gourmet hot dog-Champagne concept with a fine-dining annex, Kitchen Table.

A. Wong **428**.................Regular neighborhood
Hoppers **450**.....................................Bargain
Koya Bar **451**....................................Breakfast
Maaemo **344**.........................Worth the travel
The Quality Chop House **469**......Local favorite
Som Saa **489**.........................Wish I'd opened
Sosharu **471**....................................Late night
Sushi Tetsu **469**................................High end

FLORENCE KNIGHT
Polpetto
11 Berwick Street, London

She worked as pastry chef under Robin Gill at Raymond Blanc's The Diamond Club and as head canapé chef at Rhubarb Food Design. She became head chef at St Clement's, before opening Polpetto in Soho, London.

40 Maltby Street **460**.............Wish I'd opened
Bao **444**...Bargain
C&R **447**..Bargain
Aux Deux Amis **565**...............Worth the travel
Fernandez & Wells **448**.....................Breakfast
The Kati Roll Company **450**..............Late night
Koya Bar **451**.................Regular neighborhood
Maison Bertaux **452**...................Local favorite
Els Pescadors **603**.................Worth the travel
Quo Vadis **453**.................................Late night
ROKA **442**..High end
Septime **566**.....................................High end
St. John Bread & Wine **489**........Local favorite
Vasco & Piero's Pavilion **454**.............Regular
      neighborhood

PETER KNOGL
Cheval Blanc
Grand Hotel Les Trois Rois, Blumenrain 8, Basel
The Swiss master of Mediterranean haute cuisine, which he serves at his restaurant Cheval Blanc in Basel.
Lasarte 597.................Regular neighborhood

ONNO KOKMEIJER
Ciel Bleu
Ferdinand Bolstraat 333, Amsterdam
Dutch born and trained, since he arrived in Amsterdam in 2003, he has established Ciel Bleu as one of the city's best restaurants.
@7 519...............................Breakfast
Brasserie Bark 518.......................Late night
The Butcher 517.............................Bargain
Café Kiêbert 518........................Breakfast
Cannibale Royale 514.....................Late night
Flocons de Sel 536.............Worth the travel
Foodhallen Amsterdam 518.......Local favorite
Geranium 378..................Worth the travel
Izakaya Asian Kitchen & Bar 517........Regular neighborhood
Merlet 510....................................High end
Omelegg 517.....................Wish I'd opened
Restaurant Daalder 516.....................Regular neighborhood
Serre Restaurant 517..Regular neighborhood
The Table 624.....................Worth the travel
Visaandeschelde 519....Regular neighborhood

ANATOLY KOMM
Anatoly Komm for Raff House
25 Malaya Nikitskaya Street, Moscow
This Russian chef, who trained as a geophysicist before taking up cooking in 2000, has won acclaim by reinventing traditional Russian dishes.
Bao + Bar 708...............................Bargain
Café Pushkin 711.......................Late night
Café Pushkin 711.....................Local favorite
Il Lago 640.................................Breakfast
Ovo by Carlo Cracco 706...................High end
Restaurant A.T 554..........Worth the travel
l'Hotel de Ville Crissier 640...........High end
Restaurant Les Trois Couronnes 642.............Breakfast
Rooftop°42 640.........................Late night
Seiji 707..................Regular neighborhood
Semifreddo 707...........Regular neighborhood
Twins 710...............Regular neighborhood
Wine & Crab 714.................Wish I'd opened

JESSICA KOSLOW
Sqirl
720 North Virgil Avenue, Los Angeles
Koslow's sunny Californian empire is expanding to a takeaway joint and a massive all-day dining compound.
108 368....................Worth the travel
Asanebo 823.............................High end
BCD Tofu House 818.....................Late night
Diner 1015......................Wish I'd opened
Guisados 811...............................Bargain

Mariscos Jalisco 813.......................Bargain
The Musso & Frank Grill 818.....Local favorite
Noma 369.....................Worth the travel
PINE & CRANE 823................Wish I'd opened
Q Sushi 814.................................High end
Russ & Daughters Cafe 1009.........Breakfast
Sapp Coffee Shop 820...Regular neighborhood
Le Servan 566....................Worth the travel
Shibumi 815................................High end

ANTON KOVALKOV
Antonym
Savinskay Naberezhnay 12/8, Moscow
Anton has embarked on a series of stages at some of the world's best restaurants, including time at Noma, where he was the first Russian stagiaire.
Forest & Marcy 505..............Worth the travel
Glenuill 712..............Regular neighborhood
Madame Wong 712.......................Late night
SAVVA 713................................Breakfast
Severyane 709.............Regular neighborhood
Tartarbar 703....................Wish I'd opened
Turandot 713..............................High end
Voronezh 707................................Bargain
White Rabbit 706....................Local favorite

KWOK KEUNG TUNG
The Chairman
18 Kau U Fong, Hong Kong
Well-practised in cooking Szechuan, Cantonese, and Taiwanese cuisine, he is now the head chef at The Chairman Restaurant, Hong Kong.
Amber 220.................................High end
Amber 220................................Late night
On Lee Noodle 228..........................Bargain
Passion by Gérard Dubois 230.........Breakfast
Seventh Son Restaurant 230.....Local favorite
Seventh Son Restaurant 230.............Regular neighborhood
Ta Vie 225.......................Wish I'd opened
Waku Ghin 322...................Worth the travel

ALBERT AU KWOK KEUNG
China Tang Hong Kong
Landmark Hotel, 4F, 15 Queen's Road, Hong Kong
Honing his skills at a variety of restaurants in Hong Kong and China, he has won Michelin stars at both Island Tang and The Eight in Macau.
8½ Otto e Mezzo Bombana 220...........Regular neighborhood
China Tang 230....................Local favorite
Juxing Home 213...........................Bargain
Juxing Home 213.........................Late night
Old Bazaar Kitchen 230.........Wish I'd opened
Restaurant Green View 242...Worth the travel
Yee Hope Seafood Restaurant 218..Breakfast

MATÍAS KYRIAZIS
Paraje Arevalo
Arévalo 1502, Buenos Aires
Matías is from Buenos Aires. Now aged 40, he has more than 20 years experience working in different restaurants in Argentina and Europe. Since 2009 he has been running

Paraje Arevalo in Buenos Aires.
Aramburu 1125..........................Late night
Don Julio Parrilla 1127............Local favourite
Guido's Bar 1127.......Regular neighbourhood
Los Platitos 1124..........................Bargain
Sol de Mayo 1125........................Breakfast

MERLIN LABRON-JOHNSON
Portland
113 Great Portland Street, London
Executive chef of Portland restaurant and Clipstone restaurant in London.
A. Wong 1125....................Local favorite
Brawn 478..................Regular neighborhood
Ekstedt 357....................Worth the travel
Honey & Co 473...........Regular neighborhood
J.E.F 526.........................Wish I'd opened
Jim's Café 468..........................Breakfast
The Laughing Heart 474..........Late night
The Ledbury 423.........................High end
Sichuan Folk 489..........................Bargain
TÄTÄ Eatery 479...........Regular neighborhood

FLORENT LADEYN
Auberge du Vert Mont
1318 Rue du Mont Noir, Boescheppe
A self-taught chef, he took over the cooking in the family estaminet (cafe-bar) in 2010, later opening Bloempot in Lille, and Au Vert Mont in Boescheppe.
De Barbier 530...........................Bargain
Candide 779..................Worth the travel
Clamato 564...............................Late night
Delicatessen 711...............Worth the travel
Kadeau 368................................High end
Köks 382...................................High end
Møller - Kaffe og Køkken 377.......Breakfast
Nobelhart & Schmutzig 630...Wish I'd opened
Portland 473.....................Worth the travel
Souvenir 530............Regular neighborhood
WarPigs 381.....................Wish I'd opened

DAVID LAI
Neighborhood
61–63 Hollywood Road, Hong Kong
After training with mentors such as Chef Sylvain Portay and Julian Serrano, he returned to Hong Kong in 2003 to open Alain Ducasse's Spoon.
Chong Fat Chiu Chow 212.........Local favorite
Fong Wing Kee 212......................Late night
GODENYA 222.............................High end
Hidden 218................................Late night
Hidden 218...............Regular neighborhood
Hop Yik Tai 213.........................Breakfast
Kau Kee Restaurant 222........Wish I'd opened
Mak's Noodle 223........Regular neighborhood
Seventh Son Restaurant 230.....Local favorite
Sun Kwai Heung 227......................Bargain
Ta Vie 225..................................High end
Tasty Congee & Noodle Wantun Shop 226.......Local favorite
Yardbird 229......................Wish I'd opened
Yat Lok 226................................Bargain

YAU TIM LAI
Tim's Kitchen
84–90 Bonham Strand, Hong Kong

Chinese master chef, and founder of Tim's Kitchen, he served as an apprentice to legendary Canton chef, Choi Lee, for thirty-three years until Lee's retirement.

8½ Otto e Mezzo Bombana **220** ..Local favorite
Lin Heung Tea House **223** ....Breakfast
RAW **208** ....Worth the travel
Restaurant André **331** ....Wish I'd opened
RyuGin **215** .... High end
Se Wong Yee **219** ....Bargain
Sun Yuen **224** ....Regular neighborhood
Yuet Wah Wui Seafood Restaurant **226** ....Late night

CARLO LAMAGNA
Clyde Common
1014 SW Stark Street, Portland

Born in the Philippines, he cooked at several restaurants in Detroit before attending culinary school at the Culinary Institute of America. Now at Clyde Common, Carlo's dishes are a glimpse into his life: old-school flavor, with new-school style.

'Āina **840** ....Wish I'd opened
Asador Extebarri **575** ....Worth the travel
Ataula **846** ....Regular neighborhood
Bad Saint **864** ....Wish I'd opened
Bestia **813** ....Worth the travel
The Big Egg **860** ....Breakfast
Chesa **849** ....Regular neighborhood
Clyde Common **850** ....Local favorite
Coquine **850** ....Regular neighborhood
Dockside Saloon **851** ....Breakfast
Hartwood **1088** ....Worth the travel
Holdfast **852** ....High end
Joe Beef **779** ....Wish I'd opened
Joe Beef **779** ....Worth the travel
Kachka **853** ....Regular neighborhood
LASA **812** ....Worth the travel
Mekong Bistro **855** ....Late night
Ned Ludd **855** ....Local favorite
Nong's Khao Man Gai **856** ....Bargain
Nong's Khao Man Gai **856** ....Regular neighborhood
Au Pied de Cochon **775** ....Wish I'd opened
Pizza Jerk **858** ....Regular neighborhood
Reel M Inn **858** ....Late night
Salare **805** ....Local favorite
Zilla Sake **861** ....Regular neighborhood

FLORIAN LAMELOT
Orient8
Jalan Asia Afrika, Jakarta

He apprenticed with Jean-Marie Gauthier among others before working at Daniel Boulud in New York and latterly, Orient8 in Jakarta.

Akelarre **578** ....Worth the travel
Bandar Djakarta Ancol **299** ....Local favorite
Bar-Roque Grill **328** ....Worth the travel
Beautika **299** ....Local favorite
Cuca **294** ....Local favorite
Daniel **1045** ....Wish I'd opened
Ju-Ma-Na **298** ....High end

KU DE TA **295** ....Late night
Nyoman's Beer Garden **297** ....Bargain
SKYE **301** ....Late night
Teba Mega Café **294** ....Local favorite
Union **302** ....Local favorite
Vin+ **302** ....Bargain

RETO LAMPART
Lampart's
Oltnerstrasse 19, Hägendorf

A Swiss-born chef whose interest in architecture now informs his approach to food at the one-Michelin-starred Lampart's.

l'Hotel de Ville Crissier **640** ....High end
Maison Boulud **774** ....High end
Restaurant Blüemlismatt **641** ....Local favorite
Restaurant Camino **642** ....Regular neighborhood
Restaurant Central **638** ....Regular neighborhood
Restaurant Chappeli **641** ....Local favorite
Taverna Romana **641** ....Bargain
Da Vittorio **654** ....Worth the travel

RICHARD LANDAU
Vedge
1221 Locust Street, Philadelphia

He set up on his own in 1994, and had to expand the space three times before moving to the centre of Philadelphia, where he opened Vedge in 2011.

South Street Philly Bagels **924** ....Breakfast

FILIP LANGHOFF
Restaurant Ask
Vironkatu 8, Helsinki

Former head chef at Chez Dominique, he is currently chef and partner in Restaurant Ask, opened in 2012, and owns the food consultancy firm CIBUS.

Amber **220** ....Worth the travel
Baskeri & Basso **384** ....Late night
Chef & Sommelier **385** ....Local favorite
Gastrologik **358** ....High end
Kuppi ja Muffini **386** ....Breakfast
Latva **386** ....Bargain
Maaemo **344** ....Worth the travel
OLO **386** ....High end
Pjoltergeist **344** ....Regular neighborhood
Restaurant Grön **387** ....Local favorite
Vinkkeli **387** ....Regular neighborhood

LEO LANUSSOL
Proper
Araoz 1676, Buenos Aires

Using the local market for inspiration each day, Lanussol's menu focuses on local and seasonal food.

La Alacena **1126** ....Breakfast
Café San Juan - La Cantina **1131** ....Bargain
Elena **1130** ....High end
Gran Dabbang **1127** .....Regular neighborhood
La Mezzeta **1131** ....Late night
Lo de Charly **1131** ....Late night
El Mostrador de Santa Teresita **1119** ....
                                                  Breakfast
Nola **1128** ....Wish I'd opened

Parador La Huella **1119** ....Worth the travel
La Toscana **1120** ....Worth the travel
Tegui **1129** ....Local favorite

NORMAND LAPRISE
Toqué!
900 Place Jean-Paul-Riopelle, Montreal

A former accountant turned chef, Laprise trained at Hotel de la Cloche near Dijon before returning home to Canada and opening his flagship Toqué! and its sister restaurant Brasserie T.

L'Auberge du Pont de Collonges **534** ......Worth the travel
Barros Lucos **775** ....Bargain
Benu **840** ....Wish I'd opened
Cabane à Sucre au Pied de Cochon **752** ..Local favorite
Jun-I **777** ....Regular neighborhood
Maison Publique **778** ....Breakfast
Mirazur **545** ....High end
Montreal Plaza **781** ......Regular neighborhood
Le Vin Papillon **780** ....Late night

MIKE LATA
FIG
232 Meeting Street, Charleston

Opened Charleston's FIG bistro in 2003 with Adam Nemirow, and The Ordinary oyster bar in 2012. Lata worked across the US and France before landing in Charleston.

Butcher & Bee **1051** ....Late night
Butcher & Bee **1051** .....Regular neighborhood
Septime **566** ....Worth the travel

SASU LAUKKONEN
Chef & Sommelier
Huvilakatu 28, Helsinki

Having earned his stripes as head chef of La Petite Maison and Loft Restaurant & Lounge in Helsinki, in 2010 Laukkonen took the helm at his own restaurant and, by 2014 it had won its first Michelin star.

Basbas & Staff **384** ....Late night
Basbas & Staff **384** ......Regular neighborhood
Café Ekberg **385** ....Breakfast
Fafa's **385** ....Bargain
Maaemo **344** ....High end
Mirazur **545** ....Worth the travel
Putte's Bar & Pizza **397** ....Late night
Relæ **378** ....Wish I'd opened
Restaurant Ask **387** ....Local favorite
Restaurant Grön **387** ....Regular neighborhood

CHOONGHU LEE
Zero Complex
113 Donggwang-ro, Seoul

Following stints at Le Dauphin, Le Châteaubriand, and Michel Rostang in Paris, Lee brought this impressive experience to Seoul, where he now runs the kitchen at Zero Complex.

Bong Pi Yang **241** ....Regular neighborhood
Hadongkwan **238** ....Breakfast
Jungsik Dang **235** ....Local favorite
Seorae Jeon **240** ....Late night

COREY LEE
Benu
22 Hawthorne Street, San Francisco

A James Beard Award-winning chef who trained at seven three-Michelin-starred restaurants in England, France, and the US before opening the two-Michelin-starred Benu in 2010.

Aqua **625**..............................Worth the travel
b. Patisserie **839**..............................Breakfast
Le Calandre **671**..............................Worth the travel
L'express **776**..............................Late night
The French Laundry **797**..............................High end
Lido 84 **659**..............................Worth the travel
RONIN **229**..............................Late night
Taqueria Vallarta **836**..............................Bargain
Tartine Bakery **836**..............................Local favorite
Trou Normand **841**.......Regular neighborhood

EDWARD LEE
610 Magnolia
610 West Magnolia Avenue, Louisville

Hailing from Brooklyn before settling in Louisville, Lee's Asian-accented "New Southern" cuisine at 610 Magnolia and MilkWood has earned him a loyal following.

Eleven Madison Park **1037**..............High end
Hakata Tonton **1028**   Regular neighborhood
Hawksworth **756**..............................Worth the travel
Jack Fry's **882**..............................Local favorite
New Wonjo **1043**..............................Late night
Peg Leg Porker **936**..............Wish I'd opened
Waffle House **883**..............................Bargain
The Wieners Circle **959**..............................Breakfast

JEREMY LEE
Quo Vadis
26–29 Dean Street, London

This Scottish-born chef left London's Blueprint Café in 2011 to take the reins at Quo Vadis, bringing with him an award-winning combination of French technique and British seasonality.

Andrew Edmunds **443**..............................Bargain
Bao **472**..............................Regular neighborhood
Bao **472**..............................Local favorite
Brawn **478**..............................Regular neighborhood
Chez Bruce **429**..............................High end
The Clove Club **487**........Regular neighborhood
The Clove Club **487**..............................High end
Dooky Chase's Restaurant **986**..Worth the travel
Le Gavroche **438**..............................High end
Gerrard's Corner **449**..............................Bargain
The Ivy **434**..............................Late night
Kiln **451**..............................Local favorite
The Laughing Heart **461**..............Late night
The Ledbury **423**..............................High end
Lyle's **488**..............................Regular neighborhood
Maison Bertaux **452**..............................Breakfast
El Pastór **462**..............................Bargain
Rochelle Canteen **486**..............Local favorite
Salon **464**..............................Breakfast
St. John Bar and Restaurant **471**........Regular
                                                                neighborhood
St. John Bar and Restaurant **471**...Local favorite
Upperline **991**..............................Worth the travel
The Wolseley **443**..............Wish I'd opened

JUN LEE
Soigné
B549-17 Banpo 4-dong, Seoul

Following a period at Thomas Keller's Per Se, Lee followed Jonathan Benno as he opened Lincoln, before bringing a series of playful pop-ups to Seoul.

Amass **370**..............................Worth the travel
Kojima **235**..............................High end
Per Se **1006**..............................Worth the travel
Polestar **236**..............................Wish I'd opened
Seoraejeon **240**..............................Late night
Seoraejeon **240**..............Regular neighborhood
Shineuiju Chapssal Sundae **236**.........Bargain
Sushi Koji **236**..............Regular neighborhood
Teacher Kim **240**..............................Breakfast
Zero Complex **240**..............................Local favorite

MALCOLM LEE
Candlenut
17A Dempsey Road, Singapore

Heading up the world's first Michelin-starred Peranakan restaurant, Lee takes a contemporary yet authentic approach to traditional Straits-Chinese cuisine.

Les Amis **328**..............................High end
L'ATELIER de Joël Robuchon **324**......High end
Azurmendi **577**..............................Worth the travel
Beach Road Scissor-Cut Curry Rice **324**....Late
                                                                        night
Bo.Lan **287**..............................Worth the travel
Buko Nero **329**..............................Wish I'd opened
Keng Eng Kee Seafood **317**........Local favorite
The Ledbury **423**..............................Worth the travel
Rumah Makan Minang **333**..............Regular
                                                                neighborhood
Springleaf Prata Place **335**..............Breakfast
Wee Nam Kee **326**..............................Bargain

SUSUR LEE
Lee
601 King Street West, Toronto

A critically acclaimed Asian-fusion chef, Hong Kong-born Lee's Toronto restaurants include Lotus, Lee, and Bent, with outposts in Washington D.C. and Singapore.

Buca **767**..............................High end
Forno Cultura **769**..............................Local favorite
King's Noodle Restaurant **766**..........Bargain
Noce **770**..............................Regular neighborhood
Peoples Eatery **766**..............................Late night
Saving Grace **770**..............................Breakfast

ÁNGEL LEÓN
Aponiente
Carrer Francisco Cossi Ochoa, Cadiz

Ángel León is head chef of Aponiente, a two Michelin starred modern seafood restaurant.

Bar El Potaje **572**..............................Breakfast
Bodeguita El Adobo **572**..............Late night
Mugaritz **576**..............................High end
El Pescaíto **572**..............................Regular
                                                        neighbourhood
Quique Dacosta **591**..............................High end
Las Rejas **572**..............................Regular
                                                        neighbourhood

Restaurante El Faro de Cádiz **572**...........Local
                                                                        favourite
Romerijo **573**..............................Wish I'd opened

CHAN YAU LEUNG
Fook Lam Moon
35-45 Johnston Road, Hong Kong

He started working at Fook Lam Moon in the 1990s and now oversees their culinary team and the group's other fine Cantonese dining brand, Guo Fu Lou.

Bing Kee **229**..............................Breakfast
Jade Dragon **191**..............Wish I'd opened
Luk Yu Tea House **223**..............Local favorite
Ming's Kitchen **213**..............................Late night
Shing Kee Noodles **227**..............................Bargain
Sushi Gin **219**..............................High end
Tim Ho Wan **213**..........Regular neighborhood
Wild Rocket **333**..............................Worth the travel

JEREME LEUNG
Ufaa
Rangali Island, Maldives

A pioneer of modern Chinese cuisine, he oversees nine restaurants across the world, including sites in Singapore, Shanghai, Beijing and, most recently, Manila.

Bites & Bottle-O **197**....Regular neighborhood

TATIANA LEVHA
Le Servan
32 Rue Saint Maur, Paris

Working with her sister, the sommelier Katia Levha, this Manila-born chef uses her multicultural upbringing to influence her traditional French training at such Michelin-starred establishements as L'Astrance in Paris.

L'Arpège **556**..............................High end
L'Astrance **568**..............................High end
Le Baratin **569**..............................Local favorite
Chez Aline **564**..............................Bargain
Clamato **564**..............Regular neighborhood
Lao Siam **569**..............................Bargain
Momofuku Noodle Bar **1023**..Wish I'd opened
Noma **369**..............................Worth the travel
Rosebud **567**..............................Late night
Song Heng **553**..............................Breakfast

JOSHUA LEWIN
Juliet
257 Washington Street, Somerville

Marine-turned-chef, he worked at Momofuku
Noodle Bar before moving to Beacon Hill
Bistro where, under Jason Bond, he refined his
classical French technique and learned about
butchery, foraging, and truly seasonal cooking.

Asta 889	High end
L'Astrance 568	Worth the travel
Atelier Crenn 833	Worth the travel
Bergamot 899	Local favorite
Bijou Café 847	Breakfast
BISq 894	Regular neighborhood
Bondir 895	Local favorite
Bondir 895	High end
Buddy's Diner 899	Breakfast
Buvette 1028	Breakfast
Café Sushi 895	Local favorite
Casa B 899	Regular neighborhood
Centre Street Cafe 898	Local favorite
Clover Food Lab 895	Late night
Eastern Standard 890	Local favorite
Eastern Standard 890	Wish I'd opened
Eastern Standard 890	Late night
Fat Hen 899	Wish I'd opened
Giulia 896	Local favorite
J and J Restaurant 899	Regular neighborhood
J and J Restaurant 899	Bargain
Momofuku Ko 1023	Worth the travel
Moody's Falafel Palace 897	Late night
The Neighborhood Restaurant 900	Bargain
No. 9 Park 891	Local favorite
No. 9 Park 891	High end
Okonomi 1018	Breakfast
Petit Crenn 830	Wish I'd opened
Prune 1024	Wish I'd opened
Prune 1024	Worth the travel
La Rosettisserie 546	Worth the travel
Russ & Daughters Cafe 1009	Breakfast
Sarma 900	Regular neighborhood
Shepard 897	Local favorite
Tasting Counter 900	High end
Tupelo 897	Bargain

JOSH LEWIS
Fleet
16 The Terrace, Brunswick Heads

Formerly of the award-winning Loam in
Victoria, he now plates up dishes at table in
this tiny, sophisticated, small-plate dining spot.

beachwood cafe 84	Local favorite
Boon Café 116	Breakfast
Brae 101	Worth the travel
Dae Jang Kum 117	Late night
Federal Doma Cafe 83	Regular neighborhood
Golden Century 111	Late night
Madang 111	Late night
Milk and Honey 84	Regular neighborhood
Momofuku Seiōbo 123	High end
The Nomadic Kitchen 83	Regular neighborhood
Restaurant Hubert 112	Late night
Saint Peter 120	Wish I'd opened
The Shop 84	Bargain
Sixpenny 123	High end
Yami 82	Local favorite

PAUL LIEBRANDT

Worked for Marco Pierre White, Pierre
Gagnaire and Raymond Blanc prior to moving
Stateside where the 'Englishman in New
York' earned multiple accolades. Opened
The Elm in Brooklyn in 2013.

Balthazar 1011	Breakfast
Balthazar 1011	Late night
Blue Ribbon Sushi 1012	Regular neighbourhood
Bonchon Chicken 1038	Bargain
Gotham Bar & Grill 1025	Local favourite
Masa 1042	High end
Minetta Tavern 1026	Wish I'd opened
Tempura Kondo 573	Worth the travel

ROSS LEWIS
Chapter One
18–19 Parnell Square, Dublin

Son of a farmer, Irish-born Lewis discovered
that he wanted to cook professionally while
at university and he went on to open Chapter
One in 1992.

Bibi's Café 505	Breakfast
Bunsen 503	Bargain
China Sichuan 506	Regular neighborhood
Hang Dai 504	Late night
Osteria Francescana 650	Wish I'd opened
Queen of Tarts 504	Breakfast
Restaurant Patrick Guilbaud 504	High end
Restaurante Dani García 573	Worth the travel
The Wild Goose 505	Local favourite

HAN LIGUANG
Restaurant Labyrinth
8 Raffles Avenue, Singapore

Originally a corporate banker, he has reimagined Singaporean cuisine as a melting
pot of influences from all around the world.

Candlenut 334	High end
L'Enclume 394	Worth the travel
Freshly Made Chee Cheong Fun 322	Bargain
Fu Ming Cooked Food 317	Late night
JB Ah Meng 323	Regular neighborhood
Keng Eng Kee Seafood 317	Regular neighborhood
Lam's Noodles 324	Bargain
Maxwell Food Centre 320	Local favorite
Selera Rasa Nasi Lemak 325	Breakfast
Sin Hoi Sai 318	Late night
Tippling Club 321	High end
Toyo Eatery 307	Worth the travel

RICHIE LIN
Mume
28 Siwei Road, Taipei

Hong Kong-born, he is one of a trio of chefs
to set up a restaurant melding new Nordic
fare with Taiwanese ingredients.

DEN 368	Worth the travel
Din Tai Fung 202	Bargain
Fuhang Soy Milk 209	Breakfast
Gēn Creative 203	Regular neighborhood
Club Boys Saloon 206	Late night
Moutain and Sea House 207	Local favourite
Noma 369	Worth the travel
SPOT Taipei 204	Wish I'd opened

S.T.A.Y 206	High end
Xiaozhang's Seafood 208	Late night

MARCUS LINDNER
The Alpina Gstaad
Alpinastrasse 23, Gstaad

Fine-dining veteran Lindner has over thirty
years' experience in Europe's most renowned
hotel kitchens, and now runs three at The
Alpina in Gstaad.

Basta by Dalsass 639	Regular neighborhood
Charly's 639	Breakfast
Globus am Bellevue 642	Local favorite
Huus Hotel Gstaad 639	Breakfast
Moana Seafood 177	Worth the travel
Restaurant Chesery 639	High end
Restaurant Rialto 639	Late night
Wasserngrat Restaurant 639	Regular neighborhood

GEOFF LINDSAY
Dandelion
133 Ormond Road, Elwood

The Modern Vietnamese restaurant
Dandelion (2011) was Lindsay's first new
venture since selling the renowned Pearl.
His modern Australian take on Asian cuisine
won him plaudits from the outset.

Barley Swine 1060	Worth the travel
Café Di Stasio 153	Regular neighborhood
HuTong Dumpling Bar 144	Breakfast
Lau's family kitchen 153	Regular neighborhood
Locavore 297	High end
Da Maria 294	Late night
MoVida 144	Wish I'd opened
Sangsaka 296	Regular neighborhood
Stokehouse 153	Local favorite
Thanh Nga Nine 151	Bargain

KEN LING
Tóng Lè
60 Collyer Quay, Singapore

Having established the Club Chinois, he now
runs the prestigious Chinese restaurant,
Tóng Lè in Resorts World Sentosa, and
Tóng Lè Private Dining in the OUE Tower.

Tsubaki 251	Worth the travel
Ting Heng Seafood 318	Late night
Ang Mo Kio Market 316	Breakfast
Nakhon Kitchen 316	Bargain
Ah Heng Curry Chicken Bee Hoon Mee 319	Regular neighborhood
Jade 320	Local favorite
Lei Garden 320	Wish I'd opened

ANDREW LITTLE
Josephine
2316 12th Avenue South, Nashville

With roots in Pennsylvania's Dutch farm country
where he grew up, Little's ground-to-gourmet
style creates a visceral experience for diners.

Big Al's Deli 934	Breakfast
Biscuit Love 934	Breakfast
Biscuit Love 934	Regular neighborhood
Corner Pub 935	Late night
Husk 935	Regular neighborhood

ERIC LIU
Gēn Creative
24 Dunhua South Road, Taipei

A Taiwanese aerospace engineer graduate, Liu attended the Culinary Institute of America before he returned home to Taiwan to open Gēn Creative, a name which means "roots" in Mandarin.

L'ATELIER de Joël Robuchon **334**	High end
Le Blanc **202**	Regular neighborhood
Le Blanc **202**	Wish I'd opened
Chou Chou **202**	Wish I'd opened
Chou Chou **202**	Regular neighborhood
Din Tai Fung **202**	Worth the travel
Dragon Restaurant **209**	Local favorite
ICHI **202**	Late night
MUME **203**	Regular neighborhood
Pin Xian **203**	Bargain
Pin Xian **203**	Late night
Shin Yeh **208**	Local favorite
SPOT Taipei **204**	Regular neighborhood
Spot **204**	Breakfast
Yong He Soy Milk King **205**	Breakfast

ANITA LO
Annisa
13 Barrow Street, New York City

A second-generation Chinese-American who trained in Paris at L'Ecole Ritz-Escoffier, she opened Annisa in New York's Greenwich Village in 2000.

Amerigo **648**	Worth the travel
Aquavit **1039**	High end
Bo Innovation **230**	Worth the travel
Indian Accent **182**	Worth the travel
Le Coucou **1012**	Wish I'd opened
KOSAKA **1029**	Regular neighborhood
Manzanilla **1077**	Worth the travel
MIMI **1026**	Late night
Murray's Bagels **1026**	Breakfast
Petit Crenn **830**	Worth the travel
ramen-ya **1027**	Bargain
Rockmeisha Izakaya **1029**	Regular neighborhood
Russ & Daughters Cafe **1009**	Breakfast
Shuko **1024**	Local favorite
The Spotted Pig **1030**	Regular neighborhood
Taïm **1030**	Bargain
Via Carota **1030**	Regular neighborhood

AARON LONDON
Al's Place
1499 Valencia Street, San Francisco

Hailing from West Sonoma County, he has experience in top-tier Michelin-starred restaurants such as L' Astrance, Daniel, and Blue Hill at Stone Barns.

Aster **834**	Local favorite
Blue Hill at Stone Barns **913**	Worth the travel
Nopa **828**	Late night
The Progress **842**	Regular neighborhood
Rich Table **831**	Local favorite
Saison **841**	High end
State Bird Provisions **832**	Wish I'd opened
Woodhouse fish company **828**	Bargain

JOSUE LOPEZ
GOMA Restaurant
Stanley Place, Brisbane

With time at Maze and Noma under his belt, he was previously head chef at Brisbane restaurant Two Small Rooms and is now executive chef at the Queensland Art Gallery and Gallery of Modern Art.

1889 Enoteca **128**	Regular neighborhood
L'Arpège **556**	Worth the travel
Bird's Nest Yakitori & Bar **129**	Bargain
Brae **101**	Wish I'd opened
Esquire **130**	Local favorite
Gauge **131**	Breakfast
Gerard's Bistro **131**	Regular neighborhood
LONgTIME **133**	Late night
Le Parc **539**	Worth the travel
Trang Restaurant **135**	Bargain
The Wolfe **136**	Regular neighborhood
Urbane Restaurant **136**	High end

KATIE LORENZEN
Tavern & Table
100 Church Street, Mount Pleasant

A graduate of Le Cordon Bleu Scottsdale, she worked her way through the ranks to become executive sous chef at Elements Restaurant in Scottsdale, Arizona, then executive chef at DD's in Aspen, before moving to Tavern & Table.

Boxcar Betty's **1051**	Bargain
Butcher & Bee **1051**	Regular neighborhood
McCrady's Tavern **1055**	High end
The Ordinary **1056**	Regular neighborhood
Ox **857**	Worth the travel
Sea Biscuit Café **931**	Breakfast
Slightly North of Broad **1056**	Local favorite
Tattooed Moose **1056**	Late night
Xiao Bao Biscuit **1057**	Wish I'd opened

BRUNO LOUBET
Grain Store
Granary Square, London

Chef-owner of London's Grain Store, his restaurant serves meat and fish but gives vegetables top billing.

Andrew Edmunds **443**	Local favorite
Le Manoir aux Quat'Saisons **403**	High end
Blue Hill at Stone Barns **913**	Wish I'd opened
Clipstone **472**	Regular neighborhood
Dishoom **482**	Breakfast
Graanmarkt 13 **522**	Worth the travel
The Ledbury **423**	High end
Old Town 97 **452**	Late night
Padella **462**	Bargain

JAMES LOWE
Lyle's
56 Shoreditch High Street, London

Lowe ran proceedings at Fergus Henderson's St. John Bread & Wine, worked at The Fat Duck and Noma, and formed the chef-trio The Young Turks, before opening Lyle's in London in 2014.

40 Maltby Street **460**	Regular neighborhood
Baest **376**	Wish I'd opened
Black Axe Mangal **480**	Bargain
Café Sillon **534**	Bargain
The Clove Club **487**	High end

Fäviken Magasinet **345**	High end
Fäviken Magasinet **345**	Worth the travel
Gjusta **824**	Breakfast
Gjusta **824**	Wish I'd opened
Miyamasou **250**	Worth the travel
Hedone **413**	High end
Noma **369**	Worth the travel
P. Franco **468**	Local favorite
Padella **462**	Bargain
Palaegade **374**	Regular neighborhood
The River Café **417**	High end
Rochelle Canteen **486**	Local favorite
Rochelle Canteen **486**	Regular neighborhood
Septime **566**	Wish I'd opened
Tayyabs **494**	Late night
Umut 2000 **491**	Late night
Violet **476**	Regular neighborhood
Xi'an Impression **477**	Bargain

BRIAN LUPTAK
The Acorn Restaurant
3995 Main Street, Vancouver

Luptak spent ten years making his way across Canada cooking in hotels and resorts before starting at The Acorn as chef de cuisine.

Estela **1010**	Worth the travel
Fassil Restaurant **758**	Regular neighborhood
The Fish Counter **759**	Bargain
Gramercy Tavern **1036**	Wish I'd opened
Guu Original **761**	Late night
Kissa Tanto **756**	Local favorite
Kissa Tanto **756**	High end
Pilgrimme **746**	Local favorite
Red Wagon Café **757**	Breakfast
Sal Y Limon **759**	Regular neighborhood
The Willows Inn **800**	Wish I'd opened

CHRIS LUSK
The Caribbean Room
2031 St Charles Avenue, New Orleans

He was selected to bring New Orleans' historic Caribbean Room back to its former glory days, together with the other three restaurants in the Pontchartrain Hotel.

Beachcorner Bar & Grill **984**	Bargain
Le Bernardin **1038**	Worth the travel
Clancy's **988**	Regular neighborhood
Commander's Palace **982**	Local favorite
Coulis **988**	Breakfast
Daisy Dukes **979**	Late night
Dat Dog **981**	Wish I'd opened
Elizabeths **974**	Breakfast
Galatoire's **980**	Local favorite
Guy's Po-Boys **989**	Regular neighborhood
Herbsaint **976**	High end
Hong Kong Market **883**	Bargain
Horn's **983**	Breakfast
Junction **974**	Wish I'd opened
Midway Pizza **981**	Late night
Muriel's Jackson Square **980**	Local favorite
El Paso Restaurant **883**	Bargain
Patois **990**	Regular neighborhood
La Petite Grocery **989**	High end
Pizza Delicious **974**	Wish I'd opened
Restaurant August **976**	High end
Restaurant R'evolution **980**	High end
Tomodachi Sushi **1066**	Worth the travel
Yaffo Tel Aviv **175**	Worth the travel

ROSS LUSTED
The Bridge Room
44 Bridge Street, Sydney
Ex-Rockpool head chef, he spent a decade
in Asia working for Aman Resorts, returning
to open the Asian-inspired The Bridge Room
with John Fink (of Quay and Otto) in 2011.
10WilliamSt. 119..........Regular neighborhood
10WilliamSt. 119.............................Late night
Alimentari 119...............................Breakfast
Bennelong Restaurant 107........Local favorite
Boon Café 116................................Breakfast
Chat Thai 116................................Late night
chi SPACCA 816.....................Worth the travel
Firedoor 124............................Local favorite
La Fontelina 647....................Worth the travel
Fred's 120..................Regular neighborhood
Geist 372...........................Wish I'd opened
La Grenouillere 540...............Wish I'd opened
Henne Kirkeby Kro 365......................High end
Icebergs Dining Room & Bar 110...Local favorite
Kikunoi 247......................................High end
The NoMad Hotel 1044..........Wish I'd opened
Palace Chinese Restaurant 112..........Regular
neighborhood
Ramen Zundo 112.............................Bargain
Relæ 378.............................Worth the travel
Restaurant Hubert 112.....................Late night
Saint Peter 120...........Regular neighborhood
Waku Ghin 322..................................High end

VAUGHAN MABEE
Amisfield Bistro
10 Lake Hayes Road, Queenstown
Hunter-fisher-forager and chef, Mabee
inherited his love of cooking from his mother
and is passionate about sourcing the best
produce of New Zealand.
L'Arpège 556......................................High end
The French Laundry 797........Worth the travel
In-N-Out Burger 817.............Wish I'd opened
Jack's Point Clubhouse 159.............Breakfast
Kappa 160....................Regular neighborhood
Slow Cuts 158...................................Bargain

SANTIAGO MACÍAS
i Latina
Murillo 725, Buenos Aires
A Colombian chef who specializes in Latin
American cuisine, he has lived in Buenos
Aires for the past ten years, where he
opened i Latina in 2012.
Aramburu 1126.................................High end
Birkin 1126.....................................Breakfast
Cassis 1120.........................Worth the travel
Crizia 1127.....................................Late night
Don Julio Parrilla 1127...................Late night
Gran Dabbang 1127.....Regular neighborhood
Gran Dabbang 1127............Wish I'd opened
i Latina 1131....................................High end
La Mar 1128..................Regular neighborhood
Mishiguene 1128.....................Local favorite
Ninina 1128....................................Breakfast
Nola 1128.............................Local favorite
Nola 1128.......................................Bargain
Tegui 1129.........................Wish I'd opened

COLIN MACKAY
Blackbird
Ayala Triangle, Manila
This Scottish-born chef has spent most of
his career cooking in Asia. Now based in the
Philippines, he is cooking at People's Palace Thai,
Sala Restaurant, and Blackbird in the historic
1930s airport building at the heart of the city.
Din Tai Fung 202.............................Bargain
Monachyle Mhor 498............Worth the travel
The River Café 417.............................High end
Spring 492........................Wish I'd opened
Thip Samai 285..............................Late night
Toyo Eatery 307..........................Local favorite
Tsukiji 307...................Regular neighborhood
The Wolseley 443.............................Breakfast

WILLIAM MAHI
210° Kitchen + Drinkery
Icon Plaza, GF, 25th Street, Manila
Basque-born Mahi worked with several Michelin-
starred chefs including Ducasse and Nicolas
Le Bec. After making his name at Athens's
two-Michelin-starred Spondi he now runs his first
solo venture, 210° Kitchen + Drinkery.
Cafe Fleur 303..............Regular neighborhood
Eat First 305...................................Bargain
Flame 305......................Regular neighborhood
High Street Cafe at Shangri-La 311..Breakfast
Lucky Noodles 309........................Late night
Mantra Bistro 304.....................Local favorite
Martin Berasategui 577...................High end
Osteria Francescana 650.......Wish I'd opened
Tickets 601......................................High end
Tickets 601.........................Worth the travel
Toyo Eatery 307.......................Local favorite

CHRISTINE MANFIELD
She hosts pop-up events in Australia and
overseas, has a range of spice pastes and
condiments, and hosts bespoke gastronomic
tours to exotic destinations across the globe.
Almond Bar 114.......................Local favorite
Bar Brosé 114...........................Local favorite
Bennelong Restaurant 107.............High end
The Bridge Room 110.......................High end
Billy Kwong 121........Regular neighborhood
Boon Cafe 116..................................Bargain
Chaco Bar 115..................................Bargain
Cuisine Wat Damnak 290......Worth the travel
Ester 114........................Wish I'd opened
Fleet 82..........................Wish I'd opened
Long Chim 111...............................Late night
Monopole 122................Regular neighborhood
Morris 120.....................................Breakfast
The Salopian Inn 95.............Worth the travel

LUKE MANGAN
Glass Brasserie
488 George Street, Sydney
Australian, trained in Melbourne under
Herman Schneider and in the UK with Michel
Roux, he owns and operates twenty-one
branches within the Luke Mangan Group.
Bennelong Restaurant 107.................Regular
neighborhood

Catalina 123.........................Local favorite
Catalina 123.................Regular neighborhood
Happy Chef 117................................Bargain
Little Jean 115.................................Breakfast
Mr Wong 111..................................Late night
Mr Wong 111................Regular neighborhood

WALTER MANZKE
République
624 South La Brea Avenue, Inglewood
Born in San Diego, he first trained under
Joachim Splichal, before working in the kitchens
of Alain Ducasse and elBulli. République opened
its doors in 2013, plus he runs five Wildflour
bakeries and cafés in Manila.
Gjusta 124......................................Breakfast

GREG MARCHAND
Frenchie
5 Rue du Nil, Paris
This Nantes native travelled the globe, from
New York to Hong Kong, before returning to
his homeland to open Frenchie, which is the
nickname Jamie Oliver gave him at Fifteen.
L'Arpège 556....................................High end
Barrafina 444.....................Wish I'd opened
The Clove Club 487................Worth the travel
Le Relais Saint Germain 554......Local favorite
Holybelly 563..................................Breakfast
Luz Verde 562.................Regular neighborhood
Au Pied de Cochon 551...................Late night
Que Du Bon 569...............................Bargain

DAVID MARTIN
La Paix
49 Rue Ropsy-Chaudron, Brussels
A one-time disciple of Passard, Martin bought
the Brussels brasserie, La Paix, in 2004,
a venue where butchers who visited the
abattoir opposite had begun meeting in 1892.
5 Flavors Mmei 522...........................Bargain
Asador Etxebarri 575............Wish I'd opened
Bozar Brasserie 523....Regular neighborhood
Friture René 522.............................Late night
Hof van Cleve 527.............................High end
De Jonkman 529............Regular neighborhood
Oak 526........................Regular neighborhood
Tsukiji Fish Market 260.........Worth the travel
La Villa Emily 524.....................Local favorite
Vrijmoed 527.................Regular neighborhood

VIRGILIO MARTÍNEZ
Central
Calle Santa Isabel 376, Lima
He ran the kitchen at Gastón Acurio's
seminal haute Peruvian Astrid & Gastón,
before launching his own celebrated Lima
restaurant Central in 2010, and shortly
after, Lima Floral and Lima in Fitzrovia and
Covent Garden, London, with more branches
planned globally.
Astrid & Gastón 1101.......................High end
Cosme 1101............................Local favorite
DEN 268............................Worth the travel
Elkano 580.........................Worth the travel
Isolina 1098..................Regular neighborhood
La Mar 1099...........................Local favorite

Maido **1100**............................Late night
Mayta **1100**............................Late night
Mayta **1100**................................Bargain
Mó Café + Bistró **1098**..................Breakfast
Mugaritz **576**....................Wish I'd opened
OSSO Carnicería y Salumeria **1098**...High end
La Picantería **1101**.......Regular neighborhood
Tanta **1101**................................Breakfast
The Willows Inn **800**..............Wish I'd opened

CAMERON MATTHEWS
The Long Apron
68 Balmoral Road, Montville
A leading figure in the dynamic local food industry, his cooking is largely self-taught and delivers a menu of local seasonal produce created by a passion for his craft.
Bare Bones Society **128**..................Breakfast
Le Manoir aux Quat'Saisons **403**.....Worth the travel
Le Manoir aux Quat'Saisons **403**.....Worth the travel
Blue Hill at Stone Barns **913**..Worth the travel
Brae **101**.........................Wish I'd opened
Chez Panisse **789**..................Worth the travel
Cutler & Co. **148**........................High end
Embassy XO **87**.....................Local favorite
Enjoy Inn **130**..........................Late night
Fat Dumpling **130**.........................Bargain
Fleet **82**................................High end
Gerard's Bar **131**.......................Late night
Lake House **101**................Wish I'd opened
The Ledbury **423**...................Worth the travel
Little May Espresso **86**..................Breakfast
Mr Wong **111**............................Late night
Noosa Waterfront Restaurant & Bar **87**...Local favorite
Nu Nu **89**.......................Wish I'd opened
Paper Daisy **83**............................High end
Pitchfork **89**..................Regular neighborhood
Provenance Restaurant **101**..Wish I'd opened
Renae's Pantry **88**.........Regular neighborhood
Rick Shores **85**.................Wish I'd opened
Royal Mail Hotel **102**.....................High end
Season **87**....................Regular neighborhood
Sorellina Pizzeria **134**......................Bargain
Spirit House **89**...........Regular neighborhood
The Tamarind **86**..................Local favorite
Thomas Corner eatery **88**..............Breakfast
Urbane Restaurant **136**.................High end
Wasabi **88**......................Local favorite

IGNACIO MATTOS
Estela
47 East Houston Street, New York City
Born in Uruguay, he has called New York home since 2006. He began his career as the chef of Il Buco, before leaving in 2011 to run the kitchen at Isa. Since then he has set up a solo venture, Estela.
Balthazar **1011**...................Local favorite
Big Jones **954**............................Breakfast
O CAFE **1026**...........................Breakfast
Cafe Mogador **1022**.......................Bargain
Le Châteaubriand **564**...........Worth the travel
Contra **1007**.....................Local favorite
Dizengoff **1034**.....................Wish I'd opened

Franny's **1016**...............Regular neighborhood
Hasaki **1022**...............Regular neighborhood
JG Melon **1045**...........................Late night
Relæ **378**....................Worth the travel
Shuko **1024**.............................High end
Sunny & Annie's **1024**.....................Bargain
Sushi Seki **1045**........................Late night

TONY MAWS
Craigie on Main
853 Main Street, Cambridge
The owner of The Kirkland Tap & Trotter and Craigie on Main, which he originally ran in a different Cambridge location as the Craigie Street Bistrot (2003).
Chilli Garden **898**.........................Bargain
Coppa **889**......................Wish I'd opened
deadhorse hill **901**.............Wish I'd opened
Eventide Oyster Co. **885**.........Worth the travel
Grill 23 **890**.............................High end
Highland Kitchen **899**.................Local favorite
Lone Star Taco Bar **896**...............Late night
Lone Star Taco Bar **896**..................Bargain
Loyal Nine **896**...........Regular neighborhood
Mamaleh's **896**.........................Breakfast
Mamaleh's **896**.........Regular neighborhood
Neptune Oyster **891**...............Local favorite
Oishii Sushi **891**.........................High end
Phở- So 1 **898**...........................Bargain
Sarma **900**...................Regular neighborhood
Sarma **900**......................Wish I'd opened
State Bird Provisions **832**.....Worth the travel

ALEXANDER MAYER
Blue Mustard
Dorotheergasse 6–8, Vienna
This Styrian chef has worked in many Viennese kitchens, and now presents truly cosmopolitan fare with his food-and-cocktail approach.
L'Astrance **568**.........................High end
Auberge des Glazicks **538**.....Worth the travel
La Bastide de Moustiers **534**.Wish I'd opened
Bar Nestor **579**...........................Bargain
Bitzingers Würstelstände **679**........Late night
Bras **541**................................High end
Café Anzengruber **679**.................Late night
Café Bacco **680**...........................Bargain
Café de la Cale **537**.....................Breakfast
Le Comptoir BREIZC Café **538**..........Bargain
Le Coquillage **538**.............Worth the travel
Gasthaus Grünauer **680**...................Regular neighborhood
Ladurée Bonaparte **555**.................Breakfast
Lasarte **597**.............................High end
Lurgbauer **678**.................Local favorite
Meierei im Stadtpark **682**.............Breakfast
La Merenda **545**................Wish I'd opened
Mochi **682**...............................Bargain
O boufés **683**...........Regular neighborhood
Petz im Gusshaus **683**..Regular neighborhood
SaQuaNa **540**.................Worth the travel
Steira Wirt **676**.................Local favorite
Ströck-Feierabend **684**................Breakfast

FRANCESCO MAZZEI
Sartoria
20 Savile Row, London
Born in Calabria, he first arrived in the UK in 1996, working for restaurateurs Corbin and King and Alan Yau, before opening Sartoria in London in 2015.
Alain Ducasse **436**.......................High end
Bellanger **479**...............Regular neighborhood
Chiltern Firehouse **419**..........Wish I'd opened
Dublin Pizza Company **504**..............Late night
Noma **369**....................Worth the travel
Princi **453**...............................Bargain
The Quality Chop House **469**......Local favorite
The Wolseley **443**.......................Breakfast

SEAN MCCONNELL
Monster Kitchen and Bar
25 Edinburgh Avenue, Canberra
An avid vegetable gardener and mushroom forager, McConnell's previously nomadic lifestyle heavily influences his use of seasonal produce.
A. Baker **80**.............................Breakfast
Aubergine **82**....................Local favorite
Aubergine **82**...........................High end
Bistro Nguyen's **80**......................Bargain
Diporto **718**....................Worth the travel
Restaurant Hubert **112**.........Wish I'd opened
XO **81**....................Regular neighborhood
Zaab Street Food **82**.....................Late night

ALLEGRA MCEVEDY
Albertine
1 Wood Lane, London
Classically trained, before co-founding Leon in 2004 she worked at Rubicon and Jardinière as well as doing a stage at Chez Panisse in Berkeley. Most recently, she has re-launched her local neighborhood wine bar and eatery, Albertine.
The Anglesea Arms **416**.....................Regular neighborhood
The Brackenbury **416**.................Local favorite
Café 2000 **426**...........................Bargain
Corner Bistro **1028**...............Worth the travel
Morito **468**.....................Wish I'd opened
Pentolina **424**...........Regular neighborhood
The River Café **417**.......................High end
Snaps & Rye **424**.........................Breakfast

JOSHUA MCFADDEN
Ava Gene's
3377 SE Division Street, Portland
Trained at Cordon Bleu in Portland, Oregon, he also spent time in Rome working at the American Academy. In 2016, he and Luke Dirks acquired ownership of Ava Gene's just before opening Tusk.
Big Star **469**...................Wish I'd opened
The Boathouse at The Suttle Lodge **800**...Local favorite
Le Coucou **1012**.........................High end
Le Coucou **1012**..................Worth the travel
DAME **850**...................Regular neighborhood
Pyro Pizza **858**...........................Bargain
Tusk **860**................................Late night

MORGAN MCGLONE
Belles Hot Chicken
150–156 Gertrude Street, Melbourne
Chef-owner of Belles Hot Chicken, he is the former chef de cuisine of Husk Restaurant in Nashville.

10WilliamSt. **119**..........Regular neighborhood
Africola **90**..............................Local favorite
L'Arpège **556**.................................High end
L'Astrance **568**.............................High end
Attica **151**.....................................High end
Attica **151**...........................Local favorite
Automata **114**........Regular neighborhood
Bar Brosé **114**.........Regular neighborhood
Boon Café **116**.......Regular neighborhood
Brae **101**......................................High end
Brae **101**.............................Local favorite
chotto/Kinome **148**....................Breakfast
Crystal Jade Restaurant **142**.........Breakfast
Dolphin Hotel **124**........................Late night
Duddell's **222**....................Worth the travel
Estela **1010**......................Wish I'd opened
Fratelli Paradiso **121**....Regular neighborhood
Golden Century **111**.....................Late night
IGNI **102**..............................Local favorite
Lung King Heen **223**........Worth the travel
Maxwell Food Centre **320**...........Breakfast
Momofuku Ko **1023**.........Worth the travel
Momofuku Ko **1023**..........................High end
Mr Wong **111**..................Wish I'd opened
Noma **369**........................Worth the travel
ShanDong MaMa **145**....................Bargain
Sin Ming Roti Prata **316**..............Breakfast
Sixpenny **123**................................High end
Sushi Suzuki **259**..............Worth the travel
Sushi-ya **259**....................Worth the travel

LARRY MCGUIRE
McGuire Moorman Hospitality
104 Annie Street, Austin
Born and raised in Austin, Texas, he and three others opened Lamberts Barbecue in Austin, quickly followed by a seafood and oyster bar. He now runs seven distinct restaurants.

Le Relais Saint Germain **554**...........Breakfast
Estela **1024**.......................Wish I'd opened
Gjusta **824**........................Wish I'd opened
La Grenouille **1039**...........................High end
Güero's Taco Bar **1062**.............Local favorite
Home Slice Pizza **1062**..................Late night
Mama's Fish House **839**.....Worth the travel
Matt's El Rancho **1063**.............Local favorite
Maudie's Café **1063**.....Regular neighborhood
Peter Luger **1018**.............................High end
Smitty's Market **938**.............Local favorite
Taco More **1065**.............................Bargain
Vespaio **1066**.............Regular neighborhood

ISAAC MCHALE
The Clove Club
380 Old Street, London
A co-founder of The Young Turks chef collective, Orkney-born McHale worked at The Ledbury, Noma, and Momofuku before opening The Clove Club in 2013.

Asador Etxebarri **575**.............Wish I'd opened
Barrafina **444**............Regular neighborhood
Benu **840**......................................High end
Black Axe Mangal **480**..Regular neighborhood
Breddos Tacos **468**...................Local favorite
Casamia **390**................................High end
Coombeshead Farm **391**............Breakfast
Dumpling heart **485**.....................Bargain
Elystan Street **412**..................Local favorite
Fäviken Magasinet **345**.........Worth the travel
Golden Century **111**.............Wish I'd opened
Kagurazaka Ishikawa **272**.....Worth the travel
Kagurazaka Ishikawa **272**...........High end
Kēu **486**..Bargain
The Laughing Heart **474**.............Late night
The Ledbury **423**.........................High end
Lyle's **488**.............................Local favorite
Manresa **792**................................High end
Mirazur **545**....................Worth the travel
Mr Wong **111**.................Wish I'd opened
Needoo Grill **494**............................Bargain
Noma **369**........................Worth the travel
Perilla **491**..........................Local favorite
Rochelle Canteen **486**...........Local favorite
The Sportsman **400**..........Worth the travel
Trullo **481**...........................Local favorite
Umut 2000 **491**.............................Late night
Umut 2000 **491**..............................Bargain
Xi'an Impression **477**.....................Bargain

SARAH MCINTOSH
épicerie
3708 Robinson Avenue, Austin
After a short stint in Napa Valley, Sarah moved back to Austin, Texas. She's a Louisiana native who felt that Texas needed a little Cajun touch and she opened épicerie in 2012.

Bacchanal **974**...................Worth the travel
Contigo **1060**.................Regular neighborhood
Dai Due **1060**.......................Local favorite
Early Bird Diner **1052**..................Breakfast
Franklin Barbecue **1061**...........Local favorite
Fresa's **1061**.......................Wish I'd opened
Justine's **1062**...............................Late night
Launderette **1063**........Regular neighborhood
Marcelino Pan Y Vino **1063**..............Breakfast
Musashino Sushi Dokoro **1064**..........Regular neighborhood
Olamaie **1064**...............................High end
Olamaie **1064**..............Regular neighborhood
Ramen Tatsu-ya **1065**............Local favorite
Tacodeli **1065**.............................Bargain
Three Little Birds Café **1057**...........Breakfast
Via 313 **1066**.................................Late night

NIALL MCKENNA
James Street South
21 James Street South, Belfast
The chef-owner of Belfast's James Street South, which opened in 2003, and the Bar + Grill, launched in 2001, both of which are located in a converted linen mill in the city center.

777 **503**..............................Wish I'd opened
Barrafina **444**........................Worth the travel
Bull & Ram **503**...................Local favorite

Chez Albert **541**.................Worth the travel
Eipic **500**......................................High end
Established **500**...........................Breakfast
Forest Avenue **505**..............Wish I'd opened
General Merchants **500**...............Breakfast
Hadskis **501**................................Late night
John Longs Fish and Chips **501**.........Bargain
The Muddlers Club **502**.............Local favorite
OX **502**..........................Regular neighborhood
Sun Kee **503**................................Late night
Wine & Brine **560**.........Regular neighborhood

JP MCMAHON
Aniar
53 Lower Dominick Street, London
Heralded as "the perfect ambassador of modern Irish cuisine", restaurateur and culinary director of the EatGalway Restaurant Group McMahon opened Cava tapas restaurant in 2008 and Aniar in 2011.

Amass **370**......................Worth the travel
Ard Bia at Nimmos **506**.Regular neighborhood
Cava Bodega **506**........................Late night
Chapter One **503**...........................High end
The Dough Bros. **506**....................Bargain
Forest & Marcy **505**.............Wish I'd opened
Forest Avenue **505**................Wish I'd opened
The Greenhouse **504**.......................High end
Kai Café & Restaurant **506**............Breakfast
Kappa-ya **507**.............Regular neighborhood
Loam Restaurant **507**.............Local favorite
London Wall Bar & Kitchen **466**...........Breakfast
Sat Bains **402**..................Worth the travel
Il Vicolo **455**................................Late night

TORY MCPHAIL
Commanders Palace
1403 Washington Avenue, New Orleans
Originally hailing from Washington State, he's been calling the shots in the kitchen of New Orleans's Commander's Palace since 2002.

Bouligny Tavern **981**.......................Late night
Commander's Palace **982**..........Local favorite
The Company Burger **981**..........Bargain
Coulis **988**...................................Breakfast
Fisher's **864**....................Wish I'd opened
Here's Looking at You **818**.....Worth the travel
Restaurant August **977**....................High end
Taqueria Corona **991**....Regular neighborhood

PAVEL MENCL
Kastrol
Ohradské Náměstí 1625/2, Prague
A Prague-based chef and television personality who serves up classic Czech fare at the no-frills, produce-led, Kastrol.

Aromi **685**...................................Late night
Aromi **685**....................................High end
Aromi **685**...............Regular neighborhood
Borgo Agnese **685**.............Worth the travel
La Bottega Bistroteka **687**...............Breakfast
Café Imperial **686**.........................Breakfast
Café Louvre **686**.........................Breakfast
CottoCrudo **686**...........Regular neighborhood
CottoCrudo **686**.............................Late night
CottoCrudo **686**..............................High end
La Degustation Bohême **687**............High end

Entrée Restaurant **685**..........Worth the travel
Brasserie La Gare **687**.....................Breakfast
Grand Cru Restaurant and Bar **686**.....Regular neighborhood
Lokál Dlouhááá **688**...........................Bargain
Lokal U Bílé kuželky **688**....................Bargain
Malostranska Beseda **688**........Local favorite
Penzion V Polich **685**..............Worth the travel
SaSaZu **689**..................Regular neighborhood
SaSaZu **689**......................Wish I'd opened
Slovanský dům **687**.........Wish I'd opened
U Medvidku **689**.....................Local favorite
U Vejvodu **689**.......................Local favorite
U zlatého tygra **689**.................Local favorite
Yamato **689**................................Late night
Yamato **689**.................................High end

MARC-ALEXANDRE MERCIER
Hôtel Herman
5171 St Laurent Boulevard, Montréal
Marc-Alexandre trained in Montreal before working for chefs Samuel Pinard and Robert Belcham in Vancouver. He also co-owns the Reservoir, a brewpub in Montreal.
Bouillon Bilk **782**..............................High end
Cabane à Sucre au Pied de Cochon **752**...Local favorite
Le Chien Fumant **776**.....................Late night
Contra **1007**...........................Worth the travel
L'express **776**................................Late night
Farine **777**.....................................Breakfast
Farine **777**......................................Bargain
Fäviken Magasinet **345**.........Wish I'd opened
La Grenouillère **540**...........Worth the travel
Hof Kelsten **777**...........................Breakfast
Larrys **777**....................................Breakfast
Lawrence Restaurant **777**................Breakfast
Liverpool House **779**..............Local favorite
Le Majestique **778**........................Late night
Marché Méli-Mélo **783**....................Bargain
MonNan **774**.................................Late night
Montreal Plaza **781**......Regular neighborhood
Mugaritz **576**..................Worth the travel
Nora Gray **774**.............Regular neighborhood
Nora Gray **774**.....................Local favorite

MICHAEL MEREDITH
Merediths
365 Dominion Road, Auckland
Born in Samoa, he moved to New Zealand at thirteen and made his name at Auckland's The Grove before opening Merediths in 2007.
Apéro **164**......................Regular neighborhood
Attica **151**...........................Worth the travel
Blue Hill at Stone Barns **913**..Worth the travel
Brae **101**.........................Wish I'd opened
Cazador **165**..................Regular neighborhood
Clooney **165**........................Local favorite
The Grove **167**.....................Local favorite
The Midnight Baker **166**..................Breakfast
New Flavour **166**.........................Late night
New Flavour **166**..........................Bargain
Sepia **113**.......................Worth the travel
SIDART **167**..................................High end

ÁDÁM MÉSZÁROS
Onyx
Vörösmarty Square 7–8, Budapest
Bringing experience from elBulli and Budapest's first Michelin-starred restaurant, Costes, this Hungarian chef has worked in the kitchen at Onyx since 2011.
Borkonyha Winekitchen **690**......Local favorite
Borkonyha Winekitchen **690**......Local favorite
Eleven Madison Park **1037**....Worth the travel
Émile **690**.....................Regular neighborhood
Gerbeaud Confectionary **690**..........Breakfast
High Note Skybar **690**....................Late night
Noma **369**.....................................High end

CLAUS MEYER
Studio at the Standard
44 Havnegade, Copenhagen
A shareholder in Noma, he has interests in other Copenhagen restaurants and owns a group of branded delis and bakeries.
Arcade Bakery **1013**......................Breakfast
Atera **1013**...................................High end
Bæst **376**......................................Bargain
Bar Bolonat **1028**.................Local favorite
Barrafina **444**................................Bargain
Barrafina **444**.....................Worth the Travel
Blue Hill at Stone Barns **913**.............High end
Blue Hill at Stone Barns **913**......Local favorite
Blue Hill at Stone Barns **913**..Wish I'd opened
Brooklyn Fare **1015**.........................High end
Carbone **1025**.......................Local favorite
Chelsea Market **1034**......................Bargain
Chinese Tuxedo **1006**...............Local favorite
CHOP-SHOP **1034**........Regular neighborhood
Co. **1034**.......................Regular neighborhood
Cosme **1036**................................Late night
Le Coucou **1012**.................Wish I'd opened
Le Coucou **1012**....................Local favorite
Eleven Madison Park **1037**...............High end
Ends Meat **1015**...........................Bargain
Estela **1010**................................Late night
Estela **1010**..................................Bargain
The Four Horsemen **1016**.........Local favorite
Geranium **378**.................................High end
Gjelina **824**......................Wish I'd opened
Gramercy Tavern **1036**...........Local favorite
Grand Sichuan International **1035**.....Regular neighborhood
High Street On Hudson **1029**..........Breakfast
Ippudo **1041**..................................Late night
Jun-Men **1035**...............................High end
Kadeau **362**...................................High end
Keng Kee Seafood **317**.................Bargain
Llama Inn **1017**.....................Local favorite
Maison Troisgros **536**..................High end
Momofuku Ko **1023**....................Late night
Momofuku Nishi **1035**..Wish I'd opened
n'eat **1023**....................................Bargain
The NoMad Hotel **1044**............Local favorite
Num Pang Kitchen **1026**..................Bargain
Nur **1037**............................Local favorite
Paowalla **1013**......................Local favorite
Pok Pok **1019**......................Local favorite
Pujol **1082**....................................High end
El Quinto Pino **1036**......Regular neighborhood
El Quinto Pino **1036**.......................Late night

Relæ **378**...Bargain
Restaurant André **331**..........Worth the Travel
Saison **841**....................................High end
Saison **841**........................Worth the travel
Sin Huat Eating House **323**....Worth the Travel
Sullivan Street Bakery **1036**............Breakfast
Wee Nam Kee **326**............Worth the Travel
Wee Nam Kee **326**.........................Bargain
Wildair **1010**................................Late night
Win Son **1017**..............................Bargain
Zinc **122**.......................................Breakfast

WILL MEYRICK
Sarong
Jalan Petitenget 19, Bali
Scotsman Meyrick, aka "The Street Food Chef", traveled extensively throughout Southeast Asia, settling in Bali to bring elevated panAsian street food to Sarong (2008), Mama San, and E&O in Jakarta.
Babi Guling Candra **293**..............Local favorite
Burnt Ends **329**......................Worth the travel
Gourmet Café **294**.........................Bargain
Locavore **297**...................................Bargain
Locavore **297**.................Wish I'd opened
Petitenget **295**............Regular neighborhood
Sari Ratu Padang **296**....................Late night
Watercress Café **296**.......................Breakfast

CHRISTOPHE MICHALAK
Pâtisserie Michalak
8 Rue du Vieux Colombier, Paris
This Picardy-born pastry chef has overseen the dessert menu at Alain Ducasse au Plaza Athénée since 2000 and opened his own Parisian pâtisserie, Michalak Masterclass, in 2013.
Akrame **557**..................Regular neighborhood
Akrame **557**......................Wish I'd opened
Alain Ducasse au Plaza Athénée **557**.............Breakfast
Angelina **550**...............................Breakfast
L'ATELIER de Joël Robuchon **556**.......High end
Atelier Vivanda **568**......................Late night
Carette **568**.................................Breakfast
El Celler de Can Roca **533**.....Worth the travel
Le Cinq **557**.......................Local favorite
La Cuisine **558**.............................Breakfast
East Mamma **565**........................Bargain
Epicure **558**.......................Local favorite
Frenchie to Go **552**.......Regular neighborhood
Lazare **558**...................................Late night
Mokonuts **565**.................Wish I'd opened
Noma **751**.........................Worth the travel
Pierre Gagnaire **559**.......................High end
Porte 12 **563**.................Regular neighborhood
Le Pré Catelan **568**...............Local favorite
Le Richer **562**............Regular neighborhood
La Scène **559**...............................High end
Ultraviolet **196**....................Worth the travel
Umami Matcha Café **553**....Wish I'd opened

JAKOB MIELCKE
Mielcke & Hurtigkarl
Frederiksberg Runddel 1, Frederiksberg

Born in Aarhus, he left Denmark to work with Pierre Gagnaire, then opened Mielcke & Hurtigkarl with Jan Hurtigkarl in 2008.

Bistro Boheme 370............................Late night
Blue Hill at Stone Barns 913.............High end
Enomania 363................Regular neighborhood
Fäviken Magasinet 345.........Wish I'd opened
Geist 372..Late night
Granola 363.......................................Breakfast
Hija de Sanchez 372.............................Bargain
Kong Hans Kælder 373.Regular neighborhood
Masa 1042...High end
Noma 369....................................Local favorite
Relæ 378.....................................Local favorite
Saison 841.............................Worth the travel
Sokkelund Cafe & Brasserie 363.....Breakfast
Soujiki Nakahigashi 250........Worth the travel

THOMASINA MIERS
Wahaca
80 Wardour Street, London

After winning BBC's "Masterchef" in 2005, she opened Wahaca in 2008. She now has twelve branches across London.

Barrafina 444.....................................Late night
The Chipping Forecast 423.................Regular
neighborhood
Clipstone 472.......................Wish I'd opened
Fortnum & Mason 438..Regular neighborhood
Hereford Road 411......Regular neighborhood
Hoppers 450.......................................Late night
Jungsik 1014........................Worth the travel
Kricket Soho 451.................Wish I'd opened
The Ledbury 423................................High end
Lyle's 488............................Wish I'd opened
Marksman Public House 475.....Local favorite
Pidgin 476...........................Wish I'd opened
Portland 473.......................................High end
Portland 473.......................Wish I'd opened
Quo Vadis 453....................................Late night
Rochelle Canteen 486.........................Bargain
Rotorino 470....................................Local favorite
Rotorino 470...............Regular neighborhood
Salvation Taco 1043...............Worth the travel
Snaps & Rye 424.................................Breakfast
Spring 492..High end
Tian Fu 332....................................Local favorite
Violet 476...................Regular neighborhood
The Wolseley 443.........Regular neighborhood

CHRISTOPHER MILLAR
Stellar at 1-Altitude
1 Raffles Place, Singapore

His culinary career includes positions at award-winning, iconic restaurants in London, Melbourne, and Sydney, before he moved to Singapore to become executive chef at Stellar.

Akashi 326.......................Regular neighborhood
Allauddin's Briyani 332.......................Bargain
Beni 326..High end
Blue Hill at Stone Barns 913..Worth the travel
Brae 101............................Worth the travel
Burnt Ends 329.............Regular neighborhood

Candlenut 334..............................Local favorite
Common Man Coffee Roasters 331.....Regular
neighborhood
Lei Garden 320..............Regular neighborhood
La Grenouillere 540.............Worth the travel
Jaan 320..High end
Lan Zhou La Mian 329...Regular neighborhood
Maxwell Food Centre 319.................Late night
Moosehead 330............Regular neighborhood
No Signboard Seafood 323..Regular neighborhood
Odette 320.......................Regular neighborhood
Odette 320..High end
One Kueh at a Time 332.......................Bargain
Park Bench Deli 331.............................Bargain
Sin Huat Eating House 323...............Late night
The Summerhouse 333.........................Breakfast
Sungei Road Laksa 333.Regular neighborhood
Terra 797..High end
Ting Heng Seafood 318........................Bargain
Tippling Club 321................................High end
Waku Ghin 322...................................High end

KATY JANE MILLARD
Coquine
6839 South East Belmont Street, Portland

With experience from five Parisian Michelin-starred restaurants in five years behind her, she is well-equipped to run her first solo venture, Coquine.

Apizza Scholls 846........Regular neighborhood
Ava Gene's 846....................................High end
Ava Gene's 846...............................Local favorite
Castagna 849.......................................High end
Lovely's Fifty-Fifty 854.................Local favorite
Manresa 792...........................Worth the travel
Nodoguro 855.....................................High end
Le Pigeon 854................................Local favorite
Le Pigeon 854......................................High end
Sweedeedee 859..................................Breakfast
Teo Bun Bo Hue 860............................Bargain
Tusk 860...Late night
The Willows Inn 800..............Wish I'd opened
The Willows Inn 800..............Worth the travel

KOICHI MINAMISHIMA
Minamishima
4 Lord Street, Richmond

The sushi-master of this eponymous restaurant washed rice for the first two years of his culinary career, and then worked at Melbourne's Kenzan before setting up on his own.

Aka Siro 147....................Regular neighborhood

KANG MIN-GOO
Mingles
Nonhyun-dong 94-, Seoul

He learned his trade under Martín Berasategui and undertook stints at Nobu before returning to his native Korea and putting his skills to use at Mingles.

Byeokje Galbi 241...............................High end
Florilège 269.........................Worth the travel
Hadongkwan 238................................Breakfast
Ipari 240...Late night
Joo.OK 234.....................................Local favorite
Jungsik Dang 235........Regular neighborhood

Locanda Mong-ro 239......................Late night
Louis Cinq 235..............Regular neighborhood
Neung Ra Do 236..................................Bargain
Tutto Bene 236......................Wish I'd opened
La Yeon 238....................................Local favorite

CARLO MIRARCHI
Roberta's
261 Moore Street. New York City

Mirarchi is co-owner of the runaway Brooklyn hit Roberta's, which opened in 2008 as a no-nonsense, noreservations, rock 'n' roll bar and pizza joint, and its sister establishment Blanca.

Corner Bistro 1028........................Local favorite
Great NY Noodletown 1006..............Late night
New World Mall Food Court 1019.......Bargain
Noodle Village 1006.............................Bargain
Le Turtle 1009.................Regular neighborhood

MOLLY MITCHELL
Rose's Fine Food
10551 East Jefferson Avenue, Detroit

She began her kitchen career in a local diner, and eighteen years and almost as many kitchen jobs later, she opened Rose's with her cousin Lucy Carnaghi.

Amar Pizza 908.............Regular neighborhood
Astro Coffee 902..................................Breakfast
Baker's Keyboard Lounge 903.........Late night
Boulettes Larder 829..............Worth the travel
Duran Central Pharmacy 88...Wish I'd opened
Ivanhoe Cafe 904..........................Local favorite
Korea House 918..................Worth the travel
New Yasmeen Bakery 902....Local favorite
Pupusería y Restaurante Salvadoreño 905......
Regular neighborhood
The Red Hook 905................................Breakfast
Roast 906..High end
Taqueria el Rey 907.............................Bargain

KHALID MOHAMMED
Chaud
2 Queen's Park West, Port of Spain

He trained at New York's French Culinary Institute before opening Chaud in Trinidad and Tobago's Port of Spain in 2008.

Blue Hill at Stone Barns 913..Worth the travel
The Breakfast Shed 1074.......Breakfast
Sugarcane Raw Bar Grill 875.Worth the travel
Wings Restaurant & Bar 1075....Local favorite

MARTÍN MOLTENI
Puratierra
3 de Febrero 1167, Bueno Aires

Globe-trotting Molteni trained in Australia and France before returning to his native Argentina to showcase his homeland's produce at his restaurant Puratierra.

Aramburu 1125..................................High end
El Baqueano 1131..............................High end
Cassis 1121..........................Worth the travel
Chila 1129...High end
El Cuartito 1130...............................Late night
Don Julio Parrilla 1127...............Local favorite
Gran Dabbang 1127.............................Bargain
La Mar 1128.................Regular neighborhood

Le Pain Quotidien **1128**...................Breakfast
Panaderia La Bella Italia **1082**........Breakfast
Las Pizarras **1129**..................Wish I'd opened
Proper **1129**...........................Wish I'd opened

RUSSELL MOORE
Camino
3917 Grand Avenue, Oakland
He worked for Alice Waters at Chez Panisse
for twenty-one years, before leaving in
2008 to open Camino, where he cooks over
a coal-fired grill.

20th century cafe **830**...........Wish I'd opened
Bad Saint **864**.......................Worth the travel
Banh Mi Ba Le **793**.........................Bargain
Beauty's Bagel Shop **794**.................Breakfast
Izakaya Rintaro **835**......................High end
Kin khao **842**...............................Late night
Kin Khao **842**................................High end
Maison Premiere **1017**..........Worth the travel
Miss Ollie's **794**....................Local favorite
El Paisa **927**..........................Local favorite
Seoul Gom Tang **795**.....................Late night
Seoul Gom Tang **795**....Regular neighborhood
Sequoia Diner **795**........................Breakfast
Standard Fare **790**................Wish I'd opened

JOSE ENRIQUE MONTES
Jose Enrique
La Placita, Duffaut Street 176, San Juan
Puerto Rican Enrique returned to his
homeland after cooking across the US to
open his celebrated eponymous San Juan
restaurant in 2007, followed by Capital
and Miel. A James Beard Award Nominee
"Best Chef South" 2015, 2016, and 2017.

El Axolote **1073**............................Bargain
Bodegas Compostela **1073**....Wish I'd opened
La España **1071**..........................Breakfast
Giant **959**.......................Worth the travel
New Taste **1074**.........................Late night
El Pescador **1072**.................Local favourite
Pikayo **1074**..............................High end
Volando Bajito **1072**....Regular neighbourhood

ALEJANDRO MORALES
Parador La Huella
Calle los Cisnes, José Ignacio
With Morales running the kitchen, the
description of La Huella as a parador belies
the impact that this sophisticated beachside
grill has had on Latin America's gastronomic
reputation.

Baker's Bar **1120**.........................Late night
Escaramuza **1120**.........Regular neighborhood
Escaramuza **1120**.........................Breakfast
Jacinto **1120**.............................Late night
Toledo **1120**.................Regular neighborhood

MARTIN MORALES
Ceviche
17 Frith Street, London
He left Lima at twelve, worked as a Disney
Media executive, and helped launch iTunes in
Europe, before opening Peruvian restaurants
Ceviche (2012) and Andina (2013) in London.
1087 Bistro **1101**..................Worth the travel

Abastos 2.0 **587**...................Worth the travel
Awesome Thai **410**.......Regular neighborhood
Benaresv **437**...............................High end
Berber & Q **478**..........................Late night
Blacklock **445**.........................Local favorite
Central **1098**..............................High end
Chick 'n' Sours **432**.....................Late night
CôBa **432**.................................Late night
Crab House Café **395**...........Wish I'd opened
Dishoom **482**...............................Bargain
Faanoos **415**.................Regular neighborhood
Flat Iron **449**..............................Bargain
Gifto's Lahore Karahi **427**..............Bargain
Hanana **425**.................Regular neighborhood
Hix Oyster & Fish House **395**.Wish I'd opened
El Mercado **1099**.................Wish I'd opened
The Modern Pantry **468**................Breakfast
La Nueva Palomino **1097**......Worth the travel
La Paisana **1098**..........................Bargain
The Palomar **452**.....................Local favorite
La Picantería **1101**........................Bargain
Pickle & Rye **426**...........Regular neighborhood
Pickle & Rye **426**........................Breakfast
Riva **410**.......................Regular neighborhood
The Seahorse **394**..................Wish I'd opened
Shawarma Bar **469**......................Late night
Som Saa **489**...............................Late night
A Taberna da Rua das Flores **616**....Worth the
travel
Temper **454**............................Local favorite
The Victoria **426**...........Regular neighborhood

EDUARDO MORENO
La Isabela
Los Chorros, Caracas
This quirky Venezuelan cook operates
La Isabela, his arty Caracas restaurant, like
a private club, with reservations available
by introduction only.

Arepera Amadani **1094**...................Breakfast
Asador Etxebarri **575**....................High end
La Casa Bistro **1094**....................Breakfast
Le Gourmet **1094**..................Wish I'd opened
Guillermina Restaurant **1094**.........Late night
Julieta Pies **1094**...........................Bargain
Koy Shunka **594**......................Local favorite
Moreno **1094**.................Regular neighborhood
Nobook **598**......................Worth the travel

WILLY TRULLÁS MORENO
El Willy
22 Zhongshan Dong Er Lu, Shanghai
Trullas Moreno brings experience
from Georges Blanc and Aquavit to his
idiosyncratic Spanish kitchen based in China,
where he serves both classic tapas and
wildly flamboyant dishes.

Asador Etxebarri **575**...........Wish I'd opened
Bar Tomás **603**............................Bargain
Charmant **196**............................Late night
Gjusta **824**...............................Breakfast
Guyi **198**......................Regular neighborhood
Paco Meralgo **599**...................Local favorite
Pierre Gagnaire **559**..............Worth the travel
Pinotxo **602**..............................Breakfast
Sushi Oyama **196**.........................High end

DANIEL MORGAN
Salt
6 Rue Rochebrune, Paris
This British chef, residing in Paris, trained
at The Square in London and Sketch, and
gathered excellent experience at Narisawa
and Noma.

Clown Bar **564**...........Regular neighborhood
A Mère **562**................Regular neighborhood

JASON MORRIS
Le Fantôme
1832 Rue William, Montreal
He has teamed up with Kabir Kapoor to bring
a fresh approach to Montreal's dining scene.

Blanca **1015**.....................Worth the travel
Cosmos Snack Bar **780**..................Breakfast
L'express **776**.......................Local favorite
Kazu **782**....................Regular neighborhood
MonNan **774**..............................Late night
MonNan **774**.................Regular neighborhood
Pho Nguyen **782**............Regular neighborhood
Chalet Bar-B-Q Rotisserie **730**......Regular
neighborhood
Tacos Frida **781**...........Regular neighborhood
Le Taj **774**...................................Bargain
Toqué! **783**...............................High end
Uniburger **783**..............Regular neighborhood

ANTONIN MOUSSEAU-RIVARD
Le Mousso
1023 Ontario East Street, Montréal
A self-taught chef who started out as a
dishwasher. His artistic flair is evident in
his food, which shows a style inspired by
the automatists movement.

Beauty's **775**..............................Breakfast
Cosmos Snack Bar **780**..................Breakfast
L'Express **776**................Regular neighborhood
Joe Beef **779**........................Local favorite
Leméac **778**.................Regular neighborhood
Au Pied de Cochon **551**............Local favorite
Pho Than Long **782**........................Bargain
La Poule au Pot **551**.....................Late night
Restaurant A.T **554**...............Worth the travel
Tour d'Argent **554**.........................High end

KAMAL MOUZAWAK
Tawlet
12 Naher Street, Beirut
He founded Beirut's first farmers' market,
Souk el Tayeb, and operates Tawlet,
a farmers' kitchen that serves regional
Lebanese dishes.

Boubouffe **176**...............Regular neighborhood
Dario Doc **669**.....................Worth the travel
Fadel **177**.....................Regular neighborhood
Falafel M.Sahyoun **176**....................Bargain
Osteria da Gemma **664**.........Wish I'd opened
Le Professeur **176**.......................Breakfast
Rafic Al Rashidi **176**.....................Breakfast
Sporting Club Beach **176**...........Local favorite
Villa Clara **176**............................High End

TOM MOXON
Bone Daddies
31 Peter Street, England

Tom Moxon carried out an apprenticeship at Zuma under head chef Ross Shonhan, for whom he would later help establish the London ramen joint, Bone Daddies.

Barrafina 444	Wish I'd opened
Dishoom 448	Breakfast
Engawa 448	High end
Kerb 410	Local favorite
The Manor 414	Regular neighborhood
Patty & Bun 421	Late night
Pizza Metro 411	Regular neighborhood
Princi 453	Bargain
The Roastery 415	Breakfast
Roti King 483	Bargain
Trattoria da Papà 647	Worth the travel
Umu 442	High end

DAVID MOYLE
Franklin
30 Argyle Street, Hobart

Previously chef at the Pacific Dining Room in Byron Bay and Circa in Melbourne, he now co-owns his newest offering, which serves deceptively simple seafood.

Aløft 97	Regular neighborhood
Dier Makr 97	Regular neighborhood
Dier Makr 97	Late night
Dunalley Fish Market 96	Regular neighborhood
Fico 98	Regular neighborhood
Hamlet 98	Breakfast
Me Wah 100	High end
The Quartermasters Arms 99	Late night
I Rizzari 667	Worth the travel
The Source 871	High end
Straight Up Coffee & Food 99	Breakfast
Templo 100	Wish I'd opened
Templo 100	Regular neighborhood
Tricycle 100	Breakfast

LUKAS MRAZ
Cordobar
Grosse Hamburger Strasse 32, Vienna

This Viennese chef worked at Dutch Librije and French Arnsbourg before returning home to Cordobar, where he has been for four years.

Aroma 628	Late night
House of Small Wonder 632	Breakfast
Industry Standard 633	Local favorite
Lon Men's Noodle House 628	Regular neighborhood
Nobelhart & Schmutzig 630	Worth the travel
Restaurant Hodori 634	Bargain
Standard Serious Pizza 633	Wish I'd opened
Tim Raue 631	High end

VALDIMIR MUKHIN
White Rabbit
3 Smolenskaya Square, Moscow

His respect for tradition and interest in new culinary techniques have made him one of the leaders of Russia's New Wave. As brand-

chef of White Rabbit holdings, he supervises a handful of additional projects.

Boston Seafood and Bar 711	Late night
La Bottega Siciliana 711	High end
Chainaya. Tea & Cocktails 711	Late night
Clown Bar 564	Worth the travel
La Docena 1079	Worth the travel
Danilovsky Market 706	Bargain
Danilovsky Market 706	Regular neighborhood
Les Déserteurs 565	Worth the travel
Duran Bar 708	Late night
LavkaLavka 712	Local favorite
One Little Sister 95	Breakfast
Semifreddo 707	High end
Septime 566	Worth the travel
Severyane 709	Wish I'd opened
Severyane 709	Breakfast
Ugolek 710	Local favorite

MARCO MÜLLER
Rutz
Chausseestrasse 8, Berlin

He arrived at Rutz in Berlin in 2004, where he has since won praise for cooking that takes in German, Austrian, and Swiss infuences.

Aigner 631	Local favorite
Atera 1013	Worth the travel
Bandol sur Mer 631	High end
Geranium 378	Worth the travel
NU 628	Regular neighborhood
Restaurant Biberbau 634	Wish I'd opened
Rosenburger 632	Late night
Sets 628	Breakfast
Strandbar Mitte 633	Bargain

DHARSHAN MUNIDASA
Ministry of Crab
Old Dutch Hospital, Colombo

The Sri Lankan-Japanese founder of Nihonbashi Honten, which originally opened in Colombo in 1995, with The Ministry of Crab following in 2012.

Burnt Ends 329	Wish I'd opened
Inoue Ramen 263	Bargain
Jubako 264	High end
Nihonryori RyuGin 208	Local favorite
Ningxia Night Market 205	Late night
Tsukiji Fish Market 260	Breakfast
Umu 442	Worth the travel

DAVID MUÑOZ
DiverXO
C / Padre Damian 23, Madrid

A graduate of London's Nobu and Hakkasan's kitchens, Muñoz returned to his native Madrid in 2007 to open DiverXO, which garnered three Michelin stars in just six years.

Asturianos 588	Regular neighbourhood
Benu 840	Worth the travel
La Bomba Bistrot 588	Bargain
El Celler de Can Roca 583	High end
La Duquesita 588	Breakfast
Hakkasan 1040	Wish I'd opened
Kabuki Wellington 589	High end
Kresios 646	Worth the travel
Lakasa 589	Late night
Mugaritz 576	High end

Nahm 283	Worth the travel
New York Burger 589	Regular neighbourhood
Sacha 590	Local favourite
Santceloni 590	Late night
StreetXO 590	Bargain
La Tasquita de Enfrente 589	Local favourite
UMIKO 591	Regular neighbourhood

YOSHIHIRO MURATA
Kikunoi
459 Shimokawara-cho, Kyoto

Championing a style of traditional Japanese fare, kaiseki, Murata holds seven Michelin stars, three of which are for his flagship restaurant in Kyoto.

Gion Sasaki 247	Wish I'd opened
Hyotei 249	Breakfast
Ichi no Hunairi 248	Bargain
Kyoto Kitcho Arashiyama 250	High end
Soba Ryuryu Senkaku 247	Regular neighbourhood
Yasukawa 248	Late night
Yoshoku Ogata 249	Local favorite

BEN MURPHY
Launceston Place
1a Launceston Place, London

Mentored by Pierre Koffmann, he took on his first head chef role at The Woodford before joining D&D London as the new head chef of Launceston Place.

The Clove Club 487	Wish I'd opened
Epicure 558	Worth the travel
The Ledbury 423	High end
Noma 369	Worth the travel
	OttolenghivLocal favorite
Pitt Cue 467	Bargain
Pizza East 486	Regular neighborhood
Pizzeria Bel Sit 494	Regular neighborhood
VQ (Vingt-Quatre) 413	Late night
The Wolseley 443	Breakfast

KRISTEN D. MURRAY
MÁURICE Luncheonette
921 South West Oak Street, Portland

Building on her Norwegian heritage, love of France, and a formative opportunity she had to work with pastry guru Christine Ferber, Murray was able to open her dream restaurant, Maurice.

L'Assiette 567	Worth the travel
Atelier Crenn 833	High end
Bar Casa Vale 847	Late night
Chen's Good Taste 849	Bargain
Coquine 850	Local favorite
Coquine 850	Regular neighborhood
Expatriate 851	Late night
Luce 855	Regular neighborhood
Meat Cheese Bread 855	Breakfast
Navarre 855	Breakfast
Navarre 855	Regular neighborhood
Nong's Khao Man Gai 856	Bargain
Otium 814	Worth the travel
Trifecta Tavern 860	Late night

SHINOBU NAMAE
L'Effervescence
2-26-4 Nishiazabu Minato-ku, Tokyo
Formerly sous chef of The Fat Duck, he opened L'Effervescence in 2011 and it won a Michelin star three years later.

Bunon 262	Regular neighborhood
Le Cabaret 268	Late night
DEN 268	Local favorite
Esquisse 257	High end
Farmer's Market 269	Bargain
Florilège 269	Local favorite
Green Pastures 310	Breakfast
Kyoaji 264	High end
Libertin 270	Late night
Miyamasou 250	Worth the travel
Organ 273	Regular neighborhood
Sushi Saito 267	Local favorite
Sushi Tokami 259	Local favorite
Yakumo Saryo 261	Breakfast

ALESSANDRO NARDUCCI
Acquolina Hostaria
Via Antonio Serra 60, Rome
He moved to the kitchen only after he graduated as a professional sommelier and now he has gained his first Michelin star, aged just twenty-seven.

Coffee Pot 656	Late night
Il Convivio Troiani 656	Regular neighborhood
Enoteca Achilli al Parlamento 656	High end
Er Gambero Rotto 656	Local favorite
Ristorante Reale 646	Worth the travel
Trapizzino 657	Bargain
Trattoria da Neno 658	Late night

YOSHIHIRO NARISAWA
Narisawa
2-6-15 Minamiaoyama, Tokyo
He trained in Switzerland with Girardet, in France with Robuchon, and in Italy at Antica Osteria del Ponte, before opening Les Créations de Narisawa (now called Narisawa) in 2003.

Bulgari Restaurant 256	Local favorite
Gion MATAYOSHI 246	Regular neighborhood
Gion MATAYOSHI 246	Worth the travel
Higuchi 270	Local favorite
Nihonryori RyuGin 208	Local favorite
Sushidokoro Mekumi 246	Worth the travel
UBUKA 273	Regular neighborhood

JORDY NAVARRA
Toyo Eatery
2316 Pasong Tamo Extension, Manila
Based in Manila, he opened Toyo Eatery with his wife May in 2016 to serve traditional Filipino food in a space where diners are surrounded by local art and crafts.

Baliwag Lechon Manok 309	Bargain
The Black Pig 309	Regular neighborhood
The Curator Coffee and Cocktails 304	Breakfast
DEN 268	Wish I'd opened
Fuglen Tokyo 269	Breakfast
Gallery Vask 310	High end

Mang Raul's BBQ Haus 303	Local favorite
Nagazumi 265	Wish I'd opened
Quintessence 271	High end
Seaside Dampa on Macapagal Avenue 310	Local favorite
Tim Ho Wan 312	Late night
Wildflour Cafe + Bakery 308	Regular neighborhood
Yukino Hana 308	Late night

BRYANT NG
Cassia
1314 7th Street, Santa Monica
He was the first chef de cuisine at Pizzeria Mozza before he opened his first restaurant, The Spice Table in Los Angeles. Ng is currently the chef-proprietor of Cassia in Santa Monica.

El Huarachito 819	Breakfast
In-n-out 817	Late night
In-n-out 817	Bargain
Lawry's The Prime Rib 811	Wish I'd opened
Luscious Dumplings 822	Regular neighborhood
Mitoya 273	Worth the travel
n/naka 821	High end
Yunnan Restaurant 820	Regular neighborhood
Yunnan Restaurant 820	Local favorite

YONG BING NGEN
Majestic Restaurant
New Majestic Hotel, 31-37 Bukit Pasoh Road, Singapore
A Malaysian-born chef with over three decades of experience, Ngen pushes the boundaries of Chinese cooking with new ingredients and techniques, while staying true to its culinary roots.

Beach Road Prawn Mee Eating House 316	Breakfast
He Jia Huan Ban Mian Mee Hoon Kway 335	Late night
Lee Fun Nam Kee 335	Regular neighborhood
Man Man Japanese Unagi Restaurant 330	Wish I'd opened
Maxwell Food Centre 320	Local favorite
Sin Huat Eating House 323	High end
To-Ricos Kway Chap 324	Bargain
Ya Kun Kaya Toast 318	Breakfast

JAKE NICOLSON
Blackbird Bar & Grill
123 Eagle Street Pier, Brisbane
Executive chef of the Ghanem Group, Nicolson is responsible for all four venues, the most recent of all being Blackbird bar & grill. His work experience includes stints at elBulli, The Square, and The Ledbury.

1889 Enoteca 615	Local favorite
Bar Alto 128	Regular neighborhood
Ben's Burgers 129	Wish I'd opened
Bird's Nest Yakitori & Bar 129	Bargain
e'cco Bistro 129	Wish I'd opened
Elystan Street 412	Worth the travel
Esquire 130	High end
Funny Funny 131	Late night
Gerard's Bistro 131	Breakfast

Icebergs Dining Room & Bar 110	Worth the travel
The Ledbury 423	Worth the travel
New Shanghai 133	Regular neighborhood
Otto 134	High end
Russ & Daughters Cafe 1009	Breakfast
Stokehouse Q 135	Local favorite
Taro's Ramen & Café 135	Bargain

MAGNUS NILSSON
Fäviken Magasinet
Fäviken 216, Järpen
He trained in Paris at L'Astrance and L'Arpège, before returning to his native Sweden in 2008, to open the tiny twelve-seat restaurant, Fäviken Magasinet.

Babette 361	Regular neighborhood
Cosme 1036	Worth the travel
Gjusta 824	Breakfast
Umut 2000 491	Late night

PETTER NILSSON
Spritmuseum
Djurgårdsvägen 38, Stockholm
The Swede who cooked at Les Trois Salons in Uzès and went on to co-own and run La Gazzetta in Paris. He is now back in Stockholm to head up the new Spritmuseum restaurant.

Babette 361	Regular neighborhood
Café Nizza 359	Regular neighborhood
KafKaf 355	Breakfast
Matbygget 350	Bargain
Mugaritz 576	High end
Mugaritz 576	Wish I'd opened
Osteria Francescana 650	Worth the travel
Pelikan 360	Local favorite
Pom & Flora 360	Breakfast
Sturehof 358	Late night
Tennstopet 362	Local favorite

CHAKALL NOIR
El Bulo Social Club
Praça David Leandro Da Saliva 9, Lisbon
Chef, author, and TV presenter, Noir is a multi-talented owner of two restaurants, Sudaka in Berlin and El Bulo in Lisbon.

Dom Lourenço 607	Bargain
Flor de Lis 613	Late night
Flor-de-Lis 613	Regular neighborhood
Francucci's Ristorante 629	Regular neighborhood
Martin Berasategui 577	Worth the travel
O Poleiro 614	Local favorite
Patagonia Sur 1125	Wish I'd opened
Schwarzwaldstube 624	High end
Sudaka 634	Breakfast

GRAE NONAS

New England-born Nonas swapped the East Coast for the West after training and, while working at Son of a Gun, he met his future partner Michael Fojtasek, with whom he opened Olamaie.

Bufalina **1060**	Regular neighborhood
Casa Mono **1038**	Wish I'd opened
Clamato **564**	Worth the travel
Dai Due **1060**	Breakfast
Franklin Barbecue **1061**	Local favorite
Gray's Papaya **1045**	Late night
Guts & Glory **515**	Worth the travel
Manfreds **377**	Worth the travel
Matsuhisa **811**	High end
Ramen Tatsu-ya **1065**	Regular neighborhood
Russ & Daughters Cafe **1009**	Breakfast
Septime **566**	Wish I'd opened
Son of a Gun **810**	Wish I'd opened
Tan My **1065**	Bargain
Veracruz All Natural **1066**	Local favorite

NICOLAI NØRREGAARD

Kadeau
Wildersgade 10B, Copenhagen

He opened the produce-based restaurant Kadeau on the remote Danish island of Bornholm in 2007. A second incarnation of the Baltic-island venue opened in Copenhagen's Christianshavn in 2012.

Admiralgade 26 **370**	Breakfast
Chicky Grill **379**	Local favorite
Daniel Berlin Krog **349**	High end
Ekstedt **357**	Worth the travel
Fäviken Magasinet **345**	Worth the travel
Geist **372**	Late night
Le Grenouillere **540**	Worth the travel
Henne Kirkeby Kro **365**	High end
Honey **373**	Regular neighborhood
Maaemo **344**	Worth the travel
Nabo **369**	Local favorite
Narisawa **265**	Worth the travel
Oaxen Krog **354**	High end
Oaxen Slip **354**	High end
Papa Ramen **380**	Bargain
Rabes Have **369**	Local favorite
Le Verre Volé **563**	Wish I'd opened

JUSTIN NORTH

Hotel Centennial
88 Oxford Street, Sydney

He began his culinary career in New Zealand and travelled to Europe in 1996 to work in the kitchen of Le Manoir with Raymond Blanc. North has been executive chef at the Hotel Centennial in Sydney since 2014.

Aria **115**	Local favorite
The Boathouse **118**	Breakfast
Chat Thai **116**	Bargain
Fleet **82**	Worth the travel
Fred's **120**	Wish I'd opened
Mamak **117**	Late night
Ruby's Diner **125**	Breakfast
Sepia **113**	High end

Street Kitchen Singapore **118**	Regular neighborhood
Yasaka Ramen **43**	Regular neighborhood

BENNY NOVAK

ICI Bistro
Rua Para 34, São Paulo

Le Cordon Bleu trained, he opened ICI Bistro in 2002 and Tappo Trattoria in 2007. He is also a director and partner of CIATC, an organisation that brings together thousands of hospitality professionals.

Asador Etxebarri **575**	Worth the travel
Churrascaria Boi na Brasa **1113**	Late night
The Clove Club **487**	Worth the travel
Estadão Bar e Lanches **1112**	Late night
Kan **1114**	High end
Bar Astor **1117**	Local favorite
Mani **1114**	High end
Padaria Dengosa **1112**	Breakfast
Shin-zushi **1114**	High end
Al Sultan Midhat Restaurante **1115**	Bargain
Tan Tan Noodle Bar **1116**	Wish I'd opened
Tanuki Restaurante Sushi **1118**	Regular neighborhood
Ton Hoi **1112**	Wish I'd opened

ÉDGAR NUÑEZ

Sud 777
Boulevard de la Luz 777, Mexico City

A talented Mexican chef who has earned his stripes in kitchens across Europe, including Noma, elBulli, and the Paul Bocuse restaurants in Lyon.

Ardente **1079**	Bargain
Biko **1079**	High end
Corazón de Tierra **1077**	Worth the travel
Enrique **1080**	Breakfast
Mazurka **1081**	Wish I'd opened
El Puntal del Norte **1082**	Regular neighborhood
Quintonil **1082**	Local favorite
Sushi Kyo **1083**	Late night

SAMUEL NUTTER

Restaurant BROR
Sankt Peders Stræde 24a, Copenhagen

Partnering with a fellow ex-Noma chef to open Bror, British-born Nutter has garnered praise for cooking bold Nordic fare.

Admiralgade 26 **370**	Breakfast
Bar Brutal **594**	Bargain
Geranium **378**	High end
Kitchen Table @ Bubble Dogs **446**	Worth the travel
Magasasa **380**	Late night
Noma **369**	Local favorite
The Raby Hunt **395**	Wish I'd opened
Southern Grill & Master Sushi **368**	Bargain
Taller **375**	High end
Uformel **381**	Regular neighborhood

KARL & RUDOLF OBAUER

Restaurant Obauer
Hotel Obauer, Markt 46, Werfen

These two brothers have run the kitchen of their eponymous restaurant since it opened in 1979.

L'Auberge de l'Ill **534**	Regular neighborhood
Carpe Diem Finest Fingerfood **677**	Breakfast
Erlhof **677**	Local favorite
Gasthaus Ackermann **676**	Bargain
Gut Purbach **676**	Worth the travel
O boufés **683**	Wish I'd opened
Restaurant de l'Hotel de Ville Crissier **840**	High end
Würstelkönigin Salzburg **677**	Late night

SHUKO ODA

Koya Bar
50 Frith Street, London

She learned the art and hard graft of udon-making at Kunitoraya in Paris before opening the London Udon restaurant Koya in 2010 and then Koya Bar in 2013.

Bao **472**	Bargain
Bashan **444**	Late night
Brick House Bakery **471**	Breakfast
DEN **268**	Worth the travel
Lyle's **488**	Local favorite
Rochelle Canteen **486**	Regular neighborhood
St. John Bar and Restaurant **471**	Wish I'd opened
The Hinds Head **390**	High end

DAVIDE OLDANI

D'O
Piazza della Chiesa 14, Milan

Born in Cornaredo, near Milan, he trained with Marchesi at Le Gavroche in London and at Louis XV in Monte Carlo, opening D'O in 2003.

Alain Ducasse au Plaza Athénée **557**	Worth the travel
I Banchi di Ragusa **667**	Wish I'd opened
Da Vittorio **659**	High end
Dry **661**	Late night
La Franceschetta 58 **649**	Bargain
Marchesi 1824 **661**	Breakfast
Trattoria Masuelli San Marco **662**	Local favorite
Zer **663**	Regular neighborhood

RODRIGO OLIVEIRA

Mocotó
Avenida Nossa Senhora do Loreto 1100, São Paulo

Originally opened by his father, José Oliveira de Almeida, Rodrigo Oliveira's Mocotó in São Paulo serves authentic Amazonian cuisine.

A Casa do Porco **1116**	Local favorite
Bar Número **1113**	Late night
Carlinhos Restaurante **1115**	Bargain
Casa Garabed **1117**	Regular neighborhood
Jun Sakamoto **1115**	High end
Il Luogo di Aimo e Nadia **661**	Worth the travel
Nosu **1117**	Regular neighborhood
O Velhão **1114**	Local favorite
Padaria Jardim Brasil **1112**	Breakfast
Roberta Sudbrack **1109**	Wish I'd opened
Sushi Hiroshi **1117**	Regular neighborhood

THE CHEFS

ANDI OLIVER
Andi's
176 Stoke Newington Church Street, London

A former band member and TV presenter, Oliver had a varied career before she opened her first restaurant, The Jackdaw and Star. 2017 will see both the launch of her second restaurant and appearances on the BBC's *Great British Menu*.

Andina 484	Wish I'd opened
Aulis at Fera 437	High end
Bad Sports 477	Late night
Beagle 478	Wish I'd opened
The Canton Arms 489	Local favorite
The Dairy 414	High end
Deeney's 474	Breakfast
Escocesa 490	Regular neighborhood
Jim's Café 468	Regular neighborhood
Kêu 486	Bargain
Mangal 1 Ocakbasi 470	Local favorite
Nanban 464	Bargain
Oban Seafood Hut 496	Worth the travel
Oishi Grand 284	Worth the travel
Ranoush Juice 422	Late night
Rubedo 491	Regular neighborhood

ANDY OLIVER
Som Saa
43a Commercial Street, London

Via a place in the final of UK MasterChef, he went on to stage in a number of restaurants including Moro, Bocca di Lupo, and Nahm. He is one of a trio to co-own Som Saa, which opened following a successful crowdfunding campaign.

Black Axe Mangal 480	Late night
Bo.Lan 287	Worth the travel
Kiln 451	Regular neighborhood
Kiln 451	Wish I'd opened
The Ledbury 423	High end
Lyle's 488	Regular neighborhood
P. Franco 468	Local favorite
P. Franco 468	Regular neighborhood
P. Franco 468	Wish I'd opened
Peckham Bazaar 484	Regular neighborhood
The Sportsman 400	Worth the travel
St. John Bread & Wine 489	Breakfast
Tayyabs 494	Bargain
Towpath Café 479	Regular neighborhood
Typing Room 462	High end

ENRIQUE OLVERA
Pujol
Tennyson 133, Mexico City

One of a New Wave of Mexican chefs re-imagining indigenous cuisine by marrying it with a fine dining setting, Olvera opened Pujol in Mexico City in 2000.

Estela 1010	Breakfast
Lardo 1081	Breakfast
Rokai 1083	Regular neighborhood

UWE OPOCENSKY
Beef & Liberty
23 Wing Fung Street, Hong Kong

This German chef worked for Anton Mosimann in London and did a stint with the Shangri-La Hotel group, before joining The Mandarin Oriental, Hong Kong.

Amber 220	Regular neighborhood
Aska 1015	Wish I'd opened
Australia Dairy Company 212	Breakfast
Blue Hill at Stone Barns 913	High end
The Boathouse 118	Breakfast
Brae 101	Worth the travel
Chicken HOF & SOJU 214	Late night
Cottage Point Inn 83	Wish I'd opened
Eleven Madison Park 1037	High end
Fäviken Magasinet 345	Worth the travel
Gyoten 244	Worth the travel
Kau Kee Restaurant 222	Local favorite
Relæ 378	
Rhoda 228	Regular neighborhood
Saison 841	Wish I'd opened
Saison 841	High end
SingleThread Farms 792	High end
Sixpenny 123	Worth the travel
Tim Ho Wan 213	Bargain
Tung Po 227	Local favorite
Yardbird 229	Regular neighborhood

KEN ORINGER
Little Donkey
505 Massachussets Avenue, Cambridge

Boston born, he worked across the US before returning to open a string of restaurants, including four Boston restaurants, Earth in Maine, and Toro tapas bar in New York City, and most recently, Little Donkey.

Coop's Place 879	Late night
Grill 23 890	Local favorite
Mike's City Diner 890	Local favorite
Neptune Oyster 891	Local favorite
Oleana 897	High end
Sam LaGrassa's 892	Bargain
Shuko 1024	Worth the travel
Los Tacos No.1 1035	Regular neighborhood
Tartine Manufactory 836	Breakfast
Via Carota 1030	Regular neighborhood
Wildair 1037	Wish I'd opened

AITOR JERONIMO ORIVE
Iggy's
581 Orchard Road, Singapore

Time spent as chef de partie at The Fat Duck has influenced his culinary techniques considerably, while his idiosyncratic Australian and Spanish upbringing and love of Japanese cuisine have informed his ingredients and style.

Fayidha Restaurant 325	Regular neighborhood
FOC 329	Wish I'd opened
Geylang Famous Beef Kway Teow 323	Bargain
Imperial Treasure Super Peking Duck 319	Local favorite
Mugaritz 576	Worth the travel
Swee Choon Tim Sum Restaurant 333	Late night
La Torre Bistrot 588	High end

Wee Nam Kee 326	Regular neighborhood
Whampoa Hawker Centre 326	Breakfast
Whitegrass 322	High end

MATTHEW ORLANDO
Amass Restaurant
Refshalevej 153, Copenhagen

Californian Orlando's résumé reads like a Who's Who of the culinary world: he worked under Eric Ripert, Raymond Blanc, Heston Blumenthal, and René Redzepi, before opening his own restaurant, Amass in 2013.

Bæst 376	Regular neighborhood
Beyti 376	Late night
Bror 371	Regular neighborhood
Cafe Det Vide Hus 371	Breakfast
Christiania Falafel 368	Bargain
Contra 1007	Worth the travel
Dragsholm Slot 364	Worth the travel
Dragsholm Slot 364	High end
Hija de Sanchez 379	Bargain
Hija de Sánchez 379	Late night
Kødbyens Fiskebar 379	Local favorite
Manfreds 377	Local favorite
Noma 369	Worth the travel
Per Se 1046	Worth the travel
Relæ 378	High end
Rufino Osteria 369	Regular neighborhood
Saltimporten Canteen 348	Wish I'd opened
Spisehuset 381	Bargain

MITCH ORR
ACME
60 Bayswater Road, Sydney

After working in the lauded Sydney restaurants Pilu at Freshwater and Sepia, Orr opened Duke Bistro, where he began to make a name for himself. In 2015 he opened Acme and followed that with Bar Brosé in 2016.

Automata 114	Regular neighborhood
Automata 114	Local favorite
Boon Café 116	Breakfast
Chat Thai 116	Bargain
Chat Thai 116	Breakfast
Chat Thai 116	Late night
Contra 1007	Worth the travel
Ester 114	Local favorite
Fratelli Paradiso 121	Local favorite
Fratelli Paradiso 121	Regular neighborhood
Golden Century 111	Late night
LP's Quality Meats 114	Regular neighborhood
Lyle's 488	Worth the travel
Momofuku Seiōbo 123	High end
Room 10 122	Breakfast
Saint Peter 120	Wish I'd opened
Saint Peter 120	Regular neighborhood
Sixpenny 123	High end
Super Bowl Chinese Restaurant 135	Late night
Yardbird 229	Worth the travel
Yellow 122	Breakfast

MARTHA ORTIZ
Dulce Patria
Anatole France 100, Mexico City

She serves vibrant modern Mexican cuisine in an environment that channels Frida Kahlo. Her cooking is informed by her studies of the history of gastronomy and regional Mexican food.

Casa Merlos **1079**........Regular neighborhood

ROBERT ORTIZ
Lima
31 Rathbone Place, London

A pioneer of Peruvian cuisine, Ortiz brings the heady flavors and bright colors of his native country to his audience in Europe's first Peruvian restaurant to win a Michelin star.

Adam's Restaurant **404**....................High end
Andi's **490**.........................Wish I'd opened
Café Monico **447**.........................Breakfast
Caravaggio **464**...........Regular neighborhood
Central **1098**....................Worth the travel
Coffee Architects **404**..........................Bargain
Icon Balcony Bar **433**.....................Late night
Little Amsterdam **403**...Regular neighborhood
Northcote **401**...................Local favorite

SHANE OSBORN
Arcane
18 On Lan Street, Hong Kong

He first made a splash at London's Pied à Terre, where he became the first Australian chef to gain two Michelin stars. In 2014, he opened Arcane.

121BC **220**...................Regular neighborhood
Amber **220**..High end
Belon **220**....................Worth the travel
The Continental **218**..............Wish I'd opened
Din Tai Fung **218**.........................Local favorite
Fineprint **222**.........................Breakfast
Hooked **227**..Bargain
Kau Kee Restaurant **222**.....................Bargain
Mak's Noodle **223**...................Local favorite
Mr & Mrs Fox **227**.........................Breakfast
Tin Lung Heen **215**........................High end
Yardbird **229**.........................Late night

YOTAM OTTOLENGHI
Ottolenghi
287 Upper Street, London

The London-based Israeli chef and co-owner of the eponymous group of sleek Middle Eastern-Mediterranean deli-cafes with business partner Sami Tamimi, and Nopi restaurant, which opened in 2011.

Bao **444**..Bargain
The Coffee Jar **465**......Regular neighborhood
The Delaunay **423**.........................Breakfast
Imperial China **434**......Regular neighborhood
J Sheeky **434**.........................Late night
Jikoni **420**.........................Wish I'd opened
The Ledbury **423**........................High end
Locanda Locatelli **440**........................High end
El Parador **483**............Regular neighborhood
Portland **473**...............Regular neighborhood
Primeur **491**...............Regular neighborhood

St. John Bar and Restaurant **471**...........Local
favorite
The Walnut Tree **499**.............Worth the travel

NATHAN OUTLAW
Restaurant Nathan Outlaw
6 New Road, Port Isaac

This Cornish-based seafood specialist runs Restaurant Nathan Outlaw and Seafood & Grill. A variation of the latter opened in London at The Capital hotel in 2012.

The Beach Hut **392**.........................Breakfast
Coombeshead farm **391**.....................Regular
neighborhood
Craft Works Street Kitchen **393**..........Regular
neighborhood
Kahuna **392**.................Regular neighborhood

PAUL PAIRET
Ultraviolet
Shanghai 200001

Having worked across Asia, he arrived in Shanghai to open Jade on 36 in 2005, following that with Mr & Mrs Bund in 2009 and Ultraviolet in 2012.

Alain Ducasse au Plaza Athénée **557**.High end
Alain Ducasse au Plaza Athénée **557** Breakfast
Alléno Paris au Pavillon Ledoyen **557** High end
L'Auberge du Vieux Puits **524**.........Worth the
travel
L'Arpège **556**.........................High end
Din Tai Fung **198**...........Regular neighborhood
Din Tai Fung **198**...................Wish I'd opened
Le Grand Restaurant **558**................High end
Imperial Treasure Fine Chinese Cuisine **197**....
Local favorite
The NEST Shanghai **197**.................Bargain
UNÍCO **198**.........................Late night

BJOERN ALEXANDER PANEK
TWENTY SIX by Liberty
11 Stanley Street, Hong Kong

He learned his trade working in the kitchens of Thomas Keller and Tim Raue and was at the helm of Berlin's Restaurant Gabriele when it won its first Michelin star.

Bo Innovation **230**...................Local favorite
Chachawan **230**.........................Late night
D.O.M. Restaurante **1114**..............High end
DEN **268**.....................Regular neighborhood
Florilège **269**.................Regular neighborhood
Mercedes me Store **224**.....................Breakfast
Nobelhart & Schmutzig **230**....Wish I'd opened
Tim Raue **631**..................Worth the travel

STEVIE PARLE
Dock Kitchen
344 Ladbroke Grove, London

He previously worked at Moro and the River Café, and is now a London based chef-restaurateur who operates Dock Kitchen, Rotorino, Craft London, Sardine, and Palatino.

The Beigel Shop **484**.....................Late night
Brunswick House **493**.................Local favorite
The Clove Club **487**........................High end
Dishoom **432**.........................Wish I'd opened
Fäviken Magasinet **345**.....................High end

Fäviken Magasinet **345**.........Worth the travel
The Goods Shed Restaurant **399**........Regular
neighborhood
Lahore Kebab House **493**.........................Bargain
Pavilion Café **476**.............................Breakfast
Viet Grill **487**.................Regular neighborhood

DANIEL PATTERSON
Alta CA
1275 Minnesota Street, San Francisco

Born in Massachusetts, he moved to California in 1989. Self-taught cook Patterson is the brains behind San Francisco's COI (2006) and has since opened Plum (2010), Haven (2012), and Alta CA (2013).

Aster **834**.........................Local favorite
Benu **840**..High end
Blanca **1015**....................Worth the travel
Boot & Shoe Service **795**..Regular neighborhood
Cosecha **795**.............Regular neighborhood
LocoL Bakery **796**.........................Breakfast
Nopa **828**..Late night
Shandong **796**....................................Bargain

DAVID PELLIZZARI
Lili.Co
4675 Boulevard Saint-Laurent, Montréal

Formerly of Park Hill and The Whip, he opened his first open-kitchened solo venture in 2013 with co-owner Catherine Draws.

Beauty's **775**.........................Breakfast
Buvette Chez Simone **776**.................Late night
Lawrence Restaurant **777**....Regular neighborhood
Nora Gray **774**........................High end
Noren **778**..Bargain
Le Réservoir **778**...................Wish I'd opened
Tim Ho Wan **213**.................Worth the travel
Le Vin Papillon **780**...................Local favorite

CARLOS PEREZ
El Blok
158 Calle Flamboyan, Vieques

Puerto Rican chef, Perez is famed for working with fishermen, farmers, and urban foragers to use local produce in his food.

Montréal Plaza **781**......Regular neighborhood
CUT **810**.........................High end
Ludobird **814**....................................Bargain
Otium **814**....................Worth the travel
Osteria Mozza **816**.........................High end
Petite Trois **817**..................Wish I'd opened
Alinea **957**....................Worth the travel
Grace **966**..High end
Roister **968**...................Local favorite
Spoon & Stable **1001**........................High end
Red Rooster **1007**....Regular neighborhood
Loring Place **1025**........Regular neighborhood
Günter Seeger **1028**........................High end
Aldea **1044**..............Regular neighborhood
167 Raw **1050**............Regular neighborhood
le Farfelle **1053**...........Regular neighborhood
Fig **1053**.........................Local favorite
The Ordinary **1056**........................High end
Langdon Hall **752**...................Worth the travel
Alo Restaurant **766**........................High end

BJÖRN PERSSON
KOKA
Viktoriagatan 12, Gothenburg

Owner of the France-meets-West-Coast Swedish brasserie, Familjen, the late-night bolthole, Björns Bar, Spisa, and the modern Scandinavian Koka.

Bhoga 350....................................Local favorite
Bord 27 350.....................................Bargain
Chef's Table at Brooklyn Fare 1019..Worth the travel
Esperanto 358.....................................High end
NOOK 360...........................Wish I'd opened
Sjömagasinet 351......................Local favorite
Trattoria la Strega 351..Regular neighborhood

CAL PETERNELL
Chez Panisse
1517 Shattuck Avenue, Berkeley

Raised in New Jersey, he cooked at Biba, the Blue Room, Bix, and Bizou before joining Alice Water's Chez Panisse, where he has been since 1995.

Bollywood Theater 848..........Worth the travel
Fieldwork 789...High end
Oori Rice Triangles 788.Regular neighborhood
Pho Ao Sen 788...........Regular neighborhood
PINE & CRANE 823................Wish I'd opened
Ramen Shop 795...........................Late night
Sam's Log Cabin 789.....................Breakfast
Tacos el Autlense 789.......................Bargain

JOCKY PETRIE
Gordon Ramsay
68 Royal Hospital Road, London

Resident Scot at The Fat Duck from 2002 to 2013, he left to act as head of development at The Ledbury and is now executive group development chef of all Gordon Ramsay's UK and European restaurants.

L'Astrance 568...................................High end
Bentley's Oyster Bar & Grill 637........Regular neighborhood
The French Laundry 797........Wish I'd opened
Granger & Co 483............................Breakfast
Kanada-ya 435.............................Late night
The Ledbury 423.......................Local favorite
Pakta 599..High end
Sourced Market 483.......................Breakfast
Wexler's Deli 815...............................Bargain

JUSTIN PFAU
Harold's Cabin
247 Congress Street, Charleston

Pfau's first mentor, Andrew McCrosky, gave him his first proper knife, a Wusthof and it was after this that he was properly introduced to Southern food by Perry Hendrix.

492 1050.............................Wish I'd opened
Bear E Patch Cafe 1051..................Breakfast
Bowen's Island 931....................Local favorite
Chez Nous 1052...............................High end
Chez Nous 1052...........Regular neighborhood
Chez Nous 1052................Wish I'd opened
Dave's Carry-Out 1052..............Local favorite

EVO 885.....................Regular neighborhood
Fishnet Seafood 931....................Local favorite
Martha Lou's Kitchen 1054........Local favorite
Xiao Bao Biscuit 1057..Regular neighborhood
Xiao Bao Biscuit 1057............Wish I'd opened
Zia Tacqueria 931.........Regular neighborhood

ROBERT PHALEN
One Eared Stag
1029 Edgewood Avenue, Atlanta

It was at Mumbo Jumbo that Phalen met his mentor, Shaun Doty, whom he followed to MidCity Cuisine. He opened the intimate and refined American eatery, One Eared Stag in 2011.

Bones 943.....................................Local favorite
Canton House 944...........................Breakfast
Estela 1010.............................Worth the travel
Fred's Meat & Bread 945..Regular neighborhood
Little's Food Store 946.......................Bargain
Majestic Diner 946.........................Late night
Spring 878...........................Wish I'd opened
Sushi Hayakawa 950........................High end

PEETER PIHEL
Fäviken Magasinet
Fäviken 216, Järpen

He formerly oversaw the kitchen at Alexander, in the Pädaste Manor Hotel on Estonia's Muhu island, and Neh, in Tallinn, and is now sous chef at Magnus Nilsson's destination restaurant Fäviken Magasinet.

L'Arpège 556......................................High end
Clown Bar 564.....................Wish I'd opened
Leib Resto ja Aed 698..Regular neighborhood
Leib Resto ja Aed 698................Local favorite
La Marine 542........................Worth the travel
Paradiso 595...................................Late night
Põhjaka mõis 696............................Bargain
Restaurant Eska 688........................Breakfast

GIANFRANCO PIRRONE
Rosso
Kota BNI, Jalan Jendral Sudirman Kav. 1, Jakarta

The Sicilian chef who offers authentic Italian cuisine in Rosso at Shangri-La.

Breakfast at Cayenne 299................Breakfast
Burgreens Express 299.....................Bargain
La Buvette 655.....................Worth the travel
La Buvette 657.....................Worth the travel
Jittlada Thai Cuisine 300.................Late night
Monty's Restaurant 300.....................High end
Ristorante Dillà 657.................Local favorite
Ristorante Dillà 657.................Local favorite
Tugu Kunstkring Paleis 302.................Regular neighborhood

JOSÉ PIZARRO
Pizarro
194 Bermondsey Street, London

A Spaniard who's made London his home, Pizarro worked with Spanish food purveyors Brindisa before, in 2011, opening José and Pizarro.

Atrio 587.................................Local favorite
Atrio 587.............................Wish I'd opened

La Chapelle 488................................High end
Duck & Waffle 466............................Late night
Hoppers 450...............Regular neighborhood
MEATliquor 421................................Bargain
Paul Ainsworth at Number 6 392.....Worth the travel
The Wolseley 443..............................Breakfast

EELKE PLASMEIJER
Locavore
Jalan Dewi Sita 10, Bali

In 2011, with two Indonesian friends, he opened Locavore, where, offering just two tasting menus, locavore and herbivore, he only uses local produce from the Indonesian archipelago.

Feyloon Restaurant 294..Regular neighborhood
Fäviken Magasinet 345..........Wish I'd opened
Kebaya 292............................Worth the travel
Manresa 792...........................Worth the travel
Nasi Padang Sederhana 301..............Regular neighborhood
Noma 369..............................Worth the travel
Puteri Minang Padang Food 297 Local favorite
Tippling Club 321..............................High end
Warung Laota Jimbaran 297...........Breakfast
Warung Pulau Kelapa 298.........Local favorite

BONNY PORTER
Balls & Company
58 Greek Street, London

Hailing from Sydney, Bonny learnt her trade under Neil Perry at Rockpool Bar & Grill. After reaching the final week on *Masterchef: The Professionals* in 2013, she relocated to London, where she started Balls & Company in 2015.

Beigel Bake 485................................Late night
Dinerama 485.........................Local favorite
Dishoom 448...........................Local favorite
Flat Iron 449.......................Wish I'd opened
Flat Iron 449...............Regular neighborhood
Granger & Co 423............................Breakfast
José Tapas Bar 460......Regular neighborhood
Petit Crenn 830....................Worth the travel
The Providores 421......Regular neighborhood
Rockpool Bar & Grill 113....................High end
Tokyo Diner 436................................Bargain

MICHEL PORTOS
Le Malthazar
19 Rue Fortia, Marseille

Based in Bordeaux, and now Marseille where he runs Le Malthazar, Portos previously ran his own restaurant in Perpignan, having trained at Les Jardins de l'Opéra and Troisgros.

L'Alcyone 542	Breakfast
Café Sillon 534	Worth the travel
Chez Mémé-Jéjé le Barbu 542	Regular neighborhood
ÉPURE 214	Worth the travel
La Grenouillère 540	Worth the travel
O'Stop 543	Late night
Peron 544	Wish I'd opened
Le Petit Nice 543	High end
Pizzeria Chez Sauveur 544	Local favorite
Le Relais 50 543	Regular neighborhood
Restaurant Chez Michel 544	Local favorite
Tien Tsin Cotier 544	Bargain
La Villa Madie 543	High end

DAVID POSEY
Elske
1350 West Randolph, Chicago

Posey's introduction to the Chicago restaurant scene came via a stint at Trio, then Alinea, and finally Blackbird, before he branched out to open Elske with his wife, Anna Posey.

Big Star 969	Late night
BOKA 958	High end
Bras 541	Worth the travel
La Chaparrita 963	Bargain
Giant 959	Regular neighborhood
Le Grenouillere 540	Worth the travel
Kadeau 368	Worth the travel
Lula Cafe 959	Regular neighborhood
Olmsted 1018	Wish I'd opened
Pho Loan 965	Bargain
Please 917	Worth the travel
The Publican 968	Local favorite
Taste of Lebanon 954	Bargain
The Willows Inn 800	Worth the travel

ALFRED PRASAD

After nearly fourteen years of being an integral part of Tamarind in London, Prasad is currently working on his own restaurant project in the city and writing his first book.

Attica 151	Worth the travel
The Bangala 185	Worth the travel
Bar Italia 444	Late night
Bar Italia 444	Late night
Al Boccon di'vino 425	Regular neighborhood
Duck & Waffle 466	Local favorite
Duck & Waffle 466	Late night
Flavors of India 417	Bargain
Flavors of India 417	Regular neighborhood
The French Laundry 797	High end
The Kati Roll Company 450	Bargain
Noma 369	Wish I'd opened
The Orangery at Kew Gardens 418	Breakfast
The Original Maids of Honour 418	Breakfast
Petersham Nurseries Café 426	Regular neighborhood
Petersham Nurseries Café 426	Regular neighborhood
Room4Dessert 298	Worth the travel

WILLIAM PREISCH
Holdfast Dining
537 South East Ash, Portland

Preisch grew up around his father's 24-hour diner, where he learnt his trade. He then moved to Portland to capitalise on the fine-dining scene, finding work at Le Pigeon and Park Kitchen.

Broder 848	Breakfast
Dan and Louis 850	Wish I'd opened
Du's Grill 851	Bargain
Fuller's Coffee Shop 851	Breakfast
Noraneko 856	Late night
Le Pigeon 854	High end
Poke Mon 858	Regular neighborhood
Relæ 378	Worth the travel

JJ PROVILLE
L'Oursin
1315 East Jefferson Street, Seattle

JJ's first kitchen job was at Gramercy Tavern, where he spent two years before moving to Seattle, where he worked at the Il Corvo Pasta with chef-restaurateur Mike Easton, and then at the Art of The Table in Fremont.

Art of the Table 801	High end
Asador Etxebarri 575	Wish I'd opened
Ba Bar 801	Late night
Bakery Nouveau 801	Breakfast
Cafe Barjot 802	Breakfast
Le Caviste 804	Regular neighborhood
The Finch 1015	Worth the travel
Peloton Cafe 804	Breakfast
Seattle Deli 805	Bargain
Single Shot 805	Regular neighborhood
Sitka & Spruce 805	Local favorite
Sushi Kashiba 806	High end

CHRISTIAN F. PUGLISI
Relæ
Jægersborggade 41, Copenhagen

A Sicilian, he worked at elBulli and Taillevant before becoming sous chef at Noma, leaving to open Relæ in 2010, followed by Manfreds & Vin across the street a year later.

108 368	Local favorite
Amass 370	Local favorite
Beyti 376	Late night
Blue Hill at Stone Barns 913	Worth the travel
Copenhagen Street Food 368	Bargain
Faviken 345	Wish I'd opened
Formel B 363	High end
Gaarden og Gaden 381	Regular neighborhood
Geist 372	High end
Lyle's 488	Worth the travel
Noma	Local favorite
Noma 369	High end
Ranees 378	Regular neighborhood
Søllerød Kro 364	High end
Tartine Manufactory 836	Wish I'd opened
Torvehallerne 375	Breakfast

HELENA PUOLAKKA
Aster
150 Victoria Street, London

Executive chef for Aster, D&D London, she draws on the Nordic-style cooking of her Finnish homeland, combined with classic French culinary techniques learned during her 21 years in the kitchen.

Agern 1039	Worth the travel
Bao 444	Bargain
Elite 385	Late night
Granger & Co 423	Regular neighborhood
Hereford Road 411	Regular neighborhood
Kuurna 386	Local favorite
Olo 386	High end
La Petite Maison 441	High end
Restaurant Gösta 383	Worth the travel
Studio 375	Wish I'd opened
The Wolseley 443	Breakfast

GLYNN PURNELL
Purnell's
55 Cornwall Street, Birmingham

This loud-and-proud Brummie did his training under Ramsay, Bos, and Alastair Little, before opening the first of his three Birmingham establishments in 2007.

Sushi Passion 406	Regular neighborhood

DAVE PYNT
Burnt Ends
20 Teck Lim Road, Singapore

Pynt comes from a heavyweight culinary background, working under such legends as Tetsuya Wakuda, René Redzepi, Nuno Mendes, and Fergus Henderson. He now runs his own project, Burnt Ends, in Singapore.

L'Arpège 556	Worth the travel
Asador Etxebarri 575	Wish I'd opened
Asador Etxebarri 575	Worth the travel
Brae 101	Worth the travel
Candlenut 334	Local favorite
Chicken Up 329	Late night
Coombeshead Farm 391	Wish I'd opened
Crystal Jade Golden Palace 326	High end
Cut 319	High end
Eng's Noodle House 325	Local favorite
Hashida Sushi 327	High end
Jaan 320	High end
JB Ah Meng 323	Regular neighborhood
JB Ah Meng 323	Late night
Lao Si Chuan 330	Late night
Odette 320	High end
Ramen Keisuke Tori King 321	Bargain
Restaurant André 331	High end
Samy's Curry 335	Regular neighborhood
Sin Hoi Sai 318	Regular neighborhood
Sin Hoi Sai 318	Late night
Sin Hoi Sai 318	Local favorite
Sin Huat Eating House 323	Regular neighborhood
Super Loco 332	Breakfast

SHAUN QUADE
Lûmé
226 Coventry Street, Melbourne
Having worked at the well-established
Australian spots Quay, Biota, and Royal
Mail, Quade opened the doors of his own
restaurant in 2015, set in a terraced house
that was formerly a burlesque club.

8bit. 149	Late night
Alinea 957	Worth the travel
Brae 101	Local favorite
Brae 101	High end
Clever Polly's 142	Regular neighborhood
Embla 143	Regular neighborhood
Patricia 144	Breakfast
Pho Dzung 145	Bargain
Pidapipó 141	Wish I'd opened

PHILIP RACHINGER
Mühltalhof
Unternberg 6, Neufelden
Growing up in a family of restaurateurs, he
trained in London and Paris before returning
to Austria where he now runs the kitchen
with his father, Helmut.

Bärenwirt 676	Wish I'd opened
Bombay Palace 678	Bargain
Dollerer 676	High end
Die Donauwirtinnen 678	Local favorite
Göttfried 678	Local favorite
Grace 681	Wish I'd opened
Jausenstation Blauer Hirsch 679	Regular neighborhood
Landhaus Bacher 676	High end
Leberkas Pepi 678	Late night
Meierei im Stadtpark 682	Local favorite
Muto 679	Local favorite
Obauer 677	High end
Steirereck 684	Local favorite
Steirereck 684	High end

WAHJUDI RAHARDJA
Restaurant Emilie
Jalan Senopati 39, Jakarta
After spending the better part of a decade
honing his vision and skills with other chefs
in his kitchen, he took over the helm and
serves a cuisine that is rooted in the classics.

L'Ambroisie 553	Worth the travel
Bakmi Karet Krekot 299	Breakfast
Bakmi Karet Krekot 299	Bargain
Fong Tu 300	Local favorite
Fong Tu 300	Regular neighborhood
Locavore 297	Wish I'd opened
Maison Troisgros 536	Worth the travel
Sushi Ichi 302	Regular neighborhood
Sushi Ichi 302	High end
Tori-Ichi 302	Late night

ALEXANDRA RAIJ
El Quinto Pino
401 West 24th Street, New York City
A Jewish-American chef with Argentine roots
who runs four Iberian-focused New York
outposts – El Quinto Pino, Txikito, El Comedor,
and La Vara.

Cafe Petisco 1007	Breakfast
Cosme 1036	High end
La Isla Café 1008	Bargain
La Isla Café 1008	Breakfast
Lucali 1013	Wish I'd opened
Pujol 1082	Worth the travel
Roberta's 1017	Wish I'd opened
Russ & Daughters Cafe 1009	Local favorite
Sake Bar Decibel 1024	Late night
Los Tacos No.1 1035	Regular neighborhood

THEO RANDALL
Theo Randall at the InterContinental
1 Hamilton Place, London
This English cook with an Italian bent ran the
kitchen at the River Café in London for over a
decade, leaving in 2007 to open Theo Randall
at the InterContinental.

Le Gavroche 438	High End
The Ginger Pig 420	Bargain
Greenberry Café 425	Regular neighborhood
Greenberry Café 425	Breakfast
Mayfair Garden 440	Local favorite
Momo 440	Late Night
Osteria Del Mirasole 648	Worth the travel
La Petite Maison 441	Wish I'd opened

NEIL RANKIN
Temper
25 Broadwick Street, London
Leaving the realms of fine dining after
meeting his mentor Adam Perry Lang, the
BBQ maestro and ex-Pitt Cue Co. chef Rankin
opened Smokehouse in 2013, and more
recently Temper in 2016.

Bashan 444	Regular neighborhood
Dinerama 485	Local favorite
Dishoom 482	Late night
Hoppers 450	Regular neighborhood
Mangal 2 470	Local favorite
Princi 453	Late night

SHAUN RANKIN
Ormer
7-11 Don Street, St Helier
A passion for the local produce of Jersey in
the Channel Islands saw the County Durham-
born chef win a Michelin star at his restaurant
Ormer just four months after opening.

Acquarello Mario Gamba 624	Worth the travel
Borough Market 462	Bargain
Cecconi's 437	Regular neighborhood
The Cliff 1071	Wish I'd opened
Green Island Restaurant 496	Local favorite
Le Jules Verne 556	High end
Mews of Mayfair 440	Late night
El Tico Beach Cantina 496	Breakfast

HANS LEE RASMUSSEN
The Educational Restaurant
Colina de Mong-Há, Macau
This Macau-born chef specialises in Nordic-
French fare, having worked in multiple
Danish restaurants before he returned home
to head up the IFT Educational Restaurant.

Estabelecimento de Comidas Koon Kee 190	Late night

Jaan 320	Worth the travel
Japas Macau 191	Wish I'd opened
Loja De Doces Hang Heong Un 191	Local favorite
Old Shanghai Restaurant 191	Breakfast
Szechuan Spicy King 192	Regular neighborhood
Vida Rica Restaurant 192	High end

ALBERT RAURICH
Dos Palillos
Carrer d'Elisabets 9, Barcelona
Ferran Adrià's right-hand man at elBulli
for seven years, he left in 2007 to open
the Asian tapas bar, Dos Palillos.

Alkimia 595	Late night
Asador Etxebarri 575	Wish I'd opened
Bar Casa Xica 601	Bargain
Bodega 1900 596	Late night
Ca l'Isidre 601	Regular neighbourhood
El Celler de Can Roca 583	High end
Compartir 582	Local favourite
Compartir 582	Wish I'd opened
Coure 596	Bargain
Disfrutar 596	Local favourite
Dos Pebrots 601	Worth the travel
Enigma 603	Worth the travel
Gresca 597	Local favourite
Mugaritz 575	High end
Pastisseria Escribà 599	Breakfast
Suculent 602	Regular neighbourhood

JORGE RAUSCH
Criterión
Calle 69a 5-75, Bogotá
Rausch trained and cut his culinary teeth in
Britain and is now chef-owner of three Latin
American restaurants: Criterión, Bistronomy,
and Rausch Restaurant.

Andrés Carne de Res 1097	Local favorite
La Brasserie 1095	Wish I'd opened
Harry Sasson 1095	Regular neighborhood
Maido 1100	Worth the travel
Misia By Leo Espinosa 1096	Bargain
Restaurante Club Colombia 1096	Breakfast
Sir Frank 1091	Late night
Versión Original 1096	High end

BEN READE
Edinburgh Food Studio
158 Dalkeith Road, Edinburgh
The co-founder and chef of the Edinburgh
Food Studio, a creative space, restaurant,
and research hub, he is a graduate of the
University of Gastronomic Sciences.

Aizle 496	Regular neighborhood
Maki and Ramen 497	Regular neighborhood
Le Mousso 774	Worth the travel
Nightcap 497	Late night
Nobles 498	Local favorite
Ostara 498	Breakfast
Storries Home Bakery 497	Late night
Timberyard 497	High end
Ting Thai Caravan 497	Wish I'd opened
The Walnut 498	Bargain

MARTÍN REBAUDINE
Roux
Peña 2300, Buenos Aires
Coming from a culinary family, Rebaudino trained in some of Spain's best kitchens before becoming head chef at Oviedo. After nineteen years he opened his own place, Roux.
Aramburu 1126............Regular neighborhood
Elena 1130...Breakfast
Il Matterello Ristorante 1125..............Bargain

RENÉ REDZEPI
Noma
Refshalevej 96, Copenhagen
The Macedonian-Dane behind Noma, which opened in 2003, the Nordic-sourced agenda of which changed haute cuisine in Scandinavia and beyond forever.
Amass 370........................Local favourite
Bras 541................................Wish I'd opened
Fäviken Magniset 345.....................High end
Hija de Sanchez 372....Regular neighborhood
Hija de Sanchez 372.........................Bargain
Matsukawa 265...............................High end
Pujol 1082..........................Worth the travel
Quintonil 1082..................Worth the travel
Sushi Saito 267.................................High end
The Willows Inn 800........................High end

ADAM REID
Adam Reid at the French
Peter Street, Manchester
Manchester born and bred, Reid now runs the kitchen for Simon Rogan in the city's century-old Midland Hotel.
The Clove Club 487.........Wish I'd opened
El Gato Negro 396......................Local favorite
Hispi Bistro 397..........Regular neighborhood
Kitchen Table @ Bubble Dogs 451.......Wish I'd opened
Lily's Vegetarian Indian Cuisine 396.......Local favorite
Manchester House 397.....................High end
Mughli Charcoal Pit 397..................Late night
Rabbit In The Moon 398....................High end
Restaurant de Librije 511......Worth the travel
Rudy's Neapolitan Pizza 398..............Bargain
Siam Smiles Thai Supermarket 398.....Bargain
Umezushi 398............................Local favorite
The Waggon Inn 398....Regular neighborhood
Woolyknit Cafe 406.........................Breakfast

MICHAEL REID
M
74 Victoria Street, London
He trained at Le Gavroche and Restaurant Gordon Ramsay, under the tutelage of celebrated chefs Michel Roux Jr, Simone Zanoni, and Mr Ramsay himself, before becoming executive chef for the entire Gaucho Group.
Attica 151..........................Worth the travel
Busaba Eathai 447............................Bargain
Daisy Green 420.........Regular neighborhood
Dishoom 432...................................Breakfast

Flat Iron 449.........................Wish I'd opened
Gunpowder 488............Regular neighborhood
The Jugged Hare 466...................Local favorite
The Ledbury 423...............................High end
Mugaritz 576....................Worth the travel
Opso 421......................Regular neighborhood
Rum Kitchen 424.............................Late night
Sager + Wilde 461.............................High end

EMMANUEL RENAUT
Flocons de Sel
1175 Route du Leutaz, Megève
Born in Soisy-sous-Montmorency, he trained at London's Claridge's and worked for Marc Veyrat, before opening Flocons de Sel in 1998.
L'ATELIER de Joël Robuchon 556.......Wish I'd opened
Chez Thérèse 534..................Local favorite
Rond de Carotte 537....Regular neighborhood
La Sauvageonne 536........................Late night
Ultraviolet 196...................................High end
Villa Le Bec 196...................Worth the travel

ANDREA REUSING
Lantern
423 West Franklin Street, Chapel Hill
She opened Lantern, in North Carolina, with her brother in 2002, where she combines Asian flavors with sustainable local ingredients.
Duende 794.......................Worth the travel
The Pig 914..Bargain
Pizzeria Faulisi 914......Regular neighborhood
SALTBOX Seafood Joint 916......Local favorite
Scratch 916......................................Breakfast

ELENA REYGADAS
Rosetta
Colima 166, Mexico City
She trained at the French Culinary Institute in New York before moving to London, where she worked alongside Giorgio Locatelli for five years before Rosetta opened its doors in 2015.
Alcalde 1034......................................High end
Aleli 1078..Breakfast
AMAYA 1078...............Regular neighborhood
Blanca 1015......................Worth the travel
Contra 1007......................Worth the travel
Corazón de Tierra 1077.........Wish I'd opened
Corazón de Tierra 1077....................High end
Eleven Madison Park 1037....Worth the travel
Fonda Margarita 1080.......................Breakfast
Hartwood 1088.................................High end
Máximo Bistrot 1081....Regular neighborhood
Nicos 1081...Breakfast
Oaxaca en Mexico 1083.......................Regular neighborhood
Panadería Pancracia 1082..............Breakfast
Paramo 1082.....................................Late night
Pujol 1082.....................................Local favorite
Pujol 1082.....................................Local favorite
Quintonil 1082..............................Local favorite
Le Tachinomi Desu 1083..................Late night
Tacos Nena 1084...............................Bargain

EVAN & SARAH RICH
Rich Table
199 Gough Street, San Francisco
Evan worked at a series of high-end culinary institutions in New York and San Francisco, including Quince and COI, before opening Rich Table with his wife, Sarah, in 2012.
Brazen Head 833..............................Late night
Hartwood 1088..................Worth the travel
The House of Prime Rib 837...Wish I'd opened
Liholiho Yacht Club 832..........Wish I'd opened
Nopalito 832.................Regular neighborhood
The Progress 842....................Local favorite
Saison 841..High end
La Taqueria 885....................Local favorite
Turtle Tower 888................................Bargain
Yank Sing 841...................................Breakfast

ANDY RICKER
Pok Pok
3226 Southeast Division Street, Portland
He began the Thai-inspired Pok Pok, in Oregon, in 2006, where he also opened Whiskey Soda Lounge, Pok Pok Noi, and Sen Yai, followed by three New York outposts.
Ava Gene's 846............Regular neighborhood
Binh Minh Bakery & Deli 847............Bargain
Del Posto 1034.................................High end
Great NY Noodletown 1006.............Late night
Nahm 283.........................Worth the travel
Le Pigeon 854......................Local favorite
St. John Bar and Restaurant 471.......Wish I'd opened

BRUCE RICKETTS
Mecha Uma
RCBC Building, 25th Street, Manila
The chef-owner of Mecha Uma, which means "absurdly delicious" in Japanese, as well as Sensei, Ooma, and La Chinesca.
Gentle Giant 156............................Breakfast
Jeany's Food House Special 309.........Bargain
Kyoaji 264...............................Worth the travel
Manam 311...........................Local favorite
Mendokoro Ramenba 306..................Regular neighborhood
Pink's Hot Dogs 312...........................Late night
Sarsá Kitchen + Bar 312........Local favorite
Tenzushi 312.....................Worth the travel
Terry's 307....................Regular neighborhood
Tim Ho Wan 213...............................Late night
Wildflour Cafe + Bakery 312..........Breakfast

JAMES RIGATO
Mabel Gray
23825 John R Road, Detroit
He became the personal chef for Ed Mamou's business, Royal Oak Recycling and Royal Oak Storage in 2007, before collaborating with him to develop and open The Root, followed by Mabel Gray.
Bacco Ristorante 909.......................High end
Bacco Ristorante 909...Regular neighborhood
Eventide Oyster Co. 885........Worth the travel
L'Express 776......................Worth the travel
Momotaro 967....................Worth the travel

Nong's Khao Man Gai **856**......Worth the travel
O.W.L. **909**.................................Late night
Odd Duck **1064**..................Worth the travel
Ox **867**...............................Worth the travel
Palace Diner **884**................Wish I'd opened
Ramen Tatsu-ya **1066**...........Worth the travel
Rose's Fine Foods **906**.................Breakfast
La Salle à Manger **779**..........Worth the travel
Selden Standard **906**.....Regular neighborhood
Spring **551**........................Worth the travel
The Telway **907**.......................Late night
Trattoria Stella **910**..............Worth the travel
Vie **969**...................................High end
Vie **969**.........................Worth the travel

ERIC RIPERT
Le Bernardin
155 West 51st Street, New York City
The head chef at Le Bernardin since 1994, he
has opened a wine bar round the corner, and
is the star of the TV show, "Avec Eric".
Balthazar **1011**............Regular neighborhood
Balthazar **1011**.................Local favorite
Balthazar **1011**................Wish I'd opened
Chateau Marmont **824**................Breakfast
Chiltern Firehouse **824**..................Late Night
La Esquina **1013**...........................Bargain
Guy Savoy **555**.....................Worth the travel
Masa **1042**...............................High End
Le Petit Nice **543**.............Worth the travel
ToriShin **1043**................................Late Night

MARTINS RITINS
Vincents
Elizabetes iela 19, Riga
This Latvian chef, born in a British refugee
camp, grew up in Corby in the English
Midlands, worked in Toronto, and opened
Vincents, in Riga, in 1994.
Amass **370**......................Worth the travel
Foodbox **699**..............................Bargain
Innocent Café **699**......................Breakfast
Kukšu Muiža **701**................Wish I'd opened
Left Door Bar **699**.....................Breakfast
Muusu **700**...............................High end
Restaurant Bergs **700**..................High end
Restaurant Naples **700**.Regular neighborhood
Restaurant Riviera **700**.Regular neighborhood
Rocket Bean Roastery **700**.........Breakfast
Valtera Restaurant **700**............Local favorite

HENRIK RITZEN
Aquavit
1 Carlton Street, London
After growing up on a sheep farm on the
northwest coast of Sweden, he worked at
The Square and The Anglesey Arms before
opening The Boundary (2008). He is now
executive chef at Aquavit London.
101 Thai Kitchen **416**....Regular neighborhood
L'Amorosa **416**............Regular neighborhood
Asador Etxebarri **575**............Wish I'd opened
Barrafina **444**...............................Late night
The Fat Duck **390**..........................High end
Franco Manca **413**........................Bargain
Morito **479**................................Late night
The Ninth **452**..........................Local favorite

Oaxen Slip **354**....................Worth the travel
Olympic Studios **410**.................Breakfast

MISSY ROBBINS
Lilia
567 Union Avenue, New York City
Chef-owner Robbins earned her stripes at
Chicago's Spiaggia before moving to New
York, where she continues to cook high-end
Italian cuisine.
Blue Hill at Stone Barns **913**............High end
Blue Ribbon Sushi **1012**.................Late night
Emilio's Ballato **1010**..Regular neighborhood
Employees Only **1028**....................Late night
Gramercy Tavern **1036**...............Local favorite
I Sodi **1029**................Regular neighborhood
I Sodi **1029**.................Wish I'd opened
Ippudo **1022**..............................Bargain
Lucali Pizza **1017**..........Regular neighborhood
Marlow & Sons **1018**...................Breakfast
Momofuku Ko **1023**......................High end
Okonomi **1018**...........................Breakfast
Osteria Francescana **650**......Worth the travel
Prune **1024**.............................Breakfast
Russ & Daughters Cafe **1009**...........Breakfast
The Spotted Pig **1030**....Regular neighborhood
The Spotted Pig **1030**....................Late night
Uncle Boons **1011**........Regular neighborhood

APRIL ROBINSON
Butter Tapas
5070 International Boulevard, Charleston
Starting out as a personal chef, she later
opened Butter Cupcakes in 2012, followed by
Butter Tapas in 2016. Her newly developed pop-
up brunches have become "can't miss" events.
167 Raw **1050**..............Regular neighborhood
2Nixons **1050**...............................Bargain
Le Bernardin **1038**........................High end
Élevé **1052**...............................Breakfast
Hakkasan **1040**...........................Late night
Hall's Chophouse **1053**...............Local favorite
Hall's Chophouse **1053**..........Wish I'd opened
Nana's Seafood & Soul **1055**.............Regular
neighborhood

JOAN, JORDI & JOSEP ROCA
El Celler de Can Roca
Carrer de Can Sunyer 48, Girona
This band of talented Catalan brothers is
behind El Cellar de Can Roca: Joan, the
eldest of the trio, runs the kitchen, the middle
brother, Josep, is sommelier, and Jordi is the
pastry chef.
Astrid & Gastón **1101**...........Worth the travel
L'ATELIER de Joël Robuchon **556**.......Wish I'd
opened
Le Baratin **569**.....................Worth the travel
Ca l'Enric **587**............................Local favorite
Cal Tet **582**...............Regular neighborhood
Can Marquès **583**.......................Breakfast
Can Roca **583**............Regular neighborhood
Can Xifra **582**............Regular neighborhood
Caves Madeleine **538**............Wish I'd opened
Central **1098**.....................Worth the travel
Compartir **582**........................Local favorite
Eleven Madison Park **1037**................High end

El Motel **583**......................Local favorite
Els Casals **586**............................Bargain
Es Xarcu **574**.....................Local favorite
Koy Shunka **594**................Worth the travel
Le Louis XV **547**..........................High end
Maison Troisgros **536**....................High end
Pierre Gagnaire **559**..............Wish I'd opened
Pujol **1082**......................Worth the ravel
Restaurante Villa Más **586**....Worth the travel
Tapas 24 **600**.............................Bargain
Tickets **601**.......................Worth the travel
Toc Al Mar **582**...........................Late night
Umai **582**................................Late night

PERFECTE ROCHER
Tarsan I Jane
4012 Leary Way North West, Seattle
Born into a family that ran a wood-fired eatery,
Rocher worked in some of the world's best
restaurants including elBulli, Manresa, and
Campton Place San Francisco, before setting
up Tarsan I Jane with his wife, in Seattle.
Bacco **801**..............................Breakfast
El Celler de Can Roca **583**......Worth the travel
Chan **802**...............................Local favorite
Chiso **802**..................................Bargain
Tai Tung **806**................Regular neighborhood

THOMAS RODE ANDERSEN
Kurhotel Skodsborg
Skodsborg Strandvej 139, Skodsborg
He was head chef of Kong Hans Kælder for
eight years and is the poster boy for the
Palaeolithic movement, now hosting cookery
classes in Skodsborg.
Bistro Boheme **370**.......Regular neighborhood
Bodega 1900 **596**................Worth the travel
Cafe Det Vide Hus **371**...................Breakfast
Cantina **371**............Regular neighborhood
Chicks by Chicks **379**....................Bargain
Il Gallo d'Oro **607**...............Worth the travel
Geist **372**..................Regular neighborhood
Kadeau **368**.........................Local favorite
Kong Hans Kælder **373**.........Wish I'd opened
LeDu **281**........................Worth the travel
Marchal at Hotel d'Angleterre **373**...Breakfast
Marchal at Hotel d'Angleterre **373**.........Local
favorite
Nabo **369**.........................Local favorite
Nobelhart & Schmutzig **630** ...Worth the travel
Noma **375**...............................High end
Pakta **599**......................Worth the travel
Palægade **374**..............Regular neighborhood
Saigon Quan **363**.........................Bargain
Shawarma Grill House **374**..............Late night

NIKO ROMITO
Ristorante Reale
Contrada Santa Liberata, Castel di Sangro

He runs the two-Michelin-starred Ristorante Reale together with his own school of the culinary arts in the Valley of Castel di Sangro in the Abruzzan mountains.

L'ATELIER de Joël Robuchon 432........Wish I'd opened
Il Boscaiolo 646...........Regular neighborhood
Casa del Supplì 655.........................Bargain
Il Luogo di Aimo e Nadia 661.............High end
Mondi Caffè 656.........................Breakfast
Noma 368.........................Worth the travel
Restaurant Al Metrò 646.........................High end
Taverna de li Caldora 646..........Local favorite
Uliassi 647.........................High end

ANA ROŠ
Hiša Franko
Staro Selo 1, Kobarid

She and her husband co-own Hiša Franko, which champions Slovenian produce.
A member of the Yugoslav National Ski Team until she was eighteen, this multi-talented chef speaks five languages.

L'Argine a Vencò 652.........................High end
Bras 541.........................Wish I'd opened
Al Cacciatore 652.........................Local favorite
Al Cacciatore 652.........................Wish I'd opened
Le Calandre 671.........................High end
Cinca Marinca 692.........................Breakfast
Lido 84 659.........................High end
Mirazur 545.........................Worth the travel
Momofuku Ko 1023.........................Worth the travel
Niù 654.........................Bargain
Noma 369.........................Worth the travel
Osteria Francescana 650......Worth the travel
Parks & Rec Diner 905.........................Breakfast
Pizzeria da Luciano 654....Regular neighborhood
Pop's Place 693.........................Bargain
Restaurant Orana 93.........................Worth the travel
Sale E Pepe 654.........................Local favorite
Septime 566.........................High end
Septime 566.........................Worth the travel
Topli Val 693.........................Regular neighborhood
Trattoria ai Cacciatori 653.........................Bargain
Trattoria alla Posta 653.........................Local favorite

MARK ROSATI
Shake Shack
Various locations

The culinary director of the American burger chain, Shake Shack, Rosati has worked for the company since 2007, creating novel and award-winning dishes.

Al Arez Restaurant 424.........................Late night
Beigel Bake 486.........................Late night
Chiltern Firehouse 419.Regular neighborhood
Koya Bar 451.........................Breakfast
Mangal 1 Ocakbasi 470.........................Late night
Marksman Public House 475.............Regular neighborhood
Rochelle Canteen 486...Regular neighborhood
St. John Bar and Restaurant 750........Regular neighborhood

ANTHONY ROSE
Schmaltz Appetizing
414 Dupont Street, Toronto

Rose is chef and co-owner of Toronto's Rose and Sons smokehouse diner, Big Crow barbeque joint, and Schmaltz Appetizing bagel spot, which are his first projects since he left The Drake Hotel.

Allen's 768.........................Regular neighborhood
Barberian's Steak House 767.............High end
Brothers 768.........................Regular neighborhood
Carousel Bakery 769.........................Breakfast
Commisso Bakery 770.........................Late night
Deb's Place 752.........................Regular neighborhood
Gryfe's Bagels 768.........................Bargain
Ha'salon 172.........................Worth the travel
Pancer's Original Delicatessen 752....Wish I'd opened
United Bakers 768.........................Breakfast
Zets 752.........................Local favorite

FABIO ROSSI
Ristorante Vite
Via Montepirolo 7, Cerasolo

Former chef of the Michelin-starred Acero Rosso, Rossi has continued to champion local produce and traditions at his current restaurant, Vite.

Agriturismo CàMì 650.........................Bargain
L'ATELIER de Joël Robuchon 556........Wish I'd opened
Bar Pasticceria Lievita 651.............Breakfast
Le Calandre 671.........................High end
Cantinetta della Corte 651.........................Late night
El Celler de Can Roca 583.....Worth the travel
Magnolia Ristorante 648...........Local favorite
Osteria la Sangiovesa 652.................Regular neighborhood
Panificio Pasticceria Bianchi 651....Breakfast
QuintoQuarto 649.........................Local favorite
Ristorante Bio's Kitchen 652.............Late night
Ristorante Reale 646.........................Worth the travel
Trattoria da Savino 651 Regular neighborhood

MATHIEU ROSTAING TAYARD
Café Sillon
46 Avenue Jean Jaures, Lyon

He opened his first restaurant at 26 and, after taking some time out to travel around the world, he returned home to open the doors of Café Sillon in 2014.

Le Bistrot du Potager 534.................Regular neighborhood
La Brasserie Georges 534.............Late night
L'Ébauche 535.........................Regular neighborhood
Kitchen Café 535.........................Breakfast
Lido 84 659.........................Worth the travel
Maison Troisgros 536.........................High end
La Mère Brazier 535.........................Local favorite
Noma 369.........................Wish I'd opened
Le Troquet des Sens 535.................Bargain

JON ROTHERAM
The Marksman
254 Hackney Road, London

Co-owner of The Marksman, before that he worked for several years at St John and helped the St John Hotel to win its Michelin star.

40 Maltby Street 460....Regular neighborhood
Bad Sports 477.........................Late night
Black Axe Mangal 477.........................Bargain
Brawn 478.........................Local favorite
Chez Georges 551.........................Worth the travel
Esters 490.........................Regular neighborhood
Lyle's 488.........................Local favorite
P. Franco 468.........................Local favorite
Primeur 491.........................Regular neighborhood
The River Café 417.........................High end
Rochelle Canteen 486.........Wish I'd opened
Towpath Café 479.........................Breakfast

NIKOS ROUSSOS
Funky Gourmet
13 Paramithias Street, Athens

This New York-trained Athens native returned home via a stint at elBulli to open avantgarde Funky Gourmet with co-chef Georgianna Hiliadaki in 2009, winning it a second Michelin star in 2014.

Bournovalia 718.........................Late night
Different Beast 718.........................Breakfast
Gramercy Tavern 1036....Wish I'd opened
Kavos 1964 719.........................Local favorite
Kritikos 718.........................Regular neighborhood
Mugaritz 516.........................High end
The Press Club 146....Worth the travel
To Xeiropoiito 719.........................Bargain

JULIEN ROYER
Odette
1 St Andrews Road, Singapore

Frenchman Royer trained under Michel Bras and Bernard Andrieux among others, before moving to Singapore in 2011.

Amber 220.........................Worth the travel
L'Astrance 568.........................High end
Blue Hill at Stone Barns 913..Wish I'd opened
Bras 541.........................Wish I'd opened
Brasserie Gavroche 329.................Regular neighborhood
The Clove Club 487.........................Worth the travel
David Toutain 556.........................Worth the travel
Din Tai Fung 327.........................Local favorite
The Ledbury 423.........................Worth the travel
Luke's Oyster bar 330...Regular neighborhood
Naked Finn 317.........................Regular neighborhood
Nihonryori RyuGin 265.........................High end
Tanjong Rhu Pau 324.........................Bargain
Tim Ho Wan 328.........................Late night
Tiong Barhu Bakery 318.........................Breakfast
Ultraviolet by Paul Pairet 196.............High end
Wild Honey 328.........................Breakfast
Zam Zam 333.........................Bargain

FRANCISCO RUANO
Alcalde
Avenida Mexico 2903, Guadalajara

Ruano returned from his culinary training in Europe to his hometown Guadalajara to develop a cuisine that binds together tradition and modernity with unlikely but yet traditional flavor combinations.

AMAYA 1078	Wish I'd opened
Birrieria Don David 1084	Breakfast
Blue Hill at Stone Barns 913	Worth the travel
Cafe Caligary 1084	Breakfast
Carnes Asadas la Chuza 1085	Late night
La Docena 1085	Regular neighborhood
Hueso 1085	High end
Juniko 1086	High end
Magno Brasserie 1085	High end
Mercado de Abastos 1085	Local favorite
Mugaritz 576	Worth the travel
Noma 369	Worth the travel
PalReal 1085	Breakfast
La Panga del Impostor 1086	Regular neighborhood
Taqueria México 1086	Bargain
Tortas Ahogadas Enrique el Viejo 1086	Local favorite
Tripitas Don Ramon 1086	Late night

GABRIEL RUCKER
Le Pigeon
738 East Burnside Street, Portland

He grew up in Napa, moved to Oregon in 2003, worked at Paley's Place and the Gotham Building Tavern, before opening Le Pigeon in 2006 and Little Bird in 2010.

Ava Gene's 846	High end
Coquine 850	Breakfast
Momofuku Ko 1023	Worth the travel
Taqueria Nueve 859	Regular neighborhood
Tusk 860	Late night

BEN RUSSELL
Aria
1 Eagle Street, Brisbane

The former sous chef at Matt Moran's Aria, Sydney, he landed the head chef position at Aria, Brisbane (sister of the Sydney flagship) in 2009, delivering modern Australian fare to eager Brisbanites.

Esquire 130	High end
The Fish House 85	Worth the travel
Fleet 82	Worth the travel
Happy Boy 132	Regular neighborhood
Julius Pizzeria 132	Local favorite
Lefty's Old Time Music Hall 132	Wish I'd opened
Maru Korean BBQ 133	Late night
Otto 134	High end
Paper Daisy 83	Worth the travel
Pearl Cafe 134	Breakfast
Strauss 135	Breakfast
Taro's Ramen & Café 135	Bargain

ALFREDO RUSSO
Dolce Stil Novo
Piazza della Repubblica 4, Turin

Born in Turin, he opened Dolce Stil Novo in the Venaria Palace in 1990, having worked in many of Piedmont's best kitchens.

The Franklin 412	Breakfast
Al Garamond 665	Bargain
Le Louis XV 547	Wish I'd opened
Mugunghwa 238	Worth the travel

HENRIQUE SÁ PESSOA
Alma
Rua Anchieta 15, Lisbon

The owner of Alma, he gained experience in London and Sydney before returning to Portugal to work at Bairro Alto and Sheraton hotels.

Bairro do Avillez 617	Wish I'd opened
Bairro do Avillez 617	Local favorite
Belcanto 617	High end
Bistro 100 Maneiras 614	Late night
Casa de Chá da Boa Nova 607	Worth the travel
Cervejaria Ramiro 618	Regular neighborhood
A Cevicheria 614	Late night
Grande Palacio Hong Kong 619	Regular neighborhood
Herdade do Esporão 606	Worth the travel
Mercado da Ribeira Time Out 617	Bargain
O Asiático 615	Wish I'd opened
Ocean 606	High end
Pastelaria Benard 618	Breakfast
Tartine 618	Breakfast
Tasca da Esquina 621	Local favorite

GEORGE SABATINO
Aldine
1901 Chestnut Street, Philadelphia

This self-taught chef has worked in Philadelphia for his entire career and Aldine is his first venture as chef and owner.

David's Mai Lai Wah 920	Late night
Hungry Pigeon 922	Breakfast
Vernick Food & Drink 924	Regular neighborhood

OLDŘICH SAHAJDÁK
La Degustation Bohême
Haštalská 18, Prague

With the ambitious aim to "introduce classic Czech cuisine to the world", Sahajdák is head chef and owner of the one-Michelin-starred La Degustation in Prague's Old Town.

Brasileiro 685	Late night
Café Savoy 686	Breakfast
Café Savoy 686	Regular neighborhood
Cobra 686	Regular neighborhood
Horváth 630	Worth the travel
Krystal Bistro 687	Bargain
Lokal 687	Local favorite
Milada Bistro 688	Local favorite
Milada Bistro 688	Regular neighborhood
Sansho 689	Late night
Sansho 689	Wish I'd opened
Sansho 689	Regular neighborhood

SaSaZu 689	High end
Le Servan 566	Worth the travel

CHRIS SALANS
Mozaic
Jalan Raya Sanggingan, Ubud

The French-American chef-owner of Ubud's Mozaic Restaurant, where he attracts wide acclaim for fusing classic Le Cordon Bleu training with Balinese flavors, and Mozaic Beach Club in Seminyak.

Arena Pub and Restaurant 293	Late night
L'Arpège 556	Worth the travel
Babi Guling Ibu Oka 297	Local favorite
Babi Guling Ibu Oka 297	Regular neighborhood
Babi Guling Ibu Oka 297	Bargain
Café Batu Jimbar 293	Breakfast
Din Tai Fung 327	Worth the travel
Kura Kura 295	High end
Locavore 297	High end
Mama San 295	Wish I'd opened
Nasi Ayam Kedewatan 297	Local favorite
Spice 298	Regular neighborhood
Warung Adi 293	Bargain
Warung Mak Beng 293	Bargain
Warung Mak Beng 293	Breakfast

ROSIO SÁNCHEZ
Hija de Sanchez
Slagterboderne 8, Copenhagen

After working as head pastry chef and later test kitchen sous chef at Noma, Sánchez stayed in Copenhagen to pay tribute to her Mexican roots by creating the best tacos in Europe.

108 368	Regular neighborhood
Amass 370	Local favorite
Bæst 376	Late night
Møller - Kaffe og Køkken 377	Breakfast
Noma 369	Local favorite

CÉSAR SANTOS
Oficina do Sabor
Rua do Amparo 335, Olinda

This renowned Brazilian chef opened Oficina do Sabor ("flavour workshop") in the Pernambuco hilltop town of Olinda in 1992, pairing French technique with local ingredients. He also runs Kaamo at Kenoa Resort.

Alvorada 1106	Worth the travel
Casa de Tereza 1104	Worth the travel
Diplomata Delicatessen 1105	Breakfast
Geraldo 1105	Bargain
Ilha da Kosta II 1105	Late night
Mingus 1105	High end
Parraxaxá 1105	Local favorite
Parraxaxá 1105	Breakfast
Ponte Nova 1105	Regular neighborhood
Quina do Futuro 1106	Local favorite
Restaurante Leite 1106	Regular neighborhood
Restaurante Leite 1106	Wish I'd opened
Wiella Bistrô 1106	High end

MARK SARGEANT
Rocksalt
4–5 Fishmarket, Folkestone

In 2011, following 13 years of working on various projects with Gordon Ramsay, Sargeant opened two restaurants in Folkestone, Rocksalt and The Smokehouse, followed by a pub and a tapas joint.

A. Wong **428**..........................Wish I'd opened
The Chambers **400**..........................Late night
Chick 'n' Sours **432**.............................Bargain
Duck & Waffle **466**.........................Breakfast
Lubens **400**..............Regular neighborhood
ROKA **442**..................................High end

STEVEN SATTERFIELD
Miller Union
999 Brady Avenue Northwest, Atlanta

Satterfield, a Georgia native, renounced his music career for the heat of the kitchen, rapidly rising through the ranks to become chef and co-owner of Atlanta's farm-to-table Miller Union.

8 Arm **942**.......................................Bargain
Argosy **942**.....................................Bargain
Atlas **942**......................................High end
Bacchanalia **943**..............................High end
Blanca **1015**....................Worth the travel
Bread & Butterfly **944**.................Breakfast
Bread & Butterfly **944**..Regular neighborhood
Chez Panisse **789**..............Worth the travel
Fritti **945**...................Regular neighborhood
Gramercy Tavern **1036**..........Wish I'd opened
Octopus Bar **947**.............................Late night
Poole's Diner **916**..............Wish I'd opened
Proof Bakeshop **948**...................Breakfast
Seo Ra Beol **878**...............................Late night
Sotto Sotto **949**............Regular neighborhood
Staplehouse **950**.................Local favorite
Ticonderoga Club **950**..............Local favorite

GUY SAVOY
Restaurant Guy Savoy
18 Rue Troyon, Paris

Bourgogne-born, Savoy trained with the Troisgros brothers before opening his eponymous Paris flagship in 1980. Today he has five international outposts.

Atelier Crenn **833**..................Worth the travel
Le Café de l'Homme **550**.....................Regular neighborhood
D.O.M. Restaurante **1114**......Worth the travel
Olympe **1109**.........................Worth the travel
Le Relais Bernard Loiseau **538**..........High end
Le Restaurant Allard **565**...........Local favorite
La Senne **540**....................................Bargain

JONATHON SAWYER
The Greenhouse Tavern, Noodlecat, Trentina
5340 Hamilton Avenue, Cleveland

Sawyer worked at New York's Kitchen 22 and Parea before returning to his hometown of Cleveland, where he subsequently opened four restaurants, including his flagship, The Greenhouse Tavern.

Aubergine at L'Auberge Carmel **791**.High end

Big Al's Diner **917**........................Breakfast
Big Star **969**.............................Late night
Biga Pizzeria **919**.........Regular neighborhood
The Black Pig **919**.........Regular neighborhood
The Black Pig **919**........................Local favorite
Del Posto **1034**...............................High end
fire food and drink **917**.Regular neighborhood
Jack's Deli **917**..............................Breakfast
Li Wah Restaurant **918**.....................Breakfast
Miega Korean BBQ **918**.......................Bargain
Ohio City Provisions **918**......................Regular neighborhood
The Plum Cafe & Kitchen **918**.............Regular neighborhood
The Plum Cafe & Kitchen **918**....Local favorite
Régis et Jacques Marcon **537**...........High end
Restore Cold Pressed **918**...............Breakfast
Superior Phở **919**............................Bargain
Szechuan Gourmet **919**.......................Bargain
Taste of Kerala **919**..........................Bargain

EMANUELE SCARELLO
Agli Amici 1887
Via Liguria 252, Udine

He represents the fifth generation of his family to run Ristorante Agli Amici in Udine, which the Scarellos first opened back in 1887.

Ancona Due Ristorante Pizzeria **654**..Late night
Al Cacciatore **652**..................Local favorite
Caffetteria Torinese **654**..................Breakfast
Dal Pescatore **660**............................High end
Don Alfonso **647**............................High end
Eleven Madison Park **1037**....Worth the travel
Enoteca Pinchiorri **668**.................High end
Le Grand Restaurant **558**......Worth the travel
il Luogo di Aimo e Nadia **661**............High end
Mamm **655**.....................................Bargain
Niù **654**...Late night
La Primula **653**...........Regular neighborhood
Panificio Venier **653**......................Breakfast
Pri Lojzetu **693**...........Regular neighborhood
Trattoria Ai Ciodi **652**............Wish I'd opened
Da Vittorio **659**..................Worth the travel

JOE SCHAFER
Bacchanalia
1460 Ellsworth Industrial Boulevard Northwest, Atlanta

Georgia-born Schafer began working for Anne Quatrano in 2014, opened Little Bacch for her in early 2015, and then rose to become executive chef of Bacchanalia and the new Star Provisions by the end of the year.

Aria **942**.......................................High end
Atlas **942**......................................High end
Chinese Buddha **944**.........................Breakfast
Home grown **945**.........Regular neighborhood
Home grown **945**..........................Breakfast
Kimball house **877**............Wish I'd opened
The NoMad Hotel **1004**..........Worth the travel
Octopus Bar **947**.............................Late night
La Pastorcita **947**..........................Late night
Le Pigeon **854**...................Worth the travel
Restaurant Eugene **948**..................High end
So Ba **949**.....................................Bargain
So Ba **949**....................Regular neighborhood
Venkman's **950**.........................Local favorite

MICHA SCHÄFER
Nobelhart & Schmutzig
Friedrichstrasse 218, Berlin

He worked at the two-Michelin-starred Villa Merton before opening the kitchen for its owner, host and sommelier, Billy Wagner.

Cordobar **631**..............Regular neighborhood
Dolden Mädel **629**...............................Bargain
Forsthaus Strelitz **625**.......................High end
Hallmann & Klee **683**.......................Breakfast
Lode & Stijn **630**.............................Late night
Markthalle Neun **630**..............Local favorite
Sosein **624**..........................Wish I'd opened
Tantris **624**......................Worth the travel

JESSE SCHENKER
The Gander
15 West 18th Street, New York City

A Florida native, he opened The Gander in Flatiron in 2014, after he had gained recognition with the success of his first venture, Recette Private Dining.

Basta Pasta **1044**.........Regular neighborhood
Gramercy Tavern **1036**.............Local favorite
Gramercy Tavern **1036**...........Wish I'd opened
Jean-Georges **1046**..........................High end
Marea **1042**...............Regular neighborhood
Mt. Kisco Diner **913**.......................Breakfast
Murray's Bagels **1026**....................Breakfast
Pass and Provisions **937**........Worth the travel
Sake Bar Hagi **1043**..........................Late night
Sushi Yasuda **1043**...........................High end
Vanessa's Dumpling House **1009**........Bargain
Waverly Diner **1027**.................Local favorite

PEDRO MIGUEL SCHIAFFINO
Malabar
Camino Real 101, Lima

Open since 2004, Schiaffino uses the menu at Malabar to showcase unique ingredients native to the Amazon, together with ancient Andean cooking techniques.

Antigua Taberna Queirolo **400**.........Late night
Costanera 700 **1098**......Regular neighborhood
Grimanesa Varga Anticuchos **1099**....Bargain
El Pan de la Chola **1099**...................Breakfast
La Picantería **1101**......................Local favorite

JASPER SCHNEIDER
Reef by CuisinArt
Anguilla

Schneider is the executive chef for the Anguilla's high-end dining spots. London born and New York raised, this is the third Caribbean island on which he has worked.

Chef's Table Dining Experience **1070**.High end
E's Oven **1070**.........................Local favorite
Falcon Nest **1070**.................Wish I'd opened
Matador Room **876**.............Worth the travel
Picante **1070**.................Regular neighborhood
Tokyo Bay **1070**.............................Late night
Valley BBQ Stand **1070**........................Bargain
Yacht Club **1070**...........................Breakfast

SHAUN SEARLEY
The Quality Chop House
92–94 Farringdon Road, London

After honing his skills at the Paternoster Chop House and Bistroteque, Searley assumed cooking duties at London's seasonal, ingredient-led Quality Chop House in 2013.

40 Maltby Street **460**....Regular neighborhood
The Dairy **414**.......................Wish I'd opened
Duck & Waffle **466**...........................Late night
The Fat Duck **390**..............................High end
Hoppers **450**......................................Bargain
The Laughing Heart **474**..................Late night
Pavilion Café **476**............................Breakfast
Per Se **1046**......................Worth the travel
Rules **435**.................................Local favorite
Xi'an Impression **477**....Regular neighborhood

MASARU SEKI
Tempura Ippoh
Kojun Building, 6-8-7 Ginza, Tokyo

Seki's family is behind Osaka's oldest tempura restaurant and he follows in the footsteps of five generations.

Akasaka Asada **262**...........................High end
Daitsune Udon Ginza **257**..................Bargain
Hamada-ya **257**................................High end
Imperial Treasure Shanghai **320**.....Worth the travel
Jiang-Nan Chun **328**..............Worth the travel
Kabuto Soro **264**............................Late night
Kobiki **258**...................Regular neighborhood
Kyoaji **264**.......................Wish I'd opened
Momozon **261**............................Local favorite
Oden Ogura **258**..........Regular neighborhood
Ryu Sushi **258**.................................Breakfast
Shinbashi Kanetanaka **258**................High end
Sougo **266**.....................................Late night
Trattoria La Baracca **261**...........Local favorite

TOM SELLERS
Restaurant Story
199 Tooley Street, London

Within months of opening Story, aged just 26, Sellers received his first Michelin star. This London-based culinary wunderkind trained under luminaries including Thomas Keller, René Redzepi, and Tom Aikens.

A Wong **428**................................Local favorite
Berners Tavern **472**........................Breakfast
Eleven Madison Park **1037**....Worth the travel
Hutong **462**....................................Late Night
Jose Tapas Bar **460**......Regular neighborhood
The Ledbury **423**.............................High end
Midsummer House **391**.....................High end
Monty's Deli **479**..............................Bargain
The Regency Café **456**...............Local favorite
ROKA **492**....................Regular neighborhood
Smokestak **487**................................Bargain
StreetXO **590**......................Worth the travel

DANIEL SERFER
Blue Collar
6730 Biscayne Boulevard, Miami

Miami-native, Serfer has two local restaurants, Blue Collar and Mignonette, both serving up "no-frills, full flavor" food.

Bagel Bar East **876**........................Breakfast
Bazaar Mar **872**...............................High end
Cafe Martorano **872**.....Regular neighborhood
Cannon's BBQ & More **931**....Worth the travel
Carbone **1025**.......................Wish I'd opened
The Front Porch Cafe **876**...............Breakfast
L.C. Roti Shop **873**...........................Bargain
Petit Rouge **875**.........................Local favorite
The Seven Dials **872**......Regular neighborhood
Tapas de Rosa **875**....................Local favorite
Upland **1038**.....................................High end
Yakko-San **876**................................Late night

PETER SERPICO
Serpico
604 South Street, Philadelphia

This former Momofuku chef moved to Philadelphia to open his eponymous restaurant with Stephen Starr. It will be followed by a Korean offering from the pair in 2017.

Barclay Prime **920**...........................High end
Fitzwater Café **921**.........................Breakfast
High Street on Market **921**........Local favorite
Kanella South **922**......Regular neighborhood
Morimoto **922**.................................High end
Nam Phuong **923**............................Bargain
New Wave Café **923**.......................Late night
Tai Lake **924**..................................Late night
Vernick Food & Drink **924**......Wish I'd opened

RYAN SESSIONS
Fen
22 Sackville Street, Port Fairy

Raised in the area where he cooks, Sessions, with his wife Kirstyn, have owned and operated Port Fairy's leading restaurant for the last ten years, first at the Merrijig Inn and now at their new stomping ground Fen.

Amaru **140**.......................................High end
Coffin Sally **103**.........................Local favorite
Coffin Sally **103**...........Regular neighborhood
Conlan's Wine Store **103**..Regular neighborhood
Conlan's Wine Store **103**............Local favorite
Fen **103**..Late night
Kermonds Hamburgers **103**............Bargain
Provenance Restaurant **00**....Worth the travel
Restaurant Orana **93**.............Wish I'd opened
Rough Diamond **103**......................Breakfast
Sepia **113**.......................................High end
Sixpenny **123**.......................Worth the travel

KARAM SETHI
Gymkhana
42 Albemarle Street, London

Sethi runs Gymkhana and the British branch of the legendary Mumbai seafood specialist Trishna, having worked at the original outpost, New Delhi's Bukhara, and at London's Zuma.

Beirut Express **424**.........................Late night

Chucs Restaurant & Café **437**.............Regular neighborhood
Colbeh **425**......................................Bargain
Colbeh **425**...................Regular neighborhood
The Fat Duck **390**..................Worth the travel
The Fat Duck **390**...........................High end
La Fromagerie **420**......Regular neighborhood
kiln **451**.................................Wish I'd opened
Lahore Eastcote **425**....Regular neighborhood
Lyle's **488**...............................Local favorite
The Wolseley **443**..........................Breakfast

ALON SHAYA
Domenica
123 Baronne Street, New Orleans

The Tel Aviv-born, Philadelphia-raised chef-partner at New Orleans's Domenica, the Italian restaurant peppered with Israeli-Jewish culinary influences, which Shaya opened with Octavio Mantilla and John Besh in 2009.

Bacchanal **974**...............................Late night
The Company Burger **981**.......Wish I'd opened
Compère Lapin **976**.........................High end
Croissant d'Or Patisserie **980**.........Breakfast
Emeril's **977**.............................Local favorite
Ideal Market **985**..............................Bargain
Tan Dinh **884**..............Regular neighborhood
Willie Mae's Scotch House **907**..Local favorite

JASPER SHEN
XLB
4090 North Williams Avenue, Portland

The former chef of Aviary, who earned his stripes at the Nordic institution, Aquavit, he has branched out to open XLB, a casual traditional Chinese restaurant, where the focus is on *xiao long bao* (soup dumplings).

Ataula **846**......................................High end
Din Tai Fung **803**...................Worth the travel
Grain & Gristle **851**.........................Late night
Hat Yai **852**..................Regular neighborhood
Nong's Khao Man Gai **856**..Regular neighborhood
Overlook Restaurant **856**.................Breakfast
Le Pigeon **854**.........................Local favorite
Pine State Biscuits **857**..................Breakfast
Roake's **858**.....................................Bargain
Salt & Straw **839**..................Wish I'd opened

CHRIS SHEPHERD
Underbelly
1100 Westheimer Road, Houston

Ex-Brennan's chef Shepherd, inspired by the ethnic diversity of Houston, left boundary pushing Catalan restaurant in 2012 to take his own pioneering route, serving New American Creole cuisine at Underbelly.

Andrew Michael Italian Kitchen **932**......Worth the travel
Cafe TH **937**....................................Bargain
Coltivare **937**...........................Local favorite
Hong Kong Dim Sum **937**....................Regular neighborhood
The NoMad Hotel **1044**.....................High end
The Ordinary **1056**.................Wish I'd opened
Pho Binh by Night **937**.....................Late night
Reef **938**.................................Local favorite

BEN SHEWRY

Attica
74 Glen Eira Road, Melbourne

Born and raised on New Zealand's North Island, he is the long-time chef and new owner of Attica, widely considered one of Australia's top kitchens.

Archie's All Day 148	Breakfast
Bennelong Restaurant 107	High end
Brae 101	High end
Embla 143	Late night
Flower Drum 143	High end
Kalimera Souvlaki Art 150	Regular neighborhood
Market Lane Coffee 152	Breakfast
Mighty Boy 149	Breakfast
Ricky & Pinky 149	Local favorite
Tartine Manufactory 836	Worth the travel
Tire Shop Taqueria 816	Wish I'd opened
Tuck Shop Take Away 141	Regular neighborhood
Vue de Monde 146	High end
Wai Bo 102	Bargain

TIM SIADATAN

Padella
6 Southwark Street, London

The star graduate of the 2002 first-year intake of Jamie Oliver's Fifteen, he trained further at Moro and St John, before opening Trullo in 2010, and fresh pasta bar Padella in 2016.

Black Axe Mangal 480	Breakfast
Black Axe Mangal 480	Regular neighborhood

ALEXANDRE SILVA

Loco
Rua dos Navegantes 53-B, Lisbon

Ex-chef of Bocca and Alentejo, Silva returned to Lisbon to be the executive chef of Bica do Sapato. Soon afterwards, he opened his first restaurant, Alexandre Silva no Mercado, at Mercado da Ribeira, shortly followed by Loco.

Bica do Sapato 612	Late night
Cervejaria Ramiro 618	Bargain
Come Prima 621	Regular neighborhood
General Merchants 500	Breakfast
Maaemo 344	Worth the travel
Mercado da Ribeira Time Out 617	Late night
O Asiático 615	Wish I'd opened
Ocean 606	High end
A Taberna da Rua das Flores 616	Regular neighborhood
A Taberna da Rua das Flores 616	Local favorite
Veranda Restaurant 613	Breakfast

GEIR SKEIE

Brygga 11
Brygga 11, Sandefjord

The Norwegian winner of the 2008 Bocuse d'Or and 2009 Bocuse d'Or world final, Skeie worked at Mathuset Midtåsen Solvold before opening Brygga 11 restaurants in Sandefjord (2010) and Stord (2013).

Bølgen og Moi Ny Hellesund 345	Local favorite

D.O.M. Restaurante 1114	High end
Eleven Madison Park 1037	High end
The French Laundry 797	High end
Håndverkeren 345	Regular neighborhood
Kverneriet 345	Bargain
Liholiho Yacht Club 882	Late night
PubliKo 345	Bargain
PubliKo 344	Worth the travel
Re-naa 345	High end
Re-naa 345	High end
Statholdegården 344	High end

BEVAN SMITH

Riverstone Kitchen
1431 State Highway 1, Oamaru

A New Zealander who, in 2006, opened Riverstone Kitchen on his parents' North Otago farm, following spells in Brisbane and London.

Amisfield 158	Local favorite
Depot 164	Bargain
Floriditas 161	Breakfast
The French Café 165	High end
Pegasus Bay 154	Local favorite
Porteño 1036	Wish I'd opened
The River Café 417	Wish I'd opened
Scotts Brewing Co. 157	Regular neighborhood
Sherwood Hotel 160	Late night
Whitebait 161	Worth the travel

HOLLY SMITH

Cafe Juanita
9702 North East 120th Place, Kirkland

She opened Cafe Juanita in 2000, after several years working with Tom Douglas at the Dahlia Lounge.

Ba Bar 801	Breakfast
Kedai Makan 803	Late night
Sushi Kappo Tamura 805	Regular neighborhood
Wataru 806	Regular neighborhood

HIRO SONE

Terra
1345 Railroad Avenue, St Helena

His big break came at Wolfgang Puck's Spago in Tokyo, which eventually brought him to the Hollywood original. Sone subsequently opened Terra in Napa and Ame in San Francisco.

Bistro Jeanty 797	Regular neighborhood
Boulevard Restaurant 829	Local favorite
Calistoga Kitchen 790	Regular neighborhood
Calistoga Kitchen 790	Breakfast
Ebisu Manmaru 269	Late night
Hog Island Oyster Co. 793	Wish I'd opened
Hokushin-Zushi 250	High end
Iyasare 790	Local favorite
Kikunoi 247	High end
Quintonil 1082	Worth the travel
Restaurant Aladdin 271	High end
Wako Sushi 831	Local favorite

JOAQUIN SORIANO

CJSJ
72 Section 1 Xiangshang Road, Taichung

This dessert chef began his cooking career at Patisserie Guillet, then moved to Le Meurice, before establishing the CJSJ Dessert Concept Shop in Taichung, with his wife.

A Jiang Stir-Fried Eel 198	Late night
LaTarte 552	Breakfast
Maison Pic 537	Local favorite
Patrick Roger 559	Wish I'd opened
Le Pré Catelan 568	High end
Sushi Suzuki 199	Regular neighborhood
Tseng FeliCity 199	Bargain
Yukari 205	Worth the travel

BEN SPALDING

PuzzleProjects
435 Holloway Road, London

Spalding ran Simon Rogan's two-year London pop-up Roganic in 2011 and, after a brief stint at John Salt, he launched PuzzleProjects, which offers a fresh take on hospitality consultancy, including events, film, and catering.

Bird 480	Bargain
Bone Daddies 445	Local favorite
Bone Daddies 445	Regular neighborhood
Flesh & Buns 433	Regular neighborhood
Indian Ocean Tandoori 477	High end
Per Se 1046	Wish I'd opened
Shinobi Sushi 460	Late night
Trattoria di Via Serra 648	Worth the travel
Vagabond N7 Coffee Shop 482	Breakfast
WOLF 492	Local favorite

TIM SPEDDING

Former chef de cuisine at The Clove Club, Spedding will also bring experience from The Ledbury to the Cornish inn and restaurant he plans to open.

40 Maltby Street 460	Regular neighborhood
Bæst 376	Local favorite
Brawn 478	Regular neighborhood
Brawn 478	Local favorite
Chinese Laundry 480	Bargain
Clamato 564	Regular neighborhood
Coombeshead Farm 391	Breakfast
Coombeshead Farm 391	Worth the travel
Dandy Cafe 490	Regular neighborhood
Daniel Berlin Krog 349	Worth the travel
Henne Kirkeby Kro 365	Worth the travel
Henne Kirkeby Kro 365	Wish I'd opened
The Laughing Heart 474	Late night
The Ledbury 423	High end
Lyle's 488	Local favorite
Lyle's 488	Regular neighborhood
Manfreds 377	Regular neighborhood
Manfreds 377	Bargain
Manfreds 377	Local favorite
Marksman Public House 475	Bargain
Noma 376	Worth the travel
Ox Cave 502	Wish I'd opened
Russ & Daughers Cafe 1009	Local favorite
St. John Bread & Wine 489	Breakfast
Quintonil 1082	High end

RYAN SQUIRES
Esquire
145 Eagle Street, Brisbane
Staged at Noma, elBulli, and Per Se, before returning to Brisbane where he caused a stir with his experimental cuisine at Urbane and Buffalo Club, opening degustation-only restaurant, Esquire in 2011.

LJUBOMIR STANISIC
100 Maneiras
Rua do Teixeira 35, Lisbon
Born in Bosnia, he moved Portuguese food into avant-garde territory with his 100 Maneiras restaurants in Cascais.

TANIA STEYTLER
Snaps + Rye
93 Golborne Road, London
This self-taught Cornish seafood chef, previously at Severn & Wye Smokery, now cooks at Snaps + Rye, London's first contemporary Danish restaurant.

JARRETT STIEBER
Eat Me Speak Me
1660 McLendon Avenue, Atlanta
With experience from the kitchens of Pura Vida, Holeman and Finch, and Abbatoir, he now runs the pop-up restaurant, Eat Me Speak Me.

JOEL STOCKS
Holdfast
537 South East Ash Street, Portland
With help from the sommelier Jeff Vejr, Stocks' Holdfast hosts reservation-only tasting dinners in the front room of Fausse Piste winery, providing an intimate and unique dining experience.

ADAM STOKES
Adam's
16 Waterloo Street, Birmingham
Success has come quickly for Lincolnshire-born Stokes. Having gained his first Michelin star at the age of 29, his eponymous restaurant in Birmingham was awarded the same honour just six months after opening.

TAM STORRAR
Blanchette
204 Brick Lane, London
He worked his way up to senior sous chef at Bibendum before moving to Blanchette, where he is now executive chef and director. Le Manoir aux Quat'Saisons 403.....Worth the travel

ETHAN STOWELL
How to Cook a Wolf
2208 Queen Anne Avenue North, Seattle

The Seattle chef-restaurateur, whose highly acclaimed and growing empire of establishments include Tavolàta, How to Cook a Wolf, Anchovies & Olives, Bar Cotto, and Mkt.

Ba Bar 801................................Late night
Cafe Besalu 802.......................Breakfast
Canlis 802.................................High end
Dick's Drive-In 802....................Bargain
Green Leaf 803...........................Regular neighborhood
Ristorante Laganà 657.........Worth the travel
Sushi Kashiba 806..................Local favorite

GIULIO STURLA
Roots
8 London Street, Christchurch

Chilean-born Sturla moved to New Zealand in 2010 and opened Roots just a couple of years later. Without a set menu at any one time, the restaurant is constantly reinventing itself.

99 Restaurante 1132.............Worth the travel
Apéro 164................................Late night
Atera 1013..............................High end
BORAGó 1132..........................High end
BORAGó 1132..........................Worth the travel
Brae 101..................................High end
Brae 101..................................Wish I'd opened
Casuarina Curry 316................Breakfast
COI 829....................................High end
Freemans Dining Room 158..............Regular neighborhood
Hello Sunday 156.....................Breakfast
Kinji 157..................................Local favorite
Mugaritz 576............................Wish I'd opened
Mugaritz 576............................High end
Orphans Kitchen 165....Regular neighborhood
Pasture 166.............................Worth the travel
The Ramen Shop 161..............Bargain
Saison 841...............................High end

PEDRO SUBIJANA
Akelarre
Paseo Padre Orcoloaga 56, San Sebastián

One of the founding fathers of New Basque cooking, after training in Madrid, Subijana opened Akelarre in his native San Sebastián in 1975.

Arzak 579..................Regular neighborhood
Arzak 579.................................Wish I'd opened
Barkaiztegi 579........................Local favorite
Bernardo Etxea 579.................High end
Calonge Sagardotegia 580.........Local favorite
The Fat Duck 390....................Worth the travel
Gandarias 580.........................Late night
Kaia Kaipe 576........................High end
Martín Berasategui 577.................Regular neighborhood
Martín Berasategui 577........Wish I'd opened
Mugaritz 576................Regular neighborhood
Mugaritz 576............................Wish I'd opened
Quique Dacosta 591..............Worth the travel
Restaurante Combarro 590..............High end
Rias de Galicia 601..................High end

Zuberoa 578..............................Regular neighborhood
Zuberoa 578..............................Wish I'd opened

ROBERTA SUDBRACK
Roberta Sudbrack
Avenue Lineu de Paula Machado 916, Rio de Janeiro

Self-taught, she stood behind the stove at Brazil's presidential palace before opening her Rio restaurant in 2005. In 2012, she designed menus for Brazil's Olympic team.

Braseiro da Gávea 1107...........Local favorite
Cervantes 1107.........................Late night
Fasano al Mare 1108................High end
Gepetto 1108............................Bargain
Le Mary Celeste 553..............Wish I'd opened
Olympe 1109...........Regular neighborhood
Talho Capixaba 1109...............Breakfast

THOMAS & MATHIAS SÜHRING
Sühring
10 Yenakat Soi 3, Bangkok

After years of working across Europe and Thailand, these twin brothers are leading the way for German cuisine with their fresh, contemporary fare.

Aqua 625..................................Worth the travel
De For-rest 286...........Regular neighborhood
Dean & Deluca 280...................Breakfast
Eat Me Restaurant 280.............Late night
Gaggan 284..............................High end
Go-Ang Kaomunkai Pratunam 285......Regular neighborhood
Nahm 283.................................Local favorite
(Not Just) Another Cup 280........Breakfast
Restaurant de Librije 511.......Wish I'd opened
Sara-Jane's 286........................Bargain

BENJAMIN SUKLE
birch
200 Washington Street, Rhode Island

A graduate of Johnson and Wales University on Rhode Island, Sukle opened birch to capitalise on the local produce and Oberlin, which is a more casual restaurant focusing on the island's seafood.

Amass 370................................Worth the travel
The Capital Grille 928...............High end
Chengdu Taste 928.....Regular neighborhood
East Side Pockets 928...............Late night
Elkano 580................................Wish I'd opened
Hog Island Oyster Co. 829.....Wish I'd opened
Joe Beef 779............................Wish I'd opened
Jr's Providence 928...................Late night
King's Garden 927........Regular neighborhood
Matunuck Oyster Bar 931..........High end
Matunuck Oyster Bar 931.......Wish I'd opened
Mike's Kitchen 927......Regular neighborhood
New Rivers 929.........................Local favorite
New Rivers 929............Regular neighborhood
Nick's on Broadway 929............Breakfast
north 929......................Regular neighborhood
north bakery 929.......................Breakfast
Not Just Snacks 929....Regular neighborhood
Olneyville New York System 929......Late night
Persimmon 930.........................High end

El Rancho Grande 930..Regular neighborhood
Red Fez 930..................Regular neighborhood
Red Fez 930..............................Wish I'd opened
Red Fez 930..............................Bargain
Seaplane Diner 930....................Breakfast
Sun and Moon 930.....................Breakfast
Swan Oyster Depot 837..........Wish I'd opened
Thai Orchids 927...........Regular neighborhood
Tony's Colonial Food 930..................Regular neighborhood

JOHN SUNDSTROM
Lark
952 East Seneca Street, Seattle

Sundstrom runs Lark, Bitter/Raw, and Slab Sandwiches + Pie from the same space, while Southpaw Pizza is a casual woodfired pizza restaurant, with a focus on vegetables and locally milled flour.

Il Corvo 803................Regular neighborhood
Fonda la Catrina 803.......................Breakfast
Kedai Makan 803.......................Late night
Little Uncle 804...........................Late night
Mean Sandwich 804.....Regular neighborhood
Palace Kitchen 804....................Late night
Quinn's Pub 804........................Late night
Russ & Daughters Cafe 1009...........Breakfast
Salumi 805....................Regular neighborhood
Sqirl 815....................................Breakfast
The Wandering Goose 806...............Breakfast

DAVID SWAIN
Fino Seppeltsfield
730 Seppeltsfield Road, Seppeltsfield

This Adelaide-born chef returned to south Austraila to open Fino Willunga and Fino Seppeltsfield, after learning the trade in Melbourne.

Africola 90.....................Regular neighborhood
Brae 101...................................Wish I'd opened
CUMULUS INC. 142...............Wish I'd opened
fermentAsian 96..........Regular neighborhood
Hentley Farm 96.......................High end
Market Street Café 92...............Breakfast
peel st 92................................Local favorite
Press* 93..................................Late night
Provenance Restaurant 101..Worth the travel
St Hugo 95................................High end
Superfish 94..............................Bargain
Wah Hing 94.............................Bargain

LUIGI TAGLIENTI
Lume
Via Giacomo Watt 37, Milan

A passionate defender of Italy's gastronomic culture who considers Carlo Cracco his mentor, Taglienti won his current restaurant Lume a Michelin star within a few months of opening its doors.

Alléno Paris au Pavillon Ledoyen 557 High end
La Cantina di Manuela 660............Regular neighborhood
Le Grand Restaurant 558......Wish I'd opened
LUME 661..................................Local favorite
Papillon 569..............................Worth the travel
Ristorante Acanto 662...............Breakfast
De Santis 662...........................Late night

TAKUJI TAKAHASHI
Kinobu
416 Iwatoyamacho, Kyoto
Declared one of Japan's best chefs, Takahashi is the third-generation chef-owner at Kinobu, a Kyoto kaiseki (Japanese multi-course meal) fixture since 1935.

Apicius 256..................................High end
Chinese Dining Kyojuzen 246...........Late night
L'Ecrin 258..................................High end
Hirasansou 252....................Worth the travel
Hyotei 249...........................Local favorite
Inoda Coffee 248.......................Breakfast
Lec Court 248............................Breakfast
Mankamerou 248................Local favorite
Old Hong Kong Restaurant Kyoto 250_Regular
  neighborhood
Shofukuro 252.................Wish I'd opened
Sushikaiseki Jubei 246..........Worth the travel
Tokyo Kitcho 250.............Wish I'd opened
TRATTORIA LEONE 250 Regular neighborhood
Zenkafuku 249................................Bargain

YOSHIHIRO TAKAHASHI
Hyotei
Nanzengaku-cho, Kyoto
A 15th-generation chef, he took over Hyotei in 2015. Takahashi studies flower arranging, gardening, and traditional Japanese ceramics in order to provide a multi-sensory dining experience for his guests.
Nakamura 249.............Regular neighborhood

YOSHIAKI TAKAZAWA
Takazawa
3-5-2 Akasaka, Tokyo
He worked at a number of yakatori (charcoal grilled skewers) restaurants before opening his own place in 2005. In addition to this fine dining restaurant he recently opened Takazawabar just around the corner.

Chugoku Hanten 263.......................Late night
Gion Nishikawa 247.............Worth the travel
Harutaka 257...............Regular neighborhood
Hirasansou 252....................Worth the travel
Kawamura 252..................................High end
Nihonryori RyuGin 265.............Local favorite
Satomi 266....................Wish I'd opened
Shichifukujin 273................................Bargain
Torishige 271.............Regular neighborhood
Yakiniku Kiraku-tei 267.Regular neighborhood

SAMI TALLBERG
Following a decade in some of the world's most renowned kitchens, this expert on wild food returned to Helsinki to consult and sell wild plants to Finland's best restaurants.

Baskeri & Basso 384................Local favorite
Bocca di Lupo 445.........Wish I'd opened
Café Andante 384.......................Breakfast
Cargo 384..................Regular neighborhood
Charlie Bird 1012..........................Late night
The Clove Club 487.........Wish I'd opened
Flying Elk 355.................Worth the travel
Maison Premiere 1017......................High end
Pompier 386................Regular neighborhood

Punkaharju State Hotel 383.............High end
Restaurant Grön 387................Local favorite
Sendai Ryouri Homma 251....Worth the travel

TIPPI TAMBUNTING
M Dining
2294 Pasong Tamo Extension, Manila
The executive chef to the M Group, her flagship M Dining has recently reopened in a new location after a ten-month hiatus.

Antonio's 303..................................High end
Bale Dutung 303....................Worth the travel
Bizu Patisserie 304.......................Breakfast
Bucky's 304..................................Bargain
Cafe Via Mare 304.......................Breakfast
Hai Shin Lou 305.........Regular neighborhood
Manam 311.......................Wish I'd opened
The Mess Hall 306..................Local favorite
Recovery Food 312......................Late night
Señor Pollo 306............................Bargain
Tim Ho Wan 312..........................Late night
Tsumura 308................Regular neighborhood
Your Local 308.....................Local favorite

SAMI TAMIMI
Ottolenghi
287 Upper Street, London
Jerusalem-born Tamimi moved to London in 1997 and ran the kitchen at Baker & Spice before joining Yotam Ottolenghi in 2002 to set up their widely acclaimed deli chain.

The Duke of Sussex 413.................Regular
  neighborhood
Grain Store 482.......................Breakfast
Maramia Café 423..........................Bargain
Morito 468...................Wish I'd opened
Murano 441..................................High end
La Poule au Pot 551.......................Late night
Septime 566..................Worth the travel
Smoking Goat 454..................Local favorite

JASON TAN
Corner House
1 Cluny Road, Singapore
Formerly executive chef of Sky on 57, where he spent five years, Tan had earlier cut his teeth at prominent restaurants Les Amis in Singapore and Robuchon Au Dôme in Macau.

Beauty in the Pot 322....................Late night
Chey Sua Carrot Cake 335.........Local favorite
The Fat Duck 390....................Worth the travel
Hashida Sushi 327............................High end
Kikunoi 247....................Worth the travel
Kim Heng chicken rice 319.................Regular
  neighborhood
Pin Wei Hong Kong Style Chee Cheong fun
  324.........................Breakfast
Tickets 601............................Wish I'd opened
Grain Store 482.......................Breakfast
Maramia Café 423..........................Bargain
Morito 468...................Wish I'd opened
Murano 441..................................High end
La Poule au Pot 551.......................Late night
Septime 566..................Worth the travel
Smoking Goat 454..................Local favorite

MING TAN
Park Bench Deli
179 Telok Ayer Street, Singapore
After three years of running Singapore's Lolla, he set up the gourmet sandwich joint Park Bench Deli in 2015, and, barely six months after opening, one of its sandwiches won best dish of the year from the *Straits Times*.

Candlenut 334......................Local favorite
Corner House 334............................High end
He Ji Porridge 319............................Bargain
JB Ah Meng 323...........................Late night
Keng Eng Kee Seafood 317................Regular
  neighborhood
Lyle's 488.............................Worth the travel
Salted and Hung 321.........Wish I'd opened
Wee Nam Kee 326.......Regular neighborhood
YY Kafei Dian 322.......................Breakfast

SAMEER TANEJA
Talli Joe
152-156 Shaftesbury Avenue, London
This Delhi-born executive chef, formerly of the Michelin-starred Benares, has high-profile collaborations with Michel and Alain Roux, Pierre Koffmann, and Atul Kochhar under his belt.

Barrafina 444.......................Local favorite
Berners Tavern 472......................Breakfast
Big Easy Bar 432.........................Late night
The Clove Club 487..........................High end
Dishoom 433.............................Breakfast
Gunpowder 488................Wish I'd opened
Hedone 413................................High end
Hoppers 450..................................Bargain
Masala Wala Café 464..Regular neighborhood
Masala Wala Café 464..........Wish I'd opened
Opium 452...................................Late night
Pho & Bun 453................................Bargain
Pizarro 488.................Regular neighborhood
Tandoor Chop House 436...........Local favorite

THITID TASSANAKAJOHN
Le Du
399/3 Silom Soi 7, Bangkok

A graduate of the Culinary institute of America and certified sommelier, he has worked at New York City's Eleven Madison Park, Jean Georges, and The Modern.

Arzak 579	Worth the travel
Asador Etxebarri 575	Worth the travel
Bo.Lan 287	Regular neighborhood
Bo.Lan 287	Local favorite
Bo.Lan 287	High end
El Celler de Can Roca 583	Worth the travel
Derby King 280	Bargain
Eat Me Restaurant 280	High end
Eat Me Restaurant 280	Local favorite
Gaggan 284	Local favorite
Gaggan 284	High end
The House on Sathorn 281	High end
Issaya Siamese Club 286	High end
Joke Samyan 280	Breakfast
Luka Café 281	Breakfast
Nahm 283	High end
Nahm 283	Local favorite
Nahm 283	Wish I'd opened
Namsaah Bottling Trust 281	Local favorite
Narisawa 265	Worth the travel
Niyom 282	Late night
Le Normandie 282	High end
Saeng Chai Pochana 283	Late night
Sühring 289	Local favorite
Sühring 289	High end

JAIR TELLEZ
MeroToro
Amsterdam 204, Mexico City

Growing up in the border town of Tijuana, Tellez did an apprenticeship at Daniel. His first restaurant Laja is in the middle of nowhere while MeroToro is based in the slick metropolis of Mexico City.

Aleli 1078	Breakfast
El Bajío 1079	Breakfast
Biko 1079	High end
Bósforo 1079	Local favorite
Le Châteaubriand 564	Worth the travel
La Docena 1079	Regular neighborhood
Estela 1010	Wish I'd opened
Farmer´s Apprentice 756	Worth the travel
Hiyoko Yakitori-Ya 1080	Late night
Hotel Carlota 1080	Local favorite
El Jamil 1080	Regular neighborhood
Kaye 1080	Local favorite
Lardo 1081	Breakfast
Mia Domenicca 1081	High end
Mia Domenicca 1081	Regular neighborhood
Máximo Bistrot 1081	High end
Pujol 1082	High end
Quintonil 1082	High end
Rafael 1100	Worth the travel
El Sella 1083	Local favorite
Taqueria El Progreso 1084	Bargain

PETER TEMPELHOFF
The Greenhouse
93 Brommersvlei Road, Plettenberg Bay

He launched the London diner Automat in 2005, taking his "progressive South African" cuisine back to his native Cape Town in 2006 to oversee six restaurants within the Relais & Chateaux hotel group.

Borruso's 732	Regular neighborhood
Chefs Warehouse & Canteen 731	Local favorite
The Conservatory 733	Breakfast
Four & Twenty Café 734	Breakfast
Hallelujah 733	Regular neighborhood
Nobu 734	High end
South China Dim Sum Bar 731	Bargain
The Test Kitchen 734	Local favorite
Willoughby & Co. 734	Regular neighborhood

OLLIE TEMPLETON
Carousel
71 Blandford Street, London

Previously sous chef at Moro, Templeton has been exposed to a huge variety of high-profile chefs as he cooks alongside them as they undertake residencies at Carousel.

Beirut Express 424	Late night
Chilli Cool 482	Regular neighborhood
Hartwood 1088	Wish I'd opened
El refugio 573	Worth the travel
Regency Café 456	Breakfast
Relæ 378	High end
Silk Road 465	Bargain

PEKKA TERÄVÄ
Emo
Kasarmikatu 44, Helsinki

The Finn who cooked at Stockholm's Edsbacka Krog and the Helsinki institution, G.W. Sundmans, he now champions Modern Nordic cooking at the Olo Group's newest offering, Emo.

Café Ekberg 385	Breakfast
Hanko Sushi 385	Bargain
Klaus K Breakfast & Brunch 385	Breakfast
Mami 382	Regular neighborhood
Manala 386	Late night
Ragu 387	High end
Rapukartano 383	Local favorite
Restaurant Fuku Supreme 383	Bargain
Restaurant Gösta 383	Local favorite
Ruka Peak 383	Worth the travel
Savoy 387	High end
Smör 382	Regular neighborhood
Tintä 382	Wish I'd opened
Wanha Hullu Poro 383	Worth the travel

CSILLA THACKRAY
The Vandal
4306 Butler Street, Pittsburgh

Thackray opened The Vandal in 2015. With her Hungarian heritage and roots in Eastern European cuisine, Thackray's approach to food is simple and seasonal.

The Allegheny Wine Mixer 925	Late night
Buca 767	Worth the travel
Chengdu Gourmet 925	Regular neighborhood
Cure 926	High end
Dinette 926	Local favorite
Everyday Noodles 926	Bargain
Kádár étkezde 690	Worth the travel
Kádár étkezde 690	Worth the travel
Legume 926	Regular neighborhood
Legume 926	Wish I'd opened
Onyx 691	Worth the travel
Onyx 691	Worth the travel
Pusadee's Garden 926	Regular neighborhood
Ritter's Diner 927	Breakfast
Slice Island 927	Late night
Tail Up Goat 871	Worth the travel

NAREN THIMMAIAH
Karavalli
66 Residency Road, Bangalore

Hailing from the Coorg district of southwest India, TV favorite Thimmaiah has been the face of the iconic Bangalore restaurant Karavalli for over 20 years.

Le Cirque Signature 182	High End
Corner House 182	Late night
The Egg Factory 182	Breakfast
Garuda Mall 183	Bargain
Imperial 183	Late night
Mavalli Tiffin Room 183	Local favorite
Olive Beach 183	Regular neighborhood
Toast & Tonic 184	Regular neighborhood
The Falls 184	Wish I'd opened
Iggys 327	Worth the travel

LANDON THOMPSON
Cooks & Soldiers
691 14th Street Northwest, Atlanta

Tapping into more than eight years experience of working under great chefs, Thompson brought his Spanish cooking experience to help make the dream of Cooks & Soldiers a reality.

Acapulco Mexican Taqueria 942	Bargain
Atlas 942	High end
La Cuchara San Telmo 581	Worth the travel
Octopus Bar 947	Late night
Pijiu Belly 948	Breakfast
So Ba 949	Regular neighborhood
Staplehouse 950	Local favorite
The Wyld 879	Wish I'd opened

LEE TIERNAN
Black Axe Mangal
156 Canonbury Road, London

Former head chef of St John's Bread and Wine, Tiernan began Black Axe as a pop-up in Copenhagen, where it earned cult status before he brought it to London.

Beigel Bake 485	Late night
The Horseshoes Country Pub & Dining Room 396	Regular neighborhood
Mission Chinese 1008	Worth the travel
Pizzeria Bel Sit 494	Regular neighborhood
Russ & Daughters Cafe 1009	Breakfast
St. John Bar and Restaurant 471	Local favorite
Tas Firin 487	Bargain

BEN TISH

He launched the London tapas group Salt Yard in 2006, before he left to pursue a new adventure in 2017.

40 Maltby Street 460............Wish I'd opened
45 Jermyn Street 455............Local favorite
Bistrotheque 460........Regular neighborhood
Blanchette 445..................................Late night
E Pellici 461....................................Breakfast
Morgan Arms 463........Regular neighborhood
Morgan Arms Bow 463.Regular neighborhood
Pavilion Café 476..........................Breakfast
Scott's 442..High end
St. John Bread and Wine 489.Wish I'd opened
Tayyabs 494..Bargain
The Gunton Arms 401...........Worth the travel

HIDEKAZU TOJO
Tojo's
1133 West Broadway, Vancouver

Widely credited as the inventor of the California roll, the Japanese-born sushi chef Tojo studied in Osaka and moved to Vancouver in 1971, opening his eponymous restaurant there in 1988.

Cioppino's Mediterranean Grill 762....Regular neighborhood
Marulilu Café 759........Regular neighborhood
Marulilu Café 759........................Breakfast

YOJI TOKUYOSHI
Tokuyoshi
Via San Calocero 3, Milan

Tokuyoshi moved to Italy from Japan over a decade ago, and now serves "contaminated Italian cuisine" in his eponymous, Michelin-starred restaurant.

Caffè Sicilia 666..........................Breakfast
Casa Ramen Milano 660.................Regular neighborhood
DEN 268............................Local favorite
Kawamura Bar 252........................Late night
Marzapane 656............Regular neighborhood
Pasticceria Cucchi 661..................Breakfast
Sakeya 662......................................Late night
Trippa - Trattoria 662....Regular neighborhood

STEPHEN TOMAN
OX
1 Oxford Street, Belfast

Belfast born, Toman worked in Scottsdale's Camelback Inn, Taillevent and James Street South. He went on to open OX in 2013 with friend Alain Kerloc'h, whom he met in L'Arpège.

L'Arpège 556.......................Wish I'd opened
L'Astrance 568...............................High end
Cast & Crew 500............................Breakfast
Castle Terrace Restaurant 496........Worth the travel
Chapter One 503............................High end
Deane's at Queens Bar & Grill 500.....Bargain
Eleven Madison Park 1037....Worth the travel
Eipic 500...........................Local favorite
General Merchants 500.................Breakfast
Graze 501....................Regular neighborhood
The Greenhouse 504........................High end

Home 501................................Bargain
Howard Street 501......Regular neighborhood
Little Italy 501...............................Late night
Mission Chinese 1008..........Worth the travel
The Muddlers Club 502..............Local favorite
Noble 502..Bargain
Noma 369..........................Wish I'd opened
Permit Room 502..........................Breakfast
Relæ 378............................Wish I'd opened
Restaurant Patrick Guilbaud 504......High end
Shu restaurant 502......Regular neighborhood

SIMONE TONDO
Tondo
29 Rue de Cotte, Paris

After moving to Paris, he worked at Rino and La Gazzetta and is now returning to the former home of La Gazzetta to cook under his own name.

L'Arpège 556....................Local favorite
L'Astrance 568...............................High end
Chez Aline 564.................................Bargain
Fäviken Magasinet 345........Worth the travel
Holybelly 563.................................Breakfast
Kunitoraya II 550........Regular neighborhood
Lao Siam 569.................................Late night
Michi 552................Regular neighborhood
Relæ 378............................Wish I'd opened
Le Square Trousseau 567..............Breakfast
Starvin' Joe 566...............................Bargain

MITCH TONKS
The Seahorse
5 South Embankment, Dartmouth

A fishmonger turned restaurateur who runs Bristol's RockFish Grill & Seafood Market, The Seahorse, and RockFish Seafood in Dartmouth and Plymouth.

Beigel Bake 485.............................Late night
East in the West 395....Regular neighborhood
Al Gatto Nero 671....Worth the travel
Harbour Kitchen 395....Regular neighborhood
La Petite Maison 441........................High end
La Pineta 669....................Worth the travel
Pullman Dining Car 394.................Breakfast
Rasa Sayang 453.............................Bargain
Restaurant Nathan Outlaw 393..Local favorite
The Seafood Restaurant 392.....Local favorite
Yauatcha Soho 455......................Late night
Zuma 419..High end
Zuma 419..........................Wish I'd opened

ISAAC TOUPS
Toups' Meatery
845 North Carrollton Avenue, New Orleans

Toups represents the new guard of Cajun chefs. His "born and braised" culinary style is both the direct result of his New Orleans fine-dining experience and of growing up Cajun, and he has been heavily influenced by the cooking of both of his grandmothers.

The Avenue Pub 978........................Late night
Bayou Wine Garden 984..............Late night
Betsy's Pancake House 984............Breakfast
Brigtsen's 987............................Local favorite
Clancy's 988..............................Local favorite
The Company Burger 981......Wish I'd opened

Crescent City Steaks 974...........Local favorite
Emeril's Delmonico 977.................High end
Honey & Co 473..............................Breakfast
Joe Beef 779....................Worth the travel
Lilly's Café 982............Regular neighborhood
Maïs Arepas 977..........Regular neighborhood
Momofuku Noodle Bar 1023..Worth the travel
The Ordinary 1056................Worth the travel
Regis Huiterie 556...........Worth the travel
Restaurant R'evolution 980............High end
St. James Cheese Company 990........Regular neighborhood
Tan Dinh 884..................................Bargain

SUZANNE TRACHT
Jar
8225 Beverly Boulevard, Los Angeles

Born and raised in Phoenix, she opened her modern chophouse in 2001 with longtime chef de cuisine, Preech Narkthong.

Noshi Sushi 818...........Regular neighborhood

PASQUALE TRIMBOLI
Italian and Sons
7 Lonsdale Street, Canberra

A self-trained chef, Trimboli focuses on Italian regional food, including antipasti and hand-cut pasta.

Dar Rochford 00.............................Late night
Café Di Stasio 153................Worth the travel
Chairman & Yip 80..........................High end
eightysix 80..................................Bargain
Fratelli Paradiso 121...Regular neighborhood
Monster 81..................Wish I'd opened
Silo Bakery 81................................Breakfast
Silo Bakery 81.............Regular neighborhood
Trattoria Tonino Bassetti 658..Worth the travel

RYAN TRIMM
Sweet Grass
937 South Cooper Street, Memphis

Trimm and Glenn Hays opened the neighborhood bistro Sweet Grass in 2010. He and two partners are also opening a series of breakfast and lunch restaurants in Memphis, all with a focus on local produce and homemade meats.

ACRE Restaurant 932......................High end
Andrew Michael Italian Kitchen 932.High end
Central BBQ 932........................Local favorite
Coppa 889........................Worth the travel
Earnestine & Hazel's 933.............Late night
Elwood's Shack 933.........Wish I'd opened
Payne's Bar-B-Que 933.....................Bargain
Payne's Bar-B-Que 933...........Local favorite
Pho Saigon 933..............................Bargain
The Purple Pig 963................Worth the travel
Restaurant Iris 934.........................High end
Las Tortugas Deli Mexicana 932........Regular neighborhood

FERNANDO TROCA
Sucre
Sucre 676, Buenos Aires

Chef-owner at Sucre in northern Buenos Aires, Trocca also oversees the menu for the London-based Argentinean restaurant group, Gaucho Grill.

Allpress Roastery Cafe **470**	Breakfast
Atelier September **370**	Wish I'd opened
Chori **1126**	Bargain
Don Julio Parrilla **1127**	Late night
Mirazur **545**	Worth the travel
Parador La Huella **1119**	Local favorite
Proper **1129**	Regular neighborhood
Tegui **1129**	High end

THOMAS TROISGROS
Olympe
Rua Custodio Serrao 62, Rio de Janeiro

This fourth-generation chef from the Troisgros family has taken over the kitchen from his father, Claude, a key figure in Brazilian cuisine. Olympe first opened its doors in 1983.

Aconchego Carioca **1106**	Local favorite
Emporio Jardim **1107**	Breakfast
Estela **1010**	Worth the travel
Galeto Sat's **1108**	Late night
Hocus Pocus DNA **1108**	Wish I'd opened
Jobi **1108**	Bargain
Lasai **1108**	High end
Da Roberta **1107**	Regular neighborhood

GEORGY TROYAN
Severyane
12 Bolshaya Nikitskaya, Moscow

Trained at Le Cordon Bleu in Paris, he is now head chef at culinary duo Illya Tyutenkov and Uilliam Lamberti's newest restaurant, Severyane, where he presides over two huge Russian ovens and no stoves.

Akrame **557**	Worth the travel
Coffeemania **711**	Regular neighborhood
Delicatessen **711**	Local favorite
Dersou **567**	Worth the travel
Gjusta **824**	Worth the travel
LavkaLavka **712**	Local favorite
Nhà **713**	Late night
Pinch **709**	Regular neighborhood
Pinch **709**	Breakfast
Selfie **709**	Late night
Semifreddo **707**	High end
Septime **566**	Worth the travel
Ugolёk **710**	Regular neighborhood
Ugolёk **710**	Late night
White Rabbit **706**	Local favorite
White Rabbit **706**	High end
White Rabbit **706**	Wish I'd opened
Yam'tcha **551**	Worth the travel
Yunost' **708**	Bargain

ROBERT TRZÓPEK
Bez Gwiazdek
Wiślana 8, Warsaw

Previously executive chef at Warsaw's Westin Hotel and Tamka 43, and one-time apprentice at Noma and elBulli, Polish chef Trzópek co-created Harvest (2013) and currently runs his own restaurant, Bez Gwiazdek, in Warsaw.

Kita Koguta **691**	Late night
Mała Polana Smaków **691**	Local favorite
Nolita **692**	High end
Regina Bar **692**	Regular neighborhood
Relæ **378**	Wish I'd opened
Sato Gotuje **692**	Bargain
Secret Life Café **692**	Breakfast
Water & Wine **691**	Worth the travel

AARON TURNER
IGNI
Ryan Place, Geelong

Within nine months of opening IGNI, with its open charcoal grill, Turner won Chef of the Year at The Age Food Guide awards in 2016.

Embla **143**	Regular neighborhood
Kilgour Street Grocer & Cafe **102**	Breakfast
Sam's Café Geelong **102**	Local favorite
Supper Inn **146**	Late night

RICHARD TURNER
Hawksmoor
11 Langley Street, London

Leaving a career in the British Army, Turner began his food career at Le Gavroche, training under Albert and Michel Roux Jnr. He has been executive chef of Hawksmoor since 2009 and also co-owns Turner & George, Pitt Cue Co., and Meatopia UK.

Cervejaria Ramiro **618**	Worth the travel
Dishoom **485**	Breakfast
Dishoom **485**	Bargain
Fish Shack **574**	Worth the travel
José Tapas Bar **460**	Regular neighborhood
The Quality Chophouse **469**	Local favorite
The Waterside Inn **390**	High end

KWANG UH
Korean Uh staged at Noma before co-founding LA's fermentation-focused restaurant Baroo.

Al Wazir Chicken **816**	Regular neighborhood
Animal **810**	Local favorite
Desano Pizza **815**	Regular neighborhood
Destroyer **813**	Wish I'd opened
Erewhon Market **816**	Breakfast
Grand Central Market **813**	Breakfast
The Halal Guys **819**	Regular neighborhood
Joan's On Third **810**	Breakfast
LocoL **796**	Local favorite
LocoL **796**	Wish I'd opened
Mingles **235**	Worth the travel
New Dragon Seafood Restaurant **812**	Bargain
Night + Market Song **823**	Late night
PINE & CRANE **823**	Late night
Pollo A La Brasa **814**	Regular neighborhood
Providence **817**	High end
Ricky's Fish Tacos **820**	Bargain

Rustic Canyon **822**	Local favorite
Saison **841**	Worth the travel
Sqirl **815**	Breakfast
Sung Don Nah **819**	Late night
Taco María **812**	Local favorite
Taco María **812**	High end
Trois Mec **818**	High end

JORGE VALLEJO
Quintonil
Newton 55, Mexico City

Vallejo launched his unique and successful take on contemporary Mexican cooking, Quintonil, in 2012, having staged at Noma, worked in Madrid, and at Mexico's fine-dining Pujol.

Amaya **418**	Regular neighborhood
Blue Hill at Stone Barns **913**	Worth the travel
La Docena **1085**	Local favorite
Hiyoko Yakitori-Ya **1080**	Late night
Nicos **1081**	Breakfast

NORMAN VAN AKEN
1921 by Norman Van Aken
142 East 4th Avenue, Mount Dora

Florida-born chef, Van Aken is a champion of "fusion cooking", and has been widely credited with bringing New World Cuisine to a wider audience.

Alter **872**	Regular neighborhood
L'Avant Comptoir **554**	Wish I'd opened
Big Star **969**	Wish I'd opened
Bras **541**	Worth the travel
Brindille **962**	High end
Cake Thai Kitchen **873**	Local favorite
Cal Pep **595**	Worth the travel
Enriqueta's **873**	Breakfast
Gramercy Tavern **1036**	Regular neighborhood
Jean-Georges **1046**	High end
The Local **872**	Late night
La Mar **874**	Local favorite
Pack Supermarket **874**	Bargain
Phuc Yea **875**	Breakfast
La Sandwicherie **876**	Late night
Taqueria Viva Mexico **875**	Bargain

FRANKIE VAN LOO
Social Wine and Tapas
39 James Street, London

Van Loo has worked with Jason Atherton since 2011, cooking at Pollen Street Social and Social Eating House, before opening up Social Wine and Tapas as head chef.

Dishoom **432**	Late night
Eleven Madison Park **1037**	Worth the travel
The Haberdashery **469**	Breakfast
Holborn Dining Room **477**	Local favorite
Katz's Delicatessen **1008**	Bargain
The Ledbury **423**	High end
Rabbit **423**	Regular neighborhood
Restaurant Nathan Outlaw **393**	Worth the travel
Sat Bains **402**	Worth the travel
Yardbird **229**	Wish I'd opened

THE CHEFS

LUKE VANDORE-MACKAY
The Hour Glass
279–283 Brompton Road, London
Part-time chef, wine merchant, food writer, and businessman, he co-founded Brompton Food Market in South Kensington in 2013 before taking on The Hour Glass Pub a couple of years later.

Applecross Inn **498**..............Worth the travel
Artisan Coffee **425**........Regular neighborhood
Awesome Thai **410**........Regular neighborhood
Borough Market **462**.......................Breakfast
The Crispy Duck **447**.....................Late night
Lahore Karahi **428**........................Late night
Lahore Karahi **428**............................Bargain
The Ledbury **423**............................High end
Ngon **413**.......................................Bargain
Quo Vadis **453**......................Local favorite
The Robin Craft Café **426**..................Regular
 neighborhood
The Sportsman **400**.......................High end
Temper **454**.......................Wish I'd opened
Vinoteca **414**.......................Local favorite

MANOJ VASAIKAR
Indian Zing
236 King Street, London
Owner of Indian Zing, Indian Zilla, and Indian Zest, Vasaikar was born in Mumbai and moved to London to work at Chutney Mary and Veeraswamy.

HIX Soho **449**...............................High end
Khyber **184**...................................High end
Saravanaa Bhavan **429**....................Bargain

HUS VEDAT
Yosma
50 Baker Street, London
Born in London, Hus has Turkish origins and started out working in the family butcher shop. Former executive chef of Jamie Oliver's Barbecoa, he is now executive chef of Yosma, whose menu is inspired by the cuisine of the streets of Istanbul.

Beigel Bake **485**...........................Late night
The Drapers Arms **480**.Regular neighborhood
The Fat Duck **390**...............Worth the travel
Flat Iron **449**..................................Bargain
Ristorante Frescobaldi London **442**..High end
Hawksmoor **433**...........................Breakfast
MEATliquor **481**......................Local favorite
NobleRot **432**....................Wish I'd opened

GREG VERNICK
Vernick Food & Drink
2031 Walnut Street, Philadelphia
Once he completed his training, Vernick rose through the ranks of the Jean-George empire, serving as sous chef at Jean-Georges, Nougatine, and Spice Market, before opening the doors to his own restaurant, Vernick Food & Drink.

Ants Pants Café **920**....Regular neighborhood
Eventide Oyster Co. **855**........Worth the travel
Khyber Pass Pub **922**...................Late night
Mama's Vegetarian **922**..Regular neighborhood

Parc **923**.................Regular neighborhood
Ponzio's **912**..............................Breakfast
Reading Terminal Market **923**...........Bargain
Royal Izakaya **923**.....................Late night
Russ & Daughters Cafe **1009**............High end
Zama **925**................Regular neighborhood
Zeppoli **913**................................High end

VIKRAM VIJ
Vij's
1480 West 11th Avenue, Vancouver
Born in India, he trained in Austria before arriving in Canada in 1989 and he currently owns Vancouver's Vij's and Rangoli.

Hawksworth Restaurant **756**...........High End
Maenam **758**...............Regular neighborhood
Pidgin **757**..................Regular neighborhood
Thomas Haas **758**....................Local favorite

EVGENY VIKENTEV
Hamlet + Jacks
Volinskiy Lane 2, St Petersburg
He started at Wine Rack in 2014, and continues to run its kitchen together with the bigger, newer, Hamlet + Jacks, which offers both an unusual wine list and modern Russian cuisine.

El Copitas Bar **701**.....................Late night
Disfrutar **596**..................Wish I'd opened
Duo Gastrobar **701**......Regular neighborhood
Kokoko **714**.................................Breakfast
Niño Viejo **598**..............................Bargain
Osteria Francescana **650**.................High end
Pakta **599**......................Worth the travel
White Rabbit **706**....................Local favorite

JORDI VILÀ
Alkimia
Ronda Sant Antoni 41, Barcelona
Catalan Vilà learnt his craft in the restaurants of Barcelona, before opening his first, Alkimia, in 2002, with a Michelin star and the management of three further restaurants following.

L'Arpège **556**...............................High end
Can Castellví **584**.........................Breakfast
Els Casals **586**................Wish I'd opened
El Celler del Barri Vell **584**..............Bargain
Coure **596**...............Regular neighborhood
Dos Palillos **602**..........................Late night
Gresca **597**.........................Local favorite
Güeyu Mar **574**..............Worth the travel
Mercat de Sant Antoni **597**.............Breakfast
Mextizo **598**................................Late night
Un'Altra Storia **603**.........................Bargain
La Volàtil **600**...............Regular neighborhood

JAMES VILES
Biota
18 Kangaloon Road, Bowral
Self-proclaimed country-boy chef, Viles has a passion for foraging and wild-food. The regional location of his restaurant allows him to grow much of the produce he uses on-site.

Attica **151**.....................................High end
Automata **114**............Regular neighborhood
Bennelong Restaurant **107**.................High end

Bernie's Diner **83**.............................Bargain
Burnt Ends **329**..................Worth the travel
Ester **114**..................Regular neighborhood
Frankie's Pizza **111**......................Late night
Golden Century **111**.....................Late night
IGNI **102**....................Wish I'd opened
Mary's **119**....................................Bargain
Quay **125**............................Local favorite
Reuben Hills **124**.........................Breakfast
Room 10 **122**...............................Breakfast

CASSY VIRES
Companion Teaching Kitchen
2331 Schuetz Road, St Louis
Vires, an award-winning food magazine columnist, trained in Houston, Texas and is the manager of Companion's Teaching Kitchen.

Beast + Bottle **798**...............Worth the travel
BEAST Craft BBQ Co. **879**...................Regular
 neighborhood
Bowood Farms **911**..............Wish I'd opened
Brasserie by Niche **911**.................High end
Chris' Pancake & Dining **912**...........Breakfast
Cleveland-Heath **880**...........Local favorite
SOHA Bar & Grill **912**....................Late night
El Tapatio **912**...............................Bargain

EBBE VOLLMER
Vollmer's
Tegelgårdsgatan 5, Malmö
He returned to his Swedish hometown of Malmö to open Vollmers in 2011 after working in Asia and in the UK with Gordon Ramsay.

Amber **220**...................................High end
Dishoom **482**................Wish I'd opened
Geist **372**......................Worth the travel
Grain Store **482**.............................Bargain
Klein's Mat **347**.........Regular neighborhood
Olof Viktors **346**.........................Breakfast
Snapphane **349**.........................Late night

MATS VOLLMER
Vollmer's
Tegelgårdsgatan 5, Malmö
Mats and brother Ebbe, the fifth generation of a family of restaurateurs, launched their modern Skåne restaurant in Malmö, a hotbed of culinary attractions, in 2011.

L'Assiette Champenoise **539**..Worth the travel
Esperanto **358**............................Late night
Falafel & Burgers **347**......................Bargain
Geranium **378**...............................High end
Geranium **378**................Wish I'd opened
Kvarteret Åkern **348**....Regular neighborhood
Malmö Saluhall **348**.....................Breakfast
Saltimporten Canteen **348**.........Local favorite

VICTOR WÅGMAN
Bror
Sankt Peders Stræde 24a, Copenhagen

A Swedish graduate of Noma, he opened the restaurant Bror with his fellow New Nordic alumus Samuel Nutter in Copenhagen's Indre By in 2013.

Daniel Berlin Krog 349	Worth the travel
Democratic Coffee 371	Breakfast
Fäviken Magasinet 345	Wish I'd opened
La Galette 373	Regular neighborhood
Gasoline Grill 372	Late night
Geranium 378	High end
Noma 369	Local favorite
Slurp Ramen Joint 374	Bargain

PAUL WALSH
City Social
25 Old Broad Street, London

He worked with Marcus Wareing and at Gordon Ramsay's restaurant before taking the head chef position at Atherton's City Social. Just six months after opening, it was awarded a Michelin star.

Berners Tavern 472	Breakfast
The Dairy 414	Local favorite
Jinjuu Soho 450	Late night
Little Social 440	Regular neighborhood
Restaurant Gordon Ramsay 412	Local favorite
Sketch 438	Late night
Temple and Sons 467	Breakfast
Yauatcha Soho 455	Regular neighborhood

JAMES WALT
Araxi
4222 Village Square, Whistler

A pioneer of the farm-to-table movement, he trained at Stratford Chef's School and completed a four-year tenure at Sooke Harbour House before becoming executive chef of Araxi.

L'Abattoir 757	Local favorite
Bao Bei Chinese Brasserie 760	Wish I'd opened
Blé Sucré 566	Worth the travel
Blue Water Café 762	Local favorite
La Cantina 748	Bargain
Elements 749	Breakfast
Five Sails 756	High end
The French Laundry 797	Wish I'd opened
Gyoza King 761	Late night
Jean-Georges 1046	Worth the travel
Sachi Sushi 749	Regular neighborhood
Splitz Grill 749	Bargain
West Restaurant 756	High end

GARETH WARD
Ynyshir Restaurant and Rooms
Eglwys Fach, Machynlleth

After five years at Hambleton Hall and a stint at Sat Bains, he moved to foodie hotspot, Ynyshir Hall, in 2013 to take on his first role as head chef.

The Araki 436	Wish I'd opened
Duck & Waffle 466	Late night
Henne Kirkeby Kro 365	High end
Paul 405	Breakfast
Pho 405	Bargain

Purnell's 405	Worth the travel
Purnell's 405	High end
Pysgoty 499	Local favorite

MARCUS WAREING
Marcus
Wilton Place, London

Re-branded the Gordon Ramsay-operated Petrus as Marcus Wareing at The Berkeley (now called Marcus) in 2008. The Gilbert Scott at London's St. Pancras Renaissance followed in 2011.

Hélène Darroze 439	Late night
The Ivy 434	Regular neighbourhood
The Ivy 434	Breakfast

SARAH WELCH
Revolver
9737 Joseph Campau, Michigan

Welch grew up the West Indies before training as a chef in New York City. Former chef of Republic and Parks & Rec she now runs the chef's table at pop-up Revolver.

Benny's Family Dining 901	Breakfast
Detroit Institute of Bagels 903	Regular neighborhood
Detroit Institute of Bagels 905	Breakfast
Eventide Oyster Co. 885	Worth the travel
Grace 966	Worth the travel
Honest John's 904	Late night
Mabel Gray 908	High end
Mani Osteria & Bar 901	Regular neighborhood
Pupusería y Restaurante Salvadoreño 905	Local favorite
Rose's Fine Foods 906	Breakfast
Selden Standard 906	Regular neighborhood
Sharaku 910	High end
Spencer 901	Wish I'd opened
Telway Hamburgers 907	Bargain
Trinosophes 908	Breakfast
Trinosophes 908	Regular neighborhood

DUNCAN WELGEMOED
Africola
4 East Terrace Adelaide 5000, Adelaide

Following time spent at Le Manoir aux Quat'Saisons, Welgemoed moved to Adelaide, where he opened Bistro Dom before going solo and drawing on his South African upbringing to open Africola in 2014.

(unnamed restaurant) 1078	Worth the travel
AMAYA 1078	Worth the travel
La Buvette 91	Late night
Chin Chin 142	Wish I'd opened
Fino Seppeltsfield 95	Local favorite
Golden Boy 90	Regular neighborhood
Hartwood 1088	Wish I'd opened
Hentley Farm 90	Local favorite
Hentley Farm 96	High end
Hey Jupiter 90	Breakfast
Kutchi Deli Parwana 91	Regular neighborhood
Magill Estate Restaurant 91	High end
Market Street Café 92	Bargain
Miss Ruben 151	Breakfast
Mission Chinese 1008	Worth the travel
Nordburger 92	Late night

Nut Tree Inn 403	Worth the travel
Restaurant Hubert 112	Wish I'd opened
Restaurant Orana 93	High end
Saigon Gate 94	Bargain
Sunny's Pizza 94	Late night
Sunnys Shop 94	Bargain
T-Chow 94	Bargain
The Test Kitchen 734	Worth the travel
Ying Chow Chinese Restaurant 95	Late night

TOWNSEND WENTZ
Townsend
1623 East Passyunk Avenue, Philadelphia

He worked under Jean-Marie Lacroix at the Four Seasons Philadelphia and The Rittenhouse Hotel, before heading to New York City, Connecticut, and London, working for the MARC group. In 2014, he returned to Philadelphia to open Townsend and A Mano in early 2016.

Alinea 957	Worth the travel
Le Coucou 1012	Wish I'd opened
Daniel 1045	High end
Dizengoff 920	Bargain
The Dutch 921	Breakfast
High Street on Market 921	Breakfast
ITV 922	Local favorite
Royal Izakaya 923	Late night
Sagami 912	Regular neighborhood
Shiao Lan Kung 924	Late night
Stargazy 924	Bargain
Umu 442	Worth the travel
Vernick Food & Drink 924	Local favorite
Vietnam Restaurant 925	Regular neighborhood

KIRK WESTAWAY
JAAN
2 Stamford Road, Singapore

This Devon-born chef is skilled in the art of French cuisine and makes sure to use only the highest-quality produce in his kitchen.

Burnt Ends 329	High end
Burnt Ends 329	Wish I'd opened
The Clove Club 487	Worth the travel
Common Man coffee Roasters 331	Breakfast
Eng Seng Restaurant 322	Local favorite
Fera at Claridge's 438	Worth the travel
Luke's Oyster Bar 330	Regular neighborhood
Newton Food Centre 325	Late night
Sin Swee Kee 321	Bargain
Sin Swee Kee 321	Local favorite
Tian Tian Seafood 331	Regular neighborhood
Tippling Club 321	High end

BLAINE WETZEL
The Willows Inn
2579 West Shore Drive, Lummi Island

Growing up in Washington, Blaine started working in kitchens at 14 and never looked back. Having studied at Noma, he's now head chef at The Willow's Inn, winning numerous awards, such as James Beard Rising Star 2015.

Belltown Pizza 801	Late Night
La Mar 1099	Worth the travel
Noma 369	Wish I'd opened
Saison 841	High end

CATHY WHIMS
Nostrana
1401 Southeast Morrison Street, Portland

From her flagship Italian restaurant Nostrana, to her urban pizza and cocktail gem, Oven & Shaker, and now her most recent Spanish-inspired ham bar Hamlet, Whims' cuisine provides heaps of flavor in rustically presented dishes.

Asador Etxebarri **575**............Worth the travel
Bar Avignon **847**.................................Late night
Le Bernadin **1038**...............................High end
Burrasca **849**............Regular neighborhood
Le Calandre **671**..............................High end
Il Corvo **803**.............................Wish I'd opened
HaVL Sandwich **852**........................Breakfast
Little T Baker **854**...........................Breakfast
Lovely's Fifty-Fifty **854**........Local favorite
La Moule **854**.................................Late night
Navarre **855**........................Local favorite
Nongs Khao Man Gai **856**.................Bargain
Parm **1011**........................Wish I'd opened
Le Parùle **647**.....................Worth the travel
Pho Hung **857**..................................Bargain
La Repubblica di Perno **664**....Worth the travel
Xico **861**...................Regular neighborhood

BAS WIEGEL
De Kas
Kamerlingh Onneslaan 3, Amsterdam

Chef de cuisine at Amsterdam's greenhouse turned restaurant, De Kas. Cultivating the on-site gardens, Wiegel and founder-owner, Gert-Jan Hageman, plate the bounty the day it's picked.

L'air du Temps **528**................Worth the travel
Cafe Modern **517**......................Local favorite
Cannibale royale **514**......................Late night
Librije's Zusje **515**.............................High end
The Lobby **518**..................................Bargain
The Lobby **518**...............................Breakfast
Restaurant Breda **515**...Regular neighborhood
Restaurant Choux **516**..Regular neighborhood
Restaurant Choux **516**............Wish I'd opened
Restaurant RIJKS **518**..Regular neighborhood
Restaurant Vermeer **516**..Regular neighborhood

MARTHA WIGGINS
Sylvain
625 Chartres Street, New Orleans

In 2010, Wiggins joined the opening staff of Sylvain as the sous chef to chef Alex Harrell, before taking over as executive chef four years later.

Angeline **978**..................................Breakfast
Angeline **978**...............Regular neighborhood
Bacchanal **974**....................Wish I'd opened
Backspace Bar & Kitchen **979**.........Late night
Bayona **979**.......................................High end
Boswell's Jamaican Grill **985**..............Bargain
Cane & Table **979**.........Regular neighborhood
Coop's Place **979**.....................Local favorite
Domenica **976**...............Regular neighborhood
Domenica **976**..................................Bargain
Doris Metropolitan **979** Regular neighborhood
Doris Metropolitan **979**....................High end
Enoteca de Belem **615**..........Worth the travel

The Joint **975**............................Local favorite
Junction **974**...................................Late night
Lil' Dizzy's **986**.......................Local favorite
Lost Love Lounge **983**......................Late night
Man chu **978**..........................Local favorite
Meauxbar **987**..........Regular neighborhood
Paladar 511 **983**.................Wish I'd opened
Pêche **977**.......................................High end
La Petite Grocery **989**.......................High end
Red's Chinese **975**............................Bargain
Restaurant R'evolution **980**...............High end
Siberia **984**.....................................Late night
Sneaky Pickle **986**...........................Bargain
Stein's Market and Deli **982**.......Local favorite
Willie Mae's Scotch House **987**..Local favorite

MICHAEL WILEY
Big Tree Hospitality
88 Middle Street, Portland

The co-chef and owner of Big Tree Hospitality, Wiley's company ethos drives to create and sustain communities through its three creative and unique restaurants, Hugo's, The Honey Paw, and Eventide Oyster co.

birch **928**.........................Worth the travel
Boda **884**...Late night
Dutch's **885**....................................Breakfast
Fore Street **885**......................Local favorite
Hot Suppa **886**................................Breakfast
Miyake **886**....................................High end
Palace Diner **884**...................Wish I'd opened
Terlingua **886**..........Regular neighborhood

JAMES WILKINS
Wilks restaurant
1–3 Chandos Road, Bristol

A glittering career that has taken in stints at Midsummer House, Aubergine, and Michel Bras was followed in 2012 by the opening in Bristol of Wilkins's eponymous restaurant, and in 2014 its first Michelin star.

Wilsons Restaurant **391**...Regular neighborhood

ALYN WILLIAMS
Alyn Williams at the Westbury
37 Conduit Street, London

Londoner Williams spent six years as a ski-instructor before training with Marcus Wareing at the Berkeley. His hotel dining room at the Westbury opened in 2011.

Akash Tandoori **410**......Regular neighborhood
Alma **616**.........................Worth the travel
Burger and Lobster **437**.........Wish I'd opened
CWTCH **429**.....................................Breakfast
Dumplings' Legend **448**..................Late night
Fera at Claridge's **438**.......................High end
The Ivy **434**............................Local favorite
The Rib Man **489**............................Bargain
Santa Maria Pizzeria **416**.....Regular neighborhood

BEN WILLIS
Aubergine
18 Barker Street, Griffith

After nine years traveling and working around the world, Willis returned to Canberra to take over Aubergine in 2008. He also runs a second venture in the city centre, Temporada.

Bar Rochford **80**..............................Late night
Grease Monkey Burgers **81**..............Bargain
iPho **81**..Bargain
LuMi Dining **122**.................Worth the travel
Monster **81**.....................................Late night
ONA Manuka **82**.............................Breakfast
Restaurant Orana **93**.............Worth the travel
Silo Bakery **81**.......................Local favorite
Sixpenny **123**....................Worth the travel
XO **81**...................Regular neighborhood

MICHAEL WILSON
PHÉNIX eatery & bar
1 Changde Road, Shanghai

Australian-born Wilson became executive chef of the Michelin-starred PHÉNIX eatery and bar at Shanghai's The PuLi Hotel in 2016, having previously worked at the hotel's Jing'an restaurant and Cutler and Co and Grossi Florentino in Melbourne.

Attica **151**........................Worth the travel
The Commune Social **198**..Regular neighborhood
Cyclo **197**..Bargain
Fu He Hui **196**......................Local favorite
Hakkasan **197**..............................High end
Malabar **198**...................................Late night
Tipo 00 **146**.....................Wish I'd opened

JOHN WINTER RUSSELL
Restaurant Candide
551 Rue St Martin, Montréal

Following a series of pop-ups and collaborations in and around Montreal, Winter Russell opened the doors to his first permanent venture in 2015, which was set within a converted church.

Dinette Triple Crown **781**..Regular neighborhood
Dispatch Coffee **776**........................Breakfast
Larrys **777**.......................................Late night
Marconi **781**.....................Wish I'd opened
Montreal Plaza **781**.........................High end
Passerini **567**....................Worth the travel
La Récolte **781**..............................Breakfast
Saison **841**.......................Worth the travel
Sumac Restaurant **781**.....................Bargain
Sunday in Brooklyn **1017**.......Worth the travel
Le Vin Papillon **780**................Wish I'd opened

LEE WOLEN
Boka
1729 North Halstead Street, Chicago

He spent a year at Le Manoir aux Quat'Saisons and elBulli before becoming sous chef at Eleven Madison Park for three years. He is now the chef partner of BOKA.

Alinea **957**......................................High end
Cold Storage **966**.........Regular neighborhood
Cosme **1036**.........................Worth the travel
Dancen **961**.....................................Late night
Dizengoff **920**....................Wish I'd opened
Floriole Bakery **958**........................Breakfast
Giant **959**.......................Regular neighborhood
Lula Cafe **959**.........................Local favorite
MingHin Cuisine **956**.........................Bargain
L'Patron Tacos **960**..........................Bargain
Rustic Canyon **822**..............Worth the travel
Social Place **224**.............................Breakfast
Tartine **225**....................................Breakfast

ALLA WOLF-TASKER
Lake House
King Street, Daylesford

Credited with kickstarting "destination dining" in regional Australia, Wolf-Tasker has run the ever-popular Lake House for more than three decades.

Balthazar **1011**......................Breakfast	
Bar Liberty **148**......................Local favorite	
Biggie Smalls **147**......................Bargain	
Blue Hill at Stone Barns **913**..Wish I'd opened	
Bras **541**......................Wish I'd opened	
Café Di Stasio **153**......................Local favorite	
CUMULUS INC. **142**......Regular neighborhood	
Eleven Madison Park **1037**.....Worth the travel	
Estelle by Scott Pickett **149**......Local favorite	
The European **143**......................Late night	
The French Laundry **797**...Wish I'd opened	
Grossi Florentino **143**..Regular neighborhood	
Grossi Florentino **143**......................Local favorite	
Hélène Darroze **439**..............Worth the travel	
Jean-Georges **1046**.................Worth the travel	
The Ledbury **423**.................Worth the travel	
Ramón Freixa Madrid **589**.....Worth the travel	
Russ & Daughters Cafe **1009**..............Bargain	
Sepia **113**......................High end	
ST. ALI **152**......................Breakfast	
Vue de Monde **146**......................High end	

ANDREW WONG
A. Wong
70 Wilton Road, London

Wong tried his best to escape the family restaurant when he was young, but was drafted in to help out when his father died, and there he discovered a passion and natural talent for cooking. Since then, he has won London's Chinese Masterchef title.

Da Dong Roast Duck **190**.......Wish I'd opened	
Da Dong Roast Duck **190**.......Worth the travel	
Din Tai Fung **218**.................Worth the travel	
Hong Kong City **483**......................Bargain	
Lahore Kebab House **493**................Late night	
Reindeer Café **415**.......Regular neighborhood	
Tickets **601**......................Worth the travel	

JANICE WONG
2am: dessertbar
21a Lorong Liput, Singapore

Singaporean, she has learned from Thomas Keller and Grant Achatz, virtuoso Spanish chocolatier Oriol Balaguer, and prodigious French pastry chef Pierre Hermé. She has restaurants in Singapore, Hong Kong, and Tokyo.

Common Man Coffee Roasters **331**..Breakfast	
Corner House **334**......................High end	
DEN **268**.................Worth the travel	
Florilège **269**.................Worth the travel	
Gyoza-Ya **327**......................Bargain	
Jaggi's **332**......Regular neighborhood	
Jumbo **316**......................Local favorite	
Lei Garden **320**......................Wish I'd opened	
Lim Joo Hin Eating House **317**.........Late night	
Long Beach **334**......................Local favorite	
Mikuni **320**......Regular neighborhood	

Mrs Pho **332**......................Bargain
Odette **320**......................High end

JUSTIN WOODWARD
Castagna
1752 South East Hawthorne Boulevard, Portland

Executive chef at Castagna from 2011, Woodward staged at Noma in Denmark and Mugaritz Restaurant in San Sebastián.

Apizza Scholls **846**........Regular neighborhood	
Beast **847**......................High end	
Benu **840**.................Worth the travel	
Broder **848**......................Breakfast	
Coquine **850**......................High end	
Fuller's Coffee Shop **851**......................Breakfast	
Luc Lac Vietnamese Kitchen **854**.....Late night	
Meat Cheese Bread **855**......................Bargain	
Momofuku Ko **1023**.........Worth the travel	
Nostrana **856**.........Regular neighborhood	
Pépé le Moko **856**......................Wish I'd opened	
Le Pigeon **857**......................Local favorite	
Pok Pok **854**......................Local favorite	
Pok Pok **858**......................Wish I'd opened	
Slow Bar **859**......................Late night	
Uno Mas **861**......................Bargain	

KARL WORLEY
Biscuit Love
316 11th Avenue South, Nashville

Worley learned to cook from his grandfather in Tennessee, and honed his skills at Rioja in Denver. He founded the Biscuit Love food truck, with his wife, Sarah, in 2012. Three years later, it is now a permanent fixture in the heart of Nashville.

Bastion **934**......................Late night	
City House **935**......................Local favorite	
Gabby's Burgers and Fries **935**.........Bargain	
The Grey **879**.................Worth the travel	
Jeff Ruby's Steakhouse **935**......High end	
Josephine **936**.........Regular neighborhood	
Marché Artisan Foods **936**......Breakfast	
Nicky's Coal Fired **936**.........Wish I'd opened	

EDUARD XATRUCH
Disfrutar
Villarroel 163, Barcelona

Former head chef at elBulli who, alongside fellow Adrià disciples Mateu Casañas and Oriol Castro, opened the more informal Compartir in Cadaqués in 2012, and Barcelona's more avant-garde Disfrutar, in 2016.

Alkimia **595**......................High end	
Esportell del Bou **584**....Regular neighborhood	
Gaig **597**......................Local favorite	
Moritz **598**......................Late night	
Mugaritz **576**.................Worth the travel	
Pinotxo **602**......................Breakfast	
Porvenir **599**......................Bargain	
Rías de Galicia **601**.............Wish I'd opened	
Sergi de Meià **599**......Regular neighborhood	
La Taverna del Clínic **600**.........Local favorite	
El Velódromo **600**......................Late night	

LONG XIONG
Le Blanc
183 Daan Road, Taipei

Boston born, he has cooked at Per Se, Adour Alain Ducasse, and Del Posto, and staged at Noma, followed by a quick stint in Norway at Lysverket. He has since opened his own restaurant in Taiwan, Le Blanc.

L'ATELIER de Joël Robuchon **206**......High end	
Elixir Health Pot **207**.....Regular neighborhood	
Lin Dong Fang Beef Noodles **208**.....Late night	
Lin Dong Fang beef noodles **208**Local favorite	
Mazendo **203**......................Bargain	
MUME **203**......................Regular neighborhood	
Olmsted **1018**.................Worth the travel	
S.T.A.Y **206**......................High end	
SPOT Taipei **204**......................Breakfast	
Tian Jin Flaky Scallion Pancake **204**...Bargain	
Totto Ramen **204**......................Wish I'd opened	

CHAN YAN TAK
Lung King Heen
8 Finance Street, Hong Kong

Yan Tak, who is the first ever Chinese chef to be awarded three Michelin stars, is now the executive chef of the Regent Hong Kong.

Hong Shun Mutton Soup **190**.Worth the travel	
Kam Wah Cafe **230**......................Local favorite	
Premium Beef Hotpot Restaurant **212**.....Late night	
Siu Choi Wong **213**.......Regular neighborhood	
Sushi Tokami **215**......................High end	
Tim Ho Wan **213**......................Bargain	

KRIS YENBAMROONG
Night + Market Song
3322 West Sunset Boulevard, Los Angeles

A self-taught chef, he grew up working in his family's restaurant, Talesai, before opening the doors to his Thai restaurant, Night + Market.

Aburiya Raku **824**......Regular neighborhood	
Al & Bea's Mexican Food **811**.............Bargain	
Baroo **817**......................Local favorite	
Café Altro Paradiso **1012**......Worth the travel	
CUT **810**......................High end	
Phoenix Inn Chinese Cuisine **812**....Late night	
Rae's **823**......................Breakfast	
Sotto **821**......................Wish I'd opened	
Sotto **821**......................Regular neighborhood	

JUNGSIK YIM
Jungsik
2 Harrison Street, New York City

Yim left the army to take on apprenticeships at leading New York restaurants Aquavit, Bouley, and Spanish Akelarre. He now runs branches of Jungsik in Seoul and New York City.

Hadongkwan **238**.........Regular neighborhood	
Hadongkwan **238**......................Breakfast	
Kkanbu **238**......................Late night	
Mapo Mandu **239**......................Bargain	
Ultraviolet **196**.................Worth the travel	
Yangchonri Jeongyukjeom **239**...Local favorite	
La Yeon **238**......................High end	

HAJIME YONEDA
Hajime
9-11-1 Edobori, Osaka

An Osaka-born former electrical engineer whose restaurant Hajime won three Michelin stars just one year after opening.

Ciucate **251**......................................Late night
DEN **268**...............................Worth the travel
Honkogetsu **251**......................Local favorite
Kadoya Shokudo **252**.......................Bargain
Mizai **247**..High end
NORTHSHORE **252**.......................Breakfast
Pasania **252**................Regular neighborhood

TONY YOO
DOOREYOO
16-12 Gahoe-dong, Seoul

Yoo left behind his career as a designer to pursue his passion for food.

Acha-san Grandfather Tofu House **237**..Bargain
Blue Hill at Stone Barns **913**..Worth the travel
Doorei **237**...........................Local favorite
Epicure **558**..High end
Mingles **235**..............Regular neighborhood
Miro Sikdang **239**..........................Late night
The Parkview **238**..........................Breakfast
Senia **799**........................Wish I'd opened

ALEX YOUNG
Zingerman's Roadhouse
2501 Jackson Ave, Ann Arbor

Born in London, he moved to California with his family when he was seventeen. Currently serving up his particular style of Southern Comfort food at Zingerman's.

The Halal Guys **1040**........................Late night
Primo **1039**...........................Wish I'd opened

JOWETT YU
Ho Lee Fook
1-5 Elgin Street, Hong Kong

Born in Taiwan and raised in Canada, he apprenticed at Tetsuya's in Australia before moving to Hong Kong to set up his own shop, the name of which translates as "good fortune for your mouth".

Belon **220**..High end
Burnt Ends **329**.....................Worth the travel
Hing Kee Restaurant **214**...............Late night
Islam Food **212**.................................Bargain
Kwan Kee Claypot Rice **227**...............Bargain
Lung King Heen **223**....................Local favorite
Lyle's **448**..........................Worth the travel
Paradise of King Asia Seafood **219**..Late night
RōNIN **229**..High end
Samsen **230**..........................Wish I'd opened
Sun Hing Restaurant **226**.................Breakfast
Yan Toh Heen **215**.....................Local favorite
Yat Lok **226**.................Regular neighborhood

ROMAN ZAŠTŠERINSKI
Kohvik Moon
Võrgu 3, Tallinn

Former chef de cuisine at Tallinn's Restoran Ö, this Russian chef and his wife Jana opened fine-dining destination Kohvik Moon in 2010, with Igor Andrejev sharing kitchen duties.

Art Priori **696**....................................High end
Burger Box **696**..................................Bargain
Fabrik **697**...............Regular neighborhood
Klaus **698**..Breakfast
Leib Resto ja Aed **698**..Regular neighborhood
Manna La Roosa **698**.......................Late night
Noa Restaurant **698**.........................Late night
Põhjaka mõis **696**.................Wish I'd opened
Sfäär Resto **699**.............................Breakfast
Tchaikovsky **699**.....................Local favorite
Tian **684**............................Worth the travel

ANDREY ZHDANOV
AQ Kitchen
Bolshaya Gruzinskaya 69, Moscow

He began his culinary career in early 2000 as a line cook and worked his way up to now be a head chef of four restaurants: AQ Kitchen, ADRI, AQ Chicken, and The Sad.

Adrian Quetglas **574**.............Worth the travel
Farsh **712**...Bargain
Grand Cru **708**.............Regular neighborhood
Heart **574**.......................Wish I'd opened
Lao Lee Café **712**.........Regular neighborhood
LavkaLavka **712**........................Local favorite
Mugaritz **576**....................................High end
SAVVA **713**.......................................Breakfast
Torro Grill **713**...............................Late night

ANDREW ZIMMERMAN
Sepia
123 North Jefferson Street, Chicago

A musician turned culinary maestro, Zimmerman trained in New York, then headed to Chicago, taking up the reins at Sepia, renowned for its inventive American cuisine, in 2009.

avec **965**..Late night
Ba Le **965**...Bargain
Blackbird **966**.........................Local favorite
Dove's Luncheonette **969**...................Regular neighborhood
High Five Ramen **962**......................Late night
Lula Cafe **959**.................................Breakfast
Oriole **967**......................................High end
Rangoli **970**..................Regular neighborhood
Schwa **970**.........................Wish I'd opened
SPQR **833**...................Worth the travel

JOCK ZONFRILLO
Orana
285 Rundle Street, Adelaide

Scottish-born Zonfrillo worked his way up the ranks in London and, seduced by an antipodean sabbatical, settled in Adelaide, launching Orana and Street ADL in 2013, both of which showcase Australia's indigenous ingredients.

La Buvette **91**..................................Late night
Gin Long Canteen **90**....Regular neighborhood
Hey Jupiter **90**.............................Breakfast
Inver Restaurant **496**...........Worth the travel
Juniper & Pine **91**...........................Breakfast
Lost in a Forest **96**...................Local favorite
Osteria Oggi **92**.................Wish I'd opened
Pink Moon Saloon **93**.....................Late night
Restaurant Blackwood **93**.........Local favorite
The Summertown Aristologist **96**........Regular neighborhood
Sunnys Shop **94**................................Bargain
Timberyard **497**...................Worth the travel

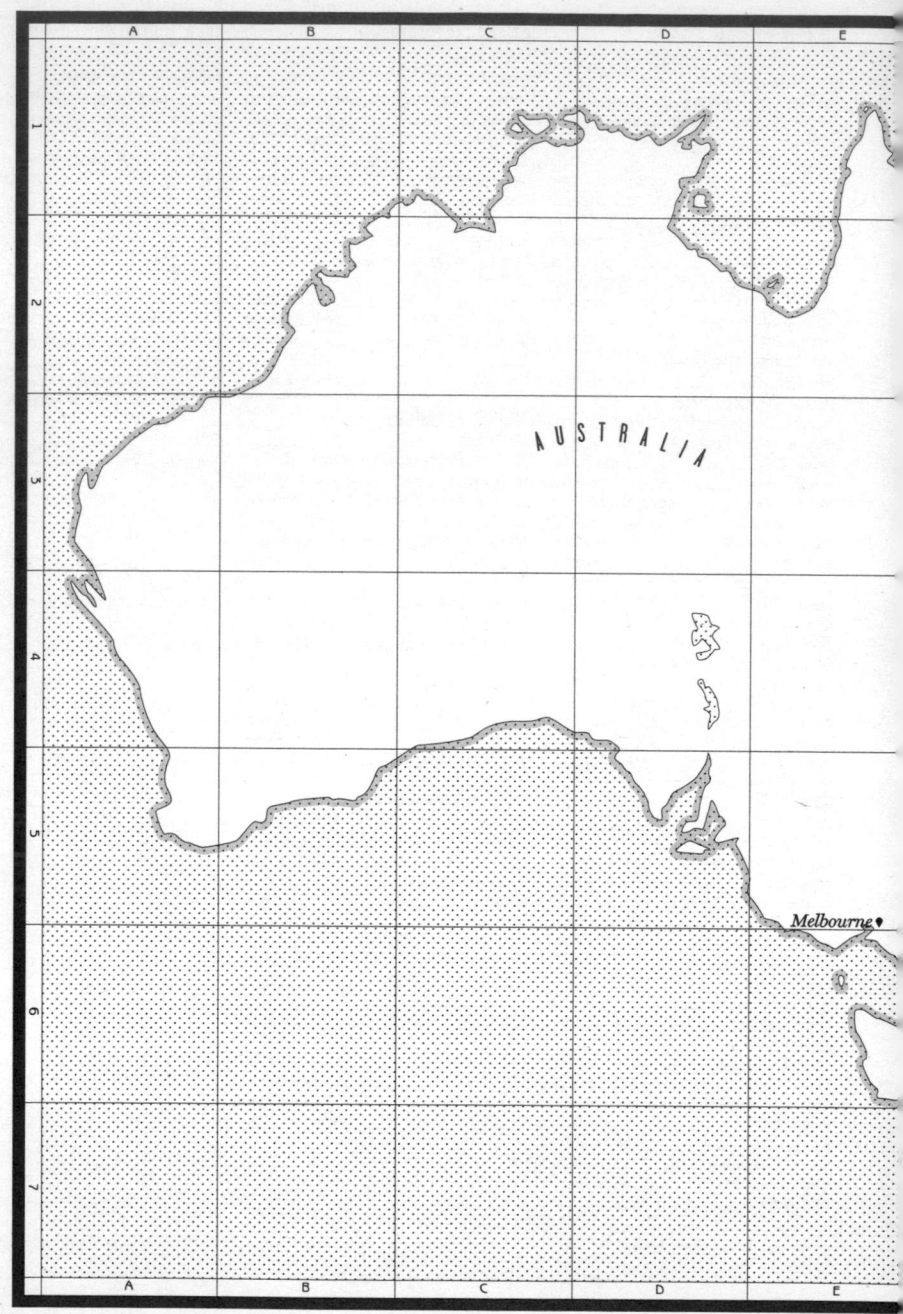

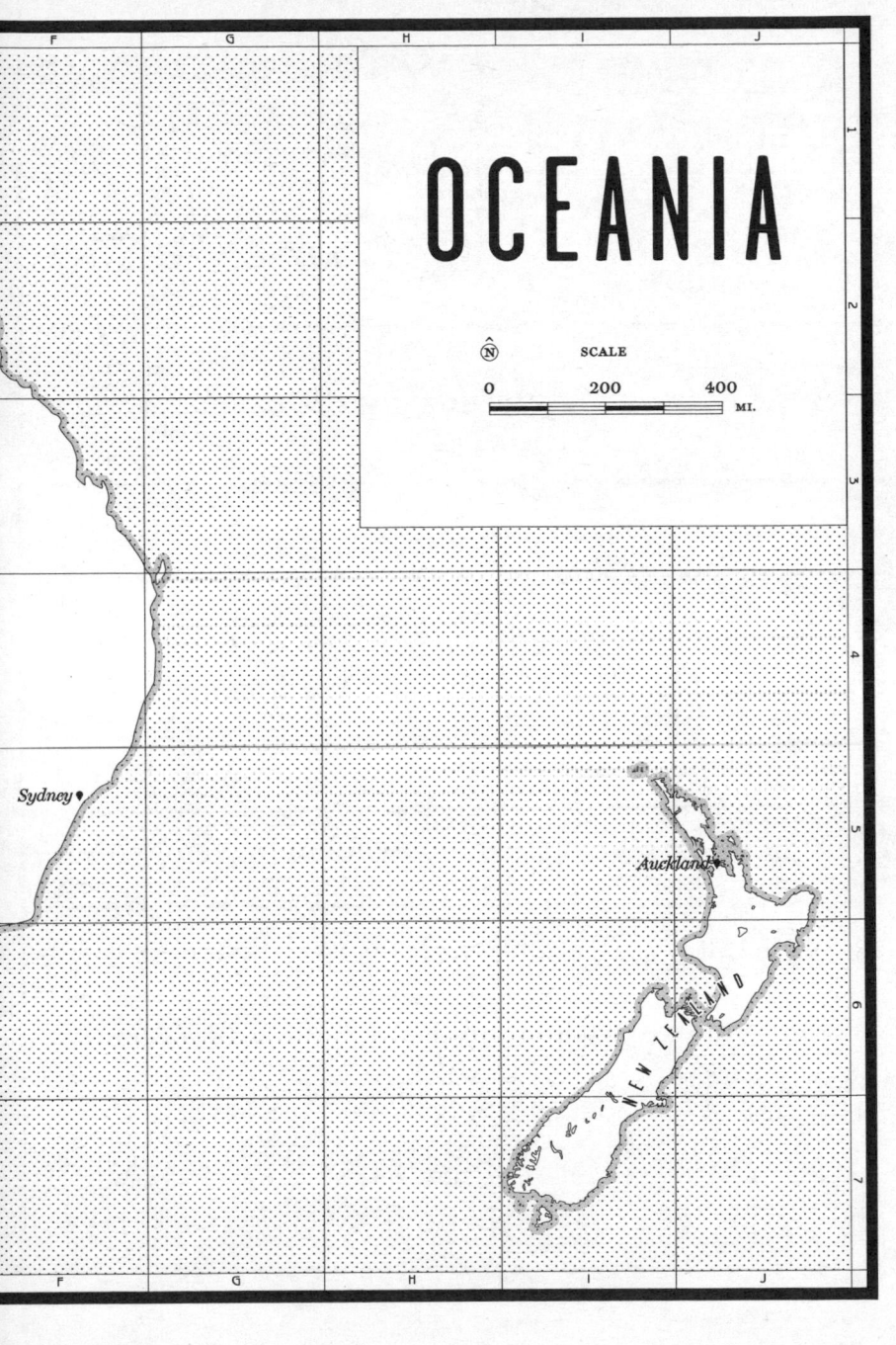

OCEANIA

Sydney

Auckland

NEW ZEALAND

"GREAT TAPAS
AND EVEN
BETTER WINE!
LOVE, LOVE,
LOVE IT!"
GEOFF LINDSAY P144

"Their
dedication
to native
ingredients is
unrivalled in
Australia."
RYAN SESSIONS P93

"Great views. Sexy chefs."
MATTHEW BREEN P97

AUSTRALIA

"The food is impeccable yet unpretentious and fun."
BEN BATTERBURY P152

"IT IS THE MOST PERSONABLE,
JOYOUS, PROFESSIONAL, AND
DELICIOUS DINING EXPERIENCE
I HAVE EVER HAD."
BEN DEVLIN P82

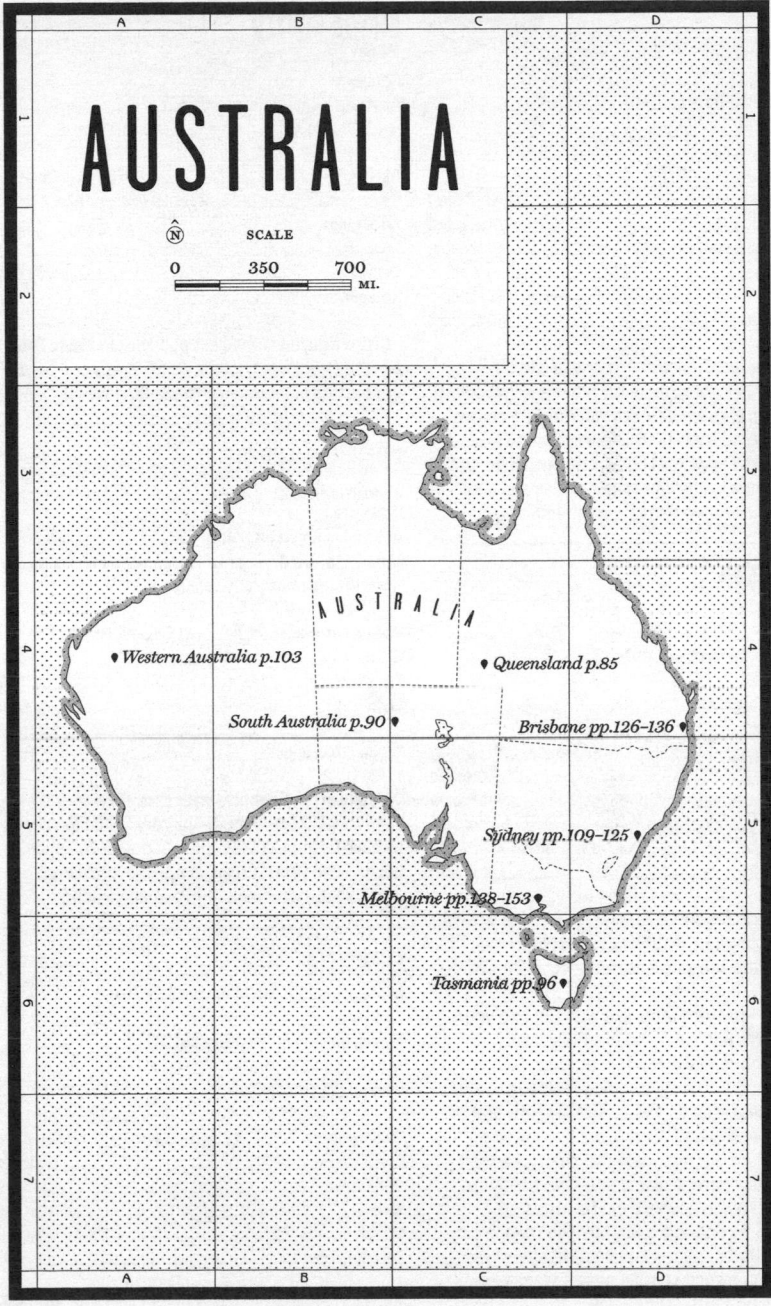

AUSTRALIA

N̂

SCALE

0   350   700
MI.

AUSTRALIA

A. BAKER

Recommended by
Sean McConnell

15 Edinburgh Avenue
Canberra
Australian Capital Territory 2601
+61 262876150
www.abaker.com.au

Opening hours	Open 7 days
Credit cards	Accepted
Price range	Affordable
Style	Casual
Cuisine	Modern Australian
Recommended for	Breakfast

"Head chef Bernd Brademann is one of the city's finest chefs. I like going there for breakfast and sitting in the courtyard, so my kids can run riot. The coffee is killer but Bernd's food is the real reason to head there. The baked eggs with nduja is my usual go-to but the smoked pork broth with soba noodles and slow cooked eggs is also up there."—Sean McConnell

BAR ROCHFORD

Recommended by
Pasquale Trimboli,
Ben Willis

65 London Circuit
Canberra
Australian Capital Territory 2601
+61 262306222
www.barrochford.com

Opening hours	Closed Monday and Sunday
Credit cards	Accepted
Price range	Affordable
Style	Smart casual
Cuisine	Bar-Modern Australian
Recommended for	Late night

"Great for cocktails and natural wine. A menu of local and seasonal produce that hits the spot between grazing bar food and substantial dinner."—Ben Willis

Entering Bar Rochford feels like walking into your coolest friend's home—familiar, warm, and just shabby enough to make you feel at ease. Set upstairs in Canberra's ramshackle Melbourne building, it embraces its 1920s architecture and adds to it by borrowing decor from subsequent decades for just the right balance. They take their drinks seriously here, evidenced by the extensive wine and cocktail list, where old favorites sit alongside twists on the traditional. The food, from a constantly updated menu, belies the size of the kitchen with the small sharing plates alone enough to tempt you up those stairs.

BISTRO NGUYEN

Recommended by
Sean McConnell

78–80 Alinga Street
Canberra
Australian Capital Territory 2601
+61 262626888

Opening hours	Open 7 days
Credit cards	Accepted but not AMEX or Diners
Price range	Budget
Style	Casual
Cuisine	Vietnamese
Recommended for	Bargain

"Bistro Nguyen is the best pho joint in town. Their *bún bò Huế* (spicy beef noodle soup) is as good as you'll get outside of Vietnam."—Sean McConnell

CHAIRMAN AND YIP

Recommended by
Pasquale Trimboli

1 Burbury Close
Canberra
Australian Capital Territory 2600
+61 261621220
www.thechairmangroup.com.au

Opening hours	Closed Monday and Sunday
Credit cards	Accepted
Price range	Affordable
Style	Smart casual
Cuisine	Cantonese
Recommended for	High end

"A stalwart in Canberra with slick service and traditional Chinese food, Chairman and Yip seems to have been at the top of its game for the past twenty-two years. Clean, simple flavors paired with exotic ingredients."—Pasquale Trimboli

EIGHTYSIX

Recommended by
Pasquale Trimboli

Mode 3, Elouera Street & Lonsdale Street
Canberra
Australian Capital Territory 2612
+61 261618686
www.eightysix.com.au

Opening hours	Open 7 days
Credit cards	Accepted
Price range	Affordable
Style	Smart casual
Cuisine	Modern Australian
Recommended for	Bargain

"A smart and casual place that delivers on all fronts. You can drop in for a quick glass of wine or a cocktail, or stay for an all-night feed."—Pasquale Trimboli

GREASE MONKEY BURGERS

Recommended by
Ben Willis

19 Lonsdale Street
Canberra
Australian Capital Territory 2612
+61 261741401
www.greasys.com.au

Opening hours	Open 7 days
Credit cards	Accepted
Price range	Budget
Style	Casual
Cuisine	Burgers
Recommended for	Bargain

"Canberra's best burgers."—Ben Willis

IPHO

Recommended by
Ben Willis

Garema Place
66–68 Bunda Street
Canberra
Australian Capital Territory 2601
+61 406776888
www.ipho.net.au

Opening hours	Open 7 days
Credit cards	Accepted but not AMEX or Diners
Price range	Budget
Style	Casual
Cuisine	Pho
Recommended for	Bargain

"Right around the corner from one of my restaurants I can get a fast, cheap bowl of beef pho that is fresh and light but filling and delicious."—Ben Willis

MONSTER

Recommended by
Pasquale Trimboli,
Ben Willis

Hotel Hotel
25 Edinburgh Avenue
Canberra
Australian Capital Territory 2601
+61 262876287
www.monsterkitchen.com.au

Opening hours	Open 7 days
Credit cards	Accepted but not Diners
Price range	Affordable
Style	Casual
Cuisine	Modern Australian
Recommended for	Wish I'd opened

"They are simply a 'Monster'. The food is fantastic and the dining room is a joy to be part of. Truly a great precinct with amazing architecture."
—Pasquale Trimboli

Monster prides itself on being a little bit different and that's evident from the moment you step in and find you'll be dining in a hotel foyer. But there are nooks and crannies aplenty, shared tables and more intimate spaces, and a central fireplace for those craving a ski lodge experience. Somehow, Monster finds a way to be all things to all people, and this carries through to Sean McConnell's food. Depending on who you speak to, Monster is a favorite breakfast hang, a wonderful place to grab a cheap lunch, a special occasion dinner venue, or a great bar with snacks. The "yabby jaffle"— a toasted sandwich of cheese, horseradish, crème fraîche, and yabby (a species of crayfish)—has been known to lure people into making the three-hour drive from Sydney all on its own.

SILO BAKERY

Recommended by
Pasquale Trimboli,
Ben Willis

36 Giles Street
Kingston
Canberra
Australian Capital Territory 2604
+61 262606060
www.silobakery.com.au

Opening hours	Closed Monday and Sunday
Credit cards	Accepted
Price range	Budget
Style	Casual
Cuisine	Bakery
Recommended for	Local favorite

"A Canberra institution. By far the best bread and pastries in Canberra and people travel some distance to get hold of them. Interesting café food that goes beyond the standard fare."—Ben Willis

XO

Recommended by
Sean McConnell,
Ben Willis

16 Iluka Street
Narrabundah
Canberra
Australian Capital Territory 2604
www.xo-restaurant.com.au

Opening hours	Closed Sunday
Credit cards	Accepted
Price range	Affordable
Style	Casual
Cuisine	Modern Southeast Asian
Recommended for	Regular neighborhood

"Casual vibe with solid cooking and bold flavors. Great staff enjoying themselves makes for a fun time."
—Ben Willis

ZAAB STREET FOOD

Recommended by
Sean McConnell

9 Lonsdale Street
Braddon
Canberra
Australian Capital Territory 2612
+61 261565638
www.zaabstreetfood.com.au

Opening hours	Open 7 days
Credit cards	Accepted but not Diners
Price range	Affordable
Style	Casual
Cuisine	Lao-Thai
Recommended for	Late night

AUBERGINE

Recommended by
Sean McConnell

18 Barker Street
Griffith
Australian Capital Territory 2603
+61 262608666
www.aubergine.com.au

Opening hours	Closed Sunday
Credit cards	Accepted
Price range	Affordable
Style	Smart casual
Cuisine	Modern Australian
Recommended for	Local favorite

"Aubergine is without doubt the best restaurant in the Australian Capital Territory. Ben's food just get's better and better, as does the service. Skilful cooking combined with locally sourced ingredients, a true representation of the Canberra region."
—Sean McConnell

ONA MANUKA

Recommended by
Ben Willis

4 Palmerston Lane
Griffith
Australian Capital Territory 2603
+61 262950057
www.onacoffee.com.au

Opening hours	Open 7 days
Reservation policy	No
Credit cards	Accepted but not Diners
Price range	Affordable
Style	Casual
Cuisine	Café
Recommended for	Breakfast

"Great coffee by a team that includes a world barista champion. Always interesting coffees and really good food. A solid local."—Ben Willis

FLEET

Recommended by
Danielle Alvarez, Matthew Breen,
Ben Devlin, Christine Manfield,
Cameron Matthews,
Justin North,
Ben Russell

2/16 The Terrace
Brunswick Heads
New South Wales 2483
+61 266851363
www.fleet-restaurant.com.au

Opening hours	Closed Tuesday and Wednesday
Credit cards	Accepted but not Diners
Price range	Affordable
Style	Smart casual
Cuisine	Modern Australian
Recommended for	Worth the travel

"This is a restaurant masquerading as a wine bar. The staff are connected personally to their suppliers, and to their guests. There is just one chef, one waitress, and one bartender. It is the most personable, joyous, professional, and delicious dining experience I have ever had."—Ben Devlin

Fleet is a master of minimalism, with seating for just twenty-two (if the weather's good —fourteen if it's not), a tightly curated wine list and a staff of four. Astrid McCormack and Josh Lewis, formerly co-owner/manager and sous-chef respectively at the now-defunct Loam in Victoria, have used their experience to create a place that, despite its bijou size, over-delivers on food, wine, service, and all-round X-factor. Lewis cooks an arm's length away from the communal table, crafting a series of concisely scribed dishes ("chicken hearts, corn, bullhorn peppers", "bonito, tuna head, egg yolk, lemon, sorrel") that surprise and intrigue; they're edgy, market-dependent, and bursting with flair and originality.

YAMI

Recommended by
Josh Lewis

2/1 Park Street
Brunswick Heads
New South Wales 2483
+61 266850186
www.yami.com.au

Opening hours	Open 7 days
Credit cards	Not accepted
Price range	Budget
Style	Casual
Cuisine	Middle Eastern-Vegetarian
Recommended for	Local favorite

"It's an institution here in Bruns—a hole-in-the-wall Middle Eastern vegetarian that turns out a wholly satisfying meal. Our menu favorite is the falafel pocket with extra chile: it's fresh, tasty, and you can eat it one-handed!"—Josh Lewis

100 MILE TABLE

Recommended by
Ben Devlin

4/8 Banksia Drive
Byron Bay
New South Wales 2481
www.100miletable.com

Opening hours	Closed Monday
Credit cards	Accepted
Price range	Affordable
Style	Casual
Cuisine	Café
Recommended for	Local favorite

THE NOMADIC KITCHEN

Recommended by
Josh Lewis

11 Inderwong Avenue
Ocean Shores
Byron Bay
New South Wales 2483
+61 405295012
www.thenomadickitchen.tumblr.com

Opening hours	Variable
Reservation policy	No
Credit cards	Not accepted
Price range	Budget
Style	Casual
Cuisine	Sicilian-Australian
Recommended for	Regular neighborhood

"It's not so much a restaurant as a weekly, roving pop-up at the region's farmers' markets. Rob, who previously worked at the River Café, cooks a fantastic Sicilian-inspired breakfast three times a week at the Byron Bay, Mullumbimby, and New Brighton markets. The menu is completely produce driven, bought from the stall holders and is available until sold out. Him and his sister Michelle, who bakes killer cakes and tarts, have developed a loyal following so you need to be quick!"—Josh Lewis

PAPER DAISY

Recommended by
Cameron Matthews,
Ben Russell

21 Cypress Cresent
Cabarita Beach
New South Wales 2488
+61 266761444
www.halcyonhouse.com.au

Opening hours	Open 7 days
Credit cards	Accepted
Price range	Expensive
Style	Smart casual
Cuisine	Modern Australian
Recommended for	High end

COTTAGE POINT INN

Recommended by
Uwe Opocensky

2 Anderson Place
Cottage Point
New South Wales 2084
+65 294561011
www.cottagepointinn.com.au

Opening hours	Closed Tuesday
Credit cards	Accepted
Price range	Expensive
Style	Smart casual
Cuisine	Australian
Recommended for	Wish I'd opened

DOMA CAFÉ

Recommended by
Josh Lewis

3–6 Albert Street
Federal
New South Wales 2480
+61 266884711

Opening hours	Closed Wednesday
Reservation policy	No
Credit cards	Accepted
Price range	Budget
Style	Casual
Cuisine	Japanese Fusion
Recommended for	Regular neighborhood

"Little Japanese café in the hills behind Byron Bay —situated in the town of Federal which consists of just a general store, a post office, and this café! Really simple, fresh produce. You can sit outside on the big picnic tables, take a bottle of wine, and just enjoy the sun."—Josh Lewis

BERNIE'S DINER

Recommended by
James Viles

402–404 Argyle Street
Moss Vale
New South Wales 2577
+61 248691502
www.berniesdiner.com.au

Opening hours	Open 7 days
Reservation policy	No
Credit cards	Accepted but not AMEX or Diners
Price range	Affordable
Style	Casual
Cuisine	American Diner
Recommended for	Bargain

"Try the house-made warm pastrami sandwich on caraway rye and onion rings in beer batter."
—James Viles

MILK AND HONEY

Recommended by
Ben Devlin,
Josh Lewis

5/59a Station Street
Mullumbimby
New South Wales 2482
+61 266841422
www.milkandhoneymullumbimby.com.au

Opening hours	Closed Monday and Sunday
Credit cards	Accepted but not AMEX or Diners
Price range	Affordable
Style	Casual
Cuisine	Italian
Recommended for	Regular neighborhood

"Small neighborhood pizza place with a complete lack of pretension. Timmy, the chef and owner, spent a large part of his career in fine dining, so applies principles of care to what he does. He raises his own pigs, grows his own pumpkins, and ferments his dough for six days, so it's tart and chewy. Bloody delicious. You can't beat it for a relaxed night."—Ben Devlin

HARVEST CAFÉ NEWRYBAR

Recommended by
Ben Devlin

18–22 Old Pacific Highway
Newrybar
New South Wales 2479
+61 266872644
www.harvestnewrybar.com.au

Opening hours	Open 7 days
Credit cards	Accepted but not Diners
Price range	Affordable
Style	Smart casual
Cuisine	Modern Australian
Recommended for	Breakfast

IZAKAYA POTTS

Recommended by
Ben Devlin

5/18 Philip Street
Pottsville
New South Wales 2489
+61 266762554

Opening hours	Closed Sunday to Tuesday
Credit cards	Accepted but not AMEX or Diners
Price range	Budget
Style	Casual
Cuisine	Japanese
Recommended for	Regular neighborhood

"Very small neighborhood Japanese restaurant, run by a bunch of Japanese surfers. Well made, friendly food."—Ben Devlin

THE SHOP

Recommended by
Josh Lewis

19 Beach Avenue
South Golden Beach
New South Wales 2483
+61 266802843

Opening hours	Open 7 days
Reservation policy	No
Credit cards	Not accepted
Price range	Budget
Style	Casual
Cuisine	Deli
Recommended for	Bargain

"If you are in the Northern Rivers you must have a fish burger from the South Golden Beach Shop. Just a hop, skip, and a jump from the beach—part pizza shop, part fish and chip, part deli, it is an absolute hidden gem. When the spanish mackerel are around, you simply cannot beat the fish burger. Ask for it grilled. The piece of fish is well cooked, incredibly generous in size and paired simply with fresh, mayo-laden coleslaw on a buttered bun. Awesome. And at A\$12 (\$9; £7) it epitomises the term 'bargain'." —Josh Lewis

SYDNEY: SEE PAGES 109-125

BEACHWOOD CAFÉ

Recommended by
Josh Lewis

22 High Street
Yamba
New South Wales 2464
+61 266469781
www.beachwoodcafé.com.au

Opening hours	Closed Monday
Credit cards	Not accepted
Price range	Affordable
Style	Casual
Cuisine	Turkish
Recommended for	Local favorite

"It's very hard to sum up our region in one restaurant; there is so much diversity, both in terms of produce and people. One of our favorites though, is Beachwood. It's a bit further afield, south of us in Yamba. A tiny café run by Sevtap Yuce, a passionate, vivacious chef. With just six tables outside, a chalkboard menu and a choice of one white, rosé or red, it is the perfect antidote to a busy week. Her menu is produce-driven with a big emphasis on seafood. When the sardines are on the menu you can't beat them."—Josh Lewis

BRISBANE: SEE PAGES 126–136

THE FISH HOUSE

Recommended by
Ben Russell

50 Goodwin Terace
Burleigh Heads
Queensland 4220
+61 755357725
www.thefishhouse.com.au

Opening hours	Closed Monday
Credit cards	Accepted
Price range	Expensive
Style	Smart casual
Cuisine	Seafood
Recommended for	Worth the travel

RICK SHORES

Recommended by
Cameron Matthews

3/43 Goodwin Terrace
Burleigh Heads
Queensland 4220
+61 756306611
www.rickshores.com.au

Opening hours	Closed Monday
Credit cards	Accepted
Price range	Affordable
Style	Casual
Cuisine	Modern Australian
Recommended for	Wish I'd opened

GANBARANBA NOODLE COLOSSEUM

Recommended by
Nick Holloway

12/20 Spence Street
Cairns
Queensland 4870
+61 740312522

Opening hours	Open 7 days
Reservation policy	No
Credit cards	Accepted but not AMEX or Diners
Price range	Affordable
Style	Casual
Cuisine	Ramen
Recommended for	Bargain

"Fast, dependable, delicious."—Nick Holloway

The name may suggest something far grander but the traditional "*Irasshaimase!*" ("Come in!") welcome at this authentic and hugely popular Japanese hole-in-the-wall couldn't be louder or warmer. Sit at one of the handful of tables or perch at the bar overlooking the fast and furious open kitchen while slurping a generous bowl of ramen.

Perfectly springy and cooked to the diner's preference (firm, medium, or soft), they come in full-flavored, slow-simmered pork *tonkotsu* (pork broth) or chicken *torigara* broth, garnished with tender slices of pork or chicken, seaweed, and a just-cooked egg. Noodle refills for just A$1.50 ($1; £1), complimentary soy sauce and a bottomless jug of cold, sweet tea make it exceptional value.

O'CHA CHA JAPANESE DINNER & TEA

Recommended by
Nick Holloway

34 Lake Street
Cairns
Queensland 4870
+61 740517055
www.dimmi.com.au

Opening hours	Closed Monday and Sunday
Credit cards	Accepted
Price range	Affordable
Style	Casual
Cuisine	Japanese
Recommended for	Regular neighborhood

PHO VIET

Recommended by
Nick Holloway

5/78 Abbot Street
Cairns
Queensland 4870
+61 740521128
www.phovietvietnamesenoodlebar.com.au

Opening hours	Open 7 days
Credit cards	Accepted
Price range	Budget
Style	Casual
Cuisine	Pho
Recommended for	Breakfast

RUSTY'S MARKET

Recommended by
Nick Holloway

57–89 Grafton Street
Cairns
Queensland 4870
+61 740402705
www.rustysmarkets.com.au

Opening hours	Closed Monday to Thursday
Reservation policy	No
Credit cards	Not accepted
Price range	Affordable
Style	Casual
Cuisine	Market
Recommended for	Breakfast

"Rusty's Market is a thriving tropical community hub—the smells, the noise, the amazing produce, and the banh mi down the back are ridiculously good."
—Nick Holloway

EDDIES GRUB HOUSE

Recommended by
Ben Devlin

171 Griffith Street
Coolangatta
Queensland 4225
+61 755992177
www.eddiesgrubhouse.com

Opening hours	Closed Monday
Reservation policy	No
Credit cards	Accepted
Price range	Budget
Style	Casual
Cuisine	Diner
Recommended for	Bargain

"A dive bar with burgers and beers."—Ben Devlin

THE TAMARIND

Recommended by
Cameron Matthews

88 Obi Lane South
Maleny
Queensland 4552
+61 1300311429
www.spicersretreats.com

Opening hours	Closed Monday
Credit cards	Accepted
Price range	Expensive
Style	Casual
Cuisine	Modern Asian
Recommended for	Local favorite

LITTLE MAY ESPRESSO

Recommended by
Cameron Matthews

174 Main Street
Montville
Queensland 4560
+61 754785015
www.littlemayespresso.com

Opening hours	Open 7 days
Credit cards	Accepted but not AMEX or Diners
Price range	Affordable
Style	Casual
Cuisine	Modern Australian
Recommended for	Breakfast

"It's easy to miss if you pass by, but this is a great little café with interesting and innovative food. The service is always exceptional and the food is delicious."
—Cameron Matthews

The venue may be small and the menu concise, but the food at this popular café, run by former fine-dining sous chef Rich Hayes, punches well above its weight. Simple and super fresh, almost everything comes from within the verdant local region or is made in-house, including their own hot chocolate powder, jam, and a tempting range of cakes and tarts. There's an organic focus at breakfast with eggs from "nomadic" chickens and organic sourdough and muesli. Their house blend coffee is served in a myriad of ways, including cold drip. Warm service exemplified by Haye's wife Hannah seals the deal and secures Little May's status as a local favorite.

SPICERS CLOVELLY ESTATE

Recommended by
Shannon Kellam

38–68 Balmoral Road
Montville
Queensland 4560
+61 375452111
www.spicersretreats.com/spicers-clovelly-estate

Opening hours	Closed Sunday
Credit cards	Accepted
Price range	Expensive
Style	Smart casual
Cuisine	Modern Australian
Recommended for	Local favorite

"Queensland hinterland and scenery, mixed with innovative cooking and fresh produce—makes for a serene experience."—Shannon Kellam

EMBASSY XO

Recommended by
Cameron Matthews

Corner of Duke Street & Bryan Street
Sunshine Beach
Noosa
Queensland 4567
+61 754554460
www.embassyxo.com.au

Opening hours	Closed Monday and Tuesday
Credit cards	Accepted
Price range	Affordable
Style	Casual
Cuisine	Asian-Australian
Recommended for	Local favorite

NOOSA HOT BREAD SHOP

Recommended by
Danielle Gjestland

60 Hastings Street
Noosa Heads
Noosa
Queensland 4567
+61 754480959
www.noosahotbreadshop.com

Opening hours	Open 7 days
Credit cards	Accepted but not AMEX or Diners
Price range	Budget
Style	Casual
Cuisine	Bakery-Patisserie
Recommended for	Breakfast

"Perfect place to pick up great bread, croissants, pastry, and nutella-filled *bomboloni* (Italian doughnuts). Add a coffee and cross the street to Main Beach to watch the waves roll in."—Danielle Gjestland

NOOSA WATERFRONT RESTAURANT

Recommended by
Cameron Matthews

142 Gympie Terrace
Noosaville
Noosa
Queensland 4566
+61 754744444
www.noosawaterfrontrestaurant.com.au

Opening hours	Open 7 days
Credit cards	Accepted
Price range	Expensive
Style	Smart casual
Cuisine	Italian
Recommended for	Local favorite

SAILS RESTAURANT

Recommended by
Danielle Gjestland

75 Hastings Street
Noosa Heads
Noosa
Queensland 4567
+61 754474235
www.sailsnoosa.com.au

Opening hours	Open 7 days
Credit cards	Accepted but not Diners
Price range	Affordable
Style	Casual
Cuisine	Modern Australian
Recommended for	Local favorite

"Perfect beachfront location for a long, lazy lunch of simply prepared seafood, watching the beach-goers' antics."—Danielle Gjestland

SEASON

Recommended by
Cameron Matthews

25 Hastings Street
Noosa Heads
Noosa
Queensland 4567
+61 754473747
www.seasonrestaurant.com.au

Opening hours	Open 7 days
Credit cards	Accepted
Price range	Affordable
Style	Smart casual
Cuisine	Modern Australian
Recommended for	Regular neighborhood

THOMAS CORNER EATERY

Recommended by
Cameron Matthews

Shop1, 201 Gympie Terrace
Noosaville
Noosa
Queensland 4566
+61 754702224
www.thomascorner.com.au

Opening hours	Open 7 days
Credit cards	Accepted but not AMEX or Diners
Price range	Affordable
Style	Casual
Cuisine	Australian
Recommended for	Breakfast

"You can always be assured that owner and chef David Rayner will create inspired dishes where he allows the freshest local produce to shine."—Cameron Matthews

Before the word "locavore" had even been coined, chef David Rayner was passionate about supporting the farmers and producers who inhabit the verdant hinterland of the Sunshine Coast. In his modern, leafy, open-plan restaurant, with expansive views across the serene Noosa River, Rayner still sticks to his ethos of minimal intervention to give those local ingredients center stage. The menu speaks intimately of the region with a natural focus on seafood, local fish, spanner crab, scallops, and more. The accommodating wine list offers Australian, New Zealand, and European wines in four different sized pours but also offers BYO.

VILLAGE BICYCLE

Recommended by
Danielle Gjestland

6/16 Sunshine Beach Road
Noosa Heads
Noosa
Queensland 4567
+61 754745343

Opening hours	Open 7 days
Credit cards	Accepted but not AMEX
Price range	Affordable
Style	Casual
Cuisine	American
Recommended for	Regular neighborhood

"Noosa's best bar scene. Tasty, well-made burgers and tacos. Every neighborhood needs one."
—Danielle Gjestland

WASABI

Recommended by
Cameron Matthews

2 Quamby Place
Noosa Heads
Noosa
Queensland 4567
+61 754492443
www.wasabisb.com

Opening hours	Closed Monday and Tuesday
Credit cards	Accepted but not Diners
Price range	Expensive
Style	Smart casual
Cuisine	Modern Japanese
Recommended for	Local favorite

"Wasabi own a farm where they grow most of their own produce, which is watered by natural springs and grown with integrity. The dishes are exquisitely presented, the view over the river is serene, and service is impeccable."—Cameron Matthews

VIVO

Recommended by
Nick Holloway

49 Williams Esplanade
Palm Cove
Queensland 4879
+61 740590944
www.vivo.com.au

Opening hours	Open 7 days
Credit cards	Accepted
Price range	Affordable
Style	Smart casual
Cuisine	Modern Australian
Recommended for	Local favorite

RENAE'S PANTRY

Recommended by
Cameron Matthews

5 The Lane
4–6 Main Street
Palmwoods
Queensland 4555
+61 754573347
www.renaespantry.com.au

Opening hours	Closed Monday and Sunday
Reservation policy	No
Credit cards	Accepted but not Amex or Diners
Price range	Budget
Style	Casual
Cuisine	Grocery-Café
Recommended for	Regular neighborhood

"Always a safe bet for a quick, casual lunch."
—Cameron Matthews

PITCHFORK

Recommended by
Cameron Matthews

5/4 Kingfisher Drive
Peregian Beach
Queensland 4573
+61 754713697
www.pitchforkrestaurant.com.au

Opening hours	Closed Monday
Credit cards	Accepted but not AMEX
Price range	Affordable
Style	Smart casual
Cuisine	Modern Australian
Recommended for	Regular neighborhood

BISTRO H

Recommended by
Nick Holloway

22 Wharf Street
Port Douglas
Queensland 4877
+61 740994011
www.bistro.pagecloud.com

Opening hours	Open 7 days
Credit cards	Accepted
Price range	Affordable
Style	Smart casual
Cuisine	Modern European
Recommended for	Local favorite

NU NU

Recommended by
Cameron Matthews

1 Veivers Road
Port Douglas
Queensland 4879
+61 740591880
www.nunu.com.au

Opening hours	Open 7 days
Credit cards	Accepted
Price range	Expensive
Style	Smart casual
Cuisine	Australian
Recommended for	Wish I'd opened

SALSA BAR & GRILL

Recommended by
Nick Holloway

26 Wharf Street
Port Douglas
Queensland 4877
+61 740994922
www.salsaportdouglas.com.au

Opening hours	Open 7 days
Credit cards	Accepted but not Diners
Price range	Affordable
Style	Casual
Cuisine	Modern Australian
Recommended for	Local favorite

"It has character, it's dependable, it's colorful, and tropical. It epitomises Far North Queensland."
—Nick Holloway

SPIRIT HOUSE

Recommended by
Cameron Matthews

20 Ninderry Road
Yandina
Queensland 4561
+61 754468994
www.spirithouse.com.au

Opening hours	Open 7 days
Credit cards	Accepted but not Diners
Price range	Affordable
Style	Smart casual
Cuisine	Modern Thai
Recommended for	Regular neighborhood

"The lush, exotic gardens and lagoon transport you to another world—pure escapism. And the modern Thai dishes burst with the freshest garden ingredients and explosions of flavor."—Cameron Matthews

AFRICOLA

Recommended by
Morgan McGlone,
David Swain

4 East Terrace
Adelaide
South Australia 5000
+61 882233885
www.africola.com.au

Opening hours	Closed Monday and Sunday
Credit cards	Accepted
Price range	Affordable
Style	Casual
Cuisine	African
Recommended for	Local favorite

"It's a crazy place—there's nothing else like it in Australia."—David Swain

Gone is the colorful clutter (and the fire pit) of a backstreet *braai* (barbecue), but Africola is still as likeable as ever. Like the decor, the menu has been reworked—the South African peri peri chicken has been joined by European and North African influences, like octopus tentacles with salted *jicama* (Mexican yam bean), lamb shawarma, and superior versions of hummus and baba ganoush, to be scooped up with grilled *injera* (East African flatbread). Vegetables have equal billing to meatier dishes—cauliflower is roasted in turmeric butter and finished with a pomegranate and tahini sauce, eggplant (aubergine) is crisp-fried, and carrots charred and dressed with feta and argan oil. Lovers of boutique wines will be gratified to find the list hasn't moved much from its left-of-field position.

GIN LONG CANTEEN

Recommended by
Jock Zonfrillo

42 O'Connell Street
Adelaide
South Australia 5006
+61 871202897
www.ginlongcanteen.com.au

Opening hours	Closed Sunday and Monday
Credit cards	Accepted but not Diners
Price range	Affordable
Style	Casual
Cuisine	Malaysian-Thai-Vietnamese
Recommended for	Regular neighborhood

"My go-to for an Asian fix—everything from delicious banh mi, and slow braised dishes, to awesome dumplings."—Jock Zonfrillo

GOLDEN BOY

Recommended by
Lachlan Colwill,
Duncan Welgemoed

309 North Terrace
Adelaide
South Australia 5000
+61 882270799
www.golden-boy.com.au

Opening hours	Closed Monday and Sunday
Credit cards	Accepted but not Diners
Price range	Affordable
Style	Casual
Cuisine	Thai
Recommended for	Regular neighborhood

"Solid Thai food, super-excellent service, delicious drinks, and one of Adelaide's busiest restaurants." —Duncan Welgemoed

HENTLEY FARM

Recommended by
Duncan Welgemoed

Gerald Roberts Road
Adelaide
South Australia 5355
+61 885628427
www.hentleyfarm.com.au

Opening hours	Open 7 days
Credit cards	Accepted
Price range	Expensive
Style	Smart casual
Cuisine	Modern Australian
Recommended for	Local favorite

HEY JUPITER

Recommended by
Duncan Welgemoed,
Jock Zonfrillo

11 Ebenezer Place
Adelaide
South Australia 5000
+61 416050721

Opening hours	Open 7 days
Reservation policy	No
Credit cards	Accepted but not AMEX or Diners
Price range	Budget
Style	Casual
Cuisine	Café
Recommended for	Breakfast

"This French café always feels like home to me—the pork sandwich is a winner!"—Jock Zonfrillo

JUNIPER & PINE

Shop 2, 450 Brighton Road
Adelaide
South Australia 5048
+61 83582453
www.juniperandpine.com.au

Opening hours	Open 7 days
Credit cards	Accepted
Price range	Budget
Style	Casual
Cuisine	Breakfast-Brunch
Recommended for	Breakfast

"Great food and great coffee in a local restaurant.
What better way to start your day?"—Jock Zonfrillo

KUTCHI DELI PARWANA

7 Ebenezer Place
Adelaide
South Australia 5000
I 61 872258586
www.kutchi.com.au

Opening hours	Closed Sunday
Reservation policy	No
Credit cards	Accepted
Price range	Affordable
Style	Casual
Cuisine	Afghan
Recommended for	Regular neighborhood

"It's Afghan party food, cooked by the most humble
family. Every chef I bring over has to eat their food
and they are blown away every time."
—Duncan Welgemoed

The Ayubi family bring a heartfelt taste of
Afghanistan to the city with Kutchi Deli, younger
sister to the much-loved Parwana in Torrensville.
The bijou diner's whimsical decor is a riot of
jewel-box colors and deliberately clashing patterns
with Afghani art and wall niches housing a collection
of eclectic ephemera. The modestly priced menu is
succinct, but traditional steamed mantu dumplings,
loosely filled with sautéed carrot and onion, and
topped with a lamb-tomato sauce are a perennial
favorite, along with banjan borane, comprising silky
eggplant (aubergine) simmered in tomato sauce
with yogurt. Immensely popular—you'll need
to sneak in before the lunch crowd if you want
to bag a seat.

LA BUVETTE

27 Gresham Street
Adelaide
South Australia 5000
+61 884108170
www.labuvettedrinkery.com.au

Opening hours	Closed Monday and Sunday
Credit cards	Accepted but not Diners
Price range	Affordable
Style	Smart casual
Cuisine	French
Recommended for	Late night

"Best natural wine list in the city."
—Duncan Welgemoed

THE LOST LOAF

1 Third Street
Adelaide
South Australia 5007
+61 0432866717

Opening hours	Closed Sunday to Tuesday, and Thursday
Reservation policy	No
Credit cards	Accepted
Price range	Budget
Style	Casual
Cuisine	Bakery
Recommended for	Breakfast

"Some of the best sourdough I've ever tasted!"
— Lachlan Colwill

MAGILL ESTATE RESTAURANT

78 Penfold Road
Adelaide
South Australia 5072
+61 883015551
www.magillestaterestaurant.com

Opening hours	Closed Sunday to Tuesday
Credit cards	Accepted but not Diners
Price range	Expensive
Style	Smart casual
Cuisine	Modern Australian
Recommended for	High end

MARKET STREET CAFÉ

Recommended by
David Swain,
Duncan Welgemoed

11 Market Street
Adelaide
South Australia 5000
+61 82315014

Opening hours	Closed Sunday
Reservation policy	No
Credit cards	Not accepted
Price range	Affordable
Style	Casual
Cuisine	French
Recommended for	Breakfast

Multifaceted Market Street Café, just a stone's throw from Adelaide's Central Markets, will sort you out for all three daily meals, plus any random hunger crises you might suffer. Don't pass on a flaky croissant, pain au chocolat, or zeppola (deep-fried dough ball), because Market Street is also the baking kitchen for Dough, an excellent local market stall. Belly-filling breakfasts or brunches include a reworking of the classic steak sandwich, coffee comes courtesy of local specialist D'Angelo, and specialty teas are sourced from Larsen & Thompson and Blooming Teas. If you're already planning your next meal, the shelves and fridge offer a comprehensive collection of premium take-home provisions.

NORDBURGER

Recommended by
Duncan Welgemoed

168 The Parade
Adelaide
South Australia 5067
www.nordburger.com

Opening hours	Open 7 days
Reservation policy	No
Credit cards	Accepted but not AMEX or Diners
Price range	Affordable
Style	Casual
Cuisine	Diner
Recommended for	Late night

OSTERIA OGGI

Recommended by
Jock Zonfrillo

76 Pirie Street
Adelaide
South Australia 5000
+61 883592525
www.osteriaoggi.com.au

Opening hours	Closed Sunday
Credit cards	Accepted
Price range	Affordable
Style	Casual
Cuisine	Italian
Recommended for	Wish I'd opened

"A brilliantly fresh Italian restaurant, great house pasta, and so much more. Beautiful room, excellent service, and great wine list."—Jock Zonfrillo

There may be elements of old-school osteria-style architecture—like tiled floors, archways, and a vine-covered indoor arbour—but they're a playful homage to the traditional, because *Oggi* (meaning "today" in Italian) is very much of the now. Dining is an upbeat and sociable affair, with seating at a 66-foot (twenty-meter) concrete bar, wooden communal tables, or semicircular booths. The kitchen is just as flexible, serving the modern Italian menu all day, so you can graze with a glass of Prosecco, devour a bowl of their seriously good pasta, made daily in-house, or simply surrender to the chef's whim with the *veloce* (fast) and *lento* (slow) tasting menus.

PEEL STREET

Recommended by
David Swain

9 Peel Street
Adelaide
South Australia 5000
+61 882318887
www.peelst.com.au

Opening hours	Closed Sunday
Credit cards	Accepted but not Diners
Price range	Affordable
Style	Casual
Cuisine	Modern Australian
Recommended for	Local favorite

PINK MOON SALOON

Recommended by
Jock Zonfrillo

21 Leigh Street
Adelaide
South Australia 5000
www.pinkmoonsaloon.com.au

Opening hours	Open 7 days
Credit cards	Accepted
Price range	Budget
Style	Casual
Cuisine	Bar-Small plates
Recommended for	Late night

"The small bar with a big heart—delicious snacks and sandwiches served until late. Love this place!"
—Jock Zonfrillo

PRESS*

Recommended by
David Swain

40 Waymouth Street
Adelaide
South Australia 5000
+61 882118048
www.pressfoodandwine.com.au

Opening hours	Closed Sunday
Credit cards	Accepted
Price range	Affordable
Style	Casual
Cuisine	Modern Australian
Recommended for	Late night

Press* promotes its food as "parochial", but with the bounty of produce available in South Australia's vast backyard, that's far from restrictive. There's a choice of dining areas—upstairs is more traditional, downstairs with its bar and shared tables offers a more casual vibe. The feed-all-appetites, please-all-palates menu has an equally democratic ethos—from delicate and fresh (kingfish sashimi with edamame and cucumber), through to heartier plates (pappardelle, blue swimmer crab, tomato, and chile), as well as a selection of beef cuts seared to juicy, smoky perfection on the wood-fired grill. Unusually, and to the delight of sweetbread lovers, there's also a section dedicated to variety meats (offal).

RESTAURANT BLACKWOOD

Recommended by
Jock Zonfrillo

285 Rundle Street
Adelaide
South Australia 5000
+61 882270344
www.restaurantblackwood.com

Opening hours	Open 7 days
Credit cards	Accepted but not Diners
Price range	Affordable
Style	Casual
Cuisine	Australian
Recommended for	Local favorite

"A true taste of Australia—upbeat food and service with a mostly natural wine list. Shouldn't be missed."
—Jock Zonfrillo

RESTAURANT ORANA

Recommended by
Ana Roš,
Ryan Sessions,
Duncan Welgemoed,
Ben Willis

285 Rundle Street
Adelaide
South Australia 5000
+61 882323444
www.restaurantorana.com

Opening hours	Closed Monday and Sunday
Credit cards	Accepted but not Diners
Price range	Expensive
Style	Smart casual
Cuisine	Modern Australian
Recommended for	Worth the travel

"Their dedication to native ingredients is unrivalled in Australia."—Ryan Sessions

Fine dining and "bush tucker" (native food from the land) may seem as incongruous a culinary partnership as street food and Michelin stars, but the gastronomic landscape is changing and chefs are starting to look to their own backyard for inspiration. Jock Zonfrillo's menu is an exemplar of true "modern Australian" cuisine, pairing wild and indigenous ingredients with innovative technique to create something both impressively high-end and with a strong sense of place. As many as twenty small plates are part of the often interactive tasting menu. If you're not local, ask for specific directions—like the unscripted menu, the un-signposted entryway gives little clue to what lies within.

SAIGON GATE

Recommended by
Duncan Welgemoed

402 Prospect Road
Adelaide
South Australia 5082
+61 882602588

Opening hours	Closed Sunday
Reservation policy	No
Credit cards	Accepted but not AMEX or Diners
Price range	Budget
Style	Casual
Cuisine	Vietnamese
Recommended for	Bargain

"Best oxtail soup anywhere in the world. For a few extra dollars add squeaky fresh tripe and soft, unctuous, tendons."—Duncan Welgemoed

SUNNY'S PIZZA

Recommended by
Duncan Welgemoed

17 Solomon Street
Adelaide
South Australia 5000
+61 404280522
www.sunnys.pizza

Opening hours	Closed Sunday to Tuesday
Reservation policy	No
Credit cards	Accepted
Price range	Budget
Style	Casual
Cuisine	Pizza
Recommended for	Late night

SUNNYS SHOP

Recommended by
Duncan Welgemoed,
Jock Zonfrillo

106b Prospect Road
Adelaide
South Australia 5082
+61 884200999
www.sunnysshop.com.au

Opening hours	Closed Sunday
Reservation policy	No
Credit cards	Accepted but not AMEX or Diners
Price range	Budget
Style	Casual
Cuisine	Asian Street Food
Recommended for	Bargain

"Asian street-food at its finest. It's authentic, colorful, and fun, and the food is just delicious."
—Jock Zonfrillo

Aaron Ratanatray's take on an Asian beachside bar burst into vibrant being in the foodie hub of Prospect in summer 2016, soothing the nostalgic hunger pains of returning Bali, Pattaya, and Da Nang holidaymakers. Retro and purposefully ramshackle, most of Sunnys' seating is hawker-style, with colorful stools set out on the street or down a laneway filled with tropical greenery. The menu takes its cues from Asian street food favorites— banh mi spiked with pork crackling, punchy Thai *larb* (meat salad), rice bowls, *laksa* (spicy noodle soup), and noodle salads, all as lively as the color scheme. The evening menu is a bit more expensive, but everything's still under A$20 ($15; £11).

SUPERFISH

Recommended by
David Swain

188 Gremfell Street
Adelaide
South Australia 5000
+61 882326900
www.super.fish

Opening hours	Closed Monday
Reservation policy	No
Credit cards	Accepted
Price range	Budget
Style	Casual
Cuisine	Seafood
Recommended for	Bargain

T-CHOW

Recommended by
Duncan Welgemoed

68 Moonta Street
Adelaide
South Australia 5000
+61 884101413
www.tchow.com.au

Opening hours	Open 7 days
Credit cards	Accepted
Price range	Budget
Style	Casual
Cuisine	Chinese
Recommended for	Bargain

WAH HING

Recommended by
David Swain

85 Gouger Street
Adelaide
South Australia 5000
+61 882120338

Opening hours	Open 7 days
Credit cards	Accepted but not AMEX or Diners
Price range	Budget
Style	Casual
Cuisine	Chinese
Recommended for	Bargain

YING CHOW CHINESE RESTAURANT
Recommended by
Duncan Welgemoed
114 Gouger Street
Adelaide
South Australia 5000
+61 882117998

Opening hours	Open 7 days
Credit cards	Accepted
Price range	Budget
Style	Casual
Cuisine	Chinese
Recommended for	Late night

SALOPIAN INN
Recommended by
Christine Manfield
Main Road
McLaren Vale
South Australia 5171
+61 883238769
www.salopian.com.au

Opening hours	Open 7 days
Credit cards	Accepted
Price range	Affordable
Style	Casual
Cuisine	Modern Australian
Recommended for	Worth the travel

"Food with a wine focus. Fabulous gin menu."
—Christine Manfield

ONE LITTLE SISTER
Recommended by
Vladimir Mukhin
4/48 Main Road
Normanville
South Australia 5204
+61 885583759
www.onelittlesister.com.au

Opening hours	Open 7 days
Reservation policy	No
Credit cards	Accepted but not AMEX or Diners
Price range	Budget
Style	Casual
Cuisine	Café
Recommended for	Breakfast

ST HUGO
Recommended by
David Swain
2141 Barossa Valley Way
Rolland Flat
South Australia 5352
+61 881159200
www.sthugo.com

Opening hours	Open 7 days
Credit cards	Accepted
Price range	Expensive
Style	Smart casual
Cuisine	Australian
Recommended for	High end

FINO SEPPELTSFIELD
Recommended by
Lachlan Colwill,
Duncan Welgemoed
730 Seppeltsfield Road
Seppeltsfield
South Australia 5355
+61 885628528
www.fino.net.au

Opening hours	Open 7 days
Credit cards	Accepted
Price range	Affordable
Style	Smart casual
Cuisine	South Australian
Recommended for	Local favorite

"Sharon Romeo and David Swain source the best local produce and booze, and deliver it in style, inside one of the most iconic venues in Australia."
—Duncan Welgemoed

The relocated Fino Restaurant (formerly in Willunga) is housed in a former bottling room dating from the mid-1800s, and enriches the experience of visiting one of the country's oldest and most historic wineries. David Swain's creative, elegant menu strongly supports local provenance—parochialism well justified in a region boasting some of Australia's finest produce and most lauded wines. Shared plates allow diners to sample a broad range of local offerings, based around sustainably farmed Port Lincoln seafood and free-range Barossan pork, goat, and chicken. The wine list, while not extensive, is carefully curated to showcase local gems with a few surprise offerings from further afield.

HENTLEY FARM

Recommended by
David Swain,
Duncan Welgemoed

Gerald Roberts Road
Seppeltsfield
South Australia 5355
+61 885628427
www.hentleyfarm.com.au

Opening hours	Closed Monday to Wednesday
Credit cards	Accepted but not Diners
Price range	Expensive
Style	Smart casual
Cuisine	Modern Australian
Recommended for	High end

"Beautiful cuisine and location."—David Swain

THE SUMMERTOWN ARISTOLOGIST

Recommended by
Jock Zonfrillo

1097 Greenhill Road
Summertown
South Australia 5141
+61 477410105
www.thesummertownaristologist.com

Opening hours	Closed Monday to Thursday
Credit cards	Accepted but not AMEX or Diners
Price range	Affordable
Style	Casual
Cuisine	Modern Australian
Recommended for	Regular neighborhood

"Natural wine producers Anton Von Klopper and
Jasper Button opened a cute little wine bar in the hills,
serving their fabulous wines and some pretty smart
eats by chef Thomas Edwards."—Jock Zonfrillo

FERMENTASIAN

Recommended by
David Swain

90 Murray Street
Tanunda
South Australia 5352
+61 885630765
www.fermentasian.com.au

Opening hours	Closed Monday and Tuesday
Credit cards	Accepted but not AMEX or Diners
Price range	Affordable
Style	Smart casual
Cuisine	Vietnamese
Recommended for	Regular neighborhood

LOST IN A FOREST

Recommended by
Jock Zonfrillo

1203 Greenhill Road
Uraidla
South Australia 5142
+61 883903444
www.lostinaforest.com.au

Opening hours	Closed Monday to Wednesday
Credit cards	Accepted but not AMEX or Diners
Price range	Budget
Style	Casual
Cuisine	Italian-Pizza
Recommended for	Local favorite

"Superb old church that has been converted into
a beautiful pizza joint and wine bar. Run by the
infamous Taras, from the wine label Ochota Barrels,
you can expect plenty of his delicious wines as well
as others he currently finds interesting. Do not miss
this!"—Jock Zonfrillo

DUNALLEY FISH MARKET

Recommended by
David Moyle

11 Fulham Road
Dunalley
Tasmania 7177
+61 362535428

Opening hours	Variable
Reservation policy	No
Credit cards	Not accepted
Price range	Budget
Style	Casual
Cuisine	Seafood
Recommended for	Regular neighborhood

"When I get a chance, I head down the peninsula, and
on the way there is a very genuine food experience
in the most incredible setting. A$10 ($7; £6), fried
fish with calamari is about the only choice, along
with whether you want lemon or vinegar. Great mixed
variety of seafood, always featuring some small and
oily fish, which is such a rarity."—David Moyle

ALØFT

Brooke Street Pier
Hobart
Tasmania 7000
+61 362231619
www.aloftrestaurant.com

Recommended by
Matthew Breen,
David Moyle

Opening hours	Closed Sunday and Monday
Credit cards	Accepted but not AMEX or Diners
Price range	Affordable
Style	Casual
Cuisine	Asian
Recommended for	High end

"Great views. Sexy chefs."—Matthew Breen

It can be hard to tear your eyes away from the seductive view of the Derwent river, its broad expanse framed by floor-to-ceiling glass, but Aløft's menu will prove a worthy distraction. Chef Christian Ryan runs the open kitchen, with the team sometimes delivering dishes to the table, Noma-style. Decor too follows the minimalist Nordic aesthetic but the exceptional and beautifully plated food takes its cues from Asia. Provenance, meanwhile, is firmly local. Order a serving of crispy pig's ear cooked in master stock and dusted in prickly ash salt, or the almost-famous shiitake dumplings, while contemplating your dining options —should you freestyle it or go with the degustation menu?

BERTA

323a Elizabeth Street
Hobart
Tasmania 7001
+61 362344844
www.bertahobart.com.au

Recommended by
Rodney Dunn

Opening hours	Open 7 days
Credit cards	Accepted but not AMEX or Diners
Price range	Affordable
Style	Casual
Cuisine	Modern Australian
Recommended for	Breakfast

**"Berta is a modern café in every sense of the word: light, airy, buzzy, with good coffee, and solidly executed dishes. I love that the menu changes and evolves. I also love that each time I go I'm torn choosing dishes as they all sound so good."
—Rodney Dunn**

CYCLO

249 Elizabeth Street
Hobart
Tasmania 7000
+61 362319946
www.cyclofood.com.au

Recommended by
Matthew Breen

Opening hours	Open 7 days
Reservation policy	No
Credit cards	Accepted
Price range	Affordable
Style	Casual
Cuisine	Vietnamese
Recommended for	Late night

"Authentic late-night banh mi."—Matthew Breen

DIER MAKR

123 Collins Street
Hobart
Tasmania 7000
+61 362888910
www.diermakr.com

Recommended by
Rodney Dunn,
David Moyle

Opening hours	Closed Monday
Credit cards	Accepted
Price range	Affordable
Style	Casual
Cuisine	Modern Australian
Recommended for	Late night

"Groovy little bar serving great cocktails and cool bites of sophisticated food using locally sourced ingredients."—Rodney Dunn

There's a relaxed, no-rules approach at this intimate, atmospheric bistro/bar/cellar. You can call in after work for creative cocktails, catch up with friends at the bar fronting the kitchen while watching chef Kobi Ruzicka magic up some drink-friendly snacks, or grab a bottle to go from the small cellar of minimal-intervention, biodynamic, and organic wines sourced from around the globe. For a more leisurely stay, dine from the creative and very reasonably priced tasting menu. Responsive to both season and market, it changes frequently, but the bare-bones descriptions ("mussels, beer") ensure whatever you order will be a surprise.

FICO

151 Macquarie Street
Hobart
Tasmania 7000
+61 262453391
www.ficofico.net

Recommended by
Matthew Breen,
David Moyle

Opening hours	Closed Monday
Credit cards	Accepted
Price range	Affordable
Style	Casual
Cuisine	European
Recommended for	Regular neighborhood

"Classic, elegant Italian."—Matthew Breen

FRANKLIN

30 Argyle Street
Hobart
Tasmania 7000
+61 362343375
www.franklinhobart.com.au

Recommended by
Matthew Breen

Opening hours	Closed Monday and Sunday
Credit cards	Accepted
Price range	Affordable
Style	Casual
Cuisine	Modern Australian
Recommended for	Local favorite

"A great use of Tasmanian produce cooked with finesse."—Matthew Breen

Franklin inhabits the ground floor of Hobart's former *Mercury* newspaper building, the appropriately industrial fit-out warmed with touches of wood, animal hides, and a huge Scotch oven used to add subtle smokiness to ingredients from both land and sea. David Moyle's tight Tasmanian menu is highly seasonal, but pristine local seafood is well represented. Periwinkles steamed in their shells and chargrilled octopus with wild fennel fronds may sound like rustic dishes from a Greek taverna but you'll find they're far more finessed here. Sit at the bar, have a glass or two from the lo-fi wine list, and watch Moyle's team work its magic—you're unlikely to see ingredients treated with such reverence again.

GINGER BROWN

464 Macquarie Street
Hobart
Tasmania 7004
+61 362233531

Recommended by
Matthew Breen

Opening hours	Open 7 days
Credit cards	Accepted but not AMEX or Diners
Price range	Affordable
Style	Casual
Cuisine	Café
Recommended for	Breakfast

"A great neighborhood café. Simple, well-cooked eggs."—Matthew Breen

Come the weekend and there's usually a line (queue) of families and couples, along with walkers fuelling up for a Mount Wellington hike. Inside, the tables are packed and the vibe is happy. Ginger Brown is one of South Hobart's best loved cafés, and for good reason. Despite an interior that looks like it's been furnished with footpath finds and grandma's cast-offs, the food is right up to date—with all-day breakfasts featuring sixty-two degree baked eggs, kimchi pancakes, and moreish house-made crumpets with lime butter, blackberry, and coconut. Equally keenly priced lunches including poke bowls and paninis are supplemented by creative weekend specials. Service, refreshingly free of hipster attitude, is swift and smiley.

HAMLET

40 Molle Street
Hobart
Tasmania 7000
+61 407169352
www.hamlet.org.au

Recommended by
David Moyle

Opening hours	Open 7 days
Credit cards	Accepted but not AMEX or Diners
Price range	Budget
Style	Casual
Cuisine	Café
Recommended for	Breakfast

LOCAL PIZZA

Recommended by
Rodney Dunn

52 Maroni Road
Hobart
Tasmania 7011
+61 362493573
www.localpizzatas.com.au

Opening hours......................Closed Monday and Tuesday
Reservation policy..No
Credit cards....................Accepted but not AMEX or Diners
Price range...Affordable
Style..Casual
Cuisine...Modern Italian
Recommended for..............................Regular neighborhood

"Wood-fired pizza using local Tasmanian ingredients accompanied by a cool selection of local wine and beer. A funky, relaxed vibe, with outdoor seating in the summer."—Rodney Dunn

THE QUARTERMASTERS ARMS

Recommended by
David Moyle

132–134 Elizabeth Street
Hobart
Tasmania 7000
| 61 362369119
www.tasmanquartermasters.com.au

Opening hours.........................Closed Monday and Sunday
Credit cards..Accepted
Price range...Affordable
Style..Casual
Cuisine...Bar-Tasmanian
Recommended for...Late night

RIN

Recommended by
Matthew Breen

167 Harrington Street
Hobart
Tasmania 7000
+61 427 634 574

Opening hours.........................Closed Monday and Sunday
Reservation policy..No
Credit cards....................Accepted but not AMEX or Diners
Price range...Affordable
Style..Casual
Cuisine...Japanese-Vegetarian
Recommended for..Bargain

THE SOURCE

Recommended by
David Moyle

655 Main Road
Hobart
Tasmania 7011
+61 362779904

www.mona.net.au

Opening hours......................Closed Monday and Tuesday
Credit cards..Accepted
Price range...Expensive
Style...Smart casual
Cuisine..French
Recommended for..High end

THE STANDARD

Recommended by
Rodney Dunn

Hudsons Lane
Liverpool Street
Hobart
Tasmania 7000
www.standard-burgers.com

Opening hours...Open 7 days
Reservation policy..No
Credit cards...Not accepted
Price range..Budget
Style..Casual
Cuisine...Burgers
Recommended for..Bargain

"The Standard is a takeout (takeaway) burger place, tucked down a laneway. There's no indoor seating, but it doesn't matter as the burgers are always good. They make their own buns and are open for lunch and dinner seven days, so always reliable. They have a creative list of burgers with equally creative names, as well as the classics."—Rodney Dunn

STRAIGHT UP COFFEE & FOOD

Recommended by
David Moyle

202a Liverpool Street
Hobart
Tasmania 7000
+61 362369237
www.straightupcoffeeandfood.com.au

Opening hours...Open 7 days
Reservation policy..No
Credit cards...Not accepted
Price range..Budget
Style..Casual
Cuisine...Café-Vegetarian
Recommended for..Breakfast

TEMPLO

Recommended by
Rodney Dunn,
David Moyle

98 Patrick Street
Hobart
Tasmania 7000
+61 362347659
www.templo.com.au

Opening hours	Closed Tuesday and Wednesday
Credit cards	Accepted but not AMEX or Diners
Price range	Affordable
Style	Casual
Cuisine	Modern Italian
Recommended for	Local favorite

"Templo is small and intimate, the service is personal, and the food is always excellent. Italian leaning in its tastes, the menu is always tiny. The best option is to have the chef's menu—a little sample of them all."
—Rodney Dunn

Seating just twenty, this tiny but elegant eatery on the fringe of Hobart's city center is a destination for worshipful diners who come for Matt Breen's Italian-inspired creativity and deft touch. The seasonally focused and market-dependent menu changes too frequently to be able to single out specific dishes, but there's fresh pasta daily—such as cloud-like gnocchi with rich, braised rabbit sauce. Templo's compact but superbly crafted wine list is an education, with something that is absolutely right for whatever's on your plate. It's a rarity in Tasmania to find stand-out, grown-up food on a Monday night so *grazie a dio* for Templo.

TRICYCLE

Recommended by
David Moyle

77 Salamanca Place
Hobart
Tasmania 7000
+61 362237228
www.salarts.org.au

Opening hours	Closed Sunday
Reservation policy	No
Credit cards	Accepted but not AMEX or Diners
Price range	Affordable
Style	Casual
Cuisine	Australian
Recommended for	Breakfast

"Adam and Megan have been serving the most delicious, nourishing food from this tiny place for a long time. It's genuinely my most visited place in Hobart and they never disappoint."—David Moyle

ME WAH

Recommended by
David Moyle

16 Magnet Court
Sandy Bay
Tasmania 7005
+61 362233688
www.mewah.com.au

Opening hours	Closed Monday
Credit cards	Accepted
Price range	Affordable
Style	Casual
Cuisine	Cantonese
Recommended for	High end

"Sunday *yum cha* with an insane Burgundy list."
— David Moyle

It's easy to spot first-timers at Me Wah—they're the ones entering tentatively, not quite convinced that this uninspiring suburban shopping center could possibly house the restaurant they've heard so much about. Soon enough though they'll be settled at one of the well-spaced, crisp-clothed tables in the sumptuous dining room, nodding in appreciation as they pop a morsel of Perkins Bay slow-cooked abalone or silky-skinned dumpling of swimmer crab into their mouths. Wine lovers will be dazzled by the lauded list—it's a veritable roll call of French wine nobility. Me Wah's exceptional Cantonese cuisine is served yum cha style (dim sum and tea) on Sundays.

LA BIMBA

Recommended by
Dan Hunter

125 Great Ocean Road
Apollo Bay
Victoria 3233
+61 352377411
www.labimba.com.au

Opening hours	Closed Tuesday
Credit cards	Accepted
Price range	Affordable
Style	Smart casual
Cuisine	Seafood
Recommended for	Local favorite

PROVENANCE RESTAURANT

Recommended by
Cameron Matthews,
Ryan Sessions,
David Swain

86 Ford Street
Beechworth
Victoria 3747
+61 357281786
www.theprovenance.com.au

Opening hours	Closed Monday
Credit cards	Accepted
Price range	Expensive
Style	Smart casual
Cuisine	Modern Australian
Recommended for	Worth the travel

"Alpine cuisine with Japanese influences."
—David Swain

In the small town of Beechworth, in a gracious, former bank with soaring ceilings and gleaming wooden tables, chef Michael Ryan and winemaker wife Jeanette Henderson have created something pretty special. And they've been recognised for it, having been awarded two "hats" by the Australian Good Food Guide six years in a row, along with many other accolades. Ryan's artfully plated, high-calibre food highlights the best local produce (and there is plenty of it), but he adds a distinctive twist with the addition of Japanese ingredients and technique—partnering meats like smoked wallaby tartare and confit goat with *umeboshi* (Japanese salt plums) and miso dressing respectively. The wine list too showcases the region, supplemented by a few intelligently chosen Europeans and, of course, some premium sake.

BIRREGURRA GENERAL STORE

Recommended by
Dan Hunter

59–61 Main Street
Birregurra
Victoria 3242
+61 352362013

Opening hours	Open 7 days
Reservation policy	No
Credit cards	Accepted but not AMEX
Price range	Budget
Style	Casual
Cuisine	Café-Deli
Recommended for	Breakfast

"Local to Brae and not a bad cheeseburger for a late morning hangover cure."—Dan Hunter

BRAE

Recommended by
Jasper Avent, Ben Devlin,
Teage Ezard, Luca Fantin, Karl Firla,
Analiese Gregory, Elizabeth Haigh,
Nick Holloway, Dan Hong,
Josh Lewis, Josue Lopez,
Cameron Matthews,
Morgan McGlone, Michael Meredith,
Christopher Millar, Uwe Opocensky,
Dave Pynt, Shaun Quade, Ben Shewry,
Giulio Sturla, David Swain

4285 Cape Otway Road
Birregurra
Victoria 3242
+61 352362226
www.braerestaurant.com

Opening hours	Closed Tuesday and Wednesday
Credit cards	Accepted but not Diners
Price range	Expensive
Style	Smart casual
Cuisine	Modern Australian
Recommended for	High end

"If Australia has a national cuisine, it is whatever Dan Hunter is serving on his menu at that time."
—Shaun Quade

Beyond the doors of this original brick farmhouse lies Brae's true focus—Chef Dan Hunter's menu. It's a tight expression of terroir, morphing daily depending on what's growing on the twelve-hectare property or on nearby farms, or has been pulled from the fishermen's nets in Apollo Bay. Produce-focused perhaps, but technique and innovation elevate each dish on the degustation menu to something singular. Take, for example, the "ice oyster"—a shell filled with oyster brine and sheep's-milk ice cream with freeze-dried sherry vinegar and dehydrated oyster powder, sprinkled with moss-green sea lettuce powder. Forget assigning a designated driver and stay over—there are now six luxury guest suites, which include an impressive collection of vinyl records, a cocktail bar, and views to the rolling hills of The Otways.

LAKE HOUSE

Recommended by
Cameron Matthews

4 King Street
Daylesford
Victoria 3460
+61 353483329
www.lakehouse.com.au

Opening hours	Open 7 days
Credit cards	Accepted
Price range	Expensive
Style	Smart casual
Cuisine	Modern Australian
Recommended for	Wish I'd opened

ROYAL MAIL HOTEL

Recommended by
Cameron Matthews

98 Parker Street
Dunkeld
Victoria 3294
+61 355772241
www.royalmail.com.au

Opening hours	Open 7 days
Credit cards	Accepted
Price range	Expensive
Style	Smart casual
Cuisine	Modern Australian
Recommended for	High end

BESPOKE HARVEST

Recommended by
Dan Hunter

16 Grant Street
Forrest
Victoria 3236
+61 352366446
www.bespokeharvest.com.au

Opening hours	Closed Tuesday to Thursday
Credit cards	Accepted
Price range	Affordable
Style	Smart casual
Cuisine	Modern Australian
Recommended for	Regular neighborhood

IGNI

Recommended by
Dan Hunter,
Morgan McGlone,
James Viles

Ryan Place
Geelong
Victoria 3220
+61 352222266
www.restaurantigni.com

Opening hours	Closed Monday to Wednesday
Credit cards	Accepted but not Diners
Price range	Expensive
Style	Smart casual
Cuisine	Australian
Recommended for	Local favorite

"These guys have it happening. Aaron's food is tasty and thoughtful."—James Viles

Igni's location, in an undistinguished city center building, doesn't do much to advertise the culinary pleasures found inside. Fortunately for its owners though, word of mouth has done a good job of that. A sophisticated little Geelong gem, Igni's austere space, in muted greys and charcoal, is smart and comfortable but doesn't draw too much attention away from the main act—Aaron Turner's exciting food. The chef-owner's impressive CV includes

stints at Noma and El Celler de Can Roca, as well as the much-loved but sadly departed Loam. Igni's food, based on the best local ingredients and served as a five- or eight-course bespoke tasting menu, supplemented with clever little snacks, can be matched with a succinct but equally intriguing selection of wine.

KILGOUR STREET GROCER & CAFÉ

Recommended by
Aaron Turner

164 Kilgour Street
Geelong
Victoria 3220
+61 439683220
www.kilgourstreetgrocer.com

Opening hours	Open 7 days
Reservation policy	No
Credit cards	Not accepted
Price range	Budget
Style	Casual
Cuisine	Café
Recommended for	Breakfast

"Simple, quick and friendly service—the way it should be."—Aaron Turner

SAM'S CAFÉ GEELONG

Recommended by
Aaron Turner

206 Moorabool Street
Geelong
Victoria 3220
+61 352224968

Opening hours	Closed Sunday
Reservation policy	No
Credit cards	Not accepted
Price range	Budget
Style	Casual
Cuisine	Lebanese
Recommended for	Local favorite

WAI BO

Recommended by
Ben Shewry

214 Pakington Street
Geelong
Victoria 3218
+61 352296838

Opening hours	Closed Monday
Credit cards	Accepted but not AMEX or Diners
Price range	Budget
Style	Casual
Cuisine	Cantonese
Recommended for	Bargain

MELBOURNE: SEE PAGES 138–153

COFFIN SALLY

Recommended by
Ryan Sessions

33 Sackville Street
Port Fairy
Victoria 3284
+61 355682618
www.coffinsally.com.au

Opening hours	Open 7 days
Credit cards	Accepted but not AMEX or Diners
Price range	Budget
Style	Casual
Cuisine	Pizza
Recommended for	Local favorite

"Great pizzas, funky little bar."—Ryan Sessions

CONLAN'S WINE STORE

Recommended by
Ryan Sessions

34 Bank Street
Port Fairy
Victoria 3284
+61 355682582
www.conlanswinestore.com.au

Opening hours	Closed Tuesday
Credit cards	Accepted
Price range	Affordable
Style	Casual
Cuisine	Modern Australian
Recommended for	Regular neighborhood

"You can walk in and grab a bottle of wine in their retail section or, for a small fee, you can drink it in the restaurant, where you can sit and eat great food in a relaxed and professional dining room."
—Ryan Sessions

FEN

Recommended by
Ryan Sessions

22 Sackville Street
Port Fairy
Victoria 3284
+61 355683229
www.fenportfairy.com.au

Opening hours	Open 7 days
Credit cards	Accepted
Price range	Affordable
Style	Smart casual
Cuisine	Modern Australian
Recommended for	Late night

KERMONDS HAMBURGERS

Recommended by
Ryan Sessions

151 Lava Street
Warrnambool
Victoria 3280
+61 355624854

Opening hours	Open 7 days
Reservation policy	No
Credit cards	Not accepted
Price range	Budget
Style	Casual
Cuisine	Fast Food
Recommended for	Bargain

"It was opened fifty years ago and hasn't changed since! It's a step back in time."—Ryan Sessions

ROUGH DIAMOND

Recommended by
Ryan Sessions

203 Koroit Street
Warrnambool
Victoria 3280
+61 355605707
www.roughdiamondcoffee.com.au

Opening hours	Closed Sunday
Reservation policy	No
Credit cards	Accepted but not AMEX or Diners
Price range	Affordable
Style	Casual
Cuisine	Modern Australian
Recommended for	Breakfast

THE ATTIC FREMANTLE

Recommended by
Alexandra Haynes

16 Bannister Street
Perth
Western Australia 6160
+61 4317500800
www.theatticfremantle.com.au

Opening hours	Closed Monday
Credit cards	Accepted but not AMEX or Diners
Price range	Budget
Style	Casual
Cuisine	Australian
Recommended for	Breakfast

"Healthy, delicious, great coffee, friendly staff."
—Alexandra Haynes

BIB & TUCKER

Recommended by
Alexandra Haynes

18 Leighton Beach Boulevard
Perth
Western Australia 6159
+61 894332147
www.bibandtucker.net.au

Opening hours	Closed Monday
Credit cards	Accepted
Price range	Affordable
Style	Casual
Cuisine	Modern Australian
Recommended for	Breakfast

BILLIE H.

Recommended by
Alexandra Haynes

34 Saint Quentin Avenue
Perth
Western Australia 6010
+61 893840808
www.billieh.com.au

Opening hours	Closed Sunday
Credit cards	Accepted but not Diners
Price range	Affordable
Style	Casual
Cuisine	Australian
Recommended for	High end

"Billie H. is like nothing else anyone is doing in Perth. The food is fantastic, and the service, venue, and music are second to none."—Alexandra Haynes

Sophisticated and moody, this Claremont wine bar calls itself "anytime dining", an agreeable concept in anyone's world. Named after Billie Holliday, a musical hero of owner Dan Godsell, both epicureans and wine lovers are provided for with generosity and finesse. The wine list spans continents and styles, including some outlier varietals you may never have heard of, while the dynamic, seasonal, Euro-influenced menu, under chef Alia Glorie, ranges from local olives and the confident pairing of oysters with orange blossom to more appetite-sating dishes like smoked pork belly with white bean, pear, and sage.

BREAD IN COMMON

Recommended by
Alexandra Haynes

43 Pakenham Street
Perth
Western Australia 6160
+61 893361032
www.breadincommon.com.au

Opening hours	Open 7 days
Credit cards	Accepted
Price range	Affordable
Style	Casual
Cuisine	Modern Australian
Recommended for	Local favorite

CLARKE'S OF NORTH BEACH

Recommended by
Shannon Kellam

97 Flora Terrace
Perth
Western Australia 6020
+61 892467621
www.clarkesofnorthbeach.com

Opening hours	Closed Monday and Sunday
Credit cards	Accepted but not Diners
Price range	Expensive
Style	Smart casual
Cuisine	Modern Australian
Recommended for	Regular neighborhood

"Well sourced produce and innovative cooking."
—Shannon Kellam

With impeccable service, crisp napery, and well-spaced candlelit tables, Clarke's has been the Perth go-to for a serious dining experience for the past fifteen years. Owner and chef Stephen Clarke has done time under Michel Roux and the famed Nico Ladenis, and partners modern accoutrements such as foams, "crumbs," and pickled vegetables with classic technique in dishes like venison *boudin* (sausage), quail roulade, and confit duck. There's a healthy focus on local provenance throughout the menu, available both as à la carte or as a tasting menu, and it's particularly strong when it comes to showcasing Western Australia's excellent seafood.

EL PÚBLICO

Recommended by
Alexandra Haynes

511 Beaufort Street
Perth
Western Australia 6003
+61 418187708
www.elpublico.com.au

Opening hours	Open 7 days
Credit cards	Accepted but not Diners
Price range	Budget
Style	Casual
Cuisine	Modern Mexican
Recommended for	Local favorite

FRANCOFORTE SPAGHETTI BAR

Recommended by
Alexandra Haynes

4/189 William Street
Perth
Western Australia 6003
+61 892279289
www.francoforte.com.au

Opening hours	Open / days
Credit cards	Accepted but not AMEX
Price range	Affordable
Style	Casual
Cuisine	Italian
Recommended for	Regular neighborhood

"Simple, delicious and affordable; very friendly and welcoming staff."—Alexandra Haynes

FUYU

Recommended by
Alexandra Haynes

26 Stirling Highway
Perth
Western Australia 6009
+61 893895517
www.fuyu.com.au

Opening hours	Closed Monday and Sunday
Credit cards	Accepted
Price range	Affordable
Style	Smart casual
Cuisine	Pan-Asian
Recommended for	High end

HAWKER'S CUISINE

Recommended by
Alexandra Haynes

40 Francis Street
Perth
Western Australia 6003
+61 893289668

Opening hours	Closed Monday
Credit cards	Accepted but not AMEX or Diners
Price range	Budget
Style	Casual
Cuisine	Asian
Recommended for	Bargain

"The food is great, and the service is organized and efficient."—Alexandra Haynes

LONG CHIM

Recommended by
Alexandra Haynes

State Buildings
Barrack Street and St Georges Terrace
Perth
Western Australia 6000
+61 86168775
www.longchimperth.com

Opening hours	Open 7 days
Credit cards	Accepted
Price range	Affordable
Style	Casual
Cuisine	Thai
Recommended for	Local favorite

Much to the chagrin of Sydneysiders, it wasn't their city (and his former home town) the venerated chef David Thompson chose as the location for his first restaurant since decamping to Bangkok nearly two decades ago—it was Perth. They've been mollified somewhat since he opened another Long Chim in an atmospheric, canteen-style space in Sydney's city center. Thai expert Thompson would never dial it down for local palates, so there's plenty of authentic, slow-burning heat; but it's expertly tempered by sweet, sour, and salty notes. Curries or punchy noodle salads are no-brainers, but if you can bear to relinquish control, the *Ma Long Chim* menu is a selection of the day's best dishes.

NAO RAMEN

Recommended by
Alexandra Haynes

191/580 Hay Street
Perth
Western Australia 6000
+61 893252090
www.naojapaneserestaurant.com.au

Opening hours	Open 7 days
Credit cards	Accepted
Price range	Budget
Style	Casual
Cuisine	Japanese
Recommended for	Regular neighborhood

NOBU

Recommended by
Alexandra Haynes

Crown Perth
Great Eastern Highway
Perth
Western Australia 6100
+61 1800954123
www.crownperth.com.au

Opening hours	Open 7 days
Credit cards	Accepted
Price range	Expensive
Style	Smart casual
Cuisine	Japanese Fusion
Recommended for	High end

ODYSSEA BEACH CAFÉ

Recommended by
Alexandra Haynes

187 Challenger Parade
Perth
Western Australia 6015
+61 893857979
www.odysseabeachcafe.com.au

Opening hours	Open 7 days
Credit cards	Accepted
Price range	Affordable
Style	Smart casual
Cuisine	Modern Australian
Recommended for	Breakfast

ROCKPOOL

Recommended by
Alexandra Haynes

Crown Perth
Great Eastern Highway
Perth
Western Australia 6100
+61 862521900
www.rockpoolbarandgrill.com.au

Opening hours	Open 7 days
Credit cards	Accepted
Price range	Expensive
Style	Smart casual
Cuisine	Steakhouse
Recommended for	High end

SHADOW WINE BAR

Recommended by
Alexandra Haynes

214 Williams Street
Perth
Western Australia 6000
+61 864304010
www.shadowwinebar.com.au

Opening hours	Open 7 days
Credit cards	Accepted
Price range	Affordable
Style	Casual
Cuisine	Modern Australian-European
Recommended for	Local favorite

"Simple, delicious food done well, and great service with personality."—Alexandra Haynes

UNCLE BILLY'S CHINESE RESTAURANT

9/66 Roe Street
Perth

Recommended by
Alexandra Haynes

Western Australia 6003
+61 892289388
www.uncle-billys.com.au

Opening hours	Open 7 days
Reservation policy	No
Credit cards	Accepted but not Diners
Price range	Expensive
Style	Casual
Cuisine	Asian
Recommended for	Late night

"It's one of the world's most iconic buildings, and now it boasts one of the best restaurants in the country."

KARL FIRLA P110

"WE LOVE THE INTIMACY OF THE SPACE AND THE TOTAL REVERENCE SHOWN TO THE PRODUCE."

JOSH LEWIS P124

SYDNEY

"These boys just seem to understand the less is more approach and execute it with consistency."

PASQUALE TRIMBOLI P108

"Amazing service, baller wines."

MITCH ORR P123

"A MUST VISIT."

JAMES VILES P114

SYDNEY

SCALE

0   600   1200   1800
—————————————— yd.

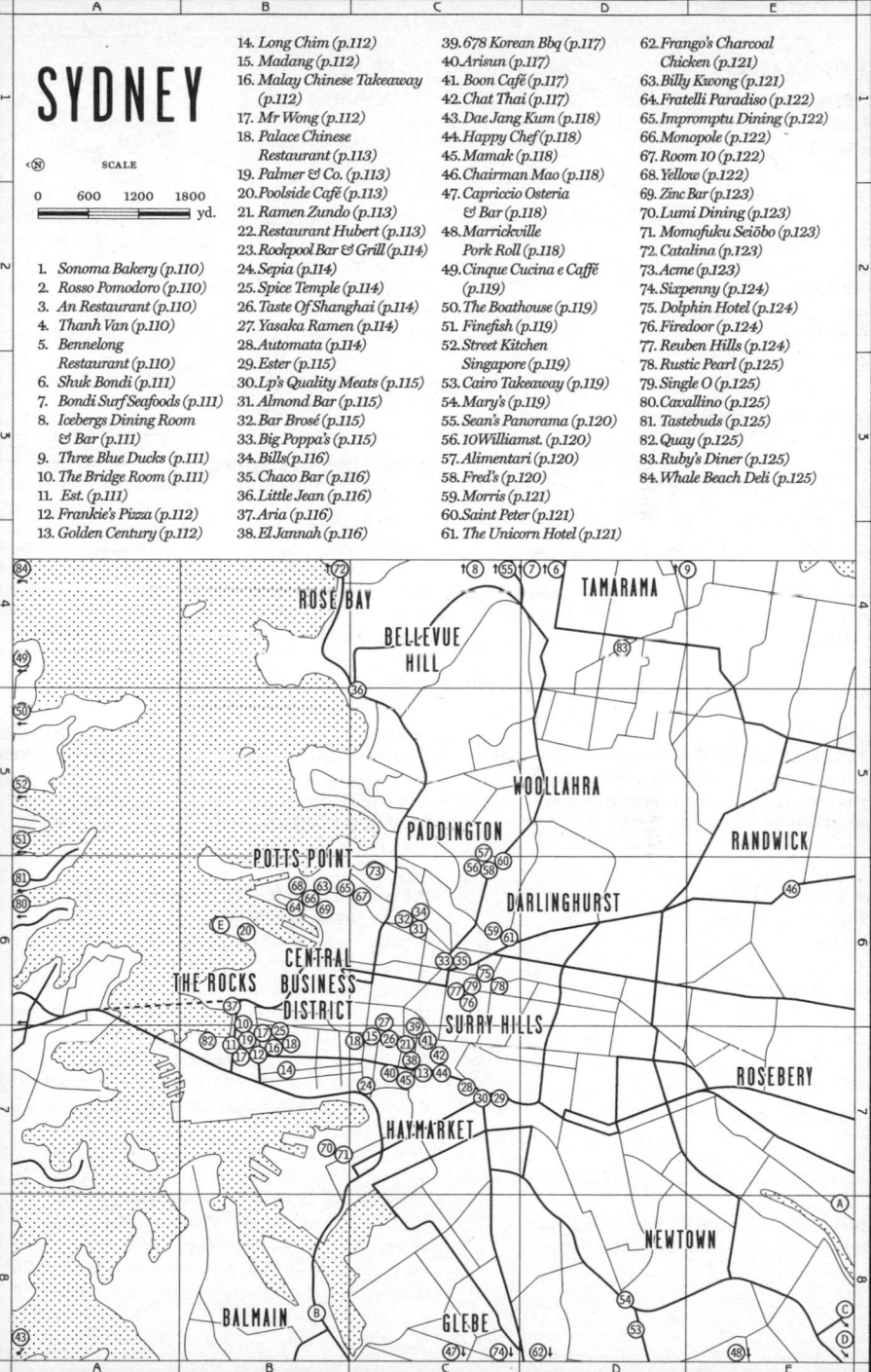

ROSE BAY
BELLEVUE HILL
TAMARAMA
WOOLLAHRA
PADDINGTON
RANDWICK
POTTS POINT
DARLINGHURST
THE ROCKS
CENTRAL BUSINESS DISTRICT
SURRY HILLS
ROSEBERY
HAYMARKET
NEWTOWN
BALMAIN
GLEBE

SONOMA BAKERY

Recommended by
Tomi Bjorck

32 Birmingham Street
Alexandria
Sydney 2015
+61 283381051
www.sonoma.com.au

Opening hours	Open 7 days
Credit cards	Accepted but not Diners
Price range	Budget
Style	Casual
Cuisine	Bakery
Recommended for	Breakfast

ROSSO POMODORO

Recommended by
Karl Firla

20–24 Buchanan Street
Balmain
Sydney 2041
+61 295555924
www.rossopomodoro.com.au

Opening hours	Closed Monday
Credit cards	Accepted but not AMEX
Price range	Budget
Style	Casual
Cuisine	Pizza
Recommended for	Regular neighborhood

"Fantastic, small, family-owned and operated pizza restaurant, using a traditional Bologna recipe without compromise. It's fun and always consistent."
—Karl Firla

AN RESTAURANT

Recommended by
Dan Hong

27 Greenfield Parade
Bankstown
Sydney 2200
+61 297967826
www.anrestaurant.com.au

Opening hours	Open 7 days
Credit cards	Not accepted
Price range	Affordable
Style	Casual
Cuisine	Pho
Recommended for	Wish I'd opened

"All they do is pho, and it's the best in Sydney. And they are so busy, all day!"—Dan Hong

THANH VAN

Recommended by
Karl Firla

327 Chapel Road South
Bankstown
Sydney 2200
+61 297082973

Opening hours	Open 7 days
Credit cards	Not accepted
Price range	Affordable
Style	Casual
Cuisine	Vietnamese
Recommended for	Bargain

"The *hủ tiếu* (clear pork broth and rice noodle soup) here is amazing!"—Karl Firla

BENNELONG RESTAURANT

Recommended by
Danielle Alvarez, Karl Firla,
Analiese Gregory, Ross Lusted,
Christine Manfield, Luke Mangan,
Ben Shewry, James Viles

Sydney Opera House
Bennelong Point
Sydney 2000
+61 292408000
www.bennelong.com.au

Opening hours	Open 7 days
Credit cards	Accepted
Price range	Expensive
Style	Smart casual
Cuisine	Modern Australian
Recommended for	High end

"It's one of the world's most iconic buildings, and now it boasts one of the best restaurants in the country."
—Karl Firla

It's a fitting place to seek the answer to the question many tourists ask and locals fiercely debate—what is Australian food? In an elegant, iridescent dining space beneath the dramatic soaring sails and steel ribs of the Sydney Opera House, acclaimed chef Peter Gilmore offers his own response to the question, with a harmonious union of native ingredients and flavors introduced by "new Australians". It's a philosophy epitomised by dishes like Cape York wild barramundi with umami butter, samphire, and native parsley, or Gilmore's playful pavlova, its sails of meringue shards an homage to the architecture of the Opera House. Whether you agree with this interpretation of "Australian" cuisine, there's no argument that dining on Gilmore's clever food while looking out to the world's most beautiful natural harbor is something of a bucket-list experience.

SHUK BONDI

Recommended by
Tomi Bjorck

2 Mitchell Street
Bondi
Sydney 2026
+61 423199859
www.shukbondi.com

Opening hours	Open 7 days
Credit cards	Accepted
Price range	Affordable
Style	Casual
Cuisine	Israeli-Mediterranean
Recommended for	Regular neighborhood

BONDI SURF SEAFOODS

Recommended by
Lucio Galletto

128 Campbell Parade
Bondi Beach
Sydney 2026
+61 291304554
www.bondisurfseafood.com.au

Opening hours	Open 7 days
Reservation policy	No
Credit cards	Accepted but not AMEX or Diners
Price range	Budget
Style	Casual
Cuisine	Seafood
Recommended for	Bargain

"Huge variety of fish, grilled, pan-fried, or deep-fried to order. Take it away and eat on the grass over the road with spectacular views of Sydney's iconic Bondi Beach."—Lucio Galletto

ICEBERGS DINING ROOM & BAR

Recommended by
Ross Lusted,
Jake Nicolson

1 Notts Avenue
Bondi Beach
Sydney 2026
+61 293659000
www.idrb.com

Opening hours	Open 7 days
Credit cards	Accepted
Price range	Expensive
Style	Smart casual
Cuisine	Modern Italian
Recommended for	Worth the travel

"The view overlooking Bondi Beach is unbelievable; the kitchen dishes out brilliant food to match. Book for lunch and stay until the sun goes down."
—Jake Nicholson

THREE BLUE DUCKS

Recommended by
Ben Greeno

141–143 Macpherson Street
Bronte
Sydney 2024
+61 293890010
www.threeblueducks.com

Opening hours	Open 7 days
Reservation policy	No
Credit cards	Accepted but not AMEX or Diners
Price range	Affordable
Style	Casual
Cuisine	Australian
Recommended for	Breakfast

"Relaxed place, friendly staff, great atmosphere, and just a short walk to the beach."—Ben Greeno

THE BRIDGE ROOM

Recommended by
Peter Gilmore,
Reon Hobson,
Christine Manfield

GF, 44 Bridge Street
Central Business District
Sydney 2000
+61 292477000
www.thebridgeroom.com.au

Opening hours	Closed Monday and Sunday
Credit cards	Accepted
Price range	Expensive
Style	Casual
Cuisine	Modern Australian
Recommended for	High end

"Stylish, considered cooking, in a class of its own. Simply knockout, every single time."
—Christine Manfield

EST.

Recommended by
Danielle Alvarez

L1, Establishment, 252 George Street
Central Business District
Sydney 2000
+61 292403000
www.merivale.com.au/est

Opening hours	Closed Sunday
Credit cards	Accepted but not Diners
Price range	Expensive
Style	Smart casual
Cuisine	Modern Australian
Recommended for	High end

"I love Peter Doyle's food, and the staff are so professional and friendly. They really know how to elevate a dining experience."—Danielle Alvarez

FRANKIE'S PIZZA

Recommended by
James Viles

50 Hunter Street
Central Business District
Sydney 2000
www.frankiespizzabytheslice.com

Opening hours	Open 7 days
Reservation policy	No
Credit cards	Not accepted
Price range	Budget
Style	Casual
Cuisine	Pizza
Recommended for	Late night

GOLDEN CENTURY

Recommended by
Danielle Alvarez, David Chang,
Karl Firla, Lucio Galletto,
Peter Gilmore, Analiese Gregory,
Ben Greeno, Reon Hobson,
Dan Hong, Dan Hunter, Josh Lewis,
Morgan McGlone, Isaac McHale,
Mitch Orr, James Viles

393–399 Sussex Street
Central Business District
Sydney 2000
+61 292123901
www.goldencentury.com.au

Opening hours	Open 7 days
Credit cards	Accepted
Price range	Affordable
Style	Casual
Cuisine	Cantonese
Recommended for	Late night

"Could be the best late-night restaurant in the world."
—Dan Hunter

LONG CHIM

Recommended by
Christine Manfield

Corner of Pitt Street & Angel Place
Central Business District
Sydney 2000
+61 292237999
www.longchimsydney.com

Opening hours	Closed Sunday
Credit cards	Accepted
Price range	Affordable
Style	Casual
Cuisine	Thai
Recommended for	Late night

"Punchy and authentic 'take no prisoners' Thai
street-food cooked with premium produce."
—Christine Manfield

MADANG

Recommended by
Josh Lewis

371a Pitt Street
Central Business District
Sydney 2000
+61 292647010

Opening hours	Open 7 days
Credit cards	Accepted but not AMEX or Diners
Price range	Budget
Style	Casual
Cuisine	Korean
Recommended for	Late night

MALAY CHINESE TAKEAWAY

Recommended by
Dan Hong

1/50–58 Hunter Street
Central Business District
Sydney 2000
+61 292316788
www.malaychinese.com.au

Opening hours	Closed Sunday
Reservation policy	No
Credit cards	Accepted but not AMEX or Diners
Price range	Budget
Style	Casual
Cuisine	Chinese
Recommended for	Bargain

MR WONG

Recommended by
Nick Holloway,
Luke Mangan,
Cameron Matthews,
Morgan McGlone,
Isaac McHale

3 Bridge Street
Central Business District
Sydney 2000
+61 292403000
www.merivale.com.au/mrwong

Opening hours	Open 7 days
Credit cards	Accepted but not Diners
Price range	Expensive
Style	Smart casual
Cuisine	Cantonese
Recommended for	Late night

"The rustic Shanghai decor over two floors is very
evocative and cool, however my preference is to sit
at the bar to watch the theater of the kitchen.
Although the dumplings and duck are personal
favorites, I order as many different bar dishes as
possible."—Cameron Matthews

PALACE CHINESE RESTAURANT

Recommended by
Analiese Gregory,
Ross Lusted

Piccadilly Tower
38/133–145 Castlereagh Street
Central Business District
Sydney 2000
+61 292836288
www.palacechinese.com.au

Opening hours	Open 7 days
Credit cards	Accepted but not AMEX or Diners
Price range	Affordable
Style	Casual
Cuisine	Cantonese
Recommended for	Bargain

PALMER & CO.

Recommended by
Jason Atherton

Abercrombie Lane
Central Business District
Sydney 2000
+61 292548088
www.merivale.com.au/palmerandco

Opening hours	Open 7 days
Credit cards	Accepted
Price range	Affordable
Style	Smart casual
Cuisine	Australian
Recommended for	Late night

POOLSIDE CAFÉ

Recommended by
Lucio Galletto

1c Mrs Macquarie's Road
Central Business District
Sydney 2000
+61 283541044
www.poolsidecafé.com.au

Opening hours	Open 7 days
Reservation policy	No
Credit cards	Accepted but not Diners
Price range	Affordable
Style	Casual
Cuisine	Modern Australian
Recommended for	Breakfast

"After an early morning swim, there are plenty of great options to fill that ravenous hunger."
—Lucio Galletto

RAMEN ZUNDO

Recommended by
Ross Lusted

World Square Shopping Centre
GF, Shop 10, 644 George Street
Central Business District
Sydney 2000
+61 292646113
www.ramenzundo.com.au

Opening hours	Open 7 days
Reservation policy	No
Credit cards	Accepted but not Diners
Price range	Affordable
Style	Casual
Cuisine	Japanese
Recommended for	Bargain

"Fast, hot, and so tasty—all the things ramen should be."—Ross Lusted

RESTAURANT HUBERT

Recommended by
Jason Atherton, Ben Devlin,
Karl Firla, Lucio Galletto,
Analiese Gregory, Philip Johnson,
Josh Lewis, Ross Lusted,
Sean McConnell,
Duncan Welgemoed

15 Bligh Street
Central Business District
Sydney 2000
+61 292320881
www.restauranthubert.com

Opening hours	Closed Sunday
Credit cards	Accepted but not Diners
Price range	Affordable
Style	Casual
Cuisine	French
Recommended for	Late night

"Descending the wood-panelled staircase into this cavern of a restaurant, you feel as if you are going back in time to 1920s Paris. It is huge, grand, and unapologetically old-school French. For some reason it makes me want to be naughty."—Analiese Gregory

Hubert hit the (under)ground running in early 2016 and all of Sydney swooned. The first full-service restaurant for young-gun duo Anton Forte and Jason Scott (owners of Shady Pines Saloon, The Baxter Inn, and Frankie's Pizza) it's a cavernous but beautiful basement space theatrically furnished with red velvet drapes, burnished wood bars, and candlelit tables. Classic cocktails and a broad wine list complement the French menu, populated by traditional Gallic dishes and impressive contemporary interpretations of them—like *oeufs en gelée* (here, a soft egg yolk and caviar set into bonito jelly). Add a generous sense of old-world hospitality and fickle Sydneysiders, who usually drop restaurants like worn-out lovers as soon as something shinier comes along, are still in thrall.

ROCKPOOL BAR & GRILL

Recommended by
Bonny Porter

66 Hunter Street
Central Business District
Sydney 2000
+61 280781900
www.rockpoolbarandgrill.com.au

Opening hours	Open 7 days
Credit cards	Accepted
Price range	Affordable
Style	Smart casual
Cuisine	Australian Grill
Recommended for	High end

"Living in London, I would happily fly halfway around the world for a David Blackmore wagyu at Rockpool Bar and Grill. I've only ever had the best service, the best food and a very impressive wine list of over 10,000 choices."—Bonny Porter

SEPIA

Recommended by
Jason Atherton, Karl Firla,
Peter Gilmore, Danielle Gjestland,
Reon Hobson, Michael Meredith,
Justin North, Ryan Sessions,
Alla Wolf-Tasker

201 Sussex Street
Central Business District
Sydney 2000
+61 292831990
www.sepiarestaurant.com.au

Opening hours	Closed Monday and Sunday
Credit cards	Accepted but not Diners
Price range	Expensive
Style	Smart casual
Cuisine	Australian-Japanese
Recommended for	High end

"Martin's dishes are beautiful, delicious, and playful, and Vicki's service team is second to none."
—Danielle Gjestland

SPICE TEMPLE

Recommended by
Peter Gilmore

10 Bligh Street
Central Business District
Sydney 2000
+61 280781888
www.spicetemple.com.au

Opening hours	Open 7 days
Credit cards	Accepted
Price range	Affordable
Style	Smart casual
Cuisine	Modern Chinese
Recommended for	Regular neighborhood

"Spice Temple for the authenticity of flavors and the variety of Chinese cuisines offered."—Peter Gilmore

114

TASTE OF SHANGHAI

Recommended by
Analiese Gregory

World Square
907/644 George Street
Central Business District
Sydney 2000
+61 292618832
www.tasteofshanghai.com.au

Opening hours	Open 7 days
Credit cards	Accepted
Price range	Affordable
Style	Casual
Cuisine	Chinese
Recommended for	Bargain

"It's in the basement of a shopping center—I come here on my day off and smash soup dumplings and other Chinese snacks with a bottle of Pet Nat—they do BYO for around A$2 ($1; £1) per person."
—Analiese Gregory

YASAKA RAMEN

Recommended by
Justin North

126 Liverpool Street
Central Business District
Sydney 2000
+61 292629027
www.yasakaramen.com.au

Opening hours	Open 7 days
Credit cards	Not accepted
Price range	Affordable
Style	Casual
Cuisine	Japanese
Recommended for	Regular neighborhood

AUTOMATA

Recommended by
Tomi Bjorck,
Paul Carmichael,
Analiese Gregory,
Morgan McGlone,
Mitch Orr,
James Viles

5 Kensington Street
Chippendale
Sydney 2008
+61 282778555
www.automata.com.au

Opening hours	Closed Monday and Sunday
Credit cards	Accepted but not Diners
Price range	Affordable
Style	Casual
Cuisine	Modern Australian
Recommended for	Local favorite

"A must visit."—James Viles

Radical, creative, distinctive—not words you'd usually find ascribed to a hotel restaurant—but chef Clayton Wells's innovative and constantly changing tasting menu has plenty of surprises, with clever snacks punctuating dishes you'll still be thinking about hours later. Part of the revamped Old Clare Hotel, the two-storey Automata (Au-TOM-ata) has a striking fit-out including a ceiling of car-piston pendants and suspended aircraft parts, but it's all eyes down when Wells's austerely beautiful, precision-plated dishes are delivered to the table. Choose the drink-matched option for tastes of the smart collection of diverse, under-the-radar European and Australian wines.

ESTER

46/52 Meagher Street
Chippendale
Sydney 2008
+61 280688279
www.ester-restaurant.com.au

Recommended by
Danielle Alvarez, Jasper Avent,
Tomi Bjorck, Peter Gilmore,
Ben Greeno, Analiese Gregory,
Dan Hong, Dan Hunter,
Christine Manfield,
Mitch Orr, James Viles

Opening hours	Closed Monday and Sunday
Credit cards	Accepted
Price range	Affordable
Style	Casual
Cuisine	Modern Australian
Recommended for	Regular neighborhood

"All the food at Ester is something you want to eat; it's delicious and interesting without being too tricky. I always find myself looking at the dishes and wishing I had come up with them first!"—Analiese Gregory

LP'S QUALITY MEATS

16/12 Chippen Street
Chippendale
Sydney 2008
+61 283990929
www.lpsqualitymeats.com

Recommended by
Tomi Bjorck,
Mitch Orr

Opening hours	Closed Monday and Sunday
Credit cards	Accepted
Price range	Affordable
Style	Casual
Cuisine	European
Recommended for	Regular neighborhood

"Luke's fine-dining training shines through in the incredible technique he uses to make fun, tasty, and approachable food. It's much, much more than just meat."—Mitch Orr

ALMOND BAR

379 Liverpool Street
Darlinghurst
Sydney 2010
+61 293805318
www.almondbar.com.au

Recommended by
Christine Manfield

Opening hours	Closed Monday
Credit cards	Accepted but not AMEX
Price range	Budget
Style	Casual
Cuisine	Syrian
Recommended for	Local favorite

"Fab Syrian food."—Christine Manfield

BAR BROSÉ

231a Victoria Street
Darlinghurst
Sydney 2010
+61 450307117
www.barbrose.com.au

Recommended by
Christine Manfield,
Morgan McGlone

Opening hours	Closed Monday
Credit cards	Accepted
Price range	Affordable
Style	Casual
Cuisine	Modern French
Recommended for	Local favorite

"Bring an appetite. Creative, inventive and packed with flavor. Don't miss the potato gnocchi and *lap cheong* sausage."—Christine Manfield

BIG POPPA'S

96 Oxford Street
Darlinghurst
Sydney 2010
+61 499052201
www.bigpoppa.com.au

Recommended by
Danielle Alvarez

Opening hours	Open 7 days
Credit cards	Accepted
Price range	Affordable
Style	Casual
Cuisine	Modern Italian
Recommended for	Late night

"A great plate of pasta, salads, grilled meat at 2.00 a.m.? You can't find that anywhere else. It's a hospitality godsend! They also play amazing hip-hop. It's pretty great."—Danielle Alvarez

BILLS

Recommended by
Ricardo Chaneton

433 Liverpool Street
Darlinghurst
Sydney 2010
+61 293609631
www.bills.com.au

Opening hours	Open 7 days
Credit cards	Accepted
Price range	Affordable
Style	Casual
Cuisine	Australian
Recommended for	Breakfast

CHACO BAR

Recommended by
Analiese Gregory,
Christine Manfield

238 Crown Street
Darlinghurst
Sydney 2010
+61 290078352
www.chacobar.com.au

Opening hours	Closed Sunday
Credit cards	Accepted but not AMEX or Diners
Price range	Budget
Style	Casual
Cuisine	Japanese
Recommended for	Bargain

"Terrific ramen."—Christine Manfield

LITTLE JEAN

Recommended by
Luke Mangan

1/1 Kiaora Lane
Double Bay
Sydney 2028
+61 293280201
www.littlejean.com.au

Opening hours	Open 7 days
Credit cards	Accepted but not Diners
Price range	Affordable
Style	Casual
Cuisine	Modern International
Recommended for	Breakfast

"Little Jean suppport local suppliers by using local products throughout the menu where they can. It takes me a lot to get excited about breakfast, but this café has a really interesting breakfast menu, including congee in twelve-hour stock."—Luke Mangan

The long, light-filled slice of space inhabited by Little Jean is split into two distinct zones—one for takeaway coffee from Single O, house-made pastries, and communal dining, the other with banquette seating for more leisurely meals. The menu eschews breakfast regulars (smashed avocado is so 2017!) for originals like brown rice porridge with white miso, maple, pears, and toasted nuts, or a corned beef and brie "Cubano" sandwich with fried egg, *piparras* (green peppers), and *aji amarillo* (yellow chile). From Wednesday to Saturday, Little Jean transforms into a bistro, with dinner dishes rangin from light—fresh tagliatelle, mint, goat's curd, pine nuts, and zucchini (courgette) to luxe (chargrilled half lobster tail, scallops, dashi, samphire, and truffle) complemented by a compact but smart all-Australian wine list.

ARIA

Recommended by
Justin North

1 Macquarie Street
East Circular Quay
Sydney 2000
+61 292402255
www.ariarestaurant.com

Opening hours	Open 7 days
Credit cards	Accepted
Price range	Expensive
Style	Smart casual
Cuisine	Australian
Recommended for	Local favorite

"Awesome food, amazing wine list and great service, all on the harbor—that's Sydney."—Justin North

EL JANNAH

Recommended by
Paul Carmichael

4–8 South Street
Granville
Sydney 2142
+61 296370977
www.eljannah.com.au

Opening hours	Open 7 days
Reservation policy	No
Credit cards	Not accepted
Price range	Budget
Style	Casual
Cuisine	Lebanese
Recommended for	Bargain

"Consistently tasty."—Paul Carmichael

678 KOREAN BBQ

Recommended by
Dan Hong

1 Pitt Street
Haymarket
Sydney 2000
+61 292818997

Opening hours	Open 7 days
Credit cards	Accepted
Price range	Affordable
Style	Casual
Cuisine	Korean Barbecue
Recommended for	Regular neighborhood

"The best Korean barbecue in Sydney, by far! The marinated shortrib and rib fingers are my favorites."
—Dan Hong

ARISUN

Recommended by
Dan Hong

35/1 Dixon Street
Haymarket
Sydney 2000
+61 292641588
www.arisunrestaurant.com

Opening hours	Open 7 days
Credit cards	Accepted
Price range	Affordable
Style	Casual
Cuisine	Korean
Recommended for	Late night

"Try the Korean fried chicken and army stew."
—Dan Hong

BOON CAFÉ

Recommended by
Danielle Alvarez, Phillip Foss,
Lennox Hastie, Dan Hong,
Josh Lewis, Ross Lusted,
Christine Manfield,
Morgan McGlone, Mitch Orr

1/425 Pitt Street
Haymarket
Sydney 2000
+61 292812114
www.booncafe.com

Opening hours	Open 7 days
Credit cards	Accepted
Price range	Affordable
Style	Casual
Cuisine	Thai
Recommended for	Breakfast

"Palisa Anderson and Amy Chanta combine Australian café culture with incredible Thai food and ingredients straight from their own farm. You can't talk about Australian cuisine without talking about Asian food, and here they do Thai excellently."—Danielle Alvarez

From the Chat Thai family dynasty, Boon is a bright and busy deli/café hybrid—a magnet for keen cooks who come to stock up on Thai groceries, and for lovers of Thai food who prefer to have it cooked for them. The café kickstarts the day with congees, Thai egg dishes, pandan custard-filled croissants, and cold pressed fruit, veg, and herb juices, supercharged with turmeric shots. The coffee comes from Aussie specialists Single O, and there's a range of traditional Thai and herbal teas. By night, Boon focuses on gutsy, spicy Isaan cuisine from the northeast of Thailand—curries, *som tum* (green papaya salad), noodles and, for the adventurous, smoky grilled secondary cuts and innards of pork or chicken.

CHAT THAI

Recommended by
Tomi Bjorck, Paul Carmichael,
Peter Gilmore, Analiese Gregory,
Ross Lusted, Justin North,
Mitch Orr

20 Campbell Street
Haymarket
Sydney 2000
+61 292111808
www.chatthai.com.au

Opening hours	Open 7 days
Credit cards	Accepted
Price range	Affordable
Style	Casual
Cuisine	Thai
Recommended for	Bargain

"Bustling, tasty, and authentic."—Mitch Orr

There are now six outlets of Chat Thai (the first opened in 1989), but that doesn't seem to have any effect on the blockbuster lines (queues), nor the expectant energy of the clientele at these cultishly popular restaurants. At the original Haymarket branch, diners are drawn by the promise of cheap, authentic street food served until the small hours. The lengthy trilingual menu delivers classics with added finesse—like pad thai with roasted boned duck, or spring rolls made with smoked fish sausage, chicken, and crab and served with a caramelized tamarind dipping sauce. There are also eight different versions of *som tum* (green papaya salad). Curries come in both tame versions and those spicy enough to satisfy even the most heat-resistant palate.

DAE JANG KUM

Recommended by
Josh Lewis

35 Goulburn Street
Haymarket
Sydney 2000
+65 292110890
www.daejangkum.com.au

Opening hours	Open 7 days
Credit cards	Accepted
Price range	Affordable
Style	Casual
Cuisine	Korean
Recommended for	Late night

"If you are looking for something to eat during the twilight hours of 2.00 a.m. and 4.00 a.m. you can't pass a Korean BBQ. The mustard and sesame seed sauce is addictive."—Josh Lewis

HAPPY CHEF

Recommended by
Danielle Alvarez,
Dan Hong,
Luke Mangan

Sussex Centre Food Court
3F, 401–403 Sussex Street
Haymarket
Sydney 2000
+61 292815832

Opening hours	Open 7 days
Reservation policy	No
Credit cards	Not accepted
Price range	Budget
Style	Casual
Cuisine	Chinese
Recommended for	Bargain

"They do the best Laksa in Sydney!"—Luke Mangan

MAMAK

Recommended by
Danielle Alvarez,
Analiese Gregory,
Justin North

15 Goulburn Street
Haymarket
Sydney 2000
+61 292111668
www.mamak.com.au

Opening hours	Open 7 days
Reservation policy	No
Credit cards	Accepted
Price range	Affordable
Style	Casual
Cuisine	Malaysian
Recommended for	Late night

"The food is super-tasty Malaysian. They make the best roti right in the window, which is such a joy to watch. They are not licensed so you're only going there for the food, which helps to keep things cheap!" —Danielle Alvarez

CHAIRMAN MAO

Recommended by
Karl Firla

189 Anzac Parade
Kensington
Sydney 2033
+61 296979189

Opening hours	Closed Tuesday
Credit cards	Accepted
Price range	Affordable
Style	Casual
Cuisine	Chinese
Recommended for	Regular neighborhood

"Great, family-run, Hunanese restaurant. Pre-order chile mud crab when you book! The smoked pork and bamboo is amazing, but always sells out."—Karl Firla

CAPRICCIO OSTERIA & BAR

Recommended by
Lucio Galletto

159 Norton Street
Leichhardt
Sydney 2040
+61 295727607
www.capriccio.sydney

Opening hours	Closed Monday
Credit cards	Accepted
Price range	Affordable
Style	Casual
Cuisine	Modern Italian
Recommended for	Local favorite

"This new restaurant is revitalising Leichhardt with modern twists on traditional Italian cuisine. Great service and wines to boot."—Lucio Galletto

MARRICKVILLE PORK ROLL

Recommended by
Dan Hong

236a Illawarra Road
Marrickville
Sydney 2204
61 420966368

Opening hours	Open 7 days
Reservation policy	No
Credit cards	Not accepted
Price range	Budget
Style	Casual
Cuisine	Vietnamese
Recommended for	Bargain

"The best Vietnamese pork rolls in the world. I like to add extra meatballs!"—Dan Hong

CINQUE CUCINA E CAFFÉ

5 Darley Street East
Mona Vale
Sydney 2103
+61 299995555
www.cinque5.com.au

Opening hours..Open 7 days
Credit cards.....................Accepted but not AMEX or Diners
Price range..Affordable
Style..Casual
Cuisine..Italian-Café
Recommended for...Breakfast

THE BOATHOUSE

2 The Esplanade
Balmoral Beach
Mosman
Sydney 2088
+61 299745440
www.theboathousebb.com.au

Opening hours..Open 7 days
Reservation policy...No
Credit cards..Accepted
Price range..Affordable
Style..Casual
Cuisine..Australian
Recommended for...Breakfast

"Amazing breakfast spread—everything from super healthy to a fried breakfast. I would argue that nobody does breakfast better than the Australians."
—Uwe Opocensky

FINEFISH

75 Grosvenor Lane
Neutral Bay
Sydney 2089
+61 299084448
www.finefish.com.au

Opening hours...Closed Sunday
Credit cards..Accepted
Price range..Affordable
Style..Casual
Cuisine..Seafood
Recommended for....................................Local favorite

STREET KITCHEN SINGAPORE

240 Military Road
Neutral Bay
Sydney 2089
+61 299082552

Opening hours..Open 7 days
Credit cards.....................Accepted but not AMEX or Diners
Price range..Budget
Style..Casual
Cuisine..Singaporean
Recommended for...........................Regular neighborhood

CAIRO TAKEAWAY

81 Enmore road
Newtown
Sydney 2042
+61 295172060
www.cairotakeaway.com

Opening hours..Open 7 days
Reservation policy...No
Credit cards.....................Accepted but not AMEX or Diners
Price range..Budget
Style..Casual
Cuisine..Egyptian
Recommended for..Bargain

"Fast, flavorful, healthy food, and great people."
—Ben Greeno

MARY'S

6 Mary Street
Newtown
Sydney 2042
www.6marystreet.com

Opening hours..Open 7 days
Reservation policy...No
Credit cards.....................Accepted but not AMEX or Diners
Price range..Budget
Style..Casual
Cuisine..Burgers
Recommended for................................Wish I'd opened

"A menu focused on burgers with five things on it. Great wine, rock music, fun atmosphere. It just makes sense. Everyone loves it."—Danielle Alvarez

SEAN'S PANORAMA

270 Campbell Parade
North Bondi
Sydney 2026
+61 293654924
www.seanspanaroma.co

Recommended by
Gabriela Cámara,
Ben Greeno

Opening hours	Closed Monday and Tuesday
Credit cards	Accepted
Price range	Affordable
Style	Smart casual
Cuisine	Australian-Mediterranean
Recommended for	Wish I'd opened

"It oversees Bondi Beach—which is a spectacular place—and the food is simply delicious. It's a lot of what I would like to make and eat every day."
—Gabriela Cámara

10WILLIAMST.

10 William Street
Paddington
Sydney 2021
+61 293603310
www.10williamst.com.au

Recommended by
Danielle Alvarez,
Analiese Gregory,
Nick Holloway,
Ross Lusted,
Morgan McGlone

Opening hours	Closed Sunday
Reservation policy	No
Credit cards	Accepted
Price range	Affordable
Style	Casual
Cuisine	Italian
Recommended for	Regular neighborhood

"On a Monday night, it's the hospitality hang-out. The vibe is excellent, the staff know what chefs and the hospitality crowd want on their day off. Good food, good wine, and keep it coming."—Danielle Alvarez

With an egalitarian no-bookings policy, it's elbow to elbow by 8.00 p.m. at this popular sibling to the venerated Fratelli Paradiso in Potts Point. The crowds are drawn by the buzz and a broad, eclectic, food-friendly wine list—or, indeed, the wine-friendly menu. Whether William Street is a wine bar with great food, or a restaurant with a superlative wine list is a moot point—what is a truism is that everyone who comes here who is not local wishes they were, thanks to the interesting wines (served by the glass), lively service, and appealing Italian-centric sharing menu. Once you've claimed your spot and ordered your whipped *bottarga* (salted fish roe) pretzels, it can be hard to find a good reason to leave.

ALIMENTARI

2 Hopetoun Street
Paddington
Sydney 2021
+61 293582142

Recommended by
Ross Lusted

Opening hours	Closed Sunday
Credit cards	Accepted
Price range	Budget
Style	Casual
Cuisine	Italian
Recommended for	Breakfast

"The food is always great, and it's in our neighborhood so we always see friends."
—Ross Lusted

FRED'S

380 Oxford Street
Paddington
Sydney 2021
+61 292403000
www.merivale.com.au/freds

Recommended by
Ross Lusted,
Justin North

Opening hours	Closed Monday and Sunday
Credit cards	Accepted
Price range	Affordable
Style	Smart casual
Cuisine	European
Recommended for	Wish I'd opened

"Simply beautiful produce, cooked well in a homely environment."—Justin North

If you had the space, money, and cooking ability, your dream kitchen would probably look a lot like the one at Fred's—posh country house, with marble-topped work benches, and a spectacular four-foot (1.25-meter) hearth centerpiece that burns night and day. Chef Danielle Alvarez comes from California's Chez Panisse stable, bringing with her the Alice Waters ethos of strong relationships with growers and a focus on the produce. The simple but tasty food is usually cooked over the coals. It feels like eating at a friend's place, with the best seats in the house being the ones set right up at a bench in the kitchen.

MORRIS

Recommended by
Christine Manfield

33 Albion Avenue
Paddington
Sydney 2021
+61 421747584
www.morris-cafe.com

Opening hours	Closed Sunday
Credit cards	Accepted
Price range	Affordable
Style	Casual
Cuisine	Modern Australian
Recommended for	Breakfast

"Healthy and imaginative. Spanking fresh produce, vibrant flavor combinations, and generous portions. Great sandwiches and salads. The best café food imaginable."—Christine Manfield

Morris, on a tree-shaded Paddington corner, is the second café venture from Georgia Woodyard and Anne Cooper, owners of the popular Scout's Honour In Redfern. It follows the same winning formula, offering a menu balanced between good and healthy on the one hand, and just plain good on the other. Like five-grain porridge (good and healthy); or bacon, provolone, and pickled slaw roll with harissa aioli (just good). There's also a very literal interpretation of fruit toast, which comes slathered with homemade *labneh* (strained yoghurt) and piled with strawberries, pear, passionfruit, and pomegranate, dressed with local honey and mint. Morris's expertly made coffee comes courtesy of Five Senses—and the pleasantly leafy outlook from a footpath table is courtesy of Mother Nature.

SAINT PETER

Recommended by
Paul Carmichael,
Ben Devlin,
Josh Lewis,
Ross Lusted,
Mitch Orr

362 Oxford Street
Paddington
Sydney 2021
+61 289372530
www.saintpeter.com.au

Opening hours	Closed Monday
Credit cards	Accepted
Price range	Affordable
Style	Casual
Cuisine	Australian Seafood
Recommended for	Regular neighborhood

"Saint Peter work with the best seafood from around Australia, and dry-age and use every part of the product they can. The food is intelligent and delicious, and the atmosphere is lively."—Ben Devlin

Named after the patron saint of fishermen, Paddington's Saint Peter doesn't so much lean towards the piscine as enthusiastically throw itself into the fishing net, grabbing it all with both hands, bycatch included. In the spirit of waste minimization, nothing is discarded—from fish scales which are served as little crunchy salt and vinegar crisps to fried fish liver. Chef-owner Josh Niland has also brought the idea of dry-aging from land to sea, with a custom-made drying cabinet. It may sound a bit oddball, but what ends up on the plate at Saint Peter is beautiful, imaginatively prepared seafood.

THE UNICORN HOTEL

Recommended by
Tomi Bjorck

106 Oxford Street
Paddington
Sydney 2012
+61 293607994
www.theunicornhotel.com.au

Opening hours	Open 7 days
Credit cards	Accepted
Price range	Affordable
Style	Casual
Cuisine	Australian
Recommended for	Late night

FRANGO'S CHARCOAL CHICKEN

Recommended by
Paul Carmichael

98 New Canterbury Road
Petersham
Sydney 2049
+61 295602369
www.frangos.com.au

Opening hours	Open 7 days
Credit cards	Accepted
Price range	Budget
Style	Casual
Cuisine	Portuguese
Recommended for	Bargain

BILLY KWONG

Recommended by
Christine Manfield

1/28 MacLeay Street
Potts Point
Sydney 2011
+61 293323300
www.billykwong.com.au

Opening hours	Open 7 days
Credit cards	Accepted but not Diners
Price range	Affordable
Style	Smart casual
Cuisine	Australian-Chinese
Recommended for	Regular neighborhood

FRATELLI PARADISO

12–16 Challis Avenue
Potts Point
Sydney 2011
+61 293571744
www.fratelliparadiso.com

Recommended by
Phillip Foss,
Lucio Galletto,
Analiese Gregory,
Morgan McGlone,
Mitch Orr,
Pasquale Trimboli

Opening hours...Open 7 days
Reservation policy..No
Credit cards...Accepted
Price range...Affordable
Style...Casual
Cuisine..Italian
Recommended for.........................Regular neighborhood

"I just simply can't get away from Italian food.
Whether at my mum's place or out and about, Italian
rules the roost for me. Hands down, these boys just
seem to understand the less is more approach and
execute it with consistency."—Pasquale Trimboli

Enrico and Giovanni "Johnny" Paradiso, along with
Marco Ambrosino, brought Italy to Sydney (via
Melbourne) almost two decades ago, establishing
Paradiso as a Pott's Point institution—a position it
shows no sign of relinquishing. The space is sexy,
dark, and frequently loud, the waiters are charming
and the food, served all day (to walk-ins only) is
trattoria-simple, bold, and authentic. A smart list
of wines from the islands, mountains, and plains of
Italy complements the food. Whether it's a lunch of
vitello tonnato (cold veal with creamy tuna sauce) or
clam linguine, a hefty *bistecca Fiorentina* (T-bone
steak) for dinner, or just an antipasto plate and a
glass of Prosecco, it's worth joining the still-
besotted locals who mill on the footpath waiting
for another taste of an old favorite.

IMPROMPTU DINING

Llankelly Place
7/24–30 Springfield Avenue
Potts Point
Sydney 2011
+61 421677089
www.impromptudining.com

Recommended by
Reon Hobson

Opening hours..........................Closed Monday and Tuesday
Credit cards...........................Accepted but not Diners
Price range...Affordable
Style...Casual
Cuisine..Australian
Recommended for.........................Regular neighborhood

"A well-executed menu. Try the pig's blood parfait
with crispy pork skin."—Reon Hobson

MONOPOLE

71a Macleay Street
Potts Point
Sydney 2011
+61 293604410
www.monopolesydney.com.au

Recommended by
Christine Manfield

Opening hours...Open 7 days
Credit cards...Accepted
Price range...Affordable
Style...Casual
Cuisine..Australian
Recommended for.........................Regular neighborhood

"Terrific wine bar showcasing boutique wines from
around the world—and snack plates too."
—Christine Manfield

ROOM 10

10 Llankelly Place
Potts Point
Sydney 2011
+61 432445342

Recommended by
Analiese Gregory,
Mitch Orr,
James Viles

Opening hours...Open 7 days
Reservation policy..No
Credit cards.....................Accepted but not AMEX or Diners
Price range...Affordable
Style...Casual
Cuisine...Modern Australian
Recommended for...Breakfast

"This is a tiny laneway café that I have been going to
since they opened. They serve Mecca coffee, very well
made, and have a solid sandwich selection, as well as
a killer breakfast rice with rhubarb, seeds, yogurt, and
honey for when I'm having a healthy day. The husband
and wife team that run it are also the cutest!"
—Analiese Gregory

YELLOW

57 Macleay Street
Potts Point
Sydney 2011
+61 293322344
www.yellowsydney.com.au

Recommended by
Mitch Orr

Opening hours...Open 7 days
Credit cards...Accepted
Price range...Affordable
Style...Casual
Cuisine.......................................Vegetarian-Australian
Recommended for...Breakfast

ZINC BAR

Recommended by
Claus Meyer

2/77 Macleay Street
Potts Point
Sydney 2011
+61 293586777

Opening hours	Open 7 days
Reservation policy	No
Credit cards	Accepted
Price range	Affordable
Style	Casual
Cuisine	Australian
Recommended for	Breakfast

LUMI DINING

Recommended by
Karl Firla,
Lennox Hastie,
Ben Willis

56 Pirrama Road
Pyrmont
Sydney 2009
+61 295711999
www.lumidining.com

Opening hours	Closed Monday and Tuesday
Credit cards	Accepted
Price range	Expensive
Style	Smart casual
Cuisine	Italian-Japanese
Recommended for	Worth the travel

"Delicious food in a relaxed, warm, and welcoming setting; inventive Italian with a Japanese influence."
—Lennox Hastie

Federico Zanellato does the seemingly impossible — he fuses two disparate cuisines into something elegantly seamless and sense-making. Born in Italy, it was working in Tokyo that ignited his love of Japanese cuisine and its techniques—and the two cultures are bought together here. At this glass-walled restaurant that seems to hover just above the water on Pyrmont Bay, Zanellato constructs a five- or eight-course tasting menu based on season and market availability, with authentic, cherry-picked ingredients. Like *chawanmushi*, a silken steamed Japanese custard flavored with Parmesan. Or delicate mushroom *agnolotti* (small ravioli) with a rye dashi. Wine can be paired with each course or Lumi's knowledgeable sommelier can help you pick from the range of sake and *umeshu* (Japanese fruit liqueur).

MOMOFUKU SEIŌBO

Recommended by
Dan Hong,
Josh Lewis,
Mitch Orr

The Star
80 Pyrmont Street
Pyrmont
Sydney 2009
www.seiobo.momofuku.com

Opening hours	Closed Sunday
Credit cards	Accepted
Price range	Expensive
Style	Smart casual
Cuisine	Australian
Recommended for	High end

"The most unique, tasty, and fun food in the city. Amazing service, baller wines."—Mitch Orr

CATALINA

Recommended by
Luke Mangan

Lyne Park
Rose Bay
Sydney 2029
+61 293710555
www.catalinarosebay.com.au

Opening hours	Open 7 days
Credit cards	Accepted
Price range	Expensive
Style	Smart casual
Cuisine	Modern Australian-European
Recommended for	Local favorite

"This is a truly iconic Sydney restaurant and one of the city's best lunch spots. The cuisine is simple and elegant, the view is amazing, and if I were to choose any one place to take a tourist, this would be the place. You can even arrive by sea plane to the restaurant's doorstep."—Luke Mangan

ACME

Recommended by
Matt Abergel

60 Bayswater Road
Rushcutters Bay
Sydney 2011
+61 435940884
www.weareacme.com.au

Opening hours	Closed Monday and Sunday
Reservation policy	No
Credit cards	Accepted but not Diners
Price range	Budget
Style	Casual
Cuisine	Italian-Asian
Recommended for	Worth the travel

SIXPENNY

83 Percival Road
Stanmore
Sydney 2048
+61 295726666
www.sixpenny.com.au

Recommended by
Luca Fantin, Peter Gilmore,
Dan Hunter, Josh Lewis,
Morgan McGlone, Uwe Opocensky,
Mitch Orr, Ryan Sessions,
Tim Spedding, Ben Willis

Opening hours..............................Closed Monday and Tuesday
Credit cards...Accepted
Price range..Expensive
Style..Smart casual
Cuisine...Australian
Recommended for..High end

"We love the intimacy of the space and the total reverence shown to the produce. Daniel Puskas has a way of presenting food that is entirely new and at the same time comfortingly familiar; always beautiful without being overworked."—Josh Lewis

Five years after it opened, the Sixpenny hype is still going strong—a rarity in a society forever hungry for the new. Tucked behind an unassuming Stanmore shopfront, the compact and understatedly elegant dining room doesn't give much away, and the degustation menu, with a choice of six or eight courses, is equally restrained. But whether it's a deceptively simple-sounding dish like potatoes with oyster and raw mushroom, or an edgy dessert of mead vinegar custard with frozen raspberry and strawberry consommé, the intrepid food, wide-ranging wine list, and amenable, polished service more than justify the continuing plaudits.

DOLPHIN HOTEL

412 Crown Street
Surry Hills
Sydney 2010
+61 293314800
www.dolphinhotel.com.au

Recommended by
Danielle Alvarez,
Morgan McGlone

Opening hours...Open 7 days
Credit cards...Accepted
Price range..Affordable
Style..Casual
Cuisine..Italian
Recommended for............................Regular neighborhood

"The food is simple, Italian-focused with great ingredients. It's the kind of food I want to eat on a long Sunday lunch after a tough week of work. Beautiful pizzas, whole grilled fish, light pastas, charcuterie, and other interesting small plates from their wine bar which is adjacent. The wine list, led by James Hird, is also amazing. Natural wine focused, which I love, but

124

still something for everyone. It's a great place for two people or a larger group. The light, open, and stylish interior makes for great ambiance."—Danielle Alvarez

The closest you'll get to a traditional "parmy" (chicken parmigiana) at the Dolphin is crumbed chicken with lemon, *guanciale* (Italian cured meat) and capers. A Surry Hills institution, the pub was bought, stripped back, and reborn as an artsy, contemporary diner under Icebergs owner Maurice Terzini and chef Monty Koludrovic. There are three different areas—the public bar that does a riff on the counter meal; the dining room, with classics like spaghetti with local blue swimmer crab and *bottarga* and a range of thin crust northern Italian pizzas; and The Wine Room, which has a raft of snacks from the retro-inspired *cabanossi* (smoked sausage), cheese, pickles, and crackers to the crispy pig's head sandwich. You'll probably need both to sustain you while perusing the lengthy and fascinating wine list.

FIREDOOR

23–33 Mary Street
Surry Hills
Sydney 2010
+61 282040800
www.firedoor.com.au

Recommended by
Massimo Bottura,
Ross Lusted

Opening hours.............................Closed Monday and Sunday
Credit cards...Accepted
Price range..Affordable
Style..Smart casual
Cuisine...Australian
Recommended for...Local favorite

REUBEN HILLS

61 Albion Street
Surry Hills
Sydney 2010
+61 292115556
www.reubenhills.com.au

Recommended by
James Viles

Opening hours...Open 7 days
Reservation policy..No
Credit cards...Accepted
Price range...Budget
Style..Casual
Cuisine...Café
Recommended for...Breakfast

"Great breakfast burritos."—James Viles

RUSTIC PEARL

Recommended by
Karl Firla

415 Crown Street
Surry Hills
Sydney 2010
+61 415102561

Opening hours	Closed Monday
Credit cards	Accepted but not AMEX or Diners
Price range	Affordable
Style	Casual
Cuisine	Turkish

SINGLE O

Recommended by
Ricardo Chaneton

60–64 Reservoir Street
Surry Hills
Sydney 2010
+61 292110665
www.singleo.com.au

Opening hours	Open 7 days
Credit cards	Accepted but not AMEX or Diners
Price range	Budget
Style	Casual
Cuisine	Café
Recommended for	Breakfast

CAVALLINO

Recommended by
Peter Gilmore

Yulong Avenue & McCarrs Creek Road
Terrey Hills
Sydney 2084
+61 294501777
www.cavallino.com.au

Opening hours	Open 7 days
Credit cards	Accepted
Price range	Affordable
Style	Casual
Cuisine	Italian-Pizza
Recommended for	Regular neighborhood

TASTEBUDS

Recommended by
Peter Gilmore

287 Mona Vale Road
Terrey Hills
Sydney 2084
+61 294500873
www.tastebudsathills.com.au

Opening hours	Open 7 days
Credit cards	Accepted
Price range	Budget
Style	Casual
Cuisine	Australian-Breakfast
Recommended for	Breakfast

QUAY

Recommended by
Dan Hong,
James Viles

Overseas Passenger Terminal
5 Hickson Road
The Rocks
Sydney 2000
+61 292515600
www.quay.com.au

Opening hours	Open 7 days
Credit cards	Accepted
Price range	Expensive
Style	Smart casual
Cuisine	Modern Australian
Recommended for	Local favorite

"Quay is a must-visit when coming to Australia. Peter Gilmore's focus on the growers and farmers of this country is inspiring and that shows through the entire restaurant. His love for food, people, and place is consuming and addictive."—James Viles

RUBY'S DINER

Recommended by
Danielle Alvarez,
Justin North

Shop 1 & 2, 179/173 Bronte Road
Waverley
Sydney 2024
+61 293865964
www.rubysdiner.com.au

Opening hours	Open 7 days
Reservation policy	No
Credit cards	Accepted but not AMEX or Diners
Price range	Budget
Style	Casual
Cuisine	Australian Café
Recommended for	Breakfast

"It has a great, laid-back 'at the beach' vibe without actually being at the beach. Coffee is excellent and food is nourishing, healthy, and tasty."—Danielle Alvarez

WHALE BEACH DELI

Recommended by
Peter Gilmore

1/231 Whale Beach Road
Whale Beach
Sydney 2107
+61 299745440
www.whalebeachdeli.com.au

Opening hours	Open 7 days
Reservation policy	No
Credit cards	Accepted but not AMEX or Diners
Price range	Affordable
Style	Casual
Cuisine	Deli
Recommended for	Breakfast

"Simply the best place to unwind."
PHILIP JOHNSON P129

"WHEN I CAN'T DECIDE WHAT I WANT, IT'S THE GO-TO, BY FAR!"
BEN BERTEI P131

BRISBANE

"This place produces some of the country's best ramen."
JAKE NICHOLSON P135

"Fresh, simple, quality pizza."
CAMERON MATTHEWS P134

"For revitalizing the soul and immersing yourself in delicate handmade parcels of sustenance, it is hard to beat this tiny family-owned café."
CAMERON MATTHEWS P130

BRISBANE

SCALE

0   525   1055   1580
YD.

1889 ENOTECA

Recommended by
Josue Lopez,
Jake Nicholson

10–12 Logan Road
Brisbane
Queensland 4102
+61 733924315
www.1889enoteca.com.au

Opening hours	Closed Monday
Credit cards	Accepted
Price range	Expensive
Style	Casual
Cuisine	Roman
Recommended for	Local favorite

"Serves traditional Roman fare—the *cacio e pepe*
(cheese and pepper pasta) is a must!"
—Jake Nicholson

ANOUK CAFÉ

Recommended by
Philip Johnson,
Shannon Kellam

212 Given Terrace
Brisbane
Queensland 4064
+61 733678663
www.anoukcafe.com

Opening hours	Open 7 days
Credit cards	Accepted but not AMEX
Price range	Affordable
Style	Casual
Cuisine	Modern Australian
Recommended for	Breakfast

"Always bustling, fast service, great selection of
fresh juices, and the breakfast choices are always
satisfying."—Philip Johnson

A decade after it opened, locals and tourists alike
still happily queue for a table at this former
apothecary with its exposed brick walls, French café
chairs, and some of the most innovative breakfasts
in town. Anouk's staff are uniformly welcoming,
the coffee is just right, and the menu—which
criss-crosses the globe for inspiration but uses
locally sourced ingredients—changes often enough
to keep regulars happy. Middle Eastern-spiced
shakshuka (baked eggs) are a favorite, but treats
like the pretty, rose petal-strewn French toast
croissant with stone fruit, torched Italian meringue,
and raspberry coulis don't help to solve the savory/
sweet breakfast conundrum.

THE APO

Recommended by
Ben Bertei

690 Ann Street
Brisbane
Queensland 4006
+61 732522403
www.theapo.com.au

Opening hours	Closed Monday
Credit cards	Accepted but not Diners
Price range	Affordable
Style	Casual
Cuisine	Modern International
Recommended for	Late night

"The fried chicken and pumpkin with yogurt sauce!
Washed down with a negroni, maybe two."
—Ben Bertei

BAR ALTO

Recommended by
Philip Johnson,
Jake Nicholson

The Powerhouse
119 Lamington Street
Brisbane
Queensland 4005
+61 733581063
www.baralto.com.au

Opening hours	Closed Monday
Credit cards	Accepted
Price range	Affordable
Style	Casual
Cuisine	Modern Italian
Recommended for	Regular neighborhood

"Perched on the edge of the Brisbane River, Bar Alto
serves consistently good food. The menu evolves, but
there are always some favorites to keep going back
for."—Philip Johnson

BARE BONES SOCIETY

Recommended by
Cameron Matthews

Jindalee Home
22/34 Goggs Road
Brisbane
Queensland 4074
+61 737155571
www.barebonessociety.com

Opening hours	Open 7 days
Credit cards	Accepted
Price range	Budget
Style	Casual
Cuisine	Breakfast-Brunch
Recommended for	Breakfast

BEN'S BURGERS

Recommended by
Jake Nicholson

5 Winn Lane
Brisbane
Queensland 4006
+61 731953094
www.bensburgers.com.au

Opening hours.................................Open 7 days
Reservation policy.......................................No
Credit cards.......................................Accepted
Price range...Budget
Style..Casual
Cuisine..Burgers
Recommended for...........................Wish I'd opened

"Hole-in-the-wall-type burger joint that quickly gained cult status for some of the city's best burgers."
—Jake Nicholson

BIRD'S NEST YAKITORI & BAR

Recommended by
Josue Lopez,
Jake Nicholson

5/220 Melbourne Street
Brisbane
Queensland 4101
+61 738444306
www.birdsnestrestaurant.com.au

Opening hours...............................Open 7 days
Credit cards..........................Accepted but not AMEX
Price range...Budget
Style..Casual
Cuisine...Japanese
Recommended for...................................Bargain

"Serves delicious chicken on sticks—think hearts, livers, and the rest—definitely for the more adventurous diner."—Jake Nicholson

BROOKLYN STANDARD

Recommended by
Philip Johnson

371 Queen Street
Brisbane
Queensland 4000
+61 428462078
www.brooklynstandard.com.au

Opening hours.................................Closed Sunday
Credit cards...................Accepted but not AMEX or Diners
Price range..Affordable
Style..Casual
Cuisine...American
Recommended for................................Late night

"Live music, great drinks, and atmosphere. Simply the best place to unwind."—Philip Johnson

E'CCO BISTRO

Recommended by
Jake Nicholson

100 Boundary Street
Brisbane
Queensland 4000
+61 738318344
www.eccobistro.com.au

Opening hours.....................Closed Monday and Sunday
Credit cards.......................................Accepted
Price range..Affordable
Style..Casual
Cuisine...Australian
Recommended for...........................Wish I'd opened

"E'cco first opened its doors in 1995 and has stood the test of time, maintaining its position at the top end of the Brisbane dining scene."—Jake Nicholson

EAT STREET NORTHSHORE

Recommended by
Philip Johnson

221d Macarthur Avenue
Brisbane
Queensland 4007
+61 411884499
www.eatstreetmarkets.com

Opening hours.....................Closed Monday to Thursday
Reservation policy.......................................No
Credit cards....................................Not accepted
Price range...Budget
Style..Casual
Cuisine...Street Food
Recommended for.............................Local favorite

"Brisbane locals love to taste flavors from all cuisines. The best way to do that in this city is at the weekend Eat Street Markets. Hundreds of stallholders open for business on Friday and Saturday nights (Sunday's in winter). The locals flock to there to graze on many different dishes, relax outdoors, and enjoy live entertainment."— Philip Johnson

ENJOY INN

Recommended by
Cameron Matthews

28/8 Harbor Road
Brisbane
Queensland 4007
+61 732527878

Opening hours	Closed Tuesday
Credit cards	Accepted
Price range	Budget
Style	Casual
Cuisine	Chinese
Recommended for	Late night

"The right amount of spice, with icy cold beers, after a long day."—Cameron Matthews

ESQUIRE

Recommended by
Elizabeth Haigh,
Philip Johnson,
Josue Lopez,
Jake Nicholson,
Ben Russell

145 Eagle Street
Brisbane
Queensland 4000
+61 732202123
www.esquire.net.au

Opening hours	Closed Monday and Sunday
Credit cards	Accepted
Price range	Expensive
Style	Smart casual
Cuisine	Modern Australian
Recommended for	High end

"Still the benchmark in Brisbane. Ryan is a local chef with some heavy-hitting international experience; his restaurant is a fine example of contemporary food with a distinctly local feel."—Ben Russell

The chic, pared-back dining room may be influenced by the design ethos of Scandinavia, but the view of the river and the Story Bridge, framed by floor-to-ceiling glass, is pure Brisbane. Esquire is an exemplar of Australian-style fine dining—upmarket but rarely uptight, equally attracting expense-account diners, celebratory couples, and fanatical foodies. Owner and chef Ryan Squires has staged at some of the world's most renowned restaurants and has acquired a well-deserved reputation for his trailblazing originality. Relax, relinquish control to the well-versed team, and be prepared to be blown away by the bold and whimsical degustation menu.

FAT DUMPLING

Recommended by
Cameron Matthews

368 Brunswick Street
Brisbane
Queensland 4006
+61 731951040
www.fatdumplingbar.com

Opening hours	Closed Monday
Credit cards	Accepted but not AMEX or Diners
Price range	Affordable
Style	Casual
Cuisine	Chinese
Recommended for	Bargain

"For revitalizing the soul and immersing yourself in delicate hand-made parcels of sustenance, it is hard to beat this tiny family-owned café."
—Cameron Matthews

FRITZENBERGER

Recommended by
Ryan Squires

52 Petrie Terrace
Brisbane
Queensland 4000
+61 735063656
www.fritzenberger.com

Opening hours	Open 7 days
Credit cards	Accepted but not AMEX or Diners
Price range	Affordable
Style	Casual
Cuisine	American
Recommended for	Late night

For decades, this Caxton Street venue was home to an attractively faded Latin American dance club, but now it's reborn as a burger joint. Unlike your typical fast-food chain though, Fritzenberger fries with love, an emotion that's reciprocated by fiercely loyal regulars who come for burgers made with grass-fed and dry-aged beef, organic ketchup, and house-made pickles. Appealing add-ons include maple syrup-candied bacon, and bacon jam. The fish burger, meanwhile, comes with a side of feel-good factor—it's made from sustainable Queensland barramundi. Roast chicken, Vegemite (Australian yeast-extract spread), beet (beetroot), shiitake mushroom, and vinegar salts cleverly elevate fries to the next level. Even the preservative-free beer, in some gratifyingly kooky flavors, is brewed in-house.

FUNNY FUNNY

Recommended by
Ben Devlin,
Jake Nicholson

85 George Street
Brisbane
Queensland 4000
+61 732113431
www.funnyfunnyrestpub.com.au

Opening hours	Open 7 days
Credit cards	Not accepted
Price range	Affordable
Style	Casual
Cuisine	Korean
Recommended for	Late night

"The fried chicken is some of the best in town.
Fill your table with a banquet of food and bring
all the mates you can—it's the perfect reward after
a big night's service in the kitchen."—Jake Nicholson

GAUGE

Recommended by
Ben Devlin,
Josue Lopez

77 Grey Street
Brisbane
Queensland 4101
+61 736380431
www.gaugebrisbane.com.au

Opening hours	Open 7 days
Credit cards	Accepted
Price range	Affordable
Style	Casual
Cuisine	Modern Australian
Recommended for	Breakfast

"In a bustling area of South Brisbane, Gauge offers
diners unexpected, intelligent dishes that taste
delicious and are good value. They also serve one of
Brisbane's best shots of coffee."—Josue Lopez

Pocket-sized Gauge's industrial-chic, coffee-shop
decor, and relaxed vibe belie the envelope-pushing
sophistication of a menu that wouldn't look out of
place in a fine-dining venue. As much as possible is
done in-house—fermenting, smoking, drying,
pickling, breaking down of beasts, baking of bread,
churning of flavored butters. Breakfast, with Marvell
Street Roasters coffee on pour, is a more casual
affair than the six-course dinner menu, but dishes
like sourdough waffles with almond, artichoke
custard, bee pollen and freeze-dried honey, or the
savory/sweet black fermented garlic bread with a
quenelle of brown butter and burned vanilla dust,
are alluring enough to entice return visits anytime.

GERARD'S BAR

Recommended by
Ben Bertei,
Cameron Matthews

13a, 23 James Street
Brisbane
Queensland 4006
+61 732522606
www.gerardsbar.com.au

Opening hours	Open 7 days
Credit cards	Accepted but not Diners
Price range	Affordable
Style	Casual
Cuisine	Tapas
Recommended for	Regular neighborhood

"Stripped-back bar with killer drinks and food that's
always on point. When I can't decide what I want, it's
the go-to, by far!"—Ben Bertei

Little sister to the acclaimed Gerard's Bistro just
across the way, Gerard's Bar, with its legs of jamón
and links of salami hanging in the front window, is
reminiscent of the bars in Barcelona or Rome—
convivial and contemporary with equal weight
assigned to food and drink. Sit at a table beneath
the shady arms of the old tree outside or perch at
the bar and watch the staff mix cocktails, ease corks
from a varied selection of wine bottles, and shuttle
out plates of premium charcuterie, cheeses, and
other substantial, drink-friendly dishes. Frequent
winemaker dinners and experimental "food lab"
degustation evenings keep things buzzing.

GERARD'S BISTRO

Recommended by
Josue Lopez,
Jake Nicholson

Gerard's Lane
14/15 James Street
Brisbane
Queensland 4006
+61 738523822
www.gerardsbistro.com.au

Opening hours	Open 7 days
Credit cards	Accepted
Price range	Affordable
Style	Smart casual
Cuisine	Middle Eastern
Recommended for	Breakfast

"Whilst Gerard's Bistro has a fantastic reputation for
their dinner meals, their fabulous weekend breakfast
menu is also spot on. It's hard to go past the Baghdad
eggs but there are plenty of other Middle Eastern
inspired dishes to tuck into."—Jake Nicholson

HAPPY BOY

Recommended by
Ben Russell

2/36 Mein Street
Brisbane
Queensland 4000
+61 413246890
www.happyboy.com.au

Opening hours	Open 7 days
Credit cards	Accepted but not AMEX
Price range	Affordable
Style	Casual
Cuisine	Chinese
Recommended for	Regular neighborhood

"High-quality Chinese cooking served from a garage in Brisbane's inner-city suburb, Spring Hill—great value for money and mostly to an unexpectedly cool soundtrack."—Ben Russell

You'd have to be a curmudgeon indeed not to leave Happy Boy with a smile. Housed in a converted garage in a Spring Hill side street with minimal signage, the decor is pared back, and the lack of soft surfaces makes for a buzz that's perfect for a convivial group outing. With dishes designed to share, the well-priced menu is a mix of classic Cantonese spiced up with Szechuan favorites and regional specialities. It doesn't change often, which is how regulars, who come for the fish-flavored eggplant (aubergine) and pork and shrimp (prawn) wontons in chile oil, like it. A succinct blackboard list offers boutique wines, most of which are under A$10 ($7; £6) a glass.

JULIUS PIZZERIA

Recommended by
Ben Russell

77 Grey Street
Brisbane
Queensland 4101
+61 738442655
www.juliuspizzeria.com.au

Opening hours	Closed Monday
Credit cards	Accepted but not Diners
Price range	Affordable
Style	Casual
Cuisine	Italian
Recommended for	Local favorite

"This place just gets all the small stuff right."
—Ben Russell

KIN & CO

Recommended by
Ben Bertei

24 Macquarie Street
Brisbane
Queensland 4005
+61 733586823
www.kinandcocafe.com

Opening hours	Open 7 days
Credit cards	Accepted
Price range	Affordable
Style	Casual
Cuisine	Café
Recommended for	Breakfast

KING OF KINGS

Recommended by
Shannon Kellam

175 Wickham Street
Brisbane
Queensland 4006
+61 738521889
www.king.letseat.at

Opening hours	Open 7 days
Credit cards	Accepted
Price range	Budget
Style	Casual
Cuisine	Chinese
Recommended for	Late night

LEFTY'S OLD TIME MUSIC HALL

Recommended by
Ben Russell

15 Caxton Street
Brisbane
Queensland 4000
www.leftysoldtimemusichall.com

Opening hours	Closed Monday
Credit cards	Accepted but not Diners
Price range	Affordable
Style	Casual
Cuisine	American
Recommended for	Wish I'd opened

"Not so much of a restaurant but a beer and whisky hall with fried food available."—Ben Russell

LONGTIME

Recommended by
Josue Lopez,
Philip Johnson

610 Ann Street
Brisbane
Queensland 4006
+61 731603123
www.longtime.com.au

Opening hours	Closed Monday
Credit cards	Accepted
Price range	Affordable
Style	Casual
Cuisine	Modern Asian
Recommended for	Late night

"Most nights LONgTIME is pumping—high impact food, fantastic drinks, and great tunes. The menu is fun, offering a twist on Southeast Asian flavors."
—Josue Lopez

A golden rickshaw in a dead-end alley marks the entry—if you can see it past the line (queue). Explosively popular since opening three years ago, LONgTIME has tapped into the zeitgeist, with its riff on Asian street food. Served in a dimly lit basement with banquette and bar seating, chef Ben Bertei's menu roams the Asian continent and is designed for sharing. Dishes come out of the frenetic open kitchen to the table at random, just as they do in Asia. Try some moreish bar snacks, like morsels of crab wrapped in betel leaf, or soft shell crab bao, while pondering the menu choices, or just surrender responsibility and go with "chef's choice". While beer might be the more traditional libation with Asian food, LONgTIME offers a smart wine list with a focus on food-friendly aromatics.

MARU KOREAN BBQ

Recommended by
Ben Russell

157 Elizabeth Street
Brisbane
Queensland 4000
+61 730129912
www.marukoreanbbq.weebly.com

Opening hours	Open 7 days
Credit cards	Accepted
Price range	Affordable
Style	Casual
Cuisine	Korean BBQ
Recommended for	Late night

"Stays open late, serving spicy fried chicken and kimchi pancakes alongside cheap Korean beers and K-Pop."—Ben Russell

MORNING AFTER

Recommended by
Ben Bertei

Vulture Street and Cambridge Street
Brisbane
Queensland 4101
+61 738440500
www.morningafter.com.au

Opening hours	Open 7 days
Reservation policy	No
Credit cards	Accepted
Price range	Affordable
Style	Casual
Cuisine	Modern Australian
Recommended for	Breakfast

"Not a bad place to watch the world pass by for an hour or two; don't miss the breakfast carbonara or the mamuffin!"—Ben Bertei

You certainly don't need to have a hangover to enjoy breakfast at Morning After, but if you do, two words: breakfast carbonara. It's just one of the indulgent options on the menu at this chic café, the vision of mother and son hospitality luminaries Soula and Yianni Passaris and an example of the change afoot in the once grungy suburb of West End as gentrification hits top gear. Morning After's designer good looks carry through to an equally stylish all-day menu. If the carbonara doesn't cure what ails you, consider *cotechino* (Italian pork sausage) with smoked corn, chorizo, chile, fried eggs, yogurt, and fried torn bread. Coffee comes courtesy of Melbourne's Five Senses and local roaster Uncle Joe's.

NEW SHANGHAI

Recommended by
Jake Nicholson

Queens Plaza
23/226 Queen Street
Brisbane
Queensland 4000
+61 731089652
www.newshanghai.com.au

Opening hours	Open 7 days
Credit cards	Accepted
Price range	Budget
Style	Smart casual
Cuisine	Shanghaiese
Recommended for	Regular neighborhood

"Serves delicious handmade dumplings and noodles alongside other awesome Shanghai-style cuisine."
— Jake Nicholson

OTTO

Recommended by
Jake Nicholson,
Ben Russell

L4, 480 Queen Street
Brisbane
Queensland 4000
+61 738352888
www.ottoristorante.com.au

Opening hours	Open 7 days
Credit cards	Accepted
Price range	Affordable
Style	Smart casual
Cuisine	Modern Italian
Recommended for	High end

"Exceptional dining room with great views of the Story Bridge. Fantastic wine list and delicious food to match."—Jake Nicholson

From its lofty perch in the heart of the city, Otto boasts sensational views over the Brisbane River and the Story Bridge, the latter especially pretty dressed up with its violet fairy light mantle at night. The Brisbane branch opened in 2016, following the original Sydney venue, both of which are creations of Fink Hospitality Group. Years of collective experience show in the attentive service and the sleek fit-out, while the food, under head chef Will Cowper, never misses a beat. Think contemporary Italian—lighter versions of traditional favorites, but with an occasional curveball local ingredient to keep things interesting. It's happily partnered by an international wine list with a concentration of both highbrow and low-fi drops that meet all budgets, expertly curated by sommelier Alan Hunter.

PEARL CAFÉ

Recommended by
Ben Russell,
Ryan Squires

28 Logan Road
Brisbane
Queensland 4102
+61 733923300

Opening hours	Open 7 days
Reservation policy	No
Credit cards	Accepted but not AMEX or Diners
Price range	Affordable
Style	Casual
Cuisine	European
Recommended for	Breakfast

SONO

Recommended by
Ryan Squires

Tattersalls
1F, Corner of Edward Street and Queen Street
Brisbane
Queensland 4000
+61 732201888
www.sonorestaurant.com.au

Opening hours	Closed Sunday
Credit cards	Accepted
Price range	Affordable
Style	Smart casual
Cuisine	Japanese
Recommended for	Bargain

SORELLINA PIZZERIA

Recommended by
Cameron Matthews

31 Logan Road
Brisbane
Queensland 4102
+61 733918459
www.sorellinapizzeria.com

Opening hours	Closed Monday
Credit cards	Accepted but not AMEX or Diners
Price range	Budget
Style	Casual
Cuisine	Pizza
Recommended for	Bargain

"Fresh, simple, quality pizza."—Cameron Matthews

SOURCED GROCER

Recommended by
Ryan Squires

11 Florence Street
Brisbane
Queensland 4006
+61 738526734
www.sourcedgrocer.com.au

Opening hours	Open 7 days
Reservation policy	No
Credit cards	Accepted
Price range	Affordable
Style	Casual
Cuisine	Café-Deli
Recommended for	Regular neighborhood

STOKEHOUSE Q

Recommended by
Jake Nicholson

Sidon Street
Brisbane
Queensland 4101
+61 730200600
www.stokehouseq.com.au

Opening hours	Open 7 days
Credit cards	Accepted but not Diners
Price range	Affordable
Style	Smart casual
Cuisine	Australian
Recommended for	Local favorite

"Beautiful restaurant for making the most of riverside dining, the menu highlights the best produce from the surrounding region with top-class service to match."
— Jake Nicholson

STRAUSS

Recommended by
Ben Russell

189 Elizabeth Street
Brisbane
Queensland 4000
+61 732365232
www.straussfd.com

Opening hours	Closed Saturday and Sunday
Reservation policy	No
Credit cards	Accepted
Price range	Affordable
Style	Casual
Cuisine	Café
Recommended for	Breakfast

"I'm not much of a breakfast person, but good coffee is high on my list of priorities and Strauss is home to some of the city's best."—Ben Russell

SUPER BOWL CHINESE RESTAURANT

Recommended by
Mitch Orr

185 Wickham Street
Brisbane
Queensland 4006
+61 732572188
www.superbowlrestaurant.com.au

Opening hours	Closed Monday
Credit cards	Accepted
Price range	Affordable
Style	Casual
Cuisine	Chinese
Recommended for	Late night

TARO'S RAMEN

Recommended by
Philip Johnson,
Jake Nicholson,
Ben Russell

L2, 480 Queen Street
Brisbane
Queensland 4000
+61 738394840
www.taros.com.au

Opening hours	Open 7 days
Reservation policy	No
Credit cards	Accepted but not AMEX or Diners
Price range	Budget
Style	Casual
Cuisine	Japanese
Recommended for	Bargain

"This place produces some of the country's best ramen, using awesome natural produce to create one of the most flavorful dishes you'll find."
—Jake Nicholson

TRANG RESTAURANT

Recommended by
Josue Lopez

2/59 Hardgrave Road
Brisbane
Queensland 4101
+61 732551610
www.trangs.com.au

Opening hours	Open 7 days
Credit cards	Accepted
Price range	Budget
Style	Casual
Cuisine	Vietnamese-Chinese
Recommended for	Bargain

"Serves Vietnamese specialties like pho, and Chinese delights like salt and pepper quail, that are always on point. It's also BYO so you can bring your own Rieslings or Gewurztraminers and have a fantastic experience."—Josue Lopez

URBANE RESTAURANT

Recommended by
Josue Lopez,
Cameron Matthews

181 Mary Street
Brisbane
Queensland 4000
+61 732292271
www.urbanerestaurant.com

Opening hours	Closed Sunday to Wednesday
Credit cards	Accepted but not Diners
Price range	Expensive
Style	Smart casual
Cuisine	Modern Australian
Recommended for	High end

"Urbane is the type of restaurant that makes you feel very special; the dining room and decor feature soft, luxurious textures and tones, and the food and wine list are some of the city's best."—Josue Lopez

THE WOLFE

Recommended by
Josue Lopez

989 Stanley Street
Brisbane
Queensland 4169
+61 738917772
www.thewolfeeastbrisbane.com.au

Opening hours	Closed Monday and Sunday
Credit cards	Accepted
Price range	Affordable
Style	Smart casual
Cuisine	Modern Australian
Recommended for	Regular neighborhood

"A quintessential suburban fine-diner. Great food and wine list, without the CBD prices."—Josue Lopez

"Classic rooftop terrace bar with views of Parliament House."
GEORGE CALOMBARIS P145

"A staple of 'best restaurant' lists for over forty years now, and it's not without reason."
TEAGE EZARD P143

MELBOURNE

"HANDS DOWN THE BEST ICE CREAM IN MELBOURNE."
SHAUN QUADE P141

"AWESOME STAFF, KARAOKE DOWNSTAIRS, THE CHICKEN AND SHRIMP DUMPLING WITH CHILE, VINEGAR AND PLENTY OF QUALITY SAKE!"
LACHLAN COLWILL P145

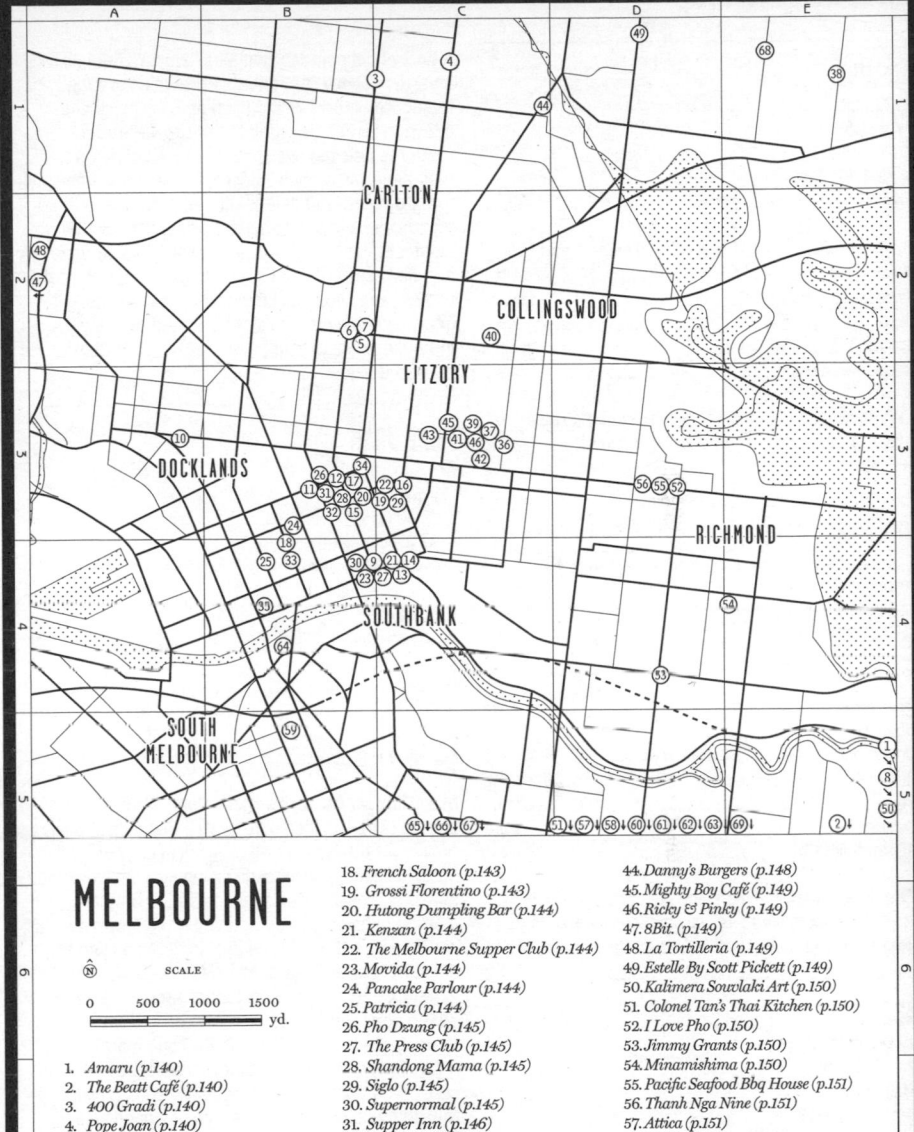

MELBOURNE

N̂

SCALE

0   500   1000   1500
yd.

AMARU

Recommended by
Ryan Sessions

1121 High Street
Armadale
Melbourne 3143
+61 398220144
www.amarumelbourne.com.au

Opening hours	Closed Monday and Sunday
Credit cards	Accepted
Price range	Expensive
Style	Smart casual
Cuisine	Modern Australian
Recommended for	High end

"It's only been going about a year—and it's some of the best food you can get in Melbourne!"
—Ryan Sessions

THE BEATT CAFÉ

Recommended by
George Calombaris

24 Beatty Avenue
Armadale
Melbourne 3143
+61 398246678
www.thebeatt.com.au

Opening hours	Open 7 days
Reservation policy	No
Credit cards	Accepted but not AMEX or Diners
Price range	Affordable
Style	Casual
Cuisine	Café
Recommended for	Breakfast

"Healthy, delicious, wholefood café and everything is real. No refined, bleached, or processed foods. Most importantly, great coffee!"—George Calombaris

400 GRADI

Recommended by
George Calombaris

99 Lygon Street
Brunswick East
Melbourne 3057
+61 393802320
www.400gradi.com.au

Opening hours	Open 7 days
Credit cards	Accepted
Price range	Budget
Style	Casual
Cuisine	Italian
Recommended for	Local favorite

"400 Gradi is an open-plan restaurant with a polished concrete floor, serving superb wood-fired Neapolitan pizza and Italian cuisine."—George Calombaris

A household name for winning "world's best pizza" awards, Johnny Di Francesco draws an urbane Melbourne crowd to the bustling Brunswick end of Lygon Street. Bursting out of the *400-gradi* (degrees Celsius) ovens come Naples-style pizzas with generously chewy bases, fruity San Marzano tomato paste, and deli-quality toppings like buffalo mozzarella and aged smoked meats. Pair with a glass of either local or Italian wine. Stick to pizza or add daily selections of seafood antipasti, rich pasta dishes, and mains including slow-cooked young goat. Sweeten up with classic Italian desserts in-house, or grab *gelati* (ice creams) next door at Zero Gradi.

POPE JOAN

Recommended by
Jasper Avent

77–79 Nicholson Street
Brunswick East
Melbourne 3057
+61 393888858
www.popejoan.com.au

Opening hours	Open 7 days
Reservation policy	No
Credit cards	Accepted but not Diners
Price range	Affordable
Style	Casual
Cuisine	Modern Australian-British
Recommended for	Breakfast

Matt Wilkinson's hardworking Pope Joan does a double shift—chilled café by day, distinctive local eatery (of the type we all pray for in our own neighborhoods) on weekday evenings. On weekends, morning crowds often spill across the footpath, waiting to have appetites tamed or hangovers soothed by a St Ali coffee and something from the all-day breakfast menu, which is supplemented, as lunchtime arrives, by substantial sandwiches like pulled pork and pickles or roast chicken with stuffing. Come sundown and the Pope morphs into a candlelit diner with a homey menu based around seasonally appropriate ingredients and, introduced this summer, plates of smoky, charry goodness from their firepit cookouts.

DONNINI'S

Recommended by
Jasper Avent

320 Lygon Street
Carlton
Melbourne 3053
+61 393473128
www.donninis.com.au

Opening hours	Open 7 days
Credit cards	Accepted
Price range	Budget
Style	Casual
Cuisine	Italian
Recommended for	Local favorite

PIDAPIPO

Recommended by
Shaun Quade

299 Lygon Street
Carlton
Melbourne 3053
+61 393474596
www.pidapipo.com.au

Opening hours	Open 7 days
Reservation policy	No
Credit cards	Accepted
Price range	Affordable
Style	Casual
Cuisine	Italian
Recommended for	Wish I'd opened

"Hands down the best ice cream in Melbourne—the flavors are clean, natural, and not heavy on sweetness, and the texture of each serve is outstanding."
—Shaun Quade

THE TOWN MOUSE

Recommended by
Alexandra Haynes

312 Drummond Street
Carlton
Melbourne 3053
+61 393473312
www.thetownmouse.com.au

Opening hours	Open 7 days
Credit cards	Accepted but not Diners
Price range	Affordable
Style	Casual
Cuisine	Modern Australian
Recommended for	Worth the travel

"Love this restaurant. The food is amazing, so different, smart, and full of flavor. The small intimate dining area looks and feels great. Excellent service too."—Alexandra Haynes

The Town Mouse feels more like a dark, glamorous wine bar than a restaurant, and you are indeed welcome to perch up at the curved, oak-topped bar with a glass of wine from the stellar list and graze —a single dressed oyster perhaps, or a plate of crisp wedges of radish to dip into creamy whipped cod roe? But if you have the time, it's recommended to take a table to experience Dave Verheul's polished, produce-forward menu in a more leisurely way. Democratically divided into "smaller" and "bigger" plates to accommodate all appetites, from the house-made sourdough with sesame butter to desserts like *feijoa* with frozen yogurt and green almond essence, the menu never misses a beat.

TUCK SHOP TAKE AWAY

Recommended by
Ben Shewry

273 Hawthorn Road
Caulfield North
Melbourne 3161
+61 431406580
www.tuckshoptakeaway.com.au

Opening hours	Closed Monday and Sunday
Reservation policy	No
Credit cards	Accepted but not AMEX or Diners
Price range	Budget
Style	Casual
Cuisine	Fast Food
Recommended for	Regular neighborhood

With its name incorporating a colloquialism for a school canteen, it's fair to say that most kids would be very happy indeed to spend their lunch money on the type of food served here. A regular on the city's "best burger" lists, Tuck Shop makes its patties with grass-fed beef and their own house-made sauce— although, shockingly, some in these parts might say, they come without beet (beetroot). There are also old-school milkshakes in flavors like "Minties" or "Redskin", as well as crisp, hot jaffles (toasted sandwiches) and hand-cut chips. Owners Clinton and Karina Serex recently opened Karton Milk Bar a couple of doors down too—a riff on the traditional milk bar, featuring pantry basics as well as candy, hot pies, house-made slushies, and ice cream sandwiches.

CHIN CHIN
Recommended by
Shannon Bennett,
Duncan Welgemoed

125 Flinders Lane
Central Business District
Melbourne 3000
+61 386632000
www.chinchinrestaurant.com.au

Opening hours..Open 7 days
Reservation policy..No
Credit cards...............................Accepted but not Diners
Price range...Affordable
Style..Casual
Cuisine...Thai
Recommended for.............................Wish I'd opened

"People complain about the lines (queues) to get in! Why? The bar downstairs is a great place to wait and the food is always generous and full of robust flavors. Great location and always open when you need it to be. Chris Lucas, the owner, looks at restaurants differently from most as he is not trained in the industry."—Shannon Bennett

CLEVER POLLY'S
Recommended by
Shaun Quade

313 Victoria Street
Central Business District
Melbourne 3003
+61 390779294
www.cleverpollys.com.au

Opening hours.............................Closed Monday and Tuesday
Credit cards...Accepted
Price range...Affordable
Style..Casual
Cuisine...Modern Australian
Recommended for.............................Regular neighborhood

"Natural wine list with delicious Japanese *omakase* (chef's choice menu). Polly is charming and gregarious when talking about the wine."—Shaun Quade

COOKIE
Recommended by
Shannon Bennett

252 Swanston Street
Central Business District
Melbourne 3000
+61 396637660
www.cookie.net.au

Opening hours..Open 7 days
Credit cards...Accepted
Price range...Affordable
Style..Casual
Cuisine...Thai
Recommended for.............................Regular neighborhood

142

CRYSTAL JADE RESTAURANT
Recommended by
Morgan McGlone

154 Little Bourke Street
Central Business District
Melbourne 3000
+61 396392633

Opening hours..Open 7 days
Credit cards...Accepted
Price range...Affordable
Style..Smart casual
Cuisine..Dim Sum
Recommended for...Breakfast

CUMULUS INC.
Recommended by
Rodney Dunn,
David Swain,
Alla Wolf-Tasker

45 Flinders Lane
Central Business District
Melbourne 3000
+61 396501445
www.cumulusinc.com.au

Opening hours..Open 7 days
Credit cards...............................Accepted but not Diners
Price range...Affordable
Style..Casual
Cuisine...International
Recommended for.............................Wish I'd opened

"Full respect needs to be paid to any restaurant doing breakfast, lunch, and dinner, seven days a week and nailing it the way Cumulus does. It draws a diverse crowd and is always busy. I love their take on food; with a little twist but nothing too crazy, very approachable."—Rodney Dunn

CUMULUS UP
Recommended by
Adam D'Sylva

45 Flinders Lane
Central Business District
Melbourne 3000
+61 396501445
www.cumulusup.com.au

Opening hours..Open 7 days
Credit cards...............................Accepted but not Diners
Price range...Affordable
Style..Casual
Cuisine..Bar-Small plates
Recommended for...Local favorite

EMBLA

Recommended by
Shaun Quade,
Ben Shewry,
Aaron Turner

122 Russell Street
Central Business District
Melbourne 3000
+61 396545923
www.embla.com.au

Opening hours	Closed Sunday
Reservation policy	No
Credit cards	Accepted but not Diners
Price range	Affordable
Style	Casual
Cuisine	Modern Australian
Recommended for	Regular neighborhood

"Love the feeling of it. It's a new place but feels old. Run by a couple of the brightest hospitality minds in Australia."—Ben Shewry

THE EUROPEAN

Recommended by
Adam D'Sylva,
Dan Hunter,
Alla Wolf-Tasker

161 Spring Street
Central Business District
Melbourne 3000
+61 396540811
www.theeuropean.com.au

Opening hours	Open 7 days
Credit cards	Accepted
Price range	Affordable
Style	Smart casual
Cuisine	European
Recommended for	Late night

"The European on Spring Street is a Melbourne icon."
—Dan Hunter

FLOWER DRUM

Recommended by
Shannon Bennett,
Adam D'Sylva,
Teage Ezard, Dan Hong,
Dan Hunter, Ben Shewry

17 Market Lane
Central Business District
Melbourne 3000
+61 396623655
www.flowerdrum.melbourne

Opening hours	Open 7 days
Credit cards	Accepted but not Diners
Price range	Expensive
Style	Smart casual
Cuisine	Chinese
Recommended for	High end

"What I find so impressive about Flower Drum isn't just the food—it's that it single-handedly managed to change the Australian perception of what Chinese food can and should be. Flower Drum has been a

staple of 'best restaurant' lists for over forty years now, and it's not without reason. It goes without saying that service is an integral part of their reputation—and with staff so skilled, you'd be cheating yourself if you ordered straight off the menu. Ditch any apprehension and leave it in their hands. You won't regret it."
—Teage Ezard

FRENCH SALOON

Recommended by
Jasper Avent

1F, 46 Hardware Lane
Central Business District
Melbourne 3000
+61 396002142
www.frenchsaloon.com

Opening hours	Closed Saturday and Sunday
Credit cards	Accepted but not Diners
Price range	Affordable
Style	Casual
Cuisine	Modern French-Australian
Recommended for	Late night

GROSSI FLORENTINO

Recommended by
Adam D'Sylva,
Alla Wolf-Tasker

80 Bourke Street
Central Business District
Melbourne 3000
+61 396621811
www.grossiflorentino.com

Opening hours	Closed Sunday
Credit cards	Accepted
Price range	Expensive
Style	Smart casual
Cuisine	Italian
Recommended for	Regular neighborhood

"Grossi Florentino is a particular favorite. Consistent and delicious."—Alla Wolf-Tasker

HUTONG DUMPLING BAR
Recommended by
Geoff Lindsay

14–16 Market Lane
Central Business District
Melbourne 3000
+61 396508128
www.hutong.com.au

Opening hours	Open 7 days
Reservation policy	No
Credit cards	Accepted
Price range	Affordable
Style	Casual
Cuisine	Chinese
Recommended for	Breakfast

"I usually have a chef's breakfast: Panadol and espresso! When I do have a day off it's usually a small sleep and then *yum cha* at Hutong, and enough *xiao long bao* (soup dumplings) and Peking duck to bring on a food coma!"—Geoff Lindsay

KENZAN
Recommended by
Shannon Bennett

45 Colins Street
Central Business District
Melbourne 3000
+61 396548933
www.kenzan.com.au

Opening hours	Closed Sunday
Credit cards	Accepted
Price range	Affordable
Style	Casual
Cuisine	Japanese
Recommended for	Wish I'd opened

THE MELBOURNE SUPPER CLUB
Recommended by
Shannon Bennett

1/161 Spring Street
Central Business District
Melbourne 3000
+61 396546300
www.melbournesupperclub.com

Opening hours	Open 7 days
Reservation policy	No
Credit cards	Accepted
Price range	Expensive
Style	Smart casual
Cuisine	Modern Australian
Recommended for	Late night

"Always great for a snack or a *mamacita* (rum cocktail), and they have late tables. I love the atmosphere. Great Mexican beers with some of the best, authentic food in town." —Shannon Bennett

MOVIDA
Recommended by
Geoff Lindsay

1 Hosier Lane
Central Business District
Melbourne 3000
+61 396633038
www.movida.com.au

Opening hours	Open 7 days
Credit cards	Accepted
Price range	Affordable
Style	Smart casual
Cuisine	Spanish
Recommended for	Wish I'd opened

"It's small, uncompromising, and has spurned many imitators but remains the best. Melbourne's favorite tapas bar now has many faces but the original, in one of Melbourne's graffiti-lined laneways, is my favorite. Great tapas and even better wine! Love, love, love it!"—Geoff Lindsay

PANCAKE PARLOUR
Recommended by
Shannon Bennett

3F, Corner of La Trobe Street and
Swanston Street
Central Business District
Melbourne 3000
+61 396543117
www.pancakeparlour.com

Opening hours	Open 7 days
Credit cards	Accepted
Price range	Affordable
Style	Casual
Cuisine	Breakfast-Brunch
Recommended for	Breakfast

PATRICIA
Recommended by
Shaun Quade

Corner of Little Bourke & Little William Street
Central Business District
Melbourne 3000
+61 96422237
www.patriciacoffee.com.au

Opening hours	Closed Saturday and Sunday
Credit cards	Accepted but not AMEX or Diners
Price range	Budget
Style	Casual
Cuisine	Café
Recommended for	Breakfast

"Standing room only for coffee, but it's the absolute best in town. And the *canelés* are always cracking."
— Shaun Quade

PHO DZUNG

Recommended by
Shaun Quade

234 Russell Street
Central Business District
Melbourne 3000
+61 396638885

Opening hours	Open 7 days
Credit cards	Accepted but not AMEX or Diners
Price range	Affordable
Style	Casual
Cuisine	Vietnamese
Recommended for	Bargain

"They serve the best pho in the CBD—no fuss or fanfare and very quick service."—Shaun Quade

THE PRESS CLUB

Recommended by
Georgianna Hiliadaki,
Nikos Roussos

72 Flinders Street
Central Business District
Melbourne 3000
+61 396779677
www.thepressclub.com.au

Opening hours	Closed Monday and Sunday
Credit cards	Accepted
Price range	Expensive
Style	Formal
Cuisine	Modern Australian
Recommended for	Worth the travel

SHANDONG MAMA

Recommended by
Dan Hunter,
Morgan McGlone

Mid City Arcade
7/200 Bourke Street
Central Business District
Melbourne 3000
+61 396503818

Opening hours	Closed Sunday
Reservation policy	No
Credit cards	Not accepted
Price range	Affordable
Style	Casual
Cuisine	Shandong Chinese
Recommended for	Bargain

"Incredible handmade dumplings, reasonably priced and delicious. Must try the mackerel dumpling."
— Morgan McGlone

The blog posts and lines (queues) testify to the fact that ShanDong MaMa, a family owned, no-frills Chinese diner in a nondescript arcade, is no longer a secret. "Mama" (chef Meiyan Wang) elevates dumpling making to an art form, her handmade wrappers coming in different thicknesses depending on the cooking method and ingredients. Specialties of the family's seafood-loving home town of Yantai on China's Shandong Peninsula are mackerel dumplings flavored with lemongrass and coriander and wrapped in a delicate translucent skin, while thicker-skinned, meat-filled dumplings come pan-fried, steamed, or *xiao long bao* (soup dumpling) style. There's a shorter version of the menu at sister venue ShanDong MaMa Mini in Centre Place laneway.

SIGLO

Recommended by
George Calombaris

2/161 Spring Street
Central Business District
Melbourne 3000
+61 396546631
www.siglobar.com.au

Opening hours	Open 7 days
Reservation policy	No
Credit cards	Accepted
Price range	Affordable
Style	Smart casual
Cuisine	Australian
Recommended for	Late night

"Classic rooftop terrace bar with views of Parliament House—serving cocktails, wine, and gourmet snacks."
—George Calombaris

SUPERNORMAL

Recommended by
Shannon Bennett,
Lachlan Colwill,
Dan Hunter

180 Flinders Lane
Central Business District
Melbourne 3000
+61 396508688
www.supernormal.net.au

Opening hours	Open 7 days
Credit cards	Accepted but not Diners
Price range	Affordable
Style	Casual
Cuisine	Pan-Asian
Recommended for	Regular neighborhood

"I'm in Melbourne regularly and cannot miss Supernormal. Awesome staff, karaoke downstairs, the chicken and shrinp (prawn) dumpling with chile, vinegar, and plenty of quality sake! Ticks all the boxes for me!"— Lachlan Colwill

SUPPER INN

Recommended by
Teage Ezard,
Aaron Turner

15 Celestial Avenue
Central Business District
Melbourne 3000
+61 396634759

Opening hours	Open 7 days
Credit cards	Accepted
Price range	Affordable
Style	Casual
Cuisine	Chinese
Recommended for	Late night

"Much like many of Chinatown's restaurants, they take a very literal 'if it ain't broke' approach—the menu, decor, and prices haven't changed much over the restaurant's thirty-plus years. Many a late-night congee has been consumed within these sparsely decorated walls."—Teage Ezard

TIM HO WAN

Recommended by
Shannon Bennett

206 Bourke Street
Central Business District
Melbourne 3000
+61 393473312
www.timhowan.com.au

Opening hours	Open 7 days
Credit cards	Accepted but not AMEX or Diners
Price range	Budget
Style	Casual
Cuisine	Dim Sum
Recommended for	Regular neighborhood

"Tim Ho Wan for dumplings—even though it's a chain it has great consistency."—Shannon Bennett

TIPO 00

Recommended by
Adam D'Sylva,
Michael Wilson

361 Bourke Street
Central Business District
Melbourne 3000
+61 399423946
www.tipo00.com.au

Opening hours	Closed Sunday
Credit cards	Accepted but not Diners
Price range	Affordable
Style	Casual
Cuisine	Italian
Recommended for	Wish I'd opened

"Tipo 00 specializes in exceptional, hand-made pasta and small plates. Fairly priced and high quality, I could eat there every day."—Michael Wilson

The name refers to the type of flour used in pasta making—a clue to what Tipo is all about. Modernist and pared back, it nevertheless emanates an old-school trattoria vibe; the welcome is warm, wine comes by the glass, bottle, or carafe, and chef Andreas Papadakis, ex-Vue de Monde, spins simple Italian staples into something next-level. There are always a couple of fish or meat dishes, along with risotto made with *carnaroli* and *vialone nano* rice but the light, silky pasta is the real diva, with dishes like the elegant squid ink *tagliolini* (thin ribbon pasta) with squid and shaved bottarga. Regulars know to pace themselves so they can finish with the delicious, theatrical "Tipomisu".

TRUNK DINER

Recommended by
Adam D'Sylva

275 Exhibition Street
Central Business District
Melbourne 3000
+61 396637994
www.trunktown.com.au

Opening hours	Open 7 days
Reservation policy	No
Credit cards	Accepted
Price range	Affordable
Style	Smart casual
Cuisine	Diner
Recommended for	Breakfast

"Eclectic range of items on the menu, from wraps to shakes. Fantastic coffee too."—Adam D'Sylva

VUE DE MONDE

Recommended by
Ben Shewry,
Alla Wolf-Tasker

L55 Rialto Towers
525 Collins Street
Central Business District
Melbourne 3000
+61 396913888
www.vuedemonde.com.au

Opening hours	Open 7 days
Credit cards	Accepted
Price range	Expensive
Style	Formal
Cuisine	Modern French
Recommended for	High end

"Destination dining. Showy and memorable."
—Alla Wolf-Tasker

It's impossible not to be impressed by the high-end flagship of Shannon Bennett's culinary empire, with its dramatic dining room and impressive panorama over Melbourne. With prices as lofty as the views, you're likely to be here for an expense account meal or a special occasion—but whether it's yours or theirs, it will be money well spent. Vue de Monde's experiential degustation menu combines contemporary technique with top-shelf and native ingredients to create unlikely sounding but ultimately revelatory partnerships. An expansive (and pricey) wine list and phenomenal attention to detail signal that this is high-end dining at its very best, but culinary whimsy, with dishes often delivered by the chefs themselves, preclude stuffiness.

AKA SIRO

106 Cambridge Street
Collingwood
Melbourne 3066
+61 394170886

Opening hours	Closed Monday and Tuesday
Credit cards	Accepted
Price range	Affordable
Style	Casual
Cuisine	Japanese
Recommended for	Regular neighborhood

"Good and simple Japanese cooking—reminds me of home."—Koichi Minamishima

BIGGIE SMALLS

86 Smith Street
Collingwood
Melbourne 3066
+61 394173531
www.biggiesmalls.com.au

Opening hours	Open 7 days
Reservation policy	No
Credit cards	Accepted but not AMEX or Diners
Price range	Affordable
Style	Casual
Cuisine	Middle Eastern
Recommended for	Bargain

Named after late rap legend Christopher Wallace, aka The Notorious B.I.G., Biggie Smalls is not your typical post-nightclub kebab joint. Owned by chef Shane Delia, the same sort of care goes into the simple food here as at his upmarket restaurant, Maha. An homage to Americana threads its way through the retro diner decor, the graffiti facade, and the pumping rap soundtrack, but the food, like Maha, takes its cues from the Middle East. Kebabs wrapped in warm, pillowy flatbread come in a choice of meats with hot sauce and sides that include moreish hot crinkle fries with harissa mayo. It's so

reasonably priced that even adding a Turkish delight ice-cream sandwich to your order will still leave you with enough for the taxi home.

LITTLE SUNFLOWER CAFÉ

15 Ormond Road
Elwood
Melbourne 3184
+61 395310399
www.littlesunflower.com.au

Opening hours	Closed Monday
Credit cards	Accepted
Price range	Affordable
Style	Casual
Cuisine	Café
Recommended for	Breakfast

"Like the name suggests, it's a little ray of sunshine, with dishes looking as good as they make you feel. For the super health-conscious, the raw granola is the pick, taking three days to make due to all the activated and broken-down nutrient components. For those who still crave a bit of protein, the Buddha bowls are massive and filling, and can be made with or without meat, and served hot or cold—perfect for when you're hungry but still want to pat yourself on the back for being healthy."—Teage Ezard

MATSUYA JAPANESE RESTAURANT

146 Station Street
Fairfield
Melbourne 3078
+61 394826088

Opening hours	Open 7 days
Credit cards	Accepted
Price range	Budget
Style	Casual
Cuisine	Japanese
Recommended for	Regular neighborhood

"Great, consistent sushi at an affordable price."
— Adam D'Sylva

ARCHIE'S ALL DAY

Recommended by
Ben Shewry

189 Gertrude Street
Fitzroy
Melbourne 3065
+61 394170066
www.archiesallday.com

Opening hours	Open 7 days
Credit cards	Accepted
Price range	Budget
Style	Casual
Cuisine	Breakfast-Brunch
Recommended for	Breakfast

BAR LIBERTY

Recommended by
Alla Wolf-Tasker

234 Johnston Street
Fitzroy
Melbourne 3065
www.barliberty.com

Opening hours	Open 7 days
Credit cards	Accepted
Price range	Affordable
Style	Casual
Cuisine	Bistro
Recommended for	Local favorite

BELLE'S HOT CHICKEN

Recommended by
Jasper Avent

150 Gertrude Street
Fitzroy
Melbourne 3065
+61 390770788
www.belleshotchicken.com

Opening hours	Open 7 days
Credit cards	Accepted but not Diners
Price range	Affordable
Style	Casual
Cuisine	American
Recommended for	Bargain

Hot young chefs crave the spicy fried chicken served up at this trendy diner in fashionable Fitzroy, with its youthful decor of pine, red paint, and bright lights. Ribs, tenders, drumsticks, and wings are served within sandwiches, burgers, and waffles. Choose a heat from "Southern" (rather spicy) to "Really F**kin Hot" (can't even) and dip into sauces like the weird-but-it-works peach-flavored barbecue. Food is served casually on plastic and paper, with a range of organic wine. To round off the meal there are fun, delicious sides like crinkle-cut fries and roast yam salad. Vegetarian? You'd better like mushrooms.

CHOTTO/KINOME

Recommended by
Morgan McGlone

35 Smith Street
Fitzroy
Melbourne 3065
+61 390415856
www.kinome.com.au

Opening hours	Closed Monday
Credit cards	Accepted
Price range	Affordable
Style	Casual
Cuisine	Modern Japanese
Recommended for	Breakfast

CUTLER & CO

Recommended by
Cameron Matthews

55–57 Gertrude Street
Fitzroy
Melbourne 3065
+61 394194888
www.cutlerandco.com.au

Opening hours	Closed Monday
Credit cards	Accepted
Price range	Expensive
Style	Smart casual
Cuisine	Modern Australian
Recommended for	High end

"The space has a cool, funky vibe set in old shop fronts. The menu is innovative but also provides classics, executed brilliantly, often with an unexpected twist. Service and wine list are outstanding."
—Cameron Matthews

DANNY'S BURGERS

Recommended by
Adam D'Sylva

360 Saint Georges Road
Fitzroy
Melbourne 3068
+61 394815847

Opening hours	Open 7 days
Reservation policy	No
Credit cards	Not accepted
Price range	Budget
Style	Casual
Cuisine	Fast Food
Recommended for	Late night

"Great burgers and steamed dim sum to fix any late-night cravings."—Adam D'Sylva

MIGHTY BOY CAFÉ

Recommended by
Ben Shewry

59–61 Gertrude Street
Fitzroy
Melbourne 3065
+61 394193686
www.mightyboyeatery.com.au

Opening hours	Open 7 days
Reservation policy	No
Credit cards	Accepted but not AMEX or Diners
Price range	Budget
Style	Casual
Cuisine	Korean
Recommended for	Breakfast

RICKY & PINKY

Recommended by
Ben Shewry

Builders Arms Hotel
211 Gertrude Street
Fitzroy
Melbourne 3065
+61 394177700
www.buildersarmshotel.com.au

Opening hours	Open 7 days
Credit cards	Accepted but not Diners
Price range	Affordable
Style	Smart casual
Cuisine	Chinese-Australian
Recommended for	Local favorite

"It feels like a very Melbourne place. It's versatile and come as you are—everybody is welcome. An informal and delicious, modern take on Chinese cooking, in a pub."—Ben Shewry

Serial restaurateur Andrew McConnell (Cumulus Inc., Cutler & Co., Supernormal and more) transformed The Builders Arms and the contemporary rear dining room, Moon Under Water, into a Chinese diner in 2016. He named it Ricky & Pinky, after the now-defunct Wan Chai tattoo parlour where he was first inked. There's a cheeky nod to the traditional Chinese restaurant, with carpeted floors, lazy Susans at the tables, fish tanks full of seafood, and fortune cookies, but chef Archan Chan's Cantonese-accented food and the smart thirty-five-page drink list have been informed by a very contemporary zeitgeist.

8BIT.

Recommended by
Shaun Quade

8 Droop Street
Footscray
Melbourne 3011
+61 396878838
www.eat8bit.com.au

Opening hours	Open 7 days
Reservation policy	No
Credit cards	Accepted but not AMEX or Diners
Price range	Affordable
Style	Casual
Cuisine	American
Recommended for	Late night

"There's a lot of competition in the burger market—and while I can't say that there's any particular formula to getting it right (it's a personal thing after all), there's something about the balance these guys manage to achieve."—Shaun Quade

LA TORTILLERIA

Recommended by
Teage Ezard

72 Stubbs Street
Kensington
Melbourne 3031
+61 393765577
www.latortilleria.com.au

Opening hours	Closed Monday
Credit cards	Accepted but not AMEX
Price range	Affordable
Style	Casual
Cuisine	Mexican
Recommended for	Bargain

"Don't leave without trying Grandma Pina's flan—and chase it with mezcal, for good measure." — Teage Ezard

ESTELLE BY SCOTT PICKETT

Recommended by
Shannon Bennett,
Alla Wolf-Tasker

245 High Street
Northcote
Melbourne 3070
+61 394894609
www.estellebysp.com

Opening hours	Closed Monday and Sunday
Credit cards	Accepted
Price range	Expensive
Style	Smart casual
Cuisine	Modern Australian
Recommended for	Local favorite

"Modern, adventurous, but well-grounded in technique. Attracts good cooks to the brigade."—Alla Wolf-Tasker

KALIMERA SOUVLAKI ART

Recommended by
Ben Shewry

41 Chester Street
Oakleigh
Melbourne 3166
+61 399393912
www.kalimerasouvlakiart.com.au

Opening hours	Closed Monday
Reservation policy	No
Credit cards	Accepted
Price range	Affordable
Style	Casual
Cuisine	Greek
Recommended for	Regular neighborhood

"It's super honest, tasty cooking. The best version of a classic Australian-Greek staple."—Ben Shewry

COLONEL TAN'S THAI KITCHEN

Recommended by
Shannon Bennett

229 Chapel Street
Prahran
Melbourne 3181
+61 395215985
www.revolverupstairs.com.au

Opening hours	Closed Monday and Sunday
Credit cards	Accepted
Price range	Affordable
Style	Casual
Cuisine	Thai
Recommended for	Regular neighborhood

"A pop-up in the back of a famous night club, with some amazing artwork from likes of Banksy and Sheppard Fairy. Great Thai street food."—Shannon Bennett

I LOVE PHO

Recommended by
Adam D'Sylva

264 Victoria Street
Richmond
Melbourne 3121
+61 394277749
www.pholove.com.au

Opening hours	Open 7 days
Credit cards	Not accepted
Price range	Budget
Style	Casual
Cuisine	Pho
Recommended for	Breakfast

"I always go here a couple of times a week. Nice, clean start to the day."—Adam D'Sylvia

JIMMY GRANTS

Recommended by
Shannon Bennett

427 Church Street
Richmond
Melbourne 3121
+61 384198808
www.jimmygrants.com.au

Opening hours	Open 7 days
Credit cards	Accepted
Price range	Affordable
Style	Casual
Cuisine	Greek
Recommended for	Late night

"Great chicken souvlaki and really tasty salads."
—Shannon Bennett

With seven venues under the banner, it's fair to say that restaurateur and MasterChef Australia judge George Calombaris has well and truly established his casual/late-night formula in the form of Jimmy Grants. His Greek heritage (the name is rhyming slang for "immigrants") inspired the cheap and cheerful clipped menu of slow-cooked meat and rotisserie chicken-filled souvlaki and accompanying dips, chips, and sides—think *saganaki* (fried cheese appetizer) with lemon and honey, hellenic slaw and taramasalata. There are draught and bottled beers and ciders, a small selection of cocktails, and a Victorian/Hellenic wine list. It's quality fast food—the perfect place to fill up before or after a big night out.

MINAMISHIMA

Recommended by
Shannon Bennett,
Adam D'Sylva

4 Lord Street
Richmond
Melbourne 3121
+61 394295180
www.minamishima.com.au

Opening hours	Open 7 days
Credit cards	Accepted
Price range	Expensive
Style	Smart casual
Cuisine	Japanese
Recommended for	High end

"Understated, yet opulent and elegant: it is the big night out restaurant that doesn't make a big deal of it. Amazing, quality ingredients curated into some of the best Japanese I have eaten. The chef and owner is as Melbourne as I am and has a loyal following since his days at Kenzan."—Shannon Bennett

If you're a fan of the ubiquitous California roll, you're probably not going to like Minamishima. For one thing, there's not a slice of avocado in sight. Secondly, an *omakase* (chef's choice) meal at this elegant, minimalist sushi restaurant is likely to set you back A$200 ($149; £115) rather than two. Chef-owner Koichi Minamishima, who famously worked his way from pot washer to sushi master, transforms both Australian seafood and seafood imported from Tokyo's Tsukiji Market into glistening jewels. Ask for a seat at the bar where you can watch his astonishing knife skills and exacting presentation. It's fine-dining Japanese style.

PACIFIC SEAFOOD BBQ HOUSE

Recommended by
Adam D'Sylva

8/240 Victoria Street
Richmond
Melbourne 3141
+61 394278225
www.pacificbbqhouse.com.au

Opening hours	Open 7 days
Credit cards	Accepted but not AMEX or Diners
Price range	Affordable
Style	Smart casual
Cuisine	Chinese
Recommended for	Bargain

"It has the best crispy pork belly, Peking duck, soy chicken, and whole steamed fish."—Adam D'Sylva

THANH NGA NINE

Recommended by
Geoff Lindsay

160 Victoria Street
Richmond
Melbourne 3121
+61 394277068

Opening hours	Open 7 days
Credit cards	Accepted
Price range	Budget
Style	Casual
Cuisine	Vietnamese
Recommended for	Bargain

"Long established Vietnamese restaurant in Victoria Street Richmond, home of Melbourne's Vietnamese community. Love the *canh chua cá* (sour fish soup) and the *cá kho tô* (caramelised fish served in a clay pot). Service is brisk, but the food wins over in the end!"—Geoff Lindsay

ATTICA

Recommended by
Dan Barber, Shannon Bennett, Ben Devlin, Rodney Dunn, Analiese Gregory, Dan Hong, Dan Hunter, Morgan McGlone, Michael Meredith, Alfred Prasad, Michael Reid, Ljubomir Stanisic, James Viles, Michael Wilson

74 Glen Eira Road
Ripponlea
Melbourne 3185
+61 395300111
www.attica.com.au

Opening hours	Closed Sunday and Monday
Credit cards	Accepted but not Diners
Price range	Expensive
Style	Casual
Cuisine	Modern Australian
Recommended for	High end

"At this level of dining it's all about the special touches and Attica has them in spades, from the juice matches for the non-drinker to the attention paid to native Australian ingredients."—Rodney Dunn

Attica's black walls and spotlighting belie the playful nature of head chef Ben Shewry's renowned Melbourne dining room, with dishes much lighter and more vibrant than the decor would have you believe. What the room might lack in personality is made up for by the food, with the famously hands-on chef often blending Asian and indigenous ingredients for interesting combos. To catch Attica at its best, head down on a Tuesday night, when the kitchen is testing and developing new menu ideas, and experience its five-course menu for a fraction of what you'd normally pay.

MISS RUBENS

Recommended by
Duncan Welgemoed

76 Glen Eira Road
Ripponlea
Melbourne 3185
+61 390425933

Opening hours	Closed Monday
Reservation policy	No
Credit cards	Accepted but not AMEX or Diners
Price range	Budget
Style	Casual
Cuisine	Deli
Recommended for	Breakfast

ST ALI

Recommended by
Alla Wolf-Tasker

12–18 Yarra Place
South Melbourne
Melbourne 3205
+61 396862990
www.stali.com.au

Opening hours	Open 7 days
Credit cards	Accepted
Price range	Affordable
Style	Casual
Cuisine	Café
Recommended for	Breakfast

DAINTY SICHUAN

Recommended by
Peter Gilmore

176 Toorak Road
South Yarra
Melbourne 3141
+61 390781686

Opening hours	Open 7 days
Credit cards	Accepted but not AMEX or Diners
Price range	Affordable
Style	Casual
Cuisine	Sichuan
Recommended for	Worth the travel

"It's the best. They serve glasses of soy milk in case the food is too spicy for you. Also the best fried eggplant (aubergine) I've ever had."—Peter Serpico

This is the top end of Sichuan dining in Melbourne. With a five star fit-out, Dainty Sichuan hosts happy diners at round tables. Haute cuisine hot pots are a hit. Choose a stock then list fresh, quality ingredients to simmer beneath. Fires burn and hot pots bubble, like the witches' cauldrons in *Macbeth*—no eyes of newt to be seen, but everything from Murray cod to hot blood curd and trotters for stirring in the pot.

MARKET LANE COFFEE

Recommended by
Ben Shewry

Shop 13, Prahran Market
163 Commercial Road
South Yarra
Melbourne 3141
+61 398047434
www.marketlane.com.au

Opening hours	Open 7 days
Credit cards	Accepted but not Diners
Price range	Affordable
Style	Casual
Cuisine	Café
Recommended for	Breakfast

MASTER ROLL VIETNAM

Recommended by
Shannon Bennett

169 Toorak Road
South Yarra
Melbourne 3141
+61 390788754
www.masterrollvietnam.com.au

Opening hours	Closed Sunday
Credit cards	Accepted but not AMEX or Diners
Price range	Budget
Style	Casual
Cuisine	Vietnamese Street Food
Recommended for	Bargain

"The best rice-paper rolls and banh mi in Melbourne. Don't get confused with the chain with a similar name, this is family run and all made to order. A chicken banh mi with duck rice-paper roll is the ultimate lunch."—Shannon Bennett

RAMBLR

Recommended by
Jasper Avent

363 Chapel Street
South Yarra
Melbourne 3141
+61 398270949
www.ramblr.com.au

Opening hours	Closed Monday
Credit cards	Accepted but not Diners
Price range	Affordable
Style	Smart casual
Cuisine	Modern Australian
Recommended for	Regular neighborhood

DINNER BY HESTON BLUMENTHAL

Recommended by
Ben Batterbury

Crown Towers Melbourne
8 Whiteman Street
Southbank
Melbourne 3006
+61 385822061
www.dinnerbyheston.com.au

Opening hours	Open 7 days
Credit cards	Accepted
Price range	Expensive
Style	Smart casual
Cuisine	European
Recommended for	Worth the travel

"As with all of Heston's restaurants, the food is impeccable yet unpretentious and fun. It is an amazing dining experience that definitely has the wow factor."—Ben Batterbury

CAFÉ DI STASIO

31 Fitzroy Street
St Kilda
Melbourne 3182
+61 295253999
www.distasio.com.au

Recommended by
Teage Ezard,
Geoff Lindsay,
Pasquale Trimboli,
Alla Wolf-Tasker

Opening hours..Open 7 days
Credit cards..Accepted
Price range..Affordable
Style..Smart casual
Cuisine..Italian
Recommended for..................Regular neighborhood

"Tradition and authenticity most succinctly sum up
Café Di Stasio, making you feel like you're in Italy
rather than Melbourne. The service is agile both
literally and figuratively—staff duck and weave
between tables, providing white-suited, unobtrusive,
but attentive service. The wine list is almost daunting,
with hundreds of bottles from both near and far
(including their own vineyard) to ensure everyone
is catered for. The fare is expected, but comforting
rather than tired. While the menu doesn't break any
new ground, it isn't trying to—it's good Italian done
great. If you miss out on a table or are simply looking
for a nightcap, like any Italian restaurant worth its salt,
there's always room at the bar."—Teage Ezard

LAU'S FAMILY KITCHEN

4 Acland Street
St Kilda
Melbourne 3182
+61 385989880
www.lauskitchen.com.au

Recommended by
Geoff Lindsay

Opening hours..Open 7 days
Credit cards..................Accepted but not AMEX or Diners
Price range..Affordable
Style...Casual
Cuisine..Cantonese
Recommended for..................Regular neighborhood

"I love Lau's family kitchen—a Cantonese restaurant
with modern styling run by the venerable Lau family.
Love the *mápó tòfu* (tofu in spicy sauce) and any
seafood dish!"—Geoff Lindsay

STOKEHOUSE

30 Jacka Boulevard
St Kilda
Melbourne 3182
+61 395255555
www.stokehouse.com.au

Recommended by
Teage Ezard,
Geoff Lindsay

Opening hours..Open 7 days
Credit cards..................................Accepted but not Diners
Price range..Affordable
Style..Smart casual
Cuisine..Modern Australian
Recommended for......................................Local favorite

"This iconic restaurant on the beach has risen from
the ashes of a devastating fire two years ago. Recently
reopened, bigger and better than ever, its dining room
is everyone's choice to celebrate, commiserate, or
entertain. On a cold winter's day, watching a storm roll
over the bay, eating, and drinking at the Stokehouse is
as Melbourne as you can get!"— Geoff Lindsay

IL PIZZAIOLO

161–163 Darebin Road
Thornbury
Melbourne 3071
+61 394848558
www.ilpizzaiolo.com.au

Recommended by
Adam D'Sylva

Opening hours............................Closed Monday and Tuesday
Credit cards..................................Accepted but not Diners
Price range..Affordable
Style...Casual
Cuisine..Pizza
Recommended for..................Regular neighborhood

BOSTON SUB

96 Chapel Street
Windsor
Melbourne 3181
+61 399399038
www.bostonsub.com.au

Recommended by
Shannon Bennett

Opening hours..Open 7 days
Credit cards..................................Accepted but not Diners
Price range..Affordable
Style...Casual
Cuisine..American
Recommended for..Bargain

"Great for a pulled-beef sandwich, especially early
or late at night when the crowds are a little less.
Great hidden bar behind the main room as well."
—Shannon Bennett

"Great bustling spot for a late night feed."

JOSH EMETT P165

NEW ZEALAND

"One of the best restaurants in Australasia."

PETER GORDON P165

"Probably the best ramen I've tried in New Zealand."

GUILIO STERLA P161

"You can't go wrong with the chipotle mayo Hereford brisket hash."

VAUGHAN MABEE P159

A B C D

1

2

Auckland pp.162–167♦

3

N E W Z E A L A N D

4

♦Wellington p.161

Canterbury p.156♦

5

♦Otago p.158

6

NEW ZEALAND

SCALE

N̂

0   80   160
▬▬▬▬▬ MI.

7

AUCKLAND: SEE PAGES 162–167

BURGERS & BEERS

Recommended by
Reon Hobson

478 Cranford Street
Redwood
Christchurch
Canterbury 8051
+64 33543336
www.burgersandbeersinc.co.nz

Opening hours	Open 7 days
Credit cards	Accepted
Price range	Affordable
Style	Casual
Cuisine	Burgers
Recommended for	Regular neighborhood

"Consistently great burgers, with the Iwi burger being a personal favorite. Don't forget to order the fries (chips) and gravy."—Reon Hobson

CHILLINGWORTH ROAD

Recommended by
Reon Hobson

2/478 Cranford Street
Redwood
Christchurch
Canterbury 8051
+64 33527784
www.chillingworthroad.co.nz

Opening hours	Closed Sunday
Credit cards	Accepted but not Diners
Price range	Expensive
Style	Smart casual
Cuisine	New Zealand Bistro
Recommended for	Local favorite

"Whether it's a meal out the front in the bistro or a gastronomic journey in the hidden room down the back, you will never leave disappointed. If time allows, do the nine courses and make a night of it."
—Reon Hobson

FIDDLESTICKS

Recommended by
Reon Hobson

48 Worcester Boulevard
Christchurch
Canterbury 8013
+64 33650533
www.fiddlesticksbar.co.nz

Opening hours	Open 7 days
Credit cards	Accepted
Price range	Affordable
Style	Smart casual
Cuisine	Modern New Zealand
Recommended for	Local favorite

"Don't forget to try the FFC—fiddlesticks fried chicken."—Reon Hobson

GENTLE GIANT

Recommended by
Bruce Ricketts

158 Ferry Road
Christchurch
Canterbury 8011
+64 33669144

Opening hours	Open 7 days
Credit cards	Accepted but not AMEX or Diners
Price range	Budget
Style	Casual
Cuisine	Café
Recommended for	Breakfast

HELLO SUNDAY

Recommended by
Giulio Sturla

6 Elgin Street
Christchurch
Canterbury 8023
+64 32601566
www.hellosundaycafe.co.nz

Opening hours	Open 7 days
Credit cards	Accepted but not AMEX or Diners
Price range	Affordable
Style	Casual
Cuisine	Breakfast
Recommended for	Breakfast

"Always delicious and consistent, changing the menu all the time. This place is also my daughter's favorite."
—Giulio Surla

Housed in a historic building that has done duty as both a post office and a Baptist Sunday school, cool little local favorite Hello Sunday makes great coffee and top-shelf brunches—like goat kofta served with *dukkah* (Egyptian spice and nut blend), roasted carrots, poached eggs, and spiced *labneh* (strained yoghurt) with flatbread and brown butter. There's also a consummate Eggs Benedict for the more conservative bruncher, as well as plenty for those with a sweet tooth. Service is as chilled as the soundtrack, and both food and drinks, including a clipped wine list, beer, and cider, are served until late afternoon. Weekends are busy so it's worth booking to ensure a table.

KINJI

Recommended by
Giulio Sturla

279B Greers Road
Christchurch
Canterbury 8053
+64 33594697
www.kinjirestaurant.com

Opening hours	Closed Sunday
Credit cards	Accepted but not AMEX or Diners
Price range	Affordable
Style	Casual
Cuisine	Japanese
Recommended for	Local favorite

"They do great Japanese food, with good technique and a variety of seafoods."—Giulio Sturla

The post-earthquake move from the city center hasn't deterred regular diners who flock to this no-longer-secret, authentic Japanese local where pristine New Zealand seafood is transformed under the experienced hands of chef Kinji Hamada. Tuna, scallops, mackerel, octopus, grouper, and more are precision-plated as flawless sashimi—squid, prawn, *tobiko* (flying fish roe), and eel wrapped in rice or as nigiri rolls. There's plenty for the carnivore too, with deeply marbled beef imported from Miyazaki prefecture, venison *tataki* (lightly seared), and the famous KFC—Kinji fried chicken. Or leave it in chef's hands with an *omakase* (chef's choice) menu. A broad range of sake is supplemented by local wines, but you can also BYO.

MAXINE'S PALACE

Recommended by
Reon Hobson

283 Lincoln Road
Christchurch
Canterbury 8024
+64 33350100
www.maxinespalace.co.nz

Opening hours	Closed Monday
Credit cards	Accepted but not AMEX or Diners
Price range	Affordable
Style	Casual
Cuisine	Chinese
Recommended for	Late night

SAMURAI BOWL

Recommended by
Reon Hobson

Shop 5
574 Colombo Street
Christchurch
Canterbury 8011
+64 33796752
www.samuraibowl.co.nz

Opening hours	Open 7 days
Credit cards	Accepted but not AMEX or Diners
Price range	Affordable
Style	Casual
Cuisine	Japanese
Recommended for	Bargain

"Spicy miso ramen is the way to go."—Reon Hobson

TOWN TONIC

Recommended by
Reon Hobson

335 Lincoln Road
Christchurch
Canterbury 8024
+64 33381150
www.towntonic.co.nz

Opening hours	Open 7 days
Credit cards	Accepted but not AMEX or Diners
Price range	Affordable
Style	Casual
Cuisine	Modern New Zealand
Recommended for	Breakfast

"Can't beat the *huevos racheros* for breakfast, and they do a freestyle Monday dinner service which shouldn't be missed."—Reon Hobson

PEGASUS BAY

Recommended by
Bevan Smith

Pegasus Bay Winery
263 Stockgrove Road
Waipara
Canterbury 7482
+64 33146869
www.pegasusbay.com

Opening hours	Open 7 days
Credit cards	Accepted
Price range	Expensive
Style	Casual
Cuisine	Modern European
Recommended for	Local favorite

**"Exemplary food and service in a stunning rural location. Everything a restaurant should be."
—Bevan Smith**

FREEMANS DINING ROOM

Recommended by
Giulio Sturla

47 London Street
Christchurch
Canterbury 8082
+64 33287517
www.freemansdiningroom.co.nz

Opening hours	Closed Monday and Tuesday
Credit cards	Accepted but not AMEX or Diners
Price range	Affordable
Style	Casual
Cuisine	Italian
Recommended for	Regular neighborhood

SLOW CUTS

Recommended by
Vaughan Mabee

46–50 Buckingham Street
Arrowtown
Otago 9302
+64 34420066

Opening hours	Open 7 days
Reservation policy	No
Credit cards	Accepted but not AMEX or Diners
Price range	Budget
Style	Casual
Cuisine	Sandwiches-Burgers
Recommended for	Bargain

"Quick and great if you've had a late night and are in need of some sustaining food."—Vaughan Mabee

THE CHOP SHOP

Recommended by
Ben Batterbury

Arrow Lane
Arrowtown
Otago 9302
+64 34421116

Opening hours	Open 7 days
Credit cards	Accepted but not AMEX or Diners
Price range	Budget
Style	Casual
Cuisine	Brunch
Recommended for	Breakfast

SCOTTS BREWING CO.

Recommended by
Bevan Smith

1 Wansbeck Street
Oamaru
Otago 9400
+64 34342244
www.scottsbrewing.co.nz

Opening hours	Open 7 days
Reservation policy	No
Credit cards	Accepted but not AMEX or Diners
Price range	Budget
Style	Casual
Cuisine	Pizza
Recommended for	Regular neighborhood

"Great vibe, no matter the time or day. Delicious pizza and a cold beer on the grass on a sunny day is hard to beat."—Bevan Smith

AMISFIELD

Recommended by
Bevan Smith

10 Lake Hayes Road
Queenstown
Otago 9371
+64 34420556
www.amisfield.co.nz

Opening hours	Open 7 days
Credit cards	Accepted
Price range	Expensive
Style	Smart casual
Cuisine	Modern New Zealand
Recommended for	Local favorite

"Exemplary food and service, delivered with passion in a stunning location."—Bevan Smith

Amisfield Winery's bistro is housed in a recycled timber building with a pitched copper roof, overlooking dramatic scenery that includes stunning views of Lake Hayes and Coronet Peak. A crackling fire warms the dining room in winter, while there are a smattering of tables outside for balmier days. The bistro offers a choice of a seasonally changing à la carte menu, with dishes designed to share, or a "Trust the Chef" option of four courses at lunch and five at dinner, that can be matched with Amisfield's own wine. Just about everything is local, from the venison (perfect with their pinot noir) to Wild Bluff oysters—and if not from a local producer, you can bet it's been made in-house or even foraged.

ATLAS BEER CAFÉ

Recommended by
Ben Batterbury

Steamer Wharf
88 Beach Street
Queenstown
Otago 9300
+64 34425995
www.atlasbeercafe.com

Opening hours	Open 7 days
Reservation policy	No
Credit cards	Accepted but not AMEX
Price range	Affordable
Style	Casual
Cuisine	Modern New Zealand
Recommended for	Local favorite

"Atlas is a great local hangout in a cool location, whether to just enjoy a cold beer or sit and have a meal. Their beer selection is awesome and the food is well priced and honest."—Ben Batterbury

BESPOKE KITCHEN

Recommended by
Josh Emett

9 Isle Street
Queenstown
Otago 9300
+64 34090552

Opening hours	Open 7 days
Reservation policy	No
Credit cards	Accepted but not AMEX or Diners
Price range	Affordable
Style	Casual
Cuisine	Café
Recommended for	Breakfast

"Great coffee and delicious, interesting breakfast dishes."—Josh Emett

FERGBURGER

Recommended by
Ben Batterbury

42 Shotover Street
Queenstown
Otago 9300
+64 34411232
www.fergburger.com

Opening hours	Open 7 days
Reservation policy	No
Credit cards	Accepted
Price range	Affordable
Style	Casual
Cuisine	Burgers
Recommended for	Late night

"Any Queenstown food guide wouldn't be complete without a mention of Fergburger. It is a living legend! Good quality burgers that are both filling and well priced, it never lets you down."—Ben Batterbury

FISHBONE

Recommended by
Ben Batterbury

7 Beach Street
Queenstown
Otago 9300
+64 34426768
www.fishbonequeenstown.co.nz

Opening hours	Open 7 days
Credit cards	Accepted but not AMEX or Diners
Price range	Affordable
Style	Casual
Cuisine	Seafood
Recommended for	High end

"For really high-end seafood, cooked simply with delicious flavors, Fishbone won't let you down. The restaurant has a really friendly feel, run by good people with a big focus on fresh local produce." —Ben Batterbury

JACK'S POINT CLUBHOUSE

Recommended by
Vaughan Mabee

McAdam Drive
Queenstown
Otago 9348
+61 43502050
www.jackspoint.com

Opening hours	Open 7 days
Credit cards	Accepted
Price range	Affordable
Style	Casual
Cuisine	Modern New Zealand
Recommended for	Breakfast

"You can't go wrong with the chipotle mayo on the Hereford beef brisket hash. Best Bloody Mary in Queenstown too."—Vaughan Mabee

KAPPA

Recommended by
Ben Batterbury,
Vaughan Mabee

36A The Mall
Queenstown
Otago 9300
+64 34411423

Opening hours	Closed Sunday
Credit cards	Accepted but not Diners
Price range	Affordable
Style	Casual
Cuisine	Sushi
Recommended for	Regular neighborhood

"Kappa is very understated, but the food is awesome and it's run by really good people."—Ben Batterbury

LA RUMBLA

Recommended by
Ben Batterbury

54 Buckingham Street
Queenstown
Otago 9302
+64 34420509

Opening hours	Closed Monday
Credit cards	Accepted but not AMEX
Price range	Affordable
Style	Casual
Cuisine	Small Plates
Recommended for	Regular neighborhood

"La Rumbla is tucked away just off the main street in Arrowtown, and has a local, hidden feel to it. The food is interesting, flavorsome, and reasonably priced and it matches an interesting wine list that has plenty of want-to-drink-it options."—Ben Batterbury

MANDU DUMPLINGS

Recommended by
Ben Batterbury

O'Connells Mall
1 Cow Lane
Queenstown
Otago 9300
+64 34412900

Opening hours	Closed Sunday
Reservation policy	No
Credit cards	Accepted but not AMEX or Diners
Price range	Budget
Style	Casual
Cuisine	Chinese
Recommended for	Bargain

SHERWOOD HOTEL

Recommended by
Bevan Smith

554 Frankton Road
Queenstown
Otago 9300
+64 34501090
www.sherwoodqueenstown.nz

Opening hours	Open 7 days
Credit cards	Accepted but not AMEX
Price range	Affordable
Style	Casual
Cuisine	Modern New Zealand
Recommended for	Late night

"Great atmosphere, with a bar you can really make yourself at home in. The food is intelligent, seasonal, unpretentious, and as much fun as the surrounds."
—Bevan Smith

VUDU CAFÉ & LARDER

Recommended by
Ben Batterbury

16 Rees Street
Queenstown
Otago 9300
+64 34418370
www.vudu.co.nz

Opening hours	Open 7 days
Reservation policy	No
Credit cards	Accepted
Price range	Budget
Style	Casual
Cuisine	Café
Recommended for	Breakfast

The second venue for the owners of Vudu Café in Beach Street, the long, narrow space of Vudu Café & Larder is dominated by a striking photograph of Queenstown from the 1950s, along with other touches of vintage—like green vinyl booth seats and the preserving-jar pendant lights. Open for breakfast and lunch, or just tea and something sweet, the menu ranges from light and simple (like toast with Queenstown honey) to hearty (smoked salmon, poached eggs, kumara (sweet potato), kale, watercress pesto, and spring onion (scallion) crème fraiche). Teatime treats change regularly but could include a pretty edible-flower-bedecked carrot and pineapple cake or a miniature chocolate and hazelnut cake. The coffee is expertly made Allpress.

YAMA EXPRESS

Recommended by
Ben Batterbury

The Pavilion
1 Beach Street
Queenstown
Otago 9300
+64 34429124

Opening hours	Open 7 days
Credit cards	Accepted
Price range	Budget
Style	Casual
Cuisine	Japanese
Recommended for	Bargain

"It's surprising to find somewhere really nice to eat within a food court in a shopping center, but this for me has some of the best sushi in town. It is good value with exceptional flavor. Even my son loves it."
—Ben Batterbury

FLORIDITAS

Recommended by
Bevan Smith

161 Cuba Street
Wellington 6011
+64 43812212
www.floriditas.co.nz

Opening hours	Open 7 days
Credit cards	Accepted
Price range	Affordable
Style	Smart casual
Cuisine	Mediterranean
Recommended for	Breakfast

"Smoked mackerel hash and good coffee is a fine way to shake out the cobwebs from the night before. Classy and consistent, it's an institution."
—Bevan Smith

THE RAMEN SHOP

Recommended by
Giulio Sturla

191 Riddiford Street
Wellington 6021
+64 43892263
www.theramenshopwellington.com

Opening hours	Open 7 days
Credit cards	Accepted but not AMEX or Diners
Price range	Budget
Style	Casual
Cuisine	Ramen Noodles
Recommended for	Bargain

"Probably the best ramen I have tried in New Zealand. They do everything, even their own noodles."
—Giulio Sturla

WHITEBAIT

Recommended by
Bevan Smith

Clyde Quay Wharf
Wellington 6011
+64 43858555
www.white-bait.nz

Opening hours	Open 7 days
Credit cards	Accepted
Price range	Affordable
Style	Smart casual
Cuisine	Seafood
Recommended for	Worth the travel

"Seafood treated with confidence and respect."
—Bevan Smith

Whitebait offers a true taste of New Zealand—from the paua shell pendant lights to the panorama over the marina, and from the menu in both English and Maori to the local, sustainable, market-dependent produce used by chef Paul Hoathe. Not unnaturally, seafood dominates, with entrées like Kapiti octopus carpaccio with diamond clam, pacific oyster, king crab, and local sea vegetables; while the Josper grill adds delicious smokiness to mains such as squid with venison *boudin noir* (blood sausage) or line-caught snapper with spanner crab, sea succulents, and a carrot confit. The dynamic wine list follows the menu's lead, focusing on organic, sustainable, and handmade wines, with a Coravin system (which allows wine to be poured without removing the cork) meaning that many rare or unusual drops are available by the glass.

"A TRUE NEIGHBORHOOD RESTAURANT."

JOSH EMMETT P166

"LOVE THE AMBIENCE AND THE BIG OPEN FIRE KITCHEN."

GIULIO STURLA P166

AUCKLAND

"GREAT FOOD AND SERVICE, AMAZING WINE LIST, AND EASY LOCATION."

MICHAEL MEREDITH P167

"Like little India in the center of Auckland."

PETER GILMORE P164

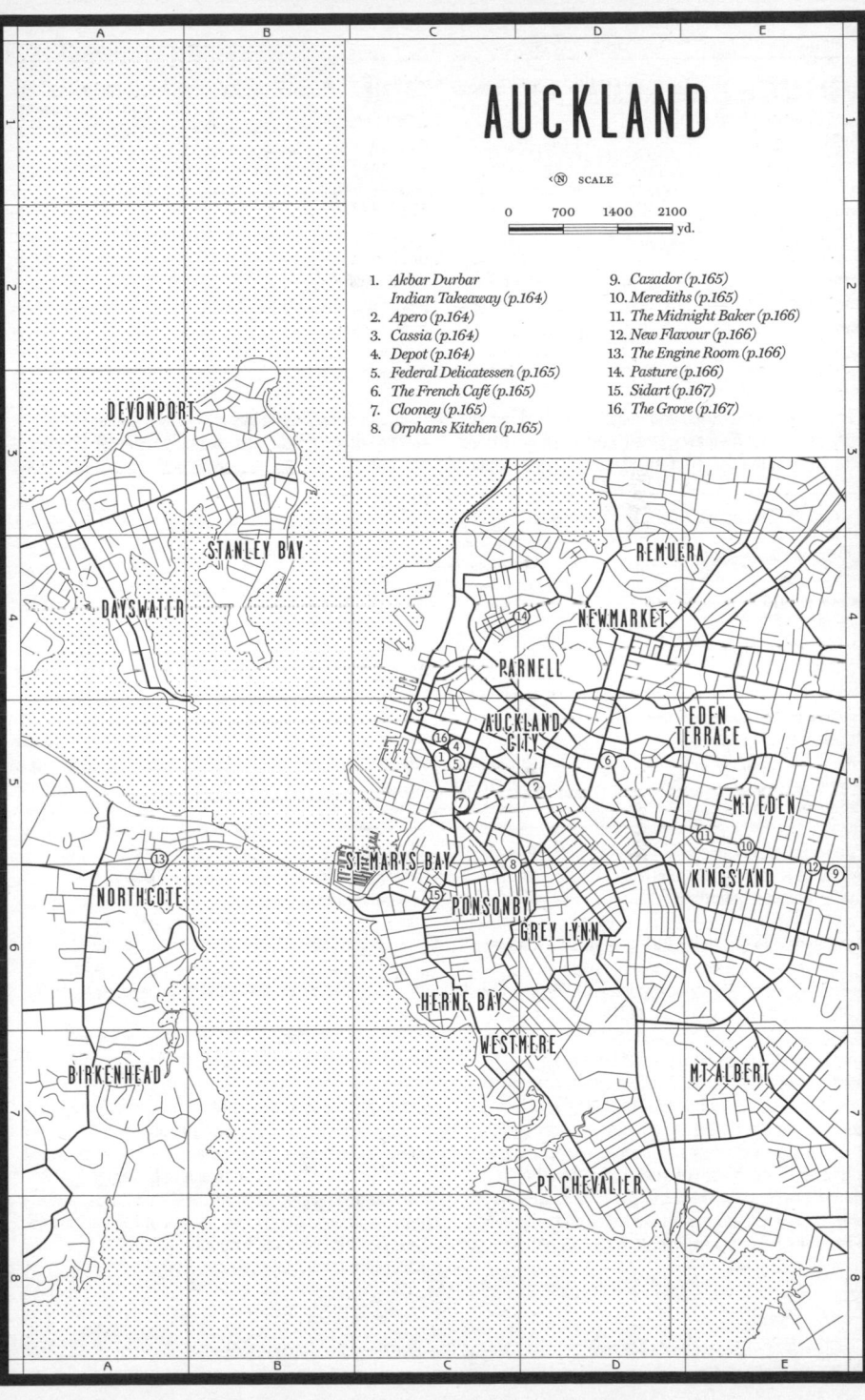

AUCKLAND

‹Ⓝ› SCALE

0   700   1400   2100
yd.

DEVONPORT

STANLEY BAY

DAYSWATER

REMUERA

NEWMARKET

PARNELL

AUCKLAND
CITY

EDEN
TERRACE

MT EDEN

THE ENGINE ROOM

NORTHCOTE

ST MARYS BAY

KINGSLAND

PONSONBY

GREY LYNN

BIRKENHEAD

HERNE BAY

WESTMERE

MT ALBERT

PT CHEVALIER

AKBAR DURBAR INDIAN TAKEAWAY

Recommended by
Peter Gilmore

51–61 Hobson Street
Auckland City
Auckland 1010
+64 93095752
www.akbardarbar.co.nz

Opening hours	Open 7 days
Credit cards	Accepted but not AMEX or Diners
Price range	Affordable
Style	Casual
Cuisine	Indian-Hyderabadi
Recommended for	Late night

"Fantastic, slow-cooked and tasty biryani and roti. A buzzing takeout (takeaway) well worth visiting. It's like little India in the center of Auckland."—Peter Gilmore

APÉRO

Recommended by
Michael Meredith,
Giulio Sturla

280 Karangahape Road
Auckland City
Auckland 1010
+64 93734778
www.apero.co.nz

Opening hours	Closed Monday and Tuesday
Credit cards	Accepted but not AMEX or Diners
Price range	Affordable
Style	Casual
Cuisine	Modern French
Recommended for	Regular neighborhood

"Delicious. New Zealand ingredients with a French influence is a perfect combination. Great wine list too."—Michael Meredith

Food and wine get equal billing at Apéro. A former tattoo bar with a karaoke bar as neighbor, it's a long, narrow, and compact space with exposed brick walls and a timber-topped bar. The menu, under chef Leslie Hottiaux, is a pleasing wander from drinking snacks (goat cheese croquettes or a plate of hand-carved Iberico ham) into more hunger-busting territory, with beef rib-eye or the bar's specialty— pork sausage ordered by the foot (quarter-meter). There are also changing blackboard specials. The infectious enthusiasm of personable sommelier and co-owner Ismo Koski (ex-maître d' at Sidart and Meredith's) will have even the most conservative wine drinker keenly exploring the exceptionally curated global list.

CASSIA

Recommended by
Peter Gilmore

5 Fort Lane
Auckland City
Auckland 1010
+64 93799702
www.cassiarestaurant.co.nz

Opening hours	Closed Monday and Sunday
Credit cards	Accepted
Price range	Affordable
Style	Smart casual
Cuisine	Modern Indian
Recommended for	Wish I'd opened

"Sid Sahrawat's more casual modern Indian restaurant, with delicious cocktails."—Peter Gilmore

DEPOT

Recommended by
Peter Gilmore,
Bevan Smith

86 Federal Street
Auckland City
Auckland 1010
+64 93637048
www.eatatdepot.co.nz

Opening hours	Open 7 days
Reservation policy	No
Credit cards	Accepted
Price range	Affordable
Style	Casual
Cuisine	New Zealand
Recommended for	Bargain

"Relaxed vibe, consistent, good service, and great food. Every city or town could use a Depot."
—Bevan Smith

From one of New Zealand's most loved chefs, Al Brown, Depot continues to woo diners with its relaxed style, unpretentious, flavor-bombed food, and unwavering consistency. There's a no-reservations policy and, even today, six years after opening, it's still so popular you'll probably have to wait for a table. Charming staff and the sharing-plate style of the seasonally changing menu mean it's always a lively and sociable place to eat. Many of the bigger dishes are cooked over charcoal or native hardwood; dishes like hapuka (fish), free-range chicken, or bones filled with rich, buttery marrow to spread on crisp slivers of toasted bread. The wine list is locally focused, with just a few disrupters from Australia and Chile.

FEDERAL DELICATESSEN

Recommended by
Josh Emett

86 Federal Street
Auckland City
Auckland 1010
+64 93637184
www.thefed.co.nz

Opening hours..Open 7 days
Reservation policy..No
Credit cards...Accepted
Price range..Budget
Style..Casual
Cuisine...Deli
Recommended for..Late Night

"Great bustling spot for a late-night feed."
—Josh Emett

THE FRENCH CAFÉ

Recommended by
Peter Gilmore,
Bevan Smith

210 Symonds Street
Eden Terrace
Auckland 1010
+64 93771911
www.thefrenchcafe.co.nz

Opening hours...............Closed Monday and Sunday
Credit cards...Accepted
Price range...Expensive
Style..Smart casual
Cuisine..Modern New Zealand
Recommended for..High end

"Simon and Creghan run one of the best restaurants
in Australasia with French-focused food in a gorgeous
dining room. Simon's never-off-the-menu confit duck
leg is always as good as the last time."—Peter Gilmore

CLOONEY

Recommended by
Michael Meredith

33 Sale Street
Freemans Bay
Auckland 1010
+64 93581702
www.clooney.co.nz

Opening hours..Open 7 days
Credit cards...Accepted
Price range...Expensive
Style..Smart casual
Cuisine..Modern New Zealand
Recommended for.......................................Local favorite

"Creative cooking using local ingredients."
—Michael Meredith

ORPHANS KITCHEN

Recommended by
Giulio Sturla

118 Ponsonby Road
Grey Lynn
Auckland 1011
+64 93787979
www.orphanskitchen.co.nz

Opening hours..Open 7 days
Credit cards...............................Accepted but not AMEX
Price range..Affordable
Style..Casual
Cuisine..Modern New Zealand
Recommended for.............................Regular neighborhood

"If I am in Auckland I go to Orphans Kitchen.
Great ethos and philosophy about their produce and
cooking style. They do breakfast, lunch, and dinner."
—Giulio Sturla

CAZADOR

Recommended by
Michael Meredith

854 Dominion Road
Mount Eden
Auckland 1041
+64 96208730
www.cazador.co.nz

Opening hours...............Closed Monday and Sunday
Credit cards....................Accepted but not AMEX or Diners
Price range..Affordable
Style..Smart casual
Cuisine...Bistro
Recommended for.............................Regular neighborhood

"It's renowned for its wild food and game dishes."
—Michael Meredith

MEREDITHS

Recommended by
Peter Gilmore,
Reon Hobson

365 Dominion Road
Mount Eden
Auckland 1024
+64 96233140
www.merediths.co.nz

Opening hours...............Closed Monday and Sunday
Credit cards...............................Accepted but not Diners
Price range...Expensive
Style..Smart casual
Cuisine...New Zealand
Recommended for..High end

"Not only is it at the forefront of New Zealand dining,
but it is led by one of the most generous human
beings you will ever meet."—Reon Hobson

THE MIDNIGHT BAKER

Recommended by
Michael Meredith

218 Dominion Road
Mount Eden
Auckland 1024
+64 962 3163
www.themidnightbaker.co.nz

Opening hours	Closed Monday
Credit cards	Accepted but not AMEX or Diners
Price range	Affordable
Style	Casual
Cuisine	Vegan Bakery-Café
Recommended for	Breakfast

"It's a great local bakery and is just up the road from us. Try the vegetarian breakfast."—Michael Meredith

It started with a loaf of bread and ended with a toast. Yeshe Dawa, aka "The Midnight Baker", began baking wheat-, gluten-, yeast-, nut-, and refined sugar-free seeded bread in 2015, selling it at markets and supplying Auckland cafés. A year later, she opened The Midnight Baker café, all based around her "Freedom Loaf". Primarily vegan, the menu features around a dozen types of toast with sweet and savory options; like smoky baked beans with kale chips, or spiced pumpkin with candied pecans, ginger, and coconut caramel. There are Latte Lab turmeric or red velvet lattes as well as Forage & Bloom tea and, for caffeine fiends, expertly made Eighthirty coffee.

NEW FLAVOUR

Recommended by
Michael Meredith

541 Dominion Road
Mount Eden
Auckland 1014
+64 96386880

Opening hours	Closed Tuesday
Reservation policy	No
Credit cards	Not accepted
Price range	Budget
Style	Casual
Cuisine	Chinese
Recommended for	Bargain

"It's a great Chinese place that's cheap and cheerful."
—Michael Meredith

THE ENGINE ROOM

Recommended by
Josh Emett

115 Queen Street
Northcote Point
Auckland 0627
+64 94809502
www.engineroom.net.nz

Opening hours	Closed Monday and Sunday
Credit cards	Accepted
Price range	Affordable
Style	Casual
Cuisine	Modern European
Recommended for	Regular neighborhood

"The engine room is a true neighborhood restaurant. Relaxed environment, knowledgeable service, and extremely consistent."—Josh Emmett

Good, honest, uncomplicated bistro food—like far better versions of the things you might make at home—is what powers local favorite The Engine Room. Inhabiting a striking art deco building in Northcote Point, the restaurant's light, airy dining room, with wooden floors and touches of greenery, has a lively and welcoming vibe enhanced by genuinely hospitable service—owner-operators Carl Koppenhagen and Natalia Schamroth take charge of the kitchen and front of house respectively. Koppenhagen's menu is populated by long-term favorites (steak with Café de Paris butter, veal schnitzel, and twice-baked goat cheese soufflé) mixed up with more contemporary dishes, and there's a compact but interesting wine list with most available by the glass.

PASTURE

Recommended by
Giulio Sturla

235 Parnell Road
Parnell
Auckland 1052
+64 93005077
www.pastureakl.com

Opening hours	Closed Monday and Tuesday
Credit cards	Accepted but not AMEX or Diners
Price range	Expensive
Style	Casual
Cuisine	Modern New Zealand
Recommended for	Worth the travel

"Very creative cooking. Simple but very focused flavors. Love the ambience and the big open fire kitchen."—Giulio Sturla

All you'll know is that there'll be six courses, with both the menu and prices dependent on what's in season, what's good at the markets, and the chef's whim. But let go and believe and you will be rewarded. The bijou-sized Pasture has a focus on ethically sourced ingredients, with food equally balanced between plant and protein cooked over flame. With the open-plan aspect of the restaurant you'll get a good view of what the kitchen is doing to your meal before chef Ed Verner or wife Laura deliver it to your table. In line with their ethos, the wine list consists of mainly local, low-intervention wines, with the addition of a few noteworthy Australians.

SIDART

Recommended by
Michael Meredith

Three Lamps Plaza
283 Ponsonby Road
Ponsonby
Auckland 1011
+64 93602122
www.sidart.co.nz

Opening hours	Closed Monday and Sunday
Credit cards	Accepted
Price range	Expensive
Style	Smart casual
Cuisine	Modern New Zealand
Recommended for	High end

"Great food and service, amazing wine list, and easy location."—Michael Meredith

A contender for one of Auckland's best restaurants (or even New Zealand's), Sidart, down an alleyway and up a staircase off Ponsonby Road, is fine dining reimagined. Sure, it ticks all the expected standards—meticulous service, a blockbuster wine list and a comfortable, elegant dining space (with the bonus of city skyline views), but there's nothing staid or fussy about Sid Sahrawat's cutting-edge, precision-plated food. A seven-course "Discovery" tasting menu comes supplemented by a selection of appetisers of the day, while the "chef's table experience" gives an insight into the creative process and techniques used in the kitchen. Tuesday nights, when the kitchen runs experimental dinners to test new dishes and prices are dropped accordingly, are insanely popular.

THE GROVE

Recommended by
Michael Meredith

Saint Patricks Square
Wyndham Street
Auckland 1010
+64 93684129
www.thegroverestaurant.co.nz

Opening hours	Closed Sunday
Credit cards	Accepted
Price range	Expensive
Style	Smart casual
Cuisine	Modern New Zealand-French
Recommended for	Local favorite

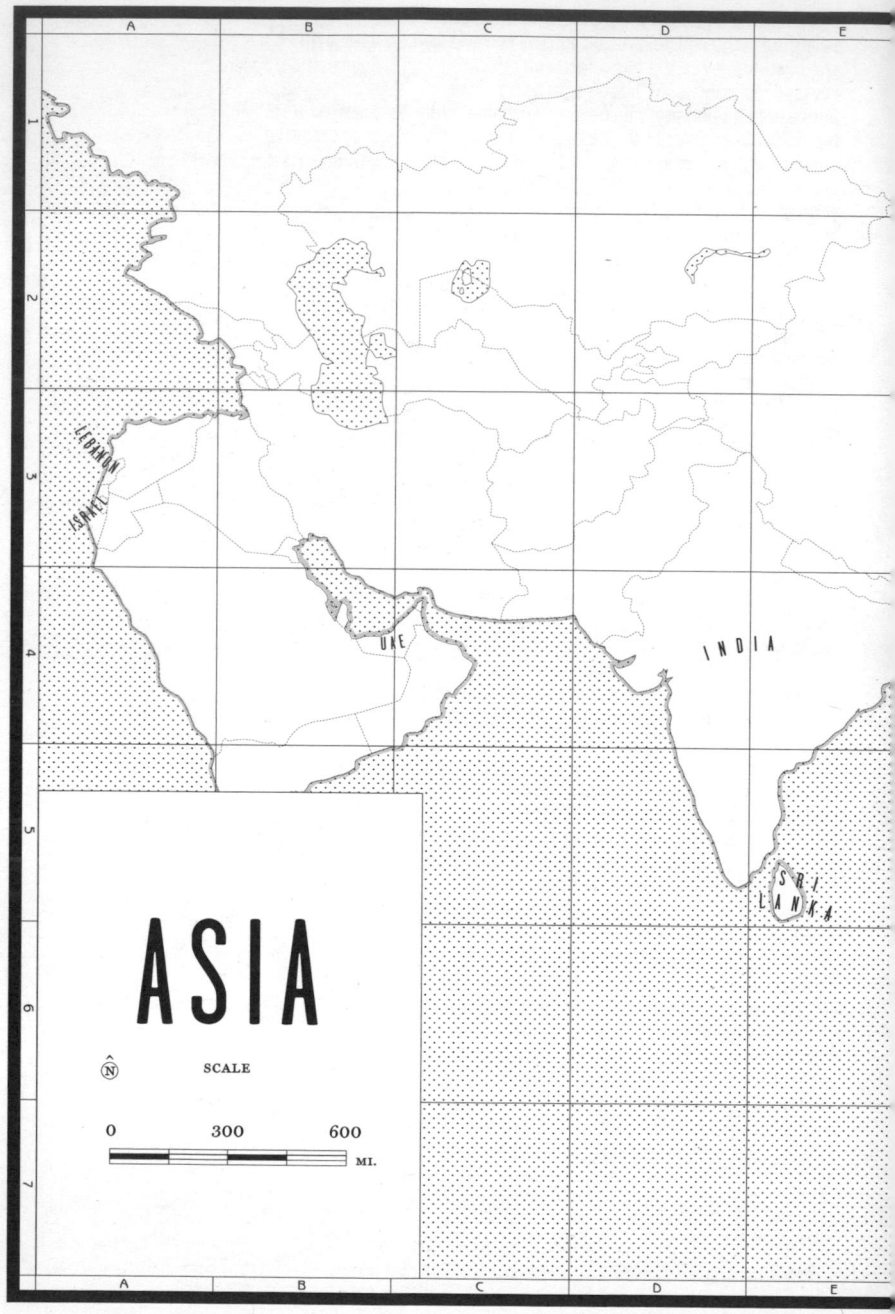

ASIA

SCALE

N

0   300   600
MI.

LEBANON

ISRAEL

UAE

INDIA

SRI LANKA

"The best place to get a sabich."

JOEL BRAHAM P174

"ONE OF THE BEST INTERPRETATIONS OF A MEZZE—FRESH INGREDIENTS AND DELICIOUS TASTES."

KAMAL MOUZAWAK P177

SOUTHWEST ASIA

"THERE IS ALWAYS A VIBRANT AND SEXY ATMOSPHERE."

MAOZ ALONIM P172

"THIS IS A HAPPY PLACE WITH INCREDIBLE FOOD, AMBIENCE, AND MUSIC."

TOMER AMEDI P175

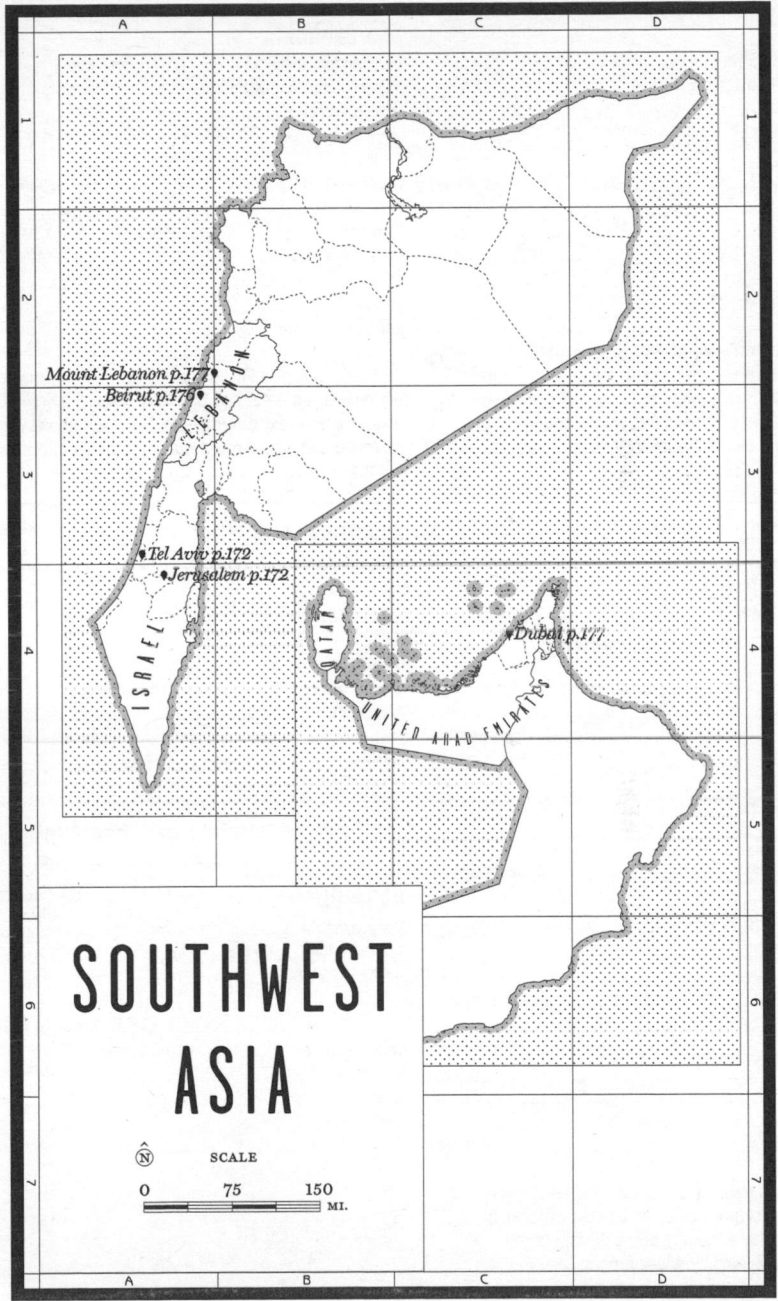

Mount Lebanon p.177
Beirut p.176

LEBANON

Tel Aviv p.172
Jerusalem p.172

ISRAEL

QATAR

Dubai p.177

UNITED ARAB EMIRATES

SOUTHWEST ASIA

Ⓝ SCALE

0   75   150
                MI.

HATZOT

Recommended by
Tomer Amedi,
Joel Braham

121 Agripas Street
Jerusalem 9430116, Israel
+972 26244014
www.hatzot.co.il

Opening hours	Open 7 days
Credit cards	Accepted
Price range	Affordable
Style	Casual
Cuisine	Israeli
Recommended for	Bargain

"This is the best Jerusalem mix in Jerusalem and the perfect food to absorb loads of booze you (might) drink on a Saturday evening. A big fluffy pitta stuffed with chicken hearts, liver, and thighs and loads of onions. What can be better than that. A true Jerusalem institution."—Tomer Amedi

MACHNEYUDA

Recommended by
Anita Lo

Beit Ya'akov Street 10
Jerusalem 9106402, Israel
+972 25333442
www.machneyuda.co.il

Opening hours	Open 7 days
Credit cards	Accepted
Price range	Affordable
Style	Smart casual
Cuisine	Israeli
Recommended for	Worth the travel

ABU HASSAN

Recommended by
Maoz Alonim

1 Ha' Dolfin Street
Tel Aviv 7541501, Israel
+972 36820387

Opening hours	Closed Saturday
Reservation policy	No
Credit cards	Accepted but not AMEX or Diners
Price range	Budget
Style	Casual
Cuisine	Israeli
Recommended for	Bargain

"A mixture of Palestinian culture and Tel Avivian vibe. Serves all kinds of hummus that will satisfy your hunger for a friendly price. Best to come during the morning."—Maoz Alonim

BAR BARBUNIA

Recommended by
Maoz Alonim

Ben Yehuda Street 163
Tel Aviv 6347601, Israel
+972 35276965
www.rol.co.il/sites/barbunya

Opening hours	Open 7 days
Reservation policy	No
Credit cards	Accepted but not AMEX or Diners
Price range	Affordable
Style	Casual
Cuisine	Seafood
Recommended for	Wish I'd opened

"Intimate bar, good music, and fresh fish. No matter what time you enter Bar Barbunia there is always a vibrant and sexy atmosphere. No reservations can be made, but all the more reason to be spontaneous."—Maoz Alonim

HANAN MARGILAN

Recommended by
Maoz Alonim

Mesilat Yesharim Street 15
Tel Aviv 6603945, Israel
+972 36873984

Opening hours	Closed Friday and Saturday
Credit cards	Accepted but not AMEX or Diners
Price range	Budget
Style	Casual
Cuisine	Israeli
Recommended for	Bargain

"Top traditional Bukharan food."—Maoz Alonim

HA'SALON

Recommended by
Anthony Rose

Ma'avar Yabok 8
Tel Aviv 6744012, Israel
+972 527035888

Opening hours	Closed Friday to Tuesday
Credit cards	Accepted but not AMEX or Diners
Price range	Affordable
Style	Casual
Cuisine	Israeli
Recommended for	Worth the travel

FALAFEL RAMBAM

Carmel Market
Rambam Street 2
Tel Aviv 6525613, Israel

Recommended by
Maoz Alonim

Opening hours	Open 7 days
Credit cards	Not accepted
Price range	Budget
Style	Casual
Cuisine	Falafel
Recommended for	Breakfast

"One man show. Not only is Elad's falafel always fresh, but there is no one in town that knows how to construct a falafel-filled pitta like he does. The market's vibrant atmosphere is an added bonus."
—Maoz Alonim

JASMINO

Allenby Street 97
Tel Aviv 6581602, Israel

Recommended by
Maoz Alonim

Opening hours	Open 7 days
Reservation policy	No
Credit cards	Not accepted
Price range	Budget
Style	Casual
Cuisine	Street Food
Recommended for	Late night

"Jasmino is a 'hole-in-the-wall' restaurant— a tiny place with a long line (queue) of customers waiting for skewers from the grill served in a pitta bread. High-quality meat, fresh salad, and a great host."—Maoz Alonim

This city-center late-night snack bar, perfectly situated in the city's busy nightlife hub, is unashamedly rough around the edges. It offers up unpretentious street food without the need for embellishment—and has earned a reputation for itself as a true Jerusalem institution. Helmed by the restaurateur Shaul Tevet, the menu doesn't stretch to more than a handful of simple-yet-sensational options: take a big fluffy pitta bread and stuff it with charcoal-grilled meats such as kebabs, chicken, homemade sausage, and spicy veal heart, then finish with fresh salad, hot peppers, grilled onions, and generous dollops of thick tahini. Fast food for the discerning foodie.

M25

HaCarmel Street 30
Tel Aviv 6525613, Israel
+972 35173086

Recommended by
John Besh

Opening hours	Closed Saturday and Sunday
Reservation policy	No
Credit cards	Accepted but not AMEX or Diners
Price range	Affordable
Style	Casual
Cuisine	Israeli-Steakhouse
Recommended for	Worth the travel

"The restaurant was created by Yaron Kestenboum. He revived an old meat market in Shuk Carmel and opened a very casual, extremely high-end steakhouse featuring only Israeli products."—John Besh

THE MINZAR

Allenby Street 60
Tel Aviv 6382160, Israel
| 972 35173015

Recommended by
Maoz Alonim

Opening hours	Open 7 days
Reservation policy	No
Credit cards	Accepted
Price range	Affordable
Style	Casual
Cuisine	Bar Snacks
Recommended for	Regular neighborhood

"Always fresh, always good, and there is always an interesting person to talk to on the bar. There is a large variety of beers on tap, a menu that changes daily, spirits at an attractive price, and you will always feel comfortable coming with your baby, sweetheart, beer buddy, or your grandma."—Maoz Alonim

MIZNON

Ibn Gabirol Street 23
Tel Aviv 6329810, Israel
+972 35081118
www.miznon.com

Recommended by
Joel Braham

Opening hours	Open 7 days
Reservation policy	No
Credit cards	Accepted
Price range	Affordable
Style	Casual
Cuisine	Israeli
Recommended for	Late night

NORTH ABRAXASS

Recommended by
Todd Ginsberg

Lilienblum Street 40
Tel Aviv 6513319, Israel
+972 35166660

Opening hours	Open 7 days
Credit cards	Accepted
Price range	Affordable
Style	Smart casual
Cuisine	Israeli-International
Recommended for	Worth the travel

"Cutting edge, traditional cuisine. Nothing molecular. Food cooked with wood burning ovens and wood burning grills. Simple, but a completely new style of food."—Todd Ginsberg

PIZZA GIUSEPPE

Recommended by
Maoz Alonim

Chayim Vital Street 1
Tel Aviv 6684025, Israel
+972 545928244
www.giuseppe.co.il

Opening hours	Closed Friday and Saturday
Credit cards	Accepted
Price range	Budget
Style	Casual
Cuisine	Pizza
Recommended for	Late night

"Traditional Italian pizza, the best slice to end the night with."—Maoz Alonim

PORT SA'ID

Recommended by
Maoz Alonim,
Joshua Katz

Har Sinai Street 5
Tel Aviv 6581602, Israel
+972 36207436

Opening hours	Open 7 days
Reservation policy	No
Credit cards	Accepted but not Diners
Price range	Affordable
Style	Casual
Cuisine	Israeli
Recommended for	Local favorite

"Port Sa'id in Tel Aviv is one of my favorite restaurants anywhere in the world, delivering fantastic food in an environment that is quintessential Tel Aviv; lively, loud, and great fun."—Joshua Katz

The top Israeli celebrity-chef Eyal Shani is known as the "cauliflower king"—his whole-roasted cauliflower recipe started a trend that elevated the much-maligned vegetable to new heights of cool. So it shouldn't come as a surprise that his restaurant in Tel Aviv, which can be found opposite the city's largest synagogue, is known as something of a hipster hangout. Inside, you'll find stacks of vinyl, an open-plan kitchen, and in-house DJ. The menu delivers new takes on classic favorites—white bean "hummus", generous plates of carpaccio, and what is said to be the best French toast in all of Tel Aviv.

SABICH

Recommended by
Joel Braham

Tchernikhovski Street 2
Tel Aviv 6329213, Israel
+972 505306654

Opening hours	Closed Saturday
Reservation policy	No
Credit cards	Not accepted
Price range	Budget
Style	Casual
Cuisine	Israeli-Street Food
Recommended for	Breakfast

"The best place in the world to get a *sabich*, the Iraqi-Jewish fried eggplant (aubergine) and egg pitta that is a staple of Tel Aviv street food."—Joel Braham

SANTA KATARINA

Recommended by
Eyal Jagermann

Har Sinai 2
Tel Aviv 6581602, Israel
+972 587820292

Opening hours	Open 7 days
Credit cards	Accepted
Price range	Affordable
Style	Smart casual
Cuisine	Mediterranean
Recommended for	Worth the travel

"The best example of modern Israeli food for me. Simply beautiful, simple, local cooking with a clever approach and renovation. An absolute must for anyone in Tel Aviv. Never miss it."—Eyal Jagermann

SHILA

Recommended by
Tomer Amedi

Ben Yehuda 182
Tel Aviv 6347601, Israel
+972 35221224
www.en.shila-rest.co.il

Opening hours	Open 7 days
Credit cards	Accepted
Price range	Affordable
Style	Smart casual
Cuisine	Modern Israeli
Recommended for	Wish I'd opened

"This is a happy place with incredible food, ambience, and music. I worked there as sous chef for a year and I just love it. Both for cooking and for eating, it was and still is a wonderful experience and really fun. They treat fish immaculately and their interpretation of modern Israeli cuisine is superb. Everything about this place is fun."—Tomer Amedi

TAIZU

Recommended by
Yair Feinberg

Levenshtein Tower
Menachem Begin Street 23
Tel Aviv 5128702, Israel
+972 35225005
www.taizu.co.il

Opening hours	Open 7 days
Credit cards	Accepted
Price range	Expensive
Style	Casual
Cuisine	Modern Asian
Recommended for	Regular neighborhood

"An interesting and modern way to look at Asian food."—Yair Feinberg

THAI HOUSE

Recommended by
Maoz Alonim

Bugrashov Street 8
Tel Aviv 6357201, Israel
+972 35178568
www.thai-house.co.il

Opening hours	Open 7 days
Credit cards	Accepted
Price range	Affordable
Style	Casual
Cuisine	Thai
Recommended for	Regular neighborhood

"Thai House has been keeping its high standards of authentic Thai food for the past twenty years. Never fails."—Maoz Alonim

YAFFO TEL AVIV

Recommended by
Chris Lusk

Rehov Yigal Alon 98
Electra Tower
Tel Aviv 6789721, Israel
+972 36249249
www.yaffotelaviv.com

Opening hours	Open 7 days
Credit cards	Accepted
Price range	Affordable
Style	Smart casual
Cuisine	Modern Israeli
Recommended for	Worth the travel

YAKIMONO

Recommended by
Maoz Alonim

Sderot Rothschild 19
Tel Aviv 4432801, Israel
+972 35175171
www.yakimono.co.il

Opening hours	Open 7 days
Credit cards	Accepted
Price range	Affordable
Style	Smart casual
Cuisine	Japanese
Recommended for	High end

"Eli Cohen chooses his fish daily for his Japanese professional sushi masters to cut the best sashimi you can get in town."—Maoz Alonim

PESCADO

Recommended by
Yair Feinberg

Martin Buber Street 1
Ashdod
Southern District 7720101, Israel
+972 88523063
www.pescado.co.il

Opening hours	Closed Friday
Credit cards	Accepted but not AMEX or Diners
Price range	Affordable
Style	Casual
Cuisine	Seafood
Recommended for	Regular neighborhood

BOUBOUFFE

Recommended by
Kamal Mouzawak

Avenue Charles Malek
Beirut 1100, Lebanon
+961 1334040

Opening hours	Open 7 days
Credit cards	Accepted
Price range	Budget
Style	Casual
Cuisine	Middle Eastern
Recommended for	Regular neighborhood

"For a perfect shawarma, meat or chicken, cooked on huge skewers in front of vertical hot coals."
—Kamal Mouzawak

FALAFEL M. SAHYOUN

Recommended by
Kamal Mouzawak

Damascus Road
Beirut 1101, Lebanon
+961 1633188

Opening hours	Open 7 days
Reservation policy	No
Credit cards	Accepted but not AMEX or Diners
Price range	Budget
Style	Casual
Cuisine	Lebanese
Recommended for	Bargain

"Best falafel in town...only in a sandwich!
Thin bread around crisp falafel, juicy tomato, a crunch of radish, mint, pickled turnip and a lot of *tarator* (tahini sauce)."—Kamal Mouzawak

RAFIC AL RASHIDI

Recommended by
Kamal Mouzawak

Monot Street
Beirut 1101, Lebanon
+961 1398800

Opening hours	Open 7 days
Reservation policy	No
Credit cards	Not accepted
Price range	Budget
Style	Casual
Cuisine	Sweets-Pastries
Recommended for	Breakfast

"For a Sunday treat: unsalted, warm, melted cheese, topped with a golden, crispy semolina dough, and soaking in syrup."—Kamal Mouzawak

LE PROFESSEUR

Recommended by
Kamal Mouzawak

Mar Elias Street
Beirut 1105, Lebanon
+961 1703935

Opening hours	Closed Sunday
Reservation policy	No
Credit cards	Not accepted
Price range	Budget
Style	Casual
Cuisine	Lebanese
Recommended for	Breakfast

"Typical Beiruti breakfast—foul, fava beans, in a warm sauce of Seville orange juice (like a warm salad), and a hint of garlic."—Kamal Mouzawak

SPORTING CLUB BEACH

Recommended by
Kamal Mouzawak

Avenue de Paris
Beirut 1103, Lebanon
+961 1742482

Opening hours	Open 7 days
Reservation policy	No
Credit cards	Not accepted
Price range	Affordable
Style	Casual
Cuisine	Middle Eastern
Recommended for	Local favorite

"It is not a restaurant—just a terrace over the sea, for a perfect beer and some fried fish and the sunset. It is not about the food, but about the people and the place that are both essentially 'Beirut'."—Kamal Mouzawak

VILLA CLARA

Recommended by
Kamal Mouzawak

Mar Mikael
Beirut, Lebanon
+961 70995739
www.villaclara.fr

Opening hours	Open 7 days
Credit cards	Accepted
Price range	Expensive
Style	Smart casual
Cuisine	French
Recommended for	High end

FADEL

Recommended by
Kamal Mouzawak

Naas
Bikfaya
Mount Lebanon 1205, Lebanon
+961 4980979

Opening hours	Open 7 days
Credit cards	Accepted
Price range	Affordable
Style	Smart casual
Cuisine	Lebanese
Recommended for	Regular neighborhood

"One of the best interpretations of a mezze—fresh ingredients and delicious tastes."—Kamal Mouzawak

AL NAFOORAH

Recommended by
Izu Ani

Jumeirah Emirates Towers
Sheikh Zayed Road
Dubai, United Arab Emirates
+971 44323232
www.jumeirah.com

Opening hours	Open 7 days
Credit cards	Accepted
Price range	Affordable
Style	Smart casual
Cuisine	Lebanese
Recommended for	Regular neighborhood

"I love 'homely' food, where time has been taken to respect the culture and ingredients used."—Izu Ani

BAZXAR

Recommended by
Izu Ani

Gate Precinct Building 4
Dubai, United Arab Emirates
+971 43551111
www.bazxar.com

Opening hours	Open 7 days
Credit cards	Accepted
Price range	Affordable
Style	Smart casual
Cuisine	International
Recommended for	Late night

"I like chilled places day and night and Bazxar is a relaxed, welcoming spot. It's not intimidating and I can eat good, simple dishes or depending on my mood, go for something a bit more complex."—Izu Ani

Bazxar (it's pronounced "bazaar", since you ask) rides the popularity of street food in Dubai by being essentially a restaurant disguised as a food court. There's a wine bar, a Vietnamese section ("wok station") serving pho and steamed bao buns, a café serving pizzas, pasta, and coffee, and a "meat station" doing burgers and hot dogs. All of which sounds like it could be a disaster, and yet the food is very good. The Vietnamese is authentic and enjoyable, and the burger in particular (stuffed with onion rings and a Portobello mushroom) is popular with the after-work crowd. It's also all pretty keenly priced.

FIREBIRD DINER

Recommended by
Izu Ani

Four Seasons Hotel
Building 9, The Gate Village
Dubai, United Arab Emirates
+971 45060100
www.firebirddubai.com

Opening hours	Open 7 days
Credit cards	Accepted but not AMEX or Diners
Price range	Affordable
Style	Casual
Cuisine	American
Recommended for	Wish I'd opened

"My kids like this place and it's one of those 'cool' hangout spots where you feel like you're in an authentic American diner on Sunset Boulevard. I admire the chef and service staff, they are consistent and have gusto—I like that!"—Izu Ani

MOANA SEAFOOD

Recommended by
Marcus G. Lindner

Sofitel Spa & Hotel
East Crescent Road
Dubai, United Arab Emirates
+971 44555656
www.sofitel-dubai-thepalm.com

Opening hours	Open 7 days
Credit cards	Accepted
Price range	Expensive
Style	Smart casual
Cuisine	French-Seafood
Recommended for	Worth the travel

"The food is varied, with excellent sushi and sashimi."—Marcus G. Lindner

PLAY RESTAURANT AND LOUNGE

Recommended by
Vineet Bhatia

H Hotel
One Sheikh Zayed Road
Dubai, United Arab Emirates
+971 43364444
www.playrestaurants.com

Opening hours	Open 7 days
Credit cards	Accepted
Price range	Expensive
Style	Smart casual
Cuisine	Mediterranean
Recommended for	Wish I'd opened

"Chef-patron Reif Othman, previously at one of Dubai's top restaurants, Zuma, is behind the recently launched PLAY. It's already been crowned Best Asian and Restaurant of the Year by *Time Out Dubai* and I don't think that anyone who visits would not be blown away by the experience and the concept."
—Vineet Bhatia

PLAY by name and play by nature—this super high-end restaurant on the 36th floor of the H Hotel has spectacular skyline views from the floor-to-ceiling windows. And the wow-factor extends, rightly so, to the kitchen: Reif Othman has stepped up his game and redefined what it means to make fusion food. He takes inspiration from the modern cuisine of Asia (largely Japan's sushi and sashimi scene) and blends his experience in that arena with the light, fresh flavors of the Mediterranean—in a cuisine he's called "Mediterrasian". On the menu, you'll find certified Japanese Sedai wagyu, black cod, fresh seasonal produce, and plenty of truffle. And the creative, sometimes deconstructed, desserts don't disappoint either.

S'WICH

Recommended by
Izu Ani

Shop 9, Marina View Towers
Dubai Marina
Dubai, United Arab Emirates
+971 80079424
www.myswich.com

Opening hours	Open 7 days
Credit cards	Accepted
Price range	Affordable
Style	Casual
Cuisine	Middle Eastern
Recommended for	Regular neighborhood

"Although it's 'fast', it's slow food; time is taken to make good quality food. Everything is so fresh, not a greasy finger in sight."—Izu Ani

ZAGOL BETEKITFO

Recommended by
Izu Ani

4B Street
Sheikh Khalifa Bin Zayed Road
Dubai, United Arab Emirates
+971 503231822

Opening hours	Open 7 days
Credit cards	Not accepted
Price range	Budget
Style	Casual
Cuisine	Ethiopian
Recommended for	Bargain

"There is this Ethiopian place in Karama, a hidden gem called Zagol Betekitfo, which is really affordable and they serve the best home-cooked food."—Izu Ani

ZUMA

Recommended by
Izu Ani

Gate Village 06
Dubai, United Arab Emirates
+971 44255660
www.zumarestaurant.com

Opening hours	Open 7 days
Credit cards	Accepted
Price range	Affordable
Style	Smart casual
Cuisine	Japanese
Recommended for	High end

"I like ZUMA because it's been consistent since the beginning, and consistency in good quality food and service is not easy to maintain. This is what makes a brand, this is what makes ZUMA a success in Dubai."—Izu Ani

"THIS IS THE ULTIMATE PLACE FOR ALL YOUR LATE-NIGHT DESSERT CRAVINGS."

NAREN THIMMAIAH P182

"KNOCKS EVERY MICHELIN-STARRED RESTAURANT I'VE BEEN TO OUT OF THE PARK."

WILL BOWLBY P185

CENTRAL & SOUTH ASIA

"THE BEST MULTI-CUISINE EATING AND DRINKING PLACE UNDER ONE ROOF."

SAMEER TANEJA P183

"An all-time favourite, this heritage center serves incredible, delectable Chettinad local fare."

ALFRED PRASAD P185

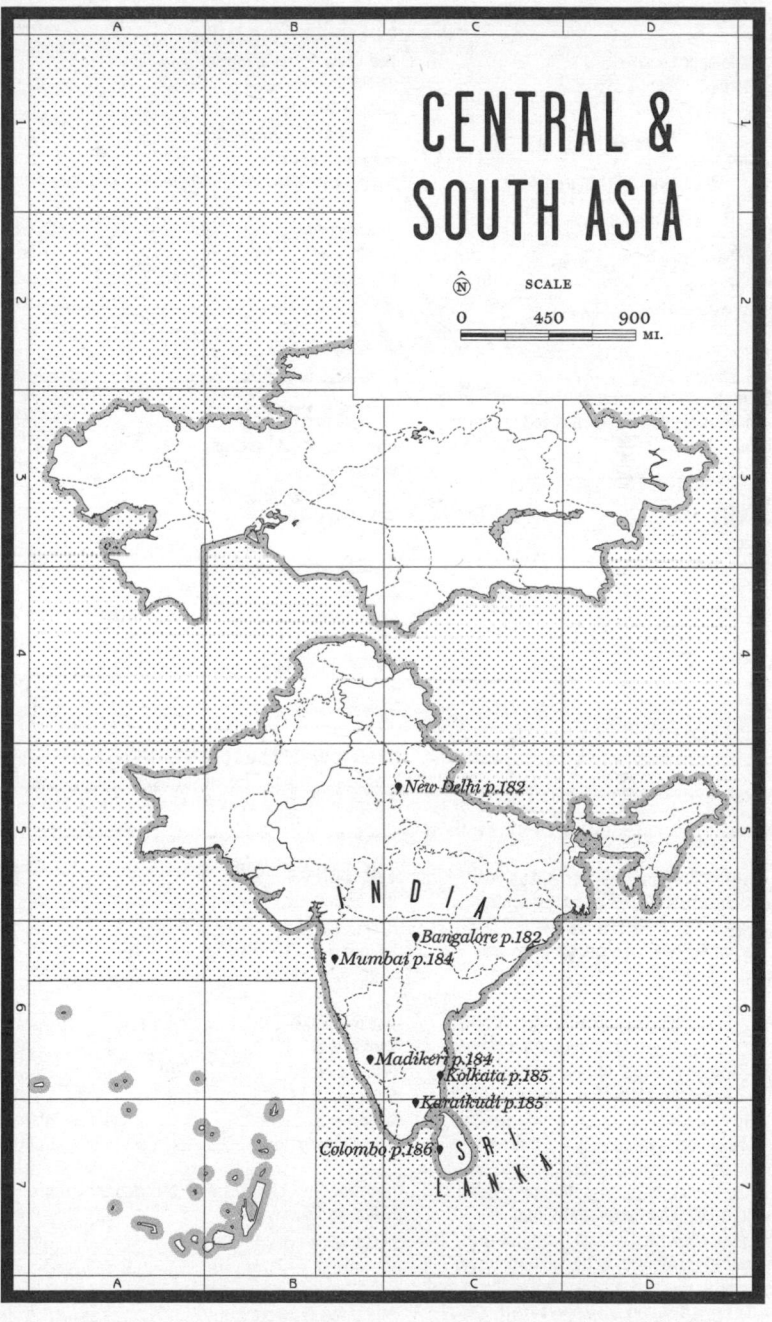

CENTRAL & SOUTH ASIA

N

SCALE

0   450   900
MI.

New Delhi p.182

I N D I A

Bangalore p.182
Mumbai p.184

Madikeri p.184
Kolkata p.185
Karaikudi p.185

Colombo p.186   S R I
L A N K A

BUKHARA

Recommended by
Rohit Ghai

ITC Maurya, Diplomatic Enclave
Sardar Patel Marg
New Delhi
Delhi 110 021, India
+91 1126112233
www.itchotels.in/dining/iconic-brands/bukhara

Opening hours	Open 7 days
Credit cards	Accepted
Price range	Affordable
Style	Smart casual
Cuisine	Northwest Indian
Recommended for	Worth the travel

"Love the aromatic flavors and authenticity of the dishes. All the ingredients and spices used are high quality."—Rohit Ghai

INDIAN ACCENT

Recommended by
Anita Lo

The Manor Hotel
77 Friends Colony West
New Delhi
Delhi 110 065, India
+91 1143235151
www.indianaccent.com

Opening hours	Open 7 days
Credit cards	Accepted
Price range	Expensive
Style	Formal
Cuisine	Modern Indian
Recommended for	Worth the travel

"I dined at the original New Delhi location a year before they opened in NYC and loved the soulful flavors juxtaposed with modern presentation and technique. It's playful, yet hasn't strayed too far from its roots."—Anita Lo

Chef Manish Mehrotra's "Modern Indian" food at The Manor Hotel's restaurant in southeast New Delhi has an "Indian Accent" but is fluent in many tongues. The Bihar-born Mehrotra, executive chef of the Old World Hospitality Group, is unafraid of stuffing *galawat* kebab with foie gras, pairing voguish pork belly with exotic bacon, walnut and *munakka* raisin korma, or putting homely *khichdi* (albeit a modern version) on an ambitious fine-dining menu. Mehrotra draws his influences from anything and anywhere, with exciting, never incoherent results. The restaurant itself is plush and glossy with its onyx bar and silver diya tree centerpieces. Excellent wine list.

LE CIRQUE SIGNATURE

Recommended by
Naren Thimmaiah

The Leela Palace Bengaluru
23 HAL Airport Road
Bangalore
Karnataka 560 008, India
+91 8030571540
www.theleela.com/en_us/hotels-in-bengaluru

Opening hours	Open 7 days
Credit cards	Accepted
Price range	Expensive
Style	Smart casual
Cuisine	French-Italian
Recommended for	High end

CORNER HOUSE

Recommended by
Naren Thimmaiah

Residency Road 1st Cross
Bangalore
Karnataka 560 001, India
+91 8025583262

Opening hours	Open 7 days
Reservation policy	No
Credit cards	Accepted but not AMEX
Price range	Budget
Style	Casual
Cuisine	Desserts
Recommended for	Late night

"This is the ultimate place for all your late-night dessert cravings. The most popular dish is 'Death By Chocolate' which is irresistible!"—Naren Thimmaiah

THE EGG FACTORY

Recommended by
Naren Thimmaiah

288 15th Cross Road
Bangalore
Karnataka 560 078, India
+91 8049653157

Opening hours	Open 7 days
Credit cards	Accepted
Price range	Affordable
Style	Casual
Cuisine	Vegetarian-International
Recommended for	Breakfast

"Bangalore's chain of egg-centric restaurants."
—Naren Thimmaiah

GARUDA MALL

Recommended by
Naren Thimmaiah

15 Magrath Road
Bangalore
Karnataka 560 025, India
+91 8040698857

Opening hours	Open 7 days
Reservation policy	No
Credit cards	Not accepted
Price range	Affordable
Style	Casual
Cuisine	International
Recommended for	Bargain

"There are various kiosks serving simple dishes including Indian, Chinese, Pan-Asian, Pizzas, Pastas, and Mexican, among others."—Naren Thimmaiah

IMPERIAL

Recommended by
Naren Thimmaiah

Building 1324
Indiranagar Double Road
Bangalore
Karnataka 560 038, India
+91 8069994888

Opening hours	Open 7 days
Credit cards	Accepted but not AMEX
Price range	Affordable
Style	Casual
Cuisine	North Indian
Recommended for	Late night

"This is a grand old restaurant for all late-nighters. They serve yummy chicken kebabs, ghee rice, and chicken curry."—Naren Thimmaiah

MAVALLI TIFFIN ROOM

Recommended by
Naren Thimmaiah

14 Lalbagh Road
Bangalore
Karnataka 560 004, India
+91 8022220022
www.mavallitiffinrooms.com/bengaluru

Opening hours	Closed Monday
Credit cards	Accepted but not AMEX
Price range	Affordable
Style	Casual
Cuisine	South Indian-Vegetarian
Recommended for	Local favorite

"This restaurant is about eighty years old and is a true custodian of Bangalore's local cuisine. A meal here is an experience in itself."—Naren Thimmaiah

The Mavalli Tiffin Room started life in 1924 with three brothers wanting to celebrate authentic South Indian cuisine in Bangalore. Almost a century later, now in the third generation of the family, this vegetarian eatery has become a legendary establishment (some patrons have been drinking their morning coffee here for over fifty years) and a global player, with several branches across Asia. The success is driven by complete faith in the brothers' original recipes that have barely changed since inception. It's all-you-can-eat, with the waiters arriving at your table to serve out an excellent selection of Karnatakan dishes, including lentil soups, beetroot and carrot curries, fried breads, and a selection of rice dishes. The *masala dosa* is undoubtedly the star, staking a strong claim to be the most renowned in India.

MONKEY BAR

Recommended by
Sameer Taneja

610 12th Main Road
Bangalore
Karnataka 560 038, India
I 91 8049653443

Opening hours	Open 7 days
Credit cards	Accepted but not AMEX
Price range	Affordable
Style	Casual
Cuisine	International
Recommended for	Worth the travel

"The best multi-cuisine eating and drinking place under one roof."—Sameer Taneja

OLIVE BEACH

Recommended by
Naren Thimmaiah

16 Wood Street
Bangalore
Karnataka 560 025, India
+91 9945565483
www.olivebarandkitchen.com

Opening hours	Open 7 days
Credit cards	Accepted but not AMEX
Price range	Expensive
Style	Smart casual
Cuisine	Mediterranian
Recommended for	Regular neighborhood

TOAST AND TONIC

Recommended by
Naren Thimmaiah

14/1 Wood Street
Bangalore
Karnataka 560 025, India
+91 8041116879
www.toastandtonic.com

Opening hours	Open 7 days
Credit cards	Accepted
Price range	Affordable
Style	Smart casual
Cuisine	European-Asian
Recommended for	Regular neighborhood

"This is a highly reputable restaurant serving European and Asian cuisine. They take pride in blending international cooking techniques with local ingredients."—Naren Thimmaiah

UMERKOT

Recommended by
Rohit Ghai

Building 30
80 Feet Main Road
Bangalore
Karnataka 560 034, India
+91 8277006586

Opening hours	Open 7 days
Credit cards	Accepted
Price range	Affordable
Style	Casual
Cuisine	Indian
Recommended for	Worth the travel

"The restaurant has Mughlai food inspired by the time of emperor Akbar, and has retained all of the old favorites. Serves a great variety of vegetarian and non-vegetarian dishes. The lovely flavors and presentation are worth the trip."—Rohit Ghai

THE FALLS

Recommended by
Naren Thimmaiah

The Tamara Coorg Resort
Kabbinkad Estate
Napoklu
Madikeri
Karnataka 571 212, India
+91 8071077700
www.thetamara.com/falls

Opening hours	Open 7 days
Credit cards	Accepted
Price range	Affordable
Style	Smart casual
Cuisine	Indian-International
Recommended for	Wish I'd opened

"This is the most lovely looking restaurant I have been to, nestled in the heart of a coffee plantation on top of a hill. Has a very good range of multi-cuisine options. You would never want to leave!"—Naren Thimmaiah

THE BOMBAY CANTEEN

Recommended by
Sameer Taneja

1 Process House
Kamla Mill
Mumbai
Maharashtra 400 013, India
+91 2249666666
www.thebombaycanteen.com

Opening hours	Open 7 days
Credit cards	Accepted
Price range	Affordable
Style	Casual
Cuisine	Indian-Café
Recommended for	Worth the travel

"Casual, modern Indian restaurant serving regional-inspired food and drink. Hottest new restaurant in India."—Sameer Taneja

Housed within a renovated bungalow, an architectural tribute to Mumbai's history, The Bombay Canteen is a nostalgia-heavy café/restaurant that has become one of the city's hippest spots. The menu has been created by local-born chef Floyd Cardoz, who built a strong reputation while training and working in the New York restaurant scene. Focusing on developing traditional regional Indian cuisine, but with Cardoz's signature modern, playful style, there is a wide range of dishes to suit all moods (it is a popular place for breakfast, lunch, and dinner) with each dish beautifully plated and bursting with invention. The restaurant has a vast cocktail and mocktail list, using classical recipes enhanced with an ingenious application of various Indian spices.

KHYBER

Recommended by
Manoj Vasaikar

145 Mahatma Gandhi Road
Mumbai
Maharashtra 400 001, India
+91 2240396666

Opening hours	Open 7 days
Credit cards	Accepted
Price range	Affordable
Style	Casual
Cuisine	North Indian
Recommended for	Worth the travel

SHREE THAKER BHOJNALAY
Recommended by
Will Bowlby

Building 31
Dadiseth Agiyari Lane
Mumbai
Maharashtra 400 002, India
+91 2222011232

Opening hours	Open 7 days
Credit cards	Accepted but not AMEX
Price range	Budget
Style	Casual
Cuisine	Indian-Vegetarian
Recommended for	Worth the travel

"The most amazing Gujarati vegetarian restaurant in the middle of Mumbai. Amazing care and love taken in every aspect of every dish. Knocks every Michelin-starred restaurant I've been to out of the park."
—Will Bowlby

Tucked away down a narrow alleyway, a short walk from the foofaraw of the busy Kalbadevi Road, is one of Mumbai's culinary hidden gems, Shree Thaker Bhojanalay. Serving traditional Gujarati vegetarian cuisine, this *thali* (set meal) restaurant has an outstanding range of hearty dishes including several types of daal, seasonal vegetables, and a series of fried breads accompanied by a range of chutneys. The only thing to look out for is portion control. There is a lot of food on the set menu and the waiters are always on hand to insist that you have your fill. You also won't want to miss out on the excellent desserts—the restaurant's proud specialty. Due to its difficult location, getting to the restaurant by car is almost impossible; parking is only available on Sunday (and good luck with that). It's recommended to take a taxi and get dropped off nearby.

THE BANGALA
Recommended by
Alfred Prasad

Devakottai Road
Sanjai
Karaikudi
Tamil Nadu 630 001, India
+91 4565220221
www.thebangala.com

Opening hours	Open 7 days
Credit cards	Accepted
Price range	Budget
Style	Casual
Cuisine	Chettinad
Recommended for	Worth the travel

"An all-time favorite, this heritage center serves incredible, delectable Chettinad local fare. The stay and meal at the Bangala offer you a great insight into Chettiar culture, history and culinary evolution."
—Alfred Prasad

DUM PUKHT
Recommended by
Harneet Baweja

ITC Sonar
1 JBS Haldane Avenue
Kolkata
West Bengal 700 046, India
+91 3323454545
www.itchotels.in/hotels/kolkata/itcsonar

Opening hours	Open 7 days
Credit cards	Accepted
Price range	Affordable
Style	Smart casual
Cuisine	Indian
Recommended for	High end

"The food and service here are incredible. My parents always took us here if they wanted to reward us, and my wife and I had our first dinner here as a couple—so this restaurant is definitely special for us. My favorite dish is the prawn *dum nisha*."—Harneet Baweja

JAI HIND DHABA
Recommended by
Harneet Baweja

41/1A Sarat Bose Road
Kolkata
West Bengal 700 020, India
+91 3324769033

Opening hours	Open 7 days
Credit cards	Not accepted
Price range	Budget
Style	Casual
Cuisine	North Indian
Recommended for	Late night

"You will get hot and fresh items from their kitchen no matter what the time. Their crispy tandoori roti (bread) with *tadka daal* (lentils) and chicken kebabs are the fix for my 2.00 a.m. curry craving."—Harneet Bhaweja

JYOTI VIHAR

Recommended by
Harneet Baweja

3a/1 Ho Chi Minh Sarani
Kolkata
West Bengal 700 071, India
+91 3322829791

Opening hours	Closed Monday
Credit cards	Not accepted
Price range	Budget
Style	Casual
Cuisine	South Indian-Vegetarian
Recommended for	Breakfast

"Fresh unfussy South Indian food. The ultimate
hangover cure. Start the meal with an idli in sambhar
and extra chutney, and finish with a raw onion *masala
dosa* and filter coffee. This place is unapologetically
vegetarian and fab. Ask the line (queue) outside."
—Harneet Baweja

A family-run restaurant that has brought authentic
South Indian breakfast and lunches to Kolkata for
generations. Situated off Little Russell Street, just
a short walk from Elliot Park and the Garer Maath,
this is the perfect launch pad for a busy day of sight-
seeing or a recovery station from the long night
before. Loved by the locals for its delicious
and fluffy *idlis*, Jyoti Vihar also serves the city's best
butter *masala dosas* and *uttapam* pancakes. You'll
want to try the variety of inventive chutneys on offer.
Their famed South-Indian style filter coffee attracts
crowds of office workers, students, and passers-by,
bemused by the large lines (queues) forming outside
this unassuming building. There is a fast turnaround
here, so even if the line (queue) is long, service will
be relatively quick.

PETER CAT

Recommended by
Harneet Baweja

18A Park Street
Kolkata
West Bengal 700 016, India
+91 3322298841

Opening hours	Open 7 days
Credit cards	Accepted but not AMEX
Price range	Budget
Style	Casual
Cuisine	North Indian-International
Recommended for	Bargain

"The food here is fantastic, if you can get in.
The original chelo kebabs, sizzlers, and half-sizzling
dum ki raan are my go to choices."—Harneet Baweja

GALLE FACE GREEN STREET MARKET

Galle Face Centre Road
Colombo
Western Province 00300, Sri Lanka

Recommended by
Dharshan Munidasa

Opening hours	Open 7 days
Reservation policy	No
Credit cards	Not accepted
Price range	Budget
Style	Casual
Cuisine	Street Food
Recommended for	Regular neighborhood

"It's street food on a sunset boulevard. Nothing beats
a *prawn vadai* (shrimp [prawn] and lentil fritter) as
the sun sets."—Dharshan Munidasa

HOTEL DE PILAWOOS

Recommended by
Dharshan Munidasa

417 Galle Road
Colombo
Western Province 00300, Sri Lanka
+94 777417417
www.pilawoos.lk/colpety

Opening hours	Open 7 days
Credit cards	Not accepted
Price range	Budget
Style	Casual
Cuisine	Sri Lankan
Recommended for	Late night

"It's a Sri Lankan institution. They gave *kottu roti*
the edge!"—Dharshan Munidasa

For a taste of Sri Lankan street food, you can't go
wrong with this nearly forty-year-old local icon.
It offers an extensive menu of wallet-friendly *kottu*,
a popular Sri Lankan dish of shredded flatbread
stir-fried with eggs, meats, vegetables, spices, and
curry sauce. If making a choice is proving difficult,
we highly recommend the cheese *kottu*.

"Simply perfection."
HANS LEE RASMUSSEN P192

"Dim sum at its best."
PAUL PAIRET P197

"THEIR ATTENTION TO DETAIL ALLOWS THE DINER TO ENJOY THE PURE FLAVORS OF THE FOOD."
JOAQUIN SORIANO P199

CHINA, MACAU, HONG KONG, TAIWAN & KOREA

"THE FOOD HERE WARMS MY SOUL."
ANDREA BONAFFINI P231

"Arguably Hong Kong's number one restaurant."
SHANE OSBORN P220

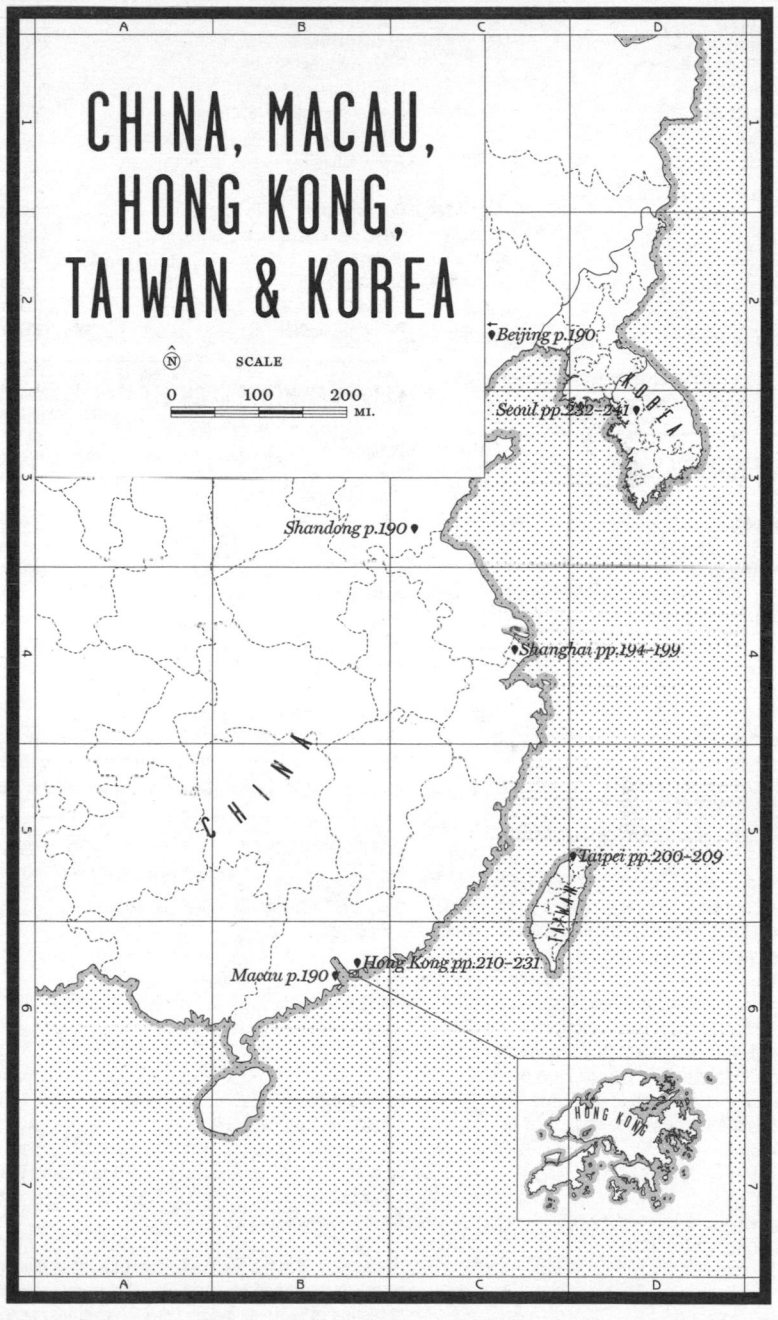

CHINA, MACAU,
HONG KONG,
TAIWAN & KOREA

N

SCALE

0   100   200
MI.

Beijing p.190

Seoul pp.232–241

KOREA

Shandong p.190

Shanghai pp.194–199

CHINA

Taipei pp.200–209

TAIWAN

Macau p.190   Hong Kong pp.210–231

HONG KONG

DA DONG ROAST DUCK

Donghua Jinjie Shopping Center
6/F, 301 Wangfujing Dajie
Beijing 100005, China
+86 1085221234
www.dadongdadong.com

Opening hours	Open 7 days
Credit cards	Not accepted
Price range	Affordable
Style	Casual
Cuisine	Chinese
Recommended for	Wish I'd opened

"Specializes in a revolutionary way of preparing Peking duck."—Andrew Wong

HONG SHUN MUTTON SOUP

Recommended by
Chan Yan-tak

Yang Shang Tang Guan
366 Nanjing Road
Qingdao
Shandong 266100, China

Opening hours	Variable
Credit cards	Not accepted
Price range	Budget
Style	Chinese
Cuisine	Qingdao
Recommended for	Worth the travel

"This is a place I usually visit when friends are taking me out to eat—some of the most authentic food leaves the deepest impression."—Chan Yan-tak

Mutton soup probably doesn't rank high up on your China eat list but when winter strikes it's not a bad idea to sample this potent, medicinal brew—and not just to keep warm. Here the broth is slow-cooked by braising mutton bones and served with a generous sprinkle of scallions (spring onions) and thick slices of mutton. It's accompanied by an intoxicating chile oil for dipping, which is laced with peppercorns, salt and MSG. To complete the meal, order a portion of stone-baked crispy dough to dunk into your hot broth. Come early for dinner as the stall closes at 8.00 p.m.

FERNANDO'S

Recommended by
Donald Berger

9 Praia de Hac Sa
Coloane Island South
Macau S.A.R. 999078, China
+853 28882264
www.fernando-restaurant.com

Opening hours	Open 7 days
Credit cards	Not accepted
Price range	Affordable
Style	Casual
Cuisine	Portuguese
Recommended for	Worth the travel

ESTABELECIMENTO KOON KEE

Recommended by
Hans Lee Rasmussen

Shop D, G/F, 28 Travessa dos Calafates
Patane
Macau S.A.R. 999078, China
+853 28238768

Opening hours	Open 7 days
Credit cards	Not accepted
Price range	Budget
Style	Casual
Cuisine	Cantonese & Sichuan
Recommended for	Late night

"Just good food with a nice menu selection, reasonable prices, close to home and very friendly staff. I especially like their roasted chicken, deep-fried tofu and sauna chicken-pot."—Hans Lee Rasmussen

GOLDEN PEACOCK

Recommended by
Guillaume Galliot

The Venetian Macao
Shop 1037, L1, Estrada da Baía de Nossa
Senhora da Esperança
Taipa
Macau S.A.R. 999078 China
+853 81189696
www.venetianmacao.com/restaurants/signature/golden-peacock

Opening hours	Open 7 days
Credit cards	Accepted
Price range	Expensive
Style	Smart casual
Cuisine	Indian
Recommended for	Late night

"For me, this is the best Indian restaurant in Macau and it has also one Michelin star. The menu has a wide selection of regional Indian food. After dinner service, it's one of the few places I can quickly eat and go home. "—Guillaume Galliot

LOJA DE DOCES HANG HEONG UN

Recommended by
Hans Lee Rasmussen

13 Travessa do Auto Novo
Macau S.A.R. 999078, China
+853 28572701

Opening hours	Open 7 days
Reservation policy	No
Credit cards	Not accepted
Price range	Affordable
Style	Casual
Cuisine	Cantonese
Recommended for	Local favorite

"I was born in Macau and my parents took me here for the first time thirty-six years ago. My earliest memory is of their fresh mango with vanilla ice cream and their old gigantic ice-cream maker. It still has the same owner today and even some of the same staff. When I visit, they remember me as the 'little fat boy' from so many years ago and they smile and remind me of how little I was back then. I find it very unusual and special to visit somewhere where they have 'known' me for my entire life and that is why this particular place is part of both my life and my Macau. Among their delicious desserts are Cantonese specialities, such as almond jelly, red bean soup, ginger milk curd etc."—Hans Lee Rasmussen

JADE DRAGON

Recommended by
Yau Leung Chan

City of Dreams
Estrada Do Istmo, L2, The Shops at the Boulevard, Cotai
Macau S.A.R. 999078, China
+853 88682822
www.cityofdreamsmacau.com

Opening hours	Open 7 days
Credit cards	Accepted
Price range	Expensive
Style	Smart casual
Cuisine	Chinese
Recommended for	Wish I'd opened

"The restaurant serves exquisite dishes made with very high quality ingredients. The ambience, decor, tableware, and presentation made it a very worth while experience for diners."—Yau Leung Chan

JAPAS MACAU

Recommended by
Hans Lee Rasmussen

165–307 Rua Do Padre Eugenio Taverna
EDIF Pat Tat Sun Chuen
Macau S.A.R. 999078, China
+853 28521199

Opening hours	Open 7 days
Credit cards	Accepted but not AMEX
Price range	Affordable
Style	Casual
Cuisine	Modern Asian
Recommended for	Wish I'd opened

"A very creative chef with an innovative menu. The decor of the restaurant is very warm with simple clean lines. There are three menus (but no à la carte menu) so service flows easily and steadily."
—Hans Lee Rasmussen

OLD SHANGHAI RESTAURANT

Recommended by
Hans Lee Rasmussen

L'Arc Macau Hotel
3/F, Alameda Dutor Carlos d'Assumpção
Macau S.A.R. 999078, China
+853 28886922
www.larcmacau.com

Opening hours	Open 7 days
Credit cards	Accepted
Price range	Affordable
Style	Casual
Cuisine	Shanghaiese
Recommended for	Breakfast

"This is, in my opinion, one of the best dim-sum restaurants I have tried in Macau. I especially like their congee with preserved eggs and, since I always eat a late breakfast, their sweet and sour soup is a 'must try' if your stomach can handle it at 11.00 a.m. in the morning."—Hans Lee Rasmussen

LIÈGE

Recommended by
Guillaume Galliot

ParknShop Taipa
Flower City (edf. Lei Tou), Rua de Évora
Macau S.A.R. 999078, China
+853 66937044

Opening hours	Open 7 days
Reservation policy	No
Credit cards	Not accepted
Price range	Budget
Style	Casual
Cuisine	Belgian
Recommended for	Breakfast

"I don't have a lot of time for breakfast, so this place offers me a quick 'grab and go', with freshly made authentic Belgian waffles that I usually have with Nutella. My late grandmother is Belgian and this reminds me of my childhood."—Guillaume Galliot

VIDA RICA RESTAURANT

Recommended by
Hans Lee Rasmussen

Mandarin Oriental Hotel
2F, 945 Avenida Dr. Sun Yat Sen
Macau S.A.R. 999078, China
+853 88058918
www.mandarinoriental.com/macau

Opening hours	Open 7 days
Credit cards	Accepted
Price range	Expensive
Style	Smart Casual
Cuisine	Chinese and Western
Recommended for	High end

"Simply perfection—a beautiful view when dining, incredibly good service, outstanding food, and, even though eating here will cost a bit of money, it is worth it."—Hans Lee Rasmussen

SZECHUAN SPICY KING

Recommended by
Hans Lee Rasmussen

Classic Bay
G/F, 1 Avenida De Demétrio Cinatti
Macau S.A.R. 999078, China
+853 28952001

Opening hours	Open 7 days
Credit cards	Not accepted
Price range	Affordable
Style	Casual
Cuisine	Szechuan
Recommended for	Regular neighborhood

"They make a very good spicy soup, with big glass noodles, fatty beef, flavorful broth, peanuts, cilantro, and a lot of chile, which is the perfect choice with an ice-cold Tsingtao beer after a long working day in the kitchen. They have a fairly lengthy menu card and the owner speaks a bit of English, which helps a lot since the menu is only avilable in Chinese. This is a cheap and clean eatery with friendly staff."
—Hans Lee Rasmussen

SHANGHAI

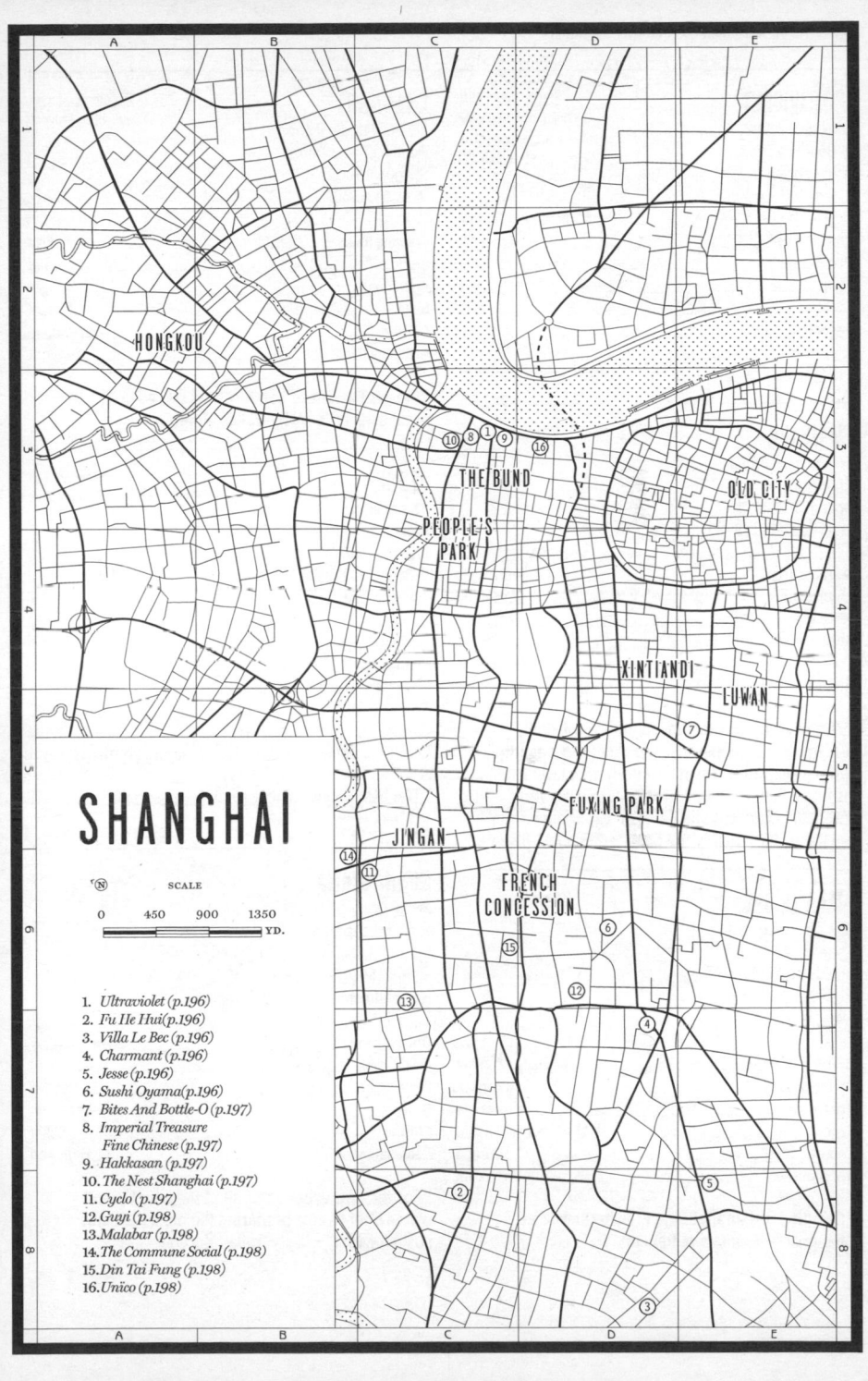

SHANGHAI

N

SCALE

0   450   900   1350

YD.

ULTRAVIOLET

Shanghai 200001
+86 2163239898
www.uvbypp.cc

Recommended by
Christophe Michalak,
Emmanuel Renaut, Julien Royer,
Jungsik Yim

Opening hours	Closed Monday and Sunday
Credit cards	Accepted
Price range	Expensive
Style	Smart casual
Cuisine	French
Recommended for	High end

"Huge, magical, and thrilling."—Christophe Michalak

FU HE HUI

1037 Yuyuan Road
Changning
Shanghai 200050
+86 2139809188

Recommended by
Michael Wilson

Opening hours	Open 7 days
Credit cards	Accepted
Price range	Expensive
Style	Smart casual
Cuisine	Vegetarian
Recommended for	Local favorite

"The name means, fortune, harmony, wisdom. It's an upscale venue in an old villa (very beautiful) and its innovative cuisine is purely vegetarian, taking its inspiration from Buddhist beliefs. It's a very interesting concept and different experience from anything I have had in the past."—Michael Wilson

VILLA LE BEC

321 Xinhua Lu
Changning
Shanghai 200052
+86 2162419100
www.lebec.com.cn

Recommended by
Emmanuel Renaut

Opening hours	Closed Monday
Credit cards	Accepted
Price range	Affordable
Style	Smart casual
Cuisine	French
Recommended for	Worth the travel

"Beautiful restaurant in the French Quarter of Shanghai."—Emmanuel Renaut

CHARMANT

1F, 1414 Huaihai Zhong Lu
French Concession
Shanghai 200030
+86 64318107

Recommended by
Willy Trullas Moreno

Opening hours	Open 7 days
Credit cards	Accepted
Price range	Budget
Style	Casual
Cuisine	Taiwanese
Recommended for	Late night

"Classic Taiwanese comfort food served until late—great sweets."—Willy Trullas Moreno

JESSE

41 Tianping Lu
French Concession
Shanghai 200000
+86 2162829260
www.xinjishi.com

Recommended by
May Chow

Opening hours	Open 7 days
Credit cards	Accepted
Price range	Affordable
Style	Casual
Cuisine	Shanghaiese
Recommended for	Worth the travel

"The best Shanghainese food I've ever had."
—May Chow

SUSHI OYAMA

2F, 20 Donghu Lu
French Concession
Shanghai 200031
+86 2154047705
www.fulufamily.com/sushioyama

Recommended by
Willy Trullas Moreno

Opening hours	Closed Sunday
Credit cards	Accepted
Price range	Expensive
Style	Smart casual
Cuisine	Sushi
Recommended for	High end

"For the best experience, sit at the counter and watch Chef Oyama preparing the most delicious sushi for you."—Willy Trullas Moreno

BITES AND BOTTLE-O

Recommended by
Jereme Leung

246 Danshui Lu
Huangpu
Shanghai 200001
+86 53085998

Opening hours	Open 7 days
Credit cards	Not accepted
Price range	Affordable
Style	Casual
Cuisine	Tapas
Recommended for	Regular neighborhood

"A tiny restaurant that serves only about twenty people in a tiny space in the old French Concession. The owner is a veteran advertising executive turned chef and the food is interesting, including light snacks and tapas with good selection of Australian wines."
—Jereme Leung

IMPERIAL TREASURE FINE CHINESE

Recommended by
Paul Pairet

99 Beijing Dong Lu
L402-403, Yi Feng Gallery
Huangpu
Shanghai 200002
+86 2153081188
www.imperialtreasure.com

Opening hours	Open 7 days
Credit cards	Accepted
Price range	Affordable
Style	Smart casual
Cuisine	Cantonese
Recommended for	Local favorite

"Excellent dim sum at lunchtime—dim sum at its best."—Paul Pairet

In Yi Feng Gallery this swish Shanghai offshoot of Singapore's Imperial Treasure restaurant group continues to impress the most discerning palates in the city. From its fourth-floor perch you get a picturesque view of the Bund to go with a menu that includes accomplished platters of roast meats, stir-fried flat rice noodles with beef, sautéed crab with turnip cake, and an extensive selection of dim sum. The service is polished and patient, and the overall attention to detail wins it a two-star rating in the inaugural Michelin guide to Shanghai.

HAKKASAN

Recommended by
Michael Wilson

Bund 18
5/F, 18 Zhongshan Dong Yi Lu
Huangpu
Shanghai 200002
+86 2163215888
www.hakkasan.com

Opening hours	Open 7 days
Credit cards	Accepted
Price range	Expensive
Style	Smart casual
Cuisine	Chinese
Recommended for	High end

"Hakkasan has the whole package—food, service, drinks, and music. I always start at the bar with a couple of cocktails before heading to my table to enjoy a Malaysian-style chile crab, which the chef prepares with steamed bread and rice, and to enjoy a nice bottle of wine while I get my hands dirty."
—Michael Wilson

THE NEST SHANGHAI

Recommended by
Paul Pairet

Zhongshi Mansion
6/F, 130 Beijing East Road
Huangpu
Shanghai 200002
+86 2163087669

Opening hours	Open 7 days
Credit cards	Accepted
Price range	Affordable
Style	Smart casual
Cuisine	European-Bar
Recommended for	Bargain

"Smart food with bold and beautiful flavors—chic bar setting, great value, and great atmosphere."
—Paul Pairet

CYCLO

Recommended by
Michael Wilson

678 Shaanxi Bei Lu
Jingan
Shanghai 200040
+86 61350150

Opening hours	Open 7 days
Credit cards	Accepted
Price range	Affordable
Style	Casual
Cuisine	Vietnamese
Recommended for	Bargain

GUYI

1F, 87 Fumin Lu
Jingan
Shanghai 200040
+86 2162495628
www.guyi2001.com

Opening hours	Open 7 days
Reservation policy	No
Credit cards	Not accepted
Price range	Budget
Style	Casual
Cuisine	Hunanese
Recommended for	Regular neighborhood

"Very good spicy Hunan-province comfort food."
—Willy Trullas Moreno

MALABAR

1081 Wuding Lu
Jingan
Shanghai 200042
+86 2152373085

Opening hours	Closed Monday
Credit cards	Accepted but not Amex
Price range	Affordable
Style	Casual
Cuisine	Tapas
Recommended for	Late night

"Super casual—a lot of the customers know
one another and the atmosphere can be like that
old TV show *Cheers*."—Michael Wilson

THE COMMUNE SOCIAL

511 Jiang Ning Lu
Jingan
Shanghai 200041
+86 2160477638
www.communesocial.com

Opening hours	Closed Monday
Reservation policy	No
Credit cards	Accepted
Price range	Affordable
Style	Casual
Cuisine	Tapas
Recommended for	Regular neighborhood

"It's a relaxed venue serving a hybrid of cuisines in
a sharing format somewhat like tapas—good service
with reasonably priced drinks and food."
—Michael Wilson

DIN TAI FUNG

2F, House 6, South Block Xintiandi
Lane 123 Xingye Road
Luwan
Shanghai 200021
+86 21 63858378
www.dintaifung.com.cn

Opening hours	Open 7 days
Credit cards	Accepted
Price range	Affordable
Style	Casual
Cuisine	Chinese-Taiwanese
Recommended for	Regular neighborhood

"Simple, well executed, consistently good quality
food and service in every branch. *Xiao long bao*
(soup dumplings), *hong you chao shou* (dumplings
with chile and spices), pork chop, stir fried spinach—
even the fried rice—everything is good
and comforting to eat."—Paul Pairet

UNÏCO

2F, 3 Zhongshan Dong Yi Lu
The Bund
Shanghai 200000
+86 2153085399
www.unicoshanghai.com

Opening hours	Closed Sunday
Credit cards	Accepted
Price range	Affordable
Style	Smart casual
Cuisine	Latin American
Recommended for	Late night

"Excellent cocktails in a beautiful bar. An interesting
bar-food menu with some delicious dishes."
—Paul Pairet

A JIANG FRIED EEL

89, Section 3 Minzu Road
West Central
Tainan 700, Taiwan
+886 937671052

Opening hours	Open 7 days
Reservation policy	No
Credit cards	Not accepted
Price range	Budget
Style	Casual
Cuisine	Taiwanese
Recommended for	Late night

"The eels are really fresh and are cooked in a simple fashion at a high temperature. They use local egg noodles from Tainan that taste so good that you can really fill up on them."—Soriano Joaquin

SUSHI SUZUKI

Recommended by
Soriano Joaquin

392 Huamei Street
West District
Taichung 403, Taiwan
+886 423202155

Opening hours	Closed Monday
Credit cards	Not accepted
Price range	Affordable
Style	Casual
Cuisine	Japanese
Recommended for	Regular neighborhood

"The method they use for curing their sashimi results produces a particularly rich and sweet flavor. Their attention to detail allows the diner to enjoy the pure flavors of the food."—Soriano Joaquin

TSENG FELICITY

Recommended by
Soriano Joaquin

18, Wuquan West 2nd Street
West District
Taichung 403, Taiwan
+886 423725518

Opening hours	Closed Sunday
Credit cards	Not accepted
Price range	Affordable
Style	Casual
Cuisine	Taiwanese
Recommended for	Bargain

"This is a really authentic Taichung snack-food restaurant. The braised food is really tasty and, when you add black vinegar and chile, this is the epitome of Taiwanese snack food."—Soriano Joaquin

YOU JIAN YI CHUI YAN

Recommended by
Shun Kai Ho

363-35 Zhongxingling
Zhongxing Village
Xinshe District
Taichung 436, Taiwan
+886 425823568

Opening hours	Open 7 days
Credit cards	Accepted but not AMEX
Price range	Affordable
Style	Smart casual
Cuisine	Japanese-Taiwanese
Recommended for	Wish I'd opened

"I love the atmospere—the scenery is beautiful and the atmosphere is peaceful."—Shun Kai Ho

"THIS RESTAURANT HAS BEEN AROUND FOR OVER 60 YEARS AND CONTINUES TO STRIVE TO UPHOLD THE INTEGRITY OF LOCAL TAIWANESE CUISINE— A BENCHMARK FOR ALL OTHERS."
ERIC LIU P208

TAIPEI

"The consistent quality of the food, service, and ambience is remarkable."
ERIC LIU P202

"NOT TO BE MISSED."
MAURO COLAGRECO P204

"Traditional Taiwanese breakfast (soy milk and fried bread) at its best!"
RICHIE LIN P209

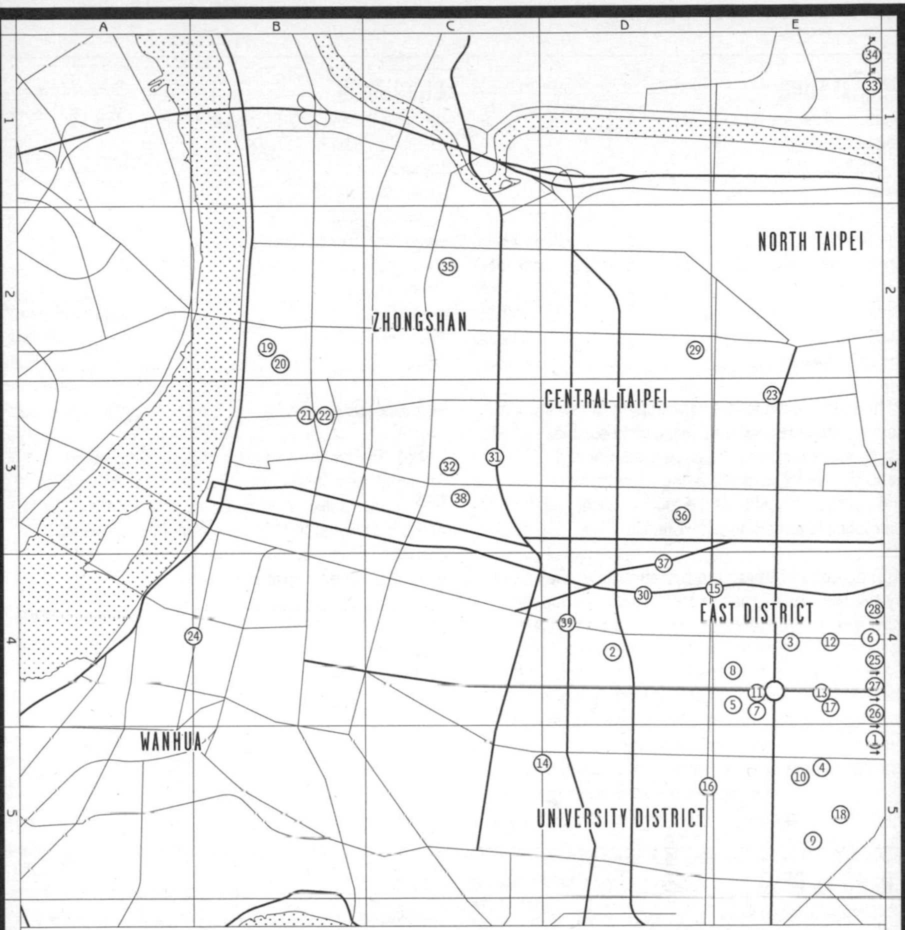

NORTH TAIPEI
ZHONGSHAN
CENTRAL TAIPEI
EAST DISTRICT
WANHUA
UNIVERSITY DISTRICT

TAIPEI

N

SCALE

0 485 970 1455 yd.

1. *Din Tai Fung (p.202)*
2. *Chang Ye Deng (p.202)*
3. *Chou Chou (p.202)*
4. *Ichi (p.202)*
5. *Le Blanc (p.202)*
6. *Mazendo (p.203)*
7. *Mume (p.203)*
8. *Orange Shabu Shabu (p.203)*
9. *Pin Xian (p.203)*
10. *Gēn Creative (p.203)*
11. *September Café (p.204)*
12. *Spot Taipei (p.204)*
13. *Sugar Pea (p.204)*
14. *Tian Jin Flaky Scallion Pancake (p.204)*
15. *Totto Ramen (p.204)*
16. *Yong He Soy Milk King (p.205)*
17. *Yukari (p.205)*
18. *Zheng Wei Yuan Seafood (p.205)*
19. *Dalongdong Baoan Temple (p.205)*
20. *Ga Er Zui (p.205)*
21. *Ningxia Night Market (p.205)*
22. *Shilin Saute Lamb (p.206)*
23. *Meowvelous Taipei Club Saloon (p.206)*
24. *Legendary Milkfish Belly (p.206)*
25. *L'atelier De Joël Robuchon (p.206)*
26. *S.t.a.y (p.206)*
27. *Taipei World Trade Center Club (p.207)*
28. *Awesome Burger (p.207)*
29. *Astar Coffee House (p.207)*
30. *Elixir Health Pot (p.207)*
31. *Ever Green (p.207)*
32. *Moutain And Sea House (p.207)*
33. *Nihonryori Ryugin (p.208)*
34. *Raw (p.208)*
35. *Shin Yeh (p.208)*
36. *Xiaozhang's Seafood (p.208)*
37. *Lin Dong Fang Beef Noodles (p.208)*
38. *Dragon Restaurant (p.209)*
39. *Fu Hang Soy Milk (p.209)*

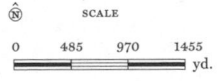

DIN TAI FUNG

Recommended by
Yannick Alléno, Richie Lin,
Eric Liu, Colin Mackay

Multiple locations
Taipei 106
+886 223218928
www.dintaifung.com.tw

Opening hours	Open 7 days
Credit cards	Accepted
Price range	Affordable
Style	Casual
Cuisine	Chinese
Recommended for	Bargain

"The best-known food establishment in Taiwan, serving Taiwanese-Shangainese style cuisine. Must-haves include pork chop fried rice and soup dumplings. Despite being a food empire, the consistent quality of the food, service, and ambiance is remarkable."—Eric Liu

Named one of the top ten restaurants in the world by the New York Times in 1993, this Taipei-based *xiao long bao* (soup dumpling) specialist is credited for starting the global craze for soup dumplings. Even though it's developed into a chain spanning more than ten countries, its standards remain exacting (each dumpling is wrapped with at least eighteen folds). Despite having multiple Michelin-starred outlets in other Asian cities, the original store on Xinyi Road has become the mecca of soup dumplings.

CHANG YE DENG

Recommended by
Shun Kai Ho

58, Section 3, Jinan Road
Da'an
Taipei 106
+886 227810887

Opening hours	Variable
Credit cards	Not accepted
Price range	Affordable
Style	Casual
Cuisine	Japanese
Recommended for	Regular neighborhood

"Open until late, this is a relaxing restaurant with good comforting food. The chefs are very funny and friendly that makes you feel like you are not in a restaurant but with a bunch of friends at home."—Shun Kai Ho

CHOU CHOU

Recommended by
Eric Liu

22, Alley 6, Lane 170, Section 4
Zhongxiao East Road
Da'an
Taipei 106
+886 0225572780
www.chouchaotzu.com

Opening hours	Open 7 days
Credit cards	Not accepted
Price range	Affordable
Style	Casual
Cuisine	Taiwanese
Recommended for	Wish I'd opened

"Chef Kin Lam used to work at Jean-Georges in Shanghai and Chou Chou offers an array of classic French bistro dishes. With a simple and well-executed approach, this restaurant has a relaxed, casual environment and its food is focused and well presented."—Eric Liu

ICHI

Recommended by
Eric Liu

40, Section 2, Anhe Road
Da'an
Taipei 106
+886 227048195
www.ichi.tw

Opening hours	Open 7 days
Credit cards	Accepted
Price range	Affordable
Style	Casual
Cuisine	Japanese
Recommended for	Late night

"This Japanese influence hangout has been around for almost ten years. Flavors are clean and food is well executed. There is a solid cocktail and sake menu with draft beers."—Eric Liu

LE BLANC

Recommended by
Andrea Bonaffini, Eric Liu

183, Section 1, Da'an Road
Da'an
Taipei 106
+886 227007770

Opening hours	Open 7 days
Credit cards	Accepted
Price range	Affordable
Style	Casual
Cuisine	Steakhouse
Recommended for	Regular neighborhood

MAZENDO

24, Lane 280, Guangfu South Road
Guangfu South Road
Da'an
Taipei 106
+886 227735559
www.mazendo.com.tw

Opening hours...Open 7 days
Credit cards...Accepted
Price range..Affordable
Style...Casual
Cuisine...Taiwanese
Recommended for...Bargain

"This small chain in Taiwan has dumplings in chile oil that are my favorite. The oil is perfectly balanced and the dumplings, which have delicious fillings, are served hot at an unbeatable price—for the quality I'd pay triple!"—Long Xiong

MUME

28 Siwei Road
Da'an
Taipei 106
+886 227000901
www.mume.tw

Opening hours...Open 7 days
Credit cards...Accepted
Price range..Affordable
Style...Casual
Cuisine...Modern European
Recommended for...............................Regular neighborhood

Owned and run by a trio of chefs—Richie Lin, Kai Ward, and Long Xiong—who cut their teeth at big-name restaurants like Noma, Per Se and Quay, this chef-driven eatery puts the spotlight on Taiwanese ingredients. It serves a strictly à la carte menu, straightforwardly categorised into snacks, small plates, larger plates and desserts. The signature wagyu tartare is seasoned with the local shrimp oil and topped with daikon, a classic Taiwanese condiment, while local tilefish arrives basking in a consommé infused with Taiwanese wild pepper. Plan to spend around NT$2,000 ($65; £53) a head.

ORANGE SHABU SHABU

135, Section 1, Da'an Road
Da'an
Taipei 106
+886 227761658
www.orangeshabu.com.tw

Opening hours...Open 7 days
Credit cards...Accepted
Price range..Expensive
Style...Casual
Cuisine..Shabu Shabu
Recommended for..Late night

"I love the quality of the food—best is the black Taiwanese chicken."—Andrea Bonaffini

PIN XIAN

68 Leli Road
Da'an
Taipei 106
+886 227358373

Opening hours...Open 7 days
Credit cards.............................Accepted but not AMEX
Price range..Affordable
Style...Casual
Cuisine...Taiwanese Seafood
Recommended for...Bargain

"Offers extremely tasty stir-fry dishes that pair well with local beer. It has a very relaxed and casual environment and is suitable for both small and large group gatherings."—Eric Liu

GEN CREATIVE

24, Lane 63, Section 2
Dunhua South Road
Da'an
Taipei 106
+886 227073348
www.gentaipei.com

Opening hours..Closed Sunday
Credit cards.............................Accepted but not AMEX
Price range..Affordable
Style...Casual
Cuisine...Modern American
Recommended for...............................Regular neighborhood

"Excellent food, always at the same standard, served in a casual atmosphere with friendly service—what more can you ask for?"—Richie Lin

SEPTEMBER CAFÉ

Recommended by
Mauro Colagreco

1, Lane 14, Siwei Road
Da'an
Taipei 106
+886 227051669
www.september.tw

Opening hours	Open 7 days
Credit cards	Accepted
Price range	Expensive
Style	Smart casual
Cuisine	Taiwanese-International
Recommended for	Breakfast

"This is a place that really nails its ambiance.
They do an amazing job with the feel of the space,
and oh yeah, the French toast is really amazing—
not to be missed."—Mauro Colagreco

SPOT TAIPEI

Recommended by
Richie Lin, Eric Liu, Long Xiong

58, Lane 233, Section 1
Dunhua South Road
Da'an
Taipei 106
+886 227754117

Opening hours	Open 7 days
Credit cards	Accepted but not AMEX
Price range	Affordable
Style	Casual
Cuisine	Modern American
Recommended for	Breakfast

"They have a large menu and yet they still somehow
manage to execute all of their dishes well. One of
my favorites is in the 'All Day Brunch' section of the
menu. A star is the Ferrero Roche French Toast, which
is even more delicious than it sounds, with its crunchy
custardy bread, filled with all that banana and Nutella.
There's some other magical stuff there but you should
eat it yourself to find out."—Long Xiong

Brunch places are a dime a dozen in Taipei, but for
New American flavors and affordable prices, head to
this industrial-chic spot tucked in an alley behind Ming
Yao Shopping Center. In a warehouse-like space
festooned with ceiling-chained lamps, hip and hungry
diners feast on hearty portions of favorites like
Ferrero Rocher French toast, crispy chicken wings
with blue cheese and sriracha sauce, and fried
chicken and waffle sandwiches. If it's your first visit,
be sure not to confuse the place with independent
movie house Spot Theatre.

SUGAR PEA

Recommended by
Mauro Colagreco

Alley 20, Lane 300, Section 4
1F, 16 Ren'ai Road
Da'an
Taipei 106
+886 2 2325 6188

Opening hours	Closed Monday and Tuesday
Credit cards	Accepted but not AMEX
Price range	Affordable
Style	Smart casual
Cuisine	International
Recommended for	Breakfast

"A beautiful restaurant and, with the pedigree of the
chef, there must be a reason I've only heard positive
things."—Mauro Colagreco

TIAN JIN FLAKY SCALLION PANCAKE

Recommended by
Long Xiong

1, Lane 6, Yong Kang Street
Da'an
Taipei 106
+886 223213768

Opening hours	Open 7 days
Reservation policy	No
Credit cards	Not accepted
Price range	Budget
Style	Casual
Cuisine	Taiwanese Street Food
Recommended for	Bargain

"A landmark on Yong Kang Street, the already
crowded area where locals head for cheap eats.
There is always a line of people, 20–30 deep.
The simple flaky scallion pancakes can be stuffed
with ham, cheese, basil, an egg or corn and, when
fully loaded with everything, they can't be beaten
on price alone!"—Long Xiong

TOTTO RAMEN

Recommended by
Long Xiong

9, Alley 5, Lane 107, Section 1
Fuxing South Road
Da'an
Taipei 106
+886 227789866
www.tottoramen.com

Opening hours	Open 7 days
Credit cards	Accepted but not AMEX
Price range	Affordable
Style	Casual
Cuisine	Japanese
Recommended for	Wish I'd opened

"It's always easy to find a delicious comforting bowl here. They also open until 4.00 a.m. on Friday and Saturday so I get the chance to look forward to my late-night fix all week long."—Long Xiong

YONG HE SOY MILK KING

Recommended by
Eric Liu

102, Section 2, Fuxing South Road
Da'an
Taipei 106
+886 227035051

Opening hours	Open 7 days
Reservation policy	No
Credit cards	Not accepted
Price range	Budget
Style	Casual
Cuisine	Taiwanese
Recommended for	Breakfast

"The traditional Northern Chinese-style breakfast served here consist of items such as soy milk, rice balls, fried pastry, soup dumplings, and fluffy egg pastries."—Eric Liu

YUKARI

Recommended by
Soriano Joaquin

4, Alley 127, Section 1
Anhe Road
Da'an
Taipei 106
+886 227008128
www.yukarigroup.com

Opening hours	Closed Monday and Sunday
Credit cards	Accepted
Price range	Affordable
Style	Smart casual
Cuisine	Japanese
Recommended for	Worth the travel

"Rich but subtle flavors and the Japanese tableware is very interesting."—Soriano Joaquin

ZHENG WEI YUAN SEAFOOD

Recommended by
Shun Kai Ho

2, Lane 171, Tonghua Street
Da'an
Taipei 106
+886 227359968

Opening hours	Open 7 days
Credit cards	Accepted but not AMEX
Price range	Affordable
Style	Casual
Cuisine	Taiwanese Seafood
Recommended for	Local favorite

DALONGDONG BAOAN TEMPLE

Recommended by
Shun Kai Ho

17, Lane 49, Bao'an Street
Datong
Taipei 103
+886 225539978

Opening hours	Open 7 days
Reservation policy	No
Credit cards	Not accepted
Price range	Budget
Style	Casual
Cuisine	Taiwanese Street Food
Recommended for	Breakfast

"This is a place full of history, where people used to gather in the olden days. It's near a pier and used to be a trading center so there are many different types of food around. Today, there are lots of stalls with different authentic Taiwanese foods."—Shun Kai Ho

GA ER ZUI

Recommended by
Shun Kai Ho

34 Ganzhou Street
Datong
Taipei 103

Opening hours	Open 7 days
Reservation policy	No
Credit cards	Not accepted
Price range	Budget
Style	Casual
Cuisine	Taiwanese
Recommended for	Bargain

"This restaurant, which has been passed down to the third generation of the same family, sells cold silver-needle noodles in the summer and hot food during winter (pork balls, fish ball, silver-needle noodles, etc.)."—Shun Kai Ho

NINGXIA NIGHT MARKET

Recommended by
Dharshan Munidasa

Ningxia Road
Datong
Taipei 103
+886 915652480
www.nx-yes.tw

Opening hours	Open 7 days
Reservation policy	No
Credit cards	Not accepted
Price range	Budget
Style	Casual
Cuisine	Taiwanese
Recommended for	Late night

SHILIN SAUTE LAMB

Recommended by
Shun Kai Ho

Shilin Night Market
101 Jihe Road
Shilin
Taipei 111
+886 288613476

Opening hours	Open 7 days
Reservation policy	No
Credit cards	Not accepted
Price range	Budget
Style	Casual
Cuisine	Taiwanese Street Food
Recommended for	Late night

"A very cool stall that is open at night and sells only sautéed lamb, beer, and rice."—Shun Kai Ho

MEOWVELOUS TAIPEI CLUB SALOON

Recommended by
Richie Lin

218 Dunhua North Road
Songshan
Taipei 105
+886 227177596

Opening hours	Open 7 days
Reservation policy	No
Credit cards	Accepted but not AMEX
Price range	Affordable
Style	Casual
Cuisine	Taiwanese Bar
Recommended for	Late night

A spin-off from owner Kuan Chen's popular first bar, Meowvelous Taipei Fan Club, this outfit offers both a restaurant and a bar and pairs Taiwanese dishes like meatballs with fried egg with a drinks list featuring craft beers and fancy cocktails (including a kimchi-flavored one). Be warned that groups are limited to no more than four people and reservations are not allowed.

LEGENDARY MILKFISH BELLY

Recommended by
Shun Kai Ho

53 Neijiang Street
Wanhua
Taipei 108
+886 223703378

Opening hours	Closed Sunday
Reservation policy	No
Credit cards	Accepted but not AMEX
Price range	Budget
Style	Casual
Cuisine	Taiwanese
Recommended for	Late night

"Delicious food but slightly pricey. The mince-pork rice is a must and the milkfish soup is light yet hearty."—Shun Kai Ho

Bubble tea and oyster *mee sua* (wheat vermicelli) are perhaps Taiwan's best-known food exports, but for the Taiwanese, milkfish is just as iconic. Anping has its own milkfish-themed museum, for example, while Kaoshiung holds an annual milkfish cultural festival. At this night-owl eatery (it only opens at 10.30 p.m.), the belly of the milkfish is either pan-fried or braised in soy sauce to produce flesh that is sweet and tender. But if the bony fish is not for you, this hangout is no one-trick pony; try the omelette, braised pork rice, or claypot three-cup clams.

L'ATELIER DE JOËL ROBUCHON

Recommended by
Eric Liu, Long Xiong

Bellavita Mall
5F, 28 Song Ren Road
Xinyi
Taipei 110
+886 287292628
www.robuchon.com.tw

Opening hours	Open 7 days
Credit cards	Accepted
Price range	Expensive
Style	Smart casual
Cuisine	French
Recommended for	High end

"A great restaurant by a French Master—a bit of a splurge, but they always deliver on their promise of a memorable meal."—Long Xiong

S.T.A.Y

Recommended by
Richie Lin, Long Xiong

Taipei 101 Mall
4F, 45 Shifu Road
Xinyi
Taipei 110
+886 28101817
www.staytaipei.com.tw

Opening hours	Open 7 days
Credit cards	Accepted
Price range	Expensive
Style	Smart casual
Cuisine	Modern French
Recommended for	High end

"A great modern French restaurant in Taipei 101. Opened by three-star Chef Yannick Alleno, you can't go wrong here. Sometimes a bit of a splurge, but worth it when Chef Yannick is in town— a great opportunity to meet and chat with the legend himself."—Long Xiong

TAIPEI WORLD TRADE CENTER CLUB
Recommended by
Richie Lin

333, Section 1
33F, Keelung Road
Xinyi
Taipei 110
+886 227232939
www.twtcclub.com.tw

Opening hours	Open 7 days
Credit cards	Accepted
Price range	Expensive
Style	Formal
Cuisine	Asian Fusion
Recommended for	Local favorite

AWESOME BURGER
Recommended by
Shun Kai Ho

11, Lane 190, Section 1
Keelung Road
Xinyi
Taipei 110
+886 227642906

Opening hours	Closed Monday
Credit cards	Accepted but not AMEX
Price range	Affordable
Style	Casual
Cuisine	Burgers
Recommended for	Bargain

"Good quality burgers at a reasonable price—juicy meat patties and bouncy burgers with crispy fries."
—Shun Kai Ho

ASTAR COFFEE HOUSE
Recommended by
Riccardo Camanini

41, Alley 13, Lane 60, Section 3
Minquan East Road
Zhongshan
Taipei
104
+886 225035856

Opening hours	Closed Monday
Credit cards	Not accepted
Price range	Budget
Style	Casual
Cuisine	Café
Recommended for	Breakfast

ELIXIR HEALTH POT
Recommended by
Long Xiong

143, Section 3, Civic Boulevard
Zhongshan
Taipei 104
+886 227317928

Opening hours	Open 7 days
Credit cards	Accepted
Price range	Affordable
Style	Smart casual
Cuisine	Mongolian-Chinese
Recommended for	Regular neighborhood

EVER GREEN
Recommended by
Shun Kai Ho

38, Section 2, Xinsheng North Rd
Zhongshan
Taipei 104
+886 225115656
www.egvr.com.tw

Opening hours	Open 7 days
Credit cards	Accepted
Price range	Affordable
Style	Smart casual
Cuisine	Vegetarian-Taiwanese
Recommended for	Local favorite

"The chef is passionate about what he is doing and, incidentally, he played a small part in Lee An's movie, *Eat Drink Man Woman*."—Shun Kai Ho

MOUTAIN AND SEA HOUSE
Recommended by
Richie Lin

16, Lane 11, Section 2
Zhongshan North Road
Zhongshan
Taipei 104
+886 225116224

Opening hours	Open 7 days
Credit cards	Accepted
Price range	Affordable
Style	Casual
Cuisine	Taiwanese
Recommended for	Local favorite

Taiwan may be synonymous with greasy street food at night-time bazaars, but ask around and those in the know will show you a more refined side. This restaurant, uses organic ingredients to re-create age-old Taiwanese dishes like chicken, bamboo shoot, and mushroom wrapped in pig's stomach, and 'leftover soup', a mixture of the remains of six banquet dishes. Yes, the bill may leave a dent in your wallet but the Taiwanese flavors will leave a lasting impression.

NIHONRYORI RYUGIN

Recommended by
Shun Kai Ho, Richie Lin

301 Lequn 3rd Road
Zhongshan
Taipei 104
+886 285015808
www.nihonryori-ryugin.com.tw

Opening hours	Closed Monday
Credit cards	Accepted
Price range	Expensive
Style	Smart casual
Cuisine	Japanese-Taiwanese
Recommended for	High end

"Excellent service, good food, and good atmosphere. They present Japanese cuisine in a different way, using Taiwanese ingredients, which the chef looks for from farm to farm and market to market. There are very passionate people behind this restaurant."
—Shun Kai Ho

RAW

Recommended by
Yau Tim Lai

301 Lequn 3rd Road
Zhongshan
Taipei 104
+886 285015800
www.raw.com.tw

Opening hours	Closed Monday and Tuesday
Credit cards	Accepted
Price range	Expensive
Style	Smart casual
Cuisine	Modern Taiwanese
Recommended for	Worth the travel

"From the leading chef, André Chiang, this restaurant uses local Taiwan ingredients and takes cooking to the next level."—Yau Tim Lai

SHIN YEH

Recommended by
Eric Liu

34-1 Shuangcheng Street
Zhongshan
Taipei 104
+886 25963255
www.shinyeh.com.tw

Opening hours	Open 7 days
Credit cards	Accepted
Price range	Affordable
Style	Casual
Cuisine	Taiwanese-Chinese
Recommended for	Local favorite

"This restaurant has been around for over sixty years and continues to strive to uphold the integrity of local Taiwanese cuisine—a benchmark for all others."
—Eric Liu

XIAOZHANG'S SEAFOOD

Recommended by
Richie Lin

73, Liaoning Street
Zhongshan
Taipei 104
+886 927808693

Opening hours	Open 7 days
Credit cards	Not accepted
Price range	Affordable
Style	Casual
Cuisine	Seafood
Recommended for	Late night

"A Taiwanese seafood joint, serving fresh local seafood everyday. The stir-fry dishes are amazing!"—Richie Lin

LIN DONG FANG BEEF NOODLES

Recommended by
Long Xiong

274, Section 2
Bade Road
Zhongshan
Taipei 104
+886 227522556

Opening hours	Closed Sunday
Reservation policy	No
Credit cards	Not accepted
Price range	Budget
Style	Casual
Cuisine	Chinese
Recommended for	Local favorite

"Beef noodles is one of, if not the, quintessential foods of Taiwan. This place hasn't been franchised and multiplied, and it hasn't been gentrified or remodeled to become trendier. It's still barely more than a stall. It is visited at all hours of the day and night. Who doesn't like a big bowl of beefy noodles at 3.30 a.m. after a long service or a late night of drinking? This is a classic that defines the city and one I always hurry back to if I've been away. Get the bowl of half-meat half-tendon if you know what's good for you."—Long Xiong

DRAGON RESTAURANT

Recommended by
Eric Liu

18, Lane 105, Section 1
Zhongshan North Road
Zhongshan
Taipei 104
+886 225639293

Opening hours	Open 7 days
Credit cards	Accepted
Price range	Affordable
Style	Casual
Cuisine	Cantonese
Recommended for	Local favorite

FU HANG SOY MILK

Recommended by
Richie Lin

108, Section 1, Zhongxiao East Road
Zhongzheng
Taipei 100
+886 223922175

Opening hours	Closed Monday
Reservation policy	No
Credit cards	Not accepted
Price range	Affordable
Style	Casual
Cuisine	Taiwanese
Recommended for	Breakfast

"Traditional Taiwanese breakfast (soy milk and fried bread) at its best!"—Richie Lin

"*Rice noodle rolls like in the old days.*"
DAVID LAI P213

HONG KONG

MAINLAND

"**PERFECT IN HONG KONG'S SWELTERING HEAT.**"
MATT ABERGEL P215

"*OPEN UNTIL 1 A.M. AND FAMOUS FOR ITS BEEF SATAY HOT POT*"
DAVID LAI P213

"*Old school... the seafood selection is top notch.*"
DAVID LAI P212

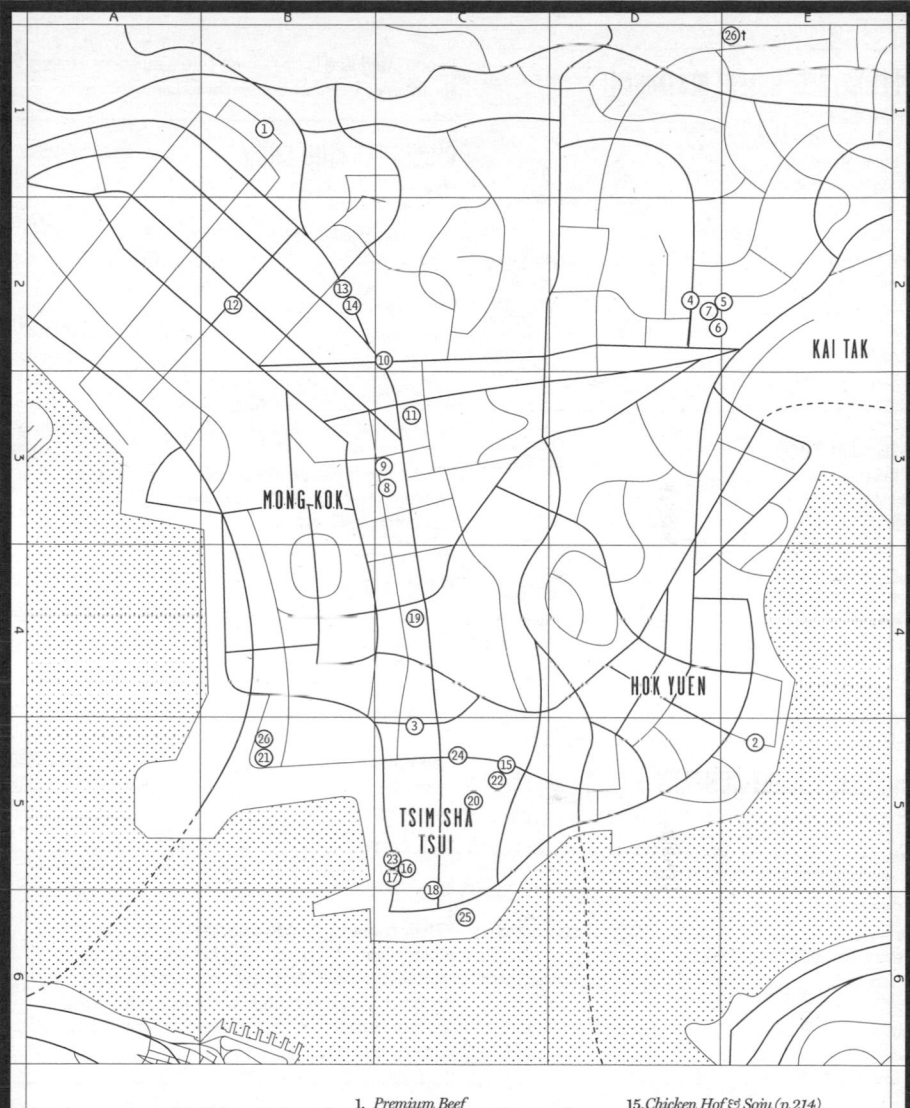

HONG KONG

MAINLAND

‹N› SCALE

0   400   800   1200
YD.

KAI TAK

MONG KOK

HOK YUEN

TSIM SHA TSUI

PREMIUM BEEF HOTPOT RESTAURANT
Recommended by
Chan Yan-tak

Tin Yu Plaza
62–168 Un Chau Street
Cheung Sha Wan
Hong Kong 999077
+852 34887818

Opening hours	Open 7 days
Credit cards	Accepted but not AMEX
Price range	Affordable
Style	Casual
Cuisine	Cantonese
Recommended for	Late night

WING LAI YUEN
Recommended by
Richard Ekkebus

7 Tak On Street
Hung Hum
Hong Kong 999077
+852 23206430

Opening hours	Open 7 days
Credit cards	Accepted
Price range	Affordable
Style	Casual
Cuisine	Noodles
Recommended for	Bargain

AUSTRALIA DAIRY COMPANY
Recommended by
Andrea Bonaffini,
Erchen Chang, Richard Ekkebus,
Todd Ginsberg, Uwe Opocensky

47 Parkes Street
Jordan
Hong Kong 999077
+852 27301356

Opening hours	Closed Thursday
Reservation policy	No
Credit cards	Not accepted
Price range	Affordable
Style	Casual
Cuisine	Hong Kongese
Recommended for	Breakfast

FONG WING KEE
Recommended by
David Lai

85–87 Hau Wong Road
Kowloon
Hong Kong 999077
+852 23821788

Opening hours	Open 7 days
Credit cards	Accepted but not AMEX
Price range	Affordable
Style	Casual
Cuisine	Chinese
Recommended for	Late night

"Fong Wing Kee is open until 1.00 a.m. and is famous for its satay beef hot pot."—David Lai

CHONG FAT CHIU CHOW
Recommended by
David Lai

60 South Wall Road
Kowloon
Hong Kong 999077
+852 23833114

Opening hours	Open 7 days
Credit cards	Not accepted
Price range	Affordable
Style	Casual
Cuisine	Chinese
Recommended for	Local favorite

"This place is like an old-school, Chinese version of a tapas restaurant. The seafood selection is top-notch."—David Lai

ISLAM FOOD
Recommended by
Vicky Cheng, Jowett Yu

1 Lung Kong Road
Kowloon
Hong Kong 999077
+852 23822822
www.islamfood.com.hk

Opening hours	Open 7 days
Credit cards	Not accepted
Price range	Budget
Style	Casual
Cuisine	Asian-Halal
Recommended for	Bargain

"Their curiously named dish 'veal goulash' is outstanding—it's a pan-fried hot pocket dumpling stuffed with beef. The juices are abundant and extremely hot. Use caution when eating this! Also worth mentioning is their Canto-Pakistani mutton curry."—Jowett Yu

MOK'S BEEF DYNASTY HOTPOT
Recommended by
Mango Tsang Chiu Lit

45 Nam Kok Road
Kowloon
Hong Kong 999077
+852 27152788

Opening hours	Open 7 days
Credit cards	Not accepted
Price range	Budget
Style	Casual
Cuisine	Hot Pot
Recommended for	Local favorite

MING'S KITCHEN
Recommended by
Chan Yau Leung
519 Shanghai Street
Mong Kok
Hong Kong 999077
+852 28712391

Opening hours..Open 7 days
Credit cards...Not accepted
Price range...Affordable
Style...Casual
Cuisine...Cantonese
Recommended for...Late night

THE PLACE
Recommended by
Mango Tsang Chiu Lit
Cordis
555 Shanghai Street
Mong Kok
Hong Kong 999077
+852 35523028

Opening hours..Open 7 days
Credit cards..Accepted
Price range..Expensive
Style..Smart casual
Cuisine...International
Recommended for..High end

JUXING HOME
Recommended by
Albert Au Kwok Keung
418 Portland Street
Prince Edward
Hong Kong 999077
+852 23929283

Opening hours..Open 7 days
Credit cards...Not accepted
Price range...Affordable
Style...Casual
Cuisine..Chinese
Recommended for...Late night

KAM WAH CAFÉ
Recommended by
Chan Yan-tak
47 Bute Street
Prince Edward
Hong Kong 999077
+852 23926830

Opening hours..Open 7 days
Reservation policy...No
Credit cards...Not accepted
Price range..Budget
Style...Casual
Cuisine...Cantonese
Recommended for....................................Local favorite

213

"In Hong Kong the first thing that comes to mind is the cafés; Kam Wah's pineapple buns and egg tarts are particularly well known."—Chan Yan-tak

HOP YIK TAI
Recommended by
David Lai
121 Kweilin Street
Sham Shui Po
Hong Kong 999077
+852 27200239

Opening hours..Open 7 days
Reservation policy...No
Credit cards...Not accepted
Price range..Budget
Style...Casual
Cuisine...Street Food
Recommended for...Breakfast

"One of the few places that still does rice noodle rolls like in the old days."—David Lai

SIU CHOI WONG
Recommended by
May Chow, Chan Yan-tak
43 Fuk Wing Street
Sham Shui Po
Hong Kong 999077
+852 27768380

Opening hours..Open 7 days
Credit cards...Not accepted
Price range..Budget
Style...Casual
Cuisine...Cantonese
Recommended for...Bargain

TIM HO WAN
Recommended by
Richard Ekkebus, Uwe Opocensky,
David Pellizzari, Bruce Ricketts,
Chan Yan-tak, Chan Yau Leung
9–11 Fuk Wing Street
Sham Shui Po
Hong Kong 999077
+852 23322896

Opening hours..Seven days
Credit cards..Accepted
Price range...Affordable
Style...Casual
Cuisine..Dim Sum
Recommended for...Bargain

It may no longer be the most affordable Michelin-starred restaurant in the world but it's still billed as Hong Kong's most famous dim-sum chain thanks to its rapid rise from a single outlet in Mongkok. The menu is headlined by the 'four heavenly kings' of baked barbecue pork buns, pan-fried radish cake, steamed egg cake and bean curd skin with pork and shrimp.

CHICKEN HOF & SOJU

82–84 Kimberley Road
Tsim Sha Tsui
Hong Kong 999077
+852 23758080

Opening hours...Open 7 days
Credit cards..Accepted
Price range..Affordable
Style...Casual
Cuisine...Korean
Recommended for...Late night

"Serves different varieties of double-fried Korean chicken, from original salt and pepper to slathered in spicy sauce. There are a few new creations too, such as honey and garlic, or chicken topped with grated cheese. Also serves draft beers, and is open until 6.00 a.m."—Uwe Opocensky

EAST OCEAN SEAVIEW RESTAURANT

1 Peking Road
Tsim Sha Tsui
Hong Kong 999077
+852 28772938
www.eastocean.com.hk

Opening hours...Open 7 days
Credit cards..Accepted
Price range..Affordable
Style...Casual
Cuisine...Cantonese
Recommended for.......................................Local favorite

"Ask for the egg tarts early so they don't run out by the time you're ready for dessert!"—Lori Granito

ÉPURE

5 Canton Road
Tsim Sha Tsui
Hong Kong 999077
+852 31858338
www.epure.hk

Opening hours...Open 7 days
Credit cards..Accepted
Price range...Expensive
Style..Smart casual
Cuisine...French
Recommended for.................................Worth the travel

GADDI'S

The Peninsula Hong Kong
Salisbury Road
Tsim Sha Tsui
Hong Kong 999077
+852 26966763
www.hongkong.peninsula.com

Opening hours...Open 7 days
Credit cards..Accepted
Price range...Expensive
Style...Formal
Cuisine...French
Recommended for..High end

HING KEE RESTAURANT

Bowa House
19 Temple St
Tsim Sha Tsui
Hong Kong 999077
+852 27220022

Opening hours...Open 7 days
Credit cards.............................Accepted but not AMEX
Price range..Affordable
Style...Casual
Cuisine...Cantonese
Recommended for...Late night

"The best typhoon-shelter crab in Hong Kong and ice cold tins of Tsing Tao to go with it. The offal platter with steamed garlic chives makes for a great start to a meal."—Jowett Yu

KIMBERLEY CHINESE RESTAURANT

The Kimberley Hotel
28 Kimberley Road

Tsim Sha Tsui
Hong Kong 999077
+852 2369 8212
www.kimberley.hk

Opening hours...Open 7 days
Credit cards..Accepted
Price range..Affordable
Style...Casual
Cuisine...Cantonese
Recommended for.......................................Local favorite

"Try the amazing pork stuffed with rice, and definitely book in advance."—Ricardo Chaneton

RYUGIN

Recommended by
Yau Tim Lai

International Commerce Center
1 Austin Road West
Tsim Sha Tsui
Hong Kong 999077
+852 23020222
www.ryugin.com.hk

Opening hours	Open 7 days
Credit cards	Accepted
Price range	Expensive
Style	Smart casual
Cuisine	Japanese
Recommended for	High end

"Contemporary Japanese *kaiseki* cuisine in Hong Kong."—Yau Tim Lai

SEORAE

Recommended by
Matt Abergel

Passkon Court
79–81 Kimberley Road
Tsim Sha Tsui
Hong Kong 999077
+852 27236692

Opening hours	Open 7 days
Credit cards	Accepted
Price range	Budget
Style	Casual
Cuisine	Korean
Recommended for	Late night

"Great place to bring all of my chefs after service. Good quality meat, and the cold noodles are perfect in Hong Kong's sweltering heat."—Matt Abergel

SUSHI TOKAMI

Recommended by
Chan Yan-tak

Ocean Center
Harbor City
Tsim Sha Tsui
Hong Kong 999077
+852 27713938
www.tokami.com.hk

Opening hours	Open 7 days
Credit cards	Accepted
Price range	Expensive
Style	Smart casual
Cuisine	Japanese
Recommended for	High end

TAI WOO RESTAURANT

Recommended by
Ricardo Chaneton

14–16 Hillwood Road
Tsim Sha Tsui
Hong Kong 999077
+852 23685420
www.taiwoorestaurant.com

Opening hours	Open 7 days
Credit cards	Accepted
Price range	Affordable
Style	Casual
Cuisine	Cantonese
Recommended for	Bargain

YAN TOH HEEN

Recommended by
Jowett Yu

Intercontinental Hong Kong
18 Salisbury Road
Tsim Sha Tsui
Hong Kong 999077
+852 23132323
www.hongkong-ic.intercontinental.com

Opening hours	Open 7 days
Credit cards	Accepted
Price range	Affordable
Style	Smart casual
Cuisine	Cantonese
Recommended for	Local favorite

TIN LUNG HEEN

Recommended by
Shane Osborn

The Ritz-Carlton
1 Austin Road West
Yau Ma Tei
Hong Kong 999077
+852 22632270
www.ritzcarlton.com

Opening hours	Open 7 days
Credit cards	Accepted
Price range	Expensive
Style	Smart casual
Cuisine	Cantonese
Recommended for	High end

Tin Lung Heen is one of the world's tallest Chinese restaurants, and the jaw-dropping view of the Hong Kong skyline from its 102-storey perch at Ritz Carlton Hong Kong is to die for. But don't get too distracted by the view—the Michelin-approved Cantonese food is just as stunning. The menu is headlined by fresh seafood and dim sum; the steamed crab claw with egg white and Hua Diao wine is noteworthy, as is the barbecue Iberico pork with honey. The chandeliered main dining room is bound to impress.

"The best congee in the world."
MIRCO KELLER P219

"It's somewhat of a chef's after-work hangout."
DAVID LAI P218

HONG KONG

ISLAND

"Best yakitori you'll ever have."
FRANKIE VAN LOO P229

"ARGUABLY HONG KONG'S NUMBER ONE RESTAURANT."
SHANE OSBORN P220

"PERFECT DIM SUM AND CRISPY-SKINNED CHICKEN."
MATT ABERGEL P221

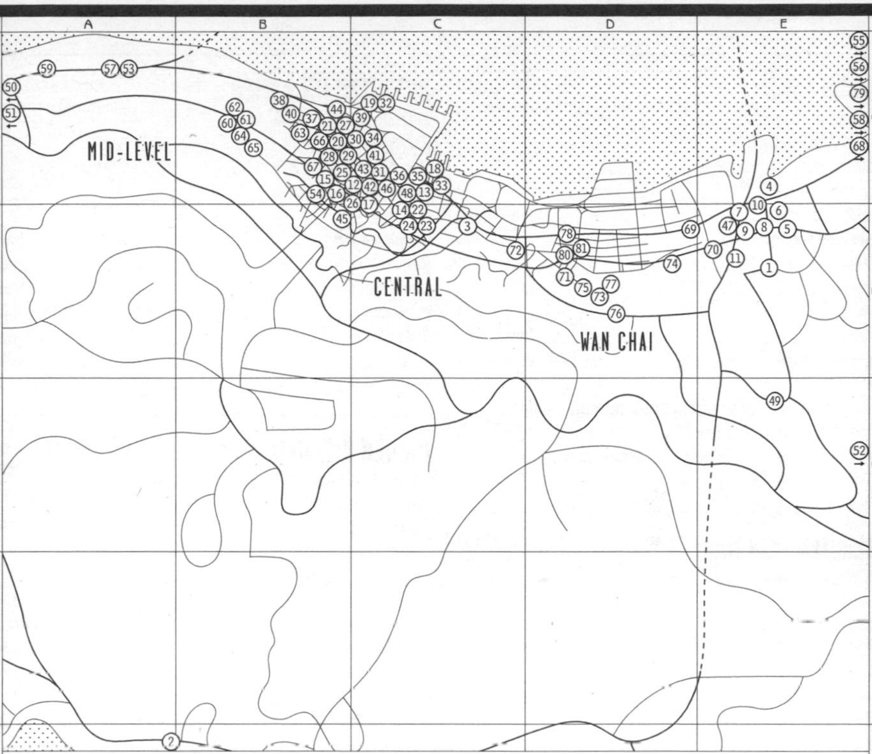

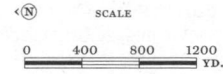

HONG KONG
ISLAND

‹Ⓝ›   SCALE

0   400   800   1200
YD.

MID-LEVEL

CENTRAL

WAN CHAI

1. *Din Tai Fung (p.218)*
2. *Aberdeen Fish Market Yee (p.218)*
3. *The Continental (p.218)*
4. *Betsutenjin Ramen (p.218)*
5. *Hidden Kitchen (p.218)*
6. *Ho Hung Kee Congee & Noodle (p.219)*
7. *Ichiran Ramen (p.219)*
8. *Kozy Okonomi-Yaki Teppan-Yaki (p.219)*
9. *Paradise Of King Asia Seafood (p.219)*
10. *Se Wong Yee (p.219)*
11. *Sushi Gin (p.219)*
12. *121 Bc (p.220)*
13. *8 ½ Otto E Mezzo Bombana (p.220)*
14. *Amber (p.220)*
15. *Belon (p.220)*
16. *Brunch Club (p.220)*
17. *Burger Circus (p.220)*
18. *Café Caussette (p.221)*
19. *Caprice (p.221)*
20. *Celebrity Cuisine (p.221)*
21. *The Chairman (p.221)*
22. *China Tang (p.221)*
23. *Ciak—In The Kitchen (p.221)*
24. *Duddell's (p.222)*
25. *Fineprint Espresso & Liquor (p.222)*
26. *The Flying Pan (p.222)*
27. *Godenya (p.222)*
28. *Ho Lee Fook (p.222)*
29. *Kau Kee Restaurant (p.222)*
30. *Lin Heung Tea House (p.223)*
31. *Luk Yu Teahouse (p.223)*
32. *Lung King Heen (p.223)*
33. *M Bar (p.223)*
34. *Mak's Noodle (p.223)*
35. *Man Wah (p.224)*
36. *Mercedes Me Store (p.224)*
37. *Sang Kee Congee Shop (p.224)*
38. *Shui Kee (p.224)*
39. *Social Place (p.224)*
40. *Sun Yuen (p.224)*
41. *Ta Vie (p.225)*
42. *Tartine (p.225)*
43. *Tsim Chai Kee Noodle Shop (p.225)*
44. *Vea (p.225)*
45. *Wagyu (p.225)*
46. *Yat Lok (p.226)*
47. *Yuet Wah Wui Seafood Restaurant (p.226)*
48. *Yung Kee (p.226)*
49. *Tasty Congee And Noodles (p.226)*
50. *Butcher And Baker Cafe (p.226)*
51. *Sun Hing Restaurant (p.226)*
52. *Sun Kwai Heung (p.227)*
53. *Lamma Rainbow (p.227)*
54. *Hooked (p.227)*
55. *Tung Po (p.227)*
56. *Mr And Mrs Fox (p.227)*
57. *Kwan Kee Claypot Rice (p.227)*
58. *On Lee Noodle (p.228)*
59. *Rhoda (p.228)*
60. *208 Duecentto Otto (p.228)*
61. *Chachawan (p.228)*
62. *Corner Kitchen Café (p.228)*
63. *Dim Sum Square (p.228)*
64. *For Kee (p.229)*
65. *Frantzén's Kitchen (p.229)*
66. *RōNin (p.229)*
67. *Yardbird (p.229)*
68. *Bing Kee (p.229)*
69. *As You Like Restaurant (p.229)*
70. *Dimdimsum Dim Sum Specialty (p.230)*
71. *Bo Innovation (p.230)*
72. *Giando (p.230)*
73. *Kam Fung Café (p.230)*
74. *Old Bazaar Kitchen (p.230)*
75. *Passion By Gerard Dubois (p.230)*
76. *Samsen (p.231)*
77. *Se Wong Sun (p.231)*
78. *Seventh Son Restaurant (p.231)*
79. *Sister Wah (p.231)*
80. *Wah Lam Noodle Restaurant (p.231)*
81. *Wing Wah Noodle Shop (p.231)*

DIN TAI FUNG

Recommended by
Gal Ben-Moshe, Umberto Bombana,
Vicky Cheng, Shane Osborn
Andrew Wong

Multiple locations
Hong Kong 999077
www.dintaifung.com.hk

Opening hours..Open 7 days
Reservation policy...No
Credit cards...Accepted
Price range...Affordable
Style...Casual
Cuisine..Taiwanese
Recommended for.....................Wish I'd opened

"They serve one of the best soup dumplings and hand-pulled noodles here. And more importantly, they do it consistently across the city, across the world."—Vicky Cheng

ABERDEEN FISH MARKET YEE

Recommended by
Albert Au,
Kwok Keung

102 Shek Pai Wan Road
Aberdeen
Hong Kong 999077
+852 21777872

Opening hours..Open 7 days
Credit cards...Not accepted
Price range...Affordable
Style...Casual
Cuisine...Chinese
Recommended for...............................Breakfast

THE CONTINENTAL

Recommended by
Shane Osborn

Pacific Place
Admiralty
Hong Kong 999077
+852 27045211
www.thecontinentalhongkong.com

Opening hours..Open 7 days
Credit cards..........................Accepted but not Diners
Price range...Affordable
Style...Casual
Cuisine.......................................Modern European
Recommended for.....................Wish I'd opened

BETSUTENJIN RAMEN

Recommended by
Ricardo Chaneton

280 Gloucester Road
Causeway Bay
Hong Kong 999077
+852 34882693

Opening hours..Open 7 days
Reservation policy...No
Credit cards...Not Accepted
Price range...Affordable
Style...Casual
Cuisine..Japanese
Recommended for.................................Bargain

HIDDEN KITCHEN

Recommended by
David Lai

54 Jardine Bazaar
Causeway Bay
Hong Kong 999077
+852 25041511

Opening hours..Closed Monday
Credit cards...Accepted
Price range...Affordable
Style...Casual
Cuisine...Japanese Izakaya
Recommended for...................Regular neighborhood

"A casual Japanese *kushiage/izakaya* joint that's open until 4.00 a.m. It's somewhat of a chef's after-work hangout."—David Lai

This compact Causeway Bay *izakaya* (formerly Hidden Kitchen) tucked away in a nondescript commercial building keeps chef-friendly hours (open until 4.30 a.m. most nights; 2.00 a.m. when they close 'early') and specializes in *kushiage* (deep-fried skewers). Grab a pew at the ten-seat counter and try sticks of whiting wrapped in Japanese chervil and scallops topped with salmon eggs. Elsewhere on the menu there's family-style heartiness to dishes such as firefly squid in miso and bowls of udon, all of which go well with one of the best shochu selections in town.

HO HUNG KEE CONGEE & NOODLE
Recommended by
Mirco Keller

500 Hennessy Road
Causeway Bay
Hong Kong 999077
+852 25776060

Opening hours	Open 7 days
Credit cards	Accepted
Price range	Budget
Style	Casual
Cuisine	Cantonese
Recommended for	Worth the travel

"The best congee in the world."—Mirco Keller

ICHIRAN RAMEN
Recommended by
Ricardo Chaneton

Lockhart House
Block A, 440 Jaffe Road
Causeway Bay
Hong Kong 999077
+852 21524040
www.ichiran.com

Opening hours	Open 7 days
Reservation policy	No
Credit cards	Accepted
Price range	Affordable
Style	Casual
Cuisine	Japanese
Recommended for	Late night

KOZY OKONOMI-YAKI TEPPAN-YAKI
Recommended by
Ricardo Chaneton,
Vicky Cheng

Circle Plaza
499 Hennessy Road
Causeway Bay
Hong Kong 999077
+852 2591 1281

Opening hours	Closed Sunday
Credit cards	Accepted but not AMEX
Price range	Affordable
Style	Casual
Cuisine	Japanese
Recommended for	Late night

"This is a restaurant I enjoy going to a lot after service, as they're open late—they serve arguably the best *okonomiyaki* (savory pancakes) in the city and it's always good fun."—Vicky Cheng

PARADISE OF KING ASIA SEAFOOD
Recommended by
Jowett Yu

31–35 Tang Lung Street
Causeway Bay
Hong Kong 999077
+852 25730552

Opening hours	Open 7 days
Credit cards	Accepted but not AMEX
Price range	Affordable
Style	Casual
Cuisine	Hot Pot
Recommended for	Late night

"It's opens late and often hosts the city's chef community. Expect live frogs, chicken testicles, and super fresh geoduck sashimi!"—Jowett Yu

SE WONG YEE
Recommended by
Yau Tim Lai

24 Percival Street
Causeway Bay
Hong Kong 999077
+852 28310163

Opening hours	Open 7 days
Reservation policy	No
Credit cards	Not accepted
Price range	Budget
Style	Casual
Cuisine	Cantonese
Recommended for	Bargain

SUSHI GIN
Recommended by
Chan Yau Leung

38 Yiu Wah Street
Causeway Bay
Hong Kong 999077
+852 21511888

Opening hours	Open 7 days
Credit cards	Accepted
Price range	Expensive
Style	Smart casual
Cuisine	Japanese
Recommended for	High end

"Sushi Gin serves *omakase* with high quality raw fish. The chef also uses interesting combinations to bring out different flavors instead of just traditional soy sauce."—Chan Yau Leung

121 BC

Recommended by
Shane Osborn

42–44 Peel Street
Central
Hong Kong 999077
+852 23950200
www.121bc.com.hk

Opening hours	Closed Sunday
Credit cards	Accepted
Price range	Affordable
Style	Casual
Cuisine	Italian
Recommended for	Regular neighborhood

"Simple, delicious Italian fare, with everything made in house. Interesting wine list specializing in natural and biodynamic wines."—Shane Osborn

8¹/₂ OTTO E MEZZO BOMBANA

Recommended by
Donald Berger,
Guillaume Galliot, Lori Granito,
Albert Au Kwok Keung,
Yau Tim Lai

Alexandra House
18 Chater Road
Central
Hong Kong 999077
+852 25378859
www.ottoemezzobombana.com

Opening hours	Closed Sunday
Credit cards	Accepted
Price range	Expensive
Style	Smart casual
Cuisine	Italian
Recommended for	High end

"A three-Michelin-starred standout in Hong Kong from an unpretentious chef. Bombana's heart comes through in every delicious bite."—Lori Granito

AMBER

Recommended by
Matt Abergel,
Ricardo Chaneton,
Vicky Cheng, Lori Granito,
Kwok Keung Tung, Filip Langhoff,
Uwe Opocensky, Shane Osborn,
Julien Royer, Ebbe Vollmer

The Landmark Mandarin Oriental
15 Queen's Road
Central
Hong Kong 999077
+852 21320066
www.amberhongkong.com

Opening hours	Open 7 days
Credit cards	Accepted
Price range	Expensive
Style	Smart casual
Cuisine	Modern French
Recommended for	High end

"Arguably Hong Kong's number one restaurant."
—Shane Osborn

BELON

Recommended by
Matt Abergel, May Chow,
Shane Osborn, Jowett Yu

41 Elgin Street
Central
Hong Kong 999077
+852 21522872
www.belonsoho.com

Opening hours	Closed Monday
Credit cards	Accepted
Price range	Expensive
Style	Casual
Cuisine	French
Recommended for	High end

"Amazing, Parisian-style neo-bistro that serves the very best French food in the city. The pigeon pithivier, foie gras torchon, and stuffed chicken wings are an exercise in excellence. There's also a comprehensive natural wine list."—Jowett Yu

BRUNCH CLUB

Recommended by
Ricardo Chaneton

70 Peel Street
Central
Hong Kong 999077
+852 25268861
www.brunch-club.org

Opening hours	Seven days
Credit cards	Accepted
Price range	Affordable
Style	Casual
Cuisine	International
Recommended for	Breakfast

"Comfort food in a cozy environment."
—Ricardo Chaneton

BURGER CIRCUS

Recommended by
Lori Granito

22 Hollywood Road
Central
Hong Kong 999077
+852 28787787
www.burgercircus.com.hk

Opening hours	Open 7 days
Reservation policy	No
Credit cards	Accepted but not AMEX
Price range	Affordable
Style	Casual
Cuisine	American
Recommended for	Late night

CAFÉ CAUSSETTE

Recommended by
Timothy Johnson

Mandarin Oriental Hotel
5 Connaught Road Central
Central
Hong Kong 999077
+852 28254005
www.mandarinoriental.com/hongkong

Opening hours	Open 7 days
Credit cards	Accepted
Price range	Affordable
Style	Casual
Cuisine	International
Recommended for	Breakfast

CAPRICE

Recommended by
Ricardo Chaneton,
Lori Granito

Four Seasons Hotel
8 Finance Street
Central
Hong Kong 999077
+852 31968888
www.fourseasons.com/hongkong/dining/restaurants/caprice

Opening hours	Open 7 days
Credit cards	Accepted
Price range	Expensive
Style	Smart Casual
Cuisine	French
Recommended for	High end

CELEBRITY CUISINE

Recommended by
Matt Abergel, Umberto Bombana,
Richard Ekkebus

Lan Kwai Fong Hotel
3 Kau U Fong
Central
Hong Kong 999077
+852 36500066
www.lankwaifonghotel.com.hk

Opening hours	Open 7 days
Credit cards	Accepted but not AMEX
Price range	Affordable
Style	Casual
Cuisine	Cantonese
Recommended for	Local favorite

"Great, classic Cantonese cuisine with a slightly more delicate touch. Perfect dim sum and the best crispy-skinned chicken."—Matt Abergel

THE CHAIRMAN

Recommended by
Matt Abergel, May Chow,
Richard Ekkebus

18 Kau U Fong
Central
Hong Kong 999077
+852 25552202
www.thechairmangroup.com

Opening hours	Open 7 days
Credit cards	Accepted
Price range	Expensive
Style	Smart casual
Cuisine	Cantonese
Recommended for	Local favorite

"Cantonese food at its finest choosing; the best ingredients executed with precision and care."
—May Chow

CHINA TANG

Recommended by
Ricardo Chaneton,
Albert Au Kwok Keung

Landmark Atrium
15 Queen's Road
Central
Hong Kong 999077
+852 25222148
www.chinatang.hk

Opening hours	Open 7 days
Credit cards	Accepted
Price range	Expensive
Style	Smart casual
Cuisine	Chinese
Recommended for	Local favorite

CIAK—IN THE KITCHEN

Recommended by
Umberto Bombana

Landmark Atrium
15 Queen's Road
Central
Hong Kong 999077
+852 25228869
www.ciakconcept.com

Opening hours	Open 7 days
Credit cards	Accepted
Price range	Affordable
Style	Casual
Cuisine	Italian
Recommended for	Regular neighborhood

DUDDELL'S

1 Duddell Street
Central
Hong Kong 999077
+852 25259191
www.duddells.co

Recommended by
Morgan McGlone

Opening hours	Open 7 days
Credit cards	Accepted
Price range	Expensive
Style	Smart casual
Cuisine	Chinese
Recommended for	Worth the travel

FINEPRINT ESPRESSO & LIQUOR

38 Peel Street
Central
Hong Kong 999077
+852 55036880

Recommended by
Shane Osborn

Opening hours	Open 7 days
Credit cards	Accepted but not Amex
Price range	Affordable
Style	Casual
Cuisine	Modern Australian
Recommended for	Breakfast

"Excellent coffee with simple breakfast items such as smashed avocado on sourdough."—Shane Osborn

THE FLYING PAN

9 Old Bailey Street
Central
Hong Kong 999077
+852 21406333
www.the-flying-pan.com

Recommended by
Lori Granito

Opening hours	Open 7 days
Credit cards	Accepted but not AMEX
Price range	Affordable
Style	Casual
Cuisine	European
Recommended for	Breakfast

GODENYA

182 Wellington Street
Central
Hong Kong 999077
www.godenya.com

Recommended by
David Lai

Opening hours	Closed Monday and Sunday
Credit cards	Accepted
Price range	Expensive
Style	Smart casual
Cuisine	Japanese
Recommended for	High end

"Consistently booked two months ahead, this place matches rare sake with an ultra seasonal Japanese menu, with local inspirations."—David Lai

HO LEE FOOK

1–5 Elgin Street
Central
Hong Kong 999077
+852 28100860
www.holeefookhk.tumblr.com

Recommended by
Matt Abergel, Ricardo Chaneton

Opening hours	Open 7 days
Credit cards	Accepted
Price range	Affordable
Style	Casual
Cuisine	Modern Cantonese
Recommended for	Local favorite

"Jowett Yu has managed to create a restaurant that really reflects Hong Kong today. He is genuinely knowledgeable and capable of interpreting classic Cantonese dishes while using the best ingredients he can source."—Matt Abergel

KAU KEE RESTAURANT

21 Gough Street
Central
Hong Kong 999077
+852 28505967

Recommended by
Ricardo Chaneton, David Lai,
Uwe Opocensky, Shane Osborn,
Mango Tsang Chiu Lit

Opening hours	Closed Sunday
Reservation policy	No
Credit cards	Not accepted
Price range	Budget
Style	Casual
Cuisine	Cantonese
Recommended for	Bargain

"This place serves probably the best beef brisket noodles in town. Incredibly good value too."
—Shane Osborn

LIN HEUNG TEA HOUSE

Recommended by
Yau Tim Lai

162 Wellington Street
Central
Hong Kong 999077
+852 25444556
www.linheung.com.hk

Opening hours	Open 7 days
Credit cards	Accepted but not AMEX
Price range	Affordable
Style	Casual
Cuisine	Cantonese
Recommended for	Breakfast

For the quintessential Hong Kong breakfast, start the day with dim sum at this famously hectic old teahouse on Wellington Street. Tables are packed back to back, while carts are stacked dangerously high with bamboo steamers. There's no host, so seat yourself and chase down a trolley with your tally card for old-fashioned treats like steamed pork meatball with quail's egg and steamed Chinese sponge cake (*mai lai gou*).

LUK YU TEAHOUSE

Recommended by
Chan Yau Leung

24-26 Stanley Street
Central
Hong Kong 999077
+852 25235464
www.lukyuteahouse.com

Opening hours	Open 7 days
Credit cards	Accepted
Price range	Affordable
Style	Casual
Cuisine	Dim Sum
Recommended for	Local favorite

LUNG KING HEEN

Recommended by
Matt Abergel, Guillaume Galliot,
Morgan McGlone, Jowett Yu

Four Seasons Hotel
8 Finance Street
Central
Hong Kong 999077
+852 31968880
www.fourseasons.com/hongkong

Opening hours	Open 7 days
Credit cards	Accepted
Price range	Expensive
Style	Smart casual
Cuisine	Cantonese
Recommended for	Local favorite

"The only place where such a high level of Cantonese food is equally complemented by perfect service.

Everything you eat here just makes you feel good about Chinese cuisine and all the beautiful tradition and history behind it."—Matt Abergel

M BAR

Recommended by
Yannick Alléno

Mandarin Oriental
5 Connaught Road
Central
Hong Kong 999077
+852 28254002
www.mandarinoriental.com/hongkong

Opening hours	Open 7 days
Reservation policy	No
Credit cards	Accepted
Price range	Affordable
Style	Smart casual
Cuisine	Bar-Small plates
Recommended for	Late night

"The view from M Bar is stunning."—Yannick Alléno

MAK'S NOODLE

Recommended by
David Lai, Shane Osborn

77 Wellington Street
Central
Hong Kong 999077
+852 28543810

Opening hours	Open 7 days
Reservation policy	No
Credit cards	Not accepted
Price range	Budget
Style	Casual
Cuisine	Noodles
Recommended for	Regular neighborhood

"I usually order the plain noodles with green onions and ginger, and a side of *gai lan* (Chinese broccoli). The soup is complex without the usual load of MSG, and everything is cooked perfectly and consistently."
—David Lai

Good things come in small packages and the tiny bowls of almost legendary wonton noodle soup served here are no exception. Originating from Guangzhou, the recipe is unique—the tiny dumplings are packed with succulent shrimps and served with a tangle of noodles in a savoury broth. The dish's success has spawned multiple outlets in Hong Kong (as well as Singapore and Macau) but the Wellington Road flagship remains popular with returning regulars. Be prepared to order at least two or more bowls to fill up.

MAN WAH

Recommended by
Richard Ekkebus

Mandarin Oriental Hong Kong
5 Connaught Road
Central
Hong Kong 999077
+852 28254003
www.mandarinoriental.com/hongkong

Opening hours	Open 7 days
Credit cards	Accepted
Price range	Expensive
Style	Smart casual
Cuisine	Asian
Recommended for	High end

MERCEDES ME STORE

Recommended by
Bjoern Alexander Panek

Entertainment Building
30 Queen's Road
Central
Hong Kong 999077
+852 28957398
www.mercedes-benz.com/hk

Opening hours	Open 7 days
Credit cards	Accepted
Price range	Expensive
Style	Smart casual
Cuisine	Spanish-Asian
Recommended for	Breakfast

"It's a beautiful spot, and the Spanish-influence food is very tasty."—Bjoern Alexander Panek

SANG KEE CONGEE SHOP

Recommended by
Richard Ekkebus

7–9 Burd Street
Central
Hong Kong 999077
+852 25411099

Opening hours	Closed Sunday
Reservation policy	No
Credit cards	Not accepted
Price range	Budget
Style	Casual
Cuisine	Congee
Recommended for	Breakfast

"For a great, authentic congee, this is probably one of the best places to go to. This simple Chinese eatery has nothing in the way of glitzy design or elegant ambience but it serves some excellent congees at a very affordable price. Variations include: pig's-heart, chicken, dried-scallop or fish-belly congee."
—Richard Ekkebus

SHUI KEE

Recommended by
Eunmi Choi

2 Gutzlaff Street
Central
Hong Kong 999077
+852 25419769

Opening hours	Closed Sunday
Credit cards	Not accepted
Price range	Budget
Style	Casual
Cuisine	Hot Pot
Recommended for	Breakfast

"They serve amazingly aromatic offal noodle soups—the heady mix of lungs, tripe, liver, and heart is incredible. And the streetside stools give a truly authentic Hong Kong experience."—Eunmi Choi

SOCIAL PLACE

Recommended by
Lee Wolen

The L. Place
139 Queen's Road
Central
Hong Kong 999077
+852 35689666
www.socialplace.hk

Opening hours	Open 7 days
Credit cards	Accepted but not AMEX
Price range	Affordable
Style	Casual
Cuisine	Chinese
Recommended for	Breakfast

"Contemporary Chinese cuisine with a modern, healthy and unique twist. Great for a late brunch."
—Lee Wolen

SUN YUEN

Recommended by
Yau Tim Lai

327–329 Queen's Road
Central
Hong Kong 999077
+852 25412207

Opening hours	Open 7 days
Reservation policy	No
Credit cards	Not accepted
Price range	Budget
Style	Casual
Cuisine	Cantonese Barbecue
Recommended for	Regular neighborhood

TA VIE

Recommended by
Kwok Keung Tung, David Lai

The Pottinger
74 Queen's Road
Central
Hong Kong 999077
+852 26686488
www.tavie.com.hk

Opening hours	Closed Sunday
Credit cards	Accepted
Price range	Expensive
Style	Smart casual
Cuisine	French-Japanese
Recommended for	Wish I'd opened

"The husband and wife team pours their heart and soul into this gem of a place. The personalized service and attention to detail is impressive. Of course the food is amazing!"—David Lai

Chef Hideaki Sato brings the high art of French-Japanese dining to an appreciative audience at his gloriously quaint, yet austere, outfit at the Pottinger Hotel. A disciple of the famed Seiji Yamamoto (of Nihonryori Ryugin in Tokyo), Sato-san was executive chef at Yamamoto's Tenku Ryugin Hong Kong before leaving to set up his own place. While still anchored in modernist *kaiseki* (Japanese multi-course dinner), Sato has developed a strong repertoire of dishes in his eight-course tasting menu. His signature dish of sweetcorn mousse with botan shrimp and shrimp broth jelly is a French-Japanese hybrid that speaks of aesthetic eloquence and sheer umami. What's not to like?

TARTINE

Recommended by
Lee Wolen

38 Lyndhurst Terrace
Central
Hong Kong 999077
+852 28080752
www.hk.thetartine.com

Opening hours	Closed Monday
Credit cards	Accepted
Price range	Affordable
Style	Casual
Cuisine	French
Recommended for	Breakfast

TSIM CHAI KEE NOODLE SHOP

Recommended by
Matt Abergel

98 Wellington Street
Central
Hong Kong 999077
+852 28506471

Opening hours	Open 7 days
Reservation policy	No
Credit cards	Not accepted
Price range	Budget
Style	Casual
Cuisine	Cantonese
Recommended for	Bargain

VEA

Recommended by
Ricardo Chaneton

198 Wellington Street
Central
Hong Kong 999077
+852 27118639
www.vea.hk

Opening hours	Closed Sunday
Credit cards	Accepted
Price range	Expensive
Style	Smart casual
Cuisine	French
Recommended for	High end

WAGYU

Recommended by
Lori Granito

60 Wyndham Street
Central
Hong Kong 999077
+852 25258805
www.casteloconcepts.com/our-venues/wagyu

Opening hours	Open 7 days
Credit cards	Accepted
Price range	Affordable
Style	Casual
Cuisine	Steakhouse-International
Recommended for	Regular neighborhood

"This is where you'd go if you don't want any surprises. Consistent food and service in an atmosphere that works well for both business lunches and casual dinners."—Lori Granito

YAT LOK

34–38 Stanley Street
Central
Hong Kong 999077
+852 25243882

Recommended by
Vicky Cheng, May Chow,
Richard Ekkebus, David Lai,
Jowett Yu

Opening hours..Open 7 days
Reservation policy..No
Credit cards..Not accepted
Price range...Affordable
Style..Casual
Cuisine..Cantonese
Recommended for....................Regular neighborhood

"It's some of the best roasted goose in Hong Kong.
Get a quarter goose and a bowl of noodles!"
—May Chow

YUET WAH WUI SEAFOOD RESTAURANT

Recommended by
Yau Tim Lai

Chung Wai Comm
447–449 Lockhart Road
Central
Hong Kong 999077
+852 23949928

Opening hours..Open 7 days
Credit cards..Not accepted
Price range...Affordable
Style..Casual
Cuisine..Cantonese
Recommended for..Late night

"Excellent seafood."—Yau Tim Lai

YUNG KEE

32–40 Wellington Street
Central
Hong Kong 999077
+852 25221624
www.yungkee.com.hk

Recommended by
Lori Granito

Opening hours..Open 7 days
Credit cards..Accepted
Price range...Affordable
Style..Casual
Cuisine..Cantonese
Recommended for....................................Local favorite

"Classic Cantonese dishes, delicious roast goose!"
—Lori Granito

TASTY CONGEE AND NOODLES

21 King Kwong Street
Happy Valley
Hong Kong 999077
+852 28383922
www.tasty.com.hk

Recommended by
David Lai

Opening hours..Open 7 days
Credit cards..Accepted
Price range...Affordable
Style..Casual
Cuisine..Cantonese
Recommended for....................................Local favorite

"Tasty Congee and Noodles covers a lot of ground in
terms of the variety of traditional, local comfort food.
It's not the cheapest but the quality is consistent and
good."—David Lai

BUTCHER AND BAKER CAFE

57–59 Cadogan Street
Kennedy Town
Hong Kong 999077
+852 25910328
www.casteloconcepts.com/our-venues/butcher-and-
baker-cafe-kennedy-town

Recommended by
Lori Granito

Opening hours..Open 7 days
Credit cards..Accepted
Price range...Affordable
Style..Casual
Cuisine..International
Recommended for..Breakfast

"Family friendly breakfast spot with a children's play
area at the back. You can watch their butcher making
home-made sausages and there's a sweet florist stand
at the front of the restaurant."—Lori Granito

SUN HING RESTAURANT

8 Smithfield Road
Kennedy Town
Hong Kong 999077
+852 28160616

Recommended by
Matt Abergel, Jowett Yu

Opening hours..Open 7 days
Credit cards..Not accepted
Price range...Affordable
Style..Casual
Cuisine..Cantonese
Recommended for..Breakfast

"This place opens at 3.00 a.m. and essentially has two
types of customers: drunk students and senior citizens

waking up. Everything is self-serve, including tea, tableware and dim sum. It may not be the best in the city, but it's definitely the most authentic Hong Kong experience. Not to mention, it's cheap and delicious."—Jowett Yu

SUN KWAI HEUNG

Recommended by
David Lai

345 Chai Wan Road
Kennedy Town
Hong Kong 999077

Opening hours	Seven days
Credit cards	Not accepted
Price range	Affordable
Style	Casual
Cuisine	Hong Kong BBQ
Recommended for	Bargain

"Their Hong Kong BBQ items are some of the best in the city, in particular the *char siu* (roast pork in a sweet and savory sauce) and pork ribs."—David Lai

LAMMA RAINBOW

Recommended by
Ricardo Chaneton

23–25 First Street
Sok Kwu Wan
Lamma Island
Hong Kong 999077
+852 29828100
www.lammarainbow.com

Opening hours	Open 7 days
Credit cards	Accepted
Price range	Affordable
Style	Casual
Cuisine	Seafood
Recommended for	Local favorite

HOOKED

Recommended by
Shane Osborn

80-88 Caine Road
Mid-Levels
Hong Kong 999077
+852 29151118
www.hooked.hk

Opening hours	Closed Monday
Reservation policy	No
Credit cards	Not accepted
Price range	Budget
Style	Casual
Cuisine	Fish and Chips
Recommended for	Bargain

"Fish and chip shop serving the best chips in Hong Kong. Perfect after a few beers."—Shane Osborn

TUNG PO

Recommended by
Ricardo Chaneton, Uwe Opocensky

99 Java Road
North Point
Hong Kong 999077
+852 28805224

Opening hours	Open 7 days
Credit cards	Not accepted
Price range	Affordable
Style	Casual
Cuisine	Chinese
Recommended for	Local favorite

MR AND MRS FOX

Recommended by
Shane Osborn

23 Tong Chong Street
Quarry Bay
Hong Kong 999077
+852 26978500
www.mrmrsfox.com

Opening hours	Open 7 days
Credit cards	Accepted
Price range	Affordable
Style	Casual
Cuisine	European
Recommended for	Breakfast

KWAN KEE CLAYPOT RICE

Recommended by
Jowett Yu

Wo Yick Mansion
253-263 Queen's Road West
Sai Ying Pun
Hong Kong 999077
+852 28037209

Opening hours	Open 7 days
Credit cards	Not accepted
Price range	Budget
Style	Casual
Cuisine	Cantonese
Recommended for	Bargain

SHING KEE NOODLES

Recommended by
Chan Yau Leung

Shop 5, Lek Yuen Estate Market
Shatin
Hong Kong 999077
+852 26926611

Opening hours	Open 7 days
Credit cards	Not accepted
Price range	Affordable
Style	Casual
Cuisine	Hot Pot
Recommended for	Bargain

ON LEE NOODLE

Recommended by
Kwok Keung Tung

22 Shau Kei Wan Main Street East
Shau Kei Wan
Hong Kong 999077
+852 25138398

Opening hours	Closed Thursday
Credit cards	Not accepted
Price range	Budget
Style	Casual
Cuisine	Noodles
Recommended for	Bargain

RHODA

Recommended by
Uwe Opocensky

345 Des Voeux Road West
Shek Tong Tsui
Hong Kong 999077
+852 21775050
www.rhoda.hk

Opening hours	Open 7 days
Reservation policy	No
Credit cards	Accepted
Price range	Affordable
Style	Casual
Cuisine	European
Recommended for	Regular neighborhood

"Beautiful open-fire cooking; honest food at a great restaurant."—Uwe Opocensky

208 DUECENTTO OTTO

Recommended by
Lori Granito

208 Hollywood Road
Sheung Wan
Hong Kong 999077
+852 25490208
www.208.com.hk

Opening hours	Open 7 days
Credit cards	Accepted
Price range	Affordable
Style	Casual
Cuisine	Italian
Recommended for	Regular neighborhood

"Above average Italian restaurant using high quality ingredients. Fantastic Happy Hour and lunch."
—Lori Granito

CHACHAWAN

Recommended by
Bjoern Alexander Panek

206 Hollywood Road
Sheung Wan
Hong Kong 999077
+852 25490020

Opening hours	Open 7 days
Reservation policy	No
Credit cards	Accepted
Price range	Affordable
Style	Smart casual
Cuisine	Isaan Thai
Recommended for	Late night

"I love Thai food and this is the perfect place for a quick night-time snack. Great location too."
—Bjoern Alexander Panek

CORNER KITCHEN CAFÉ

Recommended by
Lori Granito

226 Hollywood Road
Sheung Wan
Hong Kong 999077
+852 25478008
www.cornerkitchencafe.com

Opening hours	Open 7 days
Reservation policy	No
Credit cards	Accepted
Price range	Affordable
Style	Casual
Cuisine	International
Recommended for	Breakfast

DIM SUM SQUARE

Recommended by
May Chow

27 Hilier Street
Sheung Wan
Hong Kong 999077
+852 28518088
www.dimsumsquare.com.hk

Opening hours	Open 7 days
Reservation policy	No
Credit cards	Not accepted
Price range	Budget
Style	Casual
Cuisine	Cantonese
Recommended for	Breakfast

"Cheap but great quality dim sum place that opens early."—May Chow

FOR KEE

Recommended by
Lori Granito

200 Hollywood Road
Sheung Wan
Hong Kong 999077
+852 25468947

Opening hours	Closed Sunday
Credit cards	Not accepted
Price range	Budget
Style	Casual
Cuisine	Noodles
Recommended for	Bargain

"They've managed to keep the local flavor, even though the neighborhood around them has become gentrified. Best pork chop noodles in town! And yes, the 'guard cat' sleeping outside (or inside) is normal!"—Lori Granito

FRANTZÉN'S KITCHEN

Recommended by
Julius Jaspers

11 Upper Station Street
Sheung Wan
Hong Kong 999077
+852 25598508
www.frantzenskitchen.com

Opening hours	Closed Monday and Sunday
Credit cards	Accepted
Price range	Affordable
Style	Smart casual
Cuisine	Nordic-Asian
Recommended for	Wish I'd opened

"Great menu-concept and superb flavors out of a tiny kitchen. Very knowledgable and friendly staff too!"—Julius Jaspers

RŌNIN

Recommended by
Jonnie Boer, Ben Greeno,
Corey Lee, Jowett Yu

8 On Wo Lane
Sheung Wan
Hong Kong 999077
+852 25475263
www.roninhk.com

Opening hours	Closed Sunday
Credit cards	Accepted
Price range	Expensive
Style	Casual
Cuisine	Japanese
Recommended for	Late night

"If I dreamed up a small, intimate restaurant that served tasty, modern, Japanese-inspired food—and great highballs—this would be it."—Corey Lee

YARDBIRD

Recommended by
Jonnie Boer, Ricardo Chaneton,
Gert de Mangeleer, Richard Ekkebus,
David Lai, Uwe Opocensky,
Mitch Orr, Shane Osborn,
Frankie Van Loo

33–35 Bridges Street
Sheung Wan
Hong Kong 999077
www.yardbirdrestaurant.com

Opening hours	Closed Sunday
Credit cards	Accepted
Price range	Affordable
Style	Casual
Cuisine	Japanese
Recommended for	Late night

"The best chicken yakitori you'll ever have! Super simple concept but done so well."—Frankie Van Loo

BING KEE

Recommended by
Chan Yau Leung

5 Shepherd Street
Tai Hang
Hong Kong 999077
+852 25773117

Opening hours	Closed Monday
Reservation policy	No
Credit cards	Not Accepted
Price range	Affordable
Style	Casual
Cuisine	Hong Kongese
Recommended for	Breakfast

"This is a *dai pai dong* (tea stall) serving decadent toast, with butter and condensed milk."
—Chan Yau Leung

AS YOU LIKE RESTAURANT

Recommended by
May Chow

Fasteem Mansion
307–311 Jaffe Road
Wan Chai
Hong Kong 999077
+852 28912787

Opening hours	Open 7 days
Credit cards	Accepted but not AMEX
Price range	Affordable
Style	Casual
Cuisine	Szechuan
Recommended for	Late night

"Known for their Sichuan chicken hot pot. It's spicy and numbing, and great with beers and friends."
—May Chow

DIMDIMSUM DIM SUM SPECIALTY

Recommended by
Richard Ekkebus

7 Tin Lok Lane
Wan Chai
Hong Kong 999077
+852 28917677
www.dimdimsum.hk

Opening hours	Open 7 days
Credit cards	Not accepted
Price range	Affordable
Style	Casual
Cuisine	Cantonese
Recommended for	Local favorite

BO INNOVATION

Recommended by
Igles Corelli, Anita Lo,
Bjoern Alexander Panek

J Senses Entrance on Ship Street
60 Johnston Road
Wan Chai
Hong Kong 999077
+852 28508371
www.boinnovation.com

Opening hours	Closed Sunday
Credit cards	Accepted
Price range	Expensive
Style	Smart casual
Cuisine	Modern Chinese
Recommended for	Worth the travel

"Every time I am in Hong Kong I go to Alvin Leung's restaurant, Bo Innovation. His high-tech approach fused with traditional Asian cooking methods results in creative dishes that you will definitely remember."—Igles Corelli

GIANDO

Recommended by
Andrea Bonaffini

Tower 1, Starcrest
9 Star Street
Wan Chai
Hong Kong 999077
+852 25118912
www.giandorestaurant.com

Opening hours	Open 7 days
Credit cards	Accepted
Price range	Expensive
Style	Casual
Cuisine	Modern Italian
Recommended for	Local favorite

"One of my favorite restaurants in the world, the food here warms my soul."—Andrea Bonaffini

KAM FUNG CAFÉ

Recommended by
Vicky Cheng

Spring Garden Mansion
41 Spring Garden Lane
Wan Chai
Hong Kong 999077
+852 25720526

Opening hours	Open 7 days
Reservation policy	No
Credit cards	Not accepted
Price range	Budget
Style	Casual
Cuisine	Chinese Café
Recommended for	Breakfast

OLD BAZAAR KITCHEN

Recommended by
Albert Au Kwok Keung

32–38 Cross Lane
Wan Chai
Hong Kong 999077
+852 28711993
www.oldbazaarkitchen.com

Opening hours	Closed Sunday
Credit cards	Accepted
Price range	Affordable
Style	Casual
Cuisine	Asian
Recommended for	Wish I'd opened

PASSION BY GERARD DUBOIS

Recommended by
Kwok Keung Tung

Lee Tung Avenue
200 Queen's Road East
Wan Chai
Hong Kong 999077
+852 28336778
www.passionbygd.com

Opening hours	Open 7 days
Reservation policy	No
Credit cards	Accepted but not AMEX
Price range	Expensive
Style	Casual
Cuisine	Café-Patisserie
Recommended for	Breakfast

SAMSEN

Recommended by
Jowett Yu

68 Stone Nullah Lane
Wan Chai
Hong Kong 999077
+852 22340001

Opening hours	Closed Sunday
Credit cards	Accepted but not AMEX
Price range	Affordable
Style	Casual
Cuisine	Thai Street Food
Recommended for	Wish I'd opened

SE WONG SUN

Recommended by
Vicky Cheng

Fortune Mansion
10–12 Cross Street
Wan Chai
Hong Kong 999077
+852 28916639

Opening hours	Open 7 days
Reservation policy	No
Credit cards	Not accepted
Price range	Budget
Style	Casual
Cuisine	Snake
Recommended for	Regular neighborhood

Mention the word 'snake' and most will squirm and shudder, but in Hong Kong, the locals are sometimes known to consider it more of a delicacy than a danger. This hole-in-the-wall-style eatery, buried deep in Wan Chai, is one of just a handful of places that still serve up snake, and it attracts quite a queue. They all come for the exotic menu of hearty snake dishes like snake bisque, snake broth and snake belly claypot rice with fish maw. Turtle soup is also on the Chinese-only menu in case you're not quite brave enough to try the main attraction.

SEVENTH SON RESTAURANT

Recommended by
Kwok Keung Tung,
David Lai

The Wharney Guang Dong Hotel
57–73 Lockhart Road
Wan Chai
Hong Kong 999077
+852 28922888
www.seventhson.hk

Opening hours	Open 7 days
Credit cards	Accepted
Price range	Expensive
Style	Smart casual
Cuisine	Cantonese
Recommended for	Local favorite

SISTER WAH

Recommended by
Matt Abergel

13 Electric Road
Wan Chai
Hong Kong 999077
+852 28070181

Opening hours	Open 7 days
Reservation policy	No
Credit cards	Not accepted
Price range	Budget
Style	Casual
Cuisine	Cantonese
Recommended for	Bargain

"Their beef brisket noodles—with a side of boiled radish—are expertly crafted and never dissapoint."
—Matt Abergel

WAH LAM NOODLE RESTAURANT

Recommended by
Vicky Cheng

5–11 Thomson Road
Wan Chai
Hong Kong 999077
+852 25272478

Opening hours	Open 7 days
Reservation policy	No
Credit cards	Not accepted
Price range	Budget
Style	Casual
Cuisine	Noodles
Recommended for	Late night

WING WAH NOODLE SHOP

Recommended by
Lori Granito

89 Hennessy Road
Wan Chai
Hong Kong 999077
+852 25277476

Opening hours	Closed Sunday
Reservation policy	No
Credit cards	Not accepted
Price range	Affordable
Style	Casual
Cuisine	Noodles
Recommended for	Late night

"**The best-loved Korean street food, served twenty four hours a day.**"
JUNGSIK YIM P234

"Korean Italian foods made with local ingredients."
KANG MIN-GOO P236

SEOUL

"THIS RESTAURANT HAS BEEN SERVING CUSTOMERS FOR THIRTY YEARS AND IS FAMOUS FOR ITS NOODLES AND DUMPLINGS."
KIM BYUNG-JIN P240

"*Simply fantastic.*"
ALFREDO RUSSO P238

"REFINED ROYAL KOREAN CUISINE. PERFECTION."
KANG MIN-GOO P239

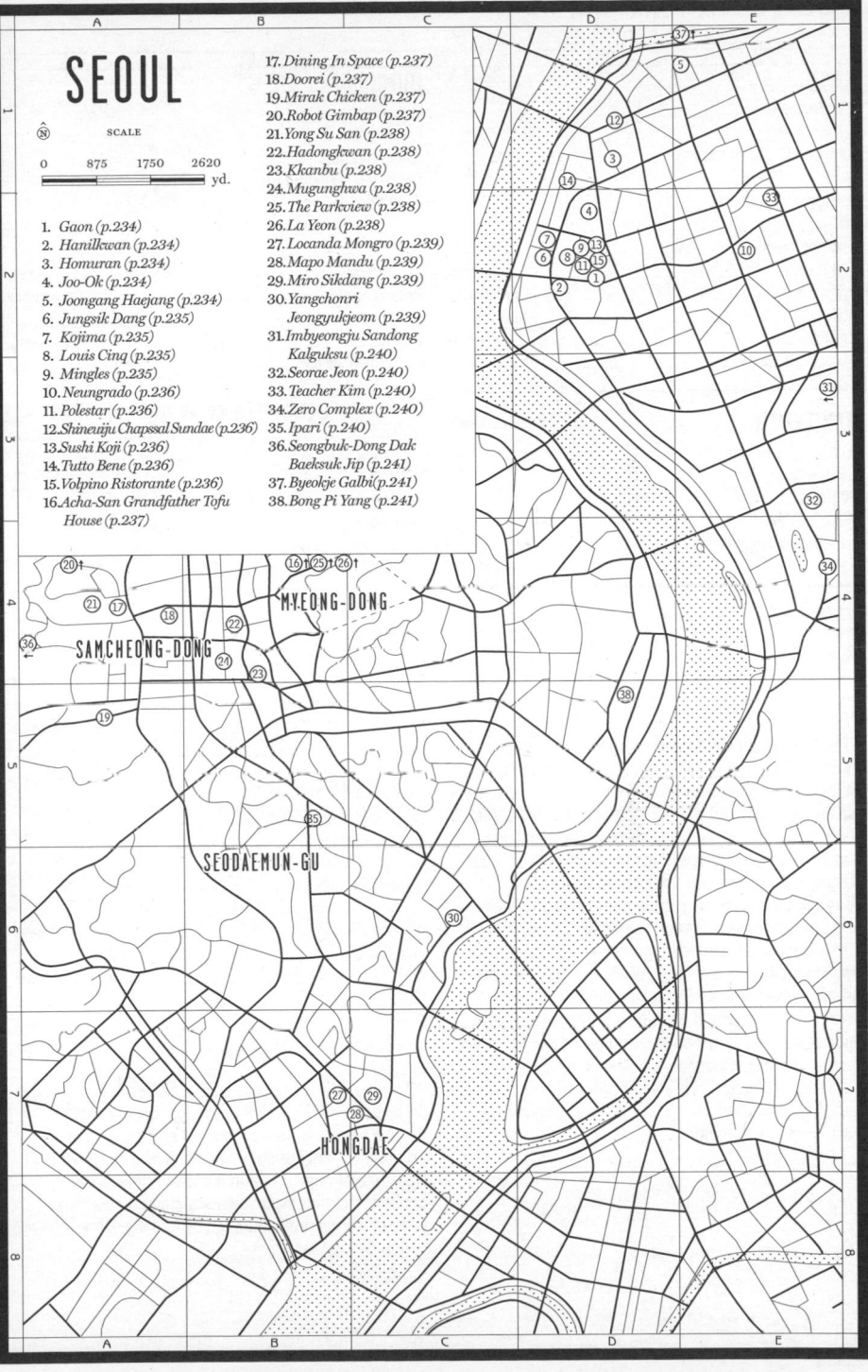

SEOUL

N̂

SCALE

0   875   1750   2620
|___|___|___|___| yd.

MYEONG-DONG

SAMCHEONG-DONG

SEODAEMUN-GU

HONGDAE

GAON

Recommended by
Kristian Baumann

317 Dosan-daero
Gangnam-gu
Seoul 6021, South Korea
+82 254598456
www.gaonkr.com

Opening hours	Closed Sunday
Credit cards	Accepted
Price range	Expensive
Style	Smart casual
Cuisine	Korean
Recommended for	Worth the travel

HANILKWAN

Recommended by
Kim Byung-jin

619-4 Shinsa-dong
Gangnam-gu
Seoul 6023, South Korea
+82 15779963
www.hanilkwan.co.kr

Opening hours	Open 7 days
Credit cards	Accepted
Price range	Affordable
Style	Smart casual
Cuisine	Korean
Recommended for	Local favorite

"This restaurant has been around for over seventy years and serves typical Seoul cuisine. A method for quickly cooking marinated slices of grilled beef (which was a royal food out of the reach of ordinary people for a long time) was developed here and Hanilkwan has established the reputation for itself as the Korean restaurant that brought 'bulgogi' to the masses. Bulgogi is prepared by cutting beef into thin slices and seasoning with a sweet soy-based sauce. The slices are then marinated together in broth and cooked on a special cooking plate. Bulgogi has now become popular in everyday Korean life, but when I was young, we would only eat it in restaurants on special days, such as holidays and birthdays. This dish remains in my memory as a food that my family would eat when we were sharing good times with each other and, for this reason, Hanilkwan is a place I like to visit." —Kim Byung-jin

HOMURAN

Recommended by
Eunmi Choi

Hakdong-ro 87 gil
Cheongdam-dong
Gangnam-gu
Seoul 6074, South Korea
+82 269471279

Opening hours	Open 7 days
Credit cards	Accepted but not AMEX
Price range	Affordable
Style	Casual
Cuisine	Japanese
Recommended for	Regular neighborhood

"Honest-to-goodness Japanese food."—Eunmi Choi

JOO-OK

Recommended by
Kang Min-goo

52-7 Seolleung-ro 148 gil
Gangnam-gu
Seoul 6064, South Korea
+82 25189393

Opening hours	Open 7 days
Credit cards	Accepted
Price range	Expensive
Style	Smart casual
Cuisine	Modern Korean
Recommended for	Local favorite

JOONGANG HAEJANG

Recommended by
Kim Byung-jin

17 Yeongdong-daero 86 gil
Gangnam-gu
Seoul 6174, South Korea
+82 25587905

Opening hours	Open 7 days
Credit cards	Accepted but not AMEX
Price range	Affordable
Style	Casual
Cuisine	Korean
Recommended for	Late night

"Open twenty-four hours a day, this restaurant focuses on its soup menu, which uses high-quality cuts of Korean beef. It is a place where I enjoy eating and drinking with my team or with friends after finishing work late at night. Though it doesn't boast fancy cooking techniques, it stakes its claim on the true taste of Korean beef supplied by Majang-Dong." —Kim Byung-jin

JUNGSIK DANG

11 Seollungro 158 gil
Gangnam-gu
Seoul 6018, South Korea
+82 25174654
www.jungsik.kr

Opening hours	Open 7 days
Credit cards	Accepted
Price range	Expensive
Style	Smart casual
Cuisine	Modern Korean
Recommended for	High end

"The food not only tastes good but also looks beautiful as the plating here is special."—Eunmi Choi

The flag-bearer for new Korean cuisine since opening in 2009, this envelope-pushing Cheongdam destination is driven by the vision of its chef-proprietor Jung Sikdang, who trained in New York at the Culinary Institute of America. He updates Hansik (traditional Korean cooking) with new techniques and ideas, such as his bibimbap with sea squirt and fried millet, and a kimchi and seaweed purée in place of traditional gochujang paste. His success at stretching the boundaries of Korean food has earned him international acclaim, spawned a second outpost in New York, and inspired a new generation of young Korean chefs.

KOJIMA

6F Boon the shop, 21 Apgujeong-ro 60-gil
Gangnam-gu
Seoul 6072, South Korea
+82 220561291
www.kojima.modoo.at

Opening hours	Closed Sunday
Credit cards	Accepted
Price range	Affordable
Style	Casual
Cuisine	Sushi
Recommended for	High end

"The quality is comparable to sushi on the Japanese mainland."—Jun Lee

LOUIS CINQ

33 Seolleung-ro 157 gil
Gangnam-gu
Seoul 6018, South Korea
+82 25471259

Opening hours	Closed Sunday
Credit cards	Accepted
Price range	Affordable
Style	Casual
Cuisine	French
Recommended for	Regular neighborhood

"A favorite place in Korea for chefs to gather and drink after work."—Kang Min-goo

It calls itself a gastropub, but this cheery eatery in Apgujeong is known more to locals as a French bistro with the odd Spanish influence and a progressive culinary approach. Chef-owner Lee You-suk cut his teeth at multiple establishments in France (including Astrance in Paris) and trained as a butcher in Spain. These experiences come together on his menu, where familiar favorites like onion soup and terrine mingle with small plates like Spanish jamon. Try 'The Fat Duck 2.0'—*confit de canard* (preserved duck) with foie gras and potatoes.

MINGLES

1F, 94-9 Nonhyun-dong
Gangnam-gu
Seoul 6064, South Korea
+82 25157306
www.restaurant-mingles.com

Opening hours	Closed Sunday
Credit cards	Accepted
Price range	Expensive
Style	Smart casual
Cuisine	Modern Korean
Recommended for	Worth the travel

Although a relative newcomer, this Gangnam eatery by Kang Min-goo has won enough accolades to earn a place alongside Jungsik on Seoul's fine-dining circuit. Its haute *hansik* (Korean cuisine) takes inspiration from his time as head chef of Nobu Bahamas and marries the culinary influences of Europe (he worked under Martín Berasategui in Spain) with his respect for Korea's culinary heritage. It's no surprise that fermentation serves as the cornerstone of this neo-Korean cuisine. The dish that embodies Kang's philosophy is the *jang* (Korean sauces) trio dessert: *doen-jang* (soybean paste), *gan-jang* (soy sauce), and *gochu-jang* (red chile paste).

NEUNGRADO

Recommended by
Kang Min-goo

655-12 Yeoksam-dong
Gangnam-gu
Seoul 6137, South Korea
+82 25698939
www.neungrado.modoo.at

Opening hours	Open 7 days
Credit cards	Accepted
Price range	Affordable
Style	Casual
Cuisine	Korean
Recommended for	Bargain

"North-Korean-style cold-noodle soup—you can
enjoy a fantastic meal for just 10 bucks."
—Kang Min-goo

POLESTAR

Recommended by
Jun Lee

10-11 Dosan-daero 45 gil
Gangnam-gu
Seoul 6020, South Korea
+82 25143450

Opening hours	Open 7 days
Reservation policy	No
Credit cards	Accepted
Price range	Expensive
Style	Smart casual
Cuisine	Bar
Recommended for	Wish I'd opened

"This classic bar has an appropriately high-quality
feel."—Jun Lee

SHINEUIJU CHAPSSAL SUNDAE

Recommended by
Jun Lee

68-7 Cheongdam-dong
Gangnam-gu
Seoul 6072, South Korea
+82 25119081

Opening hours	Open 7 days
Credit cards	Accepted but not AMEX
Price range	Affordable
Style	Casual
Cuisine	Korean
Recommended for	Bargain

"This restaurant is just in front of my house and I can
eat a hearty meal here for only 8,000 Korean won."
—Jun Lee

SUSHI KOJI

Recommended by
Jun Lee

1st Building, 2F, Cheongdam-dong 1-1
56 Dosan-daero
Gangnam-gu
Seoul 6062, South Korea
+82 25416200
www.sushikoji.co.kr

Opening hours	Open 7 days
Credit cards	Accepted
Price range	Affordable
Style	Smart casual
Cuisine	Sushi
Recommended for	Regular neighborhood

"Offers a comfortable atmosphere."—Jun Lee

TUTTO BENE

Recommended by
Kang Min-goo

118-9 Cheongdam-dong
Apgujeong-ro 77 gil
Gangnam-gu
Seoul 6011, South Korea
+82 25461489

Opening hours	Open 7 days
Credit cards	Accepted but not AMEX
Price range	Affordable
Style	Casual
Cuisine	Italian
Recommended for	Wish I'd opened

"Korean Italian food made with local ingredients."
—Kang Min-goo

VOLPINO RISTORANTE

Recommended by
Eunmi Choi

10-7 Dosan-daero 45 gil
Sinsa-dong
Gangnam-gu
Seoul 6021, South Korea
+82 1022491571

Opening hours	Open 7 days
Credit cards	Accepted but not AMEX
Price range	Affordable
Style	Smart casual
Cuisine	Italian
Recommended for	Regular neighborhood

"I like the atmosphere here."—Eunmi Choi

ACHA-SAN GRANDFATHER TOFU HOUSE

143-2 Gueui-dong
Gwangjin-gu
Seoul 4957, South Korea

Recommended by
Tony Yoo

Opening hours	Open 7 days
Reservation policy	No
Credit cards	Not accepted
Price range	Budget
Style	Casual
Cuisine	Tofu
Recommended for	Bargain

"It is a restaurant that makes tofu on the spot. The menu only has two items, tofu K5,000 ($4; £3) and soft tofu K3,000 ($3; £2), but I like the simple taste made from domestically produced beans."—Tony Yoo

DINING IN SPACE

Arario Museum in SPACE 5F
83 Yulgok-ro
Jongno-gu
Seoul 3059, South Korea
+82 27478105
www.arariomuseum.org

Recommended by
Kim Byung-jin

Opening hours	Closed Sunday
Credit cards	Accepted
Price range	Expensive
Style	Smart casual
Cuisine	French
Recommended for	High end

"This restaurant, with one Michelin star, is a place in which to relax and enjoy the elegant views of Changdeok Palace while visiting the Araria Museum. Thanks to its modern French dishes and the skill and experience of the staff, diners can focus on the essence of the ingredients used without being distracted by undue decoration."—Kim Byung-jin

DOOREI

8-7 Insa-dong
Jongno-gu
Seoul 3133, South Korea
+82 27322919
www.foodsidae.com/dure

Recommended by
Tony Yoo

Opening hours	Open 7 days
Credit cards	Accepted but not AMEX
Price range	Affordable
Style	Casual
Cuisine	Korean
Recommended for	Local favorite

"This is a traditional restaurant that has been operating for sixty years over two generations. There aren't that many old Korean restaurants in Seoul and I like the taste of its food and atmosphere, both of which have depth that comes with longevity."—Tony Yoo

MIRAK CHICKEN

17-1 Jahamun-ro
Jongno-gu
Seoul 3022, South Korea
+82 27366741

Recommended by
Eunmi Choi

Opening hours	Open 7 days
Credit cards	Accepted
Price range	Affordable
Style	Casual
Cuisine	Korean
Recommended for	Late night

"This snack bar serves fried chicken with a thin and crispy batter, which is the kind of food that Koreans enjoy as a late night meal."—Eunmi Choi

It's fried chicken galore at this dimly lit, old-fashioned pub where Korean fried chicken fans make a beeline for the star dish of garlic chicken (fried chicken soaked in a sweet glaze alongside a heaping pile of garlic cloves). Should the garlicky notes prove a little overwhelming, patrons routinely fall back on the crisp and moist regular fried chicken. Of course, don't forget to knock back a jug of beer to keep the palate refreshed.

ROBOT GIMBAP

246 Changgyeonggung-ro
Jongno-gu
Seoul 3194, South Korea
+82 236747991

Recommended by
Eunmi Choi

Opening hours	Open 7 days
Reservation policy	No
Credit cards	Accepted but not AMEX
Price range	Affordable
Style	Casual
Cuisine	Korean-Street Food
Recommended for	Bargain

"It's cheap and serves healthy food."—Eunmi Choi

YONG SU SAN

Recommended by
Eunmi Choi

2 Changdeokgung 1 gil
Jongno-gu
Seoul 3057, South Korea
+82 27435999
www.yongsusan.co.kr

Opening hours	Open 7 days
Credit cards	Accepted
Price range	Affordable
Style	Smart casual
Cuisine	Korean
Recommended for	Local favorite

"One of the first refined traditional Korean restaurants. You can experience classic Korean dishes here, and Changdeokgung, the old royal palace, is nearby."—Eunmi Choi

HADONGKWAN

Recommended by
Choonghu Lee, Kang Min-goo,
Jungsik Yim

10-4 Myeong-dong 1 ga
Jung-gu
Seoul 4534, South Korea
+82 27765656
www.hadongkwan.com

Opening hours	Open 7 days
Reservation policy	No
Credit cards	Accepted
Price range	Affordable
Style	Casual
Cuisine	Korean
Recommended for	Breakfast

"Hadongkwan specializes in *gomtang* (traditional Korean beef soup with rice) and is one of the oldest restaurant in Seoul. The soup tastes simple and is easy to eat for breakfast."—Choonghu Lee

KKANBU

Recommended by
Jungsik Yim

68-7 Taepyungno 2 ga
Jung-gu
Seoul 4526, South Korea
+82 27779282
www.kkanbu.co.kr

Opening hours	Open 7 days
Credit cards	Accepted
Price range	Affordable
Style	Casual
Cuisine	Korean
Recommended for	Late night

"Korean's all time favorite is fried chicken—and this company make the best!"—Jungsik Yim

MUGUNGHWA

Recommended by
Alfredo Russo

Lotte Hotel
38F, 30 Eulji-ro
Jung-gu
Seoul 4533, South Korea
+82 27711000
www.lottehotel.com/seoul

Opening hours	Open 7 days
Credit cards	Accepted
Price range	Expensive
Style	Smart casual
Cuisine	Modern Korean
Recommended for	Worth the travel

"Simply fantastic."—Alfredo Russo

THE PARKVIEW

Recommended by
Tony Yoo

The Shilla Seoul
249 Dongho-ro
Jung-gu
Seoul 4606, South Korea
+82 222303374
www.shilla.net

Opening hours	Open 7 days
Credit cards	Accepted
Price range	Expensive
Style	Smart casual
Cuisine	International
Recommended for	Breakfast

"You can enjoy substantial and diverse food in a warm atmosphere."—Tony Yoo

LA YEON

Recommended by
Kang Min-goo, Jungsik Yim

The Shilla Seoul
23F, 249 Dongho-ro
Jung-gu
Seoul 4606, South Korea
+82 222303367
www.shilla.net

Opening hours	Open 7 days
Credit cards	Accepted
Price range	Expensive
Style	Smart casual
Cuisine	Korean
Recommended for	Local favorite

"Refined royal Korean cuisine. Perfection."
—Kang Min-goo

Seoul may now be littered with Michelin-star restaurants but none serves up a view as enviable as this contemporary Korean stronghold perched on the twenty-third floor of The Shilla hotel. Befitting the grandeur of its location, the setting is decidedly austere—hushed surrounds, starched tablecloths, exquisite tableware—but this sets the tone for the restaurant's tasting menu-only appreciation of Hansik. Under the guiding hands of head chef Kim Sung II, Korean culinary traditions and seasonal local ingredients are masterfully melded with modernity to produce dishes like bibimbap (a Korean rice dish) served in a stone bowl with Korean abalone.

LOCANDA MONGRO

Recommended by
Kang Min-goo

18 Jandari-ro 7 gil
Mapo-gu
Seoul 3994, South Korea
+82 231448767

Opening hours	Closed Sunday
Credit cards	Accepted
Price range	Affordable
Style	Casual
Cuisine	Italian-Korean
Recommended for	Late night

MAPO MANDU

Recommended by
Jungsik Yim

393-1 Seogyo-dong
Mapo-gu
Seoul 4035, South Korea
+82 23339842

Opening hours	Open 7 days
Reservation policy	No
Credit cards	Not accepted
Price range	Budget
Style	Casual
Cuisine	Korean-Street Food
Recommended for	Bargain

"The best-loved Korean street food, served twenty-four hours a day."—Jungsik Yim

MIRO SIKDANG

Recommended by
Tony Yoo

52 Eoulmadang-ro 5 gil
Mapo-gu
Seoul 3978, South Korea
+82 23263777

Opening hours	Closed Monday and Sunday
Reservation policy	No
Credit cards	Accepted but not AMEX
Price range	Affordable
Style	Casual
Cuisine	Korean
Recommended for	Late night

"Delicious Korean snacks."—Tony Yoo

Situated a stone's throw away from Hongik University, this home-style Korean *izakaya* (Japanese-style pub) draws a healthy crowd of young adults with its no-frills menu of small plates. Scallion (spring onion) pancake and Korean beef tartare are served up with a shots of alcohol—*soju* or *makgeolli* (Korean rice liquor), your choice. Reservations aren't permitted, so come early.

YANGCHONRI JEONGYUKJEOM

Recommended by
Jungsik Yim

50-1 Yonggang-dong
Mapo-gu
Seoul 4164, South Korea
+82 27010455

Opening hours	Open 7 days
Reservation policy	No
Credit cards	Not accepted
Price range	Budget
Style	Casual
Cuisine	Korean-Barbeque
Recommended for	Local favorite

IMBYEONGJU SANDONG KALGUKSU

Recommended by
Kim Byung-jin

1365 Seocho 2-dong
Seocho-gu
Seoul 6735, South Korea
+82 0234737972

Opening hours	Open 7 days
Credit cards	Accepted but not AMEX
Price range	Affordable
Style	Casual
Cuisine	Korean
Recommended for	Bargain

"This restaurant has been serving customers for around thirty years and is famous for noodles and dumplings. I often come here with my wife on Sundays for brunch thanks to the exquisite combination of the texture of the freshly prepared noodles and refreshing clam soup. The spicy and sweet kimchi on the side adds to the taste of the noodles."—Kim Byung-jin

SEORAE JEON

Recommended by
Choonghu Lee, Jun Lee

76-4 Banpo-dong
Seocho-gu
Seoul 6577, South Korea

Opening hours	Closed Sunday
Reservation policy	No
Credit cards	Accepted but not AMEX
Price range	Budget
Style	Casual
Cuisine	Korean-Bar
Recommended for	Late night

"Their Makgeolli (a Korean alcoholic beverage, made from rice or wheat mixed with Nuruk) and *jeon* (Korean pancakes) are fantastic. I like to visit there with my colleagues after work."—Choonghu Lee

TEACHER KIM

Recommended by
Jun Lee

LG Seocho Eclat
1F, 71 Banpo-daero 14-gil
Seocho-gu
Seoul 6670, South Korea
+82 18001525
www.teacherkim.co.kr

Opening hours	Open 7 days
Reservation policy	No
Credit cards	Accepted but not AMEX
Price range	Budget
Style	Casual
Cuisine	Gimbap
Recommended for	Breakfast

"It's comfort food, but they pay close attention to the ingredients and the menu. Gimbap (or kimbap) is a Korean dish made from steamed white rice and various other ingredients, rolled in sheets of dried seaweed and served in bite-size slices. It is similar to sushi roll slices, but often contains meat and/or vegetables instead of fish."—Jun Lee

ZERO COMPLEX

Recommended by
Jun Lee

2F, 113 Donggwang-ro
Seocho-gu
Seoul 6589, South Korea
+82 25320876

Opening hours	Closed Monday and Sunday
Credit cards	Accepted
Price range	Affordable
Style	Casual
Cuisine	Neo-Bistro
Recommended for	Local favorite

"This is one of the restaurants that most resembles the atmosphere of Seorae Village and it does not adhere to fads."—Jun Lee

Given the free-style French gastronomy that it brings to Seoul, perhaps it's apt that this 'bistronomy' by chef-owner Lee Choong Hu is located in Seorae Village, Seoul's 'Little France' neighborhood. Yet there is nothing classically French about its uber-chic, steel-and-concrete-clad interior. Here, Lee's light, minimalist, and boundary-pushing plates are gaining approval from the food-loving crowd and a taste of his smoked beef tartare with pimento rice crackers is all it takes to get you on his side.

IPARI

Recommended by
Kang Min-goo

4 Yeonhui mat-ro 2F
Seodaemun-gu
Seoul 3628, South Korea
+82 1043326221

Opening hours	Closed Sunday
Credit cards	Accepted but not AMEX
Price range	Affordable
Style	Casual
Cuisine	Korean
Recommended for	Late night

"Enjoy authentic Korean food late at night."
—Kang Min-goo

SEONGBUK-DONG DAK BAEKSUK JIP

9 Seongbuk-ro 31 gil
Seongbuk-gu
Seoul 2878, South Korea

Recommended by
Eunmi Choi

Opening hours	Open 7 days
Reservation policy	No
Credit cards	Not accepted
Price range	Budget
Style	Casual
Cuisine	Traditional Korean
Recommended for	Breakfast

"Serves Korean traditional dishes such as dumplings
and *kalguksu* (noodles) served in beef-bone soup."
—Eunmi Choi

BYEOKJE GALBI

205-8 Bangi-dong
Songpa-gu
Seoul 5541, South Korea
+82 24155522
www.ibjgalbi.com

Recommended by
Kang Min-goo

Opening hours	Open 7 days
Credit cards	Accepted
Price range	Expensive
Style	Smart casual
Cuisine	Korean Barbeque
Recommended for	High end

"The best Korean beef."—Kang Min-goo

BONG PI YANG

16-9 Ichon-ro 75 gil
Yongsan-Gu
Seoul 4422, South Korea
+82 24155527
www.bonpiyang.modoo.at

Recommended by
Kim Byung-jin, Choonghu Lee

Opening hours	Open 7 days
Credit cards	Accepted but not AMEX
Price range	Affordable
Style	Casual
Cuisine	Naengmyeon, BBQ
Recommended for	Regular neighborhood

"Bon Pi Yang, which is owned and developed as
a second brand by Byeokje Galbi, focuses on a menu
of pork ribs and Pyeongyang-style cold noodles.
I am from Gangweon province, where a lot of food
is prepared with buckwheat. The food at Bon Pi Yang
connects me to my father and I eat it when I miss
him or when I am tired."—Kim Byung-jin

JAPAN

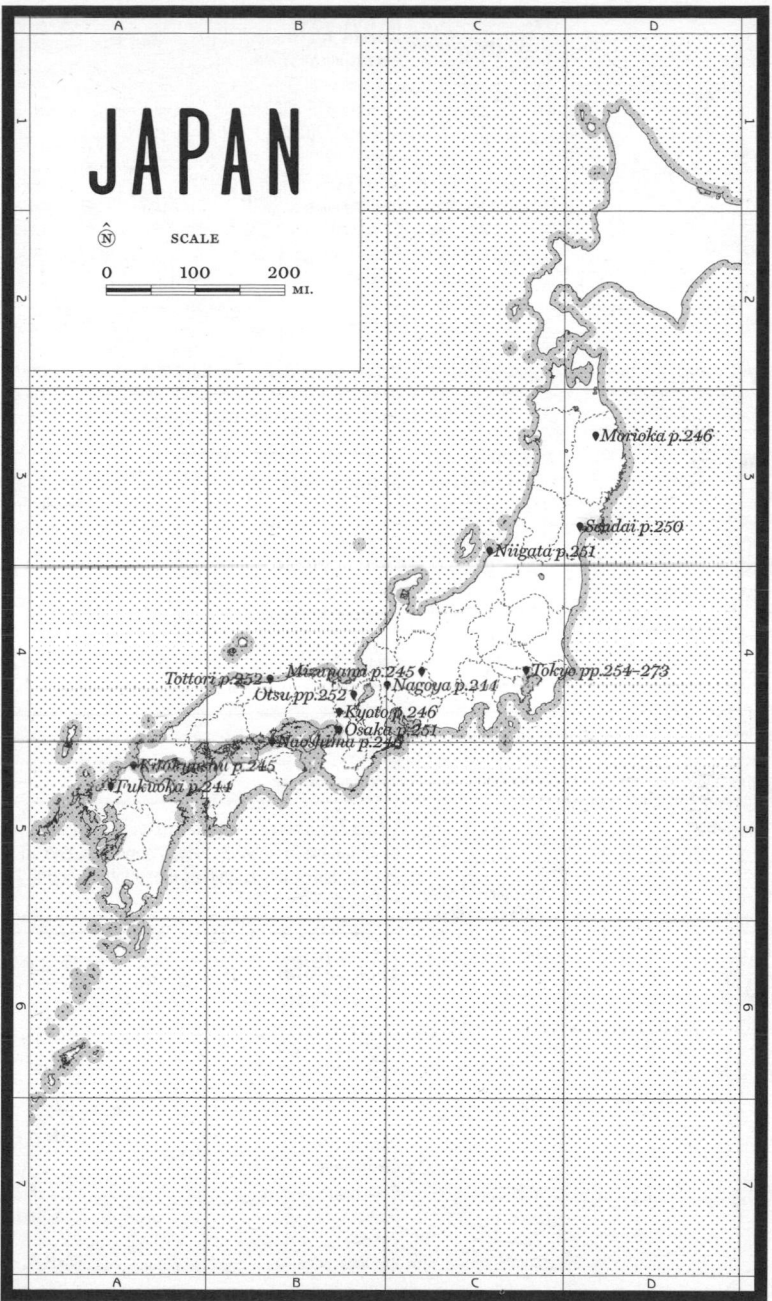

JAPAN

Morioka p.246

Sendai p.250

Niigata p.251

Tottori p.252   Mizunami p.245
Otsu pp.252   Nagoya p.214   Tokyo pp.254–273
Kyoto p.246
Osaka p.251
Naoshima p.248
Kitakyushu p.245
Fukuoka p.244

Ñ   SCALE

0   100   200
                    MI.

A   B   C   D

1   2   3   4   5   6   7

ONOMICHI

7-43 Haruokatori
Chikusa-ku
Nagoya
Aichi 464-0847
+81 527630703

Opening hours	Closed Monday
Credit cards	Accepted
Price range	Expensive
Style	Casual
Cuisine	Steakhouse
Recommended for	Worth the travel

"There is only one chef, but the braised beef tongue is superb."—Yong Bing Ngen

CHIKAMATSU

2-6-19 Yakuin
Chuo-ku
Fukuoka 810-0022
+81 927165855

Opening hours	Closed Monday
Credit cards	Accepted
Price range	Expensive
Style	Smart casual
Cuisine	Sushi
Recommended for	High end

"Everything about it is wonderful. I think it's one of the top sushi restaurants in Japan!"
—Takeshi Fukuyama

GYOTEN

Inoue
1F, 1-2-12 Hirao
Chuo-ku
Fukuoka 810-0014
+81 925212200

Opening hours	Open 7 days
Credit cards	Accepted but not Amex or Diners
Price range	Expensive
Style	Casual
Cuisine	Sushi
Recommended for	Worth the travel

HANYA KUTA

2-8 Nishinakasu
Chuo-ku
Fukuoka 810-0002
+81 927390102
www.ku-ta.net

Opening hours	Open 7 days
Credit cards	Accepted
Price range	Affordable
Style	Casual
Cuisine	Izakaya
Recommended for	Regular neighborhood

"You can eat delicious, fresh fish caught locally. Everything is delicious, whether it's sashimi, tempura, sushi, or meat."—Takeshi Fukuyama

MIHARA TOFUTEN

3-19 Nishinakasu
Chuo-ku
Fukuoka 810-0002
+81 927311108
www.miharatofu.jp

Opening hours	Closed Sunday
Credit cards	Accepted
Price range	Affordable
Style	Casual
Cuisine	Izakaya
Recommended for	Bargain

"It's a Japanese-style pub (*izakaya*) with a rich menu of Japanese food using tofu. It's modern and all the food is delicious, as well as reasonably priced!"
—Takeshi Fukuyama

SALA CARINA

3-35 Goshogadani
Chuo-ku
Fukuoka 810-0027
+81 925317722
www.salacarina.com

Opening hours	Closed Monday
Credit cards	Accepted
Price range	Expensive
Style	Smart casual
Cuisine	Italian
Recommended for	Wish I'd opened

"It's a stand-alone restaurant in a quiet, high-end residential area of Fukuoka. It offers delicious Italian cuisine and has a long history, but at the same time it's modern. I'd like to be that kind of restaurant, which has been loved by local people for many years."
—Takeshi Fukuyama

SHIN-SHIN

Recommended by
Takeshi Fukuyama

3-2-19 Tenjin
Chuo-ku
Fukuoka 810-0001
+81 927324006
www.hakata-shinshin.com

Opening hours	Closed Sunday
Credit cards	Not accepted
Price range	Budget
Style	Casual
Cuisine	Ramen noodles
Recommended for	Late night

"You can eat the Hakata (Fukuoka) specialty, *tonkotsu* ramen! Besides ramen, there's a wide-ranging menu including yakitori. You feel that you've really arrived in Fukuoka."—Takeshi Fukuyama

In Tokyo, it's sushi; but in Fukuoka, the foodie priority is Hakata-style *tonkotsu* (pork bone broth) ramen, which comes with a heap of thin noodles, slabs of *char siu* (barbecued pork) and scallions (spring onions) basking in a rich broth. While there are a plethora of ramen options dotted around the prefecture, this cash-only eatery located minutes away from Tenjin Station is a convenient stop after a jaunt to the nearby Oyafuku-dori entertainment district. They also serve a *goma* (sesame) ramen if you prefer your broth thick, black and strong.

YAKITORI HACHIBEI

Recommended by
Adam Byatt

1-4-27 Keigo
Chuo-ku
Fukuoka 810-0023
+81 927325379
www.hachibei.com

Opening hours	Open 7 days
Credit cards	Accepted
Price range	Affordable
Style	Casual
Cuisine	Yakitori
Recommended for	Worth the travel

"I took my family to this restaurant while on a recent trip to Japan. We gorged ourselves on incredible meat skewers, grilled over a first-rate charcoal stove, and

cooked by a chef who was so clearly at one with his grill. We all loved this restaurant, having been won over by both its vibe and food (especially the ramen and the chicken salad)."—Adam Byatt

CURRENT

Recommended by
Takeshi Fukuyama

2290 Shimanogita-Mukaibata
Itoshima
Fukuoka 819-1303
+81 923305789
www.bakeryrestaurantcurrent-2007.com

Opening hours	Closed Wednesday
Credit cards	Accepted
Price range	Affordable
Style	Casual
Cuisine	Bakery
Recommended for	Breakfast

"Eating breakfast while admiring the wonderful, expansive ocean view is the best!"—Takeshi Fukuyama

TENZUSHI

Recommended by
Takeshi Fukuyama,
Bruce Ricketts

3-11-9 Kyomach
Kokurakita-ku
Kitakyushu
Fukuoka 802-0002
+81 935215540

Opening hours	Closed Monday and Tuesday
Credit cards	Not accepted
Price range	Expensive
Style	Smart casual
Cuisine	Sushi
Recommended for	Worth the travel

"Amano-San makes sushi that gives me goosebumps. I find his *neta* (nigiri toppings) and the combinations of flavor very exciting and I still remember clearly how everything tasted during my first meal there."
—Bruce Ricketts

YANAGIYA

Recommended by
Kristian Baumann

573-27 Suechomachizume
Mizunami
Gifu 509-6361
+81 572652102

Opening hours	Open 7 days
Credit cards	Accepted
Price range	Expensive
Style	Smart casual
Cuisine	Japanese
Recommended for	Wish I'd opened

SUSHIDOKORO MEKUMI

4-48 Shimobayashi
Nonoichi
Ishikawa 921-8831
+81 762467781

Opening hours	Closed Monday and Tuesday
Credit cards	Accepted
Price range	Expensive
Style	Smart casual
Cuisine	Sushi
Recommended for	Worth the travel

"Amazing sushi master."—Yoshihiro Narisawa

Unlike the all-too-serious sushi-ya (sushi restaurant) joints dotted around Tokyo, this upscale sushi temple in Ishikawa serves the same top-notch sushi with the added bonus of a chance to chat with the chef. Apart from its conviviality, the biggest draw here is the bountiful array of regional seafood from Ishikawa and the adjoining Noto Peninsula. The most noteworthy example is the jumbo *botan ebi* (botan shrimp), with the tail served sashimi style, the shell grilled, and the body crafted into a nigiri complete with savory grains of *shari* (sushi rice). Thankfully, reservations are not that difficult to come by.

SUSHIKAISEKI JUBEI

14-2 Nagata-cho
Morioka
Iwate 020-0062
+81 196545235

Opening hours	Closed Sunday
Credit cards	Accepted
Price range	Affordable
Style	Casual
Cuisine	Japanese
Recommended for	Worth the travel

"It's absolutely superb during the early-September matsutake mushroom season."—Takuji Takahashi

RESTAURANT ISSEN

Benesse House Museum B1F
Naoshima
Kagawa 761-3110
+81 878923223
www.benesse-artsite.jp

Opening hours	Open 7 days
Credit cards	Accepted
Price range	Expensive
Style	Smart casual
Cuisine	Kaiseki
Recommended for	High end

"Oh my God—the setting, the art, and oh yes, the food! Classic *kaiseki* cuisine with fabulous ingredients. Would go back tomorrow in a flash—where's my sugar-daddy?"—Jean Beddington

TOKYO: SEE PAGES 254–273

CHINESE DINING KYOJUZEN

8-1 Benzaiten-cho
Higashiyama-ku
Kyoto 605-0086
+81 755259332

Opening hours	Closed Sunday
Credit cards	Not accepted
Price range	Budget
Style	Casual
Cuisine	Szechuan
Recommended for	Late night

"They're open until late, but the quality is still excellent."—Takuji Takahashi

GION MATAYOSHI

570-123 Gionmachi Minamigawa
Higashiyama-ku
Kyoto 605-0074
+81 755510117
www.gion-matayoshi.com

Opening hours	Open 7 days
Credit cards	Accepted
Price range	Expensive
Style	Smart casual
Cuisine	Kaiseki
Recommended for	Worth the travel

With only eight seats in the house, this is one *ryotei* (traditional and exclusive Japanese restaurant) that demands a fair bit of advanced planning. The good news is, those who bag a reservation at the kappo-style (multi-course, open-kitchen) counter are duly rewarded with a poetic *kyo-ryori* (traditional Kyoto cuisine) multi-course menu that changes with the season—think tilefish broth with grilled leek and jade tofu, steamed snow crab sushi, and if you're visiting in late spring, *hamo* (pike conger eel) and grilled *ayu* (sweetfish) treats.

GION NISHIKAWA

Recommended by
Yoshiaki Takazawa

473 Shimokawaracho
Higashiyama-ku
Kyoto 605-0825
+81 755251776
www.r.goope.jp/gion-nishikawa

Opening hours	Closed Monday and Sunday
Credit cards	Accepted
Price range	Expensive
Style	Smart casual
Cuisine	Kaiseki
Recommended for	Worth the travel

GION SASAKI

Recommended by
Yoshihiro Murata

566-27 Yasakadori
Higashiyama-ku
Kyoto 605-0811
+81 755515000
www.gion-sasaki.sakura.ne.jp

Opening hours	Closed Monday and Sunday
Credit cards	Accepted
Price range	Expensive
Style	Smart casual
Cuisine	Kappo
Recommended for	Wish I'd opened

"A theatrical-style restaurant in which the master chef takes center stage."—Yoshihiro Murata

This kappo-style (multi-course, open-kitchen) eatery by Hiroshi Sasaki is one of the hardest tables to book in Kyoto—and for good reason. Michelin stars aside, the seasonal, inventive *kaiseki* (traditional multi-course dinner) menu showcases Japanese seasonality in quaint antique vessels, with the added attraction of a thirty-foot (ten-meter) table made from a single piece of wood as the restaurant's centerpiece. In spring, diners look forward to dishes like stone-oven-grilled scallop with bamboo, lily bulbs, broad beans, and field mustard. If you don't have a generous budget, come at lunch—the affordable lunchtime *kaiseki* prices are hard to beat.

KIKUNOI

Recommended by
Gaggan Anand, Kyle Connaughton,
Tan Jason, Ross Lusted,
Hiro Sone

459 Shimokawara-cho
Higashiyama-ku
Kyoto 605-0825
+81 0755610015
www.kikunoi.jp

Opening hours	Open 7 days
Credit cards	Accepted but not Diners
Price range	Expensive
Style	Smart casual
Cuisine	Kaiseki-Kyotonese
Recommended for	Worth the travel

"Kikunoi's cuisine is known as 'Kyo-kaiseki' and draws on the rich traditions of Kyoto-style, multiple-course dining. Its seasonal approach, by the Master Chef Yoshihiro Murata, is so inspiring that it's a must for every chef to dine once in their life at his restaurant."—Gaggan Anand

MIZAI

Recommended by
Hajime Yoneda

Maruyama Park
613 Maruyama-cho
Higashiyama-ku
Kyoto 605-0071
+81 755513310
www.mizai.jp

Opening hours	Closed Wednesday
Credit cards	Not accepted
Price range	Expensive
Style	Smart casual
Cuisine	Kaiseki
Recommended for	High end

"He's the chef I most respect."—Hajime Yoneda

SOBA RYURYU SENKAKU

Recommended by
Yoshihiro Murata

Yasaka
1F, 10-2 Tsukimi-cho
Higashiyama-ku
Kyoto 605-0829
+81 755414815

Opening hours	Closed Wednesday
Credit cards	Not accepted
Price range	Budget
Style	Casual
Cuisine	Japanese
Recommended for	Regular neighborhood

"You can enjoy hand-made soba noodles."
—Yoshihiro Murata

YASUKAWA
Recommended by
Yoshihiro Murata

93 Yasaka Shinchisueyoshi-cho
Higashiyama-ku
Kyoto 605-0085
+81 755513390
www.oden-yasukawa.com

Opening hours	Closed Sunday
Credit cards	Not accepted
Price range	Affordable
Style	Smart casual
Cuisine	Japanese
Recommended for	Late night

"You can enjoy Kyoto *obanzai* cuisine, informally."
—Yoshihiro Murata

For a taste of Kyoto's home-style cooking, this Gion eatery is a must-visit; if only to savor the winter *oden* (one pot) dish of radish, fish cake, and boiled eggs, stewed in a dashi-flavored soy broth, and served with *karashi* (Japanese mustard). Of course, no Asian meal is complete without carbs and the Japanese fried-rice dish of *wafu* (Japanese dressing) pilaf with sardines is highly recommended. The opening hours (6.00 p.m. to 1.00 a.m.) make it appealing to nocturnal types.

MANKAMEROU
Recommended by
Takuji Takahashi

387 Ebisu-cho
Kamigyo-ku
Kyoto 602-8118
+81 754415020
www.mankamerou.com

Opening hours	Variable
Credit cards	Accepted
Price range	Expensive
Style	Smart casual
Cuisine	Kaiseki
Recommended for	Local favorite

ICHINOFUNAIRI
Recommended by
Yoshihiro Murata

537-50 Nijo-kudaru Ichinofunairi-cho
Nakagyo-ku
Kyoto 604-0924
+81 752561271
www.ichinohunairi.com

Opening hours	Closed Sunday
Credit cards	Accepted
Price range	Affordable
Style	Casual
Cuisine	Chinese
Recommended for	Bargain

INODA COFFEE
Recommended by
Takuji Takahashi

140 Douyuucho Sanjyo Sagaru
Nagakyo-ku
Kyoto 604-8118
+81 752410915
www.inoda-coffee.co.jp

Opening hours	Open 7 days
Credit cards	Accepted
Price range	Budget
Style	Casual
Cuisine	Café
Recommended for	Breakfast

Even with several outlets in Kyoto, this flagship store of the city's oldest coffee shop chain continues to draw the coffee-loving crowd. Perhaps it's the sense of history you get from the luxuriously decorated interior set in a traditional double-storey Kyoto building; or the immaculately dressed waiting staff, all of whom sport suits and bow ties. Or maybe it's simply the iconic coffee, pre-mixed with sugar and milk and paired with a menu of cakes and sandwiches, that keeps them packing in. Get your caffeine fix here.

LEC COURT
Recommended by
Takuji Takahashi

Kyoto Hotel Okura
1F, Kawaramachi-Oike
Nakagyo-ku
Kyoto 640-8558
+81 75-254-2517
www.okura.kyotohotel.co.jp

Opening hours	Open 7 days
Reservation policy	No
Credit cards	Accepted
Price range	Affordable
Style	Smart casual
Cuisine	French/International
Recommended for	Breakfast

"The French toast is delicious."—Takuji Takahashi

NAKAMURA

Recommended by
Yoshihiro Takahashi

Tominokoji Oike Sagaru
Nakagyo-ku
Kyoto 604-8093
+81 752215511
www.kyoryori-nakamura.com

Opening hours...Closed Sunday
Credit cards..Accepted
Price range...Expensive
Style...Smart casual
Cuisine...Kaiseki
Recommended for................................Regular neighborhood

"It has its own style and technique."
—Yoshihiro Takahashi

THE LOBBY LOUNGE

Recommended by
Luca Fantin

The Ritz-Carlton Kyoto
Kamogawa Nijo-Ohashi Hotori
Nakagyo-ku
Kyoto 604-0902
+81 757465522
www.ritzcarlton.com

Opening hours..Open 7 days
Credit cards..Accepted
Price range...Affordable
Style...Smart casual
Cuisine.......................International and Japanese breakfast
Recommended for...Breakfast

"Magic atmosphere and perfect quality of ingredients.
The croissant framboise is addictive."—Luca Fantin

YOSHOKU OGATA

Recommended by
Yoshihiro Murata

32-1 Tojijicho
Nakagyo-ku
Kyoto 604-0956
+81 752232230

Opening hours...Closed Tuesday
Credit cards..Accepted
Price range...Affordable
Style...Smart casual
Cuisine...Western
Recommended for..Local favorite

"You can enjoy genuine Japanese *yoshoku*
(Western-style) cuisine here."—Yoshihiro Murata

ZENKAFUKU

Recommended by
Takuji Takahashi

654 Karasuma-dori higashi-iri Inabado-cho
Nakagyo-ku
Kyoto 600-8009
+81 753446263

Opening hours...Closed Monday
Credit cards..Not accepted
Price range...Affordable
Style...Casual
Cuisine...Shanghaiese
Recommended for..Bargain

"You never tire of homely Chinese food such as
pot-braised Chinese mitten crab dumplings."
—Takuji Takahashi

HYOTEI

Recommended by
Kyle Connaughton,
Yoshihiro Murata,
Takuji Takahashi

35 Kusagawa-cho
Sakyo-ku
Kyoto 606-8437
+81 757714116
www.hyotei.co.jp

Opening hours...Closed Tuesday
Credit cards..Accepted
Price range...Expensive
Style...Smart casual
Cuisine...Kaiseki
Recommended for..Breakfast

"The building is equivalent to an important cultural
asset."—Takuji Takahashi

If you can't afford a *kaiseki* (traditional multi-
course) lunch or dinner at this 400-year-old former
teahouse near the temple of Nanzenji in Kyoto, at
least come here for breakfast. Yes, the price tag of
¥4,500 ($41; £33) for *asagayu* (breakfast rice
porridge) is by no means cheap but it's a fraction
of the lunch and dinner prices, plus breakfast is a
multi-course affair featuring numerous lacquered
trays and condiments including the century-old
signature Hyotei boiled egg. Still not convinced?
Perhaps the restaurant's recent designation as an
Intangible Cultural Property by the prefecture of
Kyoto will provide an added motivation for an
experiential breakfast there.

MIYAMASOU

375 Daihizan
Sakyo-ku
Kyoto 601-1102
+81 757460231
www.miyamasou.jp

Recommended by
Erchen Chang, Analiese Gregory,
Dan Hunter, James Lowe,
Shinobu Namae

Opening hours	Open 7 days
Credit cards	Accepted
Price range	Expensive
Style	Casual
Cuisine	Kaiseki
Recommended for	Worth the travel

"If you're already in Kyoto, make the two-hour drive out to this incredibly magical place. The food is inspiring and the setting is incredible."—James Lowe

SOUJIKI NAKAHIGASHI

32-3 Jodoji Ishibashi-cho
Sakyo-ku
Kyoto 606-8406
+81 757523500
www.soujiki-nakahigashi.co.jp

Recommended by
Kyle Connaughton,
Peter Gordon,
Jakob Mielcke

Opening hours	Closed Monday
Credit cards	Not accepted
Price range	Expensive
Style	Smart casual
Cuisine	Kaiseki
Recommended for	Worth the travel

"It is the best meal I've ever eaten. Mr Nakahigashi presided over everything and he and his team work in a beautifully calm, orchestrated way. The food is faultless and so local the fish is served with herbs picked from the same part of the river."
—Peter Gordon

OLD HONG KONG RESTAURANT KYOTO

620 Suiginya-cho
Shimogyo-ku
Kyoto 600-8411
+81 753411800
www.oldhongkong-kyoto.net

Recommended by
Takuji Takahashi

Opening hours	Open 7 days
Credit cards	Accepted
Price range	Expensive
Style	Smart casual
Cuisine	Chinese
Recommended for	Regular neighborhood

"I love that they telephone me when they've returned with some delicious ingredients from Hong Kong, such as garlic-sautéed large mantis shrimp with roe."
—Takuji Takahashi

TRATTORIA LEONE

Kyoto 1
1F, 295-1 Hanjo-cho
Shimogyo-ku
Kyoto 600-8433
+81 753513898
www.trattoria-leone.com

Recommended by
Takuji Takahashi

Opening hours	Closed Wednesday
Credit cards	Not accepted
Price range	Affordable
Style	Casual
Cuisine	Italian
Recommended for	Regular neighborhood

KYOTO KITCHO ARASHIYAMA

58 Sagatenryuji Susukinobaba-cho
Ukyo-ku
Kyoto 616-8385
+81 758811101
www.kyoto-kitcho.com

Recommended by
Yoshihiro Murata

Opening hours	Closed Wednesday
Credit cards	Accepted
Price range	Expensive
Style	Smart casual
Cuisine	Kaiseki
Recommended for	High end

"Colorful dishes in a calm space."—Yoshihiro Murata

HOKUSHIN-ZUSHI

1-1-1 Chuo
Aoba-ku
Sendai
Miyagi 980-0021
+81 222240170

Recommended by
Hiro Sone

Opening hours	Open 7 days
Reservation policy	No
Credit cards	Accepted
Price range	Affordable
Style	Casual
Cuisine	Sushi/Seafood
Recommended for	Bargain

"Located in Sendai train station. Huge selections of fish —about forty different kinds—always fresh; no seats; and a secret sake selection from Miyagi."—Hiro Sone

SENDAI RYOURI HOMMA

2-9-17 Kokubun-cho
Aoba-Ku
Sendai
Miyagi 980-0803
+81 222250125

Opening hours	Closed Sunday
Credit cards	Accepted
Price range	Affordable
Style	Smart casual
Cuisine	Modern Japanese
Recommended for	Worth the travel

"Impeccable tasting menu with local and seasonal ingredients from the woods and sea. They have a great passion for wild mushrooms and one of the signature dishes is made of ten different wild 'shrooms."
—Sami Tallberg

TSUBAKI

1981-1 Hanacho
Chuo-ku
Niigata 951-8056
+81 5055717921

Opening hours	Open 7 days
Credit cards	Accepted
Price range	Affordable
Style	Casual
Cuisine	Bistro
Recommended for	Worth the travel

"Good value for money. The beef is really worth looking out for, it has a very rich flavor and even marbling, but isn't fatty."—Ken Ling/Shaoquan Lin

CIUCATE

1-17-3 Kyomachibori
Nishi-ku
Osaka 550-0003
+81 664412202

Opening hours	Open 7 days
Credit cards	Not accepted
Price range	Affordable
Style	Casual
Cuisine	Italian
Recommended for	Late night

HAJIME RESTAURANT

1-9-11 1F Edobori
Nishi-ku
Osaka 550-0002
+81 664476688
www.hajime-artistes.com

Opening hours	Open 7 days
Credit cards	Accepted
Price range	Expensive
Style	Smart casual
Cuisine	French-Japanese
Recommended for	Worth the travel

To understand the visually stimulating French-Japanese cuisine on offer here, it's worth looking at the background of chef-owner Hajime Yoneda. A university graduate who worked as a computer engineer to save up for culinary school, Yoneda spent time as both a chef and an artist in France. One of his most iconic dishes is *Chikyu* (meaning "earth"), which features almost 100 varieties of vegetables, herbs, and grains artfully arranged on a cloud of savory clam foam; as much a feast for the eyes as it is for the palate. No wonder the restaurant won two Michelin stars within a year-and-a-half of opening.

HONKOGETSU

1-7-11 Dotonbori
Chuo-ku
Osaka 542-0071
+81 662110201

Opening hours	Closed Sunday
Credit cards	Accepted
Price range	Expensive
Style	Formal
Cuisine	Japanese
Recommended for	Local favorite

"One of the leading chefs of Japanese cuisine in Osaka."—Hajime Yoneda

Located in a cobblestone-paved street in the bustling Minami district, this Michelin-star restaurant offers one of the best *kaiseki* (traditional multi-course dinner) experiences in Osaka. Befitting the price, the setting is grand; a triple-storey house, with counter seats set against a 600-year-old cedar table on the ground floor, and traditionally decorated private rooms on the upper floors. Open only for dinner, there is one menu on offer: *omakase* (chef's choice), where zen plates feature in-season vegetables and seafood, matched with signature dishes like *karasumi* (salted mullet roe) sandwiched in *mochi* (Japanese rice cake).

KADOYA SHOKUDO

Recommended by
Hajime Yoneda

Capital Nishinagahori
1F, 4-16-13 Shinmachi
Nishi-ku
Osaka 550-0013
+81 665353633

Opening hours	Closed Tuesday
Reservation policy	No
Credit cards	Not accepted
Price range	Budget
Style	Casual
Cuisine	Ramen noodles
Recommended for	Bargain

"They make wonderful ramen."—Hajime Yoneda

NORTHSHORE

Recommended by
Hajime Yoneda

Biruma
1/2F, 1-1-28 Kitahama
Chuo-ku
Osaka 541-0041
+81 647076668
www.northshore-hanafru.com

Opening hours	Variable
Credit cards	Accepted
Price range	Affordable
Style	Casual
Cuisine	Café
Recommended for	Breakfast

PASANIA

Recommended by
Hajime Yoneda

Nakanoshima Dai
3F, 3-3-23 Nakanoshima
Kita-Ku
Osaka 530-6103
+81 662257464
www.pasania.osaka

Opening hours	Closed Wednesday
Credit cards	Accepted
Price range	Expensive
Style	Casual
Cuisine	Japanese
Recommended for	Regular neighborhood

"You can enjoy choice wines and the Osaka local specialities of *okonomiyaki* (savory pancakes) and *yakisoba* (stir-fried noodles)."—Hajime Yoneda

HIRASANSOU

Recommended by
Takuji Takahashi,
Yoshiaki Takazawa

94 Katsuragawabomura-cho
Otsu
Shiga 520-0475
+81 775992058
www.hirasansou.com

Opening hours	Closed Tuesday
Credit cards	Accepted but not Diners
Price range	Expensive
Style	Smart casual
Cuisine	Kaiseki
Recommended for	Worth the travel

"You can enjoy cuisine that uses local ingredients from deep in the mountains."—Yoshiaki Takazawa

SHOFUKURO

Recommended by
Takuji Takahashi

8-11 Yokaichi Hommachi
Higashiomi
Shiga 527-0012
+81 748220003
www.shofukuro.jp

Opening hours	Closed Monday
Credit cards	Accepted
Price range	Expensive
Style	Casual
Cuisine	Omakase-Kaiseki
Recommended for	Wish I'd opened

KAWAMURA BAR

Recommended by
Yoji Tokuyoshi

227 Yayoicho
Tottori
Tottori 680-0832
+81 857244243

Opening hours	Closed Sunday
Credit cards	Not accepted
Price range	Affordable
Style	Casual
Cuisine	Bar
Recommended for	Late night

"Tottori is my home town and each time I carry on late into the night you can find me at Kawamura Bar, where I like to drink from their selection of Japanese whiskies."—Yoji Tokuyoshi

VILLA AIDA

71-5 Kawajiri
Iwade
Wakayama 649-6231
+81 73 663 2227
villa-aida.jp

Recommended by
Hiroyasu Kawate

Opening hours	Closed Monday
Credit cards	Accepted
Price range	Affordable
Style	Smart casual
Cuisine	Italian-French-Japanese
Recommended for	Wish I'd opened

"The restaurant is located amid the fields, and it's a perfect, wonderful place."—Hiroyasu Kawate

Farm-to-table is personified by chef Kobayashi at his bijou restaurant—complete with Airbnb room—in Iwade city. Here, creative Italian cuisine is produced from herbs, fruits, and vegetables harvested either from the chef's own farm or the nearby mountains; fish, oysters, and seafood from the local fishing communities; and game meats reared by neighboring farmers. For a taste of Wakayama's terroir, try Kobayashi's radish dish, featuring eight types of black radish in a fennel broth perfumed with rosemary, lemon zest, and white balsamic vinegar.

TOKYO

TOKYO

SCALE

0 700 1400 2100 yd.

1. *Apicius (p.256)*
2. *Hibiki (p.256)*
3. *Robata Kaimaru (p.256)*
4. *Akasaka Rikyu Ginza (p.256)*
5. *Bulgaria Restaurant (p.256)*
6. *Esquisse (p.257)*
7. *Daitsune Udon Ginza (p.257)*
8. *Ginza Harutaka (p.257)*
9. *Hamadaya (p.257)*
10. *Ginza Kagari (p.257)*
11. *Kawamura (p.257)*
12. *Kobiki (p.258)*
13. *L'ecrin (p.258)*
14. *Oden Ogura (p.258)*
15. *Ryu Sushi (p.258)*
16. *Shinbashi Kanetanaka (p.258)*
17. *Shiniseya Yaesu (p.258)*
18. *Sugita (p.259)*
19. *Sukiyabashi Jiro (p.259)*
20. *Sushi Sawada (p.259)*
21. *Sushi Suzuki (p.259)*
22. *Sushi Tokami (p.259)*
23. *Sushi-Ya (p.259)*
24. *Tsukiji Sushisay (p.260)*
25. *Tempura Kondo (p.260)*
26. *Tokyo Kitcho (p.260)*
27. *Tsukiji Fish Market (p.260)*
28. *Château Robouchon (p.260)*
29. *Icaro (p.261)*
30. *Mamezon (p.261)*
31. *Le Ressort (p.261)*
32. *Trattoria La Baracca (p.261)*
33. *Yakumo Saryo (p.261)*
34. *Akanoren (p.262)*
35. *Akasaka Asada (p.262)*
36. *Akasaka Kikunoi (p.262)*
37. *La Bombance (p.262)*
38. *Bunon (p.262)*
39. *Chugoku Hanten (p.263)*
40. *Daigo (p.263)*
41. *L'effervescence (p.263)*
42. *Gaigai (p.263)*
43. *Hiroya (p.263)*
44. *Inoue Ramen (p.263)*
45. *Jubako (p.264)*
46. *Kabuite Soro (p.264)*
47. *Kanda (p.264)*
48. *Kyoaji (p.264)*
49. *Lauderdale (p.264)*
50. *Matsukawa (p.265)*
51. *Nagazumi (p.265)*
52. *Narisawa (p.265)*
53. *Nihonryori Ryugin (p.265)*
54. *Ootanino Sushi (p.265)*
55. *Satomi (p.266)*
56. *Sawamura Bakery (p.266)*
57. *Soba Roppongi (p.266)*
58. *Sougo (p.266)*
59. *Sudachi (p.266)*
60. *Sushi Saito (p.267)*
61. *Tajima Soba (p.267)*
62. *Takazawa (p.267)*
63. *Toriyoshi Nishi Azabu Yakitori (p.267)*
64. *Ushigoro (p.267)*
65. *Yakiniku Kiraku-Tei (p.267)*
66. *Yugentei Nishiazabu (p.268)*
67. *Arai (p.268)*
68. *Anis (p.268)*
69. *Le Cabaret (p.268)*
70. *Den (p.268)*
71. *Deus Ex Machina (p.269)*
72. *Ebisu Manmaru (p.269)*
73. *Florilège (p.269)*
74. *Farmer's Market (p.269)*
75. *Fuglen Tokyo (p.269)*
76. *Fuku Yakitori (p.270)*
77. *Higuchi (p.270)*
78. *Rakushokushu Maru (p.270)*
79. *Libertin (p.270)*
80. *Sushi Matsue (p.270)*
81. *Minatoya (p.270)*
82. *Restaurant Aladdin (p.271)*
83. *Sourin (p.271)*
84. *Torishige (p.271)*
85. *Quintessence (p.271)*
86. *Ajihachi Ramen (p.271)*
87. *Fungo (p.272)*
88. *Kagurazaka Ishikawa (p.272)*
89. *Kouei (p.272)*
90. *Sushi Mitani (p.272)*
91. *Toritama (p.272)*
92. *Troisgros (p.273)*
93. *Ubuka (p.273)*
94. *Mitoya (p.273)*
95. *Organ (p.273)*
96. *Shichifukujin (p.273)*

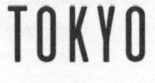

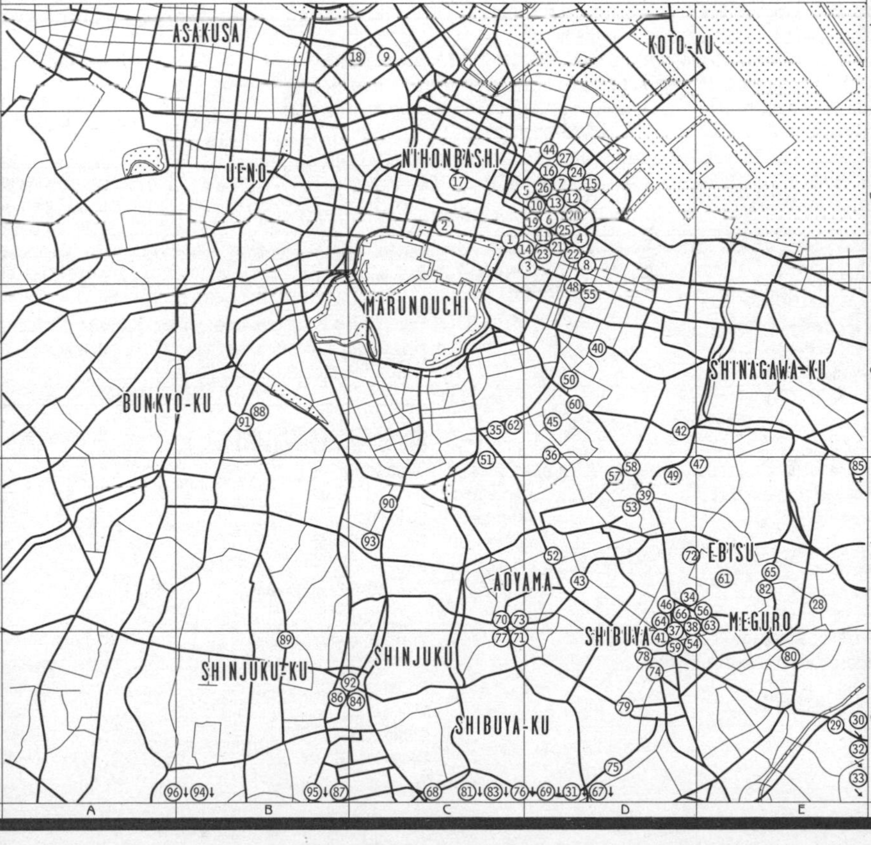

APICIUS

Recommended by
Takuji Takahashi

Sanshi-Kaikan
1BF, 1-9-4 Yuraku-cho
Chiyoda-ku
Tokyo 100-006
+81 332141361
www.apicius.co.jp

Opening hours..Closed Sunday
Credit cards..Accepted
Price range...Expensive
Style..Formal
Cuisine...French
Recommended for...High end

"They have an amazing selection of wine. Try the sautéed duck with salmis sauce."—Takuji Takahashi

With a name like this (it's named after Marcus Gavius Apicius, the Roman gourmet thought to have first produced foie gras) and an airy art-nouveau dining room adorned with artworks by Chagall and Andrew Wyeth, it's not surprising that this central Tokyo restaurant serves up one of the finest classical French meals money can buy (with white-glove service). While you tuck into signature dishes like the caviar and sea urchin with cauliflower cream mousse and consommé jelly, four sommeliers will be on hand to offer wine advice because, in case you've not heard, its cellar stocks a 50,000-bottle-strong collection.

HIBIKI

Recommended by
Andrea Ferrero

Tokyo Kaijo Nishido
1F, 1-2-1 Marunouchi
Chiyoda-ku
Tokyo 100-0005
+81 352088275
www.dynac-japan.com/hibiki

Opening hours..Closed Sunday
Credit cards..Accepted
Price range..Affordable
Style...Smart casual
Cuisine...Japanese
Recommended for...Local favorite

"Traditional Japanese cuisine in a casual atmosphere."—Andrea Ferrero

ROBATA KAIMARU

Recommended by
Danielle Gjestland

2-1-1 Yurkucho
Chiyoda-ku
Tokyo 100-0006
+81 0355324567

Opening hours...Open 7 days
Reservation policy...No
Credit cards..Accepted
Price range..Affordable
Style..Casual
Cuisine...Japanese
Recommended for...Late night

"Down a narrow alleyway under the bullet train tracks between Ginza and Shimbashi; inexpensive and good-quality dishes for the price, all grilled over smoky charcoal. It's always bustling until the trains stop running."—Danielle Gjestland

AKASAKA RIKYU GINZA

Recommended by
Hiroyasu Kawate

5F 6-8-7 Ginza
Chuo-ku
Tokyo 104-0061
+81 335692882
www.rikyu.jp/ginza

Opening hours...Open 7 days
Credit cards..Accepted
Price range...Expensive
Style...Smart casual
Cuisine...Cantonese
Recommended for...High end

"Everything is superb, from grilled dishes to *chahan* (fried rice). I recommend the whole-fried pigeon."
—Hiroyasu Kawate

BULGARIA RESTAURANT

Recommended by
Yoshihiro Narisawa

Ginza Tower
9F, 2-7-12 Ginza
Chuo-ku
Tokyo 104-0061
+81 363620555
www.bulgarihotels.com

Opening hours...........................Closed Monday and Sunday
Credit cards..Accepted
Price range...Expensive
Style..Formal
Cuisine...Italian
Recommended for...Local favorite

ESQUISSE

Recommended by
Shinobu Namae

Royal Crystal Ginza
9F, 5-4-6 Ginza
Chuo-ku
Tokyo 104-0061
+81 355375580
www.esquissetokyo.com

Opening hours	Open 7 days
Credit cards	Accepted
Price range	Expensive
Style	Formal
Cuisine	Modern French
Recommended for	High end

"Brilliant chef Lionel Beccat's story-telling and flavorsome menu will be your most memorable experiences in Tokyo. No other place marries French and Japanese cuisine so happily."—Shinobu Namae

DAITSUNE UDON GINZA

Recommended by
Masaru Seki

Daitsune 1F, 7-15-17 Ginza
Chuo-ku
Tokyo 104-0061
+81 335412227

Opening hours	Closed Saturday and Sunday
Credit cards	Not accepted
Price range	Budget
Style	Casual
Cuisine	Udon Noodles
Recommended for	Bargain

"It used to be a greengrocer in Tsukiji Market, so it specializes in unique udon using dashi and various vegetables."—Masaru Seki

GINZA HARUTAKA

Recommended by
Yoshiaki Takazawa

Tokiden
6F, 8-3-1 Ginza
Chuo-ku
Tokyo 104-0061
+81 335731144

Opening hours	Closed Sunday
Credit cards	Accepted
Price range	Expensive
Style	Smart casual
Cuisine	Sushi
Recommended for	Regular neighborhood

"It offers the highest quality fish and, as well as sushi, there are appetisers and tsumami (light snacks)."
—Yoshiaki Takazawa

HAMADAYA

Recommended by
Masaru Seki

3-13-5 Ningyo-cho
Chuo-ku
Tokyo 103-0013
+81 336615940
www.hamadaya.info

Opening hours	Closed Sunday
Credit cards	Accepted
Price range	Expensive
Style	Smart casual
Cuisine	Kaiseki
Recommended for	High end

GINZA KAGARI

Recommended by
Val Cantu

Ginza A
4-4-1 Ginza
Chuo-ku
Tokyo 104-0061
+81 335357565

Opening hours	Closed Sunday
Credit cards	Not accepted
Price range	Budget
Style	Casual
Cuisine	Ramen Noodles
Recommended for	Worth the travel

KAWAMURA

Recommended by
Yoshiaki Takazawa

Brioni
8F, 6-5-1 Ginza
Chuo-ku
Tokyo 104-0061
+81 362525011
www.bifteck.co.jp

Opening hours	Open 7 days
Credit cards	Accepted but not Mastercard
Price range	Expensive
Style	Smart casual
Cuisine	Steakhouse
Recommended for	High end

Unless you have an introduction from a regular, the hope of dining in one of the best wagyu *yoshoku* (Western-style cuisine) steakhouses in Japan will remain a pipe dream. If you do manage to bag a reservation, get ready dig deep into your wallet. But there's a reason for that: the wagyu steak cuts like butter. Given its reputation as one of Japan's biggest users of white truffles, you wouldn't want to miss the restaurant's legendary white truffle *omakase* (chef's choice) menu; though it's reportedly priced at ¥179,000 ($1,600; £1,300) a head.

KOBIKI

6-16-6 Ginza
Chuo-ku
Tokyo 104-0061
+81 335416077

Opening hours	Closed Sunday
Credit cards	Accepted
Price range	Affordable
Style	Casual
Cuisine	Izakaya
Recommended for	Regular neighborhood

"Delicious fish and seasonal vegetables."
—Masaru Seki

L'ECRIN

Mikimoto
B1F, 4-5-5 Ginza
Chuo-ku
Tokyo 104-0061
+81 335619706
www.lecringinza.co.jp

Opening hours	Closed Sunday
Credit cards	Accepted
Price range	Expensive
Style	Formal
Cuisine	French
Recommended for	High end

ODEN OGURA

Honda
1F, 6-3-6 Ginza
Chuo-ku
Tokyo 104-0061
+81 5058690590

Opening hours	Closed Sunday
Credit cards	Accepted
Price range	Affordable
Style	Smart casual
Cuisine	Kappo
Recommended for	Regular neighborhood

RYU SUSHI

Tsukiji Market Building 1
5-2-1 Tsukiji
Chuo-ku
Tokyo 104-0045
+81 335419517

Opening hours	Closed Sunday
Credit cards	Not accepted
Price range	Affordable
Style	Casual
Cuisine	Sushi
Recommended for	Breakfast

"They have some of the best ingredients in Tsukiji Market and are thorough in their work."—Masaru Seki

SHINBASHI KANETANAKA

7-18-17 Ginza
Chuo-ku
Tokyo 104-0061
+81 335412556
www.kanetanaka.co.jp

Opening hours	Variable
Credit cards	Accepted
Price range	Expensive
Style	Smart casual
Cuisine	Japanese
Recommended for	High end

SHINISEYA YAESU

3-3-4 Nihonbashi
Chuo-ku
Tokyo 103-0027
+81 0332311688
www.yaesu-shiniseya.com

Opening hours	Closed Sunday
Credit cards	Accepted
Price range	Affordable
Style	Smart casual
Cuisine	Japanese-Seafood
Recommended for	Regular neighborhood

"Typical Japanese izakaya restaurant (informal gastropub) with high quality ingredients, cozy atmosphere, friendly staff, and a good sake list."
—Andrea Ferrero

SUGITA

Recommended by
Dan Hong

3-1-3 Higashinihonbashi
Chuo-ku
Tokyo 103-0014
+81 336693855

Opening hours	Closed Monday
Credit cards	Accepted
Price range	Expensive
Style	Casual
Cuisine	Sushi
Recommended for	Worth the travel

"Simply the best sushi meal of my life."—Dan Hong

SUKIYABASHI JIRO

Recommended by
Kyle Connaughton

Tsukamoto Sogyo
B1F, 4-2-15 Ginza
Chuo-ku
Tokyo 104-0061
+81 335353600
www.sushi-jiro.jp

Opening hours	Variable
Credit cards	Accepted
Price range	Expensive
Style	Formal
Cuisine	Sushi
Recommended for	Worth the travel

SUSHI SAWADA

Recommended by
David Chang,
Kyle Connaughton,
Dylan Jones &
Songvisava Duangporn

MC
3F, 5-9-19 Ginza
Chuo-ku
Tokyo 104-0061
+81 335714711

Opening hours	Closed Monday
Credit cards	Accepted
Price range	Expensive
Style	Smart casual
Cuisine	Sushi
Recommended for	Worth the travel

SUSHI SUZUKI

Recommended by
Morgan McGlone

Nogakudo
5F, 6-5-15 Ginza
Chuo-ku
Tokyo 104-0061
+81 355376868

Opening hours	Closed Monday
Credit cards	Accepted
Price range	Expensive
Style	Smart casual
Cuisine	Sushi
Recommended for	Worth the travel

SUSHI TOKAMI

Recommended by
Kyle Connaughton,
Shinobu Namae

Seiwa Silver
B1F, 8-2-10 Ginza
Chuo-ku
Tokyo 104-0061
+81 335716005
www.sushitokami.3zoku.com

Opening hours	Variable
Price range	Accepted
Price range	Expensive
Style	Smart casual
Cuisine	Sushi
Recommended for	Local favorite

SUSHI-YA

Recommended by
Justin Cogley,
Morgan McGlone

Yugen
1F, 6-3-17 Ginza
Chuo-ku
Tokyo 104-0061
+81 335717900

Opening hours	Closed Monday
Credit cards	Accepted
Price range	Expensive
Style	Smart casual
Cuisine	Sushi
Recommended for	Worth the travel

"Amazing product and technique from a young sushi chef."—Justin Cogley

TSUKIJI SUSHISAY

Recommended by
Federico Heinzmann

4-3-19 Tsukiji Fish Market
Chuo-ku
Tokyo 104-0061
+81 0335417720
www.tsukijisushisay.co.jp

Opening hours	Closed Wednesday
Credit cards	Accepted
Price range	Affordable
Style	Casual
Cuisine	Sushi
Recommended for	Breakfast

"Yes, sushi breakfast! When we go to Tsukiji market to visit suppliers, I just love to stop by this place. Just fresh fish with green tea—brilliant. Open from 8.00 a.m."—Federico Heinzmann

Sushi Dai may be the darling of tourists who clamour for a taste of market-fresh sushi at Tsukiji market but the relentlessly long line (queue) can be quite a put-off, which is why foodies in-the-know sniff their way to this sushi-ya with not one, but two outlets located a stone's throw from each other at the outer market. The best time to savor the season's freshest catch draped over a parcel of vinegared rice is at breakfast (note one of the two outlets opens only at 8.30 am) or for an early lunch. If you know exactly what sushi you want, pick from the à la carte menu, which is available in English with pictures. Or just sit back and enjoy the *omakase* (chef's choice) set, washed down with a cup of sake.

TEMPURA KONDO

Recommended by
Josh Lewis

5-5-13 Ginza
Chuo-ku
Tokyo 104-0061
+81 355680923

Opening hours	Closed Sunday
Credit cards	Accepted
Price range	Expensive
Style	Smart casual
Cuisine	Tempura
Recommended for	Worth the travel

"One meal that really stands out was Tempura Kondo, both for the food and experience. The restaurant is booked months and months in advance. However, by some incredible stroke of luck, we turned up at the exact moment of a cancellation, which saw us being seated in front of Chef Kondo! We were blown away

by the lightness and freshness of the flavors. A very special experience."—Josh Lewis

TOKYO KITCHO

Recommended by
Takuji Takahashi

8-17-4 Ginza
Chuo-ku
Tokyo 104-0061
+81 335418228
www.kitcho.com

Opening hours	Closed Sunday
Credit cards	Accepted
Price range	Expensive
Style	Smart casual
Cuisine	Kaiseki
Recommended for	Wish I'd opened

TSUKIJI FISH MARKET

Recommended by
David Martin,
Dharshan Munidasa

5-2-1 Tsukiji
Chuo-ku
Tokyo 104-0045
+81 3-3541-2640
www.tsukiji-market.or.jp

Opening hours	Closed Sunday
Reservation policy	No
Credit cards	Not accepted
Price range	Affordable
Style	Casual
Cuisine	Seafood-Market
Recommended for	Breakfast

"Walk a bit and you will find fishmongers serving sliced up choices of fish with soy and wasabi to try!" —Dharshan Munidasa

CHÂTEAU ROBOUCHON

Recommended by
Italo Bassi

Yebisu Garden Place
1-13-1 Mita
Meguro-ku
Tokyo 153-0062
+81 35241347
www.robuchon.jp

Opening hours	Open 7 days
Credit cards	Accepted
Price range	Expensive
Style	Formal
Cuisine	Modern French
Recommended for	Wish I'd opened

"Impeccable cuisine and service."—Italo Bassi

ICARO

Recommended by
Luca Fantin

2-44-24 Kamimeguro
Meguro-ku
Tokyo 153-0005
+81 357248085

Opening hours	Closed Sunday
Credit cards	Accepted
Price range	Affordable
Style	Smart casual
Cuisine	Italian
Recommended for	Late night

"This small restaurant feels bigger than it is, thanks to the large window, and it has a casual, trattoria-style atmosphere. The chef uses his seven years of experience in Italy, and his brother, a wine connoisseur, handles the service."—Luca Fantin

MAMEZON

Recommended by
Masaru Seki

Gakugei University branch
3-9-18 Takaban
Meguro-ku
Tokyo 152-0004
T +81 3-3719-2688

Opening hours	Closed Monday
Credit cards	Accepted
Price range	Affordable
Style	Casual
Cuisine	Izakaya
Recommended for	Local favorite

LE RESSORT

Recommended by
Hiroyasu Kawate

Meiwa 1F
3-11-14 Komaba
Meguro-ku
Tokyo 153-0041
+81 334671172

Opening hours	Closed Monday
Credit cards	Not accepted
Price range	Budget
Style	Casual
Cuisine	Bakery
Recommended for	Breakfast

"I always have their breakfast pastries. Their croissants are superb."—Hiroyasu Kawate

TRATTORIA LA BARACCA

Recommended by
Masaru Seki

Tachikawa
2F, 2-11-4 Nakane
Meguro-ku
Tokyo 152-0031
+81 357014020
www.la-baracca.com

Opening hours	Closed Monday
Credit cards	Accepted
Price range	Affordable
Style	Casual
Cuisine	Italian
Recommended for	Local favorite

"A friendly Italian that makes the most of the ingredients' natural flavors. It's a space you can spend time relaxing in with friends or family."—Masaru Seki

YAKUMO SARYO

Recommended by
Alexandre Gauthier,
Shinobu Namae

3-4-7 Yakumo
Meguro-ku
Tokyo 152-0023
+81 357311620
www.yakumosaryo.jp

Opening hours	Closed Sunday
Reservation policy	No
Credit cards	Accepted
Price range	Expensive
Style	Smart casual
Cuisine	Kaiseki
Recommended for	Breakfast

"Very calm and relaxing breakfast place. Having Japanese breakfast with tea soothes your body and relaxes your mind. It makes me feel like I'm having a quiet meal in a zen temple. So, please be quiet—and your five senses are coming back to normal."—Shinobu Namae

AKANOREN

Recommended by
Matthew Crabbe

Nakaoka
1F, 3-21-24 Nishi-Azabu
Minato-ku
Tokyo 106-0031
+81 334084775
www.akanoren.com

Opening hours	Closed Sunday
Reservation policy	No
Credit cards	Not accepted
Price range	Budget
Style	Casual
Cuisine	Japanese
Recommended for	Late night

"The best late night ramen and gyoza in Tokyo."
—Matthew Crabbe

AKASAKA ASADA

Recommended by
Masaru Seki

3-6-4 Akasaka
Minato-ku
Tokyo 107-0052
+81 335856606
www.asadayaihei.co.jp

Opening hours	Open 7 days
Credit cards	Accepted
Price range	Expensive
Style	Smart casual
Cuisine	Japanese
Recommended for	High end

"It's a well-managed restaurant that pays close attention to detail, both in the food and service. You could take someone important there with peace of mind."—Masaru Seki

AKASAKA KIKUNOI

Recommended by
Byeongjin Kim

6-13-8 Akasaka
Minato-ku
Tokyo 207-0052
+81 335686055
www.kikunoi.jp

Opening hours	Closed Sunday
Credit cards	Accepted
Price range	Expensive
Style	Formal
Cuisine	Kaiseki
Recommended for	Worth the travel

"The main location in Kyoto has three Michelin stars and the Tokyo branch, with a hundred-year history,

gets two. The selection of seasonal ingredients that allow one to sense the changing of the seasons, endeavours to select the very best ingredients and the refined techniques of handling them, showcase the best feelings and memories, at every moment, through the integrated flow of expression and harmony of each item served. This restaurant is also the best place to experience the special refinement and consideration of Japanese service."—Byeongjin Kim

LA BOMBANCE

Recommended by
Matthew Crabbe

B1, 2-26-21 Nishi-azabu
Minato-ku
Tokyo 106-0031
+81 357786511
www.bombance.com

Opening hours	Closed Sunday
Credit cards	Accepted but not Diners
Price range	Expensive
Style	Smart casual
Cuisine	Japanese
Recommended for	Late night

BUNON

Recommended by
Shinobu Namae

4-2-14 Nishiazabu
Minayo-ku
Tokyo 106-0031
+81 0334062207
www.bunon.jp

Opening hours	Closed Sunday
Credit cards	Accepted
Price range	Expensive
Style	Smart casual
Cuisine	Japanese
Recommended for	Regular neighborhood

"The best post-service meal spot with the freshest seafood from the market every day, sourced by the chef himself and lots of Japanese home-style cooking. Sometimes there are surprises like shark's heart or grilled bear meat. The selection of natural wine is divine and there's good sake too."—Shinobu Namae

CHUGOKU HANTEN

Recommended by
Yoshiaki Takazawa

Oriental
1F, 1-1-5 Nishi-Azabu
Minato-ku
Tokyo 106-0031
+81 334783828
www.chuugokuhanten.com

Opening hours	Open 7 days
Credit cards	Accepted
Price range	Expensive
Style	Smart casual
Cuisine	Chinese
Recommended for	Late night

"The very best Chinese cuisine, with last orders at 3.00 a.m."—Yoshiaki Takazawa

DAIGO

Recommended by
Andrea Ferrero

Forest Tower
2F, 2-3-1 Atago
Minato-ku
Tokyo 105-0002
+81 334310811
www.atago-daigo.jp

Opening hours	Open 7 days
Credit cards	Accepted
Price range	Expensive
Style	Smart casual
Cuisine	Vegetarian Kaiseki
Recommended for	High end

"Beautiful restaurant, excellent food, and great service. Very traditional Japanese fine dining, but unusual as it's vegan."—Andrea Ferrero

L'EFFERVESCENCE

Recommended by
Sean Brock,
Kyle Connaughton

2-26-4 Nishi-azabu
Minato-ku
Tokyo 106-0031
+81 357669500
www.leffervescence.jp

Opening hours	Closed Monday and Sunday
Credit cards	Accepted
Price range	Expensive
Style	Smart casual
Cuisine	Japanese-French
Recommended for	Worth the travel

GAIGAI

Recommended by
Luca Fantin

Aporia
1F, 1-3-1 Azabujuban
Minato-ku
Tokyo 106-0045
+81 335863335
www.gaigai.jp

Opening hours	Open 7 days
Credit cards	Accepted
Price range	Affordable
Style	Smart casual
Cuisine	Yakitori
Recommended for	Bargain

HIROYA

Recommended by
Hiroyasu Kawate

1F, 3-5-3 Minami-Aoyama
Minato-ku
Tokyo 107-0062
+81 364592305

Opening hours	Variable
Credit cards	Accepted
Price range	Expensive
Style	Smart casual
Cuisine	Japanese-Fusion
Recommended for	Late night

"Their cuisine has originality, and it's convenient to eat at the counter seats."—Hiroyasu Kawate

INOUE RAMEN

Recommended by
Dharshan Munidasa

4-9-16 Tsukiji Fish Market
Chuo-ku
Tokyo 104-0045
+81 335420620

Opening hours	Closed Sunday
Reservation policy	No
Credit cards	Not accepted
Price range	Budget
Style	Casual
Cuisine	Ramen Noodles
Recommended for	Bargain

"It's the best meal one could ask for. Ramen is the soul food of the Japanese people."
—Dharshan Munidasa

JUBAKO

Recommended by
Dharshan Munidasa

2-17-61 Akasaka
Minato-ku
Tokyo 107-0052
+81 335831319
www.jubako.jp

Opening hours	Closed Sunday
Credit cards	Accepted
Price range	Expensive
Style	Smart casual
Cuisine	Unagi Ryoutei
Recommended for	High end

"A two-hundred-and-thirty-year-old restaurant, shouldering such legacy and responsibility, serves unbelievable *unagi* (eel) generation after generation. The Otani family is a living treasure, making time stand still."—Dharshan Munidasa

KABUITE SORO

Recommended by
Masaru Seki

Takahashi
1F, 1-11-10 Nishi-Azabu
Minato-ku
Tokyo 106-0031
+81 334704840

Opening hours	Closed Sunday
Credit cards	Not accepted
Price range	Affordable
Style	Casual
Cuisine	Izakaya
Recommended for	Late night

"They have plenty of food and drink on the menu, and they serve quickly too. Everything is delicious."
—Masaru Seki

With a red lantern hanging from its tiled roof, the facade of this no-frills Japanese pub at Nishi-Azabu may not stand out from the crowd, but the yakitori (charcoal-grilled chicken) and oden (one-pot winter dish) keep the night-time drinking crowd coming back. If ordering from the hand-written Japanese menu pasted on the walls is too difficult, just point at your neighbors' delicious-looking plates.

KANDA

Recommended by
Umberto Bombana

36-34 Motoazabu
Minato-ku
Tokyo 106-0046
+81 357860150
www.nihonryori-kanda.com

Opening hours	Closed Sunday
Credit cards	Accepted
Price range	Expensive
Style	Smart casual
Cuisine	Kaiseki
Recommended for	High end

KYOAJI

Recommended by
Shinobu Namae, Bruce Ricketts,
Masaru Seki

3-3-5 Shinbashi
Minato-ku
Tokyo 105-0004
+81 335913344

Opening hours	Closed Sunday
Credit cards	Not accepted
Price range	Expensive
Style	Smart casual
Cuisine	Kyotonese
Recommended for	High end

"Such a special place, and it's hard to describe what impresses me most, but I definitely admire Chef Nishi-san's heart-warming character and sharp eye on every ingredient."—Shinobu Namae

LAUDERDALE

Recommended by
Andrea Ferrero

6-15-1 Roppongi Hills
Minato-ku
Tokyo 106-0032
+81 34055533
www.lauderdale.co.jp

Opening hours	Open 7 days
Credit cards	Accepted
Price range	Affordable
Style	Smart casual
Cuisine	Western
Recommended for	Breakfast

"Very comfortable place, simple but impeccable food, nice coffee and smoothies, great pancakes and omelettes."—Andrea Ferrero

MATSUKAWA

Recommended by
Dan Hunter

Terrace House
1F, 1-11-6 Akasaka
Minato-ku
Tokyo 107-0052
+81 0362777371
www.t-matsukawa.com

Opening hours	Variable
Credit cards	Not accepted
Price range	Expensive
Style	Smart casual
Cuisine	Japanese-Omaske
Recommended for	Wish I'd opened

"Refined yet friendly and approachable but really, just great cooking."—Dan Hunter

NAGAZUMI

Recommended by
Jordy Navarra

1-5-3 Motoakasaka
Minato-ku
Tokyo 107 0051
+81 354101919

Opening hours	Variable
Credit cards	Accepted but not Diners
Price range	Expensive
Style	Smart casual
Cuisine	Kappo
Recommended for	Wish I'd opened

"We were introduced to this restaurant by our friends. Intimate space with great food and a friendly atmosphere, where you're served by the Chef Ogo Masashi. They cook fine Japanese food, refined but still homey and from the heart."—Jordy Navarra

NARISAWA

Recommended by
Fredrik Berselius, Luca Fantin,
Alexandre Gauthier,
Danielle Gjestland,
José Luis Gonzalez,
Nicolai Nørregaard,
Thitid Tassanakajohn

2-6-15 Minami Aoyama
Minato-ku
Tokyo 107-0062
+81 357850799
www.narisawa-yoshihiro.com

Opening hours	Closed Monday and Sunday
Credit cards	Accepted
Price range	Expensive
Style	Smart casual
Cuisine	Modern Japanese
Recommended for	High end

"For its inventive and imaginative take on traditional Japanese ingredients, many of them not even common to Japanese people themselves. I admire

265

Narisawasan's ability to look with fresh eyes at ingredients that are falling into disuse, in a high-end Japanese food culture that praises exact replication."
—Danielle Gjestland

NIHONRYORI RYUGIN

Recommended by
Jason Atherton, Kyle Connaughton,
Luca Fantin, José Luis Gonzalez,
Liguang Han, Dharshan Munidasa,
Yoshihiro Narisawa, Julien Royer,
Yoshiaki Takazawa

Side Roppongi
1F, 7-17-24 Roppongi
Minato-ku
Tokyo 106-0032
+81 334238006
www.nihonryori-ryugin.com

Opening hours	Open 7 days
Credit cards	Accepted
Price range	Expensive
Style	Smart casual
Cuisine	Japanese
Recommended for	Local favorite

"It's the leader in Japanese gastronomy."
—Yoshiaki Takazawa

Who would have thought that a cuisine as traditional as *kaiseki* (multi-course dinner) marries so well with cutting-edge cooking techniques? Under the stewardship of chef-owner Seiji Yamamoto, who is also a certified sommelier, modernist *kaiseki* has taken foodies by storm at this eighteen-seat eatery in Roppoingi. Reflecting the mood of the season, Yamamoto's menu changes daily. It's a discovery of in-season Japanese produce; dishes like Hokkaido monkfish liver with seasonal vegetables in miso broth are matched with a curated list of tea, sake, and wine. But you haven't truly dined here until you've tried the legendary -196°C (-321°F) seasonal fruit dessert.

OOTANINO SUSHI

Recommended by
Luca Fantin,
José Luis Gonzalez

4-11-7 Nishiazabu
Minato-ku
Tokyo 106-0031
+81 354688880
www.ootanino.com

Opening hours	Variable
Credit cards	Accepted
Price range	Expensive
Style	Smart casual
Cuisine	Sushi
Recommended for	Late night

SATOMI

Recommended by
Yoshiaki Takazawa

3-3-7 Shinbashi
Minato-ku
Tokyo 105-0004

Opening hours	Variable
Reservation policy	No
Credit cards	Not accepted
Price range	Expensive
Style	Casual
Cuisine	Japanese
Recommended for	Wish I'd opened

"The owner is single-handed and operates a referral system. It has the very best ingredients and wines."
—Yoshiaki Takazawa

SAWAMURA BAKERY

Recommended by
Matthew Crabbe

LaSaccaia-Azabu
1-2F, 5-1-6 Minamiazabu
Minato-ku
Tokyo 106-0047
+81 354218686
www.b-sawamura.com

Opening hours	Open 7 days
Credit cards	Accepted
Price range	Budget
Style	Casual
Cuisine	Bakery
Recommended for	Breakfast

"Freshly baked breads of all types. The sandwiches are always fresh and simple."—Matthew Crabbe

SOBA ROPPONGI

Recommended by
Andrea Ferrero

Roppongi Xe
7−14−3 Roppongi
Minato-ku
Tokyo 106-0032
+81 354133735

Opening hours	Open 7 days
Credit cards	Accepted
Price range	Budget
Style	Casual
Cuisine	Soba Noodles
Recommended for	Bargain

SOUGO

Recommended by
Masaru Seki

Green Building
3F, 6-1-8 Roppongi
Minato-ku
Tokyo 106-0032
+81 354141133
www.sougo.tokyo

Opening hours	Variable
Credit cards	Accepted
Price range	Affordable
Style	Smart casual
Cuisine	Vegetarian
Recommended for	Late night

The family behind the legendary—and expensive—Daigo reach out to a more mass-market audience at this casual *shojin ryori* (Buddhist vegetarian cuisine) eatery, where the lunch course starts from just ¥1,500 ($14; £11) and dinner starts at ¥6,000 ($54; £44). To cater to the drinking crowd, an à la carte bar menu is served from 10.00 p.m. to 5.00 a.m., offering items like handmade soba (buckwheat noodles), truffled fries, and salad; perfect accompaniments to your glass of wine, whisky, or shochu. If your diet means you avoid fish, eggs, or dairy products, it's wise to inform the restaurant at least two-days ahead of your visit.

SUDACHI

Recommended by
Matthew Crabbe

B1, 7-12-12 Minamiaoyama
Minato-ku
Tokyo 107-0072
+81 0364335386
www.sudachi.tokyo

Opening hours	Closed Monday, Tuesday and Friday
Credit cards	Accepted but not Diners
Price range	Expensive
Style	Smart casual
Cuisine	Mpdern Japanese
Recommended for	Local favorite

"Sudachi has a very seasonal menu with ingredients that you don't eat every day, cooked in a variety of interesting ways. The design is cool and the counter seating allows interaction with the kitchen and guests."—Matthew Crabbe

SUSHI SAITO

Ark Hills South Tower
1F, 1-4-5 Roppongi
Minato-ku
Tokyo 106-0032
+81 335894412

Opening hours................................Closed Sunday
Credit cards..Accepted
Price range..Expensive
Style...Formal
Cuisine...Sushi
Recommended for..........................Local favorite

"His nigiri is very delicate and subtle, not too overwhelming, but very true to the ingredients. His 'less is more'-minded sushi is always different even if you eat the same *neta* (nigiri toppings), which calls for regular come-back. His *aji* (horse mackerel) always blows my mind."—Shinobu Namae

TAJIMA SOBA

3-8-6 Nishiazabu
Minato-ku
Tokyo 106-0031
+81 334456617
www.sobatajima.jp

Opening hours................................Closed Sunday
Credit cards..Accepted
Price range..Affordable
Style..Smart casual
Cuisine...Soba Noodles
Recommended for...............Regular neighborhood

TAKAZAWA

Sanyo Akasaka
2F, 3-5-2 Akasaka
Minato-ku
Tokyo 107-0052
+81 335055052
www.takazawa-y.co.jp

Opening hours.......................................Variable
Credit cards..Accepted
Price range..Expensive
Style..Smart casual
Cuisine..Modern Kaiseki
Recommended for.........................Wish I'd opened

TORIYOSHI NISHI AZABU YAKITORI

Ryowa Palace
B1, 4-2-6 Nishiazabu
Minato-ku
Tokyo 106-0031
+81 354640466

Opening hours....................................Open 7 days
Credit cards..Accepted
Price range..Affordable
Style...Casual
Cuisine...Yakitori
Recommended for..............Regular neighborhood

"Great yakitori (charcoal grilled chicken) just around the corner from my house. The chicken is really fresh and all the parts are used. My favorite is the *chochin* (unfertilised egg attached to the liver)."
—Matthew Crabbe

USHIGORO

Barbizon73
1F, 2-24-14 Nishiazabu
Minato-ku
Tokyo 106-0031
+81 5058680615
www.ushigoro.com

Opening hours....................................Open 7 days
Credit cards..Expensive
Price range..Affordable
Style..Smart casual
Cuisine...........................Japanese-Korean BBQ
Recommended for..............Regular neighborhood

YAKINIKU KIRAKU-TEI

Minamiazabu
B1F, 4-11-26 Minamiazabu
Minato-ku
Tokyo 106-0047
+81 334420729

Opening hours....................................Open 7 days
Credit cards..Accepted
Price range..Affordable
Style...Casual
Cuisine...........................Japanese-Korean BBQ
Recommended for..............Regular neighborhood

YUGENTEI NISHIAZABU

Recommended by
Matthew Crabbe

Jojoen
1F, 3-24-8 Nishiazabu
Minato-ku
Tokyo 106-0031
+81 337968989
www.jojoen.co.jp

Opening hours	Open 7 days
Credit cards	Accepted
Price range	Expensive
Style	Smart casual
Cuisine	Japanese
Recommended for	Late night

ARAI

Recommended by
Diego Hernández-Velasco Baquedano

4-19-8 Kasuya
Setagaya-ku
Tokyo 157-0063
+81 353137423

Opening hours	Closed Wednesday
Credit cards	Accepted
Price range	Expensive
Style	Smart casual
Cuisine	Sushi
Recommended for	Worth the travel

"Essentially speaking, Arai is perfect: its quality, technique, aesthetic and intentions. It's a really fantastic experience."
—Diego Hernández-Velasco Baquedano

ANIS

Recommended by
Zaiyu Hasegawa

1F, 1-9-7 Hatsudai
Shibuya-ku
Tokyo 151-0061
+81 362760026
www.restaurant-anis.jp

Opening hours	Closed Monday
Credit cards	Accepted
Price range	Affordable
Style	Smart casual
Cuisine	French
Recommended for	Regular neighborhood

"The chef's meat grilling technique is amazing! It's cosy, reasonably priced and delicious. The food is unique to this place."—Zaiyu Hasegawa

LE CABARET

Recommended by
Shinobu Namae

Motoyoyogi Leaf
1F, 8-8 Motoyoyogi-cho
Shibuya-ku
Tokyo 151-0062
+81 334697466
www.restaurant-lecabaret.com

Opening hours	Closed Monday
Credit cards	Accepted
Price range	Expensive
Style	Casual
Cuisine	French Bistro
Recommended for	Late night

DEN

Recommended by
Vicky Cheng, Gert De Mangeleer,
Luca Fantin, Katsuya Fukushima,
Federico Heinzmann,
Hiroyasu Kawate,
Richie Lin, Virgilio Martínez,
Shinobu Namae, Jordy Navarra,
Shuko Oda, Bjoern Alexander Panek,
Yoji Tokuyoshi, Janice Wong,
Hajime Yoneda

Kenchikuka Kaikan JIA Wing
B1F, 2-3-18 Jingumae
Shibuya-ku
Tokyo 150-0001
+81 364555433
www.jimbochoden.com

Opening hours	Closed Sunday
Credit cards	Accepted
Price range	Expensive
Style	Casual
Cuisine	Modern Kaiseki
Recommended for	Worth the travel

"A seriously fun restaurant where the chef's rigor and own particular sense of humor is expressed in every plate."—Shuko Oda

If you have time for just one gastronomic indulgence in Tokyo, come here. Although it has recently moved to a new—and bigger—location at Jingumae, chef-owner Zaiyu Hasegawa remains firm in his belief that dining should be fun as well as delicious. Multiple courses from his modern *kaiseki* (multi-course dinner) tasting menu exhibit playful antics that diners have come to associate as "Den" hallmarks—the sticky-rice-and-turtle-meat-stuffed "Dentucky Fried Chicken", served in a mock fast-food cardboard box bearing the chef's image, and "Den's Salad", prepared with twenty different vegetables dotted with Nagano ants, are just two examples.

DEUS EX MACHINA

Recommended by
Andrea Ferrero

3-29-5 Jingumae
Shibuya-ku
Tokyo 150-0001
+81 354133949
www.deuscustoms.comu

Opening hours	Open 7 days
Credit cards	Accepted
Price range	Budget
Style	Casual
Cuisine	Café
Recommended for	Wish I'd opened

"The quality of what they make is really high even if it's a casual sandwich or a cappuccino—they put passion into the simplest things, and that is very hard to find."—Andrea Ferrero

EBISU MANMARU

Recommended by
Hiro Sone

1F, 2-11-7 Green Heights
Shibuya-ku
Tokyo 150-0013
+81 357892851

Opening hours	Open 7 days
Credit cards	Accepted
Price range	Affordable
Style	Casual
Cuisine	Japanese
Recommended for	Late night

"Whenever we are in Tokyo, we go to this place. It's open from 5.00 p.m. to 5.00 a.m. Great selection of *Shochu*, and limited but very fresh seafood and small interesting dishes."—Hiro Sone

FLORILÈGE

Recommended by
Gert De Mangeleer,
Luca Fantin, Zaiyu Hasegawa,
Mingoo Kang, Shinobu Namae,
Bjoern Alexander Panek, Janice Wong

Seizan-Gaien
B1F, 2-5-4 Jingumae
Shibuya-ku
Tokyo 150-0001
+81 364400878
www.aoyama-florilege.jp

Opening hours	Closed Wednesday
Credit cards	Accepted
Price range	Expensive
Style	Casual
Cuisine	Japanese-French
Recommended for	Local favorite

"It's always evolving. A superb restaurant."
—Zaiyu Hasegawa

There is something to be said for eating French food in Tokyo, where French techniques are combined with access to pristine Japanese ingredients. And if that sounds appealing, one of the trendiest venues to visit is this twenty-two-seat, windowless Jingumae digs set in the basement of an office building. Chef-owner Hiroyasu Kawate has embellished a cavernous, almost industrial, space with an open kitchen surrounded by a metallic counter where he dispatches dishes like beef carpaccio with beetroot (beet) puree, smoked potato puree, and apple sorbet, from an eleven-course dinner tasting menu. For the full experience, be sure to opt for wine or juice pairing.

FARMER'S MARKET

Recommended by
Shinobu Namae

United Nations University
5-53-70 Jingumae
Shibuya-ku
Tokyo 150-0001
+81 354594934
www.farmersmarkets.jp

Opening hours	Closed Monday to Friday
Reservation policy	No
Credit cards	Not accepted
Price range	Budget
Style	Casual
Cuisine	Street Food
Recommended for	Bargain

"Every Saturday and Sunday, Farmer's Market has different choices of food trucks, ranging from Japanese bento to Italian pizza, coffee, pastries, etc. using very fresh ingredients from the market. You can't experience better quality than here at any food court in Japan."—Shinobu Namae

FUGLEN TOKYO

Recommended by
Jordy Navarra

1F, 1-16-11 Tomigaya
Shibuya-ku
Tokyo 151-0063
+81 334810884
www.fuglen.com

Opening hours	Open 7 days
Reservation policy	No
Credit cards	Accepted
Price range	Budget
Style	Casual
Cuisine	Café-Bar
Recommended for	Breakfast

FUKU YAKITORI

Recommended by
Federico Heinzmann

3-23-4 Nishihara
Shibuya-ku
Tokyo 151-0066
+81 334853234

Opening hours	Closed Wednesday
Credit cards	Accepted
Price range	Affordable
Style	Casual
Cuisine	Yakitori
Recommended for	Regular neighborhood

HIGUCHI

Recommended by
Yoshihiro Narisawa

2-19-12 Jingumae
Shibuya-ku
Tokyo 150-0001
+81 334027038

Opening hours	Closed Sunday
Credit cards	Accepted
Price range	Expensive
Style	Smart casual
Cuisine	Japanese-French
Recommended for	Local favorite

RAKUSHOKUSHU MARU

Recommended by
Matthew Crabbe

5-50 Jingumae
Shibuya-ku
Tokyo 150-0001
+81 03-6418-5572
www.maru-mayfont.jp

Opening hours	Open 7 days
Credit cards	Accepted
Price range	Expensive
Style	Smart casual
Cuisine	Izakaya
Recommended for	Late night

LIBERTIN

Recommended by
Shinobu Namae

Ito
1F, 1-22-6
Shibuya-ku
Tokyo 150-0002
+81 364184885

Opening hours	Closed Sunday
Credit cards	Accepted
Price range	Affordable
Style	Smart casual
Cuisine	Bistro
Recommended for	Late night

With its trademark blue French doors, this quaint bistro and wine bar brings a late-night (it closes at 2.00 a.m.) slice of Paris to Shibuya. There's a convivial ambience about the place, and the mostly French wine list goes perfectly with the hearty portions of French comfort food like duck confit and *choucroute* (sauerkraut with meats and sausages), which are prepped with Japanese ingredients like roasted Iwachu pork. And if you like your wine natural, you've come to the right place.

SUSHI MATSUE

Recommended by
Izu Ani

2-4-1 Ebisuminami
Shibuya-ku
Tokyo 150-0022
+81 0337114364
www.matsue.cc

Opening hours	Open 7 days
Credit cards	Accepted
Price range	Expensive
Style	Smart casual
Cuisine	Sushi
Recommended for	Worth the travel

"Pure simplicity."—Izu Ani

MINATOYA

Recommended by
Hiroyasu Kawate

Okada
1F, 2-41-20 Sasazuka
Shibuya-ku
Tokyo 151-0073
+81 363833120

Opening hours	Closed Wednesday
Credit cards	Accepted
Price range	Budget
Style	Casual
Cuisine	Japanese
Recommended for	Bargain

**"The *kakigori* (shaved ice dessert) is absolutely delicious. Try the tiramisu or *imo* (potato) *kakigori*."
—Hiroyasu Kawate**

RESTAURANT ALADDIN

Recommended by
Hiro Sone

G1F, 2-22-10 Hiroo Riverside
Shibuya-ku
Tokyo 150-0013
+81 354200038
www.restaurant-aladdin.com

Opening hours	Open 7 days
Credit cards	Accepted
Price range	Expensive
Style	Smart casual
Cuisine	French
Recommended for	High end

"Chef Kawasaki's French cooking is solid, tasty, and bold. Great Burgundy wine selection."—Hiro Sone

SOURIN

Recommended by
Hiroyasu Kawate

1F, 2-30-9 Sasazuka
Shibuya-ku
Tokyo 151-0073
+81 333738374

Opening hours	Closed Monday
Credit cards	Not accepted
Price range	Affordable
Style	Casual
Cuisine	Japanese
Recommended for	Local favorite

"The hand-made soba and *tsumami* (light snacks) are superb, as are the *tenseiro* (noodles topped with tempura) and hand-made *ganmo* (deep-fried tofu)."
—Hiroyasu Kawate

TORISHIGE

Recommended by
Yoshiaki Takazawa

2-6-5 Yoyogi
Shibuya-ku
Tokyo 151-0053
+81 333795188

Opening hours	Closed Sunday
Credit cards	Not accepted
Price range	Affordable
Style	Casual
Cuisine	Yakitori
Recommended for	Regular neighborhood

QUINTESSENCE

Recommended by
Jordy Navarra

Garden City Shinagawa Gotenyama
1F, 6-7-29 Kitashinagawa
Shinagawa-ku
Tokyo 141-0001
+81 362770090
www.quintessence.jp

Opening hours	Closed Sunday
Credit cards	Accepted
Price range	Expensive
Style	Smart casual
Cuisine	French-Japanese
Recommended for	High end

"Great restaurant that just amazes with the quality of the food and service. Having a meal there was probably one of the most eye-opening experiences for me as a cook and a chef. Everything just exuded class and quality with food executed at such a high level—seasoning and taste all on point. Really beautiful experience."—Jordy Navarra

AJIHACHI RAMEN

Recommended by
Federico Heinzmann

Daikan Plaza A
1F, 7-1-7 Nishishinjuku
Shinjuku-ku
Tokyo 160-0023
+81 353304381

Opening hours	Closed Sunday
Credit cards	Not accepted
Price range	Budget
Style	Casual
Cuisine	Ramen Noodles
Recommended for	Bargain

"Just awesome ramen for Y900 ($7; £6)!"
—Federico Heinzmann

FUNGO

Recommended by
Federico Heinzmann

1F, 6-16-7 Nishishinjuku
Shinjuku-ku
Tokyo 160-0023
+81 353397123
www.fungo.com

Opening hours	Open 7 days
Credit cards	Accepted
Price range	Affordable
Style	Casual
Cuisine	Italian
Recommended for	Late night

"Great pasta everytime, very nice wine list, and open until late."—Federico Heinzmann

Located just a fifteen-minute walk from Shinjuku station and a stone's throw from Shinjuku Central Park, this Italian café-restaurant serves takeouts (takeaways) for parties, a value-for-money semi-buffet lunch, and an affordable set menu and à la carte for dinner. Come 11.00 p.m., it morphs into a bar with an impressive wine collection, closing unusually late (or early) at 5.00 a.m. Night owls take note.

KAGURAZAKA ISHIKAWA

Recommended by
Val Cantu
Björn Frantzén,
Isaac McHale

Takamura
1F, 5-37 Kagurazaka
Shinjuku-ku
Tokyo 162-0825
+81 352250173
www.kagurazaka-ishikawa.co.jp

Opening hours	Closed Sunday
Credit cards	Accepted
Price range	Expensive
Style	Smart casual
Cuisine	Kaiseki
Recommended for	Worth the travel

"The refined food of Hideki Ishikawa, the friendly interactions, and a beautiful space made this my best meal in the past twelve months."—Isaac McHale

KOUEI

Recommended by
Zaiyu Hasegawa

Okano
1F, 2-41-12 Kabuki-cho
Shinjuku-ku
Tokyo 160-0021
+81 332022005
www.shinjyuku-horumon.com

Opening hours	Open 7 days
Credit cards	Accepted
Price range	Affordable
Style	Casual
Cuisine	Korean
Recommended for	Late night

"Everything is mouth-watering."—Zaiyu Hasegawa

SUSHI MITANI

Recommended by
Alex Atala

1-22-1 Yotsuya
Shinjuku-ku
Tokyo 160-0004
+81 353660132

Opening hours	Closed Monday
Credit cards	Accepted
Price range	Expensive
Style	Smart casual
Cuisine	Sushi
Recommended for	Worth the travel

"A place that at the same time manages to be modern and cosy. Anyone who sits at the counter will journey through a universe of new concepts and innovative flavors."—Alex Atala

TORITAMA

Recommended by
Andrea Ferrero

162-0825 Tōkyō-to,
Shinjuku-ku,
Kagurazaka, 5 Chome—7
Tokyo 162-0825
+81 364575131
www.toritama.net

Opening hours	Closed Sunday
Credit cards	Not accepted
Price range	Affordable
Style	Casual
Cuisine	Yakitori
Recommended for	Late night

"Great yakitori (charcoal grilled chicken), nice staff, and good beers."—Andrea Ferrero

TROISGROS

Recommended by
Federico Heinzmann

Hyatt Regency Tokyo
1F, 2-7-2 Nishi-Shinjuku
Shinjuku-ku
Tokyo 160-0023
+81 333481234
www.troisgros.jp

Opening hours.......................Closed Tuesday and Wednesday
Credit cards...Accepted
Price range...Expensive
Style...Smart casual
Cuisine..French
Recommended for...High end

UBUKA

Recommended by
Yoshihiro Narisawa

AIES
1F, 2-14 Araki-cho
Shinjuku-ku
Tokyo 160-0007
+81 333567270
www.arakicho.com

Opening hours..................................Closed Sunday
Credit cards..Accepted
Price range...Expensive
Style...Smart casual
Cuisine.......................................Japanese Seafood
Recommended for................Regular neighborhood

"It has a firm position in Japanese food with an outstanding, crustacean-filled menu. The chef is really humble. You understand how sincerely his dishes are made when you meet him."—Yoshihiro Narisawa

MITOYA

Recommended by
Bryant Ng

1-36-7 Asagaya Minami
Suginami-ku
Tokyo 166-0004
+81 333153104

Opening hours..Open 7 days
Credit cards...Not accepted
Price range..Budget
Style...Casual
Cuisine.......................................Japanese-Italian
Recommended for..........................Worth the travel

"A restaurant in Tokyo that serves nothing but spaghetti Bolognese. There are about ten seats and two cooks. The chef/owner makes his own pasta and you can see huge pots of Bolognese cooking. It's simple, delicious, and beautiful."—Bryant Ng

ORGAN

Recommended by
Shinobu Namae

2-19-12 Nishiogi-minami
Suginami-ku
Tokyo 167-0053
+81 359415388

Opening hours....................................Closed Monday
Credit cards.......................................Not accepted
Price range..Affordable
Style..Casual
Cuisine..Modern French
Recommended for..................Regular neighborhood

"This high-end natural wine bistro stands just a tiny step away from bustling central Tokyo. Chef Konno goes to the market to get the finest products back to his kitchen. Not only his dishes, but his wine selection too, will never disappoint you. Reserve your seats beforehand."—Shinobu Namae

SHICHIFUKUJIN

Recommended by
Yoshiaki Takazawa

3-2-13 Koenji-kita
Suginami-ku
Tokyo 166-0002
+81 332238755
www.shichifukujin7.com

Opening hours..Open 7 days
Credit cards...Accepted
Price range..Affordable
Style..Casual
Cuisine..Sushi
Recommended for..Bargain

> "After a late night of drinking and dancing, nothing hits the spot better than beef brisket noodle soup and their famous baked pork buns."
> TIPPI TAMBUNTING P312

SOUTHEAST ASIA

> "The greatest selection of authentic Vietnamese food."
> DONALD BERGER P291

> "Where traditional street food is served yakitori style."
> JOSÉ LUIS GONZALEZ P307

> "FOR GIANT RIVER PRAWNS ON THE CHAO PHRAYA RIVER FOR LUNCH THIS IS A MUST."
> TIM BUTLER P276

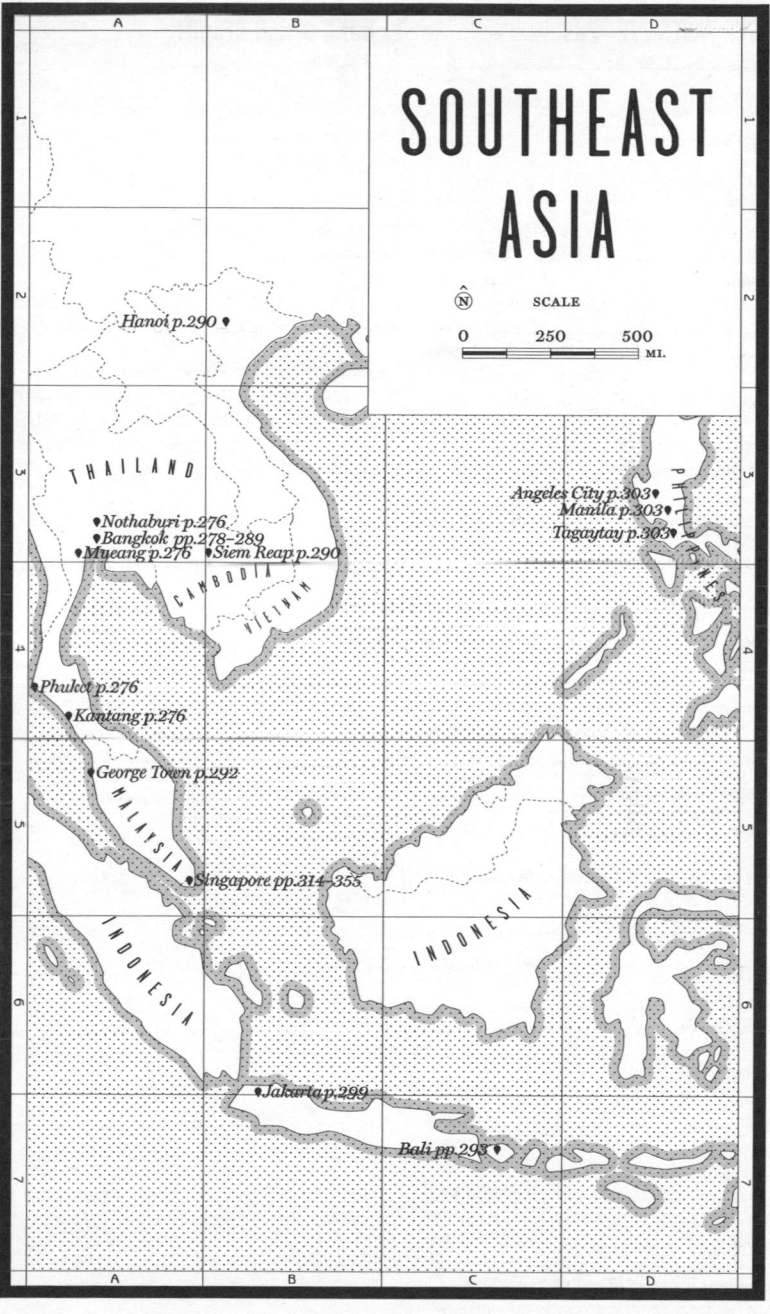

SOUTHEAST
ASIA

N   SCALE

0   250   500
MI.

Hanoi p.290

THAILAND

Nothaburi p.276
Bangkok pp.278–289
Mueang p.276   Siem Reap p.290

CAMBODIA

VIETNAM

Angeles City p.303
Manila p.303
Tagaytay p.303

Phuket p.276

Kantang p.276

George Town p.292

MALAYSIA

Singapore pp.314–355

INDONESIA

INDONESIA

Jakarta p.299

Bali pp.293

HONG SENG PHOCHANA

Recommended by
Tim Butler

280 Moo 2 Pakkret
Nonthaburi
Nonthaburi 11120, Thailand
+66 25837654

Opening hours	Open 7 days
Reservation policy	No
Credit cards	Not accepted
Price range	Budget
Style	Casual
Cuisine	Thai
Recommended for	Local favorite

"For giant river shrimp (prawns) on the Chao Phraya river for lunch this is a must."—Tim Butler

INIALA GOURMET

Recommended by
Tim Butler

49/27 Boat Avenue
Thalang
Phuket 83110, Thailand
+66 07660230
www.inialakb.com

Opening hours	Open 7 days
Credit cards	Accepted
Price range	Affordable
Style	Smart casual
Cuisine	Patisserie
Recommended for	Breakfast

"Great breads and pastries in a casual café setting."
—Tim Butler

RUAN PAN YHA

Recommended by
Dylan Jones &
Duangporn Songvisava

1300/1600 Soi Ekachai
11 Norrarach-Uthit Road
Muang
Samut Songkhram 75000, Thailand

Opening hours	Variable
Credit cards	Not accepted
Price range	Affordable
Style	Smart casual
Cuisine	Thai
Recommended for	Worth the travel

"In my opinion, this is one of (if not the) best Thai restaurants in Thailand. Go as a group as the portions are large and you want to try as much as possible."
—Dylan Jones & Duangporn Songvisava

LI BONG BEACH RESORT

Recommended by
Jason Bailey

18/3 Moo 6
Kantang
Trang 92000, Thailand
+66 075225205
www.libong-beach.com

Opening hours	Open 7 days
Credit cards	Accepted but not AMEX or Diners
Price range	Affordable
Style	Casual
Cuisine	International
Recommended for	Worth the travel

"Just meters from the beach, this restaurant serves the freshest *poo phad num prik pao* (black sea crab in a spicy chile jam and fresh red curry paste). The burn inside my mouth coupled with cold beer and a stunning beach setting will always stick in my mind."
—Jason Bailey

BANGKOK

PHRA NAKHON
PATCHATHEWI
HUAI KHWANG
KHLONG TAN NUEA
BANG RAK
THUNG ANA MEK

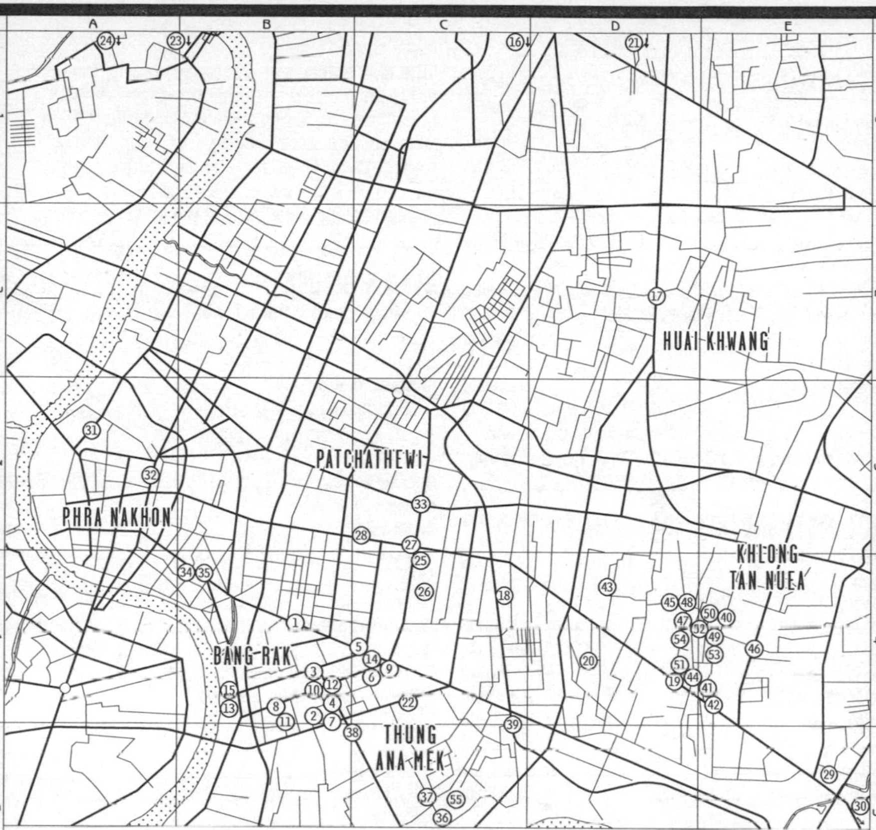

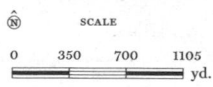

BANGKOK

N

SCALE

0 350 700 1105 yd.

1. *Joke Samyan (p.280)*
2. *(Not Just) Another Cup (p.280)*
3. *Boon Pochana (p.280)*
4. *Dean & Deluca (p.280)*
5. *Derby King (p.280)*
6. *Eat Me Restaurant (p.280)*
7. *The House On Sathorn (p.281)*
8. *Kalpapruek Restaurant (p.281)*
9. *La Table De Tee (p.281)*
10. *Ledu (p.281)*
11. *Luka (p.281)*
12. *Namsaah Bottling Trust (p.281)*
13. *Le Normandie (p.282)*
14. *Street Stalls On Convent Road (p.282)*
15. *The Verandah (p.282)*
16. *Beer Hima (p.282)*
17. *Huai Kawang Night Market (p.282)*
18. *Niyom (p.282)*
19. *Saengchai Pochana (p.283)*
20. *Xia Duck Noodles (p.283)*
21. *Khaophat Pu Mueang Thong 1 (p.283)*
22. *Nahm (p.283)*
23. *Suan Thip (p.283)*
24. *Baan Rabiang Nam (p.284)*
25. *Fei Ya (p.284)*
26. *Gaggan (p.284)*
27. *Ginza Sushi Ichi (p.284)*
28. *Oishi Grand (p.284)*
29. *Burmese Noodles (p.284)*
30. *Som Tam Khun Gan (p.285)*
31. *Kanom Jeen Banglumpoo (p.285)*
32. *Thipsamai (p.285)*
33. *Go-Ang Kaomunkai Pratunam (p.285)*
34. *Yim Yim (p.285)*
35. *Hia Tue Yaowarat (p.286)*
36. *Amantee (p.286)*
37. *De For-Rest (p.286)*
38. *Sara-Jane's (p.286)*
39. *Issaya Siamese Club (p.286)*
40. *Shukuriki 432 (p.286)*
41. *Soul Food Mahanakorn (p.287)*
42. *55 Pochana (p.287)*
43. *Appia (p.287)*
44. *Bo.lan (p.287)*
45. *Brekkie (p.287)*
46. *In The Mood For Love (p.288)*
47. *Khua Kling Pak Sod (p.288)*
48. *Klang Soi Restaurant (p.288)*
49. *Little Bao (p.288)*
50. *Little Beast (p.288)*
51. *Saew Noodles (p.289)*
52. *Suki Masa (p.289)*
53. *Took Lae Dee (p.289)*
54. *Umi (p.289)*
55. *Sühring (p.289)*

JOKE SAMYAN

Recommended by
Thitid Tassanakajohn

Udomsuk Soi 9
Bangna
Bangkok 10330
+66 0813506671

Opening hours	Open 7 days
Reservation policy	No
Credit cards	Not accepted
Price range	Budget
Style	Casual
Cuisine	Thai
Recommended for	Breakfast

"Super amazing congee. Selling from 4.00 a.m. and usually sold out by 7.00 a.m.!"—Thitid Tassanakajohn

(NOT JUST) ANOTHER CUP

Recommended by
Lucio Galletto,
Thomas & Mathias Sühring

5/1 Sathon Road 10
Bangrak
Bangkok 10500
+66 26353464

Opening hours	Open 7 days
Credit cards	Accepted
Price range	Affordable
Style	Casual
Cuisine	International
Recommended for	Breakfast

"The food is excellent, the owners and staff are very friendly, and the little side alley location and setting are very charming."—Lucio Galletto

BOON POCHANA

Recommended by
Tim Butler,
Mirco Keller

152/8–9 Silom Road
Suriyawong
Bangrak
Bangkok 10500
+66 22372764

Opening hours	Open 7 days
Credit cards	Accepted but not AMEX
Price range	Budget
Style	Casual
Cuisine	Cantonese
Recommended for	Regular neighborhood

"Late night chefs hangout open till 4.00 a.m., serving spicy Szechuan tripe and kidneys."—Tim Butler

No-nonsense Szechuan cooking, served in no-nonsense dining room off Silom Road which boasts air conditioning, bare wooden tables and little else in terms of creature comforts. Open until 4.00 a.m., there's an authentic Szechuan-style punchiness to dishes such as Mápó tòfu (tofu in spicy sauce); steamed goby fish; deep-fried squid (or frog) with chile, salt and garlic; long beans with minced pork; pepper clams; fried pig kidneys; spicy preserved egg salad; and steamed salty chicken.

DEAN & DELUCA

Recommended by
Thomas & Mathias Sühring

98 Sathorn Square Office Tower
1F, North Sathorn Road
Bangrak
Bangkok 10500
+66 21081208
www.deandeluca.com/thailand

Opening hours	Open 7 days
Reservation policy	No
Credit cards	Accepted
Price range	Affordable
Style	Casual
Cuisine	International
Recommended for	Breakfast

"We love enjoying our morning breakfast there."
—Thomas & Mathias Sühring

DERBY KING

Recommended by
Thitid Tassanakajohn

70–72 Thanon Patpong 1
Bangrak
Bangkok 10500
+66 22348354

Opening hours	Open 7 days
Credit cards	Not accepted
Price range	Budget
Style	Casual
Cuisine	Thai
Recommended for	Bargain

EAT ME RESTAURANT

Recommended by
Dylan Jones &
Duangporn Songvisava,
Thomas & Mathias Sühring,
Thitid Tassanakajohn

Soi Pipat 2
Bangrak
Bangkok 10500
+66 22380931
www.eatmerestaurant.com

Opening hours	Open 7 days
Credit cards	Accepted but not Diners
Price range	Affordable
Style	Smart casual
Cuisine	International
Recommended for	High end

"The food is great and tasty. We love to bring our team to enjoy a late dinner there after service."
—Thomas and Mathias Suhring

THE HOUSE ON SATHORN

Recommended by
Thitid Tassanakajohn

106 Si Lom
Bangrak
Bangkok 10500
+66 23444025
www.thehouseonsathorn.com

Opening hours..Open 7 days
Credit cards...Accepted
Price range..Expensive
Style..Smart casual
Cuisine...Modern Turkish
Recommended for..High end

KALPAPRUEK RESTAURANT

Recommended by
Gaggan Anand

27 Pramuan Road
Bangrak
Bangkok 10500
+66 22384002
www.kalpapruekrestaurant.com

Opening hours..Open 7 days
Credit cards................................Accepted but not AMEX
Price range..Affordable
Style...Casual
Cuisine..Thai
Recommended for..Bargain

"You get the best of local food—easy to eat yet using produce that comes from the Royal Project!"
—Thitid Tassanakajohn

LA TABLE DE TEE

Recommended by
Alexis Gauthier

69/5 Saladaeng Road Silom
Bangrak
Bangkok 10500
+66 26363220
www.latabledetee.com

Opening hours..Closed Monday
Credit cards...Accepted
Price range..Affordable
Style..Smart casual
Cuisine..Thai-French
Recommended for...............................Worth the travel

"Absolutely superb value and a lovely little place, serving food several levels above what you are paying for. It's hard to get a table but it has very friendly staff."—Alexis Gauthier

LEDU

Recommended by
Thomas Rode Anderson

399/3 Silom Soi 7
Bangrak
Bangkok 10500
+66 929199969
www.ledubkk.com

Opening hours..Closed Sunday
Credit cards........................Accepted but not AMEX or Diners
Price range..Affordable
Style...Casual
Cuisine...Modern Thai
Recommended for...............................Worth the travel

LUKA

Recommended by
Thitid Tassanakajohn

64/3 Thanon Pan
Bangrak
Bangkok 10500
+66 26378558
www.lukabangkok.format.com

Opening hours..Open 7 days
Credit cards................................Accepted but not Diners
Price range..Affordable
Style...Casual
Cuisine...American
Recommended for..Breakfast

NAMSAAH BOTTLING TRUST

Recommended by
Thitid Tassanakajohn

401 Silom Soi 7
Silom Road
Bangrak
Bangkok 10500
+66 26366622
www.namsaah.com

Opening hours..Open 7 days
Credit cards........................Accepted but not AMEX or Diners
Price range..Expensive
Style..Smart casual
Cuisine..Thai
Recommended for...............................Local favorite

LE NORMANDIE

Mandarin Oriental Hotel
48 Oriental Avenue
Bangrak
Bangkok 10500
+66 26599000
www.mandarinoriental.com/bangkok

Opening hours..Closed Sunday
Credit cards...Accepted
Price range...Expensive
Style..Smart casual
Cuisine..French
Recommended for...High end

"Amazing food, great wine list, and a spectacular
view of the river. The service is the best in town!"
—Thitid Tassanakajohn

STREET STALLS ON CONVENT ROAD

Convent Road and Sala Daeng Soi 2
Bangrak
Bangkok 10500

Opening hours..Open 7 days
Reservation policy..No
Credit cards...Not accepted
Price range...Budget
Style...Casual
Cuisine..Thai Street Food
Recommended for...Bargain

"Tons of street food that changes from lunch to dinner
and late night."—Tim Butler

THE VERANDAH

Mandarin Oriental Hotel
48 Oriental Avenue
Bangrak
Bangkok 10500
+66 6599000
mandarinoriental.com/bangkok

Opening hours..Open 7 days
Credit cards...Accepted
Price range...Expensive
Style..Smart casual
Cuisine...International
Recommended for...Breakfast

"I love the service of the Mandarin. They always
remember what you like and which eggs you prefer,
but, more importantly, I love the view of the busy
morning Chao Phraya river."—Gaggan Anand

BEER HIMA

12/21 Thetsaban Song Khro Road
Chatuchak
Bangkok 10900
+66 22105118

Opening hours..Open 7 days
Credit cards...Not accepted
Price range...Affordable
Style...Casual
Cuisine..Thai-Seafood
Recommended for.................Regular neighborhood

"Super-fresh live seafood, in a casual setting
serving some extremely spicy southern Thai
seafood dishes."—Tim Butler

HUAI KWANG NIGHT MARKET

Soi Pracha Rat Bamphen
Din Daeng
Bangkok 10400

Opening hours..Open 7 days
Reservation policy..No
Credit cards...Not accepted
Price range...Budget
Style...Casual
Cuisine..Thai Street Food
Recommended for.......................................Late night

NIYOM

174 Soi Sukhumvit 8
Khlong Toei
Bangkok 10110
+66 22340149

Opening hours..Open 7 days
Reservation policy..No
Credit cards...Not accepted
Price range...Affordable
Style...Casual
Cuisine..Chinese
Recommended for.......................................Late night

SAENGCHAI POCHANA
762 Sukumvit Road 5–6
Khlong Toei
Bangkok 10110
+66 813760150

Recommended by
Thitid Tassanakajohn

Opening hours	Open 7 days
Reservation policy	No
Credit cards	Accepted but not AMEX or Diners
Price range	Budget
Style	Casual
Cuisine	Thai-Chinese
Recommended for	Late night

"Amazing late-night food and the best pork soup with Chinese plum...period!"—Thitid Tassanakajohn

XIA DUCK NOODLES
2856 Soi Sukhumvit 22
Rama 4 Road
Khlong Toei
Bangkok 10310
+66 26713279

Recommended by
Dylan Jones &
Duangporn Songvisava

Opening hours	Closed Sunday
Reservation policy	No
Credit cards	Not accepted
Price range	Budget
Style	Casual
Cuisine	Chinese
Recommended for	Late night

"The quality of the braised duck is great and the blood cakes are unreal."
—Dylan Jones & Duangporn Songvisava

KHAOPHAT PU MUEANG THONG 1
29/69 Soi Chaeng Wattana 14
Lak Si
Bangkok 10210
+66 816463296

Recommended by
Mirco Keller

Opening hours	Open 7 days
Reservation policy	No
Credit cards	Not accepted
Price range	Budget
Style	Casual
Cuisine	Fast Food
Recommended for	Bargain

NAHM
COMO Metropolitan
27 South Sathorn Road
Nakhon
Bangkok 10120
+66 26253388
www.comohotels.com

Recommended by
Angus An,
Gaggan Anand,
José Avillez,
David Muñoz, Andy Ricker,
Thomas & Mathias Sühring,
Thitid Tassanakajohn

Opening hours	Open 7 days
Credit cards	Accepted but not Diners
Price range	Expensive
Style	Smart casual
Cuisine	Thai
Recommended for	Worth the travel

"David Thomson, the authority on Thai food, cooks old recipes from a lost era in a modern setting. A must for gourmands looking for fine Thai cuisine."
—Gaggan Anand

SUAN THIP
Chongwattana Pak Kret 3 Road
Soi Wat Koo
Bangpood
Nonthaburi
Bangkok 11120
+66 25834540
www.suanthip.com

Recommended by
Jason Bailey

Opening hours	Open 7 days
Credit cards	Accepted
Price range	Affordable
Style	Smart casual
Cuisine	Thai-Vegetarian
Recommended for	Local favorite

"This restaurant embodies the Siamese roots of central Thailand. Its stunning location beside the Chao Phraya river and its table settings located in a lush tropical garden make it unique."—Jason Bailey

BAAN RABIANG NAM

Soi 23 Wat Khae Nok
Nonthaburi
Bangkok 11000
+66 29681481
www.baanrabiangnam.com

Opening hours	Open 7 days
Credit cards	Accepted but not AMEX or Diners
Price range	Affordable
Style	Casual
Cuisine	Thai
Recommended for	Wish I'd opened

"I love the simplicity and broad range of their Thai home cooking. Set in a old teak wood home where the view up the Chao Phraya river is spectacular at sunset. The flavors are exactly as they should be."—Jason Bailey

FEI YA

518/8 Ploenchit Road
Pathum Wan
Bangkok 10330
+66 21255030

Opening hours	Open 7 days
Credit cards	Accepted
Price range	Affordable
Style	Casual
Cuisine	Chinese
Recommended for	High end

"It's high-end Chinese—the Peking duck is pretty special."—Dylan Jones & Duangporn Songvisava

GAGGAN

68/1 Soi Langsuan
Ploenchit Road
Pathum Wan
Bangkok 10330
+66 26521700
www.eatatgaggan.com

Opening hours	Open 7 days
Credit cards	Accepted
Price range	Expensive
Style	Smart casual
Cuisine	Modern Indian
Recommended for	High end

"This restaurant made a big impact on me. It surprised me in all sorts of ways, eating and seeing things for the first time. Just one word—wonderful!"
—Takeshi Fukuyama

GINZA SUSHI ICHI

Erawan Bangkok Shopping Mall
494 Ploenchit Road
Pathum Wan
Bangkok 10330
+66 22500014
www.ginza-sushiichi.jp

Opening hours	Closed Monday
Credit cards	Accepted
Price range	Expensive
Style	Smart casual
Cuisine	Sushi
Recommended for	High end

"Sushi *omakase* (chef's choice) at its best in Bangkok."—Gaggan Anand

OISHI GRAND

Siam Paragon Shopping Mall
991 Rama 1 Road
Pathum Wan
Bangkok 10330
+66 26580222
www.oishigroup.com

Opening hours	Open 7 days
Reservation policy	No
Credit cards	Accepted but not AMEX or Diners
Price range	Budget
Style	Casual
Cuisine	Japanese
Recommended for	Worth the travel

"Gorgeous sashimi and tempura—perfect."
—Andi Oliver

BURMESE NOODLES

Phra Khanong Market
Sukhumvit Road
Phra Khanong
Bangkok 10110

Opening hours	Open 7 days
Reservation policy	No
Credit cards	Not accepted
Price range	Budget
Style	Casual
Cuisine	Burmese
Recommended for	Breakfast

"My favorite dish is *Mohinga* which is Burmese cold rice noodles."—Jason Bailey

SOM TAM KHUN GAN

Recommended by
Thitid Tassanakajohn

6 Soi Wichairatanit
23 Sukhumvit 101/1
Phra Khanong
Bangkok 10260
+66 23970770

Opening hours..Open 7 days
Credit cards.........................Accepted but not AMEX or Diners
Price range...Affordable
Style..Casual
Cuisine...Thai
Recommended for.................................Regular neighborhood

"So good! North-eastern style Thai food with real flavors and no compromises."—Thitid Tassanakajohn

KANOM JEEN BANGLUMPOO

Recommended by
Jason Bailey

Chakrabongse Road
Pedestrain alley beside Tang Huan Seng
Department Store
Phra Nakhon
Bangkok 10200

Opening hours..Open 7 days
Reservation policy..No
Credit cards...Not accepted
Price range...Budget
Style..Casual
Cuisine...Thai
Recommended for..Bargain

"This is my favorite Thai curried-fermented noodle store. I love the fish curry (*naamya*) because of the *umami* balance between the fish and shrimp (prawn) paste and the aromatic herbs such as lesser ginger, lemongrass, and lemon basil leaves."—Jason Bailey

THIPSAMAI

Recommended by
Colin Mackay

313-315 Maha Chai Road
Phra Nakhon
Bangkok 10200
+66 22266666
www.thipsamai.com

Opening hours..Open 7 days
Reservation policy..No
Credit cards...Not accepted
Price range...Budget
Style..Casual
Cuisine...Thai
Recommended for...Late night

"One of the best pad Thai stalls in Bangkok. Their stir-fried noodles with seafood, egg, and onion chives is the most satisfying thing to eat at the end of a long night. Delicious."—Colin Mackay

GO-ANG KAOMUNKAI PRATUNAM

Recommended by
Thomas &
Mathias Sühring

960-962 Phetchaburi Road
Ratchathewi
Bangkok 10400
+66 817797255

Opening hours..Open 7 days
Reservation policy..No
Credit cards...Not accepted
Price range...Budget
Style..Casual
Cuisine...Thai
Recommended for.................................Regular neighborhood

"This is the Thailand we like. Fresh ingredients and prepared with passion. Their chicken rice is amazing."—Thomas & Mathias Sühring

YIM YIM

Recommended by
Mirco Keller

89 Yaowaphanit Road
Samphanthawong
Bangkok 10100
+66 22242203

Opening hours..Open 7 days
Credit cards.........................Accepted but not AMEX or Diners
Price range...Affordable
Style..Casual
Cuisine...Thai-Chinese
Recommended for...Local favorite

"It has been open for over eighty years—also serves Chinese food."—Mirco Keller

Even with the plethora of options available in Chinatown, this eighty-year-old Teochew (from the Chaosan region of China) veteran, which sits atop an old banquet hall at Yaowarat Road, remains a standout. Yes, the kitschy decor is a throwback to a past era, what with the low ceiling, plastic divider curtains, and a clutter of other knick-knacks, but the regulars are there for the food. The ham with goat's skin dipped in rice vinegar is a perennial favorite, as is the raw fish doused in a peanut-scented plum sauce. Of course, Teochew classics like sea cucumber, stewed goose feet, and crab claws with ginger are popular too.

HIA TUE YAOWARAT

Recommended by
Mirco Keller

Krungsri Ayudhya Bank
Yaowarat Road
Samphanthawong
Bangkok 10100

Opening hours	Open 7 days
Reservation policy	No
Credit cards	Not accepted
Price range	Budget
Style	Casual
Cuisine	Thai-Chinese
Recommended for	Late night

This nondescript street-side stall in front of Krungsri Ayudhya Bank on Yaowarat Road, Bangkok's Chinatown, has no address and is operated from a pushcart—but make no mistake, the Thai-style Chinese food it serves is blue-ribbon standard. Take our advice and order the steamed abalone or stir-fried crab in yellow curry powder.

AMANTEE

Recommended by
Dylan Jones &
Duangporn Songvisava

2240/12–13 Chan Kao Road
Chongnonsee
Sathom
Bangkok 10120
+66 818140920
www.amantee.com

Opening hours	Closed Monday
Credit cards	Accepted but not AMEX
Price range	Budget
Style	Casual
Cuisine	Bakery
Recommended for	Breakfast

"Technically it's not a restaurant yet, but the breads and pastries are so good it's our go-to for a western breakfast."—Dylan Jones & Duangporn Songvisava

DE FOR-REST

Recommended by
Thomas & Mathias Sühring

8/11 Nanglinchee Road
Sathon
Bangkok 10120
+66 22869200

Opening hours	Open 7 days
Credit cards	Accepted but not AMEX or Diners
Price range	Affordable
Style	Casual
Cuisine	Thai
Recommended for	Regular neighborhood

SARA-JANE'S

Recommended by
Thomas &
Mathias Sühring

88 Naradhiwas Rajanagarindra Road
Sathon
Bangkok 10120
+66 26763338

Opening hours	Open 7 days
Credit cards	Accepted but not AMEX or Diners
Price range	Affordable
Style	Casual
Cuisine	Thai
Recommended for	Bargain

"We love the authenticity of this place."
—Thomas & Mathias Sühring

ISSAYA SIAMESE CLUB

Recommended by
Thitid Tassanakajohn

4 Soi Sri Aksorn
Chua Ploeng Road
Sathorn
Bangkok 10120
+66 627878768
www.issaya.com

Opening hours	Open 7 days
Credit cards	Accepted but not AMEX or Diners
Price range	Affordable
Style	Casual
Cuisine	Thai
Recommended for	High end

SHAKARIKI 432

Recommended by
Gaggan Anand

440/7–8 Sukhumvit 55 (Thonglor)
Wattana
Bangkok 10110
+66 23818432
www.shakariki432.com

Opening hours	Open 7 days
Credit cards	Accepted
Price range	Affordable
Style	Casual
Cuisine	Japanese
Recommended for	Late night

"This great value twenty-four-hour *Izakaya* (Japanese gastropub) is the best after a late service, when you need to relax with your team."—Gaggan Anand

SOUL FOOD MAHANAKORN

56/10 Soi Thonglor
Sukhumvit Soi 55
Wattana
Bangkok 10110
+66 27147708
www.soulfoodmahanakorn.com

Recommended by
Dylan Jones &
Duangporn Songvisava

Opening hours	Open 7 days
Credit cards	Accepted
Price range	Affordable
Style	Casual
Cuisine	Thai
Recommended for	Local favorite

"Good produce, treated deftly—the seasoning is spot on and the cocktail list is smashing."
—Dylan Jones & Duangporn Songvisava

This hip venue in Thonglor, owned by a former food writer, serves jazzed-up Thai street food with local herbs and spices—and from the retro-inspired interior all the way to the spot-on kitchen execution, it ticks all the right boxes. The banana leaf-wrapped, charcoal-grilled seabass is perfectly moist and smoky, while the *yam hua plee* (banana blossom salad) is full of vibrancy and fresh flavors. It also helps that the bar serves up a great selection of locally inspired cocktails—try the Thai basil-infused "So Fashioned".

55 POCHANA

1093 Sukhumvit Road
Watthana
Bangkok 10110
+66 23912021

Recommended by
Jason Bailey

Opening hours	Open 7 days
Credit cards	Not accepted
Price range	Budget
Style	Casual
Cuisine	Thai-Chinese
Recommended for	Late night

"A wide cross section of Thai Chinese dishes."
—Jason Bailey

APPIA

20/4 Sukhumvit 31
Watthana
Bangkok 10110
+66 22612056
www.appia-bangkok.com

Recommended by
Dylan Jones &
Duangporn Songvisava

Opening hours	Closed Monday
Credit cards	Accepted but not Diners
Price range	Affordable
Style	Casual
Cuisine	Italian
Recommended for	High end

BO.LAN

24 Sukhumvit 53
Watthana
Bangkok 10110
+66 22602961
www.bolan.co.th

Recommended by
Tim Butler, Mark Dobbie,
Gary Foulkes, Malcolm Lee,
Andy Oliver,
Thitid Tassanakajohn

Opening hours	Closed Monday
Credit cards	Accepted but not Diners
Price range	Expensive
Style	Smart casual
Cuisine	Thai
Recommended for	Worth the travel

"Showcases a great combination of contemporary and traditional styles and regions of Thai food. The menu changes every quarter and it's always something to look forward to."—Malcolm Lee

BREKKIE

6/9 Sukhumvit Soi 39
Watthana
Bangkok 10110
+66 836566141
www.brekkiebangkok.com

Recommended by
Mirco Keller

Opening hours	Open 7 days
Credit cards	Accepted but not AMEX
Price range	Budget
Style	Casual
Cuisine	International
Recommended for	Breakfast

This organic all-day café offers a menu of comforting start-the-day staples: avocado on toast; baked eggs with chorizo and fluffy whole wheat pancakes. Added to that are a selection of classic sandwiches, healthy 'superfood' bowls and a whole quinoa-championing menu section (fried quinoa *tom yum* with diced salmon). The organic coffee is made with beans from Chiang Mai.

IN THE MOOD FOR LOVE

Recommended by
Jason Bailey

Ekamai Soi 1
Watthana
Bangkok 10110
+66 23928477

Opening hours	Open 7 days
Credit cards	Accepted but not Diners
Price range	Affordable
Style	Smart casual
Cuisine	Japanese
Recommended for	High end

"Without a doubt this is the best creative *omakase* in Bangkok, firmly rooted in Japanese technique."
—Jason Bailey

KHUA KLING PAK SOD

Recommended by
Gaggan Anand

98/1 Soi Thonglor 5 Sukhumvit 55 Road
Watthana
Bangkok 10110
+66 21853977
www.khuaklingpaksod.com

Opening hours	Open 7 days
Credit cards	Not accepted
Price range	Affordable
Style	Casual
Cuisine	Thai
Recommended for	Regular neighborhood

"Recipes from their home. My favorite Thai restaurant in Bangkok—the crab and the fish dishes are the best. Please book the coconut pudding in advance!"
—Gaggan Anand

KLANG SOI RESTAURANT

Recommended by
Jason Bailey

12/1 Sukhumvit 49/9 Road
Watthana
Bangkok 10110
+66 23914988

Opening hours	Closed Monday
Credit cards	Accepted but not AMEX or Diners
Price range	Affordable
Style	Casual
Cuisine	Thai
Recommended for	Regular neighborhood

"A rare example of grandma-style Thai cooking with delicate layers of flavor combinations. A refreshing difference."—Jason Bailey

LITTLE BAO

Recommended by
Lori Granito

72 Courtyard
72 Sukhumvit, 55 Thonglor
Watthana
Bangkok 10110
+66 23926922
www.little-bao.com

Opening hours	Closed Monday
Credit cards	Accepted but not AMEX or Diners
Price range	Affordable
Style	Casual
Cuisine	Modern Chinese
Recommended for	Worth the travel

"May Chow has managed to take her delicious Hong Kong bao sharing concept and transplant it to Thailand with the same delicious result."—Lori Granito

LITTLE BEAST

Recommended by
Mirco Keller

44/9–10 Thonglor 13
Watthana
Bangkok 10110
+66 21852670

Opening hours	Closed Monday
Credit cards	Accepted but not AMEX or Diners
Price range	Affordable
Style	Casual
Cuisine	French-American
Recommended for	Regular neighborhood

"French-American-style comfort food."—Mirco Keller

With young chef Rangsima "Nan" Bunyasaranand at the helm, this trendy gastro-bar has attracted plenty of attention. Born in Thailand and schooled at the Culinary Institute of America, Bunyasaranand has worked under big names like Thomas Keller and Jean-Georges Vongerichten, but Little Beast is her own labor of love. Diners come as much for the relaxed 1920s vibes (think exposed pipes and a concrete floor) as for the modern American sharing plates—charcuterie, meats, salads and, best of all, desserts (order the ice-cream sandwiches).

SAEW NOODLES

Klang Alley
Watthana
Bangkok 10110
+66 917805604

Recommended by
Jason Bailey,
Dylan Jones &
Duangporn Songvisava

Opening hours	Closed Thursday
Reservation policy	No
Credit cards	Not accepted
Price range	Budget
Style	Casual
Cuisine	Thai-Chinese
Recommended for	Bargain

"A two-generation-old noodle shop renowed for the depth of flavor in its broth and its sphere-shaped fish and shrimp balls."—Jason Bailey

SUKI MASA

113 Thong Lo 5 Alley
Watthana
Bangkok 10110
+66 23924769

Recommended by
Dylan Jones &
Duangporn Songvisava

Opening hours	Open 7 days
Credit cards	Accepted
Price range	Expensive
Style	Casual
Cuisine	Japanese
Recommended for	Regular neighborhood

"The quality of beef is pretty high."—Dylan Jones & Duangporn Songvisava

TOOK LAE DEE

87 Soi Sukhumvit 55
Watthana
Bangkok 10110
+66 23901188

Recommended by
Mirco Keller

Opening hours	Open 7 days
Reservation policy	No
Credit cards	Accepted but not AMEX or Diners
Price range	Budget
Style	Casual
Cuisine	Thai
Recommended for	Bargain

"Simple Thai food—good, cheap, and fast. This restaurant can be found inside every Foodland supermarket."—Mirco Keller

UMI

Piman 49
Soi Sukumvit 49
Watthana
Bangkok 10110
+66 26626661

Recommended by
Tim Butler

Opening hours	Closed Monday
Credit cards	Accepted but not Diners
Price range	Affordable
Style	Casual
Cuisine	Japanese
Recommended for	High end

"Super fresh *omakase* (chef's choice) menus." —Tim Butler

SÜHRING

10 Yen Akat Soi 3
Yan Nawa
Bangkok 10120
+66 022871799
www.restaurantsuhring.com

Recommended by
Mirco Keller,
Thitid Tassanakajohn

Opening hours	Open / days
Credit cards	Accepted
Price range	Expensive
Style	Smart casual
Cuisine	European
Recommended for	High end

"A strong concept—consistently good food and the wine list is very reasonably priced."—Mirco Keller

CUISINE WAT DAMNAK

Wat Damnak Market Street
Sala Kamreuk Commune
Siem Reap
Siem Reap 17259, Cambodia
+855 77347762
www.cuisinewatdamnak.com

Opening hours............................Closed Monday and Sunday
Credit cards........................Accepted but not AMEX or Diners
Price range...Affordable
Style...Casual
Cuisine...Cambodian
Recommended for..Worth the travel

"The chef, a French Cambodian resident, is
honoring local traditions with a modern
interpretation highlighting flavors and textures.
The tasting menu is a masterpiece in precision
—a real gem!"—Christine Manfield

GOLDEN DRAGON RESTAURANT

Hanoi Hotel
D8 Giảng Võ Street
Ba Đình
Hanoi 10000, Vietnam
+84 888161158
www.hanoihotel.com.vn

Opening hours...Open 7 days
Credit cards...Accepted
Price range...Affordable
Style...Casual
Cuisine..Chinese
Recommended for..Late night

"Great noodles and a lively scene."—Donald Berger

BIA HOI CORNER

20 Ta Hiên
Hoàn Kiêm
Hanoi 111500, Vietnam
+84 39260168

Opening hours...Open 7 days
Credit cards..Not accepted
Price range...Budget
Style...Casual
Cuisine..Vietnamese
Recommended for...Bargain

BÚN BÒ NAM BÔ

76 Hang Dieu Street
Hoàn Kiêm
Hanoi 111202, Vietnam
+84 439230701
www.bunbonambo.com

Opening hours...Open 7 days
Reservation policy...No
Credit cards..Not accepted
Price range...Budget
Style...Casual
Cuisine...Noodles
Recommended for...Regular neighborhood

"Eating two kinds of pork sausages with hot sauce
(fermented and cooked, both in banana leaf), and then
a bowl of stir-fried beef with garlic and beansprouts,
salad, noodles, and *gastrique* (sugar and vinegar
flavoring), with pickles, peanuts, and crispy shallots
and a beer with ice is an experience all about the
taste—sweetness, textures, aroma, and a buzz and
spiciness that just hit the spot every single time!
Not fancy, just sublime."—Donald Berger

LA BADIANE

10 Nam Ngư
Hoàn Kiêm
Hanoi 111105, Vietnam
+84 439424509
www.labadiane-hanoi.com

Opening hours...Closed Sunday
Credit cards...Accepted
Price range...Expensive
Style...Smart casual
Cuisine..French
Recommended for...High end

QUÁN AN NGON

18 Phan Bôi Châu
Hoàn Kiêm
Hanoi 111105, Vietnam
+84 439428162
www.ngonhanoi.com.vn

Opening hours...Open 7 days
Credit cards...Accepted
Price range...Affordable
Style...Casual
Cuisine..Vietnamese
Recommended for..Local favorite

WRAP AND ROLL

33 Đinh Tiên Hoàng
Hoàn Kiếm
Hanoi 100000, Vietnam
+84 438243718
www.wrap-roll.com

Opening hours	Open 7 days
Credit cards	Accepted but not AMEX or Diners
Price range	Affordable
Style	Casual
Cuisine	Vietnamese
Recommended for	Local favorite

"Wrap and Roll is a restaurant chain but my goodness they do Vietnamese food so well."—Donald Berger

Crisp rolls assembled with herbs, vegetables and an array of meats are the cornerstone of this vibrantly decorated fast food chain that boasts outlets in Ho Chi Minh City, Hanoi, and even Singapore. Apart from traditional menu items like rice paper rolls, *bánh cuốn* (steamed rice cake filled with minced mushrooms and pork), and the *nem nướng* (grilled pork sausage) wrap, the eatery also allows customers to create their own rolls. Prices can be steep for the snack-sized portions.

BÁNH CUỐN

34 Yên Phụ
Quận Ba Đình
Hanoi 118307, Vietnam

Opening hours	Open 7 days
Reservation policy	No
Credit cards	Accepted but not AMEX or Diners
Price range	Affordable
Style	Casual
Cuisine	Vietnamese
Recommended for	Breakfast

"This is where I take my lovely Vietnamese wife for a breakfast date after dropping my son at school. Delicious!"—Donald Berger

BÚN CHẢ MAI ANH

47 Xuân Diêu
Tây Hồ
Hanoi 124424, Vietnam
+84 1648186663
www.bunchata.com

Opening hours	Open 7 days
Credit cards	Accepted but not AMEX or Diners
Price range	Budget
Style	Casual
Cuisine	Vietnamese
Recommended for	Bargain

"Cheap and fast."—Donald Berger

MAISON DE TÊT DECOR

Villa 156 Tu Hoa
Tây Hồ
Hanoi 124424, Vietnam
+84 438239722
www.tet-lifestyle-collection.com

Opening hours	Open 7 days
Credit cards	Accepted
Price range	Affordable
Style	Casual
Cuisine	Café
Recommended for	Breakfast

Everything in this charming old French villa overlooking lake Hồ Tây ticks the right boxes. Spread out over three levels of wood-decorated space peppered with local art, sculptures, and fabrics, they have some of the best single origin coffee in the city, as well as a solid menu of sumptuous and wholesome food. The dishes are crafted—whenever possible —with locally sourced organic ingredients; think soups, egg dishes, pastas, and homemade burgers. There are plenty of gluten-free, dairy-free, and vegetarian options too. Extra brownie points go to the restaurant's effort in training and employing disadvantaged young people.

FRENCH GRILL

8 Đỗ Đức Road
Từ Liêm
Hanoi 129412, Vietnam
+84 438335588
www.marriott.com

Opening hours	Open 7 days
Credit cards	Accepted
Price range	Expensive
Style	Smart casual
Cuisine	Modern French
Recommended for	High end

OPERA

Park Hyatt Saigon
2 Công Trường Lam Sơn
Bến Nghé
Hô Chí Minh 710007, Vietnam
+84 838241234
www.saigon.park.hyatt.com

Opening hours	Open 7 days
Credit cards	Accepted
Price range	Expensive
Style	Smart casual
Cuisine	Italian
Recommended for	Breakfast

E.T. STEAMBOAT RESTAURANT

6 Rangoon Road
George Town
Penang 11400, Malaysia
+60 42266025

Opening hours	Closed Thursday
Credit cards	Not accepted
Price range	Affordable
Style	Casual
Cuisine	Malaysian
Recommended for	Worth the travel

"The food on offer changes every day and the flavors are so good—and so cheap for the quality."
—Mark Jarvis

KEBAYA

14a Steward Lane
George Town
Penang 10200, Malaysia
+60 42642333
www.kebaya.com.my

Opening hours	Open 7 days
Credit cards	Accepted but not AMEX or Diners
Price range	Affordable
Style	Casual
Cuisine	Peranaken
Recommended for	Worth the travel

"Modern Nyonya cuisine in an authentic setting."
—Eelke Plasmeijer

If you're looking for Peranakan food served in a refined setting, look no further than this gloriously tiled, Straits Chinese restaurant at the Seven Terraces boutique hotel. Don't come here expecting the classics, though. Kebaya serves Peranakan cuisine prepared with western techniques—think *sous-vide* (cooked in a pouch in water) organic roasted pork and grilled chicken *kapitan* (Malaysian chicken curry), plus the occasional Indo-Chinese dish like shrimp (prawn) *geng* (thick soup) or grilled *chao tom* (sugar-cane shrimp). Unless you're a hotel guest, you'll have to settle for the *prix fixe* four-course menu. Come early for an aperitif at the adjoining Kebaya and Baba Bar; one of the most stylish bars in town.

RESTAURANT GREEN VIEW

8 Jalan 19/3
Petaling Jaya
Selangor 46300, Malaysia
+60 379549363

Opening hours	Open 7 days
Credit cards	Accepted but not Diners
Price range	Affordable
Style	Casual
Cuisine	Malaysian
Recommended for	Worth the travel

ARENA PUB AND RESTAURANT

Recommended by
Chris Salans

Jalan By Pass I Gusti Ngurah Rai 115
Sanur
Denpasar
Bali 80228, Indonesia
+62 361287255
www.arenabali.com

Opening hours	Open 7 days
Credit cards	Accepted
Price range	Affordable
Style	Casual
Cuisine	German
Recommended for	Late night

"Open late. Well priced German comfort food."
—Chris Salans

BABI GULING CANDRA

Recommended by
Will Meyrick

Jalan Teuku Umar 140
Denpasar
Bali 80114, Indonesia
+62 361221278

Opening hours	Open 7 days
Reservation policy	No
Credit cards	Not accepted
Price range	Budget
Style	Casual
Cuisine	Balinese
Recommended for	Local favorite

CAFÉ BATU JIMBAR

Recommended by
Chris Salans

Jalan Danau Tamblingan 75a
Sanur
Denpasar
Bali 80228, Indonesia
+62 361287374
www.cafebatujimbar.com

Opening hours	Open 7 days
Credit cards	Accepted but not AMEX or Diners
Price range	Budget
Style	Casual
Cuisine	Café
Recommended for	Breakfast

"Down to earth place, very chilled and comfortable
where locals hang out. Good quality fare and great
value for money."—Chris Salans

WARUNG ADI

Recommended by
Chris Salans

Jalan Danau Buyan 15
Sanur
Denpasar
Bali 80227, Indonesia
+62 361286882

Opening hours	Open 7 days
Reservation policy	No
Credit cards	Not accepted
Price range	Budget
Style	Casual
Cuisine	Balinese
Recommended for	Bargain

WARUNG MAK BENG

Recommended by
Chris Salans

Jalan Hang Tuah 45
Sanur
Denpasar
Bali 80227, Indonesia
+62 361282633

Opening hours	Open 7 days
Reservation policy	No
Credit cards	Not accepted
Price range	Budget
Style	Casual
Cuisine	Balinese
Recommended for	Bargain

WARUNG WARDANI

Recommended by
Ray Adriansyah

Jalan Yudistira 2
Dangin Puri Kauh
Denpasar
Bali 80232, Indonesia
+62 361224398

Opening hours	Open 7 days
Reservation policy	No
Credit cards	Not accepted
Price range	Budget
Style	Casual
Cuisine	Balinese
Recommended for	Local favorite

CUCA

Recommended by
Ray Adriansyah,
Florian Lamelot

Jalan Yoga Perkanthi
Jimbaran
Bali 80364, Indonesia
+62 361708066
www.cucaflavor.com

Opening hours	Open 7 days
Credit cards	Accepted
Price range	Affordable
Style	Casual
Cuisine	Tapas
Recommended for	Local favorite

"I love this place. They opened in 2013 and are already well-known in Bali. Chef Kevin creates tasteful tapas and molecular dishes using local ingredients. I recommend the baby octopus or the roasted tiger prawns (shrimp). I also love their cocktails."
—Florian Lamelot

TEBA MEGA CAFÉ

Recommended by
Florian Lamelot

Jalan Four Seasons Resort
Pantai Muaya
Jimbaran
Bali 80361, Indonesia
+62 361703156
www.indo.com/restaurants/tebacafe

Opening hours	Open 7 days
Credit cards	Not accepted
Price range	Affordable
Style	Casual
Cuisine	Seafood
Recommended for	Local favorite

"Teba Mega Café is a very good seafood restaurant in south Jimbaran beach and the prices here are still very affordable compared to the north side. Perfect for sitting on the beach and eating fresh seafood, Balinese style, while enjoying the sunset."—Florian Lamelot

DA MARIA

Recommended by
Geoff Lindsay

Jalan Petitenget 170
Seminyak
Kuta
Bali 80361, Indonesia
+62 82237733099
www.damariabali.com

Opening hours	Open 7 days
Credit cards	Accepted
Price range	Affordable
Style	Smart casual
Cuisine	Italian
Recommended for	Late night

"It's a boisterous bar—great music and some delicious late-night food from chef Steve Skelly."
—Geoff Lindsay

FEYLOON RESTAURANT

Recommended by
Eelke Plasmeijer

Jalan Raya Kuta 98
Kuta
Bali 80361, Indonesia
+62 361766308
www.feyloon.wordpress.com

Opening hours	Open 7 days
Credit cards	Accepted but not AMEX or Diners
Price range	Affordable
Style	Casual
Cuisine	Chinese
Recommended for	Regular neighborhood

GOURMET CAFÉ

Recommended by
Will Meyrick

Jalan Petitenget 77a
Seminyak
Kuta
Bali 80361, Indonesia
+62 3618095188
www.balicateringcompany.com/cafe

Opening hours	Open 7 days
Reservation policy	No
Credit cards	Accepted but not AMEX or Diners
Price range	Budget
Style	Casual
Cuisine	Café
Recommended for	Bargain

KU DE TA

Recommended by
Florian Lamelot

Jalan Kayu Aya 9
Seminyak
Kuta
Bali 80361, Indonesia
+62 361736969
www.kudeta.net

Opening hours	Open 7 days
Credit cards	Accepted
Price range	Affordable
Style	Smart casual
Cuisine	Modern International
Recommended for	Late night

"The setting is gorgeous and the service efficient. The food is great too! The chef knows how to please every guest. From casual fine dining to international tapas and great cocktails, Ku De Ta is always at the top of its game."—Florian Lamelot

KURA KURA

Recommended by
Chris Salans

Oberoi Hotel
Jalan Kayu Aya
Seminyak
Kuta
Bali 80361, Indonesia
+62 361730361
www.oberoihotels.com

Opening hours	Open 7 days
Credit cards	Accepted
Price range	Affordable
Style	Smart casual
Cuisine	European-Indonesian
Recommended for	High end

MAMA SAN

Recommended by
Chris Salans

Jalan Raya Kerobokan 135
Banjar Taman
Kuta
Bali 80361, Indonesia
+62 361730436
www.mamasanbali.com

Opening hours	Open 7 days
Credit cards	Accepted
Price range	Budget
Style	Casual
Cuisine	Modern Asian
Recommended for	Wish I'd opened

"Great South East Asian fare prepared and presented in a modern way."—Chris Salans

NAUGHTY NURI'S WARUNG

Recommended by
Will Goldfarb

Jalan Mertanadi 62
Seminyak
Kuta
Bali 80361, Indonesia
+62 3618476783
www.naughtynurisseminyak.com

Opening hours	Open 7 days
Credit cards	Accepted but not AMEX or Diners
Price range	Affordable
Style	Casual
Cuisine	Balinese
Recommended for	Regular neighborhood

"My absolute haunt is Naughty Nuri's Warung, which is right next to my own restaurant. I can be found there most days having a gin martini and a pork chop."—Will Goldfarb

PETITENGET

Recommended by
Will Meyrick

Jalan Petitenget 40X
Seminyak
Kuta
Bali 80361, Indonesia
+62 3614733054
www.petitenget.net

Opening hours	Open 7 days
Credit cards	Accepted
Price range	Affordable
Style	Casual
Cuisine	International
Recommended for	Regular neighborhood

SANGSAKA

Recommended by
Ray Adriansyah,
Geoff Lindsay

Jalan Pangkung Sari 100X
Kerobokan
Kuta
Bali 80361, Indonesia
+62 81236959895
www.sangsakabali.com

Opening hours	Open 7 days
Credit cards	Accepted
Price range	Affordable
Style	Smart casual
Cuisine	Modern Indonesian
Recommended for	Regular neighborhood

"I split my time between Bali and Melbourne... so two neighborhoods. My Bali neighborhood recommendation is Sangsaka, a contemporary Indonesian restaurant run by chef Kieran Morland of more famous and much larger restaurant Merah Putih. Sangsaka is bubbling with exciting inventive dishes."—Geoff Lindsay

SARI RATU PADANG

Recommended by
Will Meyrick

Jalan Sunset Road
Jalan Sri Dewi Intersection
Kuta
Bali 80361, Indonesia
+62 3618947482

Opening hours	Open 7 days
Credit cards	Accepted but not AMEX
Price range	Budget
Style	Casual
Cuisine	Indonesian
Recommended for	Late night

SISTERFIELDS

Recommended by
Ray Adriansyah

Jalan Bayu Cendana 7
Seminyak
Kuta
Bali 80361, Indonesia
+62 361738454
www.sisterfieldsbali.com

Opening hours	Open 7 days
Reservation policy	No
Credit cards	Accepted
Price range	Affordable
Style	Casual
Cuisine	Australian
Recommended for	Breakfast

"Melbourne-style restaurant with a good selection of breakfast dishes and coffee. Family-friendly and super tasty."—Ray Adriansyah

SMOKEHOUSE BBQ BALI

Recommended by
Ray Adriansyah

Jalan Petitenget 14
Kerobokan
Kuta
Bali 80361, Indonesia
+62 87862351052
www.smokehousebali.com

Opening hours	Closed Monday
Credit cards	Accepted
Price range	Affordable
Style	Casual
Cuisine	Barbecue
Recommended for	Regular neighborhood

"Go for the beef brisket."—Ray Adriansyah

WARUNG SULAWESI

Recommended by
Ray Adriansyah

Jalan Raya Seminyak 2000X
Seminyak
Kuta
Bali 80361, Indonesia
+62 3617463052

Opening hours	Open 7 days
Credit cards	Not accepted
Price range	Budget
Style	Casual
Cuisine	Balinese
Recommended for	Local favorite

WATERCRESS CAFÉ

Recommended by
Will Meyrick

Jalan Batu Belig 21a
Kerobokan
Kuta
Bali 80361, Indonesia
+62 3617808030
www.watercressbali.com

Opening hours	Open 7 days
Credit cards	Not accepted
Price range	Affordable
Style	Casual
Cuisine	International
Recommended for	Breakfast

NYOMAN'S BEER GARDEN

Jalan Pantai Mengiat
Nusa Dua
Bali 80361, Indonesia
+62 361775746
www.sendok-bali.com

Opening hours	Open 7 days
Credit cards	Accepted
Price range	Affordable
Style	Casual
Cuisine	Balinese
Recommended for	Bargain

"A nice little restaurant located in Nusa Dua. The food is simple but delicious, and you can count on Andreas the chef-owner to take good care of you. I always go for a German specialty, like the cheese and ham *spaetzle* (egg noodle or dumpling)."—Florian Lamelot

WARUNG LAOTA JIMBARAN

Jalan By Pass Ngurah Rai 77X
Jimbaran
Nusa Dua
Bali 80361, Indonesia
+62 85103069393
www.warunglaota.id

Opening hours	Open 7 days
Credit cards	Accepted but not AMEX or Diners
Price range	Affordable
Style	Casual
Cuisine	Chinese
Recommended for	Breakfast

BABI GULING IBU OKA

Jalan Tegal
Ubud
Bali 80571, Indonesia
+62 361976345

Opening hours	Open 7 days
Reservation policy	No
Credit cards	Not accepted
Price range	Budget
Style	Casual
Cuisine	Balinese
Recommended for	Local favorite

"Spit-roasted suckling pig in Balinese spices. A typical dish which is prepared to perfection in this local chain of restaurants."—Chris Salans

LOCAVORE

Jalan Dewi Sita 10
Ubud
Bali 80571, Indonesia
+62 361977733
www.locavore.co.id

Opening hours	Closed Sunday
Credit cards	Accepted but not Diners
Price range	Affordable
Style	Casual
Cuisine	Modern Indonesian
Recommended for	High end

"This is Bali's best restaurant. Highly innovative food, all local produce, seven courses, and guaranteed to include something you have never eaten before! Amazing cocktails and wine parings. Understated but super comfortable dining room with Scandinavian stylings."—Geoff Lindsay

NASI AYAM KEDEWATAN

Jalan Kayu Jati 12
Ubud
Bali 80361, Indonesia
+62 361974795

Opening hours	Open 7 days
Reservation policy	No
Credit cards	Not accepted
Price range	Budget
Style	Casual
Cuisine	Balinese
Recommended for	Local favorite

PUTERI MINANG PADANG FOOD

Jalan Raya Ubud 77
Ubud
Bali 80571, Indonesia
+62 361975577

Opening hours	Open 7 days
Reservation policy	No
Credit cards	Not accepted
Price range	Budget
Style	Casual
Cuisine	Indonesian
Recommended for	Local favorite

"Little place were they serve proper *nasi padang* (steamed rice with vegetable and meat dishes) from Sumatra. All the dishes are set up in the window and you can pick what you like. Super tasty and available throughout the day."—Eelke Plasmeijer

PICA SOUTH AMERICAN KITCHEN

Jalan Dewi Sita
Ubud
Bali 80571, Indonesia
+62 0361971660
www.picakitchen.com

Opening hours	Closed Monday
Credit cards	Accepted but not AMEX or Diners
Price range	Affordable
Style	Casual
Cuisine	Latin American
Recommended for	Regular neighborhood

ROOM4DESSERT

Jalan Raya Sanggingan
Ubud
Bali 80561, Indonesia
+62 81236662806
www.room4dessert.asia

Opening hours	Open 7 days
Credit cards	Accepted
Price range	Budget
Style	Smart casual
Cuisine	Dessert
Recommended for	Worth the travel

"Chef Will Goldfarb has created something truly
special. I hesitatingly tried the signature tasting menu,
which features only desserts, and was quite blown
away by the sheer genius of his vision and execution.
The room is also quirky and creative, and everything
about the experience is unique and works deliciously
well."—Alfred Prasad

SPICE

Jalan Raya Ubud 23
Ubud
Bali 80571, Indonesia
+62 3614792420
www.spicebali.com

Opening hours	Open 7 days
Credit cards	Accepted but not Diners
Price range	Affordable
Style	Casual
Cuisine	Indonesian
Recommended for	Regular neighborhood

"Great fusion of Western comfort food and cocktails
with Indonesian flavors. Good value for money. Fully
air-conditioned and great tunes."—Chris Salans

THE NIGHT ROOSTER

Jalan Dewisita 10b
Ubud
Bali 80571, Indonesia
+62 361977733
www.locavore.co.id/nightrooster

Opening hours	Closed Sunday
Reservation policy	No
Credit cards	Accepted but not Diners
Price range	Affordable
Style	Smart casual
Cuisine	Indonesian
Recommended for	Late night

WARUNG PULAU KELAPA

Jalan Raya Sanggingan
Ubud
Bali 80561, Indonesia
+62 361971872
www.warungpulaukelapa.com

Opening hours	Open 7 days
Credit cards	Accepted but not AMEX or Diners
Price range	Affordable
Style	Casual
Cuisine	Indonesian
Recommended for	Local favorite

JU-MA-NA

Banjar Kelod
Ungasan
Bali 80364, Indonesia
+62 3613007000
www.banyantree.com

Opening hours	Open 7 days
Credit cards	Accepted
Price range	Expensive
Style	Smart casual
Cuisine	Indonesian
Recommended for	High end

"This stunning sea-view restaurant in the Ungasan
area offers an innovative French molecular menu.
The food is well executed and the service is efficient
and professional. You can go for their set menu or
à la carte."—Florian Lamelot

ANTIPODEAN CAFÉ

Recommended by
Petty Elliott

Hero Kemang Villa Complex
Jalan Kemang Selatan I
Jakarta 12730, Indonesia
+62 217192364
www.antipodeancoffee.com

Opening hours	Open 7 days
Reservation policy	No
Credit cards	Accepted but not AMEX or Diners
Price range	Budget
Style	Smart casual
Cuisine	European-Asian
Recommended for	Breakfast

BAKMI KARET KREKOT

Recommended by
Wahjudi Rahardja

Jalan Samanhudi 6
Jakarta 10710, Indonesia

Opening hours	Open 7 days
Reservation policy	No
Credit cards	Not accepted
Price range	Budget
Style	Casual
Cuisine	Indonesian-Chinese
Recommended for	Breakfast

"Great old-school chicken noodle joint that's only open until noon."—Wahjudi Rahardja

BANDAR DJAKARTA ANCOL

Recommended by
Florian Lamelot

Pintu Timur Taman Impian Jaya Ancol
Jakarta 14430, Indonesia
+62 216455472
www.bandar-djakarta.com

Opening hours	Open 7 days
Credit cards	Accepted
Price range	Affordable
Style	Casual
Cuisine	Seafood
Recommended for	Local favorite

"Located in south Jakarta, this place is one of a kind. Serving live Alaskan king crab, Brittany blue lobster, and most of the local live seafood that you can find in Indonesia, for up to five-thousand people a day. I go there for the freshness of the seafood, grilled the Indonesian way."—Florian Lamelot

BEAUTIKA

Recommended by
Petty Elliott,
Florian Lamelot

Jalan Hang Lekir 1
Jakarta 12120, Indonesia
+62 217226683
www.beautika-manado.com

Opening hours	Open 7 days
Credit cards	Accepted
Price range	Affordable
Style	Casual
Cuisine	Indonesian
Recommended for	Local favorite

"A well-known local restaurant serving a variety of Indonesian food from Manado, North Sulawesi. My favorite dishes are *cakalang* (tuna) and roa fish served with a traditional chile called *dabu-dabu*. Most of the dishes here are spicy but you can also experience the strong flavor of Indonesian food."—Florian Lamelot

BREAKFAST AT CAYENNE

Recommended by
Gianfranco Pirrone

Jalan Kemang Timur VIII C2
Jakarta 12730, Indonesia
+62 2171770105

Opening hours	Open 7 days
Credit cards	Accepted but not AMEX or Diners
Price range	Affordable
Style	Casual
Cuisine	International
Recommended for	Breakfast

"Very nice food and atmosphere, lovely staff."
—Gianfranco Pirrone

BURGREENS EXPRESS

Recommended by
Gianfranco Pirrone

Union Yoga
Jalan Wijaya II/73
Darmawangsa
Jakarta 12160, Indonesia
+62 87889892010
www.burgreens.com

Opening hours	Open 7 days
Credit cards	Accepted
Price range	Affordable
Style	Casual
Cuisine	Burgers
Recommended for	Bargain

FONG TU

Recommended by
Wahjudi Rahardja

Jalan Pluit Barat I 12A/B
Jakarta 14450, Indonesia
+62 216696118

Opening hours	Open 7 days
Credit cards	Not accepted
Price range	Affordable
Style	Casual
Cuisine	Chinese
Recommended for	Regular neighborhood

"An old institution that serves Indonesian-style Chinese hakka cuisines that is unique to Jakarta." —Wahjudi Rahardja

Jakarta may not be known for its Chinese food, but if that's what you're craving, there are some gems to be found in the city. One such place is this twenty-something-year-old Chinese stalwart in Pluit, Jakarta Utara, that serves Hakka delicacies like claypot pig's trotters and steamed fish. Yes, the space is a little old-school—but the mostly Chinese diners don't seem to mind.

JITTLADA THAI CUISINE

Recommended by
Gianfranco Pirrone

Senayan City Mall
Jalan Asia Afrika 19
Jakarta 20270, Indonesia
+62 2172781396
www.jittlada.com

Opening hours	Open 7 days
Credit cards	Accepted but not AMEX or Diners
Price range	Affordable
Style	Casual
Cuisine	Thai
Recommended for	Late night

LE QUARTIER RESTAURANT

Recommended by
Petty Elliott

Jalan Gunawarman 34
Kebayoran Baru
Jakarta 12110, Indonesia
+62 2172788001
www.lequartier.co.id

Opening hours	Open 7 days
Credit cards	Accepted
Price range	Affordable
Style	Smart casual
Cuisine	French
Recommended for	Breakfast

"Well-prepared modern French breakfast choices with attentive service and comfortable bench seating—equally ideal for a morning meeting or a leisurely start with friends."—Petty Elliott

MAJAPAHIT AT THE DHARMAWANGSA

Recommended by
Petty Elliott

The Dharmawangsa Jakarta
Jalan Brawijaya Raya 26
Jakarta 12160, Indonesia
+62 217258181
www.the-dharmawangsa.com

Opening hours	Open 7 days
Credit cards	Accepted but not Diners
Price range	Expensive
Style	Smart casual
Cuisine	International
Recommended for	Regular neighborhood

MONTY'S RESTAURANT

Recommended by
Gianfranco Pirrone

Jalan Raya Senopati 84
Kebayoran Baru
Jakarta 12110, Indonesia
+62 217204848
www.montys.co.id

Opening hours	Open 7 days
Credit cards	Accepted
Price range	Expensive
Style	Smart casual
Cuisine	International
Recommended for	High end

NAMAAZ

Recommended by
Petty Elliott

Jalan Gunawarman 42
Jakarta 12110, Indonesia
+62 8111557798
www.namaazdining.com

Opening hours	Closed Monday and Sunday
Credit cards	Accepted
Price range	Expensive
Style	Smart casual
Cuisine	Modern Indonesian
Recommended for	High end

"It's a super fun place to enjoy Indonesian cuisine in a modern, playful environment. Namaaz is different to other molecular gastronomy restaurants around the world—very informal and no long wine list. In fact, it's best to bring your own."—Petty Elliott

NASI PADANG SEDERHANA

Jalan Subang
Jakarta 10310, Indonesia

Opening hours	Open 7 days
Credit cards	Not accepted
Price range	Budget
Style	Casual
Cuisine	Indonesian
Recommended for	Regular neighborhood

OKU

Hotel Indonesia Kempinski
Jalan MH Thamrin 1
Jakarta 10310, Indonesia

+62 2123583800
www.kempinski.com

Opening hours	Open 7 days
Credit cards	Accepted
Price range	Affordable
Style	Smart casual
Cuisine	Modern Japanese
Recommended for	High end

"OKU easily surpasses its rivals in flavor, and playful presentations based on a 'close to nature' theme. My favorite is the 'chicken karage', which resembles a black rock atop a piece of wood, and encloses a delicious sauce made of balsamic, soya, and yuzu."
—Petty Elliott

PAGI SORE

Jalan Cipete 2
Fatmawati
Jakarta 12410, Indonesia
+62 217667000
www.pagi-sore.com

Opening hours	Open 7 days
Credit cards	Accepted but not AMEX or Diners
Price range	Affordable
Style	Casual
Cuisine	Indonesian
Recommended for	Regular neighborhood

SALT GRILL BY LUKE MANGAN

The Plaza
56F
Jalan M.H. Thamrin 28–30
Jakarta 10350, Indonesia
+62 2129922448
www.saltgrillindonesia.com

Opening hours	Open 7 days
Credit cards	Accepted
Price range	Affordable
Style	Smart casual
Cuisine	International
Recommended for	Bargain

"Salt Grill offers really nice, modern Australian cuisine, and the business lunch package is around $13 (£10) for two courses. The restaurant is located on the 56th floor and has the best view in Jakarta."
—Petty Elliott

SKYE

BCA Tower
56F
Jalan M.H. Thamrin 1
Jakarta 10310, Indonesia
+62 2123586996
www.ismaya.com

Opening hours	Open 7 days
Credit cards	Accepted
Price range	Affordable
Style	Smart casual
Cuisine	Japanese
Recommended for	Late night

"This is a stylish, unique restaurant with a 180-degree view of Jakarta. Divided in two, it has an open-air bar outside serving finger food and a Japanese restaurant indoors. The wine and drinks are a good price for Jakarta. The view and the ambience make this a stunning spot."—Florian Lamelot

SUSHI ICHI
Recommended by
Wahjudi Rahardja

Hotel Pullman
Jalan M.H. Thamrin 59
Jakarta 10350, Indonesia
+62 2139835850
www.ginza-sushiichi.jp

Opening hours	Closed Monday
Credit cards	Accepted
Price range	Affordable
Style	Casual
Cuisine	Japanese
Recommended for	Regular neighborhood

"Sushi Ichi is the finest sushi bar in Jakarta. Fresh seasonal seafood is flown in daily from Tsukiji Market in Tokyo."—Wahjudi Rahardja

THE WRITER'S BAR
Recommended by
Petty Elliott

Lotte Shopping Avenue
Ciputra Word 1
Jalan Professor Doktor Satrio Kavling 3–5
Jakarta 12940, Indonesia
+62 2129880888
www.raffles.com/jakarta/dining/writers-bar

Opening hours	Open 7 days
Reservation policy	No
Credit cards	Accepted
Price range	Affordable
Style	Smart casual
Cuisine	Asian-European
Recommended for	Late night

"For seafood laksa, late at night, The Writer's Bar is amazing. One of the best in town, in a luxurious setting with impeccable service—all without hurting your wallet."—Petty Elliott

TORI-ICHI
Recommended by
Wahjudi Rahardja

Pondok Indah Mall 2
Jalan Metro Pondok Indah
Jakarta 12310, Indonesia
+62 2121889061

Opening hours	Open 7 days
Credit cards	Accepted but not AMEX or Diners
Price range	Budget
Style	Casual
Cuisine	Japanese
Recommended for	Late night

"Late-night *Izakaya* bar specializing in yakitori and sushi."—Wahjudi Rahardja

UNION
Recommended by
Florian Lamelot

Plaza Senayan Courtyard
Jalan Asia Afrika 8
Jakarta 12220, Indonesia
+62 2157905861
www.unionjkt.com

Opening hours	Open 7 days
Credit cards	Accepted
Price range	Affordable
Style	Casual
Cuisine	Brasserie
Recommended for	Local favorite

"This New York-style brasserie serves simple but tasteful dishes with an international touch. The restaurant is busy all day. The ambience is cosmopolitan and echoes the 1920s. I recommend the whole roasted baby chicken or their pasta."—Florian Lamelot

VIN+
Recommended by
Florian Lamelot

Jalan Kemang Raya 45b
Jakarta 12730, Indonesia
+62 3614732377
www.vingroup.biz

Opening hours	Open 7 days
Credit cards	Accepted
Price range	Affordable
Style	Casual
Cuisine	International
Recommended for	Bargain

"Vin+ is a tapas restaurant with a wine cellar. Good food, affordable wine, and cosy atmosphere."—Florian Lamelot

TUGU KUNSTKRING PALEIS
Recommended by
Gianfranco Pirrone

Jalan Teuku Umar 1
Menteng
Jakarta 10350, Indonesia
+62 213900899
www.tuguhotels.com

Opening hours	Open 7 days
Credit cards	Accepted
Price range	Affordable
Style	Casual
Cuisine	Indonesian
Recommended for	Regular neighborhood

ANTONIO'S

Recommended by
Erwan Heussaff

Purok 138
Barangay Neogan
Tagaytay
Cavite 4120, Philippines
+63 9178992866
www.antoniosrestaurant.ph

Opening hours	Closed Monday
Credit cards	Accepted
Price range	Affordable
Style	Smart casual
Cuisine	International
Recommended for	Worth the travel

"Breakfast, lunch, or dinner—you can get a different experience for each meal—this forever favorite will never let you down."—Erwan Heussaff

BALAY DAKO

Recommended by
Erwan Heussaff

Tagaytay-Nasugbu Highway
beside Leslie's and Max's
Tagaytay
Cavite 4120, Philippines
+63 464134866
www.antoniosrestaurant.ph/balay-dako

Opening hours	Open 7 days
Credit cards	Accepted
Price range	Affordable
Style	Casual
Cuisine	Filipino
Recommended for	Worth the travel

BALE DUTUNG

Recommended by
Erwan Heussaff,
Tippi Tambunting

Paul Avenue
Angeles City
Pampanga 2009, Philippines
+63 456250169
www.baledutung.com

Opening hours	Variable
Credit cards	Not accepted
Price range	Affordable
Style	Casual
Cuisine	Filipino
Recommended for	Worth the travel

"No one else does Pampanga cuisine better than Claude Tayag himself. Dine in his Angeles residence as he prepares a multi-course meal and, while you're at it, see his beautiful art pieces, on which he works when he's not cooking."—Tippi Tambunting

CAFÉ FLEUR

Recommended by
William Mahi

L-463B Miranda Street
Barangay Santo Rosario
Angeles City
Pampanga 2009, Philippines
+63 995138413

Opening hours	Open 7 days
Credit cards	Accepted
Price range	Affordable
Style	Casual
Cuisine	International
Recommended for	Regular neighborhood

"Chef Sau Del Rosario is possibly the most talented chef in the country. The way he cooks is highly original, resulting in surprising and incredible tastes. He is also the most humble chef that I have ever met—French trained in the best French restaurants of his generation. He is a serious source of inspiration."—William Mahi

MANG RAUL'S BBQ HAUS

Recommended by
Jordy Navarra

CRM Avenue
BF Homes Almanza
Near Holy Family Parish
Las Piñas
Metropolitan Manila 1750, Philippines
+63 9206122150

Opening hours	Closed Monday
Credit cards	Not accepted
Price range	Budget
Style	Casual
Cuisine	Barbecue
Recommended for	Local favorite

"I grew up eating at Mang Raul's. He started out on the street in front of a house, just grilling different pieces of pork and chicken on a small makeshift charcoal grill every afternoon. He would stay open until he sold out, which would be early evenings. This is where my childhood friends and I learned how to eat different parts of the chicken and pork, like pig's ears and chicken intestines, just simply grilled over charcoal and basted with his sweet and spicy sauce. He now has a permanent storefront not far from where he set up on the street, still doing the same thing to this day."—Jordy Navarra

MANTRA BISTRO

Recommended by
William Mahi

Grand Midori, G-7
Bolanos
Legaspi Village
Manilla
Luzon 1229, Philippines
+63 9260499357

Opening hours..Closed Monday
Credit cards..Accepted but not Amex
Price range..Affordable
Style..Casual
Cuisine...Indian
Recommended for....................................Local favorite

"Excellent Indian food at affordable prices . A great
neighborhood place to go, with an Indian owner who
is always on the spot, smiling, and helpful . For me this
is the best in Manila – maybe the whole Philippines."
– William Mahi

12/10

Recommended by
Erwan Heussaff

7635 Guijo
San Antonio Village
Makati City
Metropolitan Manila 1203, Philippines
+63 9156632823

Opening hours..Closed Sunday
Credit cards...Accepted
Price range..Affordable
Style..Casual
Cuisine...Japanese-Korean
Recommended for....................................Wish I'd opened

BIZU PATISSERIE

Recommended by
Tippi Tambunting

G/L Greenbelt 2
Ayala Centre
Makati City
Metropolitan Manila 1226, Philippines
+63 27572498
www.bizupatisserie.com

Opening hours..Open 7 days
Credit cards...Accepted
Price range..Affordable
Style..Casual
Cuisine...Patisserie
Recommended for..Breakfast

BUCKY'S

Recommended by
Tippi Tambunting

5666 Don Pedro
Makati City
Metropolitan Manila 1210, Philippines
+63 9178445104

Opening hours..Closed Monday
Credit cards..Not accepted
Price range..Budget
Style..Casual
Cuisine...Bakery
Recommended for..Bargain

CAFÉ VIA MARE

Recommended by
Tippi Tambunting

Level 1, Greenbelt 1
Paseo De Roxas
Makati City
Metropolitan Manila 1226, Philippines
+63 28151918
www.viamare.com.ph

Opening hours..Open 7 days
Credit cards...Accepted
Price range..Budget
Style..Casual
Cuisine...Filipino
Recommended for..Breakfast

"An all-day breakfast joint we have frequented
since I was a little girl. It's an oldie but a goodie."
—Tippi Tambunting

THE CURATOR COFFEE AND COCKTAILS

Legazpi Parkview Condominium
134 Legazpi Street
Legazpi Village
Makati City
Metropolitan Manila 1229, Philippines
+63 9163554129

Recommended by
Jordy Navarra

Opening hours..Open 7 days
Credit cards...Accepted
Price range..Budget
Style..Casual
Cuisine...Café-Bar
Recommended for..Breakfast

"I like to wake up and have a nice coffee and
a croissant here. They roast and blend their own
beans so a cup from this place helps me start my day.
Funny thing is that, at night, the coffee bar becomes
a world-class cocktail bar."—Jordy Navarra

EAT FIRST

4726 Salamanca
Makati City
Metropolitan Manila 1210, Philippines
+63 25538605

Opening hours	Open 7 days
Credit cards	Not accepted
Price range	Budget
Style	Casual
Cuisine	Chinese
Recommended for	Bargain

"A taste of the Chinese mainland and a good compromise when you feel like having a hot pot as theirs are the best so far."—William Mahi

FLAME

Discovery Primea
16F, 6749 Ayala Avenue
Makati City
Metropolitan Manila 1226, Philippines
+62 29558888
www.discoveryprimea.com

Opening hours	Closed Sunday
Credit cards	Accepted
Price range	Expensive
Style	Smart Casual
Cuisine	Modern European
Recommended for	Regular neighborhood

"The chef, Luis Chikiamco, creates excellent and well-executed dishes without pretention."
—William Mahi

GOTO MONSTER

Corner of Pablo Ocampo Sr. Exit, La Paz
Makati City
Metropolitan Manila 1203, Philippines
+63 9163002600

Opening hours	Open 7 days
Reservation policy	No
Credit cards	Not accepted
Price range	Budget
Style	Casual
Cuisine	Filipino
Recommended for	Bargain

"It serves Filipino favorites for twenty-four hours and has an extensive Filipino breakfast menu. Its food is simple, homely, comforting, well cooked, and value for money."—José Luis Gonzalez

GRACE PARK

One Rockwell
GF, Rockwell Drive
Makati City
Metropolitan Manila 1200 ,Philippines
+63 28437275
www.margaritafores.com

Opening hours	Open 7 days
Credit cards	Accepted
Price range	Affordable
Style	Casual
Cuisine	Italian
Recommended for	Wish I'd opened

"Margarita Fores is one of the most important people in the local culinary scene—she has helped both the cuisine and products grow in prominence locally and internationally."—José Luis Gonzalez

HAI SHIN LOU

810 Arnaiz Avenue (Pasay Road)
San Lorenzo Village
Makati City
Metropolitan Manila 1223 ,Philippines
+63 28441735
www.haishinlou.com

Opening hours	Open 7 days
Credit cards	Accepted
Price range	Expensive
Style	Smart casual
Cuisine	Chinese
Recommended for	Regular neighborhood

"Always hits the spot."—Tippi Tambunting

KIKUFUJI

Little Tokyo
2277 Chino Roces Avenue
Legaspi Village
Makati City
Metropolitan Manila 1229, Philippines
+63 28937319

Opening hours	Open 7 days
Credit cards	Accepted
Price range	Affordable
Style	Casual
Cuisine	Japanese
Recommended for	Regular neighborhood

"Cosy, but chaotic during lunch time. Good Japanese food and sake selection."—Antonio Escalante

MENDOKORO RAMENBA

Recommended by
Bruce Ricketts

V Corporate Centre
Soliman Street
Makati City
Metropolitan Manila 1227, Philippines
+63 24789625

Opening hours...Open 7 days
Credit cards...Accepted
Price range..Affordable
Style...Casual
Cuisine..Japanese
Recommended for.................Regular neighborhood

"The best *tonkotsu* (breaded pork cutlet) ramen
in Manila."—Bruce Ricketts

THE MESS HALL

Recommended by
Tippi Tambunting

The Moplex
2316 Karrivin Plaza
Chino Roces Avenue Extention
Makati City
Metropolitan Manila 1232, Philippines
+63 26185388
www.momentgroup.ph

Opening hours..................Closed Saturday and Sunday
Reservation policy...No
Credit cards...Accepted
Price range...Budget
Style...Casual
Cuisine...Filipino
Recommended for.............................Local favorite

"A perfect place to go to for a quick lunch and satisfy
yourself with local favorites."—Tippi Tambunting

MILKY WAY CAFÉ

Recommended by
Erwan Heussaff

Milky Way
2F, 900 Arnaiz Avenue (Pasay Road)
Makati City
Metropolitan Manila 1200, Philippines
+63 8434124
www.cafe.milkywayrestaurant.com

Opening hours.......................................Closed Sunday
Credit cards...Accepted
Price range..Affordable
Style...Casual
Cuisine...Filipino-International
Recommended for.............................Local favorite

RAZON'S OF GUAGUA

Recommended by
Erwan Heussaff

22 Jupiter Street
Bel-Air Village
Makati City
Metropolitan Manila 1209 ,Philippines
+63 8997841
www.razonsfoodcorp.com.ph

Opening hours...Open 7 days
Credit cards...Not accepted
Price range...Budget
Style...Casual
Cuisine...Filipino
Recommended for..Bargain

"Simple and always good."—Erwan Heussaff

RICH (ROYAL INDIAN CURRY HOUSE)

Recommended by
Erwan Heussaff

5345 General Luna Street
Barangay Poblacion
Makati City
Metropolitan Manila 1208, Philippines
+63 8014435
www.jhiro10.wixsite.com

Opening hours...Open 7 days
Credit cards...Accepted
Price range..Affordable
Style...Casual
Cuisine...Indian
Recommended for..Late night

"Nothing hits the spot like curry and naans after
midnight."—Erwan Heussaff

SEÑOR POLLO

Recommended by
José Luis Gonzalez,
Tippi Tambunting

5767 Ebro Street
Barangay Poblacion
Makati City
Metropolitan Manila 1210 ,Philippines
+63 28316945

Opening hours...Open 7 days
Reservation policy...No
Credit cards...Accepted
Price range...Budget
Style...Casual
Cuisine..Latin American
Recommended for..Bargain

"One of the best deals in an area full of affordable
eats. Serving juicy and tasty birds slow roasted to
perfection, which are best eaten with the spicy rice,
plantains, and coleslaw."—Tippi Tambunting

SHI LIN

Recommended by
José Luis Gonzalez

Power Plant Mall
2F, Rockwell Center
Makati City
Metropolitan Manila 1210, Philippines
+63 28597012

Opening hours	Open 7 days
Credit cards	Accepted
Price range	Affordable
Style	Casual
Cuisine	Taiwanese
Recommended for	Regular neighborhood

"A Taiwanese-inspired restaurant local to the Philippines—I enjoy the dim sum and the Chinese menu selection."—José Luis Gonzalez

TAMBAI

Recommended by
José Luis Gonzalez

5779 Felipe Street
Barangay Poblacion
Makati City
Metropolitan Manila 1780 ,Philippines
+63 2155695

Opening hours	Open 7 days
Credit cards	Not accepted
Price range	Affordable
Style	Casual
Cuisine	Japanese
Recommended for	Local favorite

"Where traditional street food is served yakitori style."—José Luis Gonzalez

TERRY'S

Recommended by
Bruce Ricketts

BCS Prime
GF, 2297 Chino Roces Avenue Extension
Makati City
Metropolitan Manila 2297 ,Philippines
+63 7297906
www.terryselection.com

Opening hours	Open 7 days
Credit cards	Accepted
Price range	Affordable
Style	Casual
Cuisine	Spanish Basque
Recommended for	Regular neighborhood

"Whenever I crave for something comforting and consistently delicious, I always find myself gravitating toward Juan Carlos de Terry's Spanish food."
—Bruce Ricketts

TOYO EATERY

Recommended by
José Luis Gonzalez,
Erwan Heussaff,
Han Liguang,
Colin Mackay,
William Mahi

Building C, GF, Karrivin Plaza
2316 Chino Roces Ave
Makati City
Metropolitan Manila 1231, Philippines
+63 9177208630

Opening hours	Open 7 days
Credit cards	Accepted
Price range	Affordable
Style	Casual
Cuisine	Modern Filipino
Recommended for	Local favorite

"Very different from the majority of other concepts in Manila—relaxing, funky somehow, very unusual. The chef, Jordy Navarra creates dishes that might surprise you here and there—ask to meet him as he is very humble and super nice!"—William Mahi

Reinvented Filipino cuisine is on the menu at this wood-and-concrete-decked eatery by former Black Sheep chef Jordy Navarra. With his boundless kitchen wizardry, Navarra takes local ingredients and familiar Filipino flavors to new heights, all the time paying homage to his motherland's terroir. One dish, for instance, features each of the vegetables that appear in the Filipino folk song "Bahay Kubo". The best way to savor this carefully thought-out cuisine is via the tasting menu—but if you're not feeling that hungry, there's a set menu and an à la carte menu too.

TSUKIJI

Recommended by
Erwan Heussaff,
Colin Mackay

Milky Way
3F, 900 Arnaiz Avenue (Pasay Road)
Makati City
Metropolitan Manila 1200 ,Philippines
+63 28122913
www.tsukiji-restaurant.com

Opening hours	Open 7 days
Credit cards	Accepted
Price range	Expensive
Style	Smart casual
Cuisine	Japanese
Recommended for	Regular neighborhood

"Great quality sushi sourced both locally and from Japan."—Colin Mackay

TSUMURA

Recommended by
Tippi Tambunting

2F, 88 Corporate Centre
Sedeno Street
Salcedo Village
Makati City
Metropolitan Manila 1227 ,Philippines
+63 28874848

Opening hours	Open 7 days
Credit cards	Accepted
Price range	Affordable
Style	Casual
Cuisine	Japanese
Recommended for	Regular neighborhood

TUAN TUAN

Recommended by
Antonio Escalante

Power Plant Mall
3F, Rockwell Center
Makati City
Metropolitan Manila 1209, Philippines
+63 9064332196
www.tuantuan.com.ph

Opening hours	Open 7 days
Credit cards	Accepted
Price range	Affordable
Style	Casual
Cuisine	Chinese
Recommended for	Regular neighborhood

"Quick service, tasty food and value for money."
—Antonio Escalante

WILDFLOUR CAFÉ + BAKERY

Recommended by
Erwan Heussaff,
Jordy Navarra

V-Corporate Centre Salcedo Village
125 Leviste Street
Salcedo Village
Makati City
Metropolitan Manila 1227, Philippines
+62 6328087072

Opening hours	Open 7 days
Credit cards	Accepted but not Diners
Price range	Affordable
Style	Casual
Cuisine	Café-Bakery
Recommended for	Regular neighborhood

"Straightforward dishes, seasonal ingredients, always done right."—Erwan Heussaff

YOUR LOCAL

Recommended by
Tippi Tambunting

Universal LMS
GF, 106 Esteban Street
Legaspi Village
Makati City
Metropolitan Manila 1229 ,Philippines
+63 28236206
www.yourlocal.ph

Opening hours	Open 7 days
Credit cards	Accepted but not AMEX
Price range	Affordable
Style	Casual
Cuisine	Asian
Recommended for	Local favorite

YUKINO HANA

Recommended by
Jordy Navarra

Azotea De Bel-Air Condominium
5786 Polaris Street
Makati City
Metropolitan Manila 1210 ,Philippines
+63 25551547

Opening hours	Open 7 days
Credit cards	Not accepted
Price range	Budget
Style	Casual
Cuisine	Korean-Japanese
Recommended for	Late night

"A chef friend named Mikko Reyes brought me to this place for a late night fried chicken fix and I got hooked. It's crispy, sweet, spicy, and juicy. Exactly I imagine how late-night fried chicken should be."
—Jordy Navarra

Still known to many locals by its former name, the Snowman, this lively late-night *izakaya* (open until 5.00 a.m.) in the Burgos neighborhood is famed for serving up the spiciest fried chicken in Manila. Beyond that the comforting Korean-Japanese menu offers everything from fluffy, stone bowl scrambled eggs, to sweetcorn with Kewpie mayonnaise, shredded kimchi, and potatoes. If sake and soju are your poison, you're well served here.

R & J BULALOHAN

Recommended by
Erwan Heussaff

600 Bonifacio Avenue
Plainview
Mandaluyong
Metropolitan Manila 1550, Philippines
+63 27465432

Opening hours	Open 7 days
Credit cards	Not accepted
Price range	Budget
Style	Casual
Cuisine	Filipino
Recommended for	Breakfast

"I usually just take in an espresso for breakfast but, when I'm up early enough, this place hits the spot. Try the beef *tapa* (cured beef) and the famous beef *Bulalo* (Filipino beef marrow stew)."—Erwan Heussaff

THE BLACK PIG

Recommended by
Jordy Navarra

Commercenter
2F, Filinvest Avenue
Muntinlupa
Metropolitan Manila 1781, Philippines
+63 28081406
www.theblackpigbar.com

Opening hours	Open 7 days
Credit cards	Accepted
Price range	Affordable
Style	Casual
Cuisine	Tapas
Recommended for	Regular neighborhood

"A nice place to relax, have a beer, and eat tasty food done well."—Jordy Navarra

BALIWAG LECHON MANOK

Recommended by
Jordy Navarra

2313 Beata Street
Pandacan
Metropolitan Manila 1011 ,Philippines
+63 26542929
www.baliwaglechonmanok.com

Opening hours	Open 7 days
Credit cards	Not accepted
Price range	Budget
Style	Casual
Cuisine	Filipino Grill
Recommended for	Bargain

"It's tasty and cheap. My favorite is the grilled pork belly which is tender and smoky, over a bowl of rice with a vinegar and soy dipping sauce."—Jordy Navarra

JEANY'S FOOD HOUSE SPECIAL

Recommended by
Bruce Ricketts

BF Homes
President's Avenue
Parañaque
Metropolitan Manila 1720 ,Philippines

Opening hours	Open 7 days
Credit cards	Not accepted
Price range	Budget
Style	Casual
Cuisine	Filipino
Recommended for	Bargain

"It's a very honest, unpretentious place—you probably won't see people you know. They only have one thing, which is a big cauldron of beef broth, and they have different off-cuts of beef that you can choose from. They include it in your soup with lots of chiles. And it's extremely inexpensive."—Bruce Ricketts

LUCKY NOODLES

Recommended by
William Mahi

Tambô Solaire Resort and Casino
1 Solaire Boulevard
Parañaque
Metropolitan Manila 1701 ,Philippines
+63 28888888
www.solaireresort.com

Opening hours	Open 7 days
Credit cards	Accepted
Price range	Affordable
Style	Casual
Cuisine	Asian
Recommended for	Late night

"This a good compromise when you want a quick meal at a very affordable price. Good selection of dishes and excellent Laksa."—William Mahi

SEASIDE DAMPA MACAPAGAL

Recommended by
Erwan Heussaff,
Jordy Navarra

Macapagal Boulevard
Libertad
Pasay City
Metropolitan Manila 1309, Philippines

Opening hours	Open 7 days
Reservation policy	No
Credit cards	Not accepted
Price range	Budget
Style	Casual
Cuisine	Seafood
Recommended for	Local favorite

"A typical local favorite where you can hang out, drink, and enjoy karaoke while eating. It's a collection of restaurants that cook what you buy so you can choose the produce in the nearby market and then ask them to prepare your food in almost any way you like."—Jordy Navarra

ABE RESTAURANT

Recommended by
José Luis Gonzalez

GF, Serendra, Retailer Area
Bonifacio Global City
Taguig
Metropolitan Manila 1630, Philippines
+63 28560526
www.ljcrestaurants.com.ph/abe

Opening hours	Open 7 days
Credit cards	Accepted
Price range	Affordable
Style	Casual
Cuisine	Filipino
Recommended for	Regular neighborhood

"A Filipino classic—a traditional restaurant where you can really feel the heart of Filipino cuisine. Authentic and well executed."—José Luis Gonzalez

CHOTTO MATTE

Recommended by
José Luis Gonzalez

Net Park
GF, 5th Avenue
Taguig
Metropolitan Manila 1634, Philippines
+63 22820442

Opening hours	Open 7 days
Credit cards	Not accepted
Price range	Affordable
Style	Casual
Cuisine	Japanese
Recommended for	Late night

GALLERY VASK

Recommended by
Josean Alija,
Jordy Navarra

Clipp Center
5F, 11th Avenue
Taguig
Metropolitan Manila 1634, Philippines
+63 917546167
www.galleryvask.com

Opening hours	Closed Monday and Sunday
Credit cards	Accepted
Price range	Expensive
Style	Smart casual
Cuisine	Filipino
Recommended for	High end

"A top place that executes at a super high level. Using ingredients from the Philippines, they come up with a unique, must-try cuisine."—Jordy Navarra

GREEN PASTURES

Recommended by
Shinobu Namae

Net Park
GF, 5th Avenue
Taguig
Metropolitan Manila 1634, Philippines
+63 2775592

Opening hours	Open 7 days
Credit cards	Accepted
Price range	Affordable
Style	Casual
Cuisine	International
Recommended for	Breakfast

HEY HANDSOME

Recommended by
José Luis Gonzalez,
Erwan Heussaff

Net Park
GF, 5th Avenue
Taguig
Metropolitan Manila 1634, Philippines
+63 917102355

Opening hours	Closed Sunday
Credit cards	Accepted
Price range	Affordable
Style	Casual
Cuisine	Southeast Asian
Recommended for	Local favorite

"A cool, young, hip, and contemporary restaurant with Southeast Asian food and good cocktails. It's a comfortable place and everyone loves it there." —José Luis Gonzalez

Touted as 2016's best new opening in Manila, this funky Bonifacio Global City eatery, with its green-tiled walls and open-concept kitchen, serves tasty interpretations of Peranakan sharing plates. Instead of serving the classics straight up, chef-owner Nicco Santos gives them his own spin; a case in point is his *buah keluak* (Indonesian black nut) dish which comes with mutton instead of chicken, and is served alongside *nasi ulam* (a Malay/Peranakan herbed rice dish) and shrimp paste-spiked crackers. It's invention like this that means Santos's place has created quite a buzz.

HIGH STREET CAFÉ AT SHANGRI-LA

Recommended by
William Mahi

30th Street, corner of 5th Avenue
Taguig
Metropolitan Manila 1637, Philippines
+63 28200888
www.shangri-la.com/manila/shangrilaatthefort

Opening hours	Open 7 days
Credit cards	Accepted
Price range	Affordable
Style	Casual
Cuisine	International
Recommended for	Breakfast

"This the kind of place where you can eat for hours."—William Mahi

JT'S MANUKAN GRILLE

Recommended by
Antonio Escalante

F&B
32nd Avenue
Taguig
Metropolitan Manila 1637, Philippines
+63 28315787
www.jtsmanukangrille.com

Opening hours	Open 7 days
Credit cards	Not accepted
Price range	Budget
Style	Casual
Cuisine	Filipino Grill
Recommended for	Late night

MANAM

Recommended by
Bruce Ricketts,
Tippi Tambunting

Net Park
GF, 5th Avenue
Taguig
Metropolitan Manila 1634, Philippines
+63 23329390
www.momentgroup.ph/manam-comfort-filipino

Opening hours	Open 7 days
Credit cards	Accepted
Price range	Affordable
Style	Casual
Cuisine	Filipino
Recommended for	Local favorite

"Manam's version of Filipino cuisine is a slightly modern take on traditional recipes but the approach does not lose the familiar flavors that all Filipino food lovers look for."—Tippi Tambunting

MECHA UMA

Recommended by
José Luis Gonzalez

RCBC Savings Bank Corporate Center
GF, 25th Street
Taguig
Metropolitan Manila 1634, Philippines
+63 28012770
www.mechauma.ph

Opening hours	Closed Sunday
Credit cards	Accepted
Price range	Expensive
Style	Casual
Cuisine	Japanese
Recommended for	High end

"This is one of the most creative restaurants in the Philippines and is one of the few to explore new techniques, ingredients, and research—a gastronomic restaurant with a deep understanding of food. The tasting menus are exciting and fun." —José Luis Gonzalez

PINK'S HOT DOGS

Recommended by
Bruce Ricketts

Shangri-La at The Fort
30th Street
Taguig
Metropolitan Manila 1213, Philippines
+63 27721147
www.pinkshollywood.com

Opening hours...Open 7 days
Credit cards..Accepted
Price range...Budget
Style...Casual
Cuisine...American
Recommended for...Late night

RECOVERY FOOD

Recommended by
Tippi Tambunting

Crossroads
GF, 32nd Street
Taguig
Metropolitan Manila 1634, Philippines
+63 25117312
www.recoveryfood.ph

Opening hours...Open 7 days
Credit cards..Accepted
Price range...Affordable
Style...Casual
Cuisine...Filipino
Recommended for...Late night

SAMBA

Recommended by
Erwan Heussaff

Shangri-La at The Fort
30th Street
Taguig
Metropolitan Manila 1637, Philippines
+63 28208888
www.samba-fort.com

Opening hours...Open 7 days
Credit cards..Accepted
Price range...Affordable
Style...Casual
Cuisine...Latin American-Seafood
Recommended for...Wish I'd opened

SARSÁ KITCHEN + BAR

Recommended by
Erwan Heussaff,
Bruce Ricketts

Unit 1–7 Forum South Global
7th Avenue
Taguig
Metropolitan Manila 1637, Philippines
+63 8660912

Opening hours...Open 7 days
Credit cards..Accepted
Price range...Affordable
Style...Casual
Cuisine...Filipino
Recommended for..Local favorite

TIM HO WAN

Recommended by
Jordy Navarra,
Tippi Tambunting

Uptown Place Mall
GF, 36th Street
Taguig
Metropolitan Manila 1637, Philippines
+63 7769367
www.timhowan.com

Opening hours...Open 7 days
Credit cards..Accepted
Price range...Budget
Style...Casual
Cuisine...Chinese
Recommended for...Late night

"After a late night of drinking and dancing, nothing hits the spot better than beef brisket noodle soup, dumplings with pork or shrimp (prawn), and their famous baked pork buns."—Tippi Tambunting

WILD FLOUR CAFÉ + BAKERY

Recommended by
Antonio Escalante,
José Luis Gonzalez,
Bruce Ricketts

Net Lima
GF, 26th Street
Taguig
Metropolitan Manila 1634, Philippines
+63 28567600

Opening hours...Open 7 days
Credit cards..Accepted
Price range...Affordable
Style...Casual
Cuisine...Café
Recommended for...Breakfast

"A neighborhood restaurant with a homey ambiance where they have homemade pastries and bread displayed and a wide eggs menu selection with some Asian favorites."—José Luis Gonzalez

"**Beautiful flavors, presentation, service, a full-on culinary experience.**"

HANS LEE RASMUSSEN P320

"TRADITIONAL SINGAPOREAN-ASIAN FLAVORS TRANSLATED INTO A MODERN CREATIVE DISHES."

YAU LEUNG CHEN P314

SINGAPORE

"Absolutely one of the best BBQ restaurants in the world."

JOWETT YU P329

"*The best black pepper crab I've ever tasted.*"

KIRK WESTAWAY P322

"*Japanese haute-cuisine at very reasonable prices, served in a casual setting.*"

ANDRÉ CHIANG P332

SINGAPORE

SCALE

‹N›

0   700   1400   2100   YD.

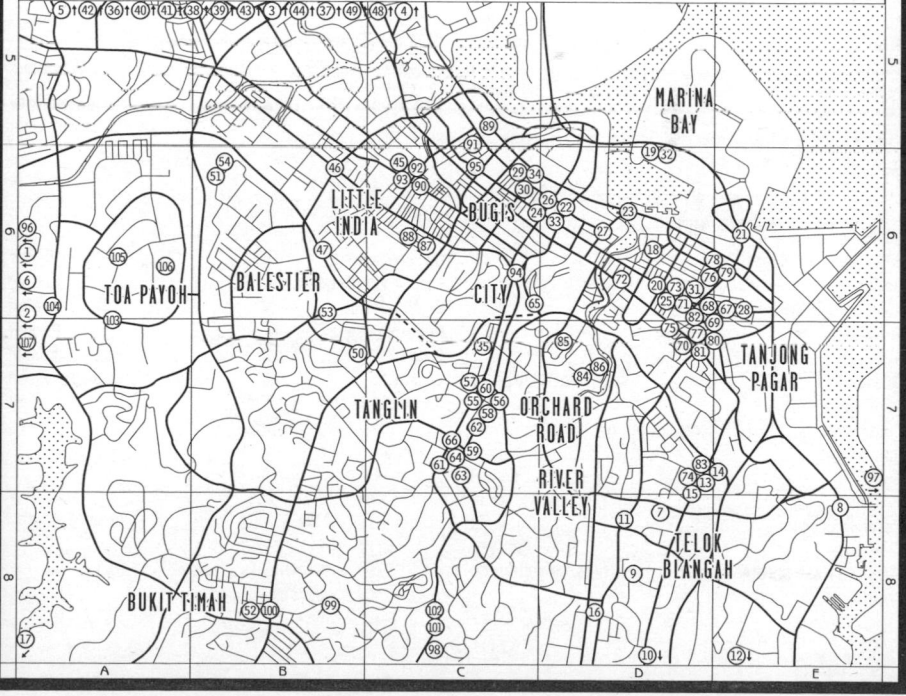

ANG MO KIO MARKET

Recommended by
Ken Ling

527 Ang Mo Kio Avenue 10
Ang Mo Kio
Singapore 560527

Opening hours	Open 7 days
Reservation policy	No
Credit cards	Not accepted
Price range	Budget
Style	Casual
Cuisine	Singaporean Street Food
Recommended for	Breakfast

"Very fragrant and richly flavored soup served with pork crackling, which offsets its fragrance. This is one of very few noodle stands in Singapore that uses pork crackling."—Ken Ling

CASUARINA CURRY

Recommended by
Giulio Sturla

136 Casuarina Road
Ang Mo Kio
Singapore 579524
+65 64559093
www.casuarinacurry.com

Opening hours	Open 7 days
Credit cards	Not accepted
Price range	Budget
Style	Casual
Cuisine	Indian
Recommended for	Breakfast

"Used to be a weekly treat as I lived across the road in my childhood."—Giulio Sturla

BEACH ROAD PRAWN MEE

Recommended by
Yong Bing Ngen

370 East Coast Road
Bedok
Singapore 428981
+65 63457196

Opening hours	Closed Tuesday
Reservation policy	No
Credit cards	Accepted but not AMEX or Diners
Price range	Budget
Style	Casual
Cuisine	Singaporean
Recommended for	Breakfast

"Try the fresh shrimp (prawns), pig's tails, or rich pork soup."—Yong Bing Ngen

JUMBO

Recommended by
Janice Wong

East Coast Seafood Center
1206 East Coast Parkway #01–07/08
Bedok
Singapore 449883
+65 64423435
www.jumboseafood.com.sg

Opening hours	Open 7 days
Credit cards	Accepted but not Diners
Price range	Budget
Style	Casual
Cuisine	Seafood
Recommended for	Local favorite

NAKHON KITCHEN

Recommended by
Ken Ling

136 Bedok North Avenue 3 #01–162
Bedok
Singapore 460136
+65 64436976

Opening hours	Open 7 days
Credit cards	Accepted but not AMEX or Diners
Price range	Budget
Style	Casual
Cuisine	Thai
Recommended for	Bargain

"Affordable and good quality."—Ken Ling

SIN MING ROTI PRATA

Recommended by
Morgan McGlone

24 Sin Ming Road #01–51
Bishan
Singapore 570024
+65 64533893

Opening hours	Open 7 days
Reservation policy	No
Credit cards	Not accepted
Price range	Budget
Style	Casual
Cuisine	Singaporean
Recommended for	Breakfast

BINCHO

Recommended by
André Chiang

78 Moh Guan Terrace
Bukit Merah
Singapore 162078
+65 64384567
www.bincho.com.sg

Opening hours	Closed Monday
Credit cards	Accepted but not Diners
Price range	Affordable
Style	Smart casual
Cuisine	Chinese-Japanese
Recommended for	Breakfast

"At breakfast they serve Chinese *mee pok* noodle and fish ball soups; lunch becomes noodles and yakitori; and at dinner it turns into a yakitori and Japanese whisky cocktail bar."—André Chiang

CYSTAL JADE DINING IN

Recommended by
Po-Sang Chan

Vivo City
1 Harbour Front Walk #01-112
Bukit Merah
Singapore 98585
+65 62785626
www.crystaljade.com

Opening hours	Open 7 days
Credit cards	Accepted
Price range	Affordable
Style	Smart casual
Cuisine	Catonese
Recommended for	High end

"It's famous for its authentic Cantonese cuisine, and great for family gatherings or business meetings."
—Po-Sang Chan

FU MING COOKED FOOD

Recommended by
Han Liguang

85 Redhill Lane
Bukit Merah
Singapore 150085
+65 96410565

Opening hours	Open 7 days
Reservation policy	No
Credit cards	Not accepted
Price range	Budget
Style	Casual
Cuisine	Singaporean Street Food
Recommended for	Late night

"The best 'carrot cake' (daikon radish omelet) in Singapore."—Han Liguang

KENG ENG KEE SEAFOOD

Recommended by
Malcolm Lee, Han Liguang,
Claus Meyer, Ming Tan

124 Bukit Merah Lane 1 #01-136
Bukit Merah
Singapore 150124
+65 62721038
www.kek.com.sg

Opening hours	Open 7 days
Credit cards	Accepted but not Diners
Price range	Affordable
Style	Casual
Cuisine	Seafood
Recommended for	Regular neighborhood

"Probably the most standout of all the casual, home-style street-food type Chinese restaurants in Singapore. Rock up in flip-flops for a lazy weekend meal, or office attire with your colleagues after a long day. Go in groups to best enjoy a larger selection of stir-fried, deep-fried, stewed, braised, and steamed dishes, paired with bowls of plain rice or elaborately layered seafood noodles. This is comfort food for four or forty."—Ming Tan

LIM JOO HIN EATING HOUSE

Recommended by
Janice Wong

715 Havelock Road
Bukit Merah
Singapore 169643
+65 62729871

Opening hours	Open 7 days
Reservation policy	No
Credit cards	Not accepted
Price range	Budget
Style	Casual
Cuisine	Chinese
Recommended for	Late night

"Best salted eggs and duck legs in Singapore."
—Janice Wong

NAKED FINN

Recommended by
Julien Royer

39 Malan Road
Bukit Merah
Singapore 109442
+65 66940807
www.nakedfinn.com

Opening hours	Closed Monday and Sunday
Credit cards	Accepted
Price range	Affordable
Style	Smart casual
Cuisine	Seafood
Recommended for	Regular neighborhood

SIN HOI SAI

55 Tiong Bahru Road #01–59
Bukit Merah
Singapore 160055
+65 62230810
www.sinhoisai.com.sg

Recommended by
Han Liguang,
Dave Pynt

Opening hours	Open 7 days
Credit cards	Accepted but not AMEX or Diners
Price range	Budget
Style	Casual
Cuisine	Seafood
Recommended for	Late night

"My favorite restaurant in Singapore. It is open 'til the early hours of the morning and you can eat some great seafood cooked fresh and have a cold beer while sitting outside with your mates."—Dave Pynt

TING HENG SEAFOOD

82 Tiong Poh Road
Bukit Merah
Singapore 160082
+65 63236830

Recommended by
Christopher Millar

Opening hours	Open 7 days
Reservation policy	No
Credit cards	Not accepted
Price range	Affordable
Style	Casual
Cuisine	Seafood
Recommended for	Bargain

Singapore has no lack of *tze char* (stir-fry) restaurants yet this pricey eatery at Tiong Poh Road attracts a sizeable crowd of foodies and *towkays* (executives). They all come for the well-executed seafood dishes headlined by delicacies like abalone, live lobster, and crab. If you're on a budget, fret not—wallet-friendly options abound too, like the wok-fried seafood *hor fun* (flat rice noodles) in a thick and savory gravy and stir-fried *chye sim* (green leaf) in garlic oil.

TIONG BARHU BAKERY

56 Eng Hoon Street #01–70
Bukit Merah
Singapore 160056
+65 62203430
www.tiongbahrubakery.com

Recommended by
Julien Royer

Opening hours	Open 7 days
Reservation policy	No
Credit cards	Accepted
Price range	Affordable
Style	Casual
Cuisine	Café-Bakery
Recommended for	Breakfast

"I love the neighborhood of Thiong Barhu area, it has a great authentic feel."—Julien Royer

YA KUN KAYA TOAST

237 Alexandra Road #03–09/10
Bukit Merah
Singapore 159929
+65 62224567
www.yakun.com

Recommended by
Po-Sang Chan,
Yong Bing Ngen

Opening hours	Open 7 days
Credit cards	Not accepted
Price range	Budget
Style	Casual
Cuisine	Café
Recommended for	Breakfast

"Really enjoy the cosy atmosphere."—Po-Sang Chan

This chain is all about the Singaporean breakfast staple of *kaya* (a sweet spread of coconut jam made with pandan leaves), served on buttered toast with soft-poached eggs and a cup of Singapore-style *kopi* (coffee roasted with margarine and sugar). The locals like to season the eggs with a dash of soy sauce and a pinch of white pepper before dipping their toast. The original stall was opened in 1944, and has since spawned an impressive empire of franchises across Asia. There's an admirable consistency across its forty or so Singapore outlets, but for ambience head to the Far East Square flagship.

KIM HENG CHICKEN RICE

Recommended by
Jason Tan

16 Teck Whye Lane
Choa Chu Kang
Singapore 680016

Opening hours	Open 7 days
Reservation policy	No
Credit cards	Not accepted
Price range	Budget
Style	Asian
Cuisine	Seafood
Recommended for	Regular neighborhood

"I particularly love their soya sauce chicken and its fragrant rice."—Jason Tan

AH HENG CURRY CHICKEN BEE HOON

Golden Shoe Car Park
50 Market Street
Downtown Core
Singapore 48940
+65 98790563

Recommended by
Ken Ling

Opening hours	Open / days
Reservation policy	No
Credit cards	Not accepted
Price range	Budget
Style	Casual
Cuisine	Singaporean
Recommended for	Regular neighborhood

"The reasons I like this place are the strong flavors of the curry, the soft but firm noodles, and the fantastic soups."—Ken Ling

CUT

Recommended by
Dave Pynt

The Shoppes at Marina Bay Sands
2 Bayfront Avenue, B1–71, Galleria Level
Downtown Core
Singapore 18972
+65 66888517
www.marinabaysands.com

Opening hours	Open 7 days
Credit cards	Accepted but not Diners
Price range	Affordable
Style	Smart casual
Cuisine	International
Recommended for	High end

HE JI PORRIDGE

Recommended by
Ming Tan

Maxwell Food Center
1 Kadayanallur Street #01–45
Downtown Core
Singapore 69184

Opening hours	Closed Sunday
Reservation policy	No
Credit cards	Not accepted
Price range	Budget
Style	Casual
Cuisine	Chinese
Recommended for	Bargain

"This hawker stall specializes in one thing. They make incredibly good Cantonese (or Hong Kong) style porridge—a thick and rich mix of broth and rice, cooked till smooth and luscious. This stall gets bonus points for being open very late too!"—Ming Tan

IMPERIAL TREASURE PEKING DUCK

Asia Square Tower
8 Marina View
Downtown Core
Singapore 18960
+65 66361868
www.imperialtreasure.com

Recommended by
Aitor Jeronimo Orive

Opening hours	Open 7 days
Credit cards	Accepted
Price range	Affordable
Style	Smart casual
Cuisine	Shanghaiese
Recommended for	Local favorite

"This place serves extremely high quality dim sum and Chinese classics. The Peking duck is extremely well done here, with very crisp skin and an option to have the meat in noodles or fried rice. The rest of the dishes are also superb, a perfect place for group dinners or brunch."—Aitor Jeronimo Orive

JAAN

Swissotel The Stamford
2 Stamford Road
Downtown Core
Singapore 178882
+65 68373322
www.jaan.com.sg

Recommended by
Christopher Millar,
Dave Pynt,
Hans Lee Rasmussen

Opening hours	Closed Sunday
Credit cards	Accepted
Price range	Expensive
Style	Formal
Cuisine	Modern European
Recommended for	High end

"Beautiful flavors, presentation, service, a full-on culinary experience."—Hans Lee Rasmussen

JADE

The Fullerton Hotel
1 Fullerton Square
Downtown Core
Singapore 49178
+65 67338388
www.fullertonhotels.com

Recommended by
Ken Ling

Opening hours	Open 7 days
Credit cards	Accepted
Price range	Expensive
Style	Formal
Cuisine	Cantonese
Recommended for	Local favorite

"Chef Leong Chee Yeng is amazing—color, fragrance, and flavor all come together. A real culinary artist."
—Ken Ling

LEI GARDEN

Chijmes
30 Victoria Street #01–24
Downtown Core
Singapore 187996
+65 63393822
www.leigarden.hk

Recommended by
Ken Ling,
Christopher Millar,
Janice Wong

Opening hours	Open 7 days
Credit cards	Accepted but not Diners
Price range	Affordable
Style	Smart casual
Cuisine	Cantonese
Recommended for	Wish I'd opened

"Modern high-quality Chinese cuisine. Exquisite decor."—Janice Wong

MAXWELL FOOD CENTRE

1 Kadayanallur Street
Downtown Core
Singapore 69184

Recommended by
Yong Bing Ngen,
Han Liguang,
Morgan McGlone,
Christopher Millar

Opening hours	Open 7 days
Reservation policy	No
Credit cards	Not accepted
Price range	Budget
Style	Casual
Cuisine	Singaporean Street Food
Recommended for	Local favorite

"The soul of Singapore's cuisine can be found in our hawkers instead of a single restaurant and Maxwell House hawker center is home to a spate of famous hawker stalls selling chicken rice, deep fried bananas, minced meat noodles, fish noodle soup, economical rice, etc."—Han Liguang

MIKUNI

Swissotel The Stamford
2 Stamford Road
Downtown Core
Singapore 178882
+65 64316156
www.swissotel.com/hotels/singapore-stamford

Recommended by
Janice Wong

Opening hours	Closed Sunday
Credit cards	Accepted
Price range	Expensive
Style	Smart casual
Cuisine	Japanese
Recommended for	Regular neighborhood

ODETTE

National Gallery
1 Saint Andrew's Road #01–04
Downtown Core
Singapore 178957
+65 63850498
www.odetterestaurant.com

Recommended by
Petty Elliott, Ramón Freixa,
Guillaume Galliot,
Shun Kai Ho,
Christopher Millar,
Dave Pynt, Janice Wong

Opening hours	Closed Sunday
Credit cards	Accepted but not Diners
Price range	Expensive
Style	Smart casual
Cuisine	Modern French
Recommended for	Worth the travel

"Beautiful restaurant with a beautiful kitchen, housed in the National Gallery of Singapore."
—Guillaume Galliot

RAMEN KEISUKE TORI KING

Recommended by
Dave Pynt

100 Tras Street #03–15
Downtown Core
Singapore 79027
+65 66046861
www.keisuke.sg

Opening hours	Open 7 days
Credit cards	Accepted
Price range	Budget
Style	Casual
Cuisine	Japanese
Recommended for	Bargain

"Quick, fast, cheap, filling, and tasty—all-you-can-eat eggs."—Dave Pynt

SALTED AND HUNG

Recommended by
Ming Tan

12 Purvis Street
Downtown Core
Singapore 188591
+65 63583130
www.saltedandhung.com.sg

Opening hours	Closed Monday
Credit cards	Accepted but not Diners
Price range	Affordable
Style	Smart casual
Cuisine	Modern Australian
Recommended for	Wish I'd opened

"A lively pre-millenial playlist, balanced menu, and refreshingly fun food—and I don't mean domes of smoke, dishes that require some sort of mixing or fiddling to combine all the elements and ingredients on the plate. Most of the dishes here have cured, pickled, or smoked ingredients, and it is a real treat trying individual components on their own, before combining them for a full-on tongue party. Dish profiles are robust but nuanced, with nothing too outlandish or wacky. Try their homemade charcuterie and deep-fried tripe. Gin-cured and torched mackerel is stunningly good."—Ming Tan

SIN SWEE KEE

Recommended by
Kirk Westaway

34–35 Seah Street
Downtown Core
Singapore 188391
+65 63377180

Opening hours	Open 7 days
Reservation policy	No
Credit cards	Accepted but not AMEX or Diners
Price range	Budget
Style	Casual
Cuisine	Singaporean
Recommended for	Local favorite

"A great restaurant—the kitchen team and I run here some afternoons for a decent feed and catch up."
—Kirk Westaway

TIPPLING CLUB

Recommended by
Han Liguang,
Christopher Millar,
Eelke Plasmeijer,
Kirk Westaway

38 Tanjong Pagar Road
Downtown Core
Singapore 88461
+65 64752217
www.tipplingclub.com

Opening hours	Closed Sunday
Credit cards	Accepted but not Diners
Price range	Expensive
Style	Smart casual
Cuisine	Modern European
Recommended for	High end

"Nice and casual, serving some interesting and—more importantly—tasty food. The sort of place were you feel at home straightaway, which I think is very important."—Eelke Plasmeijer

As far as avant-garde cuisine in Singapore goes, this green-swathed eatery at Tanjong Pagar might well be number one. Chef-owner Ryan Clift can point to an armoury of kitchen equipment—including a sound wave sonifier and a distiller—to prove his experimental credentials, but he much prefers that you focus on his food and cutting-edge cocktails. To get the full experience, come for dinner and pick the gourmand tasting menu, which comes with standout courses like razor clams in purple Brittany garlic soup and A4 Toriyama beef with homemade burrata and Japanese fruit tomato. Pick your cocktails from the new "Smell Me" menu.

WAKU GHIN

10 Bayfront Avenue #02–01
Marina Bay Sands
Downtown Core
Singapore 18956
+65 66888507
www.marinabaysands.com

Opening hours	Open 7 days
Credit cards	Accepted but not Diners
Price range	Expensive
Style	Smart casual
Cuisine	Japanese-European
Recommended for	High end

"Have a drink at Spago's on the rooftop at Marina Bay Sands then proceed to dinner at Waku Ghin with superb delicate flavors."—Christopher Millar

WHITEGRASS

30 Victoria Street #01–26/27
Downtown Core
Singapore 187996
+65 68370402
www.whitegrass.com.sg

Opening hours	Closed Monday and Sunday
Credit cards	Accepted but not Diners
Price range	Expensive
Style	Casual
Cuisine	Modern Australian
Recommended for	High end

"Executive Chef Sam Aisbett truly knows how to create stunning flavor combinations with lots of textures."—Aitor Jeronimo Orive

YY KAFEI DIAN

37 Beach Road #01–01
Downtown Core
Singapore 189678
+65 63368813

Opening hours	Open 7 days
Reservation policy	No
Credit cards	Accepted but not AMEX or Diners
Price range	Budget
Style	Casual
Cuisine	Café
Recommended for	Breakfast

"Old-school. This place does a common local breakfast dish incredibly well—kaya toast. An irresistible jam of coconut, sugar, eggs, and pandan

leaf is dolloped onto fluffy white enriched buns that have been freshly baked and then toasted. A slab of cold butter on top of the kaya seals the deal. Have this with an unsweetened strong local coffee to start your day right. They bake their bread throughout the entire day, so put your order in, breathe deep, and enjoy your coffee break."—Ming Tan

BEAUTY IN THE POT

The Centrepoint
176 Orchard Road
Geylang
Singapore 238843
+65 62353557
www.paradisegroup.com.sg

Opening hours	Open 7 days
Credit cards	Accepted
Price range	Affordable
Style	Casual
Cuisine	Hot Pot
Recommended for	Late night

ENG SENG RESTAURANT

247 Joo Chiat Place
Geylang
Singapore 427935
+65 64405560

Opening hours	Open 7 days
Reservation policy	No
Credit cards	Not accepted
Price range	Budget
Style	Casual
Cuisine	Seafood
Recommended for	Late night

"They have the best black pepper crab I've ever tasted."—Kirk Westaway

FRESHLY MADE CHEE CHEONG FUN

Old Airport Road Food Center
51 Old Airport Road #01–155
Geylang
Singapore 390051
+65 94372455

Opening hours	Open 7 days
Reservation policy	No
Credit cards	Not accepted
Price range	Budget
Style	Casual
Cuisine	Singaporean Street Food
Recommended for	Bargain

GEYLANG LOR 9 FRESH FROG

Recommended by
Po-Sang Chan

7 Lorong 9 Geylang
Geylang
Singapore 388755
+65 62505287

Opening hours	Open 7 days
Reservation policy	No
Credit cards	Accepted but not AMEX or Diners
Price range	Budget
Style	Casual
Cuisine	Chinese
Recommended for	Late night

"An ideal choice for late nights."—Po-Sang Chan

GEYLANG FAMOUS BEEF KWAY TEOW

Recommended by
Aitor Jeronimo Orive

237 Geylang Rd
Geylang
Singapore 389296

Opening hours	Open 7 days
Reservation policy	No
Credit cards	Not accepted
Price range	Budget
Style	Casual
Cuisine	Singaporean
Recommended for	Bargain

"This hole-in-the-wall serves amazing beef *kway teow* (fried noodles with beef) with the signature 'wok hei' charred notes in each strand of noodle. It is served in a black bean and chile sauce and each piece of beef is also very tender."—Aitor Jeronimo Orive

JB AH MENG

Recommended by
Han Liguang,
Dave Pynt,
Ming Tan

534 Geylang Road
Geylang
Singapore 389490
+65 67412418

Opening hours	Open 7 days
Reservation policy	No
Credit cards	Not accepted
Price range	Budget
Style	Casual
Cuisine	Chinese Street Food
Recommended for	Regular neighborhood

"The ultimate supper-after-service for chefs and their crews. Amazing dishes with all manner of textures and a heavy richness that needs pairing with a cold beer. Street-food roots are apparent everywhere, even in their new location."—Ming Tan

NO SIGNBOARD SEAFOOD

Recommended by
Po-Sang Chan,
Christopher Millar

414 Geylang Road
Geylang
Singapore 389392
+65 68423415
www.nosignboardseafood.com

Opening hours	Open 7 days
Credit cards	Accepted
Price range	Affordable
Style	Casual
Cuisine	Seafood
Recommended for	Regular neighborhood

"The restaurant is just a few steps from my home and the alfresco dining reminds me of the old days of Singapore. The renowed chile crab is really fresh, and worth a try."—Po-Sang Chan

SIN HUAT EATING HOUSE

Recommended by
Yong Bing Ngen,
Christopher Millar,
Dave Pynt

659–661 Lorong
35 Geylang Road
Geylang
Singapore 389589
+65 67449755

Opening hours	Open 7 days
Reservation policy	No
Credit cards	Not accepted
Price range	Expensive
Style	Casual
Cuisine	Seafood
Recommended for	Regular neighborhood

"Check it out, it will make you feel important!"
—Yong Bing Ngen

For all the media coverage it's attracted, including an endorsement by Anthony Bourdain on his TV show "No Reservations", this dilapidated eating house in the heart of Singapore's red-light district has its fair share of detractors. The quality of the food is not in question—take their famous crab dish, which Bourdain described as "giant Sri Lankan beasts cooked with a spicy mystery sauce and noodles"—but the astronomical price tag and dictated menu are. Still, no trip to Singapore is complete without a pilgrimage here. Start saving now.

TANJONG RHU PAU

Recommended by
Julien Royer

389 Guillemard Road
Geylang
Singapore 399788
+65 68422112

Opening hours	Open 7 days
Reservation policy	No
Credit cards	Not accepted
Price range	Budget
Style	Casual
Cuisine	Singaporean
Recommended for	Bargain

TO-RICOS KWAY CHAP

Recommended by
Yong Bing Ngen

Old Airport Road Food Centre
51 Old Airport Road #01–135/136
Geylang
Singapore 390051

Opening hours	Closed Monday
Reservation policy	No
Credit cards	Not accepted
Price range	Budget
Style	Casual
Cuisine	Singaporean
Recommended for	Bargain

"The pig's trotters and large intestines are a must, and the waiting time whilst they are being prepared is relatively good."—Yong Bing Ngen

BEACH ROAD SCISSOR-CUT CURRY

Recommended by
Malcolm Lee

229 Jalan Besar
Kallang
Singapore 208905
+65 98261464

Opening hours	Open 7 days
Reservation policy	No
Credit cards	Not accepted
Price range	Budget
Style	Casual
Cuisine	Singaporean Street Food
Recommended for	Late night

"They serve deep fried pork chops, braised soy pork belly, crispy fried tofu rolls, and more; all cut with scissors and served with rice, and drizzled with lots of curry and gravy. The ultimate comfort food."
—Malcolm Lee

LAM'S NOODLES

Recommended by
Han Liguang

460 Race Course Road
Kallang
Singapore 217800
+65 63981154
www.lamskitchen.com

Opening hours	Closed Monday
Reservation policy	No
Credit cards	Not accepted
Price range	Budget
Style	Casual
Cuisine	Noodles
Recommended for	Bargain

"The texture of the noodles coupled with the abalone sauce, and braised abalones and minced meat and chile sauce, makes for a very satisfying meal. It is also very affordable."—Han Liguang

PIN WEI HONG KONG STYLE CHEE CHEONG FUN

Recommended by
Tan Jason

Peek Kio Hawker Centre
41A Cambridge Road #01–25
Kallang
Singapore 211041

Opening hours	Open 7 days
Reservation policy	No
Credit cards	Not accepted
Price range	Budget
Style	Casual
Cuisine	Cantonese
Recommended for	Breakfast

328 KATONG LAKSA

Recommended by
Po-Sang Chan

51 East Coast Road
Marine Parade
Singapore 428770
+65 97328163

Opening hours	Open 7 days
Reservation policy	No
Credit cards	Not accepted
Price range	Budget
Style	Casual
Cuisine	Singaporean
Recommended for	Local favorite

"I really enjoy the laksa with its shrimp paste, rich coconut milk, and cockles."—Po-Sang Chan

ENG'S NOODLE HOUSE

Recommended by
Dave Pynt

287 Tanjong Katong Road
Marine Parade
Singapore 437070
+65 86882727

Opening hours	Open 7 days
Reservation policy	No
Credit cards	Not accepted
Price range	Budget
Style	Casual
Cuisine	Noodles
Recommended for	Local favorite

NEWTON FOOD CENTRE

Recommended by
Kirk Westaway

500 Clemenceau Avenue North
Newton
Singapore 229495

Opening hours	Open 7 days
Reservation policy	No
Credit cards	Not accepted
Price range	Budget
Style	Casual
Cuisine	Singaporean Street Food
Recommended for	Late night

"Huge late night selection, from satay to fried stingray
—this area ticks every box."—Kirk Westaway

FAYIDHA RESTAURANT

Recommended by
Aitor Jeronimo Orive

26 Kim Keat Road
Novena
Singapore 328807
+65 62597560

Opening hours	Open 7 days
Reservation policy	No
Credit cards	Not accepted
Price range	Budget
Style	Casual
Cuisine	Malaysian
Recommended for	Regular neighborhood

"It's a Malay-Indian place that's open twenty-four
hours a day, which is great for supper or very early-
morning bites. It's good and also very cheap. The
place serves late-night supper favorites."
—Aitor Jeronimo Orive

SELERA RASA NASI LEMAK

Recommended by
Han Liguang

Adam Road Food Center
2 Adam Road #01–02
Novena
Singapore 289876
| 65 98434509
www.selerarasa.com

Opening hours	Closed Friday
Reservation policy	No
Credit cards	Not accepted
Price range	Budget
Style	Casual
Cuisine	Malaysian
Recommended for	Breakfast

"The rice cooked in coconut milk is very fragrant
and the crispiness of the fried chicken is spot on."
—Han Liguang

This twenty-year-old hawker stall sells just one dish
but it draws one of the lengthiest lines (queues) in
all of the Adam Road Food Center. They all come for
the fragrant and fluffy *nasi lemak* (a popular Malay
dish of rice in coconut milk and pandan leaf) cooked
with basmati—rather than jasmine—rice and
served with fried anchovies, a sunny-side-up egg,
and a choice of accompaniments (grilled fish paste
with spices, fried chicken, fried potato patty, or fried
fish). The fact that the Sultan of Brunei is a regular
patron adds a feather to its cap.

WEE NAM KEE

101 Thomson Road #01–08
Novena
Singapore 307591
+65 62556396

Recommended by
Po-Sang Chan,
Malcolm Lee, Claus Meyer,
Aitor Jeronimo Orive,
Ming Tan

Opening hours	Open 7 days
Reservation policy	No
Credit cards	Accepted but not AMEX or Diners
Price range	Affordable
Style	Casual
Cuisine	Singaporean
Recommended for	Bargain

"One of the best chicken rice in Singapore and an easy fix for when you don't know what you want to eat."—Aitor Jeronimo Orive

Chicken rice is a Singaporean national obsession—ask a local for a recommendation and you'll be inundated with passionate responses. Wee Nam Kee, with four branches in Singapore, is likely to come near the top of most people's lists. Don't expect friendly banter or restaurant-quality comforts though—it's all business and bustle at this hawker stall and you'll probably have to share a table. But loyal aficionados agree it's all worth it for the tender "white" (steamed), roasted, or soya chicken that come with a bowl of fragrant broth, rice, and chile and ginger sauce for mixing and dipping.

WHAMPOA HAWKER CENTRE

91 Whampoa Drive
Novena
Singapore 320091
+65 18002255632

Recommended by
Aitor Jeronimo Orive

Opening hours	Open 7 days
Reservation policy	No
Credit cards	Not accepted
Price range	Budget
Style	Casual
Cuisine	Singaporean Street Food
Recommended for	Breakfast

"The market has something for everyone. It's both a wet market and hawker center, with many stalls serving a bunch of local cuisine. It's great for when you can't make up your mind on what you want to eat, but one of my favorite things there is the congee. It's also very close to where I live, which makes it one of my go-tos for breakfast."—Aitor Jeronimo Orive

AKASHI

Orchard Parade Hotel
1 Tanglin Road
Orchard
Singapore 247905
+65 67324438
www.akashi.com.sg

Recommended by
Christopher Millar

Opening hours	Open 7 days
Credit cards	Accepted but not Diners
Price range	Affordable
Style	Casual
Cuisine	Japanese
Recommended for	Regular neighborhood

"I love all things Japanese. And there are many great Japanese restaurants in Singapore, but not necessarily ones a humble chef can afford everyday. Akashi is affordable, super fresh, and of consistent quality—with a decent wine list too."—Christopher Millar

BENI

Mandarin Gallery
333A Orchard Road
Orchard
Singapore 238897
+65 91593177
www.beni-sg.com

Recommended by
Christopher Millar

Opening hours	Closed Sunday
Credit cards	Accepted but not Diners
Price range	Expensive
Style	Smart casual
Cuisine	Japanese-French
Recommended for	High end

CRYSTAL JADE GOLDEN PALACE

The Paragon Shopping Center
290 Orchard Road
Orchard
Singapore 238859
+65 67346866
www.crystaljade.com

Recommended by
Po-Sang Chan,
Dave Pynt

Opening hours	Open 7 days
Credit cards	Accepted
Price range	Affordable
Style	Smart casual
Cuisine	Chinese
Recommended for	High end

"The very finest *chao zhou* cuisine combined with comtemporary design to create an unforgettable dining experience."—Po-Sang Chan

DIN TAI FUNG

Recommended by
Julien Royer,
Chris Salans

The Paragon Shopping Center
290 Orchard Road
Orchard
Singapore 238859
+65 68368336
www.dintaifung.com.sg

Opening hours	Open 7 days
Reservation policy	No
Credit cards	Accepted
Price range	Affordable
Style	Casual
Cuisine	Taiwanese
Recommended for	Local favorite

"The *xiao long bao* are outstanding and very
consistent."—Julien Royer

Xiao long bao (soup dumplings) filled with savory
pork broth are the main attraction at this Singapore
offshoot of the famous Taiwanese chain. But while
the steamed soup dumplings are its raison d'être,
they are by no means the only choice on offer—the
menu teems with well-executed Chinese dishes
like braised beef noodles and fried rice. Although
there are multiple outlets dotted around the city,
the restaurant's no reservation policy means that
a healthy line (queue) builds up quickly at lunchtime.
Come early!

GYOZA-YA

Recommended by
Janice Wong

Robinsons Heeren
260 Orchard Road #B1–02A
Orchard
Singapore 238855
+65 67375581
www.gyozaya.com.sg

Opening hours	Open 7 days
Credit cards	Accepted
Price range	Budget
Style	Casual
Cuisine	Chinese
Recommended for	Bargain

"Consistently flavorful dumplings with many variations
and specials. Reasonably priced."—Janice Wong

HASHIDA SUSHI

Recommended by
Dave Pynt,
Jason Tan

Mandarin Gallery
333A Orchard Road #04–16
Orchard
Singapore 238897
+65 67332114
www.hashida.com.sg

Opening hours	Closed Monday
Credit cards	Accepted
Price range	Expensive
Style	Casual
Cuisine	Japanese
Recommended for	High end

"Just order the *omakase* (chef's choice) menu."
—Jason Tan

IGGYS

Recommended by
Naren Thimmaiah

The Hilton Hotel
581 Orchard Road
Orchard
Singapore 238883
+65 67322234
www.iggys.com.sg

Opening hours	Closed Sunday
Credit cards	Accepted
Price range	Expensive
Style	Smart casual
Cuisine	Modern European
Recommended for	Worth the travel

"The most consistent modern-European restaurant
with a distinct use of local ingredients."
—Naren Thimmaiah

IMPERIAL TREASURE SHANGHAI

Takashimaya Shopping Center
Orchard Road #04–22 391
Orchard
Singapore 238874
+65 68366909
www.imperialtreasure.com

Opening hours	Open 7 days
Credit cards	Accepted
Price range	Affordable
Style	Smart casual
Cuisine	Shanghaiese
Recommended for	Regular neighborhood

"True Shanghai cuisine with an extra fineness of care and attention—all appetisers are delicate and fresh and the signature spicy fish head and claypot rice is to die for."—André Chiang

JIANG-NAN CHUN

Four Seasons Hotel Singapore
190 Orchard Boulevard
Orchard
Singapore 248646
+65 67341110
www.fourseasons.com/singapore

Opening hours	Open 7 days
Credit cards	Accepted
Price range	Affordable
Style	Smart casual
Cuisine	Cantonese
Recommended for	Worth the travel

LES AMIS

Shaw Centre
1 Scotts Road #01–16
Orchard
Singapore 228208
+65 67332225
www.lesamis.com.sg

Opening hours	Open 7 days
Credit cards	Accepted
Price range	Affordable
Style	Smart casual
Cuisine	French
Recommended for	High end

"Absolutely stunning food and wines—great produce cooked with great precision and flavors."
—Malcolm Lee

TIM HO WAN

Plaza Singapura
68 Orchard Road #01–29A
Orchard
Singapore 238839
+65 62512000
www.timhowan.com

Opening hours	Open 7 days
Reservation policy	No
Credit cards	Accepted
Price range	Affordable
Style	Casual
Cuisine	Chinese
Recommended for	Late night

WILD HONEY

6 Scotts Square
6 Scotts Road #03–01
Orchard
Singapore 228209
+65 66361816
www.wildhoney.com.sg

Opening hours	Open 7 days
Credit cards	Accepted but not AMEX or Diners
Price range	Affordable
Style	Casual
Cuisine	Brunch
Recommended for	Breakfast

BAR-ROQUE GRILL

165 Tanjong Pagar Road
Outram
Singapore 88539
+65 64449672
www.bar-roque.com.sg

Opening hours	Closed Sunday
Credit cards	Accepted
Price range	Affordable
Style	Casual
Cuisine	International
Recommended for	Worth the travel

BRASSERIE GAVROCHE

Recommended by
Julien Royer

66 Tras Sreet
Outram
Singapore 79005
+65 62258266
www.brasseriegavroche.com

Opening hours	Closed Sunday
Credit cards	Accepted
Price range	Affordable
Style	Casual
Cuisine	Brasserie
Recommended for	Regular neighborhood

"I love going to Brasserie Gavroche—it has a home-feel like nowhere else in Singapore. Chef Frederic cooks very tasty French fare—classic and comforting, rustic yet elegant."—Julien Royer

BUKO NERO

Recommended by
Malcolm Lee

126 Tanjong Pagar Road
Outram
Singapore 88534
+65 63246225

Opening hours	Closed Monday and Sunday
Reservation policy	No
Credit cards	Accepted
Price range	Budget
Style	Casual
Cuisine	Italian
Recommended for	Wish I'd opened

"A small, cozy restaurant of only twenty seats, run by a husband and wife team. They serve a small selection of dishes—simple but delicious food."—Malcolm Lee

BURNT ENDS

Recommended by
Tim Butler, Rodney Dunn,
Will Meyrick, Christoph Millar,
Dharshan Munidasa,
Kirk Westaway,
James Viles, Jowett Yu

20 Teck Lim Road
Outram
Singapore 88391
+65 62243933
www.burntends.com.sg

Opening hours	Closed Monday and Sunday
Credit cards	Accepted
Price range	Affordable
Style	Casual
Cuisine	Modern Australian
Recommended for	Worth the travel

"Absolutely one of the best BBQ restaurants in the world. Dave Pynt is a master at grilling and uses the specially designed oven and charcoal grill to create an outstanding repertoire of BBQ meats and seafood sourced from Australia."—Jowett Yu

CHICKEN UP

Recommended by
Dave Pynt

48 Tanjong Pagar Road
Outram
Singapore 88469
+65 63271203
www.chicken-up.com

Opening hours	Open 7 days
Reservation policy	No
Credit cards	Accepted
Price range	Budget
Style	Casual
Cuisine	Korean
Recommended for	Late night

FOC

Recommended by
Aitor Jeronimo Orive

40 Hongkong Street
Outram
Singapore 59679
+65 61004040
www.focrestaurant.com

Opening hours	Closed Sunday
Credit cards	Accepted
Price range	Affordable
Style	Casual
Cuisine	Modern Spanish
Recommended for	Wish I'd opened

"Modern Spanish food interpreted in an accessible and affordable way. The space is really fun and always buzzing and the quality of food is never compromised. An all-round reliable place, especially for an everyday meal."—Aitor Jeronimo Orive

LAN ZHOU LA MIAN

Recommended by
Christopher Millar

19 Smith Street
Outram
Singapore 58933
+65 63271286

Opening hours	Open 7 days
Reservation policy	No
Credit cards	Not accepted
Price range	Budget
Style	Casual
Cuisine	Chinese
Recommended for	Regular neighborhood

LAO SI CHUAN

Recommended by
Dave Pynt

249 Outram Road
Outram
Singapore 169048
+65 62263658
www.laosichuan.com.sg

Opening hours	Open 7 days
Credit cards	Not accepted
Price range	Affordable
Style	Casual
Cuisine	Chinese
Recommended for	Late night

LIAO FAN HONG KONG

Recommended by
Guillaume Galliot

Chinatown Food Complex
78 Smith Street #02–126
Outram
Singapore 50335

Opening hours	Closed Wednesday
Reservation policy	No
Credit cards	Not accepted
Price range	Budget
Style	Casual
Cuisine	Singaporean Street Food
Recommended for	Bargain

"The world's cheapest Michelin-starred meal in Singapore."—Guillaume Galliot

LUKE'S

Recommended by
Julien Royer,
Kirk Westaway

22 Gemmill Lane
Outram
Singapore 69257
+65 62214468
www.lukes.com.sg/gemmil

Opening hours	Closed Sunday
Credit cards	Accepted but not Diners
Price range	Expensive
Style	Smart casual
Cuisine	American Seafood
Recommended for	Regular neighborhood

"Great food, consistent with its calm relaxed atmosphere—somewhere I can unwind and enjoy the view along Orchard Road."—Kirk Westaway

Although the draw at this classy American chop house is the list of bivalve molluscs headlined by varieties imported from waters around the owner's home town of Boston, you'll be missing out if you stop at the oysters. The menu is packed with comforting American classics—burgers, pot pies, crab cakes, and clam chowder—and meat, with a fine selection of classic cuts such as bone-in tenderloin *au poivre* and a fennel-spiced bone-in Kurobuta pork chop. Prices are pitched at those with expense accounts—the lobster pot pie alone will set you back SG$115 ($82; £66)—but it's a class act with smart service at both the Gemmill Lane original and its younger sibling on the Orchard Road.

MAN MAN JAPANESE UNAGI

Recommended by
Yong Bing Ngen

1 Keong Saik Road #01–01
Outram
Singapore 89109
+65 62220678

Opening hours	Closed Sunday
Reservation policy	No
Credit cards	Accepted but not AMEX or Diners
Price range	Affordable
Style	Casual
Cuisine	Japanese
Recommended for	Wish I'd opened

MOOSEHEAD

Recommended by
Christopher Millar

110 Telok Ayer Street
Outram
Singapore 68579
+65 66368055
www.mooseheadproject.com

Opening hours	Closed Sunday
Credit cards	Accepted
Price range	Affordable
Style	Casual
Cuisine	Mediterranean
Recommended for	Regular neighborhood

"Casual and hip."—Christopher Millar

PARK BENCH DELI

Recommended by
Christopher Millar

179 Telok Ayer Street
Outram
Singapore 68627
+65 68154600
www.parkbenchdeli.com

Opening hours	Closed Sunday
Reservation policy	No
Credit cards	Accepted but not AMEX or Diners
Price range	Budget
Style	Casual
Cuisine	Sandwiches
Recommended for	Bargain

"I love a good sandwich and these are made with panache—just ignore the overly hipster vibe."
—Christopher Millar

THE POPULUS CAFÉ

Recommended by
André Chiang

146 Neil Road Outram
Singapore 088875
+65 6635 8420
www.thepopuluscafe.com

Opening hours	Open 7 days
Credit cards	Accepted
Price range	Budget
Style	Casual
Cuisine	Café
Recommended for	Breakfast

RESTAURANT ANDRÉ

Recommended by
Vineet Bhatia,
Sang-Hoon Degeimbre,
Alexandre Gauthier,
Dan Graham, Yau Tim Lai,
Claus Meyer, Dave Pynt

41 Bukit Pasoh Road
Outram
Singapore 89855
+65 65348880
www.restaurantandre.com

Opening hours	Closed Monday and Sunday
Credit cards	Accepted
Price range	Expensive
Style	Smart casual
Cuisine	Modern French
Recommended for	Worth the travel

"Beautiful, nuanced food with the personality and journey of the chef really shining through."
—Dan Graham

TERRA

Recommended by
Christopher Millar

54 Tras Street
Outram
Singapore 78993
+65 62215159
www.terraseita.com

Opening hours	Closed Sunday
Credit cards	Accepted
Price range	Affordable
Style	Smart casual
Cuisine	Japanese-European
Recommended for	High end

TIAN TIAN SEAFOOD

Recommended by
Kirk Westaway

239 Outram Road
Outram
Singapore 169042
+65 63241082

Opening hours	Closed Tuesday
Reservation policy	No
Credit cards	Not accepted
Price range	Budget
Style	Casual
Cuisine	Seafood
Recommended for	Regular neighborhood

"A great late night hawker where I like to go with my kitchen team for some fantastic local food."
—Kirk Westaway

COMMON MAN COFFEE ROASTERS

Recommended by
Christopher Millar,
Kirk Westaway,
Janice Wong

22 Martin Road
River Valley
Singapore 239058
+65 68364695
www.commonmancoffeeroasters.com

Opening hours	Open 7 days
Reservation policy	No
Credit cards	Accepted
Price range	Affordable
Style	Casual
Cuisine	Café
Recommended for	Breakfast

"They offer healthy, hearty breakfast options with good coffee and fresh juices."—Janice Wong

HACHI

Recommended by
André Chiang

6 Mohamed Sultan Road #01–01
River Valley
Singapore 238956
+65 67349622
www.hachi-group.com

Opening hours	Open 7 days
Credit cards	Accepted but not Diners
Price range	Expensive
Style	Smart casual
Cuisine	Japanese
Recommended for	Regular neighborhood

"Japanese haute-cuisine at very reasonable prices, served in a casual setting."—André Chiang

SUPER LOCO

Recommended by
Enrico Cripa,
Dave Pynt

The Quayside
60 Robertson Quay #01–13
River Valley
Singapore 238252
+65 62358900
www.super-loco.com

Opening hours	Open 7 days
Credit cards	Accepted but not Diners
Price range	Affordable
Style	Casual
Cuisine	Mexican
Recommended for	Breakfast

"Great food, great service, and a relaxed environment."—Dave Pynt

ALLAUDDIN'S BRIYANI

Recommended by
Christopher Millar

Tekka Food Center
665 Buffalo Road
Rochor
Singapore 210665
+65 62966786

Opening hours	Open 7 days
Reservation policy	No
Credit cards	Not accepted
Price range	Budget
Style	Casual
Cuisine	Indian-Malaysian
Recommended for	Bargain

JAGGI'S

Recommended by
Janice Wong

37–39 Chander Road
Rochor
Singapore 219541
+65 62966141
www.jaggis.com.sg

Opening hours	Open 7 days
Credit cards	Accepted
Price range	Affordable
Style	Casual
Cuisine	Northern Indian
Recommended for	Regular neighborhood

"It's humble and simple yet it serves up some of the best flavors and textures of Northern Indian at a very reasonable price."—Janice Wong

MRS PHO

Recommended by
Janice Wong

349 Beach Road
Rochor
Singapore 199570
+65 62920018
www.mrspho.com

Opening hours	Open 7 days
Credit cards	Not accepted
Price range	Budget
Style	Casual
Cuisine	Vietnamese
Recommended for	Bargain

"Delicious Vietnamese Pho with many variations and side dishes. Its specialty is its preserved lemon drink."—Janice Wong

ONE KUEH AT A TIME

Recommended by
Christopher Millar

Berseh Food Center
166 Jalan Besar #02–61
Rochor
Singapore 208877
+65 97956119

Opening hours	Closed Monday and Tuesday
Reservation policy	No
Credit cards	Not accepted
Price range	Budget
Style	Casual
Cuisine	Singaporean
Recommended for	Bargain

RUMAH MAKAN MINANG

Recommended by
Malcolm Lee

18–18A Kandahar Street
Rochor
Singapore 198884
+65 62944805
www.minang.sg

Opening hours	Open 7 days
Reservation policy	No
Credit cards	Not accepted
Price range	Budget
Style	Casual
Cuisine	Indonesian
Recommended for	Regular neighborhood

"Reasonably priced with a huge variety of dishes."
—Malcolm Lee

SUNGEI ROAD LAKSA

Recommended by
Ray Adriansyah,
Christopher Millar

Block 27 Jalan Berseh #01–100
Rochor
Singapore 200027
www.sungeiroadlaksa.com.sg

Opening hours	Open 7 days
Reservation policy	No
Credit cards	Not accepted
Price range	Budget
Style	Casual
Cuisine	Singaporean Street Food
Recommended for	Worth the travel

"Laksa at its best for under SG$4 ($3; £2)!"
—Ray Adriansyah

SWEE CHOON TIM SUM

Recommended by
Aitor Jeronimo Orive

183–191 Jalan Besar
Rochor
Singapore 208882
+65 62257788
www.sweechoon.com

Opening hours	Closed Tuesday
Reservation policy	No
Credit cards	Not accepted
Price range	Budget
Style	Casual
Cuisine	Chinese
Recommended for	Late night

"I love how cheap the dim sum is here and it's
consistently good. As chefs, we can only go out and
eat late at night after shift, so this place is ideal as it
is open until 6.00 a.m."—Aitor Jeronimo Orive

WILD ROCKET

Recommended by
Yau Leung Chen

Hangout Hotel
10A Upper Wilkie Road
Rochor
Singapore 228119
+65 63399448
www.wildrocket.com.sg

Opening hours	Closed Sunday
Credit cards	Accepted
Price range	Affordable
Style	Casual
Cuisine	Modern Singaporean
Recommended for	Worth the travel

"Taste the traditional Singaporean/Asian flavors
translated into modern creative dishes in this
showcase of modern contemporary Singaporean
cuisine."—Yau Leung Chen

ZAM ZAM

Recommended by
Julien Royer

697–699 North Bridge Road
Rochor
Singapore 198675
+65 62986320
www.zamzamsingapore.com

Opening hours	Open 7 days
Reservation policy	No
Credit cards	Not accepted
Price range	Budget
Style	Casual
Cuisine	Indian
Recommended for	Bargain

"The atmosphere is unique with fantastic value for
money."—Julien Royer

THE SUMMERHOUSE

Recommended by
Christopher Millar

3 Park Lane
Seletar
Singapore 798387
+65 62621063
www.thesummerhouse.sg

Opening hours	Closed Monday and Tuesday
Credit cards	Accepted
Price range	Affordable
Style	Smart casual
Cuisine	Café-Bar
Recommended for	Breakfast

"An escape from the busy city—this place has a unique
heritage and garden charm."—Christopher Millar

L'ATELIER DE JOËL ROBUCHON

Recommended by
Malcolm Lee

Hotel Michael
26 Sentosa Gateway
Southern Islands
Singapore 98138
+65 65778888
www.joel-robuchon.com

Opening hours	Closed Tuesday and Wednesday
Credit cards	Accepted
Price range	Expensive
Style	Smart casual
Cuisine	French
Recommended for	High end

"Great produce cooked with precise technique and flavors. The menu changes regularly and the ambience is relaxed and casual. Understated simplicity."
—Malcolm Lee

CANDLENUT

Recommended by
Liguang Han,
Christopher Millar,
Dave Pynt,
Ming Tan

17A Dempsey Road
Tanglin
Singapore 249676
1800-304-2288 (Local calls only)
www.comodempsey.sg/candlenut

Opening hours	Open 7 days
Credit cards	Accepted
Price range	Expensive
Style	Smart casual
Cuisine	Peranakan
Recommended for	Local favorite

"Young Singaporean chef doing a modern take on Peranakan cuisine. Represents the best of Singapore —progressive and forward thinking whilst holding true to authentic cuisines."—Christopher Millar

CORNER HOUSE

Recommended by
Ming Tan,
Janice Wong

E J H Corner House
1 Cluny Road
Singapore Botanic Gardens
Tanglin
Singapore 259569
+65 64691000
www.cornerhouse.com.sg

Opening hours	Closed Monday
Credit cards	Accepted but not Diners
Price range	Expensive
Style	Smart casual
Cuisine	International
Recommended for	High end

"Set in the beautiful Singapore Botanic Gardens, Corner House makes its home in a colonial black-and-white bungalow. Every bite of food is packed with flavor—a clear reflection of the love given to the food by the team."—Ming Tan

DA PAOLO GASTRONOMIA

Recommended by
Manoella Buffara Ramos

Cluny Court 01–01
501 Bukit Timah Road
Tanglin
Singapore 259760
+65 64687010
www.dapaolo.com.sg

Opening hours	Open 7 days
Reservation policy	No
Credit cards	Accepted
Price range	Budget
Style	Casual
Cuisine	Italian
Recommended for	Breakfast

"Great pastries and snacks to go, with ideal surroundings."—Manoella Buffara Ramos

LONG BEACH

Recommended by
Janice Wong

25 Dempsey Road
Tanglin
Singapore 249670
+65 63232222
www.longbeachseafood.com.sg

Opening hours	Open 7 days
Credit cards	Accepted
Price range	Affordable
Style	Smart casual
Cuisine	Seafood
Recommended for	Local favorite

"Founded in 1945, it has maintained its consistency, serving up traditional Singaporean seafood dishes such as the black pepper and chile crab."
—Janice Wong

SAMY'S CURRY

Recommended by
Dave Pynt

25 Dempsey Road
Tanglin
Singapore 249670
+65 64722080
www.samyscurry.com

Opening hours	Closed Tuesday
Credit cards	Accepted but not AMEX or Diners
Price range	Affordable
Style	Casual
Cuisine	Indian
Recommended for	Regular neighborhood

CHEY SUA CARROT CAKE

Recommended by
Jason Tan

127 Tao Payoh
Lorong 1
Toa Payoh
Singapore 310127

Opening hours	Closed Monday
Reservation policy	No
Credit cards	Not accepted
Price range	Budget
Style	Casual
Cuisine	Singaporean Street Food
Recommended for	Local favorite

HE JIA HUAN BAN MIAN MEE HOON

Recommended by
Yong Bing Ngen

Toa Payoh Food Center
75 Toa Payoh Lorong 5 #01–14
Toa Payoh
Singapore 640496

Opening hours	Open 7 days
Reservation policy	No
Credit cards	Not accepted
Price range	Budget
Style	Casual
Cuisine	Noodles
Recommended for	Late night

LEE FUN NAM KEE

Recommended by
Yong Bing Ngen

94 Lorong 4 Toa Payoh #01–04
Toa Payoh
Singapore 310094
+65 62550891

Opening hours	Open 7 days
Reservation policy	No
Credit cards	Not accepted
Price range	Budget
Style	Casual
Cuisine	Singaporean
Recommended for	Regular neighborhood

"Although it is a Singaporean chicken rice restaurant, it also serves dishes such as roast duck, *char suey* (barbecued pork), dumpling soup, etc."—Yong Bing Ngen

SOON HENG ROJAK

Recommended by
Po-Sang Chan

480 Lorong 6 Toa Payoh
Toa Payoh
Singapore 310480

Opening hours	Open 7 days
Reservation policy	No
Credit cards	Accepted but not AMEX or Diners
Price range	Budget
Style	Casual
Cuisine	Singaporean
Recommended for	Bargain

"Extremely generous portions for only a few dollars."—Po-Sang Chan

SPRINGLEAF PRATA PLACE

Recommended by
Malcolm Lee

Springleaf Garden
1 Thong Soon Avenue
Yishun
Singapore 787431
+65 64595670
www.springleafprataplace.com

Opening hours	Open 7 days
Reservation policy	No
Credit cards	Not accepted
Price range	Budget
Style	Casual
Cuisine	Indian
Recommended for	Breakfast

"They have original and interesting takes on the traditional *roti prata*, like the 'murtaburger', 'plaster blaster', 'umami 50'. I especially like their 'plaster prata' being crispy and fluffy."—Malcolm Lee

"Great interior, amazing atmosphere, and impeccable food."

GÍSLI AUDUNSSON P340

ICELAND

"THIS PLACE TRULY SUMS UP MY CITY OF REYKJAVÍK."

GUNNAR KARL GÍSLASON P340

"REALLY HIGH-QUALITY RESTAURANT THAT HAS BEEN AROUND FOR CENTURIES."

GÍSLI AUDUNSSON P340

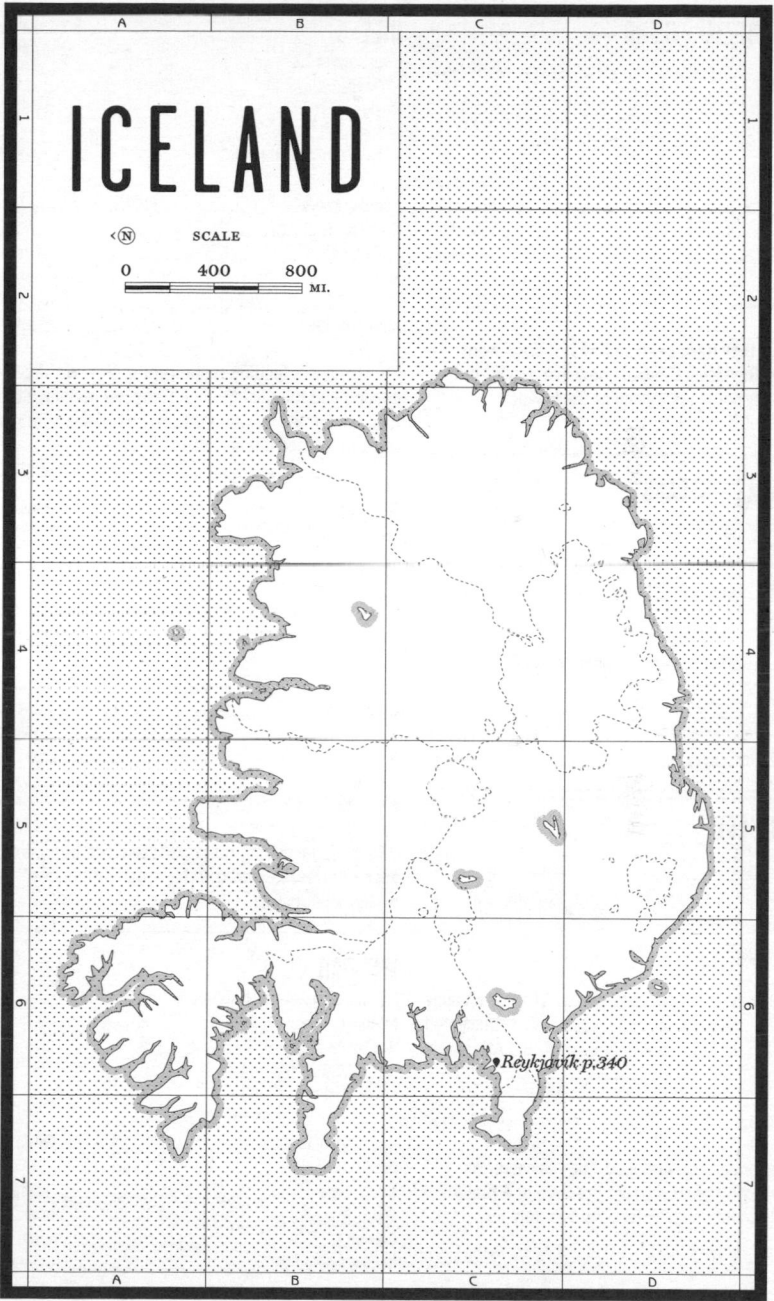

ICELAND

SCALE

0   400   800
MI.

•Reykjavik p.340

BÆJARINS BEZTU PYLSUR

Recommended by
Gísli Audunsson,
Gunnar Karl Gíslason

Tryggvagötu 1
Reykjavík 101
+354 5111566
www.bbp.is

Opening hours	Open 7 days
Credit cards	Accepted
Price range	Budget
Style	Casual
Cuisine	Hot Dogs
Recommended for	Bargain

"Since 1937, they have been selling hot dogs from that stand in Reykjavík Centre. I now live in NYC but this place truly sums up my city of Reykjavík."
—Gunnar Karl Gíslason

BURRO TAPAS + STEAKS

Recommended by
Gísli Audunsson

Veltusund 1
Reykjavík 101
+354 5527333
www.burro.is

Opening hours	Open 7 days
Credit cards	Accepted but not AMEX or Diners
Price range	Affordable
Style	Casual
Cuisine	Mexican Tapas
Recommended for	Late night

COOCOO'S NEST

Recommended by
Gísli Audunsson

Grandagarður 23
Vesturbær
Reykjavík 101
+354 5525454
www.coocoosnest.is

Opening hours	Closed Monday
Credit cards	Accepted
Price range	Affordable
Style	Casual
Cuisine	Italian-International
Recommended for	Regular neighborhood

"The restaurant is really relaxed. They serve high quality food using great organic produce in a really honest and humble way."—Gísli Audunsson

DILL

Recommended by
Gísli Audunsson

Hverfisgata 12
Miðborg
Reykjavík 101
+354 5521522
www.dillrestaurant.is

Opening hours	Closed Sunday to Tuesday
Credit cards	Accepted
Price range	Expensive
Style	Smart casual
Cuisine	Modern Nordic
Recommended for	High end

"It's Iceland's leading restaurant in New Nordic cuisine and the only Michelin-starred restaurant in Iceland. Owned by Gunnar Karl, one of the country's most renowned chefs."—Gísli Audunsson

GRILLIÐ

Recommended by
Gísli Audunsson

107 Hagatorg
Vesturbær
Reykjavík 101
+354 5259960
www.en.grillid.is

Opening hours	Closed Monday and Sunday
Credit cards	Accepted but not Diners
Price range	Expensive
Style	Smart casual
Cuisine	Modern Icelandic
Recommended for	Local favorite

"Really high-quality restaurant that has been around for centuries. Icelandic with French influences."
—Gísli Audunsson

MAT BAR

Recommended by
Gísli Audunsson

Hverfisgata 26
Miðborg
Reykjavík 101
+354 7883900
www.matbar.is

Opening hours	Open 7 days
Credit cards	Accepted
Price range	Affordable
Style	Smart casual
Cuisine	Italian-Nordic
Recommended for	Late night

"Nice atmosphere and food with Italian influences as well as Scandinavian. Great interior, amazing atmosphere, and impeccable food."—Gísli Audunsson

"THIS RESTAURANT HAS THE POTENTIAL TO BECOME A NEW CLASSIC IN HELSINKI."
FILIP LANGHOFF P387

NORWAY, SWEDEN, DENMARK & FINLAND

"THIS PLACE IS SOMETHING OUT OF A FAIRYTALE. HIS PHILOSOPHY AND PRODUCT SOURCING REACHES ANOTHER LEVEL."
MARC-ALEXANDRE MERCIER P345

"THOUGHT-PROVOKING, CASUAL FOOD THAT SURPRISES YOU WITH EVERY DISH."
OLLIE TEMPLETON P378

"IT IS TRULY ONE OF THE BEST FINE DINING EXPERIENCES IN THE NORDICS."
GUNNAR KARL GÍSLASON P349

NORWAY,
SWEDEN,
DENMARK
& FINLAND

$\hat{N}$ SCALE

0   90   180
              MI.

FAROE

Streymoy p.382

ISLANDS

Northern Ostrobothnia p.383 ◆

Jämtland p.345 ◆

FINLAND

Pirkanmaa p.383 ◆
Southern Savonia p.383 ◆

SWEDEN

Uusimaa p.383 ◆

Finland Proper p.382 ◆

NORWAY

Oslo p.344 ◆

Østfold p.344 ◆
Vestfold p.345 ◆
Rogaland p.345 ◆

Stockholm pp.352–365 ◆

Søgne pp.345 ◆

Vastra Gotaland p.350 ◆

DENMARK

Midtjylland p.364 ◆
Hovedstaden p.362 ◆
Copenhagen pp.367–381 ◆   Skania p.346 ◆
Sjælland p.364 ◆
Syddanmark p.365 ◆   Bornholm p.362 ◆

MAAEMO

Annette Thommessens Plass
Schweigaards Gate 15
Oslo, 191, Norway
+47 22179969
www.maaemo.no

Opening hours...............Closed Monday, Tuesday, and Sunday
Credit cards...Accepted
Price range...Expensive
Style...Smart casual
Cuisine...Scandinavian
Recommended for..Worth the travel

"There are not many chefs that are able to cook
with the same precision yet simplicity as Esben
Holmboe Bang. It's a pure pleasure to dine at
Maaemo."—Filip Langhoff

Old Norse for "Mother Earth", Maaemo draws
inspiration from Norway's natural environment,
creating eye-catching dishes, dramatically decorated
with foraged vegetation, that encapsulate the
country's craggy fjords and pine-covered mountains.
The brainchild of Danish-born chef, Esben Holmboe
Bang, Maaemo presents an unconventional take
on Nordic cuisine. The menu offers a series of
outstanding bite-sized dishes, including mahogany
clams (which can be up to 400 years old, if you're
keen to eat something born during the time of
Galileo), Røros butter ice cream, and their
world-famous Norwegian langoustines. With just
a handful of tables in the main dining area, and
a third Michelin star awarded in 2016, it goes
without saying to book well in advance.

PJOLTERGEIST

Rosteds Gate 15b
Oslo 178, Norway
+47 40237788
www.pjoltergeist.no

Opening hours.............................Closed Monday and Sunday
Reservation policy..No
Credit cards...Accepted but not AMEX
Price range...Affordable
Style..Casual
Cuisine...Asian-Scandinavian
Recommended for.................................Regular neighborhood

"If I still lived in Oslo I know my regular place would be
Pjoltergeist. Fantastic food and wine."—Filip Langhoff

PUBLIKO

Vibes Gate 11
Oslo 356, Norway
+47 21422880
www.publiko.no

Opening hours.............................Closed Monday and Sunday
Credit cards...Accepted
Price range..Budget
Style..Casual
Cuisine...Nordic
Recommended for...Bargain

"Great place that makes very tasty and honest food
with influences from all over the world."—Geir Skeie

STATHOLDEGÅRDEN

Rådhusgate 11
Oslo 151, Norway
+47 22418800
www.statholdergaarden.no

Opening hours..Closed Sunday
Credit cards...Accepted
Price range...Expensive
Style...Smart casual
Cuisine..Modern Norwegian
Recommended for...High end

MARCHÉ SOLLI

Solliveien 276
Greåker
Sarpsborg
Østfold 1719, Norway
+47 69 14 73 04
www.marche-restaurants.com/en/marche-solli

Opening hours...Open 7 days
Credit cards.........................Accepted but not AMEX or Diners
Price range..Budget
Style..Casual
Cuisine...Nordic
Recommended for..Worth the travel

RE-NAA

Recommended by
Geir Skeie

Steinkargata 10
Stavanger
Rogaland 4006, Norway
+47 51551111
www.restaurantrenaa.no

Opening hours............................Closed Monday and Sunday
Credit cards..................................Accepted but not AMEX
Price range...Expensive
Style...Smart casual
Cuisine...Norwegian
Recommended for...High end

BØLGEN OG MOI NY HELLESUND

Recommended by
Geir Skeie

Kapelløya 2
Ny-Hellesund
Søgne 4644, Norway
+47 40008011
www.bolgenogmoi.no

Opening hours................................Closed Monday and Sunday
Credit cards...Accepted
Price range...Expensive
Style...Smart casual
Cuisine...European
Recommended for..Local favorite

"Perfectly located on an island without cars, on the
peninsula outside Kristiansand. A very nice place
to be in summer. Good food, excellent service,
and wine list."—Geir Skeie

HÅNDVERKEREN

Recommended by
Geir Skeie

Kongensgate 17
Sandefjord
Vestfold 3211, Norway
+47 45502035
www.handverkerenkaffe.no

Opening hours..Open 7 days
Reservation policy..No
Credit cards...Accepted
Price range...Affordable
Style...Casual
Cuisine..European Bistro
Recommended for......................Regular neighborhood

"Very cosy coffee bar with good homemade
baguettes, sandwiches, and sweets. They roast their
own coffee in-house. There's also a nice ice cream
parlor in the backyard on summer days."—Geir Skeie

KVERNERIET

Recommended by
Geir Skeie

Rambergveien 15
Tønsberg
Vestfold 3115, Norway
+47 90600333
www.kverneriet.com

Opening hours...Open 7 days
Credit cards.................................Accepted but not AMEX
Price range..Affordable
Style...Casual
Cuisine...Burgers
Recommended for...Bargain

"Very good hamburgers, friendly service, and good
beers. Relaxed atmosphere on the pier."—Geir Skeie

FÄVIKEN MAGASINET

Recommended by
Tom Aikens, Kristian Baumann,
Bo Bech, Paul Berglund,
Riccardo Camanini, Paul Cunningham,
Daniel Berlin, Anton Bjuhr,
Daniel Burns, Sang-Hoon Degeimbre,
Mikael Einarsson, Katsuya Fukushima,
Erick Harvey, Jacon Holström,
Philip Howard, James Lowe,
Isaac Mchale, Marc-Alexandre Mercier,
Jakob Mielcke, Nicolai Nørregaard,
Uwe Opocensky, Stevie Parle,
Eelke Plasmeijer, Ljubomir Stanisic,
Olle T. Celton, Simone Tondo,
Victor Wågman

Fäviken 216
Järpen
Jämtland 830 05, Sweden
l 46 64740177
www.favikenmagasinet.se

Opening hours............................Closed Monday and Sunday
Credit cards...Accepted
Price range...Expensive
Style...Smart casual
Cuisine...Swedish
Recommended for......................................Worth the travel

"This place is something out of a fairytale. I don't
know anything comparable to this. His philosophy
and product sourcing reaches another level."
—Marc-Alexandre Mercier

To say that Fäviken is worth the journey is high praise
indeed when you consider that your destination is
Järpen in the unspoiled northwest of Sweden, 466
miles (750 km) north of Stockholm. It's run by farmer/
forager/hunter/chef Magnus Nilsson, who transforms
wild ingredients into an haute experience for only a
handful of guests. Almost everything served at the
strikingly intimate, twelve-seat restaurant is collected,
caught, hunted, or grown on the surrounding estate.
Show-stopping dishes include a charcoal-grilled
moose thigh bone, which is sawn in half on a block
in the dining room before having its marrow served.

OLOF VIKTORS

Recommended by
Ebbe Vollmer

Österlenvägen 86
Glemmingebro
Scania 270 21, Sweden
+46 411522020
www.olofviktors.se

Opening hours	Open 7 days
Credit cards	Accepted but not AMEX or Diners
Price range	Expensive
Style	Casual
Cuisine	Bakery
Recommended for	Breakfast

"Pastry chef Jan Hedh makes artisan bread 362 days a year with biodynamic flour."—Ebbe Vollmer

BASTARD

Recommended by
Daniel Berlin,
Olle T. Cellton,
Robert Jacobsson

Mäster Johansgatan 11
Malmö
Scania 211 21, Sweden
+46 40121318
www.bastardrestaurant.se

Opening hours	Closed Monday and Sunday
Credit cards	Accepted but not AMEX or Diners
Price range	Affordable
Style	Smart casual
Cuisine	Modern European
Recommended for	Late night

"Great, relaxed food in fantastic surroundings—loud music, big plates, and just fun."—Robert Jacobsson

Chef Andreas Dahlberg's boldly named Malmö outpost opened in late 2009. A smartly restyled tavern, all dark wood and white butcher's tiles, its doors open each night at 5.00 p.m. and the bar quickly fills up with the city's most fashionable foodies, who drink natural wine and eat charcuterie, sliced by the huge red machine that sits behind the open counter. When the kitchen proper opens at 6.00 p.m., the menu is meat-heavy with a love of variety meats (offal) and game that would please Fergus "St. John" Henderson. The kitchen is proud of its eco-credentials—a champion of local, organic, and high-welfare farming.

BORD 13

Recommended by
Daniel Berlin

Engelbrektsgatan 13
Malmö
Scania 211 33, Sweden
+46 04258788
www.bord13.se

Opening hours	Closed Monday and Sunday
Credit cards	Accepted but not AMEX
Price range	Affordable
Style	Casual
Cuisine	Swedish
Recommended for	Local favorite

BOUCHON

Recommended by
Daniel Berlin,
Olle T. Cellton

Andrélundsvägen 5
Malmö
Scania 211 52, Sweden
+46 40306850
www.bouchon.se

Opening hours	Closed Tuesday
Credit cards	Accepted but not AMEX or Diners
Price range	Expensive
Style	Casual
Cuisine	French
Recommended for	Local favorite

"A Lyonnaise bouchon in Malmö but still so much more. Everything I wish for in a local restaurant. Great produce, modest prices, and amazing food prepared simply."—Olle T. Cellton

It may take you a few attempts to find Bouchon, tucked away as it is in a secluded alleyway near Malmö town hall. But if you're looking for traditional Lyonnaise cuisine which presents a combination of quality local produce and imported French delicacies, the search will be well worth it. Bouchon, headed by chef Dennis Gustafsson, stakes its reputation on its *canard à la presse*: the duck is marinated for two days before the breast is cut into thin slices and dressed with a sauce made from the anchor-pressed carcass, cognac, red wine, port, and duck liver. The wine list covers all regions of France and is well balanced between conventional, biodynamic, and organic.

CASUAL STREETFOOD

Recommended by
Daniel Berlin,
Andreas Dahlberg

Spångatan 32
Malmö
Scania 211 53, Sweden
www.casualstreetfood.se

Opening hours	Closed Monday
Reservation policy	No
Credit cards	Accepted but not AMEX or Diners
Price range	Affordable
Style	Casual
Cuisine	Burgers
Recommended for	Regular neighborhood

"Best burgers in town and probably in the world."
—Andreas Dahlberg

FALAFEL & BURGERS

Recommended by
Andreas Dahlberg,
Olle T. Cellton,
Mats Vollmer,

Malmö Saluhall
Gibraltargatan 6
Malmö
Scania 211 18, Sweden
+46 708280210
www.malmosaluhall.se

Opening hours	Open 7 days
Reservation policy	No
Credit cards	Accepted but not AMEX
Price range	Budget
Style	Casual
Cuisine	Fast food
Recommended for	Bargain

"I grew up in Malmö and you could find me skating along the streets pretty much every day. Falafel is still my favorite comfort food to eat whilst sitting on a curb."—Olle T. Cellton

FALAFEL BAGHDAD

Recommended by
Daniel Berlin

Annelundsgatan 59
Malmö
Scania 214 44, Sweden
+46 700944922

Opening hours	Open 7 days
Reservation policy	No
Credit cards	Accepted but not AMEX
Price range	Budget
Style	Casual
Cuisine	Middle Eastern
Recommended for	Bargain

"Traditional, tasty, and just great!"—Daniel Berlin

HAGEN

Recommended by
Robert Jacobsson

Storgatan 41
Malmö
Scania 211 42, Sweden
+46 40970970
www.ihagen.se

Opening hours	Closed Sunday
Credit cards	Accepted but not AMEX or Diners
Price range	Affordable
Style	Casual
Cuisine	Swedish
Recommended for	Bargain

"Cheap, quick, tasty food for no money!"
—Robert Jacobsson

KAFFEBAREN MÖLLAN

Recommended by
Robert Jacobsson

Ystadvägen 9
Malmö
Scania 214 24, Sweden
+46 721348305

Opening hours	Open 7 days
Reservation policy	No
Credit cards	Accepted but not AMEX or Diners
Price range	Budget
Style	Casual
Cuisine	Café
Recommended for	Breakfast

"Great coffee, nice sandwiches, cool place to hang out."—Robert Jacobsson

KLEIN'S MAT

Recommended by
Ebbe Vollmer

Katrinetorps allé 1
Malmö
Scania 215 74, Sweden
+46 40467167
www.kleinsmat.se

Opening hours	Open 7 days
Credit cards	Accepted but not AMEX or Diners
Price range	Affordable
Style	Casual
Cuisine	Swedish
Recommended for	Regular neighborhood

"They have their own garden where they get all their vegetables from."—Ebbe Vollmer

KVARTERET ÅKERN

Recommended by
Daniel Berlin,
Andreas Dahlberg,
Mats Vollmer

Nobelvägen 73b
Malmö
Scania 214 33, Sweden
+46 40969600
www.kvarteretakern.com

Opening hours	Closed Monday and Sunday
Credit cards	Accepted but not AMEX or Diners
Price range	Affordable
Style	Casual
Cuisine	Swedish
Recommended for	Regular neighborhood

"Serving mostly vegetable-based dishes in a friendly environment."—Andreas Dahlberg

MALMÖ SALUHALL

Recommended by
Mats Vollmer

Gibraltargatan 6
Malmö
Scania 211 18, Sweden
+46 406267730
www.malmosaluhall.se

Opening hours	Open 7 days
Credit cards	Accepted but not AMEX or Diners
Price range	Budget
Style	Casual
Cuisine	Market
Recommended for	Breakfast

PINK HEAD NOODLE BAR

Recommended by
Andreas Dahlberg

Malmö Saluhall
Gibraltargatan 6
Malmö
Scania 211 18, Sweden
+46 406267730
www.malmosaluhall.se

Opening hours	Open 7 days
Credit cards	Accepted but not AMEX or Diners
Price range	Affordable
Style	Casual
Cuisine	Asian
Recommended for	Late night

"Amazing Asian fast-food served by our favorite Aussie, Wade Brown."—Andreas Dahlberg

RESTAURANT STURE

Recommended by
Robert Jacobsson

Adelgatan 13
Malmö
Scania 211 22, Sweden
+46 40121253
www.restaurantsture.com

Opening hours	Closed Sunday
Credit cards	Accepted
Price range	Expensive
Style	Smart casual
Cuisine	French
Recommended for	Regular neighborhood

"Fantastic French restaurant run by a passionate French chef. Classic style and fantastic service."
—Robert Jacobsson

SALTIMPORTEN CANTEEN

Recommended by
Daniel Berlin,
Olle T. Cellton,
Matthew Orlando,
Mats Vollmer

Grimsbygatan 24
Malmö
Scania 211 20, Sweden
+46 706518426
www.saltimporten.com

Opening hours	Closed Saturday and Sunday
Credit cards	Accepted but not AMEX
Price range	Budget
Style	Casual
Cuisine	Swedish
Recommended for	Local favorite

"It's a lunch spot that does one dish a day, and they do it very well, in a cool space at the end of an abandoned dock in Malmö."—Matthew Orlando

Having closed the acclaimed Trio, rising stars Ola Rudin and Sebastian Persson brought a simpler, more homely version of their New Nordic cooking to this harbor-side warehouse in 2013. Open for weekday lunches only, Saltimporten Canteen attracts a hipster crowd, many of whom make the thirty-minute crossing from Copenhagen for the two-dish menu: veal, cucumber, yogurt, and mint, perhaps, or beet (beetroot), lingonberry, mustard, and spelt. Everything—from the canteen-style tables and benches to the clean-cut compilations on the plates—is carefully pared back. And the bread alone is worth the journey. Check the website first to find out what they're serving before you head over.

SNAPPHANE

Recommended by
Ebbe Vollmer

Adelgatan 4
Malmö
Scania 211 22, Sweden
+46 40150100
www.snapphane.nu

Opening hours	Closed Monday and Sunday
Credit cards	Accepted
Price range	Expensive
Style	Smart casual
Cuisine	Scandinavian
Recommended for	Late night

VOLLMERS

Recommended by
Robert Jacobsson

Tegelgårdsgatan 5
Malmö
Scania 211 33, Sweden
+46 40579750
www.vollmers.nu

Opening hours	Variable
Credit cards	Accepted
Price range	Expensive
Style	Smart casual
Cuisine	Scandanavian
Recommended for	Local favorite

SÖDERBERG & SARA

Recommended by
Daniel Berlin

Mäster Danielsgatan 3
Malmö
Scania 211 58, Sweden
+46 40125810
www.soderbergsara.se

Opening hours	Open 7 days
Reservation policy	No
Credit cards	Accepted but not AMEX
Price range	Affordable
Style	Casual
Cuisine	Café
Recommended for	Breakfast

"Small place, intimate, serving fresh baked bread, good coffee, and juice."—Daniel Berlin

DANIEL BERLIN KROG

Recommended by
Anton Bjuhr, Fredrik Berselius,
Andreas Dahlberg, Magnus Ek,
Robert Jacobsson,
Nicolai Nørregaard, Tim Spedding,
Olle T. Cellton, Victor Wågman

Diligensvägen 21
Tomelilla
Scania 273 92, Sweden
+46 41720300
www.danielberlin.se

Opening hours	Variable
Credit cards	Accepted
Price range	Expensive
Style	Smart casual
Cuisine	Scandanavian
Recommended for	High end

"It is truly one of the best fine-dining experiences in the Nordics."—Olle T. Cellton

Daniel Berlin's parents quit their jobs to work for him in 2009. They're not the only ones to believe in the thirty-four-year-old Swede: René Redzepi himself tipped him for the top. Berlin draws his inspiration from the landscape and natural larder all around him. Diners come to the Scanian sticks expecting unusual ingredients: Berlin's roasted blackened celery root (celeriac) flesh with Västerbotten cheese, egg yolk with four kinds of cabbage, and quail eggs in local lardo (cured pork). An overnight stay at nearby Logi Gamlegård is recommended—the chef or his dad will drive you there after supper.

SOLDE KAFFEBAR

Recommended by
Andreas Dahlberg,
Robert Jacobsson

Regementsgatan 2
Malmö
Scania 211 42, Sweden
+46 739357770
www.solde.se

Opening hours	Open 7 days
Credit cards	Accepted
Price range	Affordable
Style	Casual
Cuisine	Café
Recommended for	Breakfast

"Great coffee from their own roastery, opens at 7.15 a.m. with a smile each day!"—Andreas Dahlberg

ASTRIDS ÄNGBY

Recommended by
Mikael Einarsson

Kök Färjestadsvägen 8
Bromma
Stockholm County 131 37, Sweden
+46 868428449
www.astridskok.se

Opening hours	Open 7 days
Credit cards	Accepted but not Diners
Price range	Affordable
Style	Smart casual
Cuisine	European
Recommended for	Regular neighborhood

"Where I take my family for good comfort food."
—Mikael Einarsson

ANDAMAN

Recommended by
Anton Bjuhr

Värmdövägen 119
Nacka
Stockholm County 131 37, Sweden
+46 87164022

Opening hours	Open 7 days
Credit cards	Accepted but not AMEX
Price range	Affordable
Style	Casual
Cuisine	Thai
Recommended for	Regular neighborhood

LINDEBERG BAGERI & KONDITORI

Recommended by
Anton Bjuhr

Orminge Centrum
Nacka
Stockholm County 132 30, Sweden
+46 87150448
www.lindebergbageriochkonditori.se

Opening hours	Open 7 days
Credit cards	Accepted but not AMEX
Price range	Affordable
Style	Casual
Cuisine	Bakery
Recommended for	Breakfast

"No fuss, you feel at home. You eat good, you feel good."—Anton Bjuhr

MATBYGGET

Recommended by
Petter Nilsson

Rudolf Steiner Seminariet 7
Järna
Södertälje
Stockholm County 153 91, Sweden
+46 855430215
www.jarnakafe.se

Opening hours	Closed Saturday and Sunday
Credit cards	Accepted but not AMEX
Price range	Affordable
Style	Casual
Cuisine	Swedish
Recommended for	Bargain

"It's in the countryside in an anthroposophic center and it's all that you long for in terms of vegetables for a well-priced lunch."—Petter Nilsson

STOCKHOLM: SEE PAGES 352–365

BHOGA

Recommended by
Björn Persson

Norra Hamngatan 10
Gothenburg
Vastra Gotaland 411 14, Sweden
+46 31138018
www.bhoga.se

Opening hours	Closed Monday and Sunday
Credit cards	Accepted
Price range	Affordable
Style	Smart casual
Cuisine	Modern Nordic
Recommended for	Local favorite

"Modern dining experience with local origins."
—Björn Persson

BORD 27

Recommended by
Björn Persson

Haga Kyrkogata 14
Gothenburg
Vastra Gotaland 411 23, Sweden
+46 31109050

Opening hours	Open 7 days
Credit cards	Accepted
Price range	Affordable
Style	Casual
Cuisine	Swedish-International
Recommended for	Bargain

TRATTORIA LA STREGA

Recommended by
Björn Persson

Aschebergsgatan 23b
Gothenburg
Vastra Gotaland 411 27, Sweden
+46 31181501
www.trattorialastrega.se

Opening hours	Closed Monday
Credit cards	Accepted
Price range	Affordable
Style	Casual
Cuisine	Italian
Recommended for	Regular neighborhood

"Friendly restaurant with high-quality Italian food and wine."—Björn Persson

SJÖMAGASINET

Recommended by
Björn Persson

Adolf Edelsvärds Gata 5
Klippans Kulturreservat
Gothenburg
Vastra Gotaland 414 51, Sweden
+46 317755920
www.sjomagasinet.se

Opening hours	Closed Monday and Sunday
Credit cards	Accepted but not Diners
Price range	Expensive
Style	Smart casual
Cuisine	Scandanavian
Recommended for	Local favorite

"Sjömagasinet is a classic establishment with high class food."—Björn Persson

Housed in a harbor-side, timber-clad eighteenth-century warehouse that once belonged to the Swedish East India Company, Michelin-starred Sjömagasinet first found fame as a seafood restaurant under legendary Swedish chef Leif Mannerström. It was taken over by Ulf Wagner, who runs it in partnership with fellow chef Gustav Trägårdh. The menu typically runs from a fennel-laced bouillabaisse, via razor clam and langoustine croquettes, to seafood *pot-au-feu* (French stew) or Swedish lamb three ways. Rustic and bedecked with nautical bric-a-brac, dine by the fire in winter and on the pier come summer.

"IT'S A MUST VISIT PLACE IF YOU LOVE AUTHENTIC SWEDISH FOOD."
NIKLAS EKSTEDT P356

"Fantastic, friendly restaurant—high class food at a bargain."
BJÖRN PERSSON P360

"The best bread in town and the pastries are divine."
JACOB HOLMSTRÖM P359

STOCKHOLM

"IF THERE WAS TO BE ONLY ONE RESTAURANT LEFT BEHIND WHEN THE OTHERS WHERE DEMOLISHED AND CLOSED, I HOPE IT WOULD BE BABETTE."
MAGNUS NILSSON P361

"MAGNUS EK IS THE GODFATHER OF NEW NORDIC COOKING."
NIKLAS EKSTEDT P354

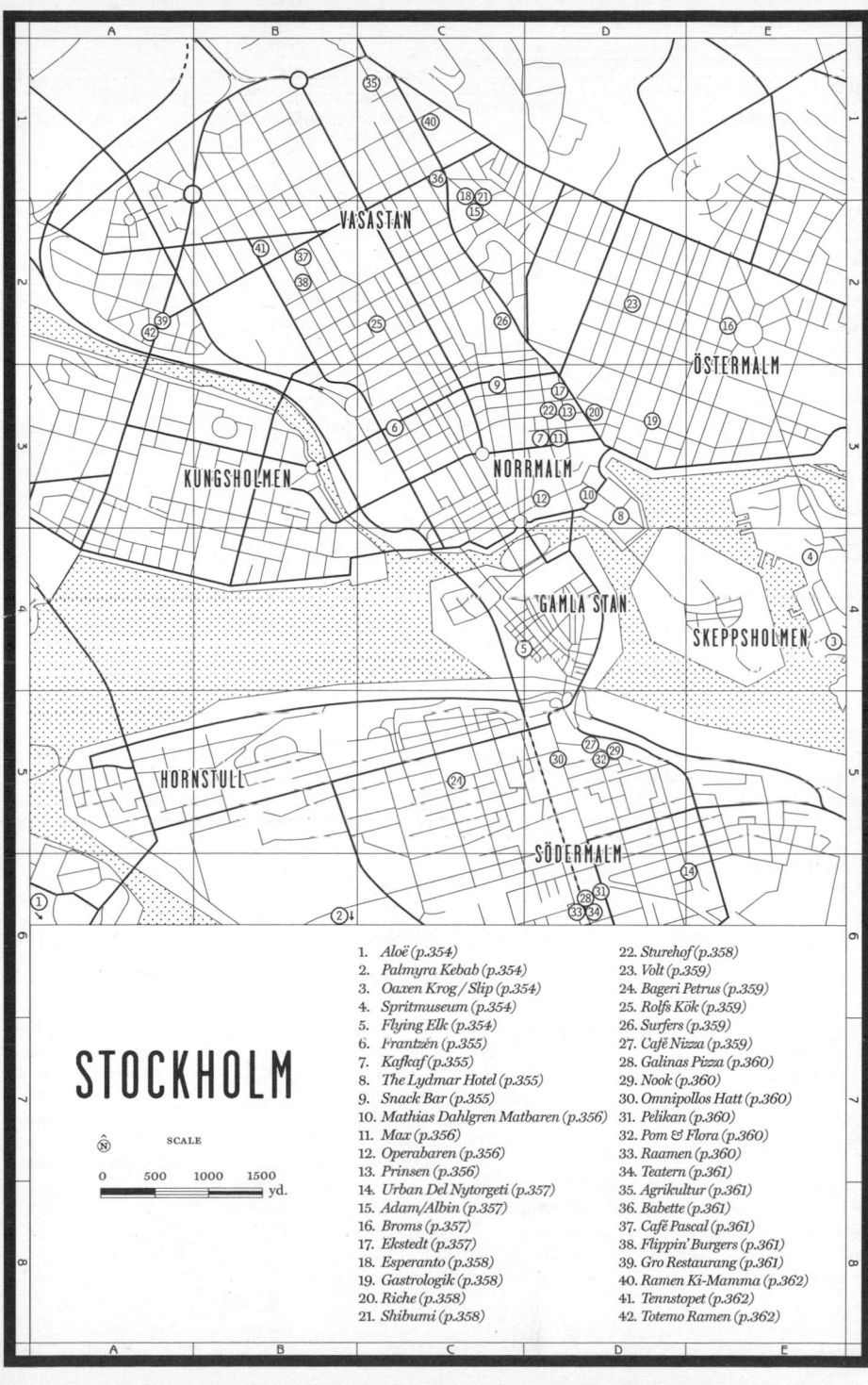

STOCKHOLM

SCALE

N̂

0   500   1000   1500   yd.

ALOË

Recommended by
Niklas Ekstedt

Svartlösavägen 52
Älvsjö
Stockholm 125 33, Sweden
+46 855636167
www.aloerestaurant.se

Opening hours	Closed Monday, Tuesday, and Sunday
Credit cards	Accepted but not AMEX
Price range	Expensive
Style	Smart casual
Cuisine	European
Recommended for	High end

PALMYRA KEBAB

Recommended by
Magnus Ek

Årstavägen 57
Årsta
Stockholm 120 54, Sweden
+46 8918012
www.palmyrakebab.se

Opening hours	Open 7 days
Reservation policy	No
Credit cards	Accepted
Price range	Budget
Style	Casual
Cuisine	Kebab-Sandwiches
Recommended for	Bargain

"Among the best kebabs in town, for a very good price."—Magnus Ek

OAXEN KROG

Recommended by
Anton Bjuhr,
Fredrik Berselius,
Niklas Ekstedt,
Nicolai Nørregaard,
Henrik Ritzen,
Tim Spedding

Beckholmsvägen 26
Djurgården
Stockholm 115 21, Sweden
+46 855153105
www.oaxen.com

Opening hours	Closed Monday and Sunday
Credit cards	Accepted
Price range	Expensive
Style	Smart casual
Cuisine	Nordic
Recommended for	High end

"Magnus Ek is the Godfather of New Nordic cooking. He was the one who started it. And if you want real New Nordic food that is not only contemporary but also very well cooked, this is the place to go."
—Niklas Ekstedt

Opened by New Nordic pioneers Magnus Ek and Agneta Green in 1994, Oaxen relocated to Djurgården in 2013 and has since gained two Michelin stars for its gourmet restaurant Oaxen Krog. The menu is inspired by the wildlife from the restaurant's original location on the rural island of Oaxen, utilizing unique ingredients from neighboring regions. The restaurant is based in a refurbished boatyard shed, with the design predictably inspired by Stockholm's marine industries. The ten-course set menu with wine pairings will set you back a hefty 3,500kr ($395; £305). However, the bistro—Oaxen Slip, housed in the same building—caters for more casual diners and is ideal for a high-quality lunch.

SPRITMUSEUM

Recommended by
Olle T. Cellton

Djurgardsvägen 38
Djurgården
Stockholm 115 21, Sweden
+46 812131309
www.spritmuseum.se

Opening hours	Open 7 days
Credit cards	Accepted but not Diners
Price range	Affordable
Style	Casual
Cuisine	Scandinavian
Recommended for	Regular neighborhood

"I'm a lunch person—I love eating a proper meal and drinking a few glasses of wine before it gets dark—and Spritmuseum is without doubt the best place to do this in Stockholm."—Olle T. Cellton

FLYING ELK

Recommended by
Sami Tallberg

Mälartorget 15
Gamla Stan
Stockholm 111 27, Sweden
+46 8208583
www.theflyingelk.se

Opening hours	Open 7 days
Credit cards	Accepted but not AMEX or Diners
Price range	Affordable
Style	Casual
Cuisine	Modern European
Recommended for	Worth the travel

FRANTZÉN

Klara Norra Kyrkogata 26
Norrmalm
Stockholm 111 22, Sweden
+46 08208580
www.studiofrantzen.com

Opening hours	Closed Monday, Tuesday, and Sunday
Credit cards	Accepted
Price range	Expensive
Style	Smart casual
Cuisine	Modern European
Recommended for	Worth the travel

"Super gastro experience. Not sure how long it will
be before he gets three stars but won't be long. He
has twenty-odd covers, which is a chef's dream to
cook for—open kitchen right in front of your guests.
It runs like clockwork and the staff are all super
pleasant and very well trained in the whole
experience." —Tom Aikens

This rapidly rising Stockholm star opened in 2008 in
the city's picturesque Old Town. It was established
as Frantzén/Lindeberg, a partnership between chef
Björn Frantzén and pastry chef Daniel Lindeberg,
before the latter left in 2013 to pursue his dream
of opening a small bakery. Raw materials are mined
from the restaurant's two gardens and from a list
of trusted local producers, farmers, and growers.
Menus are made up of whatever they have in each
day and presented in a series of bite-sized courses.
Try and book a berth at one of the four front-row
counter seats that overlook the action at the
kitchen's pass.

KAFKAF

Hamngatan 10
Norrmalm
Stockholm 111 47, Sweden
+46 86515555

Opening hours	Closed Sunday
Reservation policy	No
Credit cards	Accepted but not AMEX or Diners
Price range	Budget
Style	Casual
Cuisine	Café
Recommended for	Breakfast

"A mobile coffee bar, perfect for a quick stop on the
way to work."—Petter Nilsson

THE LYDMAR HOTEL

Södra Blasieholmshamnen 2
Norrmalm
Stockholm 103 24, Sweden
+46 8223160
www.lydmar.com

Opening hours	Open 7 days
Credit cards	Accepted but not AMEX
Price range	Affordable
Style	Smart casual
Cuisine	Swedish-French
Recommended for	Breakfast

SNACK BAR

K25, Kungsgatan 25
Norrmalm
Stockholm 111 56, Sweden
+46 87990000
www.snack-bar.se

Opening hours	Closed Sunday
Reservation policy	No
Credit cards	Accepted
Price range	Budget
Style	Casual
Cuisine	Kebab-Fast food
Recommended for	Bargain

"Great veal kebab, my favorite street food in
Stockholm."—Johan Agrell

MATHIAS DAHLGREN MATBAREN

Recommended by
Johan Agrell

Grand Hôtel
Södra Blasieholmshamnen 6
Norrmalm
Stockholm 111 48, Sweden
+46 86793584
www.mdghs.se

Opening hours	Closed Sunday
Credit cards	Accepted
Price range	Affordable
Style	Smart casual
Cuisine	Modern Swedish
Recommended for	High end

"The Ilse Crawford interior is Stockholm's most beautiful place to eat."—Johan Agrell

Of the not one but two Mathias Dahlgren restaurants at Stockholm's Grand Hôtel, Matbaren is the poor relation, with just one Michelin star to its name compared with upmarket Matsalen's two. But comparisons are odious—both 2007-vintage restaurants are high achievers, each with their own inimitable style. Buzzy, popular Matbaren ("food bar"), styled by Ilse Crawford, presents Dahlgren's unimpeachably seasonal modern Swedish in good-looking "medium-sized" plates, crafted in the impressively fast-paced open kitchen. Sample dishes include steamed beef-rib buns, salt-baked beet (beetroot) with smoked goat's cheese, and fallow deer tartare with salted roe, blood bread, raw onion, and smoked butter.

MAX

Recommended by
Anton Bjuhr

Kungsträdgårdsgatan 20
Norrmalm
Stockholm 111 47, Sweden
+46 86113810
www.max.se

Opening hours	Open 7 days
Reservation policy	No
Credit cards	Accepted
Price range	Budget
Style	Casual
Cuisine	Burgers
Recommended for	Bargain

OPERABAREN

Recommended by
Johan Agrell,
Niklas Ekstedt

The Royal Opera House
Karl XII:S Torg
Norrmalm
Stockholm 111 86, Sweden
+46 86765808
www.operakallaren.se

Opening hours	Closed Sunday
Credit cards	Accepted
Price range	Affordable
Style	Smart casual
Cuisine	Swedish
Recommended for	Local favorite

"It's a local hangout where you can always spot famous Swedish actors and musicians. The food is classic Swedish old-school cooking—it's one of the few places where they really serve this well. It's a must-visit place if you love authentic Swedish food."
—Niklas Ekstedt

Top-drawer meatballs and herring, framed by a certain degree of formality—this is, after all, Sweden's Royal Opera House—are on the menu at this bourgeois favorite, with its handsome turn-of-the-century decor, where the ruling and chattering classes break bread together. Daily specials might include Irish stew, or smoked haddock with spinach, poached egg and hollandaise; among the à la carte mains are steamed cod loin, steak tartare, and spring chicken with foie gras sauce. The same menu is served at the counter in the tiny Bakficka ("back pocket") bistro, which has outdoor seating overlooking Kungsträdgårdsgatan, the royal park—a great spot for lunch in the summer.

PRINSEN

Recommended by
Niklas Ekstedt

Mäster Samuelsgatan 4
Norrmalm
Stockholm 111 44, Sweden
+46 86111331
www.restaurangprinsen.eu

Opening hours	Open 7 days
Credit cards	Accepted
Price range	Affordable
Style	Smart casual
Cuisine	Swedish
Recommended for	Local favorite

URBAN DEL NYTORGET

Recommended by
Niklas Ekstedt

Nytorget 4
Norrmalm
Stockholm 116 40, Sweden
+46 842550030
www.urbandeli.org

Opening hours	Open 7 days
Credit cards	Accepted
Price range	Affordable
Style	Casual
Cuisine	Swedish
Recommended for	Breakfast

"Södermalm locals' favorite hang out. Always fun to meet people and always crowded."—Niklas Ekstedt

ADAM/ALBIN

Recommended by
Jacob Holmström

Rådmansgatan 16
Östermalm
Stockholm 114 25, Sweden
+46 84115535
www.adamalbin.se

Opening hours	Closed Sunday
Credit cards	Accepted
Price range	Expensive
Style	Casual
Cuisine	Swedish
Recommended for	Regular neighborhood

"World class food in a relaxed and comfy restaurant with a New York kind of feeling. Not too pricey either." —Jacob Holmström

BROMS

Recommended by
Bjorn Frantzen

Karlavägen 76
Östermalm
Stockholm 114 59, Sweden
+46 8 26 37 10
www.bromskarlaplan.se

Opening hours	Open 7 days
Credit cards	Accepted but not Diners
Price range	Affordable
Style	Casual
Cuisine	Bistro
Recommended for	Breakfast

EKSTEDT

Recommended by
Magnus Ek, Dan Graham,
Merlin Labron-Johnson,
Nicolai Nørregaard

Humlegardsgatan 17
Östermalm
Stockholm 114 46, Sweden
+46 86111210
www.ekstedt.nu

Opening hours	Closed Monday and Sunday
Credit cards	Accepted
Price range	Expensive
Style	Smart casual
Cuisine	Modern Swedish
Recommended for	Worth the travel

"Perfect, nuanced French cuisine cooked by a Viking over fire."—Dan Graham

Wanting to throw off the shackles of the "lightweight TV chef" tag and to move away from his molecular gastronomic beginnings, Niklas Ekstedt went soul-searching for his new project. He was traveling through the Ingarö Island woodlands when inspiration struck. He made it his mission to create a fine dining experience that eschewed electricity and only used open flames, taking inspiration from long-forgotten eighteenth-century cookbooks. What resulted was the culinary colossus that is Ekstedt. Constantly pushing the boundaries of open fire cooking, Ekstedt has created high-concept fine dining at its best. The proudly Nordic menu includes dried reindeer, cold smoked langoustines, birch-fired duck, and hay-flamed dairy cow—when he said 'you can create minor miracles with fire, smoke, ashes, and soot," Niklas Ekstedt wasn't overstating.

ESPERANTO

Kungstensgatan 2
Östermalm
Stockholm 114 25, Sweden
+46 86962323
www.esperantorestaurant.se

Opening hours	Closed Monday, Tuesday, and Sunday
Credit cards	Accepted
Price range	Expensive
Style	Smart casual
Cuisine	International
Recommended for	Late night

"Exceptional food, service, and wine."—Björn Persson

Swedish chef Sayan Isaksson won gold at the World Culinary Olympics in 2004, but has since shown he can create art on a plate even when there's no podium place at stake. His grand restaurant Esperanto opened in 2005 in what was the foyer of Stockholm's old Jarla Theatre (John Cale and Blondie played there in the 1970s) and was awarded a Michelin star two years later. Isaksson's cuisine is minimal-yet-flamboyant "international gastronomy without boundaries"—hence "Esperanto"—and shows marked French, Japanese and local influences. Choose from a seasonal or "dégustation" menu of, say, Swedish wagyu, served with fine wines or rare teas.

GASTROLOGIK

Artillerigatan 14
Östermalm
Stockholm 114 51, Sweden
+46 86623060
www.gastrologik.se

Opening hours	Closed Monday and Sunday
Credit cards	Accepted
Price range	Expensive
Style	Smart casual
Cuisine	Modern Swedish
Recommended for	High end

"Top experience in a very relaxed atmosphere. Fantastic local produce and perfect techniques."
—Filip Langhoff

Opened in late 2011 in Östermalm, by chefs Jacob Holmström and Anton Bjuhr, Gastrologik has quickly established a reputation as one of Stockholm's freshest, most forward-thinking restaurants. The relaxed modern dining room—a beautifully understated combination of oak floors, white walls, copper lampshades, aquamarine glass, and sturdy but stylish Scandinavian furniture—is a suitable setting for daily-changing dishes that are exercises in product-driven simplicity; hence the restaurant's playfully named "Let Today's Produce Decide" tasting menu. Next door sits Speceriet, their delicatessen, where their stone oven-baked sourdough bread is made.

RICHE

Birger Jarlsgatan 4
Östermalm
Stockholm 114 34, Sweden
+46 854503560
www.riche.se

Opening hours	Open 7 days
Credit cards	Accepted
Price range	Affordable
Style	Casual
Cuisine	Café-Bar-Bistro
Recommended for	Breakfast

SHIBUMI

Kungstensgatan 2
Östermalm
Stockholm 114 25, Sweden
+46 86962310
www.shibumi.se

Opening hours	Closed Monday and Sunday
Credit cards	Accepted
Price range	Affordable
Style	Casual
Cuisine	Japanese
Recommended for	Regular neighborhood

STUREHOF

Sturegallerian 42, Stureplan 2
Östermalm
Stockholm 114 46, Sweden
+46 84405730
www.sturehof.com

Opening hours	Open 7 days
Credit cards	Accepted
Price range	Affordable
Style	Casual
Cuisine	Seafood
Recommended for	Late night

"The kitchen is open until 1.00 a.m. so you can always get something...mostly fish and Swedish classic dishes."—Niklas Ekstedt

A night out with Stockholm's beautiful people should begin and end at Sturehof, the beating heart of Stureplan's social scene. Open 365 days a year, from mid-morning to the early hours, Sturehof is a classic seafood brasserie in a modern metropolitan vein. Opened in 1897 as a German-style beer hall by the name of Malta, it was renamed in 1905, when it became the seafood and fine wine specialist that it is today. Turbot with brown butter, lobster soup, and fried herring are among the dishes that have stood the test of time. Preening and posing abounds, both al fresco and in the bars.

VOLT

Recommended by
Jacob Holmström

Kommendörsgatan 16
Östermalm
Stockholm 114 48, Sweden
+46 86623400
www.restaurangvolt.se

Opening hours	Closed Sunday to Wednesday
Credit cards	Accepted
Price range	Expensive
Style	Casual
Cuisine	Modern Nordic
Recommended for	High end

"Super talented chefs cooking smart food. All organic."—Jacob Holmström

The cool young things at Volt have done away with the fuss of the fine dining experience to produce an ambitious restaurant with the buzz of a bistro. The kitchen embraces New Nordic, preferring ingredients that are natural and artisanal, and techniques that maximize flavor, texture, and excitement. "Fermented cod roe, onion cream, and pickled garlic" or "lamb cabbage bouillon malt" look and sound modern but there's an appealing note of nostalgia in there too. For full Volt-age, there's a nine-course menu with natural wine pairings.

BAGERI PETRUS

Recommended by
Johan Agrell,
Mikael Einarsson,
Jacob Holmström

Swedenborgsgatan 4b
Södermalm
Stockholm 118 48, Sweden
+46 864152111

Opening hours	Closed Sunday
Reservation policy	No
Credit cards	Accepted
Price range	Budget
Style	Casual
Cuisine	Bakery
Recommended for	Breakfast

"The best bread in town and the pastries are divine."
—Jacob Holmström

ROLFS KÖK

Recommended by
Björn Frantzén

Tegnérgatan 41
Norrmalm
Stockholm 111 61, Sweden
+46 (8) 10 16 96
www.rolfskok.se

Opening hours	Open 7 days
Credit cards	Accepted
Price range	Affordable
Style	Casual
Cuisine	Swedish
Recommended for	Late night

"Really good ox cheek with truffle mash."
—Björn Frantzén

SURFERS

Recommended by
Björn Frantzén

Regeringsgatan 88
Norrmalm
Stockholm 11139, Sweden
+46 8 - 21 10 03
www.surfersstockholm.se

Opening hours	Closed Monday
Credit cards	Accepted
Price range	Budget
Style	Casual
Cuisine	Chinese
Recommended for	Bargain

CAFÉ NIZZA

Recommended by
Petter Nilsson,
Olle T. Cellton

Åsögatan 171
Södermalm
Stockholm 116 32, Sweden
+46 86409950
www.cafenizza.se

Opening hours	Open 7 days
Credit cards	Accepted but not AMEX or Diners
Price range	Affordable
Style	Casual
Cuisine	French
Recommended for	Regular neighborhood

GALINAS PIZZA

Recommended by
Olle T. Cellton

Götgatan 132
Södermalm
Stockholm 118 62, Sweden
+ 46 8276760
www.galinaspizza.se

Opening hours	Open 7 days
Credit cards	Accepted
Price range	Budget
Style	Casual
Cuisine	Pizza
Recommended for	Local favorite

NOOK

Recommended by
Björn Persson

Åsögatan 176
Södermalm
Stockholm 116 32, Sweden
+46 87021222
www.nookrestaurang.se

Opening hours	Closed Monday and Sunday
Credit cards	Accepted but not Diners
Price range	Affordable
Style	Casual
Cuisine	Swedish-Asian Fusion
Recommended for	Wish I'd opened

"Fantastic, friendly restaurant—high class food at a bargain."—Björn Persson

OMNIPOLLOS HATT

Recommended by
Magnus Ek

Hökens Gata 1a
Södermalm
Stockholm 116 46, Sweden
www.omnipolloshatt.com

Opening hours	Open 7 days
Reservation policy	No
Credit cards	Accepted but not AMEX
Price range	Budget
Style	Casual
Cuisine	Pizza
Recommended for	Bargain

Noticing the giant purple psychedelic lips around the pizza oven and the neon sign that looks like it's been designed for an Eighties children's cartoon, you could be forgiven for thinking that this was a student bar. But stroll on past this place and you'll be missing out on one of Stockholm's true local gems. For all the quirkiness, Omnipollos Hatt take their food and beer very seriously. The ever-changing draft beer menu prioritizes quality and variety over

quantity and will please the most ardent connoisseurs. The pizzas are simple, but exceptional. It's packed almost all year round and with only around thirty seats, and very little standing room, you'll want to get there as early as possible.

PELIKAN

Recommended by
Petter Nilsson

Blekingegatan 40
Södermalm
Stockholm 116 62, Sweden
+46 855609090
www.pelikan.se

Opening hours	Open 7 days
Credit cards	Accepted but not Diners
Price range	Affordable
Style	Casual
Cuisine	Swedish
Recommended for	Local favorite

"An old wood-paneled restaurant serving classic Swedish food. It must have felt like this going to a restaurant in the Sixties."—Petter Nilsson

POM & FLORA

Recommended by
Petter Nilsson

Bondegatan 64
Södermalm
Stockholm 116 29, Sweden
+46 841010049
www.pomochflora.se

Opening hours	Open 7 days
Reservation policy	No
Credit cards	Accepted but not AMEX
Price range	Budget
Style	Casual
Cuisine	Café
Recommended for	Breakfast

RAAMEN

Recommended by
Niklas Ekstedt

Teatern
Götgatan 100
Södermalm
Stockholm 118 62, Sweden
+46 08206125
www.raamen.se

Opening hours	Open 7 days
Reservation policy	No
Credit cards	Accepted
Price range	Budget
Style	Casual
Cuisine	Ramen Noodles
Recommended for	Bargain

TEATERN

Recommended by
Jacob Holmström

Götgatan 100
Södermalm
Stockholm 118 62, Sweden
+46 86963031
www.ringencentrum.se

Opening hours	Open 7 days
Credit cards	Not accepted
Price range	Budget
Style	Casual
Cuisine	European
Recommended for	Bargain

"It's actually a food court. Go there for a kebab at Snackbar or a hot dog at Korvkiosk."
—Jacob Holmström

AGRIKULTUR

Recommended by
Magnus Ek,
Niklas Ekstedt

Roslagsgatan 43
Vasastan
Stockholm 113 54, Sweden
+46 8150202
www.agrikultur.se

Opening hours	Closed Saturday and Sunday
Credit cards	Accepted
Price range	Affordable
Style	Casual
Cuisine	Nordic
Recommended for	Local favorite

"Nordic, low budget, easy going. Good bang for your buck."—Magnus Ek

BABETTE

Recommended by
Mikael Einarsson, Magnus Ek,
Niklas Ekstedt,
Jacob Holmström,
Magnus Nilsson

Roslagsgatan 6
Vasastan
Stockholm 113 55, Sweden
+46 850902224
www.babette.se

Opening hours	Open 7 days
Credit cards	Accepted
Price range	Affordable
Style	Casual
Cuisine	European
Recommended for	Regular neighborhood

"If there was to be only one restaurant left behind when the others were demolished and closed, I hope it would be Babette."—Magnus Nilsson

If you're exploring the Vasastan area of Stockholm and are in need of an evening feast, your first stop should be Babette. It has the vibe and intimacy of a friendly local restaurant, but under the cosy decor is one of the best pizzerias in town. Babette believes in simple cooking with fresh ingredients, while throwing in a few off-beat flavor combinations. It's often packed, so it would be wise to phone ahead, but some walk-ins will be accepted to eat at the bar.

CAFÉ PASCAL

Recommended by
Johan Agrell

Norrtullsgatan 4
Vasastan
Stockholm 113 29, Sweden
+46 8316110
www.cafepascal.se

Opening hours	Open 7 days
Credit cards	Accepted but not AMEX or Diners
Price range	Affordable
Style	Casual
Cuisine	Café
Recommended for	Breakfast

FLIPPIN' BURGERS

Recommended by
Anton Bjuhr

Observatoriegatan 8
Vasastan
Stockholm 113 29, Sweden
www.flippinburgers.se

Opening hours	Open 7 days
Reservation policy	No
Credit cards	Accepted but not AMEX
Price range	Budget
Style	Casual
Cuisine	Burgers
Recommended for	Local favorite

"The place to be for the best burgers in town."
—Anton Bjuhr

GRO RESTAURANG

Recommended by
Jacob Holmström

Sankt Eriksgatan 67
Vasastan
Stockholm 113 32, Sweden
+46 86434222
www.grorestaurang.se

Opening hours	Closed Monday and Sunday
Credit cards	Accepted but not Diners
Price range	Affordable
Style	Smart casual
Cuisine	Modern Swedish
Recommended for	Local favorite

RAMEN KI-MAMMA

Recommended by
Johan Agrell

Birger Jarlsgatan 93
Vasastan
Stockholm 113 56, Sweden
+46 8155539

Opening hours	Open 7 days
Reservation policy	No
Credit cards	Accepted but not AMEX
Price range	Budget
Style	Casual
Cuisine	Ramen Noodles
Recommended for	Regular neighborhood

"Stockholm is cold and their Gekikara Ramen is hot.
Go for the ramen and gyoza."—Johan Agrell

TENNSTOPET

Recommended by
Petter Nilsson

Dalagatan 50
Vasastan
Stockholm 113 24, Sweden
+46 8322518
www.tennstopet.se

Opening hours	Open 7 days
Credit cards	Accepted
Price range	Affordable
Style	Smart casual
Cuisine	Swedish
Recommended for	Local favorite

"As popular as Pelikan and slightly more fancy."
—Petter Nilsson

TOTEMO RAMEN

Recommended by
Mikael Einarsson

Sankt Eriksgatan 70
Vasastan
Stockholm 113 20, Sweden
www.totemoramen.com

Opening hours	Closed Saturday and Sunday
Reservation policy	No
Credit cards	Accepted
Price range	Affordable
Style	Casual
Cuisine	Ramen Noodles
Recommended for	Regular neighborhood

KADEAU

Recommended by
Magnus Ek

Baunevej 18
Vestre Sømark
Åkirkeby
Bornholm 3720, Denmark
+45 56978250
www.kadeau.dk

Opening hours	Variable
Credit cards	Accepted
Price range	Expensive
Style	Smart casual
Cuisine	Modern Nordic
Recommended for	Worth the travel

COPENHAGEN: SEE PAGES 367–381

LAGKAGEHUSET

Recommended by
Paul Cunningham

Copenhagen Airport
Lufthavnsboulevarden 6
Kastrup
Hovedstaden 2770, Denmark
+45 72144788
www.lagkagehuset.dk

Opening hours	Open 7 days
Reservation policy	No
Credit cards	Accepted but not Diners
Price range	Affordable
Style	Casual
Cuisine	Bakery-Café
Recommended for	Breakfast

ANARKI

Recommended by
Brian Mark Hansen

Vodroffsvej 47
Frederiksberg
Hovedstaden 1900, Denmark
+45 22131134
www.restaurant-anarki.dk

Opening hours	Closed Monday
Credit cards	Accepted
Price range	Affordable
Style	Casual
Cuisine	French-Danish
Recommended for	Bargain

"Good charcuterie—fantastic food for your money."
—Brian Mark Hansen

ENOMANIA
Recommended by
Jakob Mielcke

Vesterbrogade 187
Frederiksberg
Hovedstaden 1800, Denmark
+45 33236080
www.enomania.dk

Opening hours	Closed Saturday to Monday
Credit cards	Accepted
Price range	Budget
Style	Casual
Cuisine	Italian
Recommended for	Regular neighborhood

FORMEL B
Recommended by
Christian F. Puglisi

Vesterbrogade 182
Frederiksberg
Hovedstaden 1800, Denmark
+45 33251066
www.formelb.dk

Opening hours	Closed Sunday
Credit cards	Accepted
Price range	Affordable
Style	Casual
Cuisine	Nordic-French
Recommended for	High end

GRANOLA
Recommended by
Jakob Mielcke

Værnedamsvej 5
Frederiksberg
Hovedstaden 1819, Denmark
+45 31311536
www.granola.dk

Opening hours	Open 7 days
Credit cards	Accepted
Price range	Affordable
Style	Smart casual
Cuisine	European
Recommended for	Breakfast

MIELCKE OG HURTIGKARL
Recommended by
Brian Mark Hansen

Frederiksberg Runddel 1
Frederiksberg
Hovedstaden 2000, Denmark
+45 38348436
www.mhcph.com

Opening hours	Closed Monday and Sunday
Credit cards	Accepted
Price range	Expensive
Style	Formal
Cuisine	International
Recommended for	Worth the travel

"The experience was one-of-a-kind—magic from start to finish."—Brian Mark Hansen

SAIGON QUAN
Recommended by
Thomas Rode Andersen

Godthåbsvej 48
Frederiksberg
Hovedstaden 2000, Denmark
+45 38101900
www.saigonquan.dk

Opening hours	Closed Tuesday
Credit cards	Not accepted
Price range	Budget
Style	Casual
Cuisine	Vietnamese
Recommended for	Bargain

"Saigon Quan on Godthåbsvej offers super reasonable Vietnamese cuisine with lots of taste."
—Thomas Rode Andersen

SOKKELUND CAFE & BRASSERIE
Recommended by
Jakob Mielcke

Smallegade 36
Frederiksberg
Hovedstaden 2000, Denmark
+45 38106400
www.cafe-sokkelund.dk

Opening hours	Open 7 days
Credit cards	Accepted
Price range	Affordable
Style	Smart casual
Cuisine	Danish
Recommended for	Breakfast

"A no-nonsense Danish-style diner. Serves throughout the day but I prefer it in the morning."—Jakob Mielcke

SØLLERØD KRO

Søllerød vej 35
Holte
Hovedstaden 2840, Denmark
+45 45802505
www.soelleroed-kro.dk

Recommended by
Kristian Baumann,
Christian F. Puglisi

Opening hours	Closed Monday and Tuesday
Credit cards	Accepted
Price range	Expensive
Style	Formal
Cuisine	French-Nordic
Recommended for	High end

"It's decadent and if you want to indulge this is the place."—Christian F. Puglisi

RESTAURANT SLETTEN

Gl Strandvej 137
Humlebæk
Hovedstaden 3050, Denmark
+45 49191321
www.sletten.dk

Recommended by
Brian Mark Hansen

Opening hours	Closed Monday
Credit cards	Accepted
Price range	Affordable
Style	Casual
Cuisine	Modern Nordic-French
Recommended for	Local favorite

"Nice food, down-to-earth, sweet service, and a great location."—Brian Mark Hansen

FRU LARSEN

Østergade 1
Langå
Midtjylland 8870, Denmark
+45 86468388
www.frularsen.dk

Recommended by
Rainer Gassner

Opening hours	Closed Monday and Sunday unless by appointment
Credit cards	Accepted
Price range	Affordable
Style	Casual
Cuisine	Nordic
Recommended for	Breakfast

"The food is great and the service is familiar and friendly."—Rainer Gassner

DRAGSHOLM SLOT

Dragsholm Allé
Hørve
Sjælland 4534, Denmark
+45 59653300
www.dragsholm-slot.dk

Recommended by
Matthew Orlando

Opening hours	Open 7 days
Credit cards	Accepted
Price range	Expensive
Style	Formal
Cuisine	Nordic
Recommended for	High end

"Located in a twelfth-century castle. The best ingredients in Denmark."—Matthew Orlando

DET VILDE KØKKEN

Klintevej 158
Nykøbing Sjælland
Sjælland 4500, Denmark
+45 50484564
www.detvildekoekken.com

Recommended by
Claus Henriksen

Opening hours	Closed Monday to Wednesday
Credit cards	Accepted
Price range	Affordable
Style	Casual
Cuisine	Nordic
Recommended for	Breakfast

"The kitchen is based on wild plants and herbs and Danish hygge."—Claus Henriksen

HOTEL FREDERIKSMINDE

Klosternakken 8
Præstø
Sjælland 4720, Denmark
+45 55909030
www.frederiksminde.com

Recommended by
Claus Henriksen

Opening hours	Open 7 days
Credit cards	Accepted
Price range	Affordable
Style	Smart casual
Cuisine	Danish-French
Recommended for	Local favorite

RØRVIG FISK

Toldboden 81
Rørvig
Sjælland 4581, Denmark
+45 59918133
www.roervig-fisk.dk

Recommended by
Claus Henriksen

Opening hours	Open 7 days
Credit cards	Accepted
Price range	Affordable
Style	Casual
Cuisine	Seafood
Recommended for	Bargain

MOEHR

Skomagergade 40
Roskilde
Sjælland 4000, Denmark
+45 76250301
www.moehr.dk

Recommended by
Claus Henriksen

Opening hours	Closed Sunday
Credit cards	Accepted
Price range	Affordable
Style	Smart casual
Cuisine	Danish-American
Recommended for	Wish I'd opened

TACOS

Danmarksgade 34
Fredericia
Syddanmark 7000, Denmark
+45 71717181
www.tacos7000.dk

Recommended by
Rainer Gassner

Opening hours	Open 7 days
Credit cards	Accepted
Price range	Budget
Style	Casual
Cuisine	Mexican
Recommended for	Bargain

"The food is fresh and simple. Superb guacamole."
—Rainer Gassner

HENNE KIRKEBY KRO

Strandvejen 234
Henne
Syddanmark 6854, Denmark
+45 75255400
www.hennekirkebykro.dk

Recommended by
Bo Bech,
Sang Hoon Degeimbre,
Ross Lusted,
Nicolai Nørregaard,
Tim Spedding, Gareth Ward

Opening hours	Variable
Credit cards	Accepted
Price range	Expensive
Style	Casual
Cuisine	Classic Scandinavian
Recommended for	High end

"A magical place, the beauty being in the spontaneity
with which every dinner is acted out. Every member
of staff plays their part in an all-star performance."
—Tim Spedding

On the west coast of Jutland in a late-eighteenth-
century inn, English ex-pat Paul Cunningham has
established a reputation for excellence since
relocating from Copenhagen in 2011. Open from
Easter through to mid-December, Henne Kirkeby
Kro's cooking combines Cunningham's classic
technique and eclectic tendencies. Raw materials
come from the kitchen garden (the largest in
Denmark) and the lambs, pigs, and chickens they
raise on site. You can take the boy out of Essex but
not the Essex out of the boy; so expect fish and chips
on a Friday, West Ham memorabilia, and blasts of
kitsch cockney rockers Chas & Dave from the kitchen.

> "It's the perfect combination of thought-provoking, casual food that surprises you with every dish."
> OLLIE TEMPLETON P378

> "Light, tasty, simple, and beautifully arranged."
> THOMAS RODE ANDERSEN P366

COPENHAGEN

> "FORAGED, PRESERVED, AND PICKLED THINGS THAT NEVER CEASE TO AMAZE."
> THOMAS RODE ANDERSEN P345

> "The quality of all their produce is incredible and the execution even better."
> KRISTIAN BAUMANN P366

> "Innovative and defining cuisine that rocks your senses."
> THOMAS RODE ANDERSEN P368

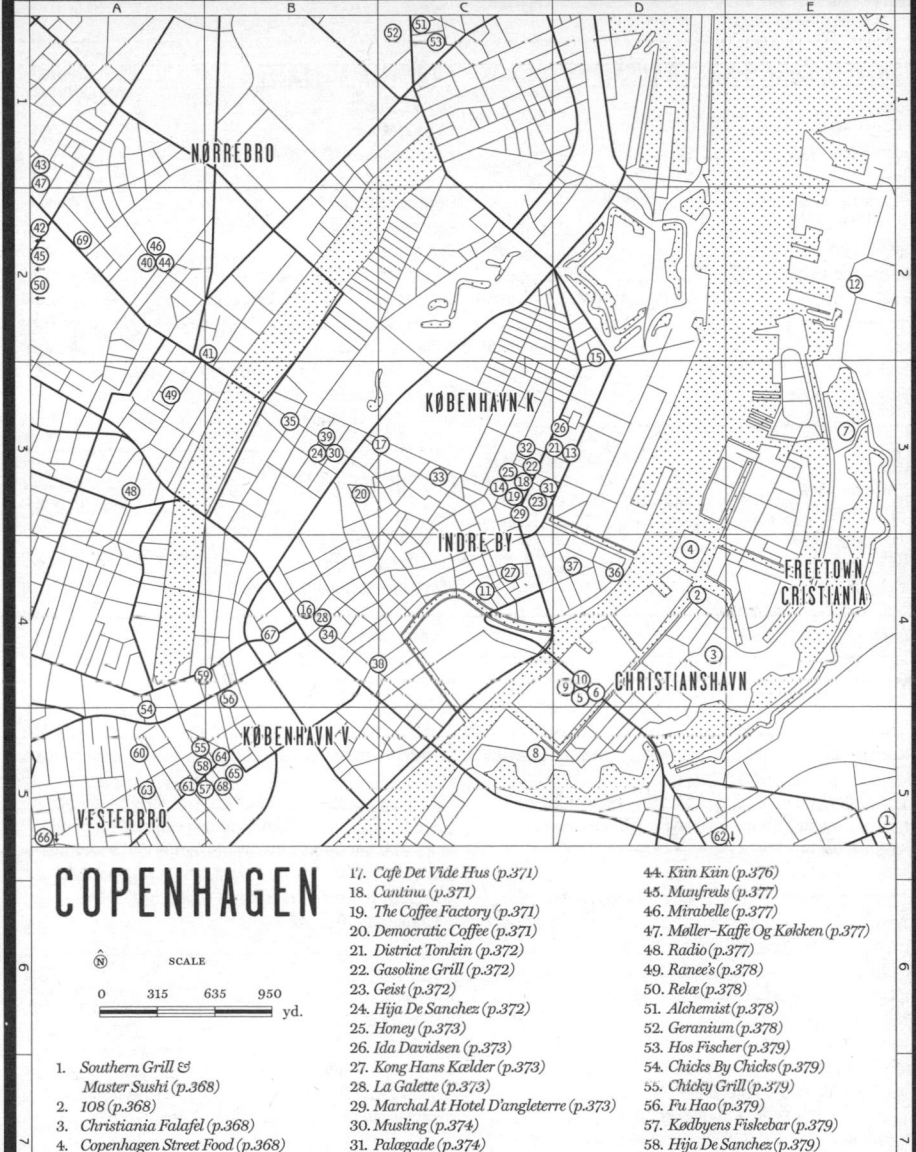

COPENHAGEN

SCALE

0   315   635   950
━━━━━━━━━━━━━━━━ yd.

SOUTHERN GRILL & MASTER SUSHI

Recommended by
Samuel Nutter

Elbagade 37
Amager East
Copenhagen 2300
+45 32553050
www.southerngrill.dk

Opening hours	Closed Monday
Reservation policy	No
Credit cards	Accepted but not AMEX or Diners
Price range	Budget
Style	Casual
Cuisine	Asian
Recommended for	Bargain

108

Recommended by
Ivan Berezutskiy, Daniel Berlin,
Jessica Koslow, Christian F. Puglisi,
Rosio Sánchez

Strandgade 108
Christianshavn
Copenhagen 1401
+45 32963292
www.108.dk

Opening hours	Open 7 days
Credit cards	Accepted
Price range	Affordable
Style	Smart casual
Cuisine	Modern Nordic
Recommended for	Worth the travel

"Great staff, good food, and amazing atmosphere. Give
it some time to find the way and it will be amazing."
—Daniel Berlin

It's a restaurant in Copenhagen so, inevitably,
there's a connection to Noma. In this case, the ties
are more than superficial, as not only is head chef
Kristian Baumann a Noma alumnus but his business
partner is none other than René Redzepi. But 108 is
most definitely its own beast—more relaxed, dare
we say more accessible, and certainly a lot easier
on the wallet than its big brother. Foraged berries,
mushrooms, and nuts are preserved for use
throughout the year, and dishes such as winter
beet (beetroot) with hot-smoked veal heart and
blackcurrants—all served in a bright, no-nonsense
warehouse space near the waterfront—sing a hymn
to the seasons.

CHRISTIANIA FALAFEL

Recommended by
Matthew Orlando

Pusher Street
Christianshavn
Copenhagen 1440

Opening hours	Variable
Reservation policy	No
Credit cards	Not accepted
Price range	Budget
Style	Casual
Cuisine	Middle Eastern-Street Food
Recommended for	Late night

"The best falafel in town, in the coolest part of town."
—Matthew Orlando

COPENHAGEN STREET FOOD

Recommended by
Christian F. Puglisi

Papirøen
Christianshavn
Copenhagen 1436
www.copenhagenstreetfood.dk

Opening hours	Open 7 days
Credit cards	Not accepted
Price range	Budget
Style	Casual
Cuisine	Street Food
Recommended for	Bargain

"It's a big eclectic mix of all sorts of street food and
you can shop around the different stalls. It's a good
place to meet larger groups of friends and everyone
can get a bit of what they want. There is good fish
and chips there and nice fresh pasta too."
—Christian F. Puglisi

KADEAU

Recommended by
Kristian Baumann,
Fredrik Berselius,
Magnus Ek, Florent Ladeyn,
Claus Meyer, David Posey,
Thomas Rode Andersen

Wildersgade 10b
Christianshavn
Copenhagen 1408
+45 33252223
www.kadeau.dk

Opening hours	Closed Sunday
Credit cards	Accepted
Price range	Expensive
Style	Casual
Cuisine	Nordic
Recommended for	High end

"A reasonable version of the taste of the Island of
Bornholm, extremely sharply executed, in both super
cosy (*hyggelig*) and gorgeous-looking ambience.
Innovative and defining cuisine that rocks your senses

and impresses with low-key, unknown raw products, foraged, preserved, pickled, and dried things that never cease to amaze."—Thomas Rode Andersen

of their high-end pop-ups in London, Tokyo, Sydney, and most recently Tulum, to Noma 2.0. Expect it to be booked-out once reservations open.

NABO

Recommended by
Nicolai Nørregaard,
Thomas Rode Andersen

Wildersgade 10a
Christianshavn
Copenhagen 1408
+45 33221002
www.nabonabo.dk

Opening hours	Closed Sunday
Credit cards	Accepted
Price range	Affordable
Style	Casual
Cuisine	Nordic Bistro
Recommended for	Local favorite

NOMA

Recommended by
Mészáros Adam, Aaron Adams,
Yannick Alléno, Kristian Baumann,
Bo Bech, Ivan Berezutskiy, Daniel Berlin,
Massimo Bottura, Daniel Burns,
Olle T. Cellton, Paul Cunningham, Luca Fantin,
Alexis Gauthier, Bertrand Grébaut,
Rodolfo Guzmán, Stephen Harris,
Zaiyu Hasegawa, Georgianna Hiliadaki,
Jessica Koslow, Tatiana Levha, Richie Lin, James Lowe,
Francesco Mazzei, Morgan McGlone, Isaac Mchale,
Christophe Michalak, Jacob Mielcke,
Ben Murphy, Samuel Nutter, Matthew Orlando,
Alfred Prasad, Eelke Plasmeijer, Christian F. Puglisi,
Thomas Rode Andersen, Niko Romito, Ana Roš, Mathieu Rostaing
Tayard, Francisco Ruano, Rosio Sánchez, Tim Spedding,
Adam Stokes, Tam Storrar, Stephen Toman, Victor Wågman

Refshalevej 96
Christianshavn
Copenhagen 1432
+45 32963297
www.noma.dk

Opening hours	Closed Monday and Sunday
Credit cards	Accepted
Price range	Expensive
Style	Smart casual
Cuisine	Modern Nordic
Recommended for	Wish I'd opened

"The one and only. It sparked the gastronomic revolution in our country that we all still thrive upon. Its evolution shows Copenhagen's readiness to change, adapt, and evolve."—Christian F. Puglisi

The old Noma, which inspired a generation of chefs, thrilled diners and won nearly as many plaudits as Copenhagen has bicycles, is no more. What we know about its new incarnation at this point is that it should be open by late 2017, located on the site of an old army bunker on the edge of Christiania. It overlooks a lake and will have an extensive vegetable garden. Beyond that, René Redzepi and his game-changing team will bring the experiences

RABES HAVE

Recommended by
Nicolai Nørregaard

Langebrogade 8
Christianshavn
Copenhagen 1411
+45 32573417
www.spiseliv.dk/rabeshave

Opening hours	Closed Monday and Tuesday
Credit cards	Accepted
Price range	Budget
Style	Casual
Cuisine	Danish
Recommended for	Local favorite

"Old-school classic Danish opened-faced sandwiches (Smørrebrød) in a mix of lunch restaurant and classic old Christianshavn pub."—Nicolai Nørregaard

RUFINO OSTERIA

Recommended by
Matthew Orlando

Strandgade 14
Christianshavn
Copenhagen 1401
+45 34120048
www.rufino-osteria.com

Opening hours	Closed Sunday
Credit cards	Accepted but not AMEX
Price range	Affordable
Style	Casual
Cuisine	Italian
Recommended for	Regular neighborhood

"Above all, these guys like to have a good time. The pasta is so good and they have some hidden gems on the wine list."—Matthew Orlando

THE CORNER

Recommended by
Kristian Baumann

Strandgade 108
Christianshavn
Copenhagen 1401
+45 32963292
www.108.dk/the-corner

Opening hours	Open 7 days
Credit cards	Accepted
Price range	Affordable
Style	Casual
Cuisine	Modern Nordic
Recommended for	Breakfast

ADMIRALGADE 26

Admiralgade 26
Indre By
Copenhagen 1066
+45 33337973
www.admiralgade26.dk

Recommended by
Angela Dimayuga,
Nicolai Nørregaard,
Samuel Nutter

Opening hours	Closed Sunday
Credit cards	Accepted but not AMEX
Price range	Affordable
Style	Casual
Cuisine	International
Recommended for	Breakfast

"I loved this little place in Copenhagen. Great wine, and lovely staff. The light in the space is gorgeous in the daytime and very close to a canal. They do a Japanese breakfast that is tasty and unique. The dinner service is casual and attentive, and the small plates are delicious without being challenging."
—Angela Dimayuga

AMASS

Refshalevej 153
Indre By
Copenhagen 1432
+45 43584330
www.amassrestaurant.com

Recommended by
Kristian Baumann, Daniel Berlin,
Daniel Burns, Analiese Gregory,
Claus Henriksen, Jun Lee,
JP McMahon, Christian F. Puglisi,
Martins Ritins, Rosio Sánchez,
Benjamin Sukle

Opening hours	Closed Monday and Sunday
Credit cards	Accepted
Price range	Expensive
Style	Smart casual
Cuisine	Modern Nordic
Recommended for	Worth the travel

"I like Amass for multiple reasons: the second-to-none hospitality, the setting, the intriguing food, the great natural wine selection, their commitment to reducing waste and promoting sustainability in restaurants, and the fact that they let me have a nap and a coffee by the fire in the garden in the middle of my meal..."—Analiese Gregory

Since launching in 2013, this venture from Matt Orlando, the American former head chef of Noma, has become one of Copenhagen's main destination restaurants. Housed in a former shipyard in the industrial area of Refshaleøen, it's a beautiful space: a vast cafeteria with soaring windows and engaging graffiti murals. The constantly changing menu has included such finely crafted inventions as crispy oats with hot-smoked foie gras and walnut marigold, and salted mackerel with grilled skin and scallion

(spring onion). Herbs are grown in the garden, where, at night, they light a bonfire.

AOC

Dronningens Tvaergade 2
Indre By
Copenhagen 1302
+45 33111145
www.restaurantaoc.dk

Recommended by
Kristian Baumann

Opening hours	Closed Monday and Sunday
Credit cards	Accepted
Price range	Expensive
Style	Smart casual
Cuisine	Modern Nordic
Recommended for	Local favorite

ATELIER SEPTEMBER

Gothersgade 30
Indre By
Copenhagen 1123
www.cafeatelierseptember.com

Recommended by
Kristian Baumann, Bo Bech,
Paul Cunningham,
Zaiyu Hasegawa,
Fernando Troca

Opening hours	Open 7 days
Reservation policy	No
Credit cards	Accepted
Price range	Budget
Style	Casual
Cuisine	Café
Recommended for	Breakfast

"Avocado on rye, chives, olive oil, and lemon—without doubt the most Instagrammed plate in Copenhagen. Superb coffee and morning pastries, green teas, and proper *matcha* too. Artistic surroundings within an antique shop, with nice jazz."—Paul Cunningham

BISTRO BOHEME

Esplanaden 8
Indre By
Copenhagen 1263
+45 33939844
www.bistroboheme.dk

Recommended by
Kristian Baumann, Bo Bech,
Paul Cunningham,
Jakob Mielcke,
Thomas Rode Andersen

Opening hours	Closed Sunday
Credit cards	Accepted
Price range	Affordable
Style	Smart casual
Cuisine	French
Recommended for	Regular neighborhood

"Seriously good, classical French cooking. Deep authentic flavors. Quaffable wines, great service."
—Paul Cunningham

BROR

Recommended by
Kristian Baumann,
Matthew Orlando

Sankt Peders Stræde 24a
Indre By
Copenhagen 1453
+45 32175999
www.restaurantbror.dk

Opening hours	Closed Monday and Tuesday
Credit cards	Accepted
Price range	Affordable
Style	Casual
Cuisine	Modern Nordic
Recommended for	Regular neighborhood

"The definition of nose-to-tail cooking, with a sense of humor."—Matthew Orlando

Bror—'brother' in Danish—is the work of English-born Samuel Nutter and Swede Victor Wågman, both former Noma sous-chefs. Opened in wood-panelled, split-level premises near Nørreport station in 2013, it's a cosy, modern Nordic bistro that pushes a compact seasonal menu. Their short list of constantly changing, tersely described, simple-sounding but technically excellent snacks—cod cheek with horseradish and dill, squid with ramson and sorrel, deep-fried bulls' balls with tartare sauce—are available either as a four- or five-course menu, each with an accompanying flight of quirky, all-natural wines.

CAFE DET VIDE HUS

Recommended by
Matthew Orlando,
Thomas Rode Andersen

Gothersgade 113
Indre By
Copenhagen 1123
+45 60612002

Opening hours	Open 7 days
Reservation policy	No
Credit cards	Accepted
Price range	Budget
Style	Casual
Cuisine	Café
Recommended for	Breakfast

"Light, tasty, simple, and beautifully arranged. GREAT coffee made by a passionate barista who happens to be the owner. He also serves a magnificent open-faced sandwich with avocado on paleo bread, with an adorable bacon-tarragon vinaigrette, that'll keep you satiated and focused all day, especially when paired up with a couple of free-range eggs. Watch out for his addictive homemade ice cream popsicles that make it extraordinarily difficult being a paleo-eating caveman!"—Thomas Rode Andersen

CANTINA

Recommended by
Thomas Rode Andersen

Borgergade 2
Indre By
Copenhagen 1300
+45 88169995
www.cantinacph.dk

Opening hours	Open 7 days
Credit cards	Accepted
Price range	Affordable
Style	Casual
Cuisine	Italian
Recommended for	Regular neighborhood

"Low-key, high quality New York-style restaurant, serving Italian food with a twist in taste and flavor way beyond what you usually see."
—Thomas Rode Andersen

THE COFFEE FACTORY

Recommended by
Paul Cunningham

Gothersgade 21
Indre By
Copenhagen 1123
+45 33141582
www.thecoffeefactory.dk

Opening hours	Open / days
Credit cards	Accepted but not AMEX or Diners
Price range	Budget
Style	Casual
Cuisine	Café
Recommended for	Breakfast

DEMOCRATIC COFFEE

Recommended by
Victor Wågman

Krystalgade 15
Indre By
Copenhagen 1172
+45 40196237

Opening hours	Closed Sunday
Credit cards	Accepted
Price range	Budget
Style	Casual
Cuisine	Café
Recommended for	Breakfast

"Keeping it local, this place is great for a coffee and a croissant early in the morning."—Victor Wågman

DISTRICT TONKIN

Recommended by
Kristian Baumann

Queen Tværgade 12
Indre By
Copenhagen 1302
+45 60888698
www.district-tonkin.com

Opening hours	Open 7 days
Reservation policy	No
Credit cards	Accepted but not AMEX or Diners
Price range	Budget
Style	Casual
Cuisine	Vietnamese
Recommended for	Late night

"Nickie Mydung cooks with love and everything here is absolutely delicious. It doesn't matter if you get takeout (takeaway) or dine at one of their two restaurants, the quality of the meal is extremely high and it's the best Vietnamese in town."
—Kristian Baumann

GASOLINE GRILL

Recommended by
Kristian Baumann,
Victor Wågman

Landgreven 10
Indre By
Copenhagen 1300

Opening hours	Open 7 days
Reservation policy	No
Credit cards	Accepted
Price range	Budget
Style	Casual
Cuisine	Burgers
Recommended for	Late night

"A very small and special little burger place. Since they do a limited amount of burgers every day it is wise not to get there too late…"—Victor Wågman

GEIST

Recommended by
Kristian Baumann,
Paul Cunningham, Rainer Gassner,
Ross Lusted, Jakob Mielcke,
Nicolai Nørregaard, Christian F. Puglisi,
Thomas Rode Andersen,
Ebbe Vollmer

Kongens Nytorv 8
Indre By
Copenhagen 1050
+45 33133713
www.restaurantgeist.dk

Opening hours	Open 7 days
Credit cards	Accepted
Price range	Affordable
Style	Casual
Cuisine	Modern Nordic
Recommended for	Late night

"International vibe and crazy good food. Bo Bech always seeks new ways of presenting dishes with a minimum of ingredients. Pioneer of minimalistic, monochrome plating. Favorite spot."
—Nicolai Nørregaard

Danish chef Bo Bech has worked with Europe's finest (including Alain Passard and Alain Senderens); he's had his own TV shows; and he's won a Michelin star (at Paustian). He brings this wealth of experience to Geist, his six-year-old restaurant on Copenhagen's Kongens Nytorv. It's a stylish and very current sort of place, touting ambitious but accessible New Nordic cooking in a multifaceted space that comprises restaurant, "food bar" and a particularly lovely courtyard. Simple-sounding dishes reveal intriguing flavor combinations—salted wasabi cream toffee, heart of lamb with red grapes and wood sorrel, avocado with lightly salted caviar—and look gorgeous too.

HIJA DE SANCHEZ

Recommended by
Anton Bjuhr

Torvehallerne
Frederiksborggade 21
Indre By
Copenhagen 1360
www.hijadesanchez.dk

Opening hours	Open 7 days
Reservation policy	No
Credit cards	Accepted
Price range	Budget
Style	Casual
Cuisine	Mexican
Recommended for	Worth the travel

"Cool place with awesome tacos."—Anton Bjuhr

What do you do if you're a Mexican expat in Copenhagen, and can't seem to find decent, fresh tacos? Well, if you're lucky enough to be as talented as Rosio Sánchez and have a few years working at Noma under your belt, the obvious solution is to open your own taco stall. Using corn imported from Mexico for the tortilla casings but filling them with the best of seasonal Danish ingredients, this modest spot in the Torvehallerne has built a loyal local following, who line up (queue) patiently rain or shine (and through harsh Copenhagen winters) for their fix of *carnitas* (braised pork belly) or *al pastor* (spit-roasted pork with pineapple and onion).

HONEY

Adelgade 12
Indre By
Copenhagen 1304
+45 22215510
www.eathoney.dk

Opening hours	Closed Monday and Sunday
Credit cards	Accepted
Price range	Affordable
Style	Casual
Cuisine	European
Recommended for	Regular neighborhood

"Easy, informal, child-friendly spot, with shared food of high quality. Make your own soft ice is the icing on the cake."—Nicolai Nørregaard

IDA DAVIDSEN

Store Kongensgade 70
Indre By
Copenhagen 1264
+45 33913655
www.idadavidsen.dk

Opening hours	Closed Saturday and Sunday
Credit cards	Accepted
Price range	Affordable
Style	Casual
Cuisine	Danish
Recommended for	Regular neighborhood

KONG HANS KÆLDER

Vingaardsstræde 6
Indre By
Copenhagen 1070
+45 33116868
www.konghans.dk

Opening hours	Closed Monday, Tuesday, and Sunday
Credit cards	Accepted
Price range	Expensive
Style	Smart casual
Cuisine	Classic French
Recommended for	High end

"Mark Lundgård cooks some of the most delicious food in Copenhagen and combined with the hospitality of Peter Pepke and the rest of the team this is a restaurant which is worth a special journey."
—Kristian Baumann

If you like your restaurants to come with a bit of history, then you'll certainly appreciate sitting down to dinner at Kong Hans Kælder, whose vaulted dining room is over 700 years old. One of the first French restaurants in Copenhagen (it opened in 1976), the food here is—perhaps unsurprisingly—traditional haute cuisine, albeit making the most of the best local produce in dishes such as Danish asparagus with golden caviar, or black lobster. Service is as slick as you'd imagine in a place with forty-one years' practice, and of course this is not a place for those on a tight budget, but for quality ingredients presented at their absolute best, there's hardly anywhere better.

LA GALETTE

Larsbjørnsstræde 9
Indre By
Copenhagen 1454
+45 33323790
www.lagalette.dk

Opening hours	Open 7 days
Credit cards	Accepted but not AMEX
Price range	Budget
Style	Casual
Cuisine	French
Recommended for	Regular neighborhood

"It's a small and very comfortable space to dine. They make pancakes but with buckwheat and it's more of a savory option. They have been around for a long time and it's a very relaxed and enjoyable place to be."
—Victor Wågman

MARCHAL AT HOTEL D'ANGLETERRE

Kongens Nytorv 34
Indre By
Copenhagen 1050
+45 33120094
www.dangleterre.com

Opening hours	Open 7 days
Credit cards	Accepted
Price range	Expensive
Style	Smart casual
Cuisine	Modern Scandinavian
Recommended for	Breakfast

"Restaurant Marchal at Hotel D'Angleterre would be the number one pick for hardcore cosmopolitans looking for an indulgent, international, haute cuisine experience, with luxurious products like truffles, caviar, and duck *a la presse* served on extravagant tableware."—Thomas Rode Andersen

MUSLING

Linnésgade 14
Indre By
Copenhagen 1361
+45 34105656
www.musling.net

Opening hours	Closed Monday and Sunday
Credit cards	Accepted but not Diners
Price range	Affordable
Style	Casual
Cuisine	Seafood
Recommended for	Local favorite

PALÆGADE

Palægade 8
Indre By
Copenhagen 1261
+45 70828288
www.palaegade.dk

Opening hours	Closed Sunday
Credit cards	Accepted
Price range	Affordable
Style	Smart casual
Cuisine	Danish
Recommended for	Regular neighborhood

"Palægade for a revamped, new wave take on Danish tradition—very good indeed."—Paul Cunningham

PLUTO

Borgergade 16
Indre By
Copenhagen 1300
+45 33160016
www.restaurantpluto.dk/forside

Opening hours	Open 7 days
Credit cards	Accepted
Price range	Affordable
Style	Casual
Cuisine	International
Recommended for	Late night

RESTAURANT GAMMEL MØNT

Gammel Mønt 41
Indre By
Copenhagen 1117
+45 33151060
www.glmoent.dk

Opening hours	Closed Monday and Sunday
Credit cards	Accepted
Price range	Affordable
Style	Smart casual
Cuisine	French-Danish
Recommended for	Regular neighborhood

"Claus Christensen is a true chef of chefs. He cooks proper old-school yet delicious food."—Bo Bech

SHAWARMA GRILL HOUSE

Frederiksberggade 36
Indre By
Copenhagen 1459
+45 33126323
www.shawarmagrillhouse.dk

Opening hours	Open 7 days
Reservation policy	No
Credit cards	Accepted but not AMEX or Diners
Price range	Budget
Style	Casual
Cuisine	Lebanese
Recommended for	Late night

"The place to go for a fast, well made shawarma. I usually ask them to leave out the pita bread and the fries but ask them for lots of tabbouleh to accompany the super tasty, awesomely seasoned, thinly cut meat." —Thomas Rode Andersen

SLURP RAMEN JOINT

Nansensgade 90
Indre By
Copenhagen 1366
+45 53708083
www.slurpramen.dk

Opening hours	Closed Monday and Sunday
Reservation policy	No
Credit cards	Accepted but not Diners
Price range	Affordable
Style	Casual
Cuisine	Ramen Noodles
Recommended for	Bargain

"Philip and his crew cook some of the best ramen outside Japan. Every little detail in this small ramen joint has been thought through and the small side dishes are just as delicious as their generous bowls of ramen."—Kristian Baumann

STUDIO

Recommended by
Kristian Baumann,
Helena Puolakka

Havnegade 44
Indre By
Copenhagen 1058
+45 72148808
www.thestandardcph.dk

Opening hours	Closed Monday and Sunday
Credit cards	Accepted
Price range	Expensive
Style	Smart casual
Cuisine	Nordic
Recommended for	Wish I'd opened

TALLER

Recommended by
Kristian Baumann,
Samuel Nutter

Tordenskjoldsgade 11
Indre By
Copenhagen 1055
+45 72140871
www.restaurant-taller.com

Opening hours	Closed Monday, Tuesday, and Sunday
Credit cards	Accepted
Price range	Expensive
Style	Smart casual
Cuisine	Modern Venezuelan
Recommended for	High end

"Not that it is outrageously expensive but it is certainly high end. This is an amazing all-round experience, the service, food, and wine are all world class. The cuisine is very personal and the dishes tell stories of childhood memories, families, and traditions and it is wonderful to be part of that for a few hours."
—Samuel Nutter

TIVOLI HALLEN

Recommended by
Paul Cunningham

Vester Voldgade 91
Indre By
Copenhagen 1552
+45 33110160
www.tivolihallen.dk

Opening hours	Closed Sunday
Credit cards	Accepted but not AMEX
Price range	Budget
Style	Casual
Cuisine	Danish
Recommended for	Regular neighborhood

Locals come to this venerable basement restaurant, which has operated continuously since 1790, for some of the best smørrebrød (open sandwiches) in Denmark. Smoked eel, salmon, or herring top rye bread with sprinklings of dill and a smooth lick of butter. The interior, with warm reds and thick tablecloths, has scarcely been updated since the 1920s, and this restaurant has remained impressively immune to the transformations Nordic cuisine has undergone in recent years. A perfect place to stop for cold beers and fresh northern fish after a morning at the nearby National Museum.

TORVEHALLERNE

Recommended by
Christian F. Puglisi

Frederiksborggade 21
Indre By
Copenhagen 1360
www.torvehallernekbh.dk

Opening hours	Open 7 days
Reservation policy	No
Credit cards	Accepted
Price range	Budget
Style	Casual
Cuisine	Market
Recommended for	Breakfast

"The market is good for The Coffee Collective coffee and the broad choice of stuff you can get there."
—Christian F. Puglisi

BÆST

Guldbergsgade 29
Nørrebro
Copenhagen 2200
+45 35350463
www.baest.dk

Opening hours	Open 7 days
Credit cards	Accepted
Price range	Affordable
Style	Casual
Cuisine	Italian
Recommended for	Late night

"They serve the best pizza, charcuterie, mozzarella, and burrata in town. The quality of all their produce is incredible and the execution even better."
—Kristian Baumann

Some people just have the Midas touch. Not content with already running two of Nørrebro's finest restaurants—the modernist Relæ and cosy bistro Manfreds over the road—restaurateurs Christian Puglisi and Kim Rossen have come up with the extraordinary Bæst, best described as a kind of Italian-Danish organic café, although that hardly does it justice. There are pizzas, made from the finest imported flour and cooked in a 500°C wood-fired oven, there's Italian-style charcuterie made from Danish pigs, there are huge slabs of premium organic meats fresh off the charcoal grill, and they even make their own mozzarella—the attention to detail is quite something.

BEYTI

Blågårdsgade 1
Nørrebro
Copenhagen 2200
+45 32170003
www.beyti.dk

Opening hours	Open 7 days
Credit cards	Accepted but not AMEX or Diners
Price range	Budget
Style	Casual
Cuisine	Middle Eastern
Recommended for	Late night

"It's close to my home and the area is quite active late at night so it is open until 6.00 a.m. on the weekends. I might in a blur from time to time have walked in to grab a falafel."—Christian F. Puglisi

CAFÉ TAXA

Hørsholmsgade 30–32
Nørrebro
Copenhagen 2200
+45 35832200
www.cafetaxa.dk

Opening hours	Open 7 days
Credit cards	Accepted
Price range	Budget
Style	Casual
Cuisine	Café
Recommended for	Breakfast

KEBABISTAN

Nørrebrogade 162
Nørrebro
Copenhagen 2200
+45 35828993

Opening hours	Open 7 days
Reservation policy	No
Credit cards	Accepted
Price range	Budget
Style	Casual
Cuisine	Turkish
Recommended for	Late night

"They make the greatest kebab in the whole of Denmark."—Brian Mark Hansen

KIIN KIIN

Guldbergsgade 21
Nørrebro
Copenhagen 2200
+45 35357555
www.kiin.dk

Opening hours	Closed Sunday
Credit cards	Accepted
Price range	Expensive
Style	Smart casual
Cuisine	Thai
Recommended for	Local favorite

MANFREDS

Jægersborggade 40
Nørrebro
Copenhagen 2200
+45 36966593
www.manfreds.dk

Recommended by
Kristian Baumann,
Grae Nonas,
Matthew Orlando,
Tim Spedding

Opening hours..Open 7 days
Credit cards...Accepted
Price range..Affordable
Style..Casual
Cuisine...Modern Scandinavian
Recommended for..............................Local favorite

"The restaurant is so very humble and charming.
The food is exquisite, carefully constructed
and delicious and it's 100 per cent sustainable.
The best tartare in the world."—Grae Nonas

Run by the team behind Relæ, which sits across
the street, Manfreds began life as more of a takeout
(takeaway) before morphing into a wine bar and
casual dining room. They have a 200-strong list of
natural wines, with the dozen or so available by the
glass displayed on the blackboard behind the bar.
Ingredients are sourced from Relæ's suppliers
and dishes are mostly tapas-sized and designed
for sharing, whether you order from the short and
snappy à la carte or go with one of their set menus.
The "Small Lunch Hunger Menu" is a steal at 195kr
($29; £23).

MIRABELLE

Guldbergsgade 29
Nørrebro
Copenhagen 2200
+45 35354724
www.mirabelle-bakery.dk

Recommended by
Kristian Baumann

Opening hours..Open 7 days
Credit cards...........................Accepted but not Diners
Price range..Affordable
Style..Casual
Cuisine...Bakery
Recommended for..Breakfast

"The restaurant is located next door to Bæst. They
actually share everything between the two places
and often you will see the same wonderful staff in
Bæst and in Mirabelle. There's a wide selection for
whatever you are in the mood for and the quality is
very high. They also serve lunch where you can get
the best pasta in town, freshly made every day."
—Kristian Baumann

MØLLER—KAFFE OG KØKKEN

Nørrebrogade 160
Nørrebro
Copenhagen 2200
+45 31505100
www.kaffeogkoekken.dk

Recommended by
Florent Ladeyn,
Rosio Sánchez

Opening hours..Open 7 days
Reservation policy...No
Credit cards...Accepted
Price range...Budget
Style..Casual
Cuisine..Café
Recommended for..Breakfast

"A bar in the center, under the street level, but with
plenty of light. Definite Copenhagen style. It's a top-
notch place, very lively, with lots of movement and
chatter that wakes me up. It's just what I need in the
morning when I'm on holiday. Organic, savory dishes.
The concept is coherent and respectful. I love having
breakfast there as soon as I get off the plane!"
—Florent Ladeyn

RADIO

Julius Thomsens Gade 12
Nørrebro
Copenhagen 1632
+45 25102733
www.restaurantradio.dk

Recommended by
Kristian Baumann

Opening hours........................Closed Monday and Sunday
Credit cards...Accepted
Price range..Affordable
Style..Casual
Cuisine...Modern Nordic
Recommended for..............................Local favorite

RANEE'S

Recommended by
Kristian Baumann,
Christian F. Puglisi

Blågårds Plads 10
Nørrebro
Copenhagen 2200
+45 35368505
www.ranees.dk

Opening hours	Closed Sunday
Credit cards	Accepted but not AMEX or Diners
Price range	Budget
Style	Casual
Cuisine	Thai
Recommended for	Regular neighborhood

"It's my neighborhood spot. It's Thai but still has the personal touch of Ranees on the food. Also a fair amount of organic produce. Really good."
—Christian F. Puglisi

RELÆ

Recommended by
Timur Abuzyarov, Aaron Adams,
Kristian Baumann,
Sergei Berezutskiy, Daniel Berlin,
Andres Bonaffini, Daniel Burns,
Andreas Dahlberg, Ben Devlin,
Erik Hascey, Sasu Laukkonen,
Ross Lusted, Ignacio Mattos,
Claus Meyer, Jakob Mielcke,
Uwe Opocensky, Matthew Orlando,
William Preisch, Tim Spedding,
Ollie Templeton, Stephen Toman,
Simone Tondo, Robert Trzópek

Jægersborggade 41
Nørrebro
Copenhagen 2200
+45 36966609
www.restaurant-relae.dk

Opening hours	Closed Monday and Sunday
Credit cards	Accepted
Price range	Expensive
Style	Smart casual
Cuisine	Modern Nordic
Recommended for	Wish I'd opened

"For me it's the perfect combination of thought-provoking, casual food that surprises you with every dish, and wines to match the experience. Also great music."—Ollie Templeton

Relæ was opened in 2010 by a pair of Noma graduates: its former head chef Christian Puglisi and Kim Rossen, who worked there as both a chef and a waiter. Their restaurant sits in Copenhagen's gentrifying but still colorful Nørrebro district. The vibe is informal, and the simply styled dining room with open kitchen is an exercise in clever Danish design; form perfectly meets function in tables with neat drawers that hold the table settings and menu. In 2016, Jonathan Tam took over as head chef from Puglisi and his cooking is expressed via a choice of the four-course "Relæ Menu" or the seven-course "Relæ Experience"—both of which showcase seriously ambitious, Michelin-starred food.

ALCHEMIST

Recommended by
Kristian Baumann

Århusgade 22
Østerbro
Copenhagen 2100
+45 51935623
www.restaurant-alchemist.dk

Opening hours	Closed Monday
Credit cards	Accepted
Price range	Expensive
Style	Smart casual
Cuisine	Modern International
Recommended for	Local favorite

GERANIUM

Recommended by
Italo Bassi,
Kristian Baumann
Sang Hoon Degeimbre, Luca Fantin,
Guillaume Galliot, Rainer Gassner,
Brian Mark Hansen,
Onno Kokmeijer, William Maki,
Claus Meyer, Marco Müller,
Samuel Nutter, Mats Vollmer,
Victor Wågman

Per Henrik Lings Allé 4, 8th Floor
Østerbro
Copenhagen 2100
+45 69960020
www.geranium.dk

Opening hours	Closed Monday, Tuesday, and Sunday
Credit cards	Accepted
Price range	Expensive
Style	Smart casual
Cuisine	Modern Scandinavian
Recommended for	High end

"Simple set-up, light dynamic space in Scandinavian design with fantastic produce and a chef with really great technique."—Guillaume Galliot

Now that Noma has shut its doors for good, perhaps it's time Geranium, in its serene space on the eighth floor of a football stadium (of all places), finally started to get the attention it deserves. After all, the food, by head chef Rasmus Kofoed, is stunning, and has even picked up the maximum three stars from the Michelin inspectors. Exquisitely presented dishes of seasonal color and immaculate technical skill—matched with pitch-perfect service—produce a restaurant experience hardly bettered anywhere in the world. A supreme achievement, and the new jewel in the crown of Copenhagen's high-flying culinary scene.

HOS FISCHER

Victor Borges Plads 12
Østerbro
Copenhagen 2100
+45 35423964
www.hosfischer.dk

Recommended by
Kristian Baumann,
Brian Mark Hansen

Opening hours	Open 7 days
Credit cards	Accepted but not AMEX
Price range	Affordable
Style	Casual
Cuisine	Italian
Recommended for	Regular neighborhood

"Fantastic Italian food and a brilliant host,
David Fischer."—Brian Mark Hansen

CHICKS BY CHICKS

Vesterbrogade 55b
Vesterbro
Copenhagen 1620
+45 88133916
www.chicksbychicks.dk

Recommended by
Thomas Rode Andersen

Opening hours	Open / days
Credit cards	Accepted
Price range	Affordable
Style	Casual
Cuisine	Rotisserie
Recommended for	Bargain

"Tasty and juicy organic rotisserie chicken! Served
with nicely seasoned sides with originality and tons
of flavor. It really tastes like chicken!"
—Thomas Rode Andersen

CHICKY GRILL

Halmtorvet 21
Vesterbro
Copenhagen 700
+45 33226696

Recommended by
Nicolai Nørregaard

Opening hours	Closed Saturday and Sunday
Credit cards	Not accepted
Price range	Budget
Style	Casual
Cuisine	Danish Rotisserie
Recommended for	Local favorite

FU HAO

Colbjørnsensgade 15
Vesterbro
Copenhagen 1652
+45 33318985
www.fuhao.dk

Recommended by
Bo Bech

Opening hours	Closed Wednesday
Credit cards	Accepted
Price range	Budget
Style	Casual
Cuisine	Chinese
Recommended for	Bargain

KØDBYENS FISKEBAR

Flæsketorvet 100
Vesterbro
Copenhagen 1711
+45 3215 5656
www.fiskebaren.dk

Recommended by
Kristian Baumann,
Matthew Orlando

Opening hours	Open 7 days
Credit cards	Accepted but not Diners
Price range	Affordable
Style	Casual
Cuisine	Seafood
Recommended for	Local favorite

"Fun, loud, and great food."—Matthew Orlando

HIJA DE SANCHEZ

Slagterboderne 8
Vesterbro
Copenhagen 1716
+45 53739510
www.hijadesanchez.dk

Recommended by
Kristian Baumann, Bo Bech,
Jakob Mielcke,
Matthew Orlando

Opening hours	Open 7 days
Reservation policy	No
Credit cards	Accepted
Price range	Budget
Style	Casual
Cuisine	Mexican
Recommended for	Bargain

"This taqueria has made it very easy to choose your
favorite place to go for tacos in Copenhagen. Former
Noma pastry chef with Mexican blood...this should
indicate where you are going."—Jacob Mielcke

ISSA

Sankt Jørgens Allé 6
Vesterbro
Copenhagen 1615
+45 31351222
www.issafoods.dk

Opening hours	Closed Tuesdays
Reservation policy	No
Credit cards	Accepted but not AMEX or Diners
Price range	Budget
Style	Casual
Cuisine	Japanese
Recommended for	Bargain

"The very best Japanese chef in Denmark, in my humble view. Underrated, understated, often missed. Wonderful, likeable character in Suzuki-San."
—Paul Cunningham

JAGGER

Istergade 62
Vesterbro
Copenhagen 1650
www.jagger.dk

Opening hours	Open 7 days
Reservation policy	No
Credit cards	Accepted
Price range	Budget
Style	Casual
Cuisine	American
Recommended for	Wish I'd opened

"Ex-multi-starred chef does probably the best burger in town. Great meat, superb bread, well exceculed in a fun space. Superb service, efficient, and friendly. Everyone likes a great burger—chicken, slaw, salads, and shakes add to the most pleasurable experience. Cheap too!"—Paul Cunningham

JUICYBURGER

Flæsketorvet 44
Vesterbro
Copenhagen 1711
+45 20222204
www.juicyb.com

Opening hours	Open 7 days
Reservation policy	No
Credit cards	Accepted but not Diners
Price range	Budget
Style	Casual
Cuisine	Burgers
Recommended for	Regular neighborhood

"JuicyBurger in Copenhagen: refreshingly different take on burgers, supreme quality."—Paul Cunningham

MAGASASA

Amagerbrogade 44
Vesterbro
Copenhagen 2300
+45 32979999
www.magasasa.dk

Opening hours	Open 7 days
Credit cards	Accepted but not AMEX or Diners
Price range	Affordable
Style	Casual
Cuisine	Chinese
Recommended for	Late night

"Great for a tasty late-night snack or meal."
—Samuel Nutter

PAPA RAMEN

Skydebanegade 16
Vesterbro
Copenhagen 1709
+45 31195436
www.paparamen.dk

Opening hours	Open 7 days
Reservation policy	No
Credit cards	Accepted but not AMEX or Diners
Price range	Affordable
Style	Casual
Cuisine	Japanese
Recommended for	Bargain

"Super tasty and easy ramen shop. Perfect for a Sunday lunch with the family."—Nicolai Nørregaard

PATÉ PATÉ

Slagterboderne 1
Vesterbro
Copenhagen 1716
+45 39695557
www.patepate.dk

Opening hours	Open 7 days
Credit cards	Accepted but not Diners
Price range	Affordable
Style	Casual
Cuisine	Modern Mediterranean
Recommended for	Regular neighborhood

"Paté Paté in Kødbyen remains a morning favorite—superb lunches."—Paul Cunningham

SPISEHUSET

Slagtehusgade 5c
Vesterbro
Copenhagen 1715
| 45 30553513
www.spisehuset.dk

Opening hours	Closed Sunday to Wednesday
Credit cards	Accepted
Price range	Affordable
Style	Casual
Cuisine	Danish
Recommended for	Local favorite

"Coolest location in the back alley of the meat packing district."—Matthew Orlando

SUPERMARCO

Støbegodsvej 1
Vesterbro
Copenhagen 2450
+45 33938293
www.supermarco.dk/da

Opening hours	Closed Sunday
Reservation policy	No
Credit cards	Accepted but not AMEX
Price range	Budget
Style	Casual
Cuisine	Café
Recommended for	Breakfast

UFORMEL

Studiestræde 69
Vesterbro
Copenhagen 1554
+45 70999111
www.uformel.dk

Opening hours	Open 7 days
Credit cards	Accepted
Price range	Affordable
Style	Casual
Cuisine	International
Recommended for	Regular neighborhood

"This is the sister restaurant of the one-Michelin-starred Formel B. It offers good value for money and above all delicious and well-cooked food!"
—Samuel Nutter

WARPIGS BREWPUB

Flæsketorvet 25
Vesterbro
Copenhagen 1711
+45 43484848
www.warpigs.dk

Opening hours	Open 7 days
Credit cards	Accepted but not Diners
Price range	Budget
Style	Casual
Cuisine	American-Danish
Recommended for	Wish I'd opened

GAARDEN & GADEN

Nørrebrogade 88
Nørrebro
Copenhagen 2200
+45 55550880
www.gaaga.dk

Opening hours	Closed Monday
Credit cards	Accepted
Price range	Affordable
Style	Casual
Cuisine	European
Recommended for	Regular neighborhood

"Gaarden & Gaden is more of a bar but they also serve simple food and the occasional oyster. It's on my way home from work and the atmosphere is great for just dropping by."—Christian F. Puglisi

KOKS

Recommended by
Florent Ladeyn

Í Geilini 13
Kirkjubøur
Kirkjubøur
Streymoy 175, Faroe Islands
+298 333999
www.koks.fo

Opening hours.............................Closed Monday and Sunday
Credit cards...Accepted
Price range..Expensive
Style...Smart casual
Cuisine...Modern Nordic
Recommended for...High end

"A revelation! Purity and simplicity in the noblest
sense. I would go to the Faroe Islands just for this.
I discovered it in a month-long pop-up opposite the
Studio restaurant in Copenhagen."—Florent Ladeyn

MAMI

Recommended by
Pekka Terävä

Linnankatu 3
Turku
Finland Proper 20100, Finland
+358 22311111
www.mami.fi

Opening hours.............................Closed Monday and Sunday
Credit cards...Accepted
Price range...Affordable
Style..Casual
Cuisine...Modern Finnish
Recommended for.........................Regular neighborhood

Situated in a previously run-down area of Turku,
Mami was a pioneer of the city's riverbank
restaurant boom back in 2007. A host of trendy
restaurants have since followed suit and opened
in the region over the last ten years, but Mami's
consistently impressive dishes have ensured its
classic status. The menu is short and seasonal,
with a focus on simple Finnish flavors cooked to
perfection and a few French twists. There's a
vegetarian, fish, and meat option in every service:
the locally sourced veal is a highlight. The view over
the river towards the cathedral is impressive, so
take your wine to the terrace if the weather allows.

SMÖR

Recommended by
Pekka Terävä

Läntinen Rantakatu 3
Turku
Finland Proper 20100, Finland
+358 25369444
www.smor.fi

Opening hours...Closed Sunday
Credit cards...Accepted
Price range...Affordable
Style...Smart casual
Cuisine..Nordic
Recommended for.........................Regular neighborhood

TINTÅ

Recommended by
Pekka Terävä

Läntinen Rantakatu 9
Turku
Finland Proper 20100, Finland
+358 22307023
www.tinta.fi

Opening hours..Open 7 days
Credit cards...Accepted
Price range...Affordable
Style..Casual
Cuisine...International
Recommended for................................Wish I'd opened

Tintå is a bistro, pizzeria, and wine bar that locals will
proudly boast of as their favorite Turku venue. Perfect
for summer dining, it's located on the leafy riverbank,
with a picture-perfect vantage point overlooking the
comers and goers across the Aura River. There are
many reasons to visit: the affordable, delicious lunch
menu; the sweet and savory pizzas (goat's cheese,
strawberry, and pistachio is a particular highlight);
and the friendly service that will provide you with
top-quality wine until the late closing time. The
relaxed atmosphere has the traits of a Parisian café,
where you can enjoy brunch, lunch, dinner, or a
late-night bite—and will never be left disappointed.

WANHA HULLU PORO

Rakkavaarantie 5
Levi
Lapland 99130, Finland
+358 166510620
www.hulluporo.fi/restaurants/wanha-hullu-poro

Opening hours.................................Open 7 days
Credit cards.....................................Accepted
Price range......................................Affordable
Style...Casual
Cuisine...Steakhouse
Recommended for............................Worth the travel

RUKA PEAK

Juhannuskalliontie 27
Rukatunturi
Northern Ostrobothnia 93825, Finland
+358 88684100
www.rukapeak.fi

Opening hours.................................Open 7 days
Credit cards.....................................Accepted
Price range......................................Affordable
Style...Casual
Cuisine...Modern Finnish
Recommended for............................Worth the travel

RESTAURANT GÖSTA

Serlachius Museum
Mänttä
Mänttä-Vilppula
Pirkanmaa 35800, Finland
+358 407085572
www.ravintolagosta.fi

Opening hours.................................Closed Monday
Credit cards.....................................Accepted
Price range......................................Affordable
Style...Casual
Cuisine...Finnish
Recommended for............................Worth the travel

"Contemporary setup in the old grounds of Serlachius Museum. Amazing, true talent behind the stove is Henry Tikkanen, one of the best chefs in Finland."
—Helena Puolakka

The four-course set menu at Gösta, titled "The Golden Age", includes traditional North European dishes such as garlic soup with chestnuts, pike loaf with pickled vegetables, and elk breast in thyme sauce, all for a reasonable €46 ($50; £39). The glass-fronted windows allow you to experience the beautiful surroundings.

RAPUKARTANO

Koivuseläntie 77
Vilppula
Mänttä-Vilppula
Pirkanmaa 35700, Finland
+358 445929429
www.rapukartano.fi

Opening hours.................................Open 7 days
Credit cards.....................................Accepted
Price range......................................Affordable
Style...Casual
Cuisine...Finnish-Seafood
Recommended for............................Local favorite

PUNKAHARJU STATE HOTEL

Harjutie 596
Punkaharju
Southern Savonia 58450, Finland
+ 358 15511311
www.hotellipunkaharju.fi

Opening hours.................................Open 7 days
Credit cards.....................................Accepted
Price range......................................Affordable
Style...Smart casual
Cuisine...Finnish
Recommended for............................High end

"A new hotel in a nature reserve in the idyllic, historically charming and beautiful lake district of Finland. I am a huge fan of Saimi Hoyer's passion for wild mushrooms which are available all year round and in vast amounts. They also have mushroom foraging courses that seem to have gurus attending from all over the world."—Sami Tallberg

RESTAURANT FUKU SUPREME

Viaporintori
Soittoniekanaukio
Espoo
Uusimaa 2600, Finland
+358 105011177
www.fukusupreme.com

Opening hours.................................Open 7 days
Credit cards.......................Accepted but not AMEX or Diners
Price range......................................Budget
Style...Casual
Cuisine...Japanese
Recommended for............................Bargain

BASBAS & STAFF

Tehtaankatu 27–29
Helsinki
Uusimaa 150, Finland
+358 442305900
www.basbas.fi

Opening hours...............Closed Monday, Tuesday, and Sunday
Credit cards...Accepted
Price range...Affordable
Style..Casual
Cuisine...Tapas
Recommended for...................................Regular neighborhood

"Natural wines, small plates, great relaxed vibe."
—Sasu Laukkonen

BASKERI & BASSO

Tehtaankatu 27–29
Helsinki
Uusimaa 150, Finland
+358 504673400
www.basbas.fi

Opening hours............Closed Monday, Saturday, and Sunday
Credit cards...Accepted
Price range...Expensive
Style..Casual
Cuisine..Bistro
Recommended for..Local favorite

"Simple and skilfully prepared comforting food +
amazing venue + hearty service + wines to sip with
enjoyment!"—Sami Talberg

Opened at the end of 2015, and beloved of Finnish
foodies ever since, Baskeri & Basso remains
a notoriously hot ticket, with reservations
recommended weeks in advance for prized Friday
and Saturday night dining. A gem in the upmarket
neighborhood of Eira, this bistro's industrial-chic
decor and candlelit tables keep the atmosphere
cosy and intimate. The flexible menu (scrawled on
a chalkboard that the waiters bring to your table)
comprises of small sharing plates and focuses on
simple, fresh ingredients prepared with skill. For
a more informal affair head next door to the sister
wine bar, BasBas, and enjoy a glass of wine and
some tapas at the bar.

CAFÉ ANDANTE

Fredrikinkatu 20
Helsinki
Uusimaa 120, Finland
+358 453235088

Opening hours............................Closed Monday and Tuesday
Credit cards...Accepted but not AMEX
Price range...Affordable
Style..Casual
Cuisine...Café
Recommended for...Breakfast

"Simple, colorful range of café goods and coffee
to die for + service with extraordinary standards."
—Sami Tallberg

CARGO

Ruoholahdenranta 8
Helsinki
Uusimaa 180, Finland
+358 449237869
www.cargohelsinki.fi

Opening hours..Open 7 days
Credit cards...Accepted but not AMEX
Price range...Affordable
Style..Casual
Cuisine..Vegetarian
Recommended for...................................Regular neighborhood

"Fuss free vegan-vegetarian restaurant made with old
shipping containers. Pure and healthy food with deep
flavors, a colorful range of funky drinks + food with
nutrition density."—Sami Tallberg

Constructed from cargo containers, this cool,
laid-back café is the perfect spot to grab a morning
latte and pastry or lunchtime salad. If you're not
pressed for time, hang out on the sunny rooftop
terrace and enjoy the exclusively vegetarian and
vegan menu of healthy and colorful soups, risottos,
small plates, and desserts. With an emphasis
on collaborating with other local food and drink
producers—the coffee is from Johan & Nyström
and they stock Helsinki Dry Gin at the bar—Cargo
also hosts an on-site repair spot with HUG BikeShop,
so bring your ride along for a quick puncture repair
while you relax over a coffee.

CHEF & SOMMELIER
Recommended by
Filip Langhoff

Huvilakatu 28
Helsinki
Uusimaa 150, Finland
+358 400959440
www.chefetsommelier.fi

Opening hours	Closed Monday and Sunday
Credit cards	Accepted
Price range	Affordable
Style	Smart casual
Cuisine	Modern Nordic
Recommended for	Local favorite

CAFÉ EKBERG
Recommended by
Sasu Laukkonen,
Pekka Terävä

Bulevardi 9
Helsinki
Uusimaa 120, Finland
+358 96811860
www.cafeekberg.fi

Opening hours	Open 7 days
Credit cards	Accepted
Price range	Affordable
Style	Casual
Cuisine	Bakery-Café
Recommended for	Breakfast

ELITE
Recommended by
Helena Puolakka

Etelainen Hesperiankatu 22
Helsinki
Uusimaa 100, Finland
+358 961285200
www.elite.fi

Opening hours	Open 7 days
Credit cards	Accepted
Price range	Expensive
Style	Smart casual
Cuisine	Finnish
Recommended for	Late night

"Cultural hub in Helsinki, classic Finnish cuisine, you can always spot an artist or two."—Helena Puolakka

FAFA'S
Recommended by
Sasu Laukkonen

Iso Roobertinkatu 2
Helsinki
Uusimaa 120, Finland
+359 73104616
www.fafas.fi

Opening hours	Open 7 days
Reservation policy	No
Credit cards	Accepted but not AMEX
Price range	Budget
Style	Casual
Cuisine	Middle Eastern
Recommended for	Bargain

"Great falafel, nice quick service."—Sasu Laukkonen

HANKO SUSHI
Recommended by
Pekka Terävä

Kaivokatu 8
Helsinki
Uusimaa 100, Finland
+358 401386223
www.hankosushi.fi

Opening hours	Open 7 days
Credit cards	Accepted
Price range	Budget
Style	Casual
Cuisine	Japanese
Recommended for	Bargain

KLAUS K BREAKFAST & BRUNCH
Recommended by
Pekka Terävä

Klaus K Hotel
Bulevardi 2–4
Helsinki
Uusimaa 120, Finland
+358 207704700
www.klauskhotel.com

Opening hours	Open 7 days
Credit cards	Accepted
Price range	Expensive
Style	Smart casual
Cuisine	Modern Nordic
Recommended for	Breakfast

KUPPI JA MUFFINI

Recommended by
Filip Langhoff

Kalevankatu 17
Helsinki
Uusimaa 100, Finland
+358 440202130
www.kuppijamuffini.fi

Opening hours	Closed Sunday
Reservation policy	No
Credit cards	Accepted but not AMEX
Price range	Budget
Style	Casual
Cuisine	Bakery-Café
Recommended for	Breakfast

"Nice small place for your organic morning coffee."
—Filip Langhoff

KUURNA

Recommended by
Helena Puolakka

Meritullinkatu 6
Helsinki
Uusimaa 170, Finland
+358 102818241
www.kuurna.fi

Opening hours	Closed Sunday
Credit cards	Accepted
Price range	Affordable
Style	Smart casual
Cuisine	Nordic
Recommended for	Local favorite

"Tiny place with balcony kitchen where you see two
chefs working. The menu changes every two weeks."
—Helena Puolakka

LATVA

Recommended by
Filip Langhoff

Korkeavuorenkatu 25
Helsinki
Uusimaa 130, Finland
+358 503818544
www.latva.fi

Opening hours	Closed Sunday
Reservation policy	No
Credit cards	Accepted
Price range	Affordable
Style	Casual
Cuisine	Finnish
Recommended for	Bargain

"The lunch at Latva is a bargain—good quality 'home'
cooking, simple and delicious. They also have very nice
wines by the glass."—Filip Langhoff

MANALA

Recommended by
Pekka Terävä

Dagmarinkatu 2
Helsinki
Uusimaa 100, Finland
+358 958077707
www.manala.fi

Opening hours	Open 7 days
Credit cards	Accepted
Price range	Affordable
Style	Casual
Cuisine	Finnish
Recommended for	Late night

OLO

Recommended by
Dmitriy Blinov,
Filip Langhoff,
Helena Puolakka

Pohjoisesplanadi 5
Helsinki
Uusimaa 170, Finland
+358 103206250
www.olo-ravintola.fi

Opening hours	Closed Monday and Sunday
Credit cards	Accepted
Price range	Affordable
Style	Smart casual
Cuisine	Finnish
Recommended for	Worth the travel

"Genius cuisine. Service and atmosphere, everything
else, is at the highest level but the main thing is the
cuisine. The food is impeccable."—Dmitriy Blinov

POMPIER

Recommended by
Sami Tallberg

Albertinkatu 29
Helsinki
Uusimaa 180, Finland
+358 9663301
www.pompier.fi

Opening hours	Open 7 days
Credit cards	Accepted but not AMEX or Diners
Price range	Affordable
Style	Casual
Cuisine	Finnish
Recommended for	Regular neighborhood

"Great mix of clientele, super positive atmosphere and
simply great lunch cooked with love."—Sami Tallberg

PUTTE'S BAR & PIZZA

Recommended by
Sasu Laukkonen

Kalevankatu 6
Helsinki
Uusimaa 100, Finland
+358 102818243
www.puttes.fi

Opening hours	Open 7 days
Reservation policy	No
Credit cards	Accepted
Price range	Budget
Style	Casual
Cuisine	Pizza
Recommended for	Late night

RAGU

Recommended by
Pekka Terävä

Ludviginkatu 3–5
Helsinki
Uusimaa 130, Finland
+358 9596659
www.ragu.fi

Opening hours	Closed Sunday
Credit cards	Accepted
Price range	Affordable
Style	Smart casual
Cuisine	Modern Finnish
Recommended for	High end

RESTAURANT ASK

Recommended by
Sasu Laukkonen

Vironkatu 8
Helsinki
Uusimaa 170, Finland
+358 405818100
www.restaurantask.com

Opening hours	Closed Monday and Sunday
Credit cards	Accepted
Price range	Expensive
Style	Smart casual
Cuisine	Modern Finnish-Nordic
Recommended for	Local favorite

"Fine dining with a deep Finnish touch."
—Sasu Laukkonen

RESTAURANT GRÖN

Recommended by
Filip Langhoff,
Sasu Laukkonen,
Sami Tallberg

Albertinkatu 36
Helsinki
Uusimaa 180, Finland
+358 942893358
www.restaurantgron.com

Opening hours	Closed Monday and Sunday
Credit cards	Accepted
Price range	Affordable
Style	Casual
Cuisine	Nordic
Recommended for	Local favorite

"New wave Nordic stuff with artistic flare and vast amounts of wild herbs used in creative ways."
—Sami Tallberg

SAVOY

Recommended by
Pekka Terävä

Eteläesplanadi 14
Helsinki
Uusimaa 130, Finland
+358 961285300
www.ravintolasavoy.fi

Opening hours	Closed Sunday
Credit cards	Accepted
Price range	Affordable
Style	Smart casual
Cuisine	Finnish
Recommended for	High end

VINKKELI

Recommended by
Filip Langhoff

Pieni Roobertinkatu 8
Helsinki
Uusimaa 130, Finland
+358 291800222
www.ravintolavinkkeli.fi

Opening hours	Closed Sunday
Credit cards	Accepted
Price range	Affordable
Style	Casual
Cuisine	Café-Brasserie
Recommended for	Regular neighborhood

"This restaurant has the potential to become a new classic in Helsinki."—Filip Langhoff

"The most amazing creations you'll ever come across."
FRANKIE VAN LOO P477

"AMONGST THE BEST IN THE WORLD."
RICHARD TURNER P390

"A TRULY WORLD CLASS DINING EXPERIENCE."
PAUL FOSTER P402

UNITED KINGDOM & REPUBLIC OF IRELAND

"I HAD THE BEST MEAL OF MY LIFE THERE."
GARETH WARD P405

"It's a local landmark and has a good seafood menu."
STEPHEN HARRIS P401

"I'M THERE AS OFTEN AS I CAN BE FOR MY EGG NAAN AND MASALA CHAI."
NEIL RANKIN P482

UNITED
KINGDOM
& REPUBLIC
OF IRELAND

Ⓝ SCALE

0   50   100
                 MI.

Highland p.498

Perthshire p.498

Argyll p.496

Edinburgh p.496

SCOTLAND

Co. Antrim p.500

Cumbria p.394

Co. Down p.503

Co. Galway p.506

Lancashire p.401

ENGLAND

Durham p.395

West Yorkshire p.406

Co. Dublin pp.503

Greater Manchester p.396

Nottinghamshire p.402

IRELAND

Norfolk p.401

Cambridge p.391

West Midlands p.404

Ceredigion p.499

Warwickshire p.403

Worcestershire p.497

Buckinghamshire p.391

Essex p.397

WALES

Oxfordshire p.403

Monmouthshire p.499

Gloucestershire p.396

Bristol p.399

London pp.409–494

Berkshire p.390

Wiltshire p.407

Surrey p.406

Kent pp.399

East Sussex p395

Devon p.394

Hampshire p.395

Dorset p.393

Cornwall p.391

Jersey p.496

THE FAT DUCK

High Street
Bray
Berkshire
England SL6 2AQ
+44 1628580334
www.thefatduck.co.uk

Opening hours	Closed Monday and Sunday
Credit cards	Accepted
Price range	Expensive
Style	Smart casual
Cuisine	Modern British
Recommended for	Worth the travel

"Heston Blumenthal's renowned temple to innovative modern British cuisine!"—George Calombaris

THE HIND'S HEAD

High Street
Bray
Berkshire
England SL6 2AB
+44 1628626151
www.hindsheadbray.com

Opening hours	Open 7 days
Credit cards	Accepted
Price range	Expensive
Style	Casual
Cuisine	Modern British
Recommended for	High end

"Heston's take on a gastropub—could be an expensive weekend depending on where you stay, but lunch or dinner here make it all worthwhile."—Shuko Oda

The Hind's Head is what happens when someone as talented and obsessive as Heston Blumenthal opens a pub. That is, we end up with something superficially resembling a pub but serving food so extraordinarily well tuned and shining with perfect technique that it's certainly a closer relation to the Fat Duck over the road than any local. Dishes are traditionally British on paper but brimming with invention—pea and ham soup arrives as an ethereally light *velouté* (French white sauce), and salmon is cold smoked in lapsang souchong tea. A recent refurb has removed the à la carte option, but the famous triple-cooked chips are still lurking on one of the set menus.

THE WATERSIDE INN

Ferry Road
Bray
Berkshire
England SL6 2AT
+44 1628620691
www.waterside-inn.co.uk

Opening hours	Closed Monday and Tuesday
Credit cards	Accepted
Price range	Expensive
Style	Smart casual
Cuisine	French
Recommended for	High end

"Amongst the best in the world; proper food."
—Richard Turner

CASAMIA

Lower Guinea Street
Bristol
England BS1 6SY
+44 1179592884
www.casamiarestaurant.co.uk

Opening hours	Closed Monday, Tuesday and Sunday
Credit cards	Accepted
Price range	Expensive
Style	Smart casual
Cuisine	Italian
Recommended for	High end

PINKMANS

85 Park Street
Bristol
England BS1 5PJ
+44 1174032040
www.pinkmans.co.uk

Opening hours	Open 7 days
Credit cards	Accepted
Price range	Affordable
Style	Casual
Cuisine	Bakery-Diner
Recommended for	Breakfast

"Busy urban bakery with delicious bread and pastries. Friendly staff, casual atmosphere, and great breakfast and lunch options."—Niall Keating

POCO

Recommended by
Joel Braham

45 Jamaica Street
Bristol
England BS2 8JP
+44 1179232233
www.pocotapasbar.com

Opening hours	Open 7 days
Credit cards	Accepted
Price range	Affordable
Style	Casual
Cuisine	North African-Spanish
Recommended for	Local favorite

WILSONS RESTAURANT

Recommended by
James Wilkins

24 Chandos Road
Bristol
England BS6 6PF
+44 1179734157
www.wilsonsrestaurant.co.uk

Opening hours	Closed Monday and Sunday
Credit cards	Accepted
Price range	Affordable
Style	Casual
Cuisine	Modern British
Recommended for	Regular neighborhood

"Fantastic English bistro run by Jan Ostle. Great seasonal, fresh ingredients, no fuss. The perfect bistro!"—James Wilkins

CHESHAM TANDOORI

Recommended by
Mark Jarvis

48 Broad Street
Chesham
Buckinghamshire
England HP5 3DX
+44 1494782669
www.cheshamtandoori.co

Opening hours	Open 7 days
Credit cards	Accepted
Price range	Budget
Style	Casual
Cuisine	Indian
Recommended for	Local favorite

"This is a restaurant I have been going to since I was fourteen-years old, in the town where I grew up. It's great Indian food and as soon as I walk in they remember me. I always order *sag gosht* (lamb and spinach curry) and garlic naan"—Mark Jarvis

MIDSUMMER HOUSE

Recommended by
Tom Sellers

Midsummer Common
Cambridge
Cambridgeshire
England CB4 1HA
+44 1223369299
www.midsummerhouse.co.uk

Opening hours	Closed Monday and Sunday
Credit cards	Accepted
Price range	Affordable
Style	Smart casual
Cuisine	Modern European
Recommended for	High end

POTAGER GARDEN & GLASSHOUSE

Recommended by
David Gingell

High Cross
Constantine
Falmouth
Cornwall
England TR11 5RF
| 44 1326341258
www.potagergarden.org

Opening hours	Closed Monday to Wednesday
Credit cards	Accepted but not AMEX or Diners
Price range	Affordable
Style	Casual
Cuisine	Modern European
Recommended for	Wish I'd opened

"It does wholesome simple food, bread, soups and salads using ingredients from the garden and surrounding farms. It does all of this with a simple charm. It's hard to put into words—it's just perfect."—David Gingell

COOMBESHEAD FARM

Recommended by
Alex Jackson, Isaac McHale,
Nathan Outlaw, Dave Pynt,
Tim Spedding

Coombeshead Farm
Lewannick
Cornwall
England PL15 7QQ
+44 1566782009
www.coombesheadfarm.co.uk

Opening hours	Closed Monday to Wednesday
Credit cards	Accepted
Price range	Affordable
Style	Casual
Cuisine	Modern British
Recommended for	Worth the travel

"Tom Adams and April Bloomfield have opened this farm, with rooms and a super restaurant. Unique with all the hospitality one would expect."—Nathan Outlaw

THE BEACH HUT

Recommended by
Nathan Outlaw

Watergate Bay Hotel
Newquay
Cornwall
England R8 4AA
+44 1637860877
www.watergatebay.co.uk

Opening hours	Open 7 days
Credit cards	Accepted but not AMEX or Diners
Price range	Affordable
Style	Casual
Cuisine	Modern Seafood
Recommended for	Breakfast

"Great views and good hospitality. Lovely full English."
—Nathan Outlaw

KAHUNA

Recommended by
Nathan Outlaw

Station Approach
Newquay
Cornwall
England TR7 2NG
+44 1637850440
www.kahunarestaurant.co.uk

Opening hours	Open 7 days
Credit cards	Accepted but not AMEX or Diners
Price range	Affordable
Style	Casual
Cuisine	Modern Asian
Recommended for	Regular neighborhood

"The most unique Asian food I've seen in Cornwall."
—Nathan Outlaw

PAUL AINSWORTH AT NUMBER 6

Recommended by
Neil Borthwick,
José Pizarro

6 Middle Street
Padstow
Cornwall
England PL28 8AP
+44 1841532093
www.paul-ainsworth.co.uk/number6

Opening hours	Closed Monday and Sunday
Credit cards	Accepted but not AMEX or Diners
Price range	Affordable
Style	Smart casual
Cuisine	Modern British
Recommended for	Worth the travel

"The food is incredible and the way they treat the
produce is unbelievable."—José Pizarro

Following a recent refurbishment, no. 6 Middle
Street is now bigger, brighter and more plush, but
fortunately still has every bit of the charm and wit
that has made it one of the very best restaurants in
the South West. The menu, short and irresistibly
accessible, features the finest local seafood (as you
might hope) and artisan producers (of which, in
Cornwall, there are no short supply) and presents
them all with energy, invention and an artist's eye.
Service, warm and attentive, is another reason the
place attracts visitors from the length and breadth
of the country.

THE SEAFOOD RESTAURANT

Recommended by
Tania Steytler, Mitch Tonks

Riverside
Padstow
Cornwall
England PL28 8BY
+44 1841532700
www.rickstein.com

Opening hours	Open 7 days
Credit cards	Accepted but not Diners
Price range	Affordable
Style	Casual
Cuisine	Modern Seafood
Recommended for	Wish I'd opened

"It's all about fish, Cornwall and being by the sea,
and making the most of it without over-complicating
things. You just want to eat there."—Tania Steytler

As far as many are concerned, this is where the
British food revolution started, when a young Rick
Stein began intercepting the fantastic fresh seafood
heading from the Padstow docks to France and
Spain, and started selling it in his seafront
restaurant. Today, it's a showcase for dishes from
his nearly three-decades on TV, from the Goan curry
with hake to the famous Singapore chile crab. As
such, it's a must-visit for the throngs of tourists that
descend on this pretty fishing village all year round.
But even TV fame aside, Stein's lasting influence on
the way the UK eats is profound.

OUTLAW'S FISH KITCHEN

1 Middle Street
Port Isaac
Cornwall
England PL29 3RH
+44 1208881183
www.outlaws.co.uk

Opening hours	Closed Sunday
Credit cards	Accepted but not Diners
Price range	Affordable
Style	Casual
Cuisine	Seafood
Recommended for	Bargain

RESTAURANT NATHAN OUTLAW

6 New Road
Port Isaac
Cornwall
England PL29 3SB
+44 1208880896
www.nathan-outlaw.com

Opening hours	Closed Sunday to Wednesday
Credit cards	Accepted but not Diners
Price range	Expensive
Style	Smart casual
Cuisine	Modern British
Recommended for	Wish I'd opened

"As a chef, the dream is to get the most amazing produce as soon as you can, and Nathan gets the first fish straight out of the sea. He's a real master with fish."—Nieves Barragán Mohacho

PORTHMINSTER BEACH CAFÉ

Porthminster Beach
Carbis Bay
Saint Ives
Cornwall
England TR26 2EB
+44 1736795352
www.porthminstercafe.co.uk

Opening hours	Closed Monday
Credit cards	Accepted but not AMEX or Diners
Price range	Affordable
Style	Casual
Cuisine	Seafood
Recommended for	Bargain

Sat right on Porthminster Beach, in the popular Cornish seaside town of Saint Ives, getting a table here in season takes a bit of forward planning. Nevertheless, with a handsome modern terrace that overlooks the immaculately clean beach, it's invariably packed throughout the summer thanks to a menu that understands its audience. Lunch offers simple seafood dishes that take in a few Asian influences, alongside a decent-sized vegetarian section and simple bowls of pasta for the kids. Things get a little more elaborate and expensive in the evening—but not prohibitively so—and the kids will still be alright.

CRAFT WORKS STREET KITCHEN

Lemon Quay House
Lemon Quay
Truro
Cornwall
England TR1 2PU
+44 7742875468
www.craftworkskitchen.co.uk

Opening hours	Open 7 days
Credit cards	Accepted but not AMEX or Diners
Price range	Budget
Style	Casual
Cuisine	Asian-Latin American
Recommended for	Regular neighborhood

"Street food done well, with an understanding of Asian cuisine."—Nathan Outlaw

L'ENCLUME

Cavendish Street
Cartmel
Cumbria
England LA11 6PZ
+44 1539536362
www.lenclume.co.uk

Recommended by
Tom Aikens, Sat Bains,
Liguang Han, Elizabeth Haigh

Opening hours	Closed Monday
Credit cards	Accepted
Price range	Expensive
Style	Smart casual
Cuisine	Modern British
Recommended for	Worth the travel

"Its cuisine showcases a great balance between bringing out the flavors of farm-fresh seasonal produce, and modern presentation and interpretation."—Liguang Han

Thanks to L'Enclume, the Lake District can offer greater culinary highlights than twee tea rooms and tourist traps churning out 'hearty' quiches for tired ramblers. Operating out of a former blacksmith's since 2006, head chef Simon Rogan was in the vanguard of the now ubiquitous approach of using local ingredients and remains one of the most innovative chefs to have graced the UK restaurant scene in the past decade. Rogan's passion for his produce, seeking out a perplexing variety of unusual herbs and vegetables, isn't yawn-inducingly worthy —nor is it PR puff. Rather, it is driven by a desire to serve decent ingredients in an eye-opening manner.

PULLMAN DINING CAR

7.30 a.m. from Newton Abbot to London
Devon
England
+44 3457000125
www.gwr.com

Recommended by
Mitch Tonks

Opening hours	Closed Saturday and Sunday
Credit cards	Accepted but not AMEX or Diners
Price range	Affordable
Style	Casual
Cuisine	British
Recommended for	Breakfast

"There is nothing like eating on the train: tablecloths, a Full English breakfast, smoked haddock or smoked salmon, heaps of fresh toast and cakes and Champagne if you wish."—Mitch Tonks

THE SEAHORSE

5 South Embankment
Dartmouth
Devon
England TQ6 9BH
+44 1803835147
www.seahorserestaurant.co.uk

Recommended by
Neil Borthwick, Henry Harris,
Martin Morales

Opening hours	Closed Monday and Sunday
Credit cards	Accepted but not Diners
Price range	Affordable
Style	Casual
Cuisine	Seafood
Recommended for	Worth the travel

"Fantastically cooked fish over coals, on the bone or off the bone but always perfectly cooked, with a view of the sea and great wines"—Neil Borthwick

The Devon flagship of accountant-turned-fishmonger-turned-self-taught-chef-and-restaurateur Mitch Tonks is, it shouldn't surprise you to hear, all about fish. While the smart-looking Seahorse on the bank of the River Dart does cater for carnivores with a couple of dishes under the heading 'Today's Meat', the majority, understandably, come here for the kitchen's way with seafood. Tonks's love of Italy comes across in a menu that features *insalata di polpo* (octopus salad), sea bream *al cartoccio* (steamed in a paper bag) and roasted ray wing with capers and aged Modena vinegar.

THE OLD INN

Drewsteignton
Exeter
Devon
England EX6 6QR
+44 1647281276
www.old-inn.co.uk

Recommended by
Shaun Hill

Opening hours	Closed Sunday to Tuesday
Credit cards	Accepted but not AMEX or Diners
Price range	Affordable
Style	Casual
Cuisine	Modern European
Recommended for	Worth the travel

"Great, unpretentious food. The real deal."
—Shaun Hill

EAST IN THE WEST

Recommended by
Mitch Tonks

75 Torquay Road
Paignton
Devon
England TQ2 2SE
+44 1803269875
www.eastinthewest.uk.com

Opening hours	Closed Sunday
Credit cards	Accepted
Price range	Affordable
Style	Smart casual
Cuisine	Indian
Recommended for	Regular neighborhood

"Easily the best curry outside of London. A totally different menu from the usual; well-made curries and homemade bread. I'm there a lot."—Mitch Tonks

HARBOUR KITCHEN

Recommended by
Mitch Tonks

16 Victoria Parade
Torquay
Devon
England Q1 2BB
+44 1803211075
www.harbourkitchen.co.uk

Opening hours	Open 7 days
Credit cards	Accepted but not AMEX or Diners
Price range	Affordable
Style	Casual
Cuisine	Seafood
Recommended for	Regular neighborhood

"Great inventive seafood."—Mitch Tonks

HIX OYSTER & FISH HOUSE

Recommended by
Martin Morales

Cobb Road
Lyme Regis
Dorset
England DT7 3JP
+44 1297446910
www.hixrestaurants.co.uk

Opening hours	Open 7 days
Credit cards	Accepted but not Diners
Price range	Affordable
Style	Casual
Cuisine	Seafood
Recommended for	Wish I'd opened

CRAB HOUSE CAFÉ

Recommended by
Martin Morales

Portland Road
Wyke Regis
Dorset
England DT4 9YU
+44 1305788867
www.crabhousecafe.co.uk

Opening hours	Closed Monday and Tuesday
Credit cards	Accepted but not AMEX or Diners
Price range	Affordable
Style	Casual
Cuisine	Seafood
Recommended for	Wish I'd opened

THE RABY HUNT

Recommended by
Samuel Nutter

Summerhouse
Darlington
Durham
England DL2 3UD
+44 1325374237
www.rabyhuntrestaurant.co.uk

Opening hours	Closed Sunday to Wednesday
Credit cards	Accepted but not Diners
Price range	Expensive
Style	Smart casual
Cuisine	Modern British
Recommended for	Wish I'd opened

"I also chose this restaurant in the last *Where Chefs Eat.* Since then James has gone on to achieve his second Michelin-star and an even busier restaurant in a very rural location. The food is fantastic and this really is a special place."—Samuel Nutter

THE LANDGATE BISTRO

Recommended by
Timothy Johnson

5–6 Landgate
Rye
East Sussex
England TN31 7LH
+44 1797222829
www.landgatebistro.co.uk

Opening hours	Closed Monday and Tuesday
Credit cards	Accepted but not Diners
Price range	Affordable
Style	Casual
Cuisine	Modern British
Recommended for	Regular neighborhood

"Good, honest food, cooked simply using local ingredients."—Timothy Johnson

THE HORSESHOES COUNTRY PUB

Recommended by
Lee Tiernan

Horseshoe Hill
Upshire
Essex
England EN9 3SN
+44 1992712745
www.thehorseshoes-countrypub.co.uk

Opening hours	Open 7 days
Credit cards	Accepted but not Diners
Price range	Affordable
Style	Casual
Cuisine	Gastropub
Recommended for	Regular neighborhood

"Perfect for a big lunch with my family before a walk in Epping Forest. We're always met with smiles and warm service."—Lee Tiernan

THE GUMSTOOL INN

Recommended by
Niall Keating

Calcot
Tetbury
Gloucestershire
England GL8 8YJ
+44 1666890391
www.calcot.co

Opening hours	Open 7 days
Credit cards	Accepted but not Diners
Price range	Affordable
Style	Casual
Cuisine	Modern British
Recommended for	Local favorite

STARGAZY FISH BAR

Recommended by
Niall Keating

London Road
Tetbury
Gloucestershire
England GL8 8JJ
+44 1666500690
www.stargazyfishbar.co.uk

Opening hours	Open 7 days
Credit cards	Accepted but not Diners
Price range	Budget
Style	Casual
Cuisine	Fish and Chips
Recommended for	Bargain

"One of the pricier chip shops, but nonetheless, a chip shop. Modern and clean, good variety, great batter and well-seasoned."—Niall Keating

TETBURY KEBAB VAN

Recommended by
Niall Keating

Tetbury Industrial Estate
Cirencester Road
Tetbury
Gloucestershire
England GL8 8
+44 7884206086

Opening hours	Open 7 days
Credit cards	Not accepted
Price range	Budget
Style	Casual
Cuisine	Fast Food
Recommended for	Late night

LILY'S VEGETARIAN INDIAN CUISINE

Recommended by
Adam Reid

75–83 Oldham Road
Ashton-under-Lyne
Greater Manchester
England OL6 7DF
+44 1613394774

Opening hours	Closed Tuesday
Credit cards	Accepted but not Diners
Price range	Budget
Style	Casual
Cuisine	Indian
Recommended for	Local favorite

EL GATO NEGRO

Recommended by
Adam Reid

52 King Street
Manchester
Greater Manchester
England M2 4LY
+44 1616948585
www.elgatonegrotapas.com

Opening hours	Open 7 days
Credit cards	Accepted but not Diners
Price range	Affordable
Style	Casual
Cuisine	Tapas
Recommended for	Local favorite

"Modern, trendy and stylish. A northerner cooking tapas—sums up the multicultural, diverse nature of Manchester."—Adam Reid

HISPI BISTRO

Recommended by
Adam Reid

1C School Lane
Manchester
Greater Manchester
England M20 6RD
+44 1614453996
www.hispi.net

Opening hours	Open 7 days
Credit cards	Accepted but not AMEX or Diners
Price range	Affordable
Style	Casual
Cuisine	Tapas
Recommended for	Regular neighborhood

MANCHESTER HOUSE

Recommended by
Adam Reid

18–22 Bridge Street
Manchester
Greater Manchester
England M3 3BZ
+44 1618352557
www.manchesterhouse.uk.com

Opening hours	Closed Monday and Sunday
Credit cards	Accepted but not Diners
Price range	Expensive
Style	Smart casual
Cuisine	Modern British
Recommended for	High end

"Adventurous cooking in a modern environment."
—Adam Reid

Aiden Byrne may want to put his televised
'Restaurant Wars' with Simon Rogan behind him,
as neither ended up with their desired Michelin
stars. But the theatrical, thoughtful dishes put out
by the open kitchens in this beautiful modern
restaurant—such as a frothy onion soup served in
an extraordinarily clever 'egg shell' made of cheese,
or butter-poached frog's legs with caviar—are well
worth any number of gongs. Leave time before (or
after) your meal for a trip up to the twelfth floor and
cocktails at the Lounge bar. The views are stunning.

MUGHLI CHARCOAL PIT

Recommended by
Adam Reid

30 Wilmslow Road
Manchester
Greater Manchester
England M14 5TQ
+44 1612480900
www.mughli.com

Opening hours	Open 7 days
Credit cards	Accepted but not AMEX
Price range	Budget
Style	Casual
Cuisine	Indian
Recommended for	Late night

"Good atmosphere with street-food style offering.
Perfect for late-night dining."—Adam Reid

POT KETTLE BLACK

Recommended by
Emily Hahn

14 Barton Arcade
Manchester
Greater Manchester
England M3 2BW
www.potkettleblackltd.co.uk

Opening hours	Open 7 days
Credit cards	Accepted but not AMEX or Diners
Price range	Budget
Style	Casual
Cuisine	Café-Bar
Recommended for	Breakfast

THE RABBIT IN THE MOON

Urbis Building
Cathedral Gardens
Todd Street
Manchester
Greater Manchester
England M4 3BG
+44 1618048560
www.therabbitinthemoon.com

Opening hours..Open 7 days
Credit cards.......................Accepted but not AMEX or Diners
Price range...Expensive
Style...Smart casual
Cuisine...Modern Asian
Recommended for...High end

If you've struggled to score a table at Michael O'Hare's flagship Man Behind the Curtain in Leeds (and you certainly aren't the only one), then chef and O'Hare protégé Luke Cockerill will show you that whatever Leeds has, Manchester can match with a similarly trailblazing menu of Asian-fusion food. Experimental to the point of surrealism, dishes such as miniature stargazy pies (where anchovies peek out of pastry casings) or squid ink bao with octopus tentacles (resembling a color-inverted hot dog) subvert and beguile, in a stark modernist room on the top of the Urbis building. A fine, and subversive, addition to the Manchester restaurant scene.

RUDY'S NEAPOLITAN PIZZA

9 Cotton Street
Manchester
Greater Manchester
England M4 5BF
+44 7931162059
www.rudyspizza.co.uk

Opening hours..Closed Monday
Reservation policy...No
Credit cards.......................Accepted but not AMEX or Diners
Price range..Budget
Style...Casual
Cuisine...Pizza
Recommended for...Bargain

SIAM SMILES THAI SUPERMARKET

48A George Street
Manchester
Greater Manchester
England M1 4HF
+44 1612371555

Opening hours..Open 7 days
Credit cards...............................Accepted but not AMEX
Price range..Budget
Style...Casual
Cuisine...Thai
Recommended for...Bargain

"Good food with absolutely no fuss."—Adam Reid

UMEZUSHI

4 Mirabel Street
Manchester
Greater Manchester
England M3 1PJ
+44 8718118877
www.umezushi.co.uk

Opening hours..Closed Monday
Credit cards.......................Accepted but not AMEX or Diners
Price range...Affordable
Style...Casual
Cuisine..Sushi
Recommended for...Local favorite

THE WAGGON INN

32–34 High Street
Uppermill
Greater Manchester
England OL3 6HR
+44 1457879106
www.thewaggoninn.co.uk

Opening hours..Open 7 days
Credit cards...Accepted
Price range...Affordable
Style...Casual
Cuisine...British
Recommended for...........................Regular neighborhood

"Informal and cosy, with good honest food and welcoming service."—Adam Reid

PULPO NEGRO

28 Broad Street
Alresford
Hampshire
England SO24 9AQ
+44 1962732262
www.pulponegro.co.uk

Opening hours	Closed Monday and Sunday
Credit cards	Accepted but not AMEX or Diners
Price range	Affordable
Style	Casual
Cuisine	Tapas
Recommended for	Regular neighborhood

"Andreas the chef-owner cooks beautiful Spanish dishes using a combination of quality Spanish produce and seasonal British ingredients."—James Durrant

THYME & TIDES DELI

The High Street
Stockbridge
Hampshire
England SO20 6HE
+44 1264810101
www.thymeandtidesdeli.co.uk

Opening hours	Open 7 days
Credit cards	Accepted but not AMEX or Diners
Price range	Affordable
Style	Casual
Cuisine	Bistro-Deli
Recommended for	Breakfast

"It's perfect for a weekend brunch with the family!"
—James Durrant

THE CHESIL RECTORY

1 Chesil Street
Winchester
Hampshire
England SO23 0HU
+44 1962851555
www.chesilrectory.co.uk

Opening hours	Open 7 days
Credit cards	Accepted
Price range	Affordable
Style	Casual
Cuisine	Modern British
Recommended for	Regular neighborhood

"I love this restaurant for their super-seasonal cooking, and the service is always great. This is an awesome neighborhood restaurant where I can happily sit back, relax and enjoy an evening off."—James Durrant

THE GOODS SHED RESTAURANT

Station Road West
Canterbury
Kent
England CT2 8AN
+44 1227459153
www.thegoodsshed.co.uk

Opening hours	Closed Monday
Credit cards	Accepted
Price range	Affordable
Style	Casual
Cuisine	British Bistro
Recommended for	Regular neighborhood

"Set in a massive warehouse near my house in Kent—it has brilliant food sellers and a wonderful, simple restaurant serving breakfast, lunch, and dinner using Kentish produce from the purveyors below."
—Stevie Parle

TED'S ROOM

11–13 Stone Street
Cranbrook
Kent
England TN17 3HF
+44 1580720880

Opening hours	Closed Sunday
Credit cards	Accepted
Price range	Budget
Style	Casual
Cuisine	Café
Recommended for	Breakfast

"Cosy and warm atmosphere with young, friendly, and helpful staff. Great coffee and bacon bagels."
—Timothy Johnson

THE CHAMBERS

Recommended by
Mark Sargeant

Cheriton Place
Folkestone
Kent
England CT20 2BB
+44 1303223333

Opening hours	Closed Sunday
Credit cards	Accepted but not Diners
Price range	Budget
Style	Casual
Cuisine	Mexican
Recommended for	Late night

"Great late-night bites and DJs."—Mark Sargeant

LUBENS

Recommended by
Mark Sargeant

24 Rendezvous Street
Folkestone
Kent
England CT20 1EZ
+44 1303487110
www.luben.co.uk

Opening hours	Open 7 days
Credit cards	Accepted but not Diners
Price range	Affordable
Style	Casual
Cuisine	Pizza
Recommended for	Regular neighborhood

"Great new local restaurant."—Mark Sargeant

THE SPORTSMAN

Recommended by
Mark Dobbie, Isaac McHale,
Andy Oliver, Luke Vandore-Mackay

Faversham Road
Seasalter
Kent
England CT5 4BP
+44 1227273370
www.thesportsmanseasalter.co.uk

Opening hours	Open 7 days
Credit cards	Accepted but not Diners
Price range	Affordable
Style	Casual
Cuisine	Gastropub
Recommended for	High end

"Whitstable is a great day trip from London. Chuck in some technically really impressive cooking with brilliant ingredients in an unpretentious atmosphere and you've got all the boxes ticked for any special occasion."—Mark Dobbie

Chef-proprietor Stephen Harris likes to describe The Sportsman as a 'grotty run-down pub by the sea', and that's exactly what it was before he took it over in 1999. Today, despite its somewhat desolate location three kilometers (two miles) outside Whitstable on the Kent coast, it has become a place of gastronomic pilgrimage based purely on the quality of its cooking. There are two menus—the daily-changing à la carte and a tasting menu that has to be ordered at least forty-eight hours in advance, and for which you'd be advised to put your name down when you book.

ELLIOT'S

Recommended by
Stephen Harris

1 Harbor Street
Whitstable
Kent
England CT5 1AG
+44 1227276608
www.no1harborstreet.co.uk

Opening hours	Open 7 days
Credit cards	Accepted but not Diners
Price range	Affordable
Style	Casual
Cuisine	Modern British
Recommended for	Breakfast

"Good coffee and food. A busy, popular place—I usually have smoked salmon and scrambled eggs."
—Stephen Harris

HARBOR STREET TAPAS

Recommended by
Stephen Harris

48 Harbor Street
Whitstable
Kent
England CT5 1AQ
+44 1227273373
www.streettapas.com

Opening hours	Closed Monday and Tuesday
Reservation policy	No
Credit cards	Accepted but not Diners
Price range	Affordable
Style	Casual
Cuisine	Tapas
Recommended for	Regular neighborhood

"It's my local and I'm very lucky to have it. No bookings, which really suits me. Food is a very good standard and the service is friendly."—Stephen Harris

TEA & TIMES

36A High Street
Whitstable
Kent
England CT5 1BQ
+44 1227262639

Opening hours	Open 7 days
Credit cards	Accepted but not Diners
Price range	Budget
Style	Casual
Cuisine	Café
Recommended for	Breakfast

WHEELERS OYSTER BAR

8 High Street
Whitstable
Kent
England CT5 1BQ
+44 1227273311
www.wheelersoysterbar.com

Opening hours	Closed Wednesday
Credit cards	Accepted but not Diners
Price range	Affordable
Style	Casual
Cuisine	Seafood
Recommended for	Regular neighborhood

"It's a local landmark and has a good seafood menu."
—Stephen Harris

THE WHITSTABLE OYSTER COMPANY

Horsebridge
Whitstable
Kent
England CT5 1BU
+44 1227276856
www.whitstableoystercompany.com

Opening hours	Open 7 days
Credit cards	Accepted but not Diners
Price range	Affordable
Style	Casual
Cuisine	Seafood
Recommended for	Local favorite

"Beautiful location with sea views. Oysters and
Guinness in the bar is a must."—Stephen Harris

NORTHCOTE

Northcote Road
Blackburn
Lancashire
England BB6 8BE
+44 1254240555
www.northcote.com

Opening hours	Open 7 days
Credit cards	Accepted but not Diners
Price range	Affordable
Style	Casual
Cuisine	Modern British
Recommended for	Local favorite

"The food is amazing and very inspiring. A huge array
of wonderful dishes created by a wonderfull team."
—Robert Ortiz

THE GUNTON ARMS

Cromer Road
Norwich
Norfolk
England NR11 8TZ
+44 1263832010
www.theguntonarms.co.uk

Opening hours	Open 7 days
Credit cards	Accepted
Price range	Affordable
Style	Casual
Cuisine	Modern British
Recommended for	Worth the travel

"Beautiful pub with rooms, with the greatest modern
art collection outside a gallery. Remote location on
a Norfolk game estate, a great area for walking. The
staff are brilliant—very professional but also fun and
friendly."—Ben Tish

BAR IBERICO

17–19 Carlton Street
Nottingham
Nottinghamshire
England NG1 1NL
+44 1159881133
www.ibericotapas.com

Opening hours	Open 7 days
Credit cards	Accepted
Price range	Affordable
Style	Casual
Cuisine	Tapas
Recommended for	Local favorite

"Great tapas bar; walk-in only, great buzz and fantastic food."— Sat Bains

THE COD'S SCALLOPS

170 Bramcote Lane
Nottingham
Nottinghamshire
England NG8 2QP
+44 1159854107
www.codsscallops.com

Opening hours	Closed Sunday
Credit cards	Accepted but not AMEX or Diners
Price range	Budget
Style	Casual
Cuisine	Fish and Chips
Recommended for	Regular neighborhood

"Brilliant local chippy, cooking fresh fish with traditional beef dripping."—Sat Bains

SAT BAINS

Lenton Lane
Nottingham
Nottinghamshire
England NG7 2SA
+44 1159866566
www.restaurantsatbains.com

Opening hours	Closed Monday, Tuesday and Sunday
Credit cards	Accepted but not AMEX
Price range	Expensive
Style	Smart casual
Cuisine	Modern British
Recommended for	Worth the travel

"This is the epitome of a destination restaurant. A truly world-class dining experience."—Paul Foster

One of the UK's most gastronomically adventurous destination restaurants is unconventionally set on the industrial outskirts of Nottingham. A modern take on the old-fashioned concept of the husband and wife-run restaurant with rooms, Sat and Amanda Bains's edgily-located, urban oasis is housed in a collection of renovated Victorian farm buildings that predate the panorama of pylons. Book a night in one of the eight rooms, plus dinner at either the 'Chef's Table' or the 'Kitchen Bench' if you want to get closer to the cutting-edge but playful cooking.

THE WOLLATON

Lambourne Drive
Nottingham
Nottinghamshire
England NG8 1GR
+44 1159288610
www.molefacepubcompany.co.uk

Opening hours	Open 7 days
Credit cards	Accepted but not AMEX
Price range	Affordable
Style	Casual
Cuisine	Gastropub
Recommended for	Regular neighborhood

"They do great breakfasts and Sunday roasts."
—Sat Bains

ZAAP THAI STREET FOOD

Bromley Place
Nottingham
Nottinghamshire
England NG1 6JG
+44 1159470204
www.zaapthai.co.uk

Opening hours	Open 7 days
Credit cards	Accepted but not AMEX
Price range	Budget
Style	Casual
Cuisine	Thai
Recommended for	Bargain

"A brilliant mix of authentic Thai street-food at great prices. It's fast and furious."—Sat Bains

LITTLE AMSTERDAM

13–14 North Bar Street
Banbury
Oxfordshire
England OX16 0TF
+44 1295279140
www.littleamsterdam.co

Opening hours	Closed Monday
Credit cards	Accepted
Price range	Budget
Style	Casual
Cuisine	Dutch
Recommended for	Regular neighborhood

LE MANOIR AUX QUAT'SAISONS

Church Road
Oxford
Oxfordshire
England OX44 7PD
+44 1844278881
www.belmond.com

Opening hours	Open 7 days
Credit cards	Accepted
Price range	Expensive
Style	Smart casual
Cuisine	French
Recommended for	Worth the travel

"Great food from a fantastic, machine of a kitchen operation. Beautiful building and surrounds make for an individual and considered dining experience."
—Christian Edwardson

NUT TREE INN

Murcott
Oxford
Oxfordshire
England OX5 2RE
+44 1865331253
www.nuttreeinn.co.uk

Opening hours	Open 7 days
Credit cards	Accepted but not AMEX or Diners
Price range	Affordable
Style	Casual
Cuisine	Gastropub
Recommended for	Worth the travel

DASTAAN

447 Kingston Road
Epsom
Surrey
England KT19 0DB
+44 2087868999
www.dastaan.co.uk

Opening hours	Closed Monday
Credit cards	Accepted but not AMEX
Price range	Budget
Style	Casual
Cuisine	Indian
Recommended for	Bargain

"Indian food with outstanding finesse and incredible value for money. One of the best in the UK."
—Neil Borthwick

THE CROSS

16 New Street
Kenilworth
Warwickshire
England CV8 2EZ
+44 1926853840
www.thecrosskenilworth.co.uk

Opening hours	Open 7 days
Credit cards	Accepted
Price range	Affordable
Style	Smart casual
Cuisine	Modern British
Recommended for	Regular neighborhood

"This pub-restaurant serves some of the best food in Warwickshire; the comfortable, warm setting is very fitting for the stunning, countryside location."
—Paul Foster

AUBREY ALLEZ

Recommended by
Paul Foster

106 Warwick Street
Royal Leamington Spa
Warwickshire
England CV32 4QP
+44 1926801933
www.aubreyallez.co.uk

Opening hours	Closed Sunday
Credit cards	Accepted
Price range	Budget
Style	Casual
Cuisine	Café
Recommended for	Breakfast

"Serves great produce, simply cooked; and really good coffee."—Paul Foster

COFFEE ARCHITECTS

Recommended by
Robert Ortiz

39 Warwick Street
Royal Leamington Spa
Warwickshire
England CV32 5JX
+44 1926339955
www.coffeearchitects.com

Opening hours	Closed Monday
Credit cards	Accepted
Price range	Budget
Style	Casual
Cuisine	Bakery-Café-Deli
Recommended for	Bargain

"Beautiful sandwiches, nice coffee, and great salads."
—Robert Ortiz

WOFON

Recommended by
Paul Foster

21 Regent Grove
Royal Leamington Spa
Warwickshire
England CV32 4NN
+44 1926330399
www.wofon.co.uk

Opening hours	Closed Sunday
Credit cards	Accepted but not AMEX or Diners
Price range	Budget
Style	Casual
Cuisine	Asian
Recommended for	Bargain

"Serves amazing noodle, ramen and rice dishes.
Great prices and massive portions."—Paul Foster

THE BOOT INN

Recommended by
Adam Stokes

Old Warwick Road
Solihull
Warwickshire
England B94 6JU
+44 1564782464
www.lovelypubs.co.uk

Opening hours	Open 7 days
Credit cards	Accepted but not AMEX or Diners
Price range	Affordable
Style	Casual
Cuisine	Gastropub
Recommended for	Regular neighborhood

THE ORANGE TREE

Recommended by
Adam Stokes

Warwick Road
Solihull
Warwickshire
England B93 0BN
+44 1564785364
www.lovelypubs.co.uk

Opening hours	Open 7 days
Credit cards	Accepted
Price range	Affordable
Style	Casual
Cuisine	Gastropub
Recommended for	Bargain

ADAM'S RESTAURANT

Recommended by
Robert Ortiz

16 Waterloo Street
Birmingham
West Midlands
England B2 5UG
+44 1216433745
www.adamsrestaurant.co.uk

Opening hours	Closed Monday and Sunday
Credit cards	Accepted
Price range	Expensive
Style	Smart casual
Cuisine	Modern British
Recommended for	High end

NOSH & QUAFF

130 Colmore Row
Birmingham
West Midlands
England B3 3AP
+44 1212364246
www.noshandquaff.co.uk

Opening hours	Open 7 days
Credit cards	Accepted
Price range	Affordable
Style	Casual
Cuisine	American
Recommended for	Late night

"The quality of the ingredients is superb and the atmosphere is amazing."—Adam Stokes

PAUL

68A East Mews
Birmingham
West Midlands
England B2 4XJ
+44 1216439085
www.paul-uk.com

Opening hours	Open 7 days
Credit cards	Accepted but not Diners
Price range	Budget
Style	Casual
Cuisine	Bakery
Recommended for	Breakfast

"Their palmiers dipped in a black coffee is the ultimate brekkie!"—Gareth Ward

PHO

Stephenson Place
Birmingham
West Midlands
England B2 4XJ
+44 1213928915
www.phocafe.co.uk

Opening hours	Open 7 days
Credit cards	Accepted but not AMEX or Diners
Price range	Budget
Style	Casual
Cuisine	Vietnamese
Recommended for	Bargain

"This is my favorite type of food and although Pho is a chain restaurant the food is amazing."—Gareth Ward

Pho is that rarest of things—a nationwide chain that doesn't seem to have sacrificed much of its attention to quality as it's grown, and has retained a loyal following for its short, focused menu. The pho —noodle soup—is the main draw, available in a variety of flavors but generally featuring a nice, rich animal-stock base, though salt-and-pepper chicken and beef in betel leaves are well worth your attention as well. Also, though the restaurants themselves are perfectly pleasant places to hang out, bear in mind their delivery option, where the pho comes cleverly packed up in a kind of self-assembly kit. Great fun.

PURECRAFT BAR AND KITCHEN

30 Waterloo Street
Birmingham
West Midlands
England B2 5TJ
+44 1212375666
www.purecraftbars.com

Opening hours	Open 7 days
Credit cards	Accepted
Price range	Affordable
Style	Casual
Cuisine	British
Recommended for	Bargain

"Homely classics like Scotch eggs and fish and chips, done in a very accurate way."— Adam Stokes

PURNELL'S

55 Cornwall Street
Birmingham
West Midlands
England B3 2DH
+44 122129799
www.purnellsrestaurant.com

Opening hours	Closed Monday and Sunday
Credit cards	Accepted
Price range	Expensive
Style	Smart casual
Cuisine	Modern British
Recommended for	High end

"I had the best meal of my life there."—Gareth Ward

RAJA MONKEY

Recommended by
Adam Stokes

1355 Stratford Road
Birmingham
West Middlands
England B28 9HW
+44 1217779090
www.rajamonkey.co.uk

Opening hours	Closed Monday
Credit cards	Accepted but not AMEX or Diners
Price range	Affordable
Style	Casual
Cuisine	Indian
Recommended for	Bargain

SUSHI PASSION

Recommended by
Glynn Purnell

Great Western Arcade
Birmingham
West Midlands
England B2 5HU
+44 1212382933
www.sushi-passion.com

Opening hours	Open 7 days
Credit cards	Accepted
Price range	Affordable
Style	Casual
Cuisine	Sushi
Recommended for	Regular neighborhood

"Without a doubt, Sushi Passion is my favorite place to eat in Birmingham. The original Sushi Passion sits within the markets, where you literally see the fish being delivered and then eat it straight away. The second restaurant is in the Great Western Arcade, and in between lunch and dinner service I often take the team there for a bite to eat. You can either sit at a table or on the floor in true Japanese style, or at the sushi bar where you can watch the chefs prepare the dishes."—Glynn Purnell

THE SPORTSMAN CLUB

Recommended by
Carl Clarke

13–15 High Street
West Bromwich
West Midlands
England B70 6PP
+44 1215531353
www.thesportsmanclub.co.uk

Opening hours	Open 7 days
Credit cards	Accepted
Price range	Affordable
Style	Casual
Cuisine	Bengali
Recommended for	Local favorite

"Proper Bengali grill in the back of an old pub where they use a charcoal oven."—Carl Clarke

WOOLYKNIT CAFE

Recommended by
Adam Reid

Unit 5 Warth Mill
Huddersfield Road
Saddleworth
West Yorkshire
England OL3 5PJ
+44 1457878660
www.woolyknit.com

Opening hours	Open 7 days
Credit cards	Accepted but not AMEX
Price range	Budget
Style	Casual
Cuisine	British-Café
Recommended for	Breakfast

"Unfussy, hearty cooking in a quaint Yorkshire mill, surrounded by the Saddleworth countryside."
—Adam Reid

THE POTTING SHED

Recommended by
Niall Keating

The Street
Crudwell
Malmsbury
Wiltshire
England SN16 9EW
+44 1666577833
www.thepottingshedpub.com

Opening hours..Open 7 days
Credit cards.....................................Accepted but not AMEX
Price range..Affordable
Style..Casual
Cuisine...Gastropub
Recommended for...............................Regular neighborhood

"Cozy, dog-friendly pub with exposed brick and wooden beams, fire places, good cask ales, hospitable staff, and good food."—Niall Keating

THE BUTCHERS ARMS

Recommended by
Shaun Hill

Lime Street
Eldersfield
Worcestershire
England GL19 4NX
+44 1452840381
www.thebutchersarms.net

Opening hours..Open 7 days
Credit cards.......................Accepted but not AMEX or Diners
Price range..Affordable
Style..Casual
Cuisine...Gastropub
Recommended for..Local favorite

"A REAL TRIP DOWN MEMORY LANE."
SAMI TAMIMI P423

"Delicious food but not fussy."
RICHARD CORRIGAN P415

"EVER-CHANGING AND CREATIVE."
TOM MOXON P410

LONDON

"One of the most technically proficient kitchens in London... exceptional quality food."
JOSHUA KATZ P412

"This place has incredible history and oozes character."
ALFRED PRASAD P418

"A gem."
HELENA PUOLAKKA P411

"It never disappoints!"
OMAR ALLIBHOY P416

LONDON

WEST

N̂

SCALE

0   400   800   1200 yd.

KERB

Recommended by
Tom Moxon

London
www.kerbfood.com

Opening hours	Variable
Credit cards	Not accepted
Price range	Affordable
Style	Casual
Cuisine	Street food
Recommended for	Local favorite

"Although it's not a restaurant as such, Kerb reflects
the diversity in London's food scene: it's ever-
changing, fast, informal, creative, with lots of different
cuisines in one place and a range of operators putting
effort into doing one thing really well."—Tom Moxon

NORTH CHINA RESTAURANT

Recommended by
Henry Harris

305 Uxbridge Road
Acton
London W3 9QU
+44 2089929183
www.northchina.co.uk

Opening hours	Open 7 days
Credit cards	Accepted
Price range	Affordable
Style	Casual
Cuisine	Chinese
Recommended for	Regular neighborhood

"Lawrence Lou understands good service and his
kitchen cooks traditional dishes very well. Jade
dumplings, grilled dumplings, salt and pepper squid
and twice-cooked pork belly with chile always nourish
and comfort."—Henry Harris

AWESOME THAI

Recommended by
Martin Morales,
Luke Vandore-Mackay

68 Church Road
Barnes
London SW13 0DQ
+44 2085637027
www.awesomethai.co.uk

Opening hours	Open 7 days
Credit cards	Accepted but not AMEX
Price range	Affordable
Style	Casual
Cuisine	Thai
Recommended for	Regular neighborhood

OLYMPIC STUDIOS

Recommended by
Henrik Ritzen

117–123 Church Road
Barnes
London SW13 9HL
+44 2089125170
www.olympicstudios.co.uk

Opening hours	Open 7 days
Credit cards	Accepted
Price range	Affordable
Style	Casual
Cuisine	Modern British Brasserie
Recommended for	Breakfast

RIVA

Recommended by
Martin Morales

169 Church Road
Barnes
London SW13 9HR
+44 2087480434

Opening hours	Open 7 days
Credit cards	Accepted
Price range	Affordable
Style	Casual
Cuisine	Italian
Recommended for	Regular neighborhood

AKASH TANDOORI

Recommended by
Alyn Williams

70 Northcote Road
Battersea
London SW11 6QL
+44 2072286434
www.akashtandoori.com

Opening hours	Open 7 days
Credit cards	Accepted but not AMEX
Price range	Affordable
Style	Casual
Cuisine	Indian
Recommended for	Regular neighborhood

PIZZA METRO

Recommended by
Tom Moxon

64 Battersea Rise
Battersea
London SW11 1EQ
+44 2072283812
www.pizzametropizza.com

Opening hours	Open 7 days
Credit cards	Accepted
Price range	Affordable
Style	Casual
Cuisine	Pizza
Recommended for	Regular neighborhood

HEREFORD ROAD

Recommended by
Henry Harris, Thomasina Miers,
Helena Puolakka, Tania Steytler

3 Hereford Road
Bayswater
London W2 4AB
+44 2077271144
www.herefordroad.org

Opening hours	Open 7 days
Credit cards	Accepted
Price range	Affordable
Style	Casual
Cuisine	British
Recommended for	Regular neighborhood

"Simple, honest, super seasonal English cooking.
A gem."—Helena Puolakka

The West London chapter of the school of St. John,
Hereford Road first brought its gutsy, no-nonsense
cooking built around British seasonal ingredients to
Notting Hill in 2007. Driven by hardworking
chef-proprietor Tom Pemberton, formerly head chef
of St. John Bread & Wine, it's housed in a Victorian
butcher's shop; open kitchen in the window where
the counter would have been, wrought ironwork on
the ceiling above the red-leather upholstered
loveseats. The daily-changing menu delivers perfect
simplicity, from whole fish and helpings of offal to
bowls of rice pudding and jam (jelly). Their set lunch
remains one of London's great bargains.

KHANS

Recommended by
Omar Allibhoy

13–15 Westbourne Grove
Bayswater
London W2 4UA
+44 2077275420
www.khansrestaurant.com

Opening hours	Open 7 days
Credit cards	Accepted
Price range	Budget
Style	Casual
Cuisine	Indian
Recommended for	Wish I'd opened

"It's a place my Indian grandfather used to visit thirty
years ago, and it's still kicking ass with the chiles.
There is a reason it's been open for so long."
—Omar Allibhoy

HUNAN

Recommended by
Cary Docherty

51 Pimlico Road
Belgravia
London SW1W 8NE
+44 2077305712
www.hunanlondon.com

Opening hours	Closed Sunday
Credit cards	Accepted
Price range	Affordable
Style	Casual
Cuisine	Chinese
Recommended for	Regular neighborhood

CAFÉ COLBERT

Recommended by
Mark Jarvis

50–52 Sloane Square
Chelsea
London SW1W 8AX
+44 2077302804
www.colbertchelsea.com

Opening hours	Open 7 days
Credit cards	Accepted
Price range	Affordable
Style	Smart casual
Cuisine	French
Recommended for	Local favorite

ELYSTAN STREET

Recommended by
Tom Aikens, Nieves Barragán Mohacho,
Adam Byatt, Richard Corrigan,
Isaac McHale, Jake Nicolson

43 Elystan Street
Chelsea
London SW3 3NT
+44 2076285005
www.elystanstreet.com

Opening hours	Open 7 days
Credit cards	Accepted
Price range	Affordable
Style	Smart casual
Cuisine	Modern British
Recommended for	Local favorite

"Phil is cooking exactly what punters want to eat. He doesn't mess around with the ingredients and he only uses the best of the best. I went in for dinner shortly after it opened and I've never felt so relaxed in a restaurant. Great wine list, great food, just sheer pleasure!"—Richard Corrigan

THE FRANKLIN

Recommended by
Alfredo Russo

24 Egerton Gardens
Chelsea
London SW3 2DB
+44 2075845533
www.thefranklinlondon.com

Opening hours	Open 7 days
Credit cards	Accepted
Price range	Expensive
Style	Smart casual
Cuisine	Modern Italian
Recommended for	Breakfast

RESTAURANT GORDON RAMSAY

Recommended by
Cary Docherty,
Paul Walsh

68 Royal Hospital Road
Chelsea
London SW3 4HP
+44 2073524441
www.gordonramsayrestaurants.com

Opening hours	Closed Saturday and Sunday
Credit cards	Accepted
Price range	Expensive
Style	Formal
Cuisine	European
Recommended for	High end

"This restaurant is still the place to go to celebrate a special occasion. Everything about it is top of the class in London. The precision in the cooking always impresses, as does the way the team in the front of house make it all look effortless."—Cary Docherty

MEDLAR

Recommended by
Joshua Katz

438 King's Road
Chelsea
London SW10 0LJ
+44 2073491900
www.medlarrestaurant.co.uk

Opening hours	Open 7 days
Credit cards	Accepted
Price range	Expensive
Style	Smart casual
Cuisine	French
Recommended for	High end

"Medlar has one of the most technically proficient kitchens in London and always turns out food of an exceptional quality."—Joshua Katz

RABBIT

Recommended by
Frankie van Loo

172 Kings Road
Chelsea
London SW3 4UP
+44 2037500172
www.rabbit-restaurant.com

Opening hours	Open 7 days
Credit cards	Accepted
Price range	Affordable
Style	Casual
Cuisine	Modern British
Recommended for	Regular neighborhood

"An amazing concept of real field-to-fork dining by the Gladwin Brothers, who between the three of them run the kitchens, front of house and their farm, which supplies the produce."—Frankie van Loo

VINEET BHATIA

Recommended by
Rohit Ghai

10 Lincoln Street
Chelsea
London SW3 2TS
+44 2072251881
www.vineetbhatia.london

Opening hours	Closed Monday
Credit cards	Accepted
Price range	Expensive
Style	Smart casual
Cuisine	Modern Indian
Recommended for	High end

"Vineet Bhatia London is the flagship restaurant from the award-winning chef and restaurateur, set within a restored Georgian townhouse, with calming light grey interspersed with splashes of yellow and ornate tiles. This is one of my favorite places. I always consider it for special occasions because they offer a tasting menu with or without wine pairing and also the staff are knowledgeable and professional."—Rohit Ghai

VQ (VINGT-QUATRE)

Recommended by
Ben Murphy

325 Fulham Road
Chelsea
London SW10 9QL
+44 2073767224
www.vqrestaurants.com

Opening hours	Open 7 days
Credit cards	Accepted
Price range	Budget
Style	Casual
Cuisine	Modern European
Recommended for	Late night

"Open twenty-four hours...need I say more! The fry-ups are great after a night out and the vibe is cool at all hours."—Ben Murphy

NGON

Recommended by
Luke Vandore-Mackay

195 Chiswick High Road
Chiswick
London W4 2DR
+44 2089949630

Opening hours	Open 7 days
Credit cards	Accepted
Price range	Budget
Style	Casual
Cuisine	Vietnamese
Recommended for	Bargain

"Big fan of Café Ngon—great pho for not much cash."
—Luke Vandore-Mackay

THE DUKE OF SUSSEX

Recommended by
Sami Tamimi

75 South Parade
Chiswick
London W4 5LF
+44 2087428801
www.thedukeofsussex.co.uk

Opening hours	Open 7 days
Credit cards	Accepted
Price range	Affordable
Style	Casual
Cuisine	English-Spanish
Recommended for	Regular neighborhood

"It's a beautiful building with a dining room and a bar with huge windows that face Acton Green. It also has a large garden, which in the summer you'll have to come in early to secure a table. Staff are super friendly. They mostly do Spanish food but also a mean Sunday roast."—Sami Tamimi

FRANCO MANCA

Recommended by
Henrik Ritzen

144 Chiswick High Road
Chiswick
London W4 1PU
+44 2087474822
www.francomanca.co.uk

Opening hours	Open 7 days
Credit cards	Accepted
Price range	Budget
Style	Casual
Cuisine	Pizza
Recommended for	Bargain

"Good quality sourdough pizza, at a good price. Kid friendly."—Henrlk Rltzen

HEDONE

Recommended by
Daniel Berlin, Stephen Harris,
James Lowe, Sameer Taneja

301–303 Chiswick High Road
Chlswlck
London W4 4HH
+44 2087470377
www.hedonerestaurant.com

Opening hours	Closed Monday and Sunday
Credit cards	Accepted
Price range	Expensive
Style	Smart casual
Cuisine	Modern European
Recommended for	High end

"Hedone is a restaurant that clearly displays the best of French and British produce alongside excellent technique."—James Lowe

Mikael Jonsson has come a long way: he was originally a lawyer and then, thanks to severe food allergies, became an ingredient-obsessed blogger. When he opened this Chiswick restaurant in 2011 it secured a Michelin star in just fourteen months. Its name roughly translating as 'pleasure', the same earnestness dictates the room's look, with bare bricks and a very open-plan kitchen. There's no fixed menu, but instead a long and elegant procession of dishes celebrating the very best British ingredients—such as wild Dorset turbot and Cornish rock oysters.

VINOTECA

Recommended by
Luke Vandore-Mackay

18 Devonshire Road
Chiswick
London W4 2HD
+44 2037018822
www.vinoteca.co.uk

Opening hours	Open 7 days
Credit cards	Accepted
Price range	Affordable
Style	Casual
Cuisine	Modern European
Recommended for	Local favorite

"I had a fantastic meal at Vinoteca on Valentine's Day.
I was furious that I had to go out on Valentine's Day
and arrived in a mood. The food, booze, and service
(and my wife) made for a great night."
—Luke Vandore-Mackay

BRICKWOOD COFFEE AND BREAD

Recommended by
Phil Carmichael

16 Clapham Common
Clapham
London SW4 7AB
+44 2078199614
www.brickwoodlondon.com

Opening hours	Open 7 days
Credit cards	Accepted but not AMEX or Diners
Price range	Affordable
Style	Casual
Cuisine	Australian
Recommended for	Breakfast

"Best coffee and breakfast in London. Busy, bustling,
always great food: the kumara (sweet potato) toast is
amazing."—Phil Carmichael

THE DAIRY

Recommended by
Tom Aikens, Adam Byatt,
Phil Carmichael, Elizabeth Haigh,
Mark Jarvis, Andi Oliver,
Shaun Searley, Paul Walsh

15 The Pavement
Clapham
London SW4 0HY
+44 2076224165
www.the-dairy.co.uk

Opening hours	Closed Monday
Credit cards	Accepted but not AMEX
Price range	Affordable
Style	Casual
Cuisine	Modern British
Recommended for	Local favorite

"Robin Gill has nailed the new bistro idea:
unbelievable food, great atmosphere, and great value
for money. A template for all local restaurants.
Unpretentious food packed with flavor and originality."
—Phil Carmichael

THE MANOR

Recommended by
Mark Jarvis,
Tom Moxon

148 Clapham Manor Street
Clapham
London SW4 6BX
+44 2077204662
www.themanorclapham.co.uk

Opening hours	Closed Monday
Credit cards	Accepted but not AMEX
Price range	Affordable
Style	Casual
Cuisine	Modern British
Recommended for	Regular neighborhood

"The Manor offers a cuisine that differs quite a bit
from what I cook at work and they come up with some
inventive flavor combinations. The food just tastes
good, it's not pretentious, the environment is laid
back, and value is surprisingly good."—Tom Moxon

MAY THE FIFTEENTH

Recommended by
Adam Byatt

47 Abbeville Road
Clapham
London SW4 9JX
+44 2087721110
www.maythe15th.com

Opening hours	Open 7 days
Credit cards	Accepted
Price range	Affordable
Style	Smart casual
Cuisine	British Bistro
Recommended for	Regular neighborhood

"May the Fifteenth is one of my favorite local
restaurants and always offers delicious, seasonal
food at a fantastic price."—Adam Byatt

THE ROASTERY

789 Wandsworth Road
Clapham
London SW8 3JQ

Opening hours	Open 7 days
Credit cards	Accepted
Price range	Budget
Style	Casual
Cuisine	Café
Recommended for	Breakfast

TRINITY RESTAURANT

4 The Polygon
Clapham
London SW4 0JG
+44 2076221199
www.trinityrestaurant.co.uk

Opening hours	Open 7 days
Credit cards	Accepted
Price range	Expensive
Style	Smart casual
Cuisine	Modern European-British
Recommended for	Regular neighborhood

"Adam Byatt really knows what people want to eat. It's delicious food but not fussy. An open kitchen really adds atmosphere to the restaurant and I always have a good time when I go."—Richard Corrigan

REINDEER CAFÉ

Unit 3, Wing Yip Business Centre
395 Edgware Road
Cricklewood
London NW2 6LN
+44 2084503330

Opening hours	Open 7 days
Credit cards	Accepted
Price range	Affordable
Style	Casual
Cuisine	Cantonese
Recommended for	Regular neighborhood

"I love their soy chicken, wonton noodles and roasted suckling pig."—Andrew Wong

ATARI-YA

1 Station Parade
Ealing
London W5 3LD
+44 2088963175
www.sushibaratariya.co.uk

Opening hours	Closed Monday and Tuesday
Credit cards	Accepted
Price range	Affordable
Style	Casual
Cuisine	Japanese
Recommended for	Local favorite

"A small, no-frills sushi spot with expertly-prepared nigiri. The relaxed environment makes a refreshing change from some of the capital's higher-end atmospheres."—Vineet Bhatia

EALING PARK TAVERN

222 South Ealing Road
Ealing
London W5 4RL
+44 2087581879
www.ealingparktavern.co.uk

Opening hours	Open 7 days
Credit cards	Accepted
Price range	Affordable
Style	Casual
Cuisine	Gastropub
Recommended for	Regular neighborhood

"Ealing Park Tavern is anything but your average gastropub. One of the best restaurants in the area, I have a special fondness for this place—it is unpretentious yet classy, offers great food that is affordable and is always incredibly charming."
—Vineet Bhatia

FAANOOS

481 Upper Richmond Road West
East Sheen
London SW14 7PU
+44 2088785738

Opening hours	Open 7 days
Credit cards	Accepted
Price range	Affordable
Style	Casual
Cuisine	Iranian-Persian
Recommended for	Regular neighborhood

LOCALE

Recommended by
Omar Allibhoy

222 Munster Road
Fulham
London SW6 6AY
+44 2073816137
www.localerestaurants.com

Opening hours................................Open 7 days
Credit cards......................................Accepted
Price range.......................................Affordable
Style..Casual
Cuisine...Italian
Recommended for............................Late night

"I always end up at this great Italian restaurant which serves a proper seafood linguine. Whenever I order that dish it never disappoints!"—Omar Allibhoy

SANTA MARIA PIZZARIA

Recommended by
Alyn Williams

94 Waterford Road
Fulham
London SW6 2HA
+44 2073842844
www.santamariapizzeria.com

Opening hours................................Open 7 days
Credit cards.....................Accepted but not Diners
Price range.......................................Affordable
Style..Casual
Cuisine...Italian
Recommended for.................Regular neighborhood

"Really good Neapolitan-style sourdough pizzas with great toppings; very lively and good service."
—Alyn Williams

101 THAI KITCHEN

Recommended by
Henrik Ritzen, Tania Steytler

352 King Street
Hammersmith
London W6 0RX
+44 2087466888
www.101thaikitchen.com

Opening hours................................Open 7 days
Credit cards......................................Accepted
Price range.......................................Affordable
Style..Casual
Cuisine...Isaan Thai
Recommended for.................Regular neighborhood

"Superb hot and authentic Isaan Thai, with Auntie Bee's Southern specialities."—Tania Steytler

L'AMOROSA

Recommended by
Henrik Ritzen

278 King Street
Hammersmith
London W6 0SP
+44 2085630300
www.lamorosa.co.uk

Opening hours...............Closed Monday and Sunday
Credit cards...............Accepted but not AMEX or Diners
Price range.......................................Affordable
Style..Casual
Cuisine...Italian
Recommended for.................Regular neighborhood

"Very good uncomplicated Italian food."
—Henrik Ritzen

THE ANGLESEA ARMS

Recommended by
Allegra McEvedy

35 Wingate Road
Hammersmith
London W6 0UR
+44 2087491291
www.angleseaarmspub.co.uk

Opening hours................................Open 7 days
Credit cards.....................Accepted but not Diners
Price range.......................................Affordable
Style..Casual
Cuisine...Gastropub
Recommended for.................Regular neighborhood

THE BRACKENBURY

Recommended by
Allegra McEvedy

129–131 Brackenbury Road
Hammersmith
London W6 0BQ
+44 2087414928
www.brackenburyrestaurant.co.uk

Opening hours...............Closed Monday and Sunday
Credit cards......................................Accepted
Price range.......................................Affordable
Style..Casual
Cuisine...................................Modern European
Recommended for............................Local favorite

"Great cooking from ex-River Café chef Humphrey and relaxed atmosphere, all at the end of my road."
—Allegra McEvedy

THE PEAR TREE

Recommended by
Cary Docherty

14 Margravine Road
Hammersmith
London W6 8HJ
+44 2073811787
www.thepeartreefulham.com

Opening hours	Closed Monday
Credit cards	Accepted
Price range	Affordable
Style	Casual
Cuisine	Gastropub
Recommended for	Breakfast

THE RIVER CAFÉ

Recommended by
Adam Byatt, Olle T. Cellton,
Samantha & Samuel Clark,
Alexis Gauthier, Philip Howard,
Alex Jackson, Eyal Jagermann,
James Lowe, Colin Mackay,
Allegra McEvedy, Jon Rotheram,
Bevan Smith

Thames Wharf
Rainville Road
Hammersmith
London W6 9HA
+44 2073864200
www.rivercafe.co.uk

Opening hours	Open 7 days
Credit cards	Accepted
Price range	Expensive
Style	Smart Casual
Cuisine	Italian
Recommended for	High end

"It serves the finest ingredients cooked with complete understanding and in so doing they deliver food that is simply wonderful to eat. It is also host to the finest front of house team in London."—Philip Howard

Italian food made by Ruth Rogers and her team with the best produce money can buy, assembled in neo-rustic style, served in a stylish modern glass-fronted canteen (originally an old oil storage facility before architect Richard Rogers got hold of it), down where the old Thames does flow. That's been the River Café's formula for success since it opened in 1988. Co-founder Rose Gray, who sadly passed away in 2010, would be pleased to see nothing has changed in her absence. Perfect setting meets perfect produce meets educated service and a wine list, aside from the odd Champagne, that is all-Italian and runs from humble bottles to Super Tuscans.

FLAVORS OF INDIA

Recommended by
Alfred Prasad

11–13 High Street
Hounslow
London TW3 1RH
+44 2085777399
www.flavorsofindia.co.uk

Opening hours	Open 7 days
Credit cards	Accepted but not AMEX or Diners
Price range	Affordable
Style	Casual
Cuisine	Indian
Recommended for	Bargain

"For a North Indian fix, Flavors of India offers great value for money. They also do the best *momos* (steamed dumplings) in London."—Alfred Prasad

DOCK KITCHEN

Recommended by
Samantha & Samuel Clark

Portobello Docks
342–344 Ladbroke Grove
Kensal Green
London W10 5BU
+44 2089621610
www.dockkitchen.co.uk

Opening hours	Open 7 days
Credit cards	Accepted
Price range	Affordable
Style	Smart casual
Cuisine	International
Recommended for	Regular neighborhood

"Stevie is a very talented chef and as he, like us, trained at the River Café, his approach and combinations feel very natural to us. The restaurant is also part of Tom Dixon's studio near Ladbroke Grove, which in itself is striking and beautiful."—Samantha & Samuel Clark

MANOS GRILL

Recommended by
Carl Clarke

1026 Harrow Road
Kensal Green
London NW10 5NN
+44 2089684140

Opening hours	Open 7 days
Credit cards	Accepted
Price range	Affordable
Style	Casual
Cuisine	Portuguese
Recommended for	Local favorite

"Local cheap-as-chips Portuguese. Best piri piri chicken in London, cooked over embers."—Carl Clarke

THE ORANGERY AT KEW GARDENS

Kew Gardens
Kew
London TW9 3AB
+44 2083325000
www.kew.org

Opening hours	Open 7 days
Credit cards	Accepted but not AMEX
Price range	Budget
Style	Casual
Cuisine	Café
Recommended for	Breakfast

"Located in Kew Gardens—one of my favorite London institutions—the Orangery offers comfort food with charm and character in a spectacular setting."
—Alfred Prasad

THE ORIGINAL MAIDS OF HONOUR

288 Kew Road
Kew
London TW9 3DU
+44 2089402752
www.theoriginalmaidsofhonour.co.uk

Opening hours	Open 7 days
Credit cards	Accepted but not AMEX or Diners
Price range	Budget
Style	Casual
Cuisine	Café
Recommended for	Breakfast

"This place has incredible history and oozes character. I always end breakfast with a delicious 'Maid of honour' custard tart."—Alfred Prasad

WOODY GRILL

211–213 Kilburn High Road
Kilburn
London NW6 7JG
+44 2032040047
www.woody-grill.com

Opening hours	Open 7 days
Credit cards	Accepted
Price range	Budget
Style	Casual
Cuisine	Kurdish
Recommended for	Late night

"Authentic grill. Love their lamb soup with kidneys. Very comforting food when you've done a few too many shifts and forgotten to eat for days." —Carl Clarke

AMAYA

Halkin Arcade
19 Motcomb Street
Knightsbridge
London SW1X 8LB
+44 2078231166
www.amaya.biz

Opening hours	Open 7 days
Credit cards	Accepted
Price range	Expensive
Style	Smart casual
Cuisine	Modern Indian
Recommended for	Regular neighborhood

BAR BOULUD

Mandarin Oriental Hyde Park
66 Knightsbridge
Knightsbridge
London SW1X 7LA
+44 2072013899
www.barboulud.com

Opening hours	Open 7 days
Credit cards	Accepted
Price range	Affordable
Style	Smart casual
Cuisine	French
Recommended for	Late night

A restaurant in a five-star hotel in the heart of Knightsbridge might seem an unlikely late-night hangout for anyone other than the supremely wealthy and unimaginative, but then Bar Boulud isn't your typical operation. Firstly, the French bistro-style food, with all manner of charcuterie and tempting titbits, is much more accessible than many hotels offer. Secondly, it does some excellent burgers, including the traditional-style 'Yankee' and the 'Piggie' (BBQ pulled pork and green chile mayonnaise). What's more, you can wash it down with one of their uncommonly large selection of draught beers.

DINNER BY HESTON BLUMENTHAL

Recommended by
Omar Allibhoy,
Sat Bains, Vineet Bhatia,
Christian Domschitz,
Dan Graham, Adam Stokes

Mandarin Oriental Hyde Park
66 Knightsbridge
Knightsbridge
London SW1X 7LA
+44 2072013833
www.dinnerbyheston.com

Opening hours	Open 7 days
Credit cards	Accepted
Price range	Expensive
Style	Smart casual
Cuisine	Modern British
Recommended for	High end

"Dinner By Heston Blumenthal is a wonderful restaurant with great service and precise, delicious food. It's everything you could hope for from a Heston restaurant. In addition it's sleek, it's sophisticated and it oozes all the glamour of its Michelin-starred heritage."—Vineet Bhatia

Heston Blumenthal's Fat Duck follow up is a bustling brasserie with a playful menu, much of it surprisingly straightforward despite being inspired by a geeky love of British food history. Overlooking Hyde Park from the handsome rear of Knightsbridge's Mandarin Oriental, its spacious dining room seats 136 at large, luxuriously spaced tables. Inside the vast, glass-fronted kitchen, a giant Swiss-watch movement turning a series of spits catches the eye. So too the now trademark 'Meat Fruit'—a chicken liver parfait made to resemble a mandarin—and the 'Tipsy Cake'—vanilla custard-filled brioche served with pineapple roasted on that showcase rotisserie.

ZUMA

Recommended by
Gert de Mangeleer, Pete Denhart,
Lori Granito, Eyal Jagermann,
Mark Jarvis, Mitch Tonks

5 Raphael Street
Knightsbridge
London SW7 1DL
+44 2075841010
www.zumarestaurant.com

Opening hours	Open 7 days
Credit cards	Accepted
Price range	Expensive
Style	Smart casual
Cuisine	Japanese
Recommended for	High end

"Great music, atmosphere, consistently good food; sushi, grills, cocktails, and an extraordinary wine list. Top place but top money."—Mitch Tonks

BISTROT DE LUXE

Recommended by
Omar Allibhoy

66 Baker Street
Marylebone
London W1U 7DJ
+44 2079354007
www.galvinrestaurants.com

Opening hours	Open 7 days
Credit cards	Accepted
Price range	Affordable
Style	Smart casual
Cuisine	French
Recommended for	Regular neighborhood

CAROUSEL

Recommended by
Elizabeth Haigh

71 Blandford Street
Marylebone
London W1U 8AB
+44 2074875564
www.carousel-london.com

Opening hours	Closed Monday and Sunday
Credit cards	Accepted but not AMEX or Diners
Price range	Affordable
Style	Smart casual
Cuisine	Modern British
Recommended for	Wish I'd opened

CHILTERN FIREHOUSE

Recommended by
Jason Atherton, Gary Foulkes,
Philip Howard, Francesco Mazzei,
Mark Rosati

1 Chiltern Street
Marylebone
London W1U 7PA
+44 2070737676
www.chilternfirehouse.com

Opening hours	Open 7 days
Credit cards	Accepted
Price range	Affordable
Style	Smart casual
Cuisine	Modern European
Recommended for	Wish I'd opened

"Chiltern Firehouse has it all. Fantastic building serving super tasty food in a lovely environment. What more do you need? The outside space is lovely in the summer, where they have an oyster trolley doing the rounds whilst you sip chilled wine. A super cool and classy place."—Gary Foulkes

DAISY GREEN

Recommended by
Michael Reid

20 Seymour Street
Marylebone
London W1H 7HX
+44 2077233301
www.daisygreenfood.com

Opening hours	Open 7 days
Credit cards	Accepted but not AMEX or Diners
Price range	Affordable
Style	Casual
Cuisine	Australian
Recommended for	Regular neighborhood

"Closest thing to an Australian breakfast and coffee in London."—Michael Reid

FISCHER'S

Recommended by
Shaun Hill

50 Marylebone High Street
Marylebone
London W1U 5HN
+44 2074665501
www.fischers.co.uk

Opening hours	Open 7 days
Credit cards	Accepted
Price range	Affordable
Style	Casual
Cuisine	Austrian
Recommended for	Wish I'd opened

LA FROMAGERIE

Recommended by
Omar Allibhoy, Karam Sethi

2–6 Moxon Street
Marylebone
London W1U 4EW
+44 2079350341
www.lafromagerie.co.uk

Opening hours	Open 7 days
Credit cards	Accepted
Price range	Affordable
Style	Casual
Cuisine	European
Recommended for	Regular neighborhood

"This is, in my opinion, the best place to buy cheese in London. You can also purchase quality, fresh produce here. The breakfast is fantastic and the best ingredients are always used. However, be warned, it's not cheap."—Omar Allibhoy

THE GINGER PIG

Recommended by
Theo Randall

8–10 Moxon Street
Marylebone
London W1U 4EW
+44 2079357788
www.thegingerpig.co.uk

Opening hours	Open 7 days
Credit cards	Accepted
Price range	Affordable
Style	Casual
Cuisine	British
Recommended for	Bargain

"Best sausage roll in the world and the pies are all excellent too. It's the best value takeaway lunch in London. Pretty good butcher as well!"—Theo Randall

THE GOLDEN HIND

Recommended by
Tom Aikens

71a–73 Marylebone Lane
Marylebone
London W1U 2PN
+44 2074863644
www.thegoldenhind.com

Opening hours	Closed Sunday
Credit cards	Accepted
Price range	Affordable
Style	Casual
Cuisine	Fish and Chips
Recommended for	Bargain

JIKONI

Recommended by
Yotam Ottolenghi

19–21 Blandford Street
Marylebone
London W1U 3DH
+44 2070341988
www.jikonilondon.com

Opening hours	Open 7 days
Credit cards	Accepted but not AMEX or Diners
Price range	Affordable
Style	Casual
Cuisine	Modern British-Asian-East African
Recommended for	Wish I'd opened

"This is exactly the sort of food I want: food that both comforts and surprises at once. I love the atmosphere of the restaurant too: so much color and comfort."
—Yotam Ottolenghi

MEATLIQUOR
74 Welbeck Street
Marylebone
London W1G 0BA
+44 2072244239
www.meatliquor.com

Opening hours	Open 7 days
Credit cards	Accepted
Price range	Budget
Style	Casual
Cuisine	Burgers
Recommended for	Late night

"Great late-night burger. It's rough and ready and the burger arrives in paper—very street-food style. My favorite is the Dead Hippie: two French mustard-fried beef patties, Dead Hippie sauce, lettuce, cheese, pickles, minced white onions. They do lots of different fries: covered in green chile sauce, for example, or melted cheddar cheese and pickled jalapeños. It's all grungy which is what you want late at night."
—Tom Aikens

OPSO
10 Paddington Street
Marylebone
London W1U 5QL
+44 2074875088
www.opso.co.uk

Opening hours	Open 7 days
Credit cards	Accepted
Price range	Affordable
Style	Casual
Cuisine	Modern Greek
Recommended for	Regular neighborhood

PATTY & BUN
54 James Street
Marylebone
London W1U 1HE
+44 2074873188
www.pattyandbun.co.uk

Opening hours	Open 7 days
Credit cards	Accepted
Price range	Budget
Style	Casual
Cuisine	Burgers
Recommended for	Bargain

"After a long day, not much beats a late night, juicy 'Jose Jose' Chilli burger from Patty & Bun. We now have two sites next to them, so it's very hard to walk past on an empty stomach."—Tom Moxon

THE PROVIDORES
109 Marylebone High Street
Marylebone
London W1U 4RX
+44 2079356175
www.theprovidores.co.uk

Opening hours	Open 7 days
Credit cards	Accepted
Price range	Affordable
Style	Smart casual
Cuisine	Tapas
Recommended for	Breakfast

"The Providores is an institution, some of the finest breakfasts around. They started the Antipodean trend of great breakfasts and coffee in London, which we have all become so familiar with now." Selin Kiazim

This Marylebone High Street establishment has been the darling of London brunchers since 2001. Come any time of day and you'll be welcomed by smiling service and knockout blends of flavor, but breakfasts in the Tapa Room will exceed your wildest dreams. Chef Peter Gordon creates true fusion food without forgetting his Kiwi roots, which is reflected in the wine list that includes a huge selection of New Zealand wine. Popular favorites include Turkish (poached) eggs with whipped yogurt and hot chile butter on sourdough, or grilled chorizo with sweet potato and miso mash, garlic labneh (strained yoghurt) and star anise cashew nut praline. A solid Bloody Mary, tamarillo and kiwi fruit smoothies, and excellent coffee provide a memorable morning hit.

RANOUSH JUICE

Recommended by
Tom Aikens, Joshua Katz,
Andi Oliver

43 Edgware Road
Marylebone
London W2 2JE
+44 2077235929
www.maroush.com

Opening hours	Open 7 days
Credit cards	Accepted
Price range	Affordable
Style	Casual
Cuisine	Lebanese
Recommended for	Late night

"Ranoush Juice on the Edgware Road, an area renowned for Middle-Eastern cuisine, is a late-night institution, specializing in mezze and shawarma wraps. It's a no-frills hole-in-the-wall kebab joint that is perfect for an end of evening stop-off or as a pit-stop to refuel before going on somewhere else. Open until 3.00 a.m."—Joshua Katz

Even East Enders on a 3.00 a.m. kebab hunt have been known to end up at this Edgware Road staple from the Maroush empire, long overlords of so-called Little Beirut. It's a little rough and ready—there are seats for twenty, but most treat it as a takeaway (takeout), and boozy queues inevitably gather in the small hours—but benefits from an expert Lebanese production line. The shawarma kebabs are first-rate, whether carved onto the plate or slathered with hummus and pickles in a sandwich, while meze, baklava and fresh fruit juices offer further fortification for those braving an all-nighter.

ROYAL CHINA CLUB

Recommended by
Mark Jarvis

40–42 Baker Street
Marylebone
London W1U 7AJ
+44 2074863898
www.theroyalchina.co.uk

Opening hours	Open 7 days
Credit cards	Accepted
Price range	Expensive
Style	Smart casual
Cuisine	Chinese
Recommended for	Regular neighborhood

"I love the dim sum here—the prawn *cheong fun* and the eel dish with black bean and garlic paste—I could eat this any day of the week."—Mark Jarvis

WINTER GARDEN

Recommended by
Lori Granito

The Landmark Hotel
222 Marylebone Road
Marylebone
London NW1 6JQ
+44 20 7631 8188
www.landmarklondon.co.uk

Opening hours	Open 7 days
Credit cards	Accepted
Price range	Expensive
Style	Smart casual
Cuisine	British
Recommended for	Wish I'd opened

WOODLANDS

Recommended by
Rohit Ghai

77 Marylebone Lane
Marylebone
London W1U 2P
+44 2074863862
www.woodlandsrestaurant.co.uk

Opening hours	Open 7 days
Credit cards	Accepted
Price range	Affordable
Style	Casual
Cuisine	Indian
Recommended for	Bargain

"Home-style South Indian food at reasonable prices."
—Rohit Ghai

108 GARAGE

Recommended by
Tom Aikens, Gary Foulkes

108 Goldborne Road
Notting Hill
London W10 5PS
+44 2089693769
www.108garage.com

Opening hours	Closed Monday and Sunday
Credit cards	Accepted
Price range	Affordable
Style	Casual
Cuisine	British-Thai
Recommended for	Breakfast

"Great, modern restaurant serving brilliant British food at crazy reasonable prices. Plus it's seriously delicious grub."—Tom Aikens

THE CHIPPING FORECAST

29 All Saints Road
Notting Hill
London W11 1HE
+44 2074602745
www.chippingforecast.com

Opening hours	Closed Monday
Credit cards	Accepted but not AMEX
Price range	Affordable
Style	Casual
Cuisine	Seafood
Recommended for	Regular neighborhood

"It stocks very fresh, line-caught fish from Cornwall and cooks the fish simply and classically. You can have delicious deep-fried scampi and chips or beautifully grilled fish with light salads or dressed crab. There is a lovely, considered choice and it is perfect for those nights when you don't want to cook but want to eat something simple and good."—Thomasina Miers

FEZ MANGAL

104 Ladbroke Grove
Notting Hill
London W11 1PY
+44 2072293010
www.fezmangal.com

Opening hours	Open 7 days
Credit cards	Accepted but not AMEX or Diners
Price range	Affordable
Style	Casual
Cuisine	Turkish
Recommended for	Bargain

"Turkish kebabs, BYOB, very busy so it's reliably fresh. Fantastic flatbreads and great lamb."—Tania Steytler

GRANGER & CO

175 Westbourne Grove
Notting Hill
London W11 2SB
+44 2072299111
www.grangerandco.com

Opening hours	Open 7 days
Reservation policy	No
Credit cards	Accepted but not Diners
Price range	Affordable
Style	Casual
Cuisine	Australian
Recommended for	Regular neighborhood

"Being an Australian in London, if there is a good breakfast spot—I know it. Bill Granger essentially founded the brunch culture back in the 2000s in Sydney so he knows his breakfast! The corn fritters are a must and the scrambled eggs a showstopper. Come for the food, stay for the sunshine and the good vibes."—Bonny Porter

THE LEDBURY

127 Ledbury Road
Notting Hill
London W11 2AQ
+44 2077929090
www.theledbury.com

Opening hours	Open 7 days
Credit cards	Accepted
Price range	Expensive
Style	Smart casual
Cuisine	Modern British
Recommended for	High end

"Give up on the rest of the day from lunchtime on because you won't leave within five hours and you won't want to. Stunning food, lots of courses, but unlike some high-end spots, you actually remember them. Attention to detail, service and timing are faultless."—Tania Steytler

MARAMIA CAFÉ

48 Golborne Road
Notting Hill
London W10 5PR
+44 2031810030
www.maramia.com

Opening hours	Closed Monday
Credit cards	Accepted
Price range	Affordable
Style	Casual
Cuisine	Palestinian
Recommended for	Bargain

"I love this place, it's the best Palestinian food in London. It's such an unassuming place with food executed to perfection. A real trip down memory lane."—Sami Tamimi

PIZZA EAST

Recommended by
David Gingell

310 Portobello Road
Notting Hill
London W10 5TA
+44 2089694500
www.pizzaeast.com

Opening hours	Open 7 days
Credit cards	Accepted
Price range	Affordable
Style	Casual
Cuisine	Pizza
Recommended for	Regular neighborhood

"Pizza East still cracks out really great eggs for brunch."—David Gingell

RUM KITCHEN

Recommended by
Michael Reid

6–8 All Saints Road
Notting Hill
London W11 1HH
+44 2036682538
www.nottinghill.therumkitchen.com

Opening hours	Open 7 days
Credit cards	Accepted
Price range	Affordable
Style	Casual
Cuisine	Caribbean
Recommended for	Late night

"Good Caribbean food that never disappoints late at night."—Michael Reid

SNAPS & RYE

Recommended by
Allegra McEvedy, Thomasina Miers

93 Golborne Rd
Notting Hill
London W10 5NL
+44 2089643004
www.snapsandrye.com

Opening hours	Closed Monday
Credit cards	Accepted
Price range	Affordable
Style	Casual
Cuisine	Danish
Recommended for	Breakfast

"This Scandinavian restaurant and deli produces beautifully-cooked food with lovely ingredients and stocks some really interesting produce and cookbooks in case you wanted to learn more about Scandinavian food. It is a real treasure."—Thomasina Miers

PENTOLINA

Recommended by
Allegra McEvedy

71 Blythe Road
Olympia
London W14 0HP
+44 2030100091
www.pentolinarestaurant.co.uk

Opening hours	Closed Monday and Sunday
Credit cards	Accepted but not AMEX
Price range	Affordable
Style	Casual
Cuisine	Italian
Recommended for	Regular neighborhood

"Lovely Italian by Italians! Baked tomino cheese with honey and almonds is an artery-busting winner!" —Allegra McEvedy

AL AREZ RESTAURANT

Recommended by
Mark Rosati

101 Edgware Road
Paddington
London W2 2HX
+44 2072624833
www.alarez.co.uk

Opening hours	Open 7 days
Credit cards	Accepted but not AMEX
Price range	Affordable
Style	Casual
Cuisine	Lebanese-European
Recommended for	Late night

BEIRUT EXPRESS

Recommended by
Karam Sethi, Ollie Templeton

112–114 Edgware Road
Paddington
London W2 2DZ
+44 2077242700
www.maroush.com

Opening hours	Open 7 days
Credit cards	Accepted
Price range	Affordable
Style	Casual
Cuisine	Lebanese
Recommended for	Late night

"Great for late-night snacks after service with the team. Eat some mezze and drink some tea." —Ollie Templeton

COLBEH

Recommended by
Karam Sethi

6 Porchester Place
Paddington
London W2 2BS
+44 2077064888
www.colbeh.co.uk

Opening hours...Open 7 days
Credit cards...Accepted
Price range..Budget
Style...Casual
Cuisine..Persian
Recommended for...Bargain

LAHORE EASTCOTE

Recommended by
Karam Sethi

99 Field End Road
Pinner
London HA5 1QG
+44 2088689800
www.lahore-restaurant.co.uk

Opening hours...Open 7 days
Credit cards...Accepted
Price range..Budget
Style...Casual
Cuisine..Pakistani
Recommended for...............................Regular neighborhood

GREENBERRY CAFÉ

Recommended by
Theo Randall

101 Regent's Park Road
Primrose Hill
London NW1 8UR
+44 2074833765
www.greenberrycafe.co.uk

Opening hours...Open 7 days
Credit cards.......................Accepted but not AMEX or Diners
Price range..Affordable
Style...Casual
Cuisine...Café
Recommended for..Breakfast

"Best kedgeree ever. Fantastic service and always packed. They allow dogs so it's the perfect place to go after a walk on Primrose Hill!"—Theo Randall

ARTISAN COFFEE

Recommended by
Luke Vandore-Mackay

203 Upper Richmond Road
Putney
London SW15 6SG
+44 7712657477
www.artisancoffee.co.uk

Opening hours...Open 7 days
Credit cards.......................Accepted but not AMEX or Diners
Price range..Budget
Style...Casual
Cuisine...Café
Recommended for...............................Regular neighborhood

"Artisan do fantastic coffee and sausage sandwiches."
—Luke Vandore-Mackay

AL BOCCON DI'VINO

Recommended by
Alfred Prasad

14 Red Lion Street
Richmond
London TW9 1RW
+44 2089409060
www.nonsolovinoltd.co.uk

Opening hours...Closed Monday
Credit cards.............................Accepted but not AMEX
Price range..Affordable
Style...Smart casual
Cuisine..Italian
Recommended for...............................Regular neighborhood

"Fabulous produce presented in a tasting menu format. They bring a non-stop array of simple, delicious food. This tiny place has loyal regulars and it's hard to get a table. But the energy and bonhomie in the room is totally unlike any other dining experience in London."—Alfred Prasad

HANANA

Recommended by
Martin Morales

49 Kew Road
Richmond
London TW9 2NQ
+44 2089488988
www.hanana.co.uk

Opening hours..Closed Sunday
Credit cards...Accepted
Price range..Affordable
Style...Casual
Cuisine..Sushi
Recommended for...............................Regular neighborhood

JACKSON + RYE

Recommended by
Lawrence Keogh

Hotham House
1 Heron Square
Richmond
London TW9 1EJ
+44 2089486951
www.jacksonrye.com

Opening hours...Open 7 days
Credit cards.......................Accepted but not AMEX or Diners
Price range...Affordable
Style...Casual
Cuisine..American
Recommended for.............................Regular neighborhood

"Excellent breakfast menu with perfect views of the river."—Lawrence Keogh

PETERSHAM NURSERIES CAFÉ

Recommended by
Adam Byatt,
Petty Elliott, Alfred Prasad

Church Lane, Petersham Road
Richmond
London TW10 7AQ
+44 2083328665
www.petershamnurseries.com

Opening hours...Closed Monday
Credit cards..Accepted
Price range..Affordable
Style...Casual
Cuisine..Modern British-Italian
Recommended for.............................Regular neighborhood

"Petersham Nurseries is one of my favorite local lunch destinations; the surroundings are really incredible, the amazing flora and plants make it an intriguing location, and of course the food is absolutely delicious!"—Adam Byatt

PICKLE & RYE

Recommended by
Martin Morales

31 Sheen Lane
Sheen
London SW14 8AB
+44 2088788982
www.pickleandrye.com

Opening hours...Open 7 days
Credit cards.................................Accepted but not AMEX
Price range..Affordable
Style...Casual
Cuisine..American
Recommended for.............................Regular neighborhood

THE ROBIN CRAFT CAFÉ

Recommended by
Luke Vandore-Mackay

38 Sheen Lane
Sheen
London SW14 8LW

Opening hours...Open 7 days
Credit cards..Accepted
Price range..Budget
Style...Casual
Cuisine..Vietnamese Café
Recommended for.............................Regular neighborhood

"Great for Vietnamese coffee and banh mi."
—Luke Vandore-Mackay

THE VICTORIA

Recommended by
Martin Morales

10 West Temple Sheen
Sheen
London SW14 7RT
+44 2088764238
www.victoriasheen.co.uk

Opening hours...Open 7 days
Credit cards.......................Accepted but not AMEX or Diners
Price range..Affordable
Style...Casual
Cuisine...Gastropub
Recommended for.............................Regular neighborhood

"A comfortable, super friendly pub that serves interesting, delicious takes on classics as well as some creative dishes."—Martin Morales

CAFÉ 2000

Recommended by
Allegra McEvedy

4 Shepherd's Bush Market
Shepherd's Bush
London W12 8DE
+44 7711037052

Opening hours...Closed Sunday
Credit cards...Not accepted
Price range..Budget
Style...Casual
Cuisine...Egyptian-Sudanese
Recommended for...Bargain

"Have the falafel wrap with all the usuals with extra chile sauce and aubergines for £3.50 ($4.50)—phenomenal!"—Allegra McEvedy

NAAMA

384 Uxbridge Road
Shepherd's Bush
London W12 7LL
+44 2087400004
www.naama.co

Opening hours	Open 7 days
Credit cards	Accepted but not AMEX
Price range	Budget
Style	Casual
Cuisine	Lebanese
Recommended for	Bargain

"It's small, so usually a takeaway option, with an on-site butcher and deli. It's not the cheapest but still a bargain and maintains quality. Kebabs and salads that are balanced, fresh and cared about."—Tania Steytler

SHIKUMEN

Dorsett Hotel
58 Shepherd's Bush Green
Shepherd's Bush
London W12 8QE
+44 2087499978
www.shikumen.co.uk

Opening hours	Open 7 days
Credit cards	Accepted
Price range	Affordable
Style	Smart casual
Cuisine	Chinese
Recommended for	Local favorite

"Expertly made dim sum. I could eat the prawn and beancurd skin *cheong fun* all day, every day. Perfect Sunday lunch spot."—Tania Steytler

TIAN FU

39 Bulwer Street
Shepherd's Bush
London W12 8AR
+44 2087404546
www.tianfulondon.com

Opening hours	Open 7 days
Credit cards	Accepted
Price range	Affordable
Style	Casual
Cuisine	Chinese
Recommended for	Local favorite

"Tian Fu does some great Szechuan cooking."
—Thomasina Miers

BRILLIANT RESTAURANT

72–76 Western Road
Southall
London UB2 5DZ
+44 2085741928
www.brilliantrestaurant.com

Opening hours	Closed Monday
Credit cards	Accepted but not AMEX or Diners
Price range	Affordable
Style	Casual
Cuisine	Indian
Recommended for	Local favorite

"As the name says, it is a brilliant family restaurant serving North Indian dishes. Love this place for its variety and consistency of food."—Rohit Ghai

The Brilliant has been a favorite of the locals of Southall for the best part of half a century, and while a recent refurb has moved the interior slightly upmarket (the flatscreen TVs showing advertorials of their cookery courses are, thankfully, no more), not much has changed where it really matters—the *methi* (fenugreek) chicken is still a must-order, the roti is still made on site and is as delicate and fluffy as ever, and the lamb chops are still among the best in town. The Anand family should be very proud indeed of what they've achieved; the Brilliant is an institution.

GIFTO'S LAHORE KARAHI

162–164 The Broadway
Southall
London UB1 1NN
+44 2088138669
www.gifto.com

Opening hours	Open 7 days
Credit cards	Accepted but not AMEX or Diners
Price range	Affordable
Style	Casual
Cuisine	Indian-Pakistani
Recommended for	Bargain

"A warm welcome awaits, at this family restaurant serving the best tandoor chicken and marinated lamb. Perfect for kids, and perfect for trying a whole variety of spicy food."—Martin Morales

MADHU'S

Recommended by
Rohit Ghai

39 South Road
Southall
London UB1 1SW
+44 2085741897
www.madhus.co.uk

Opening hours	Open 7 days
Credit cards	Accepted
Price range	Affordable
Style	Smart casual
Cuisine	Indian
Recommended for	Local favorite

THE WHARF

Recommended by
Lawrence Keogh

Manor Road
Teddington
London TW11 8BG
+44 2089776333
www.thewharfteddington.com

Opening hours	Open 7 days
Credit cards	Accepted
Price range	Affordable
Style	Smart casual
Cuisine	Gastropub
Recommended for	Regular neighborhood

"Excellent value set-lunch menu on the river."
—Lawrence Keogh

LAHORE KARAHI

Recommended by
Luke Vandore-Mackay

1 Tooting High Street
Tooting
London SW17 0SN
+44 2087672477
www.lahorekarahirestaurant.co.uk

Opening hours	Open 7 days
Credit cards	Accepted but not AMEX or Diners
Price range	Affordable
Style	Casual
Cuisine	Pakistani
Recommended for	Bargain

A. WONG

Recommended by
Massimo Bottura, Cary Docherty,
Dan Graham, James Knappett,
Merlin Labron-Johnson,
Mark Sargeant, Tom Sellers

70 Wilton Road
Victoria
London SW1V 1DE
+44 2078288931
www.awong.co.uk

Opening hours	Closed Sunday
Credit cards	Accepted but not AMEX
Price range	Affordable
Style	Casual
Cuisine	Chinese
Recommended for	Wish I'd opened

"Full-flavor, finessed food from all regions of China."
—Dan Graham

BLEECKER VICTORIA

Recommended by
Cary Docherty

205 Victoria Street
Victoria
London SW1E 5NE
www.bleeckerburger.co.uk

Opening hours	Open 7 days
Credit cards	Accepted
Price range	Budget
Style	Casual
Cuisine	Burgers
Recommended for	Bargain

"The Bleeker Black is to die for. It's my favorite burger.
I've taken loads of other chef friends there and they
always agree that it's a top, top burger. Rare, flavorful
beef and black pudding, what's not to like?"
—Cary Docherty

As most chefs will tell you, success is rarely more
than a case of starting with good ingredients and
not messing them up. The trick to Bleecker's success
is their beef, from butcher Nathan Mills; premium
grass-fed and dry-aged, and packing more flavor
into a single burger patty than most could fit in an
entire Sunday roast. Add to that a slick of proper
American cheese and a firm seeded bun and you
have one of the very best burgers in town, for less
than a tenner ($13) even with a side of fries. Oh, and
try the 'Bleecker Black'—all the above but with a
layer of black pudding. A work of near-genius.

CHEZ BRUCE

2 Bellevue Road
Wandsworth
London SW17 7EG
+44 2086720114
www.chezbruce.co.uk

Opening hours	Open 7 days
Credit cards	Accepted
Price range	Affordable
Style	Smart casual
Cuisine	Modern European
Recommended for	Regular neighborhood

"I love Chez Bruce for a long wine-fuelled lunch."
—Adam Byatt

Bruce Poole 'takes it as a compliment' that some find his food old-fashioned. He and Matt Christmas, his kitchen collaborator of over ten years, are proud to serve the French-inspired braises, offal dishes, salads and desserts that others eschew. The inspiration is classical, but the style is their own: calf's brains and Puy lentils come with sauce gribiche (a mayonnaise-style sauce) and crisp chicken skin, brandade (salt cod spread) with mussels and monk's beard, cod with truffle mash and hazelnut dressing. This Wandsworth Common restaurant (twenty-five minutes by cab from town) celebrated two decades in 2015. Its cheeseboard and wine list are now legendary.

CWTCH

Pitch 157, Old York Road
Wandsworth
London SW18 1SU
+44 2088118111
www.cwtchldn.com

Opening hours	Open 7 days
Credit cards	Not accepted
Price range	Budget
Style	Casual
Cuisine	Welsh
Recommended for	Breakfast

"It's not a restaurant at all, it's a kiosk selling some of the best coffee in London along with great homemade cereals and the best bacon butty for miles."
—Alyn Williams

SARAVANAA BHAVAN

22–22a Ealing Road
Wembley
London HA0 4TL
+44 2089008526
www.saravanabhavan.co.uk

Opening hours	Open 7 days
Credit cards	Accepted but not AMEX
Price range	Budget
Style	Casual
Cuisine	South Indian Vegetarian
Recommended for	Bargain

"For South Indian food: dosas especially."
—Manoj Vasaikar

LONDON
CENTRAL

<N> SCALE

0   150   300   450
yd.

1. *Noble Rot* (p.432)
2. *L'ATELIER De Joël Robuchon* (p.432)
3. *Big Easy Bar* (p.432)
4. *Chick 'N' Sours* (p.432)
5. *The Delaunay* (p.432)
6. *Dishoom Convent Garden* (p.432)
7. *Flesh & Buns* (p.433)
8. *Frenchie Covent Garden* (p.433)
9. *Hawksmoor Seven Dials* (p.433)
10. *Hazuki* (p.433)
11. *Homeslice* (p.433)
12. *Icon Balcony Bar* (p.433)
13. *Imperial China* (p.434)
14. *The Ivy* (p.434)
15. *The Ivy Market Grill* (p.434)
16. *J. Sheekey* (p.434)
17. *Joe Allen* (p.434)
18. *Kanada-Ya* (p.435)
19. *Margot* (p.435)
20. *Punjab* (p.435)
21. *Rules* (p.435)
22. *Shake Shack* (p.436)
23. *Tandoor Chop House* (p.436)
24. *Tokyo Diner* (p.436)
25. *Alain Ducasse* (p.436)
26. *The Araki* (p.436)
27. *Aulis At Fera* (p.437)
28. *Benares* (p.437)
29. *Bentley's Oyster Bar & Grill* (p.437)
30. *Burger And Lobster* (p.437)
31. *Cecconi's* (p.437)
32. *Chucs Restaurant & Café* (p.437)
33. *Fera At Claridge's* (p.438)
34. *Fortnum & Mason* (p.438)
35. *Four Seasons Hotel* (p.438)
36. *The Foyer & Reading Room* (p.438)
37. *The Gallery at Sketch* (p.438)
38. *Le Gavroche* (p.438)
39. *Goodman* (p.439)
40. *Gymkhana* (p.439)
41. *Hakassan* (p.439)
42. *Hawksmoor Air Street* (p.439)
43. *Hélène Darroze* (p.439)
44. *Kitty Fisher's* (p.439)
45. *Little Social* (p.440)
46. *Locanda Locatelli* (p.440)
47. *Mayfair Garden* (p.440)
48. *Mews Of Mayfair* (p.440)
49. *Momo* (p.440)
50. *Mount Street Deli* (p.440)
51. *Murano* (p.441)
52. *Nobu London* (p.441)
53. *Park Chinois* (p.441)
54. *La Petite Maison* (p.441)
55. *Pollen Street Social* (p.441)
56. *Ristorante Frescobaldi London* (p.442)
57. *Roka Mayfair* (p.442)
58. *Scott's* (p.442)
59. *Street Xo* (p.442)
60. *Umu* (p.442)
61. *Wild Honey* (p.442)
62. *The Windmill* (p.443)
63. *The Wolseley* (p.443)
64. *10 Greek Street* (p.443)
65. *Andrew Edmunds* (p.443)
66. *Le Bab* (p.443)
67. *Bao* (p.444)
68. *Bar Italia* (p.444)
69. *Bar Termini* (p.444)
70. *Barrafina* (p.444)
71. *Bashan Restaurant* (p.444)
72. *Blacklock* (p.445)
73. *Blanchette* (p.445)
74. *Bob Bob Ricard* (p.445)
75. *Bocca Di Lupo* (p.445)
76. *Bone Daddies* (p.445)
77. *Brasserie Zédel* (p.446)
78. *The Breakfast Club* (p.446)
79. *Bubble Dogs* (p.446)
80. *Burger And Lobster* (p.446)
81. *Busaba Eathai Soho* (p.447)
82. *C&R* (p.447)
83. *Café Monico* (p.447)
84. *Chotto Matte* (p.447)
85. *The Crispy Duck* (p.447)
86. *Dean Street Townhouse* (p.447)
87. *Dishoom Carnaby* (p.448)
88. *Ducksoup* (p.448)
89. *Dumplings' Legend* (p.448)
90. *Eat Tokyo* (p.448)
91. *Engawa* (p.448)
92. *Fernandez & Wells* (p.448)
93. *Flat Iron* (p.449)
94. *Four Seasons* (p.449)
95. *Gail's* (p.449)
96. *Gerrard's Corner* (p.449)
97. *The Golden Dragon* (p.449)
98. *Hix Soho* (p.449)
99. *Hoppers* (p.450)
100. *Jen Café* (p.450)
101. *Jinjuu Soho* (p.450)
102. *Joy Luck Restaurant* (p.450)
103. *The Kati Roll Company* (p.450)
104. *Kiln* (p.451)
105. *Kitchen Table @ Bubble Dogs* (p.451)
106. *Koya Bar* (p.451)
107. *Kricket Soho* (p.451)
108. *Maison Bertaux* (p.452)
109. *The Ninth* (p.452)
110. *Old Town 97* (p.452)
111. *Opium* (p.452)
112. *The Palomar* (p.452)
113. *Pho & Bun* (p.453)
114. *Princi* (p.453)
115. *Quo Vadis* (p.453)
116. *Rasa Sayang* (p.453)
117. *Roka* (p.453)
118. *Smoking Goat* (p.454)
119. *Spuntino* (p.454)
120. *Temper* (p.454)
121. *Tonkotsu* (p.454)
122. *Vasco & Piero's Pavilion* (p.454)
123. *Yauatcha Soho* (p.455)
124. *45 Jermyn Street* (p.455)
125. *The Gallery* (p.455)
126. *Il Vicolo* (p.455)
127. *Cinnamon Club* (p.455)
128. *The Goring Dining Room* (p.456)
129. *Regency Café* (p.456)

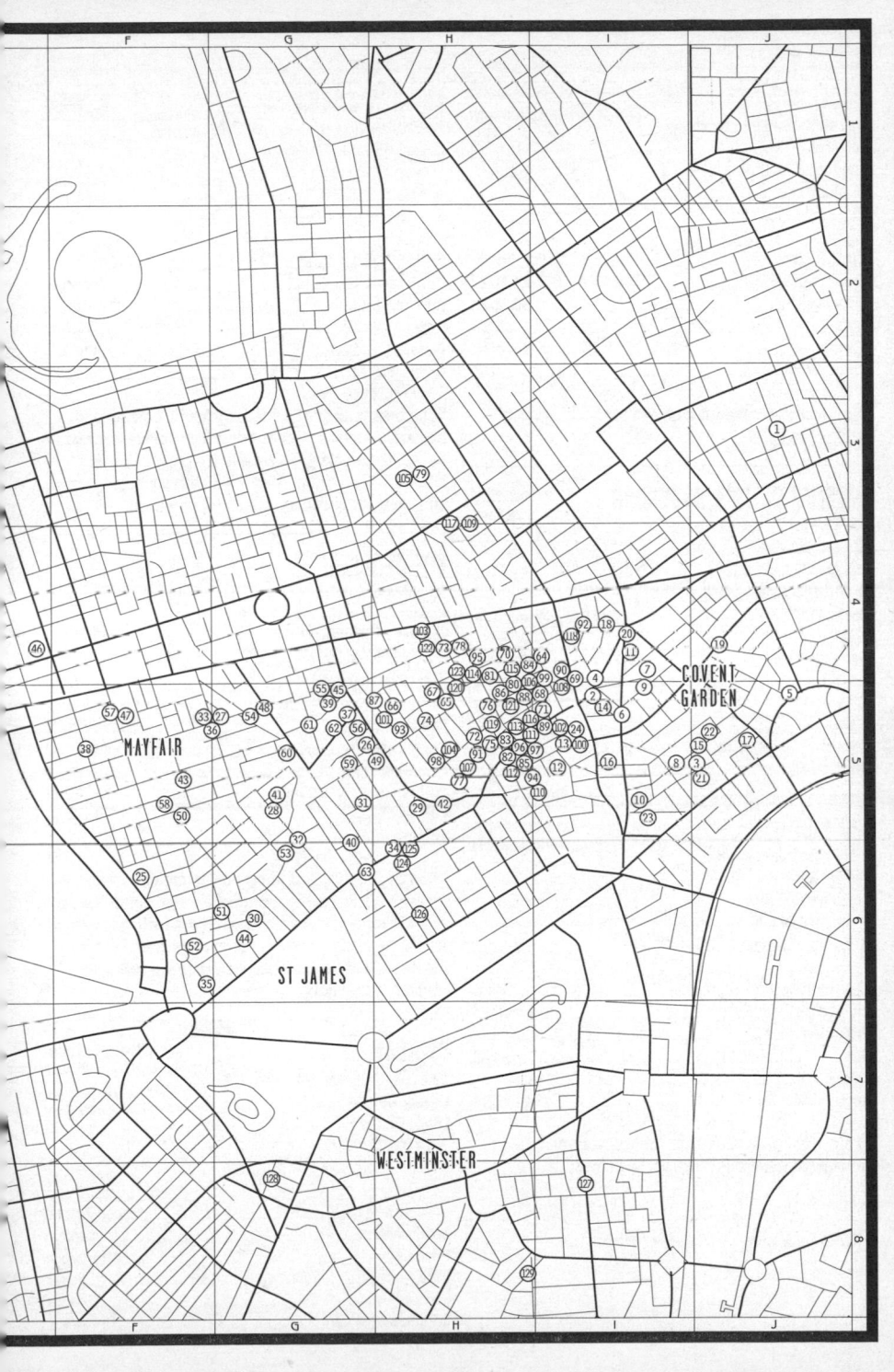

NOBLE ROT

51 Lamb's Conduit Street
Bloomsbury
London WC1N 3NB
+44 2072428963
www.noblerot.co.uk

Recommended by
Neil Borthwick, Hus Vedat

Opening hours...Closed Sunday
Credit cards..................................Accepted but not AMEX
Price range...Affordable
Style...Casual
Cuisine..Modern European
Recommended for.................................Wish I'd opened

"Consistently excellent food and awesome wine list!"—Hus Vedat

L'ATELIER DE JOËL ROBUCHON

13–15 West Street
Covent Garden
London WC2H 9NE
+44 207010860
www.joelrobuchon.co.uk

Recommended by
Sat Bains

Opening hours...Open 7 days
Credit cards...Accepted
Price range...Affordable
Style..Smart casual
Cuisine..French
Recommended for...High end

BIG EASY BAR

12 Maiden Lane
Covent Garden
London WC2E 7NA
+44 2037284888
www.bigeasy.com

Recommended by
Sameer Taneja

Opening hours...Open 7 days
Credit cards...Accepted
Price range...Affordable
Style...Casual
Cuisine..American
Recommended for..Late night

"Late-night grub at its best. No fuss, nice and easy, great meal, generous portions."—Sameer Taneja

CHICK 'N' SOURS

1a Earlham Street
Covent Garden
London WC2H 9LL
+44 2031984814
www.chicknsours.co.uk

Recommended by
Tom Aikens, Pete Denhart,
Martin Morales, Mark Sargeant

Opening hours...Open 7 days
Credit cards...Accepted
Price range...Affordable
Style...Casual
Cuisine...Chicken
Recommended for...Bargain

"The best selection of fried chicken in London and beyond, serious seasonal sides, sour cocktails, great beers, and cracking soft-serve ice cream. Burger heaven is the Korean fried thigh with gochujang mayo, chile vinegar and Asian slaw."—Tom Aikens

THE DELAUNAY

55 Aldwych London
Covent Garden
London WC2B 4BB
+44 2074998558
www.thedelaunay.com

Recommended by
Eyal Jagermann, Yotam Ottolenghi

Opening hours...Open 7 days
Credit cards...Accepted
Price range...Affordable
Style..Smart casual
Cuisine..European
Recommended for..Breakfast

"Corbin and King just know how to create restaurants that work. The food is confident enough not to have to prove itself or show off and you leave feeling set up for the day. I also love the room: it has a real sense of theater and really matches the European menu."
—Yotam Ottolenghi

DISHOOM

12 Upper Saint Martin's Lane
Covent Garden
London WC2H 9FB
+44 2074209320
www.dishoom.com

Recommended by
Henry Harris, Tom Moxon,
Stevie Parle, Michael Reid,
Frankie van Loo

Opening hours...Open 7 days
Credit cards...Accepted
Price range...Affordable
Style...Casual
Cuisine..Indian
Recommended for..Breakfast

FLESH & BUNS

41 Earlham Street
Covent Garden
London WC2H 9LX
+44 2076329500
www.bonedaddies.com

Opening hours	Open 7 days
Credit cards	Accepted
Price range	Affordable
Style	Casual
Cuisine	Japanese
Recommended for	Regular neighborhood

FRENCHIE COVENT GARDEN

16 Henrietta Street
Covent Garden
London WC2E 8QH
+44 2078364422
www.frenchiecoventgarden.com

Opening hours	Open / days
Credit cards	Accepted
Price range	Affordable
Style	Casual
Cuisine	French
Recommended for	Regular neighborhood

HAWKSMOOR

11 Langley Street
Covent Garden
London WC2H 9JG
+44 2074209390
www.thehawksmoor.com

Opening hours	Open 7 days
Credit cards	Accepted
Price range	Affordable
Style	Smart casual
Cuisine	Steakhouse
Recommended for	Breakfast

"Grilled bone marrow for breakfast is the nuts!"
—Hus Vedat

HAZUKI

43 Chandos Place
Covent Garden
London WC2N 4HS
+44 2072402530
www.hazukilondon.co.uk

Opening hours	Open 7 days
Credit cards	Accepted but not Diners
Price range	Affordable
Style	Casual
Cuisine	Japanese
Recommended for	Regular neighborhood

"Great little hide-away Japanese restaurant. Lovely set menus."—Christian Edwardson

HOMESLICE

13 Neal's Yard
Covent Garden
London WC2H 9DP
+44 2031517488
www.homeslicepizza.co.uk

Opening hours	Open 7 days
Credit cards	Accepted
Price range	Affordable
Style	Casual
Cuisine	Pizza
Recommended for	Late night

"Once I've finished a service I tend to go straight home but if I'm coming back with my wife and kids we sometimes pop into Homeslice in Covent Garden for a bite. A precise menu with toppings like wild venison and pig cheeks—who couldn't enjoy? Mark's got it right!"—Richard Corrigan

ICON BALCONY BAR

Empire Casino
5–6 Leicester Square
Covent Garden
London WC2H 7NA
+44 2036425216
www.thecasinolsq.com

Opening hours	Open 7 days
Credit cards	Accepted
Price range	Affordable
Style	Smart casual
Cuisine	Modern European
Recommended for	Late night

IMPERIAL CHINA

Recommended by
Yotam Ottolenghi

White Bear Yard
25A Lisle Street
Covent Garden
London WC2H 7BA
+44 2077343388
www.imperialchina-london.com

Opening hours	Open 7 days
Credit cards	Accepted
Price range	Affordable
Style	Smart casual
Cuisine	Chinese
Recommended for	Regular neighborhood

"I go here a lot at the moment on the weekend with Karl and our young kids. We are all mildly obsessed with dumplings and are working our way through all the melt-in-the-mouth dim sum. Steamed prawns or the pork and cabbage are current favorites. There's something hugely reassuring about Imperial China. They stick with what they know, they know what they are doing and they are doing it very well."
—Yotam Ottolenghi

THE IVY

Recommended by
Carl Clarke,
Jeremy Lee,
Marcus Wareing,
Alyn Williams

1–5 West Street
Covent Garden
London WC2H 9NQ
+44 2078364751
www.the-ivy.co.uk

Opening hours	Open 7 days
Credit cards	Accepted
Price range	Affordable
Style	Smart casual
Cuisine	British
Recommended for	Local favorite

"It's quintessential London...a lovely place to eat."
—Alyn Williams

THE IVY MARKET GRILL

Recommended by
Cary Docherty

1 Henrietta Street
Covent Garden
London WC2E 8PS
+ 44 2033010200
www.theivymarketgrill.com

Opening hours	Open 7 days
Credit cards	Accepted
Price range	Affordable
Style	Smart casual
Cuisine	Modern British
Recommended for	Wish I'd opened

"The people running The Ivy Market Grill are very talented and smart. They are rolling them out everywhere."—Cary Docherty

J. SHEEKEY

Recommended by
Yotam Ottolenghi

28–32 Saint Martin's Court
Covent Garden
London WC2N 4A
+44 2072402565
www.j-sheekey.co.uk

Opening hours	Open 7 days
Credit cards	Accepted but not Diners
Price range	Affordable
Style	Smart casual
Cuisine	Seafood
Recommended for	Late night

"This is a restaurant that knows what it's doing and does it well and has the confidence to keep doing it. It's a real haven from the busy streets of Covent Garden, as well, which feels cosy late at night."—Yotam Ottolenghi

JOE ALLEN

Recommended by
Erchen Chang

13 Exeter Street
Covent Garden
London WC2E 7DT
+44 2078360651
www.joeallen.co.uk

Opening hours	Open 7 days
Credit cards	Accepted but not Diners
Price range	Affordable
Style	Casual
Cuisine	American
Recommended for	Late night

"Sit at the bar, order the off-menu burger, get a free shot with your beer, and finish with an Old Fashioned."
—Erchen Chang

KANADA-YA

64 Saint Giles High Street
Covent Garden
London WC2H 8LE
+44 2072400232
www.kanada-ya.com

Recommended by
Jocky Petrie

Opening hours...Open 7 days
Credit cards.....................................Accepted but not Diners
Price range..Affordable
Style..Casual
Cuisine...Ramen
Recommended for..Late night

"Tiny restaurant with limited seating and brilliant tasty noodles. Midnight snacks don't come any better."
—Jocky Petrie

London's love affair with ramen only really began with the opening of this unassuming little spot in Saint Giles back in 2014. Specialists in the *tonkotsu* (pork bone) broth style, customers are not only able to choose from a list of nine different ramen options, but are also able to specify the hardness of their noodles—an attention to detail others would do well to take note of. It's wildly popular, but the queue goes pretty quickly—probably due to the cheek-by-jowl seating arrangements not encouraging lingerers—and you may have more luck later on; it's open until 10.30 p.m.

MARGOT

45 Great Queen Street
Covent Garden
London WC2B 5AA
+44 2034094777
www.margotrestaurant.com

Recommended by
Amandine Chaignot,
Hélène Darroze

Opening hours...Open 7 days
Credit cards..Accepted
Price range...Affordable
Style..Smart casual
Cuisine..Italian
Recommended for..............................Regular neighborhood

PUNJAB

80 Neal Street
Covent Garden
London WC2H 9PA
+44 2078369787
www.punjab.co.uk

Recommended by
Rohit Ghai

Opening hours...Open 7 days
Credit cards..Accepted
Price range...Affordable
Style..Casual
Cuisine...Punjabi-Indian
Recommended for...Late night

"Lovely, informal restaurant in Covent Garden. It offers home-style Punjabi food with friendly staff and flexible timings. Mostly I prefer early dinners, but sometimes I love to stop by this restaurant late at night for a taste of Punjabi food."—Rohit Ghai

RULES

34–35 Malden Lane
Covent Garden
London WC2E 7LB
+44 2078365314
www.rules.co.uk

Recommended by
Shaun Searley

Opening hours...Open 7 days
Credit cards..Accepted
Price range...Affordable
Style..Smart casual
Cuisine..British
Recommended for...Local favorite

"This is one of the oldest restaurants in London and serves traditional hearty food. Best time to go is the beginning of the game season for grouse."
—Shaun Searley

SHAKE SHACK

Recommended by
Richard Corrigan

24 Market Building
The Piazza
Covent Garden
London WC2E 8RD
+44 1923555129
www.shakeshack.com

Opening hours	Open 7 days
Credit cards	Accepted
Price range	Affordable
Style	Casual
Cuisine	American
Recommended for	Bargain

"A burger and a beer is a guilty pleasure of mine. It has to be the full monty though—rashers, cheese, onions, the lot. There's always a massive wait to get in the door, but it's worth it."—Richard Corrigan

TANDOOR CHOP HOUSE

Recommended by
Sameer Taneja

8 Adelaide Street
Covent Garden
London WC2N 4HZ
+44 2030960359
www.tandoorchophouse.com

Opening hours	Open 7 days
Credit cards	Accepted
Price range	Affordable
Style	Casual
Cuisine	Indian-British
Recommended for	Local favorite

"Premium cuts of meat, spiced and grilled over a charcoal tandoor."—Sameer Taneja

TOKYO DINER

Recommended by
Bonny Porter

2 Newport Place
Covent Garden
London WC2H 7JJ
+44 2072878777
www.tokyodiner.com

Opening hours	Closed Monday
Credit cards	Accepted but not AMEX or Diners
Price range	Affordable
Style	Casual
Cuisine	Japanese
Recommended for	Bargain

"Open till midnight, this restaurant has impeccable, fast service and serves only a small selection of dishes—sticking to what they know and doing it well.

They don't take service charge or tips and will also happily bulk out your meal if you want. More rice? No worries—won't cost you a cent. Bargain!"
—Bonny Porter

ALAIN DUCASSE

Recommended by
Francesco Mazzei

The Dorchester
53 Park Lane
Mayfair
London W1K 1QA
+44 2076298866
www.alainducasse-dorchester.com

Opening hours	Closed Monday and Sunday
Credit cards	Accepted
Price range	Expensive
Style	Smart casual
Cuisine	French
Recommended for	High end

"The stunning dining room, the service, and Monsieur Ducasse's cuisine is mind blowing."
—Francesco Mazzei

THE ARAKI

Recommended by
Erchen Chang, Gareth Ward

Unit 4, 12 New Burlington Street
Mayfair
London W1S 3BF
+44 2072872481
www.the-araki.com

Opening hours	Closed Monday
Credit cards	Accepted but not AMEX or Diners
Price range	Expensive
Style	Smart casual
Cuisine	Japanese
Recommended for	Wish I'd opened

"I have always loved the idea of cooking for about ten people on a bench all together—no real restaurant just the kitchen, the chef, and the customers."
—Gareth Ward

AULIS AT FERA

Recommended by
Andi Oliver

Claridge's
Brook Street
Mayfair
London W1K 4HR
+44 2071078860
www.aulis.feraatclaridges.co.uk

Opening hours	Closed Sunday to Wednesday
Credit cards	Accepted but not Diners
Price range	Expensive
Style	Smart casual
Cuisine	Modern British
Recommended for	High end

Food from another planet! Extraordinary creations from chef Dan Cox and his team, from the sublime to the even more sublime! They infuse all that they do with flavor, tenderness, love, and care."—Andi Oliver

BENARES

Recommended by
Martin Morales

12a Berkeley Square
Mayfair
London W1J 6BS
+44 2076298886
www.benaresrestaurant.com

Opening hours	Open 7 days
Credit cards	Accepted
Price range	Expensive
Style	Smart casual
Cuisine	Modern Indian
Recommended for	High end

"An explosion of flavors, textures, and colors at this smart Mayfair restaurant."—Martin Morales

BENTLEY'S OYSTER BAR & GRILL

Recommended by
Jocky Petrie

11–15 Swallow Street
Mayfair
London W1B 4DG
+44 2077344756
www.bentleys.org

Opening hours	Open 7 days
Credit cards	Accepted
Price range	Expensive
Style	Smart casual
Cuisine	Seafood
Recommended for	High end

"It's hard to pass by and not pop in for a cheeky oyster or two! Steeped in history and with a great ambience, especially when eating at the bar."—Jocky Petrie

BURGER AND LOBSTER

Recommended by
Alyn Williams

29 Clarges Street
Mayfair
London W1J 7EF
+44 2074091699
www.burgerandlobster.com

Opening hours	Open 7 days
Credit cards	Accepted but not Diners
Price range	Affordable
Style	Casual
Cuisine	Burgers-Seafood
Recommended for	Wish I'd opened

CECCONI'S

Recommended by
Shaun Rankin

5A Burlington Gardens
Mayfair
London W1S 3EP
+44 2074341500
www.cecconis.co.uk

Opening hours	Open 7 days
Credit cards	Accepted
Price range	Affordable
Style	Smart casual
Cuisine	Italian
Recommended for	Regular neighborhood

"Cecconi's is a modern-day classic Italian restaurant. They serve fantastic handmade pasta, seafood, and dishes from Italy using very fine ingredients."
—Shaun Rankin

CHUCS RESTAURANT & CAFÉ

Recommended by
Karam Sethi

31 Dover Street
Mayfair
London W1S 4NB
+44 2037632013
www.chucs.com

Opening hours	Open 7 days
Credit cards	Accepted
Price range	Affordable
Style	Smart casual
Cuisine	Modern European
Recommended for	Regular neighborhood

FERA AT CLARIDGE'S

Recommended by
Kirk Westaway, Alyn Williams

Claridge's
49 Brook Street
Mayfair
London W1K 4HR
+44 2071078888
www.feraatclaridges.co.uk

Opening hours	Open 7 days
Credit cards	Accepted
Price range	Affordable
Style	Smart casual
Cuisine	Modern British
Recommended for	Worth the travel

"Using vegetables personally grown on his own farm, each dish has a purpose and a reason. The service is perfect and every plate they send out follows an impressive style. One of my favorite restaurants in London."—Kirk Westaway

FORTNUM & MASON

Recommended by
Thomasina Miers

181 Picadilly
Mayfair
London W1A 1ER
+44 2077348040
www.fortnumandmason.com

Opening hours	Open 7 days
Credit cards	Accepted
Price range	Affordable
Style	Smart casual
Cuisine	British
Recommended for	Regular neighborhood

"Fortnum's delivers a first-class breakfast."
—Thomasina Miers

FOUR SEASONS HOTEL

Recommended by
Rohit Ghai

Park Lane
Mayfair
London W1J 7DR
+44 2074990888
www.fourseasons.com

Opening hours	Open 7 days
Credit cards	Accepted
Price range	Affordable
Style	Smart casual
Cuisine	British-Italian
Recommended for	Regular neighborhood

THE FOYER & READING ROOM

Recommended by
Adam Byatt,
Hélène Darroze

Claridge's
49 Brook Street
Mayfair
London W1K 4HR
+44 2076298860
www.claridges.co.uk

Opening hours	Open 7 days
Credit cards	Accepted
Price range	Expensive
Style	Smart casual
Cuisine	British
Recommended for	Local favorite

"My first job as an apprentice was at Claridge's and it really set such an incredibly high standard for their approach to food. They continually provide their guests with the highest level of cookery, and for me show-off classical British cooking at its finest."—Adam Byatt

THE GALLERY

Recommended by
Sergio Herman
Paul Walsh

Sketch
9 Conduit Street
Mayfair
London W1S 2XG
+44 2076594500
www.sketch.london

Opening hours	Open 7 days
Credit cards	Accepted
Price range	Expensive
Style	Smart casual
Cuisine	Modern European
Recommended for	High end

"It's the most contemporary, high-end concept I have ever seen. Everything is mystical and artfully addressed."—Sergio Herman

LE GAVROCHE

Recommended by
Richard Corrigan, David Gingell,
Jeremy Lee, Theo Randall

43 Upper Brook Street
Mayfair
London W1K 7QR
+44 2074080881
www.le-gavroche.co.uk

Opening hours	Closed Sunday
Credit cards	Accepted
Price range	Expensive
Style	Smart casual
Cuisine	French
Recommended for	High end

"Fantastic classic French food with service to match. Very consistent food and lovely staff."—Theo Randall

GOODMAN

Recommended by
Cary Docherty

24–26 Maddox Street
Mayfair
London W1S 1QH
+44 2074993776
www.goodmanrestaurants.com

Opening hours	Closed Sunday
Credit cards	Accepted
Price range	Affordable
Style	Smart casual
Cuisine	Steakhouse
Recommended for	Late night

"Goodman offers exceptional service. Pair that with a great burger or steak and a glass of red and you can see that it's perfect for a quick bite and a drink at the end of a long day."—Cary Docherty

GYMKHANA

Recommended by
Tam Storrar

42 Albemarle Street
Mayfair
London W1S 4JH
+44 2030115900
www.gymkhanalondon.com

Opening hours	Closed Sunday
Credit cards	Accepted but not Diners
Price range	Affordable
Style	Smart casual
Cuisine	Indian
Recommended for	Local favorite

HAKASSAN

Recommended by
Galton Blackiston, Julien Duboué,
Rohit Ghai, Philip Howard,
David Muñoz

17 Bruton Street
Mayfair
London W1J 6QB
+44 2079071888
www.hakkasan.com

Opening hours	Open 7 days
Credit cards	Accepted
Price range	Affordable
Style	Smart casual
Cuisine	Modern Cantonese
Recommended for	High end

"It just does tick all the boxes—guaranteed buzz, amazing cooking and cocktails galore!"
—Philip Howard

HAWKSMOOR AIR STREET

Recommended by
Joel Braham

5A Air Street
Mayfair
London W1J 0AD
+44 2074063980
www.thehawksmoor.com

Opening hours	Open 7 days
Credit cards	Accepted
Price range	Affordable
Style	Smart casual
Cuisine	Steakhouse
Recommended for	High end

"The British, dry-aged and charcoal-grilled steaks are the best in London. Stunning dining room, great cocktails and attentive, knowledgeable staff. It's an experience every time."—Joel Braham

HÉLÈNE DARROZE

Recommended by
Marcus Wareing,
Alla Wolf Tasker

The Connaught
Carlos Place
Mayfair
London W1K 2AL
+44 2074997070
www.the-connaught.co.uk

Opening hours	Open 7 days
Credit cards	Accepted but not Diners
Price range	Expensive
Style	Smart casual
Cuisine	French
Recommended for	Worth the travel

KITTY FISHER'S

Recommended by
Hélène Darroze

10 Shepherd Market
Mayfair
London W1J 7QF
+44 2033021661
www.kittyfishers.com

Opening hours	Closed Sunday
Credit cards	Accepted
Price range	Affordable
Style	Smart casual
Cuisine	Modern British
Recommended for	Local favorite

LITTLE SOCIAL

Recommended by
Paul Walsh

5 Pollen Street
Mayfair
London W1S 1NE
+44 2078703730
www.littlesocial.co.uk

Opening hours	Closed Sunday
Credit cards	Accepted
Price range	Expensive
Style	Smart casual
Cuisine	Modern British-French
Recommended for	Regular neighborhood

LOCANDA LOCATELLI

Recommended by
Yotam Ottolenghi

8 Seymour Street
Mayfair
London W1H 7JZ
+44 2079359088
www.locandalocatelli.com

Opening hours	Open 7 days
Credit cards	Accepted but not Diners
Price range	Expensive
Style	Smart casual
Cuisine	Italian
Recommended for	High end

"A firm favorite."—Yotam Ottolenghi

MAYFAIR GARDEN

Recommended by
Theo Randall

8–10 North Audley Street
Mayfair
London W1K 6ZD
+44 2074933223
www.mayfairgarden.co.uk

Opening hours	Open 7 days
Credit cards	Accepted
Price range	Affordable
Style	Smart casual
Cuisine	Chinese
Recommended for	Local favorite

"Great Chinese food. Lovely for Sunday lunch—start with their dim sum menu. Great quality and value for money."—Theo Randall

MEWS OF MAYFAIR

Recommended by
Shaun Rankin

10 Lancashire Court
Mayfair
London W1S 1EY
+44 2075189388
www.mewsofmayfair.com

Opening hours	Open 7 days
Credit cards	Accepted
Price range	Expensive
Style	Smart casual
Cuisine	Modern British Brasserie
Recommended for	Late night

"A great place to go and unwind after work. They do excellent pizzas in the wood-fired oven and great wines by the glass."—Shaun Rankin

MOMO

Recommended by
Theo Randall

23–25 Heddon Street
Mayfair
London W1B 4BH
+44 2074344040
www.momoresto.com

Opening hours	Open 7 days
Credit cards	Accepted
Price range	Affordable
Style	Casual
Cuisine	Moroccan
Recommended for	Late Night

"Great Moroccan food with a fantastic bar downstairs so you can dance all night after tagine and couscous. Very cool!"—Theo Randall

MOUNT STREET DELI

Recommended by
Hélène Darroze

100 Mount Street
Mayfair
London W1K 2TG
+44 2074996843
www.themountstreetdeli.co.uk

Opening hours	Closed Sunday
Credit cards	Accepted but not Diners
Price range	Affordable
Style	Casual
Cuisine	Deli
Recommended for	Breakfast

"Very simple food but very fresh and very well-executed, in the heart of cozy Mayfair."
—Hélène Darroze

MURANO

Recommended by
Tomer Amedi, Sami Tamimi

20 Queen Street
Mayfair
London W1J 5PP
+44 2074951127
www.muranolondon.com

Opening hours...Closed Sunday
Credit cards...Accepted
Price range...Affordable
Style..Casual
Cuisine...Modern European
Recommended for...High end

"It's always seasonal, unpretentious and damn good.
When I go to fine-dining restaurants I'm not looking
for the chef to prove something, I just want the food
to be beautiful and it is here."—Tomer Amedi

NOBU LONDON

Recommended by
Tam Storrar

19 Old Park Lane
Mayfair
London W1K 1LB
+44 2074474747
www.noburestaurants.com

Opening hours..Open 7 days
Credit cards...Accepted
Price range...Expensive
Style...Smart casual
Cuisine..Japanese-Peruvian
Recommended for...High end

"They know when to be elaborate and when to let the
food speak for itself."—Tam Storrar

PARK CHINOIS

Recommended by
Rohit Ghai

17 Berkeley Street
Mayfair
London W1J 8EA
+44 2072915100
www.parkchinois.com

Opening hours..Open 7 days
Credit cards...Accepted
Price range...Expensive
Style...Smart casual
Cuisine...Chinese
Recommended for.................................Wish I'd opened

"High-end Chinese restaurant with elegant interiors.
Its menu is derived from authentic Chinese with
superior quality ingredients. I love the individuality
of all the dishes on the menu."—Rohit Ghai

LA PETITE MAISON

Recommended by
Izu Ani,
Eyal Jagermann,
Helena Puolakka,
Theo Randall, Mitch Tonks

Avey House
53–54 Brooks Mews
Mayfair
London W1 4EG
+44 2074954774
www.lpmlondon.co.uk

Opening hours..Open 7 days
Credit cards...Accepted
Price range...Affordable
Style...Smart casual
Cuisine...French
Recommended for...High end

"What an amazing restaurant. Chef Raphael Duntoye
serves dishes and flavors of southern France, with
influences from the Mediterranean. Simple, clever,
sharp flavors, incredible quality of produce and
stunning execution, time and time again. Scallop
carpaccio with chives and cranberries, grilled veal
chops with aubergine sauce, lemon and garlic
chicken—everything is just perfect. The room and
atmosphere are luxurious and the service is on
point and friendly."—Eyal Jagermann

This offshoot of the famous Nice hotspot of the
same name caters for the Mayfair set by combining
a luxuriously bourgeois French menu with suave but
informal service. Dishes are designed for sharing
and arrive in their own time, from *hors d'oeuvres* to
rich mains such as pappardelle with veal ragù and
Mediterranean classics like salt-baked sea bass.
If there's a dish that sums it up, it's probably the
whole black leg chicken stuffed with foie gras—
roasted to order and well worth the hour's wait.

POLLEN STREET SOCIAL

Recommended by
Sat Bains, James Durrant

8–10 Pollen Street
Mayfair
London W1S 1NQ
+44 2072907600
www.pollenstreetsocial.com

Opening hours...Closed Sunday
Credit cards...Accepted
Price range...Expensive
Style...Smart casual
Cuisine...Modern British
Recommended for.......................................Local favorite

"It's a refined, sophisticated restaurant. I think it really
sums up the London food scene."—James Durrant

RISTORANTE FRESCOBALDI LONDON
Recommended by
Hus Vedat
15 New Burlington Place
Mayfair
London W1S 2HX
+44 2036933435
www.frescobaldi.london

Opening hours	Open 7 days
Credit cards	Accepted
Price range	Affordable
Style	Smart casual
Cuisine	Italian
Recommended for	High end

"White truffle tagliolini, when in season, is not to be missed!"—Hus Vedat

ROKA
Recommended by
Sat Bains, Hélène Darroze,
Florence Knight, Mark Sargeant
30 North Audley Street
Mayfair
London W1K 6HP
+44 2073055644
www.rokarestaurant.com

Opening hours	Open 7 days
Credit cards	Accepted
Price range	Expensive
Style	Smart casual
Cuisine	Japanese
Recommended for	High end

SCOTT'S
Recommended by
Alexis Gauthier, Ben Tish
20 Mount Street
Mayfair
London W1K 2HE
+44 2074957309
www.scotts-restaurant.com

Opening hours	Open 7 days
Credit cards	Accepted
Price range	Affordable
Style	Smart casual
Cuisine	Seafood
Recommended for	Local favorite

"Scott's is the embodiment of London restaurants, in my opinion. Perfect service, simple but excellent food, beautiful design. Enduring: how many restaurant make it past two years, let alone fifty!"—Alexis Gauthier

STREET XO
Recommended by
Tom Aikens
15 Old Burlington Street
Mayfair
London W1S 3AJ
+44 2030967555
www.streetxo.com

Opening hours	Open 7 days
Credit cards	Accepted
Price range	Affordable
Style	Smart casual
Cuisine	Spanish
Recommended for	High end

UMU
Recommended by
Hélène Darroze, Tom Moxon,
Dharshan Munidasa,
Townsend Wentz
14–16 Bruton Place
Mayfair
London W1J 6LX
+44 2074998881
www.umurestaurant.com

Opening hours	Closed Sunday
Credit cards	Accepted
Price range	Expensive
Style	Smart casual
Cuisine	Japanese
Recommended for	Worth the travel

"I love Japanese food and this restaurant uses the best products from the UK in its cuisine, particularly the amazing fish from Scotland. Yoshinori Ishii, the chef, is particularly respectful of these products but is also so creative."—Hélène Darroze

WILD HONEY
Recommended by
Jason Atherton
12 St George Street
Mayfair
London W1S 2FB
+44 2077589160
www.wildhoneyrestaurant.co.uk

Opening hours	Closed Sunday
Credit cards	Accepted
Price range	Affordable
Style	Casual
Cuisine	Modern European
Recommended for	Regular neighborhood

THE WINDMILL

Recommended by
Jason Atherton

6–8 Mill Street
Mayfair
London W1S 2AZ
+44 2074918050
www.windmillmayfair.co.uk

Opening hours	Open 7 days
Credit cards	Accepted
Price range	Affordable
Style	Casual
Cuisine	British
Recommended for	Local favorite

"Trying to get a table on pie night is impossible."
—Jason Atherton

THE WOLSELEY

Recommended by
Tom Aikens, Jason Atherton, Sat Bains,
Alexis Gauthier, David Gingell,
Peter Gordon, Philip Howard,
Jeremy Lee, Colin Mackay,
Francesco Mazzei, Thomasina Miers

160 Piccadilly
Mayfair
London W1J 9EB
+44 2074996996
www.thewolseley.com

Opening hours	Open 7 days
Credit cards	Accepted
Price range	Expensive
Style	Smart casual
Cuisine	European
Recommended for	Breakfast

"It has an amazing buzz that sets the pace for a day in the center of town—and delivers exactly what it sets out to do—a great breakfast, suitable for all tastes and budgets."—Philip Howard

Such is its overwhelming popularity as a breakfast venue, many of its loyal regulars never go to The Wolseley for either lunch or dinner, although it's typically full for both. The lengthy morning menu is packed with comfort: crumpets, kedgeree, crispy bacon rolls, Eggs Benedict, fried haggis with duck eggs, omelette Arnold Bennett (with smoked haddock, Parmesan and cream) and a fine selection of Viennese pastries—to name but a fraction of what's on offer. But it's also about the setting and the sumptuous space. Once the Piccadilly showroom for the old marque it's named after, it's now a sweeping grand café in the European style.

10 GREEK STREET

Recommended by
Shaun Hill

10 Greek Street
Soho
London W1D 4DH
+44 2077344677
www.10greekstreet.com

Opening hours	Closed Sunday
Credit cards	Accepted
Price range	Affordable
Style	Casual
Cuisine	Modern European
Recommended for	Bargain

"Great wines and interesting snacks."—Shaun Hill

ANDREW EDMUNDS

Recommended by
Alexis Gauthier, Jeremy Lee,
Bruno Loubet, Tania Steytler

46 Lexington Street
Soho
London W1F 0LP
+44 2074375708
www.andrewedmunds.com

Opening hours	Open 7 days
Credit cards	Accepted
Price range	Affordable
Style	Smart casual
Cuisine	European-British
Recommended for	Local favorite

"Andrew Edmunds is a Soho institution that's been around since the 1980s. It's a small, rambling little townhouse with a handwritten menu, serving excellent classics that aren't over-priced."—Bruno Loubet

LE BAB

Recommended by
Pete Denhart

Top Floor, Kingly Court
Carnaby Street
Soho
London W1B 5PW
+44 2074399222
www.eatlebab.com

Opening hours	Open 7 days
Credit cards	Accepted
Price range	Affordable
Style	Casual
Cuisine	Middle Eastern Kebab
Recommended for	Worth the travel

"Spiced cauliflower pastilla, fifteen-hour free range pork shawarma kebab, and double-cooked fries with fondue—it's just amazing."—Pete Denhart

BAO

53 Lexington Street
Soho
London W1F 9AS
+44 7769627811
www.baolondon.com

Opening hours	Closed Sunday
Credit cards	Accepted
Price range	Affordable
Style	Casual
Cuisine	Taiwanese
Recommended for	Bargain

"This is fast food, but not as the term would suggest. The buns are what pull people in, but it's all the sides I go back for—the aubergine mapo is incredible."
—Yotam Ottolenghi

It's a familiar route for London restaurateurs; begin as a street-food operation then progress to a bricks-and-mortar site, bringing your fan base with you. But nobody who had ever tried the admittedly lovely rice-flour buns from Netil Market could have prepared themselves for the tour-de-force of modern Taiwanese cooking that is Bao Soho, with dishes such as pig blood cake (topped with a luminous egg yolk), beef rump cap with aged soy sauce, and the instant classic Taiwanese fried chicken. Queues reflect the quality (and value) of the food, but there's a second branch now in Fitzrovia to spread the demand (where you can even book).

BAR ITALIA

22 Frith Street
Soho
London W1D 4RF
+44 2074374520
www.baritaliasoho.co.uk

Opening hours	Open 7 days
Credit cards	Accepted
Price range	Budget
Style	Casual
Cuisine	Café-Italian
Recommended for	Late night

"I love the buzz and energy, and also the history of this late-night Soho institution. It is more of a snacky eatery, and more often than not you meet some amazing characters."—Alfred Prasad

BAR TERMINI

7 Old Compton Street
Soho
London W1D 5JE
+44 7860945018
www.bar-termini.com

Opening hours	Open 7 days
Credit cards	Accepted
Price range	Affordable
Style	Casual
Cuisine	Italian
Recommended for	Breakfast

BARRAFINA

26–27 Dean Street
Soho
London W1D 3LL
www.barrafina.co.uk

Opening hours	Open 7 days
Credit cards	Accepted
Price range	Affordable
Style	Casual
Cuisine	Spanish
Recommended for	Late night

"Mouth-watering Spanish tapas served at a bar, using the most beautiful ingredients and with a really delicious wine list."—Thomasina Miers

BASHAN RESTAURANT

24 Romilly Street
Soho
London W1D 5AH
+44 2072873266
www.bashanrestaurant.co.uk

Opening hours	Open 7 days
Credit cards	Accepted but not AMEX
Price range	Affordable
Style	Casual
Cuisine	Chinese
Recommended for	Regular neighborhood

"Bashan is one of my go-to evening venues. Blisteringly good Hunanese food with lots of offal and spice on offer. Go for the fried chicken bits on a bed of chile or the whole sea bass. Also the cabbage side is way, way better than it sounds"—Neil Rankin

BLACKLOCK

24 Great Windmill Street
Soho
London W1D 7LG
+44 2034416996
www.theblacklock.com

Recommended by
Tomer Amedi, Pete Denhart,
Elizabeth Haigh, Martin Morales

Opening hours	Open 7 days
Credit cards	Accepted
Price range	Affordable
Style	Casual
Cuisine	Barbecue
Recommended for	Local favorite

"I go there whenever I crave chops. I always crave chops. Go there, eat chops!"—Tomer Amedi

There's something peculiarly attractive about anywhere with a good, solid focus. At Blacklock, the speciality is chops—pork, lamb and beef—sourced from top butchers Warrens of Cornwall and given just enough of a blast over charcoal to form a nice char while leaving them pink and juicy within. This would be enough of a reason in itself to visit this buzzy Soho basement space, but with a range of larger cuts available from time to time and an interesting drinks list, it's no wonder they're regularly queuing down the street.

BLANCHETTE

9 D'Arblay Street
Soho
London W1F 8DR
+44 2074398100
www.blanchettesoho.co.uk

Recommended by
Tomer Amedi, Ben Tish

Opening hours	Open 7 days
Credit cards	Accepted
Price range	Affordable
Style	Casual
Cuisine	French
Recommended for	Late night

"Three very cool French brothers, Yannis, Max, and Malik, have opened this funky little spot in Soho and it's my favorite place when I want to feel at home, drink good French wine and eat lots of charcuterie and cheese. They also have a fantastic à la carte menu if you are looking for more."—Tomer Amedi

BOB BOB RICARD

1 Upper James Street
Soho
London W1 9DF
+44 2031451000
www.bobbobricard.com

Recommended by
Alexis Gauthier

Opening hours	Open 7 days
Credit cards	Accepted but not Diners
Price range	Expensive
Style	Smart casual
Cuisine	British-Russian
Recommended for	Regular neighborhood

"It is the most fun you can have in a restaurant. Beautiful interior, superb service, food, and drink. All about luxury, enjoyment and comfort."
—Alexis Gauthier

BOCCA DI LUPO

12 Archer Street
Soho
London W1D 7BB
+44 2077342223
www.boccadilupo.com

Recommended by
Hélène Darroze, Adam D'Sylva,
Jarrett Stieber, Sami Tallberg

Opening hours	Open 7 days
Credit cards	Accepted
Price range	Affordable
Style	Casual
Cuisine	Italian
Recommended for	Wish I'd opened

"Simply stunning seasonal and regional Italian food, with a typical Central London non-stop-service mentality."—Sami Tallberg

BONE DADDIES

31 Peter Street
Soho
London W1F 0AR
+44 2072878581
www.bonedaddies.com

Recommended by
Miles Kirby, Ben Spalding

Opening hours	Open 7 days
Credit cards	Accepted
Price range	Affordable
Style	Casual
Cuisine	Japanese
Recommended for	Late night

BRASSERIE ZÉDEL

20 Sherwood Street
Soho
London W1F 7ED
+44 2077344888
www.brasseriezedel.com

Opening hours	Open 7 days
Credit cards	Accepted
Price range	Affordable
Style	Smart casual
Cuisine	French Brasserie
Recommended for	Bargain

"Great brasserie food, can't really fault it any time of day but also one of the only late spots in London." —Mark Dobbie

Though prices have crept up slightly in recent years at this cavernous basement brasserie, it remains one of the few Soho restaurants where you can sit down, be served a three-course meal by a smartly clad waiter, and still pay less than the price of a cinema ticket. The *prix fixe,* including *steak haché* and *frites,* comes thoroughly recommended, but do leave room for desserts; the *tarte citron* (lemon tart) is a beauty. At the Bar Americain next door you can snack and drink till the wee hours, and there's a cabaret too (Live at Zedel). An operation from an altogether more civilized age.

THE BREAKFAST CLUB

33 D'Arblay Street
Soho
London W1F 8EU
+44 2074342571
www.thebreakfastclubcafes.com

Opening hours	Open 7 days
Credit cards	Accepted but not AMEX
Price range	Budget
Style	Casual
Cuisine	Café-Bistro
Recommended for	Breakfast

"Very relaxed informal service with a high-quality breakfast, always hot, always tasty."—Adam Stokes

BUBBLE DOGS

70 Charlotte Street
Soho
London W1T 4QG
+44 2076377770
www.bubbledogs.co.uk

Opening hours	Closed Sunday
Credit cards	Accepted
Price range	Affordable
Style	Casual
Cuisine	Hot Dogs
Recommended for	Wish I'd opened

"What a brilliant concept! Sell wealthy Londoners American-style hot dogs and expensive Champagne. How witty and ironic, and hence how British. Excellent."—Matthew Kirkley

Run by an ex-Noma duo, this Champagne and hot-dog joint opened in 2012, and immediately won over both the hip and the jaded. Its concept is clever: single-estate Champagnes served not with caviar, as you'd expect, but gourmet dogs—from the 'New Yorker' (with sauerkraut and caramelized onions), to more extravagant versions like the 'BLT' (crispy bacon, caramelized lettuce and truffle mayo). Sides include potato 'tots' and fresh coleslaw. The owners' small-plate venture, Kitchen Table, is also on the premises.

BURGER AND LOBSTER

36–38 Dean Street
Soho
London W1D 4PS
+44 2074324800
www.burgerandlobster.com

Opening hours	Open 7 days
Credit cards	Accepted but not Diners
Price range	Affordable
Style	Casual
Cuisine	Burgers-Seafood
Recommended for	Wish I'd opened

BUSABA EATHAI SOHO

106–110 Wardour Street
Soho
London W1F 0TR
+44 2072558686
www.busaba.com

Recommended by
Omar Allibhoy, Michael Reid

Opening hours	Open 7 days
Credit cards	Accepted
Price range	Budget
Style	Casual
Cuisine	Thai
Recommended for	Bargain

"I've been dining here since it first opened in London over a decade ago and I believe the food is as good now as it was then. It doesn't break the bank either!" —Michael Reid

C&R

4 Rupert Court
Soho
London W1D 6DY
+44 2074341128
www.cnrrestaurant.com

Recommended by
Florence Knight

Opening hours	Open 7 days
Credit cards	Accepted
Price range	Budget
Style	Casual
Cuisine	Malaysian
Recommended for	Bargain

CAFÉ MONICO

39–45 Shaftesbury Avenue
Soho
London W1D 6LA
+44 2037276161
www.cafemonico.com

Recommended by
Robert Ortiz

Opening hours	Open 7 days
Credit cards	Accepted
Price range	Affordable
Style	Casual
Cuisine	Italian-French
Recommended for	Breakfast

CHOTTO MATTE

11–13 Frith Street
Soho
London W1D 4RB
+44 2070427171
www.chotto-matte.com

Recommended by
Peter Gordon

Opening hours	Open 7 days
Credit cards	Accepted
Price range	Affordable
Style	Casual
Cuisine	Japanese
Recommended for	Late night

THE CRISPY DUCK

27 Wardour Street
Soho
London W1D 6PW
+44 2072876578

Recommended by
Luke Vandore-Mackay

Opening hours	Open 7 days
Credit cards	Accepted but not AMEX or Diners
Price range	Affordable
Style	Casual
Cuisine	Chinese
Recommended for	Late night

"When I was much younger after a night out in the West End, I would usually end up in Chinatown by myself eating an oyster and pork belly dish in The Crispy Duck. Salty. Delicious. Hangover making." —Luke Vandore-Mackay

DEAN STREET TOWNHOUSE

69–71 Dean Street
Soho
London W1D 3SE
+44 2074341775
www.deanstreettownhouse.com

Recommended by
Alexis Gauthier

Opening hours	Open 7 days
Credit cards	Accepted but not AMEX or Diners
Price range	Affordable
Style	Smart casual
Cuisine	British
Recommended for	Breakfast

"It's everything you want a simple breakfast place to be. Good service. Good value."—Alexis Gauthier

DISHOOM

Recommended by
Pete Denhart, Bonny Porter

22 Kingly Street
Soho
London W1B 5QP
+44 2074209322
www.dishoom.com

Opening hours	Open 7 days
Credit cards	Accepted
Price range	Affordable
Style	Casual
Cuisine	Indian
Recommended for	Breakfast

"Go off-menu and order a bacon, egg and sausage naan with cream cheese, chile tomato jam and fresh herbs."—Pete Denhart

DUCKSOUP

Recommended by
Matteo Aloe

41 Dean Street
Soho
London W1D 4PY
+44 2072874599
www.ducksoupsoho.co.uk

Opening hours	Open 7 days
Credit cards	Accepted
Price range	Affordable
Style	Casual
Cuisine	Modern European
Recommended for	Late night

DUMPLINGS' LEGEND

Recommended by
Tomer Amedi, Alyn Williams

15–16 Gerrard Street
Soho
London W1D 6JE
+44 2074941200
www.dumplingslegend.com

Opening hours	Open 7 days
Credit cards	Accepted
Price range	Affordable
Style	Casual
Cuisine	Chinese
Recommended for	Bargain

"On the weekend, I think it's the only place I like to go after service. My favorite dumplings are of course the *xiao long bao*, the soup dumplings. I love the ritual, I love the way they burst in your mouth, I love eating them until I can't move. Plus it's probably the fastest service you can get anywhere."—Tomer Amedi

EAT TOKYO

Recommended by
Eyal Jagermann

16 Old Compton Street
Soho
London W1D 4TL
+44 2074399887
www.eattokyo.co.uk

Opening hours	Open 7 days
Credit cards	Accepted but not AMEX or Diners
Price range	Affordable
Style	Casual
Cuisine	Japanese
Recommended for	Regular neighborhood

"I eat quite a lot at Eat Tokyo—a simple and delicious Japanese restaurant. Sushi, sashimi, tempura and lots of Japanese classics. Great price too."
—Eyal Jagermann

ENGAWA

Recommended by
Tom Moxon

2 Ham Yard
Soho
London W1D 7DT
+44 2072875724
www.engawa.uk

Opening hours	Open 7 days
Credit cards	Accepted
Price range	Expensive
Style	Smart casual
Cuisine	Japanese
Recommended for	High end

FERNANDEZ & WELLS

Recommended by
Florence Knight

1–3 Denmark Street
Soho
London WC2H 8LP
+44 2033029799
www.fernandezandwells.com

Opening hours	Open 7 days
Credit cards	Accepted
Price range	Affordable
Style	Casual
Cuisine	Spanish Café
Recommended for	Breakfast

"The egg dishes are cooked simply on a hot plate and served with toasted and buttered sourdough. Good, strong coffee, fresh orange juice and pastries make a fine breakfast."—Florence Knight

FLAT IRON

17 Beak Street
Soho
London W1F 9RW
+44 2034870088
www.flatironsteak.co.uk

Recommended by
Joel Braham, Martin Morales,
Bonny Porter, Michael Reid,
Hus Vedat

Opening hours	Open 7 days
Credit cards	Accepted
Price range	Affordable
Style	Casual
Cuisine	Steakhouse
Recommended for	Bargain

"£10 ($13) steak, enough said."—Hus Vedat

FOUR SEASONS

23 Wardour Street
Soho
London W1D 6PW
+44 2072879995
www.fs-restaurants.co.uk

Recommended by
Phil Carmichael

Opening hours	Open 7 days
Credit cards	Accepted
Price range	Affordable
Style	Casual
Cuisine	Chinese
Recommended for	Late night

"This place has the best crispy duck in London; good for a few beers after work."—Phil Carmichael

GAIL'S

128 Wardour Street
Soho
London W1F 8ZL
+44 2072871324
www.gailsbread.co.uk

Recommended by
Matteo Aloe, Amandine Chaignot

Opening hours	Open 7 days
Credit cards	Accepted
Price range	Budget
Style	Casual
Cuisine	Bakery
Recommended for	Breakfast

GERRARD'S CORNER

30 Wardour Street
Soho
London W1D 6QW
+44 2072871878
www.gerrardscorner.co.uk

Recommended by
Jeremy Lee

Opening hours	Open 7 days
Credit cards	Accepted
Price range	Affordable
Style	Casual
Cuisine	Chinese
Recommended for	Bargain

"For quick, cheap chow, hard to beat."—Jeremy Lee

THE GOLDEN DRAGON

28–29 Gerrard Street
Soho
London W1D 6JW
+44 20 7734 1073

Recommended by
Florence Knight, Miles Kirby

Opening hours	Open 7 days
Credit cards	Accepted
Price range	Affordable
Style	Casual
Cuisine	Dim Sum
Recommended for	Late night

HIX SOHO

66–70 Brewer Street
Soho
London W1F 9UP
+44 2072923518
www.hixrestaurants.co.uk/restaurant/hix-soho

Recommended by
Manoj Vasaikar

Opening hours	Open 7 days
Credit cards	Accepted
Price range	Affordable
Style	Casual
Cuisine	Modern British
Recommended for	High end

HOPPERS

49 Frith Street
Soho
London W1D 4SG
www.hopperslondon.com

Recommended by
Nieves Barragán Mohacho, Erchen Chang,
Pete Denhart, James Knappett,
Thomasina Miers, José Pizarro,
Neil Rankin, Shaun Searley,
Tam Storrar, Sameer Taneja

Opening hours	Closed Sunday
Credit cards	Accepted
Price range	Affordable
Style	Casual
Cuisine	Sri Lankan
Recommended for	Bargain

"I'm not a huge fan of Indian food done in small-plate format and to an extent that's what Hoppers does but it's not fancy chef-y stuff. These are big, bold, thick curries packed with fat and huge flavor profiles, from bone marrow to chicken hearts. You can't eat much more than they give you and you usually over order. Almost everything is done perfectly and the attention to detail for such great-value food is stunning. I'd go there every day if I trusted myself more. Cracking roti parathas too."—Neil Rankin

JKS, the team behind Trishna, Gymkhana and a whole host of London's finest restaurants, have a knack of distilling a cuisine down to its essence, adding an on-trend twist, and then packaging it all in such a way that has them queuing down the street. Hoppers is Sri Lankan food for modern London, a mixture of the traditional (the hopper itself, a perfectly timed fried egg set in a delicate pancake) and the modern (the creative cocktail list and the inventive small plates, such as bonemarrow varuval roti). Of course, it's all wildly popular and no reservations—but they'll take your number and call you back when there's a space, and you can't say fairer than that.

JEN CAFÉ

4–8 Newport Place
Soho
London WC2H 7JP
+44 2072879708

Recommended by
Sandia Chang, Alex Jackson

Opening hours	Open 7 days
Credit cards	Accepted but not AMEX or Diners
Price range	Affordable
Style	Casual
Cuisine	Chinese
Recommended for	Bargain

"The best £5 ($6.50) plate of boiled dumplings in town. My wife orders two portions of the veg ones as standard, no sharing. Also home to excellent hand-pulled noodles with spicy minced pork and cucumber."—Alex Jackson

JINJUU SOHO

Kingly Court
15 Kingly Street
Soho
London W1B 5PS
+44 2081818887
www.jinjuu.com

Recommended by
Rohit Ghai, Paul Walsh

Opening hours	Open 7 days
Credit cards	Accepted
Price range	Affordable
Style	Casual
Cuisine	Korean
Recommended for	Late night

JOY LUCK RESTAURANT

47 Gerrard Street
Soho
London W1D 5QJ
+44 2074374170

Recommended by
Carl Clarke

Opening hours	Open 7 days
Credit cards	Accepted
Price range	Affordable
Style	Casual
Cuisine	Chinese
Recommended for	Regular neighborhood

"Family-run and from the outside doesn't seem open sometimes but go in and you will find the best hand-stretched noodles in beef broth in London, amongst other spicy delights such as pigs' ears with peanut chile and the best Singapore noodles on the planet, cooked with spam and tandoor paste."—Carl Clarke

THE KATI ROLL COMPANY

24 Poland Street
Soho
London W1F 8QL
+44 2072874787
www.thekatirollcompany.com

Recommended by
Florence Knight,
Alfred Prasad

Opening hours	Open 7 days
Credit cards	Accepted
Price range	Budget
Style	Casual
Cuisine	Indian
Recommended for	Bargain

"Kati rolls—wholemeal (wholewheat) paratha wraps filled with succulent grilled meat—are a popular

Indian street food. This restaurant does a great job of recreating the experience whilst offering really good value for money."—Alfred Prasad

KILN

58 Brewer Street
Soho
London W1F 9TL
www.kilnsoho.com

Recommended by
Jason Atherton, Nieves Barragán Mohacho, Harneet Baweja, Tom Cunanan, David Gingell, Elizabeth Haigh, Stephen Harris, Jeremy Lee, Andy Oliver, Karam Sethi

Opening hours..Open 7 days
Credit cards...Accepted
Price range..Affordable
Style...Casual
Cuisine...Thai
Recommended for.............................Wish I'd opened

"Kiln delivers all my expectations but more. My favorite part of their restaurant is how they use this small insulated burner called a 'tao' to heat up their claypots and woks. You get that sensation of the fire and smell of charcoal from their open kitchen to your table. Besides their cooking technique, the food looks awesome. The clay pot baked crab and glass noodle with mangalitsa belly this is the kind of dish that makes me say, 'Why didnt I think of this?!'"
—Tom Cunanan

KITCHEN TABLE @ BUBBLE DOGS

70 Charlotte Street
Soho
London W1T 4QQ
www.kitchentablelondon.co.uk

Recommended by
Elizabeth Haigh, Paul Foster, Samuel Nutter, Adam Reid

Opening hours..Closed Sunday
Credit cards...Accepted
Price range...Expensive
Style...Smart casual
Cuisine...Modern British
Recommended for.............................Wish I'd opened

"The cooking is very clean and you can feel that the quality of the ingredients is very high. The thing that is evident whilst dining there is the passion and time that has gone into sourcing the produce as all of the dishes are explained to you from the open kitchen."
—Samuel Nutter

KOYA BAR

50 Frith Street
Soho
London W1D 4SQ
www.koyabar.co.uk

Recommended by
Nieves Barragán Mohacho, Sandia Chang, Samantha & Samuel Clark, Carl Clarke, Pete Denhart, Cary Docherty, James Knappett, Florence Knight, Mark Rosati

Opening hours..Open 7 days
Credit cards.............................Accepted but not AMEX
Price range..Budget
Style...Casual
Cuisine..Japanese
Recommended for..Breakfast

"I like to start my day off in a calm, serene and delicious way and Koya Bar ticks all the boxes. The breakfast is a mix of wonderfully executed traditional Japanese dishes with some British inspired ones too, such as the Full English Udon, which contains a fried egg and streaky bacon. The Japanese tea selection is wonderful too."—Mark Rosati

KRICKET SOHO

12 Denman Street
Soho
London W1D 7HH
www.kricket.co.uk

Recommended by
Nieves Barragán Mohacho, Thomasina Miers

Opening hours..Closed Sunday
Credit cards...Accepted
Price range..Affordable
Style...Casual
Cuisine...British-Indian
Recommended for.......................Regular neighborhood

MAISON BERTAUX

Recommended by
Florence Knight, Jeremy Lee

28 Greek Street
Soho
London W1D 5DQ
+44 2074376007
www.maisonbertaux.com

Opening hours	Open 7 days
Credit cards	Accepted but not Diners
Price range	Affordable
Style	Casual
Cuisine	French
Recommended for	Local favorite

"Maison Bertaux is a favorite spot for an afternoon Earl Grey and chocolate eclair."—Florence Knight

This old Soho spot boasts of being London's oldest patisserie, originally opened by Communards who, having fled Paris following the failure of the Fourth French Revolution, took refuge in cake. While it's true that the service can be hit and miss, it never fails to be entertainingly theatrical. The French fancies and cream cakes, still baked daily on the premises, are a reliable source of calories and *le café au lait—c'est bon*. Whether it's from a window table at street level or out on the pavement (sidewalk), there are few better vantage points from which to watch Soho go by.

THE NINTH

Recommended by
Henrik Ritzen

22 Charlotte street
Soho
London W1T 2NB
+44 2030190880
www.theninthlondon.com

Opening hours	Closed Sunday
Credit cards	Accepted but not Diners
Price range	Affordable
Style	Smart casual
Cuisine	Modern French
Recommended for	Local favorite

"Very high-quality food in a relaxed and warm atmosphere. Good choice of sharing plates."
—Henrik Ritzen

OLD TOWN 97

Recommended by
Bruno Loubet

19 Wardour Street
Soho
London W1D 6PL
+44 2077342868

Opening hours	Open 7 days
Credit cards	Accepted
Price range	Affordable
Style	Casual
Cuisine	Chinese
Recommended for	Late night

"This place is in the center of Chinatown and open until very late, so it's perfect for when you've had a busy late shift. They do excellent tofu."—Bruno Loubet

OPIUM

Recommended by
Sameer Taneja

The Jade Door
15–16 Gerrard Street
Soho
London W1D 6JE
+44 2077347276
www.opiumchinatown.com

Opening hours	Open 7 days
Credit cards	Accepted
Price range	Affordable
Style	Casual
Cuisine	Chinese
Recommended for	Late night

THE PALOMAR

Recommended by
Matteo Aloe, Joel Braham,
Martin Morales

34 Rupert Street
Soho
London W1D 6DN
+44 2074398777
www.thepalomar.co.uk

Opening hours	Open 7 days
Credit cards	Accepted
Price range	Affordable
Style	Smart casual
Cuisine	Middle Eastern
Recommended for	Local favorite

PHO & BUN

76 Shaftsbury Avenue
Soho
London W1D 6ND
+44 2072873528
www.vieteat.co.uk

Recommended by
Sameer Taneja

Opening hours	Open 7 days
Credit cards	Accepted
Price range	Budget
Style	Casual
Cuisine	Vietnamese
Recommended for	Bargain

"Very affordable, fresh and quick. Fantastic bao and noodles."—Sameer Taneja

PRINCI

135 Wardour Street
Soho
London W1F 0UT
+44 2074788888
www.princi.com

Recommended by
Francesco Mazzei, Tom Moxon,
Neil Rankin

Opening hours	Open 7 days
Credit cards	Accepted
Price range	Affordable
Style	Casual
Cuisine	Italian-Pizza-Bakery
Recommended for	Bargain

"Princi has two major advantages for me in the morning. One: it has the best-tasting coffee in London, a far cry from the over acidic coffee we're sold with a naff design in the foam and not enough milk. Two: it has the best toilet in London. It's like a fancy spa toilet from a five-star hotel. Those two facts alone tick off my morning routine. Add to that ceps with poached eggs and toast and pastries and it's an ideal start to the day." —Neil Rankin

QUO VADIS

26–29 Dean Street
Soho
London W1D 3LL
+44 2074379585
www.quovadissoho.co.uk

Recommended by
Will Bowlby, Olle T. Cellton,
Florence Knight, Luke Vandore-Mackay,
Nieves Barragán Mohacho,
Thomasina Miers

Opening hours	Closed Sunday
Credit cards	Accepted but not Diners
Price range	Affordable
Style	Smart casual
Cuisine	British
Recommended for	Late night

"The bar is open until midnight and the food is always good. Freshly baked cheese straws are really buttery and who doesn't love a chip butty before bed?" —Florence Knight

RASA SAYANG

5 Macclesfield Street
Soho
London W1D 6AY
+44 2077341382
www.rasasayangfood.com

Recommended by
Mitch Tonks

Opening hours	Open 7 days
Credit cards	Accepted
Price range	Affordable
Style	Casual
Cuisine	Malaysian
Recommended for	Bargain

"Good curries and Malay food, you only need one plate and it's enough for a meal. The *nasi goreng* is very good. Eat early when it's all freshly prepared and ask for thighs in the chicken curry, they tend to give breast if you're not Malaysian."—Mitch Tonks

ROKA

37 Charlotte street
Soho
London W1T 1RR
+44 2075806464
www.rokarestaurant.com

Recommended by
Miles Kirby

Opening hours	Open 7 days
Credit cards	Accepted
Price range	Expensive
Style	Smart casual
Cuisine	Japanese
Recommended for	High end

"Great food, great service, great vibe. Every time." —Miles Kirby

SMOKING GOAT

Recommended by
Carl Clarke, Sami Tamimi

7 Denmark Street
Soho
London WC2H 8LZ
www.smokinggoatsoho.com

Opening hours	Open 7 days
Credit cards	Accepted
Price range	Affordable
Style	Casual
Cuisine	Thai Barbecue
Recommended for	Local favorite

"This down-to-earth restaurant offers the most delicious Thai food. Spicy, innovative and on-point."
—Sami Tamimi

SPUNTINO

Recommended by
Tom Aikens, Adam Byatt

61 Rupert Street
Soho
London W1D 7PW
www.spuntino.co.uk

Opening hours	Open 7 days
Reservation policy	No
Credit cards	Accepted
Price range	Affordable
Style	Casual
Cuisine	American-Italian
Recommended for	Late night

Russell Norman's follow-up to Polpo channels the aesthetic of a hip Brooklyn diner meets a fashion-forward Lower East Side speakeasy. It's darkly lit with artfully aged white tiles on the walls, rusty tin on the ceiling, an alt-rock soundtrack and a U-shaped, zinc-topped counter around which sit twenty-seven fixed stools. There's no telephone, no reservations, and a long wait at peak times for the menu of Italian-American small plates that take in various sliders, meatballs, and pizzette. The popcorn machine churns out complimentary cups of the salty snack laced with chile to make you thirsty for the predominantly Italian and reasonably-priced wine list.

TEMPER

Recommended by
Martin Morales, Luke Vandore-Mackay

25 Broadwick Street
Soho
London W1F 0DF
+44 2038793834
www.temperrestaurant.com

Opening hours	Open 7 days
Credit cards	Accepted
Price range	Affordable
Style	Casual
Cuisine	Barbecue
Recommended for	Wish I'd opened

"Meat and Fire. It's brilliant and Neil Rankin is a great guy."—Luke Vandore-Mackay

TONKOTSU

Recommended by
Carl Clarke

63 Dean Street
Soho
London W1D 4QG
+44 2074370071
www.tonkotsu.co.uk

Opening hours	Open 7 days
Credit cards	Accepted
Price range	Budget
Style	Casual
Cuisine	Ramen Noodles
Recommended for	Bargain

"Best ramen noodles in the UK all made in-house. Tasty broths and two of my favorite restaurant peeps in town."—Carl Clarke

VASCO & PIERO'S PAVILION

Recommended by
Florence Knight

15 Poland Street
Soho
London W1F 8QE
+44 2074378774
www.vascosfood.com

Opening hours	Closed Sunday
Credit cards	Accepted but not Diners
Price range	Affordable
Style	Casual
Cuisine	Italian
Recommended for	Regular neighborhood

"A long-standing institution in Soho. Umbrian classics make up most of the menu alongside weekly specials. The interior is comfortably dated and the service easy and old fashioned."—Florence Knight

YAUATCHA SOHO

15–17 Broadwick Street
Soho
London W1F 0DL
+44 2074948888
www.yauatcha.com

Recommended by
Sat Bains, Cary Docherty,
Alexis Gauthier, Mitch Tonks,
Paul Walsh

Opening hours	Open 7 days
Credit cards	Accepted
Price range	Affordable
Style	Smart casual
Cuisine	Chinese
Recommended for	Regular neighborhood

"I already know all my favorite dishes. I can almost order before I get there. My kids love the jasmine tea smoked ribs."—Paul Walsh

45 JERMYN STREET

45 Jermyn Street
St James's
London SW1Y 6DN
+44 207 205 4545
https://www.45jermynst.com/

Recommended by
Ben Tish

Opening hours	Open 7 days
Credit cards	Accepted
Price range	Expensive
Style	Smart Casual
Cuisine	International
Recommended for	Local favorite

"More discreet than the Wolseley but same kind of chic London vibe"—Ben Tish

THE GALLERY

Fortnum & Mason
181 Piccadilly
St James's
London W1A 1ER
+44 2077348040
www.fortnumandmason.com

Recommended by
Shaun Hill

Opening hours	Open 7 days
Credit cards	Accepted
Price range	Affordable
Style	Smart casual
Cuisine	Modern British
Recommended for	Breakfast

"Comfortably traditional and with top class ingredients."—Shaun Hill

IL VICOLO

3–4 Crown Passage
St James's
London W1Y 5PP
+44 2078393960
www.ilvicolorestaurant.co.uk

Recommended by
JP McMahon

Opening hours	Closed Sunday
Credit cards	Accepted
Price range	Affordable
Style	Smart casual
Cuisine	Italian
Recommended for	Late night

"Contemporary Italian food. Great for a bottle of wine and a cheese and meat platter."—JP McMahon

CINNAMON CLUB

The Old Westminster Library
30–32 Great Smith Street
Westminster
London SW1P 3BU
+44 2072222555
www.cinnamonclub.com

Recommended by
Rohit Ghai

Opening hours	Open 7 days
Credit cards	Accepted
Price range	Affordable
Style	Casual
Cuisine	Modern Indian
Recommended for	Breakfast

"Mostly I prefer doing breakfast at home, but whenever I get a chance I go for Cinnamon Club because of the wide range of homely breakfast dishes served with a modern twist."—Rohit Ghai

THE GORING DINING ROOM

Recommended by
Mark Dobbie

15 Beeston Place
Westminster
London SW1W 0JW
+44 2073969000
www.thegoring.com

Opening hours	Open 7 days
Credit cards	Accepted
Price range	Expensive
Style	Smart casual
Cuisine	British
Recommended for	Local favorite

"The Goring are serving up British food that is very hard to find these days. Think eggs Drumkilbo (egg mayonnaise seafood cocktail) and beef Wellington carved table-side. It's an experience that is well worth it."—Mark Dobbie

Owned and run by the Goring family for over a century, this luxury Belgravia hotel was appointed a Royal Warrant on its 100th anniversary in 2010. From serving as a plush command center for the Chief of Allied Forces during World War I, to being the bride's family base for the wedding of the Duke and Duchess of Cambridge, it has always served the establishment. Its dining room, revamped in 2005 by Viscount Linley, remains a bastion of Britishness, where lunch is still called 'luncheon' and the trolley is laden with roast lamb, steak and kidney pie or roast beef. If class and grace are boring, then The Goring is a snorefest.

REGENCY CAFÉ

Recommended by
Tom Sellers, Ollie Templeton

17–19 Regency Street
Westminster
London SW1P 4BY
+44 2078216596
www.regencycafe.co.uk

Opening hours	Closed Sunday
Credit cards	Accepted
Price range	Budget
Style	Casual
Cuisine	Café
Recommended for	Breakfast

"It's a traditional café in Westminster that has been around for years. Busiest early in the morning when the tradespeople are in."—Tom Sellers

LONDON

EAST

$\hat{N}$ SCALE

0   400   800   1200   yd.

SHINOBI SUSHI

85 Junction Rd
Archway
London N19 5QU
+44 2037950517
www.ordershinobisushi.co.uk

Opening hours	Open 7 days
Credit cards	Accepted
Price range	Affordable
Style	Casual
Cuisine	Japanese
Recommended for	Late night

40 MALTBY STREET

40 Maltby Street
Bermondsey
London SE1 3PA
+44 2072379247
www.40maltbystreet.com

Opening hours	Closed Sunday to Tuesday
Credit cards	Accepted but not AMEX
Price range	Affordable
Style	Casual
Cuisine	British
Recommended for	Regular neighborhood

"Without doubt, the best neighborhood restaurant-wine bar in the world. Consistently surprising, genuinely delicious food, crafted for enjoyment rather than to suit modern trends. Excellent selection of interesting wines that they import themselves. Lovely people and ham!"—Tim Spedding

Locals weren't too pleased when this idiosyncratic venture in a rattling railway arch began to hit the headlines, but with its serious food and no-fuss presentation, it wasn't going to stay secret for long. Maltby Street was dubbed the 'next Borough Market', and while that hasn't really happened, it has spawned good ad hoc eateries—not least this wine bar and shop with a handful of tables and limited service hours. There are unusual natural wines from France, Italy and Slovenia at goodish mark-ups, but it's the (mismatched) small plates—deep fried duck eggs, say, or glazed Yorkshire ham—which really take center stage.

JOSÉ TAPAS BAR

104 Bermondsey Street
Bermondsey
London SE1 3UB
www.josepizarro.com/jose-tapas-bar

Opening hours	Open 7 days
Credit cards	Accepted
Price range	Budget
Style	Casual
Cuisine	Tapas
Recommended for	Regular neighborhood

"At this little hole in the wall you could be forgiven for thinking you had found yourself in Barcelona or San Sebastián. As a tiny corner bar, the atmosphere is always vibrant and the food prepared à la minute before your very eyes. From melting, moorish croquettes and sun-blushed *pan con tomate* to the jaw-droppingly good Iberica pork fillet—José Tapas Bar nails it everytime! Dare I say they have the best Padrón peppers in London?!"—Bonny Porter

BISTROTHEQUE

23–27 Wadeson Street
Bethnal Green
London E2 9DR
+44 2089837900
www.bistrotheque.com

Opening hours	Open 7 days
Credit cards	Accepted
Price range	Affordable
Style	Casual
Cuisine	Modern British
Recommended for	Regular neighborhood

"Brilliant all rounder that I've visited for years—week nights, sundays...and a great bar. They also have brilliant live acts, like a classical piano player at brunch." —Ben Tish

CAFÉ 338

338 Bethnal Green Road
Bethnal Green
London E2 0AG
+44 2077290246
www.cafe338.com

Opening hours	Open 7 days
Credit cards	Accepted
Price range	Budget
Style	Casual
Cuisine	Café
Recommended for	Breakfast

"Café 338 is our neighborhood breakfast place. They do great omelettes and will stuff it with whatever your heart desires."—Harneet Baweja.

E PELLICI

332 Bethnal Green Rd
Bethnal Green
London E2 0AG
+4420 7739 4873
http://epellicci.com/

Opening hours	Closed Sunday
Reservation policy	No
Credit cards	Accepted
Price range	Budget
Style	Casual
Cuisine	Café
Recommended for	Breakfast

"Bethnal green old-school italian café—solid breakfast and lunch and very entertaining service."
—Ben Tish

LAHORE EXPRESS

265 Bethnal Green Road
Bethnal Green
London E2 6AH
+44 2070121233

Opening hours	Open 7 days
Credit cards	Not accepted
Price range	Budget
Style	Casual
Cuisine	Pakistani
Recommended for	Bargain

"You always hear about Tayyabs but this place, in my opinion, is better, with no queue and even cheaper. There is a complete ban on alcohol on the premises but the karahi and lamb chops here are seriously the best in London. Big, big call I know, but it's true."
—Alexis Gauthier

SAGER + WILDE

Arch 250 Paradise Row
Bethnal Green
London E2 9LE
+44 2076130478
www.sagerandwilde.com

Opening hours	Closed Monday
Credit cards	Accepted but not AMEX or Diners
Price range	Affordable
Style	Smart casual
Cuisine	Modern European
Recommended for	High end

TOP TASTE

129 Roman Road
Bethnal Green
London E2 0QN
+44 2089802037
www.toptaste-e2.co.uk

Opening hours	Open 7 days
Credit cards	Accepted
Price range	Budget
Style	Casual
Cuisine	Chinese
Recommended for	Bargain

TYPING ROOM

Recommended by
Tom Aikens, Andy Oliver

Town Hall Hotel
8 Patriot Square
Bethnal Green
London E2 9NF
+44 2078710461
www.typingroom.com

Opening hours	Closed Monday and Sunday
Credit cards	Accepted
Price range	Expensive
Style	Smart casual
Cuisine	Modern European
Recommended for	High end

"The Typing Room deserves way more credit than it gets!"—Andy Oliver

BOROUGH MARKET

Recommended by
Shaun Rankin, Luke Vandore-Mackay

8 Southwark Street
Borough
London SE1 1TL
+44 2074071002
www.boroughmarket.org.uk

Opening hours	Closed Sunday
Credit cards	Not accepted
Price range	Affordable
Style	Casual
Cuisine	Market-Deli
Recommended for	Breakfast

"The best breakfast in town is a fresh-from-the-oven Ginger Pig sausage roll and a Monmouth filter coffee. Happily both establishments are within spitting distance, literally. Grab both and watch the market come to life. Magic."—Luke Vandore-Mackay

EL PASTÓR

Recommended by
Jeremy Lee

6–7A Stoney Street
Borough
London SE1 9AA
www.tacoselpastor.co.uk

Opening hours	Closed Monday and Sunday
Credit cards	Accepted
Price range	Affordable
Style	Casual
Cuisine	Mexican
Recommended for	Bargain

HUTONG

Recommended by
Tom Sellers

The Shard
31 Saint Thomas Street
Borough
London SE1 9RY
+44 2030111257
www.hutong.co.uk

Opening hours	Open 7 days
Credit cards	Accepted
Price range	Expensive
Style	Smart casual
Cuisine	Chinese
Recommended for	Late Night

"The location is incredible and the view is unrivalled. At night, the whole of London is under you."
—Tom Sellers

PADELLA

Recommended by
Elizabeth Haigh, Philip Howard,
Bruno Loubet, James Lowe

6 Southwark Street
Borough
London SE1 1TQ
www.padella.co

Opening hours	Open 7 days
Credit cards	Accepted
Price range	Affordable
Style	Casual
Cuisine	Italian
Recommended for	Bargain

"I always try to get there early—there's a great spot in the window, or outside the restaurant, where you can people-watch with a big bowl of pasta and an Aperol Spritz, and I'm a happy chef."—Elizabeth Haigh

If you aren't utterly smitten with this little pasta bar, with its beautiful marble bar surfaces, its expertly pitched selection of 'Britalian' antipasti and its exquisite handmade and wallet-friendly pasta dishes, then you probably just haven't eaten there yet. Unfortunately, the Padella love affair currently sweeping London means the queues most nights at this bijou spot in Borough Market are, to say the least, prohibitive, and only the truly patient stand a chance of sampling the delights of things like the *pici cacio e pepe* (thick pasta in a lemon and pepper sauce) before the lines are closed. Hurry up and open a second branch, guys.

ROAST

Recommended by
Paul Foster

The Floral Hall
Stoney Street
Borough
London SE1 1TL
+44 2030066111
www.roast-restaurant.com

Opening hours	Open 7 days
Credit cards	Accepted
Price range	Affordable
Style	Casual
Cuisine	Gastropub
Recommended for	Breakfast

"Really good breakfast, always very tasty. Top of the range Bloody Marys to go with it."—Paul Foster

MORGAN ARMS

Recommended by
Ben Tish

43 Morgan Street
Bow
London E3 5AA
+44 2089806389
www.morganarmsbow.com

Opening hours	Open 7 days
Credit cards	Accepted
Price range	Affordable
Style	Casual
Cuisine	Gastropub
Recommended for	Regular neighborhood

LAS AMERICAS

Recommended by
Mark Dobbie

26 Pope's Road
Brixton
London SW9 8JJ
+44 2072745533

Opening hours	Closed Sunday
Credit cards	Not accepted
Price range	Budget
Style	Casual
Cuisine	Colombian
Recommended for	Bargain

"It's a Colombian deli/butchers/money exchange: a kind of all-in-one Colombian community hub. It's one of those places where you get plastic cutlery and paper plates but it doesn't matter because it's about the food being delicious and the people are super friendly. Empanadas, arepas, Colombian chorizo—it's all brilliant and dirt cheap, you can just snack or have a full meal."—Mark Dobbie

ASMARA RESTAURANT

Recommended by
Mark Dobbie

386 Coldharbour Lane
Brixton
London SW9 8LF
+44 2077374144

Opening hours	Open 7 days
Credit cards	Not accepted
Price range	Budget
Style	Casual
Cuisine	Eritrean
Recommended for	Regular neighborhood

"Eritrean food served by a lady that's extremely proud of her culture and heritage, which shows in the food. Lots of heavily spiced stews served on *injira*, a type of fermented flatbread."—Mark Dobbie

CARIOCA

Recommended by
Mark Dobbie

25–27 Market Row
Brixton
London SW9 8LB
+44 2070959052
www.cariocabrixton.com

Opening hours	Open 7 days
Credit cards	Accepted but not AMEX or Diners
Price range	Affordable
Style	Casual
Cuisine	Brazilian
Recommended for	Regular neighborhood

"They do Brazilian breakfast maize muffins with poached eggs, avocado, chorizo (the spicy kind) and salsa verde. No matter how under the weather you feel they'll fix you up."—Mark Dobbie

MAMA LAN

Recommended by
Phil Carmichael

18 Brixton Village Market
Brixton
London SW9 8PR
www.mamalan.co.uk

Opening hours	Open 7 days
Credit cards	Accepted but not AMEX or Diners
Price range	Affordable
Style	Casual
Cuisine	Chinese
Recommended for	Regular neighborhood

"Situated in the Brixton village complex, this place serves great fresh noodles. The spicy chilled noodles are a must as well as the handmade dumplings."
—Phil Carmichael

NANBAN

Recommended by
Andi Oliver

426 Coldharbour Lane
Brixton
London SW9 8LF
+44 2073460098
www.nanban.co.uk

Opening hours	Open 7 days
Credit cards	Accepted but not AMEX
Price range	Affordable
Style	Casual
Cuisine	Japanese
Recommended for	Bargain

"The most incredible ramen and side dishes. Inspired, beyond delicious, stunning flavors. Food that warms your heart and soul."—Andi Oliver

NAUGHTY PIGLETS

Recommended by
Will Bowlby

28 Brixton Water Lane
Brixton
London SW2 1PE
+44 2072747796
www.naughtypiglets.co.uk

Opening hours	Closed Monday
Credit cards	Accepted but not AMEX
Price range	Affordable
Style	Casual
Cuisine	Modern European
Recommended for	Regular neighborhood

SALON

Recommended by
Will Bowlby, Mark Dobbie,
Jeremy Lee

18 Market Row
Brixton
London SW9 8LD
+44 2075019152
www.salonbrixton.co.uk

Opening hours	Closed Monday
Credit cards	Accepted but not Diners
Price range	Affordable
Style	Casual
Cuisine	Modern British
Recommended for	Breakfast

"These handsome lads know a good breakfast: eggs and anchovies on toast—always a winner."
—Jeremy Lee

WAHACA

Recommended by
Anna Hansen

20 Atlantic Road
Brixton
London SW9 8JA
+44 2037636357
www.wahaca.co.uk

Opening hours	Open 7 days
Credit cards	Accepted
Price range	Affordable
Style	Casual
Cuisine	Mexican
Recommended for	Regular neighborhood

"Super tasty Mexican market food. Buzzy, colorful and a fun ambience. Great on your own, for sharing or with children. They always have plenty of books, crayons and paper for coloring in."—Anna Hansen

MASALA WALA CAFÉ

Recommended by
Sameer Taneja

5 Brockley Cross
Brockley
London SE4 2AB
+44 2036594055
www.masalawalacafe.co.uk

Opening hours	Closed Monday
Credit cards	Accepted but not AMEX or Diners
Price range	Affordable
Style	Casual
Cuisine	Pakistani
Recommended for	Regular neighborhood

"My local hangout. I have to visit at least once a month."—Sameer Taneja

CARAVAGGIO

Recommended by
Robert Ortiz

47 Camberwell Church Street
Camberwell
London SE5 8TR
+44 2072071612

Opening hours	Open 7 days
Credit cards	Accepted but not Diners
Price range	Affordable
Style	Casual
Cuisine	Italian
Recommended for	Regular neighborhood

"Cosy Italian restaurant with authentic dishes and unbelievable staff. I've been going there for at least fifteen years. They make it feel like home."
—Robert Ortiz

SILK ROAD

Recommended by
Harneet Baweja,
Will Bowlby, Erchen Chang,
Ollie Templeton

49 Camberwell Church Street
Camberwell
London SE5 8TR
+44 2077034832

Opening hours	Open 7 days
Credit cards	Not accepted
Price range	Budget
Style	Casual
Cuisine	Xinjiang Chinese
Recommended for	Bargain

"It is honest, soulful cooking. Every dish on its concise menu is a punch of flavor. From their home-style cabbage to their sugary, spicy, double-cooked pork, everything hits the mark. I am in love with their hand-pulled noodles."—Harneet Baweja

Camberwell's no-frills Silk Road specializes in the food of Xinjiang, China's north-west frontier province. The basic set-up of communal tables and punishingly hard benches isn't what brings London's gluttons back again and again: that would be the fascinating regional cuisine with its central Asian and Chinese influences and the great value it represents. Few leave without trying the fried pork dumplings, chile and cumin lamb skewers, and 'big plate' chicken in fiery broth, with its side of hand-pulled noodles for optimal slurping. A feast and a few Tsingtao beers still leave change from £20 ($26).

THEO'S PIZZERIA

Recommended by
Joel Braham

2 Grove Lane
Camberwell
London SE5 8SY
+44 2030264224
www.theospizzeria.com

Opening hours	Open 7 days
Credit cards	Accepted
Price range	Affordable
Style	Casual
Cuisine	Italian
Recommended for	Local favorite

"The best Neapolitan, wood-fired pizzas in London, in a stunning dining room always bustling with happy customers and attentive staff."—Joel Braham

THE COFFEE JAR

Recommended by
Yotam Ottolenghi

83 Parkway
Camden
London NW1 7PP
+44 7956032741

Opening hours	Open 7 days
Credit cards	Accepted but not AMEX or Diners
Price range	Budget
Style	Casual
Cuisine	Café
Recommended for	Regular neighborhood

"I love getting coffee and croissants from The Coffee Jar, our local cafe in Camden."—Yotam Ottolenghi

SUSHI SHOW

Recommended by
Dan Graham

28 Camden Passage
Camden
London N1 8ED
+44 2073541329

Opening hours	Open 7 days
Credit cards	Accepted
Price range	Budget
Style	Casual
Cuisine	Japanese
Recommended for	Bargain

"Great sushi and miso soup...small, authentic, delicious."—Dan Graham

WOODY GRILL

Recommended by
Tam Storrar

1 Camden Road
Camden
London NW1 9LG
+44 2086169587
www.thewoodygrill.co.uk

Opening hours	Open 7 days
Credit cards	Accepted
Price range	Budget
Style	Casual
Cuisine	Turkish-Middle Eastern
Recommended for	Late night

DUCK & WAFFLE

Heron Tower
110 Bishopsgate
City of London
London EC2N 4AY
+44 2036407310
www.duckandwaffle.com

Recommended by
Tom Aikens, Nieves Barragán Mohacho,
James Durrant, Paul Foster,
Elizabeth Haigh, José Pizarro,
Alfred Prasad, Mark Sargeant,
Shaun Searley, Gareth Ward

Opening hours...Open 7 days
Credit cards...Accepted
Price range..Affordable
Style...Smart casual
Cuisine...British-European
Recommended for..Late night

"A name that sounds like a quirky London pub, a fun approach to British classical food, open round the clock and very welcoming of other foods into their British repertoire. I can't think of another restaurant that sums up London. The talented chef Dan Doherty brings alive this relaxed, fun concept and does a great job of making it successful."—Alfred Prasad

London still doesn't have a great number of truly twenty-four-hour restaurants; certainly not many boasting breathtaking panoramic views of London from forty floors up, and certainly not any offering a menu showcasing head chef Dan Doherty's love of egg. From *shakshuka* (a North African poached egg dish) to the titular 'Duck and Waffle' with mustard maple syrup, there are plenty of inventive dishes to choose from. Whether you come for breakfast or dinner, a meal here is a real event thanks to the interesting global dishes, the experimental cocktail list (the 'inside-out' cocktail bar managed by Rich Woods is worth a trip by itself) and of course the rollercoaster of a glass lift, the fastest in Europe.

HAWKSMOOR

10 Basinghall Street
City of London
London EC2V 5BQ
+44 2073978120
www.thehawksmoor.com

Recommended by
Tomer Amedi

Opening hours.......................Closed Saturday and Sunday
Credit cards...Accepted
Price range..Affordable
Style...Smart casual
Cuisine...Steakhouse
Recommended for....................................Regular neighborhood

"After a night of drinking you need some fat and protein to help with your hangover. This is where the Hawksmoor Full English Breakfast enters.

Don't forget to add Lobster Benedict to the order. Plus a few Bloody Marys always help!"—Tomer Amedi

THE JUGGED HARE

49 Chiswell Street
City of London
London EC1Y 4SA
+44 2076140134
www.thejuggedhare.com

Recommended by
Michael Reid

Opening hours...Open 7 days
Credit cards...Accepted
Price range..Affordable
Style...Casual
Cuisine...Gastropub
Recommended for..Local favorite

"A great English pub using terrific seasonal produce."
—Michael Reid

LONDON WALL BAR & KITCHEN

150 London Wall
City of London
London EC2Y 5HN
+44 2076007340
www.benugo.com

Recommended by
JP McMahon

Opening hours...Open 7 days
Credit cards...Accepted
Price range..Affordable
Style...Casual
Cuisine...Café
Recommended for...Breakfast

MY OLD PLACE

88–90 Middlesex Street
City of London
London E1 7EZ
+44 2072472200

Recommended by
Harneet Baweja

Opening hours...Closed Sunday
Credit cards........................Accepted but not AMEX or Diners
Price range..Affordable
Style...Casual
Cuisine...Chinese
Recommended for.............................Regular neighborhood

"A must-try is the pork in chile oil and the handmade dumplings."—Harneet Baweja

PITT CUE

Recommended by
Ben Murphy

1 The Avenue
Devonshire Square
City of London
London EC2M 4YP
+44 2073247770
www.pittcue.co.uk

Opening hours	Open 7 days
Credit cards	Accepted
Price range	Affordable
Style	Casual
Cuisine	Barbecue
Recommended for	Bargain

"Great beer and meat: the perfect winning combination."—Ben Murphy

Following a successful summer residency operating out of a van on the South Bank, the Pitt Cue Co. found its first permanent home in Soho, but moved in 2016 to a new, industrial-chic premises in Spitalfields. Wherever the location, Chef Tom Adams's skill with a smoker, combined with the sourcing of the perfect cuts of pork and beef, has always made for a carnivores' Shangri-La. An extensive list of craft beers, ciders, and bourbon, rum and mezcal-based cocktails provide the liquid refreshment—try the mezcal daiquiri.

ROYAL EXCHANGE GRAND CAFÉ

Recommended by
Vineet Bhatia

The Royal Exchange
City of London
London EC3V 3LR
+44 2076182480
www.royalexchange-grandcafe.co.uk

Opening hours	Closed Saturday and Sunday
Credit cards	Accepted but not Diners
Price range	Affordable
Style	Casual
Cuisine	Café Brasserie
Recommended for	Breakfast

"I have eaten at The Grand Café on a number of occasions but my favorite meal here has always been breakfast. The breakfast menu, from the bircher muesli to the Californian-style eggs with avocado, barrel-aged feta and coriander is incredible and way better than anything you'd expect to be served in a courtyard. The staff are very approachable, and it's the kind of place you want to post up and stay for a while." —Vineet Bhatia

SWEETINGS

Recommended by
Tom Harris, Miles Kirby

39 Queen Victoria Street
City of London
London EC4N 4SF
+44 2072483062
www.sweetingsrestaurant.co.uk

Opening hours	Closed Saturday and Sunday
Credit cards	Accepted
Price range	Affordable
Style	Casual
Cuisine	Seafood
Recommended for	Local favorite

"Old-school service; old-school food."—Miles Kirby

Serving simple fish dishes in the City of London since 1889, without being pompous Sweetings revels in being fantastically old fashioned, a right earned by having survived two world wars and more financial crashes than you can a shake a skate wing at. It's the likes of crab bisque, smoked eel, potted shrimps, fried whitebait and scallops and bacon to start, with main courses running from extravagant, simply prepared catches such as turbot and Dover sole, to their infinitely more affordable fish pie and salmon cake. Puddings are hefty boarding-school classics such as baked jam (jelly) roll and spotted dick (sponge cake with dried fruit).

TEMPLE AND SONS

Recommended by
Paul Walsh

22 Old Broad Street
City of London
London EC2N 1HQ
+44 2078777710
www.templeandsons.co.uk

Opening hours	Open 7 days
Credit cards	Accepted
Price range	Affordable
Style	Smart casual
Cuisine	Modern British
Recommended for	Breakfast

JIM'S CAFÉ

Recommended by
Merlin Labron-Johnson, Andi Oliver

59 Chatsworth Road
Clapton
London E5 0LH
+44 2030264465

Opening hours	Open 7 days
Credit cards	Accepted but not AMEX or Diners
Price range	Budget
Style	Casual
Cuisine	Café
Recommended for	Breakfast

"It's the perfect place for relaxing and reading the newspapers. They serve delicious food, great coffee and juices and it's on one of my favorite streets in London—Chatsworth Road."—Merlin Labron-Johnson

P. FRANCO

Recommended by
Matteo Aloe, Sandia Chang,
Carl Clarke, Tom Harris,
James Lowe, Andy Oliver,
Jon Rotheram

107 Lower Clapton Road
Clapton
London E5 0NP
+44 2085334660
www.pfranco.co.uk

Opening hours	Closed Monday
Reservation policy	No
Credit cards	Accepted
Price range	Affordable
Style	Casual
Cuisine	Modern European
Recommended for	Local favorite

"Brilliant wines and small plates created by a different resident chef every few months."—James Lowe

BREDDOS TACOS

Recommended by
Isaac McHale

82 Goswell Road
Clerkenwell
London EC1V 7DB
+44 2035358301
www.breddostacos.com

Opening hours	Open 7 days
Credit cards	Accepted but not AMEX
Price range	Affordable
Style	Casual
Cuisine	Mexican
Recommended for	Local favorite

THE MODERN PANTRY

Recommended by
Tom Aikens, Mark Jarvis,
Martin Morales

47–48 Saint John's Square
Clerkenwell
London EC1V 4JJ
+44 2075539210
www.themodernpantry.co.uk

Opening hours	Open 7 days
Credit cards	Accepted but not Diners
Price range	Affordable
Style	Casual
Cuisine	Modern European
Recommended for	Breakfast

"Anna Hansen is the queen of fusion, blending influences from around the world as well as her native New Zealand. A relaxed and calm restaurant with some phenomenal flavors."—Martin Morales

MORITO

Recommended by
Joel Braham, Joshua Katz,
Allegra McEvedy

32 Exmouth Market
Clerkenwell
London EC1R 4QE
+44 2072787007
www.morito.co.uk

Opening hours	Open 7 days
Credit cards	Accepted
Price range	Affordable
Style	Casual
Cuisine	Tapas
Recommended for	Wish I'd opened

"Tiny, busy, delicious tapas bar with some wonderful dishes that linger in the memory...the lamb chops spring to mind. Favorite restaurant of many. Wish I'd opened it!"—Joel Braham

MORO

Recommended by
Joshua Katz, Olle T. Cellton

34–36 Exmouth Market
Clerkenwell
London EC1R 4QE
+44 2078338336
www.moro.co.uk

Opening hours	Open 7 days
Credit cards	Accepted
Price range	Affordable
Style	Casual
Cuisine	Spanish-North African
Recommended for	Wish I'd opened

"Moro is a timeless institution that is as relevant today as it was when it first opened twenty-years ago.

It serves exceptional Spanish and North African-influenced food in a beautiful room that generates such a convivial atmosphere, one where you can feel both relaxed and indulged at the same time. It is, for me, the perfect restaurant."—Joshua Katz

THE QUALITY CHOP HOUSE

Recommended by
Nieves Barragán
Mohacho, Eyal Jagermann,
Joshua Katz, James Knappett,
Francesco Mazzei, Richard Turner

88–94 Farringdon Road
Clerkenwell
London EC1R 3EA
+44 2072781452
www.thequalitychophouse.com

Opening hours	Open 7 days
Credit cards	Accepted
Price range	Affordable
Style	Casual
Cuisine	British
Recommended for	Regular neighborhood

"An old restaurant restored to greatness, serving modern British food with great wine at reasonable prices. There is something particularly London about the interiors and execution."—Joshua Katz

SASA SUSHI

Recommended by
André Chiang

422 St John Street
Clerkenwell
London EC1V 4NJ
+44 20 7837 1155
sasasushi.co.uk

Opening hours	Closed Sunday
Credit cards	Accepted but not Diners
Price range	Affordable
Style	Casual
Cuisine	Sushi
Recommended for	Worth the travel

SHAWARMA BAR

Recommended by
Miles Kirby, Martin Morales

46 Exmouth Market
Clerkenwell
London EC1R 4QE
+44 2078371726
www.shawarmabar.co.uk

Opening hours	Closed Sunday
Credit cards	Accepted
Price range	Affordable
Style	Casual
Cuisine	Middle Eastern
Recommended for	Bargain

"Everything you eat feels like a bargain—it's that good."—Miles Kirby

SUSHI TETSU

Recommended by
Elizabeth Haigh, James Knappett

12 Jerusalem Passage
Clerkenwell
London EC1V 4JP
+44 2032170090
www.sushitetsu.co.uk

Opening hours	Closed Monday and Sunday
Credit cards	Accepted
Price range	Expensive
Style	Smart casual
Cuisine	Japanese
Recommended for	High end

"This restaurant is a small seven-seat sushi bar serving the best sushi in the city for me!"
—James Knappett

BANNER'S

Recommended by
Richard Corrigan

21 Park Road
Crouch End
London N8 8TE
+44 2083482930
www.bannersrestaurant.com

Opening hours	Open 7 days
Credit cards	Accepted but not AMEX or Diners
Price range	Affordable
Style	Casual
Cuisine	Jamaican-International
Recommended for	Breakfast

"This is a great breakfast spot. When the kids are home, it's our Sunday morning go-to place. It was established around twenty-four years ago and has fantastic character. They do a mean *huevos rancheros* (rancher's eggs)."—Richard Corrigan

THE HABERDASHERY

Recommended by
Frankie van Loo

22 Middle Lane
Crouch End
London N8 8PL
+44 2083428098
www.the-haberdashery.com

Opening hours	Open 7 days
Credit cards	Accepted but not Diners
Price range	Budget
Style	Casual
Cuisine	Café
Recommended for	Breakfast

ALLPRESS ROASTERY CAFE

Recommended by
Peter Gordon,
Fernando Troca

55 Dalston Lane
Dalston
London E8 2NG
+44 2077491780
www.uk.allpressespresso.com

Opening hours	Open 7 days
Credit cards	Accepted but not AMEX
Price range	Budget
Style	Casual
Cuisine	Café
Recommended for	Breakfast

"Excellent coffee, of course, as well as a simple breakfast menu—boiled egg, avocado and provolone toast; great granola too."—Peter Gordon

ARTHUR'S

Recommended by
Carl Clarke

495 Kingsland Road
Dalston
London E8 4AU
+44 2072543391
www.arthurscafe.org.uk

Opening hours	Closed Saturday and Sunday
Credit cards	Accepted but not AMEX or Diners
Price range	Budget
Style	Casual
Cuisine	Café
Recommended for	Breakfast

"Old-school café that has been family run for eighty years. They refuse to serve bacon after 11.00 a.m.!"
—Carl Clarke

HASH E8

Recommended by
Joshua Katz

170 Dalston Lane
Dalston
London E8 1NG
www.hashe8.com

Opening hours	Closed Monday
Reservation policy	No
Credit cards	Accepted but not AMEX or Diners
Price range	Affordable
Style	Casual
Cuisine	Café-Diner
Recommended for	Breakfast

"A small, neighborhood spot that is unassuming to the eye but a best-kept secret for locals. Think pork belly, Eggs Benedict, sweet potato and chorizo hash and buttermilk pancakes."—Joshua Katz

MANGAL 1 OCAKBASI

Recommended by
Andi Oliver, Mark Rosati

10 Arcola Street
Dalston
London E8 2DJ
+44 2072758981
www.mangal1.com

Opening hours	Open 7 days
Credit cards	Accepted
Price range	Affordable
Style	Casual
Cuisine	Turkish
Recommended for	Local favorite

"Incredible yet simple beautifully grilled meat, alongside fresh vibrant salads and hot fluffy bread; no bar so you take your own drink."—Andi Oliver

MANGAL 2

Recommended by
Olle T. Cellton, Neil Rankin

4 Stoke Newington Road
Dalston
London N16 8BH
+44 2072547888
www.mangal2.com

Opening hours	Open 7 days
Credit cards	Accepted
Price range	Affordable
Style	Casual
Cuisine	Turkish
Recommended for	Local favorite

"My go-to kebab joint. Mangal 1 round the corner is a little better but their social media isn't as hilarious and Gilbert and George aren't regulars."—Neil Rankin

ROTORINO

Recommended by
Thomasina Miers

434 Kingsland Road
Dalston
London E8 4AA
+44 2072499081
www.rotorino.com

Opening hours	Open 7 days
Credit cards	Accepted
Price range	Affordable
Style	Casual
Cuisine	Southern Italian
Recommended for	Local favorite

"A delicious little Italian restaurant by Stevie Parle. Regional, southern Italian cooking, everything made from scratch, with freshly-made pasta, delectable sauces, and a beautiful wine list."—Thomasina Miers

SÖMINE

Recommended by
Samantha & Samuel Clark

131 Kingsland High Street
Dalston
London E8 2PB
+44 20 7254 7384
www.somine-restaurant.co.uk

Opening hours	Open 7 days
Credit cards	Accepted
Price range	Budget
Style	Casual
Cuisine	Turkish
Recommended for	Late night

BRICK HOUSE BAKERY

Recommended by
Shuko Oda

1 Zenoria Street
East Dulwich
London SE22 8HP
+44 2086932031
www.brickhousebread.com

Opening hours	Closed Monday
Reservation policy	No
Credit cards	Accepted but not AMEX
Price range	Affordable
Style	Casual
Cuisine	Bakery
Recommended for	Breakfast

"Good coffee and interesting brunch options, always lively and smells of baking bread in the morning."
—Shuko Oda

PRUFROCK COFFEE

Recommended by
Richard Corrigan

23–25 Leather Lane
Farringdon
London EC1N 7TE
+44 2072420467
www.prufrockcoffee.com

Opening hours	Open 7 days
Credit cards	Accepted but not AMEX or Diners
Price range	Budget
Style	Casual
Cuisine	Café
Recommended for	Regular neighborhood

"The coffee here is always good and they have a great pastry selection in the morning."—Richard Corrigan

SOSHARU

Recommended by
James Knappett

64 Turnmill Street
Farringdon
London EC1M 5RR
+44 2038052304
www.sosharuLondon.com

Opening hours	Closed Sunday
Credit cards	Accepted but not Diners
Price range	Affordable
Style	Smart casual
Cuisine	Japanese
Recommended for	Late night

"This is a great place to get late-night chef food with cold beers and great ingredients, cooked in traditional street-food style."—James Knappett

ST. JOHN BAR AND RESTAURANT

Recommended by
Matteo Aloe,
Maoz Alonim, Şemsa Denizsel,
Tom Harris, Miles Kirby,
Jeremy Lee, Shuko Oda,
Yotam Ottolenghi, Andy Ricker,
Lee Tiernan

26 Saint John Street
Farringdon
London EC1M 4AY
+44 2072510848
www.stjohngroup.uk.com

Opening hours	Open 7 days
Credit cards	Accepted
Price range	Affordable
Style	Smart casual
Cuisine	British
Recommended for	Local favorite

"Its place in the evolution of London and British dining is still undisputed. Its place in my evolution as a cook is undiminished. It is a place like no other."
—Tom Harris

Arguably the most seminal London restaurant of the last twenty years, the original branch of St. John has barely changed since it opened back in 1994. The birthplace of Fergus Henderson's famed 'nose-to-tail' philosophy, the twice-daily-changing menu is still tersely written, strictly seasonal and still likes to make use of the bits of beast that Anglo-Saxon chefs used to throw away, until Henderson made them fashionable. The other star is the Georgian building: an old smokehouse whose high ceilings, whitewashed walls and surfeit of natural light somehow manage to make it feel like nowhere else in London.

BAO

Recommended by
Jeremy Lee, Shuko Oda

31 Windmill Street
Fitzrovia
London W1T 2JN
+44 2030111632
www.baoLondon .com

Opening hours	Closed Sunday
Credit cards	Accepted
Price range	Affordable
Style	Casual
Cuisine	Taiwanese
Recommended for	Regular neighborhood

BERNERS TAVERN

Recommended by
Sat Bains, James Durrant,
Paul Hood, Tom Sellers,
Sameer Taneja, Paul Walsh

Edition Hotel
10 Berners Street
Fitzrovia
London W1T 3NP
+44 2079087979
www.bernerstavern.com

Opening hours	Open 7 days
Credit cards	Accepted
Price range	Affordable
Style	Smart casual
Cuisine	Modern British
Recommended for	Breakfast

"The room is stunning and the food is great. It always feels like an occasion to go."—Tom Sellers

Jason Atherton's glamorous all-day dining venture opened in 2013—a prolific year for the chef, who also found time to launch Soho's Little Social and the Social Eating House. Naturally enough, given its setting in Ian Schrager's £33m ($55m) Edition Hotel, it's a jaw-dropping space, with Grand Central Station-style chandeliers, walls packed with paintings, and an impressive backlit bar. With Atherton's long-time lieutenant Phil Carmichael heading up the kitchen, the inventive modern British cooking is just as stellar, balancing witty modernist touches reminiscent of Atherton's first venture, Pollen Street Social, with grass-fed Scottish steaks and crowd-pleasing roasts.

CLIPSTONE

Recommended by
Bruno Loubet, Thomasina Miers

5 Clipstone Street
Fitzrovia
London W1W 6BB
+44 2076370871
www.clipstonerestaurant.co.uk

Opening hours	Closed Sunday
Credit cards	Accepted
Price range	Affordable
Style	Casual
Cuisine	Modern British-European
Recommended for	Regular neighborhood

"Clipstone is a new restaurant that manages to be a charming neighborhood restaurant in the center of town. The quality of cooking is outstanding and I love that much of the menu is very vegetable focused."
—Bruno Loubet

ETHOS

Recommended by
Phil Carmichael

48 Eastcastle Street
Fitzrovia
London W1W 8DX
+44 2035811538
www.ethosfoods.com

Opening hours	Open 7 days
Credit cards	Accepted
Price range	Affordable
Style	Casual
Cuisine	Vegetarian
Recommended for	Bargain

"Great vegetarian restaurant that serves amazing healthy food, by weight. Super original salads and always packed!"—Phil Carmichael

HAKKASAN

Recommended by
Galton Blackiston,
Gary Foulkes

8 Hanway Place
Fitzrovia
London W1T 1HD
+44 2079277000
www.hakkasan.com

Opening hours	Open 7 days
Credit cards	Accepted
Price range	Affordable
Style	Smart casual
Cuisine	Chinese
Recommended for	Late night

"I've been coming here for many years and the food always delivers. There is always a great atmosphere in Hakkasan, whatever time of night you visit."
—Gary Foulkes

HONEY & CO

Recommended by
Merlin Labron-Johnson, Isaac Toups

25a Warren Street
Fitzrovia
London W1T 5LZ
+44 2073886175
www.honeyandco.co.uk

Opening hours	Closed Sunday
Credit cards	Accepted but not AMEX or Diners
Price range	Affordable
Style	Casual
Cuisine	Middle Eastern
Recommended for	Regular neighborhood

"Another favorite. The best cakes, Turkish coffee, and lovely service."—Merlin Labron-Johnson

LANTANA

Recommended by
Matteo Aloe

13 Charlotte Place
Fitzrovia
London W1T 1SN
+44 2076373347
www.lantanacafe.co.uk

Opening hours	Open 7 days
Credit cards	Accepted but not AMEX or Diners
Price range	Affordable
Style	Casual
Cuisine	Café
Recommended for	Regular neighborhood

PERCY & FOUNDERS

Recommended by
Christian Edwardson

1 Pearson Square
Fitzrovia
London W1W 7EY
+44 2037610200
www.percyandfounders.co.uk

Opening hours	Open 7 days
Credit cards	Accepted but not AMEX
Price range	Affordable
Style	Casual
Cuisine	Modern British-European
Recommended for	Breakfast

PORTLAND

Recommended by
Adam Byatt, Amandine Chaignot,
Florent Ladeyn, Thomasina Miers,
Yotam Ottolenghi

113 Great Portland Street
Fitzrovia
London W1W 6QQ
+44 2074363261
www.portlandrestaurant.co.uk

Opening hours	Closed Sunday
Credit cards	Accepted
Price range	Affordable
Style	Smart casual
Cuisine	Modern British
Recommended for	Worth the travel

"Where every plate of food is like a piece of art. Full of light, sparkling ingredients."—Thomasina Miers

THE RIDING HOUSE CAFÉ

Recommended by
Tom Aikens,
Christian Edwardson

43–51 Great Titchfield Street
Fitzrovia
London W1W 7PQ
+44 20792/0840
www.ridinghousecafe.co.uk

Opening hours	Open 7 days
Credit cards	Accepted
Price range	Affordable
Style	Casual
Cuisine	Brasserie
Recommended for	Regular neighborhood

BROADWAY MARKET

Recommended by
Amandine Chaignot

Broadway Market
Hackney
London E8 4QJ
www.broadwaymarket.co.uk

Opening hours	Open Saturday
Credit cards	Not accepted
Price range	Affordable
Style	Casual
Cuisine	Market-Deli
Recommended for	Bargain

DEENEY'S

Recommended by
Andi Oliver

Broadway Market
Hackney
London E8 4QJ
+44 2085584023
www.deeneys.com

Opening hours	Open Saturday
Credit cards	Not accepted
Price range	Budget
Style	Casual
Cuisine	Scottish
Recommended for	Breakfast

"Deeney's is legendary. They make a haggis toastie that blows your mind! Haggis, cheddar, caramelized onion and a massive slice of 'Oh my God it's amazing!'"
—Andi Oliver

E5 BAKEHOUSE

Recommended by
Matteo Aloe

Arch 395
Mentmore Terrace
Hackney
London E8 3PH
+44 2089869600
www.e5bakehouse.com

Opening hours	Open 7 days
Credit cards	Accepted
Price range	Bargain
Style	Casual
Cuisine	Bakery-Deli
Recommended for	Breakfast

"Good coffee to start the day, and you can find sweet pastries or salads and sandwiches, both fresh and amazing. I usually go for both."—Matteo Aloe

THE GRAND HOWL

Recommended by
Tom Harris

214 Well Street
Hackney
London E9 6QT
+44 2036599631

Opening hours	Open 7 days
Credit cards	Accepted
Price range	Affordable
Style	Casual
Cuisine	Café
Recommended for	Breakfast

"Greg is serious about his coffee, roasting his own beans on site. Poached eggs, avocado, and dukka on sourdough every time for me."—Tom Harris

HILL & SZROK

Recommended by
Peter Gordon, Eyal Jagermann

60 Broadway Market
Hackney
London E8 4QJ
+44 2072548805
www.hillandszrok.co.uk

Opening hours	Open 7 days
Reservation policy	No
Credit cards	Accepted but not AMEX
Price range	Affordable
Style	Casual
Cuisine	British Butcher
Recommended for	Regular neighborhood

"I love this little gem in Broadway Market. Specializing in high-quality British meat, this is a butcher by day with some of the best produce around, then after dark they fire up the grill and cook their best cuts, served with simple sides like buttered potatoes and French lettuce salad, combined with a great organic wine list and one of the best cheese cakes in town. This is one of my favorite places for dinner."—Eyal Jagermann

KUZU SIS GRILL & MEZE

Recommended by
Tom Harris

269 Well Street
Hackney
London E9 6RG
+44 2089850660

Opening hours	Closed Sunday
Credit cards	Not accepted
Price range	Budget
Style	Casual
Cuisine	Turkish
Recommended for	Bargain

"A long-standing family favorite."—Tom Harris

THE LAUGHING HEART

Recommended by
David Gingell, Elizabeth Haigh,
Tom Harris, Joshua Katz,
Jeremy Lee, Merlin Labron-Johnson,
Isaac McHale, Shaun Searley,
Tim Spedding

277 Hackney Road
Hackney
London E2 8NA
+44 2076869535
www.thelaughingheartLondon .com

Opening hours	Closed Monday and Tuesday
Reservation policy	No
Credit cards	Accepted but not AMEX
Price range	Budget
Style	Casual
Cuisine	Modern British
Recommended for	Late night

"Swinging wildly from cheap Tsingtao beer to one of the best wine lists in London , whilst eating extremely tasty food, is a rare treat. And if I was ten-years younger and not doing the school run the next day, I'd be there every night."—Tom Harris

LEGS

Recommended by
Matteo Aloe

120 Morning Lane
Hackney
London E9 6LH
+44 2034418765
www.legsrestaurant.com

Opening hours..............................Closed Monday and Tuesday
Credit cards....................................Accepted but not Diners
Price range..Affordable
Style...Smart casual
Cuisine.................. ,,...Modern British
Recommended for................. ,,......................Late night

"Informal, warm, cozy. The menu is seasonal and it changes daily so you can always find terrific new dishes. What I like most is the simplicity. Chef Magnus Reid's idea is to keep the best ingredients as they are. The wines are all natural and interesting: trust the guys to choose, they will never be wrong."
—Matteo Aloe

LEMLEM KITCHEN

Recommended by
Peter Gordon

Netil Market
23 Westgate Street
Hackney
London E8 3RL
www.lemlemkitchen.co.uk

Opening hours..................................Closed Sunday to Friday
Reservation policy................ ,,...No
Credit cards................................... ,,.............Accepted
Price range..Budget
Style..Casual
Cuisine...Modern African
Recommended for..Bargain

"Eritrean snack food, with injera 'bread' wrapped around braised lamb and spices."—Peter Gordon

MY NEIGHBOURS THE DUMPLINGS

Recommended by
Miles Kirby

165 Lower Clapton Road
Hackney
London
East London E5 8EQ
+44 20 3327 1556
www.myneighboursthedumplings.com

Opening hours...Closed Monday
Reservation policy...No
Credit cards...Accepted
Price range...Affordable
Style...Casual
Cuisine..Dim Sum
Recommended for..............................Regular neighborhood

MARKSMAN PUBLIC HOUSE

Recommended by
Harneet Baweja,
Henry Harris, Miles Kirby,
Thomasina Miers, Mark Rosati,
Tim Spedding

254 Hackney Road
Hackney
London E2 7SJ
+44 2077397393
www.marksmanpublichouse.com

Opening hours............................. ,,.................Open 7 days
Credit cards...Accepted but not Diners
Price range..Affordable
Style... ,,........Casual
Cuisine..British
Recommended for..............................Regular neighborhood

"Marksman Public House is another one of my favorite restaurants these days. The menu exemplifies modern British cooking at its finest, while also maintaining the charm of an old pub. Their rotating selection of pies is not to be missed, from oxtail to chicken and wild garlic, they are always masterfully crafted."
—Mark Rosati

Oddly, considering the dynamism of its restaurant scene otherwise, London does not have a great deal of gastropubs. Places where you can turn up and have a pint at the bar, maybe have a Scotch egg and, if you fancy, stay for lunch—so common up and down the country yet strangely absent in the capital. So thank the heavens for the Marksman, at once a gorgeous wood-panelled old Victorian boozer and proper restaurant, with joint head chefs Tom Harris and Jon Rotheram combining their years of experience to create an attractive—and keenly priced—menu of seasonal Modern British invention.

PACIFIC SOCIAL CLUB

Recommended by
Alex Jackson

8 Clarence Road
Hackney
London E5 8HB
+44 7816963127

Opening hours	Open 7 days
Credit cards	Not accepted
Price range	Affordable
Style	Casual
Cuisine	Café
Recommended for	Breakfast

"Since Railroad on Morning Lane closed (RIP), this is my new favorite Hackney café. Excellent music, delicious food (Bloody Mary, bacon toastie, extra cheese), bags of character. At dinner it morphs into an *okonomiyaki* (savory pancake) restaurant."—Alex Jackson

PAVILION CAFÉ

Recommended by
Stevie Parle, Shaun Searley, Ben Tish

Victoria Park
Old Ford Road
Hackney
London E9 7DE
+44 2089800030

Opening hours	Open 7 days
Credit cards	Accepted
Price range	Affordable
Style	Casual
Cuisine	British-Sri Lankan Café
Recommended for	Breakfast

"It's in my favorite London park, serves great coffee, amazing breakfasts and Sri Lankan food."—Stevie Parle

PIDGIN

Recommended by
Thomasina Miers

52 Wilton Way
Hackney
London E8 1BS
+44 2072548311
www.pidginLondon.com

Opening hours	Closed Monday and Tuesday
Credit cards	Accepted
Price range	Expensive
Style	Smart casual
Cuisine	Modern British
Recommended for	Wish I'd opened

"This restaurant really does serve the most exciting food. It is inventive, unusual, and using some of the best ingredients and techniques around. Always a delight."—Thomasina Miers

RAWDUCK

Recommended by
Tom Harris, Miles Kirby

197 Richmond Road
Hackney
London E8 3NJ
+44 2089866534
www.rawduckhackney.co.uk

Opening hours	Open 7 days
Credit cards	Accepted
Price range	Affordable
Style	Casual
Cuisine	Modern British-Asian
Recommended for	Regular neighborhood

VIOLET

Recommended by
James Lowe, Thomasina Miers

47 Wilton Way
Hackney
London E8 3ED
+44 2072758360
www.violetcakes.com

Opening hours	Closed Monday
Credit cards	Accepted
Price range	Affordable
Style	Casual
Cuisine	Café-Bakery
Recommended for	Regular neighborhood

"A real gem."—Thomasina Miers

FRANKS CANTEEN

Recommended by
Tam Storrar

86 Highbury Park
Highbury
London N5 2XE
+44 7717683651
www.frankscanteen.com

Opening hours	Closed Monday
Credit cards	Accepted
Price range	Affordable
Style	Casual
Cuisine	English
Recommended for	Breakfast

"Great small place with a menu that is constantly changing. They have classics as well as experiments with different cuisines."—Tam Storrar

HOLBORN DINING ROOM

Recommended by
Paul Foster, Frankie van Loo

252 High Holborn
Holborn
London WC1V 7EN
+44 2037478633
www.holborndiningroom.com

Opening hours..Open 7 days
Credit cards..Accepted
Price range...Affordable
Style...Casual
Cuisine...British Brasserie
Recommended for..............................Local favorite

"Great modern British brasserie but the best part is definitely the pies—the most amazing creations you'll ever come across."—Frankie van Loo

INDIAN OCEAN TANDOORI

Recommended by
Ben Spalding

359 Holloway Road
Holloway
London N7 0RN
+44 2076099963
www.indianoceanislington.co.uk

Opening hours..Open 7 days
Credit cards.......................Accepted but not AMEX or Diners
Price range...Affordable
Style...Casual
Cuisine...Indian
Recommended for..High end

"Brilliant indian cooking with highly professional staff and a charismatic owner full of stories!"
—Ben Spalding

XI'AN IMPRESSION

Recommended by
Joel Braham, Sandia Chang,
Carl Clarke, Dan Graham,
Joshua Katz, James Lowe,
Isaac McHale, Shaun Searley

117 Benwell Road
Holloway
London N7 7BW
+44 2034410191
www.xianimpression.co.uk

Opening hours..Open 7 days
Reservation policy...No
Credit cards..Not accepted
Price range..Budget
Style...Casual
Cuisine..Xi'an Chinese
Recommended for............................Regular neighborhood

"Xi'an Impression serves outstanding and unusual Chinese food that is very affordable. As is the way with food from Xi'an, the hand-pulled noodle dishes

are their speciality, specifically the Xi'an Biang Biang noodles in special chile sauce."—Joshua Katz

ZIA LUCIA

Recommended by
Tam Storrar

157 Holloway Road
Holloway
London N7 8LX
+44 2077003708
www.zialucia.com

Opening hours..Closed Monday
Credit cards.............................Accepted but not AMEX
Price range...Affordable
Style...Casual
Cuisine...Pizza
Recommended for............................Regular neighborhood

"I would say that this is the best pizza I have had in London. They make authentic pizza bases, although one creative one is made with charcoal in it."
—Tam Storrar

BAD SPORTS

Recommended by
Tom Harris, Andi Oliver,
Jon Rotheram

184 Hackney Road
Hoxton
London E2 7QL
+44 7842378220
www.badsports.co.uk

Opening hours..Closed Monday
Credit cards..Accepted
Price range...Affordable
Style...Casual
Cuisine...Mexican-American
Recommended for...Late night

"The best Mexican food I've had outside of Mexico! Bursting with flavor—incredible combinations, beautiful ingredients, authentic taste. Fabulous drinks, incredible staff and inviting energy."—Andi Oliver

BEAGLE

Recommended by
Andi Oliver

397–400 Geffrye Street
Hoxton
London E2 8HZ
+44 2076132967
www.beagleLondon.co.uk

Opening hours	Open 7 days
Credit cards	Accepted
Price range	Affordable
Style	Casual
Cuisine	Modern British
Recommended for	Wish I'd opened

"Elegant, delicious, and seasonal. Beautiful plates and delicious cocktails."—Andi Oliver

BERBER & Q

Recommended by
Martin Morales

338 Acton Mews
Hoxton
London E8 4EA
+44 2079230829
www.berberandq.com

Opening hours	Closed Monday and Sunday
Reservation policy	No
Credit cards	Accepted
Price range	Affordable
Style	Casual
Cuisine	Middle Eastern
Recommended for	Late night

BRAWN

Recommended by
Matteo Aloe, Amandine Chaignot,
Peter Gordon, Merlin Labron-Johnson,
Jeremy Lee, Jon Rotheram,
Tim Spedding

49 Columbia Road
Hoxton
London E2 7RG
+44 2077295692
www.brawn.co

Opening hours	Open 7 days
Credit cards	Accepted but not AMEX
Price range	Affordable
Style	Casual
Cuisine	Bar-Bistro
Recommended for	Regular neighborhood

"The food is always perfect—simple, gutsy, flavorsome. The wine list heads towards 'natural wines' and always offers a surprise."—Peter Gordon

The likeable follow-up to Terroirs, Brawn sits on Columbia Road, in the hip heart of the East End. Utilitarian furniture meets whitewashed walls, Pop art, amusingly random bric-a-brac and a soundtrack

that's big on reggae. It's staffed by a mixture of pretty young things and arty bearded blokes. The gutsy, daily-changing menu is made for sharing, and features the likes of Morecambe Bay oysters, veal ragù tagliatelle and pork chop with green beans and anchovy. It's all designed to go with an impressive wine list that's big on natural wines.

FRIENDS OF OURS

Recommended by
Elizabeth Haigh

61 Pitfield Street
Hoxton
London N1 6BU
www.friendsofourscafe.com

Opening hours	Open 7 days
Reservation policy	No
Credit cards	Accepted but not Diners
Price range	Affordable
Style	Casual
Cuisine	Café
Recommended for	Breakfast

"I'm married to an Australian, so this small café reminds me of being back in Melbourne, with brightly colored food, awesome coffee and super friendly staff. It's always busy on the weekend and if it's sunny I love sitting outdoors with a big bowl of satisfying food."
—Elizabeth Haigh

LANARK COFFEE

Recommended by
Tom Harris

262 Hackney Road
Hoxton
London E2 7SJ
www.lanarkcoffee.co.uk

Opening hours	Open 7 days
Reservation policy	No
Credit cards	Accepted
Price range	Budget
Style	Casual
Cuisine	Café
Recommended for	Regular neighborhood

"For delicious coffee and heart-stopping sandwiches like the 'Helicopter'."—Tom Harris

MEAT MISSION

15 Hoxton Market
Hoxton
London N1 6HG
www.meatliquor.com

Opening hours	Open 7 days
Credit cards	Accepted
Price range	Budget
Style	Casual
Cuisine	American
Recommended for	Late night

MONTY'S DELI

227–229 Hoxton Street
Hoxton
London N1 5LG
+44 2077295737
www.montys-deli.com

Opening hours	Closed Monday
Credit cards	Accepted
Price range	Affordable
Style	Casual
Cuisine	Jewish Deli
Recommended for	Bargain

"Monty's Deli for a pastrami sandwich."—Tom Sellers

MORITO

195 Hackney Road
Hoxton
London E2 8JL
+44 2076130754
www.moritohackneyroad.co.uk

Opening hours	Open 7 days
Credit cards	Accepted
Price range	Affordable
Style	Casual
Cuisine	Tapas
Recommended for	Regular neighborhood

"It's the food I love with just the right twist. Based in Hackney it's buzzing and alive. I love the atmosphere, I love the food, it's my kind of place."—Sami Tamimi

TÄTÄ EATERY

258 Kingsland Road
Hoxton
London E8 4DG
+44 2072544945
www.tataeatery.co.uk

Opening hours	Open 7 days
Credit cards	Accepted but not AMEX or Diners
Price range	Affordable
Style	Casual
Cuisine	European-Asian
Recommended for	Regular neighborhood

"It's a fusion of Chinese and Portuguese cooking and there's nothing quite like it in London."
—Merlin Labron-Johnson

TOWPATH CAFÉ

36 De Beauvoir Crescent
Hoxton
London N1 5SB
+44 2072547606

Opening hours	Closed Monday
Credit cards	Accepted but not AMEX or Diners
Price range	Affordable
Style	Casual
Cuisine	Modern European Café
Recommended for	Breakfast

"It's a café set up on the path of Regent's Canal, open from Spring to end of Summer every year. It's a perfect place to sit on a sunny day eating toasted cheese sandwiches and ice cream."—Jon Rotheram

BELLANGER

9 Islington Green
Islington
London N1 2XH
+44 2072262556
www.bellanger.co.uk

Opening hours	Open 7 days
Credit cards	Accepted
Price range	Affordable
Style	Casual
Cuisine	French
Recommended for	Regular neighborhood

"The atmosphere and food is fantastic."
—Francesco Mazzei

BIRD

Recommended by
Ben Spalding

81 Holloway Rd
Islington
London N7 8LT
+44 2031958788
www.birdrestaurants.com

Opening hours	Open 7 days
Credit cards	Accepted
Price range	Affordable
Style	Casual
Cuisine	Chicken
Recommended for	Bargain

"Impeccably cooked chicken and amazing sides, with excellent, friendly diner-style service."—Ben Spalding

BLACK AXE MANGAL

Recommended by
Nieves Barragán Mohacho,
Neil Borthwick, Erchen Chang,
Sandia Chang, David Gingell,
Elizabeth Haigh,
Christophe Hardiquest,
Tom Harris, James Lowe,
Isaac McHale, Andy Oliver, Jon Rotheram

156 Canonbury Road
Islington
London N1 2UP
www.blackaxemangal.com

Opening hours	Closed Monday and Sunday
Reservation policy	No
Credit cards	Accepted
Price range	Affordable
Style	Casual
Cuisine	Contemporary
Recommended for	Regular neighborhood

"Fun, irreverent, surprising, affordable, and always delicious. Black Axe is the nuts."—Andy Oliver

If you like your kebabs served with a healthy dollop of rock 'n' roll attitude, then this grungy spot in Highbury and Islington may be what you've been waiting for. Chef Lee Tiernan knows a bit about the application of direct heat to animal protein from his days at St. John, and his idiosyncratic style is evident in both the geographically varied, offal-heavy menu (lamb-offal flatbread, crispy pig's cheek) and the provocative interior design. True, the pounding soundtrack and penis-motif flooring won't be for everyone, but something tells us Black Axe Mangal aren't in the business of diplomacy.

CHINESE LAUNDRY

Recommended by
Tim Spedding

107 Upper Street
Islington
London N1 1QN
+44 2076866847
www.chineselaundryroom.co.uk

Opening hours	Closed Monday
Credit cards	Accepted
Price range	Affordable
Style	Casual
Cuisine	Chinese
Recommended for	Bargain

THE DRAPERS ARMS

Recommended by
Elizabeth Haigh, Hus Vedat

44 Barnsbury Street
Islington
London N1 1ER
+44 2076190348
www.thedrapersarms.com

Opening hours	Open 7 days
Credit cards	Accepted but not AMEX
Price range	Affordable
Style	Casual
Cuisine	Modern British
Recommended for	Regular neighborhood

"Always seasonal, their Sunday roasts are banging, and the landlord Nick is a great host."—Hus Vedat

THE LITTLE VIET KITCHEN

Recommended by
Gary Foulkes

2 Chapel Market
Islington
London N1 9EZ
+44 2078379779
www.thelittlevietkitchen.com

Opening hours	Open 7 days
Credit cards	Accepted
Price range	Affordable
Style	Casual
Cuisine	Modern Vietnamese
Recommended for	Regular neighborhood

"Authetic Vietnamese flavors that pack a real punch, cooked and served by friendly chef-owner Thuy Diem Pham."—Gary Foulkes

MEAT LIQUOR

133b Upper Street
Islington
London N1 1QP
+44 2037110104
www.meatliquor.com

Recommended by
Hus Vedat

Opening hours	Open 7 days
Credit cards	Accepted
Price range	Budget
Style	Casual
Cuisine	American
Recommended for	Local favorite

"I can't pass Meat Liquor without smashing a Dead Hippie...burger."—Hus Vedat

OLDROYD

344 Upper Street
Islington
London N1 0PD
+44 2086179010
www.oldroydLondon .com

Recommended by
Elizabeth Haigh

Opening hours	Open 7 days
Credit cards	Accepted
Price range	Affordable
Style	Casual
Cuisine	Modern European
Recommended for	Local favorite

OTTOLENGHI

287 Upper Street
Islington
London N1 2TZ
+44 2072881454
www.ottolenghi.co.uk

Recommended by
Amandine Chaignot, Joshua Katz,
Ben Murphy

Opening hours	Open 7 days
Credit cards	Accepted
Price range	Affordable
Style	Casual
Cuisine	Middle Eastern
Recommended for	Local favorite

"Fresh, tasty food every day, the perfect choice for those who want good food on the go...a common trait of the modern-day Londoner!"—Ben Murphy

THE PIG AND BUTCHER

80 Liverpool Road
Islington
London N1 0QD
+44 2072268304
www.thepigandbutcher.co.uk

Recommended by
Elizabeth Haigh

Opening hours	Open 7 days
Credit cards	Accepted
Price range	Affordable
Style	Casual
Cuisine	Gastropub
Recommended for	Regular neighborhood

SUNDAY CAFÉ & RESTAURANT

169 Hemingford Road
Islington
London N1 1DA
+44 2076073868

Recommended by
Joshua Katz

Opening hours	Open 7 days
Credit cards	Accepted
Price range	Affordable
Style	Casual
Cuisine	Café
Recommended for	Regular neighborhood

"Sunday Café does a fantastic selection of brunch options taking influence and inspiration from all over the world, the only drawback being it's small and very popular, making it hard to grab a table."—Joshua Katz

TRULLO

300–302 Saint Paul's Road
Islington
London N1 2LH
+44 2072262733
www.trullorestaurant.com

Recommended by
Gabriela Cámara,
Isaac McHale

Opening hours	Open 7 days
Credit cards	Accepted
Price range	Affordable
Style	Casual
Cuisine	Modern British-Italian
Recommended for	Regular neighborhood

"One of my most visited restaurants in London."
—Gabriela Cámara

VAGABOND N7 COFFEE SHOP

Recommended by
Ben Spalding

105 Holloway Road
Islington
London N7 8LT
www.vagabond.London

Opening hours	Open 7 days
Credit cards	Accepted
Price range	Budget
Style	Casual
Cuisine	British Café
Recommended for	Breakfast

CHILLI COOL

Recommended by
Ollie Templeton

15 Leigh Street
King's Cross
London WC1H 9EW
+44 2073833135
www.chillicool.co.uk

Opening hours	Open 7 days
Credit cards	Accepted
Price range	Affordable
Style	Casual
Cuisine	Chinese
Recommended for	Regular neighborhood

"I work in the area and if I crave one kind of food more than any its Szechuan. The food at Chilli Cool ticks all my boxes."—Ollie Templeton

CÔBA

Recommended by
Martin Morales

244 York Way
King's Cross
London N7 9AG
+44 7495963336
www.cobarestaurant.co.uk

Opening hours	Closed Monday and Sunday
Credit cards	Accepted but not Diners
Price range	Affordable
Style	Casual
Cuisine	Vietnamese
Recommended for	Late night

DISHOOM

Recommended by
Dan Graham, Anna Hansen,
Bruno Loubet, Martin Morales,
Neil Rankin, Ebbe Vollmer

Granary Square
5 Stable Street
King's Cross
London N1C 4AB
+44 2074209321
www.dishoom.com

Opening hours	Open 7 days
Reservation policy	No
Credit cards	Accepted
Price range	Affordable
Style	Casual
Cuisine	Indian
Recommended for	Local favorite

"I'm there as often as I can be for my egg naan and *masala chai*. It's almost a religion for me."
—Neil Rankin

Some days it feels like half of London is relying upon the bacon naan breakfast to get them through the day. The dish—bacon cured with salt and sugar then smoked over oak chips, paired with bread straight from the tandoor—is a thing of beauty, and yet hardly the only thing worth your money at this citywide group of British-Indian restaurants. Later in the day, and indeed some way into the night, their lamb chops are also legendary; similarly their rich, almost chocolatey black daal (lentil stew). It's all served in grandly stylish rooms populated by capable and amenable staff.

GRAIN STORE

Recommended by
Sami Tamimi, Ebbe Vollmer

Granary Square
1–3 Stable Street
King's Cross
London N1C 4AB
+44 2073244466
www.grainstore.com

Opening hours	Open 7 days
Credit cards	Accepted but not Diners
Price range	Affordable
Style	Casual
Cuisine	Modern European
Recommended for	Breakfast

"The decor is modern, simple and comfortable and on the weekend you can go for the classics or the classics with a twist."—Sami Tamimi

GRANGER & CO

Recommended by
Elizabeth Haigh, Jocky Petrie

Unit 1 Stanley Building
7 Pancras Square
King's Cross
London N1C 4AG
+44 2030582567
www.grangerandco.com

Opening hours...Open 7 days
Reservation policy..No
Credit cards.................................Accepted but not Diners
Price range...Affordable
Style..Casual
Cuisine..Australian
Recommended for...Breakfast

HONEST BURGERS

Recommended by
Dan Graham

251 Pentonville Road
King's Cross
London N1 9NG
+44 2033023452
www.honestburgers.co.uk

Opening hours....................................Open 7 days
Credit cards...Accepted
Price range..Budget
Style..Casual
Cuisine..Burgers
Recommended for......................Regular neighborhood

"When you find your burger place, nothing else will do."—Dan Graham

EL PARADOR

Recommended by
Yotam Ottolenghi

245 Eversholt Street
King's Cross
London NW1 1BA
+44 2073872789
www.elparadorLondon .com

Opening hours...Open 7 days
Credit cards...Accepted
Price range...Affordable
Style...Casual
Cuisine..Spanish
Recommended for.............................Regular neighborhood

ROTI KING

Recommended by
Joshua Katz, Tom Moxon

40 Doric Way
King's Cross
London NW1 1LH
+44 2073872518
www.rotiking.in

Opening hours...................................Closed Sunday
Credit cards...Accepted
Price range...Budget
Style..Casual
Cuisine...Malaysian
Recommended for.................................Bargain

"A small, hole-in-the-wall Malaysian restaurant on a back street in Euston serving excellent, authentic Malaysian food at very reasonable prices. Naturally, roti is their speciality, but everything else they serve is always very good."—Joshua Katz

SOURCED MARKET

Recommended by
Jocky Petrie

Saint Pancras International
King's Cross
London N1C 4QP
+44 2078339352
www.sourcedmarket.com

Opening hours...................................Open 7 days
Credit cards...Accepted
Price range...Affordable
Style..Casual
Cuisine...Café
Recommended for.................................Breakfast

"I pass this place every morning and evening to and from work. Great way to start a chilly winter's morning with porridge and fantastic filter coffee."
—Jocky Petrie

HONG KONG CITY

Recommended by
Andrew Wong

43 New Cross Road
New Cross
London SE14 5DS
+44 2072529888

Opening hours...................................Open 7 days
Credit cards.....................Accepted but not AMEX or Diners
Price range...Affordable
Style..Casual
Cuisine...Chinese
Recommended for.................................Bargain

BABETTE

Recommended by
Petter Nilsson

57 Nunhead Lane
Nunhead
London SE15 3TR
+44 2031722450
www.babettenunhead.com

Opening hours................................Open 7 days
Credit cards..Accepted
Price range..Affordable
Style...Casual
Cuisine....................................Modern British
Recommended for..............Regular neighborhood

M. MANZE

Recommended by
Jason Atherton

105 High Street Peckham
Peckham
London SE15 5RS
+4420 72776181
www.manze.co.uk

Opening hours..................Closed Monday and Sunday
Credit cards................Accepted but not AMEX or Diners
Price range..Budget
Style...Casual
Cuisine...British
Recommended for............................Local favorite

PECKHAM BAZAAR

Recommended by
Adam Byatt, Andy Oliver

119 Consort Road
Peckham
London SE15 3RU
+44 2077322525
www.peckhambazaar.com

Opening hours................................Open 7 days
Credit cards..................Accepted but not AMEX
Price range..Affordable
Style...Casual
Cuisine..........................Turkish-Albanian-Greek
Recommended for..............Regular neighborhood

"I tend to eat locally normally; Peckham Bazaar for
dinner always proves to be a great experience."
—Adam Byatt

THE BEIGEL SHOP

Recommended by
Stevie Parle

159 Brick Lane
Shoreditch
London E1 6SB
+44 2077290826

Opening hours................................Open 7 days
Reservation policy...No
Credit cards....................................Not accepted
Price range..Affordable
Style...Casual
Cuisine...British
Recommended for................................Late night

"The massive salt-beef bagels here are exactly what
you want late at night. I'm not sure they ever close."
—Stevie Parle

ALBION

Recommended by
Matteo Aloe

2–4 Boundary Street
Shoreditch
London E2 7DD
+44 2077291051
www.albion-uk.London

Opening hours................................Open 7 days
Credit cards..Accepted
Price range..Affordable
Style...Casual
Cuisine....................................Modern British
Recommended for..............Regular neighborhood

ANDINA

Recommended by
Andi Oliver

1 Redchurch Street
Shoreditch
London E2 7DJ
+44 2079206499
www.andinaLondon .com

Opening hours................................Open 7 days
Credit cards..Accepted
Price range..Affordable
Style...Casual
Cuisine...Peruvian
Recommended for......................Wish I'd opened

BEIGEL BAKE

159 Brick Lane
Shoreditch
London E1 6SB
+44 2077290616
www.beigelbake.com

Recommended by
Harneet Baweja, Alex Jackson,
Eyal Jagermann, Bonny Porter,
Mark Rosati, Lee Tiernan,
Mitch Tonks, Hus Vedat

Opening hours	Open 7 days
Reservation policy	No
Credit cards	Not accepted
Price range	Budget
Style	Casual
Cuisine	Bakery
Recommended for	Late night

"Hands down, the best salt beef on the planet. Get double mustard. Open 24 hours."—Lee Tiernan

A true food institution if ever there was one, the Brick Lane Beigel Bake has been feeding all sections of London society, twenty-four hours a day, seven days a week, for the best part of half a century. The beigels in question (the spelling—pronounced 'bye-gel'—is a peculiarly London Yiddish variation) are made fresh on site and are boiled before baking for that addictive chew. As for fillings, take your pick—but most would look no further than the house-cured salt beef (with mustard and pickles, of course). It's probably the finest in town—and there's some competition on that front.

DINERAMA

19 Great Eastern Street
Shoreditch
London EC2A 3EJ
www.streetfeast.com/where/dinerama

Recommended by
Bonny Porter, Neil Rankin

Opening hours	Closed Sunday to Wednesday
Reservation policy	No
Credit cards	Not accepted
Price range	Affordable
Style	Casual
Cuisine	Market-Deli
Recommended for	Local favorite

"Located smack bang in the middle of Shoreditch, Dinerama is a melting pot of creativity and like-minded individuals keen to have a good time. The food offering is street food from across the world and each stall gives fully-fledged restaurants a run for their money. Atmosphere 10, food 10, concept 10."
—Bonny Porter

DISHOOM

7 Boundary Street
Shoreditch
London E2 7JE
+44 2074209324
www.dishoom.com

Recommended by
Sameer Taneja, Richard Turner

Opening hours	Open 7 days
Reservation policy	No
Credit cards	Accepted
Price range	Affordable
Style	Casual
Cuisine	Indian
Recommended for	Breakfast

DUMPLING HEART

8 Lee Street
Shoreditch
London E8 4DY

Recommended by
Isaac McHale

Opening hours	Closed Monday and Sunday
Credit cards	Accepted but not AMEX or Diners
Price range	Affordable
Style	Casual
Cuisine	Taiwanese
Recommended for	Bargain

HOI POLLOI

100 Shoreditch High Street
Shoreditch
London E1 6JQ
+44 2088806100
www.hoi-polloi.co.uk

Recommended by
Nieves Barragán Mohacho

Opening hours	Open 7 days
Credit cards	Accepted
Price range	Affordable
Style	Casual
Cuisine	Modern British-American
Recommended for	Breakfast

"It's cool, there's always good background music, it's spacious and I can stay there after breakfast to read, work, or chill..."—Nieves Barragán Mohacho

KÊU

332 Old Street
Shoreditch
London EC1V 9DR
+44 2077391164
www.thevietnamesekitchen.co.uk

Recommended by
Elizabeth Haigh, Isaac McHale,
Andi Oliver

Opening hours	Closed Sunday
Credit cards	Accepted but not Diners
Price range	Budget
Style	Casual
Cuisine	Vietnamese
Recommended for	Bargain

"Incredible, authentic, life-saving Vietnamese banh mi!"—Andi Oliver

LEILA'S SHOP

15–17 Calvert Avenue
Shoreditch
London E2 7JP
+44 2077299789

Recommended by
Tom Harris

Opening hours	Closes Monday and Tuesday
Credit cards	Accepted but not Diners
Price range	Affordable
Style	Casual
Cuisine	Café
Recommended for	Regular neighborhood

OKLAVA

74 Luke Street
Shoreditch
London EC2A 4PY
+44 2077293032
www.oklava.co.uk

Recommended by
Peter Gordon

Opening hours	Open 7 days
Credit cards	Accepted
Price range	Affordable
Style	Casual
Cuisine	Turkish-Cypriot
Recommended for	Regular neighborhood

"Selin Kiazim is a fabulously talented Turkish-Cypriot chef who is reinventing the food of her family. She cooks the most delicious meals and combinations in this small open kitchen and her business partner Laura Christie runs a tight front of house. All the wines are Turkish and the breads are superb."
—Peter Gordon

OZONE COFFEE ROASTERS

11 Leonard Street
Shoreditch
London EC2A 4AQ
+44 2074901039
www.ozonecoffee.co.uk

Recommended by
Matteo Aloe

Opening hours	Open 7 days
Credit cards	Accepted
Price range	Affordable
Style	Casual
Cuisine	Café
Recommended for	Regular neighborhood

PIZZA EAST

56A Shoreditch High Street
Shoreditch
London E1 6PQ
+44 2077291888
www.pizzaeast.com

Recommended by
Ben Murphy

Opening hours	Open 7 days
Credit cards	Accepted
Price range	Affordable
Style	Casual
Cuisine	Pizza
Recommended for	Regular neighborhood

ROCHELLE CANTEEN

Rochelle School
Arnold Circus
Shoreditch
London E2 7ES
+44 2077295677
www.arnoldandhenderson.com

Recommended by
Harneet Baweja, Olle T. Cellton,
Peter Gordon, Alex Jackson,
Jeremy Lee, James Lowe,
Isaac McHale, Thomasina Miers,
Shuko Oda, Mark Rosati,
Jon Rotheram

Opening hours	Closed Saturday and Sunday
Credit cards	Accepted
Price range	Affordable
Style	Casual
Cuisine	Modern British
Recommended for	Local favorite

"Rochelle Canteen is another one of my favorites. Not only is the food always stellar, but there is no other restaurant the feels quite like Rochelle due its amazing setting in a courtyard hidden behind a brick wall. Love this spot especially on a lovely day in the summer."—Mark Rosati

SMOKESTAK

35 Sclater Street
Shoreditch
London E1 6LB
+44 2038731733
www.smokestak.co.uk

Recommended by
Pete Denhart, Tom Sellers

Opening hours	Open 7 days
Credit cards	Accepted
Price range	Affordable
Style	Casual
Cuisine	Barbecue
Recommended for	Bargain

"The food is really tasty, the meat is well smoked and you can tell they thought hard about putting the menu together."—Tom Sellers

TAS FIRIN

160 Bethnal Green Road
Shoreditch
London E2 6DG
+44 2077296446

Recommended by
Leo Tiernan

Opening hours	Open 7 days
Credit cards	Not accepted
Price range	Budget
Style	Casual
Cuisine	Turkish
Recommended for	Bargain

"Fresh speciality bread made to order."—Lee Tiernan

THE CLOVE CLUB

Shoredich Town Hall
380 Old Street
Shoreditch
London EC1V 9LT
+44 2077296496
www.thecloveclub.com

Recommended by
Tom Aikens, Matteo Aloe,
Olle T. Cellton, Luke Dale Roberts,
Hélène Darroze, Cary Docherty,
Konstantin Filippou, Henry Harris,
Jeremy Lee, James Lowe,
Greg Marchand

Opening hours	Closed Sunday
Credit cards	Accepted
Price range	Expensive
Style	Smart casual
Cuisine	Modern British
Recommended for	High end

"The food, service, wine, and cocktails are amazing. They get everything just right and are lovely people. You can go for a tasting menu or a few bites and a drink at the bar. They cater to whatever you're looking for, whether it's a special occasion or an impromptu get together. "—Cary Docherty

Beginning life as a cult Dalston pop-up, The Clove Club found a permanent home in a section of Shoreditch Town Hall in 2013. The space is split between bar and dinner only dining room. The latter, a handsome combination of lofty ceiling and open kitchen with show pass, serves a take-it-or-leave it five-course menu with a few snacks thrown in for fun. The cooking combines carefully sourced British produce, a Nordic sensibility and a few more far-flung influences—notably a fondness for Korean condiments. Lunch, served in the bar, offers a more pared-back menu but the full tasting can be booked ahead of time.

VIET GRILL

58 Kingsland Road
Shoreditch
London E2 8DP
+44 2077396686
www.thevietnamesekitchen.co.uk

Recommended by
Stevie Parle

Opening hours	Open 7 days
Credit cards	Accepted but not AMEX or Diners
Price range	Affordable
Style	Casual
Cuisine	Vietnamese
Recommended for	Regular neighborhood

"I go to Viet Grill quite a lot. It's always excellent."
—Stevie Parle

LYLE'S

Tea Building
56 Shoreditch High Street
Shoreditch
London E1 6JJ
+44 2030115911
www.lylesLondon .com

Recommended by
Timur Abuzyarov, Matteo Aloe,
Olle T. Cellton, Carl Clarke,
Mark Dobbie, Elizabeth Haigh,
Tom Harris, John Jackson,
Eyal Jagermann, Jeremy Lee,
Isaac McHale, Shuko Oda,
Jowett Yu

Opening hours	Closed Sunday
Credit cards	Accepted
Price range	Affordable
Style	Casual
Cuisine	British
Recommended for	Worth the travel

"I think the cooking here is one of the best anywhere in the world. James Lowe takes really amazing local produce in season, treats it carefully and simply, and what you end up with is a contemporary, sensibly creative cuisine. I think this place is flying the flag for the future of British cooking."—Jowett Yu

As soon as you step into Lyle's, with its bright white tiling and whitewashed brick walls, the connection with St. John seems obvious. But despite chef James Lowe's background (he headed Bread & Wine in Spitalfields after the Young Turks chef collective came to an end), you could never describe this remarkable restaurant as derivative. Lowe's food is inventive, colorful, seasonal and—most importantly —consistently excellent, the best of British produce married to superb kitchen technique. The evening tasting menu is something approaching a bargain at £55 ($71), but the lunch offering, with the option to pick smaller plates of unusual offal-based delicacies, is great value.

PIZARRO

194 Bermondsey Street
Southwark
London SE1 3TQ
+44 2073789455
www.josepizarro.com/pizarro-restaurant

Recommended by
Peter Gordon, Sameer Taneja

Opening hours	Open 7 days
Credit cards	Accepted
Price range	Affordable
Style	Smart casual
Cuisine	Spanish
Recommended for	Worth the travel

"Lovely simple Spanish food, great wine list, good service, and love the neighborhood."—Peter Gordon

RESTAURANT STORY

199 Tooley Street
Southwark
London SE1 2JX
+44 2071832117
www.restaurantstory.co.uk

Recommended by
Tom Aikens

Opening hours	Closed Sunday
Credit cards	Accepted
Price range	Expensive
Style	Smart casual
Cuisine	Modern British
Recommended for	High end

"Top-quality food in a great restaurant by chef Tom Sellers. Expect some great surprises and all beautifully presented with real thought, care and attention to detail."—Tom Aikens

LA CHAPELLE

35 Spital Square
Spitalfields
London E1 6DY
+44 2072990400
www.galvinrestaurants.com

Recommended by
José Pizarro

Opening hours	Open 7 days
Credit cards	Accepted
Price range	Affordable
Style	Smart casual
Cuisine	French
Recommended for	High end

GUNPOWDER

11 Whites Row
Spitalfields
London E1 7NF
+44 2074260542
www.gunpowderLondon.com

Recommended by
Michael Reid,
Sameer Taneja

Opening hours	Closed Sunday
Reservation policy	No
Credit cards	Accepted but not AMEX or Diners
Price range	Affordable
Style	Casual
Cuisine	Modern Indian
Recommended for	Regular neighborhood

"Gunpowder is my standout neighborhood restaurant of the last few years."—Michael Reid

THE RIB MAN

Recommended by
Alyn Williams

Brick Lane Market
Spitalfields
London E1 6QR
www.theribman.co.uk

Opening hours	Open Sunday
Credit cards	Not accepted
Price range	Affordable
Style	Casual
Cuisine	Barbecue
Recommended for	Bargain

"Great pork rib rolls with the Rib Man's own hot sauce."—Alyn Williams

SICHUAN FOLK

Recommended by
Merlin Labron-Johnson

32 Hanbury Street
Spitalfields
London E1 6QR
+44 2072474735
www.sichuan-folk.co.uk

Opening hours	Open 7 days
Credit cards	Accepted but not AMEX or Diners
Price range	Affordable
Style	Casual
Cuisine	Szechuan
Recommended for	Bargain

"It's the first authentic, spicy Szechuan food I've tried. I go back there often, especially for the famous Szechuan fish hotpot."—Merlin Labron-Johnson

SOM SAA

Recommended by
Will Bowlby, Gary Foulkes,
Elizabeth Haigh, James Knappett,
Martin Morales, Lee Tiernan

43A Commercial Street
Spitalfields
London E1 6BD
+44 2073247790
www.somsaa.com

Opening hours	Closed Sunday
Credit cards	Accepted but not Diners
Price range	Affordable
Style	Casual
Cuisine	Thai
Recommended for	Wish I'd opened

"Fun, sexy food, cool and stylish with a completely relaxed atmosphere, taking Thai flavors to the max." —Martin Morales

ST. JOHN BREAD & WINE

Recommended by
Matteo Aloe, Harneet Baweja,
Neil Borthwick, Olle T. Cellton,
Samantha & Samuel Clark,
Mark Dobbie, Christian Edwardson,
Henry Harris, Eyal Jagermann,
Florence Knight, Andy Oliver,
Tim Spedding

94–96 Commercial Street
Spitalfields
London E1 6LZ
+44 2072510848
www.stjohngroup.uk.com

Opening hours	Open 7 days
Credit cards	Accepted
Price range	Affordable
Style	Casual
Cuisine	British
Recommended for	Breakfast

"St. John's opening represented a turning point in British food. It married casual dining with excellent food and nose-to-tail eating."—Florence Knight

TABERNA DO MERCADO

Recommended by
Matteo Aloe

Old Spitalfields Market
107b Commercial Street
Spitalfields
London E1 6BG
+44 2073750649
www.tabernamercado.co.uk

Opening hours	Open 7 days
Credit cards	Accepted
Price range	Affordable
Style	Casual
Cuisine	Portuguese
Recommended for	Regular neighborhood

"Transported to Portugal by amazing ingredients. The *bifana* sandwich (pork sandwich) and *pastel de nata* (custard tarts) are a dream."—Matteo Aloe

THE CANTON ARMS

Recommended by
Andi Oliver

177 South Lambeth Road
Stockwell
London SW8 1XP
+44 2075828710
www.cantonarms.com

Opening hours	Open 7 days
Credit cards	Accepted but not AMEX
Price range	Affordable
Style	Casual
Cuisine	Gastropub
Recommended for	Local favorite

"Imaginative, flavorsome, colorful, heartwarming food—just gorgeous."—Andi Oliver

ANDI'S

176 Church Street
Stoke Newington
London N16 0JL
+44 2072416919
www.andis.London

Opening hours	Open 7 days
Credit cards	Accepted
Price range	Affordable
Style	Casual
Cuisine	Café-Bistro
Recommended for	Wish I'd opened

APOLLO PIZZERIA

160 Stoke Newington High Street
Stoke Newington
London N16 7JL
+44 2072411914
www.pizzeriaapollo.com

Opening hours	Open 7 days
Credit cards	Accepted but not AMEX
Price range	Affordable
Style	Casual
Cuisine	Pizza
Recommended for	Regular neighborhood

DANDY CAFE

20 Newington Green
Stoke Newington
London N16 9PU
+44 2086171930
www.dandycafe.co.uk

Opening hours	Open 7 days
Credit cards	Accepted but not AMEX or Diners
Price range	Affordable
Style	Casual
Cuisine	Café
Recommended for	Regular neighborhood

ESCOCESA

67 Church Street
Stoke Newington
London N16 0AR
+44 2078129189
www.escocesa.co.uk

Opening hours	Open 7 days
Credit cards	Accepted
Price range	Affordable
Style	Smart casual
Cuisine	Scottish-Spanish
Recommended for	Regular neighborhood

"Beautiful Scottish seafood tapas! Amazing cultural marriage of flavors and ingredients, expertly prepared and so full of flavor you're happy for hours afterwards."—Andi Oliver

ESTERS

55 Kynaston Road
Stoke Newington
London N16 0EB
+44 2072540253
www.estersn16.com

Opening hours	Closed Monday
Credit cards	Accepted
Price range	Budget
Style	Casual
Cuisine	Café
Recommended for	Regular neighborhood

ISTANBUL RESTAURANT

9 Stoke Newington Road
Stoke Newington
London N16 8BH
+44 2072547291
www.istanbulrestaurant.co.uk

Opening hours	Open 7 days
Credit cards	Accepted but not AMEX or Diners
Price range	Affordable
Style	Casual
Cuisine	Turkish
Recommended for	Late night

"Amazing authentic Turkish grill house. I'm addicted to their lamb döner which I reckon is the best in London."—Carl Clarke

PERILLA

Recommended by
Richard Corrigan, Isaac McHale

1–3 Green Lanes
Stoke Newington
London N16 9BS
+44 2073590779
www.perilladining.co.uk

Opening hours	Open 7 days
Credit cards	Accepted but not AMEX
Price range	Affordable
Style	Smart casual
Cuisine	Modern European
Recommended for	Regular neighborhood

"Great food by a young, ambitious chef—very thoughtful cooking for such a young guy. They deserve to do well."—Richard Corrigan

PRIMEUR

Recommended by
Tom Harris, Alex Jackson,
Joshua Katz, Miles Kirby,
Yotam Ottolenghi, Jon Rotheram

116 Petherton Road
Stoke Newington
London N5 2RT
+44 2072265271
www.primeurn5.co.uk

Opening hours	Closed Monday
Credit cards	Accepted but not AMEX
Price range	Affordable
Style	Casual
Cuisine	Modern European
Recommended for	Regular neighborhood

"It's a former garage which the team have converted into a friendly, neighborhood restaurant with a great interior. They have a daily changing menu with a strong French influence and a great selection of wines."—Jon Rotheram

RUBEDO

Recommended by
Andi Oliver

35 Stoke Newington Church Street
Stoke Newington
London N16 0NX
+44 2072540364
www.rubedoLondon.com

Opening hours	Closed Monday and Sunday
Credit cards	Accepted but not AMEX or Diners
Price range	Affordable
Style	Casual
Cuisine	Modern European
Recommended for	Regular neighborhood

THE SPENCE BAKERY

Recommended by
Sandia Chang

161 Stoke Newington Church Street
Stoke Newington
London N16 0UH
www.thespence.co.uk

Opening hours	Open 7 days
Credit cards	Accepted
Price range	Budget
Style	Casual
Cuisine	Café-Bakery
Recommended for	Regular neighborhood

UMUT 2000

Recommended by
Johan Agrell, Joel Braham,
James Lowe, Isaac McHale,
Magnus Nilsson, Tim Spedding

6 Crossway
Stoke Newington
London N16 8HX
+44 2072490903

Opening hours	Open 7 days
Credit cards	Not accepted
Price range	Budget
Style	Casual
Cuisine	Turkish
Recommended for	Late night

"Small and friendly Turkish charcoal grill. The huge grill dominates the café-style dining room. Lamb ribs and chicken livers are my standout favorites, with all the house salads, and the meaty bread full of all that smoke from the grill."—Joel Braham

USTUN LAHMACUN

Recommended by
David Gingell

107 Green Lanes
Stoke Newington
London N16 9BX
+44 2077040360
www.ustunlahmacun.com

Opening hours	Open 7 days
Credit cards	Not accepted
Price range	Budget
Style	Casual
Cuisine	Turkish
Recommended for	Bargain

"When we where doing the building work at Primeur we lived on *lahmacun* (meat-topped flatbread) from this place. £2 ($2.60) a pop. It's proper fast food and it's so very good."—David Gingell

WOLF

Recommended by
Ben Spalding

110 Stoke Newington High Street
Stoke Newington
London N16 7NY
+44 2072544141
www.wolf-restaurant.co.uk

Opening hours	Open 7 days
Credit cards	Accepted
Price range	Affordable
Style	Casual
Cuisine	Italian
Recommended for	Local favorite

ROKA

Recommended by
Tom Sellers

71 Aldwych
Strand
London WC2B 4HN
+44 2072947636
www.rokarestaurant.com

Opening hours	Open 7 days
Credit cards	Accepted
Price range	Expensive
Style	Smart casual
Cuisine	Japanese
Recommended for	Regular neighborhood

SPRING

Recommended by
Olle T. Cellton, Colin Mackay,
Thomasina Miers

Somerset House
Lancaster Place
Strand
London WC2R 1LA
+44 2030110115
www.springrestaurant.co.uk

Opening hours	Open 7 days
Credit cards	Accepted
Price range	Affordable
Style	Smart casual
Cuisine	Modern British
Recommended for	Wish I'd opened

"Skye Gyngell has created a beautiful dining room with a small, focused menu of fresh, interesting cooking that always hits the mark."—Colin Mackay

BRAVI RIGAZZI

Recommended by
Anna Hansen

2a Sunnyhill Road
Streatham
London SW16 2UH
+44 2087694966
www.braviragazzipizzeria.co.uk

Opening hours	Open 7 days
Credit cards	Accepted but not Diners
Price range	Affordable
Style	Casual
Cuisine	Pizza
Recommended for	Late night

"Although pizza is probably the worst thing to eat before you go to bed they make great sourdough pizza and the service is always super friendly and upbeat."—Anna Hansen

BROOKS & GAO

Recommended by
Anna Hansen

The High Parade
28 Streatham High Road
Streatham
London SW16 1EX

Opening hours	Open 7 days
Credit cards	Accepted
Price range	Affordable
Style	Casual
Cuisine	Café-Deli
Recommended for	Breakfast

"Best coffee in Streatham and they make an awesome Comte omelette. In the evenings it's perfect for a tipple and a few small plates."—Anna Hansen

BEAR + WOLF

Recommended by
Sandia Chang

153 Fortess Road
Tuffnell Park
London NW5 2HR
+44 2036011900
www.bearandwolfcafe.com

Opening hours	Open 7 days
Credit cards	Accepted
Price range	Affordable
Style	Casual
Cuisine	Café
Recommended for	Breakfast

TUFNELL PARK KEBAB & FISH BAR

233 Brecknock Road
Tuffnell Park
London N19 5AA
+44 2074857015

Opening hours	Open 7 days
Credit cards	Accepted
Price range	Budget
Style	Casual
Cuisine	Middle Eastern Kebab
Recommended for	Late night

"It's open late with great falafel wraps and it's just outside my tube station."—Sandia Chang

BRUNSWICK HOUSE

30 Wandsworth Road
Vauxhall
London SW8 2LG
+44 2077202926
www.brunswickhouse.co

Opening hours	Open 7 days
Credit cards	Accepted but not AMEX
Price range	Affordable
Style	Casual
Cuisine	Modern British
Recommended for	Local favorite

"Such a brilliantly 'London' restaurant: all my favorite things in one place and always excellently hosted by chef Jackson Boxer."—Stevie Parle

BÜHLER AND CO

8 Chingford Road
Walthamstow
London E17 4PJ
+44 2085273652
www.buhlerandco.com

Opening hours	Closed Monday
Credit cards	Accepted but not AMEX or Diners
Price range	Affordable
Style	Casual
Cuisine	Café
Recommended for	Breakfast

"I would like to say firstly that I didn't know this café was veggie or I would not have gone in but I am glad that I did. Good coffee, the odd house-baked pastry, vegetarian breakfasts, and light lunches. Also, just very nice people which is very important to me in the morning."—David Gingell

493

SODO PIZZA CAFÉ

21 Hatherley Mews
Walthamstow
London E17 4QP
+44 2085201244
www.sodopizza.co.uk

Opening hours	Closed Monday
Credit cards	Accepted but not AMEX
Price range	Affordable
Style	Casual
Cuisine	Pizzeria
Recommended for	Regular neighborhood

"They are so very good at what they do. Good pizza, a couple of good low intervention wines and hipster beers. The service is also very good. They are amazing with my three-year-old daughter, which is often overlooked by many restaurants, not with a kid's menu but with a really good margherita and some apple juice. All in all, it does what every good neighborhood restaurant should do: it makes you and the ones you love feel happy."—David Gingell

LAHORE KEBAB HOUSE

2–10 Umberston Street
Whitechapel
London E1 1PY
+44 2074819737
www.lahore-kebabhouse.com

Opening hours	Open 7 days
Credit cards	Accepted
Price range	Affordable
Style	Casual
Cuisine	Pakistani
Recommended for	Bargain

"Brilliant Pakistani grill in a huge strip-light illuminated dining room. The food here is hot and tasty. Don't miss the lamb chops."—Stevie Parle

NEEDOO GRILL

Recommended by
Isaac McHale

87 New Road
Whitechapel
London E1 1HH
+44 2072470648
www.needoogrill.co.uk

Opening hours	Open 7 days
Credit cards	Accepted but not AMEX
Price range	Affordable
Style	Casual
Cuisine	Pakistani
Recommended for	Bargain

SAKANA SUSHI

Recommended by
Neil Borthwick

43A Commercial Street
Whitechapel
London WC2E 7LB
+44 2086178181

Opening hours	Open 7 days
Credit cards	Accepted but not AMEX or Diners
Price range	Affordable
Style	Casual
Cuisine	Japanese
Recommended for	Regular neighborhood

"This is a little hidden gem of a restaurant in our neighborhood from an ex-Nobu chef who spent nineteen years in Milan."—Neil Borthwick

TAYYABS

Recommended by
Olle T. Cellton, Gary Foulkes,
Rohit Ghai, Eyal Jagermann,
Joshua Katz, James Lowe,
Andy Oliver, Ben Tish

83–89 Fieldgate Street
Whitechapel
London E1 1JU
+44 2072476400
www.tayyabs.co.uk

Opening hours	Open 7 days
Credit cards	Accepted
Price range	Budget
Style	Casual
Cuisine	Punjabi Indian
Recommended for	Bargain

"London is not about a particular cuisine or culture but a diffusion of all—a melting pot in which different people live together side by side. Indian cuisine is as prominent and integral to London as any other cuisine and Tayyabs serves the best Punjabi Indian food in the capital to queues of customers every night, and has done for years. The fast energy of the place and mix of different customers makes it a perfect example of what eating in London is all about."—Joshua Katz

No one comes to Tayyabs for the ambience. Forty years after opening, E1's worst-kept secret is more cut and thrust than ever, from the location round the back of Whitechapel High Street to the hour-plus queues (waiting lines)—and that's with a reservation—and the ferocious noise levels. However, the Punjabi food—specifically the sizzling lamb chops and groaning mixed grill plate, as well as fresh-from-the-tandoor naan—makes it all worthwhile, especially with change from £20 ($26). Don't get caught out by the BYO policy—bring an extra beer or two so you can enjoy a pre-dinner drink while you wait for a table.

PIZZERIA BEL-SIT

Recommended by
Ben Murphy, Lee Tiernan

439–441 High Road
Woodford
London IG8 0XE
+44 2085041164

Opening hours	Closed Sunday
Credit cards	Not accepted
Price range	Affordable
Style	Casual
Cuisine	Pizza
Recommended for	Regular neighborhood

GREEN ISLAND RESTAURANT

Recommended by
Shaun Rankin

Green Island
Saint Clement
Jersey
Channel Islands JE2 6LS
+44 1534857787
www.greenisland.je

Opening hours	Closed Monday
Credit cards	Accepted but not AMEX
Price range	Affordable
Style	Smart casual
Cuisine	Mediterranean
Recommended for	Local favorite

"They do a fantastic Fruit de Mer that has to be enjoyed leisurely on the terrace, overlooking the bay, with a chilled bottle of Sancerre."—Shaun Rankin

EL TICO BEACH CANTINA

Recommended by
Shaun Rankin

La Grande Route des Mielles
Saint Ouen
Jersey
Channel Islands JE3 7FN
+44 1534482009
www.elticojersey.com

Opening hours	Open 7 days
Credit cards	Accepted but not Diners
Price range	Affordable
Style	Casual
Cuisine	International
Recommended for	Breakfast

"It's relaxed, great for the kids and right on the beach at Saint Ouen."—Shaun Rankin

OBAN SEAFOOD HUT

Recommended by
Andi Oliver

1 Railway Pier
Oban
Argyll
Scotland PA34 4LW
+44 7881418565

Opening hours	Open 7 days
Credit cards	Not accepted
Price range	Affordable
Style	Casual
Cuisine	Scottish Seafood
Recommended for	Worth the travel

"A glorious celebration of Scottish seafood, literally just pulled from the sea, cooked simply and served in a polystyrene tub from a harbor-side hut. It may as

well be a palace the way you feel when you eat here! Sublime!"—Andi Oliver

INVER RESTAURANT

Recommended by
Jock Zonfrillo

Strathlachlan
Strachur
Argyll
Scotland PA27 8BU
+44 1369860537
www.inverrestaurant.co.uk

Opening hours	Closed Tuesday
Credit cards	Accepted but not AMEX or Diners
Price range	Affordable
Style	Smart casual
Cuisine	Modern Scottish
Recommended for	Worth the travel

"Much amazingness about this place: brilliant food, the finest hospitality, and a rural Scottish setting that makes you want to move there. More than worth the journey!"—Jock Zonfrillo

AIZLE

Recommended by
Ben Reade

107–109 Saint Leonard's Street
Edinburgh
Scotland EH8 9QY
+44 1316629349
www.aizle.co.uk

Opening hours	Closed Monday and Tuesday
Credit cards	Accepted
Price range	Affordable
Style	Smart casual
Cuisine	Scottish
Recommended for	Regular neighborhood

"Simple tasting menu, great flavors, and proper cooking. The price is right and the drinks are quality."—Ben Reade

CASTLE TERRACE RESTAURANT

Recommended by
Stephen Toman

33–35 Castle Terrace
Edinburgh
Scotland EH1 2EL
+44 1312291222
www.castleterracerestaurant.com

Opening hours	Closed Monday and Sunday
Credit cards	Accepted
Price range	Expensive
Style	Smart casual
Cuisine	Modern British-French
Recommended for	Worth the travel

MAKI AND RAMEN

Recommended by
Ben Reade

13 West Richmond Street
Edinburgh
Scotland
EH8 9EF
+44 7548628685
www.makimaki-restaurant.co.uk

Opening hours..Open 7 days
Credit cards........................Accepted but not AMEX or Diners
Price range..Affordable
Style..Casual
Cuisine...Japanese
Recommended for................................Regular neighborhood

"Authentic Japanese ramen bar, serving proper broth and good noodles."—Ben Reade

NIGHTCAP

Recommended by
Ben Reade

3 York Place
Edinburgh
Scotland EH1 3EB
+44 1315565481
www.nightcapbar.co.uk

Opening hours..........................Closed Monday to Wednesday
Credit cards..Accepted
Price range..Affordable
Style..Casual
Cuisine..Scottish-American
Recommended for...Late night

"Late-night food in Edinburgh is really hard—these guys do it right: good cocktails and a solid slider selection."—Ben Reade

STORRIES HOME BAKERY

Recommended by
Ben Reade

279 Leith Walk
Edinburgh
Scotland EH6 8PD

Opening hours..Open 7 days
Reservation policy...No
Credit cards...Not accepted
Price range..Budget
Style..Casual
Cuisine...Bakery
Recommended for...Late night

"Storries Home Bakery is a pie shop that opens at midnight on Leith Walk. It is the stuff of legends."
—Ben Reade

TIMBERYARD

Recommended by
Ben Reade, Jock Zonfrillo

10 Lady Lawson Street
Edinburgh
Scotland EH3 9DS
+44 1312211222
www.timberyard.co

Opening hours.............................Closed Monday and Sunday
Credit cards..Accepted
Price range..Affordable
Style..Smart casual
Cuisine..Modern European
Recommended for...................................Worth the travel

"These guys are killing it, from the natural wine list through to the quirky and often challenging dishes. Lip-smacking...go there, you won't be disappointed."
—Jock Zonfrillo

TING THAI CARAVAN

Recommended by
Ben Reade

8–9 Teviot Place
Edinburgh
Scotland EH1 2RA
+44 1312259801

Opening hours..Open / days
Reservation policy...No
Credit cards...Not accepted
Price range..Affordable
Style..Casual
Cuisine..Thai
Recommended for..................................Wish I'd opened

"The reason I wish I'd opened it is how unbelievably popular the place is. No bookings and always a queue out the door. Quite remarkable and adding something new to the Edinburgh dining scene."—Ben Reade

THE WALNUT

9 Croall Place
Edinburgh
Scotland EH7 4LT
+44 1312811236

Opening hours	Open 7 days
Credit cards	Accepted but not AMEX or Diners
Price range	Budget
Style	Casual
Cuisine	Scottish
Recommended for	Bargain

"Good produce and proper cooking. BYOB means its already budget menu is made cheaper by not needing to pay restaurant mark-ups on vino. It's always full, never pretentious and always tasty. Go for Sunday lunch, if you can get a table."—Ben Reade

NOBLES

44a Constitution Street
Leith
Edinburgh
Scotland EH6 6RS
+44 1316297215
www.new.noblesbarleith.co.uk

Opening hours	Open 7 days
Credit cards	Accepted
Price range	Affordable
Style	Casual
Cuisine	Gastropub
Recommended for	Local favorite

"Quite a remarkable, traditional Leith interior. A decent selection of whiskies, good local beer, and the food, especially the pub classics—fish and chips and burgers—is top notch."—Ben Reade

OSTARA

52 Coburg Street
Leith
Edinburgh
Scotland EH6 6HJ
+44 1312615441
www.ostaracafe.co.uk

Opening hours	Open 7 days
Credit cards	Accepted
Price range	Affordable
Style	Casual
Cuisine	Scottish
Recommended for	Breakfast

"Quality sourcing policy, great coffee, abundant portions and the perfect place to start a walk up the Water of Leith."—Ben Reade

APPLECROSS INN

Shore Street
Applecross
Strathcarron
Highland
Scotland IV54 8LR
+44 1520744262
www.applecross.uk.com

Opening hours	Open 7 days
Credit cards	Accepted
Price range	Affordable
Style	Casual
Cuisine	Scottish Seafood
Recommended for	Worth the travel

"A plate of langoustines, outside, looking over Applecross Bay from whence they were caught is a quasi-religious experience."—Luke Vandore-Mackay

ANDREW FAIRLIE AT GLENEAGLES

Gleneagles Hotel
Auchterarder
Perthshire
Scotland PH3 1NF
+44 1764694267
www.gleneagles.com

Opening hours	Closed Sunday
Credit cards	Accepted
Price range	Expensive
Style	Smart casual
Cuisine	Modern European
Recommended for	High end

MONACHYLE MHOR

Balquhidder
Lochearnhead
Perthshire
Scotland FK19 8PQ
+44 1877384622
www.mhor.net

Opening hours	Open 7 days
Credit cards	Accepted
Price range	Expensive
Style	Smart casual
Cuisine	Modern Scottish-European
Recommended for	Worth the travel

"This restaurant with rooms has great style and a relaxed atmosphere. Located in central Scotland, on the banks of a remote loch, the cooking uses local produce and vegetables and herbs from the garden. A hidden gem."—Colin Mackay

PYSGOTY

Recommended by
Gareth Ward

The Harbor
South Promenade
Aberystwyth
Ceredigion
Wales SY23 1JY
+44 1970624611
www.pysgoty.co.uk

Opening hours	Closed Monday and Sunday
Credit cards	Accepted
Price range	Affordable
Style	Smart casual
Cuisine	Seafood
Recommended for	Local favorite

"It is a tiny place with about ten seats, right on the Marina overlooking the sea, where you can watch the sunset. They serve fish straight from the boats—simple and beautiful."—Gareth Ward

THE HARDWICK

Recommended by
Shaun Hill

Old Raglan Road
Abergavenny
Monmouthshire
Wales NP7 9AA
+44 1873854220
www.thehardwick.co.uk

Opening hours	Open 7 days
Credit cards	Accepted but not AMEX
Price range	Affordable
Style	Casual
Cuisine	Modern European
Recommended for	Regular neighborhood

"It's both close and good. Out here that's a winning combination."—Shaun Hill

A London restaurant scene legend, chef Stephen Terry returned to his native Wales in 2005 to take ownership of a pub called the Horse & Jockey on the outskirts of Abergavenny, the Monmouthshire market town famous for the Walnut Tree and the annual food festival it hosts each September. Reopened as The Hardwick four weeks after he first took it over, it has since grown into an award-winning restaurant with rooms. Terry's unfussy menu makes the most of the best local ingredients, combining them with the good taste and technical ability with which he originally made his name.

THE WALNUT TREE

Recommended by
Yotam Ottolenghi

Llanddewi Skirrid
Abergavenny
Monmouthshire
Wales NP7 8AW
+44 1873852797
www.thewalnuttreeinn.com

Opening hours	Closed Monday and Sunday
Credit cards	Accepted but not Diners
Price range	Affordable
Style	Smart casual
Cuisine	Modern British
Recommended for	Worth the travel

"It's just a lovely place to go out of the way for (if you don't live in Wales). The food is Michelin-quality but the setting is informal and welcoming. The surrounding grounds and cottages also make the whole adventure one worth stretching out."
—Yotam Ottolenghi

One of Britain's great cooking heroes, Shaun Hill 'retired' to Abergavenny to take over The Walnut Tree in 2007. He formerly ran the fine and tiny Merchant House in Ludlow, where he always cooked alone. He has more help in the kitchen here, a famous dining destination on and off since the 1960s. The cooking, wonderfully straightforward but with the sort of seasoned skill that only years at the stove can bring, makes use of local produce sourced from Monmouthshire's rich pantry. Make a proper meal of it and book a room in one of their two nearby cottages.

WINE & BRINE

59 Main Street
Moira
Craigavon
Armagh
Northern Ireland BT67 0LQ
+44 2892610500
www.wineandbrine.co.uk

Opening hours	Closed Monday
Credit cards	Accepted
Price range	Affordable
Style	Casual
Cuisine	Modern European
Recommended for	Regular neighborhood

"Wine & Brine is new and the head chef and owner here, Chris McGowan, is a great friend and an old work colleague. The food is superb and old school."
—Niall McKenna

CAST & CREW

Titanic Quarter
Queens Road
Belfast
County Antrim
Northern Ireland BT3 9DH
+44 2890451400
www.castandcrewbelfast.co.uk

Opening hours	Open 7 days
Credit cards	Accepted but not AMEX or Diners
Price range	Affordable
Style	Casual
Cuisine	Gastropub
Recommended for	Breakfast

DEANE'S AT QUEENS BAR & GRILL

1 College Gardens
Belfast
County Antrim
Northern Ireland BT9 6BQ
+44 2890382111
www.michaeldeane.co.uk/deanes-at-queens

Opening hours	Open 7 days
Credit cards	Accepted
Price range	Affordable
Style	Casual
Cuisine	Modern British
Recommended for	Bargain

EIPIC

28–40 Howard Street
Belfast
County Antrim
Northern Ireland BT1 6PF
+44 2890331134
www.deaneseipic.com

Opening hours	Open 7 days
Credit cards	Accepted
Price range	Affordable
Style	Smart casual
Cuisine	Seasonal
Recommended for	High end

"One of two Michelin-starred restaurants with Dani Barry as head chef—the only Michelin-starred woman chef in Ireland—and the food is tasty, refined and very special."—Niall McKenna

ESTABLISHED

54 Hill Street
Belfast
County Antrim
Northern Ireland BT1 2LB
+44 2890319416
www.established.coffee

Opening hours	Open 7 days
Credit cards	Accepted
Price range	Affordable
Style	Casual
Cuisine	Café
Recommended for	Breakfast

"For sourdough and coffee, Established in the Cathedral Quarter is a great spot to people watch, recharge your tech and get refuelled."
—Niall McKenna

GENERAL MERCHANTS

361 Ormeau Road
Belfast
County Antrim
Northern Ireland BT7 3GL
+44 2890291007
www.generalmerchants.co.uk

Opening hours	Open 7 days
Credit cards	Accepted
Price range	Affordable
Style	Casual
Cuisine	Café
Recommended for	Breakfast

"This is a great chain of restaurants serving home-cooked food with an Australian vibe. Great pancakes and waffles for brunch."—Niall McKenna

GRAZE

Recommended by
Stephen Toman

402 Upper Newtownards Road
Belfast
County Antrim
Northern Ireland BT4 3GE
+44 2890658658
www.grazebelfast.weebly.com

Opening hours	Open 7 days
Credit cards	Accepted but not AMEX or Diners
Price range	Affordable
Style	Smart casual
Cuisine	Modern European
Recommended for	Regular neighborhood

HADSKIS

Recommended by
Niall McKenna

33 Donegall Street
Commercial Court
Belfast
County Antrim
Northern Ireland BT1 2NB
+44 2890658658
www.hadskis.co.uk

Opening hours	Open 7 days
Credit cards	Accepted
Price range	Affordable
Style	Casual
Cuisine	Café-Modern European
Recommended for	Late night

"Sit at the bar and grab the squid starter and meatballs."—Niall McKenna

HOME

Recommended by
Stephen Toman

22 Wellington Place
Belfast
County Antrim
Northern Ireland BT1 6GE
+44 2890234946
www.homebelfast.co.uk

Opening hours	Open 7 days
Credit cards	Accepted
Price range	Affordable
Style	Casual
Cuisine	International
Recommended for	Bargain

HOWARD STREET

Recommended by
Stephen Toman

56 Howard Street
Belfast
County Antrim
Northern Ireland BT1 6PG
+44 2890325444
www.howardstbelfast.com

Opening hours	Closed Monday and Sunday
Credit cards	Accepted
Price range	Affordable
Style	Casual
Cuisine	Modern European-Asian
Recommended for	Regular neighborhood

"This restaurant has a great mix of Asian and European food. Busy and great value too."
—Stephen Toman

JOHN LONGS FISH AND CHIPS

Recommended by
Niall McKenna

39 Athol Street
Belfast
County Antrim
Northern Ireland BT12 4GX
+44 2890321848
www.johnlongs.com

Opening hours	Closed Sunday
Credit cards	Accepted
Price range	Budget
Style	Casual
Cuisine	Fish and Chips
Recommended for	Bargain

"Traditional fish and chips with the ability to sit in; not shiny and new but perfect every time. Great fresh fish."—Niall McKenna

LITTLE ITALY

Recommended by
Stephen Toman

13 Amelia Street
Belfast
County Antrim
Northern Ireland BT2 7GS
+44 2890314914

Opening hours	Open 7 days
Credit cards	Accepted
Price range	Budget
Style	Casual
Cuisine	Pizza
Recommended for	Late night

"Best pizzas in town."—Stephen Toman

THE MUDDLERS CLUB

1 Warehouse Lane
Belfast
County Antrim
Northern Ireland BT1 2DX
+44 2890313199
www.themuddlersclubbelfast.com

Opening hours	Closed Monday and Sunday
Credit cards	Accepted
Price range	Affordable
Style	Smart casual
Cuisine	Modern European
Recommended for	Local favorite

"This restaurant has it all. Exciting menus, fantastic drinks list, and service to match. Try the little black book."—Stephen Toman

NOBLE

27A Church Road
Holywood
Belfast
County Antrim
Northern Ireland BT18 9BU
+44 2890425655
www.nobleholywood.com

Opening hours	Closed Monday and Tuesday
Credit cards	Accepted
Price range	Affordable
Style	Smart casual
Cuisine	Modern European
Recommended for	Bargain

"A fantastic new addition to the Northern Ireland dining scene. The food and service are faultless. The Sunday menu is a steal."—Stephen Toman

OX

1 Oxford Street
Belfast
County Antrim
Northern Ireland BT1 3LA
+44 2890314121
www.oxbelfast.com

Opening hours	Closed Monday and Sunday
Credit cards	Accepted
Price range	Affordable
Style	Casual
Cuisine	Modern European
Recommended for	Regular neighborhood

"The owner and head chef, Stephen Toman, worked with me for over ten years. It's great to have a restaurant close by which has great consistency and always makes me feel welcome."—Niall McKenna

OX CAVE

1 Oxford Street
Belfast
County Antrim
Northern Ireland BT1 3LA
+44 2890314121
www.oxbelfast.com

Opening hours	Closed Monday and Sunday
Credit cards	Accepted
Price range	Affordable
Style	Casual
Cuisine	Modern European
Recommended for	Wish I'd opened

PERMIT ROOM

Unit 6 McAuley House
Fountain Street
Belfast
County Antrim
Northern Ireland BT1 5ED
+44 2890231394
www.permitroom.co.uk

Opening hours	Open 7 days
Credit cards	Accepted but not AMEX
Price range	Affordable
Style	Casual
Cuisine	International
Recommended for	Breakfast

SHU RESTAURANT

253 Lisburn Road
Belfast
County Antrim
Northern Ireland BT9 7EN
www.shu-restaurant.com

Opening hours	Closed Sunday
Credit cards	Accepted but not AMEX
Price range	Affordable
Style	Casual
Cuisine	Modern European
Recommended for	Regular neighborhood

SUN KEE

Recommended by
Niall McKenna

43–47 Donegall Pass
Belfast
County Antrim
Northern Ireland BT7 1DQ
+44 2890312233

Opening hours	Open 7 days
Credit cards	Accepted
Price range	Affordable
Style	Casual
Cuisine	Chinese
Recommended for	Late night

"This is my local Chinese restaurant and there is nothing tastier than a bowl of the Singapore noodles with fresh pak choi."—Niall McKenna

BULL & RAM

Recommended by
Niall McKenna

1 Dromore Street
Ballynahinch
County Down
Northern Ireland BT24 8AG
+44 2897560908
www.bullandram.com

Opening hours	Open 7 days
Credit cards	Accepted
Price range	Affordable
Style	Casual
Cuisine	Modern European
Recommended for	Local favorite

"New restaurant just outside Belfast, housed in an old listed butcher's shop, which is serving some of the best cuts of Northern Irish meat available. Not for vegetarians."—Niall McKenna

CHAPTER ONE

Recommended by
JP McMahon, Stephen Toman

18–19 Parnell Square
Dublin 1
County Dublin
Republic of Ireland
+353 18732266
www.chapteronerestaurant.com

Opening hours	Closed Monday and Sunday
Credit cards	Accepted
Price range	Expensive
Style	Smart casual
Cuisine	Irish
Recommended for	High end

"A powerhouse of Irish cuisine."—JP McMahon

Ross Lewis's restaurant beneath the Dublin Writers Museum is a warm bastion of Irish hospitality at its very best. Housed in the basement of a handsome eighteenth-century townhouse, once the family home of John Jameson of the distilling dynasty, the dining room is a welcoming combination of exposed brickwork and sage-green carpet, its walls hung with work by emerging Irish artists. Lewis's menus champion the very best of Ireland's pantry, with a penchant for pork, game, and seafood in cooking that's both refined and generous. As befits the building's history, there's a lengthy list of Irish whiskeys for after dinner.

777

Recommended by
Niall McKenna

53 South Great George's Street
Temple Bar
Dublin 2
County Dublin
Republic of Ireland
+353 14254052
www.777.ie

Opening hours	Open 7 days
Credit cards	Accepted but not AMEX or Diners
Price range	Affordable
Style	Casual
Cuisine	Mexican
Recommended for	Wish I'd opened

BUNSEN

Recommended by
Ross Lewis

36 Wexford Street
Dublin 2
County Dublin
Republic of Ireland
+353 15525408
www.bunsen.ie

Opening hours	Open 7 days
Credit cards	Accepted
Price range	Budget
Style	Casual
Cuisine	Burgers
Recommended for	Bargain

"What a concept! Simple, tasty, premium burgers served in a really cool restaurant space. Best hamburger in Dublin!"—Ross Lewis

DUBLIN PIZZA COMPANY

Recommended by
Francesco Mazzei

32 Aungier Street
Dublin 2
County Dublin
Republic of Ireland
+353 15611714
www.dublinpizzacompany.ie

Opening hours	Open 7 days
Credit cards	Accepted
Price range	Budget
Style	Casual
Cuisine	Pizza
Recommended for	Late night

"I tried this street-food concept a few weeks ago when I was in Dublin and was amazed by the quality of the pizza and ingredients."—Francesco Mazzei

THE GREENHOUSE

Recommended by
JP McMahon, Stephen Toman

Off Saint Stephen's Green
Dawson Street
Dublin 2
County Dublin
Republic of Ireland
+353 16767015
www.thegreenhouserestaurant.ie

Opening hours	Closed Monday and Sunday
Credit cards	Accepted
Price range	Expensive
Style	Smart casual
Cuisine	French
Recommended for	High end

HANG DAI

Recommended by
Ross Lewis

20 Camden Street
Dublin 2
County Dublin
Republic of Ireland
+353 15458888
www.hangdaichinese.com

Opening hours	Closed Monday and Sunday
Credit cards	Accepted but not AMEX or Diners
Price range	Affordable
Style	Casual
Cuisine	Chinese
Recommended for	Late night

"Nothing beats duck roasted in a wood-burning oven—so tasty. It also offers a really good selection of contemporary Chinese food cooked in a unique way."—Ross Lewis

PICKLE

Recommended by
Rohit Ghai

43 Camden Street
Dublin 2
County Dublin
Republic of Ireland
+353 15557755
www.picklerestaurant.com

Opening hours	Closed Monday
Credit cards	Accepted
Price range	Affordable
Style	Casual
Cuisine	Indian
Recommended for	Wish I'd opened

"An authentic Indian restaurant with casual interiors. Love the warm, soothing environment."—Rohit Ghai

QUEEN OF TARTS

Recommended by
Ross Lewis

Cows Lane, Dame Street
Dublin 2
County Dublin
Republic of Ireland
+353 16334681
www.queenoftarts.ie

Opening hours	Open 7 days
Credit cards	Accepted but not AMEX or Diners
Price range	Affordable
Style	Casual
Cuisine	Irish Café
Recommended for	Breakfast

"It's such a homely and welcoming space which offers the best breakfasts and weekend brunch in Dublin."
—Ross Lewis

RESTAURANT PATRICK GUILBAUD

Recommended by
Ross Lewis,
Stephen Toman

21 Upper Merrion Street
Dublin 2
County Dublin
Republic of Ireland
+353 16764192
www.restaurantpatrickguilbaud.ie

Opening hours	Closed Monday, Tuesday and Sunday
Credit cards	Accepted
Price range	Expensive
Style	Smart casual
Cuisine	Modern French
Recommended for	High end

"It is true to itself and constantly pushes for the highest standards. Really beautiful surroundings, luxurious and elegant, and the food is quite simply outstanding." —Ross Lewis

FOREST & MARCY

Recommended by
Anton Kovalkov, JP McMahon

126 Leeson Street Upper
Dublin 4
County Dublin
Republic of Ireland
+353 16602480
www.forestandmarcy.ie

Opening hours	Closed Monday and Tuesday
Credit cards	Accepted
Price range	Affordable
Style	Smart casual
Cuisine	Irish-French
Recommended for	Worth the travel

"Small, neighborhood restaurant food served by Chef Ciaran Sweeney. The food is modern and seasonal, using the best ingredients. It's really smart, casual food."—Anton Kovalkov

FOREST AVENUE

Recommended by
Richard Corrigan, Niall McKenna,
JP McMahon

8 Sussex Terrace
Dublin 4
County Dublin
Republic of Ireland
+353 16678337
www.forestavenuerestaurant.ie

Opening hours	Closed Monday, Tuesday, and Sunday
Credit cards	Accepted
Price range	Affordable
Style	Smart casual
Cuisine	Modern Irish
Recommended for	Wish I'd opened

"Unique style of food, personal service, individual and well thought out dishes, run by a passionate husband and wife team."—Richard Corrigan

BIBI'S CAFÉ

Recommended by
Ross Lewis

14b Emorville Avenue
Dublin 8
County Dublin
Republic of Ireland
+353 14547421
www.bibis.ie

Opening hours	Open 7 days
Credit cards	Accepted
Price range	Affordable
Style	Casual
Cuisine	Modern Irish
Recommended for	Breakfast

"Bibi's is a cosy neighborhood café serving breakfast, lunch and brunch at the weekends. The ever-changing and evolving menus are driven by creativity, innovation and the use of prime produce from Ireland and abroad. Chef-owner Maisha Lenehan, working with her brother Geoff, have combined their individual skills to create a unique dining experience in the heart of Dublin 8."—Ross Lewis

THE WILD GOOSE

Recommended by
Ross Lewis

1 Sanford Road
Dublin 6
County Dublin
Republic of Ireland
+353 14912377
www.thewildgoosegrill.ie

Opening hours	Closed Monday
Credit cards	Accepted
Price range	Affordable
Style	Smart casual
Cuisine	Modern European
Recommended for	Local favorite

"It's a neighborhood restaurant in Ranelagh, a suburb of Dublin, serving really tasty, interesting food with a keen emphasis on artisan produce and sustainability. It's a warm, welcoming room with great atmosphere and its owner and chef, Kevin McMahon, is brilliant at what he does."—Ross Lewis

CHINA SICHUAN

The Forum
Ballymoss Road
Sandyford
County Dublin
Republic of Ireland
+353 12935100
www.china-sichuan.ie

Opening hours	Open 7 days
Credit cards	Accepted but not AMEX or Diners
Price range	Affordable
Style	Smart casual
Cuisine	Modern Chinese
Recommended for	Regular neighborhood

ANIAR

53 Dominick Street
Galway
County Galway
Republic of Ireland
+353 91535947
www.aniarrestaurant.ie

Opening hours	Closed Monday, Tuesday, and Sunday
Credit cards	Accepted
Price range	Expensive
Style	Smart casual
Cuisine	Modern Irish
Recommended for	Worth the travel

ARD BIA AT NIMMOS

Spanish Arch
Long Walk
Galway
County Galway
Republic of Ireland
+353 91561114
www.ardbia.com

Opening hours	Open 7 days
Credit cards	Accepted but not AMEX
Price range	Affordable
Style	Casual
Cuisine	Modern Irish
Recommended for	Regular neighborhood

"Casual dining in a historic building beside the River Corrib. Mediterranean and Middle Eastern influences with a focus on Irish produce."—JP McMahon

CAVA BODEGA

1 Middle Street
Galway
County Galway
Republic of Ireland
+353 91539884
www.cavarestaurant.ie

Opening hours	Open 7 days
Credit cards	Accepted
Price range	Affordable
Style	Casual
Cuisine	Spanish
Recommended for	Late night

"Great tapas and a Spanish wine list with a host of sherries."—JP McMahon

THE DOUGH BROS.

Unit 1 Cathedral Buildings
Middle Street
Galway
County Galway
Republic of Ireland
+35 3871761662
www.thedoughbros.ie

Opening hours	Open 7 days
Reservation policy	No
Credit cards	Accepted
Price range	Budget
Style	Casual
Cuisine	Neopolitan Pizza
Recommended for	Bargain

KAI CAFÉ & RESTAURANT

20 Sea Road
Galway
County Galway
Republic of Ireland
+353 91526003
www.kaicaferestaurant.com

Opening hours	Open 7 days
Credit cards	Accepted but not AMEX
Price range	Affordable
Style	Casual
Cuisine	Modern Irish
Recommended for	Breakfast

"Best brunch in Galway, located in the city's Westend, focusing on Irish artisan produce, local farmers, and raw milk."—JP McMahon

KAPPA-YA

Recommended by
JP McMahon

4 Middle Street Mews
Galway
County Galway
Republic of Ireland
+353 16764192

Opening hours	Closed Sunday
Credit cards	Accepted but not AMEX
Price range	Affordable
Style	Smart casual
Cuisine	Japanese
Recommended for	Regular neighborhood

KIRWANS LANE RESTAURANT

Recommended by
Ruairí de Blacam

Kirwans Lane
Galway
County Galway
Republic of Ireland
+353 91568266
www.kirwanslane.com

Opening hours	Open 7 days
Credit cards	Accepted
Price range	Affordable
Style	Smart casual
Cuisine	Seafood
Recommended for	Regular neighborhood

"It's not really my 'local' as I live on an island thirty-miles away! However, Galway is our nearest town. I regularly visit for a day trip and I usually end up in Kirwans Lane for a quick lunch. I never look at the menu, I know the chef so I simply ask, 'What's good?' I can sit up at the seafood bar and have a sole *meunière* or a simple pan-fried piece of fish with a green salad. A bottle of San Pellegrino, a quick espresso, read the headlines, and I'm outta there in thirty minutes."—Ruairí de Blacam

LOAM RESTAURANT

Recommended by
JP McMahon

Geata Na Cathrach
Fairgreen Road
Galway
County Galway
Republic of Ireland
+353 91569727
www.loamgalway.com

Opening hours	Closed Monday and Sunday
Credit cards	Accepted
Price range	Affordable
Style	Smart casual
Cuisine	Irish Seafood
Recommended for	Local favorite

"It's probably the best Dutch food in the world! Go and have a look."

DANIEL ACHILLES P511

NETHERLANDS

"Great chef, delicious food, and good atmosphere."

ONNO KOKMEIJER P510

"SMALL AND PERSONAL, GREAT BISTRO FOOD, GREAT WINES, GOOD VALUE FOR MONEY."

JULIUS JASPERS P510

NETHERLANDS

N̂ SCALE

0   25   50 mi.

Bergen p.510

Amsterdam p.512–519

Het Gooi p.510

Overijssel p.510

Sluis p.510

BISTRO LA CAVE

Kapelstraat 11
Bussum
Het Gooi 1404 HT
+31 355446571
www.bistrolacave.nl

Opening hours	Closed Monday
Credit cards	Accepted but not AMEX
Price range	Affordable
Style	Casual
Cuisine	French Bistro
Recommended for	Regular neighborhood

"Small and personal, great bistro food, great wines, good value for money."—Julius Jaspers

MERLET

Duinweg 15
Schoorl
Bergen 1871 AC
+31 725093644
www.merlet.nl

Opening hours	Closed Monday
Credit cards	Accepted
Price range	Expensive
Style	Smart casual
Cuisine	International
Recommended for	High end

"Great chef, delicious food, and good atmosphere."
—Onno Kokmeijer

DE EETBOETIEK

Beestenmarkt 2
Sluis 4524 EA
+31 117851006
www.eetboetiek.nl

Opening hours	Closed Thursday
Credit cards	Accepted but not AMEX
Price range	Affordable
Style	Casual
Cuisine	International
Recommended for	Breakfast

"Great concept where you can have breakfast or lunch and also shop for beautiful tableware."
—Sergio Herman

BAIYOK

Diezenpoortenplas 3
Zwolle
Overijssel 8011 VV
+31 384229882
www.baiyok.nl

Opening hours	Open 7 days
Credit cards	Not accepted
Price range	Affordable
Style	Casual
Cuisine	Thai
Recommended for	Regular neighborhood

"Authentic Thai food. Very nice people. One of the best Thais in the Netherlands."—Jonnie Boer

BISTRO BONNE FEMME

Samuel Hirschstraat 5
Zwolle
Overijssel 8011 PT
+31 384222780
www.bistrobonnefemme.nl

Opening hours	Open 7 days
Credit cards	Accepted but not AMEX
Price range	Affordable
Style	Casual
Cuisine	Bistro
Recommended for	Regular neighborhood

"I always eat the veal liver and freshwater eel."
—Jonnie Boer

DE GILLENDE KEUKENMEIDEN

Meerminneplein 7
Zwolle
Overijssel 8011 SW
+31 655027690
www.gillende-keukenmeiden.nl

Opening hours	Closed Monday
Credit cards	Not accepted
Price range	Affordable
Style	Casual
Cuisine	Café
Recommended for	Breakfast

RESTAURANT DE LIBRIJE

Spinhuisplein 1
Zwolle
Overijssel 8011 ZZ
+31 384212083
www.librije.com

Recommended by
Daniel Achilles,
Adam Reid,
Thomas & Mathias Sühring

Opening hours	Closed Monday and Sunday
Credit cards	Accepted
Price range	Expensive
Style	Smart casual
Cuisine	Modern European
Recommended for	Worth the travel

"It's probably the best Dutch food in the world! Go and have a look."—Daniel Achilles

> **"Elegant and understated, giving a great backdrop to the pure and unfussy dishes, with a great accent on vegetables."**
> JEAN BEDDINGTON P516

AMSTERDAM

> **"BEST RIBEYE, BEST CHICKEN, BEST WINE LIST, BEST PATRON."**
> JULIUS JASPERS P519

> *"Everything is a little different up in the north. I think it sums up Amsterdam well."*
> BAS WIEGEL P517

> **"Easy going. Healthy food items and quick service."**
> ONNO KOKMEIJER P519

> **"WOW! WORTH A DETOUR. BRILLIANT COOKING."**
> CHRISTIAN EDWARDSON P514

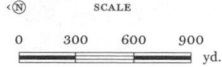

AMSTERDAM

(N) SCALE

0 300 600 900 yd.

1. *Bak Restaurant (p.514)*
2. *Bar-Becue Castel (p.514)*
3. *Bord'eau (p.514)*
4. *Brut De Mer (p.514)*
5. *Cannibale Royale (p.514)*
6. *Cannibale Royale (p.514)*
7. *The Chippy (p.515)*
8. *Guts & Glory (p.515)*
9. *Lotti's (p.515)*
10. *Librije's Zusje (p.515)*
11. *Restaurant Breda (p.515)*
12. *Restaurant Choux (p.516)*
13. *Restaurant Daalder (p.516)*
14. *Restaurant Vermeer (p.516)*
15. *The Seafood Bar (p.516)*
16. *The Butcher (p.517)*
17. *Izakaya Asian Kitchen & Bar (p.517)*
18. *Omelegg (p.517)*
19. *Serre Restaurant (p.517)*
20. *Café Modern (p.517)*
21. *The Lobby (p.518)*
22. *Foodhallen Amsterdam (p.518)*
23. *Brasserie Bark (p.518)*
24. *Café Kiêbert (p.518)*
25. *Le Garage (p.518)*
26. *Restaurant Rijks (p.518)*
27. *Rijsel (p.519)*
28. *At Seven (p.519)*
29. *Halvemaan (p.519)*
30. *Visaandeschelde (p.519)*

CENTRUM
DE PIJP
JORDAAN
OUD ZUID
WESTPARK
OUD WEST

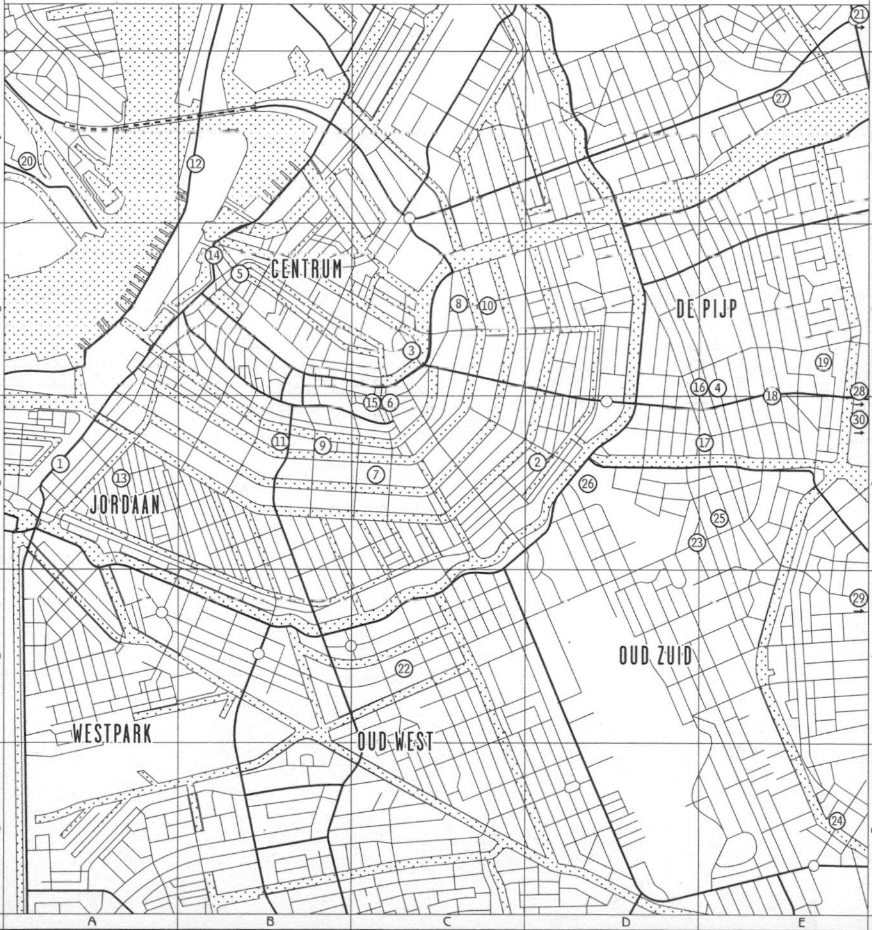

BAK RESTAURANT

Recommended by
Julius Jaspers

Van Diemenstraat 408
Centrum
Amsterdam 1013 CR
+31 207372553
www.bakrestaurant.nl

Opening hours	Closed Monday and Tuesday
Credit cards	Accepted but not AMEX or Diners
Price range	Affordable
Style	Casual
Cuisine	Modern European
Recommended for	Local favorite

BAR-BECUE CASTEL

Recommended by
Julius Jaspers

Lijnbaansgracht 252–254
Centrum
Amsterdam 1017 RK
+31 206228606
www.castellamsterdam.nl

Opening hours	Open 7 days
Credit cards	Accepted
Price range	Affordable
Style	Casual
Cuisine	Steakhouse
Recommended for	Late night

"Personal service, great steak, no fuss."
—Julius Jaspers

BORD'EAU

Recommended by
Christian Edwardson,
Julius Jaspers

Nieuwe Doelenstraat 2–14
Centrum
Amsterdam 1012 CP
+31 205311619
www.bordeau.nl

Opening hours	Closed Monday and Sunday
Credit cards	Accepted
Price range	Expensive
Style	Smart casual
Cuisine	French
Recommended for	High end

"Wow! Worth a detour. Brilliant cooking."
—Christian Edwardson

BRUT DE MER

Recommended by
Jean Beddington

Gerard Douplein 8
De Pijp
Amsterdam 1072 VE
+31-20 4714099
www.brutdemer.nl

Opening hours	Open 7 days
Credit cards	Accepted
Price range	Affordable
Style	Casual
Cuisine	Seafood
Recommended for	Regular neighbourhood

CANNIBALE ROYALE

Recommended by
Sergio Herman,
Bas Wiegel

Lange Niezel 15H
Centrum
Amsterdam 1012 GS
+31 202182120
www.cannibaleroyale.nl

Opening hours	Open 7 days
Credit cards	Accepted but not AMEX or Diners
Price range	Affordable
Style	Casual
Cuisine	American
Recommended for	Late night

"Sometimes after a hard service, you just need this."
—Bas Wiegel

CANNIBALE ROYALE

Recommended by
Onno Kokmeijer

Handboogstraat 17a
Centrum
Amsterdam 1012 XM
+31 202337160
www.cannibaleroyale.nl

Opening hours	Open 7 days
Credit cards	Accepted but not AMEX or Diners
Price range	Affordable
Style	Casual
Cuisine	American
Recommended for	Late night

THE CHIPPY

Recommended by
Jean Beddington

Pop-up: locations vary
Centrum
Amsterdam
+31 626016809
www.thechippy.nl

Opening hours	Variable
Reservation policy	No
Credit cards	Accepted
Price range	Affordable
Style	Casual
Cuisine	Fish and Chips
Recommended for	Bargain

"A taste of home with super fresh fish in a perfect crispy batter, and for those moments when only fries (chips) doused in vinegar will hit the spot."
—Jean Beddington

GUTS & GLORY

Recommended by
Groc Nonas

Utrechtsestraat 6
Centrum
Amsterdam 1017 VN
+31 203620030
www.gutsglory.nl

Opening hours	Open 7 days
Credit cards	Accepted
Price range	Affordable
Style	Casual
Cuisine	International
Recommended for	Worth the travel

With a slightly more casual atmosphere than its sister restaurant, Breda, Guts & Glory offers fine dining with experimental flair. Your options within the restaurant are limited; you can choose the five-, six-, or seven-course meal, and whether you want the wine pairing, but that's it. The rest is in the hands of the kitchen team, with each dish presented as a surprise. Every few months the chefs dramatically change the menu to celebrate a particular cuisine (Japanese, French, Latin) or to focus on a particular ingredient. Not only does the style of cooking change, but the restaurant itself transforms too, in homage to the menu being served. As the name suggests, you'll need guts here —but you'll be rewarded with a glorious dining experience.

LOTTI'S

Recommended by
Jean Beddington

The Hoxton
Herengracht 255
Centrum
Amsterdam 1016 BJ
+31 208885555
www.thehoxton.com

Opening hours	Open 7 days
Credit cards	Accepted but not Visa
Price range	Affordable
Style	Casual
Cuisine	International
Recommended for	Breakfast

LIBRIJE'S ZUSJE

Recommended by
Richard Ekkebus,
Bas Wiegel

Waldorf Astoria
Herengracht 542–556
Centrum
Amsterdam 1017 CG
+31 207184643
www.librijeszusje.nl

Opening hours	Closed Monday and Sunday
Credit cards	Accepted
Price range	Expensive
Style	Smart casual
Cuisine	Modern European
Recommended for	High end

RESTAURANT BREDA

Recommended by
Julius Jaspers,
Bas Wiegel

Singel 210
Centrum
Amsterdam 1016 AB
+31 206225233
www.breda-amsterdam.com

Opening hours	Open 7 days
Credit cards	Accepted
Price range	Affordable
Style	Smart casual
Cuisine	International
Recommended for	Regular neighborhood

On the back of the success of Guts & Glory, Amsterdam's gastronomic wunderkinds Guillaume de Beer and Freek van Noortwijk opened Breda, inspired by their southern Dutch roots. Serving deceptively complicated dishes using just a handful of seasonal ingredients, this is the perfect place for a luxury Sunday lunch. The food is so good you'll feel like you're missing out if you don't try the surprise seven- course taster menu. The wines are on the pricey side, but the nuanced pairings, chosen by the sommelier Johanneke van Iwaarden, are worth it.

RESTAURANT CHOUX

Recommended by
Bas Wiegel

De Ruyterkade 128
Centrum
Amsterdam 1011 AC
+31 202103090
www.choux.nl

Opening hours	Closed Sunday
Credit cards	Accepted but not AMEX or Diners
Price range	Affordable
Style	Smart casual
Cuisine	Modern European
Recommended for	Wish I'd opened

"Great place and the food is special and on point. They use a lot of vegetables."—Bas Wiegel

Opened just a couple of years ago, the brainchild of chef Merijn van Berlo and sommelier Figo van Onna, Choux has already made a huge impact on the Amsterdam gastronomic scene. The restaurant is situated just a five-minute walk from the ferry port and the train terminal in an unassuming, spacious industrial building decked out with chic, modern decor. You can choose three or four dishes from their seasonal menu—€31 ($34; £26) and €39 ($42; £33) respectively—or the seven-course tasting menu curated by the chef €55 ($60; £46). You'll notice the careful construction work that has gone into the staging of each plate of food —this is modern European dining at its best.

RESTAURANT DAALDER

Recommended by
Onno Kokmeijer

Lindengracht 90
Centrum
Amsterdam 1015 KK
+31 206248864
www.daalderamsterdam.nl

Opening hours	Open 7 days
Credit cards	Accepted but not AMEX
Price range	Affordable
Style	Casual
Cuisine	International
Recommended for	Regular neighborhood

RESTAURANT VERMEER

Recommended by
Jean Beddington,
Bas Wiegel

Prins Hendrikkade 59–72
Centrum
Amsterdam 1021 AD
+31 205564885
www.restaurantvermeer.nl

Opening hours	Closed Sunday
Credit cards	Accepted
Price range	Affordable
Style	Smart casual
Cuisine	Modern European
Recommended for	Wish I'd opened

"Restaurant Vermeer has just undergone a complete re-styling and now suits the cuisine of chef Christopher Naylor. Elegant and understated, giving a great backdrop to the pure and unfussy dishes, with an accent on vegetables."—Jean Beddington

Named after Johannes Vermeer, the Dutch painter of middle-class life, this spacious restaurant unravels beyond the facades of the tall old houses of five-star hotel NH Barbizon Palace (opposite Centraal station). Michelin-starred Christopher Naylor, who trained with Albert Roux, cares for vegetables; it's particularly evident in his seasonal vegetable casserole. In fact, seasonal produce—pear, mackerel, asparagus, pigeon—is a guiding influence on the menu, from which diners can choose a three-, four-, or five-course option. Competitive pricing of both food and wine, the latter packaged by sommelier Simon Veldman, makes Vermeer a favorite with Amsterdammers.

THE SEAFOOD BAR

Recommended by
Jean Beddington

Spui 15
Centrum
Amsterdam 1012 WX
+31 202337452
www.theseafoodbar.com

Opening hours	Open 7 days
Credit cards	Accepted
Price range	Affordable
Style	Casual
Cuisine	Seafood
Recommended for	Late night

"Fresh seafood and an unpretentious atmosphere." —Jean Beddington

THE BUTCHER

Recommended by
Onno Kokmeijer

Albert Cuypstraat 129
De Pijp
Amsterdam 1072 CS
+31 204707875
www.the-butcher.com

Opening hours	Open 7 days
Reservation policy	No
Credit cards	Accepted
Price range	Budget
Style	Smart casual
Cuisine	Fast Food
Recommended for	Bargain

"The best hamburgers in town."—Onno Kokmeijer

IZAKAYA ASIAN KITCHEN & BAR

Recommended by
Onno Kokmeijer

Sir Albert Hotel
Albert Cuypstraat 2–6
De Pijp
Amsterdam 1072 CT
+31 203053090
www.izakaya-restaurant.com/amsterdam

Opening hours	Open 7 days
Credit cards	Accepted
Price range	Affordable
Style	Smart casual
Cuisine	Modern Japanese
Recommended for	Regular neighborhood

"Great food, tasty cocktails, nice atmosphere—the place to be in Amsterdam. Asian in a new way."
—Onno Kokmeijer

OMELEGG

Recommended by
Onno Kokmeijer

Ferdinand Bolstraat 143
De Pijp
Amsterdam 1072 LH
+31 203701134
www.omelegg.com

Opening hours	Open 7 days
Reservation policy	No
Credit cards	Accepted
Price range	Affordable
Style	Casual
Cuisine	International
Recommended for	Wish I'd opened

"They only serve egg dishes—more than fifty different kinds of omelette."—Onno Kokmeijer

Mornings after the night before in Amsterdam need to be a rejuvenating experience. Self-described as "the Netherlands' first omelettery", this cheerful breakfast/brunch eatery is the perfect place to start your day. Celebrating the humble egg in all its glory, the menu offers a wide range of reasonably priced eggy dishes prepared with the freshest ingredients. The staff are jovial and there is a convivial atmosphere, where an egg pun is never too far away. You may have to line up (queue), especially at weekends, but there's usually a quick turn-around and a visit here comes with a guaranteed spring in your step for the day ahead.

SERRE RESTAURANT

Recommended by
Onno Kokmeijer

Hotel Okura Amsterdam
Ferdinand Bolstraat 333
De Pijp
Amsterdam 1072 LH
+31 206787450
www.okura.nl/en/culinary/serre/

Opening hours	Open 7 days
Credit cards	Accepted
Price range	Affordable
Style	Smart casual
Cuisine	International
Recommended for	Regular neighborhood

CAFÉ MODERN

Recommended by
Bas Wiegel

Meidoornweg 2
Noord
Amsterdam 1031 GG
+31 204940684
www.modernamsterdam.nl

Opening hours	Closed Sunday
Credit cards	Accepted but not AMEX or Diners
Price range	Affordable
Style	Casual
Cuisine	International
Recommended for	Local favorite

"I think it sums up Amsterdam well."— Bas Wiegel

Located in a disused bank with many of the original features still in place (the repurposing of the vaults has to be seen to be believed), Café Modern has fast become a local favorite in the Noord area of Amsterdam thanks to its modern, affordable European cuisine. It's slightly off the beaten track, but well worth visiting for its fifties decor, unpretentious ambience, and food bursting with bold, seasonal flavors. There is a set four-course menu costing around €40 ($44; £34) which changes on a weekly basis, and they're happy to accommodate specific diets.

THE LOBBY

Recommended by
Bas Wiegel

Fizeaustraat 2
Oost
Amsterdam 1097 SC
+31 207585275
www.thelobbyfizeaustraat.nl

Opening hours	Open 7 days
Credit cards	Accepted
Price range	Affordable
Style	Casual
Cuisine	Café
Recommended for	Breakfast

"Great place, nice atmosphere, good breakfast."
—Bas Wiegel

FOODHALLEN AMSTERDAM

Recommended by
Onno Kokmeijer

Bellamyplein 51
Oud West
Amsterdam 1053 AT
+31 202181774
www.foodhallen.nl

Opening hours	Open 7 days
Reservation policy	No
Credit cards	Accepted
Price range	Budget
Style	Casual
Cuisine	International
Recommended for	Local favorite

BRASSERIE BARK

Recommended by
Onno Kokmeijer

Van Baerlestraat 120
Oud Zuid
Amsterdam 1071 BD
+31 206750210
www.bark.nl

Opening hours	Open 7 days
Credit cards	Accepted
Price range	Affordable
Style	Casual
Cuisine	Brasserie
Recommended for	Late night

"Burgundy-style brasserie with a lot of *fruits de mer*."
—Onno Kokmeijer

Chef-owner Peter Janssen's busy Parisian-style brasserie, where dark banquettes flank big windows, is very popular with concertgoers before and after the main event (his kitchen stays open until half-past midnight). Janssen concentrates

on crustaceans, lobster (decadently served with Canadian scallops), native and rock oysters on ice, and Dutch shrimp cocktail. Just add Muscadet. Fleshier fish includes salmon (smoked with wasabi mayonnaise), Dover sole, and rose fish. From the land, there's grilled rib-eye steak with homemade fries, and braised veal cheek with shallots. Finish with parfait of prunes with Armagnac.

CAFÉ KIÊBERT

Recommended by
Onno Kokmeijer

Marathonweg 2
Oud Zuid
Amsterdam 1076 TE
+31 208458283
www.cafekiebert.nl

Opening hours	Open 7 days
Credit cards	Accepted but not AMEX or Diners
Price range	Affordable
Style	Casual
Cuisine	Dutch-European
Recommended for	Breakfast

LE GARAGE

Recommended by
Julius Jaspers

Ruysdaelstraat 54–56
Oud Zuid
Amsterdam 1071 XE
+31 206797176
www.restaurantlegarage.nl

Opening hours	Open 7 days
Credit cards	Accepted but not Diners
Price range	Affordable
Style	Smart casual
Cuisine	French
Recommended for	Regular neighborhood

"Always good, personal service, classical French dishes."—Julius Jaspers

RESTAURANT RIJKS

Recommended by
Jean Beddington,
Bas Wiegel

Museumstraat 2
Oud Zuid
Amsterdam 1071 XX
+31 206747555
www.rijksrestaurant.nl

Opening hours	Open 7 days
Credit cards	Accepted
Price range	Affordable
Style	Casual
Cuisine	International
Recommended for	Regular neighborhood

RIJSEL

Recommended by
Julius Jaspers

Marcusstraat 52B
Watergraafsmeer
Amsterdam 1091 TK
+31 204632142
www.rijsel.com

Opening hours	Closed Sunday
Credit cards	Accepted but not AMEX
Price range	Affordable
Style	Casual
Cuisine	Northern French
Recommended for	Local favorite

"Old school building, no fuss. Best rib-eye, best chicken, best wine list, best patron."—Julius Jaspers

AT SEVEN

Recommended by
Onno Kokmeijer

Scheldestraat 92
Zuid
Amsterdam 1078 GN
+31 206709295
www.at7online.nl

Opening hours	Open 7 days
Credit cards	Accepted but not AMEX
Price range	Budget
Style	Casual
Cuisine	Café
Recommended for	Breakfast

"Easy going. Healthy food items and quick service. Nice setting. Good value for money."—Onno Kokmeijer

At Seven is so named because it serves food seven days a week and opens at 7.00 a.m. on weekdays (the doors don't open until 8.00 a.m. and 9.00 a.m. on Saturdays and Sundays respectively). It's a bright café serving fresh coffee, homemade apple pie, muffins, wild smoked fish, and excellent brunch. But perhaps it's most famous for its Brazilian health shakes at around €5 ($5; £4) apiece. At Seven is hugely dog- and child-friendly: they'll provide water and treats for pets and there's a special play area, with toys, for youngsters. Round the corner is Amstelpark, which has a kid's playground and a city farm.

HALVEMAAN

Recommended by
Jean Beddington

Van Leijenberghlaan 320
Zuid
Amsterdam 1082 DD
+31 206440348
www.restauranthalvemaan.nl

Opening hours	Variable
Credit cards	Accepted
Price range	Affordable
Style	Smart casual
Cuisine	Modern European
Recommended for	Regular neighborhood

"The chef-owner has always been an innovative chef and continues to surprise and delight with new dishes."—Jean Beddington

VISAANDESCHELDE

Recommended by
Onno Kokmeijer

Scheldeplein 4
Zuid
Amsterdam 1078 GR
+31 206751583
www.visaandeschelde.nl

Opening hours	Open 7 days
Credit cards	Accepted
Price range	Affordable
Style	Smart casual
Cuisine	Seafood
Recommended for	Regular neighborhood

Chef Michiel Deenik's popular fish restaurant is easily reached, being opposite the RAI exhibition center. The dinner menu is split into four straightforward yet appealing sections: oysters, lobster, fish, and "classics". Dishes show Asian influences, such as the lobster with rice noodles, oriental vegetables and Malaysian sambal paste, and the soft shell crab with wasabi mayonnaise. Desserts, by contrast, are more straightforward —like the pretty fusion of blood orange, fennel, and almond sorbets.

"Flavoursome cuisine and outstanding produce."

PETER GOOSSENS P525

"This is probably my favorite restaurant."

MERLIN LABRON-JOHNSON P526

BELGIUM

"SEASONAL INGREDIENTS, NICE TECHNIQUES, SIMPLE AND TASTY."

SANG HOON DEGEIMBRE P528

"THIS IS SPECIAL. A TRIP WORTH MAKING AND A CULINARY EXPERIENCE."

BAS WIEGEL P528

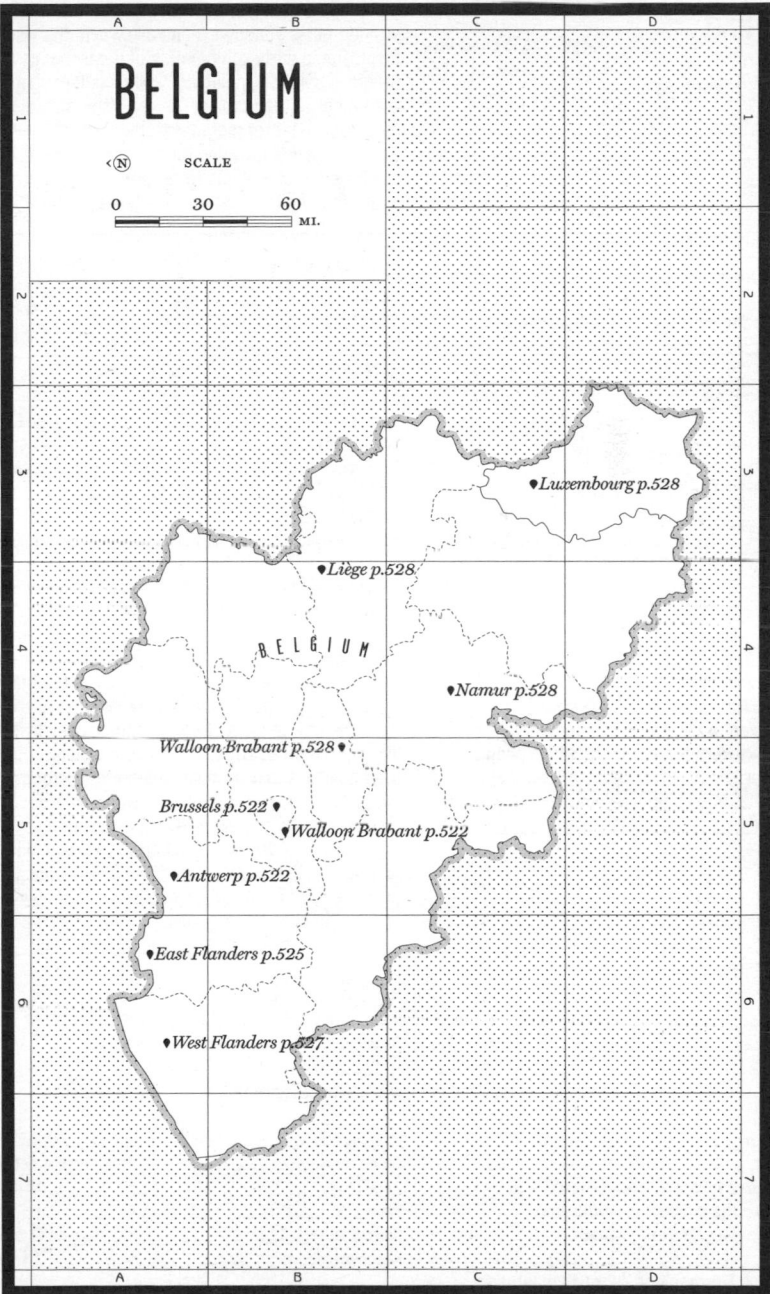

BELGIUM

N SCALE

0   30   60
MI.

Luxembourg p.528

Liège p.528

BELGIUM

Namur p.528

Walloon Brabant p.528

Brussels p.522

Walloon Brabant p.522

Antwerp p.522

East Flanders p.525

West Flanders p.527

5 FLAVORS MMEI

Volkstraat 37
Antwerp 2000, Belgium
+32 32813037

Opening hours	Closed Wednesday
Credit cards	Accepted but not AMEX
Price range	Affordable
Style	Casual
Cuisine	Cantonese
Recommended for	Bargain

"Fabulous Cantonese food."—David Martin

GRAANMARKT 13

Graanmarkt 13
Antwerp 2000, Belgium
+32 33377991
www.graanmarkt13.be

Opening hours	Closed Monday and Sunday
Credit cards	Accepted
Price range	Affordable
Style	Casual
Cuisine	Modern Belgian
Recommended for	Worth the travel

"I love Seppe Nobels' approach to cooking—
it's seasonal and modern with a focus on local
ingredients. Antwerp is a lovely city which people
don't necessarily think of as a culinary destination
but in fact it has lots of hidden gems."—Bruno Loubet

THE JANE

Paradeplein 1
Antwerp 2018, Belgium
+32 38084465
www.thejaneantwerp.com

Opening hours	Closed Monday and Sunday
Credit cards	Accepted
Price range	Expensive
Style	Casual
Cuisine	International
Recommended for	Worth the travel

"Fine dining in a futuristic and relaxing
surroundings—the concept is unique and
the food is fantastic."—Rolf Fliegauf

If chefs Sergio Herman and Nick Bril wanted to
create a religious dining experience, they found the
ideal location—a former military chapel in the
Haringrode region of Antwerp. A lot of work has
gone into creating a modern, stylish interior; the
stained-glass windows alone are worth the visit,
displaying a witty combination of gastronomic and
religious symbols including skulls, bishops' hats, ice
cream cones, and croissants. On offer is an eight- or
nine-course taster menu, with the larger-than-
average dishes meaning food is served at an
unhurried pace—it can take up to four-and-a-half
hours to complete a meal. Worth the pilgrimage.

FRITURE RENÉ

Place de la Résistance 14
Anderlecht
Brussels 1070, Belgium
+32 25232876

Opening hours	Closed Tuesday
Credit cards	Accepted but not AMEX
Price range	Affordable
Style	Casual
Cuisine	Belgian
Recommended for	Late night

"A brasserie typical of Brussels with a family
atmosphere."—David Martin

A friendly, family-run, reasonably priced bistro,
Friture René was established in 1932 in the busy
Anderlecht district (about twenty minutes by metro
from the city center). It delivers fuss-free classics,
like shrimp croquettes, steak cut to order, rugged
meatballs in tomato sauce, and garlic-scented
mussels (baked or steamed). Be sure to order
a side of twice-cooked frites—best dipped in
Béarnaise—alongside a pick from the beer, wine,
or even tea list. Soak up the night-time atmosphere
at the little bar or grab one of the small tables
covered in chequered plastic.

A LA BÉCASSE

Rue de Tabora 11
Brussels 1000, Belgium
+32 25110006
www.alabecasse.com

Opening hours	Open 7 days
Credit cards	Accepted but not AMEX
Price range	Affordable
Style	Casual
Cuisine	Belgian Gastropub
Recommended for	Late night

BOZAR BRASSERIE

Recommended by
David Martin

Rue Baron Horta 3
Brussels 1000, Belgium
www.bozarbrasserie.be

Opening hours	Closed Monday and Sunday
Credit cards	Accepted
Price range	Expensive
Style	Smart casual
Cuisine	Modern Belgian
Recommended for	Regular neighborhood

CAFFÈ AL DENTE

Recommended by
Christophe Hardiquest

Rue du Doyenné 85-87
Brussels 1180, Belgium
+32 23434523
www.caffealdente.com

Opening hours	Closed Monday and Sunday
Credit cards	Accepted but not AMEX
Price range	Affordable
Style	Casual
Cuisine	Italian
Recommended for	Regular neighborhood

"Simple cuisine with a short choice of dishes and a beautiful atmosphere."—Christophe Hardiquest

CHARLI

Recommended by
Christophe Hardiquest

Rue Sainte-Catherine 34
Brussels 1000, Belgium
+32 25136332
www.charliboulangerie.com

Opening hours	Open 7 days
Reservation policy	No
Credit cards	Accepted but not AMEX
Price range	Budget
Style	Casual
Cuisine	Bakery
Recommended for	Breakfast

"The best viennoiserie in town, croissants *au beurre*, and sourdough bread."—Christophe Hardiquest

LA FABRIQUE CHATELAIN

Recommended by
Sang Hoon Degeimbre

Rue Américaine 122
Brussels 1050, Belgium
+32 25375636
www.lafabriqueresto.be

Opening hours	Closed Monday
Credit cards	Accepted but not AMEX
Price range	Affordable
Style	Casual
Cuisine	French-International
Recommended for	Breakfast

"Perfect place to get you out of your bed on Saturday morning."—Sang Hoon Degeimbre

LA FRITERIE DE LA BARRIÈRE

Recommended by
Sang Hoon Degeimbre

Avenue du Parc 5
Brussels 1060, Belgium
+32 25375770
www.friteriedelabarriere.be

Opening hours	Open 7 days
Reservation policy	No
Credit cards	Not accepted
Price range	Budget
Style	Casual
Cuisine	Belgian
Recommended for	Late night

KAMO

Recommended by
Sang Hoon Degeimbre,
Christophe Hardiquest

Chaussée de Waterloo 550a
Brussels 1050, Belgium
+32 26487848
www.restaurant-kamo.be

Opening hours	Closed Saturday and Sunday
Credit cards	Accepted
Price range	Expensive
Style	Smart casual
Cuisine	Japanese
Recommended for	Local favorite

"The best Japanese in town, and the best value for money, with an open kitchen where you can see the cooks working."—Christophe Hardiquest

MAISON ANTOINE

Place Jourdan
Brussels 1040, Belgium
+32 22305456
www.maisonantoine.be

Opening hours	Open 7 days
Reservation policy	No
Credit cards	Not accepted
Price range	Budget
Style	Casual
Cuisine	Belgian
Recommended for	Late night

"Typical Belgian fries—some of the best in Belgium.
It's surrounded by small bars where you can eat your
fries paired with a nice Belgian beer."
—Sang Hoon Degeimbre

MARU BRUSSELS

Chaussée de Waterloo 510
Brussels 1050, Belgium
+32 23461111

Opening hours	Closed Monday
Credit cards	Accepted but not AMEX
Price range	Affordable
Style	Casual
Cuisine	Korean
Recommended for	Regular neighborhood

"Relaxed and casual with a nice selection of natural
wines. Boris is a perfect host!"
—Sang Hoon Degeimbre

LE PAIN QUOTIDIEN

Chaussée de Waterloo 123
Brussels 1410, Belgium
+32 23545990
www.lepainquotidien.be

Opening hours	Open 7 days
Reservation policy	No
Credit cards	Accepted
Price range	Budget
Style	Casual
Cuisine	Café-Bakery
Recommended for	Breakfast

PISTOLET ORIGINAL

Rue Joseph Stevens 24
Brussels 1000, Belgium
+32 28808098
www.pistolet-original.be

Opening hours	Open 7 days
Reservation policy	No
Credit cards	Not accepted
Price range	Budget
Style	Casual
Cuisine	Café-Bakery
Recommended for	Bargain

"A wide variety of Belgian specialties in a kind
of sandwich—always crunchy and fresh that day."
—Christophe Hardiquest

AU VIEUX SAINT MARTIN

Grand Sablon 38
Brussels 1000, Belgium
+32 25126476
www.auvieuxsaintmartin.be

Opening hours	Open 7 days
Reservation policy	No
Credit cards	Accepted
Price range	Affordable
Style	Casual
Cuisine	Belgian-British
Recommended for	Late night

"Very nice brasserie with little things to eat. Nice
champagne by the glass. Real Belgian ambiance."
—Christophe Hardiquest

LA VILLA EMILY

Rue de l'Abbaye 4
Brussels 1000, Belgium
+32 23181858
www.lavillaemily.be

Opening hours	Closed Monday and Sunday
Credit cards	Accepted
Price range	Affordable
Style	Smart casual
Cuisine	Belgian-French
Recommended for	Local favorite

"Elegant and refined—a cuisine with finesse."
—David Martin

WITTAMER

Place du Grand Sablon 6-12-13
Brussels 1000, Belgium
+32 25123742
www.wittamer.com

Opening hours	Open 7 days
Credit cards	Accepted
Price range	Affordable
Style	Casual
Cuisine	Bakery
Recommended for	Breakfast

"The best croissant in town with a beautiful view."
—Christophe Hardiquest

DE HERMELIJN

Wannegemdorp 7
Wannegem-Lede
Brussels 9772, Belgium
+32 93836411
www.dehermelijn.be

Opening hours	Closed Wednesday and Thursday
Credit cards	Accepted
Price range	Affordable
Style	Casual
Cuisine	Modern Flemish
Recommended for	Regular neighborhood

T HUIS VAN LEDE

Lededorp 7
Wannegem-Lede
Brussels 9772, Belgium
+32 93835096
www.thuisvanlede.be

Opening hours	Closed Monday and Sunday
Credit cards	Accepted
Price range	Affordable
Style	Casual
Cuisine	Modern Belgian
Recommended for	Regular neighborhood

"Flavorsome cuisine and outstanding produce."
—Peter Goossens

DE ZWAAN

Wannegemdorp 4
Wannegem-Lede
Brussels 9772, Belgium
+32 479803808
www.gasthofdezwaan.be

Opening hours	Closed Monday and Tuesday
Credit cards	Accepted but not AMEX
Price range	Affordable
Style	Casual
Cuisine	Belgian-French
Recommended for	Regular neighborhood

GASTHOF HALIFAX

Emiel Clauslaan 143
Deinze
East Flanders 9800, Belgium
+32 92823102
www.gasthofhalifax.be

Opening hours	Open 7 days
Credit cards	Accepted
Price range	Affordable
Style	Casual
Cuisine	French-Belgian
Recommended for	Late night

PLEIN 25

Elsegemplein 25
Elsegem
East Flanders 9790, Belgium
+32 56602525
www.plein25.be

Opening hours	Closed Wednesday and Sunday
Credit cards	Accepted
Price range	Affordable
Style	Casual
Cuisine	Bistro
Recommended for	Regular neighborhood

ABOOOV ADANACI

Recommended by
Kobe Desramaults

Geraard Mercatorstraat 2
Ghent
East Flanders 9000, Belgium
+32 485 20 54 69

Opening hours	Open 7 days
Credit cards	Not accepted
Price range	Budget
Style	Casual
Cuisine	Kebab Shop
Recommended for	Late night

HET MOMENT

Recommended by
Kobe Desramaults

Burgstraat 20
Ghent
East Flanders 9000, Belgium
+32 476 42 14 57
www.genietvanhetmoment.be

Opening hours	Closed Monday and Tuesday
Credit cards	Accepted but not Diners
Price range	Budget
Style	Casual
Cuisine	Café
Recommended for	Breakfast

J.E.F

Recommended by
Merlin Labron-Johnson

Lange Steenstraat 10
Ghent
East Flanders 9000, Belgium
+32 93368058
www.j-e-f.be

Opening hours	Closed Monday and Sunday
Credit cards	Accepted
Price range	Affordable
Style	Casual
Cuisine	Belgian
Recommended for	Wish I'd opened

"This is probably my favorite restaurant. It's run by a chef called Jason Blanckaert and his wife Famke, hence the name. It's just them and two other members of staff looking after a tiny dining room. They abstain from being in any guides or lists and do exactly what they want, which is to serve the kind of delicous and generous food that I imagine they'd like to eat themselves."—Merlin Labron-Johnson

J.E.F. is named after Jason Blanckaert and his wife Femke Dequidt, who set up the restaurant in the middle of Ghent's old town. The off-white walls and aged, bare tables give the place a clean and sturdy look—it's not fancy, but the food is innovative, on-trend, and very reasonably priced. Snails come with bone marrow and smoked bread croutons; assorted shellfish arrive with oyster tartare, samphire, and seafood broth; and there's a must-try dessert of pear with sorrel, coffee, and basil and lime sorbet. The set lunch has two choices for each course and there's a cracking selection of great Belgian beers.

MARTINO

Recommended by
Kobe Desramaults

Vlaanderenstraat 125
Ghent
East Flanders 9000, Belgium
+32 9 225 01 04

Opening hours	Closed Monday and Tuesday
Credit cards	Acceoted
Price range	Budget
Style	Casual
Cuisine	Italian
Recommended for	Late night

Martino in Ghent, an institute and favourite of mine. Be sure to order "cheese and eggs".

T NIEUW STADION

Recommended by
Peter Goossens

Brusselsesteenweg 664
Ghent
East Flanders 9050, Belgium
+32 92308833
www.nieuwstadion.be

Opening hours	Closed Monday and Tuesday
Credit cards	Accepted
Price range	Affordable
Style	Smart casual
Cuisine	Belgian
Recommended for	Bargain

OAK

Recommended by
David Martin

Hoogstraat 167/001
Ghent
East Flanders 9000, Belgium
+32 9 3539050
www.oakgent.be

Opening hours	Closed Monday and Sunday
Credit cards	Accepted
Price range	Affordable
Style	Smart casual
Cuisine	Belgian-European
Recommended for	Regular neighborhood

"Elegant, contemporary, with a strong identity.
The chef, Marcelo Baladin, offers contemporary
cuisine full of taste and flavor. A restaurant to watch!"
—David Martin

VRIJMOED

Recommended by
David Martin

Vlaanderenstraat 22
Ghent
East Flanders 9000, Belgium
Europe
+32 92799977
www.vrijmoed.be

Opening hours	Closed Saturday and Sunday
Credit cards	Accepted
Price range	Expensive
Style	Smart casual
Cuisine	Modern European
Recommended for	Regular neighborhood

HOF VAN CLEVE

Recommended by
David Martin

Riemegemstraat 1
Kruishoutem
East Flanders 9770, Belgium
+32 93835848
www.hofvancleve.com

Opening hours	Closed Monday and Sunday
Credit cards	Accepted
Price range	Expensive
Style	Smart casual
Cuisine	Modern Belgian
Recommended for	High end

"The best in Belgium, a cuisine exclusively focused on
taste, and exceptional service."—David Martin

BRASSERIE BOULEVARD

Recommended by
Peter Goossens

Kortrijksesteenweg 175
Sint-Martens-Latem
East Flanders 9831, Belgium
+32 92791200
www.blvd.be

Opening hours	Closed Sunday
Credit cards	Accepted but not AMEX
Price range	Affordable
Style	Casual
Cuisine	Belgian Brasserie
Recommended for	Bargain

BRASSERIE LATEM

Recommended by
Peter Goossens

Kortrijksesteenweg 9
Sint-Martens-Latem
East Flanders 9831, Belgium
+32 92823617
www.brasserielatem.be

Opening hours	Closed Sunday
Credit cards	Accepted
Price range	Expensive
Style	Smart casual
Cuisine	Belgian Brasserie
Recommended for	Local favorite

BOULEVARD BOUTIQUE

Recommended by
Peter Goossens

Kortrijksesteenweg 140/1
Sint-Martens-Latem
East Flanders 9830, Belgium
+32 92770272
www.blvd.boutique

Opening hours	Closed Sunday
Reservation policy	No
Credit cards	Accepted but not AMEX
Price range	Affordable
Style	Casual
Cuisine	Café-Bistro
Recommended for	Breakfast

LA MENUISERIE

Recommended by
Sang Hoon Degeimbre

Champagne 12
Waimes
Liège 4950, Belgium
+32 80444485
www.lamenuiserie.eu

Opening hours	Closed Monday and Tuesday
Credit cards	Accepted but not AMEX
Price range	Affordable
Style	Casual
Cuisine	Modern European
Recommended for	Local favorite

"Creative with a lot of local ingredients. This young dynamic couple perfectly match modern cuisine with Walloon philosophy."—Sang Hoon Degeimbre

LA GRAPPE D'OR

Recommended by
Sang Hoon Degeimbre

Rue de l'Ermitage 18
Torgny
Luxembourg 6767, Belgium
+32 63577056
www.lagrappedor.com

Opening hours	Closed Monday and Tuesday
Credit cards	Accepted but not AMEX
Price range	Affordable
Style	Casual
Cuisine	Belgian-French
Recommended for	Local favorite

L'AIR DU TEMPS

Recommended by
Bas Wiegel

Rue de la Croix Monet 2
Liernu
Namur 5310, Belgium
+32 81813048
www.airdutemps.be

Opening hours	Closed Monday and Tuesday
Credit cards	Accepted
Price range	Expensive
Style	Smart casual
Cuisine	Modern Asian
Recommended for	Worth the travel

"This is special. A trip worth making and a culinary experience."—Bas Wiegel

True to its name, L'Air du Temps is an avant-garde restaurant with a sensory mission. Having been a butcher before becoming a sommelier, Korean-born chef Sang Hoon Degeimbre then decided to move to modernist cookery methods. Fastidious research

and a menu that has been perfected over time earned him first one Michelin star, then two. Unlike that of many gastronomic innovators, Degeimbre's menu is accessible, with the likes of kimchi cleverly paired with more conventional ingredients. The menu dégustation (tasting menu) comes as a series of artfully garnished creations. Provenance is central to this develop-mental venture.

L'AMANDIER

Recommended by
Sang Hoon Degeimbre

Rue de Limalsart 9
Genval
Walloon Brabant 1332, Belgium
+32 26530671
www.amandier.be

Opening hours	Closed Wednesday
Credit cards	Accepted but not AMEX
Price range	Affordable
Style	Smart casual
Cuisine	Belgian-European
Recommended for	Local favorite

LE 1900

Recommended by
Sang Hoon Degeimbre

Grand Place 22
Perwez
Walloon Brabant 1360, Belgium
+32 81226373
www.le1900.be

Opening hours	Closed Sunday
Credit cards	Accepted but not AMEX
Price range	Affordable
Style	Casual
Cuisine	Brasserie
Recommended for	Bargain

"Seasonal ingredients, nice techniques—simple and tasty."—Sang Hoon Degeimbre

DE OESTERPUT

Recommended by
Sergio Herman

Wenduinse Steenweg 16
Blankenberge
West Flanders 8370, Belgium
+32 50411035
www.oesterput.com

Opening hours	Closed Monday and Tuesday
Reservation policy	No
Credit cards	Accepted but not AMEX
Price range	Affordable
Style	Casual
Cuisine	Seafood
Recommended for	Local favorite

IN DE ZON

Recommended by
Kobe Desramaults

Dikkebusstraat 80
De Klijte
Heuvelland
West Flanders 8958, Belgium
+32 57 21 26 26
www.indezon.be

Opening hours	Closed Monday and Tuesday
Credit cards	Accepted
Price range	Affordable
Style	Casual
Cuisine	Traditional Belgian
Recommended for	Regular neighbourhood

BOSRAND

Recommended by
Gert De Mangeleer

Koning Albert-I laan 108
Bruges
West Flanders 8200, Belgium
+32 494527552
www.frituurbosrand.be

Opening hours	Open 7 days
Reservation policy	No
Credit cards	Accepted but not AMEX
Price range	Budget
Style	Casual
Cuisine	Belgian
Recommended for	Bargain

"Best fries in town."—Gert de Mangeleer

GASTROBAR HUBERT

Recommended by
Gert De Mangeleer

Langestraat 159
Bruges
West Flanders 8000, Belgium
+32 50641009
www.gastrobar-hubert.be

Opening hours	Closed Monday, Saturday, and Sunday
Credit cards	Accepted
Price range	Affordable
Style	Casual
Cuisine	Bistro
Recommended for	Regular neighborhood

"Easy-going sharing dishes—good vibe."
—Gert de Mangeleer

DE JONKMAN

Recommended by
David Martin

Maalsesteenweg 438
Bruges
West Flanders 8310, Belgium
+32 50360767
www.dejonkman.be

Opening hours	Closed Monday, Tuesday, and Sunday
Credit cards	Accepted
Price range	Expensive
Style	Smart casual
Cuisine	Modern Belgian
Recommended for	Regular neighborhood

ROCK FORT

Recommended by
Gert De Mangeleer

Langestraat 15
Bruges
West Flanders 8000, Belgium
+32 50334113
www.rock-fort.be

Opening hours	Closed Wednesday, Saturday and Sunday
Credit cards	Accepted
Price range	Affordable
Style	Casual
Cuisine	Belgian
Recommended for	Regular neighborhood

SIPHON

Recommended by
Gert De Mangeleer,
Sergio Herman

Damse Vaart-Oost 1
Damme
West Flanders 8340, Belgium
+32 50620202
www.siphon.be

Opening hours	Closed Saturday and Sunday
Credit cards	Not accepted
Price range	Affordable
Style	Casual
Cuisine	Traditional Belgian
Recommended for	Local favorite

"Classic—where time stood still and I hope it will
stay like this. The staff, the interior, it all adds to the
atmosphere."—Sergio Herman

DE BARBIER

Recommended by
Florent Ladeyn

5 Hillestraat
Heuvelland
West Flanders 8591, Belgium
+ 32 57445924

Opening hours	Closed Monday to Thursday
Credit cards	Accepted but not AMEX
Price range	Affordable
Style	Casual
Cuisine	Traditional Belgian
Recommended for	Bargain

"A real 'estaminet', proudly lost among the fields and mountains. The decor is classy and Thierry's service is everything one would expect: warm and jokey. Igor's prawn croquettes are extraordinary!"—Florent Ladeyn

CASTOR

Recommended by
Peter Goossens

Kortrijkseweg 164
Beveren-Leie
Waregem
West Flanders 8791, Belgium
+32 56190121
www.cas-tor.be

Opening hours	Closed Monday and Sunday
Credit cards	Accepted but not AMEX
Price range	Affordable
Style	Smart casual
Cuisine	Modern French
Recommended for	Wish I'd opened

ESCABECHE

Recommended by
Peter Goossens

Stationsstraat 166
Waregem
West Flanders 8790, Belgium
+32 56328697
www.escabechedeluxe.be

Opening hours	Closed Monday and Sunday
Credit cards	Accepted but not AMEX
Price range	Affordable
Style	Casual
Cuisine	Spanish Tapas
Recommended for	Regular neighborhood

BISTRONOOM

Recommended by
Peter Goossens

Waregemseweg 155
Wortegem-Petegem
West Flanders 9790, Belgium
+32 56611122
www.bistronoom.be

Opening hours	Closed Wednesday
Credit cards	Accepted
Price range	Affordable
Style	Smart casual
Cuisine	European
Recommended for	Regular neighborhood

SOUVENIR

Recommended by
Florent Ladeyn

12 Rue de Surmont
Ypres
West Flanders 8900, Belgium
+32 57360606
www.souvenir-restaurant.be

Opening hours	Closed Monday, Thursday and Sunday
Credit cards	Accepted but not AMEX
Price range	Affordable
Style	Smart casual
Cuisine	Modern French
Recommended for	Regular neighborhood

"It's a very pretty and very cosy place, in white and wood—very Nordic. Vil is from Iceland and he settled here because his wife is from the town. The food is very inspiring. His way of cooking vegetables is fascinating."—Florent Ladeyn

HERTOG JAN

Recommended by
Christophe Hardiquest

Loppemsestraat 52
Zedelgem
West Flanders 8210, Belgium
+32 50673446
www.hertog-jan.com

Opening hours	Closed Sunday
Credit cards	Accepted
Price range	Expensive
Style	Formal
Cuisine	Modern European
Recommended for	High end

"High professionalism and high level of produce—beautiful service. I love to go whenever I can."
—Christophe Hardiquest

"*It remains today the most inspiring restaurant ever.*"
JULIEN ROYER P541

"**VERY ELEGANT AND FANCY PLACE WHERE YOU CAN ENJOY HAUTE CUISINE.**"
MATHIEU ROSTAING-TAYARD P536

"AMAZING SETTING IN THE CÔTE D'AZUR."
SASU LAUKKONEN P545

FRANCE & MONACO

"**THEY FOLLOW THE SEASONS AND COMBINE FLAVORS FROM THE SEA, THE LAND, THE WOODS, GRASSES, GRAINS, PLANTS AND SMOKE.**"
PEETER PIHEL P542

"It's untypically French—no butter, no cream, more sea water and rock pool. This is the most 'loyal to local' restaurant I've ever been to. Mind blowing."
TANIA STEYTLER P543

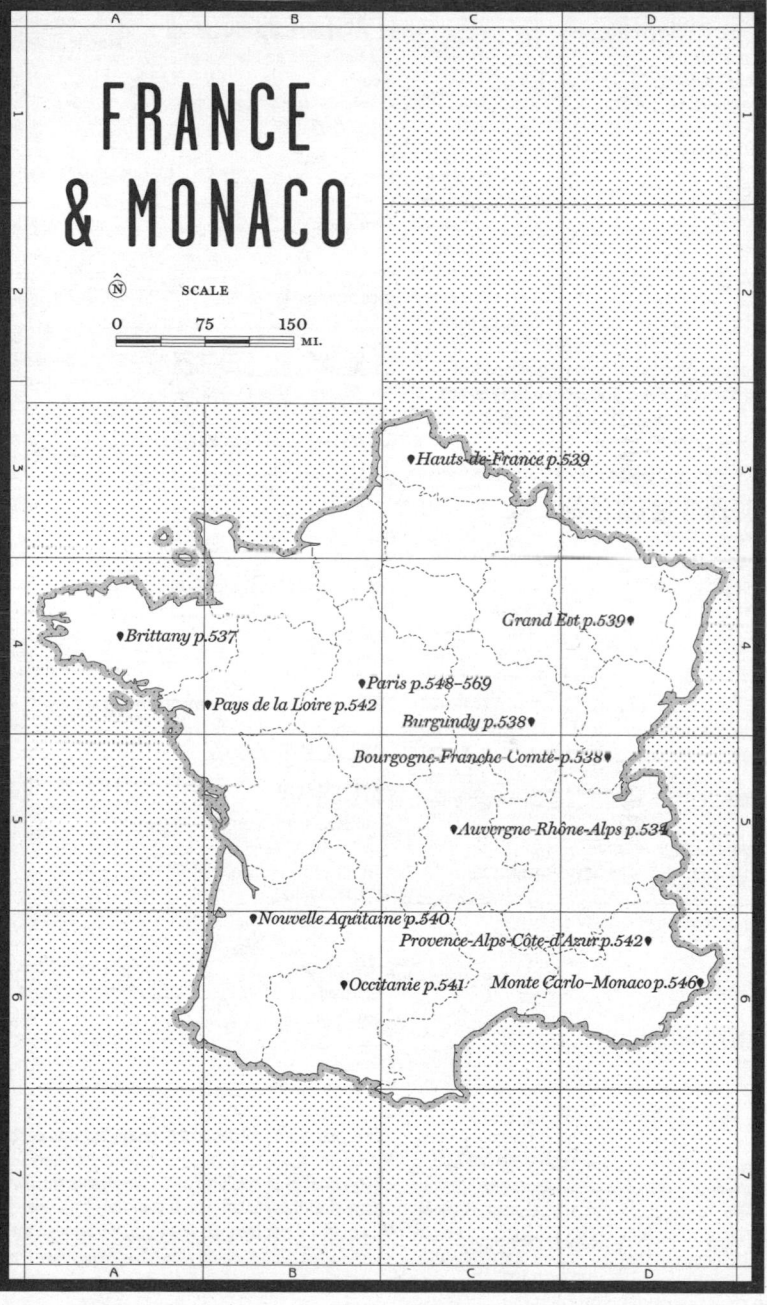

FRANCE
& MONACO

N

SCALE

0   75   150
MI.

LA BASTIDE DE MOUSTIERS

Recommended by
Alexander Mayer

Chemin de Quinson
Moustiers-Sainte-Marie
Alpes-de-Haute-Provence 04360
+33 492704747
www.bastide-moustiers.com

Opening hours	Open 7 days
Credit cards	Accepted
Price range	Affordable
Style	Casual
Cuisine	French
Recommended for	Wish I'd opened

"Amazing, peaceful place with its own gardens full of vegetables, its own bakery, and a beautiful terrace with views of the olive trees and lavender fields. Pure nature!"—Alexander Mayer

L'AUBERGE DU PONT DE COLLONGES

Recommended by
José Gutierrez,
Normand Laprise

50 Rue de la Plage
Collonges-au-Mont-d'Or
Auvergne-Rhône-Alpes 69660
+33 472429090
www.bocuse.fr

Opening hours	Open 7 days
Credit cards	Accepted
Price range	Expensive
Style	Formal
Cuisine	French
Recommended for	Worth the travel

"Three Michelin stars for over fifty years, that's what I call impressive."—Normand Laprise

CHEZ THÉRÈSE

Recommended by
Emmanuel Renaut

La Ferme du Sciozier
Route du Gâteau
Flumet
Auvergne-Rhône-Alpes 73590
+33 479317519
www.fermedusciozier.com

Opening hours	Open 7 days
Credit cards	Accepted but not AMEX
Price range	Affordable
Style	Casual
Cuisine	French
Recommended for	Local favorite

"A mountain chalet surrounded by fields." —Emmanuel Renaut

LE BISTROT DU POTAGER

Recommended by
Mathieu Rostaing-Tayard

163 Boulevard de Stalingrad
Lyon
Auvergne-Rhône-Alpes 69006
+33 478931975

Opening hours	Closed Saturday and Sunday
Credit cards	Accepted
Price range	Affordable
Style	Casual
Cuisine	French
Recommended for	Regular neighborhood

LA BRASSERIE GEORGES

Recommended by
Mathieu Rostaing-Tayard

30 Cours de Verdun Perrache
Lyon
Auvergne-Rhône-Alpes 69002
+33 472565454
www.brasseriegeorges.com

Opening hours	Open 7 days
Credit cards	Accepted
Price range	Affordable
Style	Casual
Cuisine	French
Recommended for	Late night

"Open very late and a very charming setting." —Mathieu Rostaing-Tayard

CAFÉ SILLON

Recommended by
James Lowe,
Michel Portos

46 Avenue Jean-Jaurès
Lyon
Auvergne-Rhône-Alpes 69007
+33 478720973
www.cafe-sillon.com

Opening hours	Closed Monday and Sunday
Credit cards	Accepted
Price range	Affordable
Style	Casual
Cuisine	French
Recommended for	Bargain

"This place isn't necessarily cheap, but it is certainly incredible value for money—I have never had such a high quality of cooking and ingredients for the price charged at this restaurant. It is simply brilliant. If I could, I'd eat here all the time."—James Lowe

L'ÉBAUCHE

4 Rue de la Martinière
Lyon
Auvergne-Rhône-Alpes 69001
+33 478581258

Opening hours	Closed Monday and Tuesday
Credit cards	Accepted but not AMEX
Price range	Affordable
Style	Casual
Cuisine	Modern French
Recommended for	Regular neighborhood

"Cool seasonal products, very good natural wine. Inspiring cuisine."—Mathieu Rostaing-Tayard

KITCHEN CAFÉ

34 Rue Chevreul
Lyon
Auvergne-Rhône-Alpes 69007
+33 603364275
www.lekitchencafe.com

Opening hours	Closed Monday and Tuesday
Credit cards	Accepted but not AMEX
Price range	Affordable
Style	Casual
Cuisine	Modern French
Recommended for	Breakfast

"Very good pastries and it's close to my home."
—Mathieu Rostaing-Tayard

LE SUPRÊME

106 Cours Gambetta
Lyon
Auvergne-Rhône-Alpes 69007
+33 4 78 72 32 68

Opening hours	Closed Monday and Sunday
Credit cards	Accepted but not Diners
Price range	Affordable
Style	Smart casual
Cuisine	Modern French
Recommended for	Bargain

LA MÈRE BRAZIER

12 Rue Royale
Lyon
Auvergne-Rhône-Alpes 69001
+33 478231720
www.amerebrazier.fr

Opening hours	Closed Saturday and Sunday
Credit cards	Accepted
Price range	Expensive
Style	Formal
Cuisine	French
Recommended for	Local favorite

"It's a Lyonnaise institution."
—Mathieu Rostaing-Tayard

The most remarkable thing about this restaurant isn't that it once held three Michelin stars, but that they were achieved in 1933—by a female chef. Eugénie Brazier, the restaurant's founder, was iconic as the first woman ever to be awarded three stars by the Michelin guide. After many years of success, La Mère Brazier's reputation and star status dwindled. Then, in 2008, chef Mathieu Viannay took over the kitchen and soon regained a very respectable two Michelin stars, of which Eugénie would surely be proud. You can still see the original 1933 Michelin guide in a display cabinet, and the excellent food served today more than backs up this place's historic reputation.

LE TROQUET DES SENS

34 Rue des Remparts d'Ainay
Lyon
Auvergne-Rhône-Alpes 69002
+33 478372223
www.troquet-des-sens.com

Opening hours	Closed Monday and Sunday
Credit cards	Accepted but not AMEX
Price range	Affordable
Style	Casual
Cuisine	French
Recommended for	Bargain

"Warm and friendly atmosphere with good wines and charcuterie."—Mathieu Rostaing-Tayard

LA MAISON DES BOIS

Col de la Croix-Fry
Manigod
Auvergne-Rhône-Alpes 74230
+33 450600000
www.marcveyrat.fr

Opening hours............................Closed Monday to Wednesday
Credit cards...Accepted
Price range...Expensive
Style...Smart casual
Cuisine..French
Recommended for...High end

"One of the best experiences ever."—Yannick Alléno

FLOCONS DE SEL

1775 Route du Leutaz
Megève
Auvergne-Rhône-Alpes 74120
+33 450214999
www.floconsdesel.com

Opening hours.........................Closed Tuesday and Wednesday
Credit cards...Accepted
Price range...Expensive
Style...Smart casual
Cuisine..French
Recommended for...Worth the travel

"Emmanuel Renaut is a chef who is reinterpreting
great French cuisine."—Enrico Crippa

Housed in the chalet of dreams—both woody and
chic—on the slopes above ski resort Megève,
Emmanuel Renaut's hotel and restaurant is a
distinctly Alpine retreat, complete with a wall of
cuckoo clocks. Having done time with Marc Veyrat,
master manipulator of mountain greens and flowers,
Renaut's instinct is to gather some of his own, using
them to flavor broths and even scatter on toast.
Ceps feature heavily, too, with little mushroom-
shaped wafers buried in mushroom powder. Dishes
such as salsify spaghetti with lard and black truffle,
or Lake Geneva pike and monkfish on a biscuit with
onion jus, look typically serene.

LA SAUVAGEONNE

2637 Route du Leutaz
Megève
Auvergne-Rhône-Alpes 74120
+33 450919081
www.restaurant-sauvageonne.com

Opening hours...Open 7 days
Credit cards...Accepted
Price range..Affordable
Style...Smart casual
Cuisine...French-Asian
Recommended for..Late night

MAISON TROISGROS

728 Route de Villerest
Roanne
Auvergne-Rhône-Alpes 42155
+33 477716697
www.troisgros.fr

Opening hours..............................Closed Monday and Tuesday
Credit cards...Accepted
Price range...Expensive
Style...Formal
Cuisine..French
Recommended for...High end

"Very elegant and fancy place where you can enjoy
haute cuisine."—Mathieu Rostaing-Tayard

Maison Troisgros represents the epitome of
traditional haute cuisine. The Troisgros family
is one of France's best-known culinary dynasties,
with a cooking heritage spanning more than eighty
years—of which their flagship restaurant has held
three Michelin stars for an impressive forty-five.
With Michel behind the stove the cooking has
become less fussy, but no less produce focused.
Many restaurants today make great boasts of
creating menus "according to what is available in
the market" but MT was doing it when they were
still in their infancy, and they're still the masters
of ad hoc hospitality.

RÉGIS ET JACQUES MARCON

Larsaillas
Saint Bonnet-le-Froid
Auvergne-Rhône-Alpes 43290
+33 471599372
www.regismarcon.fr

Opening hours	Closed Tuesday and Wednesday
Credit cards	Accepted
Price range	Expensive
Style	Smart casual
Cuisine	French
Recommended for	High end

In the wilds of the remote Haute-Loire, master of the mushroom, Régis Marcon, and his son Jacques create dishes that have garnered three Michelin stars, using the rich natural pantry in their midst. Such dishes as lobster cassoulet with green lentils from nearby Le Puy, mushroom tea scented with tansy served between fish and meat courses, and lamb with cep granita, are served in a sleekly modern dining room. By day this clever reinvention of the original auberge has uninterrupted views over the Ardèche River and Monts du Velay (bedrooms are sympathetically sunk into the grounds), while at night its ceiling lights sparkle. Follow on with local cheeses and rum-free, raspberry-rich baba.

ROND DE CAROTTE

50 Rue de la Vignette
Saint-Gervais-Les-Bains
Auvergne-Rhône-Alpes 74170
+33 450477639
www.ronddecarotte.fr

Opening hours	Closed Monday and Sunday
Credit cards	Accepted but not AMEX or Diners
Price range	Affordable
Style	Casual
Cuisine	French
Recommended for	Regular neighborhood

"Excellent cooking, unbeatable value for money, and superb service."—Emmanuel Renaut

MAISON PIC

285 Avenue Victor Hugo
Valence
Auvergne-Rhône-Alpes 26000
+33 475441532
www.anne-sophie-pic.com

Opening hours	Closed Monday
Credit cards	Accepted
Price range	Expensive
Style	Smart casual
Cuisine	Modern French
Recommended for	Worth the travel

"Anne-Sophie Pic is the only female three-Michelin-starred chef in France. She combines a wide variety of elements in her cooking, leaving your senses tantalised in a very delicate and feminine manner."
—Joaquin Soriano

Located on the Route Nationale 7 (the road provides the name of the trendy on-site bistro), the century-old Maison Pic has always been on the radar of gastro-tourists. Home to one of France's oldest kitchen dynasties, these days it's run by Anne-Sophie Pic—the only woman in France with three Michelin stars (although her ancestors had already won and lost that many twice). Such pedigree is worked into the boutique hotel's design, which features the Pic family's photo archive. In the restaurant, the "Menu Essentiel" exemplifies Anne-Sophie's perfectionist streak, with dishes like langoustines with aniseed and cinnamon leaf striving to outdo the overachieving Pics of the past.

CAFÉ DE LA CALE

Quai Guerveur
Belle-Ile-en-Mer
Brittany 29120
+33 297316574
www.cafedelacale.pagecom.fr

Opening hours	Open 7 days
Credit cards	Accepted
Price range	Budget
Style	Casual
Cuisine	Café
Recommended for	Breakfast

LE RELAIS BERNARD LOISEAU

Recommended by
Guy Savoy

2 Rue d'Argentine
Saulieu
Bourgogne-Franche-Comté 21210
+33 3 80 90 53 53
www.bernard-loiseau.com/en

Opening hours	Closed Tuesday and Wednesday
Credit cards	Accepted
Price range	Expensive
Style	Smart casual
Cuisine	French
Recommended for	High end

DOMAINE DE ROCHEVILAINE

Recommended by
Eric & Bruce Bromberg

Pointe de Penlan
Billiers
Brittany 56190
+33 297416161
www.domainerochevilaine.com

Opening hours	Open 7 days
Credit cards	Accepted
Price range	Expensive
Style	Casual
Cuisine	French
Recommended for	High end

"The team there beautifully transforms local ingredients into wondrous and mystical creations. Real appreciation for great produce is what is most alluring about this place."—Eric & Bruce Bromberg

AUBERGE DES GLAZICKS

Recommended by
Alexander Mayer

7 Rue de la Plage
Plomodiern
Brittany 29550
+33 298815232
www.aubergedesglazick.com

Opening hours	Closed Monday and Tuesday
Credit cards	Accepted but not AMEX or Diners
Price range	Expensive
Style	Smart casual
Cuisine	French Seafood
Recommended for	Worth the travel

"A modern version of traditional Breton cuisine— the chef is really cooking at his best at the moment." —Alexander Mayer

LE COMPTOIR BREICZ CAFÉ

Recommended by
Alexander Mayer

6 Rue de l'Orme
Saint Malo
Brittany 35400
+33 299569608
www.breizhcafe.com

Opening hours	Closed Monday and Tuesday
Credit cards	Accepted
Price range	Affordable
Style	Casual
Cuisine	French-Crêperie
Recommended for	Bargain

LE COQUILLAGE

Recommended by
Vicky Cheng,
Alexander Mayer

Château Richeux
Saint-Méloir-des-Ondes
Brittany 35350
+33 299896476
www.maisons-de-bricourt.com

Opening hours	Open 7 days
Credit cards	Accepted
Price range	Expensive
Style	Smart casual
Cuisine	French Seafood
Recommended for	Worth the travel

CAVES MADELEINE

Recommended by
Josep Roca

8 Rue Faubourg Madeleine
Beaune
Burgundy 21200
+33 380229330

Opening hours	Closed Thursday and Sunday
Credit cards	Accepted but not AMEX
Price range	Affordable
Style	Smart casual
Cuisine	Burgundian
Recommended for	Wish I'd opened

Very much off the track beaten by those devoted to the Red Guide, this rural French bistro has been popularized via word of mouth and because of an ability to pair excellent wines with brilliantly cooked classic French dishes. The usual suspects are all done very well. From confit duck to *andouille* (smoked pork sausage), and beef *bourguignon* to snail *cassolette*, the regional authenticity always feels nourishing. Net curtains drape in the windows of a fairly unassuming facade behind which diners sit cheek by jowl on communal wooden tables. Wines are available to takeout (take away)— and a mere €6 ($7; £5) corkage is charged.

L'ARNSBOURG

Recommended by
Chantel Dartnall

18 Untermuhlthal
Baerenthal
Grand Est 57230
+33 387065085
www.arnsbourg.com

Opening hours	Closed Monday and Tuesday
Credit cards	Accepted
Price range	Expensive
Style	Formal
Cuisine	Modern French
Recommended for	Wish I'd opened

"This is certainly a place of unsurpassed serenity, a truly magical culinary retreat. Definitely worth the journey."—Chantel Dartnall

L'AUBERGE DE L'ILL

Recommended by
Sergey Eroshenko,
Lori Granito,
Jean Joho,
Rudolf Obauer

2 Rue de Collonges au Mont d'Or
Illhaeusern
Grand Est 68970
+33 389718900
www.auberge-de-l-ill.com

Opening hours	Closed Monday and Tuesday
Credit cards	Accepted
Price range	Expensive
Style	Smart casual
Cuisine	Alsatian
Recommended for	Worth the travel

"My all-time favorite restaurant."—Lori Granito

LES COPAINS D'ABORD

Recommended by
Julien Duboué

32 Rue du Coetlosquet
Metz
Grand Est 57000
+33 387762146
www.restaurantlescopainsdabordmetz.fr

Opening hours	Closed Monday and Sunday
Credit cards	Accepted but not AMEX or Diners
Price range	Affordable
Style	Casual
Cuisine	Brasserie
Recommended for	Bargain

"They serve pig's feet in *escabèche* for €10 ($11; £9) on Wednesday mornings. I treat myself every time."
—Julien Duboué

LE PARC

Recommended by
Josue Lopez

Domaine Les Crayères
64 Boulevard Henry Vasnier
Reims
Grand Est 51100
+33 326249000
www.lescrayeres.com

Opening hours	Closed Monday and Tuesday
Credit cards	Accepted
Price range	Expensive
Style	Smart casual
Cuisine	French
Recommended for	Worth the travel

"Housed in the most beautiful of châteaux. Transports you somewhere else."—Josue Lopez

L'ASSIETTE CHAMPENOISE

Recommended by
Peter Goossens,
John Horne,
Mats Vollmer,

40 Avenue Paul Vaillant-Couturier
Tinqueux
Grand Est 51430
+33 326846464
www.assiettechampenoise.com

Opening hours	Closed Tuesday and Wednesday
Credit cards	Accepted
Price range	Expensive
Style	Smart casual
Cuisine	French
Recommended for	High end

"This place is off the hook. Everything was delicious, from the langoustine to the lamb. Probably one of the best dinners I've had in my life."—John Horne

LA SIRENE

Recommended by
Alexandre Gauthier

376 Rue de la Plage
Audinghen
Hauts-de-France 62179
+33 321329597
www.lasirene-capgrisnez.com

Opening hours	Closed Monday
Credit cards	Accepted but not AMEX
Price range	Affordable
Style	Casual
Cuisine	French Seafood
Recommended for	Local favorite

"Fresh fish, simply cooked, ocean view."
— Alexandre Gauthier

LA COUR DE RÉMI

Recommended by
Alexandre Gauthier

1 Rue Baillet
Bermicourt
Hauts-de-France 62130
+33 321033333
www.lacourderemi.com

Opening hours	Closed Monday
Credit cards	Accepted but not AMEX
Price range	Affordable
Style	Casual
Cuisine	French
Recommended for	Regular neighborhood

"A relaxing place in the countryside where you can escape."—Alexandre Gauthier

LE CAVEAU

Recommended by
Alexandre Gauthier

40 Place du Général de Gaulle
Montreuil
Hauts-de-France 62170
+33 321060521

Opening hours	Closed Monday
Credit cards	Accepted
Price range	Affordable
Style	Casual
Cuisine	French-Italian
Recommended for	Bargain

LE GRENOUILLERE

Recommended by
Ross Lusted,
Marc-Alexandre Mercier,
Christopher Millar,
Nicolai Nørregaard,
Michel Portos, David Posey

19 Rue de la Grenouillère
Montreuil
Hauts-de-France 62170
+33 321060722
www.lagrenouillere.fr

Opening hours	Closed Monday, Tuesday, and Wednesday
Credit cards	Accepted
Price range	Expensive
Style	Smart casual
Cuisine	Modern French
Recommended for	Worth the travel

"Very special and unique cuisine. Great taste and totally standout food. Alex is indeed a special character in the world of gastronomy. Just amazing."
—Nicolai Nørregaard

The Auberge de la Grenouillère opened in 1920 in the pretty village of Montreuil-sur-Mer, a few miles from Le Touquet. It once specialized in dishes involving frogs but, at least since 2003—when chef Alexandre Gauthier (then aged just twenty-three)

took over the kitchen from his father—the cuisine has ranged far wider. Gauthier's cooking is bold and vigorous: Norway lobster comes to the table on a bed of still-smoking juniper twigs; morel mushrooms are stuffed with sweetbreads and then covered in tiny cones of raw turnip; a white chocolate and potato shell, once broken into, reveals a sticky center of strawberry compote. One of the best restaurants in this part of France.

LA SENNE

Recommended by
Guy Savoy

4 Quai Maximin LicciardiSete
Hérault 34200
+33 9 67 53 01 91

Opening hours	Closed Sunday to Tuesday
Credit cards	Accepted but not AMEX or Diners
Price range	Affordable
Style	Smart casual
Cuisine	Seafood
Recommended for	Bargain

"For all the fish."—Guy Savoy

PARIS: SEE PAGES 548-569

SAQUANA

Recommended by
Alexander Mayer

22 Place Hamelin
Honfleur
Normandy 14600
+33 231894080
www.alexandre-bourdas.com

Opening hours	Closed Monday, Tuesday, and Wednesday
Credit cards	Accepted
Price range	Expensive
Style	Casual
Cuisine	French
Recommended for	Worth the travel

CHÂTEAU DE BRINDOS

Recommended by
Xabier Diez Esteibar

1 Allée du Château
Anglet
Nouvelle-Aquitaine 64600
+33 559238980
www.chateaudebrindos.com

Opening hours	Open 7 days
Credit cards	Accepted
Price range	Affordable
Style	Smart casual
Cuisine	French
Recommended for	Worth the travel

CHEZ ALBERT

Recommended by
Niall McKenna

51 Bis Allée Port des Pêcheurs
Biarritz
Nouvelle-Aquitaine 64200
+33 559244384
www.chezalbert.fr

Opening hours	Closed Wednesday
Credit cards	Accepted
Price range	Affordable
Style	Casual
Cuisine	French
Recommended for	Worth the travel

"Overlooking the small port in Biarritz—a great spot to relax over a bottle of wine with lots of fresh fish and shellfish."—Niall McKenna

RELAIS DE LA POSTE

Recommended by
Julien Duboué

24 Avenue de Maremne
Magescq
Nouvelle-Aquitaine 40140
+33 558477025
www.relaisposte.com

Opening hours	Closed Monday and Tuesday
Credit cards	Accepted
Price range	Expensive
Style	Smart casual
Cuisine	Modern French
Recommended for	Local favorite

"I go back every time I go down south to rediscover the authentic flavors of the land. I love it"
—Julien Duboué

L'AUBERGE DU VIEUX PUITS

Recommended by
Paul Pairet

5 Avenue Saint Victor
Fontjoncouse
Occitanie 11360
+33 468440737
www.aubergeduvieuxpuits.fr

Opening hours	Closed Monday and Tuesday
Credit cards	Accepted
Price range	Expensive
Style	Smart casual
Cuisine	French
Recommended for	Worth the travel

The cuisine of Gilles Goujon, son of a fighter pilot, is rated three stars by Michelin and therefore "worth a special journey". Satnav (GPS) is essential when making this pilgrimage. The sleepy Languedoc hamlet of Fontjoncouse is populated by fewer than a hundred—including some of the restaurant's sixteen chefs. Dishes are beautiful tableaux: from lightly poached oyster with a smoky "pearl" that must be broken with a miniature hammer, to a vol-au-vent of rabbit's kidney, and an assiette of five types of tomato. Considering the location, it is advisable to book one of the pretty rooms by the pool. The freshly baked breakfast arrives in a basket.

BRAS

Recommended by
Kyle Connaughton, Matthew Gaudet,
Analiese Gregory, John Horne,
Dylan Jones & Duangporn Songvisava,
Alexander Mayer, David Posey,
Ana Roš, Julien Royer,
Norman Van Aken, Alla Wolf-Tasker

Route de l'Aubrac
Laguiole
Occitanie 12210
+33 565511820
www.bras.fr

Opening hours	Closed Monday and Tuesday
Credit cards	Accepted
Price range	Expensive
Style	Smart casual
Cuisine	French
Recommended for	Wish I'd opened

"Bras is unique in the world and was so ahead of his time. It remains today the most inspiring restaurant ever."—Julien Royer

LE PUITS SAINT-JACQUES

Recommended by
Guillaume Galliot

57 Avenue Victor Capoul
Pujaudran
Occitanie 32600
+33 562074111
www.lepuitssaintjacques.fr

Opening hours	Closed Monday and Tuesday
Credit cards	Accepted
Price range	Affordable
Style	Smart casual
Cuisine	French
Recommended for	High end

LE PARC

Recommended by
Guillaume Galliot

Domaine les Crayères
64 Boulevard Henry Vasnier
Reims
Occitanie 51100
+33 326249000
www.lescrayeres.com

Opening hours	Closed Monday and Tuesday
Credit cards	Accepted
Price range	Expensive
Style	Smart casual
Cuisine	Modern French
Recommended for	High end

LA MARINE

Recommended by
Peeter Pihel

5 Rue Marie Lemonnier
Noirmoutier en Ile
Pays de la Loire 85330
+33 251392309
www.alexandrecouillon.com

Opening hours	Closed Tuesday, Wednesday, and Sunday
Credit cards	Accepted
Price range	Expensive
Style	Casual
Cuisine	French-Seafood
Recommended for	Worth the travel

"They follow the seasons and combine flavors from the sea, the land, the woods, grasses, grains, plants, and smoke."— Peeter Pihel

EDEN-ROC GRILL

Recommended by
Eric & Bruce Bromberg

Hotel du Cap-Eden-Roc
Boulevard J F Kennedy 29
Antibes
Provence-Alpes-Côte d'Azur 06601
+33 493615663
www.hotel-du-cap-eden-roc.com

Opening hours	Open 7 days
Credit cards	Accepted
Price range	Expensive
Style	Formal
Cuisine	French-Seafood
Recommended for	Worth the travel

"This is the classiest and most romantic place ever. Food is simple and perfectly executed, which it had better be for the prices that they charge. It really can't be surpassed anywhere in the world, though."
—Eric & Bruce Bromberg

LA GUERITE

Recommended by
Mauro Colagreco

Île Sainte-Marguerite
Lérins Islands
Cannes
Provence-Alpes-Côte d'Azur 6400
+33 4 93 43 49 30
www.restaurantlaguerite.com

Opening hours	Open 7 days
Credit cards	Accepted
Price range	Expensive
Style	Smart casual
Cuisine	Mediterranean
Recommended for	Local favourite

CHEZ MÉMÉ-JÉJÉ LE BARBU

Recommended by
Michel Portos

84 Boulevard Longchamp
Marseille
Provence-Alpes-Côte d'Azur 13001
+33 781022147

Opening hours	Closed Sunday
Credit cards	Accepted but not AMEX
Price range	Affordable
Style	Casual
Cuisine	French
Recommended for	Regular neighborhood

L'ALCYONE

Recommended by
Michel Portos

InterContinentale Marseille—Hotel Dieu
1 Place Daviel
Marseille
Provence-Alpes-Côte d'Azur 13002
+33 413424343
www.marseille.intercontinental.com

Opening hours	Closed Monday
Credit cards	Accepted
Price range	Expensive
Style	Formal
Cuisine	Seafood
Recommended for	Breakfast

"For its excellent breakfast, its location, and its terrace on a fine day."—Michel Portos

LA VILLA MADIE

Avenue de Revestel-anse de Corton
Marseille
Provence-Alpes-Côte d'Azur 13260
+33 496180000
www.lavillamadie.com

Opening hours	Closed Monday and Tuesday
Credit cards	Accepted
Price range	Expensive
Style	Formal
Cuisine	French
Recommended for	High end

"Creativity and knowledge of Mediterranean
produce, made sublime by a chef from Normandy."
—Michel Portos

LE PETIT NICE

17 Rue des Braves
Marseille
Provence-Alpes-Côte d'Azur 13007
+33 491592592
www.passedat.fr

Opening hours	Closed Monday and Sunday
Credit cards	Accepted
Price range	Expensive
Style	Formal
Cuisine	Seafood
Recommended for	Worth the travel

"Forgotten species of fish, contrasting textures,
a combination of cooked and raw, and the use of
seaweeds to create both jelly and crisp, is what's
happening here. It's untypically French—no butter
or cream, more sea water and rock pool. This is the
most 'loyal to local' restaurant I've ever been to.
Mind blowing and three stars well deserved."
—Tania Steytler

Gérald Passedat was born in this neo-Greek villa,
purchased by his grandfather, and continues to draw
inspiration from its spectacular views of the
Mediterranean. Apt to go into a paean about the
personality of the little-known fish (the "solitary"
comber, the "flirtatious" wrasse) that form the basis
of his three-star cooking, Passedat reserves his
greatest passion for his cult take on southern
favorite *bouillabaisse*. The corner table has
impressive panoramic views—as does the terrace,
where you can swim and sip pastis, should you opt
for a night in one of the hotel's restful suites.

LE RELAIS 50

Hôtel La Résidence
18 Quai du Port
Marseille
Provence-Alpes-Côte d'Azur 13002
+33 491919122
www.hotel-residence-marseille.com

Opening hours	Closed Monday and Sunday
Credit cards	Accepted
Price range	Affordable
Style	Casual
Cuisine	Modern European
Recommended for	Regular neighborhood

"Go for its retro charm, its location in the Old Port,
and its sophisticated, reasonably priced food."
—Michel Portos

O'STOP

16 Rue Saint-Saëns
Marseille
Provence-Alpes-Côte d'Azur 13001
+33 491338534

Opening hours	Open 7 days
Credit cards	Accepted but not AMEX
Price range	Affordable
Style	Casual
Cuisine	French
Recommended for	Late night

PERON

Recommended by
Michel Portos

56 Promenade de la Corniche John Kennedy
Marseille
Provence-Alpes-Côte d'Azur 13007
+33 491521522
www.restaurant-peron.com

Opening hours	Open 7 days
Credit cards	Accepted
Price range	Expensive
Style	Smart casual
Cuisine	Modern French
Recommended for	Wish I'd opened

"A restaurant overlooking the sea, with a wonderful terrace and first-rate cooking. An institution in Marseille."—Michel Portos

This restaurant is unmissable, perched as it is on jutting rocks above the ocean. The wide seascape is the perfect complement to a very modern menu of Mediterranean fish and seafood, such as red tuna sashimi with Korean black garlic and lemon caviar, and carpaccio of scallops in citrus with a red pepper sorbet. If that's all a bit extravagant, there are still classics like catch of the day and, of course, Marseille's traditional fish soup dish, bouillabaisse, which is lovingly prepared. The indoor and outdoor eating areas are stylish and surprisingly un-chintzy, with wood panelling from floor to ceiling making it feel that you're dining on the deck of a boat.

PIZZERIA CHEZ SAUVEUR

Recommended by
Michel Portos

10 Rue d'Aubagne
Marseille
Provence-Alpes-Côte d'Azur 13001
+33 491543396
www.chezsauveur.fr

Opening hours	Closed Monday and Sunday
Credit cards	Accepted but not AMEX
Price range	Affordable
Style	Casual
Cuisine	Italian
Recommended for	Local favorite

"A local institution specializing in pizza, that opened in 1943. Warm, convivial atmosphere."—Michel Portos

RESTAURANT CHEZ MICHEL

Recommended by
Michel Portos

6 Rue des Catalans
Marseille
Provence-Alpes-Côte d'Azur 13007
+33 491523063
www.restaurant-michel-13.fr

Opening hours	Open 7 days
Credit cards	Accepted
Price range	Affordable
Style	Smart casual
Cuisine	French
Recommended for	Local favorite

"Chez Michel for its *bouillabaisse*."— Michel Portos

If you want to sample the definitive *bouillabaisse*, the classic Provençal fish stew that originated in Marseille, then look no further than this smart bistro adjacent to the old port. Check out the display of fresh fish in the boat-shaped counter, then take your seat for the main event. First comes the soup: saffron-rich poaching liquor made from whole rockfish, blitzed and sieved to remove the bones. Meanwhile, white-jacketed waiters fillet prime fish tableside and present them as a platter with saffron potatoes. Other local specialities include *bourride* (fish stew thickened with garlic mayonnaise) or grilled fresh fish of your choice.

TIEN TSIN COTIER

Recommended by
Michel Portos

3 Place Jules Verne
Marseille
Provence-Alpes-Côte d'Azur 13002
+33 491904796

Opening hours	Closed Monday
Credit cards	Accepted
Price range	Affordable
Style	Casual
Cuisine	Chinese
Recommended for	Bargain

"Same owner and staff for forty years—and always the same quality."—Michel Portos

MARCO RISTORANTE

Recommended by
Mauro Colagreco

1 Quai Laurenti
Menton
Provence-Alpes-Côte d'Azur 06500
+33 493841690

Opening hours	Closed Monday and Tuesday
Credit cards	Accepted but not Diners
Price range	Expensive
Style	Smart casual
Cuisine	Italian
Recommended for	Regular neighborhood

"Fresh seafood at Port de Garavan."
—Mauro Colagreco

MIRAZUR

Recommended by
Daniel Berlin,
Stephen Harris,
Normand Laprise,
Sasu Laukkonen,
Isaac McHale, Ana Roš,
Fernando Trocca

30 Avenue Aristide Briand
Menton
Provence-Alpes-Côte d'Azur 06500
+33 492418686
www.mirazur.fr

Opening hours	Closed Monday and Tuesday
Credit cards	Accepted
Price range	Expensive
Style	Smart casual
Cuisine	French-Italian
Recommended for	Worth the travel

"Amazing setting in the Côte D'Azur, pure flavors and friendly service."—Sasu Laukkonen

Le Mirazur overlooks the gleaming Côte d'Azur, yards (metres) from Italy's border. "Food's aromas awaken the oldest memories", believes Argentinian head chef Mauro Colagreco, who left home for France to learn the "building blocks of cuisine" with Alain Ducasse, Alain Passard, and the late Bernard Loiseau. He breathed life back into a shell that had been closed for years, sowing an edible garden in the process. Colagreco's South American heritage is evident in ingredients such as quinoa, *mate* (for macaroons), and dulce de leche, although dishes such as the deconstructed Vietnamese spring roll show his increasing interest in Asia.

SINI RESTAURANT

Recommended by
Mauro Colagreco

7 Rue des Marins
Menton
Provence-Alpes-Côte d'Azur 6500
+33 4 89 98 71 77

Opening hours	Open 7 days
Credit cards	Accepted
Price range	Affordable
Style	Casual
Cuisine	Italian
Recommended for	Bargain

LA MERENDA

Recommended by
Alexander Mayer

4 Rue Raoul Bisio
Nice
Provence-Alpes-Côte d'Azur 06300
www.lamerenda.net

Opening hours	Closed Saturday and Sunday
Reservation policy	No
Credit cards	Not accepted
Price range	Affordable
Style	Casual
Cuisine	French
Recommended for	Wish I'd opened

"A very different place, with a cool concept."
—Alexander Mayer

Cash only, no phone, closed every weekend, tiny, and quirky—La Merenda in Nice's Old Town is one of a kind. Dominique Le Stanc, who previously ran the star-studded Le Chantecler, took it over in the mid-1990s as a going concern that had been serving simple Niçoise cuisine for some twenty years. He changed very little. All the cooking is done solo from the simple, open kitchen at the back. The menu, scrawled on a blackboard, is a short selection of local classics that, depending on the time of year, might include *pâtes au pistou* (pasta with pesto), *tripes à la Niçoise,* and *tarte aux blettes* (Swiss chard tart).

LA ROSETTISSERIE

Recommended by
Joshua Lewin

8 Rue Mascoinat
Nice
Provence-Alpes-Côte d'Azur 06300
+33 493761880
www.larossettisserie.com

Opening hours	Closed Sunday
Credit cards	Accepted
Price range	Affordable
Style	Casual
Cuisine	Niçoise
Recommended for	Worth the travel

"Classic rotisserie and steakhouse with the warmest service ever, where you eat dinner in the wine cellar, which is also a cave. Maybe the best meal I've had in France. Niçoise staples like pissaladière or ratatouille and lentils come first, followed by your choice of roast and potatoes, and a little lemon tart for dessert. There's also a secret little dining room on the third floor that seats maybe twelve for a nightly tasting menu."— Joshua Lewin

LE BISTROT DE PARADOU

Recommended by
Alex Jackson

Alpilles Natural Regional Park
57 Avenue de la Vallée des Baux
Paradou
Provence-Alpes-Côte d'Azur 13520
+33 490543270

Opening hours	Closed Monday and Sunday
Credit cards	Accepted but not AMEX or Diners
Price range	Affordable
Style	Casual
Cuisine	French
Recommended for	Worth the travel

"Amazing little bistro in a beautiful part of Provençe. One of the best meals I've ever had in France. Unassuming, good value, complete lack of pretension. Delicious classic Provençal magic."—Alex Jackson

LA VAGUE D'OR

Recommended by
Peter Goossens

Résidence de la Pinède
Plage de la Bouillabaisse
Saint Tropez
Provence-Alpes-Côte d'Azur 83990
+33 494559100
www.vaguedor.com

Opening hours	Open 7 days
Credit cards	Accepted
Price range	Expensive
Style	Smart casual
Cuisine	French-Mediterranean
Recommended for	Worth the travel

"Outstanding kitchen, excellent service and ambiance."—Peter Goossens

LES BACCHANALES

Recommended by
Paul Cunningham

247 Avenue de Provence
Vence
Provence-Alpes-Côte d'Azur 06140
+33 493241919
www.lesbacchanales.com

Opening hours	Closed Tuesday and Wednesday
Credit cards	Accepted but not Diners
Price range	Affordable
Style	Smart casual
Cuisine	Modern French
Recommended for	Worth the travel

JOËL ROBUCHON

Recommended by
Alexis Gauthier

4 Avenue de la Madone
Monte Carlo
Monaco 98000
+377 93151510
www.joel-robuchon.com

Opening hours	Closed Wednesday
Credit cards	Accepted
Price range	Expensive
Style	Formal
Cuisine	Mediterranean
Recommended for	Worth the travel

LE LOUIS XV

Hôtel de Paris
Place du Casino
Monte Carlo
Monaco 98000
+377 98068864
www.alain-ducasse.com

Opening hours	Closed Tuesday and Wednesday
Credit cards	Accepted
Price range	Expensive
Style	Formal
Cuisine	French
Recommended for	High end

**"From the way you are put at ease when you walk through the front door, to the menu, and the food—it's the whole package in a restaurant."
—Ben Greeno**

The ultimate expression of Monégasque glamour, Le Louis XV, an opulent Versailles grand siècle-inspired palace of pleasure which opened in 1987, is perhaps the greatest achievement and defining project of Alain Ducasse's star-studded career. Leaving aside the swan-like service, a dining room in which Marie Antoinette would have felt at home, the gilded handbag stools, the bespoke crockery and silverware, the 400,000-bottle cellar, and a mineral water list longer than the average bistro's carte du vin, it's the quality of Riviera-led cooking (which takes the very best from sea, garden, and farm) that remains at its luxurious heart.

MONTE-CARLO BAY HOTEL

40 Avenue Princesse-Grace
Monte Carlo
Monaco 98000
+377 98060360
www.montecarlobay.com

Opening hours	Open 7 days
Credit cards	Accepted
Price range	Expensive
Style	Formal
Cuisine	Modern
Recommended for	Breakfast

"I like to go on Sundays for the special brunch they do."—Mauro Colagreco

PARIS

1ER—8ÈME

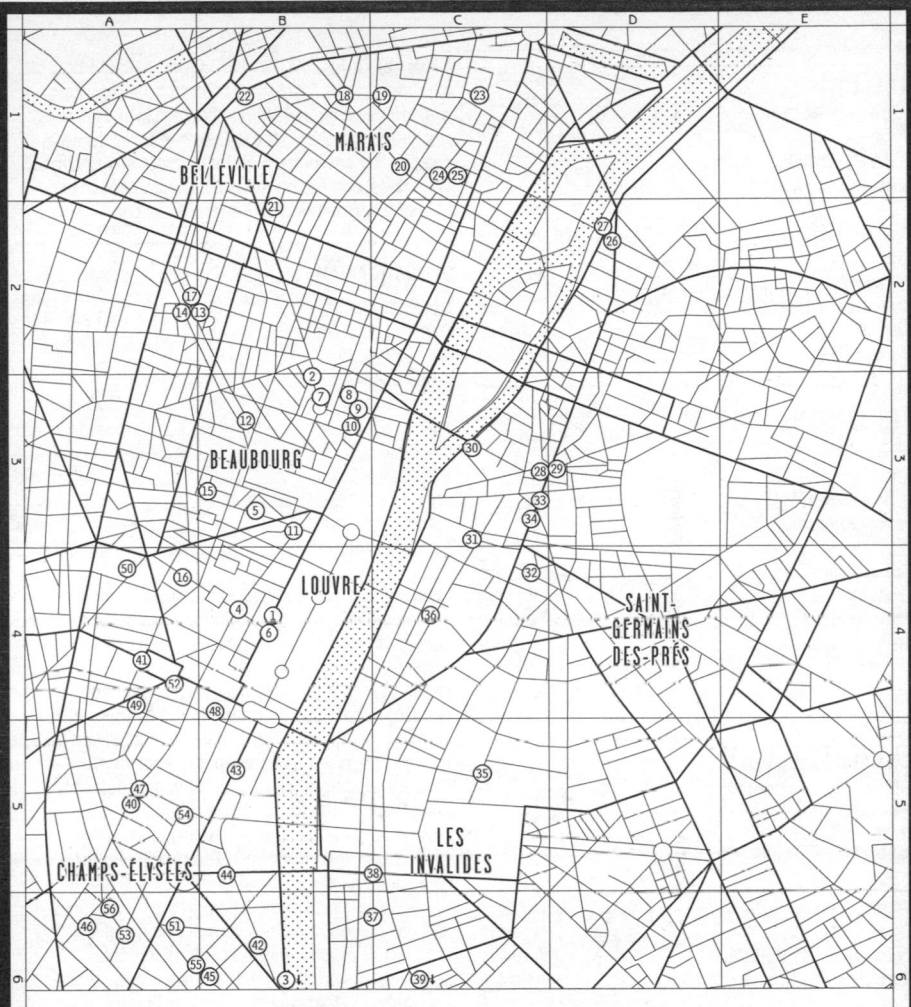

MARAIS

BELLEVILLE

BEAUBOURG

LOUVRE

SAINT-
GERMAINS
DES-PRÉS

LES
INVALIDES

CHAMPS-ÉLYSÉES

PARIS
1er–8e

SCALE

0   300   600   900   yd.

ANGELINA

Recommended by
Christophe Michalak

226 Rue de Rivoli
Paris 1st 75001
+33 142608200
www.angelina-paris.fr

Opening hours	Open 7 days
Credit cards	Accepted
Price range	Affordable
Style	Casual
Cuisine	French
Recommended for	Breakfast

LES ARTIZANS

Recommended by
Julien Duboué

30 Rue de Montorgueil
Paris 1st 75001
+33 140284474
www.lesartizans.fr

Opening hours	Open 7 days
Credit cards	Accepted but not AMEX
Price range	Affordable
Style	Casual
Cuisine	French Bistro
Recommended for	Regular neighborhood

LE CAFÉ DE L'HOMME

Recommended by
Guy Savoy

17 Place du Trocadéro
Paris 1st 75016
+33 144053015
www.cafedelhomme.comI

Opening hours	Open 7 days
Credit cards	Accepted
Price range	Affordable
Style	Smart Casual
Cuisine	Contemporary Brasserie
Recommended for	Regular neighborhood

LE CASTIGLIONE CAFÉ

Recommended by
Ruairí de Blacam

235 Rue Saint-Honoré
Paris 1st 75001
+33 142606822
www.lecastiglione.com

Opening hours	Open 7 days
Credit cards	Accepted
Price range	Affordable
Style	Smart casual
Cuisine	Café
Recommended for	Breakfast

"This café is just off Place Vendome, so it can be a bit touristy, and the fashionistas like to be seen sitting outside smoking and sipping cappuccinos. However, it's quieter before 8.00 a.m., when you can sit up at the counter and enjoy a perfect omelette with coffee, croissants, and freshly speezed orange juice in very pleasant surroundings."—Ruairí de Blacam

KUNITORAYA II

Recommended by
Sven Chartier,
Simone Tondo

5 Rue Villedo
Paris 1st 75001
+33 147030774
www.kunitoraya.com

Opening hours	Closed Monday
Credit cards	Accepted but not AMEX
Price range	Affordable
Style	Casual
Cuisine	Japanese
Recommended for	Regular neighborhood

"For the diversity and quality of Japanese food available. The room is beautiful and classic and the service is professional but warm."—Simone Tondo

In the mid-nineties Japanese chef Masafumi Nomoto introduced Parisians to the delights of slurping cheap, fat udon noodles in his packed out, no-reservations canteen, Kunitoraya. Now that there's another branch—Nomoto took over Chez Pauline, the famous ex-haut lieu of Burgundy cuisine across the street—the original has been re-christened Kunitoraya 1. The noodle, hot or cold, remains the star, but in this unlikely decor of imposing 1900s brasserie mirrors, wall clocks, and dark wood paneling you will find excellent tempura or *onigiri*. In the evenings the chef sends out his small-plate feast of sashimi, whelks, and leeks in miso sauce or grated radish with broad (fava) beans.

LE MEURICE

Recommended by
Massimiliano Alajmo

Hôtel Le Meurice
228 Rue de Rivoli
Paris 1st 75001
+33 144581055
www.alainducasse-meurice.com

Opening hours	Open 7 days
Credit cards	Accepted
Price range	Expensive
Style	Formal
Cuisine	French
Recommended for	High end

"Elegance, sophistication, and style."
—Massimiliano Alajmo

AU PIED DE COCHON

Recommended by
Eric & Bruce Bromberg,
Reid Henninger,
John Jackson,
Greg Marchand

6 Rue Coquillière
Paris 1st 75001
+33 140137700
www.pieddecochon.com

Opening hours...Open 7 days
Credit cards...Accepted
Price range...Affordable
Style...Casual
Cuisine...French
Recommended for.............................Worth the travel

"This is basically the coolest brasserie in the world.
Our dad used to take us there when we were kids.
Upon arrival in Paris, it's always been the go-to spot
for every trip over the last thirty years. Classic, beautiful,
well-prepared food."—Eric & Bruce Bromberg

LA POULE AU POT

Recommended by
Antonin Mousseau-Rivard,
Sami Tamimi

9 Rue Vauvilliers
Paris 1st 75001
+33 142363296
www.lapouleaupot.com

Opening hours..Closed Monday
Credit cards......................Accepted but not AMEX
Price range...Affordable
Style...Casual
Cuisine...French
Recommended for...Late night

"This traditional French restaurant is open until
5.00 a.m. every morning. The food is classic and
so delicious. It's noisy, has attitude, and a bohemian
atmosphere—it's exactly what you want from the
city of lights."—Sami Tamimi

SPRING

Recommended by
James Rigato

6 Rue Bailleul
Paris 1st 75001
+33 145960572
www.springparis.fr

Opening hours.....................Closed Monday and Sunday
Credit cards.................Accepted but not AMEX or Diners
Price range..Expensive
Style..Smart casual
Cuisine...French
Recommended for.............................Worth the travel

YAM'TCHA

Recommended by
Georgy Troyan

121 Rue Saint Honoré
Paris 1st 75001
+33 140260807
www.yamtcha.com

Opening hours......................Closed Sunday to Tuesday
Credit cards.................Accepted but not AMEX or Diners
Price range..Expensive
Style...Casual
Cuisine...French-Asian
Recommended for.............................Worth the travel

Adeline Grattard spent three years with Pascal Barbot
at L'Astrance, and three in restaurants in China. In
2009 she pitched her twenty-cover, verging-on-
austere restaurant perfectly, as Paris moved on from
traditional French high-end formality and woke up to
post-sushi Asian diversity and refinement. With her
husband Chi Wan, cooking from a minuscule open
kitchen, she offers just one service an evening. Like a
sommelier, Chi Wan matches his teas (there's a wine
list too) to Grattard's breathtakingly sensual cooking
—Challans duck, eggplants (aubergines) *à la
sichuanaise*, cockles sautéed with black soya.

ZEN

Recommended by
Yannick Alléno

8 Rue de L'Echelle
Paris 1st 75001
+33 142619399
www.restaurantzenparis.fr

Opening hours...Open 7 days
Credit cards......................Accepted but not AMEX
Price range..Budget
Style...Casual
Cuisine...Japanese
Recommended for..........................Regular neighborhood

CHEZ GEORGES

Recommended by
Tom Harris,
Jon Rotheram

1 Rue du Mail
Paris 2nd 75002
+33 142600711

Opening hours......................Closed Saturday and Sunday
Credit cards......................Accepted but not AMEX
Price range...Affordable
Style...Casual
Cuisine...French Bistro
Recommended for.............................Worth the travel

"A Parisian brasserie doing the classics—grilled lamb
kidneys, veal sweetbreads and morelles, *andouillettes*,
and rum baba. A real feel of Paris."—Jon Rotheram

FRENCHIE
5 Rue du Nil
Paris 2nd 75002
+33 140399619
www.frenchie-restaurant.com

Opening hours	Closed Saturday and Sunday
Credit cards	Accepted
Price range	Affordable
Style	Smart casual
Cuisine	French
Recommended for	Worth the travel

The Nantes-born chef Gregory Marchand acquired his nickname while working at Jamie Oliver's Fifteen restaurant in London: "Hey, Frenchie". The name stuck, and when he opened his own restaurant in Paris in 2009, it seemed a fitting title. Before long, the place had made a name for itself as an excellent neighborhood bistro-style restaurant, and since then, it's been next to impossible to get a table (you'll have more success going for lunch). The tiny space is decorated in the down-to-earth style that has become synonymous with low-key Parisian dining—exposed brickwork, oversized chalkboards, and nonchalant art on the walls. It's perfect for an intimate date—the food has the panache to make a Parisian proud.

FRENCHIE TO GO
9 Rue du Nil
Paris 2nd 75002
+33 140262343
www.frenchietogo.com

Opening hours	Open 7 days
Reservation policy	No
Credit cards	Accepted
Price range	Affordable
Style	Casual
Cuisine	French
Recommended for	Regular neighborhood

"Frenchie To Go for a good blowout."
—Christophe Michalak

MICHI
58 Bis Rue Sainte-Anne
Paris 2nd 75002
+33 140204993

Opening hours	Closed Monday
Credit cards	Accepted but not AMEX or Diners
Price range	Budget
Style	Casual
Cuisine	Japanese
Recommended for	Regular neighborhood

PUR'—JEAN-FRANÇOIS ROUQUETTE
Hôtel Park Hyatt Paris-Vendôme
5 Rue de la Paix
Paris 2nd 75002
+33 158711060
www.paris-restaurant-pur.fr

Opening hours	Open 7 days
Credit cards	Accepted
Price range	Expensive
Style	Formal
Cuisine	Modern French
Recommended for	Worth the travel

"Each course was impecable and the entire kitchen interacted with us and explained the philosophy and elements of each course."—Chantel Dartnall

LATARTE
5 Rue de Damiette
Paris 2nd 75002
+33 973533782
www.latarte.fr

Opening hours	Closed Saturday and Sunday
Reservation policy	No
Credit cards	Accepted but not AMEX
Price range	Affordable
Style	Casual
Cuisine	Breakfast-Brunch
Recommended for	Breakfast

"They only bake a limited number of tarts, cakes, and small desserts each day. Simple but delicious."
—Joaquin Soriano

CANDELARIA

Recommended by
Beau Clugston

52 Rue de Saintonge
Paris 3rd 75003
+33 142744128
www.quixotic-projects.com/venue/candelaria

Opening hours...Open 7 days
Reservation policy...No
Credit cards..Accepted but not AMEX
Price range..Budget
Style..Casual
Cuisine...Mexican
Recommended for..Late night

"Simple no frills tacos and nice cocktails. And you're
bound to run into people you know."—Beau Clugston

LE MARY CELESTE

Recommended by
Roberta Sudbrack

1 Rue Commines
Paris 3rd 75003
+33 142779837
www.quixotic-projects.com/venue/mary-celeste

Opening hours..Open 7 days
Credit cards........................Accepted but not AMEX or Diners
Price range..Budget
Style..Casual
Cuisine...Bar-French
Recommended for..Wish I'd opened

"A cocktail bar with divine food!"—Roberta Sudbrack

ROBERT ET LOUISE

Recommended by
Katrina Jazayeri

64 Rue Vieille du Temple
Paris 3rd 75003
+33 142785589
www.robertetlouise.com

Opening hours...Closed Monday
Credit cards........................Accepted but not AMEX or Diners
Price range..Budget
Style..Casual
Cuisine..French Steakhouse
Recommended for...Worth the travel

"There is a small wood-burning fireplace at one end
of the restaurant where most of the food is cooked,
a curving bar along one side where one or both of the
owners can be found, and small pots of Dijon mustard
sit on each table."—Katrina Jazayeri

SONG HENG

Recommended by
Tatiana Levha

3 Rue Volta
Paris 3rd 75003
+33 142783170

Opening hours...Closed Sunday
Reservation policy...No
Credit cards...Not accepted
Price range..Budget
Style..Casual
Cuisine..Vietnamese-Thai
Recommended for..Breakfast

"A very small place where you can have a Vietnamese
pho with lots of chile from 11.00 a.m. For me, the best
beef pho in Paris!"—Tatiana Levha

UMAMI MATCHA CAFÉ

Recommended by
Christophe Michalak

22 Rue Béranger
Paris 3rd 75003
+33 148040602
www.umamiparis.com

Opening hours...Closed Monday
Credit cards...Accepted
Price range..Affordable
Style..Casual
Cuisine..French-Japanese
Recommended for..Wish I'd opened

L'AMBROISIE

Recommended by
Matthew Kirkley,
Wahjudi Rahardja

9 Place des Vosges
Paris 4th 75004
+33 142785145
www.ambroisie-paris.com

Opening hours...............................Closed Monday and Sunday
Credit cards..Accepted but not AMEX
Price range..Expensive
Style...Formal
Cuisine..French
Recommended for...High end

"I still believe this is the best restaurant in the world.
Perfect cooking. Worth it at any price."
—Matthew Kirkley

L'AS DU FALLAFEL

Recommended by
Joel Braham

34 Rue des Rosiers
Paris 4th 75004
+33 148876360

Opening hours	Closed Saturday
Reservation policy	No
Credit cards	Accepted but not AMEX
Price range	Affordable
Style	Casual
Cuisine	Israeli
Recommended for	Late night

MIZNON

Recommended by
Alexandre Gauthier

22 Rue des Ecouffes
Paris 4th 75004
+33 142748358

Opening hours	Closed Saturday
Credit cards	Accepted but not Diners
Price range	Affordable
Style	Casual
Cuisine	Israeli
Recommended for	Bargain

RESTAURANT A.T

Recommended by
Anatoly Komm,
Antonin Mousseau-Rivard

4 Bis Rue du Cardinal Lemoine
Paris 5th 75005
+33 156819408
www.atsushitanaka.com

Opening hours	Closed Monday and Sunday
Credit cards	Accepted
Price range	Affordable
Style	Smart casual
Cuisine	Modern French
Recommended for	Worth the travel

"Exceptional in every way!"—Anatoly Komm

TOUR D'ARGENT

Recommended by
Antonin Mousseau-Rivard

15 Quai de la Tournelle
Paris 5th 75005
+33 143542331
www.tourdargent.com

Opening hours	Closed Monday and Sunday
Credit cards	Accepted
Price range	Expensive
Style	Formal
Cuisine	Modern French
Recommended for	High end

"It's the perfect place to spend a lot of money, and I mean a lot. With an average of €150 ($170; £130) per plate, you can turn your well-earned money into a storm of palate pleasure!"—Antonin Mousseau-Rivard

L'AVANT COMPTOIR

Recommended by
Norman Van Aken

Hôtel Relais Saint-Germain
3 Carrefour de l'Odéon
Paris 6th 75006
+33 144270797
www.hotel-paris-relais-saint-germain.com

Opening hours	Open 7 days
Reservation policy	No
Credit cards	Accepted but not AMEX
Price range	Budget
Style	Casual
Cuisine	Small plates
Recommended for	Wish I'd opened

"We were introduced to this place by a very 'in the know' woman who runs a Paris food-tour business. It's the kind of place you will hang out with local eaters, chefs, winemakers, and more. I have not enjoyed a Paris spot like this one since the first time we ate at L'Ami Louis, yet with prices far below."
—Norman Van Aken

LE RELAIS SAINT GERMAIN

Recommended by
Johan Agrell,
Alexandre Gauthier,
Greg Marchand,
Larry McGuire

Hôtel Relais Saint-Germain
9 Carrefour de l'Odéon
Paris 6th 75006
+33 144270797
www.hotel-paris-relais-saint-germain.com

Opening hours	Open 7 days
Credit cards	Accepted
Price range	Affordable
Style	Casual
Cuisine	French Bistro
Recommended for	Local favorite

"A bistro that is always very reliable, with a style all its own. Yves Camdeborde offers generous gourmet cooking and a superb wine list—all without a hint of pretension."—Greg Marchand

Yves Camdeborde is one of the founding fathers of *la bistronomie*, the movement that dismissed starry codes in favor of simple bistro cuisine made gastronomic. Camdeborde's Comptoir has been a Basque trailblazer of all things pig and has not emptied since the day it opened. Such is Camdeborde's fame and reputation, you'll be hard pushed to get a table. But he has thoughtfully opened a hotel on one side—where you can stay and wait a day or two to pounce—and the great Avant Comptoir, a small-plate and tapas stand-up counter, on the other, if you're happy to go shoulder to shoulder.

GUY SAVOY

Recommended by
Lucio Galletto,
Eric Ripert

Monnaie de Paris
11 Quai de Conti
Paris 6th 75006
+33 143804061
www.guysavoy.com

Opening hours	Closed Monday and Sunday
Credit cards	Accepted
Price range	Expensive
Style	Formal
Cuisine	French
Recommended for	High end

"The most amazing, complete package of food, wine, ambience, and incredible service that makes you feel like you are the only customers in the restaurant. Incomparable."—Lucio Galletto

Just like Pierre Gagnaire and Joël Robuchon, Guy Savoy has grown a global empire, spreading as far as Las Vegas and Singapore, from this intimate three-Michelin-starred restaurant where the service is ultra-personalized from the minute the client opens the door. Elsewhere in Paris, three modern bistros/brasseries—Le Chiberta, Les Bouquinistes, and L'Atelier Maître Albert—serve simpler versions of Savoy's classicism, but his artichoke soup with black truffles and parmesan, served with a mushroom brioche and black truffle butter, remains one of France's most celebrated dishes. Chefs return again and again to soak up the Savoy magic and inspiration.

LADURÉE BONAPARTE

Recommended by
Alexander Mayer

21 Rue Bonaparte
Paris 6th 75006
+33 144076487
www.laduree.com

Opening hours	Open 7 days
Credit cards	Accepted but not AMEX or Diners
Price range	Affordable
Style	Casual
Cuisine	French
Recommended for	Breakfast

AUX PRÉS—CYRIL LIGNAC

Recommended by
Alexandre Gauthier

27 Rue du Dragon
Paris 6th 75006
+33 145482968
www.restaurantauxpres.com

Opening hours	Open 7 days
Credit cards	Accepted
Price range	Affordable
Style	Smart casual
Cuisine	French
Recommended for	Late night

HUITRERIE REGIS

Recommended by
Isaac Toups

3 Rue de Montfaucon
Paris 6th 75006
+33 144411007
www.huitrerieregis.com

Opening hours	Open 7 days
Reservation policy	No
Credit cards	Accepted but not AMEX or Diners
Price range	Affordable
Style	Smart casual
Cuisine	French
Recommended for	Worth the travel

"I dream of their oysters."— Isaac Toups

TSUKIZI

Recommended by
Sven Chartier

2 Bis Rue des Ciseaux
Paris 6th 75006
+33 143546519

Opening hours	Closed Monday and Sunday
Credit cards	Accepted but not AMEX or Diners
Price range	Budget
Style	Casual
Cuisine	Japanese
Recommended for	Regular neighborhood

"Classic and unpretentious sushi."—Sven Chartier

L'ARPÈGE

84 Rue de Varenne
Paris 7th 75007
+33 147050906
www.alain-passard.com

Recommended by
Andrew Carmellini, Beau Clugston,
Richard Corrigan,
Helene Darroze, Matthew Gaudet,
Bertrand Grébaut, Christophe Hardiquest,
Stephen Harris, Tatiana Levha,
Josue Lopez, Vaughan Mabee,
Greg Marchand, Morgan McGlone,
Paul Pairet, Peeter Pihel, Dave Pynt, Chris Salans,
Stephen Toman, Simone Tondo, Jordi Vila

Opening hours	Closed Saturday and Sunday
Credit cards	Accepted
Price range	Expensive
Style	Formal
Cuisine	French
Recommended for	High end

"The fact Passard almost single-handedly adapted French cuisine to one purely based on vegetables is a profound concept and reflects in the cuisine he is able to produce today. Ever the showman and story teller, it is a meal I will always remember. A truly captivating experience."—Josue Lopez

In 2001, Alain Passard raised an eyebrow or two among his countrymen when he took red meat off the menu at L'Arpège, pledging instead to explore the virtues of veg. Michelin didn't seem to mind. Chef Passard kept his trio of stars, bought a kitchen garden 140 miles (230 km) outside Paris and now ferries his organic harvest to the city early each morning to grace plates in the hushed dining room the same afternoon. There's flesh too (the duck is particularly fine) and the much-imitated "hot-cold egg". It all comes at a three-star price, so it's worth noting that the lunch tasting menu, at less than half the price of the evening menu, is more affordable.

L'ATELIER DE JOËL ROBUCHON

Hôtel du Pont Royal
5 Rue Montalembert
Paris 7th 75007
+33 142225656
www. atelier-robuchon-saint-germain.com

Recommended by
Ivo Adam,
Christophe Michalak,
Emmanuel Renaut,
Jordi Roca, Fabio Rossi

Opening hours	Open 7 days
Credit cards	Accepted
Price range	Expensive
Style	Smart casual
Cuisine	French
Recommended for	Wish I'd opened

"I fell in love with this place on my first visit. I've now eaten there twice and each time was perfect. Fine flavors and succulent dishes."—Fabio Rossi

The Asian-feel, small-plate, chef-gawking counter that Robuchon created in 2003 conquered a sceptical Paris clientele. L'Atelier's door opens from the inside out, meaning staff control entry, and its booking system is a pain, but, once inside its black lacquer cocoon with the brigade busy making five-bite morsels, all's well. No wonder the Ateliers took off—the menu allows clients a bit of luxurious everything. About twenty tasting plates on one side; on the other, larger mains and desserts. After the foie gras-stuffed quail with truffled mashed potato, sweetbreads with bay and rosemary, the *chocolat tendance*—an Araguani chocolate ganache with cocoa-nib ice cream and Oreo cookies—is a no-brainer.

CHEZ L'AMI JEAN

27 Rue Malar
Paris 7th 75007
+33 147058689
www.lamijean.fr

Recommended by
Julien Duboué,
Matthew Gaudet

Opening hours	Closed Monday and Sunday
Credit cards	Accepted but not AMEX or Diners
Price range	Affordable
Style	Casual
Cuisine	French Bistro
Recommended for	Worth the travel

DAVID TOUTAIN

29 Rue Surcouf
Paris 7th 75007
+33 145501110
www.davidtoutain.com

Recommended by
Julien Royer

Opening hours	Closed Saturday and Sunday
Credit cards	Accepted but not Diners
Price range	Expensive
Style	Smart casual
Cuisine	French
Recommended for	Worth the travel

LE JULES VERNE

2ème étage Eiffel Tower
Avenue Gustave Eiffel
Paris 7th 75007
+33 145556144
www.lejulesverne-paris.com

Recommended by
Shaun Rankin

Opening hours	Open 7 days
Credit cards	Accepted
Price range	Expensive
Style	Formal
Cuisine	Modern French
Recommended for	High end

"This restaurant offers exceptional cuisine by a master of the trade. It's a really special experience at an iconic location. You can't beat the view."—Shaun Rankin

LE 114 FAUBOURG

Recommended by
Peter Goossens

Hôtel Le Bristol
114 Rue du Faubourg Saint-Honoré
Paris 8th 75008
+33 153434444
www.lebristolparis.com

Opening hours	Open 7 days
Credit cards	Accepted
Price range	Expensive
Style	Smart casual
Cuisine	Modern French
Recommended for	High end

AKRAME

Recommended by
Christophe Michalak,
Georgy Troyan

7 Rue Tronchet
Paris 8th 75008
+33 140671116
www.akrame.com

Opening hours	Closed Saturday and Sunday
Credit cards	Accepted
Price range	Expensive
Style	Smart casual
Cuisine	French
Recommended for	Regular neighborhood

"Chef Akrame Benallal's cuisine is modern and simple."—Christophe Michalak

ALAIN DUCASSE AU PLAZA ATHÉNÉE

Recommended by
Riccardo Camanini,
Konstantin Filippou,
Ramón Freixa,
Guillaume Galliot,
Peter Goossens,
Christophe Michalak,
Davide Oldani, Paul Pairet

25 Avenue Montaigne
Paris 8th 75008
+33 153676500
www.alainducasse-plazaathenee.com

Opening hours	Closed Saturday and Sunday
Credit cards	Accepted
Price range	Expensive
Style	Formal
Cuisine	French
Recommended for	High end

"Innovation and sheer brilliance."—Davide Oldani

ALLÉNO PARIS AU PAVILLON LEDOYEN

Recommended by
Daniel Humm,
Paul Pairet,
Luigi Taglienti

8 Avenue Dutuit
Paris 8th 75008
+33 153051000
www.pavillon-ledoyen.fr

Opening hours	Closed Sunday
Credit cards	Accepted
Price range	Expensive
Style	Formal
Cuisine	French
Recommended for	High end

"Yannick is one of the most talented French chefs in the world."—Daniel Humm

LE CLARENCE

Recommended by
Jason Bond

Hôtel Dillon
31 Avenue Franklin D. Roosevelt
Paris 8th 75008
+33 182821010
www.le-clarence.paris/dillon-hotel

Opening hours	Closed Monday and Sunday
Credit cards	Accepted
Price range	Expensive
Style	Smart casual
Cuisine	French
Recommended for	Worth the travel

"Amazing chef Christophe Pelé and a world-class wine list in a beautiful space. Unmatched."
—Jason Bond

LE CINQ

Recommended by
Christophe Michalak

Four Seasons Hotel Georges V
31 Avenue George V
Paris 8th 75008
+33 149527000
www.fourseasons.com/paris

Opening hours	Open 7 days
Credit cards	Accepted
Price range	Expensive
Style	Formal
Cuisine	French
Recommended for	Local favorite

LA CUISINE

Le Royal Monceau
37 Avenue Hoche
Paris 8th 75008
+33 142999880
www.raffles.com/paris

Opening hours	Open 7 days
Credit cards	Accepted
Price range	Expensive
Style	Smart casual
Cuisine	French
Recommended for	Breakfast

EPICURE

112 Rue du Faubourg Saint-Honoré
Paris 8th 75008
+33 153434340
www.lebristolparis.com

Opening hours	Open 7 days
Credit cards	Accepted
Price range	Expensive
Style	Formal
Cuisine	French
Recommended for	Local favorite

"Its beautiful, elegant interior and the food, cooked to perfection, are perfect for celebrating a special day."—Tony Yoo

The grand restaurant at L'Hôtel Le Bristol, re-launched as Epicure in 2011, in the dramatically but classically refurbished garden room of the five-star luxury hotel, is the quintessential Parisian multi-Michelin-starred haute cuisine experience. Headed up by Knight of the Legion of Honour, Eric Frechon, a friend of former French president Nicolas Sarkozy, it's the place to go for the seriously luxurious ingredients synonymous with posh French nosh: think foie gras, caviar, lobster, frog's legs, and grand cru chocolate. For sheer impact, however, try the Bresse chicken *en vessie* (stuffed with truffles and cooked inside a pig's bladder).

LA FARNESINA

9 Rue Boissy D'Anglas
Paris 8th 75008
+33 142666557
www.farnesina.fr

Opening hours	Closed Sunday
Credit cards	Accepted but not Diners
Price range	Affordable
Style	Casual
Cuisine	Italian
Recommended for	Local favorite

LE GRAND RESTAURANT

7 Rue d'Aguesseau
Paris 8th 75008
+33 153050000
www.jeanfrancoispiege.com

Opening hours	Closed Saturday and Sunday
Credit cards	Accepted but not Diners
Price range	Expensive
Style	Smart casual
Cuisine	French
Recommended for	Worth the travel

"A tranquil atmosphere combined with perfect cuisine and service. It seems classical—and yet there are some surprises. A great place to eat."
—Emanuele Scarello

LAZARE

Rue Intérieure
Paris 8th 75008
+33 144908080
www.lazare-paris.fr

Opening hours	Open 7 days
Credit cards	Accepted
Price range	Affordable
Style	Casual
Cuisine	French
Recommended for	Late night

"It never fails!"—Christophe Michalak

LA MAISON DE L'AUBRAC

Recommended by
Julien Duboué

37 Rue Marbeuf
Paris 8th 75008
+33 143590514
www.maison-aubrac.com

Opening hours	Open 7 days
Credit cards	Accepted but not Diners
Price range	Affordable
Style	Casual
Cuisine	French
Recommended for	Late night

"Its wine list makes it an ideal place for whiling away the time after a meal."—Julien Duboué

PATRICK ROGER

Recommended by
Joaquin Soriano

3 Place de la Madeleine
Paris 8th 75008
+33 142652447
www.patrickroger.com

Opening hours	Open 7 days
Credit cards	Accepted but not AMEX
Price range	Expensive
Style	Casual
Cuisine	Chocolatier
Recommended for	Wish I'd opened

"Patrick Roger is a master of French chocolate. He makes enormous sculptural installations out of chocolate. His interpretations are perfect."
—Joaquin Soriano

PIERRE GAGNAIRE

Recommended by
Manoella Buffara Ramos,
Ramón Freixa,
Matthew Gaudet,
Alexandre Gauthier,
Christophe Michalak,
Joan Roca,
Willy Trullas Moreno

6 Rue Balzac
Paris 8th 75008
+33 158361250
www.pierre-gagnaire.com

Opening hours	Closed Saturday and Sunday
Credit cards	Accepted
Price range	Expensive
Style	Formal
Cuisine	Modern French
Recommended for	High end

"I go every year and I'm always astonished. The dishes are always of a high creative level."
—Ramón Freixa

RESTAURANT LE GABRIEL

Recommended by
Lori Granito

La Réserve Paris Hotel & Spa
42 Avenue Gabriel
Paris 8th 75008
+33 158366050
www.lareserve-paris.com

Opening hours	Open 7 days
Credit cards	Accepted
Price range	Expensive
Style	Formal
Cuisine	French
Recommended for	Worth the travel

"Currently two-Michelin-starred, but I suspect they'll be receiving a third once they tweak a few things on the service side. Food already at a three-star level."
—Lori Granito

LA SCÈNE

Recommended by
Christophe Michalak

Hôtel Prince de Galles
33 Avenue George V
Paris 8th 75008
+33 153237850
www.restaurant-la-scene.fr

Opening hours	Open 7 days
Credit cards	Accepted but not AMEX
Price range	Affordable
Style	Smart casual
Cuisine	French
Recommended for	High end

"Creative cooking and wonderful decor."
—Christophe Michalak

LE TAILLEVENT

Recommended by
Guillaume Galliot

15 Rue Lamennais
Paris 8th 75008
+33 144951501
www.taillevent.com

Opening hours	Closed Saturday and Sunday
Credit cards	Accepted
Price range	Expensive
Style	Formal
Cuisine	French
Recommended for	High end

"Simply prepared with honesty and pride."

HENRY HARRIS P567

"Tiny and ever so good."

CHRISTOPHE MICHALAK P565

PARIS

9ÈME—20ÈME

"IT HAS BEEN AT THE FOREFRONT OF THE PARISIAN FOOD SCENE FOREVER."

TATIANA LEVHA P569

"BEST LUNCH OF ALL TIME."

JONATHAN BROOKS P569

"A UNIQUE, ROMANTIC, AND OLD WORLD CHARM."

CHANTEL DARTNALL P562

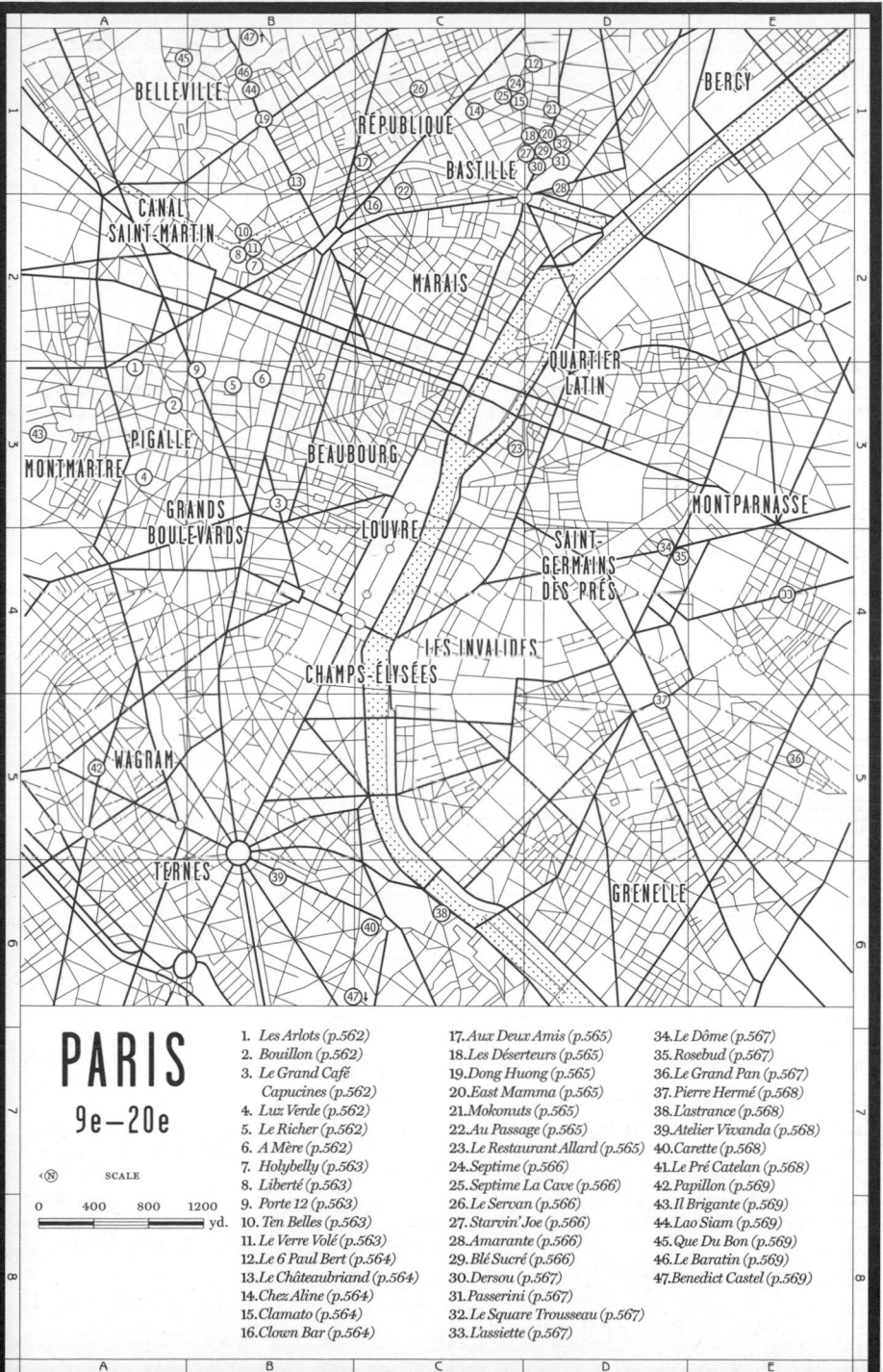

PARIS
9e–20e

1. *Les Arlots (p.562)*
2. *Bouillon (p.562)*
3. *Le Grand Café Capucines (p.562)*
4. *Luz Verde (p.562)*
5. *Le Richer (p.562)*
6. *A Mère (p.562)*
7. *Holybelly (p.563)*
8. *Liberté (p.563)*
9. *Porte 12 (p.563)*
10. *Ten Belles (p.563)*
11. *Le Verre Volé (p.563)*
12. *Le 6 Paul Bert (p.564)*
13. *Le Châteaubriand (p.564)*
14. *Chez Aline (p.564)*
15. *Clamato (p.564)*
16. *Clown Bar (p.564)*
17. *Aux Deux Amis (p.565)*
18. *Les Déserteurs (p.565)*
19. *Dong Huong (p.565)*
20. *East Mamma (p.565)*
21. *Mokonuts (p.565)*
22. *Au Passage (p.565)*
23. *Le Restaurant Allard (p.565)*
24. *Septime (p.566)*
25. *Septime La Cave (p.566)*
26. *Le Servan (p.566)*
27. *Starvin' Joe (p.566)*
28. *Amarante (p.566)*
29. *Blé Sucré (p.566)*
30. *Dersou (p.567)*
31. *Passerini (p.567)*
32. *Le Square Trousseau (p.567)*
33. *L'assiette (p.567)*
34. *Le Dôme (p.567)*
35. *Rosebud (p.567)*
36. *Le Grand Pan (p.567)*
37. *Pierre Hermé (p.568)*
38. *L'astrance (p.568)*
39. *Atelier Vivanda (p.568)*
40. *Carette (p.568)*
41. *Le Pré Catelan (p.568)*
42. *Papillon (p.569)*
43. *Il Brigante (p.569)*
44. *Lao Siam (p.569)*
45. *Que Du Bon (p.569)*
46. *Le Baratin (p.569)*
47. *Benedict Castel (p.569)*

N

SCALE

0   400   800   1200
yd.

LES ARLOTS

Recommended by
Bertrand Grébaut

136 Rue du Faubourg Poissonnière
Paris 9th 75010
+33 142829201

Opening hours	Closed Monday and Sunday
Credit cards	Accepted but not AMEX
Price range	Affordable
Style	Casual
Cuisine	French Bistro
Recommended for	Local favorite

"A bistro that excels as much in terrines and sausage with mashed potato, as it does in innovative contemporary cuisine. For me, that is what is so great about Parisian bistros these days."—Bertrand Grébaut

BOUILLON

Recommended by
Julien Duboué

47 Rue de Rochechouart
Paris 9th 75009
+33 951186659

Opening hours	Closed Monday and Sunday
Credit cards	Accepted
Price range	Affordable
Style	Casual
Cuisine	French
Recommended for	Regular neighborhood

LE GRAND CAFÉ CAPUCINES

Recommended by
Chantel Dartnall

4 Boulevard des Capucines
Paris 9th 75009
+33 143121900
www.legrandcafe.com

Opening hours	Open 7 days
Credit cards	Accepted but not Diners
Price range	Affordable
Style	Casual
Cuisine	French
Recommended for	Wish I'd opened

"It has a great location close to the Opéra Garnier, and is one of the most beautiful, classic Parisian Art Nouveau brasseries—its red velvet chairs, peacock mosaic murals, and beautiful, stained-glass ceilings give this restaurant a unique, romantic, and old world charm."—Chantel Dartnall

LUZ VERDE

Recommended by
Greg Marchand

24 Rue Henry Monnier
Paris 9th 75009
+33 170236960
www.luzverde.fr

Opening hours	Closed Monday and Sunday
Credit cards	Accepted but not AMEX or Diners
Price range	Budget
Style	Casual
Cuisine	Mexican-French
Recommended for	Regular neighborhood

"I greatly enjoy the work of Alexis Dellasaux, who used to work at Frenchie and has now opened Luz Verde to pay homage to his Mexican heritage. First-rate ceviche, tacos, and grilled meat, as well as a selection of original and delicious cocktails."—Greg Marchand

LE RICHER

Recommended by
Christophe Michalak

2 Rue Richer
Paris 9th 75009
+33 148244480
www.lericher.com

Opening hours	Open 7 days
Reservation policy	No
Credit cards	Accepted but not AMEX or Diners
Price range	Budget
Style	Casual
Cuisine	Modern Bistro
Recommended for	Regular neighborhood

"Perfect for a stylish, light lunch."
—Christophe Michalak

A MÈRE

Recommended by
Daniel Morgan

L'Échiquier
49 Rue de L'Échiquier
Paris 10th 75010
+33 148000828
www.amere.fr

Opening hours	Closed Saturday and Sunday
Credit cards	Accepted but not AMEX or Diners
Price range	Affordable
Style	Casual
Cuisine	French
Recommended for	Regular neighborhood

HOLYBELLY

Recommended by
Bertrand Grébaut,
Greg Marchand,
Simone Tondo

19 Rue Lucien Sampaix
Paris 10th 75010
+33 973601364
www.holybel.ly

Opening hours	Open 7 days
Reservation policy	No
Credit cards	Accepted but not AMEX
Price range	Affordable
Style	Casual
Cuisine	International
Recommended for	Breakfast

"It's a very informal coffee shop that serves breakfast and brunch."—Bertrand Grébaut

This narrow, elegantly tiled space along the Canal St Martin is among the most popular breakfast destinations in Paris (you'll need to arrive early and be prepared to wait in line [queue], especially for weekend brunch). But it's not croissants and croques here—on the menu is a dreamy list of Melbourne-style dishes, such as black rice porridge cooked in vanilla bean-infused coconut milk, served with puffed grains and seasonal fruit, or pancakes with fried eggs, doused in homemade bourbon butter and maple syrup. The hot drinks list is equally impressive—if you've never tried one, ask for a decidedly un-French London Fog (Earl Grey, frothy milk, and honey syrup).

LIBERTÉ

Recommended by
Julien Duboué

39 Rue des Vinaigriers
Paris 10th 75010
+33 142055176
www.libertepatisserieboulangerie.com

Opening hours	Closed Sunday
Reservation policy	No
Credit cards	Accepted but not AMEX
Price range	Budget
Style	Casual
Cuisine	Bakery
Recommended for	Breakfast

"You can eat at the bakery and watch the baker baking his bread right in front of you."—Julien Duboué

PORTE 12

Recommended by
Christophe Michalak

12 Rue Des Messageries
Paris 10th 75010
+33 142462264
www.porte12.com

Opening hours	Closed Monday and Sunday
Credit cards	Accepted but not AMEX or Diners
Price range	Affordable
Style	Smart casual
Cuisine	Modern French
Recommended for	Regular neighborhood

TEN BELLES

Recommended by
Beau Clugston

10 Rue de la Grange aux Belles
Paris 10th 75010
+33 142409078
www.tenbelles.com

Opening hours	Open 7 days
Credit cards	Accepted but not AMEX or Diners
Price range	Budget
Style	Casual
Cuisine	Café
Recommended for	Breakfast

"House-made everything, good coffee, friendly staff."
—Beau Clugston

LE VERRE VOLÉ

Recommended by
Beau Clugston,
Nicolai Nørregaard

67 Rue de Lancry
Paris 10th 75010
+33 148031734
www.leverrevole.fr

Opening hours	Open 7 days
Credit cards	Accepted but not AMEX or Diners
Price range	Affordable
Style	Casual
Cuisine	French Bistro
Recommended for	Regular neighborhood

"Natural wine and good solid bistro cooking. The perfect hangout—especially on a Sunday night."
—Nicolai Nørregaard

LE 6 PAUL BERT

6 Rue Paul Bert
Paris 11th 75011
+33 143791432
www.le6paulbert.com

Recommended by
Taras Kiriyenko

Opening hours	Closed Monday and Sunday
Credit cards	Accepted but not AMEX or Diners
Price range	Affordable
Style	Casual
Cuisine	French
Recommended for	Wish I'd opened

"Small, cosy and trendy place, serving small and modern plates."—Taras Kiriyenko

LE CHÂTEAUBRIAND

129 Avenue Parmentier
Paris 11th 75011
+33 143574595
www.lechateaubriand.net

Recommended by
Danny Bowien,
Estanislao Carenzo,
Paul Carmichael,
Ignacio Mattos,
Jair Tellez

Opening hours	Closed Monday and Sunday
Credit cards	Accepted but not AMEX or Diners
Price range	Affordable
Style	Casual
Cuisine	French
Recommended for	Worth the travel

"It was love at first sight. It feels so free and unorthodox. A truly impressive experience."
—Paul Carmichael

Sat on a sycamore-shaded avenue in Belleville, Le Chateaubriand occupies a handsome old bistro, its 1930s facade and interior largely unchanged. With its lack of airs and graces, championing of pungent natural wines, and a take-it-or-leave-it five-course fixed-price menu at dinner, there are those who don't get why it's created such a stir since opening in 2006. But that's their loss, because the cooking, which keeps things as raw and unadulterated as possible, while mixing French staples with less familiar foreign flavors, makes it clear why chef-owner Iñaki Aizpitarte has become the poster boy for the bistronomique movement.

CHEZ ALINE

85 Rue de la Roquette
Paris 11th 75011
+33 143719075

Recommended by
Tatiana Levha,
Simone Tondo

Opening hours	Closed Saturday and Sunday
Reservation policy	No
Credit cards	Accepted but not AMEX or Diners
Price range	Budget
Style	Casual
Cuisine	Café-Sandwiches
Recommended for	Bargain

"Everything is made in-house that morning, from octopus salad to roasted chicken. You can pass by this little place on a lunch break, or just to pick up a fresh sandwich—all with the cash in your pocket!"
—Simone Tondo

CLAMATO

80 Rue de Charonne
Paris 11th 75011
+33 143727453
www.septime-charonne.fr

Recommended by
Pascal Barbot, Beau Clugston,
Konstantin Filippou,
Rodolfo Guzmán, Florent Ladeyn,
Tatiana Levha, Grae Nonas,
Tim Spedding

Opening hours	Closed Monday and Tuesday
Reservation policy	No
Credit cards	Accepted
Price range	Affordable
Style	Casual
Cuisine	French-Seafood
Recommended for	Late night

"Bertrand has pulled off a wonderful tour-de-force yet again. The place is beautiful, and you would think you were miles away from Paris, even when it comes to the prices. I love it! The mussels in vin jaune—wow!"—Florent Ladeyn

CLOWN BAR

114 Rue Amelot
Paris 11th 75011
+33 143558735
www.clown-bar-paris.com

Recommended by
Sven Chartier, Daniel Morgan,
Valdimir Mukhin, Peeter Pihel,
Greg & Gabrielle Quiñónez Denton

Opening hours	Closed Monday and Tuesday
Credit cards	Accepted but not AMEX or Diners
Price range	Affordable
Style	Casual
Cuisine	French Bistro
Recommended for	Late night

While there is a certain section of Parisian society that will always spend big bucks on eating out, arguably far more exciting is what's happening at the mid-range. The bistronomie movement's latest flagship is this buzzy spot in what used to be the canteen of the Cirque d'Hiver, where the great and good of Paris's food scene gather to drink, chat, and devour stunning small plates of things like duck foie gras brioche *pithiviers* (puff pastry pies), or veal brains. The ambience is irreverent, informal, youthful, and brash—the exact opposite of the temples of gastronomy elsewhere in town, and all the better for it.

AUX DEUX AMIS

Recommended by
Florence Knight

45 Rue Oberkampf
Paris 11th 75011
+33 158303813

Opening hours	Closed Monday and Sunday
Credit cards	Accepted but not Diners
Price range	Affordable
Style	Casual
Cuisine	Spanish-International
Recommended for	Worth the travel

"Aux Deux Amis has no menu and the daily changing dishes are announced by the waiters. Food is inspirational and exceptional."—Florence Knight

LES DÉSERTEURS

Recommended by
Valdimir Mukhin

46 Rue Trousseau
Paris 11th 75011
+33 148069585

Opening hours	Closed Monday and Sunday
Credit cards	Accepted but not AMEX or Diners
Price range	Affordable
Style	Casual
Cuisine	French Bistro
Recommended for	Worth the travel

DONG HUONG

Recommended by
Iñaki Aizpitarte

16 Rue Louis Bonnet
Paris 11th 75011
+33 143382574
www.dong-huong.fr

Opening hours	Closed Tuesday
Credit cards	Accepted
Price range	Budget
Style	Casual
Cuisine	Vietnamese
Recommended for	Breakfast

EAST MAMMA

Recommended by
Christophe Michalak

133 Rue du Faubourg Saint-Antoine
Paris 11th 75011
+33 143413215
www.bigmammagroup.com

Opening hours	Open 7 days
Credit cards	Accepted but not AMEX
Price range	Affordable
Style	Casual
Cuisine	Italian
Recommended for	Bargain

MOKONUTS

Recommended by
Christophe Michalak

5 Rue Saint-Bernard
Paris 11th 75011
+33 980818285

Opening hours	Closed Saturday and Sunday
Reservation policy	No
Credit cards	Not accepted
Price range	Budget
Style	Casual
Cuisine	Café-Bakery
Recommended for	Wish I'd opened

"Tiny and ever so good."—Christophe Michalak

AU PASSAGE

Recommended by
Gary Foulkes,
Taras Kiriyenko

1 Bis Passage Saint-Sébastien
Paris 11th 75011
+33 185152274
www.restaurant-aupassage.fr

Opening hours	Closed Sunday
Credit cards	Accepted but not AMEX or Diners
Price range	Affordable
Style	Smart casual
Cuisine	Modern French
Recommended for	Worth the travel

LE RESTAURANT ALLARD

Recommended by
Guy Savoy

41 Rue Saint-André de Arts
Paris 6th 75006
+33 158002346

Opening hours	Open 7 days
Credit cards	Accepted
Price range	Expensive
Style	Smart Casual
Cuisine	French
Recommended for	Local

SEPTIME

80 Rue de Charonne
Paris 11th 75011
+33 143673829
www.septime-charonne.fr

Recommended by
Matthew Breen,
Sven Chartier, Taras Kiriyenko,
Florence Knight, James Lowe,
Valdimir Mukhin, Grae Nonas,
Ana Roš, Sami Tamimi, Georgy Troyan

Opening hours	Closed Saturday and Sunday
Credit cards	Accepted but not AMEX
Price range	Affordable
Style	Casual
Cuisine	Modern French
Recommended for	Worth the travel

"Fresh, direct cooking with bold flavors and classic
ingredients that make the meal sing."—Sami Tamimi

Rarely has a restaurant in Paris condensed and
combined so many world trends. The room is an
industrial-style loft, and the waiters are kindly, and
attentive. Chef Bernard Grébaut speaks his mind, loves
poetry, was trained by Passard, and pocketed a
Michelin star aged only twenty-seven. His gentle,
sensitive cuisine enfolds New Nordic codes in French
technique—veal with foie gras bouillon, white
asparagus, *sauce gribiche*, oysters, and flowers.
Septime is hip and hard to book but it's exhilarating
to witness the emergence of a blazing new talent.

SEPTIME LA CAVE

3 Rue Basfroi
Paris 11th 75011
+33 143671487
www.septime-charonne.fr

Recommended by
Beau Clugston

Opening hours	Open 7 days
Reservation policy	No
Credit cards	Accepted but not AMEX
Price range	Affordable
Style	Casual
Cuisine	Wine Bar
Recommended for	Wish I'd opened

LE SERVAN

32 Rue Saint-Maur
Paris 11th 75011
+33 155285182
www.leservan.com

Recommended by
Olle T. Cellton,
Alexandre Gauthier,
Bertrand Grébaut,
Jessica Koslow,
Oldřich Sahajdák

Opening hours	Closed Saturday and Sunday
Credit cards	Accepted but not AMEX
Price range	Affordable
Style	Casual
Cuisine	French-Asian
Recommended for	Worth the travel

With a CV that includes both L'Arpège and
L'Astrance, you'd expect the food cooked by sisters
Tatiana and Katia Levha to be pretty special. And
indeed it is—dishes such as fried blood sausage
wontons in bouillon, or asparagus with tandoori-
spiced *beurre blanc*, speak of a time cooking at the
very highest level and with intimate knowledge of
the finest ingredients. But this is no po-faced temple
of haute cuisine; the dining room is bright and
functional, the atmosphere informal and friendly.
And the bill is unlikely to break the bank, especially
given that the wine list includes some interesting
bottles at only around €30 ($33; £25).

STARVIN' JOE

42 Rue de Charonne
Paris 11th 75011
+33 983801719

Recommended by
Simone Tondo

Opening hours	Open 7 days
Reservation policy	No
Credit cards	Accepted but not AMEX or Diners
Price range	Budget
Style	Casual
Cuisine	Burgers
Recommended for	Bargain

AMARANTE

4 Rue Biscornet
Paris 12th 75012
+33 950809380
www.amarante.paris

Recommended by
Beau Clugston

Opening hours	Closed Wednesday and Thursday
Credit cards	Accepted but not AMEX
Price range	Affordable
Style	Casual
Cuisine	French
Recommended for	Bargain

BLÉ SUCRÉ

7 Rue Antoine Vollon
Paris 12th 75012
+33 143407773

Recommended by
James Walt

Opening hours	Closed Monday
Reservation policy	No
Credit cards	Accepted but not AMEX or Diners
Price range	Affordable
Style	Casual
Cuisine	Patisserie
Recommended for	Worth the travel

DERSOU

Recommended by
Timur Abuzyarov,
Georgy Troyan

21 Rue Saint Nicolas
Paris 12th 75012
+33 981011273
www.dersouparis.com

Opening hours	Closed Monday
Credit cards	Accepted but not Diners
Price range	Expensive
Style	Casual
Cuisine	International
Recommended for	Worth the travel

PASSERINI

Recommended by
John Winter Russell

65 Rue Traversière
Paris 12th 75012
+33 143422756
www.passerini.paris

Opening hours	Closed Monday and Sunday
Credit cards	Accepted but not AMEX or Diners
Price range	Affordable
Style	Casual
Cuisine	Italian-French
Recommended for	Worth the travel

LE SQUARE TROUSSEAU

Recommended by
Simone Tondo

1 Rue Antoine Vollon
Paris 12th 75012
+33 143430600
www.squaretrousseau.com

Opening hours	Open 7 days
Credit cards	Accepted
Price range	Affordable
Style	Casual
Cuisine	French
Recommended for	Breakfast

"The best hot chocolate in Paris."—Simone Tondo

L'ASSIETTE

Recommended by
Massimiliano Alajmo,
Ruairí de Blacam,
Linton Hopkins,
Kristen D. Murray

181 Rue du Château
Paris 14th 75014
+33 143226486
www.restaurant-lassiette.paris

Opening hours	Closed Monday and Tuesday
Credit cards	Accepted
Price range	Affordable
Style	Casual
Cuisine	French
Recommended for	Regular neighborhood

LE DÔME

Recommended by
Jonathan Brooks

108 Boulevard du Montparnasse
Paris 14th 75014
+33 143352581
www.restaurant-ledome.com

Opening hours	Open 7 days
Credit cards	Accepted
Price range	Affordable
Style	Casual
Cuisine	French Seafood
Recommended for	Worth the travel

"Best lunch of all time."—Jonathan Brooks

ROSEBUD

Recommended by
Bertrand Grébaut,
Tatiana Levha

11 Rue Delambre
Paris 14th 75014
+33 143353854

Opening hours	Open 7 days
Reservation policy	No
Credit cards	Accepted
Price range	Affordable
Style	Smart casual
Cuisine	Brasserie
Recommended for	Late night

"It has a classic brasserie menu—but you can get a great *chilli con carne* with bread and butter until 2.00 a.m."—Tatiana Levha

LE GRAND PAN

Recommended by
Henry Harris

20 Rue Rosenwald
Paris 15th 75015
+33 142500250
www.legrandpan.fr

Opening hours	Closed Saturday and Sunday
Credit cards	Accepted
Price range	Affordable
Style	Casual
Cuisine	French
Recommended for	Wish I'd opened

"Great meat and charcuterie, simply prepared with honesty and pride."—Henry Harris

PIERRE HERMÉ

Recommended by
Pascal Barbot

185 Rue Vaugirard
Paris 15th 75015
+33 147838997
www.pierreherme.com

Opening hours	Open 7 days
Reservation policy	No
Credit cards	Accepted but not AMEX
Price range	Budget
Style	Casual
Cuisine	Bakery
Recommended for	Breakfast

"Great breakfast."—Pascal Barbot

L'ASTRANCE

Recommended by
Chantel Dartnall, Sang-Hoon Degeimbre,
Björn Frantzén, Guillaume Galliot,
Tatiana Levha, Joshua Lewin,
Alexander Mayer,
Morgan McGlone,
Jocky Petrie, Julien Royer,
Stephen Toman, Simone Tondo

4 Rue Beethoven
Paris 16th 75016
+33 140508440
www.astrancerestaurant.com

Opening hours	Closed Monday, Saturday, and Sunday
Credit cards	Accepted
Price range	Expensive
Style	Smart casual
Cuisine	French
Recommended for	High end

"It's an example to all other restaurants in Paris.
One of the most humble and talented chefs in the
world, and one of the best service teams I have
encountered. What else can I say?"—Simone Tondo

This small (but tall!), out-of-the-way, airy, three-
Michelin-starred restaurant is soaked in relaxed
confidence, as is Pascal Barbot's concise cooking.
Root vegetables, flowers, and herbs are very much
the stars, sitting together raw, fermented, and
poached, or spiked with notes of smoke, citrus, and
pickle. Barbot rightly prides himself on the very
careful pairing of wine with the tasting menu
(for instance, Challans duck and raspberries paired
with a 2005 Gevrey-Chambertin Vieilles Vignes) and,
unlike many lazier grandes tables, it would be a
shame not to let yourself be guided from start to
finish here. You're in good hands.

ATELIER VIVANDA

Recommended by
Christophe Michalak

18 Rue Lauriston
Paris 16th 75016
+33 140671000
www.ateliervivanda.com

Opening hours	Closed Saturday and Sunday
Credit cards	Accepted
Price range	Affordable
Style	Casual
Cuisine	French
Recommended for	Late night

"First-rate meat, especially the Akrame-style burgers,
and a superb orange-blossom flan."
—Christophe Michalak

CARETTE

Recommended by
Christophe Michalak

4 Place du Trocadéro et du 11 Novembre
Paris 16th 75016
+33 147279885
www.carette-paris.fr

Opening hours	Open 7 days
Reservation policy	No
Credit cards	Accepted but not Diners
Price range	Affordable
Style	Casual
Cuisine	French
Recommended for	Breakfast

"Great atmosphere. Top-class pastry, especially the
apple turnover."—Christophe Michalak

LE PRÉ CATELAN

Recommended by
Peter Goossens,
Joaquin Soriano,
Christophe Michalak

Bois de Boulogne
Route de la Grande Cascade
Paris 16th 75016
+33 144144114
www.restaurant.leprecatelan.com

Opening hours	Closed Monday and Sunday
Credit cards	Accepted
Price range	Expensive
Style	Smart casual
Cuisine	Modern French
Recommended for	High end

"Combines great ambience and fantastic food. The
service and food are incredible."—Joaquin Soriano

PAPILLON

Recommended by
Luigi Taglienti

8 Rue Meissonier
Paris 17th 75017
+33 156798188
www.papillonparis.fr

Opening hours	Closed Saturday and Sunday
Credit cards	Accepted but not Diners
Price range	Affordable
Style	Casual
Cuisine	Bistro
Recommended for	Worth the travel

"Skillful cooking in an informal setting."
—Luigi Taglienti

IL BRIGANTE

Recommended by
Iñaki Aizpitarte

14 Rue du Ruisseau
Paris 18th 75018
+33 144927215

Opening hours	Closed Sunday
Credit cards	Accepted but not AMEX
Price range	Affordable
Style	Casual
Cuisine	Italian
Recommended for	Late night

LAO SIAM

Recommended by
Bertrand Grébaut,
Tatiana Levha,
Simone Tondo

49 Rue de Belleville
Paris 19th 75019
+33 140400968

Opening hours	Open 7 days
Credit cards	Accepted but not AMEX or Diners
Price range	Affordable
Style	Casual
Cuisine	Thai
Recommended for	Bargain

QUE DU BON

Recommended by
Greg Marchand

22 Rue du Plateau
Paris 19th 75019
+33 142381865
www.restaurantquedubon.fr

Opening hours	Closed Monday and Sunday
Credit cards	Accepted
Price range	Affordable
Style	Casual
Cuisine	French
Recommended for	Bargain

LE BARATIN

Recommended by
Iñaki Aizpitarte,
Tatiana Levha,
Josep Roca

3 Rue Jouye-Rouve
Paris 20th 75020
+33 143493970

Opening hours	Closed Monday and Sunday
Credit cards	Accepted but not AMEX
Price range	Affordable
Style	Casual
Cuisine	French Bistro
Recommended for	Local favorite

"It has been at the forefront of the Parisian food scene forever—great natural wine list and delicious. A French bistro with a twist."—Tatiana Levha

Raquel Carena and Philippe "Pinuche" Pinoteau have admirably ridden the wave of global fame and *New York Times* profiles to keep Le Baratin the way it has always been—a crammed, no-nonsense, local bistro with a splash of charm, plus slavish, personal devotion to the highest quality wine and ingredients. Chefs love revitalizing their tired palates with Raquel's motherly, delicate handling of fish and vegetables from Breton superstar Annie Bertin. She holds their awe and respect as much as the Passards and Ducasses for the dozens of remarkably inventive dishes that spring from her heart and tiny kitchen every day.

BENEDICT CASTEL

Recommended by
Beau Clugston

150 Rue Menilmontant
Paris 20th 75020
+33 146361382

Opening hours	Closed Monday and Tuesday
Reservation policy	No
Credit cards	Accepted
Price range	Affordable
Style	Casual
Cuisine	Bakery
Recommended for	Breakfast

"THE BEST TOMATO SALAD EVER MADE."

OLLIE TEMPLETON P573

SPAIN

"SUPER-DELICIOUS, CRAZY-PLAYFUL FOOD. IF YOU'RE LUCKY ENOUGH TO FIND YOURSELF IN THEIR WILLY WONKA-ESQUE DESSERT ROOM, BRACE YOURSELF FOR AN UNFORGETTABLE EXPERIENCE."

RICK BAYLESS P601

"The food is bright and colorful, contrary to the stark, Nordic-inspired minimalism that influences many today."

DANIELLE GJESTLAND P579

"Everything here is simply stunning."

AITOR JERONIMO ORIVE P576

"This is a restaurant for which I will gladly travel 900 km again to revisit."

CHANTEL DARTNALL P578

SPAIN

♦ Asturias p.574   ♦ Basque Country p.575
                        ♦ Catalonia p.582

♦ Galicia p.587   Barcelona pp.592–603 ♦

                        ♦ Madrid p.587   Balearic Islands p.574 ♦

            Valencian Community p.591 ♦

♦ Extremadura p.581

        Andalusia p.572 ♦

N

SCALE

0   75   150
                    MI.

BAR EL POTAJE

Calle Ribera del Río 5
El Puerto de Santa María
Cádiz
Andalusia 11500

Opening hours	Variable
Credit cards	Accepted but not AMEX or Diners
Price range	Budget
Style	Casual
Cuisine	Spanish
Recommended for	Breakfast

"Typical breakfast: authentic bread, molletes, traditional coffee and fresh orange juice at a very reasonable price. I feel at home there."—Ángel León

BODEGUITA EL ADOBO

Calle Rosario 4
Cádiz
Andalusia 11004
+34 636 81 46 75

Opening hours	Closed Tuesdays
Credit cards	Accepted but not Diners
Price range	Budget
Style	Casual
Cuisine	Seafood-Tapas
Recommended for	Late night

EL CAMPERO

Avenida Constitución Local 5c
Barbate
Cádiz
Andalusia 11160
+34 956432300
www.restauranteelcampero.es

Opening hours	Closed Monday
Credit cards	Accepted
Price range	Affordable
Style	Casual
Cuisine	Seafood
Recommended for	Worth the travel

"El Campero is in the heart of the traditional tuna fishing region of Jerez and during tuna fishing season it serves a mouth-watering tuna tasting menu."
—Samantha & Samuel Clark

LAS REJAS

Estrada El Lentiscal
El Lentiscal
Cádiz
Andalusia 11391
+34 956 68 85 46

Opening hours	Closed Tuesdays
Credit cards	Accepted but not AMEX or Diners
Price range	Affordable
Style	Casual
Cuisine	Seafood
Recommended for	Regular neighbourhood

"Right on the Bolonia beach in Cádiz. It is a family business that serves high-quality fresh ingredients, including spectacular rockfish that they bake whole in the oven... from the sea to the plate. The setting is spectacular as well."—Ángel León

EL PESCAÍTO

Calle Atalaya 9
El Puerto de Santa María
Cádiz
Andalusia 11500
+34 956 85 04 56

Opening hours	Closed Tuesdays
Credit cards	Accepted but not AMEX or Diners
Price range	Affordable
Style	Casual
Cuisine	Seafood
Recommended for	Regular neighbourhood

RESTAURANTE EL FARO DE CÁDIZ

Calle San Félix 15
El Puerto de Santa María
Cádiz
Andalusia 11002
+34 956 21 10 68
www.elfarodecadiz.com

Opening hours	Open 7 days
Credit cards	Accepted
Price range	Affordable
Style	Casual
Cuisine	Spanish-Tapas
Recommended for	Local favourite

ROMERIJO
Recommended by
Ángel León

Calle José Antonio Romero Zarazaga 1
El Puerto de Santa María
Cádiz
Andalusia 11500
+34 956 542 290
www.romerijo.com

Opening hours	Open 7 days
Credit cards	Accepted
Price range	Affordable
Style	Casual
Cuisine	Seafood
Recommended for	Wish I'd opened

NOOR
Recommended by
Oriol Castro

Alle Pablo Ruiz Picasso 8
Cañero
Córdoba
Andalusia 14014
+34 957 96 40 55
www.noorrestaurant.es

Opening hours	Closed Monday to Wednesday
Credit cards	Accepted
Price range	Expensive
Style	Smart casual
Cuisine	Andalusian
Recommended for	Worth the travel

"After an overnight visit to the Cordoba mosque, finishing at Noor is the best way to understand the culture through the kitchen."—Oriol Castro

EL REFUGIO
Recommended by
Ollie Templeton

Calle Cerro Currita 10
Zaharra de los Atunes
Andalusía 11393
+34 956439746
www.elrefugiodezahara.com

Opening hours	Open 7 days
Credit cards	Accepted but not AMEX
Price range	Affordable
Style	Casual
Cuisine	Andalusian
Recommended for	Worth the travel

"Located right on the beach on the Atlantic coast in the south of Spain. It's a place I go to as many times a year as I can, usually three. It's a family-run place where the ingredients lead. The feeling of sand beneath your feet while eating the best tomato salad ever made is nice."—Ollie Templeton

BIBO
Recommended by
Jonnie Boer

Hotel Puente Romano
Avenida Bulevar Principe Alfonso von Hohenlohe
Marbella
Andalusía 29602
+34 952820900
www.grupodanigarcia.com

Opening hours	Open 7 days
Credit cards	Accepted
Price range	Affordable
Style	Casual
Cuisine	International
Recommended for	Late night

"Good atmosphere, nice people, and good-food-quick concept."—Jonnie Boer

RESTAURANTE DANI GARCÍA
Recommended by
Ross Lewis

Hotel Puento Romano
Avenida Bulevar Príncipe Alfonso de Hohenlohe
Marbella
Andalusía 29602
+34 952764252
www.grupodanigarcia.com

Opening hours	Open 7 days
Credit cards	Accepted
Price range	Expensive
Style	Smart casual
Cuisine	Modern Spanish
Recommended for	Worth the travel

"The design of the restaurant room is so stylish and benefits from great light. The menu has been tweaked since our last visit and benefited from being slightly shorter with a great mix of Spanish influences producing some outstanding flavors."—Ross Lewis

GÜEYU MAR

Recommended by
Jordi Vilà

Playa de Vega 84
Ribadesella
Asturias 33560
+34 985860863
www.gueyumar.es

Opening hours	Open 7 days
Credit cards	Accepted but not AMEX
Price range	Affordable
Style	Casual
Cuisine	Seafood
Recommended for	Worth the travel

"Highly sensitive treatment of grilled fish, quality raw materials, and an excellent wine list."—Jordi Vilà

FISH SHACK

Recommended by
Richard Turner

Cap Martinet
Talamanca Beach
Ibiza
Balearic Islands 07819

Opening hours	Open 7 days
Credit cards	Not accepted
Price range	Affordable
Style	Casual
Cuisine	Seafood
Recommended for	Worth the travel

HEART

Recommended by
Andrey Zhdanov

Passeig Joan Carles I 17
Ibiza
Balearic Islands 07800
+34 971933777
www.heartibiza.com

Opening hours	Open 7 days
Credit cards	Accepted
Price range	Expensive
Style	Smart casual
Cuisine	Modern International
Recommended for	Wish I'd opened

"The most incredible experience of my life— a magical circus + street food + cocktails!" —Andrey Zhdanov

ES XARCU

Recommended by
Joan Roca

Cala Es Xarco
Sant Josep
Ibiza
Balearic Islands 07830
+34 971187867
www.esxarcu.com

Opening hours	Variable
Credit cards	Accepted
Price range	Affordable
Style	Casual
Cuisine	Spanish Grill
Recommended for	Local favorite

Few restaurants can boast a terrace with a view as picturesque as Es Xarcu's, which is located directly on the sandy shores of a Sant Josep cove. Locals don't just come for the view though; they also come for the traditional food, cooked simply over a flame for maximum flavor. The menu is comfortingly basic, with starters such as hand-carved *jamón*, *boquerones* (anchovies) and fresh shrimp (prawns) *a la plancha* (grilled) making way for simple mains of freshly caught fish that are merely thrown on the grill. There are no delusions of grandeur here, with the cheap plastic chairs and the daily lunchtime scramble only adding to the experience.

ADRIAN QUETGLAS

Recommended by
Andrey Zhdanov

Passeig de Mallorca
Palma
Majorca
Balearic Islands 07012
+34 971781119
www.adrianquetglas.es

Opening hours	Closed Monday and Sunday
Credit cards	Accepted
Price range	Affordable
Style	Casual
Cuisine	Modern European
Recommended for	Worth the travel

"Magical place in the heart of Majorca—it's about love and fine dining. It's also a home from home." —Andrey Zhdanov

ASADOR ETXEBARRI

Plaza de San Juan 1
Atxondo
Basque Country 48291
+34 946583042
www.asadoretxebarri.com

Recommended by
Matt Abergel, Johan Agrell,
Brian Ahern, Josean Alija,
Kristian Baumann, Daniel Berlin,
Thomas Boemer, Danny Bowien,
Tim Butler, Kevin Fink,
Analiese Gregory,
Rodolfo Guzmán, Dan Hunter,
Carlo Lamagna, David Martin, Isaac McHale,
Eduardo Moreno, Willy Trullas Moreno, Benny Novak,
JJ Proville, Dave Pynt, Albert Raurich, Henrik Ritzen,
Ljubomir Stanisic, Thitid Thassanakajohn

Opening hours	Closed Monday
Credit cards	Accepted
Price range	Affordable
Style	Casual
Cuisine	Modern Spanish
Recommended for	Wish I'd opened

"This a temple to grilling and a really unique experience. Aside from the stunning ingredients, there's something about the tranquility of the location that makes the food so special."—JJ Proville

There's no food without fire at Victor Arguinzoniz's homage to the Iberian-born tradition of the *asador* (grill restaurant). It sits in the bucolic Basque village of Axpe, nestled at the foot of Mount Anboto, halfway between San Sebastián and Bilbao. Every dish that makes it onto Arguinzoniz's strictly seasonal tasting menu is flavored with a smoky kiss from his charcoal-fired grill: seafood, marbled beef, vegetables, eggs, cheese, butter, even the desserts —smoked milk often makes an appearance. Ingredients are predominantly sourced from the surrounding, fertile Atxondo valley—even the charcoal for the grill, which is made from local oak.

BAR ROTTERDAM

Txakur Kalea 6
Bilbao
Basque Country 48005
+34 944162165

Recommended by
Josean Alija

Opening hours	Open 7 days
Credit cards	Accepted but not AMEX
Price range	Affordable
Style	Casual
Cuisine	Pintxos
Recommended for	Breakfast

"When I meet up with friends I like to have a heavier breakfast, known as *hamaiketako*, in the Rotterdam. We order casseroles and traditional dishes."
—Josean Alija

NERUA

Guggenheim Bilbao Museum
Avenida Abandoibarra 2
Bilbao
Basque Country 48009
+34 944000430
www.neruaguggenheimbilbao.com

Recommended by
Juan Mari & Elena Arzak,
Chele (José Luis) Gonzalez

Opening hours	Closed Monday
Credit cards	Accepted
Price range	Expensive
Style	Smart casual
Cuisine	Modern Basque
Recommended for	Worth the travel

BISTRÓ

Guggenheim Bilbao Museum
Avenida Abandoibarra 2
Bilbao
Basque Country 48009
+34 944239333
www.bistroguggenheimbilbao.com

Recommended by
Josean Alija

Opening hours	Closed Monday
Credit cards	Accepted
Price range	Affordable
Style	Casual
Cuisine	European
Recommended for	Bargain

"High quality in a unique space and an informal setting."—Josean Alija

TXAKOLI SIMÓN

Camino San Roque 89
Bilbao
Basque Country 48015
+39 944457499
www.txakolisimon.com

Recommended by
Josean Alija

Opening hours	Open 7 days
Credit cards	Accepted
Price range	Affordable
Style	Casual
Cuisine	Basque Grill
Recommended for	Regular neighborhood

"Very good meat, interesting wine list, informal atmosphere. It allows me to get out of the city and get in touch with nature. It's interesting to have the option of eating inside or outside."—Josean Alija

MUGARITZ

Otazulueta Baserria
Aldura Aldea 20
Errenteria
Basque Country 20100
+34 943522455
www.mugaritz.com

Recommended by
Josean Alija, Juan Mari & Elena Arzak,
Ivan Berezutskiy, Fredrik Berselius,
Massimo Bottura, Daniel Burns,
Kyle Connaughton,Luca Fantin,
Peter Gilmore,
Chele (José Luis) Gonzalez,
Dan Graham, Analiese Gregory
Rodolfo Guzmán, Martin Juneau,
Taras Kiriyenko, Ángel León, Virgilio Martínez,
Marc-Alexandre Mercier, David Muñoz, Petter Nilsson,
Aitor Jeronimo Orive, Albert Raurich, Michael Reid,
Nikos Roussos, Francisco Ruano, Giulio Sturla,
Pedro Subijana, Eduard Xatruch, Andrey Zhdanov

Opening hours	Closed Monday
Credit cards	Accepted
Price range	Expensive
Style	Casual
Cuisine	Modern Spanish
Recommended for	Worth the travel

"Everything here is simply stunning. From the location—it has beautiful scenery—to their use of local produce. The cuisine is extremely unique and experimental, so it isn't for everyone. But Chef Andoni, whom I worked with for a while, is free to do whatever he wants and that translates to boundary-pushing plates."—Aitor Jeronimo Orive

The smell of barbecue greets visitors to this cutting-edge restaurant tucked away in the hills outside San Sebastián, where head chef Andoni Luis Aduriz believes it's a universal childhood aroma. It's academic, really, as everything you're served once seated in the bright and spacious dining room is unrecognizable—designed to startle, amaze, and even to challenge the way you think about food. The techno-emotional cooking approach means a succession of wildly creative dishes (like "edible stones"). There are no Basque favorites such as hake and salsa verde on the menu. In fact, there isn't even a menu—you simply put yourself at the kitchen's mercy.

KAIA KAIPE

General Arnao 4
Getaria
Basque Country 20808
+34 943140500
www.kaia-kaipe.com

Recommended by
Pedro Subijana

Opening hours	Open 7 days
Credit cards	Accepted
Price range	Affordable
Style	Smart casual
Cuisine	Basque
Recommended for	High end

Situated about 15 miles (25 km) along the coast from San Sebastián, Getaria catches the eye from the rocky outcrop that juts out into the sea, attached by a spit of land. On this spit, overlooking the little harbor, stands Kaia Kaipe. You can imagine how fresh the fish is. If you get a table outside, you can watch it coming in. Turbot, hake, langoustines, lobster—all cooked as well as any fish you will ever have the pleasure of eating. This specialty brings in the local regulars, as well as fish fanciers from far and wide, which all makes for a very rewarding experience.

ALAMEDA

Minasoroeta Kalea 1
Hondarribia
Basque Country 20280
+34 943642789
www.restaurantealameda.net

Recommended by
Juan Mari & Elena Arzak

Opening hours	Closed Monday
Credit cards	Accepted
Price range	Affordable
Style	Casual
Cuisine	Modern Spanish
Recommended for	High end

This third-generation restaurant, run by the three Txapartegi brothers, lies in a tiny seaside hamlet, just a seven-minute ferry ride from France, that's starting to steal some of nearby San Sebastián's limelight. Chef Gorka, who trained under Martín Berasategui, is a rising star in the region thanks to his contemporary Basque cuisine—local fish paired with roasted buckwheat and seasonal vegetables, scallop carpaccio with tomato tartar and almond emulsion—which is more about respecting the local produce than indulging in experimental high jinks. The spacious dining room feels far from Donostia's madding crowd, and the food is more affordable too.

ASADOR HORMA ONDO

Caserío Legina Goika S/N
Larrabetzu
Basque Country 48195
+34 946565700
www.asadorhormaondo.com

Opening hours	Closed Monday
Credit cards	Accepted
Price range	Affordable
Style	Casual
Cuisine	Basque
Recommended for	Late night

AZURMENDI

Legina Auzoa
Larrabetzu
Basque Country 48195
+34 944558359
www.azurmendi.biz

Opening hours	Closed Monday
Credit cards	Accepted
Price range	Expensive
Style	Casual
Cuisine	Modern Basque
Recommended for	Worth the travel

With its brightly lit dining room and tall windows, Azurmendi—opened in 2005 and housed in a warehouse-style building ten minutes outside Bilbao—is an undeniably stylish and modern restaurant. Eneko Atxa is its young, passionate, and impressively earringed chef. His food is bold and experimental, as evidenced by dishes like marine turnip with herb emulsion and frozen tomato lollipop, but there are nods to a more rustic Basque heritage in a dish of red mullet with wheat stew and parsley potatoes. There's also an excellent Txacolí wine on offer, produced by the restaurant's own winery.

MARTÍN BERASATEGUI

Loidi Kalea 4
Lasarte-Oria
Basque Country 20160
+34 943366471
www.martinberasategui.com

Opening hours	Closed Monday and Tuesday
Credit cards	Accepted
Price range	Expensive
Style	Smart casual
Cuisine	Modern Spanish
Recommended for	Worth the travel

"Incredible technique, in perfect harmony with all your senses from your arrival to your departure. The staff are very knowledgable and speak several languages, which is rare. By far my favorite for years —I am always so happy to go there and enjoy Martín Berasategui's creations."—William Mahi

As if you need another reason to go to San Sebastián, a visit to Martín Berasategui is the cherry on the icing on the cake (and a warm toasted almond cake at that). Located a short drive outside the Basque capital, the restaurant is a haven of calm simplicity, while in the kitchen an orchestra of sous-chefs plays tirelessly to Berasategui's score. Not one for gilding the lily, he has become a master at extracting the maximum from his pure ingredients. Expect not a lavish feast, but delicate portions of intense flavor that melt in the mouth and leave a long-lasting impression.

MIRADOR DE ULÍA

Paseo de Ulía 193
Lasarte-Oria
Basque Country 20013
+34 943272707
www.miradordeulia.es

Opening hours	Closed Monday and Tuesday
Credit cards	Accepted
Price range	Affordable
Style	Casual
Cuisine	Modern Basque
Recommended for	Regular neighborhood

ZUBEROA

Araneder Bidea
Oiartzun
Basque Country 20180
+34 943491228
www.zuberoa.com

Recommended by
Juan Mari & Elena Arzak,
Pedro Subijana

Opening hours	Closed Wednesday
Credit cards	Accepted
Price range	Affordable
Style	Casual
Cuisine	Basque
Recommended for	Local favorite

The setting—a convivial old stone building in a 600-year-old village outside San Sebastián—may be quaint, but there is nothing quaint about the cooking. This is traditional Basque food brought right up to date by chef Hilario Arbelaitz, who stakes his reputation on the quality of his ingredients and his ability to arrange them enticingly on the plate. Seafood plays the lead role, as you would expect in this part of the world, and the flavors are rich and warming. But Arbelaitz is not afraid to throw in the odd exotic ingredient, like coconut or pineapple (or even both).

A FUEGO NEGRO

31 de Agosto Kalea 31
San Sebastián
Basque Country 20003
+34 650135373
www.afuegonegro.com

Recommended by
Juan Mari & Elena Arzak,
Xabier Diez Esteibar

Opening hours	Closed Monday
Credit cards	Accepted
Price range	Affordable
Style	Casual
Cuisine	Spanish Tapas
Recommended for	Late night

AGORREGI

Portuetxe Kalea 15
San Sebastián
Basque Country 20018
+34 943224328
www.agorregi.com

Recommended by
Xabier Diez Esteibar

Opening hours	Closed Sunday
Credit cards	Accepted but not AMEX
Price range	Affordable
Style	Casual
Cuisine	Modern Basque
Recommended for	Bargain

Gorka Arzelus (chef) and his wife Beatriz (front of house) have spent time working with Basque food giants Juan Mari Arzak and Martín Berasategui, and so, having set up their own place in the western suburbs of San Sebastián, it's probably no surprise that it's good—and popular. What is perhaps more of a surprise are the prices—usually no more than €30 ($33; £25) or so a head for a meal including the likes of "fake" black risotto (made with chopped squid in ink) or pan-fried pigeon with sage purée. Even the room—minimalist and modern—belies its budget.

AKELARRE

Paseo Padre Orcolaga 56
San Sebastián
Basque Country 20008
+34 943311209
www.akelarre.net

Recommended by
Juan Mari & Elena Arzak,
Michael Belton,
Chantel Dartnall,
Florian Lamelot

Opening hours	Closed Monday
Credit cards	Accepted
Price range	Expensive
Style	Smart casual
Cuisine	Modern Basque
Recommended for	Worth the travel

"Chef Pedro Subijana and his team managed to exceed all my expectations on both ocasions. This is a restaurant for which I will gladly travel 600 miles (900 km) again to revisit."
—Chantel Dartnall

Should you tire of San Sebastián's abundant *pintxos* (Basque tapas) bars, venture a little out of town for an altogether more ethereal and quirky demonstration of Basque hospitality. Admired by professional chefs the world over, Pedro Subijana of the three-Michelin-starred Akelarre is one of the founding fathers of New Basque cuisine. Injecting much-needed humor into high-concept cooking, his restaurant—perched above the Bay of Biscay—has pursued culinary innovation and technical perfection with tongue firmly in cheek for over thirty years. Two tasting menus, one based on *Aranori* (fish) and one on *Bekarki* (meat), are beautifully conceived and pleasingly playful.

ARZAK

Recommended by
Josean Alija,
Xabier Diez Esteibar,
Danielle Gjestland,
Pedro Subijana,
Thitid Tassanakajohn

Avenida Alcalde José Elósegui 273
San Sebastián
Basque Country 20015
+34 943278465
www.arzak.es

Opening hours	Closed Monday and Sunday
Credit cards	Accepted
Price range	Expensive
Style	Smart casual
Cuisine	Modern Basque
Recommended for	High end

"The food is bright and colorful, contrary to the stark, Nordic-inspired minimalism that influences many today. It was thoughtful but still delicious. The room felt warm and cared for because Juan Mari Arzak came to speak to each of his guests at their tables."
—Danielle Gjestland

Juan Mari and his daughter Elena preside over Arzak, the fourth generation of their family to do so in the restaurant's 120-year history. The cooking has come some distance since the building's former incarnation as a wine tavern, built by Juan Mari's grandparents; so much so that Arzak is now the proud holder of three Michelin stars. The monochrome dining room provides an urbane backdrop for the New Basque cuisine, which works classic local ingredients into avant-garde compilations: sardines and strawberries; peach curd with seaweed; "chorizo and tonic" on an upside-down Schweppes can. Fish—particularly hake—is exquisite. Book the chef's table to observe the father-daughter team at work.

ASTELENA

Recommended by
Juan Mari & Elena Arzak

Euskai Herria Kalea 3
San Sebastián
Basque Country 20003
+34 943425867
www.restauranteastelena.com

Opening hours	Closed Monday
Credit cards	Accepted
Price range	Affordable
Style	Smart casual
Cuisine	Modern Basque
Recommended for	Regular neighborhood

"Food prepared with the utmost care."
—Juan Mari & Elena Arzak

BAR NESTOR

Recommended by
Alexander Mayer

Arrandegi Kalea 11
San Sebastián
Basque Country 20003
+34 943424873

Opening hours	Closed Monday
Credit cards	Accepted but not AMEX
Price range	Affordable
Style	Casual
Cuisine	Spanish
Recommended for	Bargain

BARKAIZTEGI

Recommended by
Pedro Subijana

Barkaiztegi Bidea 42
San Sebastián
Basque Country 20014
+34 943451304
www.barkaiztegi.com

Opening hours	Closed Sunday
Credit cards	Accepted but not AMEX
Price range	Affordable
Style	Casual
Cuisine	Basque
Recommended for	Local favorite

BERNARDO ETXEA

Recommended by
Pedro Subijana

Calle del Puerto 7
San Sebastián
Basque Country 20003
+34 943422055
www.bernardoetxea.com

Opening hours	Open 7 days
Credit cards	Accepted
Price range	Affordable
Style	Casual
Cuisine	Basque
Recommended for	High end

"There aren't many expensive places in the area, you only pay a lot if you eat seafood and drink expensive wines, which you can do at Bernardo Etxea."
—Pedro Subijana

BOKADO MIKEL SANTAMARÍA

Recommended by
Juan Mari & Elena Arzak

Jacque Cousteau Plaza 1
San Sebastián
Basque Country 20003
+34 943431842
www.bokadomikelsantamaria.com

Opening hours	Closed Monday
Credit cards	Accepted but not AMEX
Price range	Affordable
Style	Casual
Cuisine	Modern Basque
Recommended for	Late night

CALONGE SAGARDOTEGIA

Recommended by
Pedro Subijana

Padre Orkolaga Ibilbidea 8
San Sebastián
Basque Country 20008
+34 943213251
www.calongesagardotegia.es

Opening hours	Closed Monday
Credit cards	Accepted
Price range	Affordable
Style	Casual
Cuisine	Basque
Recommended for	Local favorite

"This *sidrería* (cider bar) is very typical when the season starts, after Christmas."—Pedro Subijana

ELKANO

Recommended by
Josean Alija,
Juan Mari & Elena Arzak,
Analiese Gregory,
Chele (José Luis) Gonzalez,
Virgilio Martínez,
Benjamin Sukle

Herrerieta Kalea 2
Getaria
Basque Country 20808
+34 943140024
www.restauranteelkano.com

Opening hours	Closed Tuesday
Credit cards	Accepted
Price range	Affordable
Style	Casual
Cuisine	Seafood
Recommended for	Worth the travel

"It is close to the sea and it allows you to eat as if you were at home, along with good service and an excellent selection of drinks. Moreover, the head waiter is a guy who always shows you new things and it's a privilege to chat with him."—Josean Alija

The philosophy at Elkano, which sits on the seafront at Getaria, an hour west of San Sebastián, is quite simple: fresh fish, chargrilled. Except some strange

alchemy seems to occur when the piscine produce of the Guipuzcoan coast meets Pedro Arregui's coals in the open air. Superlative turbot and hake are delivered unadorned to clothed tables in the unselfconsciously old-fashioned dining room, with its terracotta tiles and dark wooden beams. Lobster, clams, baby squid, and coral-pink shrimp (prawns) all receive the same treatment, partnered by a compact selection of Spanish wines, including the region's own dry sparkling Txacolí. Round off with another local specialty—the indulgent, custard-filled *panchineta* (a traditional Basque dessert).

GANBARA JATETXEA

Recommended by
Juan Mari & Elena Arzak

Calle San Jeronimo 21
San Sebastián
Basque Country 20003
+34 943422575
www.ganbarajatetxea.com

Opening hours	Closed Monday
Credit cards	Accepted but not AMEX
Price range	Affordable
Style	Casual
Cuisine	Basque
Recommended for	Regular neighborhood

"Good produce and the possibility of eating both standing at the counter or sitting in the dining room."—Juan Mari & Elena Arzak

GANDARIAS

Recommended by
Pedro Subijana

31 de Agosto Kalea 23
San Sebastián
Basque Country 20003
+34 943426362
www.restaurantegandarias.com

Opening hours	Open 7 days
Credit cards	Accepted but not AMEX
Price range	Affordable
Style	Casual
Cuisine	Basque
Recommended for	Late night

"I don't usually eat late at night, but Gandarias in Donosti is a good place to do so."—Pedro Subijana

San Sebastián's old town is awash with atmospheric bars, their counters loaded with *pintxos* (Basque tapas) and hams hanging from their ceilings. Gandarias is one such establishment and is as essential a stop on a serious gourmet tour of the city as it is on a late-night bar crawl. Its restaurant is known for its bloody, marbled steaks and excellent wine cellar (strong on Rioja), while the always lively bar is recommended for its classic *pintxos* and blackboard specials. Specialties include the *brocheta di chipirón* (squid), *ensaladilla rusa* (Russian salad) and, of course, the celebrated acorn-fed Joselito ham.

HAIZEA BAR

Recommended by
Juan Mari & Elena Arzak

Aldamar Kalea 8
San Sebastián
Basque Country 20003
+34 943425710

Opening hours	Closed Sunday
Credit cards	Accepted
Price range	Affordable
Style	Casual
Cuisine	Basque
Recommended for	Breakfast

"It's located a stone's throw away from the Bretxa market, ideal for a *pintxo* (Basque tapas) or *Txakolí* (Basque wine)."—Juan Mari & Elena Arzak

LA CUCHARA SAN TELMO

Recommended by
Landon Thompson

31 de Agosto Kalea 28
San Sebastián
Basque Country 20003
+34 943441655
www.lacucharadesantelmo.com

Opening hours	Closed Monday
Reservation policy	No
Credit cards	Accepted
Price range	Affordable
Style	Casual
Cuisine	Basque
Recommended for	Worth the travel

"My most favorite *pintxo* (Basque tapas) bar in all of Basque country. It's certainly not gout-friendly, serving up half-lobes of seared foie gras without bating an eye, but it's damned delicious and should be your first stop if you're ever in the area."—Landon Thompson

LA RAMPA

Recommended by
Xabier Diez Esteibar

Kaika Pasealekua 26
San Sebastián
Basque Country 20003
+34 943421652
www.restaurantelarampa.com

Opening hours	Closed Wednesday
Credit cards	Accepted
Price range	Affordable
Style	Casual
Cuisine	Spanish-Basque
Recommended for	Wish I'd opened

PASTELERIA GAZTELO

Recommended by
Xabier Diez Esteibar

Zarautz Kalea 76
San Sebastián
Basque Country 20018
+34 943226584

Opening hours	Open 7 days
Reservation policy	No
Credit cards	Not accepted
Price range	Budget
Style	Casual
Cuisine	Bakery
Recommended for	Breakfast

PASTELERÍA GELTOKI

Recommended by
Juan Mari & Elena Arzak

Easo Kalea 61
San Sebastián
Basque Country 20006
+34 943450902

Opening hours	Open 7 days
Reservation policy	No
Credit cards	Not accepted
Price range	Budget
Style	Casual
Cuisine	Bakery
Recommended for	Breakfast

BARCELONA: SEE PAGES 592–603

TOC ALMAR

Recommended by
Joan Roca

Carrer de Platja d'Aiguablava 6
Begur
Catalonia 17255
+34 972113232
www.tocalmar.cat

Opening hours..Variable
Credit cards.........................Accepted but not AMEX
Price range...Affordable
Style..Casual
Cuisine...Seafood
Recommended for.......................................Late night

COMPARTIR

Recommended by
Albert Raurich,
Jordi Roca

Riera Sant Vicenç
Cadaqués
Catalonia 17488
+34 972258482
www.compartircadaques.com

Opening hours..Variable
Credit cards.........................Accepted but not AMEX
Price range...Affordable
Style..Casual
Cuisine...Modern Spanish
Recommended for...............................Local favorite

The picture-book whitewashed fishing village of
Cadaqués is a dream location, and Compartir
(Catalan for "share") could be many people's idea
of a dream restaurant. Hidden in a beautifully
restored 300-year-old house, complete with terrace
walled with local slate for when the weather is good
(unusually for Costa Brava restaurants, Compartir is
open year-round), guests enjoy innovative sharing
plates such as watermelon and tomatoes with blood
orange foam, *bacallà* (cod) with "honey air" or
mussels with Béarnaise sauce—combinations
worthy of the three founding chefs' pedigree (they
previously worked with Ferran Adrià at El Bulli).

CAN XIFRA

Recommended by
Jordi Roca

Calle Mas Artigas
Cartellà
Catalonia 17150
+34 972428546
www.canxifra.com

Opening hours......................................Closed Wednesday
Credit cards.........................Accepted but not AMEX
Price range...Affordable
Style..Casual
Cuisine..Catalan
Recommended for.................Regular neighborhood

Styled in the inviting farmhouse aesthetic of rural
Catalonia, Can Xifra has rustic terracotta-tiled
flooring, exposed brick walls, and wooden-beamed
ceilings. It's a simple affair, situated within view of
the outstanding Rocacorba mountains, about 4 miles
(7 km) outside Girona. Bold food, such as roasted
shoulder of lamb, pig trotters, and stewed rabbit,
is served in unpretentious surroundings. An obvious
aim to provide robust sustenance with unfussy
house wines is a welcome reminder that, despite
the innovation in many restaurants across Spain,
there remains a place for the hearty traditionalists.

CAL TET

Recommended by
Joan Roca

Cal Tet Hotel
Carrer Santa Anna 38
L'Estartit
Catalonia 17258
+34 972751179
www.caltet.com

Opening hours...Open 7 days
Credit cards.........................Accepted but not AMEX
Price range...Affordable
Style..Casual
Cuisine...Mediterranean
Recommended for.................Regular neighborhood

Eating out on Spain's Costa Brava is not a simple
toss-up between eye-popping molecular gastronomy
and greasy *calamares* (deep-fried squid rings) in
beachfront bars. This *marisqueria* (seafood
restaurant), in the fishing village-turned-resort of
L'Estartit, is where local families go to enjoy their
region's traditional dishes. Since 1971, the Giménez
family have staked their reputation on dazzling
shellfish from local and Galician waters, serving
Catalan classics such as *mariscada* (seafood stew
of sea snails, winkles, and mussels) and *fideuada*
(pasta 'paella'), accompanied by local Empordà wine.

EL MOTEL

Recommended by
Mateu Casañas,
Josep Roca

Hotel Empordà
Avenida Salvador Dalí i Domènech 170
Figueres
Catalonia 17600
+34 972500562
www.elmotel.cat

Opening hours	Open 7 days
Credit cards	Accepted
Price range	Affordable
Style	Casual
Cuisine	Modern Catalan
Recommended for	Local favorite

CAN MARQUÈS

Recommended by
Joan Roca,
Jordi Roca,
Josep Roca

Plaça Calvet i Rubalcaba 3
Girona
Catalonia 17001
+34 972201001
www.canmarques.com

Opening hours	Closed Sunday
Credit cards	Accepted
Price range	Affordable
Style	Casual
Cuisine	Catalan
Recommended for	Breakfast

Currently overseen by the fourth generation of the founding family, Can Marquès describes itself as "one of the most traditional restaurants in Girona". Its interior subtly pays tribute to the innovations of restaurant design, striking a careful balance between old and new with modern furniture sitting comfortably among traditional wooden dressers and cabinets stacked with wine bottles and glassware. With a dinner menu divided straightforwardly into "classics" and "meat", it is in part defined by its proximity to the city market, which lies opposite and sells a wealth of exciting produce. For breakfast try the scrambled eggs with shrimp (prawns) and garlic.

EL CELLER DE CAN ROCA

Recommended by
Gastón Acurio,
Juan Mari & Elena Arzak,
José Avillez, Ivan Berezutskiy,
Massimo Bottura, Mateu Casañas,
Christophe Michalak, David Muñoz,
Albert Raurich, Perfecte Rocher,
Fabio Rossi, Ljubomir Stanisic,
Thitid Tassanakajohn

Carrer de Can Sunyer 48
Girona
Catalonia 17007
+34 972222157
www.cellercanroca.com

Opening hours	Closed Monday and Sunday
Credit cards	Accepted
Price range	Expensive
Style	Smart casual
Cuisine	Modern Catalan
Recommended for	Worth the travel

"The best place to celebrate the unlimited horizons of pleasure."—Gastón Acurio

While molecular gastronomy fans flocked to El Bulli and The Fat Duck, the pioneering trio of brothers at El Celler de Can Roca in Girona remained Spain's little secret—until their restaurant was named the world's best in 2013 (and again in 2015). Eating in the clean-cut Scandi-style dining room is an experience that plays with mood and memory. Traditional Catalonian ingredients are given innovative treatment to create playful dishes such as caramelized olives hanging from a bonsai tree, the famous "Journey to Havana"—a tobacco-flavored "cigar" sitting on an "ashtray"—or desserts that replicate Calvin Klein or Lancôme scents. Having achieved a third star in 2009, the €180 ($198; £152) seven-course tasting menu doesn't look like bad value.

UMAI

Plaça Josep Pla I Casadevall 18
Girona
Catalonia 17001
+34 972417872
www.umaigirona.com

Opening hours	Closed Sunday
Credit cards	Accepted but not AMEX
Price range	Affordable
Style	Casual
Cuisine	Sushi
Recommended for	Late night

MIRAMAR

Passeig Marítim 7
Llançà
Catalonia 17490
+34 972 38 01 32
www.restaurantmiramar.com

Opening hours	Closed Monday
Credit cards	Accepted
Price range	Expensive
Style	Smart casual
Cuisine	Modern Spanish-Mediterranean
Recommended for	High end

"Paco and Montse are one of the strongest exponents of the cuisine and great teachers of hard work, constancy, humility, and sincerity."—Mateu Casañas

CAN CASTELLVÍ

Avenida Can Castellví
Molins de Rei
Catalonia 08750
+34 936682678
www.cancastellvi.com

Opening hours	Closed Monday and Tuesday
Credit cards	Accepted but not AMEX
Price range	Affordable
Style	Casual
Cuisine	Catalan
Recommended for	Breakfast

"It is a restaurant-farm. I like to go on weekends to have a good 'mountaineer' family breakfast and so that my daughters can enjoy the outdoors and the animals."—Jordi Vilà

Only twenty minutes' drive out of the Barcelona metropolis is picturesque restaurant-farm Can Castellví, surely one of the more delightful

breakfasting spots in the Molins de Rei. Heavily geared towards families and school parties, guests (and their minders) are encouraged first to feed the animals (ducks, geese, Vietnamese pot-bellied pigs, you name it) and then feed themselves, from a simple but hearty menu of eggs and fries (chips), local charcuterie, and *pan con tomate* (bread with tomato). It's hardly fine dining, but there can't be many kids out there who wouldn't enjoy breakfast on a farm, and there's sometimes even (season permitting) a *calçot* (Catalan scallion [spring onion]) grill—something the grown-ups would happily make the journey for.

EL CELLER DEL BARRI VELL

Carrer d'Allada 18
Palamós
Catalonia 17230
+34 972600961
www.cellerdelbarrivell.com

Opening hours	Closed Monday
Credit cards	Accepted but not AMEX
Price range	Affordable
Style	Casual
Cuisine	Seafood
Recommended for	Bargain

ESPORTELL DEL BOU

Carrer Diputat Orga 3-5
Picamoixons
Catalonia 43491
+34 977604868
www.esportelldelbou.com

Opening hours	Closed Tuesday
Credit cards	Accepted
Price range	Affordable
Style	Casual
Cuisine	Catalan
Recommended for	Regular neighborhood

"It is a restaurant with traditional cuisine, very informal, where they treat you with great affection. Its *calçotades* (Catalan-style barbecue with scallions [spring onions]) are spectacular."
—Eduard Xatruch Cerro

LAS GOLONDRINAS

Recommended by
Mateu Casañas

Carrer Sant Sebastià 63
Roses
Catalonia 17480
+34 972153705

Opening hours	Closed Wednesday
Credit cards	Accepted but not AMEX or Diners
Price range	Affordable
Style	Casual
Cuisine	Spanish
Recommended for	Regular neighbourhood

"Specialized in working with grilled meat, stone...
Alex is a character!"—Mateu Casañas

RASPA & WINE

Recommended by
Mateu Casañas

Almadraba Park Hotel
Avinguda Díaz Pacheco 70
Roses
Catalonia 17480
+34 972256550
www.raspawine.com

Opening hours	Open 7 days
Reservation policy	No
Credit cards	Accepted
Price range	Affordable
Style	Casual
Cuisine	Spanish-Seafood-Bar
Recommended for	Late night

"One of the most incredible terraces on the Gulf of
Roses. It's unpretentious, dynamic, and full of nuances
that combined with its location make it unique."
—Mateu Casañas

RESTAURANT CAL CAMPANER

Recommended by
Mateu Casañas

Carrer de Mossèn Carles Feliu 23
Roses
Catalonia 17480
+34 972256954
www.calcampaner.cat

Opening hours	Closed Sunday
Credit cards	Accepted
Price range	Affordable
Style	Casual
Cuisine	Seafood
Recommended for	Local favourite

"Exquisite family treatment and incomparable fresh
seafood. Mediterranean in its purest state.'"
—Mateu Casañas

SI US PLAU

Recommended by
Mateu Casañas

Passeig Marítim 1
Roses
Catalonia 17480
+34 659136196

Opening hours	Closed Tuesday
Credit cards	Accepted but not AMEX or Diners
Price range	Affordable
Style	Casual
Cuisine	Spanish-Mediterranean
Recommended for	Breakfast

LA SIRENA

Recommended by
Julius Jaspers

Plaça Sant Pere 7
Roses
Catalonia 17480
+34 972257294

Opening hours	Open 7 days
Credit cards	Accepted but not AMEX
Price range	Affordable
Style	Casual
Cuisine	Mediterranean-Seafood
Recommended for	Bargain

"Fresh tapas made in front of you and fantastic fish
on the *plancha* (grill). Small but inexpensive and
a good wine list."—Julius Jaspers

There are places like La Sirena the length of the
Costa Brava—unassuming little seafront bars
where you can order *calamars a la romana*
(battered squid rings, usually frozen though hardly
the worse for that), Russian salad, and an Estrella
beer without the total bill pushing much north of €20
($22; £17). Here though, the menu is embellished
with slightly more interesting tapas, such as tuna
tataki (lightly seared, Japanese-style) or veal
carpaccio, and if you're lucky, owner Jordi will be
offering fish fresh off the day boats. Understandably
popular with locals and tourists alike, you'd be well
advised to book—especially in season.

ELS CASALS

Recommended by
Josep Roca,
Jordi Vilà

Els Casals Hotel
Camí de la Guàrdia
Sagàs
Catalonia 08517
+34 938251200
www.elscasals.cat

Opening hours	Variable
Credit cards	Accepted
Price range	Expensive
Style	Smart casual
Cuisine	Modern Spanish
Recommended for	Wish I'd opened

"The restaurant is linked to a family of farmers. All the products they use belong to the same farm or to nearby farms that work in a traditional way using traditional methods."—Jordi Vilà

Head about 55 miles (90 km) north of Barcelona and you'll reach the small town of Sagàs in the Pre-Pyrenees. There you'll find this rural ten-bedroom hotel surrounded by its own farmland, which has its restaurant in a converted stable block. Dozens of varieties of vegetables and herbs, including Sant Pau beans, Blanca de Bufet potatoes, and Montserrat tomatoes, grow in the garden, and the fields are home to free-range cattle and other livestock. All of which are used well—along with other local, seasonal produce—by chef Oriol Rovira, who serves dishes like suckling pig with sweet potato salad, blood orange, hazelnut, and fennel.

RESTAURANTE VILLA MÁS

Recommended by
Josep Roca

Passeig de San Pol 95
Sant Feliu de Guíxols
Catalonia 17220
+34 972822526
www.restaurantvillamas.com

Opening hours	Variable
Credit cards	Accepted but not AMEX
Price range	Affordable
Style	Casual
Cuisine	Catalan
Recommended for	Worth the travel

An early twentieth-century modernist villa set in the bay of Sant Feliu de Guíxols, an hour north of Barcelona, is home to Restaurant Villa Más. Former DJ and now chef Carlos Orta serves the freshest seafood, such as red shrimp (prawns) from Palamos, scorpion fish, grilled grouper, and marinated sardines on potato confit. There are regional specialties, including *salmorejo* (a type of gazpacho), and inventive pairings such as pig's trotter with sea cucumber. For wine lovers there's an internationally noted selection of Burgundy vintages pegged at close-to-retail prices, although you'll still need deep pockets to enjoy them. The courtyard is perfect for summer dining.

KAK KOY

Recommended by
Oriol Castro

Carrer de Ripoll 16
Lloreda
Santa Coloma de Gramenet
Catalonia 8002
+34 933 02 84 14
www.koyshunka.com

Opening hours	Closed Monday and Sunday
Credit cards	Accepted
Price range	Affordable
Style	Casual
Cuisine	Japanese
Recommended for	Local favourite

"It's a place I usually hang out with my kids, who love Japanese cuisine."—Oriol Castro

SANT PAU

Recommended by
Ramón Freixa

Carrer Nou 10
Sant Pol de Mar
Catalonia 08395
+34 937600662
www.ruscalleda.cat/es

Opening hours	Closed Monday and Sunday
Credit cards	Accepted
Price range	Expensive
Style	Smart casual
Cuisine	Modern Catalan
Recommended for	High end

BAR SPORT TORREDEMBARRA

Recommended by
Oriol Castro

11 Carrer de la Indústria
Torredembarra
Tarragona
Catalonia 43830
+34 977 64 56 29

Opening hours	Open 7 days
Credit cards	Accepted but not AMEX or Diners
Price range	Budget
Style	Casual
Cuisine	Tapas-Seafood
Recommended for	Bargain

CA L'ENRIC

Recommended by
Jordi Roca

Carretera Camprodon
La Vall De Bianya
Catalonia 17813
+34 972290015
www.calenric.net

Opening hours	Closed Monday
Credit cards	Accepted but not AMEX
Price range	Affordable
Style	Smart casual
Cuisine	Modern Spanish
Recommended for	Local favorite

ATRIO

Recommended by
José Pizarro

Atrio Hotel
Plaza de San Mateo 1
Cáceres
Extremadura 10003
+34 927242928
www.restauranteatrio.com

Opening hours	Open 7 days
Credit cards	Accepted
Price range	Expensive
Style	Smart casual
Cuisine	Modern Spanish
Recommended for	Local favorite

"Amazing, creative food, in the old town of Cáceres.
The building was a palace and the surroundings
look back at old times. The views are also beautiful."
—José Pizarro

This incarnation of Toño Pérez and José Polo's Atrio,
designed by renowned architects Luis M. Mansilla
and Emilio Tuñón Alvarez, opened its doors in 2011.
Situated on a small square beside the convent of
San Pablo and the church of San Mateo in the
beautiful, historic part of the city, black granite
floors and white oak walls adorned with
contemporary art are the setting for Pérez's famous
creations—roast scallops with creamy boletus and
truffle, and *jamón ibérico* (Iberian ham) with lobster,
pimentón (paprika) and garlic—and Polo's
celebrated wine selection, kept in an incredible,
purpose-built cellar.

D'BERTO

Recommended by
Nieves Barragán Mohacho

Rúa Teniente Domínguez 84
O Grove
Galicia 36980
+34 986733447
www.dberto.com

Opening hours	Variable
Credit cards	Accepted but not AMEX
Price range	Affordable
Style	Casual
Cuisine	Seafood
Recommended for	Worth the travel

"Galicia is one of the best places in the world for
seafood and Berto gets the best seafood in the market.
The biggest langoustines, goose barnacles, cockles...
they taste like they've just come out of the sea."
—Nieves Barragán Mohacho

ABASTOS 2.0

Recommended by
Martin Morales

Praza de Abastos
Ameas 4
Santiago de Compostela
Galicia 15703
+34 654015937
www.abastoscompostela.com

Opening hours	Closed Monday and Sunday
Credit cards	Accepted
Price range	Affordable
Style	Casual
Cuisine	Galician
Recommended for	Worth the travel

LA TERRAZA DEL CASINO

Recommended by
Ramón Freixa

Calle de Alcalá 17
Madrid 28022
+34 915218700
www.casinodemadrid.es

Opening hours	Variable
Credit cards	Accepted
Price range	Expensive
Style	Smart casual
Cuisine	Modern Spanish
Recommended for	Late night

"Highly personal cuisine, surprising tasting menu, and
unique decoration by Jaime Hayón."—Ramón Freixa

ALABASTER

Recommended by
Ramón Freixa

Calle Montalbán 9
Madrid 28014
+34 915121131
www.restaurantealabaster.com

Opening hours	Closed Sunday
Credit cards	Accepted
Price range	Affordable
Style	Casual
Cuisine	Modern Spanish
Recommended for	Regular neighborhood

ASTUARIANOS

Recommended by
David Muñoz

Calle Vallehermoso 94
Vallehermoso
Madrid 28003
+34 915335947

Opening hours	Closed Saturday
Credit cards	Accepted
Price range	Affordable
Style	Casual
Cuisine	Asturian
Recommended for	Regular neighbourhood

LA BOMBA BISTROT

Recommended by
David Muñoz

Calle Pedro Muguruza 5
Madrid 28036
+34 913 50 30 47
www.labombabistrot.com

Opening hours	Open 7 days
Credit cards	Accepted
Price range	Affordable
Style	Smart casual
Cuisine	Spanish-European
Recommended for	Bargain

CASA DANI

Recommended by
Ramón Freixa

Calle de Ayala 28
Madrid 28001
+34 915755925

Opening hours	Closed Sunday
Reservation policy	No
Credit cards	Accepted
Price range	Affordable
Style	Casual
Cuisine	Spanish
Recommended for	Breakfast

DIVERXO

Recommended by
Ljubomir Stanisic

NH Eurobuilding
Madrid 28036
+34 915700766
www.diverxo.com

Opening hours	Closed Monday and Sunday
Credit cards	Accepted
Price range	Expensive
Style	Casual
Cuisine	Modern Spanish
Recommended for	Worth the travel

"Surprising, tasty, modern."—Ljubomir Stanisic

LA DUQUESITA

Recommended by
David Muñoz

Calle Fernando VI 2
Justicia
Madrid 28004
+34 913 08 02 31
www.laduquesita.es

Opening hours	Open 7 days
Reservation policy	No
Credit cards	Accepted
Price range	Affordable
Style	Casual
Cuisine	Patisserie
Recommended for	Breakfast

"It has one of the best pastry makers, you also do very personal things, to the front this Oriol Balaguer, who is one of the best pastry chefs in Spain"—David Muñoz

LA TORRE BISTROT

Recommended by
Aitor Jeronimo Orive

Box Art Hotel
Paseo de los Rosales 48
Madrid 28450
+34 672568729
www.elinvernadero-rdelacalle.com

Opening hours	Closed Monday to Wednesday
Credit cards	Accepted
Price range	Expensive
Style	Smart casual
Cuisine	Spanish-International
Recommended for	High end

"Rodrigo de la Calle has amazing ideas that are executed in all his dishes."—Aitor Jeronimo Orive

FISMULER

Recommended by
Ramón Freixa

Calle de Sagasta 29
Madrid 28004
+34 918277581
www.fismuler.es

Opening hours	Closed Sunday
Credit cards	Accepted
Price range	Affordable
Style	Casual
Cuisine	Spanish-Nordic
Recommended for	Bargain

"Pure cooking, fun atmosphere, and surprising ingredients with Nordic touches."—Ramón Freixa

KABUKI WELLINGTON

Recommended by
David Muñoz

Calle de Velázquez 6
Recoletos
Madrid 28001
+34 915777877
www.restaurantekabuki.com

Opening hours	Closed Sunday
Credit cards	Accepted
Price range	Affordable
Style	Smart casual
Cuisine	Japanese-Mediterranean
Recommended for	High end

LAKASA

Recommended by
David Muñoz

Plaza del Descubridor Diego de Ordás 1
Ríos Rosas
Madrid 28003
+34 915338715
www.lakasa.es

Opening hours	Closed Monday and Sunday
Credit cards	Accepted
Price range	Affordable
Style	Smart casual
Cuisine	Tapas-Spanish
Recommended for	Late night

LA TASQUITA DE ENFRENTE

Recommended by
Ramón Freixa,
David Muñoz

Calle de la Ballesta 6
Madrid 28004
+34 915325449
www.latasquitadeenfrente.com

Opening hours	Closed Sunday
Credit cards	Accepted
Price range	Affordable
Style	Casual
Cuisine	Modern Spanish
Recommended for	Local favorite

"The best from each region in Spain."—Ramón Freixa

RAMÓN FREIXA MADRID

Recommended by
Alla Wolf-Tasker

Hotel Único
Madrid 28001
+34 917818262
www.ramonfreixamadrid.com

Opening hours	Closed Monday and Sunday
Credit cards	Accepted
Price range	Expensive
Style	Smart casual
Cuisine	Modern Spanish
Recommended for	Worth the travel

Nothing says "special occasion" quite like dinner at Ramón Freixa's ravishing Madrid restaurant. Jaws hit the floor at the first sight of the chandeliers, mosaic floor, and magnificent mirrored ceiling. Classically trained Catalan chef Freixa backs up style with substance: his highly evolved cuisine was awarded two Michelin stars within two years of the restaurant opening in 2009. Both traditional and modern dishes are served—it's not often one finds hake with green peas and "variety-meat canapé" (offal) on the same menu. Cooking is in Freixa's blood—his father was a top chef and his excellent bread is served here.

NEW YORK BURGER

Recommended by
David Muñoz

General Yagüe 5
Cuatro Caminos
Madrid 28020
+34 917703079
www.newyorkburger.es

Opening hours	Closed Sunday
Credit cards	Accepted
Price range	Affordable
Style	Casual
Cuisine	Burgers
Recommended for	Regular neighbourhood

RESTAURANTE COMBARRO

Recommended by
Pedro Subijana

Calle Reina Mercedes 12
Madrid 28020
+34 915547784
www.combarro.com

Opening hours	Open 7 days
Credit cards	Accepted
Price range	Affordable
Style	Smart casual
Cuisine	Galician-Seafood
Recommended for	High end

This elegant and refined dining room close to Madrid's city center specializes in the cuisine of Galicia. Seafood is the specialty here, with a long list of *mariscos*—oysters, clams, mussels, crab— sitting alongside fish dishes like Galician hake, monkfish in garlic, and baked sea bass. There are equally attractive propositions for meat lovers, too, like the classic grilled sirloin with potatoes. You don't have to indulge in full-on fine-dining though —there's tapas in the handsome wood-panelled bar, with its impressive display of hanging hams.

SACHA

Recommended by
David Muñoz

Calle de Juan Hurtado de Mendoza 11
Nueva España
Madrid 28036
+34 913 45 59 52

Opening hours	Closed Sunday
Credit cards	Accepted
Price range	Affordable
Style	Smart casual
Cuisine	Spanish
Recommended for	Local favourite

SANTCELONI

Recommended by
David Muñoz

Paseo de la Castellana 57
Madrid28046
+34 912 10 88 40
www.restaurantesantceloni.com

Opening hours	Closed Sunday
Credit cards	Accepted
Price range	Affordable
Style	Smart casual
Cuisine	Spanish
Recommended for	Late night

STREETXO

Recommended by
Oriol Castro,
David Muñoz,
Tom Sellers

Calle de Serrano 52
Madrid 28001
+34 915319854

Opening hours	Open 7 days
Credit cards	Accepted
Price range	Affordable
Style	Casual
Cuisine	Tapas
Recommended for	Worth the travel

"Inventive food with a disciplined balance between Spanish and Asian flavors. Also, the venue is unexpected."—Tom Sellers

EL TRICICLO

Recommended by
Taras Kiriyenko

Calle Santa María 28
Madrid 28014
+34 910244798
www.eltriciclo.es

Opening hours	Closed Sunday
Credit cards	Accepted but not AMEX
Price range	Affordable
Style	Casual
Cuisine	Modern Spanish
Recommended for	Late night

"A must-go in Madrid. Beautiful restaurant with outstanding food, great for sharing."—Taras Kiriyenko

TABERNA DE LA DANIELA GOYA

Recommended by
Omar Allibhoy

Calle de General Pardiñas 21
Madrid 28001
+34 915752329
www.tabernaladaniela.com

Opening hours	Open 7 days
Credit cards	Accepted
Price range	Affordable
Style	Casual
Cuisine	Madrileno
Recommended for	Local favorite

"This restaurant serves the best *Cocido Madrileño*— a rich soup with thin angel-hair pasta, chickpeas and stewed beef in tomato sauce and seasonal greens. It's a must try if you're in Madrid."—Omar Allibhoy

UMIKO

Recommended by
David Muñoz

Calle de los Madrazo 18
Madrid 28014
+34 914938706
www.umiko.es

Opening hours	Closed Sunday
Credit cards	Accepted
Price range	Affordable
Style	Casual
Cuisine	Japanese
Recommended for	Regular neighbourhood

VIRIDIANA

Recommended by
David Muñoz

Calle Juan de Mena 14
Madrid 28014
+34 915 31 10 39
www.restauranteviridiana.com

Opening hours	Open 7 days
Credit cards	Accepted
Price range	Affordable
Style	Smart casual
Cuisine	Spanish
Recommended for	Local favourite

STREETXO

Recommended by
Oriol Castro

Calle de Serrano 52
Salamanca
Madrid 28001
+34 915319854

Opening hours	Open 7 days
Credit cards	Accepted
Price range	Affordable
Style	Casual
Cuisine	Tapas
Recommended for	Wish I'd opened

LA TABERNA DEL GOURMET

Recommended by
Mashama Bailey

Calle San Fernando 10
Alicante
Valencian Community 03002
+39 965204233
www.latabernadelgourmet.com

Opening hours	Open 7 days
Credit cards	Accepted but not Diners
Price range	Affordable
Style	Smart casual
Cuisine	Catolonian
Recommended for	Worth the travel

"I love the atmosphere and the way they went out of their way for locals but made us feel at home as well. We started with something as simple as fried eggplant (aubergine) and honey and it totally inspired me because of the simplicity and perfection of it."
— Mashama Bailey

QUIQUE DACOSTA

Recommended by
José Avillez,
Sang-Hoon Degeimbre,
Karl Firla,
Sergio Herman,
Ángel León,
Ljubomir Stanisic,
Adam Stokes, Pedro Subijana

Urbanización del Poblet
Calle Rascassa 1
Dénia
Valencian Community 03700
+34 965784179
www.quiquedacosta.es

Opening hours	Closed Monday and Tuesday
Credit cards	Accepted
Price range	Expensive
Style	Formal
Cuisine	Modern Spanish
Recommended for	Worth the travel

"Quique has his own style and vision. He plays your tastes and emotions."—Sergio Herman

Chef Quique Dacosta takes his place among the Spanish avant-garde giants thanks to his desire to create truly original dishes. Following El Bulli's closure, his Costa Blanca restaurant has become the new place of pilgrimage for globetrotting gastronomes. Inside the glass-and-concrete building, which simultaneously resembles a modern art gallery and a rustic Spanish retreat, Dacosta experiments with underutilized plants, such as cacti, as well as more traditional Spanish ingredients, in an attempt to create an "edible landscape". As you might imagine, dishes are colorful, often surprising, and occasionally crazy—but always memorable.

"LOCAL BUT NOT CONFINED. YOU FEEL AT HOME HERE."

ESTANISLAO CARENZO P597

BARCELONA

"*Blown away!*"

KARL FIRLA P596

"TOP-QUALITY, PRODUCE-DRIVEN, LOCAL TAPAS BAR IN BARCELONA."

WILLY TRULLAS MORENO P597

"I WAS UTTERLY IMPRESSED BY THE FRESHNESS. THE TASTE. THE SIMPLICITY AND THE HUMBLE PERFECTION OF THE MEAL I WAS SERVED."

THOMAS RODE ANDERSEN P596

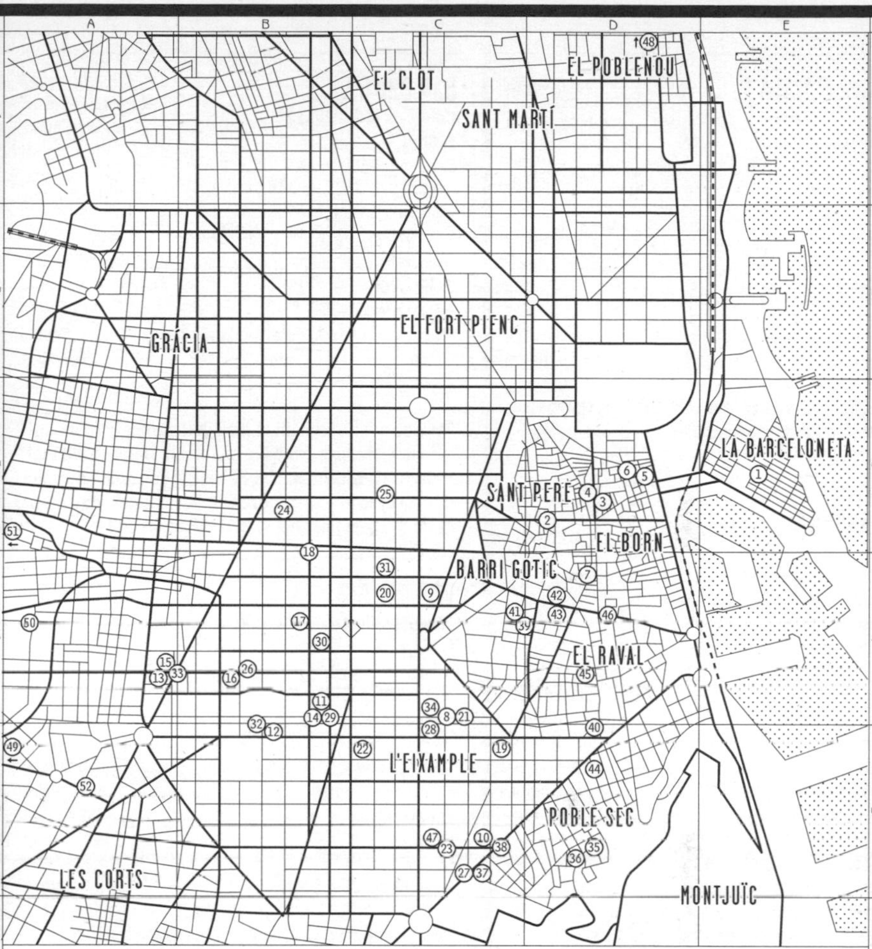

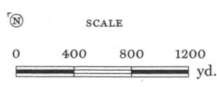

EL CLOT
EL POBLENOU
48
SANT MARTÍ
GRÁCIA
EL FORT PIENC
LA BARCELONETA
SANT PERE
EL BORN
BARRI GOTIC
EL RAVAL
L'EIXAMPLE
POBLE SEC
LES CORTS
MONTJUÏC

BARCELONA

N

SCALE

0 400 800 1200 yd.

1. *La Cova Fumada (p.594)*
2. *Koy Shunka (p.594)*
3. *Bar Brutal (p.594)*
4. *Bar Del Pla (p.594)*
5. *Cal Pep (p.595)*
6. *Paradiso (p.595)*
7. *Satans Coffee Corner (p.595)*
8. *Alkimia (p.595)*
9. *Bacoa (p.595)*
10. *Bodega 1900 (p.596)*
11. *Bar Ket (p.596)*
12. *Cloudstreet Bakery (p.596)*
13. *Coure (p.596)*
14. *Disfrutar (p.596)*
15. *Fogo (p.597)*
16. *Gaig (p.597)*
17. *Gresca (p.597)*
18. *Lasarte (p.597)*
19. *Mercat De Sant Antoni (p.597)*
20. *Mextizo (p.598)*
21. *Moritz(p.598)*
22. *Morro Fi (p.598)*
23. *Niño Viejo (p.598)*
24. *Nobook (p.598)*
25. *Norte (p.598)*
26. *Paco Meralgo (p.599)*
27. *Pakta (p.599)*
28. *Pastisseria Escribà (p.599)*
29. *Porvenir (p.599)*
30. *Sergi De Meià (p.599)*
31. *Tapas 24 (p.600)*
32. *La Taverna Del Clínic (p.600)*
33. *El Velódromo (p.600)*
34. *La Volàtil (p.600)*
35. *Xemei (p.600)*
36. *Bar Casa Xica (p.601)*
37. *Rias De Galicia (p.601)*
38. *Tickets (p.601)*
39. *Dos Pebrots (p.601)*
40. *Ca L'isidre (p.601)*
41. *Dos Palillos (p.602)*
42. *Mercat De La Boqueria (p.602)*
43. *Pinotxo (p.602)*
44. *Quimet & Quimet (p.602)*
45. *Suculent (p.602)*
46. *Rocambolesc (p.602)*
47. *Enigma (p.603)*
48. *Els Pescadors (p.603)*
49. *Bar Tomás (p.603)*
50. *Freixa Tradició (p.603)*
51. *Un'altra Storia (p.603)*
52. *Via Veneto (p.603)*

LA COVA FUMADA

Carrer del Baluart 56
La Barceloneta
Barcelona 08003
+34 932214061

Recommended by
David Gingell,
Andy Hollyday

Opening hours	Closed Sunday
Credit cards	Not accepted
Price range	Affordable
Style	Casual
Cuisine	Tapas
Recommended for	Worth the travel

"Good Spanish vibes—one of the rare restaurants in Barcelona that still feels like it's for the locals."
—David Gingell

KOY SHUNKA

Copons 7
Barri Gòtic
Barcelona 08002
+34 934127939
www.koyshunka.com

Recommended by
Eduardo Moreno,
Joan Roca,
Oriol Castro

Opening hours	Closed Monday
Credit cards	Accepted
Price range	Expensive
Style	Smart casual
Cuisine	Japanese
Recommended for	Local favorite

"It's a typical Japanese restaurant in Barcelona. The produce is its main selling point: perfect cuts and perfectly cooked, a purity and simplicity that result in unique, unforgettable dishes."—Eduardo Moreno

The narrow, low-ceilinged vaults of the Barri Gòtic could almost have been made to house sushi bars, and Koy Shunka (the grown-up brother of Shunka) feels right at home here despite serving the kind of precisely beautiful *omakase* (menu chosen by the chef) more common 6,000 miles (10,000 km) away. But actually, chef Hideki Matsuhisa's work is, despite appearances, distinctly of Barcelona— ingredients such as white asparagus from Gava or eel from Delta del Ebro are simply the best available, and though they are given the Japanese treatment, they showcase the region's producers as well as any traditional Catalan joint you could think of. Service, too, is a perfect marriage of Japanese hospitality and Catalan warmth.

BAR BRUTAL

Carrer de la Princesa 14
El Born
Barcelona 08003
+34 932954797
www.cancisa.cat

Recommended by
Estanislao Carenzo,
Samuel Nutter

Opening hours	Closed Sunday
Credit cards	Accepted
Price range	Affordable
Style	Casual
Cuisine	Wine Bar
Recommended for	Bargain

"Maybe not the cheapest meal but certainly value for money. Incredible wine list and fresh, simple food that is perfectly executed. The vibe is very special and you can easily lose a whole evening here before you know it! (In the best possible way!)"—Samuel Nutter

BAR DEL PLA

Carrer de Montcada 2
El Born
Barcelona 08003
+34 932683003
www.bardelpla.cat

Recommended by
Robert Jacobsson

Opening hours	Closed Sunday
Credit cards	Accepted
Price range	Affordable
Style	Casual
Cuisine	Tapas
Recommended for	Worth the travel

"Good food, fantastic wine, super nice ambiance."
— Robert Jacobsson

At first glance, Bar del Pla looks like any ordinary tapas joint tucked in to the medieval backstreets of El Born, with its vaulted ceiling and gaggle of happy locals occupying the marble bar. But as anyone familiar with the work of Jaume Pla (like the longstanding Restaurant Pla in the Barri Gòtic, and the now-closed Repla) will tell you, these guys don't do ordinary. The food is of an extraordinarily high standard—immaculate squid ink croquettes and *calçots* (Catalan [scallions] spring onions) at the more traditional end, or an innovative mushroom carpaccio with wasabi vinaigrette showcasing some Asian influence. The wine list, too, is well chosen and has interesting options at all budgets. Definitely worth a visit.

CAL PEP

Recommended by
Norman Van Aken

Plaça de les Olles 8
El Born
Barcelona 08003
+34 933107961
www.calpep.com

Opening hours	Closed Sunday
Credit cards	Accepted
Price range	Affordable
Style	Casual
Cuisine	Spanish Tapas
Recommended for	Worth the travel

"Noted Spanish food and wine expert and friend Gerry Dawes told us to 'go to Cal Pep'. It was just the kind of place we love! The food is cooked in front of you by people who love their work. It is a tough place to get in to so plan ahead. Counter seating with seasonal, local Spanish foods."—Norman Van Aken

PARADISO

Recommended by
Peeter Pihel

Carrer de Rera Palau 4
El Born
Barcelona 08003
+34 933607222
www.paradiso.cat

Opening hours	Open 7 days
Credit cards	Accepted but not AMEX
Price range	Budget
Style	Casual
Cuisine	Tapas
Recommended for	Late night

"The Pastrami Bar is the first permanent location from Rooftop Smokehouse, regulars from the Van Van Market. Needless to say that their €7 ($8; £6) made-in-house pastrami is a delight."—Peeter Pihel

SATANS COFFEE CORNER

Recommended by
Estanislao Carenzo

Carrer de l'Arc de Sant Ramon del Call 11
El Born
Barcelona 08002
+34 666222599
www.satanscoffee.com

Opening hours	Open 7 days
Reservation policy	No
Credit cards	Accepted but not AMEX
Price range	Budget
Style	Casual
Cuisine	Café-Bakery
Recommended for	Breakfast

"Love this place—full of energy. The coffee is so good and I thank Marcos and Ken for serving incredible, healthy, modern Japanese soul food."
—Estanislao Carenzo

ALKIMIA

Recommended by
Albert Raurich,
Eduard Xatruch Cerro

Ronda de Sant Antoni 41
L'Eixample
Barcelona 08011
+34 932076115
www.alkimia.cat

Opening hours	Closed Saturday and Sunday
Credit cards	Accepted
Price range	Expensive
Style	Smart casual
Cuisine	Modern Catalan
Recommended for	High end

"It has magnificent quality—impressive."
—Eduard Xatruch Cerro

If people still accuse Catalan cuisine of taking itself too seriously—even after the departure of El Bulli from the scene—then it's probably due to places like Alkimia, with its austere modernist decor and knowing reimagining of traditional local dishes. But chef Jordi Vilà is undoubtedly one of the most talented chefs at work today in Barcelona, and the food he produces—everything from the liquid *pan con tomate* (bread with tomato) amuse-bouche to the dance of exquisite seasonality that follows—impresses (seriously) on every level. The name of the restaurant is derived from the Arabic word *al-kimia* ("the art"), but the pun on the English "alchemy" is undoubtedly no accident—and thoroughly apt.

BACOA

Recommended by
Estanislao Carenzo

Ronda Universitat 31
L'Eixample
Barcelona 08007
+34 932507290
www.bacoaburger.com

Opening hours	Open 7 days
Credit cards	Accepted but not AMEX
Price range	Affordable
Style	Casual
Cuisine	Burgers
Recommended for	Late night

"A local burger chain that uses eco-products and works with responsibility."—Estanislao Carenzo

BODEGA 1900

Recommended by
Albert Raurich,
Thomas Rode Andersen

Carrer de Tamarit 91
L'Eixample
Barcelona 08015
+34 933252659
www.bodega1900.com

Opening hours	Closed Monday and Sunday
Credit cards	Accepted
Price range	Affordable
Style	Casual
Cuisine	Tapas
Recommended for	Worth the travel

"I was utterly impressed by the freshness, the taste, the simplicity, and the humble perfection of the meal I was served there with my family. I would love to open a restaurant like that."—Thomas Rode Andersen

BAR KET

Mercado del Ninot
Carrer de Mallorca 133
L'Eixample
Barcelona 8036
+34 933 23 49 09
www.mercatdelninot.com

Opening hours	Closed Sunday
Reservation policy	No
Credit cards	Not accepted
Price range	Budget
Style	Casual
Cuisine	Spanish-Tapas
Recommended for	Breakfast

"I always like to have a tortilla sandwich and a cut of meat after having been in the market buying product."—Oriol Castro

CLOUDSTREET BAKERY

Recommended by
Estanislao Carenzo

Carrer del Rosselló 112
L'Eixample
Barcelona 08036
+34 932505828
www.cloudstreet.es

Opening hours	Closed Sunday
Credit cards	Accepted but not AMEX
Price range	Budget
Style	Casual
Cuisine	Bakery
Recommended for	Regular neighborhood

"When I'm in a hurry, I like to grab something from Cloudstreet Bakery."—Estanislao Carenzo

COURE

Recommended by
Albert Raurich,
Jordi Vilà

Passatge de Marimon 20
L'Eixample
Barcelona 08021
+34 932007532
www.restaurantcoure.es

Opening hours	Closed Monday and Sunday
Credit cards	Accepted
Price range	Affordable
Style	Casual
Cuisine	Modern Catalan
Recommended for	Regular neighborhood

"Direct, tasty, and sincere cuisine."—Jordi Vilà

Barcelona's bistronomics movement is all about ambitious chefs serving exciting food while keeping costs to a minimum. The modern Catalan dishes chef Albert Ventura produces in his basement restaurant are aimed at the heights of Michelin-starred gastronomy, but at just €35 ($38; £30) for a seasonal menu, this classy cooking doesn't have to be a rare treat. On the ground floor are squeezed ten stools at a small tapas bar, where you can enjoy a taste of the theatrics from below—without the white tablecloths and for an even smaller chunk of cash.

DISFRUTAR

Recommended by
Karl Firla,
Chele (José Luis) Gonzalez,
Julius Jaspers,
Albert Raurich,
Evgeny Vikentev

Carrer de Villarroel 163
L'Eixample
Barcelona 08036
+34 933486896
www.ca.disfrutarbarcelona.com

Opening hours	Closed Monday and Sunday
Credit cards	Accepted
Price range	Expensive
Style	Smart casual
Cuisine	Modern Catalan
Recommended for	Worth the travel

"Blown away! The most progressive, intriguing, fun, precise meal I have had in a long time."—Karl Firla

Gastro-star trio Mateu Casañas, Oriol Castro, and Eduard Xatruch (who cut their teeth at—where else —El Bulli) opened Disfrutar in 2014, intending not to be another branch of Compartir (their stonkingly successful Cadaques restaurant) but rather a re-working of the same ideals, namely seasonal

Catalan cuisine served in a variety of surprising and avant-garde ways. The food more than lives up to the pedigree, being stunning to look at and deeply rewarding to eat, with a sense of humor and playfulness often missing from highfalutin tasting menus at this price point. A superb tribute to the El Bulli legacy, and one of modern Barcelona's finest restaurants.

FOGO

Recommended by
Ruairí de Blacam

Carrer de Còrsega 231
L'Eixample
Barcelona 08036
+34 932692830
www.alquimiafogo.com

Opening hours	Closed Monday and Sunday
Credit cards	Accepted
Price range	Affordable
Style	Casual
Cuisine	Brazilian
Recommended for	Regular neighborhood

"A modern Brazilian restaurant with an excellent chef."—Ruairí de Blacam

GAIG

Recommended by
Eduard Xatruch Cerro

Carrer de Còrsega 200
L'Eixample
Barcelona 08036
+34 934532020
www.restaurantgaig.com

Opening hours	Closed Monday
Credit cards	Accepted
Price range	Affordable
Style	Casual
Cuisine	Traditional Catalan
Recommended for	Local favorite

GRESCA

Recommended by
Estanislao Carenzo,
Albert Raurich,
Jordi Vilà

Calle Provença 230
L'Eixample
Barcelona 08036
+34 934516193
www.gresca.net

Opening hours	Closed Sunday
Credit cards	Accepted
Price range	Affordable
Style	Casual
Cuisine	Modern Catalan
Recommended for	Local favorite

"A great natural wine list, local produce, and a great cook with a flavorful, beautiful, and intelligent cuisine. Local but not confined. You feel at home here."
—Estanislao Carenzo

With just twenty-six covers, the narrow, minimalist dining room, with its white linen and white walls, focuses the diner's full attention on the plate. Which is no bad thing, as the dinnerware here is the canvas for talented and creative chef Rafael Peña. A graduate of the school of Spanish modernism sustained by both Ferran Adrià and Martín Berasategui, Peña's style of "bistronomia" fuses traditional bistro food with the haute-cuisine ideals of gastronomy to produce dishes—a flower-shaped egg-white soufflé with soft yolk center, for instance —that are as affordable as they are delicious.

LASARTE

Recommended by
Oriol Castro
Peter Knogl,
Alexander Mayer

Carrer Mallorca 259
L'Eixample
Barcelona 08008
+34 934453242
www.restaurantlasarte.com

Opening hours	Closed Monday and Sunday
Credit cards	Accepted
Price range	Expensive
Style	Smart casual
Cuisine	Modern International
Recommended for	Regular neighborhood

"For me it is pure perfection."—Peter Knogl

MERCAT DE SANT ANTONI

Recommended by
Jordi Vilà

Carrer del Comde d'Urgell 1
L'Eixample
Barcelona 08011
+34 934263521
www.mercatdesantantoni.com

Opening hours	Closed Sunday
Reservation policy	No
Credit cards	Not accepted
Price range	Affordable
Style	Casual
Cuisine	Market
Recommended for	Breakfast

MEXTIZO

Recommended by
Jordi Vilà

Carrer de la Diputació 239
L'Eixample
Barcelona 08007
+34 935414623
www.mextizo.es

Opening hours	Open 7 days
Credit cards	Accepted
Price range	Expensive
Style	Formal
Cuisine	Mexican
Recommended for	Late night

MORITZ

Recommended by
Eduard Xatruch

Ronda Sant Antoni 39
L'Eixample
Barcelona 08011
+34 934260050
www.moritz.com

Opening hours	Open 7 days
Credit cards	Accepted
Price range	Affordable
Style	Casual
Cuisine	Tapas
Recommended for	Late night

"It's an informal place with tapas and a good place to have a few drinks."—Eduard Xatruch Cerro

MORRO FI

Recommended by
Estanislao Carenzo

Carrer del Consell de Cent 171
L'Eixample
Barcelona 08015
www.morrofi.cat

Opening hours	Open 7 days
Reservation policy	No
Credit cards	Not accepted
Price range	Budget
Style	Casual
Cuisine	Tapas
Recommended for	Bargain

"Perfect place for smoked sardines, *gildas* (anchovy, olive, and pickled chile skewers) and very good *vermut* (vermouth). Barcelona every-day luxury."
—Estanislao Carenzo

NIÑO VIEJO

Recommended by
Evgeny Vikentev

Avinguda de Mistral 54
L'Eixample
Barcelona 08015
+34 933482194
www.ninoviejo.es

Opening hours	Closed Sunday
Credit cards	Accepted
Price range	Affordable
Style	Casual
Cuisine	Mexican
Recommended for	Bargain

"Mexican taqueria by Albert Adrià and Paco Méndez. A perfect balance between simple, traditional, and modern and interesting cuisine, with cocktails based on tequila and mezcal and the best tacos that I've ever eaten."—Evgeny Vikentev

NOBOOK

Recommended by
Eduardo Moreno

Carrer Provença 310
L'Eixample
Barcelona 08037
www.nobook.es

Opening hours	Closed Sunday
Reservation policy	No
Credit cards	Accepted but not AMEX
Price range	Affordable
Style	Casual
Cuisine	Asian
Recommended for	Worth the travel

"Everyday cooking taken to its utmost expression, refined technique, innovative cocktail bar, perfect service, enjoyable place with a contemporary style, good music, and prices beyond compare. All this makes it a very difficult choice to improve on."
—Eduardo Moreno

NORTE

Recommended by
Estanislao Carenzo

Carrer de la Diputació 321
L'Eixample
Barcelona 08009
+34 935287676

Opening hours	Closed Saturday and Sunday
Credit cards	Accepted
Price range	Affordable
Style	Casual
Cuisine	Catalan
Recommended for	Regular neighborhood

"I love this place. They just open for lunch, buy the best products they can find, locally sourced, respecting the season. They deliver love and you can feel how amazing these two women are. I believe that they are incredibly generous by keeping prices low. That's why you will be eating with a small crowd of local patrons almost every day." —Estanislao Carenzo

PACO MERALGO

Recommended by
Willy Trullas Moreno

Carrer de Muntaner 171
L'Eixample
Barcelona 08036
+34 934309027
www.restaurantpacomeralgo.com

Opening hours	Open 7 days
Credit cards	Accepted
Price range	Affordable
Style	Casual
Cuisine	Catalan
Recommended for	Local favorite

"Best example of a top-quality, produce-driven, local tapas bar in Barcelona."—Willy Trullas Moreno

PAKTA

Recommended by
Jocky Petrie,
Thomas Rode Andersen,
Evgeny Vikentev

Carrer Lleida 5
L'Eixample
Barcelona 08004
+34 936240177
www.es.pakta.es

Opening hours	Closed Monday and Sunday
Credit cards	Accepted
Price range	Affordable
Style	Smart casual
Cuisine	Japanese-Peruvian
Recommended for	Worth the travel

"Very trendy Nikkei cuisine in one of my favorite cities. Albert Adrià and his team reconstruct Japanese and Peruvian cuisine. Pure tastes, interesting flavor combinations, perfect service, and a contemporary interior with authentic details."—Evgeny Vikentev

PASTISSERIA ESCRIBÀ

Recommended by
Albert Raurich

Gran Via de les Corts Catalanes 546
L'Eixample
Barcelona 8011
+34 934 54 75 35
www.escriba.es

Opening hours	Open 7 days
Credit cards	Accepted
Price range	Affordable
Style	Smart casual
Cuisine	Patisserie
Recommended for	Breakfast

"Christian Escribà is one of the best pastry cooks in this country, is a specialist in pastry and uses high quality raw material."—Albert Raurich

PORVENIR

Recommended by
Eduard Xatruch

Carrer de Villarroel 157
L'Eixample
Barcelona 08036
+34 934531046
www.oretorno.es/porvenir

Opening hours	Closed Monday
Credit cards	Accepted but not AMEX
Price range	Affordable
Style	Casual
Cuisine	Galician
Recommended for	Bargain

SERGI DE MEIÀ

Recommended by
Eduard Xatruch

Carrer d'Aribau 106
L'Eixample
Barcelona 08036
+34 931255710
www.restaurantsergidemeia.cat

Opening hours	Closed Monday and Sunday
Credit cards	Accepted
Price range	Affordable
Style	Casual
Cuisine	Catalan
Recommended for	Regular neighborhood

"An informal restaurant with Catalan cuisine."
—Eduard Xatruch Cerro

TAPAS 24

Carrer de la Diputació 269
L'Eixample
Barcelona 08007
+34 934880977
www.carlesabellan.es

Opening hours	Closed Sunday
Reservation policy	No
Credit cards	Accepted
Price range	Affordable
Style	Casual
Cuisine	Tapas
Recommended for	Bargain

The Eixample tapas bar from chef Carles Abellan, who did sixteen years under you-know-who of El Bulli fame, and also runs Bravo24 in the W Hotel as well as the more experimental Commerc24. In a small, brightly lit basement, the short menu of crowd-pleasing snacks is designed as a cutlery wrapper and scrawled across mirrors and blackboards. These include classic salt-cod croquettes, Catalan favorites like tripe stew, and the posh fast-food hits that are the "Bikini"—a ham and cheese toasted sandwich flecked with black truffle—and the "McFoie Burger"—a beef and foie gras patty in a crispy bun.

LA TAVERNA DEL CLÍNIC

Carrer del Roselló 155
L'Eixample
Barcelona 08036
+34 934104221
www.latavernadelclinic.com

Opening hours	Closed Sunday
Credit cards	Accepted
Price range	Expensive
Style	Casual
Cuisine	Spanish Tapas
Recommended for	Local favorite

"Its sublime ingredients are particularly noteworthy."
—Eduard Xatruch Cerro

EL VELÓDROMO

Carrer de Muntaner 213
L'Eixample
Barcelona 08036
+34 934306022
www.moritz.com

Opening hours	Open 7 days
Credit cards	Accepted
Price range	Affordable
Style	Casual
Cuisine	Modern Catalan
Recommended for	Late night

"Eating late is quite difficult in Barcelona. El Velodromo makes me remember Buenos Aires, as it offers real food and service until late. Sometimes when I'm going home I like to stop and have a proper meal and chill."—Estanislao Carenzo

LA VOLÀTIL

Carrer Mutaner 6
L'Eixample
Barcelona 08011
+34 931721199
www.lavolatil.com

Opening hours	Open 7 days
Credit cards	Accepted
Price range	Affordable
Style	Casual
Cuisine	Spanish Tapas
Recommended for	Regular neighborhood

XEMEI

Paseo de la Exposición 85
Montjuic
Barcelona 08004
+34 935535140
www.xemei.es

Opening hours	Open 7 days
Credit cards	Accepted
Price range	Affordable
Style	Casual
Cuisine	Venetian
Recommended for	Local favorite

"It's modern Venetian cuisine, but they use a lot of local ingredients and really understand the region."
— Estanislao Carenzo

BAR CASA XICA

Recommended by
Albert Raurich

Carrer de la França Xica 20
El Poble-sec
Barcelona 8004
+34 936 00 58 58

Opening hours	Closed Sunday
Credit cards	Accepted but not AMEX or Diners
Price range	Affordable
Style	Casual
Cuisine	Spanish
Recommended for	Bargain

RIAS DE GALICIA

Recommended by
Pedro Subijana,
Eduard Xatruch

Carrer Lleida 7
El Poble-sec
Barcelona 08004
+34 934248152
www.riasdegalicia.com

Opening hours	Open 7 days
Credit cards	Accepted
Price range	Expensive
Style	Smart casual
Cuisine	Spanish-Seafood
Recommended for	Wish I'd opened

**"This is the best shellfish restaurant in Barcelona."
—Eduard Xatruch Cerro**

The late-1980s/early-1990s time warp of a dining room aside, it's hard to fault anything bar the steepness of the bill at this Galician seafood specialist. Fish this rare, though, doesn't come cheap. Aside from the vintage Joselito ham and the large range of cheeses, the only "land" food on offer is suckling pig and veal—so indulge in the lengthiest list of wacky and wonderful shellfish you're ever likely to see this side of a high-end Tokyo sushi bar.

TICKETS

Recommended by
Omar Allibhoy, Gaggan Anand,
Kristian Baumann, Rick Bayless,
John Jackson, William Mahi,
Jordi Roca, Jason Tan,
Andrew Wong

Avinguda del Paral·lel 164
El Poble-sec
Barcelona 08015
+34 606225545
www.ticketsbar.es

Opening hours	Closed Monday and Sunday
Credit cards	Accepted
Price range	Affordable
Style	Casual
Cuisine	Tapas
Recommended for	Worth the travel

"This is the most mind-blowing experience! Super-delicious, crazy-playful food. If you're lucky enough to find yourself in their Willy Wonka-esque dessert room, brace yourself for an unforgettable experience."—Rick Bayless

DOS PEBROTS

Recommended by
Albert Raurich

Carrer Doctor Dou 19
El Raval
Barcelona 8001
+34 938 539 598
www.dospebrots.com

Opening hours	Closed Monday and Tuesday
Credit cards	Accepted
Price range	Affordable
Style	Smart casual
Cuisine	Spanish
Recommended for	Worth the travel

CA L'ISIDRE

Recommended by
Albert Raurich

Carrer de les Flors 12
El Raval
Barcelona 8001
+34 934 41 11 39
www.calisidre.com

Opening hours	Closed Sunday
Credit cards	Accepted
Price range	Affordable
Style	Smart casual
Cuisine	Catalan-Mediterranean
Recommended for	Regular neighbourhood

"Nuria Girones (daughter of Isidre) has taken the reins and has taken a trip to the legendary Catalan restaurant of Barcelona, the best products of the Boqueria are in the best hands."—Albert Raurich

DOS PALILLOS

Recommended by
Jordi Vilà

Carrer d'Elisabets 9
El Raval
Barcelona 08001
+34 933040513
www.dospalillos.com

Opening hours	Closed Monday and Sunday
Credit cards	Accepted
Price range	Affordable
Style	Casual
Cuisine	Asian Fusion
Recommended for	Late night

You've been executive chef at a renowned restaurant for the best part of a decade—what do you do next? The answer for Albert Raurich, who ran the kitchen at El Bulli from 1999 until 2007, is to open an Asian-inspired tapas bar. Located beside the Casa Camper hotel, it serves small plates in its no-nonsense front bar, where you perch perilously on crates. Behind the bead curtain at the back lies a formal dining room with counter seating and a menu of Asian-Iberian dishes.

MERCAT DE LA BOQUERIA

Recommended by
Brian Ahern

Rambla 91
El Raval
Barcelona 08001
+34 933182584
www.boqueria.info

Opening hours	Closed Sunday
Reservation policy	No
Credit cards	Not accepted
Price range	Affordable
Style	Casual
Cuisine	Market
Recommended for	Worth the travel

PINOTXO

Recommended by
Ramón Freixa,
Willy Trullas Moreno,
Eduard Xatruch

Mercat de la Boqueria 466–470
La Rambla 89
El Raval
Barcelona 08002
+34 933171731
www.pinotxobar.com

Opening hours	Closed Sunday
Reservation policy	No
Credit cards	Not accepted
Price range	Affordable
Style	Casual
Cuisine	Pintxos
Recommended for	Breakfast

"This local place is perfect to have a fork-and-knife traditional breakfast with traditional Catalan cuisine dishes."—Willy Trullas Moreno

QUIMET & QUIMET

Recommended by
Oriol Castro

Carrer del Poeta Cabanyes 25
El Poble-sec
Barcelona 8004
+34 934423142

Opening hours	Closed Sunday
Reservation policy	No
Credit cards	Accepted but not AMEX or Diners
Price range	Budget
Style	Casual
Cuisine	Tapas
Recommended for	Late night

SUCULENT

Recommended by
Albert Raurich

Rambla del Raval 43
El Raval
Barcelona 8001
+34 934436579

Opening hours	Closed Monday and Tuesday
Credit cards	Accepted
Price range	Affordable
Style	Casual
Cuisine	Mediterranean
Recommended for	Regular neighborhood

**"Here we can find another reflection of what is happening in this city, which is nothing other than consolidating a fantastic level of cuisine!"
—Albert Raurich**

ROCAMBOLESC

Recommended by
Oriol Castro

La Rambla 51-59
El Raval
Barcelona 8002
www.rocambolesc.com

Opening hours	Open 7 days
Reservation policy	No
Credit cards	Accepted
Price range	Budget
Style	Casual
Cuisine	Ice Cream
Recommended for	Regular neighborhood

"They treat the ice cream as a dish, they have revolutionized the ice cream concept and allow the customer to 'create' their own."—Oriol Castro

ENIGMA

Recommended by
Albert Raurich

Carrer Sepúlveda 38-40
Sant Antoni
Barcelona 8015
www.enigmaconcept.es

Opening hours	Closed Monday and Sunday
Credit cards	Accepted
Price range	Expensive
Style	Formal
Cuisine	Modern Spanish
Recommended for	Worth the travel

ELS PESCADORS

Recommended by
Florence Knight

Plaça Prim 1
Sant Marti
Barcelona 08005
+34 932252018
www.elspescadors.com

Opening hours	Open 7 days
Credit cards	Accepted
Price range	Affordable
Style	Casual
Cuisine	Catalan
Recommended for	Worth the travel

"Beautiful food from Catalonia. Ingredient-led, simple and very elegant."—Florence Knight

BAR TOMÁS

Recommended by
Estanislao Carenzo,
Willy Trullas Moreno

Carrer Major de Sarrià 49
Sarrià-Sant Gervasi
Barcelona 08017
+34 932031077
www.eltomasdesarria.com

Opening hours	Closed Sunday
Reservation policy	No
Credit cards	Not accepted
Price range	Budget
Style	Casual
Cuisine	Tapas
Recommended for	Bargain

"Great place to go for *patatas bravas*, anchovies, and olives or for a combi-plate."—Willy Trullas Moreno

FREIXA TRADICIÓ

Recommended by
Ramón Freixa

Carrer de Sant Elies 22
Sarrià-Sant Gervasi
Barcelona 08006
+34 932252018
www.freixatradicio.com

Opening hours	Closed Monday
Credit cards	Accepted
Price range	Affordable
Style	Casual
Cuisine	Catalan
Recommended for	Local favorite

UN'ALTRA STORIA

Recommended by
Jordi Vilà

Carrer de Saragossa 122
Sarrià-Sant Gervasi
Barcelona 08006
+34 935662814
www.unaltrastoria.cat

Opening hours	Closed Monday
Credit cards	Accepted but not AMEX
Price range	Affordable
Style	Casual
Cuisine	Sicilian
Recommended for	Bargain

"Simple Italian cuisine, following traditional Sicilian recipes, carried out by a Sicilian mother and son in Barcelona."—Jordi Vilà

VIA VENETO

Recommended by
Estanislao Carenzo

Carrer de Ganduxer 10
Sarrià-Sant Gervasi
Barcelona 08021
+34 932007244
www.viaveneto.es

Opening hours	Closed Sunday
Credit cards	Accepted
Price range	Affordable
Style	Smart casual
Cuisine	European
Recommended for	High end

"A hint of how the old days used to be. Old-school luxury, *canard au sang* (pressed duck), and classic wines."—Estanislao Carenzo

PORTUGAL

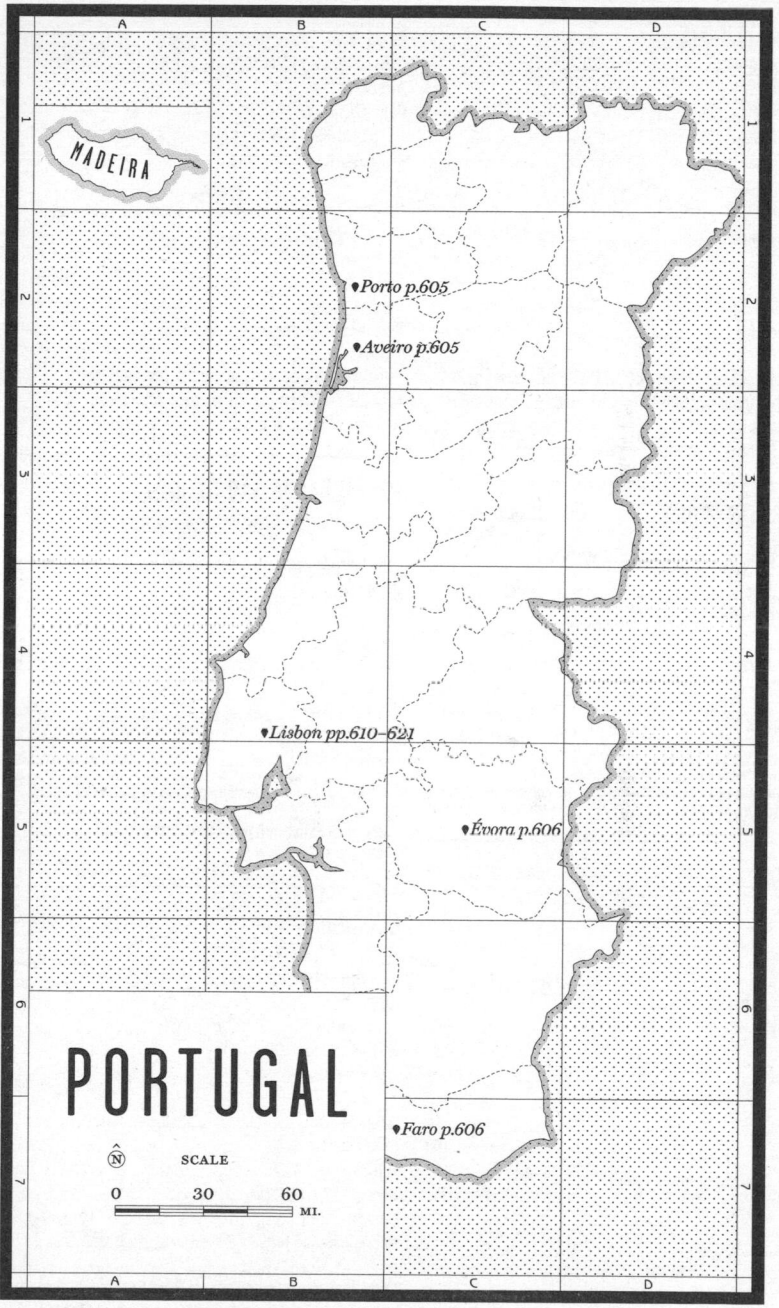

MADEIRA

♦Porto p.605

♦Aveiro p.605

♦Lisbon pp.610–621

♦Évora p.606

PORTUGAL

♦Faro p.606

N̂   SCALE

0   30   60
MI.

RESTAURANTE POTE

Recommended by
José Cordeiro

Rua do Cadaval 395
Válega
Aveiro 3880-583
+351 966627719
www.restaurantepote.com

Opening hours	Closed Sunday
Credit cards	Not accepted
Price range	Affordable
Style	Casual
Cuisine	Traditional Portuguese
Recommended for	Local favorite

"Magnificent atmosphere with a POTE charcoal grill and grilled dishes prepared as you watch. Excellent cuisine with a wood-fired oven. Exemplary table service and good wine list."—José Cordeiro

HERDADE DO ESPORÃO

Recommended by
Henrique Sá Pessoa

Apartado 31
Reguengos de Monsaraz
Évora 7200-999
+351 266509280
www.esporao.com

Opening hours	Closed Monday
Credit cards	Accepted
Price range	Affordable
Style	Casual
Cuisine	Mediterranean
Recommended for	Worth the travel

VILA JOYA

Recommended by
Ljubomir Stanisic

Vila Joya & Joy Jung Spa
Estrada da Galé
Albufeira
Faro 8200-416
+351 289591795
www.vilajoya.com

Opening hours	Variable
Credit cards	Accepted
Price range	Expensive
Style	Smart casual
Cuisine	Modern European
Recommended for	High end

GIGI'S

Recommended by
Miguel Castro e Silva

Quinta do Lago South Portugal
Almancil
Faro 8135-024
+351 964045178
www.quintadolago.com

Opening hours	Open 7 days
Credit cards	Accepted
Price range	Affordable
Style	Smart casual
Cuisine	Traditional Portuguese
Recommended for	Worth the travel

"I go there because it makes me feel good; relaxing with great views and top-class fish."
—Miguel Castro e Silva

RESTAURANTE SÃO GABRIEL

Recommended by
Miguel Castro e Silva

Estrada Vale do Lobo
Almancil
Faro 8135-106
+351 289394521
www.sao-gabriel.com

Opening hours	Closed Monday
Credit cards	Accepted
Price range	Expensive
Style	Smart casual
Cuisine	Modern European
Recommended for	High end

"Great cuisine with unusual creativity."
—Miguel Castro e Silva

OCEAN

Recommended by
Henrique Sá Pessoa,
Alexandre Silva,
Ljubomir Stanisic

Hotel Vila Vita Parc
Rua Anneliese Pohl
Alporchinhos
Faro 8400-450
+351 282310100
www.restauranteocean.com

Opening hours	Closed Monday and Tuesday
Credit cards	Accepted
Price range	Expensive
Style	Formal
Cuisine	Portuguese-Seafood
Recommended for	High end

"My favorite restaurant in Portugal, with amazing creative cuisine made with local ingredients."
—Ljubomir Stanisic

MAR DO INFERNO
Recommended by
José Avillez

Avenida Rei Humberto II de Itália
Boca do Inferno
Cascais
Lisbon 2750-800
+351 214832218
www.mardoinferno.pt

Opening hours	Closed Wednesday
Credit cards	Accepted
Price range	Expensive
Style	Casual
Cuisine	Portuguese-Seafood
Recommended for	Local favorite

"For the high quality of the seafood and fish."
—José Avillez

LISBON: SEE PAGES 610–621

DOM LOURENÇO
Recommended by
Chakall Noir

Avenida António José do Vale 4/6
Praia de Areia Branca
Lourinhã
Lisbon 2530-213
+351 261422809
www.domlourenco.com

Opening hours	Open 7 days
Credit cards	Accepted
Price range	Affordable
Style	Casual
Cuisine	Portuguese-Seafood
Recommended for	Bargain

"High-quality homemade food."—Chakall Noir

CUP OF JOE
Recommended by
José Cordeiro

Oeiras Marina
Estrada da Marginal
Oeiras
Lisbon 2780-267
+351 214412788

Opening hours	Open 7 days
Credit cards	Accepted
Price range	Budget
Style	Casual
Cuisine	Portuguese
Recommended for	Breakfast

IL GALLO D'ORO
Recommended by
Thomas Rode Andersen

The Cliff Bay Hotel
Estrada Monumental 147
Funchal
Madeira Island 9004-532
+351 291707700
www.ilgallodoro.portobay.com

Opening hours	Open 7 days
Credit cards	Accepted
Price range	Expensive
Style	Formal
Cuisine	International
Recommended for	Worth the travel

CASA DE CHÁ DA BOA NOVA
Recommended by
Henrique Sá Pessoa

Rua de Boa Nova
Leça de Palmeira
Porto 4450-705
+351 229940066
www.ruipaula.com

Opening hours	Closed Monday and Sunday
Credit cards	Accepted
Price range	Expensive
Style	Smart casual
Cuisine	Portuguese-Seafood
Recommended for	Worth the travel

"The chef's style is inspired by the produce from
the sea."—Henrique Sá Pessoa

MARISQUEIRA MARUJO
Recommended by
José Cordeiro

Rua de Tomaz Ribeiro 284
Matosinhos
Porto 4450-019
+351 224001940
www.marujomarisqueira.com

Opening hours	Open 7 days
Credit cards	Accepted
Price range	Affordable
Style	Casual
Cuisine	Portuguese-Seafood
Recommended for	Bargain

"The best little French restaurant in the northern
region. Call Senhor Carlos to make a booking.
Excellent cooking and excellent seafood."
—José Cordeiro

RESTAURANTE SAO VALENTIM

Recommended by
José Cordeiro

Rua Heróis de França 335
Matosinhos
Porto 4450-158
+351 229379204
www.saovalentim.pt

Opening hours	Open 7 days
Credit cards	Accepted
Price range	Affordable
Style	Casual
Cuisine	Portuguese-Seafood
Recommended for	Regular neighborhood

CONFEITARIA TAVI

Recommended by
José Cordeiro

Rua da Senhora da Luz 363
Porto 4150-400
+351 226180152
www.tavi.pt

Opening hours	Open 7 days
Credit cards	Accepted
Price range	Affordable
Style	Casual
Cuisine	Portuguese Patisserie
Recommended for	Breakfast

"Excellent breakfast with views of the sea."
—José Cordeiro

PEDRO LEMOS

Recommended by
Ljubomir Stanisic

Rua do Padre Luís Cabral 974
Porto 4150-459
+351 220115986
www.pedrolemos.net

Opening hours	Closed Monday
Credit cards	Accepted
Price range	Affordable
Style	Casual
Cuisine	Mediterranean
Recommended for	High end

In that modest way of so many top European chefs, Pedro Lemos claims the biggest influences on his cooking were his grandmothers, one of whom worked in the nearby city of Bragança and the other in Matosinhos. His menu contains the best traditional Portuguese flavors and fine local ingredients, but he must have also picked up something working in professional kitchens as they're all treated to the latest cooking techniques, resulting in delights such as black pork with wild mushrooms or tuna with asparagus. Choose

between three, five, or seven courses (there's no à la carte option), and if the weather's good, grab a seat on the roof terrace.

RESTAURANTE CASA INÊS

Recommended by
José Cordeiro

Rua de Miraflor 20
Porto 4300-332
+351 225106988

Opening hours	Open 7 days
Credit cards	Accepted but not AMEX
Price range	Affordable
Style	Casual
Cuisine	Portuguese
Recommended for	Regular neighborhood

"Excellent premises serving everything from traditional Portuguese hotpot on Sunday, divine tripe Porto-style, and fillets of octopus and fish that will have you crying for more."—José Cordeiro

RESTAURANTE PAJÚ

Recommended by
José Cordeiro

Rua de Faria Guimaraes 309
Porto 4000-203
+351 225021555

Opening hours	Closed Sunday
Credit cards	Accepted but not AMEX
Price range	Affordable
Style	Casual
Cuisine	European
Recommended for	Late night

WISH RESTAURANTE & SUSHI

Recommended by
José Cordeiro

Largo da Igreja 105
Porto 4150-400
+351 912375313
www.wishrestaurante.com

Opening hours	Open 7 days
Credit cards	Accepted
Price range	Affordable
Style	Smart casual
Cuisine	Mediterranean-Japanese
Recommended for	High end

"Run by the great chef António Vieira. Creative cuisine and wonderful sushi. Excellent wine list. Good atmosphere and decor by architect Paulo Lobo. Exemplary service presided over by Liliana."—José Cordeiro

THE YEATMAN
Rua do Choupelo
Vila Nova de Gaia
Porto 4400-088
+351 220133100
www.the-yeatman-hotel.com

Recommended by
Ljubomir Stanisic

Opening hours	Open 7 days
Credit cards	Accepted
Price range	Expensive
Style	Smart casual
Cuisine	Modern Portuguese
Recommended for	High end

"FINE DINING RESTAURANT IN LISBON, WITH A WARM WELCOME. EACH COURSE IS EXPLOSIVE, BUT THE CHICKPEAS AND PORK BELLY ARE STILL ON MY MIND."

MATTEO ALOE P621

LISBON

"It's the best breakfast in town."

ALEXANDRE SILVA P613

"WE DECIDED TO STAY FOR DINNER. BEST DECISION I MADE IN PORTUGAL."

MARTHA WIGGINS P614

"Portuguese ingredients taken to the next level."

LJUBOMIR STANISIC P616

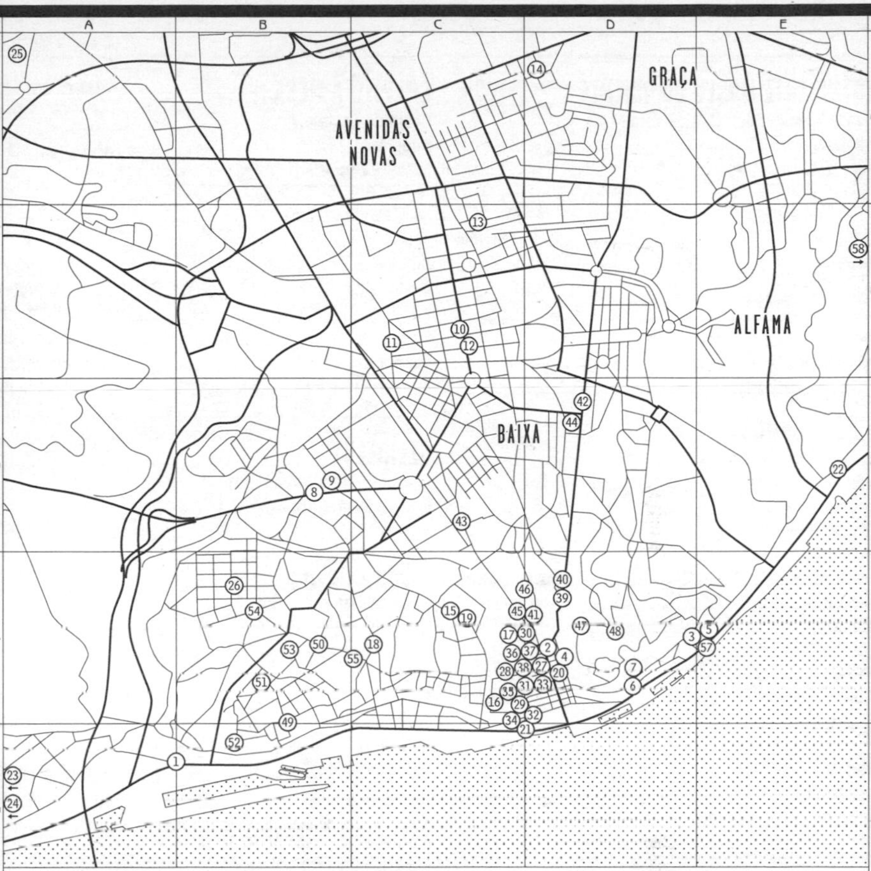

LISBON

N̂

SCALE

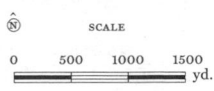

0   500   1000   1500
                          yd.

RESTAURANTE MUSEU DO ORIENTE
Recommended by
Ljubomir Stanisic

Avenida Brasília Doca de Alcântara Norte
Alcântara
Lisbon 1350-362
+351 912190320

Opening hours	Closed Monday
Credit cards	Accepted
Price range	Affordable
Style	Casual
Cuisine	Asian
Recommended for	Regular neighborhood

ZÉ DOS CORNOS
Recommended by
Ljubomir Stanisic

Beco dos Surradores 5
Alcântara
Lisbon 1100-591
+351 218869641

Opening hours	Closed Sunday
Credit cards	Not accepted
Price range	Affordable
Style	Casual
Cuisine	Portuguese-Tapas
Recommended for	Bargain

BICA DO SAPATO
Recommended by
Alexandre Silva

Avenida Infante Dom Henrique
Armazém B, Cais da Pedra
Alfama
Lisbon 1900-436
+351 218810320
www.bicadosapato.com

Opening hours	Open 7 days
Credit cards	Accepted
Price range	Affordable
Style	Casual
Cuisine	Portuguese
Recommended for	Late night

On a cobbled street in Lisbon's old town—alongside
a tramway leading to the sea—is Bica Do Sapato,
a warehouse-space restaurant, sushi bar, and
adjacent club co-owned by actor John Malkovich.
The lofty, minimalist space and Euro-vogue decor
is mirrored in the restaurant's libertarian take on
Portuguese classics. The coastal location means
that the sushi is fresh and fish, rightly, dominates
the menu. Conveniently located across the street,
for post-dinner shape-throwing, is Club Lux where
skilfully prepared cocktails and iced beverages
are served to a young and undeniably hip crowd.

CHAPITÔ À MESA
Recommended by
Ljubomir Stanisic

Costa do Castelo 7
Alfama
Lisbon 1149-079
+351 218875077
www.chapito.org

Opening hours	Open 7 days
Credit cards	Accepted
Price range	Affordable
Style	Smart casual
Cuisine	Portugese
Recommended for	Late night

DELIDELUX
Recommended by
Ljubomir Stanisic

Avenida Infante Dom Henrique
Cais da Pedra, Armazém B, Loja 8
Alfama
Lisbon 1900-264
+351 218862070
www.delidelux.pt

Opening hours	Open 7 days
Credit cards	Accepted
Price range	Affordable
Style	Casual
Cuisine	Café-Bistro
Recommended for	Regular neighborhood

PALACETE CHAFARIZ D'EL REI
Recommended by
Ljubomir Stanisic

Travessa Chafariz del Rei 6
Alfama
Lisbon 1100-140
+351 218886150
www.chafarizdelrei.com

Opening hours	Open 7 days
Credit cards	Accepted but not AMEX
Price range	Affordable
Style	Casual
Cuisine	International
Recommended for	Regular neighborhood

SANTO ANTÓNIO DE ALFAMA

Beco São Miguel 7
Alfama
Lisbon 1100-538
+351 218881328
www.siteantonio.com

Opening hours	Open 7 days
Credit cards	Accepted but not AMEX or Diners
Price range	Affordable
Style	Casual
Cuisine	Modern Portuguese
Recommended for	Late night

FLOR-DE-LIS

Avenida Engenheiro Duarte Pacheco 15
Amoreiras
Lisbon 1070-100
+351 211597300
www.lisboa.epic.sanahotels.com

Opening hours	Open 7 days
Credit cards	Accepted
Price range	Affordable
Style	Casual
Cuisine	Portuguese
Recommended for	Regular neighborhood

"Shellfish, excellent chips, egg, and steak."
—Chakall Noir

VARANDA RESTAURANT

Four Seasons Hotel Ritz
Rua Rodrigo da Fonseca 88
Amoreiras
Lisbon 1099-039
+351 213811400
www.fourseasons.com/lisbon

Opening hours	Open 7 days
Credit cards	Accepted
Price range	Expensive
Style	Smart casual
Cuisine	International
Recommended for	Breakfast

"It's the best breakfast in town."—Alexandre Silva

CHOUPANA CAFFÉ

Avenida da República 25a
Avenidas Novas
Lisbon 1050-053
+351 213570140

Opening hours	Open 7 days
Reservation policy	No
Credit cards	Accepted
Price range	Budget
Style	Casual
Cuisine	Café
Recommended for	Regular neighborhood

GO JUU

Rua Marquês Sá Da Bandeira 46
Avenidas Novas
Lisbon 1050-148
+351 218280704

Opening hours	Closed Monday
Credit cards	Accepted
Price range	Affordable
Style	Casual
Cuisine	Japanese
Recommended for	Regular neighborhood

"Traditional Japanese restaurant with the best
ingredients, a great atmosphere, and very good
service."—José Avillez

GALETO

Avenida da República 14
Avenidas Novas
Lisbon 1050-191
+351 213544444

Opening hours	Open 7 days
Credit cards	Accepted
Price range	Budget
Style	Casual
Cuisine	Portuguese
Recommended for	Late night

"Open until late. Honest cuisine, with a nice *caldo
verde* (a popular soup in Portuguese cuisine), very
comforting, made with Portuguese cabbage."
—José Avillez

O POLEIRO

Rua de Entre Campos 30
Avenidas Novas
Lisbon 1700-156
+351 217976265
www.opoleiro.com

Opening hours	Closed Sunday
Credit cards	Accepted
Price range	Affordable
Style	Casual
Cuisine	Portuguese
Recommended for	Local favorite

"Typical high-quality Portuguese food. A family restaurant with its own produce."—Chakall Noir

SALSA & COENTROS

Rua Coronel Marques Leitão 12
Avenidas Novas
Lisbon 1700-125
+351 218410990
www.salsaecoentros.pt

Opening hours	Closed Sunday
Credit cards	Accepted but not AMEX or Diners
Price range	Affordable
Style	Casual
Cuisine	Traditional Portuguese
Recommended for	Local favorite

A CEVICHERIA

Rua Dom Pedro V 129
Bairro Alto
Lisbon 1250-096
+351 218038815

Opening hours	Open 7 days
Reservation policy	No
Credit cards	Accepted
Price range	Affordable
Style	Casual
Cuisine	Ceviche
Recommended for	Late night

"Good atmosphere, friendly service, good Pisco Sours, fresh and creative ceviche."—Henrique Sá Pessoa

ÁGUA PELA BARBA

Rua do Almada 29/31
Bairro Alto
Lisbon 1200-054
+351 213461376

Opening hours	Open 7 days
Credit cards	Accepted
Price range	Affordable
Style	Casual
Cuisine	Seafood-Tapas
Recommended for	Late night

"It's a good friend's place, simple and relaxed, based on seafood tapas."—Ljubomir Stanisic

BISTRO 100 MANEIRAS

Largo da Trindade 9
Bairro Alto
Lisbon 1200-466
+351 910307575
www.100maneiras.com

Opening hours	Open 7 days
Credit cards	Accepted
Price range	Affordable
Style	Casual
Cuisine	Modern Portuguese
Recommended for	Late night

"Irreverant—good cocktails."—Miguel Castro e Silva

CAFÉ DE SÃO BENTO

Rua de São Bento 212
Bairro Alto
Lisbon 1200-821
+351 213952911
www.en.cafesaobento.com

Opening hours	Open 7 days
Credit cards	Accepted
Price range	Affordable
Style	Casual
Cuisine	Portuguese-Steakhouse
Recommended for	Late night

O ASIÁTICO

Rua da Rosa 317
Bairro Alto
Lisbon 1250-083
+351 211319369

Opening hours	Open 7 days
Credit cards	Accepted but not AMEX
Price range	Affordable
Style	Casual
Cuisine	Asian
Recommended for	Wish I'd opened

"Amazing, beautiful restaurant."—Alexandre Silva

NICOLAU LISBOA

Rua São Nicolau 15
Baixa
Lisbon 1100-026
+351 218860312

Opening hours	Open 7 days
Reservation policy	No
Credit cards	Accepted but not AMEX
Price range	Budget
Style	Casual
Cuisine	Café
Recommended for	Breakfast

"Young, relaxed, with plenty of healthy, fresh, and delicious offerings."—Ljubomir Stanisic

SOLAR DO KADETE

Cais do Sodré 2
Baixa
Lisbon 1200-450
+351 213427255

Opening hours	Closed Sunday
Credit cards	Accepted but not AMEX
Price range	Affordable
Style	Casual
Cuisine	Portuguese
Recommended for	Regular neighborhood

MARÍTIMA DE XABREGAS

Rua Manutenção 40/2
Beato
Lisbon 1900-320
+351 218682235
www.restaurantemaritimadexabregas.com.pt

Opening hours	Closed Saturday
Credit cards	Accepted
Price range	Affordable
Style	Casual
Cuisine	Portuguese
Recommended for	Local favorite

ENOTECA DE BELÉM

Travessa Marta Pinto 10
Belém
Lisbon 1300-083
+351 213631511
www.travessadaermida.com

Opening hours	Open 7 days
Credit cards	Accepted
Price range	Affordable
Style	Casual
Cuisine	Portuguese-International
Recommended for	Worth the travel

"So, a few years ago I went to Portugal with my best friend and, after a little research, we stumbled upon this gem in Belém. It couldn't have had more than twenty seats, tops. After being guided through their incredible wine selection, with taste after taste poured with genuine passion and enthusiasm, we decided to stay for dinner. Best decision I made in Portugal. The manager guided us through our entire meal with care and attention, pairing wines with every course. This was by far the most spectacular dining experience I've ever had in my life. It's the kind of restaurant that probably couldn't work in the States, or if it did, I'd never make it on the waiting list. It assumes the diner is there to eat the food the way the chef carefully prepared it, while still choreographing the meal to your desires. Amazing."—Martha Wiggins

FEITORIA

Altis Belém Hotel & Spa
Doca do Bom Sucesso
Belém
Lisbon 1400-038
+351 210400208
www.restaurantefeitoria.com

Opening hours...Closed Sunday
Credit cards..Accepted
Price range..Expensive
Style..Smart casual
Cuisine...Modern Portuguese
Recommended for..High end

"Portuguese ingredients taken to the next level."
—Ljubomir Stanisic

O GALITO

Rua Adelaide Cabete 7
Benfica
Lisbon 1500-023
+351 217111088

Opening hours...Closed Sunday
Credit cards..Accepted
Price range..Affordable
Style..Casual
Cuisine...European
Recommended for..Local favorite

MAGANO RESTAURANTE

Rua Tomás da Anunciação 52a
Campo de Ourique
Lisbon 1350-328
+351 213954522

Opening hours...Closed Sunday
Credit cards..Accepted
Price range..Affordable
Style..Casual
Cuisine...Portuguese
Recommended for..................................Regular neighborhood

"Food from the Alentejo region, with concentrated
flavors and a nice service."—José Avillez

ALMA

Rua Anchieta 15
Chiado
Lisbon 1200-023
+351 213470650
www.almalisboa.pt

Opening hours...Closed Monday
Credit cards..Accepted
Price range..Affordable
Style..Smart casual
Cuisine...Modern Portuguese
Recommended for..Worth the travel

"Very good, progressive cuisine in an interesting
environment with excellent service."—Alyn Williams

A TABERNA DA RUA DAS FLORES

Rua das Flores 103
Chiado
Lisbon 1200-015
+351 213479418

Opening hours...Closed Sunday
Reservation policy...No
Credit cards...Not accepted
Price range..Affordable
Style..Casual
Cuisine...Portuguese
Recommended for..................................Regular neighborhood

"It's a small tavern with Portuguese food and wine."
— Henrique Sá Pessoa

BAGOS CHIADO RESTAURANTE

Rua António Maria Cardoso 15b
Chiado
Lisbon 1200-026
+351 213420802

Opening hours..............................Closed Sunday and Monday
Credit cards.......................Accepted but not AMEX or Diners
Price range..Affordable
Style..Casual
Cuisine...Modern Portuguese
Recommended for..High end

"Chef Henrique Mouro makes the best rice dishes
in the world."—José Cordeiro

BAIRRO DO AVILLEZ

Recommended by
Henrique Sá Pessoa

Rua Nova da Trindade 18
Chiado
Lisbon 1200-466
+351 215830290
www.joseavillez.pt/en/bairro-do-avillez

Opening hours	Open 7 days
Credit cards	Accepted
Price range	Affordable
Style	Casual
Cuisine	Seafood
Recommended for	Local favorite

BELCANTO

Recommended by
Miguel Castro e Silva,
Henrique Sá Pessoa

Largo de São Carlos 10
Chiado
Lisbon 1200-410
+351 213420607
www.belcanto.pt

Opening hours	Closed Monday and Sunday
Credit cards	Accepted
Price range	Expensive
Style	Smart casual
Cuisine	Portuguese
Recommended for	High end

Chef José Avillez has taken over the space that formerly played host, in the form of a gentleman's club, to opera patrons and artists from the nearby Teatro Nacional de São Carlos. It has been designed to act as an arena in which this promising chef (who has worked under both Ferran Adrià and Alain Ducasse) can flourish. A formal and sophisticated makeover retained some signs of the past, such as bookshelves, wood-panelling, and grand lighting. Modern Portuguese cuisine, however, has replaced the pole dancers of old. The likes of braised red mullet with liver juice, a "dip into the sea" comprising sea bass and seaweed, and "suckling pig revisited" come from a menu that aims—ambitiously—to tell stories and stir emotions.

DUPLEX

Recommended by
Ljubomir Stanisic

Rua Nova do Carvalho 58–60
Chiado
Lisbon 1200 371
+351 915162808
www.duplexrb.pt

Opening hours	Closed Sunday
Credit cards	Accepted
Price range	Affordable
Style	Casual
Cuisine	International
Recommended for	Late night

KAFFEEHAUS

Recommended by
Ljubomir Stanisic

Rua Anchieta 3
Chiado
Lisbon 1200-023
+351 210956828
www.kaffeehaus-lisboa.com

Opening hours	Open 7 days
Credit cards	Accepted
Price range	Affordable
Style	Casual
Cuisine	Austrian
Recommended for	Regular neighborhood

MERCADO DA RIBEIRA TIME OUT

Recommended by
Henrique Sá Pessoa,
Alexandre Silva

Avenida 24 de Julho 49
Chiado
Lisbon 1200-129
+351 213951274
www.timeoutmarket.com

Opening hours	Open 7 days
Reservation policy	No
Credit cards	Accepted
Price range	Affordable
Style	Casual
Cuisine	Portuguese
Recommended for	Bargain

"It is one of the biggest food markets in the world, with great chefs and ambiance."—Alexandre Silva

MINI BAR TEATRO

Recommended by
Miguel Castro e Silva

Rua Antonio Maria Cardoso 58
Chiado
Lisbon 1200-026
+351 211305393
www.minibar.pt

Opening hours	Open 7 days
Credit cards	Accepted
Price range	Affordable
Style	Smart casual
Cuisine	Modern Portuguese Fusion
Recommended for	Wish I'd opened

"A good opportunity to try original dishes."
—Miguel Castro e Silva

O TREVO

Recommended by
José Avillez

Praça Luís de Camões 48
Chiado
Lisbon 1200-243
+351 213468092

Opening hours	Closed Sunday
Credit cards	Not accepted
Price range	Budget
Style	Casual
Cuisine	Portugese Sandwiches
Recommended for	Bargain

"Eat a pork sandwich at Trevo."—José Avillez

PASTELARIA BENARD

Recommended by
José Avillez,
Henrique Sá Pessoa

Rua Garrett 104
Chiado
Lisbon 1200-205
+351 213473133

Opening hours	Closed Sunday
Reservation policy	No
Credit cards	Accepted
Price range	Budget
Style	Casual
Cuisine	Café-Patisserie
Recommended for	Breakfast

"An emblematic place. I really like their mini veal
pastry pies."—José Avillez

TARTINE

Recommended by
Henrique Sá Pessoa

Rua Serpa Pinto 15a
Chiado
Lisbon 1200-026
+351 213429108
www.tartine.pt

Opening hours	Open 7 days
Reservation policy	No
Credit cards	Accepted but not AMEX
Price range	Affordable
Style	Casual
Cuisine	Portugese-French Patisserie
Recommended for	Breakfast

CERVEJARIA RAMIRO

Recommended by
Henrique Sá Pessoa,
Alexandre Silva,
Richard Turner,
Ljubomir Stanisic

Avenida Almirante Reis 1-H
Estefania
Lisbon 1150-007
+351 218851024
www.cervejariaramiro.pt

Opening hours	Closed Monday
Reservation policy	No
Credit cards	Accepted
Price range	Affordable
Style	Casual
Cuisine	Portuguese-Seafood
Recommended for	Worth the travel

"Perfect shellfish, simply cooked. Amongst the best
in the world."—Richard Turner

Cervejaria (meaning "beerhouse") downplays the
charms of this relaxed seafood specialist. Sure, the
scruffy neighborhood and the 1970s decor are not
particular pulls, but beer certainly isn't the main
reason that, for over fifty years, Lisboetas have
been waiting in line here. That accolade goes to the
superb seafood. Start with the house *pata negra*
(ham), before getting stuck into giant Portuguese
carabineiros (shrimp), *santola* (crab), and sea-salty
percebes (gooseneck barnacles). Leave room for the
famous *prego* steak sandwich, and wash it all down
with local beer or a bottle of ice-cold Vinho Verde.
The seasoned staff are quick (the line [queue]
moves fast) but always cheery.

COVA FUNDA

Recommended by
Ljubomir Stanisic

Travessa do Cidadão J. Gonçalves 20a
Estefania
Lisbon 1150-096
+351 218852095

Opening hours	Closed Sunday
Credit cards	Accepted
Price range	Budget
Style	Casual
Cuisine	Modern European
Recommended for	Regular neighborhood

MADMARY CUISINE

Recommended by
Ljubomir Stanisic

Rua Rodrigues Sampaio 29
Estefania
Lisbon 1150-278
+351 213540317

Opening hours	Closed Sunday
Credit cards	Accepted
Price range	Budget
Style	Casual
Cuisine	Breakfast-Brunch
Recommended for	Regular neighborhood

GAMBRINUS

Recommended by
Ljubomir Stanisic

Rua das Portas de Santo Antão 23
Estefania
Lisbon 1150-264
+351 213421466
www.gambrinuslisboa.com

Opening hours	Open 7 days
Credit cards	Accepted
Price range	Affordable
Style	Casual
Cuisine	Portuguese
Recommended for	Local favorite

MR. LU

Recommended by
Ljubomir Stanisic

Rua António Pedro 95
Estefania
Lisbon 1150-023
+351 213520613

Opening hours	Open 7 days
Credit cards	Accepted
Price range	Affordable
Style	Casual
Cuisine	Chinese
Recommended for	Bargain

GRANDE PALÁCIO HONG KONG

Recommended by
José Avillez,
Henrique Sá Pessoa

Rua Pascoal de Melo 8
Estefania
Lisbon 1170-140
+351 218123349
www.restaurante-chines.com

Opening hours	Open 7 days
Credit cards	Not accepted
Price range	Affordable
Style	Casual
Cuisine	Chinese
Recommended for	Bargain

"My favorite Chinese restaurant in Lisbon."
—José Avillez

PINÓQUIO

Recommended by
Ljubomir Stanisic

Praça dos Restauradores 79
Estefania
Lisbon 1250-188
+351 213465106
www.restaurantepinoquio.pt

Opening hours	Open 7 days
Credit cards	Accepted
Price range	Affordable
Style	Casual
Cuisine	Mediterranean
Recommended for	Local favorite

SOLAR DOS PRESUNTOS

Recommended by
Ljubomir Stanisic

Rua Portas de Santo Antão 150
Estefania
Lisbon 1150-269
+351 213424253
www.solardospresuntos.com

Opening hours	Closed Sunday
Credit cards	Accepted
Price range	Affordable
Style	Casual
Cuisine	Portuguese
Recommended for	Regular neighborhood

"Portuguese traditional food, with the best ingredients, an amazing wine list, and Portuguese hospitality, ambience, and service."
—Ljubomir Stanisic

COZINHA POPULAR DA MOURARIA

Recommended by
Ljubomir Stanisic

Rua das Olarias 5
Graça
Lisbon 1100-012
+351 926520568

Opening hours	Closed Monday, Saturday, and Sunday
Credit cards	Not accepted
Price range	Budget
Style	Casual
Cuisine	International
Recommended for	Bargain

"Simple and tasty food in a communitarian project."
—Ljubomir Stanisic

O PITÉU DA GRAÇA

Recommended by
Ljubomir Stanisic

Largo da Graça 95–96
Graça
Lisbon 1170-165
+351 218871067

Opening hours	Open 7 days
Credit cards	Not accepted
Price range	Affordable
Style	Casual
Cuisine	Portuguese
Recommended for	Local favorite

LA BOULANGERIE

Recommended by
Ljubomir Stanisic

Rua do Olival 42
Lapa
Lisbon 1200-739
+351 213951208

Opening hours	Closed Monday
Credit cards	Accepted
Price range	Budget
Style	Casual
Cuisine	Café-Bistro
Recommended for	Regular neighborhood

CABANA DA ESTRELA

Recommended by
Miguel Castro e Silva

Rua da Bela Vista à Lapa 18
Lapa
Lisbon 1200-613
+351 213971934

Opening hours	Closed Sunday
Credit cards	Accepted
Price range	Budget
Style	Casual
Cuisine	Portuguese
Recommended for	Regular neighborhood

"It's opposite my house and, for €7 ($8; £6) I get a meal so that I am able to carry on working at home."—Miguel Castro e Silva

CRISTAL 2

Recommended by
Miguel Castro e Silva

Rua Buenos Aires 30a
Lapa
Lisbon 1200-798
+351 214044848

Opening hours	Closed Sunday
Reservation policy	No
Credit cards	Not accepted
Price range	Budget
Style	Casual
Cuisine	Portuguese
Recommended for	Breakfast

"They make their own pastries and pies, they're nice people, and they're nearby."—Miguel Castro e Silva

COME PRIMA

Recommended by
Alexandre Silva

Rua do Olival 258
Lapa
Lisbon 1200-744
+351 213902457
www.comeprima.pt

Opening hours	Closed Sunday
Credit cards	Accepted
Price range	Affordable
Style	Smart casual
Cuisine	Italian
Recommended for	Regular neighborhood

"A small restaurant with Italian cuisine made in a wood-burning stove."—Alexandre Silva

LOCO

Recommended by
Matteo Aloe,
Miguel Castro e Silva,
Ljubomir Stanisic

Rua Navegantes 53
Lapa
Lisbon 1200-830
| 351 213951861
www.loco.pt

Opening hours	Closed Monday and Sunday
Credit cards	Accepted
Price range	Expensive
Style	Smart casual
Cuisine	Modern Portuguese
Recommended for	High end

"A fine dining restaurant in Lisbon, with a warm welcome. Each course is explosive, but the chickpeas and pork belly are still on my mind."—Matteo Aloe

TASCA DA ESQUINA

Recommended by
Miguel Castro e Silva,
Henrique Sá Pessoa,
Ljubomir Stanisic

Rua Domingos Sequeira 41c
Lapa
Lisbon 1350-119
+351 919837255
www.tascadaesquina.com

Opening hours	Closed Sunday
Credit cards	Accepted
Price range	Affordable
Style	Casual
Cuisine	Portuguese Tapas
Recommended for	Local favorite

Chef Vitor Sobral masterminded Tasca da Esquina, a minimalistic corner restaurant that has raised the bar of tapas joints in the capital since its inception in 2007. Sobral is largely recognized as one of the pioneers of national petiscos—the Portuguese sibling of Spanish tapas—of which there are plenty to nibble on as you watch the world go by through the restaurant's vast glass frontage. Opt either for the *Hoje Há* ("today there is") menu of daily-changing dishes or, if you want something more traditional, pick from the *Petiscos* (snacks) list, a fixed menu of classics that seldom changes.

XL RESTAURANTE

Recommended by
Miguel Castro e Silva

Calçada da Estrela 57
Lapa
Lisbon 1200-109
+351 213956118
www.xl.besttables.com

Opening hours	Closed Sunday
Credit cards	Accepted
Price range	Affordable
Style	Casual
Cuisine	Portuguese
Recommended for	Late night

CAFÉ COM CALMA

Recommended by
Ljubomir Stanisic

Rua do Açúcar 10
Marvila
Lisbon 1950-242
+351 218680398

Opening hours	Closed Sunday
Credit cards	Accepted but not AMEX
Price range	Budget
Style	Casual
Cuisine	Portuguese-Café
Recommended for	Regular neighborhood

RIVER LOUNGE RESTAURANTE

Recommended by
Ljubomir Stanisic

Hotel Myriad
Cais das Naus Lote 2.21.01
Parque das Nações
Lisbon 1990-173
+351 211107600
www.myriad.pt

Opening hours	Open 7 days
Credit cards	Accepted
Price range	Affordable
Style	Smart casual
Cuisine	European
Recommended for	Regular neighborhood

> "BEST SERVICE TEAM IN TOWN, VERY CREATIVE KITCHEN. WHAT'S NOT TO LIKE?"
> GAL BEN-MOSHE P631

GERMANY

> "Direct, frank, masculine, yet delicate too. The most important thing? It's very good."
> FLORENT LADEYN P630

> "ARGUABLY THE BEST MEAL I HAVE EVER EATEN."
> MARC DJOZLIJA P631

> "THIS IS FOR ME ONE OF THE TEN BEST RESTAURANTS IN THE WORLD!"
> OLDŘICH SAHAJDÁK P630

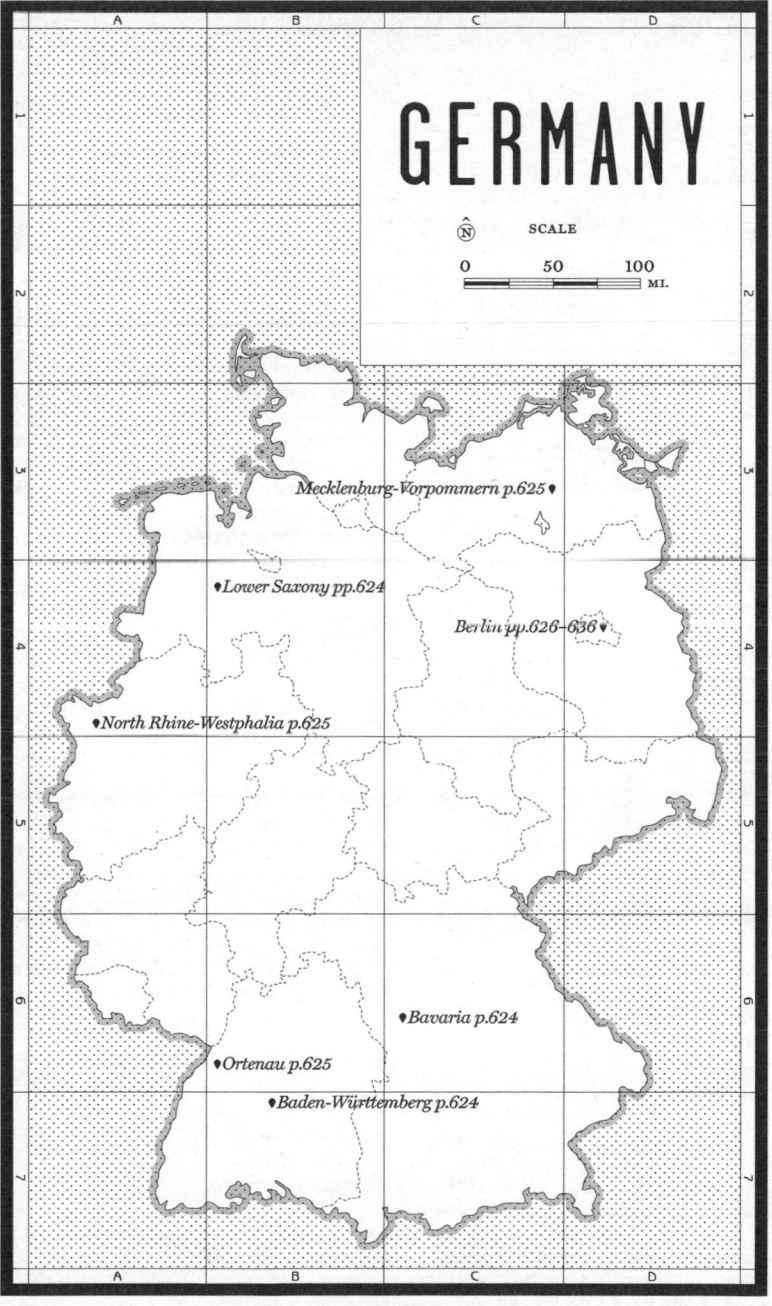

GERMANY

SCALE

0   50   100
MI.

SCHWARZWALDSTUBE

Recommended by
Chakall Noir

Hotel Traube Tonbach
Tonbachstrasse 237
Baiersbronn
Baden-Württemberg 72270
+49 74424920
www.traube-tonbach.de

Opening hours...............................Closed Monday and Tuesday
Credit cards...Accepted
Price range...Expensive
Style..Formal
Cuisine...French
Recommended for..High end

"Fantastic, refined, and original three-star restaurant."—Chakall Noir

SOSEIN

Recommended by
Micha Schäfer

Hauptstrasse 19
Heroldsberg
Bavaria 90562
+49 91195699680
www.sosein-restaurant.de

Opening hours...............................Closed Monday and Sunday
Credit cards...Accepted
Price range...Expensive
Style...Smart casual
Cuisine...Modern German
Recommended for...Wish I'd opened

"Felix Schneider cooks local cuisine in a part of Germany that has very rich resources."—Micha Schäfer

ACQUARELLO MARIO GAMBA

Recommended by
Shaun Rankin

Mühlbaurstrasse 36
Munich
Bavaria 81677
+49 894704848
www.acquarello.de

Opening hours...Open 7 days
Credit cards...Accepted but not AMEX
Price range..Affordable
Style...Smart casual
Cuisine..Italian
Recommended for...Worth the travel

"Mario is a perfectionist and his dishes are exquisite, from the small tasters to the main event. He is also passionate about wine so you will get the best recommendations for your meal. Everything you try here is a piece of art."—Shaun Rankin

SCHUMANN'S

Recommended by
Ruairí de Blacam

Odeonsplatz 6–7
Munich
Bavaria 80539
+49 89229060
www.schumanns.de

Opening hours..Open 7 days
Credit cards...Accepted but not Diners
Price range...Budget
Style..Casual
Cuisine..Italian-Bavarian
Recommended for...Late night

"This is more of a bar that serves food than a restaurant really. After a day's work that usually didn't finish up until 10.00 p.m. this used to be my go-to bar/restaurant when I was on business in Munich. The waiters wear white coats, know their job, and stay out of your hair. The kind of no nonsense quality you need after a day of nonsense! Roast beef, *Bratkartofflen*, salad, and a few decent glasses of Pils."
—Ruairí de Blacam

TANTRIS

Recommended by
Christian Domschitz,
Mirco Keller,
Micha Schäfer

Johann-Fichte-Strasse 7
Munich
Bavaria 80805
+49 893619590
www.tantris.de

Opening hours...............................Closed Monday and Sunday
Credit cards...Accepted
Price range...Expensive
Style...Smart casual
Cuisine..French-Swiss
Recommended for...Worth the travel

"A place with a history of great chefs and amazing wines. Real time travel."—Micha Schäfer

THE TABLE

Recommended by
Onno Kokmeijer

Shanghaiallee 15
Hamburg
Lower Saxony 20457
+49 4022867422
www.thetable-hamburg.de

Opening hours...............................Closed Monday and Sunday
Credit cards...Accepted
Price range...Expensive
Style...Smart casual
Cuisine..International
Recommended for...Worth the travel

AQUA

Recommended by
Corey Lee,
Thomas & Mathias Sühring

The Ritz-Carlton
Parkstrasse 1
Wolfsburg
Lower Saxony 38440
+49 5361606056
www.restaurant-aqua.com

Opening hours	Closed Monday and Sunday
Credit cards	Accepted
Price range	Expensive
Style	Formal
Cuisine	Modern European
Recommended for	Worth the travel

"This is the best gastronomic excursion from Berlin."
—Corey Lee

How good can any restaurant be, we hear you ask, when it's located in an industrial town more famous for its Volkswagen car plant than for its fine dining? Well, if the promise of not one, not two, but three Michelin stars doesn't convince you there's something special going on, the menu will: wagyu beef, Périgord truffle, and foie gras are just some of the ingredients offered seductively by chef Sven Elverfeld. His refined modern European food is certainly impressive, but it's not cheap. Five courses, with accompanying wine, costs €275 ($295; £230) per person, while the full nine courses with wine will set you back €425 ($456; £356) each.

FORSTHAUS STRELITZ

Recommended by
Micha Schäfer

Berliner Chaussee 1
Neustrelitz
Mecklenburg-Vorpommern 17235
+49 3981447135
www.forsthaus-strelitz.de

Opening hours	Closed Monday and Tuesday
Credit cards	Accepted
Price range	Affordable
Style	Casual
Cuisine	Modern German
Recommended for	High end

"It is actually not that expensive, but a perfect place if you want to treat yourself. A family business. Most of the stuff they serve is from their own farm."
—Micha Schäfer

If you're looking for an escape from the bustle of Germany's big cities, you'll find it in the northern town of Neustrelitz. And if you're looking for great food while you're there, you'll find it at this farm-to-table restaurant, headed by chef Wenzel Pankratz. It's a family affair: his sister serves his unpretentious, elegant, and reasonably priced food, while his mother and brother take care of the farm, from which most of the ingredients are sourced. There's also the option to stay the night, and the rooms are as stylish and simple as the menu. Wake up to the wide open countryside, and start the day with the resident donkeys, pigs, and sheep.

VENDÔME

Recommended by
Daniel Achilles

Schloss Bensberg Hotel
Kadettenstrasse
Bergisch Gladbach
North Rhine-Westphalia 51429
+49 2204421941
www.schlossbensberg.com

Opening hours	Closed Monday and Tuesday
Credit cards	Accepted
Price range	Expensive
Style	Formal
Cuisine	Modern German
Recommended for	High end

WALDGASTSTÄTTE PONYHOF

Recommended by
Rolf Fliegauf

Mattenhofweg 6
Gengenbach
Ortenau 77723
+49 78031469
www.ponyhof.co

Opening hours	Closed Monday
Credit cards	Accepted
Price range	Affordable
Style	Casual
Cuisine	Modern German
Recommended for	Bargain

"Very nice location and the food is really good—a lot of Black-Forest-style dishes. A very good concept."
—Rolf Fliegauf

"FANTASTIC BRUNCH."

CHAKALL NOIR P634

BERLIN

"It has an unpretentious Berliner atmosphere combined with very creative and fun cuisine."

MICHA SCHÄFER P631

"THEY DO AN EXCELLENT SCHNITZEL."

DANIEL ACHILLES P631

"The food is all about the quality of the ingredients."

MICHA SCHÄFER P630

BERLIN

‹N› SCALE

0   650   1300   1950
                        yd.

AROMA

Recommended by
Lukas Mraz

Kantstrasse 35
Charlottenburg
Berlin 10625
+49 3037591628

Opening hours	Open 7 days
Credit cards	Accepted
Price range	Affordable
Style	Casual
Cuisine	Chinese
Recommended for	Late night

"Fried tofu with pepper and salt. Closes at 3.00 a.m., which is pretty late for Berlin."—Lukas Mraz

LON MEN'S NOODLE HOUSE

Recommended by
Lukas Mraz

Kantstrasse 33
Charlottenburg
Berlin 10625
+49 3031519678

Opening hours	Open 7 days
Reservation policy	No
Credit cards	Not accepted
Price range	Budget
Style	Casual
Cuisine	Taiwanese
Recommended for	Regular neighborhood

"Order *Nudel mit scharfer Fleischsoße* (pasta with spicy meat sauce) and chile wontons."—Lukas Mraz

THE BUTCHER

Recommended by
Gal Ben-Moshe

Kantstrasse 144
Charlottenburg
Berlin 10623
+49 30323015673
www.the-butcher.com

Opening hours	Open 7 days
Credit cards	Accepted
Price range	Affordable
Style	Smart casual
Cuisine	Burgers and grill
Recommended for	Late night

"A burger place that is open late in this neighborhood (a rarity), offering a good patty, great service, great drinks, and a very cool atmosphere."—Gal Ben-Moshe

MADAME NGO

Recommended by
Gal Ben-Moshe

Kantstrasse 30
Charlottenburg
Berlin 10623
+49 3060274585
www.madame-ngo.de

Opening hours	Open 7 days
Credit cards	Accepted but not AMEX
Price range	Budget
Style	Casual
Cuisine	Vietnamese-French
Recommended for	Regular neighborhood

"In a city full of Vietnamese restaurants focusing on pho, this one shines, with cool interpretations of French-Vietnamese fusion, great pho and excellent bahn mi, which is one of my favorite lunches around."—Gal Ben-Moshe

NU

Recommended by
Marco Müller

Schlüterstrasse 55
Charlottenburg
Berlin 10629
+49 3088709811
www.nu-eat.de

Opening hours	Open 7 days
Credit cards	Accepted but not AMEX or Diners
Price range	Budget
Style	Casual
Cuisine	Asian
Recommended for	Regular neighborhood

SETS

Recommended by
Marco Müller

Schlüterstrasse 36
Charlottenburg
Berlin 10629
+49 3056738797
www.setsberlin.de

Opening hours	Open 7 days
Credit cards	Accepted but only debit cards
Price range	Budget
Style	Casual
Cuisine	Café
Recommended for	Breakfast

"Fresh breakfast and great bread."—Marco Müller

The name's an abbreviation: it stands for *sitzen*, *essen*, *trinken*, *schlafen* (sit, eat, drink, sleep), all things you can do at this brasserie, bed and breakfast. You could add "w" for "wait"—as you might well have to do if you pitch up on a Sunday, the busiest day of the week for this chic Charlottenburg breakfast destination off the Kurfürstendamm. Breakfast options vary from the robust *Bauernfrühstück* (farmer's breakfast) to bircher muesli. The beautiful people that frequent Sets also rate it for cocktails, salads, cakes, and creatively topped *Flammkuchen* (Alsatian pizza-like flatbread).

FRANCUCCI'S RISTORANTE

Recommended by
Chakall Noir

Kurfüstendamm 90
Halensee
Berlin 10709
+49 303233318
www.francucci.de

Opening hours	Open 7 days
Credit cards	Accepted
Price range	Budget
Style	Casual
Cuisine	Italian
Recommended for	Regular neighborhood

"Fantastic Italian food—one of the best that I know."
—Chakall Noir

BIG STUFF SMOKED BBQ

Recommended by
Gal Ben-Moshe

Eisenbahnstrasse 42/43
Kreuzberg
Berlin 10997
+49 1636290413
www.bigstuff.de

Opening hours	Closed Monday and Sunday
Credit cards	Not accepted
Price range	Budget
Style	Casual
Cuisine	BBQ
Recommended for	Bargain

"Best BBQ place in Berlin. Not necessarily authentic, but produce-driven, high quality, consistent, and most importantly tasty. Their ribs are probably the tastiest meal being served in Berlin."—Gal Ben-Moshe

CURRY 36

Recommended by
Mirco Keller

Mehringdamm 36
Kreuzberg
Berlin 10961
+49 302517368
www.curry36.de

Opening hours	Open 7 days
Reservation policy	No
Credit cards	Not Accepted
Price range	Budget
Style	Casual
Cuisine	German
Recommended for	Wish I'd opened

DOLDEN MÄDEL

Recommended by
Micha Schäfer

Mehringdamm 80
Kreuzberg
Berlin 10965
+49 3077326213
www.doldenmaedel-berlin.de

Opening hours	Open 7 days
Credit cards	Accepted but not AMEX
Price range	Budget
Style	Casual
Cuisine	German
Recommended for	Bargain

"Simple, classic dishes for a fair price."
—Micha Schäfer

HENNE

Recommended by
Paul Cunningham

Leuschnerdamm 25
Kreuzberg
Berlin 10999
+49 306147730
www.henne-berlin.de

Opening hours	Closed Monday
Credit cards	Not Accepted
Price range	Budget
Style	Casual
Cuisine	German
Recommended for	Wish I'd opened

HORVÁTH

Paul-Lincke-Ufer 44a
Kreuzberg
Berlin 10999
+49 3061289992
www.restaurant-horvath.de

Recommended by
Daniel Achilles,
Oldřich Sahajdák

Opening hours	Closed Monday and Tuesday
Credit cards	Accepted
Price range	Expensive
Style	Smart casual
Cuisine	International
Recommended for	Worth the travel

"This is, for me, one of the ten best restaurants in the world!"—Oldřich Sahajdák

LODE & STIJN

Lausitzer Strasse 25
Kreuzberg
Berlin 10999
+49 3065214507
www.lode-stijn.de

Recommended by
Micha Schäfer

Opening hours	Closed Monday and Sunday
Credit cards	Accepted but not AMEX
Price range	Expensive
Style	Smart casual
Cuisine	Modern European
Recommended for	Late night

"The food is all about the quality of the ingredients."
—Micha Schäfer

MARKTHALLE NEUN

Eisenbahnstrasse 42-43
Kreuzberg
Berlin 10997
www.markthalleneun.de

Recommended by
Micha Schäfer

Opening hours	Closed Sunday
Reservation policy	No
Credit cards	Not accepted
Price range	Budget
Style	Casual
Cuisine	Streetfood
Recommended for	Local favorite

"Not so much a restaurant but more of a food market. It is more or less a culinary center for Berlin."
—Micha Schäfer

It was almost all over for Berlin's historic market. Built in the nineteenth century as a masterpiece of wrought iron and wide open space, by 2009 it was run down and dismal. But it was saved by dedicated locals who saw its potential, and now Markthalle Neun is hailed as a pioneer of Berlin's street food movement. Street Food Thursdays (from 5.00 p.m. to 10.00 p.m.) draw in huge crowds, who arrive hungry to sample culinary delights from around the world—Mexico, Nigeria, Thailand—all washed down with craft beer from Heidenpeters, the on-site brewer. Don't miss the Breakfast Market on the third Sunday of each month, which has everything you need to make the most of the first meal of the day.

NOBELHART & SCHMUTZIG

Friedrichstrasse 218
Kreuzberg
Berlin 10969
+49 3025940610
www.nobelhartundschmutzig.com

Recommended by
Florent Ladeyn,
Lukas Mraz,
Bjoern Alexander Panek,
Thomas Rode Andersen,

Opening hours	Closed Monday and Sunday
Credit cards	Accepted
Price range	Expensive
Style	Smart casual
Cuisine	Modern German
Recommended for	Wish I'd opened

"A UFO behind a glass storefront on a busy shopping street. Customers eat at the bar round the kitchen, having left their phone and preconceptions in the cloakroom. The restaurant is run by Billy, a brilliant sommelier with a fiery temperament—a character to match his talent. Direct, frank, masculine, yet delicate too. The most important thing? It's very good."—Florent Ladeyn

It looks like nothing from the outside. You'll think you're at the wrong door on this busy street. But inside, there's no mistake. Everything about this acclaimed modern German restaurant is stylish and slick—on the plate and off. Billy Wagner, a sommelier-turned-restaurateur, and executive chef Micha Schäfer, "the workhorse of the kitchen", created Nobelhart & Schmutzig. Their main message is one of pared-back simplicity: on offer is a short menu of "brutally local" seasonal ingredients (no pepper, no lemons, no chocolate, no tuna—if you can't source it in Berlin, it's not worth having), served in a seriously small space.

TIM RAUE

Rudi-Dutschke Strasse 26
Kreuzberg
Berlin 10969
+49 3025937930
www.tim-raue.com

Recommended by
Daniel Achilles,
Marc Djozlija,
Lukas Mraz,
Bjoern Alexander Panek

Opening hours	Closed Monday and Sunday
Credit cards	Accepted
Price range	Expensive
Style	Smart casual
Cuisine	Modern Asian
Recommended for	Worth the travel

"Currently ranked thirty-fourth best restaurant in the world, the tasting menu at this Asian inspired restaurant in Berlin is arguably the best meal I have ever eaten."—Marc Djozlija

AIGNER

Französische Strasse 25
Mitte
Berlin 10117
+49 30203751850
www.aigner-gendarmenmarkt.de

Recommended by
Marco Müller

Opening hours	Open 7 days
Credit cards	Accepted
Price range	Affordable
Style	Smart casual
Cuisine	German
Recommended for	Local favorite

BANDOL SUR MER

Torstrasse 167
Mitte
Berlin 10115
+49 3067302051
www.bandolsurmer.de

Recommended by
Marco Müller

Opening hours	Open 7 days
Credit cards	Accepted
Price range	Affordable
Style	Smart casual
Cuisine	French Bistro
Recommended for	High end

"For me, one of the most creative kitchens in the city." —Marco Müller

BORCHARDT

Französiche Strasse 47
Mitte
Berlin 10117
+49 3081886262
www.borchardt-restaurant.de

Recommended by
Daniel Achilles

Opening hours	Open 7 days
Credit cards	Accepted
Price range	Affordable
Style	Smart casual
Cuisine	German-French
Recommended for	Wish I'd opened

"They do an excellent schnitzel."—Daniel Achilles

CORDOBAR

Grosse Hamburger Strasse 32
Mitte
Berlin 10115
+49 3027581215
www.cordobar.net

Recommended by
Rolf Fliegauf,
Micha Schäfer

Opening hours	Closed Monday and Sunday
Credit cards	Accepted
Price range	Affordable
Style	Casual
Cuisine	Modern German
Recommended for	Regular neighborhood

"It has an unpretentious Berliner atmosphere combined with very creative and fun cuisine." —Micha Schäfer

EINSUNTERNULL

Hannoversche Strasse 1
Mitte
Berlin 10115
+49 3027577810
www.einsunternull.com

Recommended by
Daniel Achilles,
Gal Ben-Moshe

Opening hours	Closed Sunday
Credit cards	Accepted
Price range	Expensive
Style	Casual
Cuisine	Modern German
Recommended for	Local favorite

"A produce-driven fine dining restaurant, looking to explore the world of regional-local ingredients, without compromising on hospitality. Best service team in town, very creative kitchen. What's not to like?"—Gal Ben-Moshe

GRILL ROYAL

Recommended by
Daniel Achilles

Friedrichstrasse 105b
Mitte
Berlin 10117
+49 3028879288
www.grillroyal.com

Opening hours	Open 7 days
Credit cards	Accepted
Price range	Affordable
Style	Smart casual
Cuisine	Modern European
Recommended for	Wish I'd opened

HOUSE OF SMALL WONDER

Recommended by
Lukas Mraz

Johannisstrasse 20
Mitte
Berlin 10117
www.houseofsmallwonder.de

Opening hours	Open 7 days
Reservation policy	No
Credit cards	Not accepted
Price range	Budget
Style	Casual
Cuisine	Japanese Fusion
Recommended for	Breakfast

"You'll see."—Lukas Mraz

The first wonder is the superbly surprising spiral staircase that invites you from the foyer to the first-floor eating area. Upstairs, the décor is New York-style palettes and plants; an obvious choice, as the original restaurant was founded in Williamsburg. The wonders keep on coming—cleverly crafted latte art, including the occasional bunny and bear. Come for the all-day brunch menu, which is decidedly European (homemade granola, croque madame, and croissant French toast), then slide into lunch and dinner, where you'll find Japanese-inspired tacos, *onigiri* rice balls with miso, and *tonkatsu* (breaded pork cutlet—as close to schnitzel as you're going to get). This is as cute and quirky a place as you could hope to find.

KUCHI

Recommended by
Daniel Achilles

Gipsstrasse 3
Mitte
Berlin 10119
+49 3028386622
www.kuchi.de

Opening hours	Open 7 days
Credit cards	Accepted
Price range	Budget
Style	Casual
Cuisine	Asian
Recommended for	Regular neighborhood

"You can eat well there—it's open on Sundays and child-friendly. 'My best friends' rolls' are my wife's favorite sushi."—Daniel Achilles

LORENZ ADLON

Recommended by
Daniel Achilles

Unter den Linden 77
Mitte
Berlin 10117
+49 3022611960
www.lorenzadlon-esszimmer.de

Opening hours	Closed Sunday to Tuesday
Credit cards	Accepted
Price range	Expensive
Style	Smart casual
Cuisine	Modern European
Recommended for	Local favorite

ROSENBURGER

Recommended by
Marco Müller

Brunnenstrasse 196
Mitte
Berlin 10119
+49 3024083037

Opening hours	Open 7 days
Reservation policy	No
Credit cards	Not accepted
Price range	Budget
Style	Casual
Cuisine	Burgers
Recommended for	Late night

"When nothing else is open you can get fresh, well-grilled burgers here."—Marco Müller

ROSENTHALER GRILL

Torstrasse 125
Mitte
Berlin 10119
+49 302832153

Opening hours................................Open 7 days
Reservation policy.......................................No
Credit cards..................................Not accepted
Price range..Budget
Style...Casual
Cuisine..Turkish
Recommended for..............................Late night

"For döner (kebabs) late at night when nowhere else is open."—Daniel Achilles

RUTZ

Chausseestrasse 8
Mitte
Berlin 210115
+49 3024628760
www.rutz-restaurant.de

Opening hours...............Closed Monday and Sunday
Credit cards......................................Accepted
Price range.......................................Expensive
Style...Formal
Cuisine..................................Modern European
Recommended for..........................Local favorite

STRANDBAR MITTE

Monbijoustrasse 3
Mitte
Berlin 10117
+49 3028385588
www.strandbar-mitte.de

Opening hours................................Open 7 days
Credit cards..................................Not accepted
Price range.....................................Affordable
Style...Casual
Cuisine...Bar
Recommended for...............................Bargain

HALLMANN & KLEE

Böhmische Strasse 13
Neukölln
Berlin 12055
+49 3023938186
www.hallmann-klee.de

Opening hours.....................Closed Monday and Tuesday
Credit cards...................................Not Accepted
Price range..Budget
Style...Casual
Cuisine..Café-Bistro
Recommended for...............................Breakfast

"A bright and cosy location. The staff are very nice and the food makes your day."—Micha Schäfer

INDUSTRY STANDARD

Sonnenallee 83
Neukölln
Berlin 12045
+49 3062727732
www.industry-standard.de

Opening hours......................Closed Monday and Tuesday
Credit cards......................................Accepted
Price range..Budget
Style...Casual
Cuisine.............................French-Mediterranean
Recommended for..........................Local favorite

STANDARD SERIOUS PIZZA

Templiner Strasse 7
Prenzlauer Berg
Berlin 10119
+49 3048625614
www.standard-berlin.de

Opening hours...................................Closed Monday
Credit cards..................Accepted but only debit cards
Price range..Budget
Style...Casual
Cuisine...Italian
Recommended for..........................Wish I'd opened

"Austrian owner who serves the best pizza in town."
—Lukas Mraz

RESTAURANT HODORI

Recommended by
Lukas Mraz

Goebenstrasse 16
Schöneberg
Berlin 10783
+49 302153562
www.restaurant-hodori.de

Opening hours	Open 7 days
Credit cards	Accepted
Price range	Budget
Style	Casual
Cuisine	Korean
Recommended for	Bargain

"Order *Schweinefleisch* (pork) with kimchi and tofu."
—Lukas Mraz

SUDAKA

Recommended by
Chakall Noir

Goltzstrasse 36
Schöneberg
Berlin 10781
+49 3021913178
www.sudaka.de

Opening hours	Closed Monday
Credit cards	Accepted
Price range	Budget
Style	Casual
Cuisine	South American
Recommended for	Breakfast

"Fantastic brunch."—Chakall Noir

BALZAC COFFEE

Recommended by
Daniel Achilles

Potsdamer Platz 10
Tiergarten
Berlin 10785
+49 403551080
www.balzaccoffee.com

Opening hours	Open 7 days
Credit cards	Accepted
Price range	Budget
Style	Casual
Cuisine	Café
Recommended for	Breakfast

FACIL

Recommended by
Daniel Achilles

Potsdamer Straße 3
Tiergarten
Berlin 10785
+49 30590051234
www.facil.de

Opening hours	Closed Saturday and Sunday
Credit cards	Accepted
Price range	Expensive
Style	Formal
Cuisine	Modern European
Recommended for	Local favorite

BENEDICT

Recommended by
Daniel Achilles
Gal Ben-Moshe

Uhlandstrasse 49
Wilmersdorf
Berlin 10719
+49 30994040997
www.benedict-breakfast.de

Opening hours	Open 7 days
Credit cards	Accepted
Price range	Affordable
Style	Casual
Cuisine	International
Recommended for	Breakfast

"A twenty-four-hour breakfast place that serves very
generous breakfasts without fuss and offers good
value for money."—Gal Ben-Moshe

RESTAURANT BIBERBAU

Recommended by
Marco Müller

Durlacher Strasse 15
Wilmersdorf
Berlin 10715
+49 308532390
www.bieberbau-berlin.de

Opening hours	Closed Saturday and Sunday
Credit cards	Accepted
Price range	Affordable
Style	Smart casual
Cuisine	International-German
Recommended for	Wish I'd opened

"A small, pleasant, family business with outstanding
cuisine."—Marco Müller

"Cool concept; classy but not presumptuous."

IVO ADAM P638

"THE CUISINE IS AS PERFECT AS A SWISS WATCH."

NENAD MLINAREVIC P640

SWITZERLAND

"Five-star hotel with a great brunch on Sunday, nice atmosphere and breathtaking view. Simply amazing."

ROLF FLIEGAUF P641

"GENUINE MARKET-FRESH CUISINE, A GREAT WINE LIST AND CHARMING HOSTS."

RETO LAMPART P642

"For the young and young-at-heart."

RUDOLF OBAUER P642

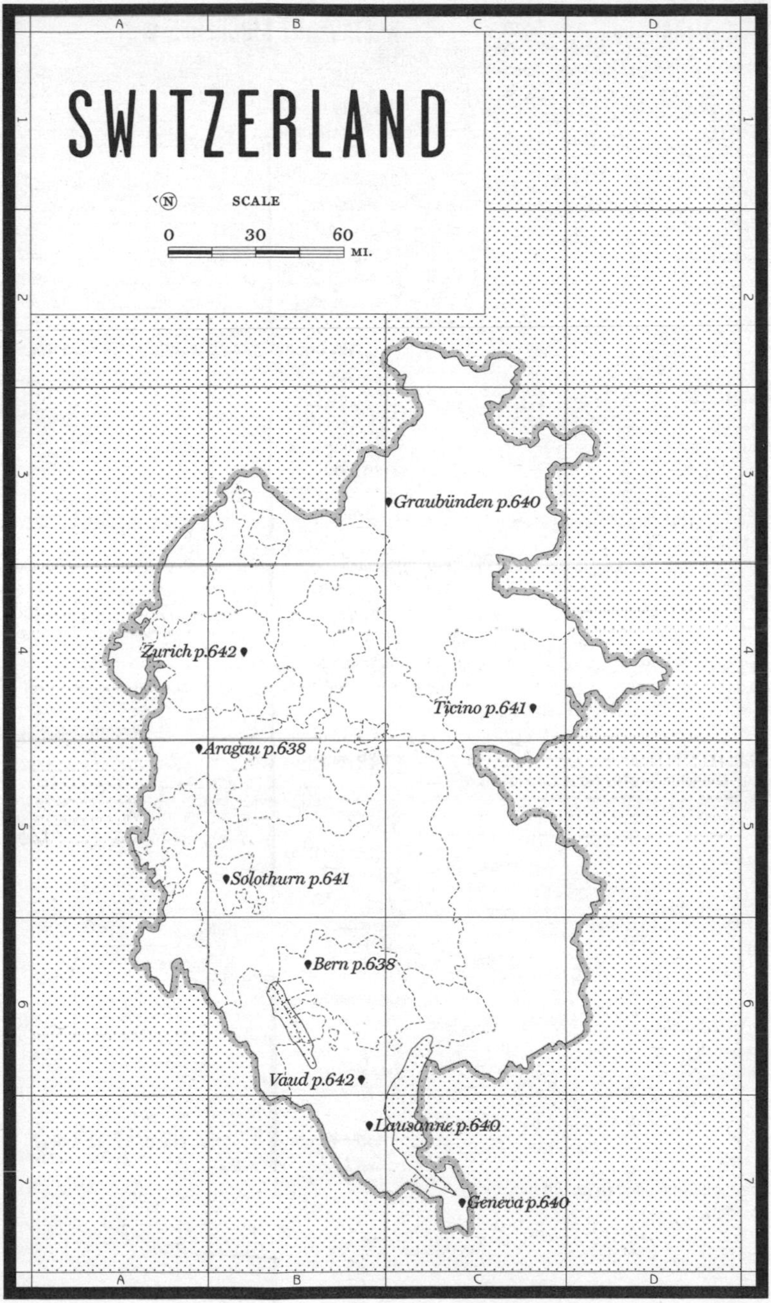
SWITZERLAND
N
SCALE
0 30 60
MI.
A
B
C
D
1
2
3
4
5
6
7
Graubünden p.640
Zurich p.642
Ticino p.641
Aragau p.638
Solothurn p.641
Bern p.638
Vaud p.642
Lausanne p.640
Geneva p.640

RESTAURANT CENTRAL

Recommended by
Reto Lampart

Dorfstrasse 18
Safenwil
Aargau 5745
+41 627970798
www.restaurant-central.ch

Opening hours	Closed Saturday and Sunday
Credit cards	Accepted
Price range	Affordable
Style	Casual
Cuisine	Swiss
Recommended for	Regular neighborhood

JACK'S BRASSERIE

Recommended by
Ivo Adam

Hotel Schweizerhof
Bahnhofplatz 11
Bern
Bern 3001
+41 313268080
www.schweizerhof-bern.ch

Opening hours	Open 7 days
Credit cards	Accepted
Price range	Expensive
Style	Smart casual
Cuisine	Swiss-French
Recommended for	Regular neighborhood

"Waiters in tails, fin-de-siècle atmosphere and
'Vive la France!' The best Wiener Schnitzel, despite
the French touch."—Ivo Adam

LÖSCHER

Recommended by
Ivo Adam

Gotthelfstrasse 29
Bern 3013
+41 774300559
www.altefeuerwehrviktoria.ch/projekt_seite/loescher

Opening hours	Closed Monday and Sunday
Credit cards	Not accepted
Price range	Affordable
Style	Casual
Cuisine	Swiss
Recommended for	Late night

"Uncomplicated, personal, and in an old fire
station."—Ivo Adam

RESTAURANT KIRCHENFELD

Recommended by
Ivo Adam

Thunstrasse 5
Bern 3005
+41 313510278
www.kirchenfeld.ch

Opening hours	Closed Monday and Sunday
Credit cards	Accepted
Price range	Expensive
Style	Smart casual
Cuisine	International
Recommended for	Local favorite

"Classic, but looks out beyond Bern."—Ivo Adam

TOI ET MOI

Recommended by
Ivo Adam

Bahnhofplatz 2
Bern 3011
+41 313124000
www.toietmoi.ch

Opening hours	Open 7 days
Credit cards	Accepted
Price range	Affordable
Style	Smart casual
Cuisine	European
Recommended for	Breakfast

"Cool concept—classy but not presumptuous."
—Ivo Adam

TULSI

Recommended by
Ivo Adam

Freiestrasse 65
Bern 3012
+41 315082202
www.tulsi-bern.ch

Opening hours	Closed Sunday
Credit cards	Accepted but not AMEX
Price range	Affordable
Style	Casual
Cuisine	Indian
Recommended for	Bargain

"Hot!—if you want a brief, cheap trip to India."
—Ivo Adam

BASTA BY DALSASS

Recommended by
Marcus G. Lindner

Hotel Bernerhof Gstaad
Bahnhofstrasse 2
Gstaad
Bern 3780
+41 337488844
www.bernerhof-gstaad.ch

Opening hours	Closed Monday and Sunday
Credit cards	Accepted
Price range	Affordable
Style	Casual
Cuisine	Italian
Recommended for	Regular neighborhood

CHARLY'S

Recommended by
Marcus G. Lindner

Promenade 76
Gstaad
Bern 3780
+41 337441544
www.charlys-gstaad.ch

Opening hours	Open 7 days
Credit cards	Accepted
Price range	Affordable
Style	Casual
Cuisine	Café-Bakery
Recommended for	Breakfast

RESTAURANT CHESERY

Recommended by
Marcus G. Lindner

Lauenenstrasse 6
Gstaad
Bern 3780
+41 337442451
www.chesery.ch

Opening hours	Closed Monday
Credit cards	Accepted
Price range	Expensive
Style	Formal
Cuisine	French-Mediterranean
Recommended for	High end

"Chef Robschi makes the best milk coffee in town."
—Marcus G. Lindner

RESTAURANT RIALTO

Recommended by
Marcus G. Lindner

Promenade 54
Gstaad
Bern 3780
+41 337443474
www.rialto-gstaad.ch

Opening hours	Open 7 days
Credit cards	Accepted
Price range	Expensive
Style	Smart casual
Cuisine	French-Mediterranean
Recommended for	Late night

WASSERNGRAT RESTAURANT

Recommended by
Marcus G. Lindner

Wasserngrat
Gstaad
Bern 3780
+41 337449622
www.wasserngrat.ch

Opening hours	Open 7 days
Credit cards	Accepted but not AMEX
Price range	Expensive
Style	Casual
Cuisine	Swiss
Recommended for	Regular neighborhood

"On the water level in Gstaad. Surprisingly light, fresh, and tasty regional cuisine with a breathtaking view."
—Marcus G. Lindner

HUUS HOTEL GSTAAD

Recommended by
Marcus G. Lindner

Schönriedstrasse 74
Saanen-Gstaad
Bern 3792
+41 337480404
www.huusgstaad.com

Opening hours	Open 7 days
Credit cards	Accepted
Price range	Expensive
Style	Smart casual
Cuisine	Swiss
Recommended for	Breakfast

"Offering fresh, local products from local producers."
—Marcus G. Lindner

EISBLUME WORB

Recommended by
Ivo Adam

Enggisteinstrasse 16A
Worb
Bern 3076
+41 318390300
www.eisblume-worb.ch

Opening hours	Closed Sunday to Wednesday
Credit cards	Accepted
Price range	Expensive
Style	Smart casual
Cuisine	Modern Swiss
Recommended for	High end

IL LAGO

Recommended by
Anatoly Komm

Four Seasons Hotel des Bergues
Quai des Bergues 33
Geneva 1201
+41 229087000
www.fourseasons.com/geneva

Opening hours	Open 7 days
Credit cards	Accepted
Price range	Expensive
Style	Smart casual
Cuisine	Italian
Recommended for	Breakfast

ROOFTOP°42

Recommended by
Anatoly Komm

Rue du Rhône 42
Geneva 1204
+41 223467700
www.rooftop42.com

Opening hours	Closed Monday and Sunday
Credit cards	Accepted
Price range	Expensive
Style	Smart casual
Cuisine	Swiss
Recommended for	Late night

SCHLOSS SCHAUENSTEIN

Recommended by
Daniel Humm

Schlossgass 77
Furstenau
Graubünden 7414
+41 816321080
www.schauenstein.ch

Opening hours	Closed Monday and Tuesday
Credit cards	Accepted
Price range	Expensive
Style	Smart casual
Cuisine	Modern Swiss
Recommended for	Worth the travel

HOTEL LAUDINELLA

Recommended by
Rolf Fliegauf

Via Tegiatscha 17
St. Moritz
Graubünden 7500
+41 818360629
www.laudinella.ch

Opening hours	Open 7 days
Credit cards	Accepted
Price range	Budget
Style	Casual
Cuisine	International
Recommended for	Late night

"Very casual and you can eat a very good pizza until five o'clock in the morning."—Rolf Fliegauf

L'HOTEL DE VILLE CRISSIER

Recommended by
Anatoly Komm,
Reto Lampart,
Rudolf Obauer

1 Rue d'Yverdon
Crissier
Lausanne 1023
+41 216340505
www.restaurantcrissier.com

Opening hours	Closed Monday and Sunday
Credit cards	Accepted
Price range	Expensive
Style	Smart casual
Cuisine	Traditional French
Recommended for	High end

"The cuisine is as perfect as a Swiss watch."
—Rudolf Obauer

Once the domain of legendary chef Frédy Girardet, Benoît Violier and wife Brigitte had a tough act to follow when they took the reins in 2012. They got off to an impeccable start though, winning three Michelin stars within a year. Set on a hill outside Lausanne, this former town hall looks more like a picture-perfect wine château than a municipal building. Inside are the white-linen, well-spaced tables, and tasteful muted decor you might expect from a pillar of haute cuisine. Created by a team of twenty-two chefs, the dishes—such as green and purple Valais asparagus served with mimosa egg—are precise, detailed, and exquisite.

RESTAURANT BLÜEMLISMATT

Recommended by
Reto Lampart

Blüemlismatt 1
Egerkingen
Solothurn 4622
+41 623981468
www.bluemlismatt.ch

Opening hours..............................Closed Monday and Tuesday
Credit cards...Accepted
Price range...Expensive
Style...Casual
Cuisine...Swiss
Recommended for...Local favorite

"Mountain restaurant with sensational views.
Classic range of food and outstanding wine list."
—Reto Lampart

RESTAURANT CHAPPELI

Recommended by
Reto Lampart

Allerheiligenstrasse 218
Grenchen
Solothurn 2540
+41 326534040
www.chappeli-grenchen.ch

Opening hours.....................Closed Tuesday and Wednesday
Credit cards...Accepted
Price range...Affordable
Style...Casual
Cuisine...Mediterranean
Recommended for...Local favorite

TAVERNA ROMANA

Recommended by
Reto Lampart

Hauptstrasse 24
Hessigkofen
Solothurn 4577
+41 323157475
www.tavernaromana.ch

Opening hours..............................Closed Monday and Tuesday
Credit cards...Accepted
Price range...Affordable
Style..Smart casual
Cuisine...Italian
Recommended for..Bargain

EDEN ROC

Recommended by
Rolf Fliegauf

Hotel Eden Roc Ascona
Via Albarelle 16
Ascona
Ticino 6612
+41 917857171
www.edenroc.ch

Opening hours...Open 7 days
Credit cards...Accepted
Price range...Expensive
Style..Smart casual
Cuisine..Modern European
Recommended for..Breakfast

"Five-star hotel with a great brunch on Sunday, nice
atmosphere, and breathtaking view. Simply amazing."
—Rolf Fliegauf

GROTTO BALDORIA

Recommended by
Rolf Fliegauf

Via Sant'Omobono 9
Ascona
Ticino 6612
+41 917913298
www.grottobaldoria.ch

Opening hours...Open 7 days
Credit cards...Not accepted
Price range...Budget
Style...Casual
Cuisine...Italian
Recommended for...Local favorite

"This is not a restaurant, it's a bit like a theater—very
easy, simple kitchen with no menu—you receive what
they serve."—Rolf Fliegauf

RISTORANTE SENSI

Recommended by
Rolf Fliegauf

Viale Verbano 9
Locarno-Muralto
Ticino 6600
+41 917431717
www.ristorante-sensi.ch

Opening hours	Open 7 days
Credit cards	Accepted
Price range	Affordable
Style	Casual
Cuisine	Italian
Recommended for	Regular neighborhood

"Very casual all-day dining with a simple but delicious kitchen and a very nice view of Lake Maggiore."
—Rolf Flieguaf

RESTAURANT LES TROIS COURONNES

Recommended by
Anatoly Komm

Rue d'Italie 49
Vevey
Vaud 1800
+41 219233200
www.hoteltroiscouronnes.ch

Opening hours	Closed Monday and Sunday
Credit cards	Accepted
Price range	Expensive
Style	Smart casual
Cuisine	International
Recommended for	Breakfast

"Great variety for any taste, from vegans to meat-lovers. Exceptional quality. Amazing pastry and homemade Swiss yogurt."—Anatoly Komm

GLOBUS AM BELLEVUE

Recommended by
Marcus G. Lindner

Theaterstrasse 12
Zürich 8001
+41 585786767
www.globus.ch

Opening hours	Open 7 days
Credit cards	Accepted
Price range	Affordable
Style	Casual
Cuisine	International
Recommended for	Local favorite

"A modern dining experience for the young and young-at-heart."—Marcus G. Lindner

RESTAURANT CAMINO

Recommended by
Reto Lampart

Freischützstrasse 4
Zürich 8004
+41 442402121
www.restaurant-camino.ch

Opening hours	Closed Saturday and Sunday
Credit cards	Accepted
Price range	Affordable
Style	Casual
Cuisine	Mediterranean
Recommended for	Regular neighborhood

"Camino is an innovative business with genuine market-fresh cuisine, a great wine list, and charming hosts."—Reto Lampart

"I eat there once a week and always feel so comfortable."
ANA ROŠ P654

"Go hungry, as you won't want to stop eating."
THEO RANDALL P648

ITALY

"A temple of Italian and Mediterranean gastronomy!"
EMANUELE SCARELLO P660

"FAMILY-RUN AND SOME OF THE BEST PASTA AND SEAFOOD I HAVE EVER EATEN. I LIKE THE SIMPLICITY OF IT, THEY LIKE COOKING FOR YOU."
MITCHELL TONKS P671

Alto Adige pp.646 ♥

Friuli-Venezia Giulia p.652 ♥

Lombardy p.659 ♥   ♥ Veneto p.659

♥ Piedmont p.663

♥ Emilia-Romagna p.650

♥ Liguria p.658

Tuscany p.665 ♥   Ancona p.647 ♥
                    Marche p.663 ♥

♥ Umbria p.670 ♥

♥ Abruzzo p.646

Lazio p.665 ♥

Benevento p.646 ♥
Campania p.617 ♥

Sardinia p.665 ♥

Sicily p.666 ♥

ITALY

⌃
N̂   SCALE

0   80   160
            MI.

IL BOSCAIOLO

Recommended by
Nikko Romito

Via Riviera 12-14
Castel di Sangro
Abruzzo 67031
+39 864847217
www.ristoranteilboscaiolo.it

Opening hours	Open 7 days
Credit cards	Accepted but not AMEX or Diners
Price range	Affordable
Style	Casual
Cuisine	Italian
Recommended for	Regular neighborhood

RISTORANTE REALE

Recommended by
Jean Beddington,
Alessandro Narducci,
Fabio Rossi

Piana Santa Liberata 21
Castel di Sangro
L'Aquila
Abruzzo 67031
+39 086469382
www.ristorantereale.com

Opening hours	Closed Monday and Tuesday
Credit cards	Accepted
Price range	Expensive
Style	Smart casual
Cuisine	Modern Italian
Recommended for	Worth the travel

"Beautiful setting and wonderful feeling of space and lightness. The food is a brilliant mix of regional and haute cuisine and the flavors are very adult. Best bread ever!"—Jean Beddington

RESTAURANT AL METRÒ

Recommended by
Nikko Romito

Via Magellano 35
San Salvo Marina
San Salvo
Abruzzo 66050
+39 873803428
www.ristorantealmetro.it

Opening hours	Closed Monday
Credit cards	Accepted
Price range	Expensive
Style	Smart casual
Cuisine	Italian-Seafood
Recommended for	High end

TAVERNA DE LI CALDORA

Recommended by
Nikko Romito

Piazza Umberto I
Pacentro
L' Aquila
Abruzzo 67030
+39 086441139

Opening hours	Closed Tuesday
Credit cards	Accepted but not AMEX or Diners
Price range	Affordable
Style	Smart casual
Cuisine	Italian
Recommended for	Local favorite

THE WINE BAR & GRILL

Recommended by
Tomaž Kavčič

Hotel Rosa Alpina
Strada Micurá de Rü 20
San Cassiano
Bolzano
Alto Adige 39036
+39 0471849500
www.rosalpina.it/norbert-niederkofler.htm

Opening hours	Open 7 days
Credit cards	Accepted
Price range	Affordable
Style	Smart casual
Cuisine	Italian
Recommended for	Late night

"The unique atmosphere with cozy corners and funky tables is topped by the simplicity and creativity of the menu that goes from pizza to homemade pasta and from mozzarella to perfectly grilled meat."
—Tomaž Kavčič

KRESIOS

Recommended by
David Muñoz

Via San Giovanni 59
Telese Terme
Benevento 82037
+39 0824940723
www.kresios.it

Opening hours	Closed Monday
Credit cards	Accepted
Price range	Expensive
Style	Smart casual
Cuisine	Modern Italian
Recommended for	Worth the travel

"It is a unique restaurant, one of the new exponents of Italian cuisine, very close to the terroir, but with a very Japanese concept in terms of shapes and background."— David Muñoz

ULIASSI

Recommended by
Matthew Accarrino

Banchina di levante 6
Senigallia
Ancona 60019
+39 07165463
www.uliassi.it

Opening hours	Closed Monday
Credit cards	Accepted
Price range	Expensive
Style	Smart casual
Cuisine	Modern Italian
Recommended for	Worth the Travel

LA FONTELINA

Recommended by
Ross Lusted

Località Faraglioni
Capri
Naples
Campania 80073
+39 0818370845
www.fontelina-capri.com

Opening hours	Open 7 days
Credit cards	Accepted
Price range	Expensive
Style	Casual
Cuisine	Modern Italian
Recommended for	Worth the travel

LE PARÙLE

Recommended by
Cathy Whims

Via Benedetto Cozzolino 70
Ercolano
Naples
Campania 80056
+39 0817396494
www.leparule.it

Opening hours	Closed Monday
Credit cards	Accepted but not AMEX or Diners
Price range	Affordable
Style	Casual
Cuisine	Italian
Recommended for	Worth the travel

"Giuseppe Pignalose is a pizza maestro, producing the lightest and most flavorful pizzas I have ever eaten. It is worth getting on a plane just to eat his pizza."—Cathy Whims

TRATTORIA DA PAPÀ

Recommended by
Tom Moxon

Via Nuova del Campo 56
Naples
Campania 80141
+39 3491416344

Opening hours	Closed Monday
Credit cards	Accepted
Price range	Affordable
Style	Casual
Cuisine	Mediterranean
Recommended for	Worth the travel

"Looking like a UPVC shed from the outside, it is in a rundown area near the airport that I stumbled across last New Year's. Hospitable owners and great, home-style Neapolitan food."—Tom Moxon

DON ALFONSO

Recommended by
Tomaž Kavčič,
Emanuele Scarello

Don Alfonso 1890
Corso Sant'Agata 11–13
Sant'Agata sui Due Golfi
Naples
Campania 80061
+39 0818780026
www.donalfonso.com

Opening hours	Closed Monday and Tuesday
Credit cards	Accepted
Price range	Expensive
Style	Formal
Cuisine	Campanian
Recommended for	High end

"The result of an all-embracing hospitality project, friendly and sophisticated: restaurant, vegetable garden, and hotel. The very highest standards throughout. The ingredients from vegetable garden and sea are the key to it all. My favorite dish? Pezzogno sausage, pistachios, mozzarella, and courgettes with 'Candida' sauce."
—Emanuele Scarello

RISTORANTE ZASS

Il San Pietro di Positano
Via Laurito 2
Positano
Salerno
Campania 84017
+39 089812080
www.ilsanpietro.it

Opening hours	Open 7 days
Credit cards	Accepted
Price range	Expensive
Style	Smart casual
Cuisine	Campanian
Recommended for	Breakfast

"The view, the service and the incredible 'elephant milk' made from fresh almond milk and lemon juice."
—Massimiliano Alajmo

TRATTORIA DI VIA SERRA

Via Luigi Serra 9b
Bologna
Emilia-Romagna 40129
+39 0516312330
www.trattoriadiviaserra.it

Opening hours	Closed Monday and Tuesday
Credit cards	Accepted but not AMEX
Price range	Affordable
Style	Casual
Cuisine	Italian
Recommended for	Worth the travel

"A masterclass in authentic, uncomplicated Italian food."—Ben Spalding

OSTERIA DEL MIRASOLE

Via Giacomo Matteotti 17
San Giovanni in Persiceto
Bologna
Emilia-Romagna 40017
+39 051821273
www.osteriadelmirasole.it

Opening hours	Open 7 days
Credit cards	Accepted but not AMEX
Price range	Expensive
Style	Casual
Cuisine	Romagnolo
Recommended for	Worth the travel

"Franco Cimini single-handedly cooks the best dishes from the wonderful region of Emilia-Romagna.

He grills delicious cuts of meat on an open hearth and his pasta is seriously good. Go hungry as you won't want to stop eating."—Theo Randall

AMERIGO

Via Guglielmo Marconi 16
Savigno
Bologna
Emilia-Romagna 40060
+39 0516708326
www.amerigo1934.it

Opening hours	Closed Monday
Credit cards	Accepted
Price range	Affordable
Style	Smart casual
Cuisine	Italian
Recommended for	Worth the travel

PASTICCERIA GUALANDI

Via Giacomo Matteotti 38
Argenta
Ferrara
Emilia-Romagna 44011
+39 0532852890

Opening hours	Closed Monday
Credit cards	Accepted
Price range	Budget
Style	Casual
Cuisine	Italian
Recommended for	Breakfast

MAGNOLIA RISTORANTE

Viale Trento 31
Angolo Via Mario Angelon
Cesenatico
Forlì-Cesena
Emilia-Romagna 47042
+39 054781598
www.magnoliaristorante.it

Opening hours	Closed Wednesday
Credit cards	Accepted
Price range	Expensive
Style	Smart casual
Cuisine	Modern Italian
Recommended for	Local favorite

"Very welcoming. The friendly atmosphere makes you feel at ease, despite the high standing of the restaurant. Very creative and imaginative. Strong, well-balanced flavors and good-sized portions."
—Fabio Rossi

QUINTOQUARTO

Recommended by
Fabio Rossi

Piazza Ciceruacchio 1
Cesenatico
Forlì-Cesena
Emilia-Romagna 47042
+39 3311476554
www.quintoquartofood.com

Opening hours	Closed Tuesday
Credit cards	Accepted but not Diners
Price range	Budget
Style	Casual
Cuisine	Italian
Recommended for	Local favorite

"A relaxed, welcoming establishment serving *piadine* (thin flatbread) and related products."—Fabio Rossi

TRATTORIA ENTRÀ

Recommended by
Johan Agrell

Via Salde Entrà 60
Finale Emilia
Modena
Emilia-Romagna 41034
+39 053597105

Opening hours	Closed Monday and Tuesday
Credit cards	Accepted
Price range	Affordable
Style	Casual
Cuisine	Italian
Recommended for	Worth the travel

"Just my kind of super rustic 'Nonna cooking'. Best gnocchi I ever had and a wine list worth coming to lunch for and staying for dinner."—Johan Agrell

LA FRANCESCHETTA 58

Recommended by
Davide Oldani

Strada Vignolese 58
Modena
Emilia-Romagna 41124
+39 0593091008
www.franceschetta58.it

Opening hours	Closed Sunday
Credit cards	Accepted but not AMEX
Price range	Affordable
Style	Casual
Cuisine	Romagnolo
Recommended for	Bargain

"For high-quality cuisine in the grand tradition."
—Davide Oldani

HOSTERIA GIUSTI

Recommended by
Daniel Costa

Via Luigi Carlo Farini 75
Modena
Emilia-Romagna 41100
+39 059222533
www.hosteriagiusti.it

Opening hours	Closed Monday and Sunday
Credit cards	Accepted
Price range	Affordable
Style	Smart casual
Cuisine	Italian Deli
Recommended for	Wish I'd opened

"I love everything about this restaurant. You walk through a salumeria to get to the five- or six-table dining room and indulge in the most delicious Modenese cuisine with Lambrusco. Absolutely perfect."—Davide Oldani

MON CAFÉ

Recommended by
Massimo Bottura

Corso Canalchiaro 128
Modena
Emilia-Romagna 41121
+39 059223257
www.mon-cafe.it

Opening hours	Closed Monday
Credit cards	Accepted but not AMFX
Price range	Affordable
Style	Casual
Cuisine	Café-Bar-Bistro
Recommended for	Breakfast

"A very elegant café. The best coffee in Modena, the best pastries, great cocktails and wines of exceptional quality"—Massimo Bottura

OSTERIA FRANCESCANA

Via Stella 22
Modena
Emilia Romagna 41121
+39 059223912
www.osteriafrancescana.it

Opening hours	Closed Monday and Sunday
Credit cards	Accepted
Price range	Expensive
Style	Smart causal
Cuisine	Modern Italian
Recommended for	High end

"A beautifully constructed restaurant, with incredible art, which makes it stylish yet warm and comfortable. Charmingly upmarket! I ate their classic tasting menu and it is food at its best, cleanly presented, artistic but with wonderfully vibrant resonating flavors."
—Ross Lewis

PASTICCERIA BAR DONDI

Strada Vignolese 578
Modena
Emilia-Romagna 41125
+39 059362248

Opening hours	Open 7 days
Reservation policy	No
Credit cards	Accepted
Price range	Budget
Style	Casual
Cuisine	Café-Bar
Recommended for	Breakfast

"Luca makes extraordinary pastry cream! When I leave on a trip, or return on a morning international flight, I stop in there to get my fill of cannoli."
—Massimo Bottura

LE GHIAINE

Via Romea Nord 180
Cervia
Ravenna
Emilia-Romagna 48015
+39 0544991696
www.ristoranteleghiaine.it

Opening hours	Open 7 days
Credit cards	Accepted but not AMEX or Diners
Price range	Affordable
Style	Casual
Cuisine	Romagnolo
Recommended for	Bargain

"Traditional Romagna-region cuisine and great piadine (thin flatbread)."—Italo Bassi

LA VOGLIA MATTA

Via Vittorio Veneto 63
Fusignano
Ravenna
Emilia-Romagna 48034
+39 0545954034
www.ristorantelavogliamatta.it

Opening hours	Closed Sunday
Credit cards	Accepted
Price range	Affordable
Style	Smart casual
Cuisine	Italian
Recommended for	Local favorite

"Reminds me of my childhood."—Italo Bassi

AGRITURISMO CÀMÌ

Via Argine Sinistro Savio 84
Ravenna
Ravenna
Emilia-Romagna 48125
+39 0544949250
www.camiagriturismo.it

Opening hours	Closed Wednesday and Thursday
Credit cards	Accepted but not AMEX
Price range	Expensive
Style	Casual
Cuisine	Modern Italian
Recommended for	Bargain

"The location, the premises, the decor make you feel at ease the moment you cross the threshold. Great attention to detail. The chef uses ingredients straight from the vegetable garden. Simple dishes, intense flavors."—Fabio Rossi

CANTINETTA DELLA CORTE

Piazzetta Salvoni 1
Coriano
Rimini
Emilia-Romagna 47853
+39 0541658117
www.cantinettadellacorte.com

Opening hours	Closed Monday
Credit cards	Accepted
Price range	Affordable
Style	Casual
Cuisine	Italian
Recommended for	Late night

"A pleasant place where you can try local produce and drink a bottle of wine without spending too much."—Fabio Rossi

Tucked beneath the Corte theater is the Cantinetta della Corte, an intimate vaulted space popular with post-theater diners and, well, more or less anyone else who finds themselves in sleepy Coriano of a Tuesday to Sunday evening. There's a small menu of standard local cheeses and meats, and a decent craft beer selection, but many will want to make the most of the wine list; over 150 bottles of, largely, the Sangiovese grape, available for a very reasonable outlay. Jazz evenings are held irregularly, and there's a small terrace alongside for the summer months.

TRATTORIA DA SAVINO

Via Cavallino 32
Coriano
Rimini
Emilia-Romagna 47853
+39 0541656206
www.trattoriadasavino.com

Opening hours	Closed Monday
Credit cards	Accepted
Price range	Budget
Style	Casual
Cuisine	Italian Bistro
Recommended for	Regular neighborhood

"It is a very relaxed, friendly place, as if you were eating at a friend's house. The food is of top quality and prices are affordable. The traditions of the Romagna region are respected. The dishes are straightforward but well prepared. They serve foods that have been forgotten elsewhere."—Fabio Rossi

BAR PASTICCERIA LIEVITA

Viale Emilia 18
Riccione
Rimini
Emilia-Romagna 47838
+39 0541645511

Opening hours	Closed Tuesday
Reservation policy	No
Credit cards	Accepted but not AMEX
Price range	Affordable
Style	Casual
Cuisine	Café
Recommended for	Breakfast

"When you go in, you are struck by the fragrance of freshly baked bread and cakes. They do a great cappuccino. The place is welcoming and they have a fine display of produce. You can watch things being made, which arouses the customers' curiosity."
—Fabio Rossi

PANIFICIO PASTICCERIA BIANCHI

Viale D'Annunzio
Riccione
Rimini
Emilia-Romagna 47838
+39 0541641351
www.bianchiriccione.it

Opening hours	Open 7 days
Reservation policy	No
Credit cards	Accepted
Price range	Affordable
Style	Casual
Cuisine	Sicilian Café-Patisserie
Recommended for	Breakfast

"In a fine position on the seafront. They serve a wide variety of top-quality sweet and savory pastries."
— Fabio Rossi

RISTORANTE BIO'S KITCHEN

Via della Fiera 66
Rimini
Emilia-Romagna 47923
+39 0541771162
www.biositalia.com

Recommended by
Fabio Rossi

Opening hours	Open 7 days
Credit cards	Accepted
Price range	Affordable
Style	Casual
Cuisine	Italian
Recommended for	Late night

"A quiet, relaxed place, just a short walk from the town center, where you can meet up with your friends after supper and at other times. As well as vegetarian and vegan dishes, they serve pizza, if you want to spend the evening out without eating a heavy meal."
—Fabio Rossi

OSTERIA LA SANGIOVESA

Via Beato Simone Balacchi 14
Sant'Arcangelo di Romagna
Rimini
Emilia-Romagna 47822
+39 0541620710

Recommended by
Fabio Rossi

Opening hours	Open 7 days
Credit cards	Accepted
Price range	Affordable
Style	Smart casual
Cuisine	Romagnolo
Recommended for	Regular neighborhood

"The eighteenth-century premises are charming, occupying old caves excavated from the tufa rock, with fine brickwork in evidence. The cuisine is typical of the Romagna region. They serve home-produced pork meats, oil, wines, and spirits."—Fabio Rossi

AL CACCIATORE

La Subida, Via Subida 52
Cormons
Gorizia
Friuli-Venezia Giulia 34071
+39 048160531
www.lasubida.it

Recommended by
Ana Roš
Emanuele Scarello

Opening hours	Closed Tuesday and Wednesday
Credit cards	Accepted
Price range	Affordable
Style	Casual
Cuisine	Northern Italian
Recommended for	Local favorite

"A family-run restaurant, also offering accommodation, in the leafy green setting of the Gorizia Hills (Collio). Hospitality here is a time-honoured ritual, reflecting the traditions of this part of Friuli. Game, Idria Valley ravioli, well-seasoned cheeses, San Daniele ham, *brovada* (a kind of turnip) and *musetto* (a spiced sausage), creamed polenta and pumpkin with smoked ricotta cheese, and *frico* (a cheese and potato pie)."—Emanuele Scarello

L'ARGINE A VENCÒ

Località Vencò 15
Dolegna del Collio
Gorizia
Friuli-Venezia Giulia 34070
+39 04811999882
www.largineavenco.it

Recommended by
Ana Roš

Opening hours	Closed Monday and Tuesday
Credit cards	Accepted
Price range	Expensive
Style	Smart casual
Cuisine	Modern Italian
Recommended for	High end

TRATTORIA AI CIODI

Isola di Anfora
Grado
Gorizia
Friuli-Venezia Giulia 65464
+39 3357522209
www.portobusoaiciodi.it

Recommended by
Emanuele Scarello

Opening hours	Open 7 days
Credit cards	Not accepted
Price range	Affordable
Style	Casual
Cuisine	Seafood
Recommended for	Wish I'd opened

"It stands on an island in my lagoon, a landscape to which I am very attached, and is open only in summer. The very simple atmosphere is an amazing contrast to the perfectly cooked seafood they serve. Seafood with some interesting features: the use of poorly rated or uncommon fish, and the chef's sensitivity in enhancing his raw materials with just the right preparation and cooking techniques."—Emanuele Scarello

LA PRIMULA

Recommended by
Emanuele Scarello

Via San Rocco 47
San Quirino
Pordenone
Friuli-Venezia Giulia 33080
+39 043491005
www.ristorantelaprimula.it

Opening hours	Closed Monday
Credit cards	Accepted
Price range	Expensive
Style	Smart casual
Cuisine	Modern Italian
Recommended for	Regular neighborhood

"The chef is outstandingly gifted and combines his ingredients perfectly. First-class wine list."
—Emanuele Scarello

EATALY

Recommended by
Tomaž Kavčič

Riva Tommaso Gulli 1
Trieste
Friuli-Venezia Giulia 34123
+39 0402465701
www.eataly.net

Opening hours	Open 7 days
Credit cards	Accepted
Price range	Affordable
Style	Casual
Cuisine	Italian
Recommended for	Bargain

"Eataly is about eating Italian food, living the Italian way. Their goal is to demonstrate that high-quality Italian products can be made available to everyone, at affordable prices, by creating a direct relationship between producers and distributors, and focusing on sustainability, responsibility, and sharing. You can get, for example, the famous durum wheat pasta from Gragnano, Piedmont's egg pasta, mineral water from the Maritime Alps, Venetian and Piedmontese wines, Ponente Riviera Ligure oil, Piedmont's *fassone* meat, and traditional Italian cheeses and cold cuts. A very interesting concept in a chain of stores and restaurants."—Tomaž Kavčič

TRATTORIA AI CACCIATORI

Recommended by
Ana Roš

Via Pradamano 28
Cerneglons
Udine
Friuli-Venezia Giulia 33047
+39 0432670132

Opening hours	Closed Monday and Tuesday
Credit cards	Accepted but not AMEX
Price range	Affordable
Style	Casual
Cuisine	Northern Italian
Recommended for	Bargain

PANIFICIO VENIER

Recommended by
Emanuele Scarello

Piazza Rizzi 32
Colugna
Udine
Friuli-Venezia Giulia 33100
+39 0432541831

Opening hours	Closed Monday
Credit cards	Not accepted
Price range	Budget
Style	Casual
Cuisine	Italian Bakery
Recommended for	Breakfast

"For an Italian-style breakfast, the Panificio Venier has light and airy pastries, and their cappuccinos are just the right temperature." —Emanuele Scarello

TRATTORIA ALLA POSTA

Recommended by
Ana Roš

Via Frazione Clodig
Grimacco
Udine
Friuli-Venezia Giulia 33040
+39 0432725000

Opening hours	Closed Tuesday and Wednesday
Credit cards	Accepted but not AMEX or Diners
Price range	Affordable
Style	Casual
Cuisine	Italian
Recommended for	Local favorite

"Great old-school local cuisine."—Ana Roš

CAFFETTERIA TORINESE

Piazza Grande 9
Palmanova
Udine
Friuli-Venezia Giulia 33057
+39 0432920732
www.caffetteriatorinese.com

Opening hours	Closed Wednesday
Reservation policy	No
Credit cards	Accepted but not Diners
Price range	Budget
Style	Casual
Cuisine	Bar-Deli
Recommended for	Breakfast

"A relaxing spot in the town square. From breakfast to evening aperitif, there's always something tasty: meats, cheeses, stuffed focaccia, raw scampi, pigeon."—Emanuele Scarello

PIZZERIA DA LUCIANO

Via Loch 41
Pulfero
Udine
Friuli-Venezia Giulia 33046
+39 0432726349

Opening hours	Closed Thursday
Credit cards	Accepted but not AMEX
Price range	Affordable
Style	Casual
Cuisine	Pizzeria
Recommended for	Regular neighborhood

"It is the best pizzeria because of great ingredients and the great hands of Luciano. An old, simple place with a fireplace. I eat there once a week and always feel so comfortable."—Ana Roš

SALE E PEPE

Via Capoluogo 19
Stregna
Udine
Friuli-Venezia Giulia 33040
+39 0432724118

Opening hours	Closed Tuesday and Wednesday
Credit cards	Accepted but not Diners
Price range	Affordable
Style	Casual
Cuisine	Traditional Italian
Recommended for	Local favorite

NIÙ

Via Nazionale 40
Tavagnacco
Udine
Friuli-Venezia Giulia 33010
+39 0432484739
www.niudine.it

Opening hours	Closed Sunday
Credit cards	Accepted
Price range	Affordable
Style	Casual
Cuisine	Italian
Recommended for	Late night

"They serve excellent panini and dishes made with local ingredients, and they have a good selection of wines, cocktails, and beers."—Emanuele Scarello

AGLI AMICI DAL 1887

Via Liguria 250
Udine
Friuli-Venezia Giulia 33100
+39 0432565411
www.agliamici.it

Opening hours	Closed Monday
Credit cards	Accepted but not Diners
Price range	Expensive
Style	Smart casual
Cuisine	Italian
Recommended for	Regular neighborhood

"At Agli Amici, Emanuele and Michela Scarello and their staff always want you to feel special. Every last detail is taken care of for you so that you are welcomed. Their cuisine tells their story, passion, and link with the country. They don't want to impress you, they just want you to feel at home."—Tomaž Kavčič

ANCONA DUE RISTORANTE PIZZERIA

Via Tricesimo 101
Udine
Friuli-Venezia Giulia 33100
+39 0432471414
www.anconadue.it

Opening hours	Closed Tuesday
Credit cards	Accepted
Price range	Affordable
Style	Smart casual
Cuisine	Pizza-Seafood
Recommended for	Late night

"The ever-cheerful atmosphere, high-quality ingredients, and convenience (easy access and parking). Pizza cooked in a wood-fired oven and seafood (a specialty is linguine with scorpion fish)."
—Emanuele Scarello

MAMM

Recommended by
Emanuele Scarello

Largo del Teatro 2
Udine
Friuli-Venezia Giulia 33100
+39 3426191801
www.mammciclofocacceria.com

Opening hours	Closed Sunday
Credit cards	Accepted
Price range	Budget
Style	Casual
Cuisine	Café-Bakery
Recommended for	Bargain

COLLINE CIOCIARE

Recommended by
Carmelo Chiaramonte,
Igles Corelli

Via Prenestina 23
Acuto
Frosinone
Lazio 03010
+39 077556049
www.salvatoretassa.it

Opening hours	Closed Monday
Credit cards	Accepted
Price range	Affordable
Style	Smart casual
Cuisine	Modern Mediterranean
Recommended for	Worth the travel

"Salvatore's cooking is reminiscent of rock music, in its infancy, when it consisted of just three instruments and vocals. The key thing is an almost shamanic combination of flavors. A restaurant where roots, berries, and other ingredients from the surrounding woods are transformed into earthy dishes with mysterious, illuminating flavors."
—Carmelo Chiaramonte

L'ARCANGELO

Recommended by
Şemsa Denizsel

Via Giuseppe Gioacchino Belli 59
Rome
Lazio 00193
+39 063210992
www.larcangelo.com

Opening hours	Closed Sunday
Credit cards	Accepted
Price range	Affordable
Style	Smart casual
Cuisine	Roman
Recommended for	Worth the travel

"For its perfect pillows of gnocchi."—Şemsa Denizsel

LA BUVETTE

Recommended by
Gianfranco Pirrone

Via Vittoria 44
Rome
Lazio 00187
+39 066790383
www.ristorantedilla.it/buvette

Opening hours	Open 7 days
Credit cards	Accepted
Price range	Affordable
Style	Smart casual
Cuisine	Italian
Recommended for	Worth the travel

"Very good food, nice ambience, and fantastic staff. Very nice cocktails as well."—Gianfranco Pirrone

CASA DEL SUPPLÌ

Recommended by
Nikko Romito

Piazza Re di Roma 20
Quartiere IX Appio Latino
Rome
Lazio 00183
+39 6 589 7110
www.lacasadelsuppli.it

Opening hours	Closed Sunday
Reservation policy	No
Credit cards	Accepted but not AMEX or Diners
Price range	Budget
Style	Casual
Cuisine	Pizza-Street Food
Recommended for	Bargain

IL CONVIVIO TROIANI

Recommended by
Alessandro Narducci

Via Vicolo dei Soldati 31
Rome
Lazio 00186
+39 066869432
www.ilconviviotroiani.it

Opening hours	Closed Sunday
Credit cards	Accepted
Price range	Expensive
Style	Smart casual
Cuisine	Roman
Recommended for	Regular neighborhood

"Roman cuisine treated with elegance and innovation.
Service and wine list of the highest level. Michelin
starred."—Alessandro Narducci

COFFEE POT

Recommended by
Alessandro Narducci

Via Michele di Lando 20
Rome
Lazio 00162
+39 0664220937
www.coffeepotcompany.com

Opening hours	Open 7 days
Credit cards	Accepted
Price range	Affordable
Style	Smart casual
Cuisine	Japanese-Mexican
Recommended for	Late night

ENOTECA ACHILLI AL PARLAMENTO

Recommended by
Alessandro Narducci

Via dei Prefetti 15
Rome
Lazio 00186
+39 066873446
www.enotecalparlamento.com

Opening hours	Closed Sunday
Credit cards	Accepted
Price range	Expensive
Style	Smart casual
Cuisine	Bar
Recommended for	High end

"Michelin starred incredible cuisine and an unique
wine list."—Alessandro Narducci

ER GAMBERO ROTTO

Recommended by
Alessandro Narducci

Via Garlasco 140
Rome
Lazio 00166
+39 63096087

Opening hours	Closed Monday and Tuesday
Credit cards	Accepted but not AMEX or Diners
Price range	Affordable
Style	Casual
Cuisine	Roman
Recommended for	Local favorite

"Authentic cuisine, ambiance of yesteryear, immortal,
unbeatable value, true story!"—Alessandro Narducci

MARZAPANE

Recommended by
Yoji Tokuyoshi

Via Velletri 39
Municipio II
Rome
Lazio 198
+39 0664781692
www.marzapaneroma.com

Opening hours	Closed Monday
Credit cards	Accepted
Price range	Expensive
Style	Smart Casual
Cuisine	Traditional Bistro
Recommended for	Regular neighborhood

"Each time I'm in Rome I cannot miss a stop to
Marzapane, run by Alba Esteve Ruiz a young and
passionate Spanish female chef. It's always a fun place
to stop by for tasty food, and I'm always inspired by
her different and creative approach."
—Yoji Tokuyoshi

MONDI CAFFÈ

Recommended by
Nikko Romito

Viale della Serenissima 12
Municipio V
Rome
Lazio 00177
+39 062593194
www.mondiroma.it

Opening hours	Closed Sunday
Reservation policy	No
Credit cards	Accepted but not AMEX or Diners
Price range	Budget
Style	Casual
Cuisine	Cafe-Bakery
Recommended for	Breakfast

LA PERGOLA

Via Alberto Cadlolo 101
Rome
Lazio 00136
+39 0635092152
www.romecavalieri.com/la-pergola

Recommended by
Luca Fantin

Opening hours	Closed Monday and Sunday
Credit cards	Accepted
Price range	Expensive
Style	Formal
Cuisine	European
Recommended for	High end

RISTORANTE DILLÀ

Via Mario de' Fiori 41
Rome
Lazio 00187
+39 0669797778
www.ristorantedilla.it

Recommended by
Gianfranco Pirrone

Opening hours	Open 7 days
Credit cards	Accepted but not Diners
Price range	Affordable
Style	Casual
Cuisine	Traditional Roman
Recommended for	Local favorite

RISTORANTE LAGANÀ

Via dell'Orso 44
Rione V Ponte
Rome
Lazio 00186
+39 0668301161
www.ristorantelagana.it

Recommended by
Ethan Stowell

Opening hours	Closed Sunday
Credit cards	Accepted but not Amex
Price range	Affordable
Style	Casual
Cuisine	Italian
Recommended for	Worth the travel

"I first stumbled across Laganà after an unsuccessful experience at another restaurant around the corner. Still hungry and drawn in by the crowd of people outside I decided to check it out. Little did I know that the crowd of people outside were not people leaving, they were people waiting to get in. An hour-and-a-half wait at midnight? It blew my mind. I almost didn't bother but I'm glad I did. It was one of the most beautiful and romantic meals I've ever had. Every time I have been back, the food has been just as good as I remember and that's hard to do."—Ethan Stowell

ROSCIOLI

Via dei Giubbonari 21
Rome
Lazio 00186
+39 066875287
www.salumeriaroscioli.com

Recommended by
Daniel Costa,
Şemsa Denizsel,
Olle T. Cellton

Opening hours	Closed Sunday
Credit cards	Accepted
Price range	Affordable
Style	Smart casual
Cuisine	Bar-Bistro-Deli
Recommended for	Worth the travel

The Roscioli name is Roman shorthand for fine food, wine, and pizza. The third generation of the family is now dispensing slices of pizza bianca and sourdough loaves at the Via dei Chiavari bakery, while the old grocery store nearby has been operating as a wine bar, restaurant, and deli since 2002. On entering, it's temptation from all sides: perfectly kept cheeses and cured meats at the counter, world-class wines (from a cellar of thousands) on every shelf, and a menu based around their produce. A contender for Rome's best carbonara, say some.

TRAPIZZINO

Piazzale Ponte Milvio 13
Rome
Lazio 00135
+39 0633221964
www.trapizzino.it

Recommended by
Alessandro Narducci

Opening hours	Open 7 days
Credit cards	Accepted
Price range	Budget
Style	Casual
Cuisine	Street Food
Recommended for	Bargain

"Intelligent, high-quality street food in a great location."—Alessandro Narducci

TRATTORIA AL MORO

Vicolo Bollette 13
Rome
Lazio 00187
+39 066783495
www.ristorantealmororoma.com

Opening hours	Closed Sunday
Credit cards	Accepted but not Diners
Price range	Expensive
Style	Formal
Cuisine	Italian
Recommended for	Wish I'd opened

TRATTORIA DA CESARE AL CASALETTO

Via del Casaletto 45
Rome
Lazio 00151
+39 06536015
www.trattoriadacesare.it

Opening hours	Closed Wednesday
Credit cards	Accepted but not AMEX or Diners
Price range	Affordable
Style	Smart casual
Cuisine	Roman
Recommended for	Worth the travel

TRATTORIA DA NENO

Via Ravenna 30
Rome
Lazio 00161
+39 0644290319
www.trattorianeno.it

Opening hours	Open 7 days
Credit cards	Accepted but not AMEX
Price range	Affordable
Style	Casual
Cuisine	Italian
Recommended for	Late night

"Simple but very well-executed dishes, and a nice place to drink."—Alessandro Narducci

TRATTORIA TONINO BASSETTI

Via Governo Vecchio 18
Rome
Lazio 00186
+39 3335870779

Opening hours	Closed Sunday
Reservation policy	No
Credit cards	Not accepted
Price range	Affordable
Style	Casual
Cuisine	Roman
Recommended for	Worth the travel

"The most unassuming little hole in the wall on one of Rome's hottest streets. Simple Roman *cucina povera* where the owners are delivering the Roman classics with passion and flavor that you can only find at mama's."—Pasquale Trimboli

LA VECCHIA OSTAIA

Via Provinciale 34
San Biagio della Cima
Imperia
Liguria 18036
+39 0184289249

Opening hours	Closed Tuesday and Wednesday
Credit cards	Accepted but not AMEX or Diners
Price range	Affordable
Style	Casual
Cuisine	Italian
Recommended for	Regular neighborhood

"It is a typical homemade Italian restaurant with a mama who cooks fresh ravioli every day. Simple and delicious!"—Mauro Colagreco

CAPANNINA CICCIO

Via C. A. Fabbricotti 71
Bocca di Magra
Spezia
Liguria 19031
+39 018765568
www.ristoranteciccio.it

Opening hours	Closed Tuesday
Credit cards	Accepted
Price range	Affordable
Style	Casual
Cuisine	Seafood
Recommended for	Wish I'd opened

"I have to declare an interest in this restaurant. It was started by my father and uncle over sixty years ago on the Ligurian Coast and I worked there as a boy and young man. It has gone from strength to strength under my cousin Mario and is the most amazing and hospitable seafood restaurant."—Lucio Galletto

DA VITTORIO

Via Cantalupa 17
Brusaporto
Bergamo
Lombardy 24060
+39 035681024
www.davittorio.com

Recommended by
Reto Lampart, Davide Oldani,
Emanuele Scarello

Opening hours	Open 7 days
Credit cards	Accepted
Price range	Expensive
Style	Smart casual
Cuisine	Lombardian
Recommended for	Worth the travel

"For the atmosphere and for their creative approach to classical Italian cuisine."—Davide Oldani

PASTICCERIA VENETO

Via Salvo D'Acquisto 8
Brescia
Brescia
Lombardy 25128
+39 030392586
www.iginiomassari.it/pasticceria-veneto

Recommended by
Riccardo Camanini

Opening hours	Closed Monday
Reservation policy	No
Credit cards	Accepted
Price range	Budget
Style	Casual
Cuisine	Italian Patisserie
Recommended for	Breakfast

LIDO 84

Corso Zanardelli 196
Gardone Riviera
Brescia
Lombardy 25083
+39 036520019
www.ristorantelido84.com

Recommended by
Corey Lee, Ana Roš,
Mathieu Rostaing Tayard

Opening hours	Closed Tuesday
Credit cards	Accepted but not AMEX
Price range	Expensive
Style	Smart casual
Cuisine	Modern Italian
Recommended for	Worth the travel

"It was one of the most thoughtful and sensitive meals I can remember."— Corey Lee

TRATTORIA RIOLET

Via Fasano di Sopra 17
Gardone Riviera
Brescia
Lombardy 25083
+39 036520545

Recommended by
Riccardo Camanini

Opening hours	Closed Wednesday
Credit cards	Accepted
Price range	Affordable
Style	Casual
Cuisine	Italian
Recommended for	Regular neighborhood

"Authentic, sustainable, organic homemade food."
—Riccardo Camanini

DAL PESCATORE

Località Runate 15
Canneto sull'Oglio
Mantua
Lombardy 46013
+39 0376723001
www.dalpescatore.com

Opening hours	Closed Monday and Tuesday
Credit cards	Accepted
Price range	Expensive
Style	Smart casual
Cuisine	Mantuan
Recommended for	High end

"A temple of Italian and Mediterranean gastronomy!"
—Emanuele Scarello

The Santini family are renowned for treating
customers like old friends at their world-class
restaurant, set in isolated splendour an hour's
drive from Milan. Dal Pescatore, originally a
humble osteria, has been in the same hands for
three generations. Serving refined Mantuan cuisine,
the three-Michelin-starred kitchen is run by Nadia
Santini, considered one of Italy's finest chefs, along
with her son Giovanni, and mother-in-law Bruna.
Produce takes pride of place, and rigorously
indigenous dishes such as *tortelli di zucca*
(pumpkin-filled pasta), snails with porcini, and
agnolini in *brodo* (stuffed pasta in broth) often
feature on the two tasting menus: the *Primavera*
and the *Campagna*.

LOCANDA DELLE GRAZIE

Via San Pio X 2
Grazie di Curtatone
Mantua
Lombardy 46010
+39 0376348038

Opening hours	Closed Tuesday and Wednesday
Credit cards	Accepted but not AMEX
Price range	Affordable
Style	Casual
Cuisine	Mantuan
Recommended for	Bargain

BEBEL

Via San Vittore 3
Milan
Lombardy 20123
+39 024812824
www.bebel.it

Opening hours	Closed Sunday
Credit cards	Accepted
Price range	Affordable
Style	Smart casual
Cuisine	Italian
Recommended for	Bargain

"You can ask these guys to do you some pizza bianca,
a ball of real buffalo mozzarella with olive oil, and
some sliced San Daniele ham with a glass of Barbera.
It shouldn't cost more than €20 ($23; £18)."
—Ruairí de Blacam

LA CANTINA DI MANUELA

Via Giulio Cesare Procaccini 41
Milan
Lombardy 20154
+39 023452034
www.lacantinadimanuela.it

Opening hours	Open 7 days
Credit cards	Accepted
Price range	Affordable
Style	Smart casual
Cuisine	Italian
Recommended for	Regular neighborhood

"Home cooking; homely welcome."—Luigi Taglienti

CASA RAMEN MILANO

Via Porro Lambertenghi 25
Isola
Milan
Lombardy 20159
+39 0239444560
www.casa-ramen.it/

Opening hours	Closed Sunday and Monday
Reservation policy	No
Credit cards	Accepted but not Amex
Price range	Affordable
Style	Casual
Cuisine	Ramen
Recommended for	Regular neighborhood

DRY

Recommended by
Davide Oldani

Via Solferino 33
Milan
Lombardy 20121
+39 0263793414
www.drymilano.it

Opening hours	Open 7 days
Credit cards	Accepted
Price range	Budget
Style	Smart casual
Cuisine	Pizzeria
Recommended for	Late night

"You can enjoy an excellent pizza while drinking a cocktail."—Davide Oldani

EMPORIO ARMANI RISTORANTE

Recommended by
Carmelo Chiaramonte

Via Croce Rossa 2
Milan
Lombardy 20121
+39 0272318683
www.armanirestaurants.com

Opening hours	Open 7 days
Credit cards	Accepted
Price range	Expensive
Style	Smart casual
Cuisine	Modern Italian
Recommended for	High end

"A young chef, Massimo Tringali, and authentic Italian cuisine. Genuine flavors and a very agreeable setting."—Carmelo Chiaramonte

LUME

Recommended by
Luigi Taglienti

Via Giacomo Watt 37
Milan
Lombardy 20143
+39 0280888624
www.lumemilano.com

Opening hours	Closed Monday
Credit cards	Accepted
Price range	Expensive
Style	Formal
Cuisine	Modern Italian
Recommended for	Local favorite

"Intimate atmosphere, innovative cuisine, fine attention to detail, and high-class service. Situated in an industrial setting, it forms part of W37, inside the former Richard Ginori factory. A shining example of industrial archaeology, luxury, and excellence."
—Luigi Taglienti

IL LUOGO DI AIMO E NADIA

Recommended by
Andrea Ferrero,
Rodrigo Oliveira,
Emanuele Scarello

Via Privata Raimondo Montecuccoli 6
Milan
Lombardy 20147
+39 02416886
www.aimoenadia.com

Opening hours	Closed Sunday
Credit cards	Accepted
Price range	Expensive
Style	Smart casual
Cuisine	Modern Italian
Recommended for	Worth the travel

"The meal of my life."—Rodrigo Oliveira

MARCHESI 1824

Recommended by
Davide Oldani

Via Montenapoleone 9
Milan
Lombardy 20121
+39 0276008238
www.pasticceriamarchesi.it

Opening hours	Open 7 days
Credit cards	Accepted
Price range	Budget
Style	Casual
Cuisine	Italian Patisserie
Recommended for	Breakfast

"They serve a perfect cappuccino with *crema di latte* (fresh cream). Their croissants are deliciously flaky."
—Davide Oldani

PASTICCERIA CUCCHI

Recommended by
Yoji Tokuyoshi

Corso Genova 1
Milan
Lombardy 20123
www.pasticceriacucchi.it

Opening hours	Open 7 days
Credit cards	Accepted
Price range	Affordable
Style	Casual
Cuisine	Classic Italian-Bar
Recommended for	Breakfast

RISTORANTE ACANTO

Recommended by
Luigi Taglienti

Hotel Principe di Savoïa
Piazza della Repubblica 17
Milan
Lombardy 20124
+39 0262302026
www.dorchestercollection.com/milan

Opening hours	Open 7 days
Credit cards	Accepted
Price range	Expensive
Style	Smart casual
Cuisine	Italian
Recommended for	Breakfast

"Historic, iconic place in Milan. Unique reception and service."—Luigi Taglienti

RISTORANTE TOKUYOSHI

Recommended by
Andrea Bonaffini,
Tomaž Kavčič

Via San Calocero 3
Milan
Lombardy 20123
+39 0284254626
www.ristorantetokuyoshi.com

Opening hours	Closed Monday
Credit cards	Accepted
Price range	Expensive
Style	Smart casual
Cuisine	Japanese-Italian
Recommended for	Worth the travel

"Love the food—a mix of Japanese and Italian. Great technique and flavor and impressive presentation."
— Andrea Bonaffini

SAKEYA

Recommended by
Yoji Tokuyoshi

Via Cesare da Sesto 1
Milan
Lombardy 20123
+39 294387836
www.sakeya.it

Opening hours	Closed Sunday and Monday
Credit cards	Accepted
Price range	Expensive
Style	Smart casual
Cuisine	Japanese
Recommended for	Late night

DE SANTIS

Recommended by
Luigi Taglienti

Corso Magenta 9
Milan
Lombardy 20123
+39 0272095124
www.paninidesantis.it

Opening hours	Open 7 days
Credit cards	Accepted
Price range	Budget
Style	Casual
Cuisine	Sandwiches
Recommended for	Late night

TRATTORIA MASUELLI SAN MARCO

Recommended by
Davide Oldani

Viale Umbria 80
Milan
Lombardy 20135
+39 0255184138
www.masuellitrattoria.com

Opening hours	Closed Sunday
Credit cards	Accepted but not Diners
Price range	Affordable
Style	Casual
Cuisine	Milanese
Recommended for	Local favorite

"For local dishes that have retained their authenticity."
—Davide Oldani

TRIPPA—TRATTORIA

Recommended by
Yoji Tokuyoshi

Via Giorgio Vasari 3
Milan
Lombardy 20135
+39 3276687908
www.trippamilano.it

Opening hours	Closed Sunday
Credit cards	Accepted
Price range	Affordable
Style	Casual
Cuisine	Modern Italian
Recommended for	Regular neighborhood

"It's an Italian 'Trattoria' with a modern philosophy, where they put a lot of effort in to source the best supplier for each ingredient. Their special dish off the day are always very fun to try; the variety meats (offal) are a must and I would highly recommend it to anyone if available."—Yoji Tokuyoshi

ZERO

Recommended by
Davide Oldani

Corso Magenta 87
Milan
Lombardy 20123
+39 0245474733
www.zero-milano.it

Opening hours	Closed Monday
Credit cards	Accepted
Price range	Expensive
Style	Smart casual
Cuisine	Modern Japanese
Recommended for	Regular neighborhood

DAL PESCATORE

Recommended by
Massimo Bottura

Località Runate 15
Canneto sull'Oglio
Mantua
Lombardy 46013
+39 0376723001
www.dalpescatore.com

Opening hours	Closed Monday and Tuesday
Credit cards	Accepted
Price range	Expensive
Style	Smart casual
Cuisine	Mantuan
Recommended for	Local favourite

"The Santini family's restaurant is not actually in the Emilia-Romagna region (it's a stone's throw from the border), but their cooking is representative of the best flavors and aromas of the Emilia-Romagna/Mantua area. An example to all restaurateurs of my generation."—Massimo Bottura

ULIASSI

Recommended by
Enrico Crippa

Banchina di Levante 6
Senigallia
Ancona
Marche 60019
+39 07165463
www.uliassi.it

Opening hours	Closed Monday
Credit cards	Accepted
Price range	Expensive
Style	Smart casual
Cuisine	Modern Italian
Recommended for	High end

"One of the outstanding restaurants we have in Italy. Mauro Uliassi is really a great chef."—Enrico Crippa

PIZZERIA RISTORANTE IL GAMBERO ROSSO

Recommended by
Massimo Bottura

Piazza S. Sebastiano 26
Cervere
Piedmont 12040
+39 0172474751

Opening hours	Closed Wednesday
Credit cards	Accepted but not AMEX or Diners
Price range	Budget
Style	Casual
Cuisine	Pizza
Recommended for	Bargain

GUSTO MADRE

Recommended by
Enrico Crippa

Via Armando Diaz 2
Alba
Cuneo
Piedmont 12051
+39 0173290915
www.gustomadre.it

Opening hours	Closed Tuesday
Credit cards	Accepted
Price range	Affordable
Style	Smart casual
Cuisine	Pizzeria
Recommended for	Bargain

"A new concept of pizzeria in Alba where you can find classic pizzas and gourmet offerings too." —Enrico Crippa

OPES

Recommended by
Enrico Crippa

Via Santa Barbara 1
Alba
Cuneo
Piedmont 12051
+39 0173470685
www.saporeconsapere.com

Opening hours	Closed Sunday
Credit cards	Accepted but not AMEX or Diners
Price range	Budget
Style	Casual
Cuisine	Café
Recommended for	Breakfast

"This is a place open from breakfast to lunch that offers a selection of vegan food, juices, and homemade pastries. Everything they serve is developed with a nutritionist."—Enrico Crippa

PIAZZA DUOMO

Piazza Risorgimento 4
Alba
Cuneo
Piedmont 12051
+39 0173366167
www.piazzaduomoalba.it

Recommended by
Andrea Bonaffini,
Luca Fantin,
Peter Gilmore

Opening hours	Closed Monday and Sunday
Credit cards	Accepted but not Diners
Price range	Expensive
Style	Formal
Cuisine	Modern Italian
Recommended for	High end

"A beautifully constructed cuisine featuring vegetables from their own garden. Impeccable service."—Peter Gilmore

Piazza Duomo, an ambitious restaurant in the heart of Alba, brings together the culinary daring of Enrico Crippa and the vision of influential wine producers the Ceretto family. Crippa's style is extraordinarily visual, a style reflected in the bold pink restaurant interior and the magnificent fresco by Francesco Clemente. Seasonal produce from the restaurant's kitchen garden is given due prominence: consider Crippa's Salad 21...31...41, with scores of rare flowers and leaves, his egg yolk and caviar *Uova e Uova* Salad, or his *Panna cotta Matisse* with its "cut-outs" of pea, raspberry, etc. Tasting menus mix new dishes and Crippa signatures.

LA REPUBBLICA DI PERNO

Vicolo Cavour 5
Perno
Cuneo
Piedmont 12065
+39 017378492
www.repubblicadiperno.it

Recommended by
Enrico Crippa,
Cathy Whims

Opening hours	Closed Wednesday and Thursday
Credit cards	Accepted but not AMEX
Price range	Affordable
Style	Casual
Cuisine	Piedmontese
Recommended for	Worth the travel

"For an elegantly simple countryside meal in Piedmont, La Republicca di Perno boasts an incredible menu from Marco Forneris, whom I consider one of the greatest chefs of the Langhe."—Cathy Whims

OSTERIA DA GEMMA

Via Guglielmo Marconi 6
Roddino
Cuneo
Piedmont 12050
+39 0173794252
www.osteriadagemma.it

Recommended by
Kamal Mouzawak

Opening hours	Closed Monday and Tuesday
Credit cards	Accepted but not AMEX or Diners
Price range	Affordable
Style	Casual
Cuisine	Italian
Recommended for	Wish I'd opened

"The best village cooks, gathered around Gemma, preparing traditional home-cooked cuisine."
—Kamal Mouzawak

TRATTORIA LA COCCINELLA

Via Provinciale 5
Serravalle Langhe
Cuneo
Piedmont 12050
+39 0173748220
www.trattoriacoccinella.com

Recommended by
Enrico Crippa

Opening hours	Closed Tuesday
Credit cards	Accepted but not AMEX or Diners
Price range	Affordable
Style	Smart casual
Cuisine	Italian
Recommended for	Local favorite

"I consider Trattoria La Coccinella a flag of Piedmontese traditional cuisine."—Enrico Crippa

COMBAL.ZERO

Piazza Mafalda di Savoia
Rivoli
Turin
Piedmont 10098
+39 0119565225
www.combal.org

Recommended by
Igles Corelli

Opening hours	Closed Monday and Sunday
Credit cards	Accepted
Price range	Expensive
Style	Smart casual
Cuisine	Modern Italian
Recommended for	Wish I'd opened

"A restaurant that mixes modernity and art with extreme creativity, in a great location in the Piedmont region."— Igles Corelli

AL GARAMOND

Recommended by
Alfredo Russo

Via Giuseppe Pomba 14
Turin
Piedmont 10123
+39 0118122781
www.algaramond.it

Opening hours	Closed Sunday
Credit cards	Accepted but not AMEX or Diners
Price range	Expensive
Style	Smart casual
Cuisine	Piedmontese-Sicilian
Recommended for	Bargain

"Good quality and attentive service."—Alfredo Russo

PASTARELL

Recommended by
Andrea Bonaffini

Piazza XVIII Dicembre
Turin
Piedmont 10122
+39 0114407696

Opening hours	Open 7 days
Credit cards	Accepted
Price range	Budget
Style	Casual
Cuisine	Neapolitan Bakery
Recommended for	Breakfast

"Very traditional Napoli-style breakfast. The homemade pastries are simply the best with great coffee."— Andrea Bonaffini

CAPITAN PIADINA

Recommended by
Igles Corelli

Via Libero Andreotti 5
Pescia
Tuscany 51017
+39 3487445205

Opening hours	Closed Monday
Credit cards	Not accepted
Price range	Budget
Style	Casual
Cuisine	Italian
Recommended for	Bargain

"They do a great *piadina*, a popular Italian flatbread sandwich that is a speciality of the Emilia-Romagna region."—Igles Corelli

INFINITY LAB PASTICCERIA

Recommended by
Igles Corelli

Via Galeotti 75
Pescia
Tuscany 51017
+39 05721901846

Opening hours	Closed Monday
Credit cards	Not accepted
Price range	Budget
Style	Casual
Cuisine	Neapolitan Bakery
Recommended for	Breakfast

"Being Italian means breakfast at the bar—the cappuccino and cornetto at this Neapolitan-style bakery are great, and the staff are welcoming as only the Neapolitans are."— Igles Corelli

THE BELVEDERE

Recommended by
Italo Bassi

Strada Provinciale 94
Località Farina
Arzachena
Porto Cervo
Sardinia 07021
+39 078996501
www.ristorantegastronomiabelvedere.com

Opening hours	Open 7 days
Credit cards	Accepted
Price range	Affordable
Style	Casual
Cuisine	Seafood
Recommended for	Regular neighborhood

MM !! TRATTORIA

Recommended by
Carmelo Chiaramonte

Via Pardo 34
Catania
Sicily 95100
+ 39 095348897
www.mmtrattoriablog.com

Opening hours	Closed Sunday
Credit cards	Accepted but not AMEX
Price range	Affordable
Style	Casual
Cuisine	Seafood
Recommended for	Regular neighborhood

"The tables of this little restaurant are arranged opposite the fishmonger's I have patronized for the last twenty years. I love eating *sardine a beccafico* (stuffed, rolled sardines) with vinegar and pecorino cheese, while observing the fish counter for inspiration. The various smells are the chief pleasure of eating this way in the open air: depending on the season, they range from iodine from the catch of the day, to fermenting fish. The last Arab corner of ancient Sicily."—Carmelo Chiaramonte

RISTORANTE MILLEFOGLIE

Recommended by
Carmelo Chiaramonte

Via Sant'Orsola 12
Catania
Sicily 95100
+39 3312505331

Opening hours	Closed Saturday and Sunday
Credit cards	Accepted but not AMEX
Price range	Budget
Style	Casual
Cuisine	Vegetarian
Recommended for	Breakfast

"Lunch only. Vegetarian cuisine."—Carmelo Chiaramonte

PASTICCERIA RUSSO

Recommended by
Carmelo Chiaramonte

Via Vittorio Emanuele 105
Santa Venerina
Catania
Sicily 95010
+39 095953202
www.dolcirusso.it

Opening hours	Closed Tuesday
Credit cards	Accepted
Price range	Budget
Style	Casual
Cuisine	Sicilian
Recommended for	Breakfast

"The last real confectioners of the towns and villages of the Etna region. As you enter, you are met by the natural aromas of historic Sicilian pastries. For breakfast, enjoy the true handmade croissant with a filling of mountain quince jam or hazelnut cream. Decadent atmosphere, art nouveau chairs, beautifully intimate. Sicilian pastries and hot snacks, including *arancini* (croquettes) with gravy."—Carmelo Chiaramonte

LA MADIA

Recommended by
Michael Anthony

Corso F. Re Capriata 22
Licata
Sicily 92027
+39 0922 771443
ristorantelamadia.it/

Opening hours	Closed Tuesday
Credit cards	Accepted
Price range	Affordable
Style	Smart casual
Cuisine	Sicilian
Recommended for	Worth the travel

CAFFÈ SICILIA

Recommended by
Yoji Tokuyoshi

Corso Vittorio Emanuele 125
Noto Siracusa
Sicily 96017
+39 0931835013

Opening hours	Open 7 days
Credit cards	Accepted but not Amex
Price range	Affordable
Style	Casual
Cuisine	Café
Recommended for	Breakfast

ACCURSIO

Recommended by
Carmelo Chiaramonte

Via Grimaldi 41
Modica
Ragusa
Sicily 87015
+39 0932941689
www.accursioristorante.it

Opening hours	Closed Monday
Credit cards	Accepted
Price range	Expensive
Style	Smart casual
Cuisine	Modern Mediterranean
Recommended for	Local favorite

"Contemporary cuisine with ultra-fresh ingredients and entertaining reinterpretations of traditional

Sicilian dishes. You leave in a buoyant, cheerful mood."— Carmelo Chiaramonte

TRATTORIA LA RUSTICANA

Recommended by
Carmelo Chiaramonte

Viale Medaglie d'Oro 34
Modica
Ragusa
Sicily 97015
+39 0932942950

Opening hours	Closed in winter
Reservation policy	No
Credit cards	Accepted but not AMEX
Price range	Affordable
Style	Casual
Cuisine	Italian
Recommended for	Bargain

"Dishes like your mother used to make, with all the beauty of simplicity and imperfection that no chef can reproduce."—Carmelo Chiaramonte

I BANCHI DI RAGUSA

Recommended by
Davide Oldani

Palazzo di Quattro
Via Orfanotrofio 39
Ragusa
Sicily 97100
+39 0932655000
www.ibanchiragusa.it

Opening hours	Closed Thursday
Credit cards	Accepted
Price range	Affordable
Style	Casual
Cuisine	Sicilian
Recommended for	Wish I'd opened

"For their informal, purely Sicilian cuisine."
—Davide Oldani

Chef patron Ciccio Sultano, who made his name at the nearby Duomo restaurant (where he has collected two Michelin stars), has taken over this stunning series of vaulted rooms at the Palazzo di Quattro and filled it with not only another restaurant but a bakery, wine cellar, delicatessen, and cookery school too—a "basilica" as he calls it, in the Roman sense, where people meet to exchange ideas as well as eat and drink. Nobody can ever accuse Sultano of lacking ambition, or indeed a passion bordering on obsessive for the very best local Sicilian produce.

I RIZZARI

Recommended by
David Moyle

Via Libertà 63
Augusta
Syracuse
Sicily 96011
+39 0931982709

Opening hours	Closed Wednesday
Credit cards	Accepted but not Diners
Price range	Affordable
Style	Casual
Cuisine	Seafood
Recommended for	Worth the travel

"Waterfront restaurant in Sicily serving very simple seafood but so beautifully cooked and treated with utter care."—David Moyle

BORGO SAN JACOPO

Recommended by
Igles Corelli

Borgo San Jacopo 62r
Florence
Tuscany 50125
+39 055281661
www.lungarnocollection.com/borgo-san-Jacopo

Opening hours	Open 7 days
Credit cards	Accepted
Price range	Expensive
Style	Smart casual
Cuisine	Italian
Recommended for	Local favorite

"Chef Peter Brunel is a great friend, add to this a great luxury hotel on the Lungarno in Florence and the mix is a winner."—Igles Corelli

CIBRÈO

Recommended by
Massimiliano Alajmo

Via dei Macci 122r
Florence
Tuscany 50122
+39 0552001492
www.edizioniteatrodelsalecibreofirenze.it

Opening hours	Closed Monday
Credit cards	Accepted
Price range	Expensive
Style	Casual
Cuisine	Florentine
Recommended for	Wish I'd opened

"Traditional Florentine cuisine served family-style at communal tables, with a theater or musical performance after dinner."—Massimiliano Alajmo

ENOTECA PINCHIORRI

Recommended by
Luca Gozzani,
Emanuele Scarello

Via Ghibellina 87
Florence
Tuscany 50122
+39 055242757
www.enotecapinchiorri.it

Opening hours	Closed Monday and Sunday
Credit cards	Accepted
Price range	Expensive
Style	Formal
Cuisine	Modern Italian
Recommended for	High end

"Simply perfection: cuisine and service, together with the fantastic hospitality of Giorgio Pinchiorri and Annie Feolde, combine to make it a divine experience."—Luca Gozzani

LA MAGNOLIA

Recommended by
Italo Bassi

Four Seasons Hotel
Borgo Pinti 99
Florence
Tuscany 50121
+39 05526261
www.fourseasons.com/florence

Opening hours	Open 7 days
Credit cards	Accepted
Price range	Affordable
Style	Smart casual
Cuisine	International
Recommended for	Breakfast

"Great charm and excellent service."—Italo Bassi

LA GIOSTRA

Recommended by
Juan Gaffuri

Borgopinti 10–18r
Florence
Tuscany 50121
+39 055241341
www.ristorantelagiostra.com

Opening hours	Closed Sunday
Credit cards	Accepted
Price range	Expensive
Style	Smart casual
Cuisine	Tuscan
Recommended for	Worth the travel

GURDULÙ

Recommended by
Italo Bassi,
Harneet Baweja

Via delle Caldaie 12r
Florence
Tuscany 50125
+39 055282223
www.gurdulu.com

Opening hours	Closed Monday
Credit cards	Accepted
Price range	Affordable
Style	Smart casual
Cuisine	Modern Italian
Recommended for	Late night

"Modern and trendy with a first-class bar." —Italo Bassi

IL SANTO BEVITORE

Recommended by
Harneet Baweja

Via di Santo Spirito 64–66r
Florence
Tuscany 50125
+39 055211264
www.ilsantobevitore.com

Opening hours	Open 7 days
Credit cards	Accepted but not AMEX or Diners
Price range	Affordable
Style	Smart casual
Cuisine	Italian
Recommended for	Worth the travel

"The flavors are superb and the ambience incredible. They've managed to create the perfect experience without overdoing anything. Trust the team's suggestion for the perfect wine pairing." —Harneet Bajewa

IL TRIPPAIO DI SAN FREDIANOV

Recommended by
Matteo Aloe

Piazza dei Nerli
Florence
Tuscany 50124
+39 3358216880

Opening hours	Open 7 days
Credit cards	Not accepted
Price range	Budget
Style	Casual
Cuisine	Florentine
Recommended for	Bargain

"Do you know the *Lampredotto* Sandwich? If not, race to Florence tomorrow and grab a couple. *Lampredotto* is the cow's stomach. It is served in a sandwich with green sauce (parsley and garlic). You can't stop asking Simone for more."—Matteo Aloe

DARIO DOC

Via XX Luglio 11
Panzano in Chianti
Florence
Tuscany 50022
+39 055852020
www.dariocecchini.com

Opening hours	Closed Sunday
Reservation policy	No
Credit cards	Accepted
Price range	Affordable
Style	Casual
Cuisine	Italian Grill
Recommended for	Worth the travel

"The total passion of a man—around life and meat!"—Kamal Mouzawak

TEATRO DEL SALE

Via dei Macci 111r
Florence
Tuscany 50122
+39 055 200 1492
www.teatrodelsale.com

Opening hours	Closed Monday
Credit cards	Accepted
Price range	Affordable
Style	Smart casual
Cuisine	Italian
Recommended for	Wish I'd opened

LA PINETA

Via dei Cavalleggeri Nord 27
Marina di Bibbona
Livorno
Tuscany 57020
+39 0586600016
www.lapinetadizazzeri.it

Opening hours	Closed Monday
Credit cards	Accepted but not Diners
Price range	Expensive
Style	Smart casual
Cuisine	Modern Mediterranean
Recommended for	Wish I'd opened

"One of the finest examples of an award-winning restaurant. A relaxed, beach-side atmosphere. Simple, joyous cooking by Luciano Zazzari. Watching the waves as you cook, real magic!"
—Carmelo Chiaramonte

PESCE BRIACO

Via della Pieve Santo Stefano 967C
Lucca
Tuscany 55100
+39 0583332091
www.pescebriaco.it

Opening hours	Open 7 days
Credit cards	Accepted
Price range	Expensive
Style	Smart casual
Cuisine	Italian Seafood
Recommended for	Regular neighborhood

"Chefs Maurizio Marsili and Alessandro Lucchinelli have a simple but original cooking style. They source great ingredients for their dishes and are inspired by a great Italian Maestro, Chef Angelo Paracucchi."
—Igles Corelli

RISTORANTE GIGLIO

Piazza del Giglio 2
Lucca
Tuscany 55100
+39 0583494058
www.ristorantegiglio.com

Opening hours	Closed Tuesday
Credit cards	Accepted
Price range	Affordable
Style	Casual
Cuisine	Modern Italian
Recommended for	Regular neighborhood

IL CANNICCIO

Via della Costituzione 1
Lamporecchio
Pistoia
Tuscany 51035
+39 057382192

Opening hours	Open 7 days
Credit cards	Accepted but not Diners
Price range	Affordable
Style	Casual
Cuisine	Tuscan
Recommended for	Late night

"Great, simple, Tuscan cooking and, if you prefer, they make a great pizza too."—Igles Corelli

DA DELFINA

Recommended by
Olle T. Cellton

Via della Chiesa 1
Artimino
Prato
Tuscany 59015
+39 0558718074
www.dadelfina.it

Opening hours	Closed Monday
Credit cards	Accepted but not AMEX
Price range	Affordable
Style	Casual
Cuisine	Italian
Recommended for	Wish I'd opened

CASA VISSANI

Recommended by
Igles Corelli

Strada Statale 448
Baschi Km 6.600
Terni
Umbria 05023
+39 0744950206
www.casavissani.it

Opening hours	Closed Wednesday
Credit cards	Accepted
Price range	Expensive
Style	Casual
Cuisine	Modern Italian
Recommended for	High end

"Gianfranco is one of best Italian chefs and a great friend of mine."—Igles Corelli

BIASETTO

Recommended by
Massimiliano Alajmo

Via Jacopo Facciolati 12
Padua
Veneto 35126
+39 049802442
www.pasticceriabiasetto.it

Opening hours	Closed Monday
Credit cards	Accepted but not AMEX
Price range	Expensive
Style	Casual
Cuisine	Italian Patisserie
Recommended for	Breakfast

LA FOLPERIA

Recommended by
Massimiliano Alajmo

Piazza della Frutta
Padua
Veneto 35139
+39 3475701232

Opening hours	Open 7 days
Reservation policy	No
Credit cards	Not accepted
Price range	Affordable
Style	Casual
Cuisine	Italian
Recommended for	Bargain

"Max and Barbara serve small boiled octopus (known in the local dialect as *folpo*) from their street cart, which is parked in Padua's main square."
—Massimiliano Alajmo

RISTORANTE MARIO E MERCEDES

Recommended by
Ruairí de Blacam

Via San Giovanni di Verdara 13
Padua
Veneto 35137
+39 0498719731
www.marioemercedes.it

Opening hours	Closed Monday
Credit cards	Accepted but not AMEX
Price range	Affordable
Style	Smart casual
Cuisine	Venetian
Recommended for	Worth the travel

"This is a comfortable, local, family-run restaurant. Really good food and service. I like to be fed good food and wine, to be professionally served by genuine and pleasant staff and to have my bottle of wine left on the table. Good Italian family-run restaurants understand this more than most. Padua is a really nice town to visit, you can go to the main piazza before your meal, get some boiled polipo with olive oil from a street stall, and bring it to the bar across the piazza where you should order a prosecco to wash it down. Then you can proceed to the restaurant on foot. I have very simple tastes and, to my mind, this is the height of luxury."—Ruairí de Blacam

LE CALANDRE

Via Liguria 1
Sarmeola di Rubano
Padua
Veneto 35030
+39 049630303
www.alajmo.it

Recommended by
Andrea Bonaffini,
Corey Lee, Ana Roš,
Fabio Rossi, Cathy Whims

Opening hours	Closed Monday and Sunday
Credit cards	Accepted
Price range	Expensive
Style	Smart casual
Cuisine	Modern Italian
Recommended for	High end

"A fascinating place. They are always one step ahead of everybody else. Their philosophy and enthusiasm for what they are doing is palpable. Outstanding welcome and first-class organization. Massimiliano is a genius, able to surprise and fascinate you with apparently simple dishes. A devotee of first-class raw materials, with the technical skills to get the best from every ingredient."—Fabio Rossi

Helmed by Massimiliano Alajmo, the youngest ever chef to receive three Michelin stars, Le Calandre has "foodie pilgrimage" written all over it. Ignore the unlovely location in the Paduan suburbs and you'll find regional classics given a molecular spin, such as the Veneto staple risotto with a sprinkling of powdered liquorice. For more experimental fare, there's the "In.gredienti" menu: this is also the name of the restaurant's gourmet store, which stocks pure essences produced in collaboration with a master perfumer. Alajmo's mother Rita taught him everything he knows: head next door to the casual sibling venue Il Calandrino for her famous *zuccotto* (a traditional dessert made with brandy, cake, and ice cream).

AL GATTO NERO

Via Giudecca 88
Burano
Venice
Veneto 30142
+39 041730120
www.gattoncro.com

Recommended by
Mitchell Tonks

Opening hours	Closed Monday
Credit cards	Accepted
Price range	Affordable
Style	Casual
Cuisine	Seafood
Recommended for	Worth the travel

"Family-run and some of the best pasta and seafood I have ever eaten. I like the simplicity of it—they like cooking for you."—Mitchell Tonks

DA ROMANO

Via San Martino Destra 221
Burano
Venice
Veneto 30012
+39 041730030
www.daromano.it

Recommended by
Massimiliano Alajmo

Opening hours	Closed Tuesday
Credit cards	Accepted
Price range	Affordable
Style	Casual
Cuisine	Venetian
Recommended for	Local favorite

"Classic Venetian cuisine. Sit outside and enjoy the colorful houses."—Massimiliano Alajmo

HARRY'S BAR

Calle Vallaresso 1323
San Marco
Venice
Veneto 30124
+39 0415285777
www.harrysbarvenezia.com

Recommended by
Massimiliano Alajmo,
Konstantin Filippou

Opening hours	Open 7 days
Credit cards	Accepted
Price range	Expensive
Style	Smart casual
Cuisine	Bar-Bistro
Recommended for	Wish I'd opened

"It's not new. It's old. But it's the best ever. It's just a great, simple concept that I love."
— Konstantin Filippou

ENOTECA MASCARETA

Recommended by
Massimiliano Alajmo

Calle Lunga Santa Maria Formosa 5183
Venice
Venice
Veneto 5183
+39 415230744
www.ostemaurolorenzon.com

Opening hours	Open 7 days
Credit cards	Accepted but not Diners
Price range	Budget
Style	Casual
Cuisine	Venetian
Recommended for	Late night

"The owner, Mauro Lorenzon, is the best host
in the world."—Massimiliano Alajmo

The offspring of established Venetian osteria,
Al Mascaron, this intimate *enoteca* (wine bar) has
over time proved more popular than its forebear.
Owner Mauro Lorenzon, famously charismatic and
always wearing a bow tie, will match your choice
of *cicchetti* (Venetian tapas) with the perfect wine.
Many rave about the prosciutto here, not to mention
the cheeseboard, crostini, traditional bean soups,
cuttlefish pasta, and *baccalà* (cod) served in
antipasti-sized portions. Whether it's a late-night
bite and *ombra* (literally "shadow"; a white wine
to follow food) or anything else from a hefty wine
list, menu and ambience conspire for fun well into
the early hours.

RISTORANTE ALLA BORSA

Recommended by
Riccardo Camanini

Via Goito 2
Valeggio sul Mincio
Verona
Veneto 37067
+39 457950093
www.ristoranteborsa.it

Opening hours	Closed Wednesday
Credit cards	Accepted but not AMEX
Price range	Expensive
Style	Smart casual
Cuisine	Italian
Recommended for	Local favorite

"The pasta is the best!"—Riccardo Camanini

AUSTRIA, CZECH REPUBLIC, HUNGARY, POLAND & SLOVENIA

Masovia p.691

Lublin p.691

P O L A N D

Cicovice p.685
Prague p.685

Moravia p.685

Brno p.685

C Z E C H   R E P U B L I C

Upper Austria p.867
Lower Austria p.676
Vienna p.679
Burgenland p.676

Salzburg p.676

A U S T R I A

Goriška p.692
Vipava p.693

S L O V E N I A

Ljubljana
p.693

AUSTRIA,
CZECH REPUBLIC,
HUNGARY,
POLAND
& SLOVENIA

SCALE

N

0   90   180
                        MI.

GUT PURBACH

Recommended by
Rudolf Obauer

Hauptgasse 64
Purbach am Neusiedler
Burgenland 7083
Austria
+43 268356086
www.gutpurbach.at

Opening hours	Closed Tuesday and Wednesday
Credit cards	Accepted
Price range	Expensive
Style	Smart casual
Cuisine	Austrian
Recommended for	Worth the travel

"Max Stiegl doing his thing in a perfect way."
—Rudolph Obauer

LANDHAUS BACHER

Recommended by
Philip Rachinger

Südtiroler Platz 2
Mautern an der Donau
Lower Austria 3512
Austria
+43 273282937
www.landhaus-bacher.at

Opening hours	Closed Monday and Tuesday
Credit cards	Accepted but not AMEX
Price range	Expensive
Style	Smart casual
Cuisine	Modern European
Recommended for	High end

STEIRA WIRT

Recommended by
Alexander Mayer

Trautmannsdorf 6
Trautmannsdorf an der Leitha
Lower Austria 8343
Austria
+43 31594106
www.steirawirt.at

Opening hours	Closed Tuesday and Wednesday
Credit cards	Accepted but not AMEX or Diners
Price range	Expensive
Style	Smart casual
Cuisine	Modern European
Recommended for	Local favorite

GASTHAUS ACKERMANN

Recommended by
Rudolf Obauer

Graben 11
Bischofshofen
Salzburg 5500
Austria
+43 64622477
www.gasthaus-ackermann.at

Opening hours	Closed Tuesday and Wednesday
Credit cards	Accepted but not AMEX
Price range	Budget
Style	Casual
Cuisine	Austrian
Recommended for	Bargain

DÖLLERER

Recommended by
Philip Rachinger

Markt 56
Golling an der Salzach
Salzburg 5440
Austria
+43 62444220
www.doellerer.at

Opening hours	Closed Monday and Sunday
Credit cards	Accepted
Price range	Expensive
Style	Smart casual
Cuisine	Modern Austrian
Recommended for	High end

BÄRENWIRT

Recommended by
Philip Rachinger

Müllner Hauptstrasse 8
Salzburg 5020
Austria
+43 662422404
www.baerenwirt-salzburg.at

Opening hours	Open 7 days
Credit cards	Accepted but not AMEX or Diners
Price range	Affordable
Style	Casual
Cuisine	Austrian
Recommended for	Wish I'd opened

CARPE DIEM FINEST FINGERFOOD

Recommended by
Rudolf Obauer

Getreidegasse 50
Salzburg 5020
Austria
+43 662848800
www.carpediemfinestfingerfood.com

Opening hours	Open 7 days
Credit cards	Accepted
Price range	Expensive
Style	Smart casual
Cuisine	Modern Austrian
Recommended for	Breakfast

Carpe Diem Finest Fingerfood, on the famous Getreidegasse Boulevard, was set up by Dietrich Mateschitz, the inventor of Red Bull—so the playfulness at the heart of this Michelin-starred dining concept, where tasty morsels of "finger food" are packed into waffle cones, should come as no surprise. There are classics like beef hamburger with cheddar cheese in a rosemary cone, or snazzier combos such as two kinds of eel, cucumber, and mango in a curry cone. It sounds gimmicky, but in fact the food is seasonal and sophisticated. There's also a gourmet menu of main courses (served on plates).

WÜRSTELKÖNIGIN SALZBURG

Recommended by
Rudolf Obauer

Ferdinand-Hanusch-Platz
Salzburg 5020
Austria
+43 662237059
www.sbg-wuerstelkoenigin.at

Opening hours	Open 7 days
Reservation policy	No
Credit cards	Not accepted
Price range	Affordable
Style	Casual
Cuisine	Sausages
Recommended for	Late night

"Perfect snack after midnight."— Rudolf Obauer

OBAUER

Recommended by
Philip Rachinger

Hotel Obauer
Markt 42
Werfen
Salzburg 5450
Austria
+43 646852120
www.obauer.com

Opening hours	Closed Monday and Tuesday
Credit cards	Accepted but not AMEX
Price range	Expensive
Style	Smart casual
Cuisine	Austrian
Recommended for	High end

"Two brothers are smashing it still after thirty years! A genius in the kitchen—just really amazing!"
—Philip Rachinger

In the shadow of majestic Schloss Hohenwerfen in Austria's Salzach Valley lies the pretty market town of Werfen, home to Restaurant-Hotel Obauer. Brothers Karl and Rudi Obauer began the ongoing modernization of their family's restaurant in 1979, gaining exposure to other chefs and cuisines as they went along, via internships at Troisgros, Alain Chapel, and Au Crocodile. The Obauers give local ingredients a starring role: trout strudel and *Werfen* lamb are classics, while chile tripe with cockscombs, and wild mushroom soup with goose breast, dates, and sauerkraut reveal their bolder side. The hotel's breakfasts are magnificent too.

ERLHOF

Recommended by
Rudolf Obauer

Erlhofweg 11
Zell am See
Salzburg 5700
Austria
+43 654256637
www.erlhof.at

Opening hours	Closed Wednesday
Credit cards	Accepted but not AMEX or Diners
Price range	Affordable
Style	Casual
Cuisine	Austrian
Recommended for	Local favorite

"The owner represents the region in a perfect way."
— Rudolf Obauer

LURGBAUER

Lurg 1
Sankt Sebastian
Styria 8630
Austria
+43 38823718
www.lurgbauer.at

Opening hours	Variable
Credit cards	Accepted but not AMEX
Price range	Expensive
Style	Casual
Cuisine	Modern Austrian
Recommended for	Local favorite

"Beef is the star of this beautiful old farm with modern architectural details, located in a meadow surrounded by the Styrian forest. It's a family business—Junior is the chef and Senior is the Lord of the Cattle, running the Black Angus breeding farm, their own slaughterhouse, the restaurant, and a few romantic rooms in the former farm building, with Philippe Stark elements. Beautiful view from the amazing terrace."—Alexander Mayer

BOMBAY PALACE

Goethestrasse 34
Linz
Upper Austria 4020
Austria
+43 732658605
www.bombaypalace.at

Opening hours	Closed Monday
Credit cards	Accepted
Price range	Affordable
Style	Casual
Cuisine	Indian
Recommended for	Bargain

"The best Indian place in Austria."—Philip Rachinger

DIE DONAUWIRTINNEN

Webergasse 2
Linz
Upper Austria 4040
Austria
+43 732737706
www.diedonauwirtinnen.at

Opening hours	Closed Monday and Tuesday
Credit cards	Not accepted
Price range	Affordable
Style	Casual
Cuisine	Austrian
Recommended for	Bargain

"Really good food for a really good price!"
—Philip Rachinger

GÖTTFRIED

Hofgasse 5
Linz
Upper Austria 4020
Austria
+43 732997023
www.goettfried.at

Opening hours	Closed Monday and Sunday
Credit cards	Accepted
Price range	Expensive
Style	Smart casual
Cuisine	Modern Austrian
Recommended for	Local favorite

LEBERKAS PEPI

Rathausgasse 3
Linz
Upper Austria 4020
Austria
+43 73279686820
www.leberkaspepi.at

Opening hours	Closed Sunday
Reservation policy	No
Credit cards	Not accepted
Price range	Budget
Style	Casual
Cuisine	Austrian
Recommended for	Late night

"They offer twelve different types of meatloaf—it might look a bit strange if you've never had it before, but it's delicious."—Philip Rachinger

MUTO

Altstadt 7
Linz
Upper Austria 4020
Austria
+43 732770377
www.mutolinz.at

Opening hours	Closed Sunday
Credit cards	Accepted but not AMEX or Diners
Price range	Expensive
Style	Smart casual
Cuisine	Modern European
Recommended for	Local favorite

JAUSENSTATION BLAUER HIRSCH

Sonnenwald 8
Ulrichsberg
Upper Austria 4161
Austria
+43 72882250

Opening hours	Closed Monday and Tuesday
Credit cards	Not accepted
Price range	Budget
Style	Casual
Cuisine	Austrian-Bohemian
Recommended for	Regular neighborhood

"Run by a couple who traveled a lot to Africa and many other places in the world. Now she cooks typical Bohemian classics and he's in the front of house. Sometimes grumpy but you will always get a pint of the local monastery brewery (Stift Schlägl)!"
—Philip Rachinger

ANSARI

Praterstrasse 15
Vienna 1020
Austria
+43 12765102
www.cafeansari.at

Opening hours	Open 7 days
Credit cards	Accepted but not AMEX or Diners
Price range	Budget
Style	Casual
Cuisine	Austrian
Recommended for	Breakfast

BITS & BITES

Webgasse 27
Vienna 1060
Austria
+43 660 8372509
www.bitsandbites.at

Opening hours	Closed Monday and Tuesday
Credit cards	Accepted but not AMEX or Diners
Price range	Affordable
Style	Casual
Cuisine	French
Recommended for	Local favorite

BITZINGERS WÜRSTELSTÄNDE

Albertinaplatz
Vienna 1010
Austria
+43 68184231474
www.bitzinger-wien.at

Opening hours	Open 7 days
Credit cards	Not accepted
Price range	Budget
Style	Casual
Cuisine	Austrian
Recommended for	Late night

CAFÉ ANZENGRUBER

Schleifmühlgasse 19
Vienna 1040
Austria
+43 15878297

Opening hours	Closed Sunday
Reservation policy	No
Credit cards	Not accepted
Price range	Affordable
Style	Casual
Cuisine	Austrian
Recommended for	Late night

"An institution for more than forty years—a meeting point for chefs, actors, and writers but also workers, politicians, and football fans. A crazy mix, lead by a sympathetic family with Croatian roots. Homemade cooking 'mama'-style, like filled peppers, pasta fagioli, goulash—simple and honest cuisine."
—Alexander Mayer

CAFÉ BACCO

Margaretenstrasse 25
Vienna 1040
Austria
+43 15866692

Recommended by
Alexander Mayer

Opening hours	Closed Saturday and Sunday
Reservation policy	No
Credit cards	Accepted but not AMEX or Diners
Price range	Budget
Style	Casual
Cuisine	Italian
Recommended for	Bargain

"One of the most sympathetic Italian guys in town, Signore Alberto Stefanelli is from Tuscany. This chef is a one-man show and a great autodidact and a wine specialist. Simple, honest, Tuscan cuisine with authentic products from his region, amazing charcuterie, pastas, and vegetable dishes."
—Alexander Mayer

CAFÉ BALTHAZAR

Praterstrasse 38
Vienna 1020
Austria
+43 6643816855
www.balthasar.at

Recommended by
Konstantin Filippou

Opening hours	Closed Sunday
Reservation policy	No
Credit cards	Not accepted
Price range	Budget
Style	Casual
Cuisine	Café
Recommended for	Breakfast

CAFÉ GRIENSTEIDL

Michaelerplatz 2
Vienna 1010
Austria
+45 153526920
www.cafegriensteidl.at

Recommended by
Konstantin Filippou

Opening hours	Open 7 days
Credit cards	Accepted but not AMEX or Diners
Price range	Affordable
Style	Casual
Cuisine	Viennese Café
Recommended for	Breakfast

CAFÉ LANDTMANN

Universitätsring 4
Vienna 1010
Austria
+43 124100120
www.landtmann.at

Recommended by
Konstantin Filippou

Opening hours	Open 7 days
Credit cards	Accepted
Price range	Affordable
Style	Smart casual
Cuisine	Viennese Café
Recommended for	Breakfast

KAFFEMIK

Zollergasse 5
Vienna 1070
Austria
www.kaffemik.at

Recommended by
Konstantin Filippou

Opening hours	Open 7 days
Reservation policy	No
Credit cards	Accepted but not AMEX or Diners
Price range	Budget
Style	Casual
Cuisine	Café
Recommended for	Breakfast

GASTHAUS GRÜNAUER

Herrmanngasse 32
Vienna 1070
Austria
+43 15264080
www.gasthaus-gruenauer.com

Recommended by
Alexander Mayer

Opening hours	Closed Saturday and Sunday
Credit cards	Accepted but not AMEX or Diners
Price range	Affordable
Style	Casual
Cuisine	Austrian
Recommended for	Regular neighborhood

GASTHAUS WOLF

Recommended by
Christian Domschitz

Grosse Neugasse 20
Vienna 1040
Austria
+43 15811544
www.gasthauswolf.at

Opening hours	Closed Monday and Sunday
Credit cards	Not accepted
Price range	Affordable
Style	Casual
Cuisine	Viennese
Recommended for	Regular neighborhood

"Classic Viennese cuisine from nose to tail, with a focus on giblets."—Christian Domschitz

THE GUESTHOUSE BRASSERIE

Recommended by
Christian Domschitz,
Konstantin Filippou

Führichgasse 10
Vienna 1010
Austria
+43 15121320
www.theguesthouse.at

Opening hours	Open 7 days
Credit cards	Accepted
Price range	Affordable
Style	Smart casual
Cuisine	International
Recommended for	Breakfast

"The breakfast is simply amazing. The variety ranges from great egg dishes (Eggs Benedict served over smoked salmon) to nice traditional Austrian breakfast dishes. The bread is made in-house and just great."
—Konstantin Filippou

GOLDFISCH

Recommended by
Konstantin Filippou

Lerchenfelder Street 16
Vienna 1080
Austria
+43 06642549596
www.goldfisch.wien

Opening hours	Closed Monday and Sunday
Credit cards	Accepted but not AMEX or Diners
Price range	Budget
Style	Casual
Cuisine	Seafood
Recommended for	Local favorite

GRACE

Recommended by
Konstantin Filippou,
Philip Rachinger

Danhausergasse 3
Vienna 1040
Austria
+43 15031022
www.grace-restaurant.at

Opening hours	Closed Monday and Sunday
Credit cards	Accepted but not AMEX or Diners
Price range	Affordable
Style	Casual
Cuisine	International
Recommended for	Regular neighborhood

"A cozy and stylish restaurant run by former Steirereck sous-chef Oliver Lucas. They serve set menus only, the dishes are fantastic, natural wines are on the wine list. Very nice place."—Konstantin Filippou

JOSEPH BROT

Recommended by
Konstantin Filippou

Landstrasser Haupstrasse 4
Vienna 1030
Austria
+43 17102881
www.joseph.co.at

Opening hours	Open 7 days
Reservation policy	No
Credit cards	Accepted but not AMEX or Diners
Price range	Affordable
Style	Casual
Cuisine	Bakery-Austrian
Recommended for	Breakfast

KIANG DINE AND WINE

Recommended by
Konstantin Filippou

Grünentorgasse 19
Vienna 1090
Austria
+43 6645153633
www.kiangwine-dine.com

Opening hours	Closed Monday and Sunday
Credit cards	Not accepted
Price range	Affordable
Style	Casual
Cuisine	Austrian-Asian
Recommended for	Regular neighborhood

"A really small Chinese hole-in-the-wall kind of place. I mostly eat the starters."—Konstantin Filippou

LÉONTINE

Recommended by
Konstantin Filippou

Reisnerstrasse 39
Vienna 1030
Austria
+43 17125430
www.leontine.at

Opening hours	Closed Monday and Sunday
Credit cards	Accepted but not AMEX or Diners
Price range	Affordable
Style	Casual
Cuisine	French-Bistro
Recommended for	Regular neighborhood

MARCO SIMONIS

Recommended by
Konstantin Filippou

Dominikanerbastei 10
Vienna 1010
Austria
+43 15122010
www.marcosimonis.com

Opening hours	Closed Saturday and Sunday
Credit cards	Accepted
Price range	Affordable
Style	Casual
Cuisine	International
Recommended for	Breakfast

MEIEREI IM STADTPARK

Recommended by
Alexander Mayer,
Philip Rachinger

Am Heumarkt 2A
Vienna 1030
Austria
+43 1713316810
www.steirereck.at/meierei

Opening hours	Open 7 days
Credit cards	Accepted
Price range	Expensive
Style	Smart casual
Cuisine	Austrian-European
Recommended for	Local favorite

"Wonderful location in the Stadtpark. During summer
you can sit on the terrace with a view of the Vienna
river. Very large menu for breakfast and brunch and
an amazing selection of cheese."—Alexander Mayer

MERCADO

Recommended by
Konstantin Filippou

Stubenring 18
Vienna 1010
Austria
+43 15122505
www.mercado.at

Opening hours	Open 7 days
Credit cards	Accepted
Price range	Affordable
Style	Casual
Cuisine	Modern Latin American
Recommended for	Regular neighborhood

MIZNON

Recommended by
Christian Domschitz

Schulerstrasse 4
Vienna 1010
Austria
+43 1 5121053

Opening hours	Open 7 days
Reservation policy	No
Credit cards	Accepted
Price range	Affordable
Style	Casual
Cuisine	Israeli
Recommended for	Bargain

MOCHI

Recommended by
Konstantin Filippou,
Alexander Mayer

Praterstrasse 15
Vienna 1020
Austria
+43 19251380
www.mochi.at

Opening hours	Closed Sunday
Credit cards	Not accepted
Price range	Affordable
Style	Casual
Cuisine	Japanese Fusion
Recommended for	Bargain

O BOUFÉS

Dominikanerbastei 17
Vienna 1010
Austria
+43 1512222910
www.konstantinfilippou.com

Recommended by
Alexander Mayer,
Rudolf Obauer

Opening hours	Closed Sunday
Credit cards	Accepted but not Diners
Price range	Expensive
Style	Smart casual
Cuisine	Modern European
Recommended for	Wish I'd opened

"A modern Mediterranean bistro with Greek roots, specializing in natural and orange wines."
—Alexander Mayer

The name of this high-end bistro and wine bar in the center of Vienna translates as "buffet" in Greek, but the dining experience here is about as far from a traditional stand-in-line buffet as you can imagine. Instead, there's a short selection of sophisticated small plates bursting with flavor, influenced by chef Konstantin Filippou's Greek heritage—octopus *saganaki* (fried cheese appetizer), bratwurst with mustard caviar and mustard foam, and a dessert of spicy pineapple with Jerusalem artichoke and salted almond ice cream. The space is super stylish and sleek, and the wine they stock is exclusively natural.

PETZ IM GUSSHAUS

Gusshausstrasse 23
Vienna 1040
Austria
+43 15044750
www.gusshaus.at

Recommended by
Konstantin Filippou,
Alexander Mayer

Opening hours	Closed Monday and Sunday
Credit cards	Accepted
Price range	Affordable
Style	Casual
Cuisine	Austrian
Recommended for	Regular neighborhood

"Christian Petz, a good friend of mine, is the chef of this inn/restaurant. I like the chef's table in the entrance part of the restaurant, which includes the bar, and the typcial Viennese atmosphere. The restaurant is a meeting point for a lot of chefs in town after hours."—Alexander Mayer

PIZZA MARI

Leopoldsgasse 23A
Vienna 1020
Austria
+43 6766874994
www.pizzamari.at

Recommended by
Konstantin Filippou

Opening hours	Closed Monday
Credit cards	Not accepted
Price range	Budget
Style	Casual
Cuisine	Italian
Recommended for	Bargain

"Very typical pizzeria—like in Napoli."
—Konstantin Filippou

PLACHUTTA

Wollzeile 38
Vienna 1010
Austria
+43 15121577
www.plachutta.at

Recommended by
Eyal Jagermann

Opening hours	Open / days
Credit cards	Accepted
Price range	Affordable
Style	Smart casual
Cuisine	Viennese
Recommended for	Worth the travel

"Viennese cuisine at its finest and the home of *Tafelspitz*, an Austrian beef stew served in a broth with potato salad and creamy spinach—an all-time classic. Brilliant every time and so comforting. Do not miss out on their *Wiener schnitzel* as well."—Eyal Jagermann

RESTAURANT HANSEN

Wipplingerstrasse 34
Vienna 1010
Austria
+43 015320542
www.hansen.co.at

Recommended by
Christian Domschitz

Opening hours	Closed Sunday
Credit cards	Accepted but not Diners
Price range	Expensive
Style	Smart casual
Cuisine	Mediterranean
Recommended for	Breakfast

RUDI'S BEISL

Recommended by
Konstantin Filippou

Wiedner Hauptstrasse 88
Vienna 1050
Austria
+43 15445102
www.rudisbeisl.at

Opening hours	Closed Saturday and Sunday
Credit cards	Not accepted
Price range	Affordable
Style	Smart casual
Cuisine	Austrian
Recommended for	Local favorite

SHIKI

Recommended by
Konstantin Filippou

Krugerstrasse 3
Vienna 1010
Austria
+43 15127397
www.shiki.at

Opening hours	Closed Sunday
Credit cards	Accepted but not Diners
Price range	Expensive
Style	Formal
Cuisine	Japanese
Recommended for	High end

"Japanese fine dining at its best."
—Konstantin Filippou

STEIRERECK

Recommended by
Christian Domschitz,
Philip Rachinger

Am Heumarkt 2A
Vienna 1010
Austria
+43 17133168
www.steirereck.at

Opening hours	Closed Saturday and Sunday
Credit cards	Accepted
Price range	Expensive
Style	Smart casual
Cuisine	Modern Austrian
Recommended for	High end

"Best restaurant in Austria—outstanding."
—Christian Domschitz

STRÖCK-FEIERABEND

Recommended by
Alexander Mayer,
Konstantin Filippou

Landstrasse Hauptstrasse 82
Vienna 1030
Austria
+43 1204399993057
www.stroeck-feierabend.at

Opening hours	Open 7 days
Credit cards	Accepted but not AMEX or Diners
Price range	Affordable
Style	Casual
Cuisine	French Patisserie
Recommended for	Breakfast

"Offering one of the best croissants in town."
—Alexander Mayer

TIAN

Recommended by
Roman Zastserinski

Himmelpfortgasse 23
Vienna 1010
Austria
+43 18904665
www.taste-tian.com

Opening hours	Closed Monday and Sunday
Credit cards	Accepted
Price range	Expensive
Style	Smart casual
Cuisine	Vegetarian
Recommended for	Worth the travel

"Innovative and meat-free—absolutely heavenly."
—Roman Zastserinski

ZUM SCHARFEN RENE

Recommended by
Konstantin Filippou

Schwarzenbergplatz 15
Vienna 1010
Austria
+43 69917999888
www.zumscharfenrene.com

Opening hours	Closed Sunday
Credit cards	Not accepted
Price range	Budget
Style	Casual
Cuisine	Sausages
Recommended for	Late night

"Vienna's great tradition is sausage places. *Zum Scharfen Rene*, translated as 'At Hot Rene's', is one of my favorites."—Konstantin Filippou

ZUR HERKNERIN

Recommended by
Konstantin Filippou

Wiedner Hauptstrasse 36
Vienna 1040
Austria
+43 69915220522
www.zurherknerin.at

Opening hours	Closed Monday, Saturday, and Sunday
Credit cards	Not accepted
Price range	Affordable
Style	Casual
Cuisine	Traditional Austrian
Recommended for	Local favorite

BORGO AGNESE

Recommended by
Pavel Mencl

Kopečná 43
Brno 602 00
Czech Republic
+420 515537500
www.borgoagnese.cz

Opening hours	Open 7 days
Credit cards	Accepted
Price range	Expensive
Style	Smart casual
Cuisine	European
Recommended for	Worth the travel

PENZION V POLICH

Recommended by
Pavel Mencl

Malé čičovice 26
Čičovice 252 68
Czech Republic
+420 233313841
www.penzionvpolich.cz

Opening hours	Variable
Credit cards	Accepted
Price range	Affordable
Style	Casual
Cuisine	European
Recommended for	Worth the travel

ENTRÉE RESTAURANT

Recommended by
Pavel Mencl

Ostravská 1
Olomouc
Moravia 779 00
Czech Republic
+420 585312440
www.entree-restaurant.cz

Opening hours	Open 7 days
Credit cards	Accepted
Price range	Affordable
Style	Casual
Cuisine	European
Recommended for	Worth the travel

AROMI

Recommended by
Pavel Mencl

Náměstí Míru 6
Prague 2, 120 00
Czech Republic
+420 222713222
www.aromi.cz

Opening hours	Open 7 days
Credit cards	Accepted
Price range	Affordable
Style	Casual
Cuisine	Italian-Seafood
Recommended for	Regular neighborhood

"A fish-specialist restaurant with an Italian chef, Riccardo. Nice interior, perfect service, and always great, surprising food."—Pavel Mencl

BRASILEIRO

Recommended by
Oldřich Sahajdák

U Radnice 8
Prague 1, 110 00
Czech Republic
+420 224234474
www.brasileiro-uradnice.ambi.cz

Opening hours	Open 7 days
Credit cards	Accepted
Price range	Affordable
Style	Casual
Cuisine	Brazilian
Recommended for	Late night

"Real Brazil in a small town in the middle of Europe."
—Oldřich Sahajdák

CAFÉ IMPERIAL

Recommended by
Pavel Mencl

Na Poříčí 15
Prague 1, 110 00
Czech Republic
+420 246011440
www.cafeimperial.cz

Opening hours	Open 7 days
Credit cards	Accepted
Price range	Affordable
Style	Smart casual
Cuisine	Czech Brasserie
Recommended for	Breakfast

"Amazing interior—perfect food and service."
—Pavel Mencl

CAFÉ LOUVRE

Recommended by
Pavel Mencl

Národní 22
Prague 1, 110 00
Czech Republic
+420 724054055
www.cafelouvre.cz

Opening hours	Open 7 days
Credit cards	Accepted
Price range	Affordable
Style	Casual
Cuisine	International
Recommended for	Breakfast

CAFÉ SAVOY

Recommended by
Oldřich Sahajdák

Vítězná 5
Prague 5, 150 00
Czech Republic
+420 257311562
www.cafesavoy.ambi.cz

Opening hours	Open 7 days
Credit cards	Accepted
Price range	Affordable
Style	Casual
Cuisine	European
Recommended for	Breakfast

"I feel like the time has stopped in 1900 there—the design and the food are so traditional!"
—Oldřich Sahajdák

COBRA

Recommended by
Oldřich Sahajdák

Milady Horákové 8
Prague 7, 170 00
Czech Republic
+420 778470515
www.barcobra.cz

Opening hours	Open 7 days
Credit cards	Accepted
Price range	Affordable
Style	Casual
Cuisine	International
Recommended for	Regular neighborhood

COTTOCRUDO

Recommended by
Pavel Mencl

Veleslavínova 1098/2a
Prague 1, 110 00
Czech Republic
+420 221426880
www.cottocrudo.cz

Opening hours	Open 7 days
Credit cards	Accepted
Price range	Expensive
Style	Smart casual
Cuisine	Italian
Recommended for	High end

GRAND CRU RESTAURANT AND BAR

Recommended by
Pavel Mencl

Lodecká 4
Prague 1, 110 00
Czech Republic
+420 775044076
www.grand-cru.cz

Opening hours	Closed Sunday
Credit cards	Accepted
Price range	Affordable
Style	Smart casual
Cuisine	International
Recommended for	Regular neighborhood

"Inspired, surprising food."—Pavel Mencl

SLOVANSKÝ DŮM
Recommended by
Pavel Mencl

Na Prikope 22
Prague 1, 110 00
Czech Republic
+420 221451258
www.kogo.cz

Opening hours	Open 7 days
Credit cards	Accepted
Price range	Affordable
Style	Smart casual
Cuisine	Mediteranean
Recommended for	Wish I'd opened

"Great place in the center, with a charming garden terrace and Mediterranean food."—Pavel Mencl

KRYSTAL BISTRO
Recommended by
Oldřich Sahajdák

Sokolovská 99/101
Prague 8, 186 00
Czech Republic
+420 222318152
www.krystal-bistro.cz

Opening hours	Open 7 days
Credit cards	Accepted
Price range	Affordable
Style	Casual
Cuisine	Modern Czech-French
Recommended for	Bargain

"It is a real bistro, with local ingredients, a seasonal menu, and very friendly staff. The owner is the head chef as well."—Oldřich Sahajdák

LA BOTTEGA BISTROTEKA
Recommended by
Pavel Mencl

Dlouhá 39
Prague 1, 110 00
Czech Republic
+420 222311372
www.bistroteka.cz

Opening hours	Open 7 days
Credit cards	Accepted but not AMEX or Diners
Price range	Affordable
Style	Casual
Cuisine	Italian
Recommended for	Breakfast

LA DEGUSTATION BOHÊME
Recommended by
Pavel Mencl

Hastalska 18
Prague 1, 110 00
Czech Republic
+420 222311234
www.ladegustation.cz

Opening hours	Open 7 days
Credit cards	Accepted
Price range	Expensive
Style	Smart casual
Cuisine	Modern Czech
Recommended for	High end

"Michelin-starred restaurant offering multiple degustation courses. Food, service, and interior merit the stars."—Pavel Mencl

BRASSERIE LA GARE
Recommended by
Pavel Mencl

V Celnici 3
Prague 1, 110 00
Czech Republic
+420 222313712
www.brasserielagare.cz

Opening hours	Open 7 days
Credit cards	Accepted but not AMEX or Diners
Price range	Affordable
Style	Casual
Cuisine	Brasserie
Recommended for	Breakfast

LOKÁL
Recommended by
Oldřich Sahajdák

Nad Královskou Oborou 232
Prague 7, 170 00
Czech Republic
+420 220912319
www.lokal-nadstromovkou.ambi.cz

Opening hours	Open 7 days
Credit cards	Accepted but not AMEX or Diners
Price range	Affordable
Style	Casual
Cuisine	Czech
Recommended for	Local favorite

"Czech cuisine—soups, pork, cabbage, and lots of beer—you will find it all here."—Oldřich Sahajdák

LOKÁL U BÍLÉ KUŽELKY

Recommended by
Pavel Mencl

Míšeňska 12
Prague 1, 118 00
Czech Republic
+420 257212014
www.lokal-ubilekuzelky.ambi.cz

Opening hours	Open 7 days
Credit cards	Accepted but not AMEX or Diners
Price range	Affordable
Style	Casual
Cuisine	Czech
Recommended for	Bargain

LOKÁL DLOUHÁÁÁ

Recommended by
Pavel Mencl

Dlouhá 33
Prague 1, 110 00
Czech Republic
+420 222316265
www.lokal-dlouha.ambi.cz

Opening hours	Open 7 days
Credit cards	Accepted
Price range	Budget
Style	Casual
Cuisine	Czech
Recommended for	Bargain

"Typical Czech pub in a modern style. Good quality food at a fair price, perfect beer, quick service, and a funny interior."—Pavel Mencl

MALOSTRANSKA BESEDA

Recommended by
Pavel Mencl

Malostranské Náměstí 35/21
Prague 1, 118 00
Czech Republic
+420 257409112
www.malostranska-beseda.cz

Opening hours	Open 7 days
Credit cards	Not Accepted
Price range	Budget
Style	Casual
Cuisine	Czech
Recommended for	Local favorite

MILADA BISTRO

Recommended by
Oldřich Sahajdák

Šmeralova 22
Prague 7, 170 00
Czech Republic
+420 222520419

Opening hours	Closed Monday, Saturday, and Sunday
Credit cards	Accepted but not AMEX or Diners
Price range	Affordable
Style	Smart casual
Cuisine	Modern Bistro
Recommended for	Local favorite

"A modern Neo-bistro—it is almost like being in Paris."—Oldřich Sahajdák

It's billed as the first Czech neo-bistro—and it certainly ticks all the boxes. The interior is minimalist and light, the menu concise (three starters, three mains, three desserts—who needs choices, anyway?), and the small plates of seasonal food that arrive at the table are carefully considered and artfully constructed, with clever combinations of textures and tastes —such as scallops with turnip and *ponzu* (Japanese citrus sauce). It's a simple set-up, and unstuffy, with one set of cutlery for the whole meal. And the final tick is that it's not even central—instead, it's located just off the beaten track, over the river, in the up-and-coming Prague 7 district.

RESTAURANT ESKA

Recommended by
Peeter Pihel

Pernerova 49
Prague 8, 186 00
Czech Republic
+420 731140884
www.eska.ambi.cz

Opening hours	Open 7 days
Credit cards	Accepted but not AMEX or Diners
Price range	Affordable
Style	Casual
Cuisine	Bakery
Recommended for	Breakfast

"Eska is a restaurant with a bakery that combines the old and the new."—Peeter Pihel

SANSHO

Recommended by
Oldřich Sahajdák

Petrská 25
Prague 1, 110 00
Czech Republic
+420 222317425
www.sancho.cz

Opening hours..............................Closed Monday and Sunday
Credit cards...Accepted
Price range..Affordable
Style...Casual
Cuisine...Pan-Asian
Recommended for..Wish I'd opened

"You eat at a large table with people you don't know
and you have great fun there! And the food of course
is great."—Oldřich Sahajdák

SASAZU

Recommended by
Pavel Mencl,
Oldřich Sahajdák

Bubenské Nábřeží 306
Prague 1, 170 04
Czech Republic
+420 284097455
www.sasazu.com

Opening hours...Open 7 days
Credit cards...Accepted
Price range..Affordable
Style..Smart casual
Cuisine..Asian
Recommended for..High end

"It is in a large hall where butchers used to slaughter
animals (about a hundred years ago) but it still has the
atmosphere. The food is Asian and very, very good."
—Oldřich Sahajdák

U MEDVÍDKŮ

Na Perštýně 7
Prague 1, 110 01
Czech Republic
+420 224211916
www.umedvidku.cz

Opening hours...Open 7 days
Credit cards...Accepted
Price range..Affordable
Style...Casual
Cuisine..Old Bohemian
Recommended for..Local favorite

U VEJVODŮ

Recommended by
Pavel Mencl

Jilská 4
Prague 1, 110 00
Czech Republic
+420 224219999
www.restauraceuvejvodu.cz

Opening hours...Open 7 days
Credit cards...Accepted
Price range..Affordable
Style...Casual
Cuisine..Bohemian-International
Recommended for..Local favorite

U ZLATÉHO TYGRA

Recommended by
Pavel Mencl

Husova 228/17
Prague 1, 110 00
Czech Republic
+420 222221111
www.uzlatehotygra.cz

Opening hours..Open / days
Credit cards...Not accepted
Price range..Budget
Style...Casual
Cuisine...Beer hall-European
Recommended for..Local favorite

"Well-known typical Czech brewery in town. You will
find genius local beer and the best Pilsner. Limited
food offering and a lot of people. Always crowded."
—Pavel Mencl

YAMATO

Recommended by
Pavel Mencl

U Kanálky 14
Prague 2, 120-00
Czech Republic
+420 222212617
www.yamato.cz

Opening hours..Closed Sunday
Credit cards...Accepted
Price range...Expensive
Style..Smart casual
Cuisine...Japanese
Recommended for..Late night

BORKONYHA WINEKITCHEN

Sas Utca 3
Budapest
Central Hungary 1051
Hungary
+36 12660835
www.borkonyha.hu

Opening hours	Open 7 days
Credit cards	Accepted but not AMEX or Diners
Price range	Affordable
Style	Smart casual
Cuisine	French-Hungarian
Recommended for	Local favorite

"Winekitchen is a blend of French-style bistro and contemporary family restaurant, offering the best of Hungarian cuisine. The concept is based on the wide and diverse wine list, the delicious food, and the personal and relaxed service. The wine assortment includes two hundred different, mostly Hungarian, wines."—Adam Mészáros

ÉMILE

Orló Utca 1
Budapest
Central Hungary 1026
Hungary
+36 305850602
www.emile.hu

Opening hours	Closed Monday
Credit cards	Accepted but not AMEX or Diners
Price range	Affordable
Style	Casual
Cuisine	Hungarian
Recommended for	Regular neighborhood

"The style of Émile restaurant is unique: it is neither fine dining nor bistro fare; you can simply enjoy the flavors and the one-of-a-kind service."
—Adam Mészáros

GERBEAUD CONFECTIONARY

Vörösmarty Tér 7–8
Budapest
Central Hungary 1050
Hungary
+36 14299000
www.gerbeaud.hu/confectionery

Opening hours	Open 7 days
Credit cards	Accepted
Price range	Affordable
Style	Casual
Cuisine	International
Recommended for	Breakfast

"Taste as many cakes, pastries, and confections as you can to get a feel for the flavors of Gerbeaud and the city, and to take pleasure in the sweet life of Budapest."—Adam Mészáros

HIGH NOTE SKYBAR

Aria Hotel
Hercegpímás Utca 5
Budapest
Central Hungary 1051
Hungary
+36 204388648
www.highnoteskybar.hu

Opening hours	Open 7 days
Credit cards	Accepted
Price range	Affordable
Style	Smart casual
Cuisine	Bar
Recommended for	Late night

"This is a beautiful sky bar on the top of Hotel Aria. Very cosy and comfortable, with amazing views of Budapest, especially the Basilica. You can leave everything behind after a hard day."—Adam Mészáros

KÁDÁR ÉTKEZDE

Klauzál Tér 9
Budapest
Central Hungary 1072
Hungary
+36 13213622

Opening hours	Closed Monday and Sunday
Credit cards	Not accepted
Price range	Budget
Style	Casual
Cuisine	Jewish-Hungarian
Recommended for	Worth the travel

"Quaint Jewish luncheon spot in Budapest. Stuffed cabbage, soups, chicken paprikash, and checkered table cloths galore. It was everything I ever dreamed of in terms of what your Hungarian grandmother would serve you if you still lived in Budapest."
—Csilla Thackray

ONYX

Recommended by
Csilla Thackray

Vörösmarty Tér 7
Budapest
Central Hungary 1051
Hungary
+36 305080622
www.onyxrestaurant.hu

Opening hours	Closed Monday and Sunday
Credit cards	Accepted
Price range	Expensive
Style	Formal
Cuisine	Hungarian-International
Recommended for	Worth the travel

"Michelin-starred in Budapest."—Csilla Thackray

Onyx is a sumptuous, art deco-style restaurant: imagine plenty of marble, grand chandeliers, gold accents, and, of course, dark onyx features. It was the second of Budapest's eating establishments to hold a Michelin star (Costes received the first, in 2010). The food is an experimental, modern take on traditional Hungarian cuisine, with dishes such as water buffalo tartar, garlic panna cotta and rice crisps; goose liver with pistachio and green apple; and twenty-first-century Somló sponge cake. It's all presented with an immaculate eye for detail, and arrives by way of white-gloved servers. The wine list comes on an iPad and covers hundreds of labels, with notable Hungarian options.

WATER & WINE

Recommended by
Robert Trzópek

Drzewce 35
Nałęczów
Lublin 24-150
Poland
+48 691770435
www.waterandwine.pl

Opening hours	Variable
Credit cards	Accepted
Price range	Expensive
Style	Smart casual
Cuisine	Polish
Recommended for	Worth the travel

"Unique concept based in a water-bottling factory. They have their own garden and lakes from where the majority of their produce comes. It's three hours from Warsaw but worth every minute of your travel."
—Robert Trzópek

KITA KOGUTA

Recommended by
Robert Trzópek

Ulica Krucza 6/14
Warsaw
Masovia 00-950
Poland
+48 512307284
www.kitakoguta.pl

Opening hours	Closed Monday
Credit cards	Accepted but not AMEX or Diners
Price range	Affordable
Style	Casual
Cuisine	Bar
Recommended for	Late night

"Kita Koguta is one of the best cocktail bars in Warsaw. They also offer some simple but original snacks. My tip: the drinks menu is available but it's best to ask a bartender for a signature cocktail according to your preference."—Robert Trzópek

MAŁA POLANA SMAKÓW

Recommended by
Robert Trzópek

Ulica Belwederska 13/44
Warsaw
Masovia 00-743
Poland
+48 224008048
www.polanasmakow.pl

Opening hours	Open 7 days
Credit cards	Accepted but not AMEX
Price range	Affordable
Style	Casual
Cuisine	Modern Polish
Recommended for	Local favorite

"Small but worth visiting. Classic Polish with a slight signature twist by the chef, Andrzej Polan. Highly recommended for those who want to taste real Polish food."—Robert Trzópek

NOLITA

Recommended by
Robert Trzópek

Ulica Wilcza 46
Warsaw
Masovia 00-679
Poland
+48 222920424
www.nolita.pl

Opening hours	Closed Sunday
Credit cards	Accepted
Price range	Affordable
Style	Smart casual
Cuisine	Modern French-Polish
Recommended for	High end

"This is the best fine-dining place in Warsaw, in my opinion. Chef Jacek Grochowina used to work at the Ritz in London. You can truly see the influence on his food."—Robert Trzópek

REGINA BAR

Recommended by
Robert Trzópek

Koszykowa 1
Warsaw
Masovia 00-564
Poland
+48 226214258

Opening hours	Open 7 days
Credit cards	Accepted but not AMEX
Price range	Affordable
Style	Casual
Cuisine	Asian-Italian
Recommended for	Regular neighborhood

"Trisno Hamid offers original Asian fusion in Warsaw. Regina Bar is inspired by Little Italy and China Town in Manhattan."—Robert Trzópek

SATO GOTUJE

Recommended by
Robert Trzópek

Adolfa Pawińskiego 24
Warsaw
Masovia 02-106
Poland
+48 517961514

Opening hours	Closed Monday and Sunday
Credit cards	Accepted
Price range	Budget
Style	Casual
Cuisine	Japanese
Recommended for	Bargain

"Japanese izakaya-style place in the middle of nowhere in Warsaw, but it's worth visiting for its great food. You can spend as little as €20 ($22; £17) and leave full and happy."—Robert Trzópek

This authentic Japanese restaurant in Warsaw's Ochota district is something of a hidden gem and is popular with locals, but off the tourist radar. It serves up the sophisticated flavors of the Far East, right in the center of the Polish capital. The owner, Satoru Yaegashi, who is also the chef, moved from Japan to Poland a few years ago and opened Sato Gotuje, which means "Sato cooks". On the menu you'll find mouth-watering small plates, such as fried oysters with panko breadcrumbs, braised duck breast, and marinated chicken livers. But most people still come for the expertly prepared, hand-cut udon.

SECRET LIFE CAFÉ

Recommended by
Robert Trzópek

Ulica Słowackiego 15/19
Warsaw
Masovia 01-592
Poland
+48 507226552

Opening hours	Open 7 days
Credit cards	Accepted but not AMEX or Diners
Price range	Budget
Style	Casual
Cuisine	Café
Recommended for	Breakfast

"All the ingredients are organic here. The owners pay special attention to high-quality, healthy food. The breakfast is always accompanied by a great coffee, usually using alternative brewing methods." —Robert Trzópek

CINCA MARINCA

Recommended by
Ana Roš

Trg Svobode 10
Kobarid
Goriška 5222
Slovenia

Opening hours	Open 7 days
Credit cards	Accepted
Price range	Affordable
Style	Casual
Cuisine	Café-Bar
Recommended for	Breakfast

"In the center of Kobarid we all know each other —you never drink your coffee alone."—Ana Roš

TOPLI VAL

Recommended by
Ana Roš

Hotel Hvala
Trg Svobode 1
Kobarid
Goriška 5222
Slovenia
+386 53899300
www.hotelhvala.si

Opening hours	Variable
Credit cards	Accepted but not Diners
Price range	Affordable
Style	Smart casual
Cuisine	Seafood
Recommended for	Regular neighborhood

"I always eat the spaghetti *scoglio,* slightly spicy."
—Ana Roš

Despite being in the middle of Slovenia's mountainous Soča Valley area, the focus of this family-run hotel restaurant is the seafood—fresh every day from the local rivers, lakes, and the Adriatic Sea. On the menu you'll find oysters, octopus, raw scampi, and lobster, alongside land-based delicacies like wild duck, steak, and Carniolan sausage. For good reason, the food is rated as some of the best the country has to offer, rivaling the best restaurants in Europe. For dessert, try the traditional Kobarid-style *štruklji* dumplings or the *gibanica* (layers of filo pastry with walnuts, apples, cottage cheese, and poppy seeds). The wine list includes Slovenian wines, too, which can be exceptionally good value for money.

POP'S PLACE

Recommended by
Ana Roš

Cankarjevo Nabrežje 3
Ljubljana 1000
Slovenia
+386 59042856

Opening hours	Open 7 days
Credit cards	Accepted but not Diners
Price range	Affordable
Style	Casual
Cuisine	Burgers
Recommended for	Bargain

VANDER URBANI RESORT

Recommended by
Tomaž Kavčič

Krojaška Ulica 6–8
Ljubljana 1000
Slovenia
+386 12009000
www.vanderhotel.com

Opening hours	Open 7 days
Credit cards	Accepted
Price range	Affordable
Style	Smart casual
Cuisine	Slovenian
Recommended for	Breakfast

"The Hotel Vander nestles under Castle Hill on the banks of the River Ljubljanica. From the outside, it looks like the other town houses in the old city, but it has been intricately re-designed with contemporary passion. The sunny roof-top terrace with a swimming pool is very intimate. You are instantly overtaken by the panorama of tiled roofs and lively streets, which makes you feel that you have found your place in the world."—Tomaž Kavčič

PRI LOJZETU

Recommended by
Emanuele Scarello

Dvorec Zemono 7
Vipava 5271
Slovenia
+386 53687007
www.zemono.si

Opening hours	Closed Monday and Tuesday
Credit cards	Accepted but not Diners
Price range	Expensive
Style	Smart casual
Cuisine	Modern Slovenian-European
Recommended for	Regular neighborhood

"They pay real, sincere attention to their guests, their cuisine is genuine, and there is a breathtaking view over the Vipacco Valley."—Emanuele Scarello

> "THE BEST ASIAN FOOD IN TALLINN, WITH A GREAT CHEF. MY FAVOURITE IS THE SEAFOOD DIM SUM."
>
> VLADISLAV DJATSUK P713

ESTONIA, LATVIA & RUSSIA

> "IT'S ALL ABOUT MEAT. I LIKE TO GO THERE AFTER A SHIFT WITH THE LADS, HAVE A STEAK AND BEER AND JUST CHILL."
>
> ANDREY ZHDANOV P713

> "A NEW VISION OF ESTONIAN CUISINE, AND GREAT WINE."
>
> VLADISLAV DJATŠUK P698

> "A menu with surprises."
>
> ROMAN ZASTSERINSKI P696

Harjumaa p.696
Raplamaa p.696
St Petersburg p.701
Järvamaa p.696
ESTONIA
Tukums p.701
Riga p.699
LATVIA

RUSSIA

Moscow Oblast pp.704–715

ESTONIA,
LATVIA &
RUSSIA

N   SCALE

0   140   280
                MI.

ÖÖBIKU GASTRONOMY FARM

Recommended by
Vladislav Djatšuk

Kuimetsa küla
Kaiu
Raplamaa 79302, Estonia
+372 56935515
www.oobiku.ee

Opening hours	Closed Monday and Tuesday
Credit cards	Accepted but not AMEX
Price range	Affordable
Style	Casual
Cuisine	Estonian
Recommended for	Worth the travel

PÕHJAKA MÕIS

Recommended by
Vladislav Djatšuk,
Peeter Pihel,
Roman Zastserinski

Mäeküla
Paide
Järvamaa 72604, Estonia
+372 5267795
www.pohjaka.ee

Opening hours	Closed Monday and Tuesday
Credit cards	Accepted
Price range	Affordable
Style	Casual
Cuisine	Modern Estonian
Recommended for	Wish I'd opened

"The restaurant was opened in 2010. By now the chefs have proven to everyone (themselves included) that is it possible to prepare delicious food using nothing else but local Estonian raw material, being thus wholly dependent on seasons. Therefore, in the winter, more filling meals are prepared, during summertime they serve lighter food—all the fresh and green that our fields and forests have to offer. And they grow much of the food themselves. Respect!"—Roman Zastserinski

In 2007, a trio of chefs began to breathe life back into a derelict nineteenth-century manor house between Tallinn and Tartu—the result was Põhjaka Mõis. The majority of typically Estonian dishes here cost less than €10 ($11; £8) and are served to a 1980s soundtrack (from vinyl LPs). The dishes include marinated lamprey eels, home-cured and smoked charcuterie with black bread, rabbit stew, fillet of wild boar with mushroom sauce and roast onion, and Pavlova with sea buckthorn sauce. The millefeuille (vanilla pastry, known here as Napoleon cake) is a staple. Ingredients are mostly sourced from the manor's garden (for their jams and compotes, for example) and also their farm, roamed by hens and pigs.

ART PRIORI

Recommended by
Roman Zastserinski

Olevimägi 7
Tallinn
Harjumaa 10123, Estonia
+372 6003353
www.artpriori.ee

Opening hours	Closed Sunday
Credit cards	Accepted
Price range	Affordable
Style	Smart casual
Cuisine	Nordic Fusion
Recommended for	High end

"High class restaurant, gourmet modern food; a menu with surprises."—Roman Zastserinski

BURGER BOX

Recommended by
Roman Zastserinski

Kopli 4
Tallinn
Harjumaa 10412, Estonia

Opening hours	Closed Monday
Reservation policy	No
Credit cards	Not accepted
Price range	Budget
Style	Casual
Cuisine	Burgers
Recommended for	Bargain

"Fast food restaurant, making homemade burgers and kimchi fries. Tasty every time!"
—Roman Zastserinski

JOSEPHINE

Recommended by
Vladislav Djatšuk

Vene 16
Tallinn
Harjumaa 10140, Estonia
+ 372 6418291
www.pierre.ee

Opening hours	Open 7 days
Credit cards	Accepted
Price range	Affordable
Style	Casual
Cuisine	French-Estonian
Recommended for	Breakfast

"Great place to have a morning coffee and a light meal."—Vladislav Djatšuk

CHEDI
Recommended by
Vladislav Djatšuk

Sulevimägi 1
Tallinn
Harjumaa 10123, Estonia
+372 6461676
www.chedi.ee

Opening hours	Open 7 days
Credit cards	Accepted but not AMEX
Price range	Affordable
Style	Smart casual
Cuisine	Asian
Recommended for	Wish I'd opened

"The best Asian food in Tallinn, with a great chef. My favorite is the seafood dim sum."—Vladislav Djatšuk

CRU
Recommended by
Vladislav Djatšuk

Viru 8
Tallinn
Harjumaa 10140, Estonia
+372 6140085
www.crurestoran.eu

Opening hours	Open 7 days
Credit cards	Accepted but not AMEX
Price range	Affordable
Style	Smart casual
Cuisine	Modern Estonian
Recommended for	Wish I'd opened

ESTONIAN BURGER FACTORY
Recommended by
Vladislav Djatšuk

Pärnu Maantee 41a
Tallinn
Harjumaa 10119, Estonia
+372 59082626
www.ebf.ee

Opening hours	Open 7 days
Credit cards	Accepted but not AMEX
Price range	Affordable
Style	Casual
Cuisine	Burgers
Recommended for	Late night

"Best burgers in Tallinn."—Vladislav Djatšuk

FABRIK
Recommended by
Roman Zastserinski

Vabriku 6
Tallinn
Harjumaa 10411, Estonia
+372 6445743
www.fabrik.ee

Opening hours	Closed Monday and Sunday
Credit cards	Accepted but not AMEX
Price range	Affordable
Style	Casual
Cuisine	Modern Estonian-Nordic
Recommended for	Regular neighborhood

GIANNI
Recommended by
Vladislav Djatšuk

Jõe 4a
Tallinn
Harjumaa 10151, Estonia
+372 6263684
www.gianni.ee

Opening hours	Open 7 days
Credit cards	Accepted but not AMEX
Price range	Affordable
Style	Smart casual
Cuisine	Italian
Recommended for	High end

"Great Italian restaurant with a very warm ambience and very friendly service."—Vladislav Djatšuk

KAKS KOKKA
Recommended by
Vladislav Djatšuk

Mere Puiestee 6e
Tallinn
Harjumaa 10111, Estonia
+372 6616151
www.kakskokka.ee

Opening hours	Open 7 days
Credit cards	Accepted
Price range	Affordable
Style	Smart casual
Cuisine	Estonian-Nordic
Recommended for	Bargain

"They have one kitchen with two restaurants: one is the best Nordic fine dining and the other, very simple and tasty food for everyday life!"—Vladislav Djatšuk

KLAUS

Recommended by
Roman Zastserinski

Kalasadama 8
Tallinn
Harjumaa 10415, Estonia
+372 56919010
www.klauskohvik.ee

Opening hours	Open 7 days
Credit cards	Accepted but not AMEX or Diners
Price range	Affordable
Style	Casual
Cuisine	Estonian
Recommended for	Breakfast

LEIB RESTO JA AED

Recommended by
Vladislav Djatšuk, Peeter Pihel,
Roman Zastserinski

Uus 31
Tallinn
Harjumaa 10111, Estonia
+372 6119026
www.leibresto.ee

Opening hours	Closed Sunday
Credit cards	Accepted
Price range	Affordable
Style	Casual
Cuisine	European
Recommended for	Regular neighborhood

"Good old Estonian black bread—fresh, warm, simple, and honest—it's what we grow up with and what we dream about when we're away. It's what we, Estonians, are really. They use simple Estonian ingredients to build a creative, seasonal menu here."—Peeter Pihel

Dominated by its grill, the grassy terrace with comfy, fleece-wrapped seats makes Leib Resto ja Aed mighty popular with locals. Leib, meaning bread (traditionally black in Estonia), is a great accompaniment to hearty dishes such as creamy onion broth, pan-fried pike perch with cauliflower cream, or slow-cooked pork cheek with roasted kale and caramelized salsify. Follow on with crème brûlée or baked chocolate ganache with honey sauce and meringue. Expect a carefully stocked cellar too, seeing as Kristjan Peäske (co-owner with Janno Lepik, ex-Rhodes W1) is a multi-award-winning sommelier.

MANNA LA ROOSA

Recommended by
Roman Zastserinski

Vana-Viru 15
Tallinn
Harjumaa 10111, Estonia
+372 6200249
www.mannalaroosa.com

Opening hours	Open 7 days
Credit cards	Accepted
Price range	Affordable
Style	Casual
Cuisine	European
Recommended for	Late night

NOA CHEFS HALL

Recommended by
Vladislav Djatšuk,
Roman Zastserinski

Ranna Tee 3
Tallinn
Harjumaa 12112, Estonia
+372 5080589
www.noaresto.ee

Opening hours	Closed Monday, Tuesday, and Sunday
Credit cards	Accepted
Price range	Expensive
Style	Smart casual
Cuisine	Modern Nordic
Recommended for	Local favorite

"The most beautiful place in Tallinn with the best view, very tasty food, a creative chef and a great atmosphere."—Vladislav Djatšuk

Ö RESTAURANT

Recommended by
Vladislav Djatšuk

Mere Puiestee 6e
Tallinn
Harjumaa 10111, Estonia
+372 661 6150
www.restoran-o.ee

Opening hours	Closed Sunday
Credit cards	Accepted
Price range	Expensive
Style	Smart casual
Cuisine	Modern Estonian
Recommended for	High end

"Very talented head chef/owners with high-level cuisine and great service. They make this one of the top Estonian restaurants, with a new vision of Estonian cuisine, a degustation menu, and great wine selection."—Vladislav Djatšuk

This restaurant is named in honour of one of Estonia's hardest-to-pronounce vowels: "Õ". Once you've mastered the art of saying it with pursed lips (the noise you need to make is supposedly the same as the "i" sound in "bird"), turn your attention to the menu, where you'll find delightfully modern Estonian dishes. "Taste journeys" include combinations such as perch with fresh cabbage and algae, and horseradish with caramel and buckwheat, served with flair and finesse. The restaurant is understated and stylish, fitting for a former warehouse space, and the influences of Estonia's neighbors—Russia, Scandinavia, and other Baltic states—can all be detected on the plate.

SFÄÄR RESTO

Recommended by
Roman Zastserinski

Mere Puiestee 6e
Tallinn
Harjumaa 10111, Estonia
+372 56992200
www.sfaar.ee

Opening hours	Closed Monday
Credit cards	Accepted
Price range	Affordable
Style	Casual
Cuisine	Modern Nordic
Recommended for	Breakfast

"For the variety of breakfast dishes and the most amazing news—on weekends the late breakfast is until 3.00 p.m."—Roman Zastserinski

TCHAIKOVSKY

Recommended by
Roman Zastserinski

Telegraaf Hotel
Vene 9
Tallinn
Harjumaa 10123, Estonia
+372 6000610
www.telegraafhotel.com

Opening hours	Open 7 days
Credit cards	Accepted
Price range	Affordable
Style	Smart casual
Cuisine	French-Russian
Recommended for	Local favorite

"Super interior, and chef Vladislav Djatšuk's mixed cuisine of Russian and French classics. Marvellous."
— Roman Zastserinski

FOODBOX

Recommended by
Martins Ritins

Antonijas Ielā 6a
Riga 1010, Latvia
+371 28205998
www.foodbox.lv

Opening hours	Closed Sunday
Credit cards	Not accepted
Price range	Budget
Style	Casual
Cuisine	Turkish
Recommended for	Bargain

"It's authentic, independent, and the Turkish chef makes his own kebabs and breads. Nothing industrial here."—Martins Ritins

INNOCENT CAFÉ

Recommended by
Martins Ritins

Blaumaņa Ielā 34
Riga 1011, Latvia
+371 29349507
www.innocent.lv

Opening hours	Open 7 days
Credit cards	Accepted
Price range	Budget
Style	Casual
Cuisine	European
Recommended for	Breakfast

LEFT DOOR BAR

Recommended by
Martins Ritins

Antonijas Iela 12
Riga 1010, Latvia
+371 26300368
www.theleftdoorbar.lv

Opening hours	Closed Sunday
Credit cards	Accepted
Price range	Affordable
Style	Casual
Cuisine	International
Recommended for	Breakfast

MUUSU

Recommended by
Martins Ritins

Skārņu iela 6
Riga 1050, Latvia
+371 25772552
www.muusu.lv

Opening hours	Closed Monday
Credit cards	Accepted
Price range	Expensive
Style	Smart casual
Cuisine	Modern European-Scandanavian
Recommended for	High end

RESTAURANT NAPLES

Recommended by
Martins Ritins

Andrejostas iela 2
Riga 1045, Latvia
+371 25775540
www.naples.lv

Opening hours	Open 7 days
Credit cards	Accepted
Price range	Affordable
Style	Casual
Cuisine	Italian Fusion
Recommended for	Regular neighborhood

"One of the rare restaurants on the waterfront in Riga; very casual, tasty, freshly cooked food by a proper chef. It's good value for money, has a relaxed, unhurried atmosphere, welcoming staff, and a nostalgic proprietor, Ivo. Good fish bar and aged beef but maybe the best pizza in town, especially the Latvian traditional dark rye pizza."—Martins Ritins

RESTAURANT BERGS

Recommended by
Martins Ritins

Bergs Bazaar
83–85 Elizabetes Iela
Riga 1050, Latvia
+371 67770957
www.hotelbergs.lv

Opening hours	Open 7 days
Credit cards	Accepted
Price range	Affordable
Style	Smart casual
Cuisine	International-French
Recommended for	High end

"Bergs is top quality. Fine dining at its best."
—Martins Ritins

RESTAURANT RIVIERA

Recommended by
Martins Ritins

Dzirnavu iela 31
Riga 1010, Latvia
+371 26605930
www.rivierarestorans.lv

Opening hours	Open 7 days
Credit cards	Accepted
Price range	Affordable
Style	Smart casual
Cuisine	Mediterranean
Recommended for	Regular neighborhood

"Very popular, vibrant and busy! They've just opened an additional oyster and dry-aged beef menu."
—Martins Ritins

ROCKET BEAN ROASTERY

Recommended by
Martins Ritins

Miera Iela 29
Riga 1001, Latvia
+371 20215120
www.rocketbean.lv

Opening hours	Open 7 days
Credit cards	Accepted
Price range	Budget
Style	Casual
Cuisine	Café-European
Recommended for	Breakfast

"From porridge to Eggs Benedict and the greatest coffees, with their own coffee roastery. And everyone goes there, from hipsters to chefs and bankers!"
— Martins Ritins

VALTERA RESTAURANT

Recommended by
Martins Ritins

Miesnieku iela 8
Riga 1050, Latvia
+371 29529200
www.valterarestorans.lv

Opening hours	Open 7 days
Credit cards	Accepted
Price range	Affordable
Style	Casual
Cuisine	Modern Latvian
Recommended for	Local favorite

"Small, intimate and one hundred per cent local."
— Martins Ritins

KUKŠU MUIŽA

Recommended by
Martins Ritins

Kukšas
Tukums 3128, Latvia
+371 63181545
www.kuksumuiza.lv

Opening hours	By appointment
Credit cards	Accepted but not AMEX
Price range	Affordable
Style	Casual
Cuisine	European
Recommended for	Wish I'd opened

"The owner is also the chef, the waiter, the sommelier, and the gardener. And the candlestick maker. Breakfast, lunch, and romantic dinners with the best antiques and silver."—Martins Ritins

MOSCOW: SEE PAGES 704–715

DUO GASTROBAR

Recommended by
Timur Abuzyarov,
Ivan Berezutskiy,
Sergey Berezutskiy,
Evgeny Vikentev

Kirochnaya Ulitsa 8b
St Petersburg, 191028, Russia
+7 9219471290
www.duobar.ru

Opening hours	Open 7 days
Credit cards	Accepted but not AMEX
Price range	Affordable
Style	Casual
Cuisine	Modern European
Recommended for	Bargain

"Interesting neo-bistro with perfect service and convenient location."—Evgeny Vikentev

Duo is a simple, stylish gastrobar that helped put an otherwise quiet, residential area on the culinary map. Kirochnaya Street may be off St Petersburg's busy tourist trail, but it's worth a detour for Duo's modern menu and fresh interiors: whitewashed brick walls, wooden tables, and colorful banquettes. The duo behind Duo are friends Renat Malikov and Dmitry Blinov, who opened the hip space in 2014. Its short fusion menu pairs unexpected ingredients, such as burrata with black pudding, bone marrow with ginger sauce, and bruschetta with crab. It sounds complicated, but it's actually all very honest, simple and original.

EL COPITAS BAR

Recommended by
Evgeny Vikentev

Kolokolnaya Ulitsa 2
St Petersburg, 191025, Russia
+7 8129417168

Opening hours	Closed Monday to Wednesday and Sunday
Credit cards	Not accepted
Price range	Affordable
Style	Casual
Cuisine	Mexican
Recommended for	Late night

"A small, cosy place in the very heart of St Petersburg, that is really difficult to find, with unusual drinks and simple Mexican cuisine. It was started with a tiny budget by three bartenders and is getting stronger and stronger every day. The menus are changed every week and the bar has a unique atmosphere and ideal hospitality."—Evgeny Vikentev

GRAS

Recommended by
Timur Abuzyarov

Inzhenernaya Ulitsa 7
St Petersburg, 191011, Russia
+7 8129281818
www.gras-restaurant.ru

Opening hours	Open 7 days
Credit cards	Accepted but not AMEX or Diners
Price range	Budget
Style	Casual
Cuisine	Nordic-Russian
Recommended for	Wish I'd opened

"Small, Nordic-style restaurant."—Timur Abuzyarov

HAMLET & JACKS

Recommended by
Dmitriy Blinov

Volynskiy Pereulok 2
St Petersburg, 191186, Russia
+7 8129070735
www.hamletandjacks.ru

Opening hours	Open 7 days
Credit cards	Accepted but not AMEX or Diners
Price range	Affordable
Style	Casual
Cuisine	Modern Russian
Recommended for	Regular neighborhood

JEROME

Recommended by
Dmitriy Blinov

Bolshaya Morskaya Ulitsa 25
St Petersburg, 190000, Russia
+7 8129186920
www.probka.org

Opening hours	Open 7 days
Credit cards	Accepted but not AMEX or Diners
Price range	Affordable
Style	Casual
Cuisine	Italian
Recommended for	Regular neighborhood

MOROSHKA DLYA PUSHKINA

Recommended by
Ivan Berezutskiy,
Dmitriy Blinov

Embankment River Moyka 3A
St Petersburg, 191186, Russia
+7 9219472500

Opening hours	Closed Monday and Sunday
Credit cards	Accepted but not AMEX or Diners
Price range	Expensive
Style	Smart casual
Cuisine	Modern Russian
Recommended for	High end

"A world-class restaurant; Scandinavian cuisine and the best wines in the country."—Dmitriy Blinov

The name is certainly a bit of a mouthful. Moroshka dlya Pushkina means "cloudberry for Pushkin" and was chosen in homage to the legendary Russian writer and Romantic poet, Alexander Pushkin. The fine dining on offer in this uber-stylish monochrome space is just as unexpected. It's billed as a contemporary Russian rendering of Scandinavian cuisine—so, expect unusual combinations of simple, native produce. Crayfish feature prominently on the menu, and the chef takes pride in flying them in from a secret mountain lake in Altai. Every dish is presented with great attention to detail and artistic flourish.

PEDRO & GOMEZ U LARISY

Recommended by
Dmitriy Blinov

Rubinshteyna Ulitsa 29
St Petersburg, 191002, Russia
+7 9219034490

Opening hours	Open 7 days
Reservation policy	No
Credit cards	Not accepted
Price range	Budget
Style	Casual
Cuisine	Bar-Grill
Recommended for	Bargain

"A delicious variety of street food from a Norwegian chef."—Dmitriy Blinov

RUSSKAYA RYUMOCHNAYA #1

Recommended by
Ivan Berezutskiy

Konnogvardeiskiy Bulvar 4
St Petersburg, 190000, Russia
+7 8125706420
www.vodkaroom.ru

Opening hours	Open 7 days
Credit cards	Accepted
Price range	Affordable
Style	Smart casual
Cuisine	Russian
Recommended for	Local favorite

**"Authentic Russian food. I showed it to all the chefs who visited St Petersburg and everybody liked it."
—Ivan Berezutskiy**

SMOKE BBQ

Recommended by
Dmitriy Blinov

Rubinshteyna Ulitsa 11
St Petersburg, 191002, Russia
+7 8129055372
www.beercard.ru

Opening hours	Open 7 days
Credit cards	Accepted but not AMEX
Price range	Affordable
Style	Casual
Cuisine	Barbecue
Recommended for	Regular neighborhood

"Realy good texas BBQ—and a big choice of wines and beers."—Dmitriy Blinov

TARTARBAR

Vilenskiy Ulitsa 15
St Petersburg, 191014, Russia
+7 8129945443
www.tartarbar.ru

Opening hours	Open 7 days
Credit cards	Accepted but not AMEX or Diners
Price range	Affordable
Style	Smart casual
Cuisine	Russian
Recommended for	Wish I'd opened

"The soul of the restaurant is the chef/owner,
Dmitriy Blinov. His cuisine gently interweaves
with the atmosphere of the restaurant. Amazing wine
list and smart service, too."—Anton Kovalkov

"THIS IS A REALLY BEAUTIFUL PLACE, WITH GREAT RUSSIAN FOOD AND ALWAYS THAT KIND OF MOOD WHERE YOU JUST HAVE TO HAVE A SHOT OF VODKA FOR BREAKFAST!"
ANDREY ZHDANOV P713

MOSCOW

"A little bit orthodox but as Russian as you can get."
ANTON KOVALKOV P704

"A MUST-SEE DURING A VISIT TO MOSCOW."
ANTON KOVALKOV P704

"*Moscow pastrami, sausages, and burgers —all the guilty pleasures are there.*"
ANTON KOVALKOV P707

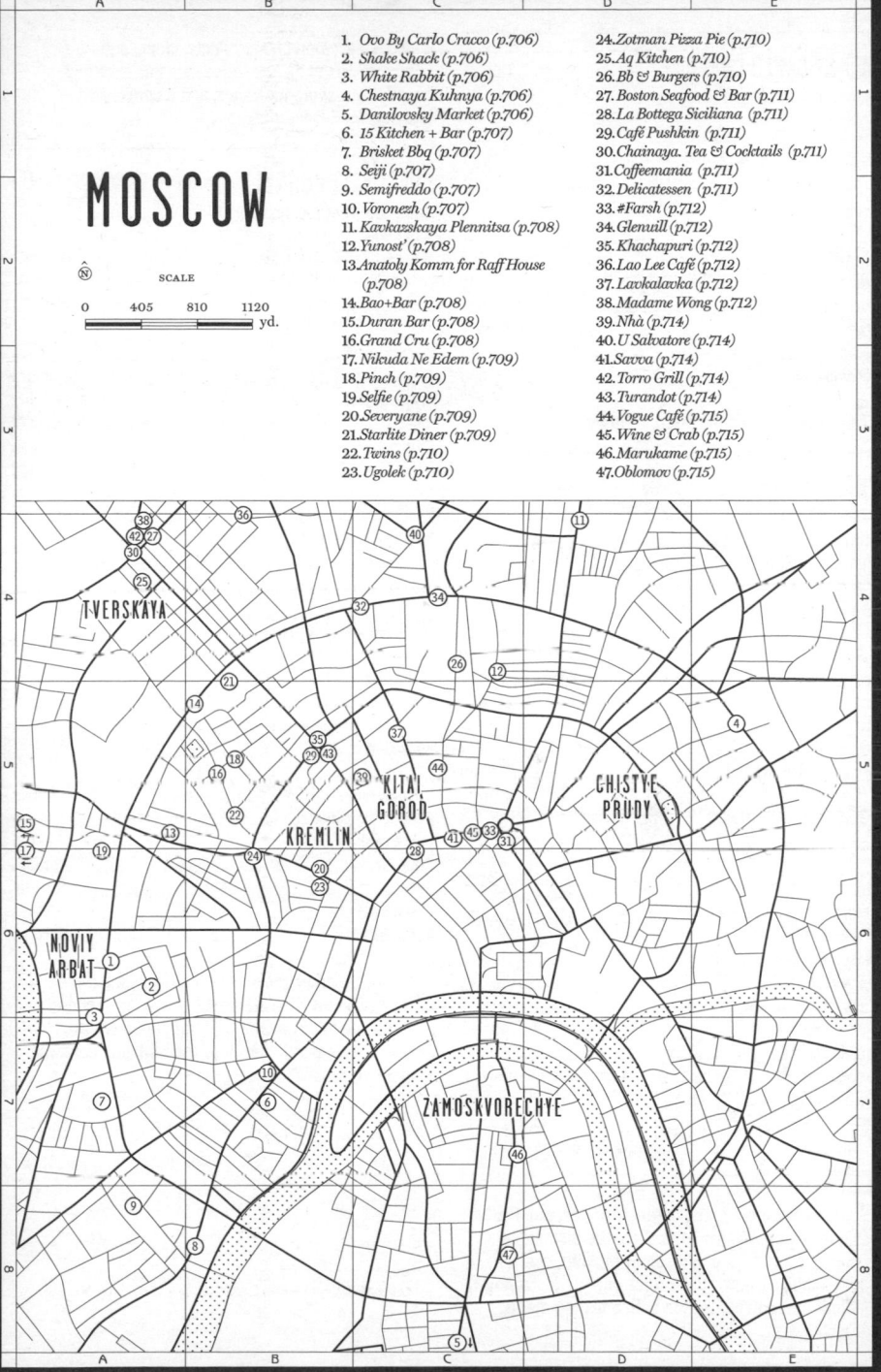

MOSCOW

N

SCALE

0   405   810   1120
yd.

1. *Ovo By Carlo Cracco* (p.706)
2. *Shake Shack* (p.706)
3. *White Rabbit* (p.706)
4. *Chestnaya Kuhnya* (p.706)
5. *Danilovsky Market* (p.706)
6. *15 Kitchen + Bar* (p.707)
7. *Brisket Bbq* (p.707)
8. *Seiji* (p.707)
9. *Semifreddo* (p.707)
10. *Voronezh* (p.707)
11. *Kavkazskaya Plennitsa* (p.708)
12. *Yunost'* (p.708)
13. *Anatoly Komm for Raff House* (p.708)
14. *Bao+Bar* (p.708)
15. *Duran Bar* (p.708)
16. *Grand Cru* (p.708)
17. *Nikuda Ne Edem* (p.709)
18. *Pinch* (p.709)
19. *Selfie* (p.709)
20. *Severyane* (p.709)
21. *Starlite Diner* (p.709)
22. *Twins* (p.710)
23. *Ugolek* (p.710)
24. *Zotman Pizza Pie* (p.710)
25. *Aq Kitchen* (p.710)
26. *Bb & Burgers* (p.710)
27. *Boston Seafood & Bar* (p.711)
28. *La Bottega Siciliana* (p.711)
29. *Café Pushkin* (p.711)
30. *Chainaya. Tea & Cocktails* (p.711)
31. *Coffeemania* (p.711)
32. *Delicatessen* (p.711)
33. *#Farsh* (p.712)
34. *Glenuill* (p.712)
35. *Khachapuri* (p.712)
36. *Lao Lee Café* (p.712)
37. *Lavkalavka* (p.712)
38. *Madame Wong* (p.712)
39. *Nhà* (p.714)
40. *U Salvatore* (p.714)
41. *Savva* (p.714)
42. *Torro Grill* (p.714)
43. *Turandot* (p.714)
44. *Vogue Café* (p.715)
45. *Wine & Crab* (p.715)
46. *Marukame* (p.715)
47. *Oblomov* (p.715)

TVERSKAYA

KITAI GOROD

CHISTYE PRUDY

KREMLIN

NOVIY ARBAT

ZAMOSKVORECHYE

OVO BY CARLO CRACCO

Lotte Hotel
Novinsky Bulvar 8/2
Arbat
Moscow, 121099, Russia
+7 4952870515
www.lottehotel.com

Opening hours	Open 7 days
Credit cards	Accepted
Price range	Affordable
Style	Casual
Cuisine	Modern Italian
Recommended for	High end

"The value matches the price."—Anatoly Komm

SHAKE SHACK

Recommended by
Taras Kiriyenko

38 Arbat Street
Arbat
Moscow, 119002, Russia
+7 4952323143
www.shakeshack.com

Opening hours	Open 7 days
Credit cards	Accepted but not AMEX or Diners
Price range	Budget
Style	Casual
Cuisine	American Burgers
Recommended for	Bargain

"Good value for money."—Taras Kiriyenko

WHITE RABBIT

Recommended by
Timur Abuzyarov,
Sergey Eroshenko,
Anton Kovalkov,
Georgy Troyan,
Evgeny Vikentev

Smolenskaya Square 3
Arbat
Moscow, 121099, Russia
+7 4956633999
www.whiterabbitmoscow.ru

Opening hours	Open 7 days
Credit cards	Accepted but not AMEX
Price range	Expensive
Style	Smart casual
Cuisine	Modern Russian
Recommended for	Local favorite

"Seasonal local products, original recipes, and finely designed combinations—those are the distinctive features of the cuisine of Vladimir Mukhin, chef of White Rabbit. Following the rules of high gastronomy, Vladimir opens every season with a tasting menu, which is based on new products, ideas, and combinations of flavors. This place has excellent hospitality, panoramic views, and a convenient location."—Evgeny Vikentev

CHESTNAYA KUHNYA

Recommended by
Ivan Berezutskiy,
Sergey Berezutskiy

Sadovaya-Chernogryazskaya Ulitsa 10
Basmanny
Moscow, 107078, Russia
+7 4956075090
www.chestnayakuhnya.ru

Opening hours	Open 7 days
Credit cards	Accepted but not Diners
Price range	Affordable
Style	Casual
Cuisine	Modern Russian
Recommended for	Regular neighborhood

"The food is always good and honest. The chef is a hunter so there is always something interesting with game in the seasonal menu."—Sergey Berezutskiy

DANILOVSKY MARKET

Recommended by
Valdimir Mukhin

Mytnaya Ulitsa 74
Danilovsky
Moscow, 115191, Russia
+7 4951201801
www.danrinok.ru

Opening hours	Open 7 days
Reservation policy	No
Credit cards	Not accepted
Price range	Budget
Style	Casual
Cuisine	Market
Recommended for	Bargain

"I like this market because of the many small food corners. My favorite is Dagestanskaya lava serving amazing, delicious *pelmeni* (dumplings), *chudu* (meat-filled pastry), herb tea, and fantastic baklava."
—Vladimir Mukhin

15 KITCHEN + BAR
Recommended by
Sergey Berezutskiy

Pozharskiy Pereulok 15
Khamovniki
Moscow, 119034, Russia
+7 9857671066
www.15kitchenbar.ru

Opening hours	Closed Monday
Credit cards	Accepted but not AMEX
Price range	Affordable
Style	Smart casual
Cuisine	Bar
Recommended for	Late night

"The concept is pretty unique for Moscow—this is a serial pop-up restaurant where the chef changes every 3–4 months, and with a fantastic bar."
—Sergey Berezutskiy

BRISKET BBQ
Recommended by
Timur Abuzyarov

Smolensky Bulvar 15
Khamovniki
Moscow, 119121, Russia
+7 9646470107
www.novikovgroup.ru

Opening hours	Open 7 days
Reservation policy	No
Credit cards	Accepted
Price range	Affordable
Style	Casual
Cuisine	American
Recommended for	Late night

SEIJI
Recommended by
Anatoly Komm

Komsomolskiy Pereulok 5/2
Khamovniki
Moscow, 119021, Russia
+7 4992467624
www.seiji.ru

Opening hours	Open 7 days
Credit cards	Accepted but not Diners
Price range	Budget
Style	Casual
Cuisine	Japanese Sushi
Recommended for	Regular neighborhood

SEMIFREDDO
Recommended by
Sergey Eroshenko,
Anatoly Komm,
Valdimir Mukhin,
Georgy Troyan

Timura Frunze Ulitsa 11, Building 55
Khamovniki
Moscow, 119021, Russia
+7 4951815555
www.semifreddo-group.com/venue/semifreddo

Opening hours	Open 7 days
Credit cards	Accepted
Price range	Expensive
Style	Formal
Cuisine	Italian
Recommended for	High end

"My favorite restaurant in the whole of Moscow! Basically, I would eat only here if I could choose one place!"—Valdimir Mukhin

Run by chef Nino Graziano, holder of two Michelin stars, Semifreddo Mulinazzo is one of Moscow's best-known restaurants. And it has won the admiration of the city's discerning diners and top-100 list compilers over the past ten years not by serving modern Russian food, but by serving Italian. The restaurant's name is a nod to the first restaurant Graziano, opened in 1988, and to the classic Italian dessert that he still prepares with a recipe passed down from his grandmother. The high-end menu includes dishes such as fresh Sicilian red shrimp with apple and celery tartar and braised veal with Nero d'Avola sauce, but there are simpler Italian dishes too, such as homemade ravioli and rabbit ragù. Not to be missed.

VORONEZH
Recommended by
Anton Kovalkov

Prechistenka Ulitsa 4
Khamovniki
Moscow, 119034, Russia
+7 4956950641
www.voronej.com

Opening hours	Open 7 days
Credit cards	Accepted but not AMEX
Price range	Affordable
Style	Smart casual
Cuisine	Russian
Recommended for	Bargain

"Huge three-floor restaurant based on local meat. The best meal is on the first floor in the bistro. Moscow pastrami, sausages, and burgers—all the guilty pleasures are there."—Anton Kovalkov

KAVKAZSKAYA PLENNITSA

Recommended by
Sergey Eroshenko

Mira Prospekt 36
Meshchansky
Moscow, 129090, Russia
+7 4951146170
www.kavkazskaya-plennitsa.ru

Opening hours	Open 7 days
Credit cards	Accepted
Price range	Affordable
Style	Casual
Cuisine	Georgian
Recommended for	Regular neighborhood

"Good quality products and delicious food, and the restaurant is suitable to visit with children."
—Sergey Eroshenko

YUNOST'

Recommended by
Georgy Troyan

Trubnaya Ulitsa 20/2
Meshchansky
Moscow, 119048, Russia
+7 4992424861
www.hotelyunost.com

Opening hours	Open 7 days
Credit cards	Accepted but not AMEX
Price range	Affordable
Style	Casual
Cuisine	Bar-Grill
Recommended for	Bargain

"New, cool, cheap place—good brunches and lots of tasty meat including perfect pastrami and brisket. One of the few restaurants that buy a carcass and use it entirely."—Georgy Troyan

ANATOLY KOMM FOR RAFF HOUSE

Recommended by
Timur Abuzyarov

Malaya Nikitskaya Ulitsa 25
Presnensky
Moscow, 121069, Russia
+7 4957753718
www.raffhouse.com

Opening hours	Closed Monday and Sunday
Credit cards	Accepted but not Diners
Price range	Expensive
Style	Formal
Cuisine	Russian-European
Recommended for	High end

BAO+BAR

Recommended by
Anatoly Komm

Sadovaya-Kudrinskaya Ulitsa 32c1
Presnensky
Moscow, 123001, Russia
+7 4993473001
www.baobar.ru

Opening hours	Open 7 days
Reservation policy	No
Credit cards	Accepted but not AMEX or Diners
Price range	Affordable
Style	Casual
Cuisine	Taiwanese
Recommended for	Bargain

"Exceptional value for money."—Anatoly Komm

DURAN BAR

Recommended by
Valdimir Mukhin

Rochdelskaya Ulitsa 15, 19/20
Presnensky
Moscow, 123022, Russia
+7 9651392929
www.duranbar.ru

Opening hours	Closed Monday and Sunday
Credit cards	Accepted but not AMEX or Diners
Price range	Expensive
Style	Smart casual
Cuisine	Modern Russian
Recommended for	Late night

GRAND CRU

Recommended by
Andrey Zhdanov

Malaya Bronnaya Ulitsa 22
Presnensky
Moscow, 123104, Russia
+7 4956500118
www.grandcru.ru

Opening hours	Open 7 days
Credit cards	Accepted but not AMEX or Diners
Price range	Affordable
Style	Smart casual
Cuisine	Russian-Spanish
Recommended for	Regular neighborhood

"I like to go there if I just want simple food with good wine, beautifully presented. It's simple gastronomy and an amazing wine list just around the corner from home."—Andrey Zhdanov

NIKUDA NE EDEM

Recommended by
Ivan Berezutskiy,
Sergey Berezutskiy

Rochdelskaya Ulitsa 15/8
Presnensky
Moscow, 123022, Russia
+7 4959262322
www.nikudaneedem.ru

Opening hours	Open 7 days
Credit cards	Accepted but not AMEX or Diners
Price range	Affordable
Style	Smart casual
Cuisine	Russian-International
Recommended for	Local favorite

"Creative, unusual food from one of the best
Russian chefs."—Sergey Berezutskiy

PINCH

Recommended by
Timur Abuzyarov,
Georgy Troyan

Bolshoy Palashevskiy Pereulok 2
Presnensky
Moscow, 123104, Russia
+7 4956919988

Opening hours	Open 7 days
Credit cards	Accepted but not AMEX or Diners
Price range	Affordable
Style	Smart casual
Cuisine	International
Recommended for	Breakfast

"Bistro serving breakfast from 8.30 a.m. until
4.00 p.m. The breakfasts are not traditional,
but they're outstanding."—Georgy Troyan

Heavy on style and heavy on substance, Pinch
really packs a punch. It's trendy and elegant, in a
Williamsburg kind of way, with its subtle tones and
natural materials (but with a very Russian twist of
purple lighting under the bar). Located in a bustling
part of the city, its doors are often flung open so
people can sit out on the street, on small wooden
stools, and soak up the vibrant atmosphere. The
kitchen serves "soul food"—hearty ingredients
dished up in ways you can't help but enjoy,
presented with the care of a chef who clearly
wants his plates to be admired.

SELFIE

Recommended by
Georgy Troyan

Novinsky Shopping Center
Novinsky Bulvar 31
Presnensky
Moscow, 123242, Russia
+7 4959958503
www.selfiemoscow.ru

Opening hours	Open 7 days
Credit cards	Accepted
Price range	Affordable
Style	Casual
Cuisine	Modern Russian
Recommended for	Late night

SEVERYANE

Recommended by
Timur Abuzyarov,
Anton Kovalkov,
Valdimir Mukhin

Bolshaya Nikitskaya Ulitsa 12
Presnensky
Moscow, 125009, Russia
+7 4997000898
www.severyane.moscow

Opening hours	Open 7 days
Credit cards	Accepted but not AMEX or Diners
Price range	Affordable
Style	Casual
Cuisine	Modern Russian
Recommended for	Breakfast

"Severyane is an ambitious project with a unique
design and authentic ovens. The food comes from
wood ovens which our grandmothers used to use,
but with the modern touch of chef Georgy Troyan."
—Anton Kovalkov

STARLITE DINER

Recommended by
Sergey Eroshenko

Bolshaya Sadovaya Ulitsa 16
Presnensky
Moscow, 125047, Russia
+7 4956500246
www.starlite.ru

Opening hours	Open 7 days
Reservation policy	No
Credit cards	Accepted
Price range	Budget
Style	Casual
Cuisine	Diner
Recommended for	Breakfast

"In this restaurant, everything is done to make it
quicker—they aim for speed."—Sergey Eroshenko

TWINS

Recommended by
Anatoly Komm

Malaya Bronnaya Ulitsa 13
Presnensky
Moscow, 123104, Russia
+7 4956954510
www.twinsmoscow.ru

Opening hours	Open 7 days
Credit cards	Accepted
Price range	Affordable
Style	Casual
Cuisine	Modern Russian
Recommended for	Regular neighborhood

UGOLEK

Recommended by
Valdimir Mukhin,
Georgy Troyan

Bolshaya Nikitskaya Ulitsa 12
Presnensky
Moscow, 125009, Russia
+7 4956290211
www.ugolek.moscow

Opening hours	Open 7 days
Credit cards	Accepted but not AMEX or Diners
Price range	Affordable
Style	Casual
Cuisine	Bar-Grill
Recommended for	Regular neighborhood

Ugolek translates as "ember" and this bustling brasserie is definitely on fire. Ilya Tyutenkov and chef Uilliam Lamberti founded it in 2014, and the place now attracts a trendy, artsy-hipster crowd, as well as people who go to admire the swanky modernist interior which includes raw concrete, exposed brickwork, huge floor-to-ceiling windows, and patches of living moss growing vertically alongside the uncovered pipes. Dishes are cooked on an antique open charcoal oven, giving the food a delicious smokiness. Lamberti loves to subvert expectations, as seen in his ironic black Caesar salad—a twist on the traditional.

ZOTMAN PIZZA PIE

Recommended by
Timur Abuzyarov

Bolshaya Nikitskaya 23/14/9
Presnensky
Moscow, 119019, Russia
+7 4992700807
www.zotman.ru

Opening hours	Open 7 days
Reservation policy	No
Credit cards	Accepted but not AMEX or Diners
Price range	Budget
Style	Casual
Cuisine	American-Italian
Recommended for	Late night

"One of the best Brooklyn-style pizzas in Moscow."
—Timur Abuzyarov

AQ KITCHEN

Recommended by
Timur Abuzyarov,
Sergey Eroshenko,
Taras Kiriyenko

Bolshaya Gruzinskaya Ulitsa 69
Tverskoy
Moscow, 123056, Russia
+7 4993933224
www.aq.kitchen

Opening hours	Open 7 days
Credit cards	Accepted but not AMEX
Price range	Affordable
Style	Casual
Cuisine	European
Recommended for	Regular neighborhood

"Amazing food and nice atmosphere—a trendy place, with a good wine selection."—Taras Kiriyenko

BB & BURGERS

Recommended by
Timur Abuzyarov

Tsvetnoy Bulvar 7
Tverskoy
Moscow, 127051, Russia
+7 9653833033
www.bbburgers.ru

Opening hours	Open 7 days
Credit cards	Accepted
Price range	Budget
Style	Casual
Cuisine	Burgers
Recommended for	Bargain

BOSTON SEAFOOD & BAR

Recommended by
Timur Abuzyarov,
Ivan Berezutskiy,
Valdimir Mukhin

Lesnaya Ulitsa 7
Tverskoy
Moscow, 125047, Russia
+7 4952284600
www.boston-restaurant.ru

Opening hours	Closed Friday and Saturday
Credit cards	Accepted but not AMEX or Diners
Price range	Affordable
Style	Casual
Cuisine	Seafood
Recommended for	Regular neighborhood

"Good atmosphere! Simple, delicious food and big choice of seafood."—Timur Abuzyarov

LA BOTTEGA SICILIANA

Recommended by
Valdimir Mukhin

Okhotny Ryad Ulitsa 2
Tverskoy
Moscow, 125009, Russia
+7 4956600383
www.semifreddo-group.com

Opening hours	Closed Sunday
Credit cards	Accepted but not AMEX or Diners
Price range	Affordable
Style	Casual
Cuisine	Italian
Recommended for	High end

CAFÉ PUSHKIN

Recommended by
Timur Abuzyarov,
Sergey Eroshenko,
Anatoly Komm

Tverskoy Bulvar 26a
Tverskoy
Moscow, 125009, Russia
+7 4957390033
www.cafe-pushkin.ru

Opening hours	Open 7 days
Credit cards	Accepted
Price range	Expensive
Style	Formal
Cuisine	Russian
Recommended for	Local favorite

"It's a little bit orthodox but as Russian as you can get."—Anatoly Komm

CHAINAYA. TEA & COCKTAILS

Recommended by
Timur Abuzyarov,
Valdimir Mukhin

1-ya Tverskaya-Yamskaya Ulitsa 29
Tverskoy
Moscow, 125047, Russia
+7 4959673052

Opening hours	Closed Monday and Sunday
Reservation policy	No
Credit cards	Accepted but not AMEX or Diners
Price range	Expensive
Style	Smart casual
Cuisine	Bar-Chinese
Recommended for	Late night

COFFEEMANIA

Recommended by
Ivan Berezutskiy,
Sergey Berezutskiy,
Georgy Troyan

Malyy Cherkasskiy Pereulok 2
Tverskoy
Moscow, 109012, Russia
+7 4959602295
www.coffeemania.ru

Opening hours	Open 7 days
Credit cards	Accepted but not AMEX
Price range	Affordable
Style	Casual
Cuisine	Café
Recommended for	Breakfast

"Just very good breakfast for the last ten years."
—Ivan Berezutskiy

DELICATESSEN

Recommended by
Florent Ladeyn,
Georgy Troyan

Building 2
Sadovaya-Karetnaya Ulitsa 20
Tverskoy
Moscow, 127051, Russia
+7 4956993952
www.newdeli.ru

Opening hours	Closed Monday
Credit cards	Accepted but not AMEX or Diners
Price range	Budget
Style	Casual
Cuisine	Deli
Recommended for	Worth the travel

"Basement restaurant, old-fashioned bar, and cosy atmosphere. They serve the best cocktails I've ever tasted in my life! Chef Ivan Shishkin is the master of fermentation, from pasta to pizza. He can grow onion sprouts in a week and ferment them. He's an expert, very precise and really good!"—Florent Ladeyn

#FARSH

Recommended by
Ivan Berezutskiy,
Taras Kiriyenko,
Andrey Zhdanov

Nikolskaya Ulitsa 12
Tverskoy
Moscow, 109012, Russia
+7 4952584205
www.novikovgroup.ru/restaurants/farsh/

Opening hours	Open 7 days
Reservation policy	No
Credit cards	Accepted but not AMEX or Diners
Price range	Budget
Style	Casual
Cuisine	American Burgers
Recommended for	Bargain

"Best bargain burgers in Moscow."—Ivan Berezutskiy

GLENUILL

Recommended by
Dmitriy Blinov,
Taras Kiriyenko,
Anton Kovalkov

Sadovo-Samotechnaia Ulitsa 20
Tverskoy
Moscow, 127151, Russia
+7 4957247627

Opening hours	Open 7 days
Credit cards	Accepted
Price range	Affordable
Style	Casual
Cuisine	International
Recommended for	Local favorite

"One of the first gastropubs in Moscow, opened by an Australian but with Russian atmosphere and warm hospitality. Chef Andrey catches the Australian wave but with some local produce."—Anton Kovalkov

KHACHAPURI

Recommended by
Taras Kiriyenko

Bolshoi Gnezdnikovskiy Ulitsa 10
Tverskoy
Moscow, 103009, Russia
+7 9857643118
www.hacha.ru

Opening hours	Open 7 days
Credit cards	Accepted but not Diners
Price range	Budget
Style	Casual
Cuisine	Café-Pizza
Recommended for	Bargain

LAO LEE CAFÉ

Recommended by
Andrey Zhdanov

Miusskaya Place 9/11
Tverskoy
Moscow, 125047, Russia
+7 9651627877

Opening hours	Open 7 days
Reservation policy	No
Credit cards	Accepted but not AMEX or Diners
Price range	Budget
Style	Casual
Cuisine	Vietnamese
Recommended for	Regular neighborhood

"A really awesome Vietnamese just nearby!"
—Andrey Zhdanov

LAVKALAVKA

Recommended by
Valdimir Mukhin,
Georgy Troyan,
Andrey Zhdanov

Petrovka Street Ulitsa 21/2
Tverskoy
Moscow, 107031, Russia

+7 4956212036
www.restoran.lavkalavka.com

Opening hours	Open 7 days
Credit cards	Accepted but not AMEX
Price range	Affordable
Style	Casual
Cuisine	Modern Russian
Recommended for	Local favorite

"It's a local cuisine restaurant. It has a wonderful atmosphere and is the only place where you can try real Russian ingredients that are in season."
—Andrey Zhdanov

MADAME WONG

Recommended by
Anton Kovalkov

Lesnaya Ulitsa 7
Tverskoy
Moscow, 125047, Russia
+7 4952801566
www.madamewong.ru

Opening hours	Open 7 days
Credit cards	Accepted but not Diners
Price range	Affordable
Style	Casual
Cuisine	Asian
Recommended for	Late night

"The modern Chinese cuisine consolidates vast territories, starting from the southern regions of

China, to Hong Kong, and ending with Malaysia, Singapore, and Japan, with original interpretations by Chef Dmitry Zotov."—Anton Kovalkov

NHÀ

Recommended by
Georgy Troyan

Stoleshnikov Pereulok 6/3
Tverskoy
Moscow, 125009, Russia
+7 9850141848

Opening hours	Open 7 days
Reservation policy	No
Credit cards	Accepted but not AMEX or Diners
Price range	Budget
Style	Casual
Cuisine	Vietnamese
Recommended for	Late night

"This place has a lot of different pho that can bring you to life at the end of the working day. On the weekend they work till 6.00 a.m."—Georgy Troyan

U SALVATORE

Recommended by
Sergey Berezutskiy

Amotechnaya Ulitsa 13
Tverskoy
Moscow, 127473, Russia
+7 4956811326
www.usalvatore.ru

Opening hours	Open 7 days
Credit cards	Accepted but not AMEX or Diners
Price range	Budget
Style	Casual
Cuisine	Italian
Recommended for	Breakfast

"Simple Italian recipes in a cozy, nice place."
—Sergey Eroshenko

SAVVA

Recommended by
Ivan Berezutskiy,
Sergey Berezutskiy,
Sergey Eroshenko,
Taras Kiriyenko,
Anton Kovalkov,
Andrey Zhdanov

Metropol Hotel
Teatralny Pereulok 2
Tverskoy
Moscow, 109012, Russia
+7 4992701062
www.savvarest.ru

Opening hours	Open 7 days
Credit cards	Accepted but not Diners
Price range	Affordable
Style	Smart casual
Cuisine	Russian-European
Recommended for	Breakfast

"I very rarely have breakfast, so whenever I do I like to have it somewhere special. This is a really beautiful place, with great Russian food and always that kind of mood where you just have to have a shot of vodka for breakfast!"—Andrey Zhdanov

TORRO GRILL

Recommended by
Timur Abuzyarov,
Sergey Eroshenko,
Andrey Zhdanov

White Square Business Center
Lesnaya Ulitsa 5b
Tverskoy
Moscow, 125047, Russia
+7 4959210475
www.torrogrill.ru

Opening hours	Open 7 days
Credit cards	Accepted but not AMEX or Diners
Price range	Affordable
Style	Casual
Cuisine	Steakhouse
Recommended for	Late night

"It's all about meat—and it's right around the corner from my own restaurant. I like to go there after a shift with the lads, have a steak and beer and just chill."
— Andrey Zhdanov

TURANDOT

Recommended by
Anton Kovalkov

Tverskoy Bulvar 26/3
Tverskoy
Moscow, 125009, Russia
+7 4957390011
www.turandot-palace.ru

Opening hours	Open 7 days
Credit cards	Accepted but not Diners
Price range	Expensive
Style	Formal
Cuisine	Pan-Asian
Recommended for	High end

"This is one restaurant that's a must-see during a visit to Moscow."—Anton Kovalkov

VOGUE CAFÉ

Recommended by
Sergey Eroshenko

Kuznetsky Most Ulitsa 7/9
Tverskoy
Moscow, 107031, Russia
+7 4956231701
www.novikovgroup.ru

Opening hours	Open 7 days
Credit cards	Accepted but not Diners
Price range	Affordable
Style	Smart casual
Cuisine	European-Asian
Recommended for	Wish I'd opened

"For many years I've admired the restaurant Vogue
Café. The cuisine is very varied: pan-Asian, Russian,
European, seafood, and elegant desserts. This is a
restaurant where you can feel the touch of the chef,
which maintains quality and comes up with new dishes.
I really like this restaurant." —Sergey Eroshenko

WINE & CRAB

Recommended by
Anatoly Komm

Nikolskaya Ulitsa 19-21/1
Tverskoy
Moscow, 109012, Russia
+7 4956217329
www.winecrab.ru

Opening hours	Open 7 days
Credit cards	Accepted but not AMEX
Price range	Expensive
Style	Smart casual
Cuisine	Seafood
Recommended for	Wish Id opened

"Great concept based on crabs on the menu and the
extensive wine list to go with it."—Anatoly Komm

MARUKAME

Recommended by
Timur Abuzyarov

Pyatnizkaya Ulitsa 29
Zamoskvorechye
Moscow, 115035, Russia
+7 9636018270
www.marukame.ru

Opening hours	Open 7 days
Reservation policy	No
Credit cards	Not accepted
Price range	Budget
Style	Casual
Cuisine	Japanese
Recommended for	Bargain

"Cheap prices and good quality."—Timur Abuzyarov

OBLOMOV

Recommended by
Sergey Eroshenko

1-y Monetchikovskiy Pereulok 5
Zamoskvorechye
Moscow, 115054, Russia
+7 4958568578
www.restoblomov.ru

Opening hours	Open 7 days
Credit cards	Accepted but not Diners
Price range	Affordable
Style	Smart casual
Cuisine	Russian
Recommended for	Late night

"Good quality, comfortable, very good service, and
most importantly, many restaurants have a reduced
menu at night but, at Oblomov, the night menu is the
same as the day."—Sergey Eroshenko

BIG WINE FREAKS

Recommended by
Dmitriy Blinov

Instrumentalnaya Ulitsa 3
St Petersburg, 197022, Russia
+7 9219386063

Opening hours	Closed Monday and Sunday
Credit cards	Accepted but not AMEX
Price range	Affordable
Style	Casual
Cuisine	Bar
Recommended for	Late night

"The best selection of wines in town, great
atmosphere, music, and one of the best cuisines
in town."—Dmitriy Blinov

KOKOKO

Recommended by
Dmitriy Blinov, Evgeny Vikentev

Voznesensky Prospekt 6
St Petersburg, 198000, Russia
+7 8124182060
www.kokoko.spb.ru

Opening hours	Open 7 days
Credit cards	Accepted
Price range	Affordable
Style	Smart casual
Cuisine	Modern Russian
Recommended for	Breakfast

"Modern Russian breakfasts, exciting food pairings
with spectacular plating."—Evgeny Vikentev

"There is no doubt that Sardunya is the best fish restaurant for me."
MUSTAFA CIHAN KIPÇAK P719

"A HIGHLIGHT IS THE PASTA WITH FRESH GREEK RAZOR CLAMS. THE FISH ON THE GRILL IS ALSO AMAZING."
NIKOS ROUSSOS P719

"For the most wonderful seafood mezzes and foraged greens."
ŞEMSA DENIZSEL P719

GREECE & TURKEY

"Traditionally local place— spectacular experience."
MUSTAFA CIHAN KIPÇAK P719

"THE FOOD IS SIMPLE BUT EXCELLENT AND THE AMBIENCE IS UNLIKE ANYTHING YOU'LL EXPERIENCE ELSEWHERE."
SEAN MCCONNELL P718

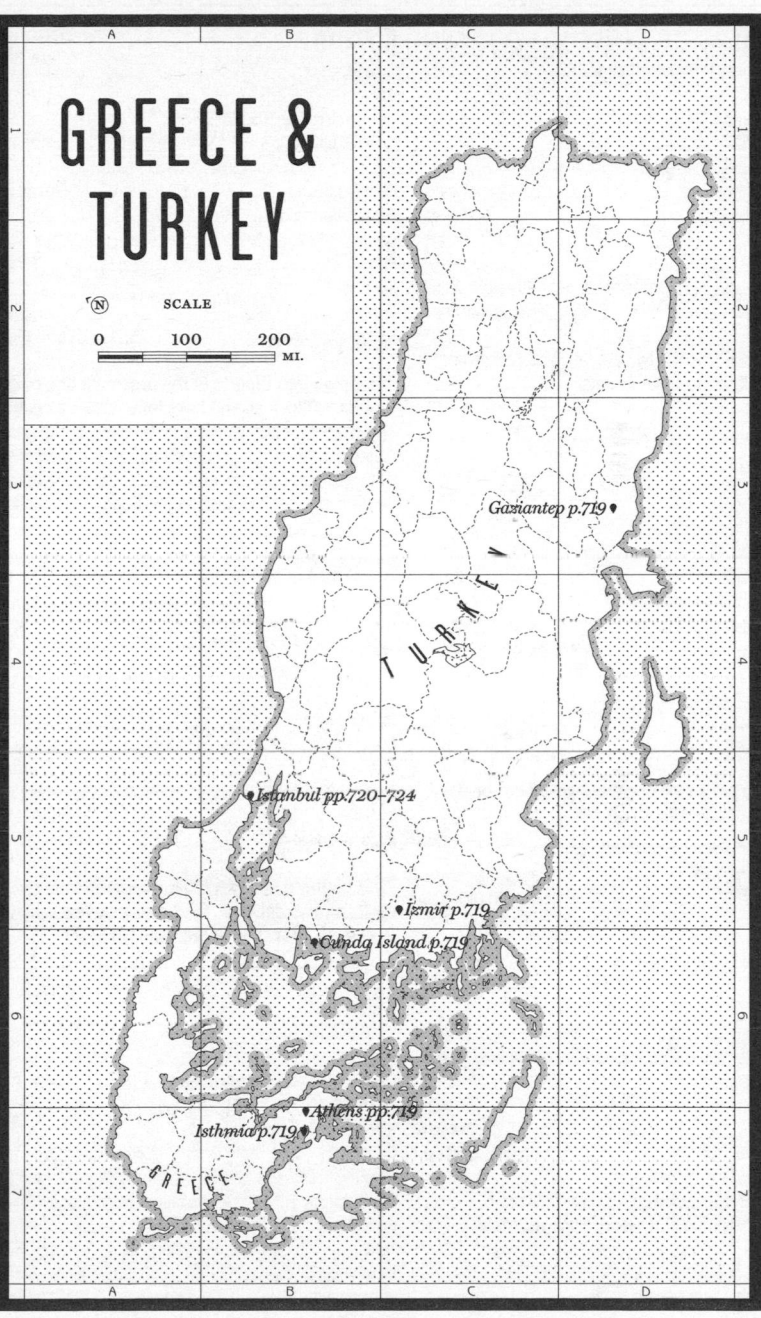

GREECE & TURKEY

SCALE

0   100   200
MI.

Gaziantep p.719 ♦

T U R K E Y

♦ Istanbul pp.720-724

♦ Izmir p.719

♦ Cunda Island p.719

♦ Athens pp.719

Isthmia p.719 ♦

G R E E C E

BARBOUNAKI

Recommended by
George Calombaris

Leoforos Dimarchou Aggelou Metaxa 48
Athens
Central Greece 166 74, Greece
+30 2109680651

Opening hours	Open 7 days
Credit cards	Accepted
Price range	Affordable
Style	Casual
Cuisine	Mediterranean-Greek Seafood
Recommended for	Regular neighborhood

"It's my all-time favorite traditional, local restaurant, nearby my holiday home in Athens."
—George Calombaris

BOURNOVALIA

Recommended by
Georgianna Hiliadaki,
Nikos Roussos

Agias Sofias 93
Athens
Central Greece 171 23, Greece
+30 2109311125

Opening hours	Closed Monday
Credit cards	Accepted but not AMEX
Price range	Affordable
Style	Casual
Cuisine	Greek-Turkish
Recommended for	Late night

"Definitely try the kebab and the Black Angus beef chunks on a stick."—Nikos Roussos

DIFFERENT BEAST

Recommended by
Georgianna Hiliadaki,
Nikos Roussos

Kassaveti 19
Athens
Central Greece 145 62, Greece
+30 2167004556

Opening hours	Closed Monday
Credit cards	Accepted but not AMEX
Price range	Budget
Style	Casual
Cuisine	Café-Brunch
Recommended for	Breakfast

"Relaxed and laid-back atmosphere, nice staff, nice crowd, lovely food."—Georgianna Hiliadaki

DIPORTO

Recommended by
Sean McConnell

Sokratous 9
Athens
Central Greece 105 52, Greece
+30 2103211463

Opening hours	Closed Sunday
Reservation policy	No
Credit cards	Not accepted
Price range	Affordable
Style	Casual
Cuisine	Greek
Recommended for	Worth the travel

"Stepping into Diporto in the basement of a building that looks like it should have fallen down a century ago is an experience. It's a lo-fi tavern in the heart of Athens right by the produce market. The food is simple but excellent and the ambience is unlike anything you'll experience elsewhere."—Sean McConnell

KRITIKOS

Recommended by
Georgianna Hiliadaki,
Nikos Roussos

Eolou 49
Athens
Central Greece 153 51, Greece
+30 2106659061

Opening hours	Open 7 days
Credit cards	Accepted
Price range	Affordable
Style	Casual
Cuisine	Greek-Steakhouse
Recommended for	Regular neighborhood

"It is mainly a meat tavern in an unpretentious environment, delicious food, and excellent quality. Best lamb chops!"—Georgianna Hiliadaki

SUSHIMOU

Recommended by
Georgianna Hiliadaki

Skoufou 6
Athens
Central Greece 105 57, Greece
+30 2114078457
www.sushimou.gr

Opening hours	Closed Saturday and Sunday
Credit cards	Accepted but not AMEX or Diners
Price range	Affordable
Style	Casual
Cuisine	Japanese
Recommended for	Worth the travel

"Chef Antonis is a sushi master indeed, preparing everything in front of you."—Georgianna Hiliadaki

TO XEIROPOIITO

Ethnikis Antistaseos 26
Athens
Central Greece 152 35, Greece
+30 2106848062

Opening hours	Open 7 days
Credit cards	Accepted
Price range	Affordable
Style	Casual
Cuisine	Greek
Recommended for	Bargain

"Here you can try good quality souvlaki without pitta, and amazing lamb kebabs."—Georgianna Hiliadaki

KAVOS 1964

Kavos
Isthmia
Corinthia 201 00, Greece
+30 2741037906
www.kavos1964.gr

Opening hours	Open 7 days
Credit cards	Accepted
Price range	Affordable
Style	Casual
Cuisine	Greek
Recommended for	Local favorite

"A highlight is the pasta with fresh Greek razor clams. The fish on the grill is also amazing."—Nikos Roussos

BAY NIHAT LALE RESTORAN

Mithatpasa Mahallesi
Mevlana Caddesi
Cunda Island
Balıkesir 10405, Turkey
+90 2663271063
www.baynihat.com.tr

Opening hours	Open 7 days
Credit cards	Accepted but not AMEX
Price range	Affordable
Style	Smart casual
Cuisine	Turkish-Seafood
Recommended for	Worth the travel

"For the most wonderful seafood mezzes and foraged greens."—Şemsa Denizsel

METANET LOKANTASI

Kozluca Caddesi 11
Sahinbey
Gaziantep 27240, Turkey
+90 3422314666

Opening hours	Open 7 days
Reservation policy	No
Credit cards	Not accepted
Price range	Budget
Style	Casual
Cuisine	Turkish
Recommended for	Worth the travel

"They make the most wonderful *beyran*, a local breakfast staple, which is a spicy rice and lamb soup with loads of garlic."—Şemsa Denizsel

ISTANBUL: SEE PAGES 720-724

SÖĞÜŞCÜM

Ilıca Mahallesi 5074
Çesme
İzmir 35930, Turkey
+90 2327232309

Opening hours	Open 7 days
Credit cards	Not accepted
Price range	Affordable
Style	Casual
Cuisine	Turkish
Recommended for	Late night

"A spectacular experience." —Mustafa Cihan Kıpçak

SARDUNYA RESTAURANT

Selîmiye Mahallesi
Marmaris
Mugla 34427, Turkey
+90 2122491092
www.sardunya.info

Opening hours	Open 7 days
Credit cards	Accepted but not AMEX or Diners
Price range	Affordable
Style	Casual
Cuisine	Turkish
Recommended for	Worth the travel

"Sardunya uses fresh fish from the Aegean sea, which is in front of the restaurant, and they get all their ingredients from Selimiye Village. Because of this it's ecological and organic."—Mustafa Cihan Kıpçak

"YOU CAN HAVE BREAKFAST IN THE OLD OTTOMAN TERRITORY OF "EMIRGAN" AND WATCH THE SHIPS WHILE SITTING UNDER THE TREES."

MUSTAFA CIHAN KIPÇAK P722

"Delicious pastries to take away."

MUSTAFA CIHAN KIPÇAK P724

ISTANBUL

"I like Mikla's style, which is a modern twist with local ingredients. Also, they have a rooftop lounge for cocktails with the best Istanbul views."

MUSTAFA CIHAN KIPÇAK P722

"KILLER LOCATION BY THE BOSPHORUS AND COOL VIBES..."

MEHMET GÜRS P722

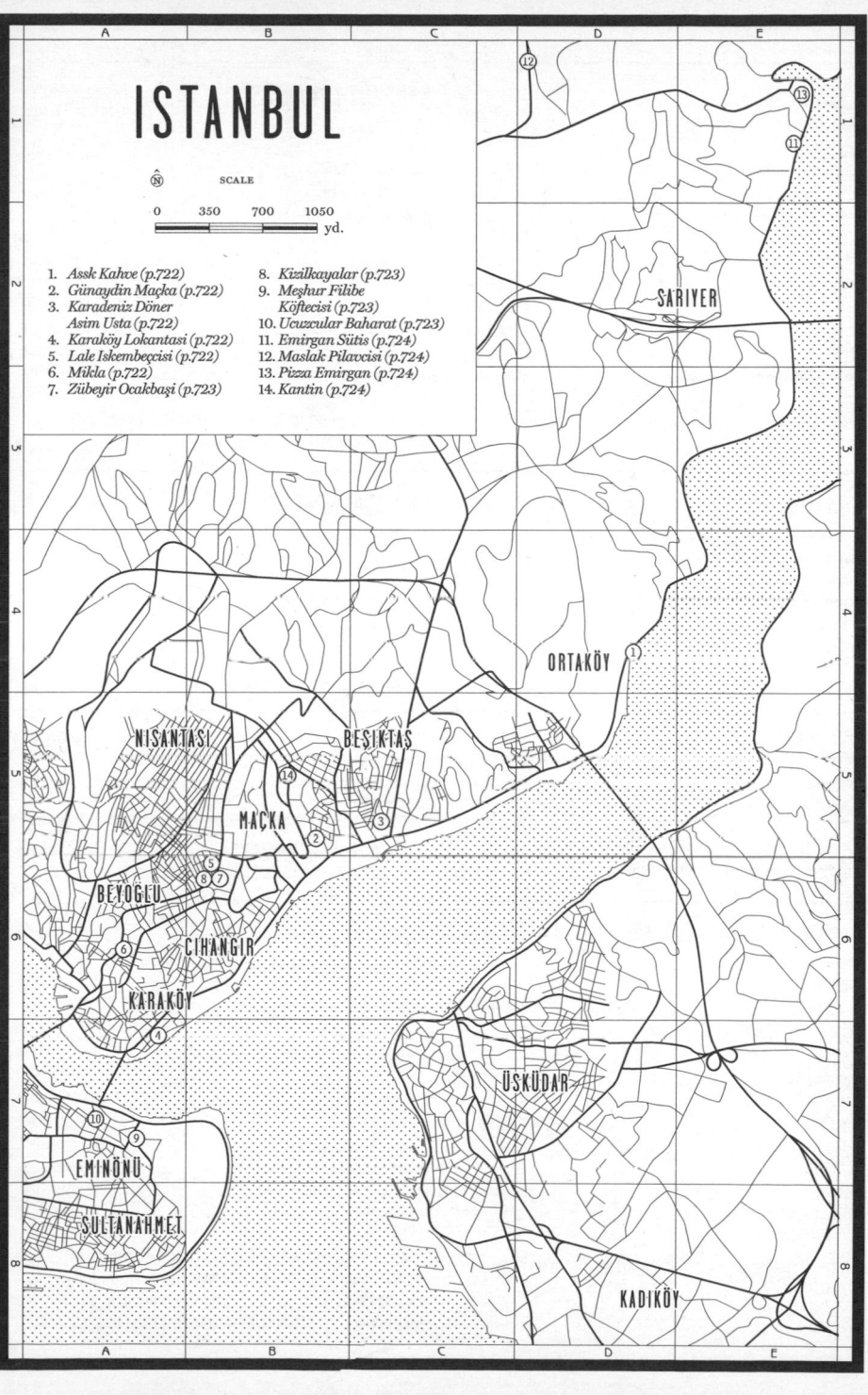

ISTANBUL

$\hat{N}$

SCALE

0   350   700   1050
yd.

SARIYER

ORTAKÖY

NIŞANTAŞI

BEŞIKTAŞ

MAÇKA

BEYOĞLU

CIHANGIR

KARAKÖY

ÜSKÜDAR

EMINÖNÜ

SULTANAHMET

KADIKÖY

AŞŞK KAHVE

Recommended by
Mehmet Gürs

Muallim Naci Caddesi 64
Beşiktaş
Istanbul 34330
+90 2122654734
www.asskkahve.com

Opening hours	Open 7 days
Credit cards	Accepted
Price range	Affordable
Style	Casual
Cuisine	International
Recommended for	Breakfast

"Killer location by the Bosphorus and cool vibes."
— Mehmet Gürs

GÜNAYDIN MAÇKA

Recommended by
Mustafa Cihan Kıpçak

Swissotel The Bosphorus
Bayıldım Caddesi 2 Maçka
Beşiktaş
Istanbul 34357
+90 122581203
www.gunaydinet.com

Opening hours	Open 7 days
Credit cards	Accepted
Price range	Expensive
Style	Smart casual
Cuisine	Turkish Kebab
Recommended for	Regular neighborhood

"Kind service and good food—always the same
quality."—Mustafa Cihan Kıpçak

KARADENIZ DÖNER ASIM USTA

Recommended by
Mustafa Cihan Kıpçak

Mumcu Bakkal Sokak 6
Sinanpaşa Mahallesi
Besiktas
Istanbul 34353

Opening hours	Open 7 days
Reservation policy	No
Credit cards	Not accepted
Price range	Budget
Style	Casual
Cuisine	Turkish
Recommended for	Bargain

"It is cheap and good."—Mustafa Cihan Kıpçak

KARAKÖY LOKANTASI

Recommended by
Mustafa Cihan Kıpçak

Kemankeş Caddesi 37a
Beyoğlu
Istanbul 34425
+90 2122924455
www.karakoylokantasi.com

Opening hours	Open 7 days
Credit cards	Accepted
Price range	Affordable
Style	Smart casual
Cuisine	Turkish
Recommended for	Local favorite

"Every time I go to Karaköy Lokantası I eat fresh
food."—Mustafa Cihan Kıpçak

LALE İŞKEMBEÇCISI

Recommended by
Şemsa Denizsel

Tarlabaşı Bulvarı 13
Beyoğlu
Istanbul 34437
+90 2122526969
www.laleiskembecisi.com.tr

Opening hours	Open 7 days
Reservation policy	No
Credit cards	Accepted but not AMEX
Price range	Budget
Style	Casual
Cuisine	Turkish
Recommended for	Late night

"Serves very garlicky tripe soup."—Şemsa Denizsel

MIKLA

Recommended by
Mustafa Cihan Kıpçak,
Şemsa Denizsel

The Marmara Pera Hotel
Meşrutiyet Caddesi 15
Beyoğlu
Istanbul 34430
+90 2122935656
www.miklarestaurant.com

Opening hours	Closed Sunday
Credit cards	Accepted
Price range	Expensive
Style	Smart casual
Cuisine	Modern Anatolian
Recommended for	High end

"I like Mikla's style, which is a modern twist with
local ingredients. Also, they have a rooftop lounge
for cocktails with the best Istanbul views. It is
expensive but worth it."—Mustafa Cihan Kıpçak

ZÜBEYIR OCAKBAŞI

Şehit Muhtar Mahallesi Bekar Sokak 28
Beyoğlu
Istanbul 34435
+90 2122933951
www.zubeyirocakbasi.com.tr

Recommended by
Mehmet Gürs

Opening hours	Open 7 days
Credit cards	Accepted but not AMEX
Price range	Affordable
Style	Casual
Cuisine	Kebab
Recommended for	Regular neighborhood

"Straightforward, good *ocakbasi*."—Mehmet Gürs

"Cosy" is a word often used to describe Zübeyir—sometimes affectionately, sometimes less so. It's true they do like to pack 'em in to this Beyoğlu joint—three floors of boisterous dining space hung with charcoal smoke—especially the sought-after seats surrounding the *ocakbaşı* (charcoal grill) on the ground floor. But it's popular for a very good reason—the food is great, from delicately balanced *adana* (minced lamb) to their signature *gavurdag* salad containing finely diced herbs and tomatoes in a pomegranate molasses dressing. Yes, it's busy, but you'll be sharing elbow space with journalists, writers, actors, and various other sections of bohemian Istanbul society—everyone's in the same boat.

KIZILKAYALAR

Siraselviler Caddesi 2/C
Cihangir
Istanbul 34433
+90 2164111177
www.kizilkayalar.com.tr

Recommended by
Şemsa Denizsel

Opening hours	Open 7 days
Reservation policy	No
Credit cards	Not accepted
Price range	Budget
Style	Casual
Cuisine	Fast Food
Recommended for	Late night

**""Wet burgers that are very garlicky."
—Şemsa Denizsel**

Kizilkayalar first managed to distinguish itself from Istanbul's vast sea of fast food stands in the late 1970s, when some bright spark, noting that the doner market was somewhat flooded, came up with the concept of the *Islak* burger (wet burger).

Their sweetly pungent smell first hits you in the long line (queue) outside. The burgers are doused in an oily tomato sauce, containing relationship-ending quantities of garlic, then steamed for several hours inside their sticky bun to produce the world's slipperiest slider. Order two right from the start, as putting your hand back into your pocket after your first is a very messy business.

MEŞHUR FILIBE KÖFTECISI

Paşa, No3 34112, Fatih Sultan Caddesi,
34425 Beyoğlu
Istanbul 34110
+90 2125193976
www.meshurfilibekoftecisi.com

Recommended by
Şemsa Denizsel

Opening hours	Closed Sunday
Reservation policy	No
Credit cards	Not accepted
Price range	Budget
Style	Casual
Cuisine	Turkish
Recommended for	Bargain

"Delicious, cheap, and satisfying. It serves simply grilled meatballs with a bean salad."—Şemsa Denizsel

UCUZCULAR BAHARAT

Stall 51, Spice Bazaar
Rüstem Paşa Mahallesi
Fatih
Istanbul 34330
+90 2125282895
www.ucuzcular.com.tr

Recommended by
George Calombaris

Opening hours	Open 7 days
Reservation policy	No
Credit cards	Not accepted
Price range	Budget
Style	Casual
Cuisine	Bazaar
Recommended for	Wish I'd opened

"The best spice shop in the world! In one of the spice capitals of the world. You go in there to buy the most incredible cinnamon you'll ever taste, and walk out pretty much buying the entire shop because everything is delicious."—George Calombaris

EMIRGAN SÜTIŞ

Sakıp Sabancı Caddesi 46
Sarıyer
Istanbul 34467
+90 2123235030
www.sutis.com.tr

Opening hours	Open 7 days
Credit cards	Accepted
Price range	Affordable
Style	Casual
Cuisine	Patisserie
Recommended for	Breakfast

"I think most importantly they are using high-quality products. It may not be boutique but it is delicious and the service is impressive. The location is superb as it is so close to the Bosphorus—you can have breakfast in the old Ottoman territory of 'Emirgan' and watch the ships while sitting under the trees."
—Mustafa Cihan Kıpçak

MASLAK PILAVCISI

Maslak
Aos 53. Sokak
Sarıyer
Istanbul 34398
+90 2123460803

Opening hours	Open 7 days
Reservation policy	No
Credit cards	Not accepted
Price range	Budget
Style	Casual
Cuisine	Turkish
Recommended for	Bargain

"Rice, chicken, and chickpeas with an *ayran* (yogurt drink) for €1.50 ($2; £1). Can't beat it."
—Mehmet Gürs

PIZZA EMIRGAN

Sakıp Sabancı Caddesi 14
Sarıyer
Istanbul 34467
+90 2122778887

Opening hours	Open 7 days
Credit cards	Accepted
Price range	Affordable
Style	Casual
Cuisine	Pizza
Recommended for	Late night

KANTIN

Akkavak Sokak 30
Şişli
Istanbul 34365
+90 2122192807
www.kantin.biz

Opening hours	Closed Sunday
Credit cards	Accepted
Price range	Affordable
Style	Casual
Cuisine	Modern Turkish
Recommended for	Local favorite

"Kantin makes fresh foods daily, based on seasonal menus. They have a simple and smart manner in the restaurant and you can find a variety of organic products. Downstairs they have delicious pastries to take away."—Mustafa Cihan Kıpçak

Semsa Denizsel is often referred to as the "Turkish Alice Waters", her ingredient-led, farm-to-table food philosophy bearing much in common with the famous Californians. Kantin, as its name suggests, is an upmarket local canteen for professionals in the smart Nişantaşi district. Downstairs is a deli with a handsome garden; upstairs is a dining room with crisp linen and cut flowers on the tables. Dishes, chalked on the blackboard, might include tabbouleh with modern accents such as candied almonds and oat-crusted chicken schnitzel, or perhaps a bonito shish kebab.

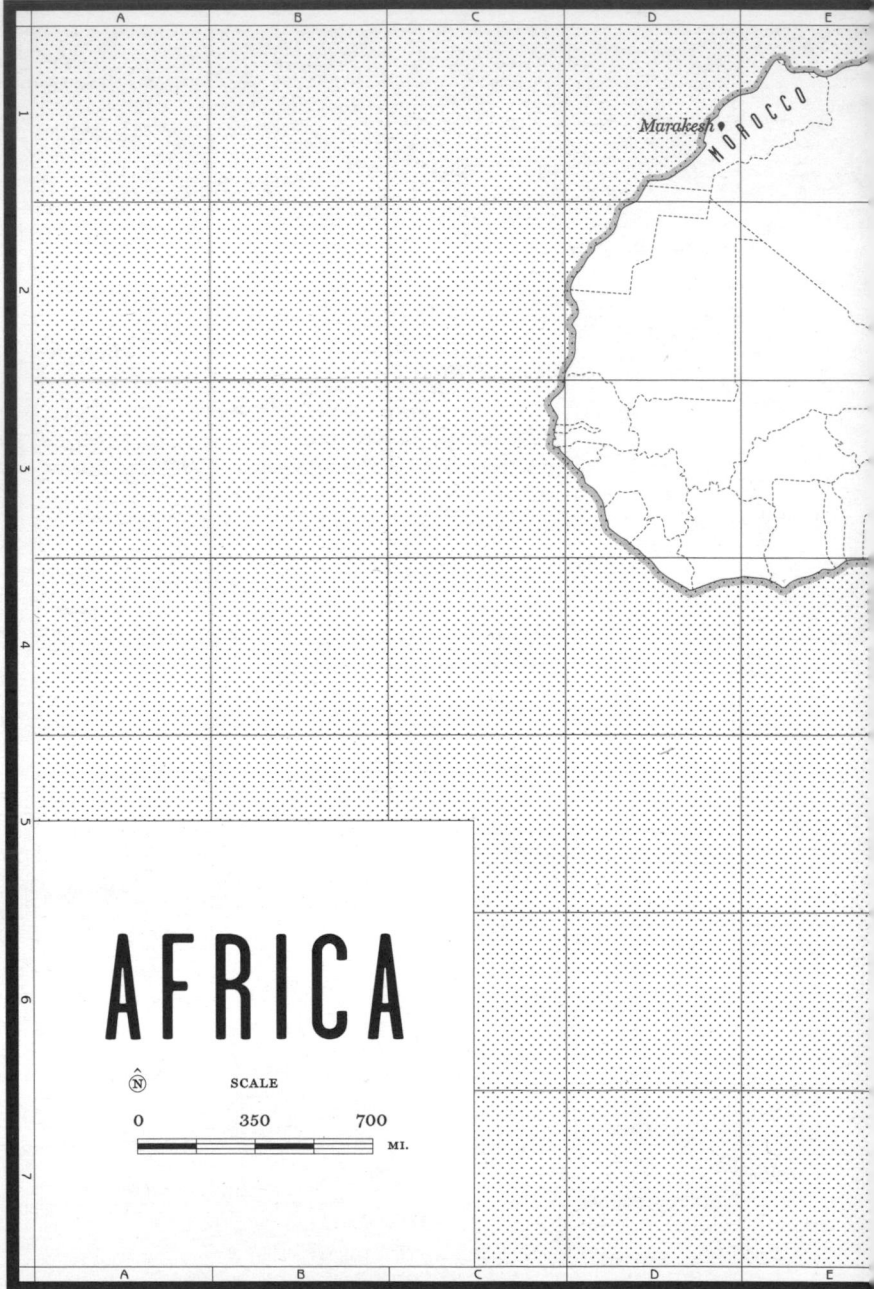

Marakesh

MOROCCO

AFRICA

N

SCALE

0   350   700

MI.

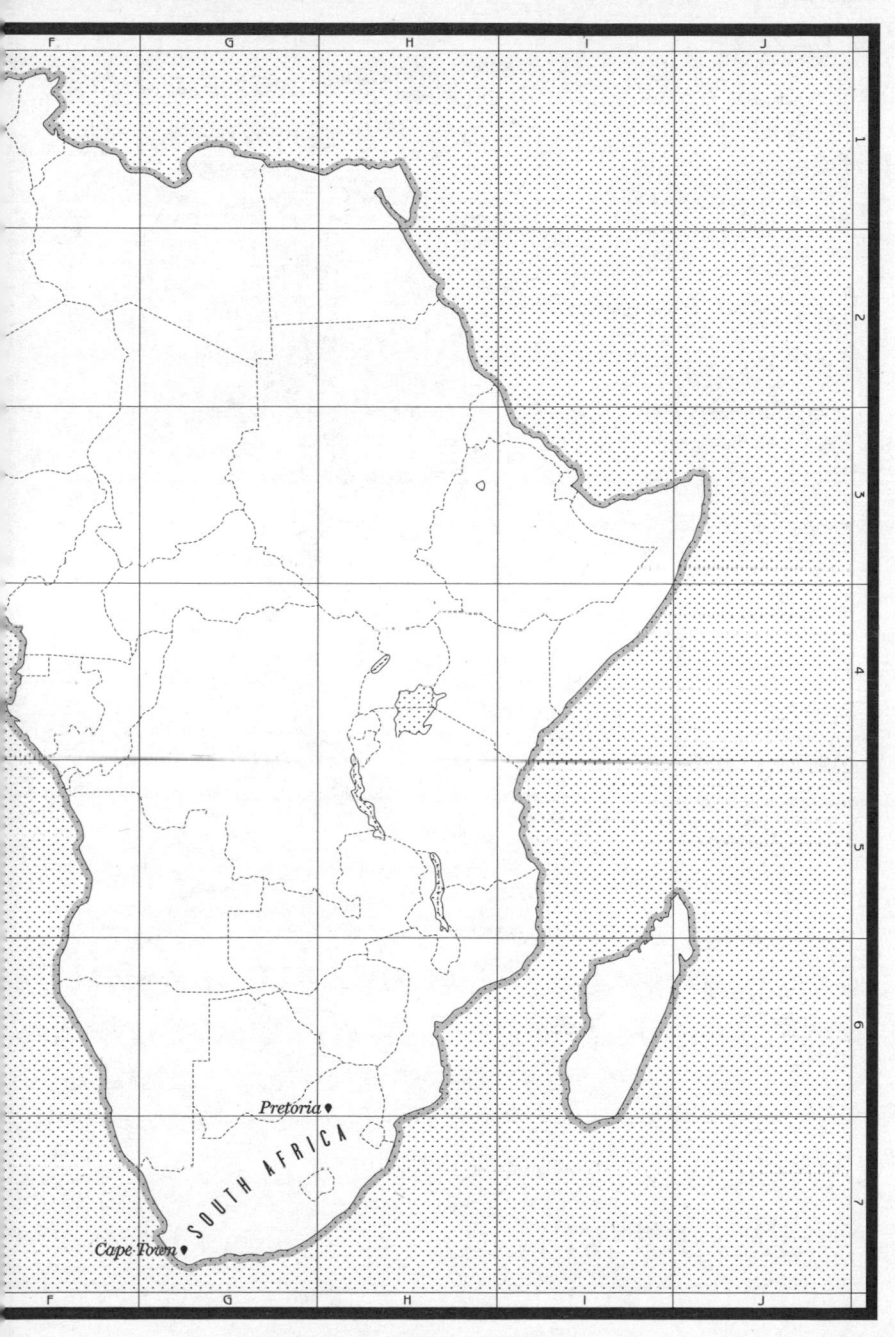

"It's bright and breezy with a friendly buzz."
CHANTEL DARTNELL P730

"An awesome restaurant with a very eclectic menu."
LUKE DALE-ROBERTS P731

"ALWAYS DELIVERS A CONSISTENTLY HIGH LEVEL OF CUISINE."
LUKE DALE-ROBERTS P734

SOUTH AFRICA & MOROCCO

"Continually pushing the boundaries of South African–Asian cooking."
CHRISTIAN DOMSCHITZ P734

"AWESOME, AUTHENTIC DIM SUM SERVED IN A CASUAL, RELAXED ENVIRONMENT."
PETER TEMPELHOFF P731

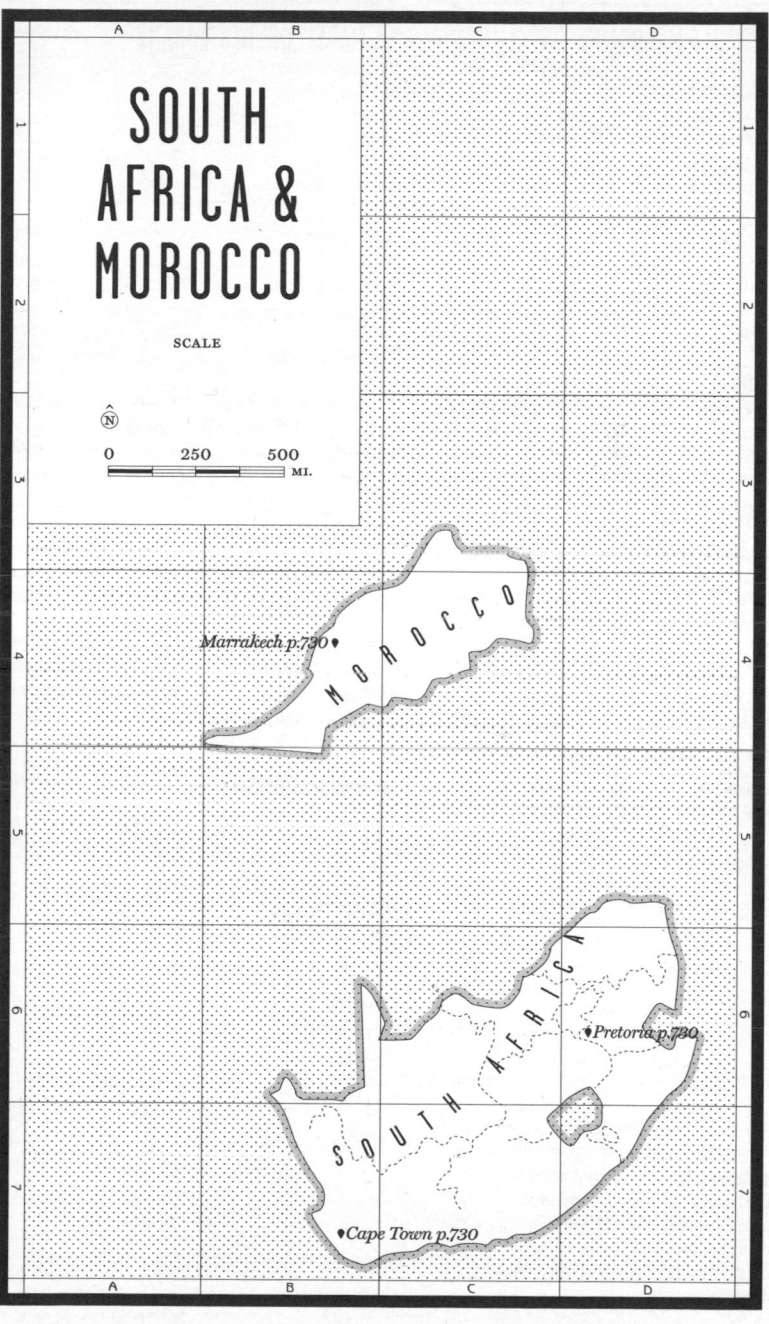

SOUTH AFRICA & MOROCCO

SCALE

0   250   500
MI.

MOROCCO

Marrakech p.730 ♦

SOUTH AFRICA

♦ Pretoria p.730

♦ Cape Town p.730

LA GRANDE TABLE MAROCAINE

Recommended by
Guillaume Galliot

Arsat Gestion
Rue Abou Abbas el Sebti
Marrakech 40 000, Morocco
+212 0529808080
www.royalmansour.com

Opening hours	Open 7 days
Credit cards	Accepted
Price range	Expensive
Style	Casual
Cuisine	Moroccan
Recommended for	Worth the travel

Situated a leisurely ten-minute walk away from the hubbub of the Jemaa el-Fnaa souk, La Grande Table Marocaine represents the very finest in Moroccan gastronomy. A part of triple Michelin-starred chef Yannick Alléno's global stable, this hotel restaurant combines traditional, locally sourced Moroccan flavors with Alléno's customary flair. The garlic and cumin-crusted Méchoui lamb (slow-cooked for thirty-six hours) is a must, as is saving enough room for the exquisite dessert trolley, which offers delicately crafted makrouts (North African pastries). The restaurant is far enough away from the alcohol-free Medina to enjoy a spicy Bloody Mary in its opulent, lantern-lit surroundings.

PURE CAFÉ

Recommended by
Chantel Dartnall

137 Thompson Street
Colbyn
Pretoria
Gauteng 0121, South Africa
+27 0123421443
www.purecafe.co.za

Opening hours	Closed Sunday
Credit cards	Accepted
Price range	Budget
Style	Casual
Cuisine	Café
Recommended for	Breakfast

"Regretfully I don't often have the opportunity to go out for breakfast, but if I do venture into town I enjoy going to Pure Café. It's bright and breezy with a friendly buzz and they offer a wonderful selection of breakfast options. My favorite is the Omega Kick-Start: a slice of rye toast and fluffy scrambled eggs with smoked salmon, lemon-zest cream cheese, and capers."—Chantel Dartnall

LA MADELEINE RESTAURANT

Recommended by
Chantel Dartnall

122 Priory Road
Lynnwood Ridge
Pretoria
Gauteng 0040, South Africa
+27 0123613667
www.lamadeleine.co.za

Opening hours	Closed Monday
Credit cards	Accepted
Price range	Affordable
Style	Smart casual
Cuisine	French-Belgian
Recommended for	Regular neighborhood

"This was the first restaurant where I saw a 'real' Chef at the age of six, when my parents first took me to La Madeleine. I was completely mesmerized by the presence of Chef Danielle as he explained the menu at our table. In those years La Madeleine was situated in Sunnyside, Pretoria, where Chef Danielle Leusch and his wife Karine cooked their beautiful classic French and Belgian dishes. The restaurant relocated to Lynnwood in 1999 where they continued their tradition. Now, three decades after the restaurant first opened, the Leuche's daughter Anne has taken over from her mother and is fully in charge of the kitchen where she continues the tradition laid down by her parents."—Chantel Dartnall

ASH RESTAURANT

Recommended by
Luke Dale-Roberts

81 Church Street
City Center
Cape Town
Western Cape 8000, South Africa
+27 0214247204
www.ashrestaurant.co.za

Opening hours	Closed Sunday
Credit cards	Accepted but not AMEX or Diners
Price range	Affordable
Style	Casual
Cuisine	Charcoal Grill
Recommended for	Local favorite

CHEFS WAREHOUSE & CANTEEN

Recommended by
Luke Dale-Roberts,
Peter Tempelhoff

92 Bree Street
City Center
Cape Town
Western Cape 8001, South Africa
+27 0214220128
www.chefswarehouse.co.za

Opening hours................................Closed Sunday
Reservation policy...No
Credit cards.......................Accepted but not AMEX or Diners
Price range...Affordable
Style...Casual
Cuisine.................................International small plates
Recommended for...............................Local favorite

"Chefs Warehouse & Canteen at Beau Constantia is an awesome restaurant. It has a very eclectic menu."—Peter Tempelhoff

Confidently located on Cape Town's hippest foodie strip, Bree Street, this no-frills fine-dining restaurant serves South African-style (read: generously portioned) seasonal tapas. Diners are presented with a radically different menu every day, designed by the team of chefs the previous night. Tapas for two people over three courses costs R650 ($49; £38) and includes an eclectic range of seafood, vegetarian, meat, and poultry options. A strict no-reservation policy at this firm local favorite means you may have to arrive early and prepare for a wait—but you won't be disappointed. If you do prefer to book ahead though, you could try the group's sister restaurant at Beau Constantia.

LA TÊTE

Recommended by
Luke Dale-Roberts

17 Bree Street
City Center
Cape Town
Western Cape 8001, South Africa
+27 0214181299
www.latete.co.za

Opening hours................................Closed Monday and Sunday
Credit cards.......................Accepted but not AMEX
Price range...Affordable
Style...Smart casual
Cuisine...Modern British
Recommended for...............................Wish I'd opened

"Good, solid, hearty food."—Luke Dale-Roberts

SOUTH CHINA DIM SUM BAR

Recommended by
Peter Tempelhoff

289 Long Street
City Center
Cape Town
Western Cape 8000, South Africa
+27 0788463656

Opening hours................................Closed Monday and Sunday
Credit cards.......................Accepted but not AMEX
Price range...Budget
Style...Casual
Cuisine...Asian
Recommended for...............................Bargain

"Awesome, authentic dim sum served in a casual, relaxed environment."—Peter Tempelhoff

THE SHORTMARKET CLUB

Recommended by
Luke Dale-Roberts

88 Shortmarket Street
City Center
Cape Town
Western Cape 8000, South Africa
+27 0214472874
www.theshortmarketclub.co.za

Opening hours................................Closed Sunday
Credit cards.......................................Accepted
Price range...Expensive
Style...Casual
Cuisine...Modern South African
Recommended for...............................Breakfast

**"Upmarket grand affair breakfast."
—Luke Dale-Roberts**

THE SNEAKY SAUSAGE

1st Floor, 84 Shortmarket Street
City Center
Cape Town
Western Cape 8000, South Africa
+27 0214261759

Opening hours	Closed Monday and Sunday
Reservation policy	No
Credit cards	Accepted but not AMEX
Price range	Budget
Style	Casual
Cuisine	Sausages
Recommended for	Late night

"A new late-night eatery."—Luke Dale-Roberts

Perfect for late-night grub, this German beer-hall-inspired eatery serves a robust selection of pork sausages, seasonal salads, pretzels, and beer. From the team behind Shortmarket Street's other trendy hotspots, The House of Machines and Outrage of Modesty, The Sneaky Sausage presents simple food, with high-quality ingredients, to be shared among friends. The long tables, tongue-in-cheek sense of humor and beer by the jug make for a riotous communal dining experience. You can't go wrong with their flagship currywurst and an ice cold weissbier (wheat beer), but the real treats here are the deep-fried sides: risotto balls, sweet potato fries and jalapeño wontons.

THE AVENUE RESTAURANT & GRILL

43 2nd Avenue
Harfield Village
Claremont
Cape Town
Western Cape 7708, South Africa
+27 0216710623
www.theavenuerestaurant.co.za

Opening hours	Closed Sunday
Credit cards	Accepted
Price range	Affordable
Style	Casual
Cuisine	South African
Recommended for	Bargain

"Great steaks and local food at a cheap price. Good for a bite before dinner service."—Luke Dale-Roberts

BORRUSO'S

Corner of Main Road & Main Avenue
Kenilworth
Claremont
Cape Town
Western Cape 7800, South Africa
+ 27 0217615822

Opening hours	Open 7 days
Reservation policy	No
Credit cards	Accepted but not AMEX
Price range	Budget
Style	Casual
Cuisine	Pizza
Recommended for	Regular neighborhood

"Great pizza and Calzone and kid-friendly."
—Peter Tempelhoff

A TAVOLA

Library Square
Wilderness Road
Claremont
Cape Town
Western Cape 7735, South Africa
+27 0216711763
www.atavola.co.za

Opening hours	Closed Sunday
Credit cards	Accepted
Price range	Affordable
Style	Smart casual
Cuisine	Italian
Recommended for	Regular neighborhood

"Good, traditional Italian cuisine."
—Luke Dale-Roberts

BEAU CONSTANTIA

ERF1026 Constantia Main Road
Glen Alpine
Constantia
Cape Town
Western Cape 7806, South Africa
+27 0217948632
www.beauconstantia.com

Opening hours	Closed Monday
Credit cards	Accepted but not AMEX
Price range	Affordable
Style	Casual
Cuisine	South African small plates
Recommended for	Worth the travel

"Best upcoming restaurant—Chef Ivor Jones is one to watch."—Luke Dale-Roberts

FOXCROFT

Shop 8/9
High Constantia Center
Constantia
Cape Town
Western Cape 7806, South Africa
+27 0212023304
www.foxcroft.co.za

Opening hours	Open 7 days
Credit cards	Accepted but not AMEX or Diners
Price range	Affordable
Style	Smart casual
Cuisine	French
Recommended for	Regular neighborhood

JONKERSHUIS RESTAURANT

Groot Constantia Estate
Groot Constantia Road
Constantia
Cape Town
Western Cape 7806, South Africa
+27 0217946255
www.grootconstantia.co.za

Opening hours	Open 7 days
Credit cards	Accepted
Price range	Affordable
Style	Casual
Cuisine	South African
Recommended for	Breakfast

THE CONSERVATORY

93 Brommersvlei Road
Constantia Heights
Constantia
Cape Town
Western Cape 7806, South Africa
+27 0217942137
www.collectionmcgrath.com

Opening hours	Open 7 days
Credit cards	Accepted
Price range	Affordable
Style	Smart casual
Cuisine	European
Recommended for	Breakfast

"Great buffet and the hot breakfast is pretty well executed."—Peter Tempelhoff

This stylish, glass-fronted restaurant sits atop a hillside with outstanding panoramic views of the Beau Constantia wine farm. Renowned for its award-winning wines, you'd be more than happy enjoying the spectacular scenery with a world-class charcuterie board in the tasting room—but you'd be missing out on the main restaurant. It serves locally sourced South African tapas, like flash-cured blesbok, springbok-liver parfait, and eland marrow, and the menu runs along a similar format to that of its stablemate, Chefs Warehouse & Canteen, where eight tapas dishes between two are served as a set menu. Unlike the other restaurants in the group though, you can book ahead here. A taxi to and from the restaurant is advised, especially if you want to make full use of the exemplary wine selection.

HALLELUJAH

11D Kloof Nek Road
Gardens
Cape Town
Western Cape 8001, South Africa
+27 0798392505
www.hallelujahhallelujah.co.za

Opening hours	Closed Sunday to Tuesday
Reservation policy	No
Credit cards	Accepted but not AMEX
Price range	Affordable
Style	Casual
Cuisine	Asian small plates
Recommended for	Regular neighborhood

"A great place to enjoy Asian small plates."
—Peter Tempelhoff

THE RESTAURANT AT WATERKLOOF

Recommended by
Chantel Dartnall

Sir Lowry's Pass Village Road
Somerset West
Cape Town
Western Cape 7129, South Africa
+27 0218581491
www.waterkloofwines.co.za

Opening hours..Variable
Credit cards..Accepted
Price range..Affordable
Style...Smart casual
Cuisine.................................Modern International
Recommended for.............................Local favorite

"When I have time to travel down to the Cape,
I rarely miss the oportunity to enjoy a meal
at The Restaurant at Waterkloof. Chef Gregory
Czarnecki has an exeptional talent for transforming
the most humble and honest of seasonal ingredients
into beautifully elegant creations, bursting with
flavor."—Chantel Dartnall

NOBU

Recommended by
Luke Dale-Roberts,
Peter Tempelhoff

One&Only Cape Town
Dock Road
V & A Waterfront
Cape Town
Western Cape 8001, South Africa
+27 0214314511
www.noburestaurants.com

Opening hours...Open 7 days
Credit cards..Accepted
Price range..Expensive
Style...Smart casual
Cuisine.................................Modern Japanese
Recommended for..................................High end

"Nobu always delivers a consistently high level
of cuisine."—Luke Dale-Roberts

WILLOUGHBY & CO.

Recommended by
Peter Tempelhoff

6132 Victoria Wharf Shopping Center
Breakwater Boulevard
V & A Waterfront
Cape Town
Western Cape 8001, South Africa
+27 0214186115
www.willoughbyandco.co.za

Opening hours...Open 7 days
Reservation policy..No
Credit cards..Accepted
Price range..Affordable
Style...Casual
Cuisine...Japanese
Recommended for...................Regular neighborhood

"They have great modern sushi."—Peter Tempelhoff

THE TEST KITCHEN

Recommended by
Marc Djozlija,
Peter Tempelhoff,
Duncan Welgemoed

The Old Biscuit Mill
375 Albert Road
Woodstock
Cape Town
Western Cape 7915, South Africa
+27 0214472337
www.thetestkitchen.co.za

Opening hours..............................Closed Monday and Sunday
Credit cards.......................Accepted but not AMEX or Diners
Price range..Expensive
Style...Casual
Cuisine.................................South African-Asian
Recommended for.............................Local favorite

"Continually pushing the boundaries of South African-
Asian cooking."—Peter Tempelhoff

FOUR & TWENTY CAFÉ

Recommended by
Luke Dale-Roberts,
Peter Tempelhoff

23 Wolfe Street
Chelsea Village
Wynberg
Cape Town
Western Cape 7800, South Africa
+27 0217620975
www.fourandtwentycafe.co.za

Opening hours...Closed Monday
Credit cards.............................Accepted but not AMEX
Price range...Budget
Style...Casual
Cuisine..Cafe-Bistro
Recommended for..Breakfast

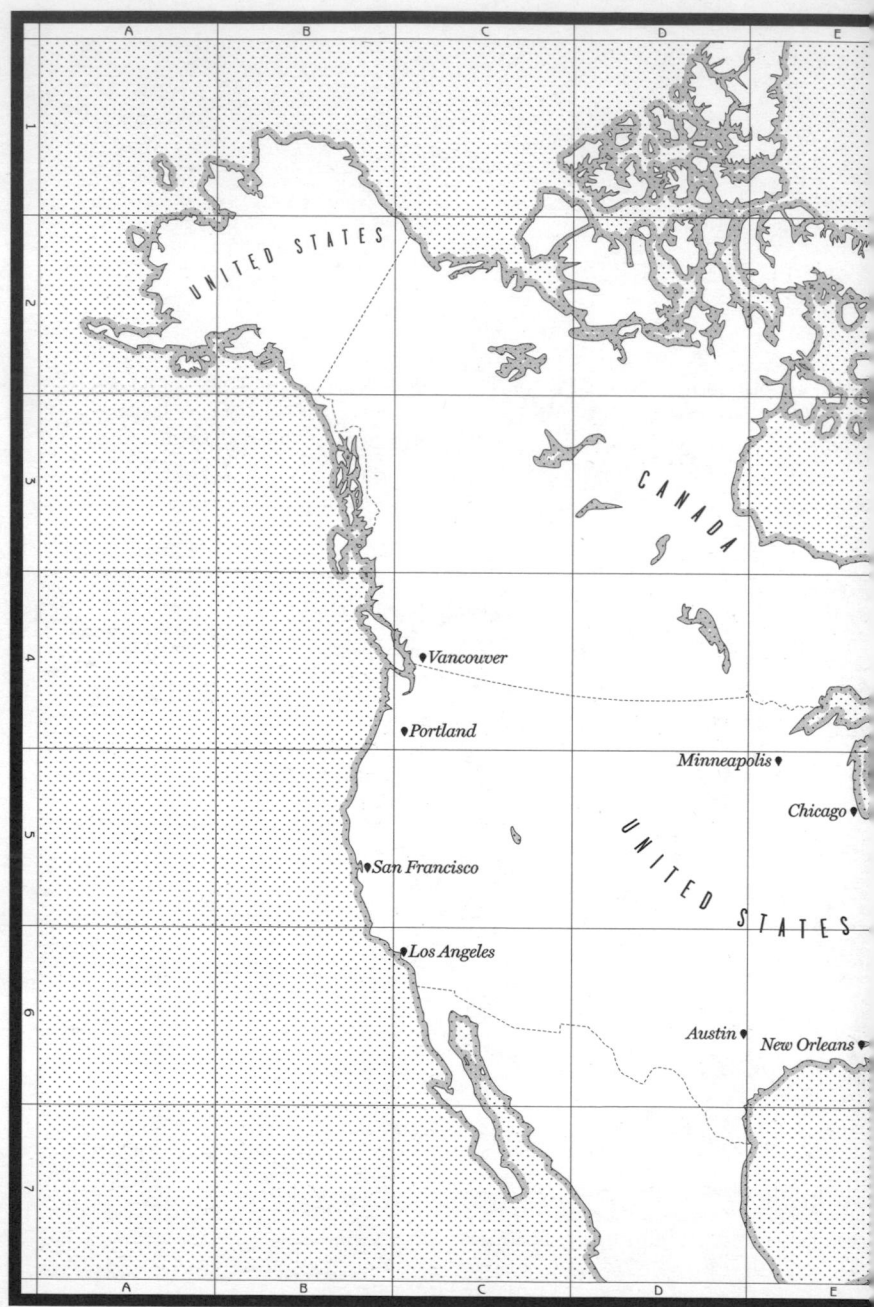

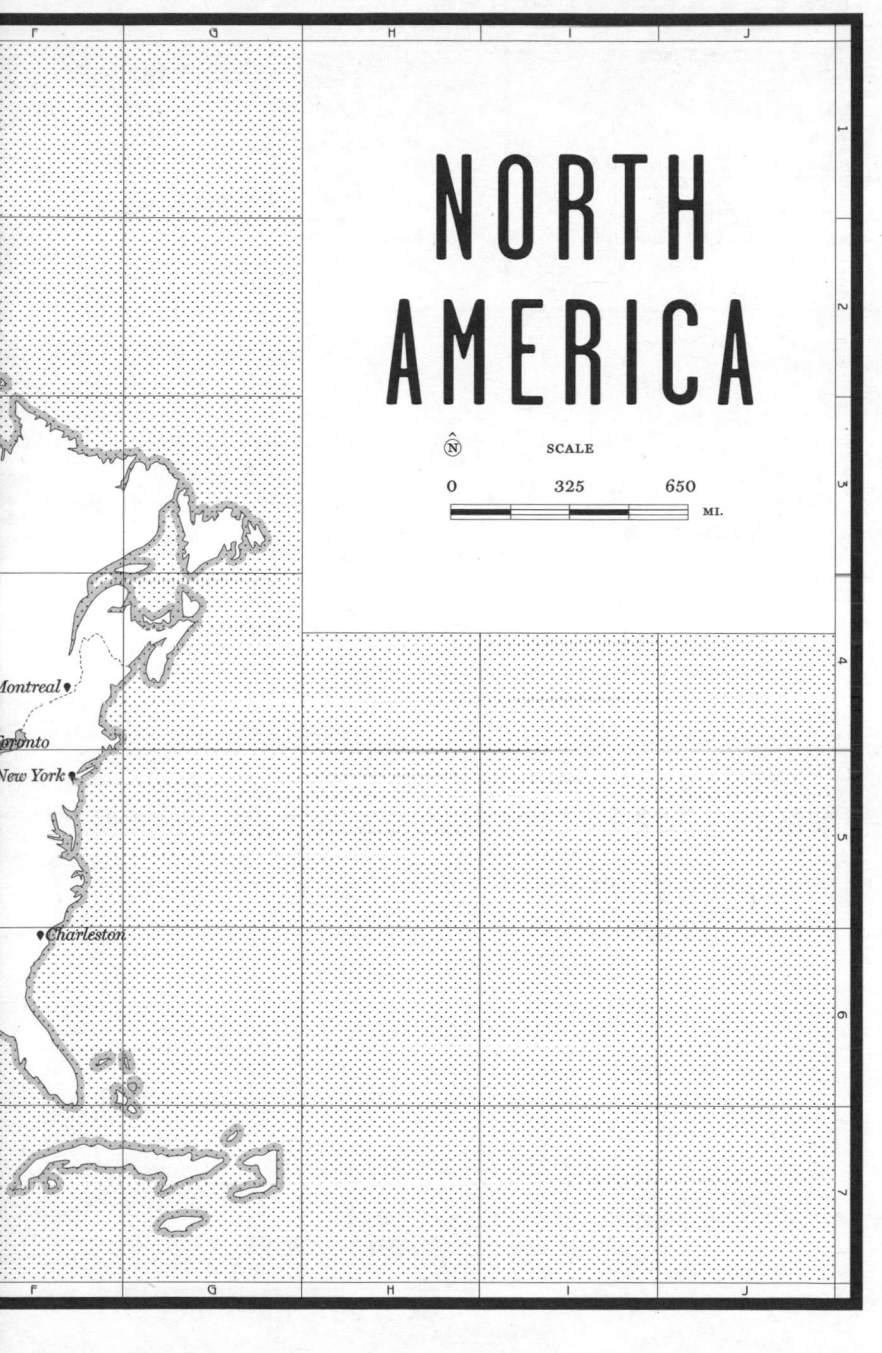

NORTH AMERICA

N

SCALE

0   325   650

MI.

Montreal

Toronto

New York

Charleston

"NO MATTER WHEN OR WHY I GO, I ALWAYS LEAVE SATISFIED."
SUSUR LEE P767

"AN ABSOUTELY PERFECT RESTAURANT."
DAVID PELLIZZARI P774

CANADA

"Wild foods from the ocean and the forest."
SAM HARRIS P746

"The best high-end restaurant in the city."
MARTIN JUNEAU P783

"SOURCING THE INGREDIENTS THAT THEY DO WITHOUT LIMITATIONS, LIKE MOOSE, WILD HARE OR PTARMIGAN, AS WELL AS ALL THE FRESH SEAFOOD, IS INCREDIBLE."
JOHN HORNE P751

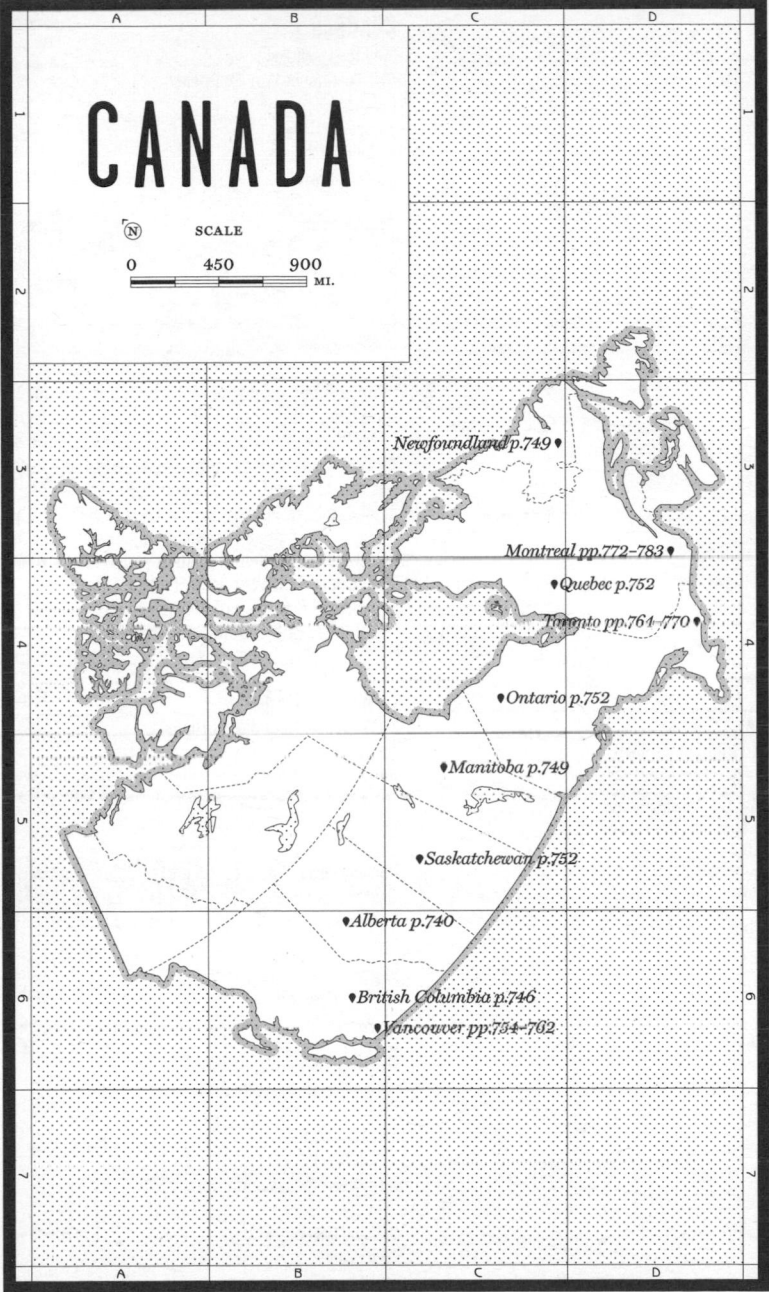

CANADA

SCALE

0   450   900 MI.

ALLOY

220 42nd Avenue Southeast
Calgary
Alberta T2G 1Y4
+1 4032879255
www.alloydining.com

Opening hours	Open 7 days
Credit cards	Accepted
Price range	Affordable
Style	Casual
Cuisine	Modern Canadian
Recommended for	Regular neighborhood

ANJU

344 17th Avenue Southwest
Calgary
Alberta T2S 0A5
+1 4034603341
www.anju.ca

Opening hours	Open 7 days
Credit cards	Accepted
Price range	Affordable
Style	Casual
Cuisine	Modern Korean
Recommended for	Late night

BLINK RESTAURANT & BAR

111 8th Avenue Southwest
Calgary
Alberta T2P 1B4
+1 4032635330
www.blinkcalgary.ca

Opening hours	Closed Sunday
Credit cards	Accepted
Price range	Affordable
Style	Casual
Cuisine	International
Recommended for	Regular neighborhood

CHARBAR

Simmons Building
618 Confluence Way Southeast
Calgary
Alberta T2G 0G1
+ 1 4034523115
www.charbar.ca

Opening hours	Open 7 days
Credit cards	Accepted but not Diners
Price range	Affordable
Style	Casual
Cuisine	Argentine Grill
Recommended for	Late night

"The culinary influence of Argentina is evident throughout the menu, with the personalized touch of tableside preparation for dishes like *ceviche mixto*. The extensive raw bar pays homage to the fresh, sustainable, West Coast seafood that is readily available here. Vegetarian cuisine is celebrated too—almost half of the options are vegetarian, particularly the small plates meant to share, such as the pistachio and avocado bruschetta, grilled provoleta, and sourdough fugazza with Roman broccoli."
—John Jackson & Connie DeSousa

CONTAINER BAR

1131 Kensington Road Northwest
Calgary
Alberta T2N 3P4
+1 4034574148
www.containerbaryyc.com

Opening hours	Open 7 days
Credit cards	Accepted
Price range	Budget
Style	Casual
Cuisine	Bar
Recommended for	Regular neighborhood

DEANE HOUSE

806 9th Avenue Southeast
Calgary
Alberta T2G 0S2
+1 4032640595
www.deanehouse.com

Opening hours	Closed Monday
Credit cards	Accepted
Price range	Affordable
Style	Casual
Cuisine	Canadian
Recommended for	Regular neighborhood

MODEL MILK

Recommended by
John Jackson &
Connie DeSousa

308 17th Avenue Southwest
Calgary
Alberta T2S 0A8
+1 4032657343
www.modelmilk.ca

Opening hours	Open 7 days
Credit cards	Accepted
Price range	Budget
Style	Smart casual
Cuisine	Modern Canadian
Recommended for	Regular neighborhood

Justin Leboe is a chef with an established haute pedigree, his CV including The French Laundry, Daniel, and, closer to home, Accolade in Toronto. But in 2011, when he opened Model Milk, housed in a converted art deco dairy in uptown Calgary, he switched to serving up southern fried chicken, waffles and gravy, and "Sunday suppers" of BBQ ribs. On his menu, which offers sharing plates and traditional mains, easy comforts sit alongside the more grown-up likes of handmade cavatelli, wagyu beef tartare, and little gem lettuce with Asturian aioli. A fine modern wine list and an extensive list of cocktails encourage lingering into the early hours.

THE NASH

Recommended by
John Jackson &
Connie DeSousa

925 11th Street Southeast
Calgary
Alberta T2G 0R4
+1 4039843365
www.thenashyyc.com

Opening hours	Closed Monday
Credit cards	Accepted but not AMEX
Price range	Affordable
Style	Casual
Cuisine	Modern Canadian
Recommended for	Regular neighborhood

NATIVE TONGUES TAQUERIA

Recommended by
John Jackson &
Connie DeSousa

235 12th Avenue Southwest
Calgary
Alberta T2R 1H7
+1 4032639444
www.nativetongues.ca

Opening hours	Open 7 days
Credit cards	Accepted
Price range	Budget
Style	Casual
Cuisine	Mexican
Recommended for	Regular neighborhood

NOTABLE

Recommended by
John Jackson &
Connie DeSousa

4611 Bowness Road Northwest
Calgary
Alberta T3B 0B2
+1 4032884372
www.notabletherestaurant.ca

Opening hours	Closed Monday
Credit cards	Accepted but not AMEX
Price range	Affordable
Style	Smart casual
Cuisine	Modern Canadian
Recommended for	Regular neighborhood

OX BAR DE TAPAS

Recommended by
John Jackson &
Connie DeSousa

528 17th Avenue Southwest
Calgary
Alberta T2S 0B1
+1 4034571432
www.oxtapas.com

Opening hours	Open 7 days
Credit cards	Accepted
Price range	Affordable
Style	Casual
Cuisine	Spanish Tapas
Recommended for	Regular neighborhood

PIGEONHOLE

Recommended by
Matt Abergel,
John Jackson &
Connie DeSousa

306 17th Avenue Southwest
Calgary
Alberta T2S 0A8
+1 4034524694
www.pigeonholeyyc.ca

Opening hours	Closed Sunday
Credit cards	Accepted
Price range	Affordable
Style	Casual
Cuisine	International-Small plates
Recommended for	Worth the travel

"Coming back home and having a meal of this quality,
with a surprising focus on vegetables, gives me hope
for the restaurant scene in Calgary today."
—Matt Abergel

RIVER CAFÉ

Recommended by
John Jackson &
Connie DeSousa

25 Prince's Island Park
Calgary
Alberta T2P 0R1
+1 4032617670
www.river-cafe.com

Opening hours	Open 7 days
Credit cards	Accepted
Price range	Expensive
Style	Smart casual
Cuisine	Modern Canadian
Recommended for	Local favorite

"River Café has created a beautiful place in an
extraordinary setting and has tended to the details
that make you feel at home—staff who care, chefs
who are passionate about quality, and regional,
seasonal ingredients that bring to your palate a sense
of place."—John Jackson & Connie DeSousa

ROUGE RESTAURANT

Recommended by
John Jackson &
Connie DeSousa

1240 8th Avenue Southeast
Calgary
Alberta T2G 0M7
+1 4035312768
www.rougecalagary.com

Opening hours	Closed Sunday
Credit cards	Accepted but not AMEX
Price range	Affordable
Style	Smart casual
Cuisine	Modern Canadian
Recommended for	Regular neighborhood

SHOKUNIN

Recommended by
John Jackson &
Connie DeSousa

2016 4th Street Southwest
Calgary
Alberta T2S 1W3
+1 4032293444
www.shokuninyyc.ca

Opening hours	Open 7 days
Credit cards	Accepted
Price range	Affordable
Style	Casual
Cuisine	Modern Japanese
Recommended for	Late night

"Crafted cocktails give way to charred yakitori and
small plates shared among friends with a bottle of
sake. Seasonal and local ingredients are combined
with traditional Japanese techniques and flavor
profiles to create a truly contemporary dining
experience."—John Jackson & Connie DeSousa

SIDEWALK CITIZEN

Recommended by
John Jackson &
Connie DeSousa

Simmons Building
618 Confluence Way Southeast
Calgary
Alberta T2G 0G1
+1 4034572245
www.sidewalkcitizenbakery.com

Opening hours	Open 7 days
Reservation policy	No
Credit cards	Accepted
Price range	Budget
Style	Casual
Cuisine	Bakery-Café
Recommended for	Breakfast

"Their menu and flavors change daily according
to seasonal ingredients and the creativity of Aviv,
the head baker and owner. Everything is made from
scratch. They use organic produce—eggs, grains,
local flour, herbs, and non-GMO oils."
—John Jackson & Connie DeSousa

TEN FOOT HENRY

Recommended by
John Jackson &
Connie DeSousa

1209 1st Street Southwest
Calgary
Alberta T2R 0V3
+1 4034755537
www.tenfoothenry.com

Opening hours	Open 7 days
Credit cards	Accepted but not AMEX
Price range	Affordable
Style	Casual
Cuisine	Modern International
Recommended for	Regular neighborhood

UNA PIZZA + WINE

Recommended by
John Jackson &
Connie DeSousa

618 17th Avenue Southwest
Calgary
Alberta T2S 0B4
+1 4034531183
www.unapizzeria.com

Opening hours	Open 7 days
Reservation policy	No
Credit cards	Accepted
Price range	Affordable
Style	Casual
Cuisine	Pizza
Recommended for	Regular neighborhood

BAIJIU BAR

Recommended by
Daniel Costa

Mercer Building
10363 104th Street
Edmonton
Alberta T5J 1B9
+1 7804217060
www.baijiuyeg.com

Opening hours	Closed Monday
Reservation policy	No
Credit cards	Accepted
Price range	Affordable
Style	Smart casual
Cuisine	Pan-Asian
Recommended for	Late night

"Baijiu serves great cocktails and fun, Asian-inspired small plates."—Daniel Costa

BAR CLEMENTINE

Recommended by
Daniel Costa

11957 Jasper Avenue
Edmonton
Alberta T5K 0P1
+1 7807564570
www.barclementine.ca

Opening hours	Closed Monday
Credit cards	Accepted but not AMEX
Price range	Affordable
Style	Smart casual
Cuisine	Bar-Small plates
Recommended for	Late night

CAFÉ LINNEA

Recommended by
Daniel Costa

10932 119th Street Northwest
Edmonton
Alberta T5H 3P5
+1 7807581160
www.cafelinnea.ca

Opening hours	Closed Tuesday and Wednesday
Credit cards	Accepted
Price range	Affordable
Style	Casual
Cuisine	Scandinavian-French
Recommended for	Breakfast

"It features a very open and clean design with loads of sunlight. All of their food is delicious—I especially love the complete galette. They also have great juices made to order, and great cocktails."—Daniel Costa

CORSO 32

Recommended by
John Jackson &
Connie DeSousa

10345 Jasper Avenue
Edmonton
Alberta T5J 1Y7
+1 7804214622
www.corso32.com

Opening hours	Open 7 days
Credit cards	Accepted
Price range	Affordable
Style	Casual
Cuisine	Modern Italian
Recommended for	Worth the travel

DUCHESS BAKE SHOP

10717 124th Street Northwest
Edmonton
Alberta T5M 0H1
+1 7804884999
www.duchessbakeshop.com

Opening hours	Closed Monday
Reservation policy	No
Credit cards	Accepted
Price range	Budget
Style	Casual
Cuisine	Café-Bakery
Recommended for	Breakfast

"I love going there and grabbing a mountain of fresh croissants in the morning."—Daniel Costa

MAYDAY DOGS

10363 104th Street
Edmonton
Alberta T5J 1B9
+1 5879895456
www.maydaydogs.com

Opening hours	Closed Monday and Sunday
Reservation policy	No
Credit cards	Accepted
Price range	Budget
Style	Casual
Cuisine	Hot Dogs
Recommended for	Bargain

"Innovative and fun hot dog stand, with interesting combinations for cheap eats."—Daniel Costa

IZAKAYA TOMO

3738 99th Street
Edmonton
Alberta T6E 6C8
+1 7804409152
www.izakayatomo.net

Opening hours	Closed Monday
Credit cards	Accepted but not AMEX
Price range	Affordable
Style	Casual
Cuisine	Japanese
Recommended for	Late night

NORTH 53

10240 124th Street
Edmonton
Alberta T5N 3W6
+1 5875245353
www.north53.com

Opening hours	Closed Monday
Credit cards	Accepted but not AMEX
Price range	Budget
Style	Casual
Cuisine	Modern Canadian
Recommended for	Late night

LEVA

11053 86th Avenue Northwest
Edmonton
Alberta T6G 0X1
+1 7804795382
www.cafeleva.com

Opening hours	Open 7 days
Reservation policy	No
Credit cards	Accepted but not AMEX
Price range	Affordable
Style	Casual
Cuisine	Café-Bar
Recommended for	Regular neighborhood

"Leva is an Italian café that serves simple pizza and fritti. They also own a roastery called Ace Coffee which is also fantastic."—Daniel Costa

RED OX INN

9420 91st Street
Edmonton
Alberta T6C 1Z5
+1 7804655727
www.theredoxinn.com

Opening hours	Closed Monday
Credit cards	Accepted
Price range	Affordable
Style	Smart casual
Cuisine	Canadian
Recommended for	High end

"A very intimate, relaxing restaurant with seasonal and delicious 'Canadiana' food."—Daniel Costa

RGE RD

Recommended by
Daniel Costa

10643 123rd Street Northwest
Edmonton
Alberta T5N 1P3
+1 7804474577
www.rgerd.ca

Opening hours	Closed Sunday
Credit cards	Accepted
Price range	Affordable
Style	Casual
Cuisine	Canadian
Recommended for	Local favorite

"Blair Lebsack's cuisine is the perfect representation of Alberta. The food is innovative and revolves around local Albertan ingredients."—Daniel Costa

ROSTIZADO

Recommended by
John Jackson &
Connie DeSousa

Mercer Warehouse
102, 10359 104th Street
Edmonton
Alberta T5J 1B9
l 1 7807610911
www.rostizado.com

Opening hours	Closed Sunday
Reservation policy	No
Credit cards	Accepted but not AMEX
Price range	Affordable
Style	Casual
Cuisine	Modern Mexican
Recommended for	Worth the travel

SHANGHAI 456

Recommended by
Daniel Costa

14456 118th Avenue Northwest
Edmonton
Alberta T5L 2M5
+1 7804518333
www.shanghai456.com

Opening hours	Closed Wednesday
Credit cards	Accepted
Price range	Budget
Style	Casual
Cuisine	Chinese
Recommended for	Bargain

TANH TANH

Recommended by
Daniel Costa

10718 101th Street Northwest
Edmonton
Alberta T5H 2S3
+1 7804265068
www.thanthanh.ca

Opening hours	Closed Monday and Sunday
Credit cards	Accepted
Price range	Budget
Style	Casual
Cuisine	Noodles
Recommended for	Bargain

THE MARC

Recommended by
Daniel Costa

9940 106th Street Northwest
Edmonton
Alberta T5K 2N2
+1 7804292828
www.themarc.ca

Opening hours	Closed Sunday
Credit cards	Accepted
Price range	Budget
Style	Smart casual
Cuisine	French
Recommended for	Local favorite

THREE BOARS

Recommended by
Daniel Costa

8424 109th Street Northwest
Edmonton
Alberta T6G 1E2
+1 7807572600
www.threeboars.ca

Opening hours	Open 7 days
Credit cards	Accepted
Price range	Affordable
Style	Casual
Cuisine	Canadian-Tapas
Recommended for	Late night

"Three Boars is an intimate and fun restaurant with great small plates and cocktails. A definite industry favorite."—Daniel Costa

TRES CARNALES TAQUERIA

Recommended by
Daniel Costa

10119 100a Street Northwest
Edmonton
Alberta T5J 0R5
+1 7804290911
www.trescarnales.com

Opening hours	Closed Sunday
Reservation policy	No
Credit cards	Accepted but not AMEX
Price range	Budget
Style	Casual
Cuisine	Mexican
Recommended for	Regular neighborhood

"Tres Carnales is a traditional Mexican taqueria. It has great energy and delicious food. I love popping in for a plate of *tacos al pastor* (spicy pork) and a beer."
— Daniel Costa

PILGRIMME

Recommended by
Andrea Carlson,
Brian Luptak

2806 Montague Road
Galiano Island
British Columbia V0N 1P0
+1 2505395392
www.pilgrimme.ca

Opening hours	Closed Tuesday to Thursday
Credit cards	Accepted
Price range	Expensive
Style	Smart casual
Cuisine	Modern Canadian
Recommended for	Local favorite

"The food is true to the coast, the region, and the people who provide the food. Clean, simple, and perfect."—Brian Luptak

WILD MOUNTAIN RESTAURANT

Recommended by
Brad Holmes

1831 Maple Avenue South
Sooke
British Columbia V9Z 0N9
+1 2506423596
www.wildmountaindinners.com

Opening hours	Closed Sunday to Tuesday
Credit cards	Accepted
Price range	Affordable
Style	Casual
Cuisine	West Coast Canadian
Recommended for	Local favorite

"They use a great mix of wild and cultivated foods from the area. Always seasonal and showcasing many unknown local edibles."—Brad Holmes

From the world around them, chef/farmer Oliver Kienast and his wife/sommelier Brooke Fader craft the menu for their idiosyncratic, totally charming, and terroir-rich restaurant in Sooke, the picturesque wharf town on the southern tip of Vancouver Island. Growing up on a honey farm, Kienast has long let his senses lead him. That means the menu, including crispy Saanich polenta with pickled vegetable mayo, and local octopus with house-made salami, burdock and borage, is constantly changing as he sifts through his surroundings. The restaurant, open from May to October, is itself unfussy and, with a terrace overlooking the waters of the Strait of Juan de Fuca, as open to the world as its owners are.

WOLF IN THE FOG

Recommended by
Sam Harris

150 4th Street
Tofino
British Columbia V0R 2Z0
+1 2507259653
www.wolfinthefog.com

Opening hours	Open 7 days
Credit cards	Accepted but not AMEX or Diners
Price range	Expensive
Style	Casual
Cuisine	Tofitian
Recommended for	Worth the travel

"Wild foods from the ocean and the forest, cooked with style and skill."—Sam Harris

VANCOUVER: SEE PAGES 754–762

AGRIUS

Recommended by
Brad Holmes

732 Yates Street
Victoria
British Columbia V8W 1L4
+1 7782656312
www.agriusrestaurant.com

Opening hours	Closed Monday and Sunday
Credit cards	Accepted
Price range	Expensive
Style	Smart casual
Cuisine	Canadian-French
Recommended for	Late night

"A beautiful restaurant that also houses their bakery, Fol Epi. The house-cured meats program is great."
—Brad Holmes

FOUNTAIN RESTAURANT

Recommended by
Sam Harris

2680 Blanshard Street
Victoria
British Columbia V8T 5E1
+1 2503813318

Opening hours	Open 7 days
Credit cards	Accepted
Price range	Affordable
Style	Casual
Cuisine	Chinese
Recommended for	Late night

JASMINE FAMILY RESTAURANT

Recommended by
Sam Harris

1752 Island Highway
Victoria
British Columbia V9B 1H8
+1 2503918648

Opening hours	Open 7 days
Credit cards	Accepted
Price range	Affordable
Style	Casual
Cuisine	Diner
Recommended for	Breakfast

"The perfect diner, family owned and operated. Get the French mix."—Sam Harris

LITTLE JUMBO

Recommended by
Brad Holmes

506 Fort Street
Victoria
British Columbia V8W 1E6
+1 7784335535
www.littlejumbo.ca

Opening hours	Open 7 days
Credit cards	Accepted
Price range	Budget
Style	Casual
Cuisine	Modern Canadian
Recommended for	Late night

OLO

Recommended by
Sam Harris

509 Fisgard Street
Victoria
British Columbia V8W 2P3
+1 2505908795
www.olorestaurant.com

Opening hours	Open 7 days
Credit cards	Accepted
Price range	Affordable
Style	Casual
Cuisine	Canadian
Recommended for	Local favorite

PART & PARCEL

Recommended by
Brad Holmes

2656 Quadra Street
Victoria
British Columbia V8T 4E4
+1 7784060888
www.partandparcel.ca

Opening hours	Closed Sunday
Reservation policy	No
Credit cards	Accepted
Price range	Affordable
Style	Casual
Cuisine	Modern Canadian
Recommended for	Regular neighborhood

"A casual, counter-service restaurant serving imaginative food using local, ethically sourced products."—Brad Holmes

RELISH FOOD & COFFEE

Recommended by
Brad Holmes

920 Pandora Avenue
Victoria
British Columbia V8V 3P3
+1 2505908464
www.relishfoodcoffee.com

Opening hours	Open 7 days
Reservation policy	No
Credit cards	Accepted but not AMEX or Diners
Price range	Affordable
Style	Casual
Cuisine	International
Recommended for	Breakfast

"Open in the daytime and using local, organic ingredients. They have a changing menu that offers breakfast and lunch items."—Brad Holmes

THE RUBY

642 Johnson Street
Victoria
British Columbia V8W 1M6
+1 7782658750
www.therubyvictoria.com

Opening hours	Open 7 days
Credit cards	Accepted
Price range	Affordable
Style	Casual
Cuisine	Modern Canadian
Recommended for	Breakfast

STAGE WINE BAR

1307 Gladstone Avenue
Victoria
British Columbia V8R 1R9
+1 2503884222
www.stagewinebar.com

Opening hours	Open 7 days
Credit cards	Accepted
Price range	Affordable
Style	Casual
Cuisine	European small plates
Recommended for	Regular neighborhood

"Dope small plates, great selection of wines by the glass, and a cheeky Irish bartender named Quigley."
—Sam Harris

STANDARD PIZZA

1515 Cook Street
Victoria
British Columbia V8T 5E5
+1 2505902363
www.standardpizza.ca

Opening hours	Closed Monday and Tuesday
Reservation policy	No
Credit cards	Accepted
Price range	Affordable
Style	Casual
Cuisine	Pizza
Recommended for	Wish I'd opened

"Wood-fired pizza with many creative and delicious toppings."—Brad Holmes

UCHIDA EATERY

633 Courtney Street
Victoria
British Columbia V8W 1C1
+1 2503887383

Opening hours	Closed Monday and Sunday
Credit cards	Accepted but not AMEX
Price range	Affordable
Style	Casual
Cuisine	Japanese
Recommended for	Bargain

"Organic Japanese lunch spot hidden down an alley by the bug zoo. Incredible flavor and value. Very good."
—Sam Harris

UCHIDA SHOKUDO

633 Courtney Street
Victoria
British Columbia V8W 1C1
+1 2503887383

Opening hours	Closed Monday and Sunday
Reservation policy	No
Credit cards	Accepted
Price range	Affordable
Style	Casual
Cuisine	Japanese
Recommended for	Regular neighborhood

LA CANTINA

4340 Lorimer Road
Whistler
British Columbia V0N 1B4
+1 6049629950
www.tacoslacantina.ca

Opening hours	Open 7 days
Credit cards	Accepted but not AMEX
Price range	Affordable
Style	Casual
Cuisine	Mexican
Recommended for	Bargain

"It has very tasty, authentic tacos. My kids love the pulled pork one."—James Walt

ELEMENTS

Recommended by
James Walt

Suite 102b, 4359 Main Street
Whistler
British Columbia V0N 1B4
+1 6049325569
www.elementswhistler.com

Opening hours	Open 7 days
Reservation policy	No
Credit cards	Accepted
Price range	Affordable
Style	Casual
Cuisine	Canadian
Recommended for	Breakfast

"They have a great selection of breakfast and brunch items. Good value too. It's where the locals go."
—James Walt

SACHI SUSHI

Recommended by
James Walt

Suite 106, 4359 Main Street
Whistler
British Columbia V0N 1B4
+1 6049355649
www.sachisushi.com

Opening hours	Open 7 days
Credit cards	Accepted
Price range	Affordable
Style	Casual
Cuisine	Japanese
Recommended for	Regular neighborhood

"It has really good sushi and noodle dishes, and is very fresh. "—James Walt

SPLITZ GRILL

Recommended by
Sam Harris,
James Walt

4369 Main Street
Whistler
British Columbia V0N 1B4
+1 6049389300
www.splitzgrill.com

Opening hours	Open 7 days
Reservation policy	No
Credit cards	Accepted
Price range	Budget
Style	Casual
Cuisine	Burgers
Recommended for	Bargain

"Splitz Grill has the best burgers around."
—Sam Harris

DEER & ALMOND

Recommended by
John Jackson &
Connie DeSousa

85 Princess Street
Winnipeg
Manitoba R3B 1K4
+1 2045048562
www.deerandalmond.com

Opening hours	Closed Sunday
Credit cards	Accepted
Price range	Affordable
Style	Casual
Cuisine	Modern Canadian
Recommended for	Worth the travel

BONAVISTA SOCIAL CLUB

Recommended by
Timothy Charles

Newmans Cove
Upper Amherst Cove
Bonavista
Newfoundland and Labrador A0C 2A0
+1 709 445-5556
www.bonavistasocialclub.com

Opening hours	Closed Monday and Tuesday
Credit cards	Accepted but not AMEX or Diners
Price range	Budget
Style	Casual
Cuisine	Newfoundland-Bakery
Recommended for	Wish I'd Opened

"The brilliant location and the obvious love for the produce that they serve."—Timothy Charles

THE COD JIGGER

Recommended by
Timothy Charles

3 Central, Main Street
Central Fogo Island
Fogo Island
Newfoundland and Labrador A0G 2W0
+1 709-266-1200

Opening hours	Open 7 days
Reservation policy	No
Credit cards	Accepted but not AMEX or Diners
Price range	Budget
Style	Casual
Cuisine	Newfoundland
Recommended for	Regular neighbourhood

"They have a simple fried cod sandwich that's a great lunch on a day away from work."
—Timothy Charles

GROWLERS

Recommended by
Timothy Charles

125 Main Road
Joe Batt's Arm
Fogo Island
Newfoundland and Labrador A0G 2X0

Opening hours	Closed Monday and Tuesday
Reservation policy	No
Credit cards	Not accepted
Price range	Budget
Style	Casual
Cuisine	Ice Cream
Recommended for	Regular neighbourhood

"Be sure to take a walk down to Growlers for a treat after lunch or dinner."—Timothy Charles

NICOLE'S CAFÉ

Recommended by
Timothy Charles

Highway 334
Joe Batt's Arm
Fogo Island
Newfoundland and Labrador A0G 2XO
+1 709-658-3663
www.nicolescafe.ca

Opening hours	Closed Monday and Sunday
Credit cards	Accepted but not AMEX or Diners
Price range	Affordable
Style	Casual
Cuisine	Newfoundland
Recommended for	Regular neighbourhood

"Great summer spot to have a salad and a glass of wine on a sunny afternoon"—Timothy Charles

ADELAIDE OYSTER HOUSE

Recommended by
Timothy Charles

334 Water Street
St. John's
Newfoundland and Labrador A1C 1C1
+1 709-722-7222

Opening hours	Open 7 days
Credit cards	Accepted
Price range	Affordable
Style	Casual
Cuisine	Seafood
Recommended for	Local favourite

BLUE ON WATER

Recommended by
Timothy Charles

319 Water Street
St. John's
Newfoundland and Labrador A1C 1B9 −3890
www.blueonwater.com

Opening hours	Open 7 days
Credit cards	Accepted
Price range	Affordable
Style	Smart casual
Cuisine	Newfoundland
Recommended for	Local favourite

CINCHED BISTRO

Recommended by
Timothy Charles

7 Queen Street
St. John's
Newfoundland and Labrador A1C 4K2
+1 709.722.3100
www.chinchedbistro.com

Opening hours	Closed Monday and Sunday
Credit cards	Accepted
Price range	Affordable
Style	Casual
Cuisine	Canadian Bistro
Recommended for	Local favourite

MALLARD COTTAGE

Recommended by
Timothy Charles,
John Horne,
John Jackson &
Connie DeSousa

8 Barrows Road
St. John's
Newfoundland and Labrador A1A 1G8
+1 7092377314
www.mallardcottage.ca

Opening hours	Open 7 days
Credit cards	Accepted
Price range	Affordable
Style	Casual
Cuisine	East Coast Canadian
Recommended for	Breakfast

"I'm not a breakfast guy. I hate breakfast. But when you travel, it's nice to find a good spot for brunch—especially when you're a little hungover. The brunch here is amazing. They do this massive spread of house-baked pastries and the view over Quidi Vidi harbor is second to none. It's the place for brunch." —John Horne

Chef Todd Perrin, his wife Kim Doyle, and business partner Stephen Lee spent years painstakingly restoring this handsome eighteenth-century Irish cottage in the quaint St. John's fishing village of Quidi Vidi. It opened as Mallard Cottage in late 2013 on a winning ticket of sparkling local produce, craft beer, and fun. Expect live music sessions, crackling fires, hearty weekend brunches, and scrawled daily menus that take pride in their no-nonsense gutsiness. Typical dishes include coldwater shrimp, caramelised onion fritters, salt cod napes with garlic cream and potato, and lobster thermidor with turnip potato hash.

MOHAMED ALI

Recommended by
Timothy Charles

177 Duckworth Street
Downtown
St. John's
Newfoundland and Labrador A1C 1G4
+1 (709) 221-8313
www.mohamed-ali.ca/mohamedali

Opening hours	Open 7 days
Credit cards	Accepted
Price range	Budget
Style	Casual
Cuisine	Middle Eastern
Recommended for	Bargain

"It is a calm space, never too loud even when it is busy. The service is prompt and kind too."
—Timothy Charles

RAYMONDS

Recommended by
Timothy Charles,
John Horne,
John Jackson &
Connie DeSousa

95 Water Street
St. John's
Newfoundland and Labrador A1C 1A4
+1 7095795800
www.raymondsrestaurant.com

Opening hours	Closed Monday and Sunday
Credit cards	Accepted
Price range	Expensive
Style	Smart casual
Cuisine	East Coast Canadian
Recommended for	Wish I'd opened

"It's located in a historic spot with virtually unlimited resources in the area and you're allowed to serve wild game, unlike anywhere else in Canada. For me, Raymonds has the ability to become the Noma of Canada. The chef, Jeremy Charles, is doing amazing things. Sourcing the ingredients that they do without limitations, like moose, wild hare, or ptarmigan, as well as all the fresh seafood, is incredible—to be able to step outside your front door and catch wild cod is pretty crazy."—John Horne

There is Raymonds and then there are all the other restaurants in Canada. Credit the proximity to

Canada's best ingredients. Credit the region's laws, which allow for the sale of truly wild game, or the charm of downtown St. John's, where Raymonds occupies a former bank overlooking the harbor. But credit most of all to chef Jeremy Charles, his maniacal sourcing, and his partner Jeremy Bonia, who manages the impeccable wine list. In a confidently formal setting, Raymonds translates the wild bounty of Canada into refined plates of foraged chanterelles, Newfoundland moose loin with gnocchi, and cod so fresh it doesn't seem to have come to terms yet with its own mortality.

THE COSTAL CAFÉ

Recommended by
Timothy Charles

2731 Robie Street
North End
Halifax
Nova Scotia B3K 4P1
+1 902 405 4022
www.thecoastal.ca

Opening hours	Closed Wednesday
Reservation policy	No
Credit cards	Accepted but not AMEX or Diners
Price range	Budget
Style	Casual
Cuisine	Café
Recommended for	Breakfast

It was the first restaurant of it's kind in Halifax, easy and unpretentious yet they are always consistent in delivering great flavours and fun combinations.

TONY'S

Recommended by
Timothy Charles

2390 Robie Street
North End
Halifax
Nova Scotia B3K 4M7
+1 902 404-8669
www.tonysdonair.ca

Opening hours	Open 7 days
Reservation policy	No
Credit cards	Accepted but not Diners
Price range	Budget
Style	Casual
Cuisine	Pizza
Recommended for	Bargain

Ahhhh, so many come to mind, so I will keep it simple, you are ever visiting Halifax N.S. be sure to go to Tony's Pizza and have a donair.

DEB'S PLACE
Recommended by
Anthony Rose

352 Huronia Road
Barrie
Ontario L4N 8Y9
+1 7057271361

Opening hours	Open 7 days
Credit cards	Accepted
Price range	Affordable
Style	Casual
Cuisine	International
Recommended for	Regular neighborhood

"As consistent and delicious as it gets. I go with my son, Simon, everytime we are at our cottage. Best, best, best Eggs Benedict you ever did have."
—Anthony Rose

LANGDON HALL
Recommended by
Carlos Perez

1 Langdon Drive
Cambridge
Ontario N3H 4R8
+1 5197402100
www.langdonhall.ca

Opening hours	Open 7 days
Credit cards	Accepted
Price range	Expensive
Style	Smart casual
Cuisine	Modern Canadian
Recommended for	Worth the travel

ZETS
Recommended by
Anthony Rose

6445 Airport Road
Mississauga
Ontario L4V 1E4
+1 9056781114
www.zets.ca

Opening hours	Open 7 days
Reservation policy	No
Credit cards	Not accepted
Price range	Budget
Style	Casual
Cuisine	Greek
Recommended for	Local favorite

PANCER'S ORIGINAL DELICATESSEN
Recommended by
Anthony Rose

3856 Bathurst Street
North York
Ontario M3H 3N3
+1 4166361230
www.pancersoriginaldeli.com

Opening hours	Open 7 days
Reservation policy	No
Credit cards	Accepted
Price range	Affordable
Style	Casual
Cuisine	Jewish Deli
Recommended for	Wish I'd opened

"Generations of deliciousness; corned beef to die for."
—Anthony Rose

TORONTO: SEE PAGE 764–770

MONTREAL: SEE PAGE 772–783

CABANE À SUCRE AU PIED DE COCHON

11382 Rang de la Fresnière
Saint-Benoît de Mirabel
Quebec J7N 2R9
+1 5148452322
www.cabane.aupieddecochon.ca

Recommended by
Normand Laprise,
Marc-Alexandre Mercier

Opening hours	Closed Monday to Wednesday
Credit cards	Accepted
Price range	Expensive
Style	Smart casual
Cuisine	Canadian
Recommended for	Local favorite

"You cannot get more authentic!"—Normand Laprise

AYDEN KITCHEN AND BAR
Recommended by
John Jackson &
Connie DeSousa

265 3rd Avenue South
Saskatoon
Saskatchewan S7K 1M3
+1 3069542590
www.aydenkitchenandbar.com

Opening hours	Closed Sunday
Credit cards	Accepted
Price range	Affordable
Style	Casual
Cuisine	Canadian
Recommended for	Wish I'd opened

"Being from Saskatchewan myself this restaurant totally hits home. Chef Dale and team are crushing it and have created a true food destination for the prairies."—John Jackson

LITTLE GROUSE ON THE PRAIRIE

167 3rd Avenue South
Saskatoon
Saskatchewan S7K 1L6
+1 3069790100
www.littlegrouse.com

Recommended by
John Jackson &
Connie DeSousa

Opening hours	Closed Monday
Credit cards	Accepted
Price range	Affordable
Style	Smart casual
Cuisine	International
Recommended for	Wish I'd opened

"This place uses great, local and sustainable seafood, and the fried oyster po-boy is out of this world."

BRIAN LUPTAK P759

"STUNNING ROOM AND FOOD TO MATCH. SMART, FUN, COOL AND NICE."

SAM HARRIS P756

VANCOUVER

"Features all that is great about the West Coast."

JAMES WALT P756

"THE BENCHMARK IN VANCOUVER FOR EXCELLENCE IN SERVICE, FOOD, AND CELLARS."

ANDREA CARLSON P756

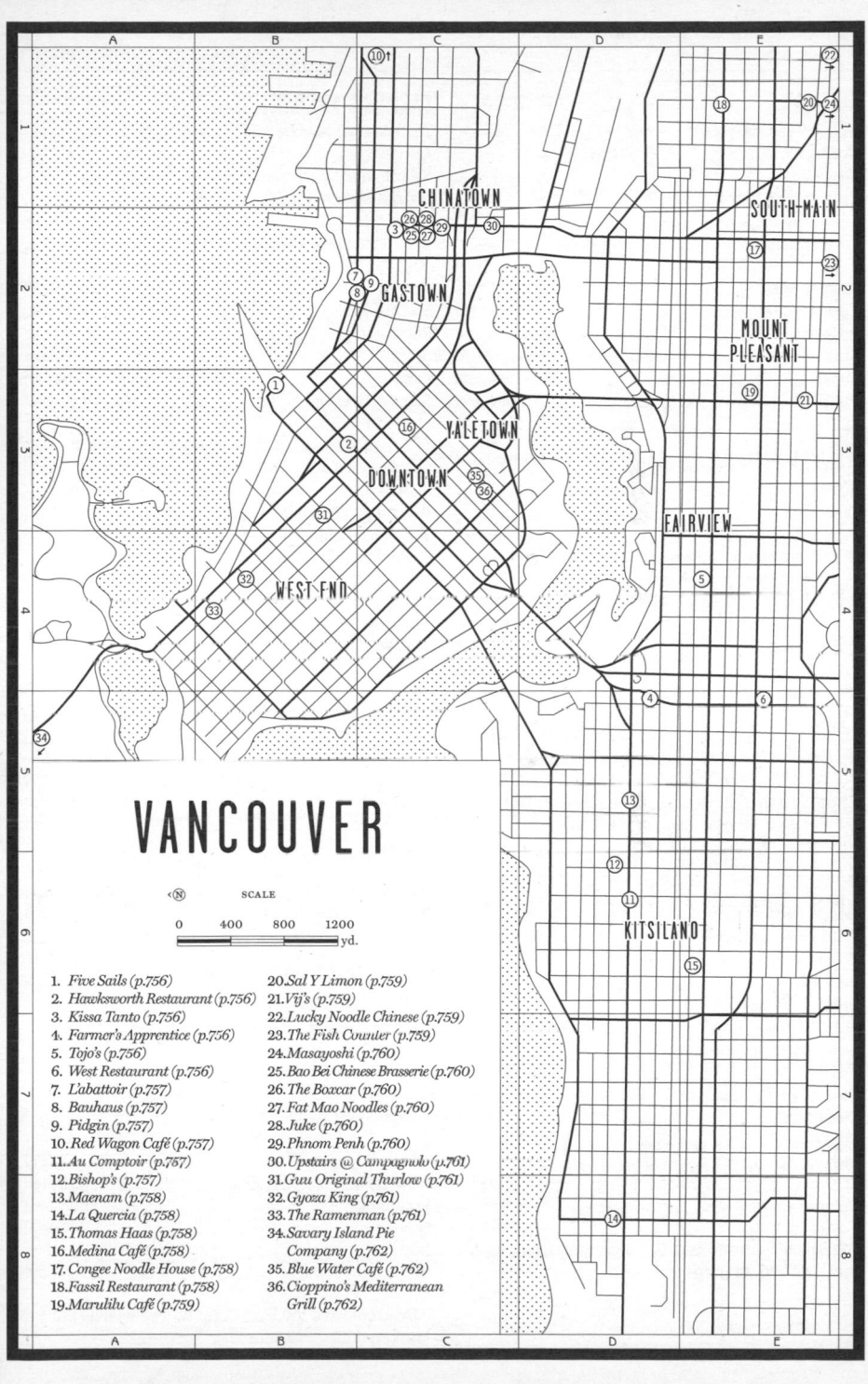

VANCOUVER

SCALE

0   400   800   1200
yd.

FIVE SAILS

Recommended by
James Walt

410, 999 Canada Place
Downtown
Vancouver
British Columbia V6C 3E1
+1 6048442855
www.fivesails.ca

Opening hours	Open 7 days
Credit cards	Accepted
Price range	Expensive
Style	Smart casual
Cuisine	Modern Canadian
Recommended for	High end

HAWKSWORTH RESTAURANT

Recommended by
Andrea Carlson,
Brad Holmes,
John Jackson &
Connie DeSousa,
Edward Lee,
Vikram Vij

801 West Georgia Street
Downtown
Vancouver
British Columbia V6C 1P7
+1 6046737000
www.hawksworthrestaurant.com

Opening hours	Open 7 days
Credit cards	Accepted
Price range	Expensive
Style	Formal
Cuisine	Modern Canadian
Recommended for	High end

"Hawksworth is the benchmark in Vancouver for excellence in service, food, and cellars."
—Andrea Carlson

KISSA TANTO

Recommended by
Sam Harris,
Brian Luptak

263 East Pender Street
Downtown East Side
Vancouver
British Columbia V6A 1T8
+1 7783798078
www.kissatanto.com

Opening hours	Closed Monday and Sunday
Credit cards	Accepted
Price range	Affordable
Style	Smart casual
Cuisine	Japanese-Italian
Recommended for	High end

"Stunning room and food to match. Smart, fun, cool, and nice."—Sam Harris

FARMER'S APPRENTICE

Recommended by
Angus An,
Jair Tellez

1535 West 6th Avenue
Fairview
Vancouver
British Columbia V6J 1R1
+1 6046202070
www.farmersapprentice.ca

Opening hours	Open 7 days
Credit cards	Accepted
Price range	Affordable
Style	Casual
Cuisine	Modern Canadian
Recommended for	Worth the travel

"I've had some of the most emotionally-charged simple meals at this small intimate restaurant. It takes a lot of guts to ride the wave he rides. Flavors are delicate, ingredients pristine, and amazing execution. This is a great example of effortless simplicity."
—Jair Tellez

TOJO'S

Recommended by
Paul Berglund

1133 West Broadway
Fairview
Vancouver
British Columbia V6H 1G1
+1 6048728050
www.tojos.com

Opening hours	Closed Sunday
Credit cards	Accepted
Price range	Affordable
Style	Casual
Cuisine	Sushi
Recommended for	Worth the travel

WEST RESTAURANT

Recommended by
James Walt

2881 Granville Street
Fairview
Vancouver
British Columbia V6H 3J4
+1 6047388938
www.westrestaurant.com

Opening hours	Open 7 days
Credit cards	Accepted
Price range	Expensive
Style	Smart casual
Cuisine	West Coast Canadian
Recommended for	High end

"They represent the West Coast so well with all the local products."—James Walt

L'ABATTOIR

Recommended by
James Walt

217 Carrall Street
Gastown
Vancouver
British Columbia V6B 2J2
+1 6045681701
www.labattoir.ca

Opening hours	Open 7 days
Credit cards	Accepted
Price range	Affordable
Style	Smart casual
Cuisine	Canadian-French
Recommended for	Local favorite

BAUHAUS

Recommended by
Andrea Carlson

1 West Cordova Street
Gastown
Vancouver
British Columbia V6B 2J2
+1 6049741147
www.bauhaus.ca

Opening hours	Open 7 days
Credit cards	Accepted
Price range	Expensive
Style	Smart casual
Cuisine	German
Recommended for	High end

"Chef Stephan aims high and provides an excellent dining experience in a modern room."
—Andrea Carlson

PIDGIN

Recommended by
Vikram Vij

350 Carrall Street
Gastown
Vancouver
British Columbia V6B 2J3
+1 6046209400
www.pidginvancouver.com

Opening hours	Open 7 days
Credit cards	Accepted
Price range	Affordable
Style	Casual
Cuisine	Asian-Fusion
Recommended for	Regular neighborhood

RED WAGON CAFÉ

Recommended by
Brian Luptak

2296 East Hastings Street
Grandview-Woodland
Vancouver
British Columbia V5L 1V4
www.redwagoncafe.com

Opening hours	Open 7 days
Credit cards	Accepted but not AMEX
Price range	Affordable
Style	Casual
Cuisine	Diner
Recommended for	Breakfast

"Great, all-day breakfast spot. Serves amazing pancakes and thick-cut pork belly."—Brian Luptak

AU COMPTOIR

Recommended by
Andrea Carlson

2278 West 4th Avenue
Kitsilano
Vancouver
British Columbia V6K 1N8
+1 6045692278
www.aucomptoir.ca

Opening hours	Closed Tuesday
Reservation policy	No
Credit cards	Accepted but not AMEX
Price range	Affordable
Style	Casual
Cuisine	French
Recommended for	Breakfast

"Best French café in Vancouver with Parisian-style service and well-executed bistro classics."
—Andrea Carlson

BISHOP'S

Recommended by
Sam Harris

2183 West 4th Avenue
Kitsilano
Vancouver
British Columbia V6K 1N7
+1 6047382025
www.bishopsonline.com

Opening hours	Closed Monday
Credit cards	Accepted but not AMEX
Price range	Affordable
Style	Casual
Cuisine	Modern Canadian
Recommended for	High end

MAENAM

Recommended by
Vikram Vij

1938 West 4th Avenue
Kitsilano
Vancouver
British Columbia V6J 1M5
+1 6047305579
www.maenam.ca

Opening hours	Open 7 days
Credit cards	Accepted
Price range	Budget
Style	Casual
Cuisine	Thai
Recommended for	Regular neighborhood

LA QUERCIA

Recommended by
Andrea Carlson

3689 West 4th Avenue
Kitsilano
Vancouver
British Columbia V6R 1P2
+1 6046761007
www.laquercia.ca

Opening hours	Closed Monday
Credit cards	Accepted
Price range	Affordable
Style	Smart casual
Cuisine	Italian
Recommended for	Wish I'd opened

"Family run and deeply passionate about Italian food. Naturally expanded into neighboring space with a wine bar. Ensconced in a neighborhood traditionally challenging for restaurants to thrive in."
—Andrea Carlson

THOMAS HAAS

Recommended by
Vikram Vij

2539 West Broadway Avenue
Kitsilano
Vancouver
British Columbia V6K 2E9
+1 6047361848
www.thomashaas.com

Opening hours	Closed Monday and Sunday
Reservation policy	No
Credit cards	Accepted
Price range	Budget
Style	Casual
Cuisine	Café-Bakery
Recommended for	Local favorite

MEDINA CAFÉ

Recommended by
Angus An

780 Richards Street
Library District
Vancouver
British Columbia V6B 3A4
+1 6048793114
www.medinacafe.com

Opening hours	Open 7 days
Reservation policy	No
Credit cards	Accepted
Price range	Budget
Style	Casual
Cuisine	Brunch
Recommended for	Breakfast

CONGEE NOODLE HOUSE

Recommended by
Angus An

141 East Broadway
Mount Pleasant
Vancouver
British Columbia V5T 1W1
+1 6048798221

Opening hours	Open 7 days
Reservation policy	No
Credit cards	Not accepted
Price range	Affordable
Style	Casual
Cuisine	Chinese
Recommended for	Breakfast

"Traditional Chinese breakfast, lots of congees to choose from."—Angus An

FASSIL RESTAURANT

Recommended by
Brian Luptak

5, 736 East Broadway
Mount Pleasant
Vancouver
British Columbia V5T 1X9
+1 6048792001
www.fassil.ca

Opening hours	Open 7 days
Credit cards	Accepted but not AMEX
Price range	Affordable
Style	Casual
Cuisine	Ethiopian
Recommended for	Regular neighborhood

"The best spot if you're feeling like heart-warming curry. Chef and owner Daresse makes you feel at home as soon as you enter this small Ethiopian restaurant. The Kitfo 'steak tartare' is so good."—Brian Luptak

MARULILU CAFÉ

Recommended by
Hidekazu Tojos

451 West Broadway
Mount Pleasant
Vancouver
British Columbia V5Y 1R4
+1 6045684211

Opening hours	Open 7 days
Reservation policy	No
Credit cards	Accepted
Price range	Affordable
Style	Casual
Cuisine	Japanese
Recommended for	Breakfast

SAL Y LIMON

Recommended by
Brian Luptak

701 Kingsway Street
Mount Pleasant
Vancouver
British Columbia V5T 2RJ
+1 6046774247
www.salylimon.ca

Opening hours	Open 7 days
Reservation policy	No
Credit cards	Accepted
Price range	Budget
Style	Casual
Cuisine	Mexican
Recommended for	Regular neighborhood

"When I'm feeling like a quick and delicious meal,
I head over to Sal y Limon for the cochinita burrito."
—Brian Luptak

VIJ'S

Recommended by
John Jackson &
Connie DeSousa

3106 Cambie Street
Mount Pleasant
Vancouver
British Columbia V5Z 2W2
+1 6047366664
www.vijsrestaurant.ca

Opening hours	Open 7 days
Reservation policy	No
Credit cards	Accepted
Price range	Affordable
Style	Casual
Cuisine	Indian
Recommended for	Worth the travel

LUCKY NOODLE CHINESE

Recommended by
Angus An

3377 Kingsway
Renfrew-Collingwood
Vancouver
British Columbia V5R 5K6
+1 6044308818

Opening hours	Closed Tuesday
Reservation policy	No
Credit cards	Not accepted
Price range	Budget
Style	Casual
Cuisine	Chinese
Recommended for	Bargain

"The best Hunan-style Chinese food—super spicy,
super delicious."—Angus An

THE FISH COUNTER

Recommended by
Brian Luptak

3825 Main Street
Riley Park
Vancouver
British Columbia V5V 3P1
+1 6048763474
www.thefishcounter.com

Opening hours	Open 7 days
Reservation policy	No
Credit cards	Accepted but not AMEX
Price range	Budget
Style	Casual
Cuisine	Seafood
Recommended for	Bargain

"This place uses great, local and sustainable seafood,
and the fried oyster po-boy is out of this world."
—Brian Luptak

MASAYOSHI

Recommended by
Angus An

4376 Fraser Street
Riley Park
Vancouver
British Columbia V5V 4G3
+1 6044286272
www.masayoshi.ca

Opening hours	Closed Sunday
Credit cards	Accepted
Price range	Expensive
Style	Smart casual
Cuisine	Sushi
Recommended for	Regular neighborhood

"Some of the best nigiri outside of Tokyo."—Angus An

BAO BEI CHINESE BRASSERIE

Recommended by
James Walt

163 Keefer Street
Strathcona
Vancouver
British Columbia V6A 1X3
+1 6046880876
www.bao-bei.ca

Opening hours	Open 7 days
Reservation policy	No
Credit cards	Accepted
Price range	Affordable
Style	Casual
Cuisine	Chinese
Recommended for	Wish I'd opened

"It's a great idea, blending Chinese and Western cuisine, and Joel is a really good chef."—James Walt

THE BOXCAR

Recommended by
Andrea Carlson

923 Main Street
Strathcona
Vancouver
British Columbia V6A 2V8
+1 6043984010
www.thecobalt.ca/the-boxcar

Opening hours	Open 7 days
Credit cards	Accepted
Price range	Budget
Style	Casual
Cuisine	Bar
Recommended for	Late night

"The bar has a great vibe and lets you order in pizza from neighboring Pizza Farina—some of the best pizza in town."—Andrea Carlson

FAT MAO NOODLES

Recommended by
Angus An

217 East Georgia Street
Strathcona
Vancouver
British Columbia V6A 1Z6
+1 6045698192
www.fatmaonoodles.com

Opening hours	Open 7 days
Credit cards	Accepted
Price range	Affordable
Style	Casual
Cuisine	Noodles
Recommended for	Bargain

JUKE

Recommended by
Sam Harris

182 Keefer Street
Strathcona
Vancouver
British Columbia V6A 3B3
+1 6043365853
www.jukefriedchicken.com

Opening hours	Open 7 days
Reservation policy	No
Credit cards	Accepted
Price range	Affordable
Style	Casual
Cuisine	Chicken-Fast Food
Recommended for	Wish I'd opened

"Fried chicken joint that delivers casual and fun food to a high standard."—Sam Harris

PHNOM PENH

Recommended by
John Horne

244 East Georgia Street
Strathcona
Vancouver
British Columbia V6A1Z7
+1 6046825777

Opening hours	Open 7 days
Credit cards	Accepted
Price range	Affordable
Style	Casual
Cuisine	Vietnamese-Cambodian
Recommended for	Bargain

"My wife is from Vancouver, so she told me about this place. It's been there for years. We love the chicken wings, rare beef carpaccio, hot and sour soup, and the beef with egg on rice. We go every time we're in Vancouver."—John Horne

UPSTAIRS @ CAMPAGNOLO

Recommended by
Andrea Carlson

1020 Main Street
Strathcona
Vancouver
British Columbia V6A 2W1
+1 6044846018
www.campagnolorestaurant.ca

Opening hours	Open 7 days
Reservation policy	No
Credit cards	Accepted
Price range	Affordable
Style	Casual
Cuisine	Bar
Recommended for	Late night

"Upstairs at Campagnolo, Peter runs a bar with an eclectic mix of fine cocktails and a tight list of natural wines. Chef Robert Belcham curates some of the best charcuterie in town, as well as some decadent carnivorous items like whole confit duck and the famous double-patty dirty burger."—Andrea Carlson

GUU ORIGINAL THURLOW

Recommended by
Brian Luptak

838 Thurlow Street
West End
Vancouver
British Columbia V6E 1W2
+1 6046858817
www.guu-izakaya.com

Opening hours	Open 7 days
Credit cards	Accepted
Price range	Affordable
Style	Casual
Cuisine	Japanese
Recommended for	Late night

"Guu is open late, the atmosphere is great, there's cold beer, and the food is spot on and delicious. The chefs have a one-page written menu of specials and if you can sit at the bar I recommend doing so, because it's a good crew to watch cook."—Brian Luptak

GYOZA KING

Recommended by
James Walt

1508 Robson Street
West End
Vancouver
British Columbia V6G 1C2
+1 6046698278
www.gyokingroup.com

Opening hours	Closed Monday and Tuesday
Credit cards	Accepted
Price range	Affordable
Style	Casual
Cuisine	Japanese
Recommended for	Late night

"It's open late and has very good gyoza. It's a good place to hang out with other industry people after work as well."—James Walt

THE RAMENMAN

Recommended by
Andrea Carlson

841 Bidwell Street
West End
Vancouver
British Columbia V6G 2J7
+1 6046208806

Opening hours	Closed Monday
Credit cards	Accepted but not AMEX
Price range	Affordable
Style	Casual
Cuisine	Japanese
Recommended for	Bargain

"Modern cooking methods, house-made noodles, and amazing umami flavor combos, such as the chicken broth with clam, truffle oil, and chive ramen. Add the egg and do NOT miss the gyoza!"—Andrea Carlson

SAVARY ISLAND PIE COMPANY
Recommended by
Andrea Carlson

1533 Marine Drive
West Vancouver
Vancouver
British Columbia V7V 1H9
+1 6049264021
www.savaryislandpiecompany.com

Opening hours	Open 7 days
Reservation policy	No
Credit cards	Accepted
Price range	Budget
Style	Casual
Cuisine	Pie Shop
Recommended for	Breakfast

"Gulf Island vibes. Consistently modest and delicious omelettes with fabulous soda bread."
—Andrea Carlson

Founded by an impoverished baker named Eileen Walkem-Hall in 1989, this Ambleside bakery still serves sweet pies bursting with fresh blueberries, rhubarb, raspberries, and apples and savory ones including *tourtière* (classic Quebec pork pie) and a chicken pot pie of great renown. To walk into the bakery is to walk into the beating heart of the community. The warmth comes not just from the freshly made loaves and muffins lining sheet trays but from the interactions with the regulars and, frankly, because it's hard not to be joyful in a pie shop.

BLUE WATER CAFÉ
Recommended by
James Walt

1095 Hamilton Street
Yaletown
Vancouver
British Columbia V6B 5T4
+1 6046888078
www.bluewatercafe.net

Opening hours	Open 7 days
Credit cards	Accepted
Price range	Expensive
Style	Smart casual
Cuisine	Seafood
Recommended for	Local favorite

"Features all that is great about the West Coast. Amazingly fresh seafood, and very good sushi and Japanese preparations. Frank Pabst is an exceptional chef."—James Walt

CIOPPINO'S MEDITERRANEAN GRILL
Recommended by
Angus An,
Hidekazu Tojos

1133 Hamilton Street
Yaletown
Vancouver
British Columbia V6B 5P6
+1 6046887466
www.cioppinosyaletown.com

Opening hours	Closed Sunday
Credit cards	Accepted
Price range	Affordable
Style	Casual
Cuisine	Mediterranean
Recommended for	Regular neighborhood

"Chef Pino is the godfather of Italian cooking. I love his modern take on Italian classics."—Angus An

Chef Giuseppe "Pino" Posteraro is known for his light touch and modest demeanour, so you won't hear him shouting about local sourcing or creative innovation. But, since he opened Cioppino's in 1999, he's been widely considered as Vancouver's godfather of Italian cuisine. In an elegant, warm, and unpretentious dining room that looks into his gleaming steel kitchen, the lightest of pastas appear —spaghetti *alla vongole* (with clams), served here with Baynes Sound Manila clams, has never seemed so ethereal—and so do Italian classics like wild boar (from Alberta), served both braised and crispy.

"I CAN ALWAYS GO THERE FOR A DRINK AND A BITE AFTER A BUSY NIGHT IN THE KITCHEN."

SUSUR LEE P766

"AMAZING FOR FRIED CHICKEN, RIBS AND BURGERS."

JOHN HORNE P769

TORONTO

"*My new favorite, bar none. So very good.*"

ANTHONY ROSE P768

"THE FOOD IS OUTSTANDING; SIMPLY DONE WITH FANTASTIC INGREDIENTS. IF A CHEF IS VISITING FROM OUT OF TOWN, THIS IS THE FIRST PLACE I RECOMMEND."

JOHN HORNE P768

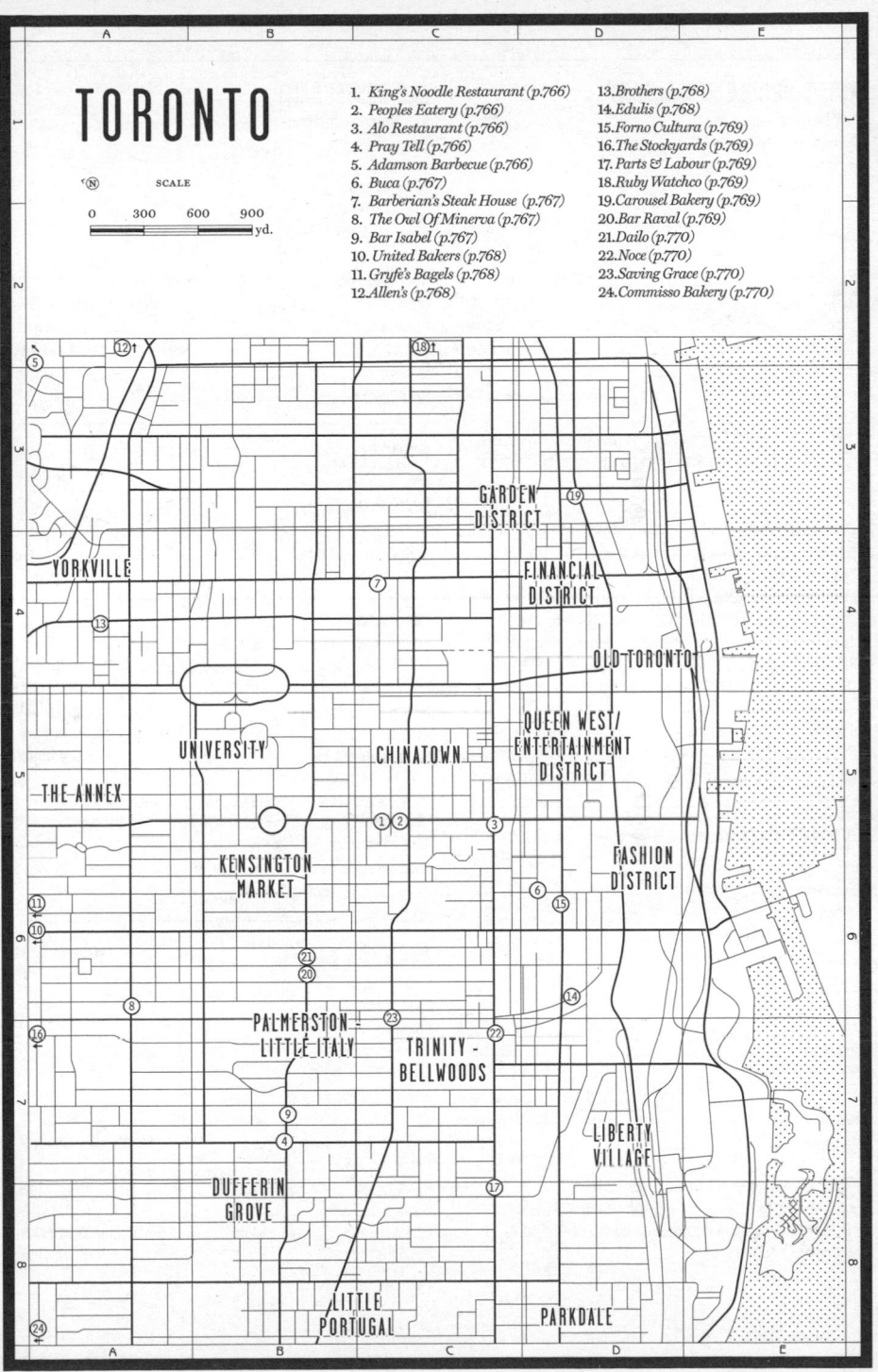

KING'S NOODLE RESTAURANT

Recommended by
Susur Lee

296 Spadina Avenue
Chinatown
Toronto
Ontario M5T 2E7
+1 4165981817
www.kingsnoodle.ca

Opening hours	Closed Wednesday
Credit cards	Not accepted
Price range	Budget
Style	Casual
Cuisine	Chinese
Recommended for	Bargain

"King's Noodle is like going home. I go so often, all of the staff know me and I get to eat the food I grew up on."—Susur Lee

A long-standing, reliable, and affordable Cantonese in the heart of Chinatown that stays open from congee at breakfast (9.00 a.m.) to noodles in the small hours (1.00 a.m.). So brightly lit since its refurbishment several years ago that the photosensitive should bring their shades. It can get chaotically busy at peak times, with long lines (queues) not uncommon during the lunch rush and late at night. The various barbecued meats in the window are not just there for display—the duck and pork come highly recommended. Be prepared to share if you're put on one of the communal tables.

PEOPLES EATERY

Recommended by
Susur Lee

307 Spadina Avenue
Chinatown
Toronto
Ontario M5T 2E6
+1 4167921784
www.peopleseatery.com

Opening hours	Open 7 days
Credit cards	Accepted
Price range	Affordable
Style	Casual
Cuisine	Canadian-International
Recommended for	Late night

"This place is owned by my good friend Dustin. I can always go there for a drink and a bite after a busy night in the kitchen, see some old friends and relax."—Susur Lee

ALO RESTAURANT

Recommended by
Carlos Perez

163 Spadina Avenue
Downtown
Toronto
Ontario M5V 2L6
+1 4162602222
www.alorestaurant.com

Opening hours	Closed Monday and Sunday
Credit cards	Accepted but not AMEX
Price range	Expensive
Style	Smart casual
Cuisine	French
Recommended for	High end

PRAY TELL

Recommended by
Timothy Charles

838 College Street
Dufferin Grove
Toronto
Ontario M6H 1A2
www.praytellbar.com

Opening hours	Open 7 days
Reservation policy	No
Credit cards	Accepted but not AMEX or Diners
Price range	Affordable
Style	Casual
Cuisine	Canadian-International
Recommended for	Late night

"The ambiance is fantastic; people pack into a well decorated space, everyone laughing and talking. The food is delicious and the cocktails are on point too. Be sure to try all the menu— The pizza pocket is genius."—Timothy Charles

ADAMSON BARBECUE

Recommended by
John Horne

176 Wicksteed Avenue
East York
Toronto
Ontario M4G 2B6
+1 6475592080
www.adamsonbarbecue.com

Opening hours	Closed Monday and Sunday
Credit cards	Accepted
Price range	Affordable
Style	Casual
Cuisine	Texas Barbecue
Recommended for	Regular neighborhood

"It's very rare to be able to find real, down and dirty Texas barbecue north of the border. There can be a bit of a wait here, and when they run out they run out, so I'd recommend getting there early. You can get meat by the pound on a plate with sides, or in a bun. I love the ribs, *kielbasa*, brisket, cheese curd sausage, as well as the coleslaw and baked beans."
—John Horne

BUCA

Recommended by
John Jackson &
Connie DeSousa,
Susur Lee,
Csilla Thackray

604 King Street West
Fashion District
Toronto
Ontario M5V 1M6
+1 4168651600
www.buca.ca

Opening hours	Open 7 days
Credit cards	Accepted
Price range	Affordable
Style	Smart casual
Cuisine	Italian
Recommended for	Worth the travel

"Another of my favorite Italian restaurants—I can go for a nice, light lunch or a family-style feast but, no matter when or why I go, I always leave satisfied."
—Susur Lee

BARBERIAN'S STEAK HOUSE

Recommended by
Anthony Rose

7 Elm Street
Garden District
Toronto
Ontario M5G 1H1
+1 4165970335
www.barberians.com

Opening hours	Open 7 days
Credit cards	Accepted
Price range	Expensive
Style	Smart casual
Cuisine	Steakhouse
Recommended for	High end

"I recommend drinking martinis at the corner table where it's really dark."—Anthony Rose

The maple-leaf flag waves proudly outside Barberian's, which has stood in the same spot, and been owned by the same family, since Harry Barberian opened a teetotal steakhouse here in 1959. Since then the owners have obtained an alcohol licence—just as well, since the 800-bin wine list now needs to be housed in a two-storey cellar. The rather masculine menu recalls an earlier era

of dining out, with oysters, snails, and Caesar salad as starters and chocolate mousse, New York cheesecake, and frozen chocolate eclair for dessert. As well as a broad range of different cuts and sizes of steak, specials such as grilled capon and salmon complete the picture.

THE OWL OF MINERVA

Recommended by
John Horne

700 Bloor Street West
Koreatown
Toronto
Ontario M6G 1L5
+1 4165383030

Opening hours	Open 7 days
Reservation policy	No
Credit cards	Accepted
Price range	Affordable
Style	Casual
Cuisine	Korean
Recommended for	Late night

"Fast and tasty. Open twenty-four hours a day so you can hit it any time. The food is amazing in the dead of Canadian winter. I love the pork bone soup and short ribs."—John Horne

BAR ISABEL

Recommended by
Suzanne Goin

797 College Street
Little Italy
Toronto
Ontario M6G 1CG
+1 4165322222
www.barisabel.com

Opening hours	Open 7 days
Credit cards	Accepted
Price range	Affordable
Style	Smart Casual
Cuisine	Spanish
Recommended for	Worth the travel

"The space is really beautiful. I had the most amazing grilled octopus!"—Suzanne Goin

UNITED BAKERS

Recommended by
Anthony Rose

506 Lawrence Avenue West
Midtown
Toronto
Ontario M6A 1A1
+1 4167890519
www.unitedbakers.ca

Opening hours	Open 7 days
Credit cards	Accepted but not AMEX
Price range	Affordable
Style	Casual
Cuisine	Diner
Recommended for	Breakfast

GRYFE'S BAGELS

Recommended by
Anthony Rose

3421 Bathurst Street
North York
Toronto
Ontario M6A 2C1
+1 4167831552

Opening hours	Open 7 days
Reservation policy	No
Credit cards	Not accepted
Price range	Budget
Style	Casual
Cuisine	Jewish
Recommended for	Bargain

"Blueberry buns and bagel pizzas."—Anthony Rose

ALLEN'S

Recommended by
Anthony Rose

143 Danforth Avenue
Old Toronto
Toronto
Ontario M4K 1N2
+1 4164633086
www.allens.to

Opening hours	Open 7 days
Credit cards	Accepted
Price range	Budget
Style	Casual
Cuisine	International
Recommended for	Regular neighborhood

"Allen's is my mainstay forever and ever."
—Anthony Rose

BROTHERS

Recommended by
Anthony Rose

1240 Bay Street
Old Toronto
Toronto
Ontario M5R 2A7
+1 416.804.6066
www.brotherstoronto.com

Opening hours	Closed Sunday
Credit cards	Accepted but not AMEX
Price range	Affordable
Style	Smart casual
Cuisine	Modern Canadian
Recommended for	Regular neighborhood

"Brothers is my new favorite, bar none. So very good."
—Anthony Rose

EDULIS

Recommended by
Andrea Carlson,
John Horne

169 Niagara Street
Old Toronto
Toronto
Ontario M5V 1C9
+1 4167034222
www.edulisrestaurant.com

Opening hours	Closed Monday and Tuesday
Credit cards	Accepted
Price range	Expensive
Style	Smart casual
Cuisine	Modern Canadian
Recommended for	Local favorite

"It's hands down my favorite restaurant in Toronto. The food is outstanding—simply done with fantastic ingredients. If a chef is visiting from out of town, this is the first place I recommend. It feels like a homey, neighborhood spot but they execute Michelin-star food. They're very good at knowing what's in season and preparing ingredients that make any dish shine."
—John Horne

FORNO CULTURA

Recommended by
Susur Lee

609 King Street West
Old Toronto
Toronto
Ontario M5V 1M5
+1 4166038305
www.fornocultura.com

Opening hours	Closed Monday
Reservation policy	No
Credit cards	Accepted
Price range	Budget
Style	Casual
Cuisine	Italian
Recommended for	Local favorite

"This home-style Italian bakery is right next to my flagship restaurant, Lee. They have everything from biscotti to bombolone and they make fresh sandwiches every day."—Susur Lee

THE STOCKYARDS

Recommended by
John Horne

699 Saint Clair Avenue West
Old Toronto
Toronto
Ontario M6C 1B2
+1 4166589666
www.thestockyards.ca

Opening hours	Closed Monday
Reservation policy	No
Credit cards	Accepted
Price range	Affordable
Style	Casual
Cuisine	Diner
Recommended for	Regular neighborhood

"The Stockyards is amazing for fried chicken, barbecue ribs, and burgers."—John Horne

PARTS & LABOUR

Recommended by
John Jackson &
Connie DeSousa

1566 Queen Street West
Parkdale
Toronto
Ontario M6R 1A6
+1 4165887750
www.partsandlabour.ca

Opening hours	Closed Monday
Credit cards	Accepted
Price range	Budget
Style	Smart casual
Cuisine	Modern Canadian
Recommended for	Worth the travel

RUBY WATCHCO

Recommended by
John Jackson &
Connie DeSousa

730 Queen Street East
Riverdale
Toronto
Ontario M4M 1H2
+1 4164650100
www.rubywatcho.ca

Opening hours	Closed Monday
Credit cards	Accepted
Price range	Affordable
Style	Smart casual
Cuisine	Modern Canadian
Recommended for	Worth the travel

CAROUSEL BAKERY

Recommended by
John Horne,
Anthony Rose

Unit 42, 92–95 Front Street East
St. Lawrence
Toronto
Ontario M5E 1C3
+1 4163634247

Opening hours	Closed Monday and Sunday
Reservation policy	No
Credit cards	Not accepted
Price range	Budget
Style	Casual
Cuisine	Canadian
Recommended for	Bargain

"Their peameal bacon sandwich is iconic."
—John Horne

BAR RAVAL

Recommended by
Timothy Charles,
John Jackson &
Connie DeSousa,
Carlos Perez

505 College Street
Trinity-Bellwoods
Toronto
Ontario M6G 1A4
+1 6473448001
www.thisisbarraval.com

Opening hours	Open 7 days
Reservation policy	No
Credit cards	Accepted
Price range	Budget
Style	Casual
Cuisine	Tapas Bar
Recommended for	Late night

DAILO

Recommended by
John Jackson &
Connie DeSousa

503 College Street
Trinity-Bellwoods
Toronto
Ontario M6J 2J3
+1 6473418882
www.dailoto.com

Opening hours	Closed Monday
Credit cards	Accepted
Price range	Budget
Style	Casual
Cuisine	Cantonese
Recommended for	Worth the travel

NOCE

Recommended by
Susur Lee

875 Queen Street West
Trinity-Bellwoods
Toronto
Ontario M6J 1G5
+1 4165043463
www.nocerestaurant.ca

Opening hours	Closed Monday
Credit cards	Accepted
Price range	Affordable
Style	Smart casual
Cuisine	Italian
Recommended for	Regular neighborhood

"It's right up the street from my house; I love just walking in to grab a nice home-cooked Italian meal."
—Susur Lee

SAVING GRACE

Recommended by
Susur Lee

907 Dundas Street West
Trinity-Bellwoods
Toronto
Ontario M6J 1V9
+1 4167037368

Opening hours	Closed Tuesday
Reservation policy	No
Credit cards	Accepted
Price range	Affordable
Style	Casual
Cuisine	Breakfast-Brunch
Recommended for	Breakfast

"Nice small restaurant—it feels like you're having brunch in your friend's kitchen. If you can get a spot, as there's always a line (queue)!"—Susur Lee

COMMISSO BAKERY

Recommended by
Anthony Rose

8 Kincort Street
York
Toronto
Ontario M6M 3E1
+1 4166517671
www.commissobakery.com

Opening hours	Open 7 days
Reservation policy	No
Credit cards	Accepted
Price range	Affordable
Style	Casual
Cuisine	Italian
Recommended for	Late night

"For veal sandwiches and they are always open, never closed."—Anthony Rose

Commisso Bros. began serving Italian-Canadians the tastes of the old country back in 1957—and this bakery continues to do so round the clock, seven days a week, 365 days a year. Persistent rumours of mob links (one former owner was shot dead outside the store in 2002) do little to dissuade customers from trooping through the door night after night for veal Parmigiana, porchetta, pizzas, and the store's own artisan breads. A large parking lot means there's always space, and you'll even find an olive bar and, in the summer, fresh gelato. A proud nugget of blue-collar Canadiana.

"IT'S MONTREAL AT ITS BEST: BOTH FRENCH AND ANGLO CULTURE IN ONE PLACE, WITH THE HOSPITALITY WE ARE RENOWNED FOR IN THE CITY."

ANTONIN MOUSSEAU-RIVARD P779

MONTREAL

"*The best lunch in town for under $10.*"

MARTIN JUNEAU P780

"REALLY GOOD, SIMPLE BRUNCH CLASSICS."

JOHN HORNE P778

"OPEN EARLY AND CLOSING LATE. IT'S PERFECT AFTER A LONG NIGHT IN MONTREAL."

COREY LEE P776

MONTREAL

N

SCALE

0   400   800   1200
yd.

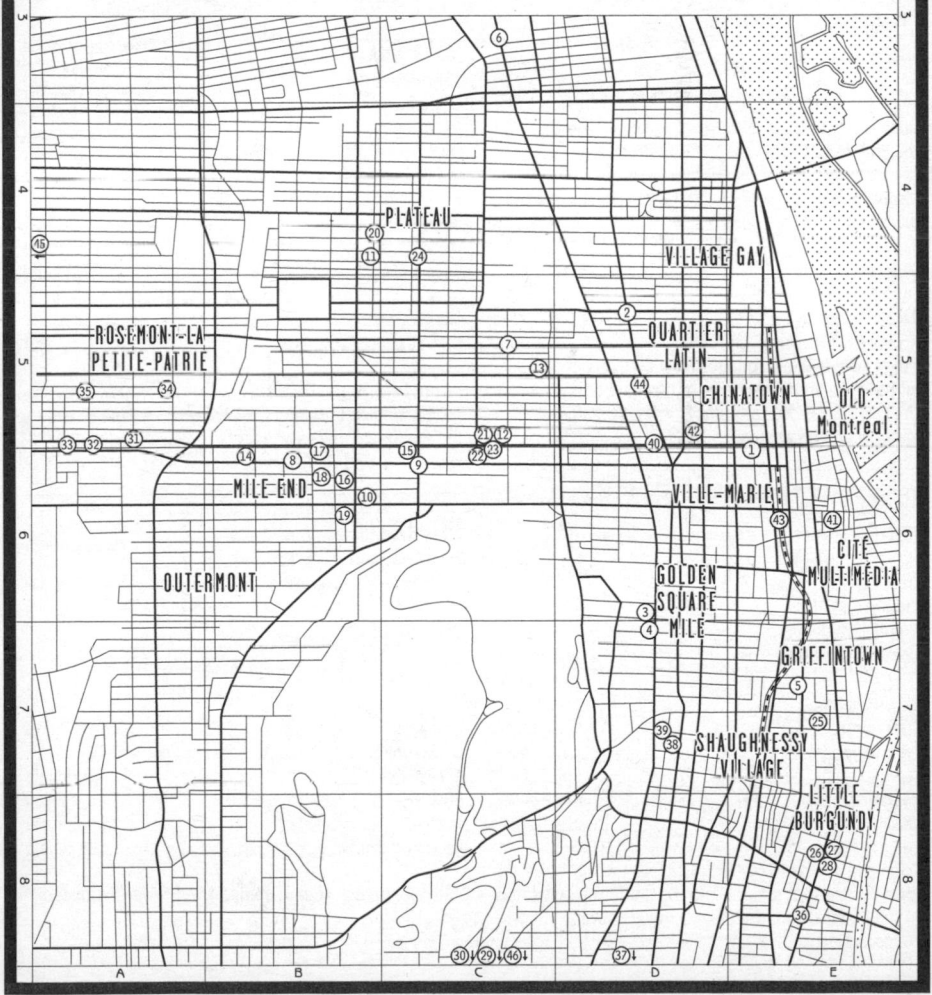

MON NAN

43 Rue de la Gauchetière Est
Chinatown
Montreal
Quebec H2Z 1K3
+1 5148667123
www.restaurantmonnan.com

Recommended by
Marc-Alexandre Mercier,
Jason Morris

Opening hours..Open 7 days
Credit cards...Accepted
Price range...Affordable
Style...Casual
Cuisine..Cantonese-Szechuan
Recommended for..Late night

LE MOUSSO

1023 Rue Ontario Est
Gay Village
Montreal
Quebec H2L 1P8
+1 4383847410

Recommended by
Martin Juneau,
Ben Reade

Opening hours.................................Closed Sunday to Tuesday
Credit cards...Accepted
Price range...Expensive
Style...Smart casual
Cuisine...Modern Canadian
Recommended for...................................Worth the travel

"Very tasty, brilliant, beautifully plated, quality
ingredients, and great pairings. Brilliant options
of extra food and drinks, super-friendly staff, and
an all-round great vibe."—Ben Reade

LE TAJ

2077 Rue Stanley
Golden Square Mile
Montreal
Quebec H3A 1R7
1 5148459015
www.restaurantletaj.com

Recommended by
Jason Morris

Opening hours..Open 7 days
Credit cards...Accepted
Price range...Affordable
Style...Smart casual
Cuisine...North Indian
Recommended for..Bargain

"Something like C$20 ($15; £11) for the buffet lunch;
drop some carrot pickles into the dahl soup and some
of the crumbs from the pakora tray—heaven!"
—Jason Morris

MAISON BOULUD

Ritz-Carlton Montreal
1228 Rue Sherbrooke Ouest
Golden Square Mile
Montreal
Quebec H3G 1H6
+1 5148424224
www.maisonboulud.com

Recommended by
Reto Lampart

Opening hours..Open 7 days
Credit cards...Accepted
Price range...Expensive
Style...Smart casual
Cuisine...Modern French
Recommended for..High end

NORA GRAY

1391 Rue Saint-Jacques
Griffintown
Montreal
Quebec H3C 1H2
+1 5144196672

Recommended by
John Jackson &
Connie DeSousa,
Marc-Alexandre Mercier,
David Pellizzari

Opening hours.............................Closed Monday and Sunday
Credit cards...Accepted
Price range...Affordable
Style...Smart casual
Cuisine..Italian
Recommended for..High end

"Nora Gray is an absoutely perfect restaurant. The
food is unquestionable, the service is charming, and
the ambience makes you feel like you never want to
leave."—David Pellizzari

MIAMI DELI

3090 Rue Sherbrooke Est
Hochelaga-Maisonneuve
Montreal
Quebec H1W 1B5
+1 5145250600
www.miamideli.com

Recommended by
Martin Juneau

Opening hours..Open 7 days
Credit cards...........................Accepted but not AMEX or Diners
Price range...Affordable
Style...Casual
Cuisine..International
Recommended for..Breakfast

"Perfect greasy spoon, open 24/7."—Martin Juneau

AU PIED DE COCHON

Recommended by
Carlo Lamagna,
Antonin Mousseau-Rivard

536 Avenue Duluth Est
Le Plateau-Mont-Royal
Montreal
Quebec H2L 1A9
+1 5142811114
www.aupieddecochon.ca

Opening hours	Closed Monday and Tuesday
Credit cards	Accepted
Price range	Affordable
Style	Casual
Cuisine	French Canadian
Recommended for	Local favorite

"Another Montreal must go—Gargantuan portions of pure love-food and an impressive wine selection make it one of my favorite places to bring friends who are visiting."—Antonin Mousseau-Rivard

Martin Picard's cult Québécois outpost has carved out a decadent reputation for itself since opening in 2001. Picard made his name here with his pork and foie gras-fixated menu, which incorporates these ingredients into everything, including the local delicacy poutine (fries [chips] topped with cheese curd and gravy), burgers, more typically French applications such as terrines and *boudin noir* (blood sausage) tarts—and stuffing it generously inside the restaurant's namesake. Meanwhile, Picard's famous duck-in-a-can is magret (breast) and more foie gras, cooked and brought to the table in said can and dumped on toast topped with celery root (celeriac) purée.

BARROS LUCOS

Recommended by
Normand Laprise

5201 Rue Saint-Urbain
Le Plateau-Mont-Royal
Montreal
Quebec H2T 2W8

Opening hours	Closed Monday
Credit cards	Accepted
Price range	Budget
Style	Casual
Cuisine	Chilean
Recommended for	Bargain

"You have to try the *barros jarpa*. It's delicious and I've been eating it for twenty five years. Same with the empanadas."—Normand Laprise

BEAUTY'S

Recommended by
Antonin Mousseau-Rivard,
David Pellizzari

93 Avenue du Mont-Royal
Le Plateau-Mont-Royal
Montreal
Quebec H2T 2S5
+1 5148498883
www.beautys.ca

Opening hours	Open 7 days
Credit cards	Accepted
Price range	Affordable
Style	Casual
Cuisine	Diner
Recommended for	Breakfast

"Beauty's is a Montreal institution serving the best brunch in town. Authentic old-school decor, classics like the bagel and lox sandwich, and the famous mish-mash omelette are just a few reasons why people are willing to wait in line to get in."
—Antonin Mousseau-Rivard

Little has changed at Beauty's since it opened in 1942. Hymie Skolnick, the kindly proprietor whose bowling nickname, "Beauty", gave the diner its name, is still there on the first stool at the bar. But what started as a lunch canteen for local garment workers has become a must-stop for Montrealers, who hunger for Skolnick's creations—like "superbeauty #2" (two eggs, fried potatoes, bacon, and sausage) and a hot dog-stuffed omelette dubbed the "Mish Mash". There are melts and burgers too. Now in his nineties, Skolnick may be greyer and slower than he was when he opened the place, but these days he's surrounded by grand-children too, to whom he's imparted the wisdom of breakfast and the benedictions of brunch.

BUVETTE CHEZ SIMONE

Recommended by
David Pellizzari

4869 Avenue Du Parc
Le Plateau-Mont-Royal
Montreal
Quebec H2V 4E7
+1 5147506577
www.buvettechezsimone.com

Opening hours	Open 7 days
Reservation policy	No
Credit cards	Accepted
Price range	Affordable
Style	Smart casual
Cuisine	International small plates
Recommended for	Late night

"I adore the owners of this place. The kitchen is open late and I can always count on discovering a new wine to love each visit."—David Pellizzari

The French have as many words for bar as the Inuit do for snow. A buvette, for instance, is a sort of late-night, always-packed, always-comfortable wine bar. This also describes Buvette Chez Simone, a mainstay for Montrealers, in Outremont. The wine selection is vast, well priced, and impeccably curated, but Frédéric Bourgault's food is also impressively good. From rotisserie chicken with crisp, fragrant skin and tender meat to more ambitious plates like deer loin with juniper and celery root (celeriac), the menu is a crowd-pleaser—and what crowds there are! Buvette Chez Simone packs the night owls in well into the evening, loathe to head home after such conviviality.

LE CHIEN FUMANT

Recommended by
Marc-Alexandre Mercier

4710 Lanaudiere Street
Le Plateau-Mont-Royal
Montreal
Quebec H2J 3P7
+1 5145242444
www.lechienfumant.com

Opening hours	Closed Monday
Credit cards	Accepted
Price range	Affordable
Style	Casual
Cuisine	International
Recommended for	Late night

DISPATCH COFFEE

Recommended by
John Winter Russell

4021 Boulevard Saint-Laurent
Le Plateau-Mont-Royal
Montreal
Quebec H2W 1Y4
+1 5145876463
www.dispatchcoffee.ca

Opening hours	Open 7 days
Reservation policy	No
Credit cards	Accepted but not AMEX
Price range	Budget
Style	Casual
Cuisine	Café
Recommended for	Breakfast

L'EXPRESS

Recommended by
Jason Morris,
Corey Lee,
Marc-Alexandre Mercier,
Antonin Mousseau-Rivard,
James Rigato

3927 Rue Saint-Denis
Le Plateau-Mont-Royal
Montreal
Quebec H2W 2M4
+1 5148455333
www.restaurantlexpress.com

Opening hours	Open 7 days
Credit cards	Accepted but not AMEX
Price range	Expensive
Style	Casual
Cuisine	French Bistro
Recommended for	Regular neighborhood

"L'Express is a timeless bistro that offers classic, hard-to-come-by fare like *rognons de veau* (veal kidneys). Open early and closing late, it's perfect after a long night in Montreal."—Corey Lee

Many swear by the steak *onglet* (hanger steak) with shallot butter and a side of fries at this iconic Parisian-style bistro. But the restaurant, which has served French classics seven days a week, nineteen hours a day for nearly the last forty years, has more to swear allegiance to. The onion soup, the calf's liver with tarragon, the ham-studded quiche, the creamy leek vinaigrette—each has its own faction. Then there's the 11,000-strong wine cellar, filled with rare Raveneau and other finds. Yes, the floor is black-and-white chequered and the waiters are black-and-white vested. But so fierce are the passions of the diners who find themselves at L'Express, among old friends and fresh flavors, there is plenty of color to be found.

FARINE

102 Rue Saint-Viateur Ouest
Le Plateau-Mont-Royal
Montreal
Quebec H2T 2L1
+1 5144399223
www.farinemontreal.com

Recommended by
Marc-Alexandre Mercier

Opening hours	Open 7 days
Reservation policy	No
Credit cards	Accepted
Price range	Budget
Style	Casual
Cuisine	Italian
Recommended for	Bargain

"Chef Juan, known as papichulo, is a great cook. He is the Italian grandma I never had. Small neighborhood joint serving comforting food."
—Marc-Alexandre Mercier

HOF KELSTEN

4524 Bouevard Saint-Laurent
Le Plateau-Mont-Royal
Montreal
Quebec H2T 1R4
+1 5146497991
www.hofkelsten.com

Recommended by
Marc-Alexandre Mercier

Opening hours	Closed Monday and Sunday
Reservation policy	No
Credit cards	Not accepted
Price range	Budget
Style	Casual
Cuisine	Modern Jewish-Eastern European
Recommended for	Breakfast

JUN I

156 Avenue Laurier Ouest
Le Plateau-Mont-Royal
Montreal
Quebec H2T 2N7
+1 5142765864
www.juni.ca

Recommended by
Normand Laprise

Opening hours	Closed Sunday
Credit cards	Accepted
Price range	Affordable
Style	Casual
Cuisine	Sushi
Recommended for	Regular neighborhood

LARRYS

9 Fairmount Avenue Est
Le Plateau-Mont-Royal
Montreal
Quebec H2T 1S4
www.larrys.website

Recommended by
Marc-Andre Jette,
Marc-Alexandre Mercier,
John Winter Russell

Opening hours	Closed Sunday
Reservation policy	No
Credit cards	Accepted
Price range	Affordable
Style	Casual
Cuisine	International Small plates
Recommended for	Late night

"I don't often eat out late, but this would be the place if and when I do. Simple food and plenty of good wine."—John Winter Russell

LAWRENCE RESTAURANT

5201 Boulevard Saint-Laurent
Le Plateau-Mont-Royal
Montreal
Quebec H2T 2L9
+1 5145031070
www.lawrencerestaurant.com

Recommended by
Marc-Alexandre Mercier
David Pellizzari

Opening hours	Closed Monday
Credit cards	Accepted
Price range	Affordable
Style	Casual
Cuisine	Bistro
Recommended for	Regular neighborhood

"Marc Cohen's food is straightforward, very honest, and consistently delicious. The service is professional and knowledgeable. It's an all-round win every time. Marc's food comes off as traditional English fare but the quality of the products he's sourced is very evident. An English traditionalist using Québec's best to make his food shine."—David Pellizzari

Shabby chic meets industrial cool at this popular forty-seat neighborhood bistro. Exposed pipework and yards of gunmetal-grey paintwork are the setting for bare wood tables, simple bistro chairs, and the odd wooden bench. Weekend brunch is hugely popular, with everything from scones to boiled egg and anchovy toast on offer—but meat lovers will save their appetite for dinner. British-born chef Marc Cohen has his own butchery in the restaurant's basement, meaning there's plenty of nose-to-tail action on the menu, including confit pork with lentils, cabbage and mustard, and ox heart with fiddleheads and fresh cheese.

LEMÉAC

Recommended by
Antonin Mousseau-Rivard

1045 Avenue Laurier Ouest
Le Plateau-Mont-Royal
Montreal
Quebec H2V 2L1
+1 5142700999
www.restaurantlemeac.com

Opening hours	Open 7 days
Credit cards	Accepted
Price range	Expensive
Style	Smart casual
Cuisine	French Bistro
Recommended for	Regular neighborhood

"It's one of those places where you always feel at home even though you're in a chic and distinguished decor. The food is classic French with a modern twist and the service is extremely friendly. Great wine list also."—Antonin Mousseau-Rivard

MAISON PUBLIQUE

Recommended by
John Horne,
John Jackson &
Connie DeSousa,
Normand Laprise

4720 Rue Marquette
Le Plateau-Mont-Royal
Montreal
Quebec H2J 3Y6
+1 5145070555
www.maisonpublique.com

Opening hours	Closed Monday and Tuesday
Reservation policy	No
Credit cards	Accepted
Price range	Affordable
Style	Casual
Cuisine	French
Recommended for	Breakfast

"Really good, simple, brunch classics, executed well, with a French, West Coast feel."—John Horne

This neighborhood pub-restaurant's British connections stretch beyond its slicked-up boozer aesthetic—it's backed by Jamie Oliver. But the gutsy menu is very much the work of local chef-owner Derek Dammann (an Oliver alumnus), whose love of seasonal gastropub cooking is evident in the likes of Welsh rarebit, Charlevoix pork with salsa verde, and fried rabbit. There's an all-Canadian wine list, a line-up of ciders, and a popular weekend brunch featuring an English breakfast loaded with blood pudding, bone marrow, and pork chops—variety meats (offal) is a specialty here. Maison Publique (geddit?) doesn't take reservations, so pitch up and grab a seat at the long counter where you can watch the chefs at work.

LE MAJESTIQUE

Recommended by
Marc-Alexandre Mercier

4105 Boulevard Saint-Laurent
Le Plateau-Mont-Royal
Montreal
Quebec H2W 1Y7
+1 5144391850
www.restobarmajestique.com

Opening hours	Open 7 days
Reservation policy	No
Credit cards	Accepted but not AMEX
Price range	Affordable
Style	Casual
Cuisine	Seafood-Bar
Recommended for	Late night

NOREN

Recommended by
David Pellizzari

77 Rue Rachel
Le Plateau-Mont-Royal
Montreal
Quebec H2W 1G2
+1 5143971141

Opening hours	Closed Monday and Tuesday
Reservation policy	No
Credit cards	Accepted but not AMEX
Price range	Affordable
Style	Casual
Cuisine	Japanese
Recommended for	Bargain

"The best *takoyaki* I've ever had in my life, *okonomiyaki* with either pork or shiitakes, and then a couple of small lunch plates that change once a week. Its consistency is amazing, and the flavors are always rich and well developed, and with the plates going from C$9–12 ($7–9; £5–8), I almost feel embarassed to not pay more each time I go."—David Pellizzari

RÉSERVOIR

Recommended by
David Pellizzari

9 Avenue Duluth Est
Le Plateau-Mont-Royal
Montreal
Quebec H2W 1G6
+1 5148497779
www.brasseriereservoir.ca

Opening hours	Open 7 days
Reservation policy	No
Credit cards	Accepted
Price range	Affordable
Style	Casual
Cuisine	Brasserie
Recommended for	Wish I'd opened

"The new partnership with the gang at Hotel Herman is super exciting and definitely something that I think most chefs would have loved to take on. The established brasserie already making some of Montreal's best beer, now open to making some great food to accompany those efforts is something that will bring many new clients in the door, including myself." —David Pellizzari

LA SALLE À MANGER

Recommended by
James Rigato

1302 Mont-Royal Avenue Est
Le Plateau-Mont-Royal
Montreal
Quebec H2J 1Y5
+1 5145220777
www.lasalleamanger.ca

Opening hours	Open 7 days
Credit cards	Accepted but not AMEX
Price range	Budget
Style	Casual
Cuisine	French
Recommended for	Worth the travel

CANDIDE

Recommended by
Florent Ladeyn

551 Rue Saint-Martin
Little Burgundy
Montreal
Quebec H3J 2L6
+1 5144472717
www.restaurantcandide.com

Opening hours	Closed Monday and Tuesday
Credit cards	Accepted but not AMEX
Price range	Affordable
Style	Smart casual
Cuisine	French Canadian
Recommended for	Worth the travel

JOE BEEF

Recommended by
Bo Bech, Sean Gray,
John Jackson &
Connie DeSousa,
Carlo Lamagna,
Antonin Mousseau-Rivard,
Benjamin Sukle,
Isaac Toups

2491 Rue Notre-Dame Ouest
Little Burgundy
Montreal
Quebec H3J 1N6
+1 5149356504
www.joebeef.ca

Opening hours	Closed Monday and Sunday
Reservation policy	No
Credit cards	Accepted but not AMEX
Price range	Affordable
Style	Casual
Cuisine	Steakhouse-Seafood
Recommended for	Worth the travel

"It's Montreal at its best—both French and Anglo culture in one place, with the hospitality we are renowned for in the city. The food is generous and the service is top notch! And the local produce used is incredible. Make sure to go in the summer and eat on their lovely terrace."—Antonin Mousseau-Rivard

Joe Beef opened in 2005 and it's easy to forget there's an actual restaurant there, underneath all the praise heaped on it. But there is, and it deserves the valedictions. At Frederic Morin and David McMillan's lively Little Burgundy restaurant, under the gaze of taxidermied beasts, the owners have pioneered a sort of glorious, gluttonous, non-stop feast. Dinner (no reservations) is a melange of high-quality ingredients, expert preparation, and lavish fun. Guests order from large black chalkboards on which are written, in neat chalk letters, carnal pleasures like lobster and bacon-studded spaghetti. The wine list is mostly natural, a little strange, and, like practically everything else at Joe Beef, the best in Canada.

LIVERPOOL HOUSE

Recommended by
Marc-Alexandre Mercier

2501 Rue Notre-Dame Ouest
Little Burgundy
Montreal
Quebec H3J 1N6
+1 5143136049
www.joebeef.ca

Opening hours	Closed Monday and Sunday
Credit cards	Accepted
Price range	Affordable
Style	Casual
Cuisine	European-Canadian
Recommended for	Local favorite

"Love this place! Feel good as I walk in. Great comforting food. Chris and James will take good care of you. Sit at the bar."—Marc-Alexandre Mercier

LE VIN PAPILLON

2519 Rue Notre-Dame Ouest
Little Burgundy
Montreal
Quebec H3J 1N4
+1 5144396494
www.vinpapillon.com

Recommended by
Andy Hollyday,
Normand Laprise,
David Pellizzari,
John Winter Russell

Opening hours	Closed Monday and Sunday
Reservation policy	No
Credit cards	Accepted
Price range	Affordable
Style	Casual
Cuisine	Modern Canadian
Recommended for	Local favorite

"Zero pretentiousness, super creative, fun environment. They don't take reservations, so it's first come first served. The use of the small space they keep for projects, like the trout pond with floating watercress garden, is super impressive. It really is Montreal in a nutshell for me. I still talk about the carrot 'pastrami' on a choux pastry I ate there like a year ago. It's all small sharing-type plates that accompany one of the best wine programs in the city."—David Pellizzari

In the heart of Griffintown, this bar à vin from the owners of Joe Beef is as freewheeling, though slightly lighter, than its forebear. The menu changes daily, with small plates—ranging from carrot pastrami on choux pastry to *plateaux de fruit de mer* (seafood plates)—that look ripped from a Caravaggio painting. Of course the wine list, curated by Vanya Filipovic and full of Champagnes and obscure Rieslings, is as wild and wonderful as any you'll find. It's especially among the best in the city when its contents are drunk on the charming terrace (if the weather allows).

CHALET BAR-B-Q ROTISSERIE

5456 Rue Sherbrooke Ouest
Notre-Dame-de-Grâce
Montreal
Quebec H4A 1V9
+1 5144897235
www.chaletbbq.com

Recommended by
Jason Morris

Opening hours	Open 7 days
Reservation policy	No
Credit cards	Accepted
Price range	Budget
Style	Casual
Cuisine	Barbecue
Recommended for	Regular neighborhood

COSMOS SNACK BAR

5843 Rue Sherbrooke Ouest
Notre-Dame-de-Grace
Montreal
Quebec H4A 1X4
+1 5144863814

Recommended by
Jason Morris,
Antonin Mousseau-Rivard

Opening hours	Open 7 days
Reservation policy	No
Credit cards	Not accepted
Price range	Budget
Style	Casual
Cuisine	Diner
Recommended for	Breakfast

"The ultimate greasy spoon. I used to go there alone when I was ten years old, to eat not one, but always three plates of chef Tony's classics—like his special creation sandwich on challah bread or the famous mish-mash. People often wait in line for more than an hour to eat at the ten-seat counter."
—Antonin Mousseau-Rivard

DÉPANNEUR LALIME

6436 Boulevard Saint-Laurent
Rosemont-La Petite-Patrie
Montreal
Quebec H2S 3C4
+1 5142734477
www.depanneurlalime.ca

Recommended by
Martin Juneau

Opening hours	Open 7 days
Reservation policy	No
Credit cards	Accepted but not AMEX
Price range	Budget
Style	Casual
Cuisine	Deli-Sandwiches
Recommended for	Bargain

"They do great sandwiches—it's the best lunch in town for under C$10 ($7; £6)."—Martin Juneau

DINETTE TRIPLE CROWN

Recommended by
John Winter Russell

6704 Clark Street
Rosemont-La Petite-Patrie
Montreal
Quebec H2S 3E9
+1 5142722617
www.dinettetriplecrown.com

Opening hours	Closed Tuesday and Wednesday
Credit cards	Accepted
Price range	Affordable
Style	Casual
Cuisine	Southern American
Recommended for	Regular neighborhood

"It's wonderful in its simplicity; great ingredients cooked with love. Don't get too tempted by the fried chicken—try the specials and anything they do with vegetables!"—John Winter Russell

MARCONI

Recommended by
Martin Juneau,
John Winter Russell

45 Avenue Mozart Ouest
Rosemont-La Petite-Patrie
Montreal
Quebec H2S 1C1
+1 5144900777
www.marconimontreal.com

Opening hours	Closed Monday and Tuesday
Credit cards	Accepted
Price range	Affordable
Style	Smart casual
Cuisine	Bistro
Recommended for	Wish I'd opened

"Superb cocktails and ambiance."—Martin Juneau

MONTREAL PLAZA

Recommended by
Marc-Andre Jette,
Martin Juneau,
Normand Laprise,
Marc-Alexandre Mercier,
Carlos Perez,
John Winter Russell

6230 Rue Saint-Hubert
Rosemont-La Petite-Patrie
Montreal
Quebec H2S 2M2
+1 5149036230
www.montrealplaza.com

Opening hours	Open 7 days
Credit cards	Accepted
Price range	Affordable
Style	Smart casual
Cuisine	Modern Canadian
Recommended for	Regular neighborhood

"First place I go when I have a chance to eat out. Love this place, the people, the food. Cheryl and Charles are awesome."—Marc-Alexandre Mercier

LA RÉCOLTE

Recommended by
John Winter Russell

764 Rue Bélanger
Rosemont-La Petite-Patrie
Montreal
Quebec H2S 1G6
+1 5145085450
www.la-recolte.ca

Opening hours	Closed Monday and Tuesday
Credit cards	Accepted
Price range	Affordable
Style	Casual
Cuisine	European
Recommended for	Breakfast

"It's only open for brunch on the weekend, but this is the brunch restaurant for me. They do wonderful dinners as well!"—John Winter Russell

SUMAC RESTAURANT

Recommended by
John Winter Russell

3618 Rue Notre-Dame Ouest
Saint-Henri
Montreal
Quebec H4C 1P5
+1 5149351444
www.sumacrestaurant.com

Opening hours	Closed Monday and Sunday
Reservation policy	No
Credit cards	Accepted but not AMEX
Price range	Affordable
Style	Casual
Cuisine	Middle Eastern
Recommended for	Bargain

TACOS FRIDA

Recommended by
Jason Morris

4350 Rue Notre-Dame Ouest
Saint-Henri
Montreal
Quebec H4C 2W6
+1 5143163255

Opening hours	Closed Sunday
Credit cards	Accepted
Price range	Budget
Style	Casual
Cuisine	Mexican
Recommended for	Regular neighborhood

KAZU

1862 Rue Sainte-Catherine Ouest
Shaughnessy Village
Montreal
Quebec H3H 1M1
+1 5149372333
www.kazuMontreal.com

Opening hours	Closed Tuesday and Wednesday
Reservation policy	No
Credit cards	Not accepted
Price range	Affordable
Style	Casual
Cuisine	Japanese
Recommended for	Regular neighborhood

PHO NGUYEN

1452a Rue Saint Mathieu
Shaughnessy Village
Montreal
Quebec QC H3H
+1 5148466688

Opening hours	Open 7 days
Reservation policy	No
Credit cards	Accepted but not AMEX
Price range	Budget
Style	Casual
Cuisine	Vietnamese
Recommended for	Regular neighborhood

BOUILLON BILK

1595 Boulevard Saint-Laurent
Ville-Marie
Montreal
Quebec H2X 2S9
+1 5148451595
www.bouillonbilk.com

Opening hours	Open 7 days
Credit cards	Accepted
Price range	Expensive
Style	Smart casual
Cuisine	Modern International
Recommended for	High end

"Classy and professional with neat and precise food."
—Marc-Alexandre Mercier

Stand-up comics talk about not stepping on a joke by rushing it with another. At Bouillon Bilk, chef François Nadon knows the value of limiting his whimsy. Except for the outside sign for the former tenant, an electronic repair shop, there's little that seems playful about this spare industrial space in Le Plateau. But the plates that emerge from the kitchen —like a perfect circle of venison tartare topped with mustard seeds, or beef playing hide and seek underneath a garden of fiddlehead ferns and sugar snap peas—are among the city's most thoughtful, creative, and even joyful. At lunch, the place is filled with the sounds of fork on plate and business chatter. At night, with warm light and thin-stemmed glassware, it echoes with bonhomie and laughter. Nadon knows his punchlines, after all.

OLIVE ET GOURMANDO

351 Rue Saint-Paul Ouest
Ville-Marie
Montreal
Quebec H2Y 2A7
+1 5143501083
www.oliveetgourmando.com

Opening hours	Open 7 days
Reservation policy	No
Credit cards	Accepted but not AMEX
Price range	Affordable
Style	Casual
Cuisine	Café-Bakery
Recommended for	Breakfast

PHO THAN LONG

103 Rue Sainte-Catherine Est
Ville-Marie
Montreal
Quebec H2X 1K5
+1 5148480521

Opening hours	Closed Sunday
Reservation policy	No
Credit cards	Accepted but not AMEX
Price range	Affordable
Style	Casual
Cuisine	Vietnamese
Recommended for	Bargain

"It's the perfect place to eat for a few bucks. Not only do they serve the best pho in Montreal, they also have a great selection of Vietnamese classics. Located right next to the Quartier des Spectacles, it's always full of life during the festival season."
—Antonin Mousseau-Rivard

TOQUÉ!

Recommended by
Jason Morris,
John Jackson &
Connie DeSousa,
Martin Juneau,
Daniel Boulud

900 Place Jean-Paul-Riopelle
Ville-Marie
Montreal
Quebec H2Z 2B2
+1 5144992084
www.restaurant-toque.com

Opening hours	Closed Monday and Sunday
Credit cards	Accepted
Price range	Expensive
Style	Smart casual
Cuisine	French-Canadian
Recommended for	High end

"The best high-end restaurant in the city—maybe even in Canada."—Martin Juneau

Opened in 1993, Normand Laprise and Christine Lamarche's Toqué! is the Abraham of Québécois fine dining. Its descendants have been as numerous as the stars (and, as the top restaurant according to "Canada's 100 Best", its stars have been as numerous as the stars too). Today, in the heart of the Quartier Internationale, the hushed dining room, with its padded walls and white tablecloths, continues to shine as a beacon of Laprise's locally focused haute cuisine. All hailing from Quebec, guinea fowl breast with beet (beetroot) purée, suckling pig with beluga lentils, and halibut with herring roe are just some of the dazzling array of dishes that keep Toqué! at the top of its game.

UNIBURGER

Recommended by
Jason Morris

302 Rue Ontario Est
Ville-Marie
Montreal
Quebec H2X 1H6
+1 5144196555
www.uniburger.com

Opening hours	Open 7 days
Reservation policy	No
Credit cards	Accepted
Price range	Budget
Style	Casual
Cuisine	Fast Food–Burgers
Recommended for	Regular neighborhood

**"It's the closest thing to Shake Shack in Montreal."
—Jason Morris**

MARCHÉ MÉLI-MÉLO

Recommended by
Marc-Alexandre Mercier

640 Rue Jarry Est
Villeray
Montreal
Quebec H2P 1V7
+1 5142776409
www.melimelocaraibes.com

Opening hours	Open 7 days
Reservation policy	No
Credit cards	Not accepted
Price range	Budget
Style	Casual
Cuisine	Haitian
Recommended for	Bargain

**"Small Haitian market with a classic Haitian food offering. You get your money's worth."
—Marc-Alexandre Mercier**

Haitians began settling in Montreal in the 1960s, fleeing the political persecution of François "Papa Doc" Duvalier. Many settled in the northern quarter of the city, and that's where Marché Méli-Mélo occupies a corner, near the Parc Jarry. Mostly a supermarket, doing a brisk trade in fufu flour, dried cod, chayote, and goat, as well as shampoos, relaxers, brushes, and combs, from a small counter in the back comes some of Montreal's best Haitian cuisine. *Griot* (marinated pork with a spicy sauce), crispy fried yucca, fluffy rice—not even the white styrofoam (polystyrene) takeout (takeaway) containers can stint the powerful flavors and immense charm of lunch here.

PARK RESTAURANT

Recommended by
John Jackson &
Connie DeSousa

378 Avenue Victoria
Westmount
Montreal
Quebec H3Z 2N4
+1 5147507534
www.parkresto.com

Opening hours	Closed Sunday
Credit cards	Accepted but not AMEX
Price range	Affordable
Style	Casual
Cuisine	Japanese Fusion
Recommended for	Worth the travel

"If money was no object, I would go here for lunch every day."

ALEXIS GAUTHIER P789

"Probably the best fine-dining restaurant in the country right now."

DANIEL PATTERSON P840

USA WEST

"THIS IS THE ONE PLACE I ALWAYS TAKE MY FRIENDS VISITING FROM OUT OF TOWN."

COREY LEE P821

"I had one of the best meals I've ever had here. It cost more than rent, but was worth every penny."

JOHN WINTER RUSSELL P784

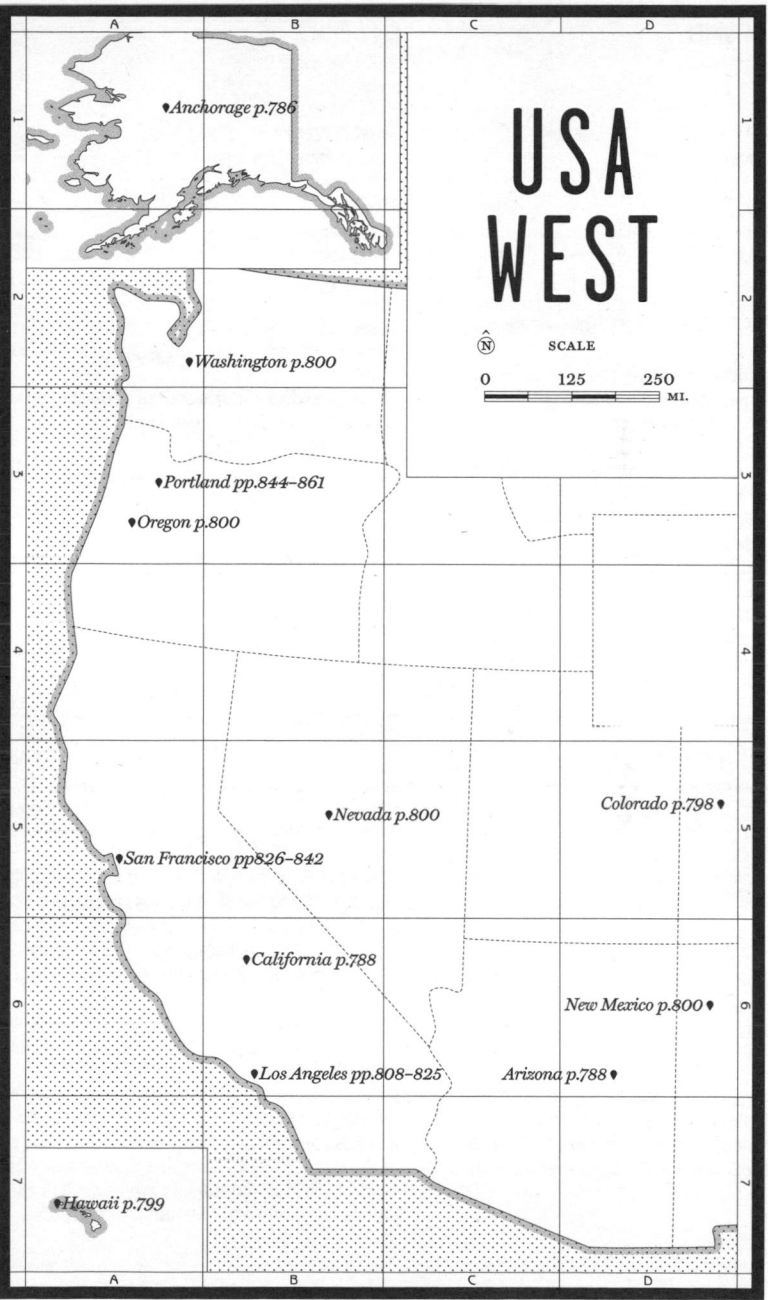

USA
WEST

Ⓝ SCALE

0   125   250
MI.

●*Anchorage p.786*

●*Washington p.800*

●*Portland pp.844–861*

●*Oregon p.800*

●*Nevada p.800*

Colorado p.798 ●

●*San Francisco pp.826–842*

●*California p.788*

New Mexico p.800 ●

●*Los Angeles pp.808–825*

Arizona p.788 ●

●*Hawaii p.799*

BEAR TOOTH GRILL

Recommended by
Drew Johnson

1230 West 27th Avenue
Anchorage
Alaska 99503
+1 9072764200
www.beartoothgrill.net

Opening hours	Open 7 days
Credit cards	Accepted
Price range	Affordable
Style	Casual
Cuisine	Mexican-Alaskan
Recommended for	Regular neighborhood

"Consistently delicious. Always has unique and creative specials. Good cocktails and tequila list too."—Drew Johnson

Founded by two rock climbers turned restaurateurs, this casual grill attached to a cinema is a local favorite, and a good place to sample an Alaskan brew before catching a flick. The southwestern-inspired menu can scratch an itch for warmer climes: tequila-lime Alaska shrimp tostadas, Peruvian satay, and the ambiguously named "Latin Mixed Grill", along with top-notch burgers. This being Alaska, seafood is a specialty, and many ingredients are proudly Alaska-grown.

BRIDGE SEAFOOD RESTAURANT

Recommended by
Drew Johnson

221 West Ship Creek Avenue
Anchorage
Alaska 99501
+1 9076448300
www.bridgeseafood.com

Opening hours	Open 7 days
Credit cards	Accepted
Price range	Expensive
Style	Smart casual
Cuisine	Seafood
Recommended for	Local favorite

"This restaurant serves masses of local seafood, prepared simply but with finesse. It's very cool and has a unique design, and you can watch the salmon swim upstream while you dine!"—Drew Johnson

CITY DINER

Recommended by
Drew Johnson

3000 Minnesota Drive
Anchorage
Alaska 99503
+1 9072772489
www.citydineranchorage.com

Opening hours	Open 7 days
Reservation policy	No
Credit cards	Accepted
Price range	Budget
Style	Casual
Cuisine	Diner
Recommended for	Breakfast

"Great breakfast classics cooked perfectly, and very generous portions too. Diner food done right!"—Drew Johnson

CROW'S NEST

Recommended by
Drew Johnson

The Hotel Captain Cook
939 West 5th Avenue
Anchorage
Alaska 99501
+1 9072766000
www.captaincook.com

Opening hours	Closed Sunday
Credit cards	Accepted
Price range	Expensive
Style	Smart casual
Cuisine	French-American
Recommended for	High end

"The food is upscale, with a focus on high-quality ingredients, and the wine pairings are always perfect thanks to their wonderful sommelier. You also cannot beat the view of Anchorage from the top of the Captain Cook Hotel."—Drew Johnson

Chef Reuben Gerber studied organic farming in Israel, several climate zones from Alaska, where he works now. But the experience had a clear influence on his passion for sustainability in fine dining. The elegant Crow's Nest soars over Tower III in Anchorage's downtown, but the panoramic views of the Chugach Mountains and the restaurant's respect for local ingredients are reminders that nature and culture are beautifully compatible.

F STREET STATION

Recommended by
Drew Johnson

325 F Street
Anchorage
Alaska 99501
+1 9072725196

Opening hours	Open 7 days
Credit cards	Accepted
Price range	Affordable
Style	Casual
Cuisine	American
Recommended for	Late night

"Great bar that also has awesome food. Very simple,
but perfectly prepared. Great clams and oysters."
—Drew Johnson

HEARTH ARTISAN PIZZA

Recommended by
Drew Johnson

1200 West Northern Lights Boulevard F
Anchorage
Alaska 99503
+1 9072220888

Opening hours	Open 7 days
Credit cards	Accepted
Price range	Affordable
Style	Casual
Cuisine	Pizza
Recommended for	Regular neighborhood

PANGEA RESTAURANT & LOUNGE

Recommended by
Drew Johnson

508 West 6th Avenue
Anchorage
Alaska 99501
+1 9072223949
www.pangearestaurantandlounge.com

Opening hours	Open 7 days
Credit cards	Accepted
Price range	Affordable
Style	Casual
Cuisine	International
Recommended for	Wish I'd opened

"The chef at this restaurant is extremely creative
and has a great eye for detail. Their dishes are well
thought out and extremely well composed. They
have an eclectic menu offering world cuisine."
—Drew Johnson

SOUTHSIDE BISTRO

Recommended by
Drew Johnson

1320 Huffman Park Drive
Anchorage
Alaska 99515
+1 9073480088
www.southsidebistro.com

Opening hours	Closed Monday and Sunday
Credit cards	Accepted
Price range	Affordable
Style	Casual
Cuisine	Modern-American
Recommended for	Local favorite

"Serves awesome local seafood."—Drew Johnson

TOMMY'S BURGER STOP

Recommended by
Drew Johnson

1106 West 29th Place
Anchorage
Alaska 99503
+1 9075615696
www.tommysburgerstop.com

Opening hours	Open 7 days
Reservation policy	No
Credit cards	Accepted
Price range	Budget
Style	Casual
Cuisine	Burgers
Recommended for	Bargain

"Tommy's Burger Stop has amazing gourmet
burgers!"—Drew Johnson

TACO KING

Recommended by
Drew Johnson

3003 Tanglewood Drive
Anchorage
Alaska 99517
+1 9077716059
www.tacokingak.com

Opening hours	Open 7 days
Reservation policy	No
Credit cards	Accepted
Price range	Budget
Style	Casual
Cuisine	Mexican
Recommended for	Bargain

"Serves authentic Mexican cuisine with a focus
on some of my favorites like *adobada* and *lengua*."
—Drew Johnson

TEQUILA 61

Recommended by
Drew Johnson

445 West 4th Avenue
Anchorage
Alaska 99501
+1 9072747678
www.tequila61.com

Opening hours	Closed Sunday
Credit cards	Accepted
Price range	Affordable
Style	Casual
Cuisine	Mexican-Gastropub
Recommended for	Wish I'd opened

"A beautiful restaurant with great décor."
—Drew Johnson

TRATTO

Recommended by
Kevin Fink

4743 North 20th Street
Phoenix
Arizona 85016
+1 6022967761
www.trattophx.com

Opening hours	Closed Monday and Sunday
Credit cards	Accepted
Price range	Affordable
Style	Casual
Cuisine	Italian
Recommended for	Worth the travel

"Everything on Tratto's small menu is well curated. The care is evident in the sourcing and the respect of the ingredients. Tratto is a restaurant that is comfortable enough to eat in everyday but delicious enough for a treasured meal."—Kevin Fink

Head chef and owner Chris Bianco describes Tratto as a "trattoria Americana", bringing together a homely Italian cooking style while collaborating with local farmers, ranchers, and millers to showcase authentically southwestern produce. The menu changes each week, depending on seasonality, but always includes a variety of antipasti, pasta, and meat dishes. Bianco has already made a profound impact on the Phoenix restaurant scene with a series of world-class pizzerias, leading some to suggest, with much New Yorker pearl-clutching, that the city is the pizza capital of the US. Trying to repeat the success with other Italian classics, Tratto marks a different direction for the legendary chef, but one that will cement his reputation as a culinary heavyweight.

PIZZERIA BIANCO

Recommended by
Kevin Hickey

623 East Adams Street
Phoenix
Arizona 85004
+1 6022588300
www.pizzeriabianco.com

Opening hours	Open 7 days
Credit cards	Accepted
Price range	Affordable
Style	Casual
Cuisine	Italian
Recommended for	Worth the travel

OORI RICE TRIANGLES

Recommended by
Cal Peternell

1247 Solano Avenue
Albany
California 94709
+1 5105268663
www.oorifoods.com

Opening hours	Closed Sunday
Reservation policy	No
Credit cards	Accepted
Price range	Budget
Style	Casual
Cuisine	Japanese
Recommended for	Regular neighborhood

"These made-to-order rice triangles are tasty and fresh. I like the spicy kimchi and tofu versions."
—Cal Peternell

PHO AO SEN

Recommended by
Cal Peternell

655 San Pablo Avenue
Albany
California 94706
+1 5106795000
www.phoaosen.com

Opening hours	Closed Wednesday
Reservation policy	No
Credit cards	Accepted
Price range	Affordable
Style	Casual
Cuisine	Vietnamese
Recommended for	Regular neighborhood

"The crispy egg roll wrapped in lettuce leaves and herbs, and dipped in fish sauce is the best!"
—Cal Peternell

SAM'S LOG CABIN

Recommended by
Cal Peternell

945 San Pablo Avenue
Albany
California 94706
+1 5105580502
www.samslogcabin.net

Opening hours	Closed Monday
Credit cards	Accepted
Price range	Affordable
Style	Casual
Cuisine	Breakfast-Brunch
Recommended for	Breakfast

"Well-sourced local ingredients cooked up into tasty, classic breakfast fare. The coffee's good and it's cool, even if you have to wait out back for a table."
—Cal Peternell

TACOS EL AUTLENSE

Recommended by
Cal Peternell

601 San Pablo Avenue
Albany
California 94706
+1 5107760701

Opening hours	Open 7 days
Reservation policy	No
Credit cards	Not accepted
Price range	Budget
Style	Casual
Cuisine	Taco Truck
Recommended for	Bargain

CLARO'S DELI

Recommended by
Ted Hopson

19 East Huntington Drive
Arcadia
California 91106
+1 6264460275
www.claros.mobi

Opening hours	Closed Wednesday
Reservation policy	No
Credit cards	Accepted
Price range	Budget
Style	Casual
Cuisine	Italian Deli
Recommended for	Bargain

"The sandwich here is what I ate all through high school, college, and my adult life. It's cheap enough to get all the time, and good enough that you just want more. I still buy them by the bunch for my crew at the restaurant."—Ted Hopson

CHEZ PANISSE

Recommended by
Gabriela Cámara,
Olle T. Cellton,
Michael Friedman,
Alexis Gauthier,
Cameron Mathews,
Steven Satterfield

1517 Shattuck Avenue
Berkeley
California 94709
+1 5105485525
www.chezpanisse.com

Opening hours	Closed Sunday
Credit cards	Accepted
Price range	Expensive
Style	Smart casual
Cuisine	Modern-American
Recommended for	Worth the travel

"If money was no object, I would go here for lunch every day and let them interpret beautiful Californian produce slowly following the seasons."
—Alexis Gauthier

This legendary restaurant, founded by Alice Waters in 1971, has always been well ahead of its time. Chez Panisse re-drew the template for restaurateurs for generations to come, and set the bar high—long before it was standard practice to serve seasonal, organic food, or eschew complicated techniques in favor of fresh ingredients, or connect directly with a network of local farmers and suppliers. This neighborhood bistro is named after Honoré Panisse, a character from a French 1930s movie trilogy. Waters was among the first wave of restaurant owners to open a casual offshoot; the upstairs Chez Panisse Café, which opened in 1980, offers a menu that's as creative as the restaurant's.

FIELDWORK

Recommended by
Cal Peternell

1160 Sixth Street
Berkeley
California 94710
+1 5108981203
www.fieldworkbrewing.com

Opening hours	Open 7 days
Reservation policy	No
Credit cards	Accepted
Price range	Affordable
Style	Casual
Cuisine	Beer
Recommended for	High end

IYASARE

Recommended by
Hiro Sone

1830 Fourth Street
Berkeley
California 94710
+1 5108458100
www.iyasare-berkeley.com

Opening hours	Open 7 days
Credit cards	Accepted
Price range	Expensive
Style	Smart casual
Cuisine	Japanese
Recommended for	Local favorite

STANDARD FARE

Recommended by
Russell Moore

2701 Eighth Street
Berkeley
California 94710
+1 5103562261
www.standardfareberkeley.com

Opening hours	Closed Sunday
Reservation policy	No
Credit cards	Accepted
Price range	Expensive
Style	Casual
Cuisine	Café-Deli
Recommended for	Wish I'd Opened

BIG SUR BAKERY

Recommended by
Joel Braham,
Justin Cogley

47540 California 1
Big Sur
California 93920
+1 8316670520
www.bigsurbakery.com

Opening hours	Open 7 days
Credit cards	Accepted
Price range	Affordable
Style	Casual
Cuisine	Modern American
Recommended for	Regular neighborhood

"Breakfast sourdough pizza from the wood-fired oven is a must."—Joel Braham

FISHERMAN'S COVE

Recommended by
Danielle Gjestland

1850 Bay Flat Road
Bodega Bay
California 94923
+1 7073774238
www.fishermanscovebodegabay.com

Opening hours	Open 7 days
Reservation policy	No
Credit cards	Accepted
Price range	Affordable
Style	Casual
Cuisine	Seafood
Recommended for	Bargain

For its fried oysters and the cold, foggy ocean breeze. We are usually here after a long city stint and the fast moving salt-air is like a reset button. The smell of it reminds me of home."—Danielle Gjestland

CALISTOGA KITCHEN

Recommended by
Hiro Sone

1107 Cedar Street
Calistoga
California 94515
+1 7079426500
www.calistogakitchen.com

Opening hours	Closed Monday to Wednesday
Credit cards	Accepted
Price range	Affordable
Style	Casual
Cuisine	Modern American
Recommended for	Regular neighborhood

"Casual friendly service and consistently great food. Love their seasonal American bistro menu."
—Hiro Sone

CULTURA

Recommended by
Justin Cogley

100 Dolores Street
Carmel-by-the-Sea
California 93923
+1 8312507005
www.culturacarmel.com

Opening hours	Closed Wednesday
Credit cards	Accepted
Price range	Affordable
Style	Casual
Cuisine	Oaxacan
Recommended for	Late night

"The only place for late night food and mezcal."
—Justin Cogley

For a long time, Carmel-by-the-Sea was as close to a one-restaurant town as you'd expect a tiny resort on the California coast to be. All things culinary revolved around Justin Cogley and his restaurant at L'Auberge. But last year, a trio from Sierra Mar, the fine-dining restaurant in Big Sur, opened up a place called Cultura, serious about both food and drink. Here you'll find wagyu *barbacoa enchiladas* and Monterey abalone with charred pasilla pepper being consumed way into the night alongside a stellar list of mezcals.

AUBERGINE AT L'AUBERGE CARMEL

Recommended by
Jonathon Sawyer

Monte Verde Street at 7th Avenue
Carmel-by-the-Sea
California 93921
+1 8316248578
www.auberginecarmel.com

Opening hours	Open 7 days
Credit cards	Accepted
Price range	Expensive
Style	Smart casual
Cuisine	Modern American-French
Recommended for	High end

"Can't be more thoughtful and bespoke than a dinner with Justin Cogley and co. at Aubergine. The plates, the silver, the service, the abalone, and everything is done with purpose. Truly one of the greatest meals I've ever enjoyed."—Jonathon Sawyer

CARMEL BELLE

Recommended by
Justin Cogley

Doud Craft Studios
San Carlos Street
Carmel-by-the-Sea
California 93921
+1 8316241600
www.carmelbelle.com

Opening hours	Open 7 days
Reservation policy	No
Credit cards	Accepted
Price range	Budget
Style	Casual
Cuisine	Modern American
Recommended for	Breakfast

TACO MARIA

Recommended by
Sarah Grueneberg

3313 Hyland Avenue
Costa Mesa
California 92626
+1 7145388444
www.tacomaria.com

Opening hours	Closed Monday
Credit cards	Accepted
Price range	Expensive
Style	Casual
Cuisine	Mexican
Recommended for	Worth the travel

"The best shrimp *quesadilla* I've ever had."
—Sarah Grueneberg

KOI PALACE

Recommended by
Ravi Kapur

365 Gellert Boulevard
Daly City
California 94015
+1 6509929000
www.koipalace.com

Opening hours	Open 7 days
Credit cards	Accepted
Price range	Affordable
Style	Smart casual
Cuisine	Dim Sum
Recommended for	Breakfast

BERGAMOT ALLEY

Recommended by
Kyle Connaughton

328A Healdsburg Avenue
Healdsburg
California 95448
+1 7074338720
www.bergamotalley.com

Opening hours	Closed Monday
Reservation policy	No
Credit cards	Accepted
Price range	Affordable
Style	Casual
Cuisine	Modern American
Recommended for	Late night

"Amazing, eclectic wine list and unique grilled cheeses."—Kyle Connaughton

SHED

Recommended by
Kyle Connaughton

25 North Street
Healdsburg
California 95448
+1 7074317433
www.healdsburgshed.com

Opening hours	Open 7 days
Credit cards	Accepted
Price range	Affordable
Style	Casual
Cuisine	Modern American
Recommended for	Local favorite

"Uniquely tied to the local produce and seasons of Sonoma."—Kyle Connaughton

SINGLE THREAD FARMS

Recommended by
Sat Bains, Gavin Kaysen,
Uwe Opocensky

131 North Street
Healdsburg
California 95448
+1 7077234646
www.singlethreadfarms.com

Opening hours	Closed Monday
Credit cards	Accepted
Price range	Expensive
Style	Casual
Cuisine	Modern American
Recommended for	Worth the travel

"I have never seen such a complete restaurant built from scratch before at the level Kyle and Cantina have obtained. Phenomenal food and service down to the finest detail."—Sat Bains

LOS ANGELES: SEE PAGES 808–825

MANRESA

Recommended by
Matthew Accarrino, Val Cantu,
Mauro Colagreco,
Alexandre Gauthier, Alex Harrell,
Isaac McHale, Katy Jane Millard,
Eelke Plasmeijer

320 Village Lane
Los Gatos
California 95030
+1 4083544330
www.manresarestaurant.com

Opening hours	Closed Monday and Tuesday
Credit cards	Accepted
Price range	Expensive
Style	Smart casual
Cuisine	Modern American
Recommended for	Worth the travel

"This was one of the most thoughtful and delicious dining experiences of my life. Seasonal food with a sense of place few are capable of."—Katy Jane Millard

EQUATOR COFFEE

Recommended by
Matthew Accarrino

244 Shoreline Highway
Mill Valley
California 94941
+1 4152093733
www.equatorcoffees.com

Opening hours	Open 7 days
Reservation policy	No
Credit cards	Accepted
Price range	Affordable
Style	Casual
Cuisine	Modern American
Recommended for	Breakfast

"This is a great place for a morning coffee and a light pastry. It's a spot I often find myself on morning bike rides from the city. Plenty of outdoor seating and a relaxed atmosphere for easing into the day."
—Matthew Accarrino

SOL FOOD

Recommended by
Matthew Accarrino

401 Miller Avenue
Mill Valley
California 94941
+1 4153801986
www.solfoodrestaurant.com

Opening hours	Open 7 days
Reservation policy	No
Credit cards	Accepted but not AMEX or Diners
Price range	Affordable
Style	Casual
Cuisine	Latin American
Recommended for	Bargain

"A great place to grab a quick inexpensive bite on the way out or into the city. Puerto Rican-inspired food using the best ingredients and with everything made fresh. I like the wraps filled with rice or quinoa and you can add protein to them or not. My favorite is the chipotle wrap."—Matthew Accarrino

SARDINE FACTORY

701 Wave Street
Monterey
California 93940
+1 8313733775
www.sardinefactory.com

Opening hours	Open 7 days
Credit cards	Accepted
Price range	Affordable
Style	Smart casual
Cuisine	Seafood
Recommended for	Local favorite

"An institution in the area."—Justin Cogley

FIRST AWAKENINGS

125 Ocean View Boulevard
Monterey
California 93950
+1 8313721125
www.firstawakenings.net

Opening hours	Open 7 days
Reservation policy	No
Credit cards	Accepted
Price range	Affordable
Style	Casual
Cuisine	Breakfast-Brunch
Recommended for	Worth the travel

COMPAGNO'S MARKET AND DELI

2000 Prescott Avenue
Monterey
California 93940
+1 8313755987
www.compagnos.com

Opening hours	Open 7 days
Reservation policy	No
Credit cards	Accepted
Price range	Budget
Style	Casual
Cuisine	Deli-Café
Recommended for	Bargain

HOG ISLAND OYSTER CO.

610 1st Street #22
Napa
California 94559
+1 7072518113
www.hogislandoysters.com

Opening hours	Open 7 days
Reservation policy	No
Credit cards	Accepted
Price range	Affordable
Style	Casual
Cuisine	Seafood
Recommended for	Bargain

BOON FLY CAFÉ

4048 Sonoma Highway
Napa
California 94559
+1 707299 4870
www.boonflycafe.com

Opening hours	Open 7 days
Credit cards	Accepted
Price range	Affordable
Style	Casual
Cuisine	American
Recommended for	Regular neighborhood

"A great place to stop on the drive back from Napa
to SF. Their fried chicken is really good."
—Matthew Accarrino

BANH MI BA LE

1909 International Boulevard
Oakland
California 94606
+1 5102619800

Opening hours	Closed Monday
Reservation policy	No
Credit cards	Accepted
Price range	Budget
Style	Casual
Cuisine	Vietnamese
Recommended for	Bargain

"Excellent banh mi. My favorite in the bay."
—Russell Moore

BEAUTY'S BAGEL SHOP

Recommended by
Russell Moore,
Ravi Kapur

3838 Telegraph Avenue
Oakland
California 94609
+1 5107886098
www.beautysbagelshop.com

Opening hours	Closed Monday
Reservation policy	No
Credit cards	Accepted
Price range	Affordable
Style	Casual
Cuisine	Bagels
Recommended for	Breakfast

BROWN SUGAR KITCHEN

Recommended by
Val Cantu

2435 Mandela Parkway
Oakland
California 94607
+1 5108397685
www.brownsugarkitchen.com

Opening hours	Closed Monday
Reservation policy	No
Credit cards	Accepted
Price range	Affordable
Style	Casual
Cuisine	Breakfast-Brunch
Recommended for	Breakfast

CAMINO

Recommended by
Olle T. Cellton

3917 Grand Avenue
Oakland
California 94610
+1 5105475035
www.caminorestaurant.com

Opening hours	Closed Tuesday
Credit cards	Accepted
Price range	Affordable
Style	Casual
Cuisine	Modern American
Recommended for	Worth the travel

COMMIS

Recommended by
Erick Harcey

3859 Piedmont Avenue
Oakland
California 94611
+1 5106533902
www.commisrestaurant.com

Opening hours	Closed Monday and Tuesday
Credit cards	Accepted
Price range	Expensive
Style	Smart casual
Cuisine	Modern American
Recommended for	Worth the travel

DUENDE

Recommended by
Andrea Reusing

468 19th Street Oakland
Oakland
California 94612
+1 5108930174
www.duendeoakland.com

Opening hours	Closed Tuesday
Credit cards	Accepted
Price range	Affordable
Style	Casual
Cuisine	Modern Spanish
Recommended for	Worth the travel

"Paul Canales' long awaited Duende is a party every
night. But with really exciting food and kind, smart
service."—Andrea Reusing

MISS OLLIE'S

Recommended by
Russell Moore

901 Washington Street
Oakland
California 94607
+1 5102856188
www.realmissolliesoakland.com

Opening hours	Closed Monday and Sunday
Reservation policy	No
Credit cards	Accepted
Price range	Affordable
Style	Casual
Cuisine	Caribbean
Recommended for	Local favorite

"Sarah Kirnon always makes delicious food in a fun,
non-fancy environment. The salt fish with rice and
peas, and soups are always great."—Russell Moore

THE RAMEN SHOP

5812 College Avenue
Oakland
California 94618
+1 5106405034
www.ramenshop.com

Opening hours	Open 7 days
Reservation policy	No
Credit cards	Accepted
Price range	Affordable
Style	Casual
Cuisine	Japanese
Recommended for	Late night

PIZZAIOLO

5008 Telegraph Avenue
Oakland
California 94609
+1 5106524888
www.pizzaiolooakland.com

Opening hours	Open 7 days
Credit cards	Accepted
Price range	Affordable
Style	Casual
Cuisine	Italian
Recommended for	Worth the travel

SEOUL GOM TANG

3801 Telegraph Avenue
Oakland
California 94609
+1 5105979989
www.seoulgomtang.com

Opening hours	Open 7 days
Credit cards	Accepted
Price range	Affordable
Style	Casual
Cuisine	Korean
Recommended for	Late night

"They specialize in classic Korean beef broth soups but I really like the homey specials."—Russell Moore

SEQUOIA DINER

3719 MacArthur Boulevard
Oakland
California 94619
+1 5104823719
www.sequoiadiner.com

Opening hours	Closed Monday and Tuesday
Reservation policy	No
Credit cards	Accepted
Price range	Affordable
Style	Casual
Cuisine	Diner
Recommended for	Breakfast

"Really fun, inexpensive food."—Russell Moore

COSECHA

907 Washington Street
Oakland
California 94607
+1 5104525900
www.cosechacafe.com

Opening hours	Closed Sunday
Reservation policy	No
Credit cards	Accepted
Price range	Affordable
Style	Casual
Cuisine	Mexican
Recommended for	Regular neighborhood

"Great ingredients and tasty cooking in an open marketplace. It's close to home, fun, and our kids love it."—Daniel Patterson

BOOT & SHOE SERVICE

3308 Grand Avenue
Oakland
California 94610
+1 5107632668
www.bootandshoeservice.com

Opening hours	Closed Monday
Credit cards	Accepted
Price range	Affordable
Style	Casual
Cuisine	Pizza
Recommended for	Regular neighborhood

LOCOL

Recommended by
Val Cantu,
Kwang Uh

2214 Broadway Street
Oakland
California 94612
www.welocol.com

Opening hours	Open 7 days
Reservation policy	No
Credit cards	Accepted
Price range	Affordable
Style	Casual
Cuisine	Modern American
Recommended for	Local favorite

LOCOL BAKERY

Recommended by
Daniel Patterson

3446 Market Street
Oakland
California 94608
www.welocol.com

Opening hours	Open 7 days
Reservation policy	No
Credit cards	Accepted
Price range	Affordable
Style	Casual
Cuisine	American
Recommended for	Breakfast

"Delicious, inexpensive coffee and pastries."
—Daniel Patterson

SHANDONG

Recommended by
Daniel Patterson

328 10th Street
Oakland
California 94607
+1 5108392299
www.sd.222.to

Opening hours	Closed Monday
Reservation policy	No
Credit cards	Accepted
Price range	Affordable
Style	Casual
Cuisine	Chinese
Recommended for	Bargain

"Handmade noodles in deeply flavored broths."
—Daniel Patterson

SIR AND STAR

Recommended by
Matthew Accarrino

10000 Sir Francis Drake Boulevard
Olema
California 94950
+1 415663.034
www.sirandstar.com

Opening hours	Closed Monday and Tuesday
Credit cards	Accepted
Price range	Affordable
Style	Casual
Cuisine	Modern American
Recommended for	Regular neighborhood

"You could drive or ride your bike past this place
hundreds of times, as I did, but, once I had noticed it,
what I found was a restaurant focusing on Marin and
hyper-local ingredients—that alone makes it worth
a visit."—Matthew Accarrino

SAN FRANCISCO: SEE PAGES 826–842

HUI TOU XIANG

Recommended by
Josef Centeno

704 West Las Tunas Drive Ste #5
San Gabriel
California, 91776
+1 6262819888
www.huitouxiang.com

Opening hours	Open 7 days
Reservation policy	Accepted
Price range	Budget
Style	Casual
Cuisine	Asian
Recommended for	Breakfast

HACHI JU HACHI

Recommended by
Thomas Kim

14480 Big Basin Way
Saratoga
California 95070
+1 4086472258

Opening hours	Open 7 days
Credit cards	Accepted
Price range	Affordable
Style	Casual
Cuisine	Japanese
Recommended for	Worth the travel

EL MOLINO CENTRAL

Recommended by
Kyle Connaughton

11 Central Avenue
Sonoma
California 95476
+1 7079391010
www.elmolinocentral.com

Opening hours	Open 7 days
Reservation policy	No
Credit cards	Accepted
Price range	Affordable
Style	Casual
Cuisine	Mexican
Recommended for	Bargain

"Incredible, authentic Mexican food—thoroughly researched and traditionally prepared."
—Kyle Connaughton

TERRA RESTAURANT

Recommended by
John Jackson

1345 Railroad Avenue
St Helena
California 94574
+1 7079638931
www.terrarestaurant.com

Opening hours	Closed Tuesday and Wednesday
Credit cards	Accepted
Price range	Expensive
Style	Smart casual
Cuisine	English
Recommended for	Worth the travel

"Husband and wife team Hiro and Lissa are two of the most talented and genuine people I have ever had the pleasure to meet. I would travel a million miles to eat a meal that they were preparing."—John Jackson

THE RESTAURANT AT MEADOWOOD

Recommended by
Gavin Kaysen

900 Meadowood Lane
St Helena
California 94574
+1 7079671205
www.therestaurantatmeadowood.com

Opening hours	Closed Monday and Tuesday
Credit cards	Accepted
Price range	Expensive
Style	Formal
Cuisine	Modern American
Recommended for	Worth the travel

"Fine dining in a way we want to eat—approachable, delicate, and delicious."—Gavin Kaysen

SICHUAN IMPRESSION

Recommended by
Josef Centeno

13816 Red Hill Avenue
Tustin
California 92780
+1 7145059070

Opening hours	Open 7 days
Reservation policy	No
Credit cards	Accepted
Price range	Budget
Style	Casual
Cuisine	Chinese
Recommended for	Local favourite

BISTRO JEANTY

Recommended by
Hiro Sone

6510 Washington Street
Yountville
California 94599
+1 7079440103
www.bistrojeanty.com

Opening hours	Open 7 days
Credit cards	Accepted
Price range	Expensive
Style	Smart casual
Cuisine	French
Recommended for	Regular neighborhood

THE FRENCH LAUNDRY

Recommended by
Matthew Accarrino, Tom Aikens,
Anton Bjuhr, Phil Carmichael,
Paul Cunningham, Paul Foster,
Brian Mark Hansen, Corey Lee,
Vaughan Mabee, Jocky Petrie,
Alfred Prasad, Geir Skeie,
Alla Wolf Tasker, James Walt

6640 Washington Street
Yountville
California 94599
+1 7079442380
www.thomaskeller.com/tfl

Opening hours	Open 7 days
Credit cards	Accepted
Price range	Expensive
Style	Formal
Cuisine	French
Recommended for	Wish I'd opened

"Thomas Keller's book *The French Laundry* was inspirational to chefs everywhere and he has done incredible things for Modern American Cusine through this restaurant."—Jocky Petrie

BAR DOUGH

Recommended by
Jennifer Jasinski

2227 West 32nd Avenue
Denver
Colorado 80211
+1 7206688506
www.bardoughdenver.com

Opening hours	Open 7 days
Credit cards	Accepted
Price range	Affordable
Style	Casual
Cuisine	Italian
Recommended for	Regular neighborhood

"Great Italian food. Amazing hand-made pastas and delicate salads at a good price point."
—Jennifer Jasinski

BEAST + BOTTLE

Recommended by
Jennifer Jasinski,
Cassy Vires

719 East 17th Avenue
Denver
Colorado 80203
+1 3036233223
www.beastandbottle.com

Opening hours	Open 7 days
Credit cards	Accepted
Price range	Affordable
Style	Casual
Cuisine	American
Recommended for	Worth the travel

"Really fun food, but still delicious and recognizable. The staff are friendly and warm, and their restaurant space is cozy and inviting."—Cassy Vires

EUCLID HALL BAR & KITCHEN

Recommended by
Jennifer Jasinski

1317 14th Street
Denver
Colorado 80202
+1 3035954255
www.euclidhall.com

Opening hours	Open 7 days
Credit cards	Accepted
Price range	Affordable
Style	Casual
Cuisine	American
Recommended for	Late night

"Full menu served late every night! Killer sausages, schnitzel, poutines!! And the chefs are rowdy and fun."—Jennifer Jasinski

FRUITION

Recommended by
Jennifer Jasinski

1313 East 6th Avenue
Denver
Colorado 80218
+1 3038311962
www.fruitionrestaurant.com

Opening hours	Open 7 days
Credit cards	Accepted
Price range	Expensive
Style	Smart casual
Cuisine	Modern American
Recommended for	High end

JJ CHINESE RESTAURANT

Recommended by
Jennifer Jasinski

2500 West Alameda Avenue
Denver
Colorado 80219
+1 3039348888
www.jjrestaurant.com

Opening hours	Open 7 days
Credit cards	Accepted
Price range	Affordable
Style	Casual
Cuisine	Chinese-Seafood
Recommended for	Late night

LINGER

Recommended by
Jennifer Jasinski

2030 West 30th Avenue
Denver
Colorado 80211
+1 3039933120
www.lingerdenver.com

Opening hours	Open 7 days
Credit cards	Accepted
Price range	Affordable
Style	Casual
Cuisine	International Street Food
Recommended for	Wish I'd opened

"I love the design and its super cool location, with a killer roof-top deck overlooking Denver."
—Jennifer Jasinski

NEW SAIGON

Recommended by
Jennifer Jasinski

630 South Federal Boulevard
Denver
Colorado 80219
+1 3039364954
www.newsaigon.com

Opening hours	Closed Monday
Credit cards	Accepted
Price range	Affordable
Style	Casual
Cuisine	Vietnamese
Recommended for	Bargain

"Killer Vietnamese food—the whole menu is super delicious so don't be afraid to try something weird!" —Jennifer Jasinski

PATZCUARO'S MEXICAN RESTAURANT

Recommended by
Jennifer Jasinski

2616 West 32nd Avenue
Denver
Colorado 80211
+1 3034554389
www.patzcuaros.com

Opening hours	Open 7 days
Reservation policy	No
Credit cards	Accepted
Price range	Affordable
Style	Casual
Cuisine	Mexican
Recommended for	Local favorite

SUSHI DEN

Recommended by
Jennifer Jasinski

1487 South Pearl Street
Denver
Colorado 80210
+1 3037770826
www.sushiden.net

Opening hours	Open 7 days
Credit cards	Accepted
Price range	Affordable
Style	Smart casual
Cuisine	Japanese
Recommended for	High end

"Sit at the counter and let the sushi chefs make you an *omakase* (chef's choice) menu!"—Jennifer Jasinski

MAMA'S FISH HOUSE

Recommended by
Larry McGuire

799 Poho Place
Paia
Hawaii 96779
+8 085798488
www.mamasfishhouse.com

Opening hours	Open 7 days
Credit cards	Accepted
Price range	High end
Style	Smart casual
Cuisine	Hawaiian Seafood
Recommended for	Worth the travel

SENIA

Recommended by
Tony Yoo

75 North King Street
Honolulu
Hawaii 96817
+1 8082005412
www.restaurantsenia.com

Opening hours	Closed Sunday
Credit cards	Accepted
Price range	Expensive
Style	Casual
Cuisine	Modern American-Hawaiian
Recommended for	Wish I'd opened

"I like its food, which is certainly delicious and trendy, and I like the comfortable, warm feeling it provides." —Tony Yoo

TIN ROOF

Recommended by
Emily Hahn

360 Papa Place, Suite Y
Maui
Hawaii 96732
+1 8088680753
www.tinroofmaui.com

Opening hours	Closed Sunday
Reservation policy	No
Credit cards	Accepted
Price range	Affordable
Style	Casual
Cuisine	Hawaiian
Recommended for	Worth the travel

E BY JOSÉ ANDRÉS

Recommended by
Christian Domschitz

3708 South Las Vegas Boulevard
Las Vegas
Nevada 89109
+1 7026987000
www.ebyjoseandres.com

Opening hours.............................Closed Monday and Tuesday
Credit cards..Accepted
Price range..Expensive
Style...Smart casual
Cuisine..Modern Spanish
Recommended for..Worth the travel

"The most exciting experience I ever had."
—Christian Domschitz

DURAN CENTRAL PHARMACY

Recommended by
Molly Mitchell

1815 Central Avenue Northwest
Albuquerque
New Mexico 87104
+1 5052474141
www.duransrx.com

Opening hours..Open 7 days
Reservation policy..No
Credit cards..Accepted
Price range..Affordable
Style...Casual
Cuisine..Modern Mexican
Recommended for....................................Wish I'd opened

DUH KUH BEE

Recommended by
José Chesa

12590 Southwest 1st Street
Beaverton
Oregon 97005
+1 5036435388

Opening hours..Closed Sunday
Reservation policy..No
Credit cards..Accepted
Price range..Affordable
Style...Casual
Cuisine...Asian Fusion
Recommended for..........................Regular neighborhood

PORTLAND: SEE PAGES 844–861

OLD OREGON SMOKEHOUSE

Recommended by
Joel Stocks

120 US 101 Rockaway Beach
Rockaway Beach
Oregon 97136
+1 5033552817

Opening hours..Open 7 days
Reservation policy..No
Credit cards..Accepted
Price range..Affordable
Style...Casual
Cuisine...Seafood
Recommended for....................................Wish I'd opened

"Perfect coastal chowder shack. Just making big
batches of chowder, cooking crab, and smoking fish
sounds like a great day job."—Joel Stocks

THE BOATHOUSE SUTTLE LODGE

Recommended by
Joshua McFadden

13300 US Highway 20
Sisters
Oregon 97759
+1 5416387001
www.thesuttlelodge.com

Opening hours..Open 7 days
Credit cards..Accepted
Price range..Affordable
Style...Casual
Cuisine...Seafood
Recommended for....................................Local favorite

THE WILLOWS INN

Recommended by
Paul Berglund, Gabriela Cámara,
Sean Gray, Brian Luptak,
Virgilio Martínez, Katy Jane Millard,
David Posey, Joel Stocks

2579 West Shore Drive
Lummi Island
Washington 98262
+1 3607582620
www.willows-inn.com

Opening hours..Open 7 days
Credit cards..Accepted
Price range..Expensive
Style...Casual
Cuisine...American
Recommended for..Worth the travel

"I love the way it cooks everything that is around
it—and the island is magical."—Virgilio Martinez

Chef Blaine Wetzel's time at Noma certainly
influenced the sense of place he creates at

The Willows Inn, but here, on a remote island in Puget Sound, the land and waters offer a seasonal bounty impossible in Copenhagen. Wetzel works closely with heirloom-focused farms and fishermen on Lummi Island and also forages, which means that the vast majority of ingredients on the menu will come from the island itself. Dinner here seems like magic—vivid and hours long, the saline air and fading sunset as much participants in the meal as the succession of exquisite dishes (rhubarb in angelica, wild beach peas, barely cured rockfish, aged venison).

ART OF THE TABLE

Recommended by
JJ Proville

3801 Stone Way North Suite AFremont
Seattle
Washington 98103
+1 2062820942
www.artofthetable.net

Opening hours	Closed Monday and Tuesday
Credit cards	Accepted
Price range	Expensive
Style	Smart casual
Cuisine	Modern American
Recommended for	High end

BA BAR

Recommended by
JJ Proville,
Holly Smith,
Ethan Stowell

550 12th Avenue
Seattle
Washington 98122
+1 2063282030
www.babarseattle.com

Opening hours	Closed Monday
Reservation policy	No
Credit cards	Accepted
Price range	Affordable
Style	Casual
Cuisine	Vietnamese
Recommended for	Breakfast

"Ba Bar is a super-cool, all-day, all-night Vietnamese spot that serves great food and cocktails. There's always a bunch of restaurant folk there as well."
—Ethan Stowell

A love letter to Vietnamese street food, Ba Bar has won the hearts of Seattle residents for both brunch and late-night eating. Two locations serve lip-smacking, slurpable, street-style classics that employ locally sourced ingredients. Besides the city's best pho, there are roasted chicken, pork belly, and duck basted in their own juices, vermicelli bowls piled high, and almost a dozen small plates

(pâté chaud—savory puff pastry—fried frog legs, steamed manila clams). Powerhouse cocktails pair perfectly with the kitchen's sparkling, herbal heat, and by the end of the night, it may be hard to say which order prompted which.

BACCO

Recommended by
Perfecte Rocher

86 Pine Street
Seattle
Washington 98101
+1 2064435443
www.baccocafe.com

Opening hours	Open 7 days
Reservation policy	No
Credit cards	Accepted
Price range	Affordable
Style	Casual
Cuisine	American
Recommended for	Breakfast

BAKERY NOUVEAU

Recommended by
JJ Proville

137 15th Avenue East
Seattle
Washington 98112
+1 2068586957
www.bakerynouveau.com

Opening hours	Open 7 days
Reservation policy	No
Credit cards	Accepted
Price range	Budget
Style	Casual
Cuisine	French bakery
Recommended for	Breakfast

"This place just slays the French bakery concept on every level."—JJ Proville

BELLTOWN PIZZA

Recommended by
Blaine Wetzel

2422 1st Avenue
Belltown
Seattle
Washington 98121
+1 2064412653
www.belltownpizza.net

Opening hours	Open 7 days
Reservation policy	No
Credit cards	Accepted
Price range	Budget
Style	Casual
Cuisine	Pizza
Recommended for	Late Night

CAFÉ BARJOT

Recommended by
JJ Proville

711 Bellevue Avenue East
Seattle
Washington 98102
+1 2064575424
www.barjotseattle.com

Opening hours	Open 7 days
Reservation policy	No
Credit cards	Accepted
Price range	Affordable
Style	Casual
Cuisine	Modern American Cafe
Recommended for	Breakfast

"Go for the life-giving cold brew and gruyère croissants."—JJ Proville

CAFÉ BESALU

Recommended by
Ethan Stowell

5909 24th Ave Northwest
Seattle
Washington 98107
+1 206 789 1463
www.cafebesalu.com

Opening hours	Closed Monday and Tuesday
Credit cards	Accepted
Price range	Affordable
Style	Casual
Cuisine	Bakery
Recommended for	Breakfast

"Besalu is a small pastry shop in Ballard, a great neighborhood in Seattle, that serves the best croissants I have ever had. I've tried to find a better croissant and it just hasn't happened."—Ethan Stowell

CANLIS

Recommended by
Jason Bond,
Ethan Stowell

2576 Aurora Avenue North
Seattle
Washington 98109
+1 2062833313
www.canlis.com

Opening hours	Closed Sunday
Credit cards	Accepted
Price range	Expensive
Style	Formal
Cuisine	Modern American
Recommended for	Worth the travel

"Seattle's one true fine-dining restaurant. The food is fantastic, the service is great, the wine list is stellar, and the view can't be beat."—Ethan Stowell

CHAN

Recommended by
Perfecte Rocher

86 Pine Street
Seattle
Washington 98101
+1 2064435443
www.chanseattle.com

Opening hours	Closed Monday and Sunday
Reservation policy	No
Credit cards	Accepted
Price range	Affordable
Style	Casual
Cuisine	Korean
Recommended for	Local favorite

"It's approachable, Korean comfort food made with ingredients from the Pacific Northwest."
—Perfecte Rocher

CHISO

Recommended by
Perfecte Rocher

3520 Fremont Avenue North
Seattle
Washington 98103
+1 2066323430
www.chisofremont.com

Opening hours	Open 7 days
Credit cards	Accepted
Price range	Affordable
Style	Casual
Cuisine	Japanese
Recommended for	Bargain

DICK'S DRIVE-IN

Recommended by
Ethan Stowell

500 Queen Anne Ave North
Seattle
Washington 98109
+1 2062855155
www.ddir.com

Opening hours	Open 7 days
Credit cards	Accepted
Price range	Budget
Style	Casual
Cuisine	Burgers
Recommended for	Bargain

"You'll only get this answer if you're from Seattle—it's a great burger, but it's less about the burger and more about the history of Dick's in Seattle."—Ethan Stowell

DIN TAI FUNG

Recommended by
Jasper Shen

2621 Northeast 46th Street
Seattle
Washington 98105
+1 2065250958
www.dintaifungusa.com

Opening hours	Open 7 days
Reservation policy	No
Credit cards	Accepted
Price range	Affordable
Style	Casual
Cuisine	Chinese
Recommended for	Worth the travel

"The best soup dumplings around."—Jasper Shen

FONDA LA CATRINA

Recommended by
John Sundstrom

5905 Airport Way South
Seattle
Washington 98108
+1 2067672787
www.fondalacatrina.com

Opening hours	Open 7 days
Reservation policy	No
Credit cards	Accepted
Price range	Affordable
Style	Casual
Cuisine	Mexican
Recommended for	Breakfast

GREEN LEAF

Recommended by
Ethan Stowell

418 8th Avenue
Seattle
Washington 98104
+1 2063401388
greenleaftaste.com

Opening hours	Open 7 days
Credit cards	Accepted
Price range	Affordable
Style	Casual
Cuisine	Vietnamese
Recommended for	Regular neighborhood

"The lunch spot I eat at most regularly. I love
Vietnamese cuisine and culture and, having spent
some time there (best vacation spot ever), I have a
huge amount of respect for how regional, seasonal,
and traditional the cuisine is. Green Leaf lives up to
the sense of fresh, modest, and delicious food that
I found throughout my travels."—Ethan Stowell

IL CORVO

Recommended by
John Sundstrom,
Cathy Whims

217 James Street
Seattle
Washington 98104
+1 2065380999
www.ilcorvopasta.com

Opening hours	Closed Saturday and Sunday
Reservation policy	No
Credit cards	Accepted
Price range	Affordable
Style	Casual
Cuisine	Italian
Recommended for	Wish I'd opened

"A tiny hole-in-the-wall pasta restaurant with a
rotating selection of three different daily pastas,
a casual atmosphere, and very fast service—even
though there is always a line (queue) out the door.
Mike Easton's reverence of pasta is manifested in every
bowl. I wish I had opened it myself."—Cathy Whims

KEDAI MAKAN

Recommended by
John Sundstrom,
Holly Smith

1802 Bellevue Avenue
Seattle
Washington 98122
+1 2065555555
www.kedaimakansea.com

Opening hours	Closed Monday and Tuesday
Reservation policy	No
Credit cards	Accepted
Price range	Affordable
Style	Casual
Cuisine	Malaysian
Recommended for	Late night

"Do not miss any of the rotis and the fried chicken
is out of this world!"—John Sundstrom

LE CAVISTE

Recommended by
JJ Proville

1919 7th Avenue
Seattle
Washington 98101
+1 2067282657
www.lecavisteseattle.com

Opening hours	Closed Sunday
Credit cards	Accepted
Price range	Affordable
Style	Casual
Cuisine	French
Recommended for	Regular neighborhood

"A place of legend. The owner, David Butler, is a much-loved industry figure, and his beef tartare and charcuterie boards are the best in the city, amid his impeccable wines. Perfect for a date, or just a solo mission with a charcuterie board."—JJ Proville

LITTLE UNCLE

Recommended by
John Sundstrom

1523 East Madison Street #101
Seattle
Washington 98122
+1 2065496507
www.littleuncleseattle.com

Opening hours	Closed Monday and Sunday
Reservation policy	No
Credit cards	Accepted
Price range	Affordable
Style	Casual
Cuisine	Thai
Recommended for	Regular neighborhood

"A little bit of Thailand. Wiley and PK are fantastic cooks, serving up authentic, family-style Thai cuisine."—John Sundstrom

MEAN SANDWICH

Recommended by
John Sundstrom

1510 Northwest Leary Way
Seattle
Washington 98107
+1 2067899999
www.meansandwich.com

Opening hours	Closed Monday
Reservation policy	No
Credit cards	Accepted
Price range	Affordable
Style	Casual
Cuisine	Sandwiches
Recommended for	Regular neighborhood

PALACE KITCHEN

Recommended by
John Sundstrom

2030 5th Avenue
Seattle
Washington 98121
+1 2064482001
www.palacekitchen.com

Opening hours	Open 7 days
Credit cards	Accepted
Price range	Affordable
Style	Casual
Cuisine	Gastropub
Recommended for	Late night

PELOTON CAFÉ

Recommended by
JJ Proville

1220 East Jefferson Street
Seattle
Washington 98122
+1 2065694265
www.pelotonseattle.com

Opening hours	Closed Sunday and Monday
Reservation policy	No
Credit cards	Accepted
Price range	Budget
Style	Casual
Cuisine	American
Recommended for	Breakfast

"I'm consistently blown away by Peloton's little touches—like the generous pile of dressed arugula (rocket) that comes with braised brisket sandwiches on grain bread, or the addictive little radish, lime, and cilantro (coriander) julienne that will accompany an expertly crafted breakfast burrito."—JJ Proville

QUINN'S PUB

Recommended by
John Sundstrom

1001 East Pike Street
Seattle
Washington 98122
+1 2063257711
www.quinnspubseattle.com

Opening hours	Open 7 days
Reservation policy	No
Credit cards	Accepted
Price range	Affordable
Style	Casual
Cuisine	Gastropub
Recommended for	Late night

"Quinn's pub for wild boar sloppy joe, Scotch eggs, and pretzels and beer cheddar fondue."
—John Sundstrom

SALARE

Recommended by
Carlo Lamagna

2404 Northeast 65th Street
Seattle
Washington 98115
+1 2065562192
www.salarerestaurant.com

Opening hours	Closed Monday and Tuesday
Credit cards	Accepted
Price range	Affordable
Style	Casual
Cuisine	Modern American
Recommended for	Local favorite

"Eduardo Jordan up in Seattle does an amazing job of bringing his roots to the plate at his restaurant."
—Carlo Lamanga

SALUMI

Recommended by
John Sundstrom

309 3rd Avenue South
Seattle
Washington 98104
+1 2066218772
www.salumicuredmeats.com

Opening hours	Closed Saturday and Sunday
Reservation policy	No
Credit cards	Accepted
Price range	Affordable
Style	Casual
Cuisine	Sandwiches
Recommended for	Regular neighborhood

"For sandwiches, you can never go wrong with Batali family-run Salumi."—John Sundstrom

SEATTLE DELI

Recommended by
JJ Proville

225 12th Avenue #101
Seattle
Washington 98144
+1 2063280106

Opening hours	Open 7 days
Reservation policy	No
Credit cards	Not accepted
Price range	Budget
Style	Casual
Cuisine	Vietnamese
Recommended for	Bargain

"It doesn't get cheaper than this—$3 (£2.50) banh mi sandwiches! These are the best ones around. A go-to is tofu or the grilled pork."—JJ Proville

SINGLE SHOT

Recommended by
JJ Proville

611 Summit Avenue East
Seattle
Washington 98102
+1 2064202238
www.singleshotseattle.com

Opening hours	Open 7 days
Credit cards	Accepted
Price range	Affordable
Style	Casual
Cuisine	Modern American Bar
Recommended for	Regular neighborhood

SITKA & SPRUCE

Recommended by
JJ Proville

1531 Melrose Avenue
Seattle
Washington 98122
+1 2063240662
www.sitkaandspruce.com

Opening hours	Open 7 days
Credit cards	Accepted
Price range	Affordable
Style	Smart casual
Cuisine	Modern American
Recommended for	Local favorite

"The ingredients, technique, and vibe of this restaurant represent the Pacific Northwest for me."
—JJ Proville

SUSHI KAPPO TAMURA

Recommended by
Holly Smith

2968 Eastlake Avenue East
Seattle
Washington 98102
+1 2065470937
www.sushikappotamura.com

Opening hours	Open 7 days
Credit cards	Accepted
Price range	Expensive
Style	Smart casual
Cuisine	Japanese
Recommended for	Regular neighborhood

"Pristine, sustainable seafood handled with care and expertise."—Holly Smith

SUSHI KASHIBA

Recommended by
JJ Proville,
Ethan Stowell

86 Pine Street
Seattle
Washington 98101
+1 2064418844
www.sushikashiba.com

Opening hours	Open 7 days
Credit cards	Accepted
Price range	Expensive
Style	Smart casual
Cuisine	Japanese
Recommended for	Local favorite

"Shiro has been making sushi in Seattle for at least thirty years. He has worked at, influenced, or started all of the best sushi restaurants in the city. He's our most iconic, and in my opinion, best chef working here today. Try and get a spot at the counter."—Ethan Stowell

TAI TUNG

Recommended by
Perfecte Rocher

655 South King Street
Seattle
Washington 98104
+1 2066227372
www.taitungrestaurant.com

Opening hours	Open 7 days
Credit cards	Accepted
Price range	Affordable
Style	Casual
Cuisine	Chinese
Recommended for	Regular neighborhood

"It has big, bold flavors and the sliced cod with black bean sauce is a dish I go back to over and over again."—Perfecte Rocher

THE WANDERING GOOSE

Recommended by
John Sundstrom

403 15th Avenue East
Seattle
Washington 98112
+1 2063239938
www.thewanderinggoose.com

Opening hours	Open 7 days
Reservation policy	No
Credit cards	Accepted
Price range	Affordable
Style	Casual
Cuisine	South American
Recommended for	Breakfast

"Chef/owner Heather Ernhardt is the embodiment of Southern hospitality, serving up a generous hangtown fry of pork belly, fried oysters, and poached eggs. The biscuits are amazing, and her coconut and brownstone cakes are legendary!"—John Sundstrom

WATARU

Recommended by
Holly Smith

2400 Northeast 65th Street
Seattle
Washington 98115
+1 2065252073
www.wataruseattle.com

Opening hours	Closed Monday
Credit cards	Accepted
Price range	Expensive
Style	Smart Casual
Cuisine	Sushi
Recommended for	Regular neighborhood

"Quaint space and fantastic food, but it's the chef and general manager that totally make the whole experience."

TORY MCPHAIL P818

"Looking at the menus makes me feel like a kid again, in the best possible way."

TORY MCPHAIL P814

"Those Shrimp tacos are things of fantasy."

JESSICA KOSLOW P811

LOS ANGELES

"It's humbling to eat such delicious food for so little money."

BEN SHEWRY P816

"The best secret menu item in Los Angeles."

BRYANT NG P819

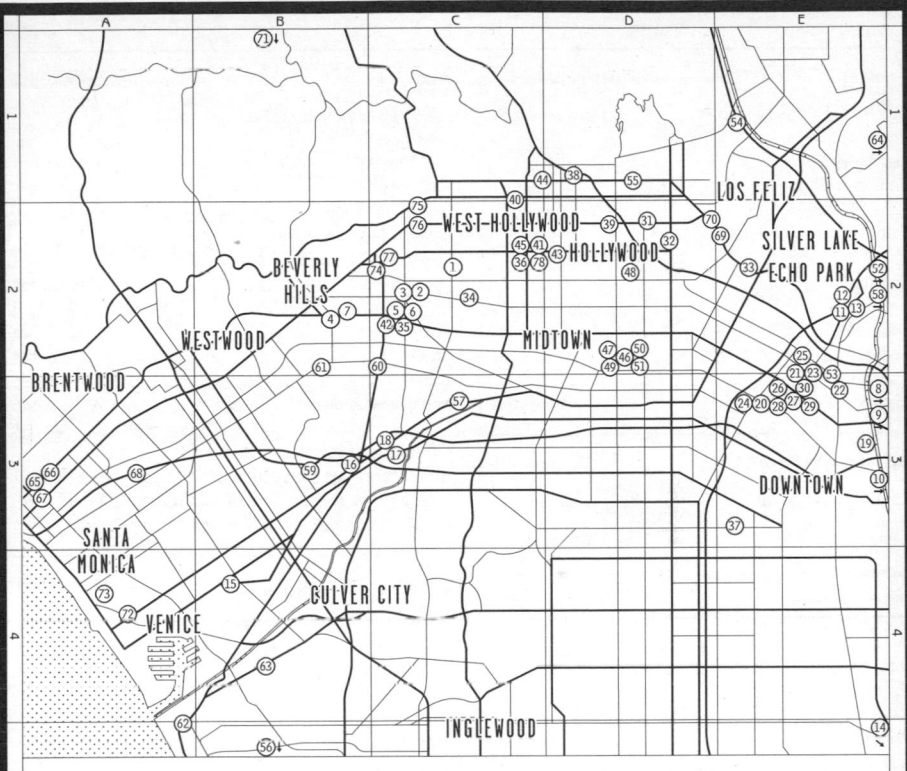

LOS ANGELES

Map labels: WEST-HOLLYWOOD, HOLLYWOOD, LOS FELIZ, SILVER LAKE, ECHO PARK, BEVERLY HILLS, WESTWOOD, MIDTOWN, BRENTWOOD, DOWNTOWN, SANTA MONICA, VENICE, CULVER CITY, INGLEWOOD

N̂ SCALE

0   1500   3000   4500
                          yd.

ANIMAL

Recommended by
Kwang Uh

435 North Fairfax Avenue
Beverly Grove
Los Angeles
California 90036
+1 3237829225
www.animalrestaurant.com

Opening hours	Open 7 days
Credit cards	Accepted
Price range	Affordable
Style	Casual
Cuisine	American
Recommended for	Local favorite

JOAN'S ON THIRD

Recommended by
Kwang Uh

8350 West 3rd Street
Beverly Grove
Los Angeles
California 90048
+1 3236552285
www.joansonthird.com

Opening hours	Open 7 days
Reservation policy	No
Credit cards	Accepted
Price range	Affordable
Style	Casual
Cuisine	Café
Recommended for	Breakfast

SON OF A GUN

Recommended by
Grae Nonas

8370 West 3rd Street
Beverly Grove
Los Angeles
California 90048
+1 3237829033
www.sonofagunrestaurant.com

Opening hours	Open 7 days
Credit cards	Accepted
Price range	Affordable
Style	Casual
Cuisine	Seafood
Recommended for	Wish I'd opened

CUT

Recommended by
Carlos Perez,
Kris Yenbamroong

9500 Wilshire Boulevard
Beverly Hills
Los Angeles
California 90212
+1 3102768500
www.wolfgangpuck.com

Opening hours	Closed Sunday
Credit cards	Accepted
Price range	Expensive
Style	Formal
Cuisine	Steakhouse
Recommended for	High end

"The level of hospitality at Cut is really special. And there's always a sense of occasion when I walk in the dining room. There's no place I'd rather spend $1,000 (£780) on a steak dinner!"—Kris Yenbamroong

LAWRY'S THE PRIME RIB

Recommended by
Bryant Ng

100 North La Cienega Boulevard
Beverly Hills
Los Angeles
California 90211
+1 3106522827
www.lawrysonline.com

Opening hours	Open 7 days
Credit cards	Accepted
Price range	Expensive
Style	Smart casual
Cuisine	Steakhouse
Recommended for	Wish I'd opened

Chicago's loyalty to Lawry's knows no bounds. The upmarket chophouse, an offshoot of the Beverly Hills original, has been serving up roasted prime rib of beef to locals and visiting carnivores since 1984. The original was opened in 1938, which explains the time-warp feel of the place, from the mansion setting—you might have stepped into the White House circa 1950—to the kitsch staff uniforms and tableside rituals. But when the meat is this good, who cares? It's carved into telephone directory-thick slabs from silver carts and served with lashings of mash, gravy, and Yorkshire pudding.

MATSUHISA

Recommended by
Grae Nonas

129 North La Cienega Boulevard
Beverly Hills
Los Angeles
California 90211
+1 3106599639
www.matsuhisarestaurants.com

Opening hours	Open 7 days
Credit cards	Accepted
Price range	Expensive
Style	Smart casual
Cuisine	Japanese
Recommended for	High end

"Legendary, iconic, and the quality is incredible."
—Grae Nonas

SPAGO

Recommended by
Suzanne Goin

176 North Canon Drive
Beverly Hills
Los Angeles
California 90210
+1 3103850880
www.wolfgangpuck.com

Opening hours	Open 7 days
Credit cards	Accepted
Price range	Expensive
Style	Smart casual
Cuisine	Modern American
Recommended for	Local favorite

AL & BEA'S MEXICAN FOOD

Recommended by
Kris Yenbamroong

2025 East 1st Street
Boyle Heights
Los Angeles
California 90033
+1 2322678810

Opening hours	Open 7 days
Credit cards	Accepted
Price range	Budget
Style	Casual
Cuisine	Mexican
Recommended for	Bargain

"The bean and cheese burritos are my go-to here.
They're so satisfying! "—Kris Yenbamroong

GUISADOS

Recommended by
Josef Centeno,
Jessica Koslow

2100 East Cesar East Chavez Avenue
Boyle Heights
Los Angeles
California 90033
+1 3232647201
www.guisados.co

Opening hours	Open 7 days
Credit cards	Accepted
Price range	Budget
Style	Casual
Cuisine	Mexican
Recommended for	Bargain

MARISCOS JALISCO

Recommended by
Jessica Koslow

3040 East Olympic Boulevard
Boyle Heights
Los Angeles
California
+1 3235286701

Opening hours	Open 7 days
Reservation policy	No
Credit cards	Not accepted
Price range	Budget
Style	Casual
Cuisine	Mexican
Recommended for	Bargain

"Those shrimp (prawn) tacos are things of fantasy."
—Jessica Koslow

LASA

Recommended by
Carlo Lamagna

727 North Broadway #120
Chinatown
Los Angeles
California 90012
+1 2134436163
www.lasa-la.com

Opening hours	Closed Monday
Credit cards	Accepted
Price range	Affordable
Style	Casual
Cuisine	Filipino
Recommended for	Worth the travel

NEW DRAGON SEAFOOD RESTAURANT

Recommended by
Kwang Uh

934 North Hill Street
Chinatown
Los Angeles
California 90012
+1 2136266050

Opening hours	Open 7 days
Credit cards	Accepted
Price range	Affordable
Style	Casual
Cuisine	Chinese
Recommended for	Bargain

PHOENIX INN CLASSIC CHINESE

Recommended by
Kris Yenbamroong

301 Ord Street
Chinatown
Los Angeles
California 90012
+1 2136292812
www.phoenixfood.us

Opening hours	Open 7 days
Credit cards	Accepted
Price range	Affordable
Style	Casual
Cuisine	Chinese
Recommended for	Late night

"Simple, no frills, classic Chinatown vibe. I have been going there since I was a kid. I always order the duck congee and the salt-and-pepper chicken wings. That's exactly what I need late at night!"—Kris Yenbamroong

TACO MARIA

Recommended by
Kwang Uh

3313 Hyland Avenue
Costa Mesa
Los Angeles
California 92626
+1 7145388444
www.tacomaria.com

Opening hours	Closed Monday
Credit cards	Accepted
Price range	Affordable
Style	Casual
Cuisine	Mexican
Recommended for	Local favorite

"For any taco lover that wants to experience next-level taco game in a fine-dining set-up."—Kwang Uh

A-FRAME

Recommended by
Massimo Bottura

12565 West Washington Boulevard
Culver City
Los Angeles
California, 90066
+1 310 398 7700
www.aframela.com

Opening hours	Open 7 days
Credit cards	Accepted
Price range	Budget
Style	Casual
Cuisine	Hawaiian
Recommended for	Bargain

THE WALLACE

Recommended by
Ted Hopson

3833 Main Street
Culver City
Los Angeles
California 90232
+1 3102026400
www.thewallacela.com

Opening hours	Open 7 days
Credit cards	Accepted
Price range	Affordable
Style	Casual
Cuisine	Modern American
Recommended for	Regular neighborhood

"I love how innovative the food is. The menu changes often and has a great mix of traditional flavors and new techniques."—Ted Hopson

DESTROYER

Recommended by
Kwang Uh

3578 Hayden Avenue
Culver City
Los Angeles
California 90232
www.destroyer.la

Opening hours	Closed Saturday and Sunday
Reservation policy	No
Credit cards	Accepted
Price range	Affordable
Style	Casual
Cuisine	Modern American
Recommended for	Wish I'd opened

LUKSHON

Recommended by
Diego Hernández-Velasco Baquedano

3239 Helms Avenue
Culver City
Los Angeles
California 90232
+1 3102026808
www.lukshon.com

Opening hours	Closed Monday and Sunday
Credit cards	Accepted
Price range	Expensive
Style	Casual
Cuisine	Asian Fusion
Recommended for	Expensive

BESTIA

Recommended by
Miles Kirby, Carlo Lamagna,
Michael Friedman

2121 East 7th Place
Downtown
Los Angeles
California 90021
+1 2135145724
www.bestiala.com

Opening hours	Open 7 days
Credit cards	Accepted
Price range	Expensive
Style	Casual
Cuisine	Italian
Recommended for	Worth the travel

"Energy, a family vibe, and intensely flavored food, all in a beautifully understated setting."—Miles Kirby

BROKEN SPANISH

Recommended by
Marc Djozlija, Cosmo Goss

1050 South Flower Street
Downtown
Los Angeles
California 90015
+1 2137491460
www.brokenspanish.com

Opening hours	Open 7 days
Credit cards	Accepted
Price range	Expensive
Style	Casual
Cuisine	Mexican
Recommended for	Worth the travel

"I wasn't assuming anything when I went, but literally everything on the menu was mind-blowing. Super simple but done in surprising ways."—Cosmo Goss

GRAND CENTRAL MARKET

Recommended by
Kwang Uh

317 South Broadway
Downtown
Los Angeles
California 90013
+1 2136242378
www.grandcentralmarket.com

Opening hours	Open 7 days
Reservation policy	No
Credit cards	Accepted
Price range	Affordable
Style	Casual
Cuisine	Restaurant Marketplace
Recommended for	Breakfast

KAGAYA

Recommended by
Josef Centeno

418 East 2nd Street
Downtown
Los Angeles
California, 90012
+1 2136171016

Opening hours	Closed Monday
Credit cards	Accepted
Price range	Affordable
Style	Casual
Cuisine	Japanese
Recommended for	High end

KNEAD & CO PASTA BAR

Recommended by
Ted Hopson

317 South Broadway
Downtown
Los Angeles
California 90013
+1 2132237592
www.kneadpasta.com

Opening hours	Open 7 days
Reservation policy	No
Credit cards	Accepted
Price range	Affordable
Style	Casual
Cuisine	Italian
Recommended for	Wish I'd opened

"Bruce is doing the food that I love—the food I grew up on. Looking at his menus makes me feel like a kid again, in the best possible way."—Ted Hopson

LUDOBIRD

Recommended by
Carlos Perez

1111 South Figueroa Street
Downtown
Los Angeles
California 90015
+1 2137427100
www.ludolefebvre.com

Opening hours	Closed Monday and Tuesday
Credit cards	Accepted
Price range	Affordable
Style	Casual
Cuisine	American
Recommended for	Bargain

OTIUM

Recommended by
Kristen D. Murray, Carlos Perez

222 South Hope Street
Downtown
Los Angeles
California 90012
+1 2139358500
www.otiumla.com

Opening hours	Closed Monday
Credit cards	Accepted
Price range	Expensive
Style	Casual
Cuisine	American Fusion
Recommended for	Worth the travel

"It was beautiful, playful, seasonally focused, and delicious."—Kristen D. Murray

There are two reasons why food critic Jonathan Gold called Otium LA's "most ambitious restaurant in years". The first is the space—trendy, sleek, modern, and with a touch of sparkle thanks to custom brass lighting and a stunning suspended glass sculpture. And don't forget the open kitchen, which brings the cooking into the dining room in a way like no other. The second reason, though, is that the dishes can be dazzling. They're unexpected but familiar, straight from California's open heart, with influences from Japan, Southeast Asia, and the Middle East. Kale salad with peanuts coexists with foie gras funnel cake, and both delight.

Q SUSHI

Recommended by
Jessica Koslow

521 West 7th Street
Downtown
Los Angeles
California 90017
+1 2132256285
www.qsushila.com

Opening hours	Closed Monday and Sunday
Credit cards	Accepted
Price range	Expensive
Style	Smart casual
Cuisine	Japanese
Recommended for	High end

RICEBAR
Recommended by
Josef Centeno

419 7th Street
Downtown
Los Angeles
California 90014
+1 2138075341
www.ricebarla.com

Opening hours	Closed Sunday
Credit cards	Accepted
Price range	Affordable
Style	Casual
Cuisine	Filipino
Recommended for	Bargain

SHIBUMI
Recommended by
Jessica Koslow

815 Hill Street
Downtown
Los Angeles
California 90014
+1 2132657923
www.shibumidtla.com

Opening hours	Closed Monday
Credit cards	Accepted
Price range	Expensive
Style	Casual
Cuisine	Japanese
Recommended for	High end

TERRONI
Recommended by
Josef Centeno

802 S Spring Street
Downtown
Los Angeles
California, 90014
+1 2132217234
www.te-nyc.com

Opening hours	Open 7 days
Credit cards	Accepted
Price range	Affordable
Style	Smart casual
Cuisine	Italian
Recommended for	Wish I'd opened

WEXLER'S DELI
Recommended by
Jocky Petrie

Grand Central Market
317 South Broadway
Downtown
Los Angeles
California 90013
+1 2136200633
www.wexlersdeli.com

Opening hours	Open 7 days
Reservation policy	No
Credit cards	Accepted
Price range	Affordable
Style	Casual
Cuisine	Jewish Deli
Recommended for	Bargain

"The finest pastrami Rubén I have had to date."
—Jocky Petrie

DESANO PIZZA
Recommended by
Kwang Uh

4959 Santa Monica Boulevard
East Hollywood
Los Angeles
California 90029
+1 3239137000
www.desanopizza.com

Opening hours	Open 7 days
Reservation policy	No
Credit cards	Accepted
Price range	Affordable
Style	Casual
Cuisine	Italian
Recommended for	Regular neighborhood

SQIRL
Recommended by
John Sundstrom,
Kwang Uh

720 North Virgil Avenue #4
East Hollywood
Los Angeles
California 90029
+1 3232848147
www.sqirlla.com

Opening hours	Open 7 days
Reservation policy	No
Credit cards	Accepted
Price range	Affordable
Style	Casual
Cuisine	Breakfast-Brunch
Recommended for	Breakfast

"Go for the famous ricotta and jam toast or a socca
pancake."—John Sundstrom

COSA BUONA
Recommended by
Josef Centeno

2100 West Sunset Boulevard
Echo Park
Los Angeles
California, 90026
+1 2139085211
www.cosabuona.com

Opening hours	Closed Tuesday
Reservation policy	Accepted
Price range	Affordable
Style	Casual
Cuisine	Italian-Pizza
Recommended for	Bargain

EREWHON MARKET
Recommended by
Kwang Uh

7660 Beverly Boulevard
Fairfax
Los Angeles
California 90036
+1 3239370777
www.erewhonmarket.com

Opening hours	Open 7 days
Reservation policy	No
Credit cards	Accepted
Price range	Affordable
Style	Casual
Cuisine	Café
Recommended for	Breakfast

CHI SPACCA
Recommended by
Ross Lusted

6610 Melrose Avenue
Hancock Park
Los Angeles
California 90038
+1 3232971133
www.chispacca.com

Opening hours	Open 7 days
Credit cards	Accepted
Price range	Expensive
Style	Casual
Cuisine	Italian
Recommended for	Worth the travel

OSTERIA MOZZA
Recommended by
Carlos Perez

6602 Melrose Avenue
Hancock Park
Los Angeles
California 90038
+1 3232970100
www.la.osteriamozza.com

Opening hours	Open 7 days
Credit cards	Accepted
Price range	Expensive
Style	Formal
Cuisine	Italian
Recommended for	High end

TIRE SHOP TAQUERIA
Recommended by
Ben Shewry

4069 South Avalon Boulevard
Historic South Central
Los Angeles
California 90011
www.tireshoptaqueria.com

Opening hours	Closed Tuesday and Wednesday
Reservation policy	No
Credit cards	Not accepted
Price range	Budget
Style	Casual
Cuisine	Mexican
Recommended for	Wish I'd opened

"It's humbling to eat such delicious food for so little
money. I love the freedom that the people that run
it have—it's barely a restaurant, more of a series
of small tents in a car park in South Central LA."
—Ben Shewry

AL WAZIR CHICKEN
Recommended by
Kwang Uh

6051 Hollywood Boulevard
Hollywood
Los Angeles
California 90028
+1 3238560660

Opening hours	Open 7 days
Credit cards	Accepted
Price range	Affordable
Style	Casual
Cuisine	Middle-Eastern
Recommended for	Regular neighborhood

BAROO

Recommended by
Kevin Fink,
Kris Yenbamroong

5706 Santa Monica Boulevard
Hollywood
Los Angeles
California 90038
+1 3239299288
www.baroola.strikingly.com

Opening hours	Closed Monday and Sunday
Reservation policy	No
Credit cards	Accepted
Price range	Affordable
Style	Casual
Cuisine	Korean-Italian-American
Recommended for	Local favorite

"Los Angeles right now is all about freedom, and
Baroo typifies that. The vibe is minimalist, and the
decor and menu are limited, which makes this
restaurant an oasis."—Kris Yenbamroong

IN-N-OUT BURGER

Recommended by
Daniel Burns,
Vaughan Mabee

7009 Sunset Boulveard
Hollywood
Los Angeles
California 90028
+1 8007861000
www.in-n-out.com

Opening hours	Open 7 days
Reservation policy	No
Credit cards	Accepted
Price range	Budget
Style	Casual
Cuisine	Burgers
Recommended for	Wish I'd opened

PETIT TROIS

Recommended by
Daniel Boulud,
Diego Hernández-Velasco Baquedano,
Carlos Perez

718 Highland Avenue
Hollywood
Los Angeles
California 90038
+1 3234688916
www.petittrois.com

Opening hours	Open 7 days
Credit cards	Accepted
Price range	Expensive
Style	Casual
Cuisine	French
Recommended for	Wish I'd opened

PIZZERIA MOZZA

Recommended by
Massimo Bottura,
Suzanne Goin

641 North Highland Avenue
Hollywood
Los Angeles
California 90036
+1 3232970101
www.pizzeriamozza.com

Opening hours	Open 7 days
Credit cards	Accepted
Price range	Affordable
Style	Casual
Cuisine	Pizza
Recommended for	Regular neighborhood

PROVIDENCE

Recommended by
Diego Hernández-Velasco Baquedano,
Jennifer Jasinski,
Kwang Uh

5955 Melrose Avenue
Hollywood
Los Angeles
California 90038
+1 3234604170
www.providencela.com

Opening hours	Open 7 days
Credit cards	Accepted
Price range	Expensive
Style	Smart casual
Cuisine	Modern American Seafood
Recommended for	High end

"The chef, Michael Ciramusti, has created an exciting
cuisine with the best ingredients in Los Angeles.
His series of amuse-bouches are direct hits of flavor
that prepare the palate for the dishes that follow,
comprising a specialized menu of sustainable seafood.
It's a must-visit in Los Angeles."
—Diego Hernández-Velasco Baquedano

THE MUSSO & FRANK GRILL

Recommended by
Jessica Koslow

6667 Hollywood Boulevard
Hollywood
Los Angeles
California 90028
+1 3234677788
www.mussoandfrank.com

Opening hours	Closed Monday
Credit cards	Accepted
Price range	Expensive
Style	Smart casual
Cuisine	Steakhouse
Recommended for	Local favorite

"Best martini you'll ever have. I recommend sharing
the wedge salad and the porterhouse. And get fries
(not thick cut) and creamed spinach. Peek into the
kitchen—it's the kitchen every chef dreams of."
—Jessica Koslow

TROIS MEC

Recommended by
Jennifer Jasinski,
Kwang Uh

716 Highland Avenue
Hollywood
Los Angeles
California 90038
+1 2134621344
www.troismec.com

Opening hours	Closed Saturday and Sunday
Credit cards	Accepted
Price range	Expensive
Style	Casual
CCuisine	French
Recommended for	Worth the travel

"An LA-minded fine-dining experience with a modern
French chef's twist."—Kwang Uh

BCD TOFU HOUSE

Recommended by
Ted Hopson,
Jessica Koslow

3575 Wilshire Boulevard
Koreatown
Los Angeles
California 90010
+1 2133826677
www.bcdtofu.com

Opening hours	Open 7 days
Reservation policy	No
Credit cards	Accepted
Price range	Affordable
Style	Casual
Cuisine	Korean
Recommended for	Late night

"There is nothing as comforting as a bowl of boiling
soon tofu, a Korean stew. You eat all the banchan, and
crack an egg into your stew, and enjoy. It warms you
up in all the right ways."—Ted Hopson

BCD Tofu House opened its original Western Avenue
location in 1996 and now boasts a dozen, including
in New York and New Jersey. The franchise has
gained a reputation for its soon tofu, or spicy tofu
stew, with a variety of options including fermented
soy, seafood, ham and sausage, and "original"
(beef and pork). It arrives searingly hot, still
bubbling, and can prove a maddening exercise
in patience. No longer exclusively attracting a
Korean-American clientele, BCD Tofu House has
also justifiably become a favorite for late-night
eating, a delicious way to fortify before collapsing
back at home.

HERE'S LOOKING AT YOU

Recommended by
Tory McPhail

3901 West 6th Street
Koreatown
Los Angeles
California 90020
+1 2135683573
www.hereslookingatyoula.com

Opening hours	Closed Tuesday
Credit cards	Accepted
Price range	Expensive
Style	Casual
Cuisine	Modern American
Recommended for	Worth the travel

"Quaint space and fantastic food, but it's the chef
and general manager that totally make the whole
experience."—Tory McPhail

NOSHI SUSHI

Recommended by
Suzanne Tracht

4430 Beverly Boulevard
Koreatown
Los Angeles
California 90004
+1 3234693458
www.noshisushila.com

Opening hours	Closed Monday
Reservation policy	No
Credit cards	Not accepted
Price range	Affordable
Style	Casual
Cuisine	Sushi
Recommended for	Regular neighborhood

"Have to go there and get my fix at least once a week. Love the spicy tuna and baked crab hand rolls."
—Suzanne Tracht

POLLO A LA BRASA

Recommended by
Kwang Uh

764 South Western Avenue
Koreatown
Los Angeles
California 90005
+1 2133871531

Opening hours	Closed Tuesday
Reservation policy	No
Credit cards	Accepted
Price range	Affordable
Style	Casual
Cuisine	Latin American
Recommended for	Regular neighborhood

SUN NONG DAN

Recommended by
Kwang Uh

3470 West 6th Street
Koreatown
Los Angeles
California 90020
+1 2133650303
www.sunnongdan.com

Opening hours	Open 7 days
Reservation policy	No
Credit cards	Accepted
Price range	Affordable
Style	Casual
Cuisine	Korean
Recommended for	Late night

"I go here for family meal feast on weekends after a busy, busy night."—Kwang Uh

THE HALAL GUYS

Recommended by
Kwang Uh

3432 Wilshire Boulevard
Koreatown
Los Angeles
California 90010
+1 2134807738
www.koreatownlaca.thehalalguys.com

Opening hours	Open 7 days
Reservation policy	No
Credit cards	Accepted
Price range	Affordable
Style	Casual
Cuisine	Middle Eastern-Asian
Recommended for	Regular neighborhood

"For a quick Middle Eastern fix."—Kwang Uh

EL HUARACHITO

Recommended by
Bryant Ng

3010 North Broadway
Lincoln Heights
Los Angeles
California 90031
+1 3232230476

Opening hours	Open 7 days
Reservation policy	No
Credit cards	Not accepted
Price range	Budget
Style	Casual
Cuisine	Mexican
Recommended for	Breakfast

"Our favorite breakfast place is El Huarachito. Their tacos al gobernador (crispy shrimp [prawn] taco filled with cheese and shrimp wrapped in a corn tortilla shell encased in crispy griddled cheese) is the best secret menu item in Los Angeles. Also their milanesa con papas is the perfect pounded breaded beef steak. Chilaquiles rojos are ideal."—Bryant Ng

DAIKOKUYA

Recommended by
Josef Centeno

27 East 1st Street
Little Tokyo
Los Angeles
California, 90012
+1 2136261680
www.daikoku-ten.com

Opening hours	Open 7 days
Reservation policy	No
Credit cards	Not accepted
Price range	Budget
Style	Casual
Cuisine	Japanese
Recommended for	Late night

RICKY'S FISH TACOS

Recommended by
Kwang Uh

3201 Riverside Drive
Los Feliz
Los Angeles
California 90027
+1 3233956233

Opening hours	Closed Monday and Tuesday
Reservation policy	No
Credit cards	Accepted
Price range	Budget
Style	Casual
Cuisine	Tacos
Recommended for	Bargain

SAPP COFFEE SHOP

Recommended by
Jessica Koslow

5183 Hollywood Boulevard
Los Feliz
Los Angeles
California 90027
+1 3236651035
www.sapp.menutoeat.com

Opening hours	Closed Wednesday
Reservation policy	No
Credit cards	Accepted
Price range	Budget
Style	Casual
Cuisine	Thai
Recommended for	Regular neighborhood

"Thai breakfast restaurant. Hard chairs and minimal care given to the decor—it's all about the food. I always get the jade noodles and/or the boat noodles."—Jessica Koslow

THE ARTHUR J

Recommended by
Ted Hopson

903 Manhattan Avenue
Manhattan Beach
Los Angeles
California 90266
+1 3108789620
www.thearthurj.com

Opening hours	Open 7 days
Credit cards	Accepted
Price range	Expensive
Style	Smart casual
Cuisine	Steakhouse
Recommended for	High end

"When we celebrate, we want steak—and not just any will do, only the best. This traditional steak house has it all, and you can spend time walking the beach

before and after dinner. There's no better place to feel like 'I've earned this'."—Ted Hopson

LEO'S TACOS TRUCK

Recommended by
George Calombaris

1515 South La Brea Avenue
Mid-City
Los Angeles
California 90019
+1 3233462001
www.leostacostruck.com

Opening hours	Open 7 days
Reservation policy	No
Credit cards	Not accepted
Price range	Budget
Style	Casual
Cuisine	Mexican
Recommended for	Bargain

"A food van I stumbled across in LA—they do the best taco in the world!"—George Calombaris

YUNNAN RESTAURANT

Recommended by
Bryant Ng

301 North Garfield Avenue
Monterey Park
Los Angeles
California 91754
+1 6265718387
www.yunnanmontereypark.com

Opening hours	Open 7 days
Credit cards	Accepted
Price range	Budget
Style	Casual
Cuisine	Chinese
Recommended for	Regular neighborhood

"There are plenty of other regional Chinese restaurants in the San Gabriel Valley, but few are as consistent and varied as this one. The La Zi Ji (spicy chicken cubes) is the best version I've had in the US and in Asia—it's like eating spicy pieces of crispy chicken skin soaked in Sichuan chile oil, garlic, and ginger. Their deli case has a great depth of flavors and variety, ranging from pickled green beans, julienne potatoes, young soybeans with greens, spicy headcheese (brawn), cured pig tongue, tripe, sauteed peanuts, to spicy duck heads."—Bryant Ng

N/NAKA

Recommended by
Bryant Ng

3455 Overland Avenue
Palms
Los Angeles
California 90034
+1 3108366252
www.n-naka.com

Opening hours	Closed Monday and Sunday
Credit cards	Accepted
Price range	Expensive
Style	Smart casual
Cuisine	Japanese Kaiseki
Recommended for	High end

Creativity needs constraint. At least this has proven true for chef Niki Nakayama, whose food sings within the formal structure of *kaiseki*, a traditional multi-course Japanese meal with set progressions. Chef Nakayama's plates are exquisite compositions, each of thirteen seasonal courses unfolding as one story. Despite the fact that Nakayama remains in the kitchen, out of view, dining here is intensely personal, with each guest's menu carefully tailored (so reservations must be made well in advance). Dining here is an intimate, unique experience.

MEXIKOSHER

Recommended by
Emily Hahn

8832 West Pico Boulevard
Pico-Robertson
Los Angeles
California 90035
+1 3102710900
www.mexikosher.com

Opening hours	Closed Saturday
Reservation policy	No
Credit cards	Accepted
Price range	Affordable
Style	Casual
Cuisine	Kosher Mexican
Recommended for	Worth the travel

SOTTO

Recommended by
Kris Yenbamroong

9575 West Pico Boulevard
Pico-Robertson
Los Angeles
California 90035
+1 3102770210
www.sottorestaurant.com

Opening hours	Open 7 days
Credit cards	Accepted
Price range	Expensive
Style	Casual
Cuuisine	Italian
Recommended for	Wish I'd opened

"Sotto isn't the new kid on the block, but it's always packed, and the vibe is somewhere between buzzy and neighborhood go-to. I go here for date night, but I also bring any family visiting from out of town."
—Kris Yenbamroong

PLAYA PROVISIONS

Recommended by
Emily Hahn

119 Culver Boulevard
Playa del Rey
Los Angeles
California 90293
+1 3106835019
www.playaprovisions.com

Opening hours	Open 7 days
Credit cards	Accepted
Price range	Affordable
Style	Casual
Cuisine	Modern American
Recommended for	Worth the travel

DA KIKOKIKO

Recommended by
Emily Hahn

12746 West Jefferson Boulevard
Playa Vista
Los Angeles
California 90094
+1 4248354192
www.dakikokiko.com

Opening hours	Open 7 days
Credit cards	Accepted
Price range	Affordable
Style	Casual
Cuisine	Hawaiian
Recommended for	Wish I'd opened

LUSCIOUS DUMPLINGS

704 West Las Tunas Drive #4
San Gabriel
Los Angeles
California 91776
+1 6262828695
www.lusciousdumplings.com

Opening hours	Closed Monday
Reservation policy	No
Credit cards	Not accepted
Price range	Budget
Style	Casual
Cuisine	Chinese
Recommended for	Regular neighborhood

"As the name implies, the dumplings are quite luscious. We order the fried sole, pork and napa dumplings, and the chive dumplings filled with pork, egg, and shrimp. Stick to ordering the dumplings and you'll have a great meal."—Bryant Ng

CASSIA

1314 7th Street
Santa Monica
Los Angeles
California 90401
+1 3103936699
www.cassiala.com

Opening hours	Open 7 Days
Credit cards	Accepted
Price range	Affordable
Style	Casual
Cuisine	Southeast Asian
Recommended for	Wish I'd opened

"I love their modern approach to Vietnamese. Coming from Houston, Vietnamese is my favorite ethnic cuisine and I would love to open a restaurant one day with those flavors and dishes."—Sarah Grueneberg

RUSTIC CANYON

1119 Wilshire Boulevard
Santa Monica
Los Angeles
California 90401
+1 3103937050
www.rusticcanyonwinebar.com

Opening hours	Open 7 days
Credit cards	Accepted
Price range	Affordable
Style	Casual
Cuisine	Modern American
Recommended for	Local favorite

"Jeremy Fox is creating some of the best simple, local, and perfect food in the city. I think what he is doing there really captures LA—it's diverse, local, and amazing."—Ted Hopson

WEXLER'S DELI

616 Santa Monica Boulevard
Santa Monica
Los Angeles
California 90401
+1 4247448671
www.wexlersdeli.com

Opening hours	Open 7 Days
Reservation policy	No
Credit cards	Accepted
Price range	Affordable
Style	Casual
Cuisine	Jewish Deli
Recommended for	Breakfast

"I love starting my mornings with a bagel and smoked fish. I usually switch it up with the smoked salmon and the smoked sturgeon. It is a perfect simple breakfast."
—Ted Hopson

RAE'S

Recommended by
Kris Yenbamroong

2901 Pico Boulevard
Santa Monica
Los Angeles
California 90405
+1 3108287937

Opening hours	Open 7 days
Reservation policy	No
Credit cards	Not accepted
Price range	Affordable
Style	Casual
Cuisine	Diner
Recommended for	Breakfast

"First and foremost I love Rae's because the food is delicious. It's an old-school diner that's been around forever—this is as authentic as it gets. I order the Club Sandwich #1 on white toast with mayo and a side of french fries and ranch dressing for the fries. Classic!"
—Kris Yenbamroong

NIGHT + MARKET SONG

Recommended by
Josef Centeno
Kwang Uh

3322 Sunset Boulevard
Silver Lake
Los Angeles
California 90069
+1 3102759724
www.nightmarketsong.com

Opening hours	Closed Sunday
Reservation policy	No
Credit cards	Accepted
Price range	Affordable
Style	Casual
Cuisine	Thai
Recommended for	Late night

PINE & CRANE

Recommended by
Jessica Koslow,
Cal Peternell,
Kwang Uh

1521 Griffith Park Boulevard
Silver Lake
Los Angeles
California 90026
+1 3236681128
www.pineandcrane.com

Opening hours	Closed Tuesday
Reservation policy	No
Credit cards	Accepted
Price range	Affordable
Style	Casual
Cuisine	Taiwanese-Chinese
Recommended for	Wish I'd opened

"Whenever I go to LA, I go to Pine & Crane."
—Cal Peternell

ASANEBO

Recommended by
Jessica Koslow

11941 Ventura Boulevard
Studio City
Los Angeles
California 91604
+1 8187603348
www.asanebo-restaurant.com

Opening hours	Open 7 Days
Credit cards	Accepted
Price range	Affordable
Style	Smart casual
Cuisine	Japanese
Recommended for	High end

"It's been around for over twenty years and the quality of their fish and the technique has stayed at masterful levels. It's wonderful."—Jessica Koslow

Viewed from outside, Asanebo, tucked into a Studio City shopping mall, betrays little sign that its inspired *omakase* (Japanese "chef's choice" dining) is among LA's best. The high quality of its seafood, much of it from Tsukiji, has won Asanebo patrons in Hollywood, but the restaurant remains as focused as when it opened in 1991. There is expert sashimi and sushi, accented by turns with beautiful examples of *tare*, *ponzu*, and *yuzu kosho* (Japanese condiments). But chef Tetsuya Nakao's skill is on brightest display in the cooked dishes—trembling *chawanmushi* (savory egg custard), unctuous and saline with *uni* (sea urchin) and abalone; Japanese conch simmering on its plate; or Hokkaido hairy crab barely steamed, its sweetness clear against its briny *kani miso* (crab brain). Here is a chef to whom one happily surrenders.

GJELINA

1429 Abbot Kinney Boulevard
Venice
Los Angeles
California 90291
+1 3104501429
www.gjelina.com

Recommended by
Josef Centeno,
Ben Greeno,
Sarah Grueneberg,
Kevin Hickey

Opening hours	Open 7 days
Credit cards	Accepted
Price range	Affordable
Style	Smart casual
Cuisine	Modern American
Recommended for	Worth the travel

"The things they do with vegetables are truly amazing. It's the epitome of Cal-Ital (Californian/Italian cuisine). Their pizza crust is so delicate but balanced with the hearty toppings."
—Sarah Grueneberg

GJUSTA

320 Sunset Avenue
Venice
Los Angeles
California 90291
+1 3103140320
www.gjusta.com

Recommended by
Ravi Kapur, James Lowe,
Walter Manzke, Larry McGuire,
Willy Trullas Moreno,
Magnus Nilsson,
Georgy Troyan

Opening hours	Open 7 days
Reservation policy	No
Credit cards	Accepted
Price range	Budget
Style	Casual
Cuisine	American
Recommended for	Breakfast

"A big restaurant that does a number of things—coffee, breads, deli-style sandwiches, flatbreads, and more. But unlike everyone else who try to do so many things, and fail miserably, everything they do is amazing. Last time I was in LA for four days I went three times!"—James Lowe

Peak hours at Gjusta, Venice's breakfast and lunch destination, can be crushing. Thank goodness for the LA sun, which makes takeout (takeaway) possible. The lucky ones will, after struggling to order from the lengthy menu, eventually make it to the end of the long counter and into the yard to enjoy some shade, if not much quiet. Still, it's impossible to be grumpy about the wait because this is LA, and at Gjusta, spirits soar and vegetables are uncannily vibrant. Toothsome breads are sliced and piled with smoked fish and bright pickles, fresh

juices sparkle with perfectly ripe fruit, and it seems like all the world's delis—American Jewish, Italian, Middle Eastern, French—have met in heaven.

ABURIYA RAKU

521 North La Cienega Boulevard
West Hollywood
Los Angeles
California 90048
+1 2133089393
www.aburiyarakula.wixsite.com/weho

Recommended by
Kris Yenbamroong

Opening hours	Closed Sunday
Credit cards	Accepted
Price range	Affordable
Style	Casual
Cuisine	Japanese Izakaya
Recommended for	Regular neighborhood

"Everything about the restaurant is pristine. From the execution of the sashimi plates to the flavors of the cooked dishes, Chef Matt knows how to make a memorable meal."—Kris Yenbamroong

Aburiya Raku became famous when its original location opened in Las Vegas in 2008. There chef Mitsuo Endo served inventive *izakaya* in a restaurant neatly tucked away from the Strip. In 2015, with chef Matthew Weaver also on board, Endo opened an outpost in West Hollywood. Like the original, the menu of the diminutive and somewhat austere restaurant takes full advantage of charcoal (Aburiya Raku means "charcoal grill house enjoyment"). The air is fragrant from the chicken meatballs (called *tsukune*), crispy salmon belly, and unctuous pig ear cooking on the robata. But Weaver has a tender touch and a sharp knife for sashimi too. And Endo's masterful homemade agedashi tofu quivers in the hills of Los Angeles as it did in the desert of Vegas before it.

CHATEAU MARMONT

8221 Sunset Boulevard
West Hollywood
Los Angeles
California 90046
+1 3236561010
www.chateaumarmont.com

Recommended by
Kris Yenbamroong,
Eric Ripert

Opening hours	Open 7 days
Credit cards	Accepted
Price range	Expensive
Style	Smart casual
CCuisine	Modern American
Recommended for	Breakfast

"I always get breakfast in-room. I feel at home here, the only difference is that I'm not cooking, and I'm very pampered. I love the vibe. I can take my time and read the papers, just like I do at home."—Eric Ripert

CONNIE & TED'S

Recommended by
Cosmo Goss

8171 Santa Monica Boulevard
West Hollywood
Los Angeles
California 90046
+1 3238482722
www.connieandteds.com

Opening hours	Open 7 days
Credit cards	Accepted
Price range	Expensive
Style	Casual
Cuisine	Seafood
Recommended for	Worth the travel

LUCQUES

Recommended by
Michael Friedman

8474 Melrose Avenue
West Hollywood
Los Angeles
California 90069
+1 3236556277
www.lucques.com

Opening hours	Open 7 days
Credit cards	Accepted
Price range	Expensive
Style	Smart casual
Cuisine	Modern American
Recommended for	Worth the travel

"IT IS LIKE GOING TO THE OPERA OR THE THEATER. POETRY. EVERY DETAIL IS SOULFUL AND ELEGANT. TRULY SPECIAL."

KRISTEN D. MURRAY P833

"This super cool space channels the essence of Japan into a Northern Californian setting."

OLLE T. CELLTON P835

SAN FRANCISCO

"For jam-filled corn muffins and great in-house roasted coffee."

MATTHEW ACCARRINO P838

"CHEF DRIVEN BREAKFAST BY ONE OF THE NICEST CHEFS IN THE CITY."

VAL CANTU P838

"THE MOST DELICIOUS TACOS EVER."

EVAN & SARAH RICH P835

SAN FRANCISCO

SCALE

0   500   1000   1500
                        yd.

1. *Nopa (p.828)*
2. *The Mill (p.828)*
3. *Mama Ji's (p.828)*
4. *Woodhouse Fish Company (p.828)*
5. *Akiko's (p.828)*
6. *Mister Jiu's (p.828)*
7. *Boulevard Restaurant (p.829)*
8. *Boulettes Larder (p.829)*

9. *Ferry Building Farmer's Market (p.829)*
10. *Hog Island Oyster Co (p.829)*
11. *Coi (p.829)*
12. *Quince (p.830)*
13. *20ᵗʰ Century Cafe (p.830)*
14. *Blue Bottle Coffee (p.830)*
15. *Cala (p.830)*
16. *Monsieur Benjamin (p.830)*
17. *Petit Crenn (p.830)*
18. *Rich Table (p.831)*
19. *Souvla (p.831)*
20. *Zuni Café (p.831)*
21. *Wako Sushi (p.831)*
22. *Art's Café (p.831)*
23. *Izakaya Sozai (p.832)*
24. *Yummy Yummy (p.832)*
25. *State Bird Provisions (p.832)*
26. *Ijji Sushi (p.832)*
27. *Nopalito (p.832)*
28. *Liholiho Yacht Club (p.832)*
29. *Out The Door (p.833)*
30. *Spqr (p.833)*
31. *Atelier Crenn (p.833)*
32. *Brazen Head (p.833)*

33. *Abv (p.834)*
34. *Al's Place (p.834)*
35. *Aster (p.834)*
36. *Belmar La Gallinita Meat Market (p.834)*
37. *Flour + Water (p.834)*
38. *Izakaya Rintaro (p.835)*
39. *La Taqueria (p.835)*
40. *Lazy Bear (p.835)*
41. *Mau (p.835)*
42. *Mission Chinese (p.835)*
43. *Motze (p.836)*
44. *Namu Gaji (p.836)*
45. *Taqueria Guadalajara (p.836)*
46. *Taqueria Vallarta (p.836)*
47. *Tartine Bakery (p.836)*
48. *Tartine Manufactory (p.836)*
49. *Wesburger N'more (p.837)*
50. *Wise Sons (p.837)*
51. *Yamo (p.837)*
52. *Lord Stanley (p.837)*
53. *Swan Oyster Depot (p.837)*
54. *The House of Prime Rib (p.837)*

55. *Sam's Burgers (p.838)*
56. *Tosca Café (p.838)*
57. *Turtle Tower (p.838)*
58. *Andytown Coffee Roasters (p.838)*
59. *Toyose (p.838)*
60. *Outerlands (p.838)*
61. *B. Patisserie (p.839)*
62. *Salt And Straw (p.839)*
63. *Breakfast at Tiffany's (p.839)*
64. *Aina (p.839)*
65. *Plow (p.839)*
66. *Saint Frank (p.840)*
67. *Benu (p.840)*
68. *Cockscomb (p.840)*
69. *In-Situ (p.840)*
70. *Saison (p.840)*
71. *Trou Normand (p.841)*
72. *Yank Sing (p.841)*
73. *Lers Ros (p.841)*
74. *Saigon Sandwich (p.841)*
75. *Del Popolo (p.841)*
76. *Kin Khao (p.842)*
77. *The Progress (p.842)*

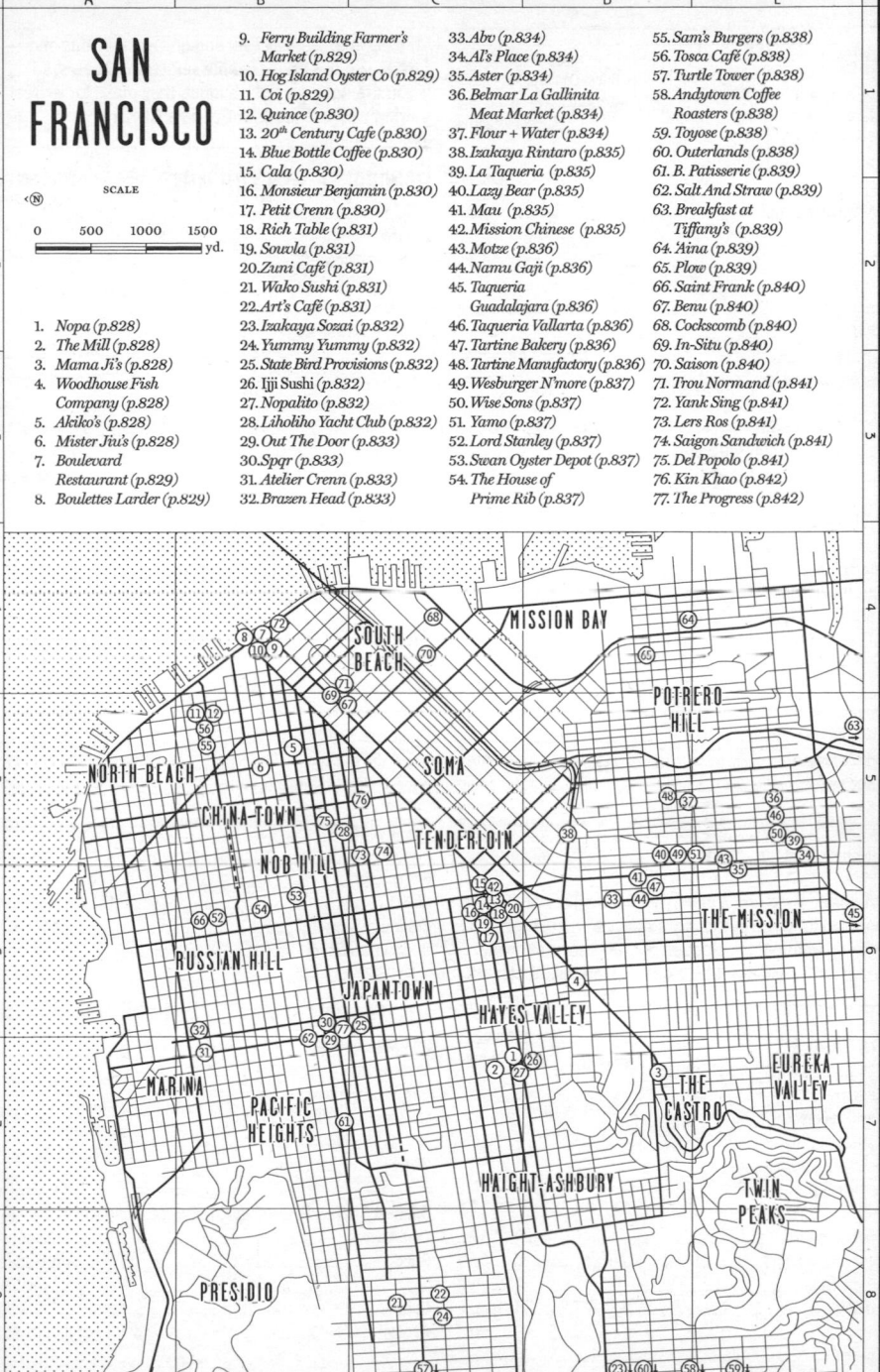

NOPA

Recommended by
Gabriela Cámara, Val Cantu,
Ravi Kapur, Aaron London,
Daniel Patterson

560 Divisadero Street
Alamo Square
San Francisco
California 94117
+1 4158648643
www.nopasf.com

Opening hours	Open 7 days
Credit cards	Accepted
Price range	Affordable
Style	Casual
Cuisine	Modern American
Recommended for	Late night

"It's an SF institution. Great burger, pork chop, and salads."—Daniel Patterson

THE MILL

Recommended by
Matthew Accarrino

736 Divisadero Street
Alamo Square
San Francisco
California 94117
+1 4153451953
www.themillsf.com

Opening hours	Open 7 days
Reservation policy	No
Credit cards	Accepted
Price range	Affordable
Style	Casual
Cuisine	Coffee
Recommended for	Regular neighborhood

"A coffee shop and a bakery all in one. They also serve my favorite pizza in the city six days a week, together with an interesting selection of craft beers and wine. Great for a casual get together."—Matthew Accarrino

MAMA JI'S

Recommended by
Gabriela Cámara

416 18th Street
Castro
San Francisco
California 94114
+1 4156264416
www.mamajissf.com

Opening hours	Open 7 days
Reservation policy	No
Credit cards	Accepted
Price range	Affordable
Style	Casual
Cuisine	Chinese
Recommended for	Bargain

"It's close to where I live, and always delicious and fast. It also has an incredible selection of beers, so if you are not on a tight budget, they make for a great pairing with the food."—Gabriela Cámara

WOODHOUSE FISH COMPANY

Recommended by
Aaron London

2073 Market Street
Castro
San Francisco
California 94114
+1 4154372722
woodhousefish.com

Opening hours	Open 7 days
Reservation policy	No
Credit cards	Accepted
Price range	Affordable
Style	Casual
Cuisine	Seafood
Recommended for	Bargain

"I'm a sucker for their clam chowder."—Aaron London

AKIKO'S

Recommended by
Gabriela Cámara

431 Bush Street
Chinatown
San Francisco
California 94108
+1 4153973218
www.akikosrestaurant.com

Opening hours	Closed Sunday
Credit cards	Accepted
Price range	Affordable
Style	Casual
Cuisine	Japanese
Recommended for	High end

MISTER JIU'S

Recommended by
Val Cantu

28 Waverly Place
Chinatown
San Francisco
California 94108
+1 4158579688
www.misterjius.com

Opening hours	Closed Monday and Sunday
Credit cards	Accepted
Price range	Affordable
Style	Casual
Cuisine	Chinese
Recommended for	Regular neighborhood

BOULEVARD RESTAURANT

Recommended by
Hiro Sone

1 Mission Street
Embarcadero
San Francisco
California 94105
+1 4155436084
www.boulevardrestaurant.com

Opening hours	Open 7 days
Credit cards	Accepted
Price range	Expensive
Style	Smart casual
Cuisine	Modern American
Recommended for	Local favorite

Only a handful of restaurants are lucky enough to welcome guests into spaces as splendid as their cooking. Boulevard, which has called this Beaux Arts building home since 1993, is one of them. It's almost enough just to be in this vaulted space with views of Bay Bridge—but the food is equally as impressive. Chef Nancy Oakes is one of America's most daring. Meals are bold—luxury as satisfaction, not piousness—and flash their French pedigree while trumpeting top-quality ingredients.

BOULETTES LARDER

Recommended by
Molly Mitchell

1 Ferry Building, Suite 48
Embarcadero
San Francisco
California 94111
+1 4153991155
www.bouletteslarder.com

Opening hours	Closed Monday
Credit cards	Accepted
Price range	Affordable
Style	Casual
Cuisine	Mediterrean
Recommended for	Worth the travel

"Boulette's Larder in the Ferry Building in San Francisco is just incredible. The atmosphere is relaxed and the food is simple but perfectly executed."
—Molly Mitchell

FERRY BUILDING FARMER'S MARKET

Recommended by
Gabriela Cámara

1 Ferry Building
Embarcadero
San Francisco
California 94111
+1 4159838030
www.ferrybuildingmarketplace.com

Opening hours	Open 7 days
Credit cards	Not accepted
Price range	Affordable
Style	Casual
Cuisine	Market
Recommended for	Regular neighborhood

"Great food for breakfast, from Mexican *chilaquiles* and *tamales* to a porchetta sandwich that is out of control."—Gabriela Cámara

HOG ISLAND OYSTER CO

Recommended by
Benjamin Sukle

1 Ferry Building
Embarcadero
San Francisco
California 94111
+1 4153917117
www.hogislandoysters.com

Opening hours	Open 7 days
Reservation policy	No
Credit cards	Accepted
Price range	Affordable
Style	Casual
Cuisine	Seafood
Recommended for	Wish I'd opened

COI

Recommended by
Giulio Sturla

373 Broadway
Financial District
San Francisco
California 94133
+1 4153939000
www.coirestaurant.com

Opening hours	Closed Tuesday and Wednesday
Credit cards	Accepted
Price range	Expensive
Style	Formal
Cuisine	Seafood
Recommended for	High end

QUINCE

Recommended by
Val Cantu,
Daniel Costa,
Linton Hopkins

470 Pacific Avenue
Financial District
San Francisco
California 94133
+1 4157758500
www.quincerestaurant.com

Opening hours	Closed Sunday
Credit cards	Accepted
Price range	Expensive
Style	Formal
Cuisine	Californian
Recommended for	High end

"I love the tasting menu and wine pairing with the extra cheese course. Every bite is spectacular."
—Daniel Costa

20TH CENTURY CAFE

Recommended by
Gabriela Cámara,
Russell Moore

198 Gough Street
Hayes Valley
San Francisco
California 94102
+1 4156212380
www.20thcenturycafe.com

Opening hours	Open 7 days
Credit cards	Accepted
Price range	Affordable
Style	Casual
Cuisine	Eastern European
Recommended for	Regular neighborhood

"Everything in the café is of extraordinary quality. Michelle, the owner, is an amazing pastry chef, but her savory dishes are also exceptionally good. I am obsessed with the bagels they bake there."
—Gabriele Camara

BLUE BOTTLE COFFEE

Recommended by
Gabriela Cámara

315 Linden Street
Hayes Valley
San Francisco
California 94102
+1 5106533394
www.bluebottlecoffee.com

Opening hours	Open 7 days
Credit cards	Accepted
Price range	Affordable
Style	Casual
Cuisine	Coffee
Recommended for	Regular neighborhood

CALA

Recommended by
Olle T. Cellton

149 Fell Street
Hayes Valley
San Francisco
California 94102
+1 4156607701
www.calarestaurant.com

Opening hours	Open 7 days
Credit cards	Accepted
Price range	Affordable
Style	Casual
Cuisine	Mexican
Recommended for	Worth the travel

MONSIEUR BENJAMIN

Recommended by
Matthew Kirkley

451 Gough Street
Hayes Valley
San Francisco
California 94102
+1 4154032233
www.monsieurbenjamin.com

Opening hours	Open 7 days
Credit cards	Accepted
Price range	Affordable
Style	Smart casual
Cuisine	French Bistro
Recommended for	Regular neighborhood

"When my wife and I ask one another where we want to eat on our day off, more often than not we end up concluding that we just want to go back here again. French bistro fare is deeply comforting to me, and Corey Lee and his team execute the classics excellently."—Matthew Kirkley

PETIT CRENN

Recommended by
Joshua Lewin,
Anita Lo,
Bonny Porter

609 Hayes Street
Hayes Valley
San Francisco
California 92102
+1 4158641744
www.petitcrenn.com

Opening hours	Closed Monday
Credit cards	Accepted
Price range	Expensive
Style	Smart casual
Cuisine	French
Recommended for	Worth the travel

"Give yourself over to the chefs. You know that they are going to serve the freshest of ingredients and they

do so with a set menu designed to be shared. I came here with six friends and each course was delectable. My favorite was a baby gem salad in a huge bowl which was passed around and we served ourselves."
—Bonny Porter

RICH TABLE

Recommended by
Ravi Kapur,
Aaron London

199 Gough Steet
Hayes Valley
San Francisco
California 94102
+1 4153559085
www.richtablesf.com

Opening hours	Open 7 days
Credit cards	Accepted
Price range	Affordable
Style	Casual
Cuisine	Modern American
Recommended for	Regular neighborhood

"Thoughtful, creative, cuisine. Elevated service, a sophisticated beverage program, and exceptional desserts."—Ravi Kapur

SOUVLA

Recommended by
Gabriela Cámara,
Val Cantu

517 Hayes Street
Hayes Valley
San Francisco
California 94102
+1 4154005458
www.souvlasf.com

Opening hours	Open 7 days
Reservation policy	No
Credit cards	Accepted
Price range	Affordable
Style	Casual
Cuisine	Greek
Recommended for	Regular neighborhood

"A newish chain serving Greek wraps and salads which is the smartest concept I've seen since Shake Shack—always is what it is, and it's good."
—Gabriela Cámara

ZUNI CAFÉ

Recommended by
Gabriela Cámara,
Olle T. Cellton,
Michael Friedman,
Matthew Kirkley

1658 Market Street
Hayes Valley
San Francisco
California 94102
+1 4155522522
www.zunicafe.com

Opening hours	Closed Monday
Credit cards	Accepted
Price range	Affordable
Style	Casual
Cuisine	Californian
Recommended for	Local favorite

"A total classic—fresh and delicious Californian cuisine at its best, served in an outstandingly beautiful and sexy space. It's in the middle of the city, and it's always a delight to spend time there. For me this is one of the best restaurants in the world, without a doubt."—Gabriela Cámara

WAKO SUSHI

Recommended by
Val Cantu,
Hiro Sone

211 Clement Street
Inner Richmond
San Francisco
California 49118
+1 4156824875
www.sushiwakosf.com

Opening hours	Closed Monday and Sunday
Credit cards	Accepted
Price range	Expensive
Style	Casual
Cuisine	Japanese
Recommended for	Local favorite

"The best sushi!"—Hiro Sone

ART'S CAFÉ

Recommended by
Val Cantu

747 Irving Street
Inner Sunset
San Francisco
California 94122
+1 4156657440

Opening hours	Closed Monday
Reservation policy	No
Credit cards	Not accepted
Price range	Affordable
Style	Casual
Cuisine	American
Recommended for	Breakfast

IZAKAYA SOZAI

1500 Irving Street
Inner Sunset
San Francisco
California 94122
+1 4157425122
www.izakayasozai.com

Recommended by
Chris Cosentino

Opening hours	Open 7 days
Credit cards	Accepted
Price range	Affordable
Style	Casual
Cuisine	Japanese
Recommended for	Regular neighborhood

YUMMY YUMMY

1015 Irving Street
Inner Sunset
San Francisco
California 94122
+1 4155664722
www.yummyyummyrestaurant.net

Recommended by
Chris Cosentino

Opening hours	Closed Tuesday
Reservation policy	No
Credit cards	Accepted
Price range	Affordable
Style	Casual
Cuisine	Vietnamese
Recommended for	Regular neighborhood

"The *pho* broth is the best I have had outside
Vietnam."—Chris Cosentino

STATE BIRD PROVISIONS

1529 Fillmore street
Japantown
San Francisco
California 94115
+1 4157951272
www.statebirdsf.com

Recommended by
Andreas Dahlberg,
Brad Holmes,
John Jackson, Jennifer Jasinski,
Aaron London, Tony Maws

Opening hours	Open 7 days
Credit cards	Accepted
Price range	Expensive
Style	Smart casual
Cuisine	Modern American
Recommended for	Wish I'd opened

"This restaurant rocks—always fun and a really great
concept."—Aaron London

IJJI SUSHI

252 Divisadero Street
Lower Haight
San Francisco
California 94117
+1 4156587388
www.ijjisf.com

Recommended by
Val Cantu

Opening hours	Closed Monday and Tuesday
Credit cards	Accepted
Price range	Expensive
Style	Casual
Cuisine	Japanese
Recommended for	Local favorite

NOPALITO

306 Broderick Street
Lower Haight
San Francisco
California 94117
+1 4154370303
www.nopalitosf.com

Recommended by
Evan & Sarah Rich

Opening hours	Open 7 days
Reservation policy	No
Credit cards	Accepted
Price range	Affordable
Style	Casual
Cuisine	Mexican
Recommended for	Regular neighborhood

"Always delicious, and great mezcal margaritas.
The perfect place to take the whole family."
—Evan & Sarah Rich

LIHOLIHO YACHT CLUB

871 Sutter Street
Lower Nob Hill
San Francisco
California 94109
+1 4154405446
www.liholihoyachtclub.com

Recommended by
Val Cantu,
Evan & Sarah Rich,
Geir Skeie

Opening hours	Closed Sunday
Credit cards	Accepted
Price range	Expensive
Style	Smart casual
Cuisine	Modern Hawaiian
Recommended for	Wish I'd opened

"Fun vibe, good cocktails, friendly service, and the
food is delicious."—Evan & Sarah Rich

Hawaiian cuisine seems to be right on trend at the moment, but any notion that Oahu-native Ravi Kapur is simply riding the recent aloha wave should be cast aside at Liholiho Yacht Club, a graphic, modern restaurant that opened in 2015 in Nob Hill. Kapur's cooking, on cheerful display in the open kitchen, is as precise as it is playful, and is genuinely designed to share. A smart wine list and refreshing selection of sake and cocktails make refreshing accompaniments to a menu that speaks equally of family and reinvention. One snack, popcorn dressed with butter and *togarashi* (Japanese spice), is a call-back to Hurricane Popcorn, the Hawaiian childhood staple. The reference may tickle those in the know, but even those who aren't can see it's delicious.

OUT THE DOOR

Recommended by
Matthew Accarrino

2232 Bush Street
Lower Pacific Heights
San Francisco
California 94115
+1 4159239575
www.outthedoors.com

Opening hours	Open 7 days
Credit cards	Accepted
Price range	Affordable
Style	Casual
Cuisine	Vietnamese
Recommended for	Local favorite

"A Californian take on Vietnamese food. The menu is seasonal, changes frequently, and is inexpensive. It's conveniently right around the corner from SPQR, since I'm there most of the time, we grab quick lunches for meetings, takeout (takeaway), or early dinners there."—Matthew Accarrino

SPQR

Recommended by
Andrew Zimmerman

1191 Fillmore Street
Lower Pacific Heights
San Francisco
California 94115
+1 4157717779
www.spqrsf.com

Opening hours	Open 7 days
Credit cards	Accepted
Price range	Affordable
Style	Casual
uisine	Italian
Recommended for	Worth the travel

"Fantastic modern Italian—Matt Accarino makes honestly delicious food."—Andrew Zimmerman

ATELIER CRENN

Recommended by
Aaron Adams, Tom Aikens,
Val Cantu, John Jackson,
Joshua Lewin, Kristen D. Murray,
Manoella Buffara Ramos,
Guy Savoy

3127 Fillmore Street
Marina
San Francisco
California 94123
+1 4154400460
www.ateliercrenn.com

Opening hours	Closed Monday and Sunday
Credit cards	Accepted
Price range	Expensive
Style	Smart casual
Cuisine	French
Recommended for	High end

"It is like going to the opera or the theater—yet feeling like you are held close by the beautiful and spectacular production. Poetry. Every detail is soulful and elegant. Truly special."—Kristen D Murray

French chef Dominique Crenn is a striking figure. San Pellegrino deemed her the World's Best Female Chef in 2016, and she was the first woman in the US to be awarded two Michelin stars, for her restaurant Atelier Crenn, in 2012. Her food is revered, and her dishes draw deeply on poignant memories, nature, and her childhood in Versailles. Each dish on the highly innovative multi-course tasting menu has a story to tell, and is presented as a line from a poem—"Where the broad ocean leans against a Spanish land", for example, is a rather unique take on surf 'n' turf.

BRAZEN HEAD

Recommended by
Evan & Sarah Rich

3166 Buchanan street
Marina
San Francisco
California 94123
+1 4159217600
www.brazenheadsf.com

Opening hours	Open 7 days
Reservation policy	No
Credit cards	Not accepted
Price range	Affordable
Style	Casual
Cuisine	French
Recommended for	Late night

"You can get classics like escargot at 1.00 a.m. Amazing!"—Evan & Sarah Rich

ABV

3174 16th Street
Mission
San Francisco
California 94103
+1 4154004748
www.abvsf.com

Recommended by
Ravi Kapur

Opening hours	Open 7 days
Reservation policy	No
Credit cards	Accepted
Price range	Affordable
Style	Smart casual
Cuisine	Bar
Recommended for	Late night

"Amazing bartenders. Skilled, and showing great hospitality. No pretense but really well made drinks and food."—Ravi Kapur

AL'S PLACE

1499 Valencia Street
Mission
San Francisco
California 94110
+1 4154166136
www.alsplacesf.com

Recommended by
Val Cantu

Opening hours	Closed on Monday and Tuesday
Credit cards	Accepted
Price range	Affordable
Style	Casual
Cuisine	Modern American
Recommended for	Local favorite

ASTER

1001 Guerrero Street
Mission
San Francisco
California 94110
+1 4158759810
astersf.com

Recommended by
Aaron Adams,
Aaron London,
Daniel Patterson

Opening hours	Open 7 days
Credit cards	Accepted
Price range	Affordable
Style	Casual
Cuisine	Californian
Recommended for	Worth the travel

"The food was top-notch, and ridiculously good-value, especially for San Fransisco. One of the best all-round dining experiences in a long time."
—Aaron Adams

Since opening in 2015, Aster has become a go-to in the San Francisco dining scene for thoughtful and inventive northern California cooking. Chef Brett Cooper draws inspiration from Japanese cuisine, and in deeper ways than most—he even air-preserves local persimmon in-house (the kitchen does much of its own fermenting, using traditional methods). In a wood-dominated dining room with a view to the open kitchen, diners order à la carte or opt for the four-course tasting menu. Most ingredients are sourced from small farms that have relationships with the restaurant. True to the moment, the drinks list features lively, natural wines, many by the glass.

BELMAR LA GALLINITA MEAT MARKET

Recommended by
Gabriela Cámara

2989 24th Street
Mission
San Francisco
California 94110
+1 4158264600

Opening hours	Open 7 days
Reservation policy	No
Credit cards	Accepted
Price range	Budget
Style	Casual
Cuisine	Mexican
Recommended for	Bargain

"It's actually a meat market, but the food they serve there is really tasty and authentic, simple Mexican fare. I have a weak spot for it."—Gabriela Cámara

FLOUR + WATER

2401 Harrison Street
Mission
San Francisco
California 94110
+1 4158267000
www.flourandwater.com

Recommended by
Val Cantu

Opening hours	Open 7 days
Credit cards	Accepted
Price range	Affordable
Style	Casual
Cuisine	Italian
Recommended for	Regular neighborhood

IZAKAYA RINTARO

82 14th Street
Mission
San Francisco
California 94103
+1 4155897022
www.izakayarintaro.com

Recommended by
Gabriela Cámara, Olle T. Cellton,
Ravi Kapur,
Russell Moore

Opening hours	Open 7 days
Credit cards	Accepted
Price range	Affordable
Style	Casual
Cuisine	Japanese
Recommended for	Local favorite

"This super-cool space channels the essence of Japan into a northern Californian setting—but don't come looking for traditional sushi. The Kyoto-born chef Sylvan Mishima Brackett works with deft precision, serving up plates of minced Sonoma liberty duck, Japanese fried-chicken wings, excellent udon noodles, and other selections of fried, skewered, and grilled items. Look out for the elegant, arched, slightly charred ceiling beams—they've been preserved after a fire destroyed the previous restaurant that occupied this space."—Olle T. Cellton

LA TAQUERIA

2889 Mission Street
Mission
San Francisco
California 94110
+1 4152857117

Recommended by
Evan & Sarah Rich

Opening hours	Closed Monday
Reservation policy	No
Credit cards	Not accepted
Price range	Affordable
Style	Casual
Cuisine	Mexican
Recommended for	Local favorite

"The most delicious tacos ever."
—Evan & Sarah Rich

LAZY BEAR

3416 19th Street
Mission
San Francisco
California 94110
+1 4158749921
www.lazybearsf.com

Recommended by
Matthew Accarrino

Opening hours	Closed Monday and Sunday
Credit cards	Accepted
Price range	Expensive
Style	Casual
Cuisine	Modern American
Recommended for	High end

MAU

665 Valencia Street
Mission
San Francisco
California 94110
+1 4159348889
www.eatmau.com

Recommended by
Ravi Kapur

Opening hours	Open 7 days
Reservation policy	No
Credit cards	Accepted
Price range	Affordable
Style	Casual
Cuisine	Vietnamese
Recommended for	Bargain

"Delicious, fresh Vietnamese using quality ingredients."—Ravi Kapur

MISSION CHINESE

2234 Mission Street
Mission
San Francisco
California 94110
+1 4158632800
www.missionchinesefood.com

Recommended by
Riccardo Camanini

Opening hours	Open 7 days
Credit cards	Accepted
Price range	Affordable
Style	Casual
Cuisine	Chinese contemporary
Recommended for	Wish I'd opened

MŌTZE

983 Valencia Street
Mission
San Francisco
California 94110
+1 4154841206
www.motze.xyz

Recommended by
Val Cantu

Opening hours	Closed Monday and Sunday
Credit cards	Accepted
Price range	Affordable
Style	Casual
Cuisine	Japanese
Recommended for	Regular neighborhood

NAMU GAJI

499 Dolores Street
Mission
San Francisco
California 94110
+1 415431-6268
www.namusf.com

Recommended by
Ravi Kapur

Opening hours	Closed Monday
Credit cards	Accepted
Price range	Affordable
Style	Casual
Cuisine	Korean
Recommended for	Breakfast

TAQUERIA GUADALAJARA

4798 Mission Street
Mission
San Francisco
California 94112
+1 4154695480

Recommended by
Val Cantu

Opening hours	Open 7 days
Reservation policy	No
Credit cards	Accepted
Price range	Budget
Style	Casual
Cuisine	Mexican
Recommended for	Late night

TAQUERIA VALLARTA

3033 24th Street
Mission
San Francisco
California 94110
T+1 415-826-8116

Recommended by
Corey Lee

Opening hours	Open 7 days
Reservation policy	No
Credit cards	Accepted
Price range	Budget
Style	Casual
Cuisine	Mexican
Recommended for	Bargain

"I always visit for two *tacos de lengua* with their salsa verde."—Corey Lee

TARTINE BAKERY

600 Guerrero Street
Mission
San Francisco
California 94110
+1 4154872600
www.tartinebakery.com

Recommended by
Corey Lee

Opening hours	Open 7 days
Reservation policy	No
Credit cards	Accepted
Price range	Budget
Style	Casual
Cuisine	Cafe-Bakery
Recommended for	Local favorite

"A modern, San Francisco classic, this is the one place I always take my friends visiting from out of town."
—Corey Lee

TARTINE MANUFACTORY

595 Alabama Street
Mission
San Francisco
California 94110
+1 4155750007
www.tartinemanufactory.com

Recommended by
Gabriela Cámara,
Olle T. Cellton,
Andreas Dahlberg,
Ken Oringer,
Christian F. Puglisi,
Ben Shewry

Opening hours	Open 7 days
Reservation policy	No
Credit cards	Accepted
Price range	Affordable
Style	Casual
Cuisine	Californian
Recommended for	Breakfast

"The best sourdough bread in the US, if not the world. This place hits the nail on the head with an airy, creative approach to breakfast."—Ken Oringer

WESBURGER N'MORE

Recommended by
Ravi Kapur

2240 Mission Street
Mission
San Francisco
California 94110
+1 4157459371
www.wesburgernmore.com

Opening hours	Closed Monday
Reservation policy	No
Credit cards	Accepted
Price range	Affordable
Style	Casual
Cuisine	American
Recommended for	Bargain

WISE SONS

Recommended by
Joel Braham

3150 24th Street
Mission
San Francisco
California 94110
+1 4157873354
www.wisesonsdeli.com

Opening hours	Open 7 days
Credit cards	Accepted
Price range	Affordable
Style	Casual
Cuisine	Jewish Deli
Recommended for	Worth the travel

"A New York Jewish deli in sunny California—they get the classics right and the modern twists too. Awesome coffee and babka!"—Joel Braham

YAMO

Recommended by
Val Cantu

3406 18th Street
Mission
San Francisco
California 94110
+1 4155538911

Opening hours	Closed Sunday
Reservation policy	No
Credit cards	Not accepted
Price range	Affordable
Style	Casual
Cuisine	Burmese
Recommended for	Bargain

"Hole-in-the-wall Burmese food."—Val Cantu

LORD STANLEY

Recommended by
Val Cantu

2065 Polk Street
Nob Hill
San Francisco
California 94109
+1 4158725512
www.lordstanleysf.com

Opening hours	Closed on Monday and Sunday
Credit cards	Accepted
Price range	Affordable
Style	Smart casual
Cuisine	European
Recommended for	Local favorite

SWAN OYSTER DEPOT

Recommended by
Benjamin Sukle

1517 Polk Street
Nob Hill
San Francisco
California 94109
+1 4156731101

Opening hours	Closed Sunday
Reservation policy	No
Credit cards	Not accepted
Price range	Affordable
Style	Casual
Cuisine	Seafood
Recommended for	Wish I'd opened

THE HOUSE OF PRIME RIB

Recommended by
Evan & Sarah Rich

1906 Van Ness Avenue
Nob Hill
San Francisco
California 94109
+1 4158854605
www.houseofprimerib.net

Opening hours	Open 7 days
Credit cards	Accepted
Price range	Affordable
Style	Casual
Cuisine	American
Recommended for	Wish I'd opened

SAM'S BURGERS

Recommended by
Matthew Kirkley

618 Broadway
North Beach
San Francisco
California 94133
+1 4153911539

Opening hours	Open 7 days
Credit cards	Accepted
Price range	Affordable
Style	Casual
Cuisine	Burgers
Recommended for	Late night

"I've come to love this little place. Just up the street from COI, Sam's is the quintessential hole-in-the-wall, greasy-spoon burger joint. Open until 2.00 a.m., you will find many a restaurant worker here past midnight. Friendly staff, good burgers, beers."—Matthew Kirkley

TOSCA CAFÉ

Recommended by
Gabriela Cámara

242 Columbus Avenue
North Beach
San Francisco
California 94133
+1 4159869651
www.toscacafesf.com

Opening hours	Open 7 days
Credit cards	Accepted
Price range	Affordable
Style	Casual
Cuisine	Italian
Recommended for	Late night

TURTLE TOWER

Recommended by
Gabriela Cámara,
Evan & Sarah Rich

5716 Geary Boulevard
Outer Richmond
San Francisco
California 94121
+1 4152219890
www.turtletowersf.com

Opening hours	Closed Wednesday
Reservation policy	No
Credit cards	Accepted
Price range	Affordable
Style	Casual
Cuisine	Vietnamese
Recommended for	Bargain

"Great pho, no fuss."—Evan & Sarah Rich

ANDYTOWN COFFEE ROASTERS

Recommended by
Matthew Accarrino

3655 Lawton Street
Outer Sunset
San Francisco
California 94122
+1 4157539775
www.andytownsf.com

Opening hours	Open 7 days
Credit cards	Accepted
Price range	Affordable
Style	Casual
Cuisine	Coffee
Recommended for	Local favorite

"For jam-filled corn muffins and great in-house roasted coffee."—Matthew Accarrino

TOYOSE

Recommended by
Gabriela Cámara,
Val Cantu,

3814 Noriega Street
Outer Sunset
San Francisco
California 94122
+1 4157310232

Opening hours	Open 7 days
Credit cards	Accepted
Price range	Affordable
Style	Casual
Cuisine	Korean
Recommended for	Late night

OUTERLANDS

Recommended by
Val Cantu

4001 Judah Street
Outer Sunsets
San Francisco
California 94122
+1 4156616140
www.outerlandssf.com

Opening hours	Open 7 days
Reservation policy	No
Credit cards	Accepted
Price range	Affordable
Style	Casual
Cuisine	Modern American
Recommended for	Breakfast

"Chef-driven breakfast by one of the nicest chefs in the city."—Val Cantu

B. PATISSERIE

Recommended by
Matthew Accarrino,
Corey Lee

2821 California Street
Pacific Heights
San Francisco
California 94115
+1 4154401700
www.bpatisserie.com

Opening hours	Closed Monday
Reservation policy	No
Credit cards	Accepted
Price range	Budget
Style	Casual
Cuisine	Café-Patisserie
Recommended for	Breakfast

"It's great to start the day in Pac Heights with Belinda Leong's *kouign amann* (Breton cake) and a coffee."
—Corey Lee

SALT AND STRAW

Recommended by
Jasper Shen

2201 Fillmore Street
Pacific Heights
San Francisco
California 94115
+1 4158292803
www.saltandstraw.com

Opening hours	Open 7 days
Reservation policy	No
Credit cards	Accepted
Price range	Affordable
Style	Casual
Cuisine	Ice cream
Recommended for	Wish I'd opened

"A great idea and business model."—Jasper Shen

BREAKFAST AT TIFFANY'S

Recommended by
Val Cantu

2499 San Bruno Avenue
Portola
San Francisco
California 94134
+1 4154688805
www.breakfastattiffanyssf.com

Opening hours	Open 7 days
Credit cards	Accepted
Price range	Affordable
Style	Casual
Cuisine	American
Recommended for	Breakfast

'AINA

Recommended by
Carlo Lamagna

900 22nd Street
Potrero Hill
San Francisco
California 94107
+1 4158143815
www.ainasf.com

Opening hours	Closed on Monday
Credit cards	Accepted
Price range	Affordable
Style	Casual
Cuisine	Hawaiian
Recommended for	Wish I'd opened

"Takes an elevated approach to Hawaiian food in a beautifully designed restaurant."—Carlo Lamagna

Aina, like the Brazilian word *saudade*, is hard to translate. It is Hawaiian for "land", but that's just the beginning. *Aina* is a connection with the land and a trust in its munificence, and is an integral cultural trait for Hawaiians. It's also the name of this small Dogpatch restaurant opened by Big Island-born chef Jordan Keao in 2016. Keao was lured to Northern California by the siren song of the tech sector (he was previously a chef at Google and Airbnb), and found there the farms and purveyors that would lend their products to a menu that includes Portuguese, Japanese, and American influences. There are spam bao, shoyu-cured short rib, and French toast made from bread flown in from Punalu'u Bakery; perhaps one reason brunch lines (queues) last two hours.

PLOW

Recommended by
Gabriela Cámara

1299 18th Street
Potrero Hill
San Francisco
California 94107
+1 4158217569
www.eatatplow.com

Opening hours	Open 7 days
Reservation policy	No
Credit cards	Accepted
Price range	Affordable
Style	Casual
Cuisine	Modern American
Recommended for	Breakfast

"The food is delicious and the place is sunny and simple. Breakfast is my favorite meal, and it's a treat to take the time to eat outside of the house. I always feel happy when I go to Plow."—Gabriela Cámara

SAINT FRANK

Recommended by
Matthew Accarrino

2340 Polk Street
Russian Hill
San Francisco
California 94109
+1 4157751619
www.saintfrankcoffee.com

Opening hours	Open 7 days
Reservation policy	No
Credit cards	Accepted
Price range	Budget
Style	Casual
Cuisine	Coffee
Recommended for	Regular neighborhood

"A coffee shop with the best almond-milk cappuccinos in the city (they make their almond milk daily and also use macadamia nuts in it). I find myself there several times a week."—Matthew Accarrino

BENU

22 Hawthorne Street
SoMa
San Francisco
California 94105
+1 4156854860
www.benusf.com

Recommended by
Tom Aikens, Sat Bains,
Diego Hernández-Velasco Baquedano,
Gabriela Cámara, Val Cantu, David Chang,
Kyle Connaughton, Richard Ekkebus,
Gary Foulkes, Alexandre Gauthier,
Mehmet Gürs, Normand Laprise,
Isaac Mchale, David Muñoz,
Daniel Patterson, Joel Stocks,
Justin Woodward

Opening hours	Closed Monday
Credit cards	Accepted
Price range	Expensive
Style	Smart casual
Cuisine	Modern Asian-American
Recommended for	Wish I'd opened

"Probably the best fine-dining restaurant in the country right now. Corey Lee's cooking is extraordinary, and the service and wine program are great as well."
—Daniel Patterson

COCKSCOMB

Recommended by
Paul Cunningham, Michael Friedman

564 Fourth Street
SoMa
San Francisco
California 94107
+1 4159740700
www.cockscombsf.com

Opening hours	Closed Sunday
Credit cards	Accepted
Price range	Affordable
Style	Casual
Cuisine	Modern American
Recommended for	Worth the travel

IN-SITU

151 Third Street
SoMa
San Francisco
California 94103
+1 4159416050
www.insitu.sfmoma.org

Recommended by
Paul Cunningham,
Mehmet Gürs

Opening hours	Closed Wednesday
Credit cards	Accepted
Price range	Affordable
Style	Casual
Cuisine	Modern American
Recommended for	Worth the travel

SAISON

178 Townsend Street
SoMa
San Francisco
California 94107
+1 4158287990
www.saisonsf.com

Recommended by
Jason Atherton, Kristian Baumann,
Bo Bech, Tomi Bjorck,
Val Cantu, Danielle Gjestland,
Ravi Kapur, Aaron London,
Claus Meyer, Jakob Mielcke,
Uwe Opocensky, John Winter Russell,
Evan & Sarah Rich,
Giulio Sturla, Kwang Uh

Opening hours	Closed Sunday and Monday
Credit cards	Accepted
Price range	Expensive
Style	Smart casual
Cuisine	Modern American
Recommended for	High end

"Last time I was in SF I had one of the best meals I've ever had here. It cost more than rent, but was worth every penny."—John Winter Russell

TROU NORMAND

Recommended by
Corey Lee

140 New Montgomery Street
SoMa
San Francisco
California 94105
+1 4159750876
www.trounormandsf.com

Opening hours	Open 7 days
Credit cards	Accepted
Price range	Affordable
Style	Casual
Cuisine	Bar Charcuterie
Recommended for	Regular neighborhood

"A place to go to for well-executed, simple food, and great drinks."—Corey Lee

YANK SING

Recommended by
Evan & Sarah Rich

101 Spear Street
SoMa
San Francisco
California 94105
+1 4157811111
www.yanksing.com

Opening hours	Open 7 days
Credit cards	Accepted
Price range	Affordable
Style	Casual
Cuisine	Dim Sum
Recommended for	Breakfast

"Always great dim sum—great variety and lots of fun."—Evan & Sarah Rich

LERS ROS

Recommended by
Val Cantu

730 Larkin Street
Tenderloin
San Francisco
California 94109
+1 4159316917
www.lersros.com

Opening hours	Open 7 days
Credit cards	Accepted
Price range	Affordable
Style	Casual
Cuisine	Thai
Recommended for	Bargain

SAIGON SANDWICH

Recommended by
Val Cantu

560 Larkin Street
Tenderloin
San Francisco
California 94102
+1 4154745698

Opening hours	Open 7 days
Reservation policy	No
Credit cards	Not accepted
Price range	Budget
Style	Casual
Cuisine	Vietnamese
Recommended for	Bargain

DEL POPOLO

Recommended by
Val Cantu

855 Bush Street
Union Square
San Francisco
California 94108
www.delpopolosf.com

Opening hours	Closed Monday
Credit cards	Accepted
Price range	Affordable
Style	Casual
Cuisine	Pizza
Recommended for	Regular neighborhood

KIN KHAO

55 Cyril Magnin Street
Union Square
San Francisco
California 94102
+1 4153627456
www.kinkhao.com

Recommended by
Russell Moore

Opening hours	Open 7 days
Credit cards	Accepted
Price range	Affordable
Style	Casual
Cuisine	Thai
Recommended for	Late night

THE PROGRESS

1525 Fillmore Street
Western Addition
San Francisco
California 94115
+1 4156731294
www.theprogress-sf.com

Recommended by
Kyle Connaughton,
Aaron London,
Evan & Sarah Rich

Opening hours	Open 7 days
Credit cards	Accepted
Price range	Expensive
Style	Smart casual
Cuisine	Modern American
Recommended for	Regular neighborhood

"Incredible cooking and atmosphere from a progressive chef."—Kyle Connaughton

> "A DIVE BAR WITH SOME OF THE BEST FRIED CHICKEN YOU'LL COME ACROSS."
>
> CARLO LAMANGA P858

> "Casual, cool, and just plain good!"
>
> CAL PETERNELL P848

PORTLAND

> "CLYDE IS CONSIDERED THE LIVING ROOM OF PORTLAND, WHERE EVERYONE COMES TOGETHER AND ENJOYS A COCKTAIL AND UNIQUE FOOD."
>
> CARLO LAMAGNA P850

> "Italian food—like an Italian grandmother would make."
>
> KRISTEN D. MURRAY P855

PORTLAND

$\hat{N}$ SCALE

0   730   1460   2185
yd.

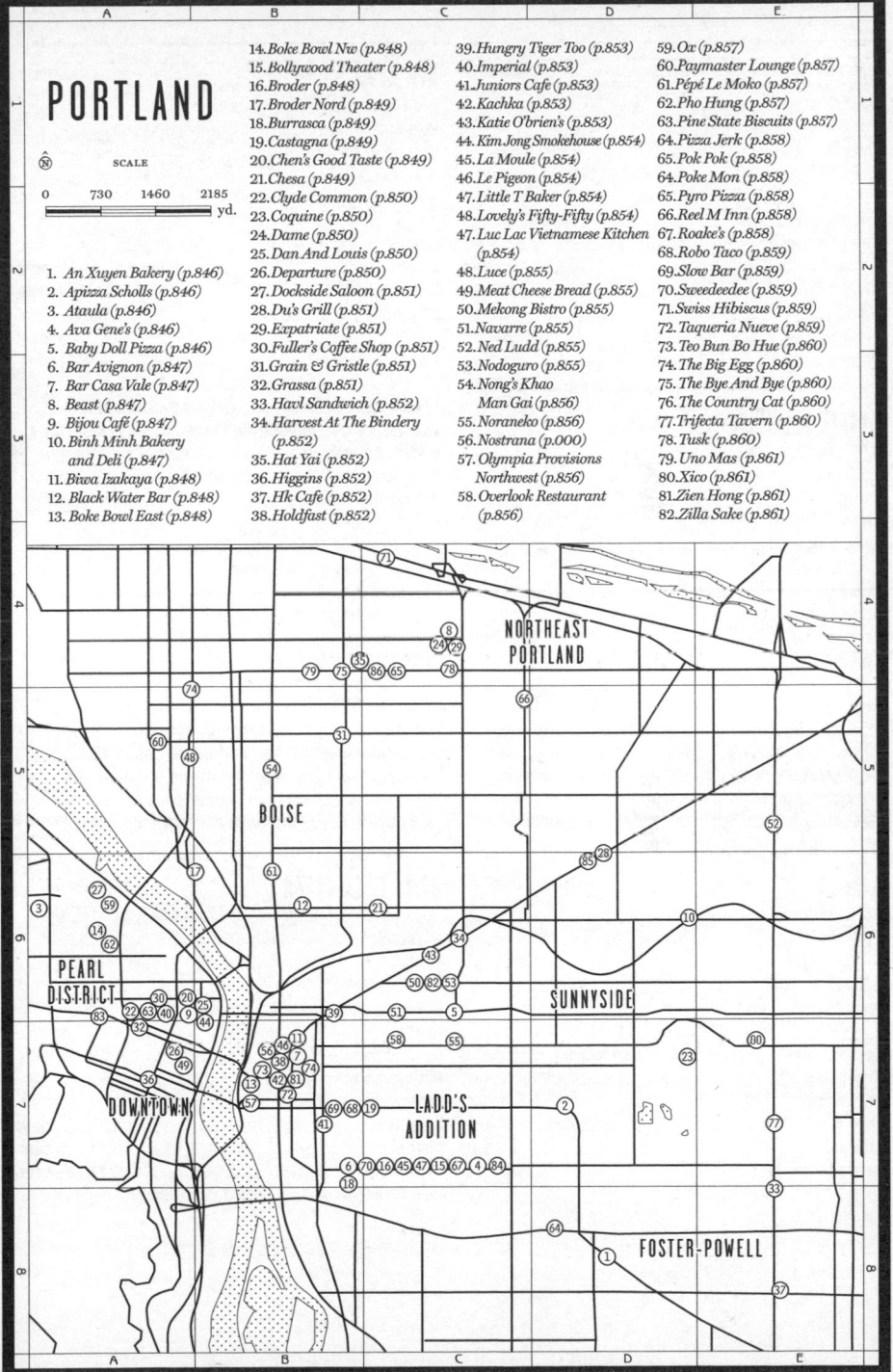

AN XUYEN BAKERY

5345 Southeast Foster Road
Portland
Oregon 97206
+1 5037880866

Opening hours	Closed Monday
Reservation policy	No
Credit cards	Accepted
Price range	Budget
Style	Casual
Cuisine	Bakery
Recommended for	Bargain

APIZZA SCHOLLS

4741 Southeast Hawthorne Boulevard
Portland
Oregon 97215
+1 5032331286
www.apizzascholls.com

Opening hours	Open 7 days
Credit cards	Accepted
Price range	Affordable
Style	Casual
Cuisine	Pizza
Recommended for	Regular neighborhood

"They serve my favorite pizza in Portland. They always have great beers on tap, and my little boy, Hugo, is always welcome here. The crunch-to-chew ratio on their crust in awe-inspiring."—Katy Jane Millard

ATAULA

1818 Northwest 23rd Place
Portland
Oregon 97210
+1 5038948904
www.atulapdx.com

Opening hours	Closed Monday and Sunday
Credit cards	Accepted
Price range	Affordable
Style	Casual
Cuisine	Spanish
Recommended for	High end

AVA GENE'S

3377 Southeast Division Street
Portland
Oregon 97202
+1 9712290571
www.avagenes.com

Opening hours	Open 7 days
Credit cards	Accepted
Price range	Affordable
Style	Smart casual
Cuisine	Italian
Recommended for	Local favorite

"From start to finish, they deliver an incredible experience. It's impossible to say no to all of the little extras. An aperitif, a gorgeous bottle of wine, grappa or amaro, espresso, gelato, an extra bowl of pasta."
—Katy Jane Millard

Ava Gene's isn't just any old pasta joint—here, they serve Roman-inspired cuisine that is locally sourced and strictly seasonal. This does include plates piled high with fresh, homemade rigatoni, tagliatelle, linguine, spaghetti, and ravioli (all served nicely *al dente*, of course); but it also means generous portions of fresh fish, local salumi meats, and Italian cheeses. The executive chef Joshua McFadden and his team do very innovative things with vegetables, as demonstrated in the half-dozen colorful and hearty *giardini* (garden) salads on the menu—ingredients include fava leaves, sprouted barley, raw cavolo nero, and poppy seeds.

BABY DOLL PIZZA

2835 Southeast Stark Street
Portland
Oregon 97214
+1 5034594450
www.babydollpizza.com

Opening hours	Open 7 days
Reservation policy	No
Credit cards	Accepted
Price range	Budget
Style	Casual
Cuisine	Pizza
Recommended for	Regular neighborhood

BAR AVIGNON

Recommended by
Cathy Whims

2138 Southeast Division Street
Portland
Oregon 97202
+1 5035170808
www.baravignon.com

Opening hours	Open 7 days
Credit cards	Accepted
Price range	Affordable
Style	Casual
Cuisine	Modern American Bistro
Recommended for	Late night

"This long-standing bistro has an impeccably well-curated wine list with knowledgable and welcoming staff. The produce is creatively and religiously sourced from local farms. It's my favorite late-night place and it's a five-minute walk from my house."
—Cathy Whims

BAR CASA VALE

Recommended by
Kristen D. Murray

215 Southeast 9th Avenue
Portland
Oregon 97214
+1 5034779081
www.barcasavale.com

Opening hours	Closed Monday and Sunday
Reservation policy	No
Credit cards	Accepted
Price range	Affordable
Style	Casual
Cuisine	Tapas
Recommended for	Late night

BEAST

Recommended by
Justin Woodward

5425 North East 30th Avenue
Portland
Oregon 97211
+1 5038416968
www.beastpdx.com

Opening hours	Closed Monday and Tuesday
Credit cards	Accepted
Price range	Expensive
Style	Smart casual
Cuisine	French-American
Recommended for	High end

"Going out to a nice meal, I like to get taken care of and not have to make too many decisions. I just want to enjoy the experience. They do that here."
—Justin Woodward

BIJOU CAFÉ

Recommended by
Joshua Lewin

132 Southwest 3rd Avenue
Portland
Oregon 97204
+1 5032223187
www.bijoucafepdx.com

Opening hours	Open 7 days
Credit cards	Accepted
Price range	Affordable
Style	Casual
Cuisine	Brunch
Recommended for	Breakfast

"It is simple, they use great ingredients, and it feels old and new at the same time—it's the perfect breakfast moment that every city has, and this is Portland's."—Joshua Lewin

BINH MINH BAKERY & DELI

Recommended by
Andy Ricker

6812 North East Broadway Street
Portland
Oregon 97213
+1 5032573868

Opening hours	Closed Monday
Reservation policy	No
Credit cards	Accepted
Price range	Budget
Style	Casual
Cuisine	Vietnamese
Recommended for	Bargain

"Best *banh mi* in Portland, which is saying something considering how many places are dedicated to the Vietnamese torpedo of awesomeness. They make their own baguette: light, crispy crust, soft crumb, and narrow profile. The sandwich itself has a small amount of everything: meat, *cu cai* (radish), raw chile, cilantro (coriander), cucumber, a smear of sketchy pâté, and a squirt of soy sauce in perfect ratio to the bread. This makes it the closest to the *banh mi* I've eaten in Vietnam."—Andy Ricker

BIWA IZAKAYA

Recommended by
Aaron Adams

215 Southeast 9th Avenue
Portland
Oregon 97214
+1 5032398830
www.biwaizakaya.com

Opening hours	Open 7 days
Credit cards	Accepted
Price range	Affordable
Style	Casual
Cuisine	Japanese Gastropub
Recommended for	Regular neighborhood

"Informal enough for an impromptu night out, but nice enough for date night."—Aaron Adams

BLACK WATER BAR

Recommended by
Aaron Adams

835 North East Broadway Street
Portland
Oregon 97232
+1 5032810439

Opening hours	Open 7 days
Reservation policy	No
Credit cards	Accepted
Price range	Budget
Style	Casual
Cuisine	Vegan-Vegetarian
Recommended for	Bargain

"Black Water is a punk bar, so of course I feel right at home. Where else can I get an amazingly delicious vegan burger while Rudimentary Peni is blasting on the sound system? The Bougie Burger is my favorite by far. I don't know what they put in that thing, but I'm addicted."—Aaron Adams

BOKE BOWL EAST

Recommended by
Aaron Adams

1028 Southeast Water Avenue
Portland
Oregon 97214
+1 5037195698
www.bokebowl.com

Opening hours	Open 7 days
Reservation policy	No
Credit cards	Accepted
Price range	Affordable
Style	Casual
Cuisine	Ramen Noodles
Recommended for	Regular neighborhood

"Absolutely delicious, quick, and hand-made. And they always have a great vegan option, including their amazing steam buns. I usually get the smoked tofu rice bowl with avocado, piled high with pickled vegetables, glazy eggplant, bamboo shoots, kimchi, and mushrooms. It's what a counter service restaurant ought to be."—Aaron Adams

BOKE BOWL NW

Recommended by
Scott Dolich

1201 Northwest 18th Street
Portland
Oregon 97209
+1 5037195698
www.bokebowl.com

Opening hours	Open 7 days
Reservation policy	No
Credit cards	Accepted
Price range	Affordable
Style	Casual
Cuisine	Japanese
Recommended for	Bargain

BOLLYWOOD THEATER

Recommended by
Cal Peternell

3010 Southeast Division Street
Portland
Oregon 97202
+1 5034776699
www.bollywoodtheaterpdx.com/

Opening hours	Open 7 days
Reservation policy	No
Credit cards	Accepted
Price range	Affordable
Style	Casual
Cuisine	Indian
Recommended for	Worth the travel

"Casual, cool, and just plain good!"—Cal Peternell

BRODER

Recommended by
William Preisch,
Justin Woodward

2508 Southeast Clinton Street
Portland
Oregon 97202
+1 5037363333
www.broderpdx.com

Opening hours	Open 7 days
Reservation policy	No
Credit cards	Accepted
Price range	Affordable
Style	Casual
Cuisine	Swedish
Recommended for	Breakfast

"Great Swedish breakfast joint. Amazing *dill aquavit* bloody mary and their *pitt y panna* (hash) is great."
—William Preisch

BRODER NORD

Recommended by
Joel Stocks

2240 North Interstate Avenue #160
Portland
Oregon 97227
+1 5032825555
www.broderpdx.com

Opening hours	Open 7 days
Reservation policy	No
Credit cards	Accepted
Price range	Affordable
Style	Casual
Cuisine	Swedish
Recommended for	Breakfast

"Broder Nord is a great spot and is usually less crowded than its sister restaurant, Broder."—Joel Stocks

BURRASCA

Recommended by
Cathy Whims

2032 Southeast Clinton Street
Portland
Oregon 97202
+1 5032367791
www.burrascapdx.com

Opening hours	Closed Monday
Credit cards	Accepted
Price range	Affordable
Style	Casual
Cuisine	Italian
Recommended for	Regular neighborhood

"Burrasca is a step back in time, as if you are walking into a Florentine trattoria in the 1970s. The food is religiously authentic and everything is hand-made from scratch. Chef and owner Paolo Calamai surprises you with specials like hand-rolled pici with comforting Tuscan ragu and dishes little known outside of Tuscany such as La Francesina, leftover boiled beef stewed with tomato and love."—Cathy Whims

CASTAGNA

Recommended by
Katy Jane Millard,
Joel Stocks

1752 Southeast Hawthorne Boulevard
Portland
Oregon 97214
+1 5032317373
www.castagnarestaurant.com

Opening hours	Closed Sunday to Tuesday
Credit cards	Accepted
Price range	Expensive
Style	Smart casual
Cuisine	Modern American
Recommended for	High end

CHEN'S GOOD TASTE

Recommended by
Kristen D. Murray

22 Northwest 4th Avenue
Portland
Oregon 97209
+1 5032233838

Opening hours	Open 7 days
Credit cards	Accepted
Price range	Budget
Style	Casual
Cuisine	Chinese
Recommended for	Bargain

"Love that the staff sit on the back table assembling dumplings between business rushes. Best wonton soup and delicious roast duck."—Kristen D. Murray

CHESA

Recommended by
Carlo Lamagna

2218 North East Broadway Street
Portland
Oregon 97232
+1 5034779521
www.chesapdx.com

Opening hours	Closed Monday and Sunday
Credit cards	Accepted
Price range	Expensive
Style	Casual
Cuisine	Tapas
Recommended for	Regular neighborhood

CLYDE COMMON

Recommended by
Carlo Lamagna

1014 Southwest Stark Street
Portland
Oregon 97205
+1 5032283333
www.clydecommon.com

Opening hours	Open 7 days
Credit cards	Accepted
Price range	Affordable
Style	Casual
Cuisine	Modern European
Recommended for	Local favorite

"Clyde is considered the living room of Portland, where everyone comes together from different walks of life, and enjoys a cocktail and unique food."
—Carlo Lamagna

COQUINE

Recommended by
Carlo Lamagna,
Kristen D. Murray,
Gabriel Rucker,
Justin Woodward,

6839 Southeast Belmont
Portland
Oregon 97215
+1 5033842483
www.coquinepdx.com

Opening hours	Open 7 days
Credit cards	Accepted
Price range	Affordable
Style	Casual
Cuisine	American-French
Recommended for	Local favorite

"It's a neighborhood restaurant, run by a husband and wife team. Everything is incredibly curated, local, and executed in a humble yet graceful, convivial manner. You feel like you are in their home and are thrilled for the sweet invite."—Kristen D. Murray

Coquine is a French word that, when directed at a mischievous little girl, is a light-hearted chide—and when directed at a woman means something a little more flirtatious. This restaurant successfully entices and seduces its diners with all the right flavors in all the right places. The chef Katy Millard began Coquine as a Portland pop-up in 2012 and opened the permanent neighborhood restaurant three years later. Manila clams, guinea hen, potxa beans, and cerignola olives grace the seasonal, sophisticated menu—and don't miss the award-winning Coquine cookies, made with smoked almonds, salted caramel, and "really good" chocolate (they can be ordered in advance by the dozen).

DAME

Recommended by
Joshua McFadden

2930 North East Killingsworth Street
Portland
Oregon 97211
+1 5032272669
www.damerestaurant.com

Opening hours	Closed Tuesday
Credit cards	Accepted
Price range	Affordable
Style	Casual
Cuisine	Modern American
Recommended for	Regular neighborhood

"It's perfect. Dana, the owner-sommelier is amazing. It feels like a modern version of Cheers, but with the best wine and really perfect food. I wish I lived closer—it's the type of restaurant every neighborhood should have. It's the way it used to be, small, focused, and with genuine interest in hospitality."
—Joshua McFadden

DAN AND LOUIS

Recommended by
William Preisch

208 Southwest Ankeny Street
Portland
Oregon 97204
+1 5032275906
www.danandlouis.com

Opening hours	Open 7 days
Credit cards	Accepted
Price range	Affordable
Style	Casual
Cuisine	Seafood
Recommended for	Wish I'd opened

"A crusty old oyster joint, in the best possible way. And one of the oldest restaurants in Portland."
—William Preisch

DEPARTURE

Recommended by
José Chesa

525 Southwest Morrison Street
Portland
Oregon 97204
+1 5038025370
www.departureportland.com

Opening hours	Open 7 days
Credit cards	Accepted
Price range	Affordable
Style	Casual
Cuisine	Asian
Recommended for	Regular neighborhood

"The ambience is relaxed and modern, yet very family friendly. The food is always impecable."—José Chesa

DOCKSIDE SALOON

2047 Northwest Front Avenue
Portland
Oregon 97209
+1 5032416433
www.docksidesaloon.com

Opening hours..Open 7 days
Credit cards...Accepted
Price range...Affordable
Style...Casual
Cuisine...Diner
Recommended for.....................................Breakfast

"An awesome greasy spoon that's been around for a while. A no-frills place that just hits the spot. The corned-beef hash is a must have."—Carlo Lamagna

DU'S GRILL

5365 North East Sandy Boulevard
Portland
Oregon 97213
+1 5032841773
www.dusgrill.com

Opening hours.............................Closed Saturday and Sunday
Reservation policy..No
Credit cards...Accepted
Price range...Budget
Style...Casual
Cuisine...Asian Fusion
Recommended for...Bargain

"Crazy-good teriyaki. Oddly, it's better when you get it to go. Great shredded iceberg salad with a poppyseed dressing."—William Preisch

EXPATRIATE

5424 North East 30th Avenue
Portland
Oregon 97211
+1 5038675309
www.expatriatepdx.com

Opening hours..Open 7 days
Reservation policy..No
Credit cards...Accepted
Price range...Affordable
Style...Casual
Cuisine...Burmese
Recommended for.......................................Late night

FULLER'S COFFEE SHOP

136 Northwest 9th Avenue
Portland
Oregon 97209
+1 5032225608

Opening hours..Closed Monday
Reservation policy..No
Credit cards...Accepted
Price range...Budget
Style...Casual
Cuisine..Coffee Shop
Recommended for.....................................Breakfast

"An old school lunch counter serving simple diner fare. The breakfast here is always hot, generous, and well-seasoned."—Greg Denton & Gabrielle Quiñónez Denton

GRAIN & GRISTLE

1473 Northeast Prescott Street
Portland
Oregon 97211
+1 5032884740
www.grainandgristle.com

Opening hours..Open 7 days
Credit cards...Accepted
Price range...Affordable
Style...Casual
Cuisine...Gastropub
Recommended for......................................Late night

GRASSA

1205 Southwest Washington Street
Portland
Oregon 97205
+1 5032411133
www.grassapdx.com

Opening hours..Open 7 days
Credit cards...Accepted
Price range...Affordable
Style...Casual
Cuisine...Italian
Recommended for.......................Regular neighborhood

HAVL SANDWICH
Recommended by
Jason French,
Cathy Whims

738 Southeast 82nd Avenue #103
Portland
Oregon 97266
+1 5037720103

Opening hours	Closed Tuesday
Reservation policy	No
Credit cards	Accepted
Price range	Budget
Style	Casual
Cuisine	Vietnamese
Recommended for	Breakfast

"Most people don't think of pho as a breakfast food, but HaVL's busiest times are before 11.00 a.m. They offer two different soups everyday with homemade broth. It's the most comforting breakfast on a blustery fall day in the Pacific Northwest."—Cathy Whims

HARVEST AT THE BINDERY
Recommended by
Aaron Adams

3101 Northeast Sandy Boulevard
Portland
Oregon 97232
+1 5038949172
www.harvestatthebindery.com

Opening hours	Closed Monday
Credit cards	Accepted
Price range	Affordable
Style	Casual
Cuisine	Modern American
Recommended for	Breakfast

"I love their biscuits and gravy."—Aaron Adams

HAT YAI
Recommended by
Greg Denton &
Gabrielle Quiñónez Denton,
Jasper Shen

1605 Northeast Killingsworth Street
Portland
Oregon 97211
+1 5037649701
www.hatyaipdx.com

Opening hours	Closed Monday
Credit cards	Accepted
Price range	Affordable
Style	Casual
Cuisine	Thai
Recommended for	Regular neighborhood

"This place is quickly becoming well known for its southern Thai-style fried chicken, and rightly so. But we can't eat here without also ordering the seriously spicy ground pork with turmeric and lemongrass.

The soy-cured short rib in coconut milk is another favorite."—Greg Denton & Gabrielle Quiñónez Denton

HIGGINS
Recommended by
Aaron Adams

1239 Southwest Broadway
Portland
Oregon 97205
+1 5032229070
www.higginsportland.com

Opening hours	Open 7 days
Credit cards	Accepted
Price range	Affordable
Style	Casual
Cuisine	Modern American
Recommended for	Local favorite

"Higgins is the original. He really brought the local-farm-to-table story to Portland and remains relevant after all these years, delivering a high level of cuisine and service, paired with great Oregon wines and beers."—Aaron Adams

HK CAFE
Recommended by
Scott Dolich

4410 Southeast 82nd Avenue
Portland
Oregon 97266
+1 5037718866
www.hkcafeportland.com

Opening hours	Open 7 days
Credit cards	Accepted
Price range	Budget
Style	Casual
Cuisine	Dim Sum
Recommended for	Regular neighborhood

"A bright, big, and busy restaurant in Portland's de facto 'Chinatown'. Funny and engaging staff push dim-sum carts all afternoon, everyday."—Scott Dolich

HOLDFAST
Recommended by
Carlo Lamagna

537 Southeast Ash Street
Portland
Oregon 97214
+1 5035049448
www.holdfastdining.com

Opening hours	Closed Monday to Thursday
Credit cards	Accepted
Price range	Expensive
Style	Smart casual
Cuisine	Modern American
Recommended for	High end

"Chefs Joel Stocks and Will Preisch put together an amazing tasting menu that really pushes the boundaries of your palate and is flawlessly executed. Pair that with amazing wines selected by Jeff Vejr and you have a fabulous, all around, intimate experience."
—Carlo Lamagna

HUNGRY TIGER TOO

207 Southeast 12th Avenue
Portland
Oregon 97214
+1 5032384321
www.hungrytigerpdx.com

Opening hours	Open 7 days
Reservation policy	No
Credit cards	Accepted
Price range	Affordable
Style	Casual
Cuisine	Diner
Recommended for	Late night

"Go for great mac and cheese, vegan corn dogs, and hot wings."—Joel Stocks

IMPERIAL

410 Southwest Broadway
Portland
Oregon 97205
+1 5032287222
www.imperialpdx.com

Opening hours	Open 7 days
Credit cards	Accepted
Price range	Affordable
Style	Casual
Cuisine	Modern American
Recommended for	Breakfast

JUNIORS CAFE

1742 Southeast 12th Avenue
Portland
Oregon 97214
+1 5034674971
www.juniorscafepdx.com

Opening hours	Open 7 days
Credit cards	Accepted
Price range	Budget
Style	Casual
Cuisine	American
Recommended for	Breakfast

"Feels like the old Portland I fell in love with. Plates are heaped with vegan French toast, garden sausage, and tofu scrambles. The high-decibel music, Victorian wallpaper, sparkly gold booths, and friendly waitstaff makes Junior's my all time favorite breakfast spot."
—Aaron Adams

KACHKA

720 Southeast Grand Avenue
Portland
Oregon 97214
+1 5032350059
www.kachkapdx.com

Opening hours	Open 7 days
Credit cards	Accepted
Price range	Affordable
Style	Casual
Cuisine	Russian
Recommended for	Regular neighborhood

"An amazing Russian restaurant from Bonnie and Israel Morales. They took an often overlooked cuisine and are showing the wide range that it has to offer."
—Carlo Lamagna

KATIE O'BRIEN'S

2809 Northeast Sandy Boulevard
Portland
Oregon 97232
+1 5032348573

Opening hours	Open 7 days
Reservation policy	No
Credit cards	Accepted
Price range	Budget
Style	Casual
Cuisine	American-Irish Pub

"Really solid and cheap breakfast food—one of the best spots to watch sports on the weekend."
—Joel Stocks

KIM JONG SMOKEHOUSE

126 Southwest 2nd Avenue
Portland
Oregon 97204
+1 5035555555
www.kimjongsmokehouse.com

Recommended by
Emily Hahn

Opening hours	Open 7 days
Credit cards	Accepted
Price range	Affordable
Style	Casual
Cuisine	Korean-Southern American
Recommended for	Worth the travel

LA MOULE

2500 Southeast Clinton Street
Portland
Oregon 97202
+1 9713392822
www.lamoulepdx.com

Recommended by
Greg Denton &
Gabrielle Quiñónez Denton,
Cathy Whims

Opening hours	Open 7 days
Credit cards	Accepted
Price range	Affordable
Style	Smart casual
Cuisine	Belgian
Recommended for	Late night

"A great little Belgian brasserie known for its craft cocktails and moules frites. We recommend snacking on the steak tartare with bone marrow while you wait for your mussels to steam."
—Greg Denton & Gabrielle Quiñónez Denton

LE PIGEON

738 East Burnside Street
Portland
Oregon 97214
+1 5035468796
www.lepigeon.com

Recommended by
Scott Dolich, Katy Jane Millard,
William Preisch, Andy Ricker,
Joe Schafer, Jasper Shen,
Justin Woodward

Opening hours	Open 7 days
Credit cards	Accepted
Price range	Expensive
Style	Smart casual
Cuisine	Modern French-American
Recommended for	Local favorite

"This is (and long has been) Portland's poster-child restaurant. Young, funky energy in the kitchen, a pervasive cuisine, local ingredients on the menu, and a great wine list."—Katy Jane Millard

LITTLE T BAKER

2600 Southeast Division Street
Portland
Oregon 97202
+1 5032383458
www.littletbaker.com

Recommended by
Cathy Whims

Opening hours	Open 7 days
Reservation policy	No
Credit cards	Accepted
Price range	Budget
Style	Casual
Cuisine	Bakery
Recommended for	Breakfast

"I love well made espresso and savory sides. The house-cured lox (smoked salmon) on homemade spelt-loaf bread is my favorite. I wish they served it at lunch, and not just at breakfast!"—Cathy Whims

LOVELY'S FIFTY-FIFTY

4039 North Mississippi Avenue
Portland
Oregon 97217
+1 5032814060
www.lovelysfiftyfifty.wordpress.com

Recommended by
Katy Jane Millard,
Cathy Whims

Opening hours	Closed Monday
Reservation policy	No
Credit cards	Accepted
Price range	Affordable
Style	Casual
Cuisine	Pizza
Recommended for	Local favorite

"Sarah Minnick's pizzas are constantly inspired by what's the freshest at the farmer's market and she is always experimenting with heirloom grains to perfect her pizza crust. Her restaurant oozes the Portland vibe."—Cathy Whims

LUC LAC VIETNAMESE KITCHEN

835 Southwest 2nd Avenue
Portland
Oregon 97204
+1 5032220047
www.luclackitchen.com

Recommended by
Justin Woodward

Opening hours	Open 7 days
Credit cards	Accepted
Price range	Affordable
Style	Casual
Cuisine	Vietnamese
Recommended for	Late night

LUCE

Recommended by
Kristen D. Murray

2140 East Burnside Street
Portland
Oregon 97214
+1 5032367195
www.luceportland.com

Opening hours	Open 7 days
Reservation policy	No
Credit cards	Accepted
Price range	Affordable
Style	Casual
Cuisine	Italian
Recommended for	Regular neighborhood

"It is warm, simple, delicious, and honest. Italian food—like an Italian grandmother would make."
—Kristen D. Murray

MEAT CHEESE BREAD

Recommended by
Kristen D. Murray,
Justin Woodward

1406 Southeast Stark Street
Portland
Oregon 97214
+1 5032341700
www.meatcheesebread.com

Opening hours	Open 7 days
Reservation policy	No
Credit cards	Accepted
Price range	Budget
Style	Casual
Cuisine	Sandwiches
Recommended for	Breakfast

"I swoon over the breakfast burrito!"
—Kristen D. Murray

MEKONG BISTRO

Recommended by
Carlo Lamagna

8200 Northeast Siskiyou Street
Portland
Oregon 97220
+1 5032658972
www.mekongbistro.com

Opening hours	Open 7 days
Credit cards	Accepted
Price range	Affordable
Style	Casual
Cuisine	Cambodian
Recommended for	Late night

"Serves delicious Cambodian food late into the wee hours."—Carlo Lamagna

NAVARRE

Recommended by
Kristen D. Murray,
Cathy Whims

10 Northeast 28th Avenue
Portland
Oregon 97232
+1 5032323555
www.navarreportland.com

Opening hours	Open 7 days
Reservation policy	No
Credit cards	Accepted
Price range	Affordable
Style	Smart casual
Cuisine	European
Recommended for	Breakfast

"I treat myself to brunch here at least once a month. I crave a pretty glass of wine on my day off and they have the best small plates loaded with seasonal vegetables. As well as a potato terrine that will keep you coming back for more."—Kristen D. Murray

NED LUDD

Recommended by
Carlo Lamagna,
Joel Stocks

3925 Northeast Martin Luther King Jr. Boulevard
Portland
Oregon 97212
+1 5032886900
www.nedluddpdx.com

Opening hours	Open 7 days
Credit cards	Accepted
Price range	Affordable
Style	Casual
Cuisine	Modern American
Recommended for	Local favorite

"Ned Ludd ties together the total Oregon experience. From wood-fire cooking to utilizing local and seasonal ingredients, the food and ambiance reflect what the PNW is—refined rustic."—Carlo Lamanga

NODOGURO

Recommended by
Katy Jane Millard

2832 Southeast Belmont
Portland
Oregon 97214
www.nodoguropdx.com

Opening hours	Closed Monday and Tuesday
Credit cards	Accepted
Price range	Expensive
Style	Smart casual
Cuisine	Japanese
Recommended for	High end

NONG'S KHAO MAN GAI

Recommended by
Greg Denton &
Gabrielle Quiñónez Denton,
Carlo Lamagna, Kristen D. Murray,
James Rigato, Jasper Shen,
Joel Stocks, Cathy Whims

609 Southeast Ankeny Street
Portland
Oregon 97214
+1 5037402907
www.khaomangai.com

Opening hours	Open 7 days
Credit cards	Accepted
Price range	Budget
Style	Casual
Cuisine	Thai
Recommended for	Regular neighborhood

"Wonderful if you want to eat healthily on a budget. Their famous dish is poached chicken, rice, steamed vegetables, and a magical caramelized garlic sauce that far outshines the traditional peanut sauce."
—Cathy Whims

By now, the Nong's Khao Man Gai origin story is something of a legend, but it bears repeating. Nong Poonsukwattana arrived in Portland from Bangkok in 2003, with only $70 (£50) in her pocket. She now owns and runs a mini chicken and rice empire (two food trucks and one full restaurant in southeast Portland). The original dish is a study in perfect simplicity: tender chicken poached with ginger, pandan, and garlic, served over aromatic jasmine rice, with a few refreshing sides and Nong's tangy signature sauce. While the restaurant now has an expanded menu, *khao man gai* is still the main event, and it's comforting to know that something this simple and nourishing can also be revelatory.

NORANEKO

Recommended by
Jason French,
William Preisch

1430 Southeast Water Avenue
Portland
Oregon 97214
+1 5032386356
www.noranekoramen.com

Opening hours	Open 7 days
Reservation policy	No
Credit cards	Accepted
Price range	Affordable
Style	Casual
Cuisine	Japanese
Recommended for	Regular neighborhood

"This is the ramen arm of Gabe Rosen and Kina Voelz, who opened Biwa in 2007. It is simple, delicious, and an ideal stop after work or for lunch! The ramen is great."—Jason French

NOSTRANA

Recommended by
Justin Woodward

1401 Southeast Morrison Street
Portland
Oregon 97214
+1 5032342427
www.nostrana.com

Opening hours	Open 7 days
Credit cards	Accepted
Price range	Affordable
Style	Casual
Cuisine	Italian
Recommended for	Regular neighborhood

"I love the bread—I usually get a Negroni and a simple pizza."—Justin Woodward

OLYMPIA PROVISIONS NORTHWEST

Recommended by
Scott Dolich

1632 Northwest Thurman Street
Portland
Oregon 97209
+1 5038948136
www.olympiaprovisions.com

Opening hours	Open 7 days
Credit cards	Accepted
Price range	Affordable
Style	Casual
Cuisine	European
Recommended for	Regular neighborhood

OVERLOOK RESTAURANT

Recommended by
Jasper Shen

1332 North Skidmore Street
Portland
Oregon 97217
+1 5032880880

Opening hours	Open 7 days
Reservation policy	No
Credit cards	Accepted
Price range	Budget
Style	Casual
Cuisine	Diner-Café
Recommended for	Breakfast

"One of the few old-school diners left. They serve breakfast all day and have a ridiculously large menu."—Jasper Shen

OX

Recommended by
Katie Lorenzen,
James Rigato

2225 Northeast Martin Luther King Jr
Boulevard
Portland
Oregon 97212
+1 5032843366
www.oxpdx.com

Opening hours	Open 7 days
Credit cards	Accepted
Price range	Expensive
Style	Casual
Cuisine	Steakhouse
Recommended for	Worth the travel

PAYMASTER LOUNGE

Recommended by
Scott Dolich

1020 Northwest 17th Street
Portland
Oregon 97209
+1 5039432780
www.paymasterlounge.com

Opening hours	Open 7 days
Reservation policy	No
Credit cards	Accepted
Price range	Affordable
Style	Casual
Cuisine	Burgers
Recommended for	Late night

"Solid burger. A friendly neighborhood dive bar."
—Scott Dolich

PEPE LE MOKO

Recommended by
Justin Woodward

407 Southwest 10th Avenue
Portland
Oregon 97205
+1 5035468537
www.pepelemokopdx.com

Opening hours	Open 7 days
Credit cards	Accepted
Price range	Affordable
Style	Casual
Cuisine	Bar
Recommended for	Wish I'd opened

"I love the vibe at this tiny place."—Justin Woodward

Beneath the Ace Hotel, in an intimate speakeasy
with a domed ceiling, it's possible to order a Blue
Hawaii and feel no shame. Jeffrey Morgenthaler
showcased his classic cocktail prowess at Clyde
Common, and here the emphasis is on the

electric-sweet drinks of 1980s suburbia: long
island iced tea, amaretto sours, grasshoppers,
daiquiris, and martinis flavored with Kahlua.
Morgenthaler is an expert mixologist, so while
it's all in good fun, the drinks are balanced and
dangerously moreish. Nate Tilden's bar menu
includes devilled eggs, shrimp chips, and *bocadillos*
(baguette sandwiches), including
one with Nutella and sea salt.

PHO HUNG

Recommended by
Cathy Whims

4717 Southeast Powell Boulevard
Portland
Oregon 97206
+1 5037753170

Opening hours	Open 7 days
Reservation policy	No
Credit cards	Accepted
Price range	Budget
Style	Casual
Cuisine	Vietnamese
Recommended for	Bargain

"Vietnamese beef noodle soup is a staple when it
comes to cheap eats. Star anise, ginger scented broth,
and sashimi-like rare beef-eye of round is always
soothing, as witnessed by all the local high-school
students and families that grab after-school snacks
here."—Cathy Whims

PINE STATE BISCUITS

Recommended by
Jasper Shen

2204 Northeast Alberta Street
Portland
Oregon 97211
+1 5034776605
www.pinestatebiscuits.com

Opening hours	Open 7 days
Reservation policy	No
Credit cards	Accepted
Price range	Affordable
Style	Casual
Cuisine	Southern American
Recommended for	Breakfast

PIZZA JERK

Recommended by
Carlo Lamagna

5028 Northeast 42nd Avenue
Portland
Oregon 97218
+1 5032849333
www.pizzajerkpdx.com

Opening hours	Open 7 days
Credit cards	Accepted
Price range	Affordable
Style	Casual
Cuisine	Pizza
Recommended for	Regular neighborhood

"This is a pizzeria that really emulates an old-school vibe with well-executed food. Their pizza is some of the best I've had since NY with a crisp crust and delicious toppings. The other items, like spaghetti and meatballs and the salads, are not just thrown together but thoughtfully created, with great flavors."
—Carlo Lamagna

POK POK

Recommended by
Scott Dolich,
Justin Woodward

3226 Southeast Division Street
Portland
Oregon 97202
+1 5032321387
www.pokpokpdx.com

Opening hours	Open 7 days
Credit cards	Accepted
Price range	Affordable
Style	Casual
Cuisine	Thai
Recommended for	Local favorite

"Authentic Thai food."—Scott Dolich

POKE MON

Recommended by
Jason French,
William Preisch

1485 Southeast Hawthorne Boulevard
Portland
Oregon 97214
+1 5038949743
www.pokemonpdx.com

Opening hours	Open 7 days
Reservation policy	No
Credit cards	Accepted
Price range	Budget
Style	Casual
Cuisine	Hawaiian
Recommended for	Regular neighborhood

"Beautiful and simple—great light in the day and a really nice place for a midday meal for me and my family. The quality of the fish and great flavors have made it a weekly go-to."—Jason French

PYRO PIZZA

Recommended by
Joshua McFadden

1204 Southeast Hawthorne Boulevard
Portland
Oregon 97214
+1 5039291404
www.pyropizzacart.com

Opening hours	Open 7 days
Reservation policy	No
Credit cards	Accepted
Price range	Budget
Style	Casual
Cuisine	Pizza
Recommended for	Bargain

"I am not a big fan of food carts, but this hits the spot—wood burning pizzas, very inexpensive, and great ingredients, I really love it!"—Joshua McFadden

REEL M INN

Recommended by
Carlo Lamagna

2430 Southeast Division Street
Portland
Oregon 97202
+1 5032313880

Opening hours	Open 7 days
Reservation policy	No
Credit cards	Not accepted
Price range	Affordable
Style	Casual
Cuisine	Bar
Recommended for	Late night

"A dive bar with some of the best fried chicken you'll come across."—Carlo Lamagna

ROAKE'S

Recommended by
Jasper Shen

1760 Northeast Lombard Place
Portland
Oregon 97211
+1 5032893557
www.roakesthehotdogfolks.com

Opening hours	Closed Sunday
Credit cards	Accepted
Price range	Budget
Style	Casual
Cuisine	American
Recommended for	Bargain

"Hot dogs and hamburgers without pretension."
—Jasper Shen

ROBO TACO

Recommended by
Joel Stocks

607 Southeast Morrison Street
Portland
Oregon 97214
+1 5032323707
www.robotacopdx.com

Opening hours	Open 7 days
Credit cards	Accepted
Price range	Budget
Style	Casual
Cuisine	Mexican
Recommended for	Late night

"A good place to stop after service for a late-night burrito on the way home."—Joel Stocks

SLOW BAR

Recommended by
Justin Woodward

533 Southeast Grand Avenue
Portland
Oregon 97214
+1 5032307767
www.slowbar.net

Opening hours	Open 7 days
Credit cards	Accepted
Price range	Affordable
Style	Casual
Cuisine	Burgers
Recommended for	Late night

"It is dark with big booths and serves great burgers. The jukebox is filled with a lot of my favorites."
—Justin Woodward

SWEEDEEDEE

Recommended by
José Chesa,
Jason French,
Katy Jane Millard,
Joel Stocks

5202 North Albina Avenue
Portland
Oregon 97217
+1 5039468087
www.sweedeedee.com

Opening hours	Open 7 days
Reservation policy	No
Credit cards	Accepted
Price range	Affordable
Style	Casual
Cuisine	Breakfast-Brunch
Recommended for	Breakfast

"A beautiful little spot with a simple approach to fresh baked bread, simple European breakfast, and the most amazing honey pie!"—Jason French

Sweedeedee is that rare type of place: intimate and reliable, and better than home. This tiny bakery and café in north Portland serves breakfast and lunch, including house-made breads and preserves, and a popular (and rammed) Sunday brunch. But the real draw is the pie, with all-butter crusts and Bob's Red Mill flour, which is baked in glass pans (there's a $5 (£4) pie-plate deposit). To settle into one of the wooden chairs, a book waiting beside a cup of coffee, and a generous slice of salted honey or marionberry—this is one Portland's quiet pleasures.

SWISS HIBISCUS

Recommended by
Greg Denton &
Gabrielle Quiñónez Denton

4950 Northeast 14th Avenue
Portland
Oregon 97211
+1 5034779224
www.swisshibiscus.com

Opening hours	Closed Monday and Sunday
Credit cards	Accepted
Price range	Affordable
Style	Casual
Cuisine	Swiss
Recommended for	Regular neighborhood

"We love this little place—the only thing better than the Alpine food at this Swiss restaurant is the beautiful and kind women who run it."
—Gerg Denton & Gabrielle Quiñónez Denton

TAQUERIA NUEVE

Recommended by
Gabriel Rucker

727 Southeast Washington Street
Portland
Oregon 97214
+1 5039541987
www.taquerianueve.com

Opening hours	Closed Monday
Credit cards	Accepted
Price range	Affordable
Style	Casual
Cuisine	Mexican
Recommended for	Regular neighborhood

"This is my go-to spot with my family—our favorite Mexican in town."—Gabriel Rucker

TEO BUN BO HUE

Recommended by
Katy Jane Millard

8220 Southeast Harrison Street Unit 230
Portland
Oregon 97216
+1 5032083532

Opening hours	Open 7 days
Reservation policy	No
Credit cards	Accepted
Price range	Affordable
Style	Casual
Cuisine	Vietnamese
Recommended for	Bargain

"They have two soups that are both delicious. Always."
—Katy Jane Millard

THE BIG EGG

Recommended by
José Chesa,
Carlo Lamagna

3039 Northeast Alberta Street
Portland
Oregon 97211
+1 5039468087
www.thebigegg.com

Opening hours	Closed Saturday and Sunday
Reservation policy	No
Credit cards	Accepted
Price range	Affordable
Style	Casual
Cuisine	Sandwiches
Recommended for	Breakfast

"This place is just delicious! They make egg
sandwiches using seasonal ingredients as
flavorings. You may wait for up to 15-minutes
for your sandwich but they are worth waiting for."
—José Chesa

THE BYE AND BYE

Recommended by
Aaron Adams

1011 Northeast Alberta Street
Portland
Oregon 97211
+1 5032810537
www.thebyeandbye.com

Opening hours	Open 7 days
Credit cards	Accepted
Price range	Affordable
Style	Casual
Cuisine	Vegan Bar
Recommended for	Late night

"I love getting the Brussels bowl here, with BBQ tofu,
peppered Brussels, and brown rice."—Aaron Adams

THE COUNTRY CAT

Recommended by
Greg Denton &
Gabrielle Quiñónez Denton

7937 Southeast Stark Street
Portland
Oregon 97215
+1 5034081414
www.thecountrycat.net

Opening hours	Open 7 days
Credit cards	Accepted
Price range	Affordable
Style	Casual
Cuisine	American
Recommended for	Breakfast

TRIFECTA TAVERN

Recommended by
Kristen D. Murray

726 Southeast 6th Avenue
Portland
Oregon 97214
+1 5038416675
www.trifectapdx.com

Opening hours	Open 7 days
Credit cards	Accepted
Price range	Affordable
Style	Casual
Cuisine	Modern American Bar
Recommended for	Late night

"A mean martini and a pretty smashing burger!"
—Kristen D. Murray

TUSK

Recommended by
Joshua McFadden,
Katy Jane Millard,
Gabriel Rucker

2448 East Burnside Street
Portland
Oregon 97214
+1 5038948082
www.tuskpdx.com

Opening hours	Open 7 days
Credit cards	Accepted
Price range	Affordable
Style	Smart casual
Cuisine	Middle Eastern
Recommended for	Late night

"They have great cocktails and a wonderful
atmosphere that feels like home. Vegetables are
the star of the show and their late-night menu
satisfies cravings."—Katy Jane Millard

Tusk is of the current generation of California-
dreaming restaurants whose aesthetic is all
off-white, rose and gold, and whose flavor-packed
food manages both wholesomeness and pleasure.

It advertises itself on the menu as locally sourced and "aggressively seasonal", and so it is, but such tongue-in-cheek swagger belies the beauty of what's happening here. Middle Eastern-inspired it may be, but the point is ultimately to eat and drink exactly what you want, without knowing it was what you wanted, in good company.

UNO MAS

Recommended by
Justin Woodward

1914 West Burnside Street
Portland
Oregon 97209
+1 5037194768
www.unomastaquiza.com

Opening hours	Open 7 days
Reservation policy	No
Credit cards	Accepted
Price range	Budget
Style	Casual
Cuisine	Mexican
Recommended for	Bargain

XICO

Recommended by
Cathy Whims

3715 Southeast Division Street
Portland
Oregon 97202
+1 5035486343
www.xicopdx.com

Opening hours	Open 7 days
Credit cards	Accepted
Price range	Affordable
Style	Casual
Cuisine	Mexican
Recommended for	Regular neighborhood

ZIEN HONG

Recommended by
Aaron Adams

5314 Northeast Sandy Boulevard
Portland
Oregon 97213
+1 5032884743

Opening hours	Open 7 days
Reservation policy	No
Credit cards	Accepted
Price range	Affordable
Style	Casual
Cuisine	Chinese-Vietnamese
Recommended for	Late night

"When you walk into a place and the family is all together cleaning green beans or making dumplings at the front table, you know it's going to be good. Zien

Hong, open until midnight, offers up some of the best late-night options in Portland. The service is friendly and quick and I love the funky old dining room straight out of the 1970s, complete with acoustic ceiling and carpeting."—Aaron Adams

ZILLA SAKE

Recommended by
Carlo Lamagna

1806 Northeast Alberta Street
Portland
Oregon 97211
+1 5032888372
www.zillasake.com

Opening hours	Open 7 days
Credit cards	Accepted
Price range	Affordable
Style	Casual
Cuisine	Japanese
Recommended for	Regular neighborhood

"Probably one of the best places for sushi around town with the best sake selection in Oregon and possibly the West Coast."—Carlo Lamagna

"YOU GET VISION, EXECUTION, AND SOURCING."

SPIKE GJERDE P866

"You're not a true Chicagoan if you haven't eaten a Polish sausage at 4 a.m. at Jim's Original."

KEVIN HICKEY P965

USA EAST

"GET THE HOT FISH, THANK ME LATER..."

CHRISTOPHER HODGSON P919

"A Miami staple."

MICHAEL BELTRAN P873

"If I lived closer I'd be there five times a week."

DANIEL SERFER P872

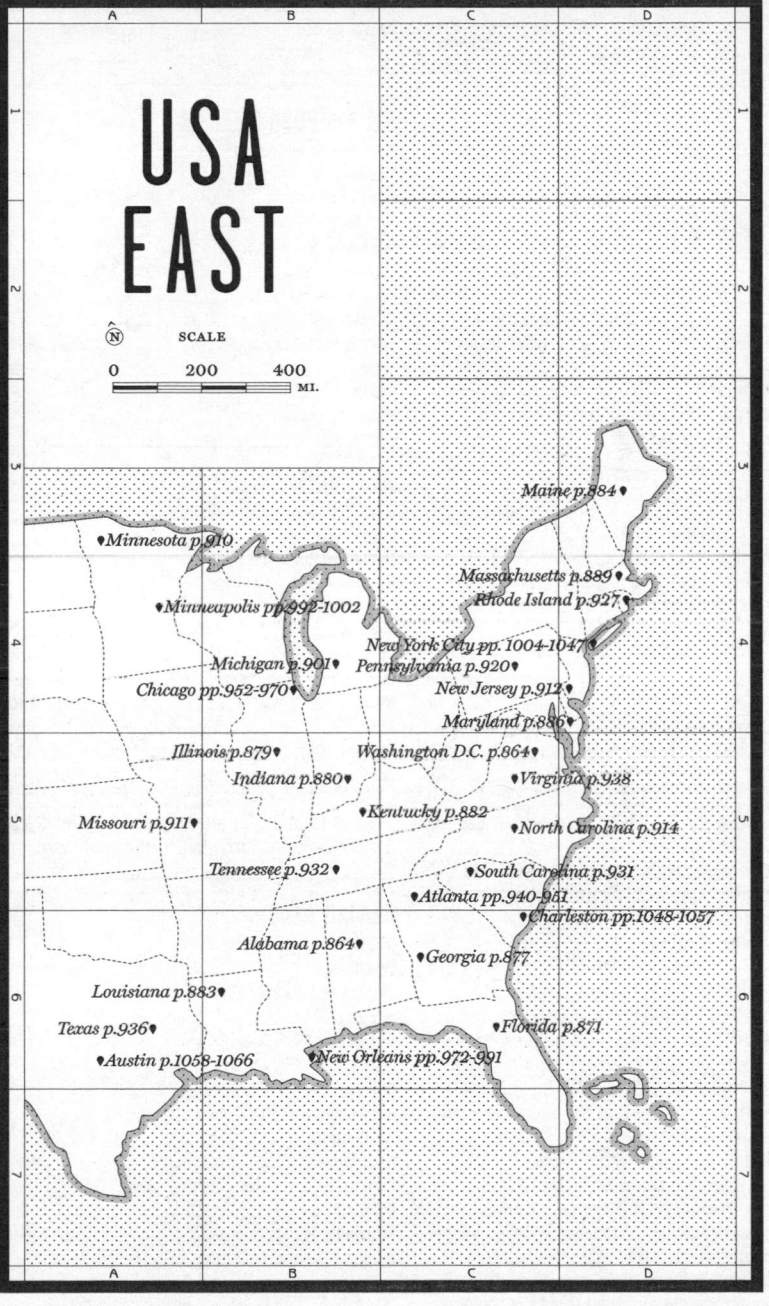

USA
EAST

$\widehat{N}$ SCALE

0   200   400
MI.

♦Minnesota p.910

♦Minneapolis pp.992-1002

Maine p.884♦

Massachusetts p.889♦
Rhode Island p.927♦

New York City pp.1004-1047♦
Michigan p.901♦   Pennsylvania p.920♦
Chicago pp.952-970♦   New Jersey p.912♦

Maryland p.886♦

Illinois p.879♦   Washington D.C. p.864♦
Indiana p.880♦   ♦Virginia p.938

Missouri p.911♦   ♦Kentucky p.882   ♦North Carolina p.914

Tennessee p.932♦   ♦South Carolina p.931

♦Atlanta pp.940-951
♦Charleston pp.1048-1057

Alabama p.864♦   ♦Georgia p.877

Louisiana p.883♦

Texas p.936♦   ♦Florida p.871
♦Austin p.1058-1066   ♦New Orleans pp.972-991

FISHER'S

Recommended by
Tory McPhail

Orange Beach Marina
27075 Marina Road
Orange Beach
Alabama 36561
+1 2519817305
www.fishersobm.com

Opening hours	Open 7 days
Credit cards	Accepted
Price range	Affordable
Style	Casual
Cuisine	Southern American-Seafood
Recommended for	Wish I'd opened

"This restaurant is designed beautifully and is located right on a marina with beautiful water views and a relaxed vibe."—Tory McPhail

2AMYS

Recommended by
Tom Cunanan

3715 Macomb Street Northwest
Washington
District of Columbia 20016
+1 2028855700
www.2amysdc.com

Opening hours	Open 7 days
Reservation policy	No
Credit cards	Accepted
Price range	Budget
Style	Casual
Cuisine	Pizza
Recommended for	Regular neighborhood

"It's a restaurant that attracts locals, families, and people who work in the industry who care about consistent service and food in a warm casual ambiance."—Tom Cunanan

Only three years after the Italian government bestowed the DOC appellation on Neapolitan pizza, DC chef Peter Pastan opened the city's first true Neapolitan pizzeria in 2001. Named after his wife, Amy, and her friend, Amy, 2Amys led the pizza revolution with pies caught taut between crispy and tender, fresh mozzarella on the cusp of cream and house-made tomato sauce with a touch of sweetness. Though the wood-fired oven dominates, there's plenty of room on the menu in this low-key, perpetually packed place for small plates like *suppli al telefono* and salt cod croquettes, whose diminutive nature belie an ambitious dedication to high-quality ingredients and time-tested techniques. Plus, there's homemade ice cream and a bar with strong drinks (to weather the long waits) in the

back, porchetta on the weekends (after 4.00 p.m.), and a cinnamon donut in the mornings worth endless encomia.

ALL-PURPOSE PIZZERIA

Recommended by
Michael Friedman

1250 9th Street Northwest
Washington
District of Columbia 20001
+1 2028496174
www.allpurposedc.com

Opening hours	Open 7 days
Credit cards	Accepted
Price range	Affordable
Style	Casual
Cuisine	Italian-American
Recommended for	Local favorite

BAD SAINT

Recommended by
Michael Friedman,
Carlo Lamagna,
Russell Moore

3226 11th Street Northwest
Washington
District of Columbia 20010
www.badsaintdc.com

Opening hours	Closed Tuesday
Reservation policy	No
Credit cards	Accepted
Price range	Affordable
Style	Casual
Cuisine	Filipino
Recommended for	Worth the travel

"Fun atmosphere, interesting, delicious food, and a completely engaged staff."—Russell Moore

BANTAM KING

Recommended by
Michael Friedman

501 G Street Northwest
Washington
District of Columbia 20003
+1 2027332612
www.bantamking.com

Opening hours	Open 7 days
Reservation policy	No
Credit cards	Accepted
Price range	Affordable
Style	Casual
Cuisine	Japanese
Recommended for	Local favorite

BISTROT LEPIC & WINE BAR

Recommended by
Michael Friedman

1736 Wisconsin Avenue Northwest
Washington
District of Columbia 20007
+1 2023330111
www.bistrotlepic.com

Opening hours	Open 7 days
Credit cards	Accepted
Price range	Expensive
Style	Smart casual
Cuisine	French Bistro
Recommended for	Local favorite

BUTTERCREAM BAKESHOP

Recommended by
Michael Friedman

1250 9th Street Northwest
Washington
District of Columbia 20001
+1 2027350102
www.buttercreamdc.com

Opening hours	Open 7 days
Reservation policy	No
Credit cards	Accepted
Price range	Budget
Style	Casual
Cuisine	Bakery
Recommended for	Regular neighborhood

CLYDE'S OF GALLERY PLACE

Recommended by
Katsuya Fukushima

707 7th Street Northwest
Washington
District of Columbia 20001
+1 2023493700
www.clydes.com

Opening hours	Open 7 days
Credit cards	Accepted
Price range	Affordable
Style	Casual
Cuisine	American Seafood
Recommended for	Late night

"It's very close to Daikaya and I like to take my crew there to eat and drink and hang out."
—Katsuya Fukushima

CONVIVIAL

Recommended by
Michael Friedman

801 O Street Northwest
Washington
District of Columbia 20001
+1 2025252870
www.convivaldc.com

Opening hours	Open 7 days
Credit cards	Accepted
Price range	Affordable
Style	Casual
Cuisine	French-American
Recommended for	Regular neighborhood

COPYCAT CO.

Recommended by
Tom Cunanan

1110 H Street North East
Washington
District of Columbia 20002
+1 2022411952
www.copycatcompany.com

Opening hours	Open / days
Credit cards	Accepted
Price range	Affordable
Style	Casual
Cuisine	Chinese
Recommended for	Late night

"Copycat is a great late-night hang out for industry people. It's a perfect place to grab a drink and small bites before last call. My go-to is an old fashioned cocktail and lamb skewers. The rich and fatty lamb are dusted with cumin and fresh chile flakes, which gives the lamb a neat, sort of crispy texture. I crave it every week!"—Tom Cunanan

LITTLE SEROW

Recommended by
Massimo Bottura

1511 17th Street Northwest
Washington
District of Columbia 20036
www.littleserow.com

Opening hours	Closed Monday and Sunday
Reservation policy	No
Credit cards	Accepted
Price range	Affordable
Style	Casual
Cuisine	Thai
Recommended for	Bargain

THE DABNEY

Recommended by
Michael Friedman,
Spike Gjerde

122 Blagden Alley Northwest
Washington
District of Columbia 20001
+1 2024501015
www.thedabney.com

Opening hours	Closed Monday
Credit cards	Accepted
Price range	Affordable
Style	Casual
Cuisine	Mid-Atlantic
Recommended for	Worth the travel

"Thankfully I don't have to travel far to go to
The Dabney in DC. You get vision, execution, and
sourcing all in one place."—Spike Gjerde

DAIKAYA

Recommended by
Michael Friedman,
Jarrett Stieber

705 6th Street Northwest
Washington
District of Columbia 20001
+1 2025891600
www.daikaya.com

Opening hours	Open 7 days
Reservation policy	No
Credit cards	Accepted
Price range	Affordable
Style	Casual
Cuisine	Japanese
Recommended for	Regular neighborhood

"Every time my wife and I get the chance to escape,
I always want to head to Daikaya. This Japanese
spot serves *izakaya*-inspired cuisine. Everything is
delicious, seasoned perfectly, and the textures are
wild. You can't go wrong with the sake list, or their
Japanese beer selection."—Michael Friedman

DEL CAMPO

Recommended by
Michael Friedman

777 I Street Northwest
Washington
District of Columbia 20001
+1 2022897377
www.delcampodc.com

Opening hours	Open 7 days
Credit cards	Accepted
Price range	Affordable
Style	Smart casual
Cuisine	South American
Recommended for	Local favorite

DGS DELICATESSEN

Recommended by
Michael Friedman

1317 Connecticut Avenue Northwest
Washington
District of Columbia 20036
+1 2022934400
www.dgsdelicatessen.com

Opening hours	Open 7 days
Credit cards	Accepted
Price range	Affordable
Style	Casual
Cuisine	Deli
Recommended for	Local favorite

LE DIPLOMATE

Recommended by
Tom Cunanan,
Michael Friedman

1601 14th Street Northwest
Washington
District of Columbia 20009
+1 2023323333
www.lediplomatedc.com

Opening hours	Open 7 days
Credit cards	Accepted
Price range	Affordable
Style	Smart casual
Cuisine	French
Recommended for	Regular neighborhood

"Le Diplomate serves classic French food, which was
the first cuisine I began cooking. As soon as you walk
in, the front of house staff are very attentive. The food
is executed well and has been consistent since they
opened in 2014."—Tom Cunanan

ESTADIO

Recommended by
Michael Friedman

14th Street Northwest
Washington
District of Columbia 20005
+1 2023191404
www.estadio-dc.com

Opening hours	Open 7 days
Credit cards	Accepted
Price range	Affordable
Style	Casual
Cuisine	Spanish
Recommended for	Regular neighborhood

FIOLA MARE

Recommended by
Tom Cunanan

3050 K Street Northwest
Washington
District of Columbia 20007
+1 2026280065
www.fiolamaredc.com

Opening hours	Open 7 days
Credit cards	Accepted
Price range	Affordable
Style	Smart casual
Cuisine	Italian Seafood
Recommended for	High end

"Everything from the ambiance to the friendly staff at first impressions is notable. Fabio Trabocchi has a great ability to sense the freshness of ingredients for his raw bar and chooses unique seasonal products. The extensive wine list pertains to the large menu."
—Tom Cunanan

JALEO

Recommended by
Michael Friedman

480 7th Street Northwest
Washington
District of Columbia 20004
+1 2026287949
www.jaleo.com

Opening hours	Open 7 days
Credit cards	Accepted
Price range	Affordable
Style	Casual
Cuisine	Spanish
Recommended for	Regular neighborhood

KAPNOS

Recommended by
Michael Friedman

2201 14th Street Northwest
Washington
District of Columbia 20009
+1 2022345000
www.kapnosdc.com

Opening hours	Open 7 days
Credit cards	Accepted
Price range	Affordable
Style	Smart casual
Cuisine	Greek
Recommended for	Regular neighborhood

KINSHIP

Recommended by
Michael Friedman

1015 7th Street Northwest
Washington
District of Columbia 20001
+1 2027377700
www.kinshipdc.com

Opening hours	Open 7 days
Credit cards	Accepted
Price range	Expensive
Style	Smart casual
Cuisine	Modern American
Recommended for	High end

KOMI

Recommended by
Michael Friedman

1509 17th Street Northwest
Washington
District of Columbia 20036
+1 2023329200
www.komirestaurant.com

Opening hours	Closed Monday and Sunday
Credit cards	Accepted
Price range	Expensive
Style	Smart casual
Cuisine	Greek
Recommended for	High end

"Johnny Monis is, in my opinion, one of the best chefs in the city. His take on Greek food at Komi is second to none, and one of my favorite meals I've ever had!"
—Michael Friedman

LEDO PIZZA

Recommended by
Tom Cunanan,
Katsuya Fukushima

7435 Georgia Avenue Northwest
Washington
District of Columbia 20012
+1 2027265336
www.ledopizza.com

Opening hours	Open 7 days
Reservation policy	No
Credit cards	Accepted
Price range	Budget
Style	Casual
Cuisine	American-Italian
Recommended for	Local favorite

"I grew up down the road from the original Ledo Restaurant, a family-owned pizzeria that opened in 1955. It's a local institution, especially for folks like me who love thin-crust pizza. I've got a weakness for their Hawaiian pizza with pineapple, sweet sauce, and salty ham."—Tom Cunanan

MANDU

453 K Street Northwest
Washington
District of Columbia 20001
+1 2022896899
www.mandudc.com

Opening hours	Open 7 days
Credit cards	Accepted
Price range	Affordable
Style	Casual
Cuisine	Korean
Recommended for	Late night

"Eating at Mandu is like eating at a Korean grandmother's house. That's probably because Danny Lee's mom is working the woks in the kitchen most days. The food is wholesome, delicious, spicy, and I always need another bite (especially after a couple beers)."—Michael Friedman

MARCEL'S

2401 Pennsylvania Avenue Northwest
Washington
District of Columbia 20037
+1 2022961166
www.marcelsdc.com

Opening hours	Open 7 days
Credit cards	Accepted
Price range	Expensive
Style	Smart casual
Cuisine	French-Belgian
Recommended for	High end

MEATS AND FOODS

247 Florida Avenue Northwest
Washington
District of Columbia 20001
+1 2025051384
www.meatsandfoods.com

Opening hours	Closed Monday and Tuesday
Reservation policy	No
Credit cards	Accepted
Price range	Budget
Style	Casual
Cuisine	Deli-Café
Recommended for	Bargain

"This little shop makes the best high-quality sausages in the city at a bargain. You can choose from bratwurst, chorizo, veggie sausage, and more. My favorite is the halfsmoke, with their house-made chile, cheddar, and topped with Gordy's pickles. I'm also addicted to their chilito, which is their house chile with hand-shredded cheddar cheese, wrapped in a warm flour tortilla. I usually order three!"
—Tom Cunanan

MÉTIER

1015 7th Street Northwest
Washington
District of Columbia 20001
+1 2027377500
www.metierdc.com

Opening hours	Open 7 days
Credit cards	Accepted
Price range	Expensive
Style	Formal
Cuisine	Modern American
Recommended for	High end

MINIBAR BY JOSÉ ANDRÉS

855 East Street Northwest
Washington
District of Columbia 20004
+1 2023930812
www.minibarbyjoseandres.com

Opening hours	Closed Monday and Sunday
Credit cards	Accepted
Price range	Expensive
Style	Smart casual
Cuisine	Modern Canadian
Recommended for	High end

NEW BIG WONG

610 H Street Northwest
Washington
District of Columbia 20001
+1 2026280491
www.newbigwong.com

Opening hours	Open 7 days
Credit cards	Accepted
Price range	Affordable
Style	Casual
Cuisine	Chinese
Recommended for	Late night

OLD EBBITT GRILL

Recommended by
Katsuya Fukushima

675 15th Street Northwest
Washington
District of Columbia 20005
+1 2023474800
www.ebbitt.com

Opening hours	Open 7 days
Credit cards	Accepted
Price range	Affordable
Style	Casual
Cuisine	American
Recommended for	Local favorite

OYAMEL COCINA MEXICANA

Recommended by
Michael Friedman

401 7th Street Northwest
Washington
District of Columbia 20004
+1 2026281005
www.oyamel.com

Opening hours	Open / days
Credit cards	Accepted
Price range	Affordable
Style	Smart casual
Cuisine	Modern Mexican
Recommended for	Regular neighborhood

PANDA GOURMET

Recommended by
Katsuya Fukushima

2700 New York Avenue Northeast
Washington
District of Columbia 20002
+1 2025341620
www.pandagourmetdc.net

Opening hours	Open 7 days
Credit cards	Accepted
Price range	Affordable
Style	Casual
Cuisine	Chinese
Recommended for	Regular neighborhood

"It's a no-nonsense type of restaurant serving cheap, delicious food. And not too many people know about this place."—Katsuya Fukushima

PERRY'S

Recommended by
Katsuya Fukushima

1811 Columbia Road Northwest
Washington
District of Columbia 20009
+1 2022346218
www.perrysam.com

Opening hours	Open 7 days
Credit cards	Accepted
Price range	Affordable
Style	Casual
Cuisine	Japanese
Recommended for	Breakfast

"Perry's for 'drag queen' brunch."
—Katsuya Fukushima

PHO VIET

Recommended by
Tom Cunanan

3513 14th Street Northwest
Washington
District of Columbia 20010
+1 2026292839
www.phovietwdc.com

Opening hours	Closed Tuesday
Reservation policy	No
Credit cards	Accepted
Price range	Affordable
Style	Casual
Cuisine	Vietnamese
Recommended for	Regular neighborhood

"I usually get #13 which comes with beef-eye round and well-done brisket. I get it half spicy so it doesn't overwhelm the broth that tastes like its been simmering all night long."—Tom Cunanan

PINEAPPLE AND PEARLS

Recommended by
Greg Denton & Gabrielle
Quiñónez Denton,
Kevin Fink,
Michael Friedman

715 8th Street Southeast
Washington
District of Columbia 20003
+1 2025957375
www.pineappleandpearls.com

Opening hours	Closed Monday and Sunday
Credit cards	Accepted
Price range	Expensive
Style	Smart casual
Cuisine	Modern American
Recommended for	Wish I'd opened

"We were so impressed with this restaurant as soon as we walked through the door. Great reception, refined and cozy ambiance, professional (but not stuffy) service, fun and creative dishes. Our minds were blown at least three times throughout the meal."
—Greg Denton & Gabrielle Quiñónez Denton

Opened in April 2016, Pineapple and Pearls already enjoys a near mythic status among Washington restaurant-goers. With an eleven-course taster menu $280 (£216)—including tax, gratuity, and wine pairings), owner and chef Aaron Silverman and his team have created a series of bite-sized masterpieces, which take familiar tastes and push them to the next level. Dishes of note include a fennel absinthe bonbon, a dairy cow steak—which could be the best steak in the city—and the extraordinary potato ice-cream dessert. Designed to make the evening as pleasant as possible, the bill is paid upon reservation, removing the pain of settling up at the end of an enchanting dining experience.

PRIME RIB

Recommended by
Katsuya Fukushima

2020 K Street Northwest
Washington
District of Columbia 20006
+1 2024668811
www.theprimerib.com

Opening hours	Closed Sunday
Credit cards	Accepted
Price range	Expensive
Style	Formal
Cuisine	Steakhouse
Recommended for	High end

"I love the vibe, the food, the decor, the service—I'd love to own a place like Prime Rib."
—Katsuya Fukushima

PROOF

Recommended by
Michael Friedman

775 G Street Northwest
Washington
District of Columbia 20001
+1 2027377663
www.proofdc.com

Opening hours	Open 7 days
Credit cards	Accepted
Price range	Expensive
Style	Smart casual
Cuisine	Modern American
Recommended for	Regular neighborhood

ROSE'S LUXURY

Recommended by
Michael Friedman, Jarrett Stieber

715 8th Street Southeast
Washington
District of Columbia 20003
+1 2025808889
www.rosesluxury.com

Opening hours	Closed Sunday
Reservation policy	No
Credit cards	Accepted
Price range	Affordable
Style	Casual
Cuisine	Modern American Tapas
Recommended for	Worth the travel

"Every detail, from the interior-design work to the way the cooks run their wide open kitchen, is flawless. They made us feel like we had known the crew for our whole lives, despite being from out of town and not knowing anyone there personally."—Jarrett Stieber

SAKEDOKORO MAKOTO

Recommended by
Katsuya Fukushima

4822 MacArthur Boulevard Northwest
Washington
District of Columbia 20007
+1 2022986866
www.sakedokoromakoto.com

Opening hours	Closed Monday and Sunday
Credit cards	Accepted
Price range	Expensive
Style	Smart casual
Cuisine	Japanese
Recommended for	High end

"I adore this restaurant. It's tiny. For a short time it takes me away to Japan. I wish I could go all the time."—Katsuya Fukushima

THE SOURCE

Recommended by
Michael Friedman

575 Pennsylvania Avenue Northwest
Washington
District of Columbia 20565
+1 2026376100
www.wolfgangpuck.com

Opening hours	Closed Sunday
Credit cards	Accepted
Price range	Expensive
Style	Smart casual
Cuisine	Asian Fusion
Recommended for	Local favorite

SUNDEVICH

Recommended by
Michael Friedman

1314 9th Street Northwest
Washington
District of Columbia 20001
+1 2023191086
www.sundevich.com

Opening hours	Closed Sunday
Credit cards	Accepted
Price range	Affordable
Style	Casual
Cuisine	Sandwiches
Recommended for	Regular neighborhood

TAIL UP GOAT

Recommended by
Csilla Thackray

1827 Adams Mill Road Northwest
Washington
District of Columbia 20009
+1 2029869600
www.tailupgoat.com

Opening hours	Open 7 days
Credit cards	Accepted
Price range	Affordable
Style	Casual
Cuisine	Bistro
Recommended for	Worth the travel

ZAYTINYA

Recommended by
Michael Friedman

701 9th Street Northwest
Washington
District of Columbia 20001
+1 2026380800
www.zaytinya.com

Opening hours	Open 7 days
Credit cards	Accepted
Price range	Affordable
Style	Smart casual
Cuisine	Greek-Mediterranean Tapas
Recommended for	Wish I'd opened

"Zaytinya is a labor of love towards Greek, Turkish, and Lebanese cuisine. Its location is amazing and its decor is inviting. The food is unique and, more importantly, absolutely delicious. Their use of spices and herbs is something I love and, if I had more experience with the cuisine, I'd open up a small joint of my own highlighting the food of these amazing cultures."
—Michael Friedman

HILLSTONE

Recommended by
Michael Beltran

201 Miracle Mile
Coral Gables
Florida 33134
+1 3055290141
www.hillstonerestaurant.com

Opening hours	Open 7 days
Credit cards	Accepted
Price range	Expensive
Style	Smart casual
Cuisine	American
Recommended for	Wish I'd opened

"The service and food consistency is out of this world. Attention to detail is amazing."—Michael Beltran

THE LOCAL

Recommended by
Michael Beltran,
Norman Van Aken

150 Giralda Avenue
Coral Gables
Florida 33134
+1 3056485687
www.thelocal150.com

Opening hours	Closed Monday
Credit cards	Accepted
Price range	Affordable
Style	Casual
Cuisine	Modern American
Recommended for	Regular neighborhood

"Chef Phil's food is always new and interesting, the vibe is super laid back. Their in-house program of vinegars, hot sauce, bread-making, and sausage work is all very impressive."—Michael Beltran

This gastropub goes the extra mile, with a wide range of cocktails and small-batch craft wines, and a rotating selection of seasonal craft beers across eighteen taps. A commitment to "local", stated right up there in the name, is at the heart of everything this restaurant does—with an emphasis on sourcing fresh ingredients from nearby farms. Don't miss "Roast and Toast", the monthly brew-paired brunch series, which combines delicious food—such as pulled hen and buttermilk dumplings, the limited-edition all-American burger, and the catch (and cut) of the day—with beers from guest breweries.

SEVEN DIALS

Recommended by
Daniel Serfer

2030 Douglas Road
Coral Gables
Florida 33134
+1 7865421603
www.sevendialsmiami.com

Opening hours	Open 7 days
Credit cards	Accepted
Price range	Affordable
Style	Casual
Cuisine	American Gastropub
Recommended for	Regular neighborhood

"If I lived closer I'd be there five times a week."
—Daniel Serfer

CAFÉ MARTORANO'S

Recommended by
Daniel Serfer

3343 East Oakland Park Boulevard
Fort Lauderdale
Florida 33308
+1 9545612554
www.cafemartorano.com

Opening hours	Closed Monday
Credit cards	Accepted
Price range	Expensive
Style	Smart casual
Cuisine	Italian-American
Recommended for	Regular neighborhood

"The pastas keep me coming back. No one does linguini with clams so well."—Daniel Serfer

ALTER

Recommended by
Norman Van Aken

223 Northwest 23rd Street
Miami
Florida 33127
+1 3055735996
www.altermiami.com

Opening hours	Closed Monday
Credit cards	Accepted
Price range	Affordable
Style	Smart casual
Cuisine	Modern American
Recommended for	Regular neighborhood

"He is a very thoughtful chef with strong technique and will go far in our industry."—Norman Van Aken

BAZAAR MAR

Recommended by
Daniel Serfer

1300 South Miami Avenue
Miami
Florida 33130
+1 3052391320
www.sbe.com

Opening hours	Open 7 days
Credit cards	Accepted
Price range	Expensive
Style	Smart casual
Cuisine	Seafood
Recommended for	High end

"The grilled oysters are really phenomenal. Not to mention, it's beautiful."—Daniel Serfer

CAKE THAI KITCHEN

Recommended by
Norman Van Aken

7910 Biscayne Boulevard
Miami
Florida 33138
+1 7865347906
www.cakethaikitchen.com

Opening hours	Open 7 days
Credit cards	Accepted
Price range	Budget
Style	Casual
Cuisine	Thai street food
Recommended for	Local favorite

"Explosively flavored, classic and modern Thai food."—Norman Van Aken

CASOLA'S PIZZA

Recommended by
Michael Beltran

2437 Southwest 17th Avenue
Miami
Florida 33145
+1 3058580090
www.casolas.com

Opening hours	Open 7 days
Reservation policy	No
Credit cards	Accepted
Price range	Budget
Style	Casual
Cuisine	Pizza
Recommended for	Late night

"A Miami staple."—Michael Beltran

ENRIQUETA'S

Recommended by
Michael Beltran,
Norman Van Aken

186 Northeast 29th Street
Miami
Florida 33137
+1 3055734681

Opening hours	Closed Sunday
Reservation policy	No
Credit cards	Accepted
Price range	Budget
Style	Casual
Cuisine	Cuban
Recommended for	Breakfast

"It's classic Miami, honest Cuban fare. You get café con leche, amazing ham croquettas, and Cuban toast."—Michael Beltran

FOOQ'S

Recommended by
Michael Beltran

1035 North Miami Avenue
Miami
Florida 33136
+1 7865362749
www.fooqsmiami.com

Opening hours	Closed Monday
Credit cards	Accepted
Price range	Affordable
Style	Casual
Cuisine	Persian
Recommended for	Regular neighborhood

"Chef Bryan Rojas does an amazing job with his menu, serving great product in a simple and elegant fashion."—Michael Beltran

HARRY'S PIZZERIA

Recommended by
Michael Beltran

3918 North Miami Avenue
Miami
Florida 33127
+1 7862754963
www.harryspizzeria.com

Opening hours	Open 7 days
Reservation policy	No
Credit cards	Accepted
Price range	Affordable
Style	Casual
Cuisine	Pizza
Recommended for	Wish I'd opened

"Amazing vibe and food in that place."
—Michael Beltran

L.C. ROTI SHOP

Recommended by
Daniel Serfer

19505 Northwest 2nd Avenue
Miami
Florida 33169
+1 3056518924

Opening hours	Closed Sunday
Reservation policy	No
Credit cards	Not accepted
Price range	Budget
Style	Casual
Cuisine	Trinidadian
Recommended for	Bargain

"The roti is cooked to order and the conch-shrimp-duck combo is the best. It's nap-inducing, so if I want to get a good sleep, I'll eat there."—Daniel Serfer

MACCHIALINA

Recommended by
Nina Compton

820 Alton Road
Miami
Florida 33139
+1 3055342124
www.macchialina.com

Opening hours	Open 7 days
Credit cards	Accepted
Price range	Affordable
Style	Casual
Cuisine	Italian
Recommended for	Worth the travel

"The atmosphere is intimate and charming and the food is some of the best rustic Italian food I've had. Everything is fresh and run by a husband and wife team."—Nina Compton

Exposed brick and leather banquettes speak more to old New York than lean-eating South Beach, and at Macchialina, it's even possible to be transported as far as Italy. Chef Michael Pirolo knows how to make great pasta, which he tosses with fresh, seasonal ingredients to satisfying effect. The simple *spaghetti pomodoro* (spaghetti with tomatoes) has maximalist flavor, while *spaghetti con gamberi* showcases the sweetness of local shrimp (prawns). Salumi and cheeses imported from Italy, fried olives, Peroni on tap, and a thoughtful, food-friendly wine list combine to make this a neighborhood favorite.

LA MAR

Recommended by
Norman Van Aken

500 Brickell Key Drive
Miami
Florida 33131
+1 3059138358
www.mandarinoriental.com

Opening hours	Open 7 days
Credit cards	Accepted
Price range	Expensive
Style	Smart casual
Cuisine	International Fusion
Recommended for	Local favorite

"In a city so filled with ethnic diversity, young chef Diego Oka, under the guidance of Gastón Acurio, gets the fusion right. The room is overly large for me but the food commands your absolute attention when it arrives. Go with a group that loves to taste many flavors!"—Norman Van Aken

MICHAEL'S GENUINE FOOD & DRINK

Recommended by
Michael Beltran

130 Northeast 40th Street
Miami
Florida 33137
+1 3055735550
www.michaelsgenuine.com

Opening hours	Open 7 days
Credit cards	Accepted
Price range	Affordable
Style	Casual
Cuisine	Modern American
Recommended for	Local favorite

"Seasonal, local products, good wine list, good cocktails, and solid service."—Michael Beltran

EL NUEVO SIGLO

Recommended by
Michael Beltran

1305 Southwest 8th Street
Miami
Florida 33135
+1 3058541916

Opening hours	Open 7 days
Reservation policy	No
Credit cards	Accepted
Price range	Budget
Style	Casual
Cuisine	Cuban
Recommended for	Bargain

"It's a market in the heart of Little Havana that has the most amazing lunch counter in the city. You can get braised oxtail, rice, plantains, and avocado salad for $10 (£8)."—Michael Beltran

PACK SUPER MARKET

Recommended by
Norman Van Aken

8235 Northeast 2nd Avenue
Miami
Florida 33138
+1 3057574777

Opening hours	Open 7 days
Reservation policy	No
Credit cards	Not accepted
Price range	Budget
Style	Casual
Cuisine	Haitian
Recommended for	Bargain

"This is a Little Haiti three-decades-old treasure serving food from early mornings to late afternoon. Fried chicken with the Haitian slaw named pikliz is a must."—Norman Van Aken

PAO

Recommended by
Michael Beltran

3201 Collins Avenue
Miami
Florida 33140
+1 7866555630
www.faena.com/miami-beach

Opening hours	Open 7 days
Credit cards	Accepted
Price range	Expensive
Style	Smart casual
Cuisine	Modern Asian
Recommended for	High end

"Chef Paul Qui—the man is a beast—his food
is absolutely amazing."—Michael Beltran

PETIT ROUGE

Recommended by
Daniel Serfer

12409 Biscayne Boulevard
Miami
Florida 33181
+1 3058927676
www.petitrougebistro.com

Opening hours	Closed Sunday
Credit cards	Accepted
Price range	Expensive
Style	Casual
Cuisine	French Bistro
Recommended for	Local favorite

"Great, small, local French bistro."—Daniel Serfer

PHUC YEA

Recommended by
Norman Van Aken

7100 Biscayne Boulevard
Miami
Florida 33138
+1 3056023710
www.phucyea.com

Opening hours	Closed Monday
Credit cards	Accepted
Price range	Affordable
Style	Casual
Cuisine	Vietnamese-American
Recommended for	Breakfast

"Actually it's brunch and they do a fusion of Cajun-
Vietnamese that is perfect for that meal too."
—Norman Van Aken

SUGARCANE RAW BAR GRILL

Recommended by
Khalid Mohammed

3252 Northeast 1st Avenue
Miami
Florida 33137
+1 7863690353
www.sugarcanerawbargrill.com

Opening hours	Open 7 days
Credit cards	Accepted
Price range	Affordable
Style	Casual
Cuisine	Asian-Latin American
Recommended for	Worth the travel

TAPAS DE ROSA

Recommended by
Daniel Serfer

449 Southwest 8th Street
Miami
Florida
33130
+1 3058569788
www.tapasderosa.com

Opening hours	Open 7 days
Credit cards	Accepted
Price range	Affordable
Style	Casual
Cuisine	Spanish Tapas
Recommended for	Local favorite

"Gloria and her mom are always so nice and it's the
one place I've found that I can consistently get *secreto*
(pork shoulder) and *pata negra* (Spanish ham)."
—Daniel Serfer

TAQUERIA VIVA MEXICO

Recommended by
Norman Van Aken

502 Southwest 12th Avenue
Miami
Florida 33130
+1 7863506360

Opening hours	Closed Monday
Reservation policy	No
Credit cards	Not accepted
Price range	Budget
Style	Casual
Cuisine	Mexican
Recommended for	Bargain

"A taco place that is not afraid to serve the 'off-cuts'
that are the true Mexican nose-to-tail cooking—tripe,
lingua (tongue), *buche* (stomach), *maciza* (pork
shoulder), to name some. A tiny place that spills on
to the sidewalk, also selling Jarritos and Mexican
Cokes."—Norman Van Aken

YAKKO-SAN

Recommended by
Michael Beltran,
Daniel Serfer

3881 Northeast 163rd Street
Miami
Florida 33160
+1 3059470064
www.yakko-san.com

Opening hours	Open 7 days
Reservation policy	No
Credit cards	Accepted
Price range	Affordable
Style	Casual
Cuisine	Japanese
Recommended for	Late night

"It's like a cult following type of place—it's always shocking when people have not heard of it. Triggerfish jerky, seaweed salad, crispy bok choy, and tofu kimchee."—Michael Beltran

Everything about this north Miami Beach Japanese restaurant is big, from its grandiose strip-mall entrance to the dramatic blue lighting under the bar. If it feels a bit like a club, it's no accident: this Miami-inflected *izakaya* (Japanese-style pub) and sushi bar has a popular happy hour that starts at 11.00 p.m. No matter what the hour, Yakko-San delivers meticulous preparations of familiar Japanese dishes, as well as more adventurous options like the day's catch served whole and cooked (or prepared as sashimi) according to one's whim.

BAGEL BAR EAST

Recommended by
Daniel Serfer

1990 Northeast 123rd Street
Miami Beach
Florida 33181
+1 3058957022
www.bagelbareastmiami.com

Opening hours	Open 7 days
Reservation policy	No
Credit cards	Accepted
Price range	Budget
Style	Casual
Cuisine	Deli
Recommended for	Breakfast

FRONT PORCH

Recommended by
Daniel Serfer

1458 Ocean Drive
Miami Beach
Florida 33139
+1 3055318300
www.frontporchoceandrive.com

Opening hours	Open 7 days
Reservation policy	No
Credit cards	Accepted
Price range	Affordable
Style	Casual
Cuisine	American
Recommended for	Breakfast

"I like sitting outside for breakfast and their breakfast potatoes are always right. For some reason, the eggs always taste better there."—Daniel Serfer

MATADOR ROOM

Recommended by
Jasper Schneider

2901 Collins Avenue
Miami Beach
Florida 33140
+1 7862574600
www.matadorroom.com

Opening hours	Open 7 days
Credit cards	Accepted
Price range	Expensive
Style	Smart casual
Cuisine	Spanish-American
Recommended for	Worth the travel

"The flavors of the food, the freshness, and the quality of the product, keeping it simple. Amazing cocktail list."—Jasper Schneider

LA SANDWICHERIE

Recommended by
Norman Van Aken

229 14th Street
Miami Beach
Florida 33139
+1 3055328934
www.lasandwicherie.com

Opening hours	Open 7 days
Reservation policy	No
Credit cards	Accepted
Price range	Budget
Style	Casual
Cuisine	French-American
Recommended for	Late night

"Open until 4.00 a.m. It's an open-air place with just stools that let you watch the cooks make big, French-style sandwiches, etc. You might be tumbling out of the famed 'Mac's Club Deuce' bar just across the street. Legendary."—Norman Van Aken

ATLANTA: SEE PAGES 940–951

CAKES & ALE

Recommended by
Todd Ginsberg,
Jarrett Stieber

155 Sycamore Street
Decatur
Georgia 30030
+1 4043777994
www.cakesandalerestaurant.com

Opening hours	Closed Monday and Sunday
Credit cards	Accepted
Price range	Affordable
Style	Casual
Cuisine	Modern American
Recommended for	Local favorite

"I have a deep respect for Billy Allin's attention to detail, his enthusasiam for elegance, his ability to coax flavor out of the simplest of ingredients, and his work ethic. I love everything about what he does at Cakes & Ale, which has been our city's version of Chez Panisse or Prune for as long as it's been open."
—Jarrett Stieber

Don't be misled—it's not all about sweet things and beer at Cakes & Ale. The dinner menu is a generous offering of carefully considered and constructed dishes, including crispy shrimp (prawn) with broccoli and beets (beetroot), and yellowedge grouper. The room, like the food, is colorful and shows off the owners' imaginative streak. The overall effect is comfortable, wholesome, and welcoming. The desserts, of course, don't fail to impress, and exude a confident simplicity—you're likely to find flourless chocolate cake, a simple praline tart, and the classic sticky toffee pudding. There's also a neighboring sister café, for a quicker hit of the action.

KIMBALL HOUSE

Recommended by
Joe Schafer

303 East Howard Avenue
Decatur
Georgia 30030
+1 4043783502
www.kimball-house.com

Opening hours	Open 7 days
Credit cards	Accepted
Price range	Expensive
Style	Casual
Cuisine	European-American
Recommended for	Wish I'd opened

"European-inspired menu featuring a lot of local foraged items and probably the best cocktail program in the city."—Joe Schafer

EL REY DEL TACO

Recommended by
Chris Hall
Jarrett Stieber

5288 Buford Highway Northeast
Doraville
Georgia 30340
+1 7709860032
www.elreydeltacoatl.com

Opening hours	Open 7 days
Reservation policy	No
Credit cards	Accepted
Price range	Affordable
Style	Casual
Cuisine	Mexican
Recommended for	Late night

"*Queso fundido* (melted cheese and chorizo) and a mariachi band at 4.00 a.m.."—Chris Hall

SEO RA BEOL

3040 Steve Reynolds Boulevard
Duluth
Georgia 30096
+1 7704971155
www.seorabeolusa.com

Opening hours	Open 7 days
Credit cards	Accepted
Price range	Affordable
Style	Casual
Cuisine	Korean Barbecue
Recommended for	Late night

"Open twenty-four hours—a fun place to go with my kitchen staff. Awesome pork belly, short rib, and shrimp cooked on natural charcoal."
—Steven Satterfield

BRANDI'S WORLD FAMOUS HOT DOGS

1377 Church Street Extension Northeast
Marietta
Georgia 30060
+1 7704223681

Opening hours	Closed Saturday and Sunday
Reservation policy	No
Credit cards	Not accepted
Price range	Budget
Style	Casual
Cuisine	Hot Dogs
Recommended for	Bargain

"For chile slaw dogs."—Chris Hall

SPRING

90 Marietta Station Walk
Marietta Square
Georgia 30060
+1 6785402777
www.springmarietta.com

Opening hours	Closed Sunday and Monday
Credit cards	Accepted
Price range	Expensive
Style	Smart casual
Cuisine	Modern American
Recommended for	Wish I'd opened

"It's a small, neighborhood restaurant located in the historic Marietta Square, serving an ever-changing menu. It's a hidden gem run by some old employees of mine. Brian is killing it there—simple food done with no fuss and always delicious."—Robert Phalen

TASTY CHINA

585 Franklin Road
Marietta
Georgia 30067
+1 7704199849
www.tastychina.net

Opening hours	Open 7 days
Credit cards	Accepted
Price range	Affordable
Style	Casual
Cuisine	Szechuan
Recommended for	Regular neighborhood

B'S CRACKLIN' BBQ

12409 White Bluff Road
Savannah
Georgia 31419
+1 9123306921
www.bscracklinbbq.com

Opening hours	Closed Monday
Reservation policy	No
Credit cards	Accepted
Price range	Affordable
Style	Casual
Cuisine	Southern American
Recommended for	Regular neighborhood

CRYSTAL BEER PARLOR

301 West Jones Street
Savannah
Georgia 31401
+1 9123491000
www.crystalbeerparlor.com

Opening hours	Open 7 days
Credit cards	Accepted
Price range	Affordable
Style	Casual
Cuisine	Burgers
Recommended for	Regular neighborhood

"It is a true local spot with the atmosphere to back it up. You can get a burger, a salad, and a locally crafted beer with no fuss or pretense. The Greek wings are my jam."—Mashama Bailey

THE GREY

Recommended by
Karl Worley

109 Martin Luther King Junior Boulevard
Savannah
Georgia 31401
+1 9126625999
www.thegreyrestaurant.com

Opening hours	Closed Monday
Credit cards	Accepted
Price range	Expensive
Style	Smart casual
Cuisine	Southern American
Recommended for	Worth the travel

"Housed in the old Greyhound station, this restaurant, led by Chef Mashama Bailey, blew our minds. Every bite was better than the last. It also helps that the ambiance was killer, the service staff stellar, and no detail went left unattended to."—Karl Worley

NAROBIA'S GRITS & GRAVY

Recommended by
Mashama Bailey

2019 Habersham Street
Savannah
Georgia 31401
+1 9122310563

Opening hours	Closed Sunday
Reservation policy	No
Credit cards	Accepted
Price range	Budget
Style	Casual
Cuisine	Southern American
Recommended for	Breakfast

"The name says it all really. Family run, excellent Southern breakfast with a laid back atmosphere. You'll be hard pressed to find a tourist in here."
—Mashama Bailey

Mornings seem extra promising when they begin with a cloudlike circle of creamy grits, white as snow, topped with shrimp and gravy, and served with two sunny eggs. But in this tiny open kitchen, scents of home-cooked soul food may sow the seeds of jealousy for a neighbor's order of French toast, "so good," Narobia's claims outside, "you don't need syrup!" The Sterns, the undisputed authority on home-town eats, judged Narobia's Grits & Gravy one of the best, and it's easy to agree that in this unassuming, single-storey building, there simmers a certain magic.

THE WYLD

Recommended by
Landon Thompson

2740 Livingston Avenue
Savannah
Georgia 31406
+1 9126921219
www.thewylddockbar.com

Opening hours	Closed Monday
Reservation policy	No
Credit cards	Accepted
Price range	Affordable
Style	Casual
Cuisine	Modern American Seafood
Recommended for	Wish I'd opened

"They cover all the important factors with room to spare. The food, drinks, service, and location are all phenomenal. Eat day-boat fresh seafood, while sipping on masterfully concocted drinks, sitting over the water, watching shrimp boats pass just feet from the dock— that's Savannah living!"
—Landon Thompson

BEAST CRAFT BBQ CO.

Recommended by
Cassy Vires

20 South Belt West
Belleville
Illinois 62220
+1 6182579000
www.beastcraftbbq.com

Opening hours	Open 7 days
Reservation policy	No
Credit cards	Accepted
Price range	Affordable
Style	Casual
Cuisine	Barbecue
Recommended for	Regular neighborhood

"The food is always amazing. It's a forty-minute drive from my house and I am there at least once a week. The pulled pork is extremely tender and the burnt ends are killer."—Cassy Vires

FOR CHICAGO: SEE PAGES 952–971

CLEVELAND-HEATH

106 North Main Street
Edwardsville
Illinois 62025
+1 6183074830
www.clevelandheath.com

Opening hours	Closed Sunday
Reservation policy	No
Credit cards	Accepted
Price range	Affordable
Style	Smart casual
Cuisine	American
Recommended for	Local favorite

"Excellent food, casual environment, with prices to match. They source a lot of local ingredients and have the approach of really letting the ingredients speak for themselves."—Cassy Vires

THE GOLDEN

898 Harrison Street
Fort Wayne
Indiana 46802
+1 2607108368
www.goldenfw.com

Opening hours	Closed Monday
Reservation policy	No
Credit cards	Accepted
Price range	Affordable
Style	Casual
Cuisine	Modern American
Recommended for	Wish I'd opened

"Killer changing menu, cocktails, happy staff, and everything served with humor."—Jonathan Brooks

The food here is an eclectic bunch of fun flavors and farm-to-fork, fresh ingredients. Not in the mood for Barnstable lady oysters with spicy green garlic mignonette? Then have the bratwurst oat porridge with green garlic and "frog juice". As the latter might indicate, you'll have to ask the waiter about (or Google) half the things on this very modern, very creative menu, but the resulting explosion of flavor will be well worth it. There are, of course, more subtle dishes on the menu too, and desserts are up there with the very best of them.

BLUEBEARD

653 Virginia Avenue
Indianapolis
Indiana 46203
+1 3176861580
www.bluebeardindy.com

Opening hours	Open 7 days
Reservation policy	No
Credit cards	Accepted
Price range	Affordable
Style	Casual
Cuisine	Modern American
Recommended for	Late night

CERULEAN

339 South Delaware Street
Indianapolis
Indiana 46225
+1 3178701320
www.ceruleanrestaurant.com

Opening hours	Closed Sunday
Credit cards	Accepted
Price range	Expensive
Style	Smart casual
Cuisine	Modern American
Recommended for	High end

"Cerulean is a great place to impress a date, and has probably the best dessert program in Indianapolis." —Jonathan Brooks

EGGROLL #1

4540 South Emerson Avenue
Indianapolis
Indiana 46203
+1 3177872225
www.eggroll1.com

Opening hours	Closed Sunday
Reservation policy	No
Credit cards	Accepted
Price range	Budget
Style	Casual
Cuisine	Asian Fusion
Recommended for	Breakfast

"I love to wake up after a night out and get a Pho for breakfast at Eggroll #1."—Jonathan Brooks

LEONARDO'S MEXICAN FOOD

Recommended by
Jonathan Brooks

8431 North Michigan Road
Indianapolis
Indiana 46268
+1 3173379022
www.leonardosmexicanfood.com

Opening hours	Open 7 days
Reservation policy	No
Credit cards	Accepted
Price range	Budget
Style	Casual
Cuisine	Mexican
Recommended for	Late night

"This is a bit of a drive from where I live but an Uber there has saved me many a hangover after a night out. Open 24-hours a day, they serve breakfast burritos, tortas, and operate a 'drive thru'!"—Jonathan Brooks

PEPPY'S GRILL

Recommended by
Jonathan Brooks

1004 Virginia Avenue
Indianapolis
Indiana 46203
+1 3176371158

Opening hours	Open 7 days
Reservation policy	No
Credit cards	Accepted
Price range	Budget
Style	Casual
Cuisine	Diner
Recommended for	Late night

"A 24-hour joint that's been around forever and will empathetically serve you burgers or pancakes despite your behavior."—Jonathan Brooks

ROOK

Recommended by
Jonathan Brooks

501 Virginia Avenue #101
Indianapolis
Indiana 46203
+1 3177372293
www.rookindy.com

Opening hours	Closed Sunday
Credit cards	Accepted
Price range	Affordable
Style	Casual
Cuisine	Asian Fusion
Recommended for	Regular neighborhood

"Chef Carlos Salazar is doing amazing things with Filipino street food."—Jonathan Brooks

ST. ELMO STEAKHOUSE

Recommended by
Jonathan Brooks

127 South Illinois Street
Indianapolis
Indiana 46225
+1 3176350636
www.stelmos.com

Opening hours	Open 7 days
Credit cards	Accepted
Price range	Expensive
Style	Smart casual
Cuisine	Steakhouse
Recommended for	High end

"Old-school steakhouse and Indianapolis landmark, famous for its shrimp cocktail and enormous wine list."—Jonathan Brooks

STEER-IN

Recommended by
Jonathan Brooks

5130 East 10th Street
Indianapolis
Indiana 46219
+1 3173560996
www.steerin.net

Opening hours	Open 7 days
Reservation policy	No
Credit cards	Accepted
Price range	Budget
Style	Casual
Cuisine	American
Recommended for	Breakfast

"An awesome American greasy-spoon breakfast joint, where I can order a Big Mac-ish burger for breakfast at 9.00 a.m. and no one judges me—the best in Indianapolis! I love their double burger and their straightforward homemade breakfast food."
—Jonathan Brooks

SUBITO

Recommended by
Jonathan Brooks

44 Virginia Avenue
Indianapolis
Indiana 46204
+1 3172208211
www.subitosoups.com

Opening hours	Closed Saturday and Sunday
Reservation policy	No
Credit cards	Accepted
Price range	Budget
Style	Casual
Cuisine	American
Recommended for	Regular neighborhood

"Very simple soups and sandwiches created from scratch—it's located right below the tattoo shop I frequent!"—Jonathan Brooks

TEX MEX

Recommended by
Jonathan Brooks

1104 Southeast Street #1
Indianapolis
Indiana 46225
+1 3179160979

Opening hours	Open 7 days
Credit cards	Accepted
Price range	Budget
Style	Casual
Cuisine	Mexican
Recommended for	Bargain

"It barely seems like you can spend enough to fulfill their $5 (£4) minimum for credit-card purchases."
—Jonathan Brooks

TIAN FU

Recommended by
Jonathan Brooks

3508 West 86th Street
Indianapolis
Indiana 46268
+1 3178726888
www.tianfuasianbistro.com

Opening hours	Open 7 days
Credit cards	Accepted
Price range	Affordable
Style	Casual
Cuisine	Chinese
Recommended for	Regular neighborhood

"There's a secret menu of traditional Chinese food that is exceptional, with West Lake soup and 'ants climbing a tree' being among my favorites. My five-year-old son loves the smoked duck as well!"
—Jonathan Brooks

GRAY BROTHERS CAFETERIA

Recommended by
Jonathan Brooks

555 South Indiana Street
Mooresville
Indiana 46158
+1 3178317234
www.graybroscafe.com

Opening hours	Open 7 days
Reservation policy	No
Credit cards	Accepted
Price range	Affordable
Style	Casual
Cuisine	American
Recommended for	Local favorite

"Huge cafeteria serving fried chicken livers, meatloaf, and noodles—and more pies than you can imagine."
—Jonathan Brooks

DECCA

Recommended by
Emily Hahn

812 East Market Street
Louisville
Kentucky 40206
+1 5027498128
www.deccarestaurant.com

Opening hours	Closed Sunday
Credit cards	Accepted
Price range	Expensive
Style	Casual
Cuisine	Modern American
Recommended for	Worth the travel

JACK FRY'S

Recommended by
Edward Lee

1007 Bardstown Road
Louisville
Kentucky 40204
+1 5024529244
www.jackfrys.com

Opening hours	Open 7 days
Credit cards	Accepted
Price range	Affordable
Style	Casual
Cuisine	Modern American
Recommended for	Local favorite

This Louisville Highlands stalwart wears its history with pride. The days of backroom bootlegging and bookmaking are well gone, immortalized now in the black and white pictures that line the walls of the handsome dining room—these days, it's a more genteel affair. This is good old-fashioned fine dining: high-end, French-influenced dishes such as escargots (snails) in garlic butter with croutons and Parmesan populate the menu, with the likes of shrimp and grits adding some Southern flavor. Don't expect hushed tones and starchy service though—locals love Jack Fry's for its relaxed atmosphere and live jazz.

WAFFLE HOUSE

Recommended by
Edward Lee

4320 Bishop Lane
Louisville
Kentucky 40218
+1 5024586434
www.wafflehouse.com

Opening hours	Open 7 days
Reservation policy	No
Credit cards	Accepted
Price range	Budget
Style	Casual
Cuisine	Diner
Recommended for	Bargain

"Jukebox, home fries, and a hell of a greasy burger."
—Edward Lee

MIDDENDORF'S

Recommended by
Edgar Caro

30160 US-51
Akers
Louisiana 70421
+1 9853866666
www.middendorfsrestaurant.com

Opening hours	Closed Monday and Tuesday
Reservation policy	No
Credit cards	Accepted
Price range	Affordable
Style	Casual
Cuisine	American Seafood
Recommended for	Worth the travel

GERALD'S DONUT & BURGER

Recommended by
Alex Harrell

6901 Saint Claude Avenue
Arabi
Louisiana 70032
+1 5042770030
www.geraldsdonuts.com

Opening hours	Open 7 days
Reservation policy	No
Credit cards	Accepted
Price range	Budget
Style	Casual
Cuisine	American
Recommended for	Late night

HONG KONG MARKET

Recommended by
Alex Harrell,
Chris Lusk

925 Behrman Highway #3
Gretna
Louisiana 70056
+1 5043947075
www.hongkongmarketnola.com

Opening hours	Open 7 days
Reservation policy	No
Credit cards	Accepted
Price range	Budget
Style	Casual
Cuisine	Market
Recommended for	Bargain

EL PASO RESTAURANT

Recommended by
Chris Lusk

2005 Belle Chasse Highway
Gretna
Louisiana 70053
+1 5043665104

Opening hours	Open 7 days
Reservation policy	No
Credit cards	Accepted
Price range	Affordable
Style	Casual
Cuisine	Mexican
Recommended for	Bargain

"Traditional Mexican food that is very good and really inexpensive."—Chris Lusk

TAN DINH

Recommended by
Alon Shaya,
Isaac Toups

1705 Lafayette Street
Gretna
Louisiana 70053
+1 5043618008

Opening hours	Closed Tuesday
Reservation policy	No
Credit cards	Accepted
Price range	Affordable
Style	Casual
Cuisine	Vietnamese
Recommended for	Bargain

"Classics mixed with some new-school Vietnamese dishes. They are an awesome representation of our really awesome Vietnamese community in Nola."
—Isaac Toups

PERINO'S BOILING POT

Recommended by
Edgar Caro

3754 Westbank Expressway
Harvey
Louisiana 70058
+1 5043405560
www.perinosboilingpot.com

Opening hours	Open 7 days
Reservation policy	No
Credit cards	Accepted
Price range	Affordable
Style	Casual
Cuisine	Cajun
Recommended for	Local favorite

"Crawfish boudin, boiled crawfish, and Dungeness crab."—Edgar Caro

SAL & JUDYS

Recommended by
Edgar Caro

27491 Highway 190 Lacombe
Lacombe
Louisiana 70445
+1 9858829443
www.salandjudysrestaurant.com

Opening hours	Closed Monday and Tuesday
Credit cards	Accepted
Price range	Affordable
Style	Casual
Cuisine	Italian
Recommended for	Worth the travel

"Great atmosphere. The veal lasagne is my favorite dish."—Edgar Caro

NEW ORLEANS: SEE PAGES 972–991

PALACE DINER

Recommended by
James Rigato,
Michael Wiley

18 Franklin Street
Biddeford
Maine 04005
+1 2072840015
www.palacedinerme.com

Opening hours	Open 7 days
Reservation policy	No
Credit cards	Not accepted
Price range	Affordable
Style	Casual
Cuisine	American
Recommended for	Wish I'd opened

"A tiny, unassuming diner car that happens to be churning out some badass food and drink with a rather nonchalant attitude that comes off as someone who is satisfied with themselves rather than pretentious. A step up from punk rock but still anti-establishment. I loved it."—James Rigato

BODA

Recommended by
Michael Wiley

671 Congress Street
Portland
Maine 04101
+1 2073477557
www.bodamaine.com

Opening hours	Open 7 days
Reservation policy	No
Credit cards	Accepted
Price range	Affordable
Style	Casual
Cuisine	Thai
Recommended for	Late night

"Great Thai food, awesome cocktails, and it's hard to beat the location."—Michael Wiley

DUTCH'S

Recommended by
Michael Wiley

28 Preble Street
Portland
Maine 04101
+1 2077612900
www.dutchsportland.com

Opening hours	Closed Monday
Reservation policy	No
Credit cards	Accepted
Price range	Affordable
Style	Casual
Cuisine	Café-Deli
Recommended for	Breakfast

"Their menu is thoughtful and delicious—it's one of those places where anything you order is going to be solid."—Michael Wiley

EVENTIDE OYSTER CO.

Recommended by
Tony Maws,
James Rigato,
Greg Vernick,
Sarah Welch

86 Middle Street
Portland
Maine 04101
+1 2077748538
www.eventideoysterco.com

Opening hours	Open 7 days
Credit cards	Accepted
Price range	Affordable
Style	Casual
Cuisine	Seafood
Recommended for	Worth the travel

"Eventide is hands down the best meal I have had in the United States. The food is incredibly fresh, the service is charming and prompt. Most importantly, their lobster roll makes me uncomfortable with its deliciousness. It may be the single best bite of food I've ever had. It makes me question how many I could actually eat before I'd become physically ill, and after much contemplation I've decided whatever the number, it still would not be enough."—Sarah Welch

Maine is proud of its lobster, of course, but also its granite—which might explain why a big block of it makes up Eventide's raw bar. It's a forgivable extravagance in a place that treats all its seafood with an elemental respect. Since the overnight success of its opening in 2012, people have come from far and wide for sweet-saline quohogs (clams), briny local oysters just as good with a slap of horseradish ice as without, and tender lobster glistening with browned butter. The cocktails, like the "Celery Gimlet" and "Negroni Bianco", seem fiendishly designed to whet the appetite. The raw bar features a wide selection of Maine oysters, but there are also salads, chowders, classic seafood bakes, and lobster rolls served in steamed buns.

EVO

Recommended by
Justin Pfau

443 Fore Street
Portland
Maine 04101
+1 2073587830
www.evoportland.com

Opening hours	Closed Monday
Credit cards	Accepted
Price range	Affordable
Style	Casual
Cuisine	Mediterranean
Recommended for	Regular neighborhood

FORE STREET

Recommended by
Michael Wiley

288 Fore Street
Portland
Maine 04101
+1 2077752717
www.forestreet.biz

Opening hours	Open 7 days
Credit cards	Accepted
Price range	Affordable
Style	Smart casual
Cuisine	Modern American
Recommended for	Local favorite

"Fore Street really cornered the market on the Maine culinary tradition. Local produce, simple preparations, wood-fired grill—it's become a cliché, but Fore Street really is the quintessential Portland restaurant."
—Michael Wiley

HOT SUPPA

Recommended by
Michael Wiley

703 Congress Street
Portland
Maine 04102
+1 2078715005
www.hotsuppa.com

Opening hours	Open 7 days
Reservation policy	No
Credit cards	Accepted
Price range	Affordable
Style	Casual
Cuisine	Southern American
Recommended for	Breakfast

"Their corned-beef hash is perfect—the Platonic ideal—it cannot be improved upon. And their patty-melt is likewise, not to be missed."—Michael Wiley

MIYAKE

Recommended by
Michael Wiley

468 Fore Street
Portland
Maine 04101
+1 2078719170
www.miyakerestaurants.com

Opening hours	Closed Sunday
Credit cards	Accepted
Price range	Expensive
Style	Smart casual
Cuisine	Japanese
Recommended for	High end

"The best sushi in Portland! Fantastic sake program and excellent service."—Michael Wiley

PRIMO RESTAURANT

Recommended by
Tim Butler

2 Main Street
Rockland
Maine 04841
+1 2075960770
www.primorestaurant.com

Opening hours	Closed Tuesday
Credit cards	Accepted
Price range	Expensive
Style	Smart casual
Cuisine	Italian
Recommended for	Worth the travel

"Primo Restaurant is one of the founding farm restaurants in the country"—Tim Butler

TERLINGUA

Recommended by
Michael Wiley

52 Washington Avenue
Portland
Maine 04101
+1 2078088502
www.terlingua.me

Opening hours	Open 7 days
Reservation policy	No
Credit cards	Accepted
Price range	Affordable
Style	Casual
Cuisine	Southern American
Recommended for	Regular neighborhood

"They smoke meat on Big Green Eggs and serve untraditional barbecue!"—Michael Wiley

B BISTRO

Recommended by
Reid Henninger

1501 Bolton Street
Baltimore
Maryland 21217
+1 4103838600
www.b-bistro.com

Opening hours	Closed Monday
Credit cards	Accepted
Price range	Affordable
Style	Casual
Cuisine	Modern American
Recommended for	Wish I'd opened

DYLAN'S OYSTER CELLAR

Recommended by
Spike Gjerde

3601 Chestnut Avenue
Baltimore
Maryland 21211
+1 4438531952
www.dylansoyster.com

Opening hours	Closed Monday
Reservation policy	No
Credit cards	Accepted
Price range	Affordable
Style	Casual
Cuisine	Seafood
Recommended for	High end

"Not necessarily high-end but I love Dylan's."
—Spike Gjerde

FAIDLEY SEAFOOD

203 North Paca Street
Baltimore
Maryland 21201
+1 4107274898
www.faidleyscrabcakes.com

Opening hours	Closed Sunday
Reservation policy	No
Credit cards	Accepted
Price range	Affordable
Style	Casual
Cuisine	Seafood
Recommended for	Local favorite

"They're still serving the freshest fish and shellfish from the Bay and every bit as good as a multi-generational, family-run institution can be."
—Spike Gjerde

GRANO'S PASTA BAR

1031 West 36th Street
Baltimore
Maryland 21211
+1 4105450444
www.granopastabar.com

Opening hours	Open 7 days
Reservation policy	No
Credit cards	Accepted
Price range	Affordable
Style	Casual
Cuisine	Italian
Recommended for	Bargain

"My kids are not into drawn-out dining experiences, so the counter service here is their idea of perfect."
—Spike Gjerde

JOE SQUARED

33 West North Avenue
Baltimore
Maryland 21201
+1 4105450444
www.joesquared.com

Opening hours	Open 7 days
Reservation policy	No
Credit cards	Accepted
Price range	Affordable
Style	Casual
Cuisine	Italian
Recommended for	Regular neighborhood

"Another favorite neighborhood pizza joint."
—Spike Gjerde

THE LOCAL OYSTER

520 Park Avenue
Baltimore
Maryland 21201
+1 8447482537
www.thelocaloyster.com

Opening hours	Open 7 days
Reservation policy	No
Credit cards	Accepted
Price range	Affordable
Style	Casual
Cuisine	Seafood
Recommended for	High end

PATISSERIE POUPON

820 East Baltimore Street
Baltimore
Maryland 21202
+1 4103320390
www.patisseriepoupon.net

Opening hours	Closed Sunday
Reservation policy	No
Credit cards	Accepted
Price range	Budget
Style	Casual
Cuisine	French
Recommended for	Breakfast

"It's a world-class French pastry shop on an unexpected corner of East Baltimore Street."
—Spike Gjerde

PAULIE GEE'S

3535 Chestnut Avenue
Baltimore
Maryland 21211
+1 4108891048
www.pauliegee.com/hampden

Opening hours	Closed Monday
Reservation policy	No
Credit cards	Accepted
Price range	Affordable
Style	Casual
Cuisine	Pizza
Recommended for	Regular neighborhood

THAMES STREET OYSTER HOUSE

Recommended by
Spike Gjerde

1728 Thames Street
Baltimore
Maryland 21231
+1 4434497726
www.thamesstreetoysterhouse.com

Opening hours	Open 7 days
Credit cards	Accepted
Price range	Affordable
Style	Smart casual
Cuisine	Seafood
Recommended for	High end

"There are few things better than a properly shucked oyster—especially when someone else is doing the shucking."—Spike Gjerde

It's almost unthinkable now that before the Thames Street Oyster House opened its doors in 2011, the historic coastal area of Fell's Point could not boast a good, mid-range seafood restaurant. Owner Candace Beattie has transformed a two-storey, harbor-adjacent store house into one of Baltimore's best restaurants, and with it has transformed the gastronomic landscape of the area. The breadth of choice on the raw bar menu is astonishing, with over ten types of oyster and a rich variety of crab and lobster claws on offer. It's all served with a panache that will please connoisseurs and casual diners alike. Upstairs dining offers pretty views of the harbor and on sunny days the rear courtyard is an island of serenity away from the busy seafront.

VERDE

Recommended by
Spike Gjerde

641 South Montford Avenue
Baltimore
Maryland 21224
+1 4105221000
www.verdepizza.com

Opening hours	Open 7 days
Credit cards	Accepted
Price range	Affordable
Style	Casual
Cuisine	Pizza
Recommended for	Regular neighborhood

"We now have so many great pizza places in Baltimore and it's where I always go with my kids."
—Spike Gjerde

WICKED SISTERS

Recommended by
Spike Gjerde

3845 Falls Road
Baltimore
Maryland 21211
+1 4108780884
www.wickedsistershampden.com

Opening hours	Open 7 days
Credit cards	Accepted
Price range	Affordable
Style	Casual
Cuisine	American
Recommended for	Late night

"Some nights it feels like they're keeping the kitchen open late just for the Woodberry Kitchen crew."
—Spike Gjerde

WOODBERRY KITCHEN

Recommended by
Michael Friedman

2010 Clipper Park Road
Baltimore
Maryland 21211
+1 4104648000
www.woodberrykitchen.com

Opening hours	Open 7 days
Credit cards	Accepted
Price range	Affordable
Style	Casual
Cuisine	American
Recommended for	Local favorite

"Spike Gjerde has been doing a great job for a long time—promoting Maryland product to its highest level. His version of terroir is so specific and delicious, that it's hard not to love this restaurant."
—Michael Friedman

GEORGETOWN BAGELRY

Recommended by
Michael Friedman

5227 River Road
Bethesda
Maryland 20816
+1 3016574442
www.georgetownbagelry.com

Opening hours	Open 7 days
Reservation policy	No
Credit cards	Accepted
Price range	Budget
Style	Casual
Cuisine	Jewish
Recommended for	Breakfast

"My Jewish roots sing when I get a chance to wait in line for bagels and lox at Georgetown Bagelry. They are constantly cooking bagels, which means they're always hot. Just a good schmear of cream cheese, buttery slices of smoked salmon, red onion, tomato, and a squeeze of lemon. That's how I wanna go out."
—Michael Friedman

WOODMONT GRILL

Recommended by
Michael Friedman

7715 Woodmont Avenue
Bethesda
Maryland 20814
www.woodmontgrill.com

Opening hours	Open 7 days
Credit cards	Accepted
Price range	Affordable
Style	Smart casual
Cuisine	American
Recommended for	Local favorite

PHO 75

Recommended by
Michael Friedman

771 Hungerford Drive
Rockville
Maryland 20850
+1 3013098873

Opening hours	Open 7 days
Reservation policy	No
Credit cards	Not accepted
Price range	Budget
Style	Casual
Cuisine	Vietnamese
Recommended for	Bargain

"Amazing Vietnamese pho. Classic. Cheap. Delicious."
—Michael Friedman

BLUE RIBBON BBQ

Recommended by
Matthew Gaudet

908 Massachusetts Avenue
Arlington
Massachusetts 02476
+1 7816487427
www.blueribbonbbq.com

Opening hours	Open 7 days
Reservation policy	No
Credit cards	Accepted
Price range	Affordable
Style	Casual
Cuisine	American Barbecue
Recommended for	Late night

ASTA

Recommended by
Daniel Bojorquez,
Jason Bond,
Joshua Lewin

47 Massachusetts Avenue
Boston
Massachusetts 02115
+1 6175859575
www.astaboston.com

Opening hours	Closed Monday and Sunday
Credit cards	Accepted
Price range	Expensive
Style	Casual
Cuisine	Modern American
Recommended for	Wish I'd opened

"Asta is a very creative tasting-menu restaurant. While not in Cambridge where I live, it's just over the bridge and I feel lucky whenever I can get there."
—Jason Bond

COPPA

Recommended by
Erick Harcey,
Tony Maws,
Ryan Trimm

253 Shawmut Avenue
Boston
Massachusetts 02118
+1 6173910902
www.coppaboston.com

Opening hours	Open 7 days
Credit cards	Accepted
Price range	Affordable
Style	Casual
Cuisine	Italian
Recommended for	High end

"If money is no object, I'll pay for flights as well."
—Erick Harcey

EASTERN STANDARD

528 Commonwealth Avenue
Boston
Massachusetts 02215
+1 6175329100
www.easternstandardboston.com

Recommended by
Daniel Bojorquez,
Katrina Jazayeri,
Joshua Lewin

Opening hours	Open 7 days
Credit cards	Accepted
Price range	Affordable
Style	Casual
Cuisine	Bistro-Brasserie
Recommended for	Late night

"It's sturdy, elegant, and dependable. I love ending a long day with a dozen oysters and a roasted chicken in the perfectly dark, always energetic bar."
—Katrina Jazayeri

Located in the shadow of baseball's most famous stadium, Fenway Park, this lively neighborhood brasserie and cocktail bar will be your go-to food and drink pit-stop for any occasion, serving a wide range of traditional dishes from breakfast until late at night. Eastern Standard prides itself on a feel-at-home vibe, with an attentive and knowledgeable staff ready to make you feel welcome. The cocktails are exceptional and the mixologists have more than enough skill to deal with any off-menu orders. The street-facing patio has a sizzling atmosphere, especially when the Sox are in town—though it'll get particularly busy when they are, so be prepared to wait for a short while.

FRANKLIN CAFÉ

278 Shawmut Avenue
Boston
Massachusetts 02118
+1 6173500010
www.franklincafe.com

Recommended by
Matthew Gaudet

Opening hours	Open 7 days
Reservation policy	No
Credit cards	Accepted
Price range	Affordable
Style	Casual
Cuisine	Modern American-Bar
Recommended for	Late night

"It's where I met my wife."—Matthew Gaudet

GRILL 23

161 Berkeley Street
Boston
Massachusetts 02116
+1 6175422255
www.grill23.com

Recommended by
Tony Maws,
Ken Oringer

Opening hours	Open 7 days
Credit cards	Accepted
Price range	Expensive
Style	Smart casual
Cuisine	Steakhouse-Seafood
Recommended for	High end

"Best steak in town, a terrific wine list, and attentive and professional (but not overbearing) service."
—Tony Maws

MIKE'S CITY DINER

1714 Washington Street
Boston
Massachusetts 02118
www.mikescitydiner.com

Recommended by
Ken Oringer

Opening hours	Open 7 days
Credit cards	Accepted
Price range	Budget
Style	Casual
Cuisine	Diner
Recommended for	Local favorite

"Mike's City Diner for old-school New England breakfast."—Ken Oringer

MYERS AND CHANG

1145 Washington Street
Boston
Massachusetts 02118
+1 6175425200
www.myersandchang.com

Recommended by
Daniel Bojorquez

Opening hours	Closed Monday
Credit cards	Accepted
Price range	Affordable
Style	Casual
Cuisine	Modern Southeast Asian
Recommended for	Regular neighborhood

"Unpretentious and just really great food. Inventive takes on traditional dishes and high-quality ingredients."—Daniel Bojorquez

NEPTUNE OYSTER

63 Salem Street
Boston
Massachusetts 02113
+1 6177423474
www.neptuneoyster.com

Opening hours	Open 7 days
Reservation policy	No
Credit cards	Accepted
Price range	Affordable
Style	Casual
Cuisine	Seafood
Recommended for	Local favorite

"Hidden in the historic North End, it's a classic-looking, tiny restaurant with the best oysters and chowder in the city."—Tony Maws

If you want to perch at Neptune's marble counter you're going to have to get in line. It's strictly no reservations for its sixteen stools and handful of banquettes. The market-priced raw bar offers the best shellfish in season, from finest East and West Coast oysters to razor clams, crab claws, and littleneck and cherrystone clams. The menu occasionally acknowledges the North End neighborhood's Italian heritage—a lobster spaghettini or a *vitello tonnato* (veal with tuna sauce) sandwich—alongside more eclectic influences—mackerel with Puya chiles and chimichurri. Their Maine lobster roll, served either hot with butter or cold with mayo, has a cult following.

NO. 9 PARK

9 Park Street
Boston
Massachusetts 02108
+1 6177429991
www.no9park.com

Opening hours	Open 7 days
Credit cards	Accepted
Price range	Affordable
Style	Smart casual
Cuisine	French-Italian
Recommended for	High end

"Well, it's just my favorite place around! When money is no object, saunter your way out of the bar room and into the carpetted dining room, order the wine, have all the courses, and don't skip the cheese."
—Joshua Lewin

O YA

9 East Street
Boston
Massachusetts 02111
+1 6176549900
www.oyarestaurantboston.com

Opening hours	Closed Monday and Sunday
Credit cards	Accepted
Price range	Expensive
Style	Smart casual
Cuisine	Japanese
Recommended for	High end

"Incredible sushi and Japanese small plates, extremely creative, lovely decor and service."—Joanne Chang

OISHII SUSHI

1166 Washington Street #110
Boston
Massachusetts 02118
+1 6174828868
www.oishiiboston.com

Opening hours	Closed Monday
Credit cards	Accepted
Price range	Affordable
Style	Casual
Cuisine	Japanese
Recommended for	High end

PEACH FARM

4 Tyler Street
Boston
Massachusetts 02111
+1 6174823332
www.peachfarmboston.com

Opening hours	Open 7 days
Reservation policy	No
Credit cards	Accepted but not AMEX
Price range	Affordable
Style	Casual
Cuisine	Chinese
Recommended for	Late night

"Best Chinese food and open late! Great XO sauce—extremely fresh seafood."—Matthew Gaudet

PHO PASTEUR

Recommended by
Matthew Gaudet

682 Washington Street
Boston
Massachusetts 02111
+1 6174827467
www.phopasteurboston.net

Opening hours	Open 7 days
Credit cards	Accepted
Price range	Budget
Style	Casual
Cuisine	Vietnamese
Recommended for	Bargain

SALTIE GIRL

Recommended by
Katrina Jazayeri

281 Dartmouth Street
Boston
Massachusetts 02116
+1 6172670691
www.saltiegirl.com

Opening hours	Closed Monday
Reservation policy	No
Credit cards	Accepted
Price range	Expensive
Style	Casual
Cuisine	Seafood
Recommended for	Wish I'd opened

"We fell in love with tinned fish in Barcelona, so I think it's great this concept exists here—but I'm a bit envious because I'm not sure the Boston area has appetite for two tinned fish joints ... at least for now."
—Katrina Jazayeri

SAM LAGRASSA'S

Recommended by
Ken Oringer

44 Province Street
Boston
Massachusetts 02108
+1 6173576861
www.samlagrassas.com

Opening hours	Closed Saturday and Sunday
Reservation policy	No
Credit cards	Not accepted
Price range	Budget
Style	Casual
Cuisine	Sandwiches
Recommended for	Bargain

"Their pastrami sandwiches are amazing. They hand-carve hot pastrami, made in-house, and it tastes unbelievable."—Ken Oringer

SAM'S

Recommended by
Joanne Chang

60 Northern Avenue
Boston
Massachusetts
+1 6172950191
www.samsatlouis.com

Opening hours	Open 7 days
Credit cards	Accepted
Price range	Affordable
Style	Casual
Cuisine	Modern American
Recommended for	Regular neighborhood

"Amazing views, the best service, and I want to eat everything on the menu."—Joanne Chang

SORELLINA

Recommended by
Joanne Chang

1 Huntington Avenue
Boston
Massachusetts 02111
+1 6174124600
www.sorellinaboston.com

Opening hours	Open 7 days
Credit cards	Accepted
Price range	Expensive
Style	Formal
Cuisine	Modern Italian
Recommended for	Wish I'd opened

"The service is impeccable, it's the most beautiful and elegant dining room in town, the food is always great, and it's always busy."—Joanne Chang

TAIWAN CAFÉ

Recommended by
Joanne Chang

34 Oxford Street
Boston
Massachusetts 02111
+1 6174268181

Opening hours	Open 7 days
Credit cards	Not accepted
Price range	Budget
Style	Casual
Cuisine	Taiwanese
Recommended for	Bargain

"Their *mápó tòfu* (tofu in spicy sauce), pea tendrils, and Hakka-style aubergine (eggplant) are among my favorite dishes in the world."—Joanne Chang

TASTY BURGER

Recommended by
Matthew Gaudet

1301 Boylston Street
Boston
Massachusetts 02215
+1 6174254444
www.tastyburger.com

Opening hours	Open 7 days
Reservation policy	No
Credit cards	Accepted
Price range	Budget
Style	Casual
Cuisine	Burgers
Recommended for	Late night

TOWNSMAN

Recommended by
John Besh

120 Kingston Street
Boston
Massachusetts 02111
+1 6179930750
www.townsmanboston.com

Opening hours	Closed Sunday
Credit cards	Accepted
Price range	Expensive
Style	Casual
Cuisine	Brasserie
Recommended for	Worth the travel

WINSOR DIM SUM CAFÉ

Recommended by
Joanne Chang

10 Tyler Street
Boston
Massachusetts 02111
+1 6173381688
www.winsordimsumcafe.com

Opening hours	Open 7 days
Reservation policy	No
Credit cards	Accepted
Price range	Budget
Style	Casual
Cuisine	Dim Sum
Recommended for	Breakfast

"Dim sum made to order."—Joanne Chang

THE ABBEY CAMBRIDGE

Recommended by
Jason Bond

1755 Massachusetts Avenue
Cambridge
Massachusetts 02140
+1 6177144944
www.abbeyrestaurant.com

Opening hours	Open 7 days
Reservation policy	No
Credit cards	Accepted
Price range	Affordable
Style	Casual
Cuisine	American
Recommended for	Late night

"The people are amazingly friendly, even at chef hours. Great food, also rare to find at chef hours."
—Jason Bond

ALGIERS COFFEE HOUSE

Recommended by
Jason Bond

40 Brattle Street
Cambridge
Massachusetts 02138
+1 6174921557
www.harvardsquare.com

Opening hours	Open 7 days
Reservation policy	No
Credit cards	Accepted
Price range	Budget
Style	Casual
Cuisine	Mediterranean
Recommended for	Bargain

"Algiers Coffee House has just reopened and thankfully has not changed. I like to get a pot of Arabic coffee and the merguez (sausage) sandwich."—Jason Bond

ALIVE AND KICKING LOBSTER

Recommended by
Katrina Jazayeri

269 Putnam Avenue
Cambridge
Massachusetts 02139
+1 6178760451
www.aliveandkickinglobsters.com

Opening hours	Open 7 days
Reservation policy	No
Credit cards	Accepted
Price range	Affordable
Style	Casual
Cuisine	Seafood
Recommended for	Local favorite

"This a fish shop that serves three to four dishes, lobster sandwiches, seafood soup, steamers, and mussels. There is only outdoor seating on picnic tables and folding chairs—and in the dead of winter, there are people in parkas sitting around these dunking steamer clams in broth and melted butter. Nothing gets in the way of seafood in these parts."—Katrina Jazayeri

AREA 4

Recommended by
Jason Bond

500 Technology Square
Cambridge
Massachusetts 02139
+1 6177584444
www.areafour.com

Opening hours	Open 7 days
Credit cards	Accepted
Price range	Affordable
Style	Casual
Cuisine	Pizza
Recommended for	Wish I'd opened

"Straightforward, well-done food from wood-burning ovens. It must be as satisfying to cook as it is to eat. I love this place."—Jason Bond

BISQ

Recommended by
Katrina Jazayeri,
Joshua Lewin

1071 Cambridge Street
Cambridge
Massachusetts 02139
+1 6177143693
www.bisqcambridge.com

Opening hours	Open 7 days
Credit cards	Accepted
Price range	Affordable
Style	Casual
Cuisine	American small plates
Recommended for	Regular neighborhood

"BISq is a wine bar that really knows how to be a neighborhood spot. Warm, friendly, knowledgeable service. If you want to learn something about wine here, you can. If you don't feel like it, you don't have to. The food is understated but incredibly professional. Expectations are high and they always beat them; charcuterie, salumi, and small plates. They host pig roasts if you plan ahead."—Joshua Lewin

From the same team that have successfully run nearby local favorite Bergamot (BISq stands for "Bergamot Inman Square", rather than being a clever soup pun), this wine bar and date-night restaurant has a more casual, unpretentious ambience, serving a range of stylishly presented sharing plates. The menu is an adventurous mix of locally caught shellfish and charcuterie platters sourced from nearby farms. The produce is perfectly showcased in the six-dish taster menu, which features an outstanding version of barbecued shrimp (prawn) toast. Although usually open for evening dining, BISq welcomes patrons for a hearty brunch between 10.00 a.m. and 3.00 p.m. on the last Sunday of every month. Inman Square is developing a strong reputation as a gastronomic hot spot—and BISq is at the forefront of it all.

BLUE ROOM

Recommended by
Jason Bond

1 Kendall Square
Cambridge
Massachusetts 02139
+1 6174949034
www.theblueroom.net

Opening hours	Open 7 days
Credit cards	Accepted
Price range	Affordable
Style	Casual
Cuisine	Modern American
Recommended for	Local favorite

"Blue Room is a classic Cambridge restaurant with a beautiful room and a magnificent wine list."
—Jason Bond

BONDIR

Recommended by
Joshua Lewin

279A Broadway
Cambridge
Massachusetts 02139
+1 6176610009
www.bondircambridge.com

Opening hours	Closed Tuesday
Credit cards	Accepted
Price range	Expensive
Style	Casual
Cuisine	Modern American
Recommended for	Local favorite

CAFÉ SUSHI

Recommended by
Jason Bond,
Katrina Jazayeri,
Joshua Lewin

1105 Massachusetts Avenue
Cambridge
Massachusetts 02138
+1 6174920434
www.cafesushicambridge.com

Opening hours	Open 7 days
Credit cards	Accepted
Price range	Affordable
Style	Smart casual
Cuisine	Japanese
Recommended for	High end

"The quality is always superb, and the chefs take an inventive but reliably excellent approach to sashimi and sushi. The *omakase* (chef's choice menu) is a real treat for a special occasion."—Katrina Jazayeri

One of Boston's true hidden treasures, this unassuming sushi bar—a stone's throw away from the Harvard University campus—comfortably fills the middle ground between the city's fine dining, but expensive, sushi restaurants, and the friendly, familiar local Japanese takeaways. Chef and owner Seizi Imura is committed to providing dishes that aren't too showy but are prepared using simple methods and high-quality produce. To assure diners of the freshness of the ingredients on offer, there's a black chalkboard behind the sushi counter that lists the fish that have arrived that day, ready for preparation. Imura's signature maki (sushi and raw vegetables wrapped in seaweed) are ingeniously created, with an assortment of textures in each bite.

CLOVER FOOD LAB

Recommended by
Jason Bond,
Joshua Lewin

496 Massachusetts Avenue
Cambridge
Massachusetts 02139
www.cloverfoodlab.com

Opening hours	Open 7 days
Reservation policy	No
Credit cards	Accepted
Price range	Budget
Style	Casual
Cuisine	Vegetarian
Recommended for	Bargain

"It's one of those rare places where you won't realize it's vegetarian because the food is so good. Great menu and probably good for you too."—Jason Bond

CRAIGIE ON MAIN

Recommended by
Jason Bond

853 Main Street
Cambridge
Massachusetts 02139
+1 6174975511
www.craigieonmain.com

Opening hours	Closed Monday
Credit cards	Accepted
Price range	Expensive
Style	Smart casual
Cuisine	French-American
Recommended for	Local favorite

"Craigie has always been about Cambridge. From its original location in a weird little apartment complex to the middle of Central Square now, this has always been a place supported by Cambridge. The dining room any night of the week will be a snap shot of who's in Cambridge and also a 'who's who' of Cambridge."—Jason Bond

THE DRUID

Recommended by
Jason Bond

1357 Cambridge Street
Cambridge
Massachusetts 02139
+1 6174970965
www.druidpub.com

Opening hours	Open 7 days
Reservation policy	No
Credit cards	Accepted
Price range	Affordable
Style	Casual
Cuisine	Irish Pub
Recommended for	Regular neighborhood

GIULIA

Recommended by
Joshua Lewin

1682 Massachusetts Avenue
Cambridge
Massachusetts 02138
+1 6174412800
www.giuliarestaurant.com

Opening hours	Closed Sunday
Credit cards	Accepted
Price range	Affordable
Style	Casual
Cuisine	Italian
Recommended for	Local favorite

LONGFELLOW COFFEE

Recommended by
Jason Bond

284 Broadway
Cambridge
Massachusetts 02139
www.longfellowscambridge.com

Opening hours	Open 7 days
Reservation policy	No
Credit cards	Accepted
Price range	Budget
Style	Casual
Cuisine	Coffee Shop
Recommended for	Regular neighborhood

"Lamplighter Brewery and Longfellow Coffee share
a space on Broadway and both focus on high-quality
ingredients, handled with skill by the owner-
operators."—Jason Bond

LONE STAR TACO BAR

Recommended by
Tony Maws

635 Cambridge Street
Cambridge
Massachusetts 02141
+1 8572856179
www.lonestar-boston.com

Opening hours	Open 7 days
Reservation policy	No
Credit cards	Accepted
Price range	Affordable
Style	Casual
Cuisine	Tex-Mex
Recommended for	Late night

"Totally serviceable tacos and guacamole with a great
beer list."—Tony Maws

LORD HOBO

Recommended by
Jason Bond

92 Hampshire Street
Cambridge
Massachusetts 02139
+1 6172508454
www.lordhobo.com

Opening hours	Open 7 days
Reservation policy	No
Credit cards	Accepted
Price range	Affordable
Style	Casual
Cuisine	Bar
Recommended for	Late night

"A very friendly crew, amazing beer selection, and
good cooking late at night."—Jason Bond

LOYAL-NINE

Recommended by
Tony Maws

660 Cambridge Street
Cambridge
Massachusetts 02141
+1 6179452576
www.loyalninecambridge.com

Opening hours	Open 7 days
Credit cards	Accepted
Price range	Affordable
Style	Casual
Cuisine	Modern American
Recommended for	Regular neighborhood

"Loyal-Nine for terrific coffee."—Tony Maws

MAMALEH'S

Recommended by
Tony Maws

1 Kendall Square
15 Hampshire Street
Cambridge
Massachusetts 02139
+1 6179583354
www.mamalehs.com

Opening hours	Closed Monday
Credit cards	Accepted
Price range	Affordable
Style	Casual
Cuisine	Jewish Deli
Recommended for	Breakfast

"Modern take on an old-school Jewish deli. Close to
my house and I love their smoked fish."—Tony Maws

MASS AVE DINER

Recommended by
Jason Bond

906 Massachusetts Avenue
Cambridge
Massachusetts 02139
+1 6178645301
www.massavediner.com

Opening hours...Open 7 days
Reservation policy...No
Credit cards...Accepted
Price range...Budget
Style...Casual
Cuisine...Diner
Recommended for...Breakfast

MOODY'S FALAFEL PALACE

Recommended by
Joshua Lewin

25 Central Square
Cambridge
Massachusetts 02139
+1 6178640827
www.falafelpalace.net

Opening hours...Open 7 days
Reservation policy...No
Credit cards...Not accepted
Price range...Budget
Style...Casual
Cuisine...Middle-Eastern
Recommended for...Late night

OLEANA

Recommended by
Ken Oringer

134 Hampshire Street
Cambridge
Massachusetts
www.oleanarestaurant.com

Opening hours...Open 7 days
Credit cards...Accepted
Price range..Expensive
Style...Smart casual
Cuisine..Turkish-Middle Eastern
Recommended for...High end

"My ideal special-occasion celebration is sitting in the Oleana garden, drinking rosé and eating mezze. My favorite dish of theirs is the whipped feta with urfa peppers."—Ken Oringer

SHEPARD

Recommended by
Joshua Lewin

1 Shepard Street
Cambridge
Massachusetts 02138
+1 6177145295
www.shepardcooks.com

Opening hours...Open 7 days
Credit cards...Accepted
Price range..Affordable
Style...Casual
Cuisine..French-American
Recommended for.......................................Local favorite

TUPELO

Recommended by
Katrina Jazayeri,
Joshua Lewin

1193 Cambridge Street
Cambridge
Massachusetts 02139
+1 6178680004
www.tupelo02139.com

Opening hours..Closed Monday
Credit cards...Accepted
Price range..Affordable
Style...Casual
Cuisine..Southern American
Recommended for...............................Regular neighborhood

"Tupelo is maybe not known for being a cheap spot, generally, but one of our favorite Sunday night traditions is a huge bowl of mussels and fries at the bar for $15 (£12). It's on their appetizer menu, but big enough for an entrée."—Joshua Lewin

HI-RISE BAKERY

Recommended by
Matthew Gaudet

208 Concord Avenue
Cambridge
Massachusetts 02138
+1 6178768766
www.hi-risebread.com

Opening hours...Open 7 days
Reservation policy...No
Credit cards...Accepted
Price range...Budget
Style...Casual
Cuisine...Bakery
Recommended for...Breakfast

TATTE BAKERY AND CAFÉ

Recommended by
Jason Bond

101 Main Street
East Cambridge
Cambridge
Massachusetts, 02142
+1 617 577 1111
www.tattebakery.com

Opening hours	Closed Saturday and Sunday
Reservation policy	No
Credit cards	Accepted
Price range	Budget
Style	Casual
Cuisine	Bakery
Recommended for	Breakfast

PHỞ SỐ 1

Recommended by
Tony Maws

223 Adams Street
Dorchester
Massachusetts 02122
+1 6174368888

Opening hours	Open 7 days
Reservation policy	No
Credit cards	Accepted
Price range	Budget
Style	Casual
Cuisine	Vietnamese
Recommended for	Bargain

J.T. FARNHAM'S

Recommended by
Matthew Gaudet

88 Eastern Avenue
Essex
Massachusetts 01929
+1 9787686643
www.jtfarnhams.com

Opening hours	Open 7 days
Reservation policy	No
Credit cards	Not accepted
Price range	Affordable
Style	Casual
Cuisine	Seafood
Recommended for	Local favorite

"Quintessential coastal New England seafood shack serving lobster rolls and fried clams—the best."
—Matthew Gaudet

HALIBUT POINT

Recommended by
Matthew Gaudet

289 Main Street
Gloucester
Massachusetts 01930
+1 9782811900
www.halibutpointrestaurant.com

Opening hours	Open 7 days
Credit cards	Accepted
Price range	Affordable
Style	Casual
Cuisine	American-Seafood
Recommended for	Regular neighborhood

CENTER STREET CAFÉ

Recommended by
Joshua Lewin

669A Center Street
Jamaica Plain
Massachusetts 02130
+1 6175249217
www.centerstreetcafejp.com

Opening hours	Open 7 days
Credit cards	Accepted
Price range	Affordable
Style	Casual
Cuisine	Italian
Recommended for	Local favorite

CHILE GARDEN

Recommended by
Tony Maws

41 Riverside Avenue
Medford
Massachusetts 02115
+1 7813968488
www.chilegardenmedford.com

Opening hours	Open 7 days
Credit cards	Accepted
Price range	Affordable
Style	Casual
Cuisine	Chinese
Recommended for	Bargain

"They have an authentic Szechuan menu that is absolutely delicious—fiery hot, extremely flavorful, and consistent."—Tony Maws

BERGAMOT

Recommended by
Joshua Lewin

118 Beacon Street
Somerville
Massachusetts 02143
+1 6175767700
www.bergamotrestaurant.com

Opening hours	Open 7 days
Credit cards	Accepted
Price range	Affordable
Style	Casual
Cuisine	Modern American
Recommended for	Local favorite

BUDDY'S DINER

Recommended by
Katrina Jazayeri,
Joshua Lewin

113 Washington Street
Somerville
Massachusetts 02143
+1 6176239725

Opening hours	Open 7 days
Reservation policy	No
Credit cards	Not accepted
Price range	Budget
Style	Casual
Cuisine	Diner
Recommended for	Breakfast

"Buddy's is zero frills. One big griddle, right behind the seating counter. One server, one cook. Big pot of coffee. Menu written on a line of paper plates tacked to the wall. I grew up working in a place like this. I eat the same thing at Buddy's as I did every day after work there. Egg sandwich, bulkie roll, sausage patty, American cheese."—Joshua Lewin

CASA B

Recommended by
Joshua Lewin

253 Washington Street
Somerville
Massachusetts 02143
+1 6177642180
www.casabrestaurant.com

Opening hours	Open 7 days
Credit cards	Accepted
Price range	Affordable
Style	Casual
Cuisine	Latin American Tapas
Recommended for	Regular neighborhood

"Unexpectedly good cooking at this Puerto Rican-inspired tapas restaurant. The dining room is beautiful and modern but there's also a 'secret' bar downstairs where the atmosphere is lively."—Joshua Lewin

FAT HEN

Recommended by
Joshua Lewin

126 Broadway
Somerville
Massachusetts 02145
+1 6177641612
www.fathenboston.com

Opening hours	Closed Monday
Credit cards	Accepted
Price range	Affordable
Style	Smart casual
Cuisine	Italian
Recommended for	Wish I'd opened

HIGHLAND KITCHEN

Recommended by
Tony Maws

150 Highland Avenue
Somerville
Massachusetts 02143
+1 6176251131
www.highlandkitchen.com

Opening hours	Open 7 days
Reservation policy	No
Credit cards	Accepted
Price range	Affordable
Style	Casual
Cuisine	American
Recommended for	Local favorite

J AND J RESTAURANT

Recommended by
Katrina Jazayeri,
Joshua Lewin

157 Washington Street
Somerville
Massachusetts 02143
+1 6176253978
www.jandjrestaurant.com

Opening hours	Open 7 days
Reservation policy	No
Credit cards	Accepted
Price range	Affordable
Style	Casual
Cuisine	Portuguese-American
Recommended for	Bargain

"This restaurant looks like a convenience store from the outside, but behind a display of Portuguese rolls and coffee is a hidden dining room serving roasted chickens, bacalhau, and my favorite dish, clams with cubed pork and pickled veggies."—Katrina Jazayeri

THREE LITTLE FIGS

Recommended by
Katrina Jazayeri

278 Highland Avenue
Somerville
Massachusetts 02143
+1 6176233447
www.3littlefigs.com

Opening hours	Open 7 days
Reservation policy	No
Credit cards	Accepted
Price range	Affordable
Style	Casual
Cuisine	Greek-Mediterranean
Recommended for	Breakfast

"Three Little Figs is a charming café with great coffee and simple but delicious food. Josh and I have a Friday morning tradition of starting our day here with the paper, a book, or sometimes a crossword."
—Katrina Jazayeri

THE NEIGHBORHOOD RESTAURANT

Recommended by
Joshua Lewin

25 Bow Street
Somerville
Massachusetts 02143
+1 6176239710
www.theneighborhoodrestaurant.com

Opening hours	Open 7 days
Reservation policy	No
Credit cards	Not accepted
Price range	Affordable
Style	Casual
Cuisine	Portuguese-American
Recommended for	Bargain

PHO 'N RICE

Recommended by
Matthew Gaudet

289 Beacon Street
Somerville
Massachusetts 02143
+1 6178648888
www.phonricema.com

Opening hours	Open 7 days
Credit cards	Accepted
Price range	Budget
Style	Casual
Cuisine	Vietnamese-Thai
Recommended for	Regular neighborhood

SARMA

Recommended by
Joshua Lewin,
Tony Maws

249 Pearl Street
Somerville
Massachusetts 02145
+1 6177644464
www.sarmarestaurant.com

Opening hours	Open 7 days
Credit cards	Accepted
Price range	Affordable
Style	Casual
Cuisine	Middle Eastern
Recommended for	Regular neighborhood

"It's close to our house and has terrific food! What more can you ask for?"—Tony Maws

TAPATIO

Recommended by
Daniel Bojorquez

82 Broadway
Somerville
Massachusetts 02145
+1 6176254119

Opening hours	Open 7 days
Reservation policy	No
Credit cards	Accepted
Price range	Budget
Style	Casual
Cuisine	Mexican
Recommended for	Bargain

TASTING COUNTER

Recommended by
Joshua Lewin

14 Tyler Street
Somerville
Massachusetts 02143
+1 6172996362
www.tastingcounter.com

Opening hours	Closed Monday and Sunday
Credit cards	Accepted
Price range	Expensive
Style	Smart casual
Cuisine	Modern American
Recommended for	High end

TRINA'S STARLITE LOUNGE

Recommended by
Daniel Bojorquez

3 Beacon Street
Somerville
Massachusetts 02143
+1 6175760006
www.trinastarlitelounge.com

Opening hours	Open 7 days
Reservation policy	No
Credit cards	Accepted
Price range	Affordable
Style	Casual
Cuisine	American
Recommended for	Breakfast

"It's the quintessential neighborhood spot. Comfortable, welcoming, and good food and drink." —Daniel Bojorquez

DEADHORSE HILL

Recommended by
Tony Maws

281 Main Street
Worcester
Massachusetts
+1 7744207107
www.deadhorsehill.com

Opening hours	Open 7 days
Credit cards	Accepted
Price range	Expensive
Style	Casual
Cuisine	Modern American
Recommended for	Wish I'd opened

BENNY'S DINER

Recommended by
Sarah Welch

1952 South Industrial Highway
Ann Arbor
Michigan 48104
+1 7346636302

Opening hours	Open 7 days
Reservation policy	No
Credit cards	Accepted
Price range	Budget
Style	Casual
Cuisine	American Diner
Recommended for	Breakfast

"When I am out of Detroit in my hometown of Ann Arbor, Benny's Diner is THE place I go. Exactly what you expect and need from a neighborhood greasy spoon."—Sarah Welch

MANI OSTERIA AND BAR

Recommended by
Sarah Welch

341 East Liberty Street
Ann Arbor
Michigan 48104
+1 7347696700
www.maniosteria.com

Opening hours	Closed Monday
Credit cards	Accepted
Price range	Affordable
Style	Casual
Cuisine	Modern American-Italian
Recommended for	Regular neighborhood

"This restaurant uses wood-fire cooking, something I learned a great deal about while working there and miss working with now. The food is simple, perfectly seasoned, and completely approachable." —Sarah Welch

SPENCER

Recommended by
Sarah Welch

113 East Liberty
Ann Arbor
Michigan 48104
+1 7343693979
www.spencerannarbor.com

Opening hours	Closed Tuesday
Reservation policy	No
Credit cards	Accepted
Price range	Affordable
Style	Casual
Cuisine	Modern American
Recommended for	Wish I'd opened

"Abby and Steve are old friends (biased again) and the food they make is so clearly crafted with love. They operate a counter-service-style restaurant that also does wine retail and, to me, it screams comfort and accessibility."—Sarah Welch

DEARBORN MEAT MARKET

Recommended by
Andy Hollyday

7721 Schaefer Road
Dearborn
Michigan 48126
+1 3135818820
www.dearbornmeatmarket.com

Opening hours	Open 7 days
Reservation policy	No
Credit cards	Accepted
Price range	Budget
Style	Casual
Cuisine	Middle Eastern
Recommended for	Local favorite

"It's not so much that beef kebabs and kafta sum up southeast Michigan, but great ethnic food at very reasonable prices is something we have in abundance across the region, and it's not something that a lot of outsiders understand. Madison Heights is a suburb known for Vietnamese, southwest Detroit has a lot of Mexican and other Latin flavors, and Dearborn has a sizeable Arab-American population. Dearborn Meat Market is a family-owned spot where they're grilling over hardwood embers and just making great, simple food. I just had the raw kafta with jalapeño and a drizzle of olive oil the other day, and it's outstanding."—Andy Hollyday

NEW YASMEEN BAKERY

Recommended by
Molly Mitchell

13900 Warren Avenue
Dearborn
Michigan 48126
+1 3135826035
www.yasmeenbakery.com

Opening hours	Open 7 days
Reservation policy	No
Credit cards	Accepted
Price range	Budget
Style	Casual
Cuisine	Middle Eastern
Recommended for	Local favorite

"What makes Detroit an amazing town is the diversity of people. Metro Detroit is home to one of the largest Middle Eastern populations in the US. New Yasmeen has the best chicken shawarma sandwich and you can also pick up baklava and pittas in the attached grocery store."—Molly Mitchell

ASTRO COFFEE

Recommended by
Andy Hollyday,
Molly Mitchell

2124 Michigan Avenue
Detroit
Michigan 48216
+1 3138080351
www.astrodetroit.com

Opening hours	Closed Monday
Reservation policy	No
Credit cards	Accepted
Price range	Affordable
Style	Casual
Cuisine	Café
Recommended for	Breakfast

"Astro is a genuinely cozy, warm, neighborhood café. It's been featured in publications from *Bon Appetit* to *Kinfolk* and it's never changed from all the attention. They rotate through an excellent selection of coffee from local and national roasters, but it's really the atmosphere and food that make it special. From the generally Australian/English-style pastries to seasonal egg sandwiches, to grain and legume salads, it's remarkably healthy, flavorful food in a perfect little neighborhood spot."—Andy Hollyday

BACCO

Recommended by
Andy Hollyday

29410 Northwestern Highway
Detroit
Michigan 48034
+1 2483566600
www.baccoristorante.com

Opening hours	Closed Sunday
Credit cards	Accepted
Price range	Expensive
Style	Smart casual
Cuisine	Italian
Recommended for	High end

"Bacco is one of the longest standing fine-dining spots in metro Detroit. Superb Italian food made with outstanding ingredients. Chef Luciano was doing farm-to-table before it was a buzzword and before anyone in Detroit cared what that meant, let alone before everyone realized that 'farm-to-table' just means 'good common-sense sourcing'."
—Andy Hollyday

BAKER'S KEYBOARD LOUNGE
Recommended by
Molly Mitchell

20510 Livernois Avenue
Detroit
Michigan 48221
+1 3133456300
www.theofficialbakerskeyboardlounge.com

Opening hours...Closed Monday
Credit cards..Accepted
Price range..Affordable
Style..Smart casual
Cuisine...Southern American
Recommended for...Late night

"One of the oldest jazz clubs in the country, where you can fill up on fried chicken, mac and cheese, pinto beans, and collard greens."—Molly Mitchell

BUCHAREST GRILL
Recommended by
Marc Djozlija

2684 East Jefferson Avenue
Detroit
Michigan 48207
+1 3139653111
www.bucharestgrill.com

Opening hours..Open 7 days
Reservation policy...No
Credit cards..Accepted
Price range...Budget
Style..Casual
Cuisine.................................Middle Eastern-Romanian
Recommended for...Bargain

"Delicious shawarmas and fresh fattoush salads."
—Marc Djozlija

BUDDY'S PIZZA
Recommended by
Andy Hollyday

17125 Conant Street
Detroit
Michigan 48212
+1 3138929001
www.buddyspizza.com

Opening hours..Open 7 days
Reservation policy...No
Credit cards..Accepted
Price range..Affordable
Style..Casual
Cuisine..Pizza
Recommended for..Local favorite

"A classic 'Detroit style' pizza spot that's been franchised, but the original is still great."
—Andy Hollyday

CHARTREUSE KITCHEN & COCKTAILS
Recommended by
Andy Hollyday

Suite D
15 East Kirby Street
Detroit
Michigan 48202
+1 3138183915
www.chartreusekc.com

Opening hours.......................Closed Monday and Sunday
Credit cards..Accepted
Price range..Affordable
Style..Casual
Cuisine...Modern American
Recommended for...............................Regular neighborhood

"I'm fortunate that it's walking distance from my house and I love that Chef Doug shares a lot of the same relationships with local farmers that I have. Everything is very fresh, very seasonal, and well executed. Sandy and Heather, the owners, are two of the nicest, most generous people in the business, and it shows in the attitude of everyone who works there. It's a genuine treat having this so nearby."
—Andy Hollyday

DETROIT INSTITUTE OF BAGELS
Recommended by
Sarah Welch

1236 Michigan Avenue
Detroit
Michigan 48226
+1 3134449342
www.detroitinstituteofbagels.com

Opening hours..Open 7 days
Reservation policy...No
Credit cards..Accepted
Price range...Budget
Style..Casual
Cuisine...Bagels
Recommended for...............................Regular neighborhood

"I LOVE Detroit Institute of Bagels for a quick bite."
—Sarah Welch

DULY'S PLACE

Recommended by
Marc Djozlija

5458 Vernor Highway
Detroit
Michigan 48209
+1 3135543076

Opening hours	Open 7 days
Reservation policy	No
Credit cards	Not accepted
Price range	Budget
Style	Casual
Cuisine	Diner
Recommended for	Late night

"Small, twenty-four-hour diner in southwest Detroit with great cheap eats."—Marc Djozlija

EL ASADOR

Recommended by
Marc Djozlija,
Andy Hollyday

1312 Springwells Street
Detroit
Michigan 48655
+1 3132972360
www.elasadordetroit.com

Opening hours	Open 7 days
Credit cards	Accepted
Price range	Affordable
Style	Casual
Cuisine	Mexican
Recommended for	Local favorite

"Southwest Detroit has a huge Latino population and this restaurant is the best. *Queso fundido* (melted cheese with chorizo), tortilla soup, and lobster quesadilla are a must."—Marc Djozlija

HONEST JOHN'S

Recommended by
Marc Djozlija
Sarah Welch

488 Selden Street
Detroit
Michigan 48201
+1 3138325646
www.honestjohnsdetroit.com

Opening hours	Open 7 days
Reservation policy	No
Credit cards	Accepted
Price range	Affordable
Style	Casual
Cuisine	American
Recommended for	Late night

"Honest John's is a stand-by for late-night sandwiches, or even tater-tot nachos or 'tatchos' (which I should be embarrassed about ordering, but

am totally not). Otherwise, late-night food is a Detroit category in desperate need of expansion."
—Sarah Welch

HYGRADE DELI

Recommended by
Marc Djozlija

3640 Michigan Avenue
Detroit
Michigan 48216
+1 3138946620
www.hygradedeli.com

Opening hours	Closed Sunday
Reservation policy	No
Credit cards	Accepted
Price range	Budget
Style	Casual
Cuisine	Diner-Deli
Recommended for	Breakfast

"I love the corned beef there, especially in the corned beef and American cheese omelette—I could eat it every day."—Marc Djozlija

IVANHOE CAFÉ

Recommended by
Molly Mitchell

5249 Joseph Campau Avenue
Detroit
Michigan 48211
+1 3139255335

Opening hours	Closed Saturday to Monday
Credit cards	Accepted
Price range	Affordable
Style	Casual
Cuisine	Polish-American
Recommended for	Local favorite

"Ivanhoe Café is tucked away in the North Poletown neighborhood. The walls are covered in memorabilia and you get pickles and coleslaw automatically with your meal."—Molly Mitchell

LAFAYETTE CONEY ISLAND

Recommended by
Marc Djozlija,
Andy Hollyday

118 West Lafayette Boulevard
Detroit
Michigan 48226
+1 3139648198

Opening hours	Open 7 days
Reservation policy	No
Credit cards	Not accepted
Price range	Budget
Style	Casual
Cuisine	Diner
Recommended for	Late night

"The classic late-night food in Detroit is the coney dog. You can find countless arguments online and in print about Lafayette coneys versus American coneys versus Duly's Tavern's coneys. And everyone has their opinion on why Lafayette is the best or why Duly's doesn't get enough love. There are reasons to love all three, but if you can only try one, head to Lafayette."
—Andy Hollyday

LONDON CHOP HOUSE

Recommended by
Marc Djozlija

155 Congress Street
Detroit
Michigan 48226
+1 3139620277
www.thelondonchophouse.com

Opening hours	Closed Sunday
Credit cards	Accepted
Price range	Affordable
Style	Smart casual
Cuisine	Steakhouse
Recommended for	High end

"Old-school steakhouse with big steaks and big red wines. Elegant setting, located in the basement of a historic building with a cigar bar upstairs"
—Marc Djozlija

NEMO'S

Recommended by
Marc Djozlija

1384 Michigan Avenue
Detroit
Michigan 48226
+1 3139653180
www.nemosdetroit.com

Opening hours	Open 7 days
Reservation policy	No
Credit cards	Accepted
Price range	Budget
Style	Casual
Cuisine	American Sports Bar
Recommended for	Wish I'd opened

"My father used to frequent here when it was down the street from the old Tiger Stadium. A quintessential sports bar—a Detroit staple with the best burger in town."—Marc Djozlija

PARKS & REC DINER

Recommended by
Ana Roš

1942 Grand River Avenue
Detroit
Michigan 48226
+1 3134468370
www.parksandrecdiner.com

Opening hours	Open 7 days
Credit cards	Accepted
Price range	Affordable
Style	Casual
Cuisine	Diner
Recommended for	Breakfast

"At Parks & Rec Diner, the food is more inventive and a little less traditional."—Ana Roš

PUPUSERÍA Y SALVADOREÑO

Recommended by
Molly Mitchell,
Sarah Welch

3149 Livernois Avenue
Detroit
Michigan 48210
+1 3138994020

Opening hours	Open 7 days
Reservation policy	No
Credit cards	Accepted
Price range	Budget
Style	Casual
Cuisine	Salvadoran
Recommended for	Local favorite

"Detroit is pretty widely known for its large Hispanic population. After experiencing my first *pupusa* (corn tortilla with a savory filling) in New York, I have been on a mission to try the huge variety of *pupusas* out there. These are some of my favorites I've come across. They are HUGE, soft and full of whatever you choose to put in them."—Sarah Welch

RED HOOK

Recommended by
Molly Mitchell

8025 Agnes Street
Detroit
Michigan 48214
+1 7189643729

Opening hours	Open 7 days
Reservation policy	No
Credit cards	Accepted
Price range	Budget
Style	Casual
Cuisine	Café
Recommended for	Breakfast

"A cozy neighborhood spot."—Molly Mitchell

ROAST

Recommended by
Molly Mitchell

1128 Washington Boulevard
Detroit
Michigan 48226
+1 3139612500
www.roastdetroit.com

Opening hours	Open 7 days
Credit cards	Accepted
Price range	Expensive
Style	Smart casual
Cuisine	Steakhouse
Recommended for	High end

"We used to go to Roast all the time because my cousin worked there and would give us a great deal on drinks. I recommend the burger, which is so tender and well-seasoned."—Molly Mitchell

ROSE'S FINE FOODS

Recommended by
James Rigato,
Sarah Welch

10551 Jefferson Avenue East
Detroit
Michigan 48214
+1 3133097947
www.rosesfinefood.com

Opening hours	Open 7 days
Reservation policy	No
Credit cards	Accepted
Price range	Affordable
Style	Casual
Cuisine	Diner
Recommended for	Breakfast

"A rehabbed diner that serves local and seasonal fare with a focus on pastry, preservation, and a commitment to neighborhood improvement." —James Rigato

Established by cousins Molly Mitchell and Lucy Carnaghi, and with a menu inspired by gatherings on their grandparents' farm, Rose's Fine Foods is unashamedly a family affair. There is everything you'd expect from a local diner but here, it's elevated to a much higher standard. As well as the usual fare, the lunch menu provides dishes such as apple-braised cider chicken with barbecue mustard (called "The Mustard Cluck"—the goofy names are part of its "mom-and-pop" charm). You cannot leave without trying the signature dessert, "Crybabies"—house-baked potato donuts glazed with maple and orange zest or wild raspberries. The diner's commitment to paying employees a living wage is admirable; tips are distributed evenly among the back-room and front-house staff, with a portion sent to Detroit-based charities.

SELDEN STANDARD

Recommended by
Marc Djozlija,
James Rigato,
Sarah Welch

3921 Second Avenue
Detroit
Michigan 48201
+1 3134385055
www.seldenstandard.com

Opening hours	Open 7 days
Credit cards	Accepted
Price range	Affordable
Style	Casual
Cuisine	European-American
Recommended for	Regular neighborhood

"Chef Andy carries the torch of a Detroit destination, chef-owned restaurant, with a seasonal and ethically sourced menu. As crazy as my schedule is I'll sometimes find myself eating there twice a week." —James Rigato

A few years ago, no one could have predicted that out of a neglected, graffitied, corner block would spring one of the city's finest restaurants, leading a gastronomic revival throughout Detroit. No one, perhaps, except Selden Standard's enthusiastic owners Andy Hollyday and Evan Hansen. With a focus on reinventing the term "New American cuisine", and a rigid farm-to-fork policy, the menu offers a selection of small plates made with seasonal, rustic produce. The dishes are bite-sized, and for good reason: you'll want to share as much as possible to get the full breadth of what is on offer. The wines are as carefully chosen as the ingredients, with a good selection from smaller, more artisan vineyards. It's easy to see why Selden Standard was awarded Detroit's restaurant of the year in 2015 and 2016 by Detroit Free Press and Hour Detroit respectively.

SHANGRI LA MIDTOWN

Recommended by
Marc Djozlija

4710 Class Avenue
Detroit
Michigan 48201
+1 3139747669
www.midtownshangri-la.com

Opening hours	Closed Sunday
Credit cards	Accepted
Price range	Budget
Style	Casual
Cuisine	Cantonese
Recommended for	Regular neighborhood

"I like to have lunch there on a regular basis. Quick, easy, cheap, and good."—Marc Djozlija

SLOWS BARBEQUE

Recommended by
Marc Djozlija

2138 Michigan Avenue
Detroit
Michigan 48216
+1 3139629828
www.slowsbarbq.com

Opening hours	Open 7 days
Credit cards	Accepted
Price range	Affordable
Style	Casual
Cuisine	American Barbecue
Recommended for	Regular neighborhood

SUPINO PIZZERIA

Recommended by
Marc Djozlija,
Andy Hollyday

2457 Russell Street
Detroit
Michigan 48207
+1 3135677879
www.supinopizzeria.com

Opening hours	Closed Sunday and Monday
Credit cards	Accepted
Price range	Affordable
Style	Casual
Cuisine	Pizza
Recommended for	Regular neighborhood

"On the less expensive side, Supino Pizzeria in Detroit's Eastern Market makes some of the best pizza in the United States, no question. It's not a New York-style pie, nor is it traditionally Italian. Dave, the owner-chef, really has made his own style of pie that's delicious."—Andy Hollyday

TAQUERIA EL REY

Recommended by
Molly Mitchell

4730 West Vernor Highway
Detroit
Michigan 48209
+1 3133573094
www.taqueria-elrey.com

Opening hours	Open 7 days
Reservation policy	No
Credit cards	Not accepted
Price range	Budget
Style	Casual
Cuisine	Mexican
Recommended for	Bargain

"Great beans and you can get a half-chicken dinner for $7 (£5)—can't beat that."—Molly Mitchell

THE TELWAY

Recommended by
James Rigato

27000 John R Road
Detroit
Michigan 48071
+1 2485457962

Opening hours	Open 7 days
Reservation policy	No
Credit cards	Not accepted
Price range	Budget
Style	Casual
Cuisine	Diner
Recommended for	Late night

"A decades-old institution with the best sliders around."—James Rigato

TELWAY HAMBURGERS

Recommended by
Sarah Welch

6820 Michigan Avenue
Detroit
Michigan 48210
+1 3138432146

Opening hours	Open 7 days
Reservation policy	No
Credit cards	Not accepted
Price range	Budget
Style	Casual
Cuisine	Burgers
Recommended for	Bargain

"$7 (£5) hamburgers served twenty-four hours a day. Need I say more? Oh, coffee and sweet rolls too."
—Sarah Welch

THUY TRANG

Recommended by
Andy Hollyday

30491 John R Road
Detroit
Michigan 48071
+1 2485887823

Opening hours	Closed Tuesday
Reservation policy	No
Credit cards	Accepted
Price range	Budget
Style	Casual
Cuisine	Vietnamese
Recommended for	Local favorite

TRINOSOPHES

Recommended by
Sarah Welch

1464 Gratiot Avenue
Detroit
Michigan 48207
+1 3137376606
www.trinosophes.com

Opening hours	Closed Monday
Reservation policy	No
Credit cards	Accepted
Price range	Affordable
Style	Casual
Cuisine	Modern American
Recommended for	Breakfast

"Well, I will be honest, my best friend is the chef so I am probably biased but the food is somehow ALWAYS exactly what I am in the mood for. She sources locally, uses grains and legumes in ways I did not know possible, and always hooks me up with extra eggs (I am addicted)."—Sarah Welch

AMAR PIZZA

Recommended by
Molly Mitchell

12195 Joseph Campau Avenue
Hamtramck
Michigan 48212
+1 3133660980
www.amarpizza.com

Opening hours	Open 7 days
Reservation policy	No
Credit cards	Accepted
Price range	Affordable
Style	Casual
Cuisine	Pizza
Recommended for	Regular neighborhood

"Amar Pizza in Hamtramck is amazing. I love the spicy beef pizza with plenty of cilantro (coriander)."
—Molly Mitchell

YEMEN CAFE

Recommended by
Andy Hollyday

8740 Joseph Campau Avenue
Hamtramck
Michigan 48212
+1 3138714349

Opening hours	Open 7 days
Reservation policy	No
Credit cards	Accepted
Price range	Affordable
Style	Casual
Cuisine	Yemeni
Recommended for	Bargain

"Yemen Café is a true original. While they recently relocated to a bigger space with a bigger menu, the focus is still on traditional cuisine and on serving Yemeni men from the neighborhood during dinner hours. It's open late and it's become a cult favorite in town for its singular approach: lamb cooked in a million ways; poultry; beans; and eggs for breakfast. It's inexpensive for the quality and quantity."—Andy Hollyday

LUIGI'S ORIGINAL

Recommended by
Andy Hollyday

36691 Jefferson Avenue
Harrison Township
Michigan 48045
+1 5864687711
www.luigisoriginal.com

Opening hours	Open 7 days
Reservation policy	No
Credit cards	Accepted
Price range	Affordable
Style	Casual
Cuisine	Pizza
Recommended for	Local favorite

"East-siders will tell you it's the best."—Andy Hollyday

LOUI'S PIZZA

Recommended by
Andy Hollyday

23141 Dequindre Road
Hazel Park
Michigan 48030
+1 2485471711
www.louispizza.net

Opening hours	Closed Monday and Tuesday
Reservation policy	No
Credit cards	Accepted
Price range	Affordable
Style	Casual
Cuisine	Pizza
Recommended for	Local favorite

MABEL GRAY

Recommended by
Andy Hollyday,
Sarah Welch

23825 John R Road
Hazel Park
Michigan 48030
+1 2483984300
www.mabelgraykitchen.com

Opening hours	Closed Monday and Sunday
Credit cards	Accepted
Price range	Affordable
Style	Smart casual
Cuisine	Modern American
Recommended for	High end

"Mabel Gray epitomizes good sourcing and letting the product drive the menu. James changes it frequently—sometimes daily—based on what's available and on his limited storage space. He's a creative chef with a diverse approach to food. It's kind of an old converted diner-style space, much like a lot of our spots. It's a casual restaurant, but his thoughtfulness, creativity, and quality of food, accompanied by a solid wine program puts it in the uppermost echelon of Michigan restaurants."—Andy Hollyday

Alice Mabel Gray was a folklore legend known as "Diana of the Dunes" who, unwilling to be bound by society's mores, lived alone in the Michigan woods. Chef James Rigato's homage to her is equally free spirited. Housed in a former diner in a blue-collar Detroit suburb, Rigato's focus is both on showcasing the bounty of Michigan and its farms and telling his own hardscrabble story. There's no set menu in the forty-three-seat restaurant. But over eight courses for the tasting menu (recommended) Rigato serves pork belly with green apple, mustard, fennel, and beet (beetroot) miso; or Sunseed Farm carrots with beer glaze, pickled mustard seeds, dill, and powdered vinegar, depending on what arrives that morning.

AJISHIN

Recommended by
Andy Hollyday

42270 Grand River Avenue
Novi
Michigan 48375
+1 2483809850

Opening hours	Open 7 days
Reservation policy	No
Credit cards	Accepted
Price range	Affordable
Style	Casual
Cuisine	Japanese
Recommended for	Local favorite

O.W.L.

Recommended by
James Rigato

27302 Woodward Avenue
Royal Oak
Michigan 48067
+1 2488086244

Opening hours	Open 7 days
Reservation policy	No
Credit cards	Accepted
Price range	Budget
Style	Casual
Cuisine	Mexican-Diner
Recommended for	Late night

"Twenty-four hour Mexican diner with counter seating and daily tacos. Chef Pedro is a beast and everything from their chilaquiles to their tortas and salsas are perfect for late-night nosh."—James Rigato

BACCO RISTORANTE

Recommended by
James Rigato

29410 Northwestern Highway
Southfield
Michigan 48034
+1 2483566600
www.baccoristorante.com

Opening hours	Closed Sunday
Credit cards	Accepted
Price range	Affordable
Style	Smart casual
Cuisine	Italian
Recommended for	High end

"Amazing Italian food with phenomenal service and a stellar wine program."—James Rigato

VENTIMIGLIA ITALIAN FOODS

Recommended by
Andy Hollyday

35197 Dodge Park
Sterling Heights
Michigan 48312
+1 5869790828
www.ventimigliafoods.com

Opening hours	Open 7 days
Reservation policy	No
Credit cards	Accepted
Price range	Budget
Style	Casual
Cuisine	Italian-Deli
Recommended for	Wish I'd opened

"I love pasta. We make it all by hand at our restaurant and I have to hold myself back from putting too much on the menu. And more than that, I just love that hand-made, old-school Italian-market way of doing things. And that's what Ventimiglia is—it's a market where old Italian home cooks can buy their semolina in bulk and where you can find great oils, but it's also got a great deli counter and foods section where you can get those homemade pastas and where they have a video about making arancini on their website. I'd love to have a little spot like this."—Andy Hollyday

TRATTORIA STELLA

Recommended by
James Rigato

1200 West 11th Street
Traverse City
Michigan 49684
+1 2319298989
www.offthemaphospitality.com

Opening hours	Open 7 days
Credit cards	Accepted
Price range	Affordable
Style	Casual
Cuisine	Mediterranean
Recommended for	Worth the travel

SHAKE SHACK

Recommended by
Val Cantu,
Doug Flicker

332 North Garden
East Bloomington
Bloomington
Minnesota 55425
+1 952-466-6056
www.shakeshack.com

Opening hours	Open 7 days
Reservation policy	No
Credit cards	Accepted
Price range	Budget
Style	Casual
Cuisine	American
Recommended for	Wish I'd opened

"Even more American than guns and apple pie are Shacks and burgers. I'm fascinated by what went from a cart in Central park to a worldwide success. The brilliance of Danny Meyer's ability to create Eleven Madison Park and Shake Shack is nuts."—Doug Flicker

SHARAKU

Recommended by
Sarah Welch

6159 Haggerty Road
West Bloomfield Township
Michigan 48322
+1 2489601888

Opening hours	Open 7 days
Credit cards	Accepted
Price range	Affordable
Style	Smart casual
Cuisine	Japanese-Sushi
Recommended for	High end

"Perfectly seasoned sushi rice, beautifully cut fish, and the two sweetest old men preparing your meal for you with effortless grace. I love treating myself to sushi here whenever I can. A truly hidden gem."
—Sarah Welch

GRAND SZECHUAN

Recommended by
Doug Flicker

Valley West Shopping Center
10602 France Avenue South
Bloomington
Minnesota 55437
+1 9528886507
www.grandszechuanmn.com

Opening hours	Open 7 days
Credit cards	Accepted
Price range	Budget
Style	Casual
Cuisine	Szechuan
Recommended for	Regular neighborhood

"I was brought up on truly bad American-Chinese food—always take out (take away), no less. When I started cooking and exploring food it was the logical first step. Szechuan cuisine just hits a cord with me. It's visually stunning and amazingy complex. The cooking at Grand Szechuan is simply top notch."
—Doug Flicker

KAFFE STUGA

Recommended by
Erick Harcey

43821 Forest Boulevard
Harris
Minnesota 55032
+1 6516749958

Opening hours	Open 7 days
Credit cards	Accepted
Price range	Affordable
Style	Casual
Cuisine	American-Swedish
Recommended for	Regular neighborhood

"It was started by my grandpa Willard. Eating here brings me back to so many memories growing up."
—Eric Harcey

MINNEAPOLIS: SEE PAGES 992–1003

COOK

Recommended by
Thomas Boemer

1124 Payne Avenue
St. Paul
Minnesota 55130
+1 6517561787
www.cookstp.com

Opening hours	Open 7 days
Reservation policy	No
Credit cards	Accepted
Price range	Affordable
Style	Casual
Cuisine	American-Korean
Recommended for	Breakfast

"A righteous cross-section of classic American breakfast and Korean fare. Incredible pancakes!"
—Thomas Boemer

MUCCI'S ITALIAN

Recommended by
Thomas Boemer

786 Randolph Avenue
St. Paul
Minnesota 55102
+1 6513302245
www.muccisitalian.com

Opening hours	Closed Monday
Reservation policy	No
Credit cards	Accepted
Price range	Affordable
Style	Casual
Cuisine	Italian-American
Recommended for	Wish I'd opened

"This is a great 'red sauce' Italian American restaurant with lasagne, deep-fried pizzas, and hand-made pastas. The right blend of comfort, culinary skill, and genuine service that really speaks to me."
—Thomas Boemer

THE STRIP CLUB MEAT & FISH

Recommended by
Thomas Boemer

378 Maria Avenue
St. Paul
Minnesota 55106
+1 6517936247
www.domeats.com

Opening hours	Closed Monday and Sunday
Credit cards	Accepted
Price range	Affordable
Style	Smart casual
Cuisine	Modern American
Recommended for	Regular neighborhood

"Incredible food and genuine hospitality for both brunch and dinner. We always feel like old friends when we dine there."—Thomas Boemer

BOWOOD FARMS

Recommended by
Cassy Vires

4605 Olive Street
St. Louis
Missouri 63108
+1 3144546868
www.bowoodfarms.com

Opening hours	Open 7 days
Credit cards	Accepted
Price range	Affordable
Style	Casual
Cuisine	Café
Recommended for	Wish I'd opened

"It is a combination garden shop, gift store, and café. The food is clean, simple, and served in the most beautiful of settings."—Cassy Vires

BRASSERIE BY NICHE

Recommended by
Cassy Vires

4580 Laclede Avenue
St. Louis
Missouri 63108
+1 3144540600
www.brasseriebyniche.com

Opening hours	Open 7 days
Credit cards	Accepted
Price range	Affordable
Style	Smart casual
Cuisine	French
Recommended for	High end

"Classic French cuisine, a great wine list and impeccable service. It's where we always go for a special occasion."—Cassy Vires

CHRIS' PANCAKE & DINING

Recommended by
Cassy Vires

5980 Southwest Avenue
St. Louis
Missouri 63139
+1 3146452088
www.chrispancakeanddining.com

Opening hours	Open 7 days
Reservation policy	No
Credit cards	Accepted
Price range	Budget
Style	Casual
Cuisine	American
Recommended for	Breakfast

"Great neighborhood spot. The food is hot and fast and the service staff know you by name."—Cassy Vires

SOHA BAR & GRILL

Recommended by
Cassy Vires

2605 Hampton Avenue
St. Louis
Missouri 63139
+1 3148027877
www.sohabar.com

Opening hours	Open 7 days
Credit cards	Accepted
Price range	Affordable
Style	Casual
Cuisine	American
Recommended for	Late night

"This place takes typical 'bar food' and improves it ten-fold! The tater tots, chicken wings, and mac and cheese are all fun and delicious."—Cassy Vires

EL TAPATIO

Recommended by
Cassy Vires

3279 Hampton Avenue
St. Louis
Missouri 63139
+1 3146457676

Opening hours	Open 7 days
Reservation policy	No
Credit cards	Accepted
Price range	Budget
Style	Casual
Cuisine	Mexican
Recommended for	Bargain

"Monday nights are $2 (£1.50) margaritas and $1 (80p) tacos. Can't beat that."—Cassy Vires

FRANK'S DELI & RESTAURANT

Recommended by
Matthew Gaudet

1406 Main Street
Asbury Park
New Jersey 07712
+1 7327756682
www.franksdelinj.com

Opening hours	Open 7 days
Reservation policy	No
Credit cards	Not accepted
Price range	Budget
Style	Casual
Cuisine	Breakfast-Deli
Recommended for	Breakfast

PONZIO'S

Recommended by
Greg Vernick

7 West Route 70
Cherry Hill
New Jersey 08034
+1 8564284808
www.ponzios.com

Opening hours	Open 7 days
Reservation policy	No
Credit cards	Accepted
Price range	Affordable
Style	Casual
Cuisine	Diner
Recommended for	Breakfast

"This place is the most perfect diner—I grew up going here and I still take my family."—Greg Vernick

SAGAMI

Recommended by
Townsend Wentz

37 West Crescent Boulevard
Collingswood
New Jersey 08108
+1 8568549773

Opening hours	Open 7 days
Credit cards	Accepted
Price range	Affordable
Style	Casual
Cuisine	Japanese
Recommended for	Regular neighborhood

"The sushi chefs at Sagami have been there for forty years, work six-days a week, lunch and dinner, and turn out pristine fish pieces. It's inspiring to watch."
—Townsend Wentz

ZEPPOLI

Recommended by
Greg Vernick

618 West Collings Avenue
Collingswood
New Jersey 08107
+1 8568542670
www.zeppolirestaurant.com

Opening hours	Closed Tuesday
Credit cards	Accepted
Price range	Affordable
Style	Smart casual
Cuisine	Italian
Recommended for	High end

"This isn't a blow-out price point, but it's where I go for special occasions—it's a cozy little Italian BYO."
—Greg Vernick

MOUNT KISCO DINER

Recommended by
Jesse Schenker

252 Main Street
Mount Kisco
New York 10549
+1 9146665676
www.mtkiscodiner.com

Opening hours	Open 7 days
Credit cards	Accepted
Price range	Affordable
Style	Casual
Cuisine	Diner
Recommended for	Breakfast

"Great quality, kid friendly, comfortable atmosphere."
—Jesse Schenker

NEW YORK CITY: SEE PAGES 1004–1047

BLUE HILL AT STONE BARNS

Recommended by
Angus An,
Sergey Berezutskiy, Fredrik Berselius,
Massimo Bottura, Sean Brock,
Daniel Burns, Andrea Carlson,
Enrico Crippa, Michael Friedman,
Peter Gilmore, Dan Graham,
Mehmet Gürs, Stephen Harris,
Sang Hoon Degeimbre, Daniel Humm, Aaron London,
Bruno Loubet, Cameron Mathews, Michael Meredith, Claus Meyer,
Jakob Mielcke, Christopher Millar, Khalid Mohammed,
Uwe Opocensky, Christian F. Puglisi, Missy Robbins,
Julien Royer, Francisco Ruano, Jorge Vallejo, Alla Wolf Tasker

630 Bedford Road
Pocantico Hills
New York 10591
+1 9143669600
www.bluehillfarm.com

Opening hours	Open 7 days
Credit cards	Accepted
Price range	Expensive
Style	Smart casual
Cuisine	Modern American
Recommended for	Worth the travel

"I find its philosophy and approach very inspiring. It's on a working farm so they have a very close relationship to their ingredients. Sustainability and land preservation are key to Dan Barber. I had the privilege of working with him one night at his wastED pop-up in London. I think the Blue Hill at Stone Barns approach has a lot to teach us and will ultimately inform the future restaurant industry."—Bruno Loubet

At his ten-year-old "farm-to-table" restaurant (the follow up to Blue Hill New York), Dan Barber sources ingredients solely within the Hudson Valley and mainly from the working farm and educational center on which the restaurant is based. Talk about fresh: guests even "cut their own" greens at the table. Barber's not called the "high priest of locavorism" for nothing. Menus arrive in list form, as an inventory of the day's harvest that reveals itself in a succession of elegant vegetable-led small plates. As a gastronomic experience, it's uplifting, edifying and lengthy: clear at least four hours for your multi-course Farmers' Feast.

BUXTON HALL BBQ

Recommended by
Jarrett Stieber

32 Banks Avenue
Asheville
North Carolina 28801
+1 8282327216
www.buxtonhall.com

Opening hours	Open 7 days
Credit cards	Accepted
Price range	Affordable
Style	Casual
Cuisine	American Barbecue
Recommended for	Worth the travel

PIZZERIA FAULISI

Recommended by
Andrea Reusing

215 East Chatham Street
Cary
North Carolina 27511
www.pizzeriafaulisi.com

Opening hours	Closed Monday and Tuesday
Reservation policy	No
Credit cards	Accepted
Price range	Affordable
Style	Casual
Cuisine	American-Italian
Recommended for	Regular neighborhood

"Extremely delicious and thoughtful American Italian with amazing vegetables. The pizzas are made from a combination of freshly milled local grains and Caputo flour."—Andrea Reusing

THE PIG

Recommended by
Andrea Reusing

630 Weaver Dairy Road #101
Chapel Hill
North Carolina 27514
+1 9199421133
www.thepigrestaurant.com

Opening hours	Closed Sunday
Reservation policy	No
Credit cards	Accepted
Price range	Budget
Style	Casual
Cuisine	American Barbecue
Recommended for	Bargain

"Pitmaster Sam Suchoff has dedicated The Pig to thoughtfully sourced meat and vegetables and also features eighteen-month country hams, hot dogs, bologna, country-fried tofu, and barbecued tempeh."—Andrea Reusing

ALEXANDER MICHAEL'S

Recommended by
Chris Coleman

401 West 9th Street
Charlotte
North Carolina 28202
+1 7043326789
www.almikestavern.com

Opening hours	Closed Sunday
Credit cards	Accepted
Price range	Affordable
Style	Casual
Cuisine	American-Pub
Recommended for	Regular neighborhood

"Great neighborhood tavern."—Chris Coleman

THE DIAMOND

Recommended by
Chris Coleman

1901 Commonwealth Avenue
Charlotte
North Carolina 28205
+1 7043758959
www.diamondcharlotte.com

Opening hours	Open 7 days
Reservation policy	No
Credit cards	Accepted
Price range	Affordable
Style	Casual
Cuisine	Diner
Recommended for	Late night

"I've never had anything here but the burger. It's fantastic."—Chris Coleman

EARL'S GROCERY

Recommended by
Chris Coleman

1609 Elizabeth Avenue
Charlotte
North Carolina 28204
+1 7043332757
www.earlsgrocery.com

Opening hours	Open 7 days
Reservation policy	No
Credit cards	Accepted
Price range	Affordable
Style	Casual
Cuisine	Modern American
Recommended for	Bargain

"The breakfast grits bowl is amazing and fairly cheap. You get old fashioned stone-ground grits, cheese, and a chow chow for $6 (£4), and can add an egg or bacon for $1 (80p)."—Chris Coleman

MIGUEL'S

Recommended by
Chris Coleman

4252 Business Center Drive
Charlotte
North Carolina 28214
+1 7043933890
www.miguelscharlotte.com

Opening hours	Open 7 days
Reservation policy	No
Credit cards	Accepted
Price range	Affordable
Style	Casual
Cuisine	Tex-Mex
Recommended for	Regular neighborhood

"Simple food at a family-friendly, family-run, hole in the wall. The salsa changes a little every time, which some see as inconsistent, but I see it as a sign they are making it fresh in-house."—Chris Coleman

NANA'S SOUL FOOD

Recommended by
Sean Brock

2908 Oaklake Boulevard
Charlotte
North Carolina 28208
+1 704-357-3700
www.nanassoulfoodkitchen.com

Opening hours	Open 7 days
Credit cards	Accepted
Price range	Budget
Style	Casual
Cuisine	American-Soul
Recommended for	Bargain

SHUFFLETOWN GRILL

Recommended by
Chris Coleman

10220 Rozzelles Ferry Road
Charlotte
North Carolina 28214
+1 7043991968
www.shuffletowngrill.com

Opening hours	Closed Sunday
Reservation policy	No
Credit cards	Accepted
Price range	Budget
Style	Casual
Cuisine	Diner
Recommended for	Breakfast

"Old school mom-and-pop diner. Great biscuits and gravy."—Chris Coleman

STAGIONI

Recommended by
Chris Coleman

715 Providence Road
Charlotte
North Carolina 28207
+1 7043728110
www.stagioniclt.com

Opening hours	Closed Sunday
Credit cards	Accepted
Price range	Affordable
Style	Smart casual
Cuisine	Modern Italian
Recommended for	High end

"We like to go here, get a bottle or two of great wine, and just graze through the menu. Fantastic modern Italian, house-made everything, open kitchen, and great space."—Chris Coleman

KINDRED

Recommended by
Chris Coleman

131 North Main Street
Davidson
North Carolina 28036
+1 9802315000
www.kindreddavidson.com

Opening hours	Closed Monday and Sunday
Credit cards	Accepted
Price range	Affordable
Style	Casual
Cuisine	Modern American
Recommended for	Local favorite

"Husband and wife team run Kindred, the most charming neighborhood restaurant ever. The food is killer, the atmosphere stellar, the service is warm and friendly."—Chris Coleman

GRADY'S BARBECUE

Recommended by
Paul Berglund

3096 Arrington Bridge Road
Dudley
North Carolina 28333
+1 9197357243

Opening hours	Closed Sunday to Tuesday
Reservation policy	No
Credit cards	Not accepted
Price range	Budget
Style	Casual
Cuisine	American Barbecue
Recommended for	Worth the travel

"The chopped pork platter at Grady's might be the single best meal I can think of."—Paul Berglund

SALTBOX

Recommended by
Andrea Reusing

608 North Mangum Street
Durham
North Carolina 27701
+1 9199088970
www.saltboxseafoodjoint.com

Opening hours	Closed Monday and Sunday
Reservation policy	No
Credit cards	Accepted
Price range	Affordable
Style	Casual
Cuisine	Seafood
Recommended for	Local favorite

"Chef Ricky Moore serves some of the best food in
North Carolina and he does it from a small seafood
shack with picnic tables and just one other cook.
Incredibly fresh fish (they close when they run out)
from the North Carolina coast. Fried mullet, flounder,
black drum, and specials like rockfish stew."
—Andrea Reusing

SCRATCH

Recommended by
Andrea Reusing

111 Orange Street
Durham
North Carolina 27701
+1 9199565200
www.piefantasy.com

Opening hours	Open 7 days
Reservation policy	No
Credit cards	Accepted
Price range	Affordable
Style	Casual
Cuisine	American
Recommended for	Breakfast

"Pie, pie, pie, with top-notch coffee and tea. And
every morning, freshly made Spanish tortilla, eggs
with kimchi, warm donuts, and empanadas."
—Andrea Reusing

POOLE'S DINER

Recommended by
Steven Sattersfield

426 South McDowell Street
Raleigh
North Carolina 27601
+1 9198324477
www.ac-restaurants.com

Opening hours	Open 7 days
Reservation policy	No
Credit cards	Accepted
Price range	Affordable
Style	Casual
Cuisine	Modern American
Recommended for	Wish I'd opened

Launched in 2007 by chef Ashley Christensen,
this downtown hot spot takes its name and diner
aesthetic from the building's original occupant—
a pie shop that was among the district's first
eateries. Christensen, who honed her talents in the
region's top kitchens, is one of the Southeast's most
hardworking young stars (with a local mini-empire
stretching to six venues), and here she turns out
an evolving chalkboard menu of unpretentious,
high-flavor, comfort food based on local seasonal
ingredients. Snug red-leather banquettes and
a double horseshoe-shaped bar underscore the
joint's appealing retro-chic vibe.

HERITAGE FOOD & DRINK

Recommended by
Chris Coleman

201 West South Main Street
Waxhaw
North Carolina 28173
+1 7048435236
www.heritagefoodanddrink.com

Opening hours	Closed Monday
Credit cards	Accepted
Price range	Affordable
Style	Smart casual
Cuisine	Modern American
Recommended for	Local favorite

"Paul Verica sources everything he serves from
as close to his location as possible (he's twenty
minutes from Charlotte in the small town, Waxhaw).
His style is playful, inventive, but not overly fussy
or staged. He represents the best of the local dining
movement."—Chris Coleman

YOURS TRULY

Recommended by
Christopher Hodgson

30 North Main Street
Chagrin Falls
Ohio 44022
+1 4402473232
www.ytr.com

Opening hours	Open 7 days
Reservation policy	No
Credit cards	Accepted
Price range	Affordable
Style	Casual
Cuisine	Breakfast
Recommended for	Breakfast

"Great small-town feel, in the heart of Chagrin falls.
The food is always incredible and after breakfast
you can walk it off by the falls and feed the ducks
whatever's left over."—Christopher Hodgson

PLEASE

Recommended by
David Posey

1405 Clay Street
Cincinnati
Ohio 45202
+1 5134058859
www.pleasecincinnati.com

Opening hours	Closed Sunday to Tuesday
Credit cards	Accepted
Price range	Expensive
Style	Smart casual
Cuisine	Modern American
Recommended for	Worth the travel

BIG AL'S DINER

Recommended by
Jonathon Sawyer

12600 Larchmere Boulevard
Cleveland
Ohio 44120
+1 2167918550

Opening hours	Open 7 days
Reservation policy	No
Credit cards	Accepted
Price range	Budget
Style	Casual
Cuisine	Diner
Recommended for	Breakfast

"Big Al's when hungover or sick for some soul
dinner fare or Bubbies pickles and matza."
—Jonathon Sawyer

THE BLACK PIG

Recommended by
Jonathon Sawyer

2801 Bridge Avenue
Cleveland
Ohio 44113
+1 2168627551
www.blackpigcle.com

Opening hours	Closed Monday
Credit cards	Accepted
Price range	Affordable
Style	Casual
Cuisine	French-American
Recommended for	Regular neighborhood

FIRE FOOD AND DRINK

Recommended by
Jonathon Sawyer

13220 Shaker Square
Cleveland
Ohio 44120
+1 2169213473
www.firefoodanddrink.com

Opening hours	Closed Monday
Credit cards	Accepted
Price range	Affordable
Style	Smart casual
Cuisine	Modern American
Recommended for	Regular neighborhood

"Chef Katz and Co. are some of the best-sourcing
chefs in Cleveland. From Aaron Miller's grass-fed
beef to bespoke onions, Fire has long been the most
consistent dinner in Cleveland. His team
is passionate."—Jonathon Sawyer

JACK'S DELI

Recommended by
Jonathon Sawyer

14490 Cedar Road
Cleveland
Ohio 44121
+1 2163825350
www.jacksdeliandrestaurant.com

Opening hours	Open 7 days
Reservation policy	No
Credit cards	Accepted
Price range	Affordable
Style	Casual
Cuisine	Deli
Recommended for	Breakfast

"A Cleveland guardian of time passed."
—Jonathon Sawyer

KOREA HOUSE

Recommended by
Molly Mitchell

3700 Superior Avenue
Cleveland
Ohio 44114
+1 2164310462
www.koreahousecleveland.com

Opening hours	Closed Monday
Credit cards	Accepted
Price range	Affordable
Style	Casual
Cuisine	Korean
Recommended for	Worth the travel

"Friends in Cleveland took me to this gem with the friendliest staff and incredible pickles. I can't stop getting the *dolsot* (Koren stone) bowl because it always comes out raging hot, so gets really crispy rice on the bottom."—Molly Mitchell

LI WAH DIM SUM

Recommended by
Jonathon Sawyer

2999 Payne Avenue #102
Cleveland
Ohio 44114
+1 2165899552
www.liwahrestaurant.com

Opening hours	Open 7 days
Credit cards	Accepted
Price range	Affordable
Style	Casual
Cuisine	Chinese
Recommended for	Breakfast

"The house-made soy milk is a must, and the bao buns and tendon salad."—Jonathon Sawyer

MIEGA KOREAN GRILL

Recommended by
Jonathon Sawyer

3820 Superior Avenue
Cleveland
Ohio 44114
+1 2164329200

Opening hours	Closed Monday
Credit cards	Accepted
Price range	Affordable
Style	Casual
Cuisine	Korean
Recommended for	Bargain

OHIO CITY PROVISIONS

Recommended by
Jonathon Sawyer

3208 Lorain Avenue
Cleveland
Ohio 44113
+1 2164652762
www.ohiocityprovisions.com

Opening hours	Open 7 days
Reservation policy	No
Credit cards	Accepted
Price range	Affordable
Style	Casual
Cuisine	Butcher-Grocery
Recommended for	Regular neighborhood

THE PLUM CAFÉ & KITCHEN

Recommended by
Jonathon Sawyer

4133 Lorain Avenue
Cleveland
Ohio 44113
+1 2169388711
www.theplumcafeandkitchen.com

Opening hours	Closed Sunday
Credit cards	Accepted
Price range	Affordable
Style	Casual
Cuisine	Modern American
Recommended for	Local favorite

"The Plum is a labour of love. The kitchen is led by Brett Sawyer, no relation to me, but a team alumni. The food is quirky, fun, and often fried with Japanese Michelin precision but hipster-stoner flair. Get anything Brett does with chicken skin, eggs, and order cocktails."—Jonathon Sawyer

RESTORE COLD PRESSED

Recommended by
Jonathon Sawyer

1001 Huron Road East
Cleveland
Ohio 44115
+1 2162176689
www.restorecoldpressed.com

Opening hours	Open 7 days
Reservation policy	No
Credit cards	Accepted
Price range	Affordable
Style	Casual
Cuisine	Vegan
Recommended for	Breakfast

"Seaweed, ginger, and tumeric shots; avocado toast; smoothie bowls and old-school oatmeal; Fetch Coffee from Duck-Rabbit roasters, and more. Always detox before you retox. They're great people, finding organic goods to press, blend, and pour in to your body for a bright and alert morning."—Jonathon Sawyer

SUPERIOR PHO

Recommended by
Jonathon Sawyer

3030 Superior Avenue #105
Cleveland
Ohio 44114
+1 2167817462
www.superiorpho.com

Opening hours	Closed Monday
Reservation policy	No
Credit cards	Accepted
Price range	Budget
Style	Casual
Cuisine	Vietnamese
Recommended for	Bargain

SZECHUAN CAFÉ

Recommended by
Christopher Hodgson

2999 Payne Avenue #142
Cleveland
Ohio 44114
+1 2165151111
www.szechuancafecleveland.com

Opening hours	Open 7 days
Credit cards	Accepted
Price range	Affordable
Style	Casual
Cuisine	Asian
Recommended for	Bargain

"Get the hot fish, thank me later."
—Christopher Hodgson

SZECHUAN GOURMET

Recommended by
Jonathon Sawyer

1735 East 36th Street
Cleveland
Ohio 44114
+1 2168819688

Opening hours	Open 7 days
Credit cards	Accepted
Price range	Budget
Style	Casual
Cuisine	Szechuan
Recommended for	Bargain

"Szechuan Gourmet speaks the fiery South Central Chinese provinces truth. Do not expect to be hand-held during this total immersion into Chinese Cleveland culture. Order more than you need (the leftovers are rivaled only by cold fried chicken) and if

you like the look of a plate on an adjoining table, ask for one. There are no courses or single portions, it's all meant to be shared. Definitely order the chilled beef tendon, cucumber salad, roasted peanuts, mustard green soup, sautéed snow pea shoots, cumin lamb shoulder, and mapo tofu. Get some cheap beers, jasmin tea, and you're dancing."—Jonathon Sawyer

TASTE OF KERALA

Recommended by
Jonathon Sawyer

5850 Mayfield Road
Cleveland
Ohio 44118
+1 4404619212
www.tasteofkeralam.com

Opening hours	Closed Monday
Reservation policy	No
Credit cards	Accepted
Price range	Budget
Style	Casual
Cuisine	Indian
Recommended for	Bargain

USHABU

Recommended by
Christopher Hodgson

2173 Professor Avenue
Cleveland
Ohio 44113
+1 2167131741
www.ushabu.com

Opening hours	Closed Monday
Credit cards	Accepted
Price range	Expensive
Style	Casual
Cuisine	Japanese
Recommended for	Late night

"It's amazing—hot pot but with incredible small plates. Unique flavors, and different from anything else around."—Christopher Hodgson

BIGA PIZZERIA

Recommended by
Jonathon Sawyer

9145 Chilecothe Road
Kirtland
Ohio 44094
+1 4403797313
www.bigapizzeria.net

Opening hours	Closed Monday and Sunday
Credit cards	Accepted
Price range	Affordable
Style	Casual
Cuisine	Pizza
Recommended for	Regular neighborhood

FLOUR

Recommended by
Christopher Hodgson

34205 Chagrin Boulevard
Moreland Hills
Ohio 44022
+1 2164643700
www.flourrestaurant.com

Opening hours	Open 7 days
Credit cards	Accepted
Price range	Affordable
Style	Casual
Cuisine	Italian
Recommended for	Regular neighborhood

"Great atmosphere and amazing food. Always some of the best Italian around. One of my favorite things is that they take new-age ways of cooking and blend them with classic preparations and dishes to create something familiar yet intriguing. They are also great with my daughter who has many food allergies—she loves going in and every time we drive by she begs to stop!"—Christopher Hodgson

CHEZ FRANCOIS

Recommended by
Christopher Hodgson

555 Main Street
Vermillion
Ohio 44089
+1 4409670630
www.chezfrancois.com

Opening hours	Closed Monday
Credit cards	Accepted
Price range	Expensive
Style	Formal
Cuisine	French
Recommended for	High end

"Best damn French and wine around! Right on the water, impeccable service."—Christopher Hodgson

ANTS PANTS CAFE

Recommended by
Greg Vernick

2212 South Street
Philadelphia
Pennsylvania 19146
+1 2158758002
www.antspantscafe.com

Opening hours	Open 7 days
Credit cards	Accepted
Price range	Affordable
Style	Casual
Cuisine	Australian Café
Recommended for	Regular neighborhood

BARCLAY PRIME

Recommended by
Peter Serpico

237 South 18th Street
Philadelphia
Pennsylvania 19103
+1 2157327560
www.barclayprime.me

Opening hours	Open 7 days
Credit cards	Accepted
Price range	Expensive
Style	Formal
Cuisine	American Steakhouse
Recommended for	High end

"It's a blow-out steakhouse. Tomahawk chops, Wagyu steaks, and a cheesesteak for over $100 (£80)."
—Peter Serpico

DAVID'S MAI LAI WAH

Recommended by
George Sabatino

1001 Race Street
Philadelphia
Pennsylvania 19107
+1 2156272610

Opening hours	Open 7 days
Reservation policy	No
Credit cards	Accepted
Price range	Affordable
Style	Casual
Cuisine	Chinese
Recommended for	Late night

"Ribs, dumplings, ginger and garlic sauce. And a shit ton of drunk assholes after 1.00 a.m.."—George Sabatino

DIZENGOFF

Recommended by
Townsend Wentz, Lee Wolen

1625 Sansom Street
Philadelphia
Pennsylvania 19103
+1 2158678181
www.dizengoffhummus.com

Opening hours	Open 7 days
Reservation policy	No
Credit cards	Accepted
Price range	Affordable
Style	Casual
Cuisine	Israeli
Recommended for	Wish I'd opened

"It's the best hummus I've ever had. It's an amazing concept that America has not seen before and done the right way with fantastic ingredients. I was able to work the pitta station for about thirty minutes while in town for a collaboration dinner and couldn't keep up with the demand, since they are packed out the door from the second they open."—Lee Wolen

THE DUTCH

Recommended by Townsend Wentz

1527 South 4th Street
Philadelphia
Pennsylvania 19147
+1 2157555600
www.thedutchphilly.com

Opening hours	Closed Monday
Reservation policy	No
Credit cards	Accepted
Price range	Affordable
Style	Casual
Cuisine	Dutch
Recommended for	Breakfast

"The creamed chipped beef on a waffle is the perfect breakfast."—Townsend Wentz

Born out of late-night, Champagne-fueled omelette contests—yes, these things happen—in 2016, two chefs opened a modest breakfast spot, since turned breakfast Mecca. The chefs—Lee Styer of Fond and Joncarl Lachman of Noord—weave together their own stories deliciously. Lachman is from Amsterdam. Styer is from Pennsylvania Dutch Country, a swath of tremendous farming land in the state's center. At The Dutch, they reinvent traditional Pennsylvania Dutch cooking with a northern European twist. Bologna finds a new home, with cream cheese, in a fluffy omelette. Big skillet-cooked Dutch pancakes sate those who wait in orderly lines. But dinner is not neglected. Crowded into baby-blue church-pew banquettes, locals dig into chow-chow and mac-and-cheese cornbread, and devour expert burgers and crispy chicken and buttermilk waffles.

FITZWATER CAFÉ

Recommended by Peter Serpico

728 South 7th Street
Philadelphia
Pennsylvania 19147
+1 2156290428

Opening hours	Open 7 days
Credit cards	Not accepted
Price range	Affordable
Style	Casual
Cuisine	Café-Bakery
Recommended for	Breakfast

"Fitzwater feels like an old-school neighborhood Philly breakfast spot. No bells and whistles, just nicely

cooked food at a very reasonable price. They only do breakfast and lunch every day and are cash only."
—Peter Serpico

HIGH STREET ON MARKET

Recommended by Peter Serpico, Townsend Wentz

308 Market Street
Philadelphia
Pennsylvania 19106
+1 2156250988
www.highstreetonmarket.com

Opening hours	Open 7 days
Credit cards	Accepted
Price range	Affordable
Style	Casual
Cuisine	American
Recommended for	Local favorite

"High Street is an all-day restaurant serving high-quality breakfast, lunch, and dinner. They do a great job on all fronts, while showcasing local farms and creativity during every meal."—Peter Serpico

"Grains, wonderful grains" might be the opening line in a celebratory ode to restaurateur Ellen Yin and chef Eli Kulp's temple to bread, High Street on Market. But what begins in the pre-dawn hours, when baker Alex Bois begins work on his imaginative pastries—like chocolate cream cheese croissants and kale and ricotta hand pies—extends through the day, getting more and more creative as the hours roll by. Breakfast sandwiches include the Hickory Town, featuring Lancaster bologna, a farm egg, Amish horseradish cheddar, and gherkin mayo. Lunch includes what is widely thought of as the country's best pastrami on rye sandwich and a genre-bending charred broccoli salad. And at night, the cosy wood-heavy room, dominated by a map of historic Philadelphia, is filled with adventurous diners drawn to Kulp's clever menu (farmer's cheese dumpling pasta with rabbit sausage and absinthe broth, anyone?) The map may be old but this room contains the future of Philadelphia dining.

HUNGRY PIGEON

Recommended by
George Sabatino

743 South 4th Street
Philadelphia
Pennsylvania 19147
+1 2152782736
www.hungrypigeon.com

Opening hours	Open 7 days
Reservation policy	No
Credit cards	Accepted
Price range	Affordable
Style	Casual
Cuisine	American
Recommended for	Breakfast

"Unbelievable pastries. Like, really unbelievable."
—George Sabatino

ITV

Recommended by
Townsend Wentz

1615 East Passyunk Avenue
Philadelphia
Pennsylvania 19148
+1 2678580669
www.itvphilly.com

Opening hours	Closed Sunday
Credit cards	Accepted
Price range	Affordable
Style	Casual
Cuisine	Bar-Small plates
Recommended for	Local favorite

"A fantastic, elegant bar by Chef Nick Elmi. Excellent cocktails, wine, and food makes this an easy spot to stop in for any reason."—Townsend Wentz

KANELLA

Recommended by
Peter Serpico

757 Front Street
Philadelphia
Pennsylvania 19147
+1 2156448949

Opening hours	Closed Monday
Credit cards	Accepted
Price range	Affordable
Style	Casual
Cuisine	Cypriot
Recommended for	Regular neighborhood

"Konstantinos' food is pure and delicious. It's everyday food in a casual setting, and the staff are always friendly."—Peter Serpico

KHYBER PASS PUB

Recommended by
Greg Vernick

56 South Second Street
Philadelphia
Pennsylvania 19106
+1 2152385888
www.khyberpasspub.com

Opening hours	Open 7 days
Reservation policy	No
Credit cards	Accepted
Price range	Affordable
Style	Casual
Cuisine	American Gastropub
Recommended for	Late night

MAMA'S VEGETARIAN

Recommended by
Greg Vernick

18 South 20th Street
Philadelphia
Pennsylvania 19103
+1 2157510477

Opening hours	Closed Saturday
Reservation policy	No
Credit cards	Not accepted
Price range	Budget
Style	Casual
Cuisine	Middle Eastern-Vegetarian
Recommended for	Regular neighborhood

MORIMOTO

Recommended by
Peter Serpico

723 Chestnut Street
Philadelphia
Pennsylvania 19106
+1 2154139070
www.morimotorestaurant.com

Opening hours	Open 7 days
Credit cards	Accepted
Price range	Expensive
Style	Smart casual
Cuisine	Japanese
Recommended for	High end

"It's the original one in Philly. The best sushi, with seasonal Tsukiji Market fish always available."
—Peter Serpico

NAM PHUONG

Recommended by
Peter Serpico

1100 Washington Avenue
Philadelphia
Pennsylvania 19147
+1 2154680410
www.namphuongphilly.com

Opening hours	Open 7 days
Credit cards	Accepted but not AMEX
Price range	Affordable
Style	Casual
Cuisine	Vietnamese
Recommended for	Bargain

"$5 (£3) roast pork banh mi on house-made bread."
—Peter Serpico

NEW WAVE CAFÉ

Recommended by
Peter Serpico

784 South 3rd Street
Philadelphia
Pennsylvania 19147
+1 2159228484
www.newwavecafe.com

Opening hours	Open 7 days
Reservation policy	No
Credit cards	Accepted
Price range	Affordable
Style	Casual
Cuisine	American Bar
Recommended for	Late night

"They have such genuine staff at New Wave.
The owners are always working and it's a great
Philadelphia establishment that's been open
for over thirty years."—Peter Serpico

PARC

Recommended by
Greg Vernick

227 South 18th Street
Philadelphia
Pennsylvania 19103
+1 2155452262
www.parc-restaurant.com

Opening hours	Open 7 days
Credit cards	Accepted
Price range	Affordable
Style	Casual
Cuisine	French
Recommended for	Regular neighborhood

READING TERMINAL MARKET

Recommended by
Greg Vernick

51 North 12th Street
Philadelphia
Pennsylvania 19107
+1 2159222317
www.readingterminalmarket.org

Opening hours	Open 7 days
Reservation policy	No
Credit cards	Accepted
Price range	Affordable
Style	Casual
Cuisine	Chinese
Recommended for	Bargain

"I go to Sang Kee—a great noodle soup counter—and
get the roast duck or pork and put it in soup. It was my
wife's number one craving when she was pregnant."
—Greg Vernick

ROYAL IZAKAYA

Recommended by
Greg Vernick,
Townsend Wentz

780 South 2nd Street
Philadelphia
Pennsylvania 19147
+1 2679099002
www.royalsushiandizakaya.com

Opening hours	Open 7 days
Reservation policy	No
Credit cards	Accepted
Price range	Affordable
Style	Casual
Cuisine	Japanese
Recommended for	Late night

"Royal Izakaya is a new spot and is rivaling others for
best Japanese, best sushi, and best late-night."
—Townsend Wentz

SHIAO LAN KUNG

Recommended by
Townsend Wentz

930 Race Street
Philadelphia
Pennsylvania 19107
+1 215928-0282

Opening hours	Closed Monday
Credit cards	Accepted
Price range	Affordable
Style	Casual
Cuisine	Cantonese
Recommended for	Late night

"After a long service, this is the spot for late-night Cantonese. We have turned our entire team onto the place, and often wind up there after Saturday service. It's also BYO, so you can bring your own beer."
—Townsend Wentz

SOUTH STREET PHILLY BAGELS

Recommended by
Richard Landau

613 South 3rd Street
Philadelphia
Pennsylvania 19147
+1 2156276277
www.southstphillybagel.com

Opening hours	Open 7 days
Reservation policy	No
Credit cards	Accepted
Price range	Budget
Style	Casual
Cuisine	Bagels
Recommended for	Breakfast

"Just the most amazing bagels in Philly. We often order them in the morning when we are prepping at Vedge. The salt crusted bagel is sick."
—Richard Landau

STARGAZY

Recommended by
Townsend Wentz

1838 East Passyunk Avenue
Philadelphia
Pennsylvania 19148
+1 2153092761

Opening hours	Closed Monday
Reservation policy	No
Credit cards	Accepted
Price range	Affordable
Style	Casual
Cuisine	British
Recommended for	Bargain

"There is nothing better than a hearty beef and onion pie, mash, and parsley liquor on a cold, grey day!"
—Townsend Wentz

Perhaps the last thing people go to Philly for are Cornish pasties and East End pie and mash. And yet when Norwich-born chef Sam Jacobson opened a splinter of a bakery on East Passyunk called Stargazy, he bent his mind and considerable talent to constructing flaky pastry envelopes filled with the most delicious combinations. Beef and onion with parsley liquor; daily specials like short rib and cheddar; and an ever-changing vegetarian option. Recently, it was red kale and ramps (wild garlic) with brie and donko shiitake. Customers grab to go or else hang around for cups of tea which cost, according to the charmingly informal menu on the wall, "Nada/Nuffink/Zilch".

TAI LAKE

Recommended by
Peter Serpico

134 North 10th Street
Philadelphia
Pennsylvania 19107
+1 2159220698
www.tailakeseafoodrest.com

Opening hours	Open 7 days
Credit cards	Accepted
Price range	Affordable
Style	Casual
Cuisine	Chinese
Recommended for	Late night

"Tai Lake for live-tank seafood. Get the steamed whole fish with ginger and scallion (spring onion), and the live shrimp (prawn)."—Peter Serpico

VERNICK FOOD & DRINK

Recommended by
George Sabatino,
Peter Serpico,
Townsend Wentz

2031 Walnut Street
Philadelphia
Pennsylvania 19103
+1 2676396644
www.vernickphilly.com

Opening hours	Closed Monday
Credit cards	Accepted
Price range	Affordable
Style	Casual
Cuisine	Modern American
Recommended for	Regular neighborhood

"Chef Greg Vernick pulls off a rare feat—a set of unique dishes that feel like they've been your favorite for as long as you can remember. It's a well-done, but not over-done, restaurant where the bar is as good as a table, and service is seamless."—Townsend Wentz

It's not often you find a restaurant where an entire section of the menu is dedicated to toast, but that's exactly what this Philly restaurant does to perfection—slices of Metropolitan Bakery sourdough, grilled to the right shade of brown and piled high with a wealth of delicious toppings like smoked trout, Maryland crab, charred spinach, and foie gras. There are plenty of other dishes on the menu too, all of which fall into the bracket of "American cuisine" and are lovingly prepared by chef Gregory Vernick—think elegant small plates (charcoal-grilled octopus niçoise), hearty large dishes (veal flank steak with white asparagus), and meat and poultry roasted on a wood-fire oven.

VIETNAM RESTAURANT

Recommended by
Townsend Wentz

221 North 11th Street
Philadelphia
Pennsylvania 19107
+1 2155921163
www.eatatvietnam.com

Opening hours	Open 7 days
Reservation policy	No
Credit cards	Accepted
Price range	Affordable
Style	Casual
Cuisine	Vietnamese
Recommended for	Regular neighborhood

"Vietnam Restaurant is a go-to for pho and crispy spring rolls."—Townsend Wentz

ZAMA

Recommended by
Greg Vernick

128 South 19th Street
Philadelphia
Pennsylvania 19103
+1 2155681027
www.zamaphilly.com

Opening hours	Open 7 days
Credit cards	Accepted
Price range	Expensive
Style	Casual
Cuisine	Japanese
Recommended for	Regular neighborhood

THE ALLEGHENY WINE MIXER

Recommended by
Csilla Thackray

5326 Butler Street
Pittsburgh
Pennsylvania 15201
+1 4122522337
www.alleghenywinemixer.com

Opening hours	Closed Monday
Reservation policy	No
Credit cards	Accepted
Price range	Affordable
Style	Casual
Cuisine	Wine Bar
Recommended for	Late night

"Lovely meat and cheese selection, toasties, and wine."—Csilla Thackray

CHENGDU GOURMET

Recommended by
Csilla Thackray

5840 Forward Avenue
Pittsburgh
Pennsylvania 15217
+1 4125212088
www.chengdugourmetpittsburgh.com

Opening hours	Open 7 days
Credit cards	Accepted
Price range	Affordable
Style	Casual
Cuisine	Chinese
Recommended for	Regular neighborhood

"Real deal Szechuan."—Csilla Thackray

CURE

Recommended by
Csilla Thackray

5336 Butler Street
Pittsburgh
Pennsylvania 15201
+1 4122522595
www.curepittsburgh.com

Opening hours	Closed Tuesday
Credit cards	Accepted
Price range	Affordable
Style	Smart casual
Cuisine	Mediterranean
Recommended for	High end

"Chef-owner Justin is one of the first in the city
to push the boundaries of what new-age fine dining
looks like. Mediterranean inspired, Justin's strongest
showing is in meat and seafood charcuterie.
A beautiful tasting menu is always an option, but
if you want to go all out, start with the large salumi
board. After that, I recommend a few snacks, two
pastas, an entrée, and two bottles of wine. Go for it!"
—Csilla Thackray

DINETTE

Recommended by
Csilla Thackray

5996 Center Avenue
Pittsburgh
Pennsylvania 15206
+1 4123620202
www.dinette-pgh.com

Opening hours	Closed Monday and Sunday
Credit cards	Accepted
Price range	Affordable
Style	Casual
Cuisine	Italian
Recommended for	Local favorite

"Sonja, the chef/owner, was one of the first to open
a chef-driven, seasonal-produce-focused restaurant
in Pittsburgh. She was a force in moving the city
towards what it has become today in terms of culinary
achievement. Sonja's food is honest and beautiful,
pulling produce straight from the restaurant's
roof-top garden."—Csilla Thackray

EVERYDAY NOODLES

Recommended by
Csilla Thackray

5875 Forbes Avenue
Pittsburgh
Pennsylvania 15217
+1 4124216668
www.everydaynoodles.net

Opening hours	Open 7 days
Reservation policy	No
Credit cards	Accepted
Price range	Affordable
Style	Casual
Cuisine	Chinese
Recommended for	Bargain

"Affordable Chinese food with the extra special
addition of house-made noodles. Noodle soups
and dumplings are a guaranteed win, especially
in the colder months."—Csilla Thackray

LEGUME

Recommended by
Csilla Thackray

214 North Craig Street
Pittsburgh
Pennsylvania 15213
+1 4126212700
www.legumebistro.com

Opening hours	Open 7 days
Reservation policy	No
Credit cards	Accepted
Price range	Affordable
Style	Casual
Cuisine	French-Eastern European
Recommended for	Regular neighborhood

"Trevett's food is honest and without pretense. His
dedication to local sourcing goes above and beyond
so you're guaranteed a truly seasonal meal. I love that
there are no-frills and how heavily the menu depends
on their fermentation program."—Csilla Thackray

PUSADEE'S GARDEN

Recommended by
Csilla Thackray

5321 Butler Street
Pittsburgh
Pennsylvania 15201
+1 4127818724
www.pusadeesgarden.com

Opening hours	Open 7 days
Credit cards	Accepted
Price range	Affordable
Style	Casual
Cuisine	Thai
Recommended for	Regular neighborhood

RITTER'S DINER

Recommended by
Csilla Thackray

5221 Baum Boulevard
Pittsburgh
Pennsylvania 15224
+1 4126824852

Opening hours	Open 7 days
Reservation policy	No
Credit cards	Not accepted
Price range	Budget
Style	Casual
Cuisine	Diner
Recommended for	Breakfast

"Ritter's is a total dive but a great representation of old generation Pittsburg. It's definitely a greasy spoon so don't expect much by way of fine dining. Do expect waitresses in scrubs, formica, and laminated menus."—Csilla Thackray

SLICE ISLAND

Recommended by
Csilla Thackray

242 51st Street
Pittsburgh
Pennsylvania 15201
+1 4125864441
www.spiritpgh.com

Opening hours	Closed Monday
Reservation policy	No
Credit cards	Not accepted
Price range	Budget
Style	Casual
Cuisine	Pizza
Recommended for	Late night

"Slice Island knows how to sling a solid pizza. Meat, veg, a couple of sides, the guys keep it straight to the point. They do bike deliveries and exist within a two-story bar/music-venue power house. It's basically a late-night recreational center." —Csilla Thackray

EL PAISA

Recommended by
Russell Moore

598 Dexter Street
Central Falls
Rhode Island 02853
+1 4017268864
www.elpaisa.com

Opening hours	Open 7 days
Credit cards	Accepted
Price range	Affordable
Style	Casual
Cuisine	Colombian
Recommended for	Local favorite

KING'S GARDEN

Recommended by
Benjamin Sukle

90 Rolfe Square
Cranston
Rhode Island 02910
+1 4014610646
www.kingsgardencranston.com

Opening hours	Open 7 days
Credit cards	Accepted
Price range	Affordable
Style	Casual
Cuisine	Chinese
Recommended for	Regular neighborhood

MIKE'S KITCHEN

Recommended by
Benjamin Sukle

170 Randall Street
Cranston
Rhode Island 02920
+1 4019465320

Opening hours	Closed Sunday
Reservation policy	No
Credit cards	Accepted
Price range	Affordable
Style	Casual
Cuisine	Italian
Recommended for	Regular neighborhood

THAI ORCHIDS

Recommended by
Benjamin Sukle

800 Park Avenue
Cranston
Rhode Island 02910
+1 4017808889

Opening hours	Closed Sunday
Credit cards	Accepted
Price range	Affordable
Style	Casual
Cuisine	Thai
Recommended for	Regular neighborhood

CHENGDU TASTE

Recommended by
Benjamin Sukle

701 Main Street
Pawtucket
Rhode Island 02860
+1 4017295699

Opening hours	Open 7 days
Reservation policy	No
Credit cards	Accepted
Price range	Affordable
Style	Casual
Cuisine	Szechuan
Recommended for	Regular neighborhood

BIRCH

Recommended by
Benjamin Sukle,
Michael Wiley

200 Washington Street
Providence
Rhode Island 02903
+1 4012723105
www.birchrestaurant.com

Opening hours	Closed Tuesday and Wednesday
Credit cards	Accepted
Price range	Expensive
Style	Casual
Cuisine	Modern American
Recommended for	Worth the travel

"Birch is relentlessly creative, and they've got a great wine list."—Benjamin Sukle

Rhode Island has long been a food lover's state, made all the more discoverable because of its small size. A case in point is Providence's Birch, which seats only twenty around its bar for four-course dinners that highlight local ingredients with a quiet originality. Chef Benjamin Sukle makes good use of Rhode Island's bounty, from Point Judith bycatch squid, fluke, and scup to cabbages and radishes, as well as seaweed that Sukle forages himself. In true New England style, this is food that never begs attention, yet it arrests: raw lobster with spring vegetables and tomato vinegar, or rhubarb with cured cherry blossom, yogurt, and malted corn. Complementary "whoopie pies"—classic American cookie cakes—at meal's end are just as they've been for generations. Why complicate what's already good?

THE CAPITAL GRILLE

Recommended by
Benjamin Sukle

10 Memorial Boulevard
Providence
Rhode Island 02903
+1 4015215600
www.thecapitalgrille.com

Opening hours	Open 7 days
Credit cards	Accepted
Price range	Affordable
Style	Smart casual
Cuisine	Steakhouse
Recommended for	High end

"Just to be clear, this was the first Capital Grille, so it wasn't some chain. It's classic steak-house food that is very consistent."—Benjamin Sukle

EAST SIDE POCKETS

Recommended by
Benjamin Sukle

278 Thayer Street
Providence
Rhode Island 02906
+1 4014531100
www.eastsidepocket.com

Opening hours	Open 7 days
Reservation policy	No
Credit cards	Accepted but not AMEX or Diners
Price range	Budget
Style	Casual
Cuisine	Middle Eastern
Recommended for	Late night

JR'S PROVIDENCE

Recommended by
Benjamin Sukle

371 Richmond Street
Providence
Rhode Island 02903
+1 4014214577
www.jrsprovidence.com

Opening hours	Open 7 days
Reservation policy	No
Credit cards	Accepted
Price range	Budget
Style	Casual
Cuisine	American
Recommended for	Late night

NEW RIVERS

Recommended by
Benjamin Sukle

7 Steeple Street
Providence
Rhode Island 02903
+1 4017510350
www.newriversrestaurant.com

Opening hours	Closed Sunday
Credit cards	Accepted
Price range	Affordable
Style	Smart casual
Cuisine	Modern American
Recommended for	Local favorite

"One of the oldest, and pioneers of farm-to-table food. It's relaxing and comforting where you can get classics and newer dishes constantly. It's always changing without losing its vision."—Benjamin Sukle

NICK'S ON BROADWAY

Recommended by
Benjamin Sukle

500 Broadway
Providence
Rhode Island 02909
+1 4014210286
www.nicksonbroadway.com

Opening hours	Closed Monday and Tuesday
Credit cards	Accepted
Price range	Affordable
Style	Casual
Cuisine	Modern American
Recommended for	Breakfast

NORTH

Recommended by
Benjamin Sukle

3 Luongo Memorial Square
Providence
Rhode Island 02903
+1 4014211100
www.foodbynorth.com

Opening hours	Open 7 days
Reservation policy	No
Credit cards	Accepted
Price range	Affordable
Style	Casual
Cuisine	Asian Fusion
Recommended for	Regular neighborhood

"James is my best friend and is trying to make a difference. His food is always true to him and properly sourced. Whether it be the dining scene in Rhode Island or the working environment, he's always looking to be better."—Benjamin Sukle

NORTH BAKERY

Recommended by
Benjamin Sukle

70 Battey Street
Providence
Rhode Island 02903
+1 4014214062
www.northbakery.com

Opening hours	Open 7 days
Reservation policy	No
Credit cards	Accepted
Price range	Affordable
Style	Casual
Cuisine	Bakery
Recommended for	Breakfast

NOT JUST SNACKS

Recommended by
Benjamin Sukle

833 Hope Street
Providence
Rhode Island 02906
+1 4018311150
www.notjustsnacks.com

Opening hours	Open 7 days
Reservation policy	No
Credit cards	Accepted
Price range	Affordable
Style	Casual
Cuisine	Indian
Recommended for	Regular neighborhood

OLNEYVILLE NEW YORK SYSTEM

Recommended by
Benjamin Sukle

18 Plainfield Street
Providence
Rhode Island 02909
+1 4016219500
www.olneyvillenewyorksystem.com

Opening hours	Open 7 days
Credit cards	Accepted
Price range	Budget
Style	Casual
Cuisine	American
Recommended for	Late night

"You get two all the way and a mousetrap: sometimes a bacon cheeseburger."—Benjamin Sukle

PERSIMMON

99 Hope Street
Providence
Rhode Island 02906
+1 4014327422
www.persimmonbristol.com

Opening hours	Closed Monday and Sunday
Credit cards	Accepted
Price range	Expensive
Style	Smart casual
Cuisine	Modern American
Recommended for	High end

EL RANCHO GRANDE

311 Plainfield Street
Providence
Rhode Island 02909
+1 4012750808
www.elranchogranderestaurant.com

Opening hours	Open 7 days
Reservation policy	No
Credit cards	Accepted
Price range	Budget
Style	Casual
Cuisine	Mexican
Recommended for	Regular neighborhood

RED FEZ

49 Peck Street
Providence
Rhode Island 02903
+1 4018613825

Opening hours	Closed Monday and Sunday
Reservation policy	No
Credit cards	Accepted
Price range	Affordable
Style	Casual
Cuisine	American-Pub
Recommended for	Regular neighborhood

"It's the anti-restaurant, opened by godfather Ed Reposa. I love it so, so, so, so much."—Benjamin Sukle

SEAPLANE DINER

307 Allens Avenue
Providence
Rhode Island 02905
+1 4019419547

Opening hours	Open 7 days
Reservation policy	No
Credit cards	Accepted
Price range	Budget
Style	Casual
Cuisine	Diner
Recommended for	Breakfast

"Classic diner food—that's really all there is to it."
—Benjamin Sukle

SUN AND MOON

95 Warren Avenue
Providence
Rhode Island 02914
+1 4014350214
www.sunandmoonkorean.com

Opening hours	Closed Monday
Credit cards	Accepted but not AMEX
Price range	Affordable
Style	Casual
Cuisine	Korean
Recommended for	Breakfast

TONY'S COLONIAL FOOD

311 Atwells Avenue
Providence
Rhode Island 02903
+1 4016218675
www.tonyscolonial.mybigcommerce.com

Opening hours	Open 7 days
Reservation policy	No
Credit cards	Accepted
Price range	Affordable
Style	Casual
Cuisine	Italian-Grocery
Recommended for	Regular neighborhood

MATUNUCK OYSTER BAR

629 Succotash Road
South Kingstown
Rhode Island 02876
+1 4017834202
www.rhodyoysters.com

Opening hours	Open 7 days
Credit cards	Accepted
Price range	Affordable
Style	Casual
Cuisine	Seafood
Recommended for	High end

"It isn't expensive but I make it very, very expensive for myself."—Benjamin Sukle

CHARLESTON: SEE PAGES 1048–1057

BOWENS ISLAND

1870 Bowens Island Road
Bowen Island
Folly Beach
South Carolina 29412
+1 8437952757
www.bowensisland.biz

Opening hours	Closed Monday and Sunday
Reservation policy	No
Credit cards	Accepted
Price range	Affordable
Style	Casual
Cuisine	Seafood
Recommended for	Wish I'd opened

"Just outside Charleston. Great oysters and seafood. The atmosphere could not be more beautiful on the inner coastal waterway."—Brian Ahern

SEA BISCUIT CAFE

21 J C Long Boulevard
Isle of Palms
South Carolina 29451
+1 8438864079

Opening hours	Open 7 days
Reservation policy	No
Credit cards	Not accepted
Price range	Affordable
Style	Casual
Cuisine	Café
Recommended for	Breakfast

"A local spot forever, with a consistently great breakfast."—Katie Lorenzen

ZIA TAQUERIA

1956A Maybank Highway
James Island
South Carolina 29412
+1 8434068877
www.ziataco.com

Opening hours	Open 7 days
Credit cards	Accepted
Price range	Budget
Style	Casual
Cuisine	Mexican
Recommended for	Regular neighborhood

"This is the closest thing to authentic Latin food that I can find in Charleston. It reminds me of the the Latin neighborhoods in Chicago where I used to live. And the margaritas are awesome."—Justin Pfau

FISHNET SEAFOOD

3832 Savannah Highway
Johns Island
South Carolina 29455
+1 8435712423

Opening hours	Closed Sunday
Reservation policy	No
Credit cards	Accepted
Price range	Budget
Style	Casual
Cuisine	Seafood Market
Recommended for	Local favorite

CANNON'S BBQ & MORE

1903 Nursery Road
Little Mountain
South Carolina 29075
+1 8039451080

Opening hours	Closed Monday and Sunday
Reservation policy	No
Credit cards	Accepted
Price range	Affordable
Style	Casual
Cuisine	American Barbecue
Recommended for	Worth the travel

"The best fried bologna sandwich."—Daniel Serfer

LAS TORTUGAS DELI MEXICANA

1215 South Germantown Road
Germantown
Tennessee 38138
+1 9017511200
www.delimexicana.com

Opening hours	Closed Sunday
Credit cards	Accepted
Price range	Budget
Style	Casual
Cuisine	Mexican
Recommended for	Regular neighborhood

"Jonathan and Pepe serve some of the most unique and fresh food in the city. They work hard to preserve consistency in the quality that is presented to each guest. This used to be a hidden treasure in Memphis, but now, although still a treasure, it is not hidden by any means."—Ryan Trimm

ACRE RESTAURANT

690 South Perkins Road
Memphis
Tennessee 38117
+1 9018182273
www.acrememphis.com

Opening hours	Closed Sunday
Credit cards	Accepted
Price range	Affordable
Style	Casual
Cuisine	Modern American
Recommended for	Regular neighborhood

"Very professional chef, great ingredients, perfect presentation, and incredible flavors."—José Gutierrez

Acre refers both to the plot of land in East Memphis, on which the restaurant (a collaboration between Andrew Adams and Mississippi's legendary chef Wally Joe) sits, and to the pair's longstanding dedication to showcasing Tennessee's natural bounty. Joe, born in Hong Kong and raised in tiny Cleveland, TN, sparked the Southern renaissance in the 1980s at KC's and here, in the light wood and welcoming rooms, the South is reimagined again. Grilled pork flat-iron is augmented with sweet potato hash, sweet and sour cabbage, and umeboshi sauce; sorghum noodles arrive with avocado and charred okra. Acre opened in 2011 in a renovated mid-century home, and that feeling, of sophisticated comfort, is suffused both inside and in the garden patio out back.

ANDREW MICHAEL ITALIAN KITCHEN

712 West Brookhaven Circle
Memphis
Tennessee 38117
+1 9013473569
www.andrewmichaelitaliankitchen.com

Opening hours	Closed Monday and Sunday
Credit cards	Accepted
Price range	Affordable
Style	Smart casual
Cuisine	Italian
Recommended for	High end

"They consistently put out the most innovative and delectable cuisine in town."—Ryan Trimm

With the mighty Mississippi River and a bustling railroad, Memphis has long drawn newcomers. In the 1900s, the city was second only in the South to New Orleans for Italian immigration. So thank the railroad and river, perhaps, for the presence of Andrew Michael Italian Kitchen, the James Beard-nominated restaurant from chefs Andrew Ticer and Michael Hudman. For it was their grandmothers who combined Italian technique with Southern ingredients, leading to the dishes that their grandsons present on the menu of one of Memphis's most elegant and steadfast restaurants. Whether it's *casonsei* with rutabaga (turnip), satsuma, and confit chicken, or *corvina* with stracciatella and lima beans, at Andrew Michael, southern Italy meets the American South in ways delicious and surprising.

CENTRAL BBQ

2249 Central Avenue
Memphis
Tennessee 38104
+1 9012729377
www.cbqmemphis.com

Opening hours	Open 7 days
Reservation policy	No
Credit cards	Accepted
Price range	Affordable
Style	Casual
Cuisine	Barbecue
Recommended for	Local favorite

"Memphis is known for its barbecue but there are a lot of tourist traps out there. These guys are legit."
—Ryan Trimm

EARNESTINE & HAZEL'S

Recommended by
Ryan Trimm

351 South Main Street
Memphis
Tennessee 38103
+1 9015239754
www.earnestineandhazelsjukejoint.com

Opening hours	Open 7 days
Reservation policy	No
Credit cards	Accepted
Price range	Budget
Style	Casual
Cuisine	Burgers
Recommended for	Late night

"Soul Burgers, Soul Burgers, Soul Burgers!"
—Ryan Trimm

ELWOOD'S SHACK

Recommended by
Ryan Trimm

4523 Summer Avenue
Memphis
Tennessee 38122
+1 9017619898
www.elwoodsshack.com

Opening hours	Open 7 days
Credit cards	Accepted
Price range	Affordable
Style	Casual
Cuisine	American
Recommended for	Wish I'd opened

"The concept is perfect. Good food, no frills."
—Ryan Trimm

In a shopping center parking lot in Memphis, there is a tiny building with a barrel smoker in the back, which cranks out an impressive amount of Memphis-style barbecue for breakfast and lunch. This city is known for its pork, in "dry" or "wet" styles, but owners Scott Scheno and Tim Bednarski's beef and chicken have also won regulars. Here is a place to come truly hungry and expect to leave truly full. There are expertly calibrated sandwiches and subs, smoked meat piled in hot dog buns, enormous barbecue tacos, barbecue pizza, and, of course, lunch plates—all served on chequered paper-lined plastic trays to match the linoleum floor.

PAYNE'S BAR-B-QUE

Recommended by
Ryan Trimm

1762 Lamar Avenue
Memphis
Tennessee 38114
+1 9012721523

Opening hours	Closed Monday and Sunday
Reservation policy	No
Credit cards	Not accepted
Price range	Budget
Style	Casual
Cuisine	American
Recommended for	Bargain

"The smoked sausage or the pulled-pork sammies are both amazing. Their slaw just mixes with their sauce perfectly."—Ryan Trimm

THE PEABODY HOTEL

Recommended by
José Gutierrez

149 Union Avenue
Memphis
Tennessee 38103
+1 9015294000
www.peabodymemphis.com

Opening hours	Open 7 days
Credit cards	Accepted
Price range	Affordable
Style	Smart Casual
Cuisine	American
Recommended for	Breakfast

PHO SAIGON

Recommended by
Ryan Trimm

2946 Poplar Avenue
Memphis
Tennessee 38111
+1 9014581644

Opening hours	Open 7 days
Reservation policy	No
Credit cards	Accepted
Price range	Budget
Style	Casual
Cuisine	Vietnamese
Recommended for	Bargain

"Pho Saigon's $3.99 (£3) banh mi is tough to beat."
—Ryan Trimm

RESTAURANT IRIS

Recommended by
Ryan Trimm

2146 Monroe Avenue
Memphis
Tennessee 38104
+1 9015902828
www.restaurantiris.com

Opening hours	Closed Sunday
Credit cards	Accepted
Price range	Expensive
Style	Smart casual
Cuisine	Cajun-Creole
Recommended for	High end

RIVER OAKS

Recommended by
José Gutierrez

5871 Poplar Avenue
Memphis
Tennessee 38119
+1 9016839305
www.riveroaksrestaurant.com

Opening hours	Closed Sunday
Credit cards	Accepted
Price range	Affordable
Style	Smart casual
Cuisine	French-American
Recommended for	Local favorite

"The menu has something for everyone."
—José Gutierrez

BASTION

Recommended by
Karl Worley

434 Houston Street
Nashville
Tennessee 37203
+1 6154908434
www.bastionnashville.com

Opening hours	Closed Monday
Credit cards	Accepted
Price range	Affordable
Style	Casual
Cuisine	American
Recommended for	Late night

"Ok, full disclosure, this is a bar with a restaurant
attached. But sit in the bar, grab a cocktail, and order
the nachos—they are the best in town."—Karl Worley

BIG AL'S DELI

Recommended by
Andrew Little

1828 4th Avenue North
Nashville
Tennessee 37208
+1 6152428118
www.bigalsdeliandcatering.com

Opening hours	Closed Sunday
Reservation policy	No
Credit cards	Accepted
Price range	Budget
Style	Casual
Cuisine	Southern American-Deli
Recommended for	Breakfast

"I love no-frills places and Big Al's is that place."
—Andrew Little

BISCUIT LOVE

Recommended by
Andrew Little

316 11th Avenue South
Nashville
Tennessee 37203
+1 6154909584
www.biscuitlove.com

Opening hours	Open 7 days
Reservation policy	No
Credit cards	Accepted
Price range	Affordable
Style	Casual
Cuisine	Southern American
Recommended for	Breakfast

"It's the perfect place for an amazing cup of coffee
and plates upon plates of food. Karl and Sarah Worley
are pros. Everything is delicious—the 'Bonuts' are my
absolute favorite!"—Andrew Little

Owned and operated by husband-and-wife team
Karl and Sarah Worley, this brunch restaurant has
become a steadfast favorite of Nashville natives.
They've earned the admiration of the community
with their commitment to championing produce from
the local area and to serving a variety of sweet and
savory biscuits in the style of traditional Southern
cooking. Biscuit Love's specialty, "Bonuts" (fried
biscuit dough, topped with lemon mascarpone and
blueberry compote), are carefully hand-made each
day, and are likely to sell out if you're not quick. In
fact, it's always best to arrive early to avoid
disappointment—there are no reservations and
lines (queues) often snake around the block
(prepare to wait up to an hour on weekends).

CITY HOUSE

Recommended by
Linton Hopkins,
Karl Worley

1222 4th Avenue North
Nashville
Tennessee 37208
+1 6157365838
www.cityhousenashville.com

Opening hours	Closed Tuesday
Credit cards	Accepted
Price range	Affordable
Style	Casual
Cuisine	Italian
Recommended for	Local favorite

"City House was one of the first places in town to take on the big chains that were typical dining establishments ten years ago. Tandy and his team took traditional Italian techniques and applied local ingredients to create a fine example of what Nashville's food scene is all about."—Karl Worley

CORNER PUB

Recommended by
Andrew Little

8058 Tennessee 100
Nashville
Tennessee 37221
+1 6152989698
www.cornerpubtn.com

Opening hours	Open 7 days
Credit cards	Accepted
Price range	Affordable
Style	Casual
Cuisine	American
Recommended for	Late night

"Super solid pub grub. Great wings, baskets of cheese beans (like cheese sticks, but smaller and with cheddar), and cold beer."—Andrew Little

GABBY'S BURGERS AND FRIES

Recommended by
Karl Worley

493 Humphreys Street
Nashville
Tennessee 37203
+1 6157333119
www.gabbysburgersandfries.com

Opening hours	Closed Sunday
Reservation policy	No
Credit cards	Accepted
Price range	Budget
Style	Casual
Cuisine	Burgers
Recommended for	Bargain

"Gabby's is one of those joint places to grab a burger and hand-cut fries. Try the sweet potato, delicious! Our six-year-old loves it, how can we resist?"—Karl Worley

HUSK

Recommended by
Michael Friedman,
Andrew Little

37 Rutledge Street
Nashville
Tennessee 37210
+1 6152566565
www.husknashville.com

Opening hours	Open 7 days
Credit cards	Accepted
Price range	Affordable
Style	Casual
Cuisine	Modern Southern American
Recommended for	Regular neighborhood

"They are always working with the best ingredients in the most innovative ways. It just feels like home to sit at their bar and enjoy thoughtful food."—Andrew Little

JEFF RUBY'S STEAKHOUSE

Recommended by
Karl Worley

300 4th Avenue North
Nashville
Tennessee 37219
+1 6154344300
www.jeffruby.com/nashville

Opening hours	Closed Sunday
Credit cards	Accepted
Price range	Expensive
Style	Formal
Cuisine	Steakhouse
Recommended for	High end

"So, they are a steakhouse, and they are also a chain —but they are everything you want in a steakhouse. Waiters in tails, incredible raw bar, and old-school, flaming desserts. "—Karl Worley

JOSEPHINE

Recommended by
Karl Worley

2316 12th Avenue South
Nashville
Tennessee 37204
+1 6152927766
www.josephineon12th.com

Opening hours	Open 7 days
Credit cards	Accepted
Price range	Affordable
Style	Casual
Cuisine	American
Recommended for	Regular neighborhood

"From the minute you walk in, Andy and Karen's attention to detail and hospitality are second to none. It's comfortable and comforting—.like walking into a friend's home."—Karl Worley

MARCHÉ ARTISAN FOODS

Recommended by
Karl Worley

1000 Main Street
Nashville
Tennessee 37206
+1 6152621111
www.marcheartisanfoods.com

Opening hours	Closed Monday
Reservation policy	No
Credit cards	Accepted
Price range	Affordable
Style	Casual
Cuisine	Café
Recommended for	Breakfast

"When you walk into Marché you feel transported to a French café. Lively and bustling, the ambiance matches the food. Don't miss the hot chocolate, which comes with its own house-made marshmallow." —Karl Worley

NICKY'S COAL FIRED

Recommended by
Karl Worley

5026 Centennial Boulevard
Nashville
Tennessee 37209
+1 6156784289
www.nickysnashville.com

Opening hours	Open 7 days
Credit cards	Accepted
Price range	Affordable
Style	Casual
Cuisine	Italian
Recommended for	Wish I'd opened

PEG LEG PORKER

Recommended by
Edward Lee

903 Gleaves Street
Nashville
Tennessee 37203
+1 6158296023
www.peglegporker.com

Opening hours	Closed Sunday
Reservation policy	No
Credit cards	Accepted
Price range	Budget
Style	Casual
Cuisine	Barbecue
Recommended for	Wish I'd Opened

"It's just no fuss, great barbecue. And they have a sliding ceiling-hook system for transporting pigs from the walk-in to the smoker that goes through the dining room. Genius."—Edward Lee

AUSTIN: SEE PAGES 1058–1067

FT33

Recommended by
Erick Harcey

1617 Hi Line Drive
Dallas
Texas 75207
+1 2147412629
www.ft33dallas.com

Opening hours	Closed Monday and Sunday
Credit cards	Accepted
Price range	Expensive
Style	Smart casual
Cuisine	Modern American
Recommended for	Worth the travel

"Chef Matt is brilliant with his cuisine and sources everything from three hundred miles from his restaurant."—Erick Harcey

KNIFE DALLAS

Recommended by
Emily Hahn

5300 East Mockingbird Lane
Dallas
Texas 75206
+1 2144439339
www.knifedallas.com

Opening hours	Open 7 days
Credit cards	Accepted
Price range	Expensive
Style	Smart casual
Cuisine	Steakhouse
Recommended for	Worth the travel

CAFÉ TH

Recommended by
Chris Shepherd

2108 Pease Street
Houston
Texas 77003
+1 7132254766
www.cafeth.com

Opening hours	Closed Sunday
Credit cards	Accepted
Price range	Budget
Style	Casual
Cuisine	Vietnamese
Recommended for	Bargain

COLTIVARE

Recommended by
Chris Shepherd

3320 White Oak Drive
Houston
Texas 77007
+1 7136374095
www.agricolehospitality.com/coltivare

Opening hours	Closed Tuesday
Reservation policy	No
Credit cards	Accepted
Price range	Affordable
Style	Casual
Cuisine	Italian
Recommended for	Local favorite

"Chef Ryan Pera harvests ingredients from his 3,000-square-foot garden, and they're on the menu that night. His technique and attention to detail is incredible."—Chris Shepherd

HK DIM SUM

Recommended by
Chris Shepherd

Suite 110, 9889 Bellaire Boulevard
Houston
Texas 77036
+1 7137777029
www.hkdimsumcity.com

Opening hours	Open 7 days
Reservation policy	No
Credit cards	Accepted but not AMEX
Price range	Budget
Style	Casual
Cuisine	Chinese
Recommended for	Regular neighborhood

"For the quality of ingredients, the textures and flavors."—Chris Shepherd

THE PASS AND PROVISIONS

Recommended by
Jesse Schenker

807 Taft Street
Houston
Texas 77019
+1 7136289020
www.passandprovisions.com

Opening hours	Closed Sunday
Credit cards	Accepted
Price range	Expensive
Style	Smart casual
Cuisine	Modern American
Recommended for	Worth the travel

"Seth and Terrence are really talented chefs. Great concept. Great food."—Jesse Schenker

After meeting while working in one of Gordon Ramsay's kitchens, chefs Terrence Gallivan and Seth Siegel-Gardner decided to combine their experience and passion to created what's now one of Houston's most celebrated dining establishments, The Pass and Provisions. The concept is unusual: it's essentially two restaurants, with two chefs and a shared kitchen. The Pass, with its minimalist decor, serves an exquisitely constructed, five-course omnivore and vegetarian tasting menu for $65 (£50), or $105 (£80) with pairings. The food is distinctly avant-garde, with surprises packed on to every plate. On the other hand, swapping tablecloths for exposed wood and paper menus, Provisions has the more relaxed atmosphere of a neighborhood bar, serving pizzas, meatball subs and a variety of lip-smacking pasta dishes, all prepared with the same vibrancy as its sibling next door.

PHO BINH BY NIGHT

Recommended by
Chris Shepherd

Suite 101, 12148 Bellaire Boulevard
Houston
Texas 77072
+1 8323512464
www.phobinh.com

Opening hours	Closed Monday
Reservation policy	No
Credit cards	Accepted
Price range	Budget
Style	Casual
Cuisine	Pho
Recommended for	Late night

"The flavor of their broth is unparalleled. Combine that with the fresh herbs and you can't beat it."
—Chris Shepherd

REEF

Recommended by
Chris Shepherd

2600 Travis Street
Houston
Texas 77006
+1 7135268282
www.reefhouston.com

Opening hours	Open 7 days
Credit cards	Accepted
Price range	Affordable
Style	Smart casual
Cuisine	Modern American
Recommended for	Local favorite

"It shows what Gulf Coast seafood is all about."
—Chris Shepherd

SMITTY'S MARKET

Recommended by
Larry McGuire

208 South Commerce Street
Lockhart
Texas 78644
+1 5123989344
www.smittysmarket.com

Opening hours	Open 7 days
Credit cards	Accepted
Price range	Affordable
Style	Casual
Cuisine	Barbecue
Recommended for	Local favorite

"This is the quintessential Central Texas barbecue spot. Open since 1948 and the first place I take people for real barbecue."—Larry McGuire

LA BANDERA MOLINO

Recommended by
Jesse Griffiths

2619 North Zarzamora
San Antonio
Texas 78201
+1 2104340631

Opening hours	Closed Monday
Reservation policy	No
Credit cards	Accepted
Price range	Budget
Style	Casual
Cuisine	Tex-Mex
Recommended for	Breakfast

"Authentic San Antonio-style hangover Mexican tacos: the perfect bean and cheese taco."—Jesse Griffiths

APIS

Recommended by
Kevin Fink

23526 Highway 71 West
Spicewood
Texas 78669
+1 5124368918
www.apisrestaurant.com

Opening hours	Closed Sunday to Tuesday
Credit cards	Accepted
Price range	Affordable
Style	Smart casual
Cuisine	Modern American
Recommended for	High end

The honeycomb on the ceiling will erase any doubt that Apis Restaurant and Apiary is all about honey. Indeed, chef Taylor Hall tends about two-dozen hives here on this six-acre property that abuts the winding Pedernales River, about thirty minutes outside Austin. The hives supply the restaurant with its signature ingredient, which imparts floral sweetness to glazes, cocktails, and desserts, while buoying the local bee population. Since 2015, Hall has delivered elegant, contemporary tasting and *prix fixe* menus that take inspiration from Asia and Europe while staying true to Texas Hill Country's fine ingredients.

RAVI KABOB

Recommended by
Katsuya Fukushima

305 North Glebe Road
Arlington
Virginia, 22203
www.ravikabobusa.com

Opening hours	Open 7 days
Reservation policy	No
Credit cards	Accepted
Price range	Affordable
Style	Casual
Cuisine	Pakistani
Recommended for	Bargain

TAYLOR GOURMET

Arlington
Virginia
www.taylorgourmet.com

Opening hours	Open 7 days
Reservation policy	No
Credit cards	Accepted
Price range	Budget
Style	Casual
Cuisine	Sandwiches
Recommended for	Local favorite

TACO BAMBA

Falls Church
Virginia
www.tacobamba.com

Opening hours	Open 7 days
Reservation policy	No
Credit cards	Accepted
Price range	Affordable
Style	Casual
Cuisine	Mexican
Recommended for	Local favorite

"SALTYARD IS AN UNDER-THE-RADAR GEM IN ATLANTA."

JARRETT STIEBER P949

"All you have to do is trust chef Atsushi 'Art' Hayakawa."

ROBERT PHALEN P950

"Everything is simple but perfectly done."

ROBERT PHAEL P945

ATLANTA

"IT'S AS GOOD AS THE FOOD I EXPERIENCED IN VIETNAM, IF NOT BETTER."

TODD GINSBERG P947

"CLASSIC DINER FOOD WITH SOUTHERN CHARM."

ROBERT PHALEN P946

ATLANTA

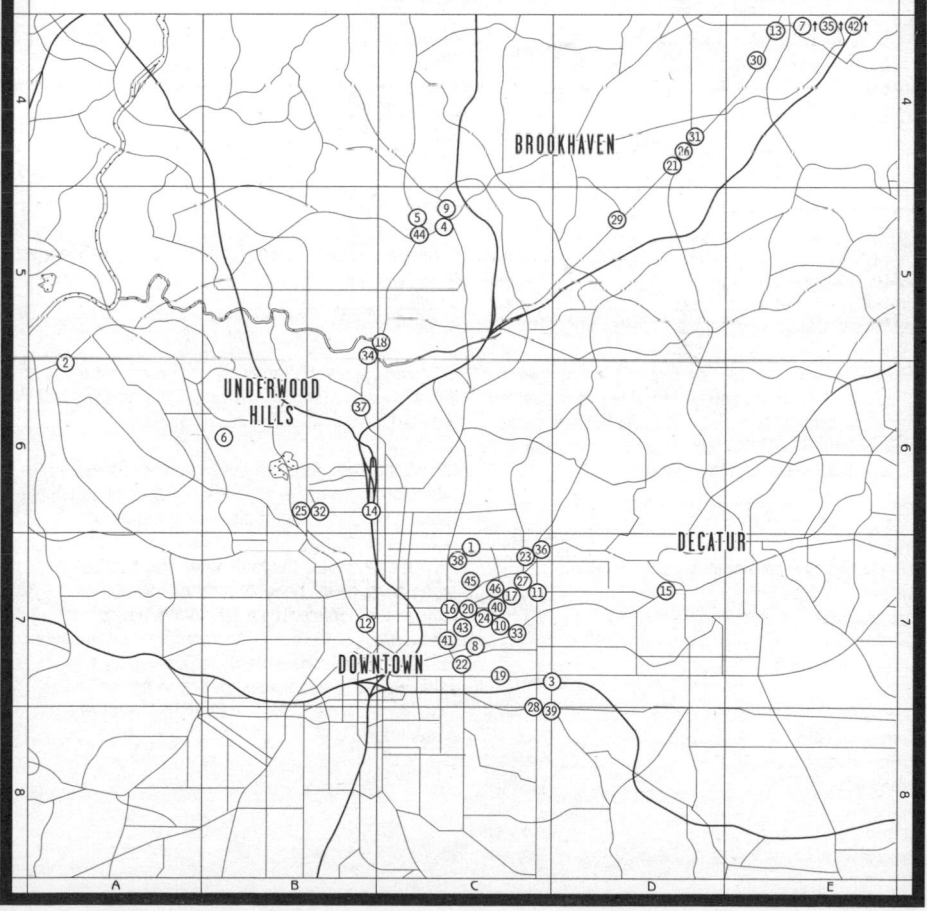

SCALE

0   1500   3000   4450
yd.

8 ARM

710 Ponce De Leon Avenue
Atlanta
Georgia 30306
+1 4708755856
www.8armatl.com

Recommended by
Steven Satterfield,
Jarrett Stieber

Opening hours	Open 7 days
Credit cards	Accepted
Price range	Budget
Style	Casual
Cuisine	Café
Recommended for	Regular neighborhood

"We love going to 8 Arm in Poncy Highlands, for simple and well prepared locally-sourced food. It's a great option for lunch when you want stuff that isn't just a sandwich or bar food."—Jarrett Stieber

ACAPULCO MEXICAN TAQUERIA

2102 Hollywood Road Northwest
Atlanta
Georgia 30318
+1 4049417865

Recommended by
Landon Thompson

Opening hours	Closed Tuesday
Reservation policy	No
Credit cards	Accepted
Price range	Budget
Style	Casual
Cuisine	Mexican
Recommended for	Bargain

"A tiny little hole-in-the-wall taqueria in Riverview. Absolutely killer tacos and an adorable family working the whole establishment. Hands down the best cheap meal around, $2 (£1.50) tacos that blow away the competition!"—Landon Thompson

ARGOSY

470 Flat Shoals Avenue Southeast
Atlanta
Georgia 30316
+1 4045770407
www.argosy-east.com

Recommended by
Steven Satterfield

Opening hours	Open 7 days
Reservation policy	No
Credit cards	Accepted
Price range	Affordable
Style	Casual
Cuisine	Gastropub
Recommended for	Bargain

ARIA

490 East Paces Ferry Road Northeast
Atlanta
Georgia 30305
+1 4042337673
www.aria-atl.com

Recommended by
Joe Schafer

Opening hours	Closed Sunday
Credit cards	Accepted
Price range	Affordable
Style	Formal
Cuisine	American
Recommended for	High end

"Aria has consistently been at the top of the Atlanta dining scene. Gerry Klaskala offers simple, well-executed food. Truffled celeriac soup is not to be missed."—Joe Schafer

ATLAS

88 West Pace Ferry Road
Atlanta
Georgia 30305
+1 4046006471
www.atlasrestaurant.com

Recommended by
Steven Satterfield, Joe Schafer,
Jarrett Stieber, Landon Thompson

Opening hours	Open 7 days
Credit cards	Accepted
Price range	Expensive
Style	Smart casual
Cuisine	Modern American
Recommended for	High end

"The service is very formal and expensive but the dining room is stunning, the wine list is amazing and the food is meticulous."—Jarrett Stieber

Copper bar, gougères (cheese choux pastries), white tablecloths, paintings by Picasso, Bacon and Chagall. Helmed by chef Christopher Grossman, Atlas, at Buckhead's St. Regis hotel, pulls off a fine-dining revival that hits all the high notes and escapes stodginess, never begging attention for its impeccable service. It's the kind of place to linger over a glass of Burgundy and contemplate the poetic restraint of a Georges Bank sea scallop, or this season's white asparagus, or brown butter, or Blue Ridge trout. A place to dine effortlessly, for at least a few hours.

BACCHANALIA

Recommended by
Steven Satterfield

1198 Howell Mill Road
Atlanta
Georgia 30318
+1 4043650410
www.starprovisions.com/bacchanalia

Opening hours	Closed Sunday
Credit cards	Accepted
Price range	Expensive
Style	Smart casual
Cuisine	Southern American
Recommended for	High end

"It has set the standard for Atlanta fine dining for the past twenty years and continues to do so as they evolve into their new space."—Steven Satterfield

BO BO GARDEN

Recommended by
Jarrett Stieber

5181 Buford Highway Northeast
Atlanta
Georgia 30340
+1 6785471881

Opening hours	Open 7 days
Credit cards	Accepted
Price range	Affordable
Style	Casual
Cuisine	Chinese
Recommended for	Late night

"Bo Bo Garden is a very good Chinese restaurant on Buford Highway that's also open super late."
—Jarrett Stieber

BOCCALUPO

Recommended by
Todd Ginsberg, Chris Hall,
Jarrett Stieber

753 Edgewood Avenue Northeast
Atlanta
Georgia 30307
+1 4045772332
www.boccalupoatl.com

Opening hours	Closed Monday and Sunday
Credit cards	Accepted
Price range	Affordable
Style	Casual
Cuisine	Italian-American
Recommended for	Wish I'd opened

"This restaurant manages to both be a neighborhood spot, fiercely supported every night by residents of Inman Park, and a destination restaurant for people coming in from the suburbs or out of town. BoccaLupo also manages to somehow be casual and formal at the same time, with elevated food and service mixing together with a laid back vibe. It's approachable without being boring or dated and much of the food is sourced from local producers. Atlanta is a city that doesn't support full-on fine dining well, but there is a ton of great food to be had in less formal settings like at BoccaLupo."—Jarrett Stieber

This neighborhood spot in Inman Park calls itself 'Italian-American', but it's a contemporary interpretation, the kind of American versed in kimchi and ramen as well as bolognese. But any suspicion that chef Bruce Logue's daringly untraditional comfort foods are all bells and whistles is swiftly dispelled. The dynamic seasonal menus—built around pasta, much of it hand-made in-house—deliver skilful, harmonious balances of texture and flavor. The octopus and mortadella spiedino (skewer) is a prime example.

BONES

Recommended by
Linton Hopkins, Robert
Phalen, Jarrett Stieber

3130 Piedmont Road Northeast
Atlanta
Georgia 30305
+1 4042372663
www.bonesrestaurant.com

Opening hours	Open 7 days
Credit cards	Accepted
Price range	Expensive
Style	Smart casual
Cuisine	Steakhouse
Recommended for	Local favorite

"Bones is the place you go and splurge and the service is impeccable. Everything here is perfection."
—Robert Phalen

BREAD & BUTTERFLY

Recommended by
Todd Ginsberg, Steven
Satterfield, Jarrett Stieber

290 Elizabeth Street
Atlanta
Georgia 30307
+1 6785154536
www.bread-and-butterfly.com

Opening hours	Closed Monday
Reservation policy	No
Credit cards	Accepted
Price range	Affordable
Style	Casual
Cuisine	French-American
Recommended for	Breakfast

"Execution is running at peak performance at this little Inman Park French bistro. Bitter salad greens, toast with sliced cured ham and fried egg with gruyere...it's not your grits and eggs kind of place. It's sophisticated without any pretense."—Todd Ginsberg

All the trappings of a French café-bistro can be found in the cheerfully tiled Bread & Butterfly, owned by Billy and Kristin Allin: copper ceiling tiles, marble counters, fresh croissants, menu scrawled in curly writing on the mirror. The omelettes du jour are perfect, as is the steak tartare, and fresh baked goods from neighboring Proof (which the pair also own) are stocked daily. The wine list is mostly French, with special love shown to the Loire.

BREWHOUSE CAFÉ

Recommended by
Jarrett Stieber

401 Moreland Avenue Northeast
Atlanta
Georgia 30307
+1 4045257799
www.brewhousecafe.com

Opening hours	Open 7 days
Reservation policy	No
Credit cards	Accepted
Price range	Affordable
Style	Casual
Cuisine	Bar
Recommended for	Late night

WAFFLE HOUSE

Recommended by
Chris Hall

135 Andrew Young International Boulevard NW
Central Park District
Atlanta
Georgia 30303
+1 4045229873
www.wafflehouse.com

Opening hours	Open 7 days
Reservation policy	No
Credit cards	Accepted
Price range	Budget
Style	Casual
Cuisine	American
Recommended for	Breakfast

"Quick, consistent—the two main needs at breakfast."
—Chris Hall

CANTON HOUSE

Recommended by
Robert Phalen

4825 Buford Highway Northeast
Buford Highway
Atlanta
Georgia 30341
+1 7709369030
www.cantonhouserestaurant.com

Opening hours	Open 7 days
Credit cards	Accepted
Price range	Affordable
Style	Casual
Cuisine	Dim Sum
Recommended for	Breakfast

"The dim sum here is the best in the city. It's our family's favorite Sunday brunch spot."—Robert Phalen

CHINESE BUDDHA

Recommended by
Joe Schafer

100 10th Street Northwest
Atlanta
Georgia 30309
+1 4048745158
www.chinesebuddhaatlantaga.com

Opening hours	Open 7 days
Credit cards	Accepted
Price range	Affordable
Style	Casual
Cuisine	Chinese
Recommended for	Late night

DISH DIVE

Recommended by
Jarrett Stieber

2233 College Avenue Northeast
Atlanta
Georgia 30317
+1 4049577918
www.dishdivekitchen.com

Opening hours	Closed Monday and Sunday
Credit cards	Accepted
Price range	Affordable
Style	Casual
Cuisine	American
Recommended for	Local favorite

Dish Dive is a quirky little spot that's a lot of fun!
It's a tiny restaurant with a small menu of affordable
sharing plates, plus they're BYO which helps save
money."—Jarrett Stieber

FRED'S MEAT & BREAD

Recommended by
Robert Phael

99 Krog Street
Atlanta
Georgia 30307
+1 4046883733
www.fredsmeatandbread.com

Opening hours	Open 7 days
Reservation policy	No
Credit cards	Accepted
Price range	Budget
Style	Casual
Cuisine	Sandwiches
Recommended for	Regular neighborhood

"Everything is simple but perfectly done. The Italian
grinder is heaven!"—Robert Phael

FRITTI

Recommended by
Steven Satterfield

309 North Highland Avenue Northeast
Atlanta
Georgia 30307
+1 4048809559
www.frittiatl.com

Opening hours	Open 7 days
Credit cards	Accepted
Price range	Affordable
Style	Casual
Cuisine	Neopolitan Pizza
Recommended for	Regular neighborhood

"Walking distance from my house—Fritti has thin,
crispy Neapolitan-style pizza."—Steven Satterfield

HOLEMAN AND FINCH

Recommended by
Todd Ginsberg

2277 Peachtree Road Northeast
Atlanta
Georgia 30309
+1 4049481175
www.holeman-finch.com

Opening hours	Open 7 days
Credit cards	Accepted
Price range	Affordable
Style	Casual
Cuisine	Gastropub
Recommended for	Late night

HOME GROWN

Recommended by
Joe Schafer

968 Memorial Drive Southeast
Atlanta
Georgia 30316
+1 4042220455
www.homegrownga.com

Opening hours	Open 7 days
Credit cards	Accepted
Price range	Budget
Style	Casual
Cuisine	Southern American
Recommended for	Breakfast

"Casual, great breakfast and brunch items. And it's my
daughter's favorite place to eat."—Joe Schafer

KEVIN RATHBUN STEAK

Recommended by
Todd Ginsberg

154 Krog Street
Atlanta
Georgia 30307
+1 4045245600
www.kevinrathbunsteak.com

Opening hours	Closed Sunday
Credit cards	Accepted
Price range	Expensive
Style	Smart casual
Cuisine	Steakhouse
Recommended for	High end

"Great dry-aged meats, impeccable service, amazing
sides and really delicious desserts."—Todd Ginsberg

LEE'S BAKERY

Recommended by
Todd Ginsberg,
Jarrett Stieber

4005 Buford Highway Northeast
Atlanta
Georgia 30345
+1 4047281008

Opening hours	Open 7 days
Reservation policy	No
Credit cards	Accepted
Price range	Budget
Style	Casual
Cuisine	Vietnamese
Recommended for	Bargain

"They bake their own bread in-house for their banh mi sandwiches, make their French-influenced Vietnamese pastries, make their head cheese, their paté, their bologna, etc, all from scratch! The sandwiches are between $3–5 (£2–4) each and if you buy five you get a sixth one free. The noodle bowls are delicious, too, with rich, warming broths."—Jarrett Stieber

LITTLE'S FOOD STORE

Recommended by
Robert Phalen

198 Carroll Street South
Atlanta
Georgia 30312
+1 4049637012
www.littlesfoodstore.com

Opening hours	Open 7 days
Reservation policy	No
Credit cards	Accepted
Price range	Budget
Style	Casual
Cuisine	Burgers
Recommended for	Bargain

"The little burgers are excellent, hand patted to order. It's very easy to put away four of them at a time."
—Robert Phalen

MAJESTIC DINER

Recommended by
Robert Phalen

1031 Ponce De Leon Avenue Northeast
Atlanta
Georgia 30306
+1 4048750276
www.majesticdiner.com

Opening hours	Open 7 days
Reservation policy	No
Credit cards	Accepted
Price range	Affordable
Style	Casual
Cuisine	Southern American-Diner
Recommended for	Late night

"This place is great after a long night of drinking—classic diner food with southern charm."
—Robert Phalen

MF SUSHI

Recommended by
Todd Ginsberg

299 North Highland Avenue Northeast
Atlanta
Georgia 30307
+1 6785757890
www.mfsushiusa.com

Opening hours	Open 7 days
Credit cards	Accepted
Price range	Affordable
Style	Smart casual
Cuisine	Sushi
Recommended for	Regular neighborhood

"It's top sushi right around the corner from my place."
—Todd Ginsberg

MILLER UNION

Recommended by
Todd Ginsberg,
Jarrett Stieber

999 Brady Avenue Northwest
Atlanta
Georgia 30318
+1 6787338550
www.millerunion.com

Opening hours	Closed Sunday
Credit cards	Accepted
Price range	Affordable
Style	Casual
Cuisine	Southern American
Recommended for	Local favorite

"It is the restaurant that best represents the current mood of Southern cuisine in the South. No one is doing it as well and with so much conviction. The service, the wine list and the food are about as good

as you can get in this city. It's been like this since the restaurant opened six or seven years ago."
—Todd Ginsberg

Miller Union makes its home in a reclaimed warehouse, but spend any amount of time here and the inevitable impression is not of industry but soul. Opened in 2009, the restaurant was one of the first in the current movement of back-to-the-farm southern cooking. But the farm-to-table message is only a piece of the picture here. Chef Steven Satterfield, who won a James Beard Foundation Award in 2017, doesn't merely respect Georgia's ingredients, he loves them; as evidenced in grit fritters with country ham, luscious braised rabbit brightened with ramps and radishes, quail glazed with sorghum, burned onion cream, and on.

NAM PHUONG RESTAURANT

Recommended by
Todd Ginsberg

4051 Buford Highway Northeast
Atlanta
Georgia 30345
+1 4046332400

Opening hours	Open 7 days
Reservation policy	No
Credit cards	Accepted
Price range	Affordable
Style	Casual
Cuisine	Vietnamese
Recommended for	Bargain

"It's as good as the food I experienced in Vietnam, if not better. So simple and straightforward. Hot tea and some Vietnamese comfort food make any rainy day better."—Todd Ginsberg

THE NORTH HIGHLAND PUB

Recommended by
Jarrett Stieber

469 North Highland Avenue Northeast
Atlanta
Georgia 30307
+1 4045224600
www.northhighlandpub.com

Opening hours	Open 7 days
Reservation policy	No
Credit cards	Accepted
Price range	Affordable
Style	Casual
Cuisine	American Pub
Recommended for	Late night

"North Highland Pub has solid bar food late at night."
—Jarrett Stieber

OCTOPUS BAR

Recommended by
Steven Satterfield,
Joe Schafer,
Landon Thompson

560 Gresham Avenue Southeast
Atlanta
Georgia 30316
+1 4046279911
www.octopusbaratl.com

Opening hours	Closed Sunday and Monday
Reservation policy	No
Credit cards	Accepted
Price range	Affordable
Style	Casual
Cuisine	Asian
Recommended for	Late night

"I love the vibe and the fact that it's open until 2.30 a.m. I love seeing all my industry buddies there as we swap war stories and decompress. But most of all, I like the food. It's funky, full flavored, sporadic and somewhat schizophrenic. It's pretty much always exactly what I want at the end of a long shift or a night out. Angus Brown is, was, and always will be one of Atlanta's greats."—Landon Thompson

Chef Angus Brown's untimely death in January 2017 cast a shadow over this late-night hot spot, opened in 2012 by Brown and Nhan Le. The restaurant scene still feels the loss of Brown, one of Atlanta's larger-than-life talents. It's fitting, then, that Octopus Bar rages on. Built by and for chefs, it has a reputation for delicious, original food, serving up a changing menu of seafood-centric dishes and powerful, creative cocktails.

LA PASTORCITA

Recommended by
Joe Schafer

3304 Buford Highway Northeast
Atlanta
Georgia 30329
+1 6787058162

Opening hours	Open 7 days
Reservation policy	No
Credit cards	Accepted
Price range	Affordable
Style	Casual
Cuisine	Mexican
Recommended for	Late night

PHO 24

Recommended by
Jarrett Stieber

4646 Buford Highway
Atlanta
Georgia 30341
+1 7707100178

Opening hours	Open 7 days
Credit cards	Accepted
Price range	Budget
Style	Casual
Cuisine	Vietnamese
Recommended for	Late night

"It's not the best Vietnamese restaurant on Buford Highway—Atlanta's finest food resource overall, which is brimming with amazing ethnic food—but it is really good and open twenty-four hours a day. When you get off work super late and don't want heavy bar food or pizza, a hot bowl of pho, a crunchy banh mi and some spring rolls or raw beef salad are just what you need!"—Jarrett Stieber

PHO DAI LOI 2

Recommended by
Todd Ginsberg

4186 Buford Highway Northeast
Atlanta
Georgia 30345
+1 4046332111

Opening hours	Open 7 days
Reservation policy	No
Credit cards	Accepted
Price range	Budget
Style	Casual
Cuisine	Vietnamese
Recommended for	Bargain

PIJU BELLY

Recommended by
Landon Thompson

678 10th Street Northwest
Atlanta
Georgia 30381
+1 4043436828
www.pijubelly.com

Opening hours	Closed Monday
Reservation policy	No
Credit cards	Accepted
Price range	Affordable
Style	Casual
Cuisine	American-Asian
Recommended for	Breakfast

"I can get ramen for breakfast and the $4 (£3) mimosas are poured tall and stout!"
—Landon Thompson

PROOF BAKESHOP

Recommended by
Steven Satterfield

100 Hurt Street Northeast
Atlanta
Georgia 30307
+1 6787053905
www.proofbakeshop.com

Opening hours	Open 7 days
Reservation policy	No
Credit cards	Accepted
Price range	Budget
Style	Casual
Cuisine	Bakery
Recommended for	Breakfast

RESTAURANT EUGENE

Recommended by
Joe Schafer

2277 Peachtree Road
Atlanta
Georgia 30309
+1 4043550321
www.restauranteugene.com

Opening hours	Closed Monday and Tuesday
Credit cards	Accepted
Price range	Expensive
Style	Smart casual
Cuisine	Modern American
Recommended for	High end

EL REY DEL TACO

Recommended by
Chris Hall, Jarrett Stieber

5288 Buford Highway Northeast
Atlanta
Georgia 30340
+1 7709860032
www.elreydeltacoatl.com

Opening hours	Open 7 days
Reservation policy	No
Credit cards	Accepted
Price range	Affordable
Style	Casual
Cuisine	Mexican
Recommended for	Late night

"*Queso fundido* (melted cheese and chorizo) and a mariachi band at 4.00 a.m.."—Chris Hall

THE RIGHTEOUS ROOM
Recommended by
Jarrett Stieber

1051 Ponce De Leon
Atlanta
Georgia 30306
+1 4048740939
www.stayrighteous.com

Opening hours	Open 7 days
Reservation policy	No
Credit cards	Accepted
Price range	Affordable
Style	Casual
Cuisine	American
Recommended for	Late night

"The wings get the dive-bar food job done very well."
—Jarrett Stieber

SALTYARD
Recommended by
Jarrett Stieber

1820 Peachtree Road Northwest
Atlanta
Georgia 30309
+1 4043828088
www.saltyardatlanta.com

Opening hours	Open 7 days
Credit cards	Accepted
Price range	Affordable
Style	Casual
Cuisine	International Small plates
Recommended for	Regular neighborhood

"Saltyard is an under-the-radar gem in Atlanta;
chef Nick Leahy and his crew truly understand what
hospitality is."—Jarrett Stieber

SIMPLY SEOUL KITCHEN
Recommended by
Linton Hopkins

Ponce City Market
675 Ponce de Leon Avenue Northeast
Atlanta
Georgia 30308
+1 4048531681
www.simplyseoulkitchen.com

Opening hours	Open 7 days
Reservation policy	No
Credit cards	Accepted
Price range	Affordable
Style	Casual
Cuisine	Korean
Recommended for	Bargain

SO BA
Recommended by
Joe Schafer, Landon Thompson

560 Gresham Avenue
Atlanta
Georgia 30316
+1 4046279911
www.soba-eav.com

Opening hours	Open 7 days
Credit cards	Not accepted
Price range	Affordable
Style	Casual
Cuisine	Vietnamese
Recommended for	Regular neighborhood

"So Ba has great pho and my wife and I's absolute
favorite charbroiled pork springrolls. It's become a
tradition of ours to make So Ba our first stop anytime
we fly back to Atlanta. It makes us feel like we're back
home, safe and sound."—Landon Thompson

SOTTO SOTTO
Recommended by
Steven Satterfield

313 North Highland Avenue Northeast
Atlanta
Georgia 30307
+1 4045236678
www.urestaurants.com

Opening hours	Open 7 days
Credit cards	Accepted
Price range	Affordable
Style	Casual
Cuisine	Italian
Recommended for	Regular neighborhood

"Sotto Sotto has an incredible Italian wine list and
hand-made pastas. It's been open for almost twenty
years."—Steven Satterfield

STAPLEHOUSE

541 Edgewood Avenue Southeast
Atlanta
Georgia 30312
+1 4045245005
www.staplehouse.com

Recommended by
Chris Hall,
Steven Satterfield,
Jarrett Stieber,
Landon Thompson

Opening hours	Closed Monday and Tuesday
Credit cards	Accepted
Price range	Affordable
Style	Casual
Cuisine	Modern American
Recommended for	Local favorite

"The passion for food there is obvious and contagious across the entire city. Ryan has a vision and talent that few can compare to and has assembled a mighty team of commis to faithfully execute his menu for those lucky enough to get a seat."—Landon Thompson

It's common now for restaurants to claim they'll make you feel like you're visiting someone's home—yet at Staplehouse, which began as a supper club, it's true. Chef Ryan Smith serves a menu of imaginative, southern-influenced food, and the accessible wine list is organized by style rather than region—a helpful detail that encourages discovery. This is a place with an adventurous and approachable spirit, and a heartfelt desire to nurture friends and family. The company can almost make you take the excellent food for granted.

SUSHI HAYAKAWA

5979 Buford Highway Northeast
Atlanta
Georgia 30340
+1 7709860010
www.atlantasushibar.com

Recommended by
Robert Phalen

Opening hours	Closed Monday and Tuesday
Credit cards	Accepted
Price range	Affordable
Style	Smart casual
Cuisine	Sushi
Recommended for	High end

"All you have to do is trust chef Atsushi 'Art' Hayakawa—his passion for his craft is great and so is the quality of his food!"—Robert Phalen

TICONDEROGA CLUB

99 Krog Street Northeast
Atlanta
Georgia 30307
+1 4044584534
www.ticonderogaclub.com

Recommended by
Todd Ginsberg,
Steven Satterfield

Opening hours	Closed Wednesday
Reservation policy	No
Credit cards	Accepted
Price range	Affordable
Style	Casual
Cuisine	American
Recommended for	Late night

"Best clam roll outside of New England, great veggie stir-fry and an incredible ode to the Salisbury steak. I haven't had a better chopped salad anywhere. Incredible sweetbreads and foie gras...I hope you get the point, no matter what the chef wants to cook, he kills it with a well-thought-out game plan and love."—Todd Ginsberg

UMI

3050 Peachtree Road
Atlanta
Georgia 30305
+1 4048410040
www.umiatlanta.com

Recommended by
Chris Hall

Opening hours	Closed Sunday
Credit cards	Accepted
Price range	Expensive
Style	Smart casual
Cuisine	Modern Japanese
Recommended for	High end

VENKMAN'S

Recommended by
Joe Schafer

740 Ralph McGill Boulevard Northeast
Atlanta
Georgia 30312
+1 4702256162
www.venkmans.com

Opening hours	Closed Monday
Credit cards	Accepted
Price range	Affordable
Style	Casual
Cuisine	Southern American-International
Recommended for	Local favorite

"Rooted in the South but draws influence from lots of different cuisines without coming across as a 'fusion' restaurant."—Joe Schafer

VICTORY SANDWICH BAR

Recommended by
Todd Ginsberg

913 Bernina Avenue Northeast
Atlanta
Georgia 30307
+1 4049631742
www.vicsandwich.com

Opening hours	Open 7 days
Reservation policy	No
Credit cards	Accepted
Price range	Budget
Style	Casual
Cuisine	Sandwiches
Recommended for	Late night

"*Fantastic tonkotsu ramen, great broth... and spicy.*"

ANDREW ZIMMERMAN P962

"THE HIGHEST QUALITY FISH IN THE CITY SERVED BY AN INCREDIBLY TALENTED CHEF."

KEVIN HICKEY P990

CHICAGO

"*The highest quality fish in the city served by an incredibly warm and talented sushi chef.*"

KEVIN HICKEY P968

"It's still one of my favorite restaurants in the city and it continues to define new Chicago."

COSMO GOSS P958

CHICAGO

<N>

SCALE

0   800   1600   2400
└─────┴─────┴─────┘ yd.

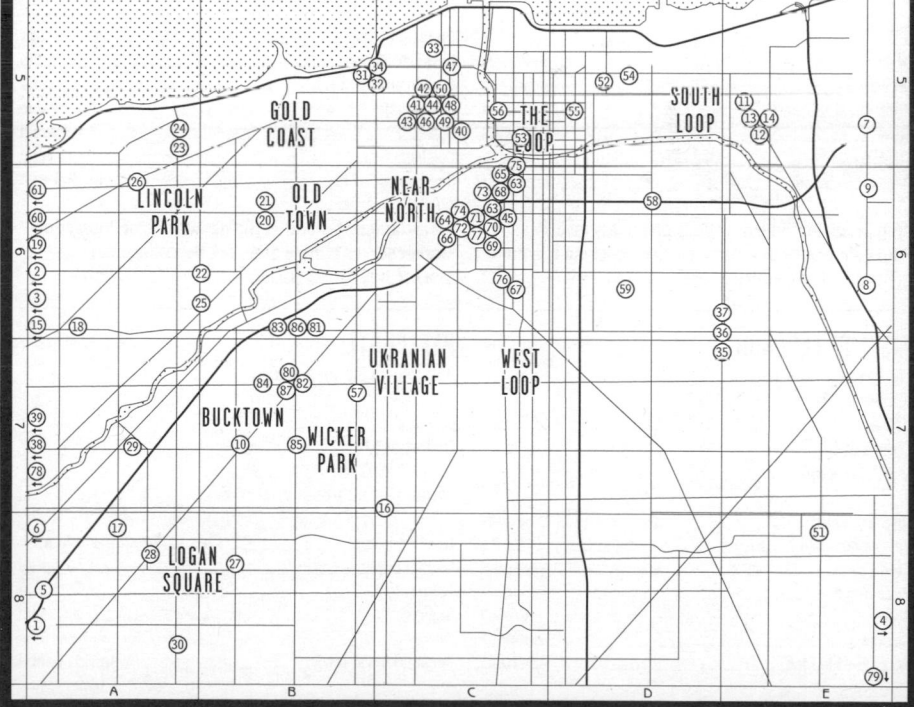

CHICAGO KALBI

Recommended by
Cosmo Goss

3752 West Lawrence Avenue
Albany Park
Chicago
Illinois 60625
+1 7736048183
www.chicago-kalbi.com

Opening hours	Closed Tuesday
Credit cards	Accepted
Price range	Affordable
Style	Casual
Cuisine	Japanese-Korean BBQ
Recommended for	Regular neighborhood

"Korean BBQ—very unpretentious, with delicious food. The place is a little goofy when you walk in—it used to be a sushi restaurant and the cases are filled with signed baseballs now."—Cosmo Goss

BIG JONES

Recommended by
Ignacio Mattos

5347 North Clark Street
Andersonville
Chicago
Illinois 60640
+1 7732755725
www.bigjoneschicago.com

Opening hours	Open 7 days
Credit cards	Accepted
Price range	Affordable
Style	Casual
Cuisine	Southern American
Recommended for	Breakfast

"Big Jones in Andersonville is one of my favorites. Paul Fehribach's Southern-inspired cooking is among the best in the country."—Ignacio Mattos

TASTE OF LEBANON

Recommended by
David Posey

1509 West Foster Avenue
Andersonville
Chicago
Illinois 60640
+1 7733341600

Opening hours	Closed Sunday
Reservation policy	No
Credit cards	Not accepted
Price range	Budget
Style	Casual
Cuisine	Lebanese
Recommended for	Bargain

BIRRIERIA ZARAGOZA

Recommended by
Kevin Hickey

4854 South Pulaski Road
Archer Heights
Chicago
Illinois 60632
+1 7735233700
www.birrieriazaragoza.com

Opening hours	Open 7 days
Reservation policy	No
Credit cards	Accepted
Price range	Affordable
Style	Casual
Cuisine	Mexican
Recommended for	Regular neighborhood

"Birrieria Zaragoza on Chicago's West Side serves the best goat stew in Chicago."—Kevin Hickey

JOONG BOO MARKET

Recommended by
Kevin Hickey

3333 North Kimball Avenue
Avondale
Chicago
Illinois 60618
+1 7734785566
www.joongboomarket.com

Opening hours	Open 7 days
Reservation policy	No
Credit cards	Accepted
Price range	Affordable
Style	Casual
Cuisine	Korean
Recommended for	Bargain

"The dumpling stand in the parking lot of Joong Boo Market serves kimchi and pork dumplings the size of a softball for $2 (£1.50) each."—Kevin Hickey

PARACHUTE

Recommended by
Rick Bayless

3500 North Elston Avenue
Avondale
Chicago
Illinois 60618
+1 7736541460
www.parachuterestaurant.com

Opening hours	Closed Monday and Sunday
Credit cards	Accepted
Price range	Affordable
Style	Casual
Cuisine	Korean-American
Recommended for	Wish I'd opened

"I could never cook this food—I admire Beverly Kim and Johnny Clark so much. They bring nuance and depth to their cooking. Just a fantastic place."
—Rick Bayless

FRANCO'S RISTORANTE

Recommended by
Kevin Hickey

300 West 31st Street
Bridgeport
Chicago
Illinois 60616
+1 7732259566
www.francoschicago.com

Opening hours	Open 7 days
Credit cards	Accepted
Price range	Affordable
Style	Casual
Cuisine	Italian
Recommended for	Regular neighborhood

"Franco's in Bridgeport is doing classic Italian-American food in a very traditional Italian neighborhood that strangely, doesn't have many Italian restaurants."—Kevin Hickey

MEXICO STEAK HOUSE

Recommended by
Kevin Hickey

2983 South Archer Avenue
Bridgeport
Chicago
Illinois 60608
+1 7732545151
www.chicagomexicosteakhouse.com

Opening hours	Closed Monday
Reservation policy	No
Credit cards	Accepted
Price range	Affordable
Style	Casual
Cuisine	Mexican
Recommended for	Breakfast

"I've been going there since I was born. The chilaquiles are my favorite along with the *carne asada* (grilled beef) and eggs. Mostly I go because the waitresses have been feeding me since I was a baby."—Kevin Hickey

NORTHERN CITY

Recommended by
Kevin Hickey

742 West 31st Street
Bridgeport
Chicago
Illinois 60616
+1 3128429677
www.northerncity.com

Opening hours	Open 7 days
Credit cards	Accepted but not AMEX or Diners
Price range	Budget
Style	Casual
Cuisine	Northern Chinese
Recommended for	Regular neighborhood

"Not your typical Chinese fare. High-quality ingredients, and substantial portions."—Kevin Hickey

ARTURO'S TACOS

Recommended by
Cosmo Goss

2001 North Western Avenue
Bucktown
Chicago
Illinois
www.arturos-tacos.com

Opening hours	Open 7 days
Credit cards	Accepted
Price range	Budget
Style	Casual
Cuisine	Mexican
Recommended for	Bargain

"It reminds me of the great taco places in California, where I'm from. Milanesa Torta—get it every time."
—Cosmo Goss

CAI

Recommended by
Cosmo Goss

2100 South Archer Avenue
Chinatown
Chicago
Illinois 60616
+1 3123266888
www.caichicago.com

Opening hours	Open 7 days
Credit cards	Accepted
Price range	Affordable
Style	Casual
Cuisine	Asian
Recommended for	Late night

"Open late, with a live seafood tank. I love picking a bunch of different things and they'll just cook it right up. "—Cosmo Goss

MINGHIN CUISINE

2168 South Archer Avenue
Chinatown
Chicago
Illinois 60616
+1 3128081999
www.minghincuisine.com

Opening hours	Open 7 days
Credit cards	Accepted
Price range	Affordable
Style	Smart casual
Cuisine	Chinese
Recommended for	Regular neighborhood

"I like going to MingHin for its authenticity. The dim sum is great, with really wonderful dumplings (shrimp with pea tip, shrimp with chives) Macao-style pork belly, XO noodle roll and egg rolls that remind me of my childhood. The dim sum crepes filled with seafood are another hit."—Sarah Grueneberg

STRINGS RAMEN

2141 South Archer Avenue
Chinatown
Chicago
Illinois 60616
+1 3123473450
www.ramenchicago.com

Opening hours	Open 7 days
Reservation policy	No
Credit cards	Accepted
Price range	Affordable
Style	Casual
Cuisine	Ramen Noodles
Recommended for	Late night

"House-made noodles, great broth, a variety of toppings, and friendly service until 2.00 a.m."
—Kevin Hickey

XI'AN CUISINE

225 West Cermak Road
Chinatown
Chicago
Illinois 60616
+1 3123263171
www.xiancuisinechicago.com

Opening hours	Open 7 days
Reservation policy	No
Credit cards	Accepted
Price range	Budget
Style	Casual
Cuisine	Chinese
Recommended for	Bargain

"Authentic, affordable and delicious. The lamb flat-bread is the dish to order."—Sarah Grueneberg

MAMA'S SOUL KITCHEN

Douglas Park
Chicago
Illinois

Opening hours	Variable
Credit cards	Not accepted
Price range	Budget
Style	Casual
Cuisine	Soul food
Recommended for	Regular neighborhood

"We don't really have too much of a neighborhood where I live above our restaurant in the little known neighborhood of Douglas Park, but Mama's Soul Kitchen on our block makes some badass eats on Thursday nights."—Phillip Foss

ROOTSTOCK

954 North California Avenue
Humboldt Park
Chicago
Illinois 60622
+1 7732921616
www.rootstockbar.com

Opening hours	Open 7 days
Reservation policy	No
Credit cards	Accepted
Price range	Affordable
Style	Casual
Cuisine	Wine Bar
Recommended for	Late night

FAT RICE

Recommended by
Cosmo Goss

2957 West Diversey Avenue
Lake View
Chicago
Illinois 60647
+1 7736619170
www.eatfatrice.com

Opening hours	Closed Monday
Credit cards	Accepted
Price range	Affordable
Style	Casual
Cuisine	Asian Fusion
Recommended for	Wish I'd opened

"Not just traditional chinese and it's not in a great part of town, which is difficult and doing a cookbook is tough too. I just really admire what they're doing with food and their business."—Cosmo Goss

REDHOT RANCH

Recommended by
Brian Ahern

3057 North Ashland Avenue
Lake View
Chicago
Illinois 60657
+1 7736619377

Opening hours	Open 7 days
Reservation policy	No
Credit cards	Not accepted
Price range	Budget
Style	Casual
Cuisine	Hot Dogs
Recommended for	Late night

"A little, awesome hot dog stand. The griddle burger is delicious and addictive."—Brian Ahern

TOONS BAR & GRILL

Recommended by
Brian Ahern

3857 North Southport
Lake View
Chicago
Illinois 60613
+1 7739351919
www.chicagotoons.com

Opening hours	Open 7 days
Reservation policy	No
Credit cards	Accepted
Price range	Affordable
Style	Casual
Cuisine	American Bar
Recommended for	Local favorite

"A little sports bar by my old house with great bar food. Best wings in Chicago hands down."
—Brian Ahern

ALINEA

Recommended by
Tomer Amedi, Kristian Baumann,
Rick Bayless, Kyle Connaughton,
Rolf Fliegauf, Phillip Foss,
Sarah Grueneberg, Gavin Kaysen,
Carlos Perez, Shaun Quade,
Ljubomir Stanisic, Townsend
Wentz, Lee Wolen

1723 North Halsted Street
Lincoln Park
Chicago
Illinois 60614
+1 3128670110
www.alinearestaurant.com

Opening hours	Closed Monday and Tuesday
Credit cards	Accepted
Price range	Expensive
Style	Smart casual
Cuisine	Modern American
Recommended for	Worth the travel

"Recently, I was fortunate enough to dine at Alinea and experience the creativity of Grant and his team first-hand. The one thing that struck me, aside from the creativity of the dishes, was simply how much fun I had in a formal dining setting. I laughed at some points in the meal and felt goosebumps on my arms at others. It kept me completely transfixed for four and a half hours."—Shaun Quade

Before Grant Achatz and Nick Kokonas opened the restaurant in May 2005, Alinea was known as the lesser used term for a paragraph symbol (the word comes from Latin, meaning 'off the line'.) But today it is synonymous with Achatz's singularly creative and virtuosic coupling of food and science. From green apple balloons to desserts prepared literally on the table, the restaurant continues to be a beacon of creativity shining from the interior of the United States into kitchens across the country and beyond. After a recent gut renovation, which juxtaposes classical elements with contemporary flourishes, there are three menus from which to choose. For parties of six or more, there's the Alinea Kitchen Table, the highest expression of Achatz's fancy; then there's the Gallery Menu, with sixteen to eighteen courses, and the Salon menu, with ten to twelve.

BOKA

Recommended by
Cosmo Goss, David Posey

1729 North Halsted Street
Lincoln Park
Chicago
Illinois 60614
+1 313376070
www.bokachicago.com

Opening hours	Open 7 days
Credit cards	Accepted
Price range	Expensive
Style	Formal
Cuisine	Modern American
Recommended for	High end

"The food is great and simple—it's not trying to be anything it's not. It's still one of my favorite restaurants in the city and it continues to define new Chicago."—Cosmo Goss

All the modern American dishes listed on the menu of this one-Michelin star restaurant sound elegant, appetizing and a little quirky—you might find roasted Spanish octopus with fennel and kumquat, roasted dry-aged duck with foie gras sausage and rhubarb, or mouth-watering desserts such as grilled pineapple with fernet and butterscotch. Quite unusually, there's also a rich selection of hand-selected teas to accompany your meal (including magnolia blossom oolong and Sicilian blood orange green). The restaurant's name is a combination of the surnames of its founders, Kevin Boehm and Rob Katz—but Boka has made a name for itself since it opened in 2003, and continues to dazzle diners and critics alike.

FLORIOLE BAKERY

Recommended by
Lee Wolen

1220 West Webster Avenue
Lincoln Park
Chicago
Illinois 60614
+1 7738831313
www.floriole.com

Opening hours	Open 7 days
Reservation policy	No
Credit cards	Accepted
Price range	Budget
Style	Casual
Cuisine	Bakery
Recommended for	Breakfast

"They have amazing pastries and savory breakfast items, such as quiche, ham and cheese croissants, as well as savory vegetarian options." —Lee Wolen

MON AMI GABI

Recommended by
Jean Joho

2300 North Lincoln Park West
Lincoln Park
Chicago
Illinois 60614
+1 7733488886
www.monamigabi.com

Opening hours	Open 7 days
Credit cards	Accepted
Price range	Expensive
Style	Smart casual
Cuisine	French Bistro
Recommended for	Late night

"French fare in a great ambiance."—Jean Joho

NAOKI

Recommended by
Jean Joho

2300 North Lincoln Park West
Lincoln Park
Chicago
Illinois 60614
+1 7738680002
www.naoki-sushi.com

Opening hours	Closed Monday and Sunday
Credit cards	Accepted
Price range	Expensive
Style	Smart casual
Cuisine	Sushi
Recommended for	Regular neighborhood

PEQUOD'S PIZZERIA

Recommended by
Phillip Foss

2207 North Clybourn Avenue
Lincoln Park
Chicago
Illinois 60614
+1 7733271512
www.pequodspizza.com

Opening hours	Open 7 days
Credit cards	Accepted
Price range	Affordable
Style	Casual
Cuisine	Pizza
Recommended for	Bargain

"If you can get past the fact that deep-dish is more like pizza lasagne than actual pizza, then this one is excellent. The lunch special at $5 (£3), with a soft drink, is a crazy good bargain."—Phillip Foss

THE WIENERS CIRCLE

Recommended by
Phillip Foss, Edward Lee

2622 North Clark Street
Lincoln Park
Chicago
Illinois 60614
+1 7734777444

Opening hours	Open 7 days
Reservation policy	No
Credit cards	Not accepted
Price range	Budget
Style	Casual
Cuisine	Hot Dogs
Recommended for	Bargain

"The Weiners Circle's char-dogs are really delicious and underrated, but the real treats are the vulgar cashiers. Make sure you ask for one of their $20 (£16) milkshakes. It may sound steep, but it's one of the best bargains in town for sure!"—Phillip Foss

In a city where there's said to be more hot dog stands than branches of all the big fast food brands combined, Lincoln Park's Wieners Circle has found fame—much of it for the X-rated patter of the ladies that work the counter. That's not to say that if you order 'the works'—a grilled Vienna Beef on a warm poppy seed bun, topped with mustard, onions, relish, dill pickle spears, tomato slices, peppers and celery salt—you'll be disappointed. Open until 5.00 a.m. on Fridays and Saturdays, it's popular with weary bar-hoppers who prefer their dog with a side of small-hours verbal abuse.

GIANT

Recommended by
Brian Ahern, Sarah Grueneberg,
David Posey, Lee Wolen

3209 West Armitage Avenue
Logan Square
Chicago
Illinois 60647
+1 7732520997
www.giantrestaurant.com

Opening hours	Closed Monday
Credit cards	Accepted
Price range	Affordable
Style	Casual
Cuisine	American
Recommended for	Regular neighborhood

"Delicious creative food that packs a punch. The pasta is incredible as well as the vegetable dishes."
—Lee Wolen

LULA CAFE

Recommended by
Brian Ahern, Rick Bayless,
Cosmo Goss, David Posey,
Lee Wolen, Andrew Zimmerman

2537 North Kedzie Avenue
Logan Square
Chicago
Illinois 60647
+1 7734899554
www.lulacafe.com

Opening hours	Closed Tuesday
Credit cards	Accepted
Price range	Affordable
Style	Casual
Cuisine	American
Recommended for	Breakfast

"Creative, well-executed and market-driven menu of local food, delivered with friendly service. It's a positively Midwestern experience."—Rick Bayless

A pioneer of the farm-to-table movement in Chicago, Lula sees itself as something of a renegade on the city's dining scene. Simple sophistication is what's on offer here. Brushed concrete and exposed ducts meet modern art and elegant drapes in the dining room, and colorful seasonal dishes are peppered with unusual components: nettle-crusted New York strip steak with black lentils and smoked date, or salmon steamed in ramp leaves with English peas and goat's milk yoghurt. To experience the chefs in full flow, pitch up for the Monday night 'Farm Dinner', but even the brunch, which runs until 2.30 p.m., is full of surprises. Save room for dessert—it's the stuff of local legend.

OWEN & ENGINE

Recommended by
Rick Bayless

2700 North Western Avenue
Logan Square
Chicago
Illinois 60647
+1 7732352930
www.owenandengine.com

Opening hours	Open 7 days
Credit cards	Accepted
Price range	Affordable
Style	Casual
Cuisine	British Bistro
Recommended for	Regular neighborhood

"This is the type of place that would be at home in a bustling downtown, but it's that much better because it's in a neighborhood. The menu here goes way above and beyond. It's pub food, but they support local farmers and that makes it all the better. Plus, there's a great beer list."—Rick Bayless

L'PATRON TACOS

Recommended by
Lee Wolen

3749 West Fullerton Avenue
Logan Square
Chicago
Illinois 60647
+1 7732526335

Opening hours	Closed Tuesday
Reservation policy	No
Credit cards	Not accepted
Price range	Budget
Style	Casual
Cuisine	Mexican
Recommended for	Bargain

"L'Patron tacos are my favorite tacos in Chicago
as well."—Lee Wolen

GIBSONS

Recommended by
Kevin Hickey

1028 North Rush Street
Near North
Chicago
Illinois 60611
+1 3122668999
www.gibsonssteakhouse.com

Opening hours	Open 7 days
Credit cards	Accepted
Price range	Affordable
Style	Smart casual
Cuisine	Steakhouse
Recommended for	Local favorite

"I was born and raised in Chicago but lived around
the world for thirteen years. Whenever I came
home Gibsons was a must. It feels like the whole
city is centered there—politicians, professional
athletes, cops and celebrities, all eating giant food—
quintessential Chicago!"—Kevin Hickey

NICO OSTERIA

Recommended by
Michael Friedman

1015 North Rush Street
Near North
Chicago
Illinois 60611
+1 3129947100
www.nicoosteria.com

Opening hours	Open 7 days
Credit cards	Accepted
Price range	Expensive
Style	Smart casual
Cuisine	Italian
Recommended for	Worth the travel

LES NOMADES

Recommended by
Kevin Hickey

222 East Ontario Street
Near North
Chicago
Illinois 60611
+1 3126499010
www.lesnomades.net

Opening hours	Closed Monday and Sunday
Credit cards	Accepted
Price range	Expensive
Style	Formal
Cuisine	French
Recommended for	Local favorite

"Les Nomades has been celebrating fine French
cuisine in one form or another for over three
decades."—Kevin Hickey

SPIAGGIA

Recommended by
Michael Friedman

980 North Michigan Avenue
Near North
Chicago
Illinois 60611
+1 3122802750
www.spiaggiarestaurant.com

Opening hours	Open 7 days
Credit cards	Accepted
Price range	Expensive
Style	Smart casual
Cuisine	Italian
Recommended for	Worth the travel

5 RABANITOS

Recommended by
Kevin Hickey

1758 West 18th Street
Pilsen
Chicago
Illinois 60608
+1 3122852710
www.5rabanitosdotcom.wordpress.com

Opening hours	Closed Monday
Credit cards	Accepted
Price range	Affordable
Style	Casual
Cuisine	Mexican
Recommended for	Regular neighborhood

"5 Rabinitos in the Pilsen neighborhood of Chicago
is doing very good Mexican food with modern
preparations and flavors."—Kevin Hickey

CARNITAS URUAPAN

Recommended by
Rick Bayless

1725 West 18th Street
Pilsen
Chicago
Illinois 60608
+1 3122262654
www.carnitasuruapanchi.com

Opening hours	Open 7 days
Reservation policy	No
Credit cards	Accepted
Price range	Budget
Style	Casual
Cuisine	Mexican
Recommended for	Bargain

"Simply put, you can get a lot of classic carnitas—crispy, golden, perfect—for not a lot of money. When I'm in Pilsen, it's a must-visit."—Rick Bayless

TAQUERIA LOS COMALES

Recommended by
Kevin Hickey

1544 West 18th Street
Pilsen
Chicago
Illinois 60623
+1 3126662251
www.loscomales.com

Opening hours	Open 7 days
Reservation policy	No
Credit cards	Accepted
Price range	Budget
Style	Casual
Cuisine	Mexican
Recommended for	Late night

"Los Comales for late-night torts"—Kevin Hickey

DANCEN

Recommended by
Lee Wolen

5114 North Lincoln Avenue
Ravenswood
Chicago
Illinois 60625
+1 7738782400

Opening hours	Open 7 days
Reservation policy	No
Credit cards	Accepted
Price range	Affordable
Style	Casual
Cuisine	Korean
Recommended for	Late night

"I think it's a cool up-beat atmosphere. The chef cooks in front of you. They also have interesting dishes such as double-fried pork skin in chile sauce which is pretty unhealthy but pretty mind-blowing at the same time."—Lee Wolen

SAN SOO GAB SAN

Recommended by
Kevin Hickey

5247 North Western Avenue
Ravenswood
Chicago
Illinois 60625
+1 7733341589

Opening hours	Open 7 days
Credit cards	Accepted
Price range	Affordable
Style	Casual
Cuisine	Korean
Recommended for	Regular neighborhood

"San Soo Gab San is the Korean standard bearer in Chicago, as well as the cafeteria at Joong Boo Food Market."—Kevin Hickey

BAVETTE'S

Recommended by
Sarah Grueneberg

218 West Kinzie Street
River North
Chicago
Illinois 60654
+1 3126248154
www.bavetteschicago.com

Opening hours	Open 7 days
Credit cards	Accepted
Price range	Affordable
Style	Smart casual
Cuisine	Steakhouse
Recommended for	High end

"I love to order the grand shellfish platter and instead of lobster get the king crab. Then we'll order the forty-two-day dry aged bone-in rib eye. Always save room for the chocolate cream pie. I also really enjoy going here because it has a romantic atmosphere without being stuffy."—Sarah Grueneberg

BEATRIX

Recommended by
Jean Joho

529 North Clark Street
River North
Chicago
Illinois 60654
+1 3122841377
www.beatrixchicago.com

Opening hours	Open 7 days
Credit cards	Accepted
Price range	Affordable
Style	Casual
Cuisine	American
Recommended for	Breakfast

BOHEMIAN HOUSE

Recommended by
Kevin Hickey

11 West Illinois Street
River North
Chicago
Illinois 60654
+1 3129550439
www.bohochicago.com

Opening hours	Open 7 days
Credit cards	Accepted
Price range	Expensive
Style	Casual
Cuisine	Eastern European
Recommended for	Wish I'd opened

"I thought it was pretty ballsy to open an unabashedly Eastern European restaurant in a neighborhood full of nightclubs and chain restaurants. The food is well-executed modern interpretations of the Polish, German and Lithuanian cuisine that I grew up on."
—Kevin Hickey

BRINDILLE

Recommended by
Kevin Hickey, Norman Van Aken

534 North Clark Street
River North
Chicago Illinois
+1 3125951616
www.brindille-chicago.com

Opening hours	Closed Sunday
Credit cards	Accepted
Price range	Expensive
Style	Smart casual
Cuisine	French
Recommended for	High end

"This is a Michelin-starred restaurant run by the amazing Chef Carrie Nahabedian. The place is stunning and her food is timeless."—Norman Van Aken

FRONTERA GRILL

Recommended by
Kevin Hickey

445 North Clark Street
River North
Chicago
Illinois 60654
+1 3126611434
www.rickbayless.com/restaurants/frontera-grill

Opening hours	Closed Monday and Sunday
Credit cards	Accepted
Price range	Affordable
Style	Casual
Cuisine	Mexican
Recommended for	Local favorite

"Frontera Grill has been serving elevated Mexican cuisine for over twenty-five years."—Kevin Hickey

HIGH FIVE RAMEN

Recommended by
Andrew Zimmerman

112 North Green Street
River North
Chicago
Illinois 60607
+1 3127540431
www.highfiveramen.com

Opening hours	Open 7 days
Reservation policy	No
Credit cards	Accepted
Price range	Affordable
Style	Casual
Cuisine	Japanese
Recommended for	Late night

"Fantastic *tonkotsu* ramen, great broth...and spicy."
—Andrew Zimmerman

NAHA

Recommended by
Kevin Hickey

500 North Clark Street
River North
Chicago
Illinois 60654
+1 3123216242
www.naha-chicago.com

Opening hours	Closed Sunday
Credit cards	Accepted
Price range	Expensive
Style	Smart casual
Cuisine	Modern American
Recommended for	Local favorite

"Naha has been a standard bearer for approachable fine dining and a family favorite."—Kevin Hickey

THE PURPLE PIG

Recommended by
Thomas Kim, Ryan Trimm

500 North Michigan Avenue
River North
Chicago
Illinois 60611
+1 3124641744
www.thepurplepigchicago.com

Opening hours	Open 7 days
Reservation policy	No
Credit cards	Accepted
Price range	Expensive
Style	Casual
Cuisine	Italian-American
Recommended for	Worth the travel

"The Purple Pig uses quality products to create really flavorful and memorable dishes. The food coming out of their kitchen is food that I could eat everyday. The space is fairly intimate and you have a full view of the kitchen so you feel part of the action."—Thomas Kim

RAMEN-SAN

Recommended by
Jean Joho

59 West Hubbard Street
River North
Chicago
Illinois 60654
+1 3123779950
www.ramensan.com

Opening hours	Open 7 days
Credit cards	Accepted
Price range	Affordable
Style	Casual
Cuisine	Ramen Noodles
Recommended for	Regular neighborhood

RPM STEAK

Recommended by
Jean Joho

66 West Kinzie Street
River North
Chicago
Illinois 60654
+1 3122844990
www.rpmrestaurants.com/rpmsteak/chicago

Opening hours	Open 7 days
Credit cards	Accepted
Price range	Expensive
Style	Smart casual
Cuisine	Steakhouse
Recommended for	Wish I'd opened

TOPOLOBAMPO

Recommended by
Kevin Hickey

445 North Clark Street
River North
Chicago
Illinois 60610
+1 3126611434
www.rickbayless.com/restaurants/topolobampo

Opening hours	Closed Monday and Sunday
Credit cards	Accepted
Price range	Expensive
Style	Smart casual
Cuisine	Mexican
Recommended for	Local favorite

LA CHAPARRITA

Recommended by
David Posey

2500 South Whipple Street
South Lawndale
Chicago
Illinois 60623
+1 7732471402

Opening hours	Closed Thursday
Reservation policy	No
Credit cards	Accepted
Price range	Budget
Style	Casual
Cuisine	Mexican
Recommended for	Bargain

DEVIL DAWGS

Recommended by
Sarah Grueneberg

767 South State Street
The Loop
Chicago
Illinois 60605
www.devildawgs.com

Opening hours	Open 7 days
Reservation policy	No
Credit cards	Accepted
Price range	Budget
Style	Casual
Cuisine	American
Recommended for	Bargain

"Great Chicago-style hot dogs with green chile cheese fries. The fried chicken sandwich is really good too."
—Sarah Grueneberg

THE EASTMAN EGG COMPANY

Recommended by
Sarah Grueneberg

23 North Upper Wacker Drive
The Loop
Chicago
Illinois 60606
+1 3123841011
www.eastmanegg.com

Opening hours	Closed Saturday and Sunday
Reservation policy	No
Credit cards	Accepted
Price range	Budget
Style	Casual
Cuisine	International
Recommended for	Breakfast

ELEVEN CITY DINER

Recommended by
Sarah Grueneberg

1112 South Wabash Avenue
The Loop
Chicago
Illinois 60605
+1 3122121112
www.elevencitydiner.com

Opening hours	Open 7 days
Reservation policy	No
Credit cards	Accepted
Price range	Affordable
Style	Casual
Cuisine	Diner-Deli
Recommended for	Breakfast

"The freaking latkes (potato pancakes), smoked salmon and bagels are all delicious. I also love the fish plate, the matzo ball soup is one of the best in Chicago, and the 'Schwartz' smoked beef brisket on a challah roll and then add chopped chicken liver to it."—Sarah Grueneberg

EVEREST

Recommended by
Jean Joho

440 South LaSalle
The Loop
Chicago
Illinois 60605
+1 3126638920
www.everestrestaurant.com

Opening hours	Closed Monday
Credit cards	Accepted
Price range	Expensive
Style	Formal
Cuisine	French
Recommended for	High end

"Top culinary experience in fine dining in the Midwest."—Jean Joho

M BURGER

Recommended by
Jean Joho

100 West Randolph Street
The Loop
Chicago
Illinois 60601
www.mburger.com

Opening hours	Open 7 days
Reservation policy	No
Credit cards	Accepted
Price range	Budget
Style	Casual
Cuisine	Burger
Recommended for	Bargain

PUB ROYALE

Recommended by
Sarah Grueneberg,
Kevin Hickey

2049 West Division Street
Ukrainian Village
Chicago
Illinois 60622
+1 7736616874
www.pubroyale.com

Opening hours	Open 7 days
Credit cards	Accepted
Price range	Affordable
Style	Casual
Cuisine	Anglo-Indian
Recommended for	Late night

"One of my favorite places to go to after a long day in the kitchen. Don't miss the lamb dumplings, salt cod samosas and cucumber raita. They also have twenty-four global beers on draft!"—Sarah Grueneberg

JIM'S ORIGINAL

Recommended by
Kevin Hickey

1250 South Union Avenue
University Village
Chicago
Illinois 60607
+1 3127337820
www.jimsoriginal.com

Opening hours	Open 7 days
Reservation policy	No
Credit cards	Accepted
Price range	Budget
Style	Casual
Cuisine	American
Recommended for	Late night

"You're not a true Chicagoan if you haven't eaten a Polish sausage at 4.00 a.m. at Jim's Original."
—Kevin Hickey

STAX CAFE

Recommended by
Kevin Hickey

1401 West Taylor Street
University Village
Chicago
Illinois 60607
+1 3127339871
www.staxcafe.com

Opening hours	Open 7 days
Reservation policy	No
Credit cards	Accepted
Price range	Affordable
Style	Casual
Cuisine	Breakfast-Brunch
Recommended for	Breakfast

"Stax for the short rib hash."—Kevin Hickey

BA LE

Recommended by
Andrew Zimmerman

5014 North Broadway
Uptown
Chicago
Illinois 60640
www.balesandwich.com

Opening hours	Open 7 days
Credit cards	Accepted
Price range	Budget
Style	Casual
Cuisine	Vietnamese
Recommended for	Bargain

"Amazing banh mi sandwiches."—Andrew Zimmerman

PHO LOAN

Recommended by
David Posey

1114 West Argyle Street
Uptown
Chicago
Illinois 60640
+1 7733344500
www.pholoanchicago.com

Opening hours	Closed Thursday
Reservation policy	No
Credit cards	Accepted
Price range	Affordable
Style	Casual
Cuisine	Vietnamese
Recommended for	Bargain

AU CHEVAL

Recommended by
Phillip Foss, Sarah Grueneberg,
Chris Hall

800 West Randolph Street
West Loop
Chicago
Illinois 60607
+1 3129294580
www.auchevalchicago.com

Opening hours	Open 7 days
Reservation policy	No
Credit cards	Accepted
Price range	Affordable
Style	Casual
Cuisine	Modern American
Recommended for	Worth the travel

"A diner on steroids. Fun, honest and delicious food and drink."—Chris Hall

A Mecca for the hip, the hungry and the downright gluttonous, Chicago's Au Cheval pulls none of its punches. Full-bore diner dishes might take their cues from Europe, but the presentation—loaded with cheese and eggs—and the unashamedly supersize portions are all American. Locals queue out the door for the city's best cheeseburger (a single packs two patties, a double three) and the beast of a bologna sandwich, delivered by staff who, like the cooking, are both laid back and on point. The joint is at its jumping best in the early hours—slide into one of the studded leather booths for a ball-breaker of a cocktail and a hefty pile of chilaquiles (smothered tortilla chips), only served after midnight.

AVEC

Recommended by
Brian Ahern, Cosmo Goss,
Andrew Zimmerman

615 West Randolph Street
West Loop
Chicago
Illinois 60661
+1 3123772002
www.avecrestaurant.com

Opening hours	Open 7 days
Credit cards	Accepted
Price range	Affordable
Style	Casual
Cuisine	Mediterranean
Recommended for	Late night

"Terrific late-night small plates and great beers."
—Andrew Zimmerman

THE AVIARY

955 West Fulton Market
West Loop
Chicago
Illinois 60607
+1 3122260868
www.theaviary.com

Opening hours	Open 7 days
Credit cards	Accepted
Price range	Expensive
Style	Smart casual
Cuisine	Bar-Small plates
Recommended for	Late night

"Grant Achatz's Aviary is a must-go for the coolest drinks and inspired bites at any hour."—Phillip Foss

BLACKBIRD

619 West Randolph Street
West Loop
Chicago
Illinois 60661
+1 3127150708
www.blackbirdrestaurant.com

Opening hours	Open 7 days
Credit cards	Accepted
Price range	Affordable
Style	Smart casual
Cuisine	American
Recommended for	High end

"Like Chicago, Blackbird is a classic that finds ways to reinvent itself while staying true to its roots in Midwestern cuisine and Midwestern farms."
—Andrew Zimmerman

COLD STORAGE

1000 West Fulton Market
West Loop
Chicago
Illinois 60607
+1 3126386280
www.coldstoragechicago.com

Opening hours	Open 7 days
Credit cards	Accepted
Price range	Affordable
Style	Casual
Cuisine	American Seafood
Recommended for	Regular neighborhood

"I love being able to eat at a classic East Coast oyster bar that's chef driven but still has the classic dishes of an old-school oyster bar. Whether it's the vegetable inspired dishes or the roasted crab knuckles, you can't go wrong."—Lee Wolen

ELSKE

1350 West Randolph Street
West Loop
Chicago
Illinois 60607
+1 3127331314
www.elskerestaurant.com

Opening hours	Closed Monday and Tuesday
Credit cards	Accepted
Price range	Expensive
Style	Smart casual
Cuisine	Modern American
Recommended for	High end

"I love the owners and I can't wait to go back. They're trying to push tasting menus only, which is a dying breed of restaurant."—Cosmo Goss

GRACE

652 West Randolph Street
West Loop
Chicago
Illinois 60661
+1 3122349494
www.grace-restaurant.com

Opening hours	Closed Monday and Sunday
Credit cards	Accepted
Price range	Expensive
Style	Formal
Cuisine	Modern American
Recommended for	High end

"I was extremely impressed by Grace. I dined alone and, while I find dining is much better with company, I was made to feel welcome by the servers and the chef, who allowed me to dabble between both their Flora and Fauna menus. The food was exceptional too, of course."—Sarah Welch

Great things were expected of Curtis Duffy when, late in 2012, he opened Grace, his earnest—in the true sense of the word—contribution to the culinary arts in Chicago's West Loop. He hasn't disappointed since. Duffy earned his stripes at Chicago's finest—Charlie Trotter's, Trio, Alinea, Avenues—and is now in the same league himself. Grace is an apt name: a serene space, seventeen linen-dressed tables, sixty-four soft white leather chairs, plush carpet and a contrastingly hard-edged, glass-walled kitchen. Choose between two elaborately presented, nine-course menus: $235 each (£180) that meld modern haute technique with inspiration from Japan —the vegetarian 'Flora' or the omnivorous 'Fauna'.

LEÑA BRAVA

Recommended by
Cosmo Goss

900 West Randolph Street
West Loop
Chicago
Illinois 60607
+1 3127331975
www.rickbayless.com/restaurants/lena-brava

Opening hours	Closed Monday
Credit cards	Accepted
Price range	Affordable
Style	Casual
Cuisine	Mexican-Seafood
Recommended for	Regular neighborhood

MAUDE'S LIQUOR BAR

Recommended by
Rick Bayless

840 West Randolph Street
West Loop
Chicago
Illinois 60607
+1 3122439712
www.maudesliquorbar.com

Opening hours	Open 7 days
Credit cards	Accepted
Price range	Affordable
Style	Casual
Cuisine	French
Recommended for	Late night

"Maude's always beckons with the promise of good cocktails and classic French food."—Rick Bayless

MOMOTARO

Recommended by
Phillip Foss, Andy Hollyday,
James Rigato

820 West Lake Street
West Loop
Chicago
Illinois 60607
+1 3127334818
www.momotarochicago.com

Opening hours	Open 7 days
Credit cards	Accepted
Price range	Expensive
Style	Smart casual
Cuisine	Japanese
Recommended for	Worth the travel

"Special shout-out to the *izakaya* and *mentaiko* (pollock) spaghetti by Chef Mark Hellyar at Momotaro."
—Phillip Foss

NEXT

Recommended by
Angus An, Kristian Baumann,
Kyle Connaughton,
Gal Ben-Moshe

953 West Fulton Market
West Loop
Chicago
Illinois 60607
+1 3122260858
www.nextrestaurant.com

Opening hours	Closed Monday and Tuesday
Credit cards	Accepted
Price range	Expensive
Style	Smart casual
Cuisine	International
Recommended for	Wish I'd opened

"The ultimate challenge for a chef—to reinvent a whole kitchen every three months."—Gal Ben-Moshe

ORIOLE

Recommended by
Phillip Foss, Andrew Zimmerman

661 West Walnut Street
West Loop
Chicago
Illinois 60661
+1 3128775339
www.oriolechicago.com

Opening hours	Closed Monday and Sunday
Credit cards	Accepted
Price range	Expensive
Style	Smart casual
Cuisine	Modern American
Recommended for	High end

"I'm very excited about some newcomers to our fine-dining arena. Noah Sandoval earned two-Michelin-stars straight out of the gate at Oriole."
—Phillip Foss

ROISTER

Recommended by
Daniel Boulud,
Sarah Grueneberg,
Carlos Perez

951 West Fulton Market
West Loop
Chicago
Illinois 60607
www.roisterrestaurant.com

Opening hours	Open 7 days
Credit cards	Accepted
Price range	Expensive
Style	Casual
Cuisine	Modern American
Recommended for	Local favorite

"Chefs Grant Achatz and Andrew Brochu are doing some interesting dishes cooked over open fire. I recommend the buttered pipe noodles and the clams with a green chile ragout and finger lime. The Yukon fries have a unique approach with smoky bonita flakes. Top off the meal with the whole chicken, which shows the best way to cook the bird—braised, fried and poached."—Sarah Grueneberg

SEPIA

Recommended by
Brian Ahern

123 North Jefferson Street
West Loop
Chicago
Illinois 60661
+1 3124411920
www.sepiachicago.com

Opening hours	Open 7 days
Credit cards	Accepted
Price range	Expensive
Style	Smart casual
Cuisine	Modern American
Recommended for	High end

SMYTH

Recommended by
Brian Ahern, Jonathan Brooks
Phillip Foss, Erick Harcey

177 North Ada Street
West Loop
Chicago
Illinois 60607
+1 7739133773
www.smythandtheloyalist.com

Opening hours	Closed Monday and Sunday
Credit cards	Accepted
Price range	Expensive
Style	Casual
Cuisine	Modern American
Recommended for	High end

"Had my favorite meal of 2016 here and maybe the most casual and delicious tasting menu of my life."
—Jonathan Brooks

THE PUBLICAN

Recommended by
Brian Ahern, Sarah Grueneberg,
David Posey

837 West Fulton Market
West Loop
Chicago
Illinois 60607
+1 3127339555
www.thepublicanrestaurant.com

Opening hours	Open 7 days
Credit cards	Accepted
Price range	Affordable
Style	Casual
Cuisine	American
Recommended for	Local favorite

"Tried and true—it's become an institution in Chicago. Perfect combination of house-made charcuterie, solid vegetable dishes and hearty food, ideal for the Midwest."—Sarah Grueneberg

Known in particular for its amazingly good brunches, this stripped-back, beer-led restaurant is all about immaculate produce served at its simplest and best. It comes courtesy of the team behind Chicago's much-loved, James Beard-nominated Blackbird restaurant, but with a stark, hall-like interior, farmhouse fare and a vast beer list. The dinner menu is split into pork-heavy 'meat', 'fish' and 'vegetable', with each section revealing impeccably sourced ingredients—be it the cuttlefish shipped over from the Aegean Sea, or the 'country rib' from the Slagel Family Farm in Illinois.

KATSU

Recommended by
Kevin Hickey

2651 West Peterson Avenue
West Ridge
Chicago
Illinois 60659
+1 7737843383

Opening hours	Closed Monday and Tuesday
Credit cards	Accepted
Price range	Affordable
Style	Smart casual
Cuisine	Japanese
Recommended for	High end

"The highest quality fish in the city served by an incredibly warm and talented sushi chef. It can be quite pricey but the place still manages to feel like a mom-and-pop, albeit a Japanese one."—Kevin Hickey

VIE

Recommended by
James Rigato

4471 Lawn Avenue
Western Springs
Chicago
Illinois 60558
+1 7082462082
www.vierestaurant.com

Opening hours	Open 7 days
Credit cards	Accepted
Price range	Expensive
Style	Smart casual
Cuisine	Modern American
Recommended for	High end

"Paul Virant is an absolute prophet of preservation and refined cooking."—James Rigato

BIG STAR

Recommended by
Phillip Foss, Joshua McFadden,
David Posey, Jonathon Sawyer,
Norman Van Aken

1531 North Damen Avenue
Wicker Park
Chicago
Illinois 60622
+1 7732354039
www.higstarchicago.com

Opening hours	Open 7 days
Reservation policy	No
Credit cards	Not accepted
Price range	Affordable
Style	Casual
Cuisine	Tacos
Recommended for	Late night

"Paul Kahan or God or Lemmy? Trick question: PK, of course. Son of Chicago, smoked meat and fish man, PK has changed how the Americans dine forever, mastering a blend of stunning food, non-intrusive yet supremely educated service, and all at value pricing. Get a bunch of tacos, a Tecate Light can and some Elijah Craig 23 Year—a classic high-low combo of super rare bourbon and cheap Mexican beer."
—Jonathon Sawyer

There's a reason that Big Star's expansive patio is always packed on sunny days. This little corner of Texas at the heart of Wicker Park provides locals with a huge outdoor dining area, an inventive taco menu and a first-rate bar. Don't be put off by its knowing hipster vibe—chef Paul Kahan has created a truly excellent, Mexican-influenced menu, with the *taco al pastor* (spit-roasted pork with pineapple and onion) and *taco de chorizo cordero* (spicy lamb and pork chorizo) particular highlights. The bar has a substantial variety of drinks to suit any mood, with many different artisan

whiskeys, craft beers, tequilas and cocktails (handily available by the pitcher for larger parties). It's worth noting that Big Star is cash only, and you might have to wait a while to be seated, especially during the summer months.

CARNICERIA GUANAJUATO

Recommended by
Kevin Hickey

1436 North Ashland
Wicker Park
Chicago
Illinois

Opening hours	Open 7 days
Credit cards	Accepted
Price range	Budget
Style	Casual
Cuisine	Mexican
Recommended for	Bargain

"Actually a grocery store that has a taco stand inside it. Delicious cheap tacos—get the tripe."
—Kevin Hickey

DOVE'S LUNCHEONETTE

Recommended by
Andrew Zimmerman

1545 North Damen Avenue
Wicker Park
Chicago
Illinois 60622
+1 7736454060
www.doveschicago.com

Opening hours	Open 7 days
Credit cards	Accepted
Price range	Affordable
Style	Casual
Cuisine	Mexican-American
Recommended for	Regular neighborhood

"Great Tex-Mex breakfast."—Andrew Zimmerman

HOLLYWOOD GRILL

Recommended by
Phillip Foss

1601 West North Avenue
Wicker Park
Chicago
Illinois 60622
+1 7733951818
www.hollywood-grill.com

Opening hours	Open 7 days
Reservation policy	No
Credit cards	Accepted
Price range	Affordable
Style	Casual
Cuisine	Diner
Recommended for	Breakfast

"Simple diner food without fuss. Always clean, always a smile with the service and a full coffee cup, and it's twenty-four hours so it's good for breakfast for early risers or late-night revelers."—Phillip Foss

MINDY'S HOT CHOCOLATE

Recommended by
Rick Bayless

1747 North Damen Avenue
Wicker Park
Chicago
Illinois 60647
+1 7734891747
www.hotchocolatechicago.com

Opening hours	Closed Monday and Tuesday
Credit cards	Accepted
Price range	Affordable
Style	Casual
Cuisine	Modern American
Recommended for	Breakfast

"Chef Mindy Segal's food is just so consistently great. She supports Midwest farmers and Hot Chocolate focuses on being a chef-run restaurant. There's a great neighborhood vibe that really shines during the incredible brunch—those chocolate babkas! Those donuts!"—Rick Bayless

RANGOLI

Recommended by
Andrew Zimmerman

2421 West North Avenue
Wicker Park
Chicago
Illinois 60647
+1 7736977114
www.rangolifeast.com

Opening hours	Closed Monday
Credit cards	Accepted
Price range	Affordable
Style	Casual
Cuisine	Indian
Recommended for	Regular neighborhood

"It is far and away the best Indian food near where I live."—Andrew Zimmerman

SCHWA

Recommended by
Phillip Foss,
Andrew Zimmerman

1466 North Ashland Avenue
Wicker Park
Chicago
Illinois 60622
+1 7732521466
www.schwarestaurant.com

Opening hours	Closed Monday and Sunday
Credit cards	Accepted
Price range	Expensive
Style	Casual
Cuisine	Modern American
Recommended for	Wish I'd opened

"Super creative food with a completely punk-rock aesthetic."—Andrew Zimmerman

URBANBELLY

Recommended by
Sarah Grueneberg

1542 North Damen Avenue
Wicker Park
Chicago
Illinois 60622
+1 7739048606
www.urbanbellychicago.com

Opening hours	Open 7 days
Reservation policy	No
Credit cards	Accepted
Price range	Affordable
Style	Casual
Cuisine	Asian Fusion
Recommended for	Regular neighborhood

"UrbanBelly in the West Loop of Chicago for the coconut pho curry."—Sarah Grueneberg

NEW ORLEANS

NEW ORLEANS

N SCALE
0 700 1400 2100 yd.

1. *Crescent City Steaks (p.974)*
2. *Bacchanal (p.974)*
3. *Elizabeth's (p.974)*
4. *Junction (p.974)*
5. *Pizza Delicious (p.974)*
6. *Red's Chinese (p.975)*
7. *Satsuma (p.975)*
8. *The Joint (p.975)*
9. *Maple Street Patisserie (p.975)*
10. *Acme Oyster House (p.975)*
11. *Balise (p.975)*
12. *Cleo's (p.976)*
13. *Cochon Butcher (p.976)*
14. *Compère Lapin (p.976)*
15. *Domenica (p.976)*
16. *Herbsaint (p.976)*
17. *La Boca (p.976)*
18. *Pêche (p.977)*
19. *Restaurant August (p.977)*
20. *Willa Jean (p.977)*
21. *Central City Bbq (p.977)*
22. *Emeril's Delmonico (p.977)*
23. *Maïs Arepas (p.977)*
24. *Primitivo (p.978)*
25. *The Avenue Pub (p.978)*
26. *1000 Figs (p.978)*
27. *Liuzza's By The Track (p.978)*
28. *Manchu (p.978)*
29. *Angeline (p.978)*
30. *Backspace Bar & Kitchen (p.979)*
31. *Bayona (p.979)*
32. *Cane & Table (p.979)*
33. *Coop's Place (p.979)*
34. *Daisy Dukes (p.979)*
35. *Doris Metropolitan (p.979)*
36. *Galatoire's (p.980)*
37. *Croissant D'or Patisserie (p.980)*
38. *Muriel's Jackson Square (p.980)*
39. *Restaurant R'evolution (p.980)*
40. *Sylvain (p.980)*
41. *The Court Of Two Sisters (p.980)*
42. *The Company Burger (p.981)*
43. *Dat Dog (p.981)*
44. *High Hat Cafe (p.981)*
45. *Midway Pizza (p.981)*
46. *Bouligny Tavern (p.981)*
47. *Commander's Palace (p.982)*
48. *District Donuts (p.982)*
49. *Hivolt (p.982)*
50. *Lilly's Café (p.982)*
51. *Stein's Market And Deli (p.982)*
52. *Turkey And The Wolf (p.982)*
53. *Gene's Po-Boys (p.983)*
54. *Horn's (p.983)*
55. *Lost Love Lounge (p.983)*
56. *Mimi's In The Marigny (p.983)*
57. *Paladar 511 (p.983)*
58. *Siberia (p.984)*
59. *Bayou Wine Garden (p.984)*
60. *Beachcorner Bar & Grill (p.984)*
61. *Betsy's Pancake House (p.984)*
62. *Bevi Seafood Co (p.984)*
63. *Blue Dot Donuts (p.984)*
64. *Boswell's Jamaican Grill (p.985)*
65. *Ideal Market (p.985)*
66. *Mandina's Restaurant (p.985)*
67. *Mopho (p.985)*
68. *Dong Phuong (p.985)*
69. *Sneaky Pickle (p.986)*
70. *Shawarma On The Go (p.986)*
71. *Dookey Chase's Restaurant (p.986)*
72. *Lil' Dizzy's (p.986)*
73. *Meauxbar (p.987)*
74. *Willie Mae's Scotch House (p.987)*
75. *Ancora (p.987)*
76. *Avo (p.987)*
77. *Brigtsen's (p.987)*
78. *Camellia Grill (p.988)*
79. *Casamento's (p.988)*
80. *Clancy's (p.988)*
81. *Coulis (p.988)*
82. *The Delachaise (p.989)*
83. *Domilise's Po-Boy And Bar (p.989)*
84. *Guy's Po-Boys (p.989)*
85. *La Boulangerie (p.989)*
86. *La Petite Grocery (p.989)*
87. *Lilette (p.989)*
88. *Patois (p.990)*
89. *Pho Cam Ly (p.990)*
90. *Shaya (p.990)*
91. *St. James Cheese Company (p.990)*
92. *Taceaux Loceaux Food Truck (p.991)*
93. *Taqueria Corona (p.991)*
94. *Upperline (p.991)*

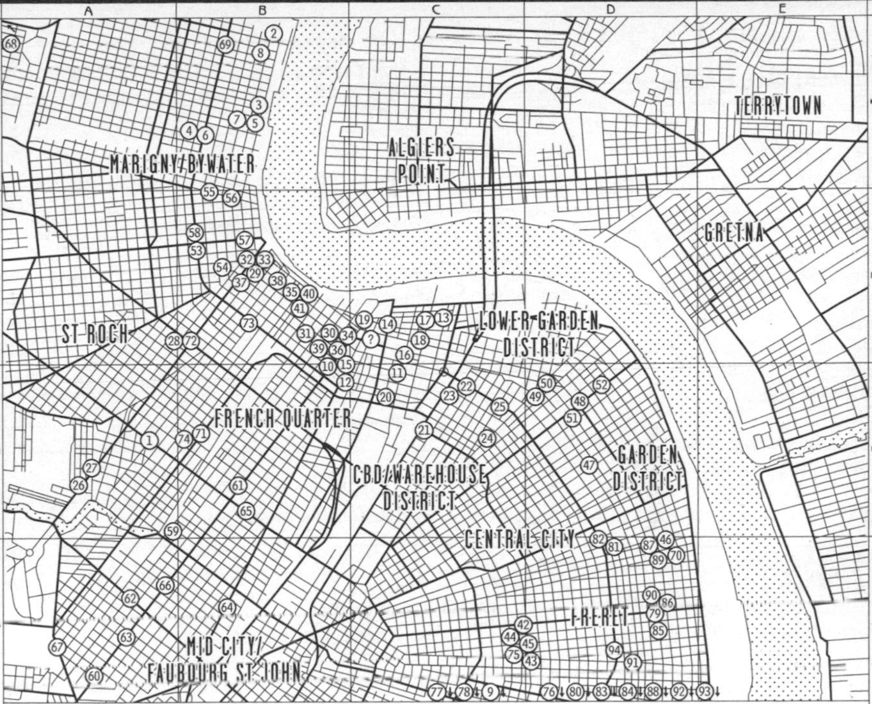

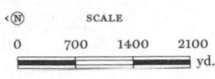

CRESCENT CITY STEAKS

Recommended by
Isaac Toups

1001 North Broad Street
Bayou St. John
New Orleans
Louisiana 70119
+1 5048213271
www.crescentcitysteaks.com

Opening hours	Closed Monday
Credit cards	Accepted
Price range	Affordable
Style	Casual
Cuisine	Steakhouse
Recommended for	Local favorite

"This is the epitome of old-school New Orleans restaurants. It's steeped in New Orleans history. The menu hasn't changed in decades. You can go there, get a consistent steak and a stiff drink."—Isaac Toups

BACCHANAL

Recommended by
Sarah Mcintosh, Alon Shaya,
Martha Wiggins

600 Poland Avenue
Bywater
New Orleans
Louisiana 70117
+1 5049489111
www.bacchanalwine.com

Opening hours	Open 7 days
Reservation policy	No
Credit cards	Accepted
Price range	Affordable
Style	Casual
Cuisine	Creole
Recommended for	Worth the travel

"Amazing atmosphere. Totally captures the vibe of New Orleans. Great music, huge wine selection. Makes me love that city even more!"—Sarah Mcintosh

Bacchanal has it all: an upstairs bar, al fresco drinking with live jazz, an impressive selection of Old World wines from small producers and delicious eats by chef Joaquin Rodas. It began in 2002 as a quirky wine shop that, thanks to its backyard parties, swiftly became a cultural destination. After Katrina, it provided a space to laugh and connect with this resilient community—in true NOLA style, of course, with booze, bands and great food. Today it's a local hero, providing a romantic, energetic place to party in the Upper Ninth Ward.

ELIZABETH'S

Recommended by
Chris Coleman,
Chris Lusk

601 Gallier Street
Bywater
New Orleans
Louisiana 70117
+1 5049449272
www.elizabethsrestaurantnola.com

Opening hours	Open 7 days
Reservation policy	No
Credit cards	Accepted
Price range	Affordable
Style	Casual
Cuisine	Southern American
Recommended for	Breakfast

JUNCTION

Recommended by
Chris Lusk, Martha Wiggins

3021 Saint Claude Avenue
Bywater
New Orleans
Louisiana 70117
+1 5042720205
www.junctionnola.com

Opening hours	Open 7 days
Reservation policy	No
Credit cards	Accepted
Price range	Affordable
Style	Casual
Cuisine	Bar
Recommended for	Late night

"One of my favorite hamburgers in New Orleans. The beer selection is very good as well."—Chris Lusk

PIZZA DELICIOUS

Recommended by
Chris Lusk

617 Piety Street
Bywater
New Orleans
Louisiana 70117
+1 5046768482
www.pizzadelicious.com

Opening hours	Closed Monday
Reservation policy	No
Credit cards	Accepted
Price range	Affordable
Style	Casual
Cuisine	Pizza
Recommended for	Wish I'd opened

RED'S CHINESE

Recommended by
John Besh, Martha Wiggins

3048 Saint Claude Avenue
Bywater
New Orleans
Louisiana 70117
+1 5043046030
www.redschinese.com

Opening hours	Open 7 days
Reservation policy	No
Credit cards	Accepted
Price range	Affordable
Style	Casual
Cuisine	Chinese
Recommended for	Late Night

"Fun, funky Chinese restaurant that doesn't take themselves too seriously."—John Besh

SATSUMA

Recommended by
John Besh

3218 Dauphine Street
Bywater
New Orleans
Louisiana 70117
+1 5043045962
www.satsumacafe.com

Opening hours	Open 7 days
Reservation policy	No
Credit cards	Accepted
Price range	Affordable
Style	Casual
Cuisine	Breakfast-Brunch
Recommended for	Breakfast

"I love the arugula (rocket), fried egg and avocado sandwich. It is casual, locally conscious and delicious."
—John Besh

THE JOINT

Recommended by
Martha Wiggins

701 Mazant Street
Bywater
New Orleans
Louisiana 70117
+1 5049493232
www.alwayssmokin.com

Opening hours	Closed Sunday
Reservation policy	No
Credit cards	Accepted
Price range	Affordable
Style	Casual
Cuisine	American Barbecue
Recommended for	Local favorite

MAPLE STREET PATISSERIE

Recommended by
Edgar Caro

7638 Maple Street
Carrollton
New Orleans
Louisiana 70118
+1 5043041526
www.cargocollective.com/maplestreetpatisserie

Opening hours	Closed Monday
Reservation policy	No
Credit cards	Accepted
Price range	Budget
Style	Casual
Cuisine	Patisserie
Recommended for	Breakfast

ACME OYSTER HOUSE

Recommended by
Christopher Hodgson

724 Iberville Street
Central Business District
New Orleans
Louisiana 70130
+1 5045225973
www.acmeoyster.com

Opening hours	Open 7 days
Reservation policy	No
Credit cards	Accepted
Price range	Affordable
Style	Casual
Cuisine	Creole
Recommended for	Worth the travel

"Never had roasted oysters like these before. They chargrill them, then finish with seasoned butter and Parmesan. I ordered a dozen and could have kept going—amazing!"—Christopher Hodgson

BALISE

Recommended by
John Besh

640 Carondelet Street
Central Business District
New Orleans
Louisiana 70130
+1 5044594449
www.balisenola.com

Opening hours	Open 7 days
Credit cards	Accepted
Price range	Affordable
Style	Casual
Cuisine	Modern Creole
Recommended for	Regular neighborhood

CLEO'S

Recommended by
Alex Harrell

165 Roosevelt Way
Central Business District
New Orleans
Louisiana 70112
+1 5045224504

Opening hours	Open 7 days
Reservation policy	No
Credit cards	Accepted
Price range	Affordable
Style	Casual
Cuisine	Mediterranean
Recommended for	Late night

COCHON BUTCHER

Recommended by
Edgar Caro, Nina Compton

930 Tchoupitoulas Street
Central Business District
New Orleans
Louisiana 70130
+1 5045882123
www.cochonbutcher.com

Opening hours	Open 7 days
Credit cards	Accepted
Price range	Affordable
Style	Casual
Cuisine	Cajun-Creole
Recommended for	Local favorite

"Donald Link's sandwich shop. Le Pig Mac is amazing."
—Nina Compton

COMPÈRE LAPIN

Recommended by
John Besh, Alon Shaya

535 Tchoupitoulas Street
Central Business District
New Orleans
Louisiana 70130
+1 5046992119
www.comperelapin.com

Opening hours	Open 7 days
Credit cards	Accepted
Price range	Expensive
Style	Casual
Cuisine	Caribbean-Creole
Recommended for	High end

"Chef Nina Compton and her husband Larry Miller
have created one of the best restaurants in New
Orleans. Nina's food is so well-thought-out and
beautifully presented. Larry runs the dining room and
will keep everyone at the table entertained with great
stories and funny jokes."—Alon Shaya

DOMENICA

Recommended by
Martha Wiggins

123 Baronne Street
Central Business District
New Orleans
Louisiana 70112
+1 5046486020
www.domenicarestaurant.com

Opening hours	Open 7 days
Credit cards	Accepted
Price range	Affordable
Style	Casual
Cuisine	Italian
Recommended for	Regular neighborhood

HERBSAINT

Recommended by
Chris Lusk

701 Saint Charles Avenue
Central Business District
New Orleans
Louisiana 70130
+1 5045244114
www.herbsaint.com

Opening hours	Closed Sunday
Credit cards	Accepted
Price range	Expensive
Style	Smart casual
Cuisine	French-Southern American
Recommended for	High end

LA BOCA

Recommended by
Edgar Caro

870 Tchoupitoulas Street
Central Business District
New Orleans
Louisiana 70130
+1 5045258205
www.labocasteaks.com

Opening hours	Closed Sunday
Credit cards	Accepted
Price range	Expensive
Style	Smart casual
Cuisine	Argentinian Steakhouse
Recommended for	High end

PÊCHE

Recommended by
Jennifer Jasinski,
Martha Wiggins

800 Magazine Street
Central Business District
New Orleans
Louisiana 70130
+1 5045221744
www.pecherestaurant.com

Opening hours	Open 7 days
Credit cards	Accepted
Price range	Affordable
Style	Casual
Cuisine	Seafood
Recommended for	High end

"Pêche isn't overly expensive but there are always so many things on the menu that are up my alley that I tend to go overboard. It's a seafood restaurant with a raw bar and the whole fish is a must have! The food is fresh, delicious and consistent. Solid."
—Martha Wiggins

RESTAURANT AUGUST

Recommended by
Chris Lusk, Tory McPhail

301 Tchoupltoulas Street
Central Business District
New Orleans
Louisiana 70130
+1 5042999777
www.restaurantaugust.com

Opening hours	Open 7 days
Credit cards	Accepted
Price range	Affordable
Style	Smart casual
Cuisine	Creole-French
Recommended for	High end

"A John Besh restaurant that really put him on the map in New Orleans."—Tory McPhail

WILLA JEAN

Recommended by
Nina Compton

611 O'Keefe Avenue
Central Business District
New Orleans
Louisiana 70113
+1 5045097334
www.willajean.com

Opening hours	Open 7 days
Credit cards	Accepted
Price range	Affordable
Style	Casual
Cuisine	Southern American
Recommended for	Breakfast

"One of John Besh's restaurants and they have amazing baked goods and delicious breakfast. I love the chicken and biscuits there."—Nina Compton

CENTRAL CITY BBQ

Recommended by
Edgar Caro, Alex Harrell

1201 South Rampart Street
Central City
New Orleans
Louisiana 70113
+1 5045584276
www.centralcitybbq.com

Opening hours	Closed Monday and Tuesday
Reservation policy	No
Credit cards	Accepted
Price range	Affordable
Style	Casual
Cuisine	American Barbecue
Recommended for	Regular neighborhood

"The best barbecue in town."—Edgar Caro

EMERIL'S DELMONICO

Recommended by
Nina Compton, Alon Shaya,
Isaac Toups

1300 Saint Charles Avenue
Central City
New Orleans
Louisiana 70130
+1 5045254937
www.emerilsrestaurants.com

Opening hours	Open 7 days
Credit cards	Accepted
Price range	Expensive
Style	Casual
Cuisine	Creole
Recommended for	Local favorite

"Emeril's is quintessential New Orleans. The service is top notch and Chef David Slater is so talented. I love the barbecue shrimp there."—Nina Compton

MAÏS AREPAS

Recommended by
Isaac Toups

1200 Carondelet Street
Central City
New Orleans
Louisiana 70130
+1 5045236247

Opening hours	Closed Monday
Credit cards	Accepted
Price range	Affordable
Style	Casual
Cuisine	Colombian
Recommended for	Regular neighborhood

PRIMITIVO
Recommended by
Alex Harrell

1800 Oretha Castle Haley Boulevard
Central City
New Orleans
Louisiana 70113
+1 5048811775
www.primitivonola.com

Opening hours	Closed Monday
Credit cards	Accepted
Price range	Affordable
Style	Casual
Cuisine	American
Recommended for	Wish I'd opened

"The heart of the restaurant is a huge open hearth where they prepare all the food over wood coals. Everything from meat, vegetables and seafood is cooked over the coals and it imparts the food with depth of flavor from the fire."—Alex Harrell

THE AVENUE PUB
Recommended by
Isaac Toups

1732 Saint Charles Avenue
Central City
New Orleans
Louisiana 70130
+1 5045869243
www.theavenuepub.com

Opening hours	Open 7 days
Reservation policy	No
Credit cards	Accepted
Price range	Affordable
Style	Casual
Cuisine	Pub
Recommended for	Late night

1000 FIGS
Recommended by
Edgar Caro

3141 Ponce De Leon Street #1
Fairgrounds
New Orleans
Louisiana 70119
+1 5043010848
www.1000figs.com

Opening hours	Closed Monday and Sunday
Reservation policy	No
Credit cards	Accepted
Price range	Affordable
Style	Casual
Cuisine	Vegetarian-Middle Eastern
Recommended for	Regular neighborhood

"Great Middle-Eastern vegetable dishes."—Edgar Caro

LIUZZA'S BY THE TRACK
Recommended by
Alex Harrell

1518 North Lopez Street
Fairgrounds
New Orleans
Louisiana 70119
+1 5042187888
www.liuzzasnola.com

Opening hours	Closed Sunday
Reservation policy	No
Credit cards	Accepted
Price range	Affordable
Style	Casual
Cuisine	Southern American
Recommended for	Local favorite

"Liuzza's is a great New Orleans neighborhood spot. Their clientele is mostly locals and always as diverse as the city. Fun and casual with cold beers and what I think is the best shrimp po-boy in New Orleans."
—Alex Harrell

MANCHU
Recommended by
Martha Wiggins

1413 North Claiborne Avenue
Fairgrounds
New Orleans
Louisiana 70116
+1 5049475507
www.manchuchicken.com

Opening hours	Open 7 days
Reservation policy	No
Credit cards	Accepted
Price range	Budget
Style	Casual
Cuisine	Asian-American
Recommended for	Local favorite

ANGELINE
Recommended by
Martha Wiggins

1032 Chartres Street
French Quarter
New Orleans
Louisiana 70116
+1 5043083106
www.angelinenola.com

Opening hours	Closed Monday and Tuesday
Credit cards	Accepted
Price range	Affordable
Style	Casual
Cuisine	Southern American
Recommended for	Breakfast

"It's the real deal. The food is true Southern cuisine at its finest, influenced by cuisines and techniques from all over the world. All product is made from scratch with the most beautiful, thoughtfully and locally sourced ingredients and with refined attention to detail. With all that being said, it is as comforting and approachable as sitting at your grandma's kitchen table."—Martha Wiggins

BACKSPACE BAR & KITCHEN

Recommended by
Martha Wiggins

139 Chartres Street
French Quarter
New Orleans
Louisiana 70130
+1 5043222281
www.backspacenola.com

Opening hours	Open 7 days
Reservation policy	No
Credit cards	Accepted
Price range	Affordable
Style	Casual
Cuisine	American
Recommended for	Late night

BAYONA

Recommended by
Martha Wiggins

430 Dauphine Street
French Quarter
New Orleans
Louisiana 70112
+1 5045254455
www.bayona.com

Opening hours	Open 7 days
Credit cards	Accepted
Price range	Expensive
Style	Casual
Cuisine	Modern Creole
Recommended for	High end

CANE & TABLE

Recommended by
Martha Wiggins

1113 Decatur Street
French Quarter
New Orleans
Louisiana 70116
+1 5045811112
www.caneandtablenola.com

Opening hours	Open 7 days
Credit cards	Accepted
Price range	Affordable
Style	Casual
Cuisine	Bar
Recommended for	Regular neighborhood

COOP'S PLACE

Recommended by
Ken Oringer, Martha Wiggins

1109 Decatur Street
French Quarter
New Orleans
Louisiana 70116
+1 5045259053
www.coopsplace.net

Opening hours	Open 7 days
Reservation policy	No
Credit cards	Accepted
Price range	Affordable
Style	Casual
Cuisine	Cajun
Recommended for	Late night

"Killer fried chicken."—Ken Oringer

DAISY DUKES

Recommended by
Chris Lusk

121 Chartres Street
French Quarter
New Orleans
Louisiana 70130
+1 5045615171
www.daisydukesrestaurant.com

Opening hours	Open 7 days
Reservation policy	No
Credit cards	Accepted
Price range	Affordable
Style	Casual
Cuisine	Cajun-Creole
Recommended for	Late night

DORIS METROPOLITAN

Recommended by
Martha Wiggins

620 Chartres Street
French Quarter
New Orleans
Louisiana 70130
+1 5042673500
www.dorismetropolitan.com

Opening hours	Open 7 days
Credit cards	Accepted
Price range	Expensive
Style	Casual
Cuisine	Steakhouse
Recommended for	Regular neighborhood

"It's an Israeli steakhouse. The food is bold and spicy and unapologetic, presentation is over the top and the atmosphere is lively and seductive. I'm always welcomed like family but definitely a place for any special occasion."—Martha Wiggins

GALATOIRE'S

Recommended by
John Besh, Chris Lusk

209 Bourbon Street
French Quarter
New Orleans
Louisiana 70130
+1 5045252021
www.galatoires.com

Opening hours	Closed Monday
Credit cards	Accepted
Price range	Expensive
Style	Formal
Cuisine	Modern Creole
Recommended for	High End

"Birthdays are often celebrated at Galatoire's for Friday lunch that turn into dinner. Ask for my favorite waiter Cajun John and have him order for you."
—John Besh

CROISSANT D'OR PATISSERIE

Recommended by
Alon Shaya

617 Ursulines Avenue
French Quarter
New Orleans
Louisiana 70116
+1 5045244663
www.croissantdornola.com

Opening hours	Closed Tuesday
Credit cards	Accepted
Price range	Budget
Style	Casual
Cuisine	Patisserie
Recommended for	Breakfast

"I like getting their warm blueberry croissant. It's the perfect little neighborhood bakery and if you show up early enough, the croissants are still warm out of the oven."—Alon Shaya

MURIEL'S JACKSON SQUARE

Recommended by
Chris Lusk

801 Chartres Street
French Quarter
New Orleans
Louisiana 70116
+1 5045681885
www.muriels.com

Opening hours	Open 7 days
Credit cards	Accepted
Price range	Affordable
Style	Casual
Cuisine	Creole
Recommended for	Local favorite

RESTAURANT R'EVOLUTION

Recommended by
Chris Lusk, Isaac Toups,
Martha Wiggins

777 Bienville Street
French Quarter
New Orleans
Louisiana 70130
+1 5045532277
www.revolutionnola.com

Opening hours	Open 7 days
Credit cards	Accepted
Price range	Expensive
Style	Smart casual
Cuisine	French-Creole
Recommended for	High end

"They really think about every single detail in a fine-dining experience. It's not for every day but a really nice treat occasionally."—Isaac Toups

SYLVAIN

Recommended by
Alex Harrell

625 Chartres Street
French Quarter
New Orleans
Louisiana 70130
+1 5042658123
www.sylvainnola.com

Opening hours	Open 7 days
Credit cards	Accepted
Price range	Affordable
Style	Smart casual
Cuisine	Modern American
Recommended for	Late night

"Chef Martha Wiggins' food is tremendous, the vibe is cool and the music is always great."—Alex Harrell

THE COURT OF TWO SISTERS

Recommended by
Eric & Bruce Bromberg

613 Royal Street
French Quarter
New Orleans
Louisiana 70130
+1 5045227261
www.courtoftwosisters.com

Opening hours	Open 7 days
Credit cards	Accepted
Price range	Affordable
Style	Smart casual
Cuisine	Creole
Recommended for	Breakfast

"The Court of Two Sisters is the perfect spot for an over-the-top breakfast experience. Elegant and fun, the jazz band playing and crawfish *étouffée* (crayfish stew) combat even a proper Crescent City hangover." —Eric & Bruce Bromberg

THE COMPANY BURGER

Recommended by
Tory McPhail, Alon Shaya,
Isaac Toups

4600 Freret Street
Freret
New Orleans
Louisiana 70115
+1 5042670320
www.thecompanyburger.com

Opening hours	Open 7 days
Reservation policy	No
Credit cards	Accepted
Price range	Affordable
Style	Casual
Cuisine	Burgers
Recommended for	Wish I'd opened

"I think Adam did a brilliant job marketing a fast food burger to the masses using quality ingredients." —Isaac Toups

DAT DOG

Recommended by
Chris Lusk

5030 Feret Street
Freret
New Orleans
Louisiana 70115
+1 5048996883
www.datdog.com

Opening hours	Open 7 days
Credit cards	Accepted
Price range	Budget
Style	Casual
Cuisine	American
Recommended for	Wish I'd opened

HIGH HAT CAFE

Recommended by
Alex Harrell

4500 Freret Street
Freret
New Orleans
Louisiana 70115
+1 5047541336
www.highhatcafe.com

Opening hours	Open 7 days
Reservation policy	No
Credit cards	Accepted
Price range	Affordable
Style	Casual
Cuisine	Southern American
Recommended for	Regular neighborhood

MIDWAY PIZZA

Recommended by
Chris Lusk

4725 Freret Street
Freret
New Orleans
Louisiana 70115
+1 5043222815
www.midwaypizzanola.com

Opening hours	Open 7 days
Reservation policy	No
Credit cards	Accepted
Price range	Affordable
Style	Casual
Cuisine	Pizza
Recommended for	Late night

"New Orleans take on deep-dish pizza."—Chris Lusk

BOULIGNY TAVERN

Recommended by
Edgar Caro, Tory McPhail

3641 Magazine Street
Garden District
New Orleans
Louisiana 70115
+1 5048911810
www.boulignytavern.com

Opening hours	Closed Sunday
Reservation policy	No
Credit cards	Accepted
Price range	Affordable
Style	Casual
Cuisine	International Small plates
Recommended for	Late night

"Great tapas menu, hand-crafted cocktails and interesting wines."—Tory McPhail

COMMANDER'S PALACE

Recommended by
Nina Compton, Chris Lusk,
Tory McPhail

1403 Washington Avenue
Garden District
New Orleans
Louisiana 70130
+1 5048998221
www.commanderspalace.com

Opening hours	Open 7 days
Credit cards	Accepted
Price range	Expensive
Style	Formal
Cuisine	Modern Creole
Recommended for	Local favorite

"Commander's is an institution—a place you go if you have friends visiting, are celebrating a special occasion, or just want a five-star fine-dining meal. Whether you go for dinner, Friday lunch or Sunday jazz brunch, you can't go wrong."—Nina Compton

DISTRICT DONUTS

Recommended by
Alex Harrell

2209 Magazine Street
Garden District
New Orleans
Louisiana 70130
+1 5045706945
www.districtdonuts.com

Opening hours	Open 7 days
Reservation policy	No
Credit cards	Accepted
Price range	Budget
Style	Casual
Cuisine	Café
Recommended for	Breakfast

HIVOLT

Recommended by
Alex Harrell

1829 Sophie Wright Place
Garden District
New Orleans
Louisiana 70130
+1 5043248818
www.hivoltcoffee.com

Opening hours	Open 7 days
Reservation policy	No
Credit cards	Accepted
Price range	Affordable
Style	Casual
Cuisine	Café
Recommended for	Breakfast

LILLY'S CAFÉ

Recommended by
Isaac Toups

1813 Magazine Street
Garden District
New Orleans
Louisiana 70130
+1 5045999999

Opening hours	Closed Sunday
Reservation policy	No
Credit cards	Accepted
Price range	Affordable
Style	Casual
Cuisine	Vietnamese
Recommended for	Regular neighborhood

STEIN'S MARKET AND DELI

Recommended by
Alex Harrell,
Martha Wiggins

2207 Magazine Street
Garden District
New Orleans
Louisiana 70130
+1 5045270771
www.steinsdeli.net

Opening hours	Closed Monday
Reservation policy	No
Credit cards	Accepted
Price range	Affordable
Style	Casual
Cuisine	Jewish-Italian Deli
Recommended for	Breakfast

TURKEY AND THE WOLF

Recommended by
Alex Harrell

739 Jackson Avenue
Garden District
New Orleans
Louisiana 70130
+1 5042187428
www.turkeyandthewolf.com

Opening hours	Closed Tuesday
Reservation policy	No
Credit cards	Accepted
Price range	Affordable
Style	Casual
Cuisine	Sandwiches
Recommended for	Regular neighborhood

GENE'S PO-BOYS

Recommended by
Nina Compton

1040 Elysian Fields Avenue
Marigny
New Orleans
Louisiana 70117
+1 5049433861

Opening hours	Open 7 days
Reservation policy	No
Credit cards	Accepted
Price range	Budget
Style	Casual
Cuisine	Sandwiches
Recommended for	Late night

"Great any time of day, but particularly a late-night favorite. The hot sausage and cheese po-boy is terrific!"—Nina Compton

HORN'S

Recommended by
Chris Lusk

1940 Dauphine Street
Marigny
New Orleans
Louisiana 70116
+1 5044594676
www.hornsnola.com

Opening hours	Open 7 days
Reservation policy	No
Credit cards	Accepted
Price range	Affordable
Style	Casual
Cuisine	Breakfast-Brunch
Recommended for	Breakfast

LOST LOVE LOUNGE

Recommended by
Martha Wiggins

2529 Dauphine Street
Marigny
New Orleans
Louisiana 70117
+1 5049492009
www.lostlovelounge.com

Opening hours	Open 7 days
Reservation policy	No
Credit cards	Accepted
Price range	Affordable
Style	Casual
Cuisine	Vietnamese
Recommended for	Late night

MIMI'S IN THE MARIGNY

Recommended by
Alex Harrell

2601 Royal Street
Marigny
New Orleans
Louisiana 70117
+1 5048729868
www.mimismarigny.com

Opening hours	Open 7 days
Reservation policy	No
Credit cards	Not accepted
Price range	Affordable
Style	Casual
Cuisine	Bar-Tapas
Recommended for	Late night

PALADAR 511

Recommended by
Martha Wiggins

511 Marigny Street
Marigny
New Orleans
Louisiana 70117
+1 5045096782
www.paladar511.com

Opening hours	Closed Tuesday
Credit cards	Accepted
Price range	Affordable
Style	Casual
Cuisine	Italian-American
Recommended for	Wish I'd opened

"It's a beautiful, modern space with an open kitchen and seats right up to it. I admire this place because it's always busy but the staff cooking right in front of you maintain this poise and calm that is beyond impressive. I love watching them go—managers, owners, cooks, bartenders are indistinguishable at times, working seamlessly side by side, like a machine. I don't know how they pull it off, appearing not to break a sweat, but they do, and then some. The food is beautifully and subtlely presented with the flavor to back it up. It's unpretentious and affordable."
—Martha Wiggins

SIBERIA

Recommended by
Martha Wiggins

2227 Saint Claude Avenue
Marigny
New Orleans
Louisiana 70117
+1 5042658855
www.siberianola.com

Opening hours	Open 7 days
Reservation policy	No
Credit cards	Accepted
Price range	Affordable
Style	Casual
Cuisine	Bar
Recommended for	Late night

BAYOU WINE GARDEN

Recommended by
Isaac Toups

315 North Rendon Street
Mid-City
New Orleans
Louisiana 70119
+1 5048262925
www.bayouwinegarden.com

Opening hours	Open 7 days
Reservation policy	No
Credit cards	Accepted
Price range	Affordable
Style	Casual
Cuisine	Bar
Recommended for	Late night

"They serve really late. It's nice to be able to get something decent to eat after a shift. Really nice staff and great atmosphere."—Isaac Toups

BEACHCORNER BAR & GRILL

Recommended by
Chris Lusk

4905 Canal Street
Mid-City
New Orleans
Louisiana 70118
+1 5044887357
www.beachcornerbarandgrill.com

Opening hours	Open 7 days
Reservation policy	No
Credit cards	Accepted
Price range	Affordable
Style	Casual
Cuisine	American Bar
Recommended for	Bargain

BETSY'S PANCAKE HOUSE

Recommended by
Isaac Toups

2542 Canal Street
Mid-City
New Orleans
Louisiana 70119
+1 5048220213

Opening hours	Closed Saturday
Reservation policy	No
Credit cards	Accepted
Price range	Budget
Style	Casual
Cuisine	Diner
Recommended for	Breakfast

"It's a simple greasy spoon. The same servers have worked there as long as I have been going. I can get my eggs, bacon and grits. I am a simple man."
—Isaac Toups

BEVI SEAFOOD CO

Recommended by
Alex Harrell

236 Carrollton Avenue
Mid-City
New Orleans
Louisiana
70119
+1 5044887503
www.beviseafoodco.com

Opening hours	Open 7 days
Reservation policy	No
Credit cards	Accepted
Price range	Affordable
Style	Casual
Cuisine	Seafood
Recommended for	Local favorite

BLUE DOT DONUTS

Recommended by
Alex Harrell

4301 Canal Street
Mid-City
New Orleans
Louisiana 70119
+1 5042184866
www.bluedotdonuts.com

Opening hours	Closed Monday
Reservation policy	No
Credit cards	Accepted
Price range	Budget
Style	Casual
Cuisine	Bakery
Recommended for	Breakfast

BOSWELL'S JAMAICAN GRILL

Recommended by
Martha Wiggins

3521 Tulane Avenue
Mid-City
New Orleans
Louisiana 70119
+1 5044826600

Opening hours	Closed Sunday
Reservation policy	No
Credit cards	Accepted
Price range	Affordable
Style	Casual
Cuisine	Caribbean
Recommended for	Bargain

IDEAL MARKET

Recommended by
Alon Shaya

250 South Broad Street
Mid-City
New Orleans
Louisiana 70119
+1 5048228861
www.laidealmarket.com

Opening hours	Open 7 days
Reservation policy	No
Credit cards	Accepted
Price range	Budget
Style	Casual
Cuisine	Central American
Recommended for	Bargain

"It's a Central American grocery that has a large hotfood section with amazing women cooking barbacoa, Spanish rice, jalapeño-and-onion-grilled chicken, hand-made tortillas, and much more all from scratch. For $9 (£7), you get dinner for two that will keep you full for the following day!"—Alon Shaya

MANDINA'S RESTAURANT

Recommended by
John Besh

3800 Canal Street
Mid-City
New Orleans
Louisiana 70119
+1 5044829179
www.mandinasrestaurant.com

Opening hours	Open 7 days
Reservation policy	No
Credit cards	Accepted
Price range	Affordable
Style	Casual
Cuisine	Italian-Creole
Recommended for	Local favorite

"A joint I grew up with where you have Creole classics intertwined with Sicilian classics, really highlighting the cultures that came to settle in New Orleans."
—John Besh

MOPHO

Recommended by
Alex Harrell

514 City Park Avenue
Mid-City
New Orleans
Louisiana 70119
+1 5044826845
www.mophonola.com

Opening hours	Open 7 days
Credit cards	Accepted
Price range	Affordable
Style	Casual
Cuisine	Vietnamese-Creole
Recommended for	Regular neighborhood

DONG PHUONG

Recommended by
John Besh, Alex Harrell

14207 Chef Menteur Highway
New Orleans East
New Orleans
Louisiana 70129
+1 5042540214
www.dpbanhmi.com

Opening hours	Closed Tuesday
Reservation policy	No
Credit cards	Accepted
Price range	Affordable
Style	Casual
Cuisine	Chinese-Vietnamese
Recommended for	Bargain

"They bake their own bread and everything they serve is made at the restaurant. I always get a Vietnamese roast pork and a vegetarian banh mi dressed with aioli, jalapeños, pickled daikon and carrots, cilantro (coriander) and cucumbers. It's fast, fresh and always delicious. You can't find a better meal anywhere for $3 (£2)."—Alex Harrell

SNEAKY PICKLE

Recommended by
Martha Wiggins

4017 Saint Claude Avenue
St. Claude
New Orleans
Louisiana 70117
+1 5042185651
www.yousneakypickle.com

Opening hours	Open 7 days
Reservation policy	No
Credit cards	Accepted
Price range	Affordable
Style	Casual
Cuisine	Vegetarian-Vegan
Recommended for	Bargain

"Chef Ben Tabor opened this home-grown, vegan-ish spot on St. Claude with a small budget, lots of hard work and help from friends. The Pickle offers affordable, inspired, delicious and moderately healthy food. It has a lively and fun-loving atmosphere, with ever-changing specials using locally-sourced products anywhere from beetroot (beets), to tofu, to waygu beef. The food is slammin' and inventive and appropriately priced, end of story. Try the beet flatbread!"—Martha Wiggins

SHAWARMA ON THE GO

Recommended by
Edgar Caro

3720 Magazine Street
Touro
New Orleans
Louisiana, 70115
+1 504 269 6427
www.shawarmaonthego.com

Opening hours	Open 7 days
Reservation policy	No
Credit cards	Accepted
Price range	Budget
Style	Casual
Cuisine	Middle-Eastern
Recommended for	Bargain

DOOKEY CHASE'S RESTAURANT

Recommended by
Jeremy Lee

2301 Orleans Avenue
Tremé
New Orleans
Louisiana 70119
+1 5048210600
www.dookychaserestaurant.com

Opening hours	Closed Saturday to Monday
Credit cards	Accepted
Price range	Affordable
Style	Casual
Cuisine	Creole
Recommended for	Worth the travel

"This dining room was the first to lay white table cloths for black folks to sit and eat at, and was at the forefront of civil rights in the US. The food is great too."—Jeremy Lee

LIL' DIZZY'S

Recommended by
Martha Wiggins

1500 Esplanade Avenue
Tremé
New Orleans
Louisiana 70116
+1 5045698997
www.lildizzyscafe.net

Opening hours	Open 7 days
Reservation policy	No
Credit cards	Accepted
Price range	Affordable
Style	Casual
Cuisine	Southern American
Recommended for	Local favorite

"It's a soul food buffet owned by Wayne Baquet, the son of Eddie, the namesake of the legendary 7th Ward restaurant Eddie's. It's also my favorite fried chicken and gumbo in town. The place is always packed with a mix of born-and-raised New Orleanians, tourists, groups of people on bike tours, NOPD, politicians and people in their Sunday best."—Martha Wiggins

MEAUXBAR

Recommended by
Martha Wiggins

942 North Rampart Street
Tremé
New Orleans
Louisiana 70116
+1 5045699979
www.meauxbar.com

Opening hours	Open 7 days
Credit cards	Accepted
Price range	Expensive
Style	Casual
Cuisine	French
Recommended for	Regular neighborhood

WILLIE MAE'S SCOTCH HOUSE

Recommended by
Alon Shaya,
Martha Wiggins

2401 Saint Ann Street
Tremé
New Orleans
Louisiana 70119
+1 5048229503
www.williemaesnola.com

Opening hours	Closed Sunday
Reservation policy	No
Credit cards	Accepted
Price range	Affordable
Style	Casual
Cuisine	Southern American
Recommended for	Local favorite

"Run by a third-generation family member, Carrie Seaton, they serve up the best fried chicken, red beans and rice, and cornbread in town."—Alon Shaya

ANCORA

Recommended by
Alex Harrell

4508 Freret Street
Uptown
New Orleans
Louisiana 70115
+1 5043241636
www.ancorapizza.com

Opening hours	Open 7 days
Credit cards	Accepted
Price range	Affordable
Style	Casual
Cuisine	Neapolitan
Recommended for	Regular neighborhood

"Ancora specializes in traditional wood-fired Neapolitan pizza and so much more. I love their house-cured salumi, gnocchi, and any of the seasonal sides. They make everything in-house and source from small local farms, so not only is it delicious but you can also feel good eating there."—Alex Harrell

AVO

Recommended by
Alex Harrell

5908 Magazine Street
Uptown
New Orleans
Louisiana 70115
+1 5045096550
www.restaurantavo.com

Opening hours	Closed Sunday
Credit cards	Accepted
Price range	Affordable
Style	Smart casual
Cuisine	Modern Italian
Recommended for	High end

"I love Chef Nick Lama's sensibility with food. He cooks with soul and creativity that I really enjoy. It's the perfect place for a date night with my wife."
—Alex Harrell

BRIGTSEN'S

Recommended by
Isaac Toups

723 Dante Street
Uptown
New Orleans
Louisiana 70118
+1 5048617610
www.brigtsens.com

Opening hours	Closed Monday and Sunday
Credit cards	Accepted
Price range	Expensive
Style	Casual
Cuisine	Creole
Recommended for	Local favorite

CAMELLIA GRILL

Recommended by
Andy Hollyday

626 South Carrollton Avenue
Uptown
New Orleans
Louisiana 70118
+1 5043092679

Opening hours	Open 7 days
Reservation policy	No
Credit cards	Accepted
Price range	Budget
Style	Casual
Cuisine	Diner
Recommended for	Breakfast

In the twenty months between the Camellia Grill (established 1946) closing post-Katrina and reopening in 2007, New Orleanians would pin notes of support on the legendary diner's door, pining for a slice of grilled pecan pie. Reopened under new ownership, it soon got its groove back. The showmanship of the bow-tied waiters remains undiminished, the omelettes are still huge, and there's always a line for a stool at the marble counter. With its nostalgic diner menu that does everything from eggs any style to waffles, grits and burgers, the Camellia Grill manages to please the tourists and keep the locals happy.

CASAMENTO'S

Recommended by
Alex Harrell

4330 Magazine Street
Uptown
New Orleans
Louisiana 70115
+1 5048959761
www.casamentosrestaurant.com

Opening hours	Closed Monday to Wednesday
Reservation policy	No
Credit cards	Not accepted
Price range	Affordable
Style	Casual
Cuisine	Seafood
Recommended for	Local favorite

CLANCY'S

Recommended by
Chris Lusk, Isaac Toups

6100 Annunciation Street
Uptown
New Orleans
Louisiana 70118
+1 5048951111
www.clancysneworleans.com

Opening hours	Closed Sunday
Credit cards	Accepted
Price range	Expensive
Style	Casual
Cuisine	Creole Seafood
Recommended for	Regular neighborhood

"Everyone knows about Clancy's and Brightsen's. They are great old-school Creole restaurants that speak to the amazing local culinary history, past and present."—Isaac Toups

COULIS

Recommended by
Chris Lusk, Tory McPhail

3625 Prytania Street
Uptown
New Orleans
Louisiana 70115
+1 5043044265
www.coulisnolas.com

Opening hours	Open 7 days
Reservation policy	No
Credit cards	Accepted
Price range	Budget
Style	Casual
Cuisine	Southern American
Recommended for	Breakfast

"It's in the location of the old Bluebird Café and has a great vibe. The food is traditional breakfast fare, done very well, with a few twists on the classics."
—Chris Lusk

THE DELACHAISE
Recommended by
Edgar Caro
3442 Saint Charles Avenue
Uptown
New Orleans
Louisiana 70115
+1 5048950858
www.thedelachaise.com

Opening hours	Open 7 days
Reservation policy	No
Credit cards	Accepted
Price range	Affordable
Style	Casual
Cuisine	International
Recommended for	Late night

DOMILISE'S PO-BOY AND BAR
Recommended by
Nina Compton
5240 Annunciation Street
Uptown
New Orleans
Louisiana 70115
+1 5048999126
www.domilisespoboys.com

Opening hours	Closed Sunday
Reservation policy	No
Credit cards	Accepted
Price range	Affordable
Style	Casual
Cuisine	Southern American
Recommended for	Bargain

"This walk-up counter serves some of the best po-boys in the city and has my favorite muffaletta (New Orleans sandwich) in town. Great food, cheap prices and no-nonsense."—Nina Compton

GUY'S PO-BOYS
Recommended by
Chris Lusk
5259 Magazine Street
Uptown
New Orleans
Louisiana 70115
+1 5048915025

Opening hours	Closed Sunday
Reservation policy	No
Credit cards	Not accepted
Price range	Budget
Style	Casual
Cuisine	Creole-Cajun Sandwiches
Recommended for	Regular neighborhood

LA BOULANGERIE
Recommended by
Edgar Caro
4600 Magazine Street
Uptown
New Orleans
Louisiana 70115
+1 5042693777
www.laboulangerienola.com

Opening hours	Open 7 days
Reservation policy	No
Credit cards	Accepted
Price range	Budget
Style	Casual
Cuisine	French Bakery
Recommended for	Breakfast

"La Boulangerie for the ham and cheese croissant."
—Edgar Caro

LA PETITE GROCERY
Recommended by
Chris Lusk, Martha Wiggins
4238 Magazine Street
Uptown
New Orleans
Louisiana 70115
+1 5048913377
www.lapetitegrocery.com

Opening hours	Open 7 days
Credit cards	Accepted
Price range	Affordable
Style	Smart casual
Cuisine	Southern American
Recommended for	High end

"Really great food and excellent service."—Chris Lusk

LILETTE
Recommended by
Edgar Caro
3637 Magazine Street
Uptown
New Orleans
Louisiana 70115
+1 5048951636
www.liletterestaurant.com

Opening hours	Closed Sunday
Credit cards	Accepted
Price range	Affordable
Style	Smart casual
Cuisine	French-Italian
Recommended for	High end

"Hearts of Palm salad Gnochetti."—Edgar Caro

PATOIS

Recommended by
Andy Hollyday, Chris Lusk

6078 Laurel Street
Uptown
New Orleans
Louisiana 70118
+1 5048959441
www.patoisnola.com

Opening hours	Closed Monday
Credit cards	Accepted
Price range	Affordable
Style	Casual
Cuisine	French-Southern American
Recommended for	Regular neighborhood

Patois's concept announces itself in its name—this is a Louisianan take on classic French cooking, from New Orleans native Aaron Burgau. A France-meets-NOLA dining room, replete with white tablecloths, wooden trim and with a copper bar, sets the scene for steak tartare with soy-cured egg, pork confit rillette, a fried oyster salad with Meyer lemon, and crayfish ramen with local pork belly. Patois is also a favorite Sunday brunch destination for its buttermilk biscuit alone, which comes with fried rabbit.

PHO CAM LY

Recommended by
Edgar Caro

3814 Magazine Street
Uptown
New Orleans
Louisiana 70115
+1 5046444228
www.phocamly.com

Opening hours	Closed Tuesday
Reservation policy	No
Credit cards	Accepted
Price range	Budget
Style	Casual
Cuisine	Vietnamese
Recommended for	Regular neighborhood

"It's near one of my restaurants and the bone marrow broth with brisket is amazing. It's easy to get in, fast and inexpensive."—Edgar Caro

SHAYA

Recommended by
Nick Anderer, Nina Compton

4213 Magazine Street
Uptown
New Orleans
Louisiana 70115
+1 5048914213
www.shayarestaurant.com

Opening hours	Open 7 days
Credit cards	Accepted
Price range	Affordable
Style	Casual
Cuisine	Modern Israeli
Recommended for	Regular neighborhood

"Alon Shaya is an incredibly talented chef doing a modern take on Israeli cuisine. I love everything there but the cauliflower hummus is my favorite." —Nina Compton

It's a good idea to visit Shaya with as many friends as possible, so as to eat more things. Chef Alon Shaya, who won a James Beard Foundation Award in 2016 for best new restaurant, doesn't seem capable of releasing anything from his kitchen that is not double-take exemplary; even something as seemingly simple as za'atar-infused olive oil, or pitta bread (which, thanks to being baked to order in the wood-fire oven, might just be the best you've ever had). Raised in Israel, Alon is taking Middle Eastern culinary tradition and drawing it through Louisiana's agricultural abundance to bring a new soul food to New Orleans.

ST. JAMES CHEESE COMPANY

Recommended by
Isaac Toups

5004 Prytania Street
Uptown
New Orleans
Louisiana 70115
+1 5048994737
www.stjamescheese.com

Opening hours	Open 7 days
Reservation policy	No
Credit cards	Accepted
Price range	Budget
Style	Casual
Cuisine	Deli
Recommended for	Regular neighborhood

"It's where we source our cheeses for both restaurants. We love eating here because you can get simple charcuterie, great cheese and a nice bottle of wine."—Isaac Toups

TACEAUX LOCEAUX FOOD TRUCK
Recommended by
Alex Harrell

5535 Tchoupitoulas Street
Uptown
New Orleans
Louisiana 70115
+1 5043074747

Opening hours	Open 7 days
Reservation policy	No
Credit cards	Accepted
Price range	Budget
Style	Casual
Cuisine	Mexican
Recommended for	Bargain

TAQUERIA CORONA
Recommended by
Tory McPhail

5932 Magazine Street
Uptown
New Orleans
Louisiana 70115
+1 5048973974
www.taqueriacorona.com

Opening hours	Open 7 days
Reservation policy	No
Credit cards	Accepted
Price range	Affordable
Style	Casual
Cuisine	Mexican
Recommended for	Regular neighborhood

"Simple and very well done Mexican food—they're
famous for their fish tacos."—Tory McPhail

UPPERLINE
Recommended by
Jeremy Lee

1413 Upperline Street
Uptown
New Orleans
Louisiana 70115
+1 5048919822
www.upperline.com

Opening hours	Closed Monday and Tuesday
Credit cards	Accepted
Price range	Expensive
Style	Smart casual
Cuisine	Cajun-Creole
Recommended for	Worth the travel

"**An old-school steakhouse where the meat is king and the whiskey is neat.**"
THOMAS KIM P998

"DINER FOOD DONE WITH A CHEF'S TOUCH. AMAZING STEAK TARTARE, BLUE PLATE SPECIALS, AND A KILLER BURGER."
JORGE GUZMAN P999

MINNEAPOLIS

"*Killer hidden cocktail room with great pizza and fire cooked foods.*"
THOMAS BOEMER P1002

"*It doesn't get more Minnesota than that.*"
THOMAS KIM P1000

"**MICHELLE GAYER JUST MAKES THE BEST BREAKFAST PASTRIES.**"
ERICK HARCEY P1000

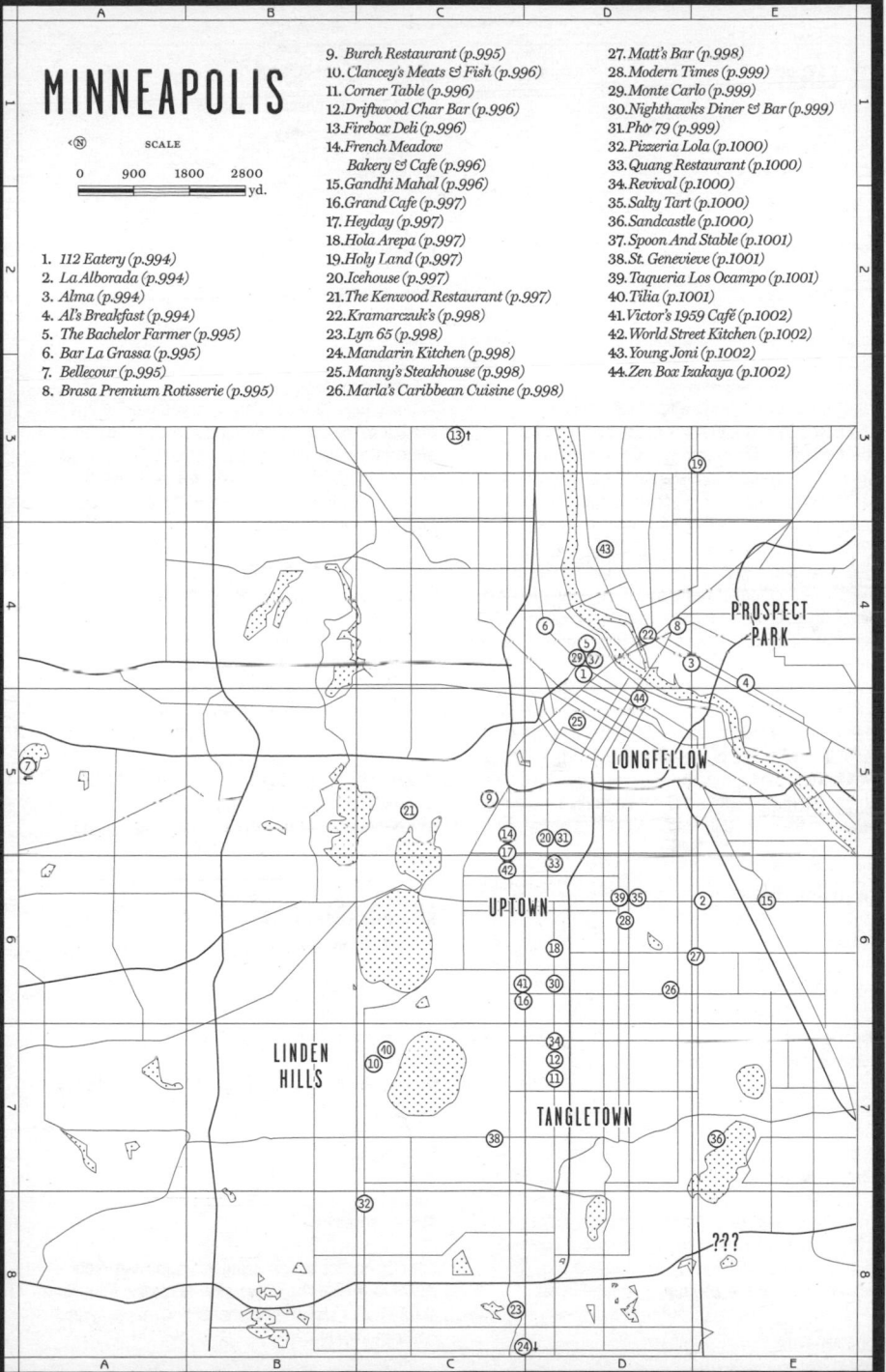

MINNEAPOLIS

‹N›   SCALE

0   900   1800   2800   yd.

PROSPECT PARK

LONGFELLOW

UPTOWN

LINDEN HILLS

TANGLETOWN

???

112 EATERY

112 North 3rd Street
Minneapolis
Minnesota 55401
+1 6123437696
www.112eatery.com

Recommended by
Jorge Guzman,
Thomas Kim

Opening hours	Open 7 days
Credit cards	Accepted
Price range	Affordable
Style	Casual
Cuisine	American
Recommended for	Late night

"Ambiance is dark, romantic, always bustling.
The best seat in the place is at the bar; it makes
you feel like you're in Tom Waits's version of
Nighthawks at the Diner. The food is amazing and
never disappoints. Strong cocktails, great wine list
and great service."—Jorge Guzman

Few could know that when chef Isaac Becker opened
the avowedly modest restaurant 112 eatery in 2005,
his stringozzi (ribbon pasta) with lamb ragu would
become the stuff of legend in the city. But from the
small kitchen in this warm and unpretentious
downtown eatery, Becker's well-trained hand turns
out both exceptional classics like the stringozzi as
well as more modern takes on the Italian kitchen (viz.
tagliatelle with foie gras meatballs). The menu goes
well beyond pasta, too. The cheeseburger—served on
an English muffin with an almost equally thick slab of
brie— is often cited as one of the city's best.

LA ALBORADA

1855 East Lake Street
Minneapolis
Minnesota 55407
+1 6122760490

Recommended by
Doug Flicker

Opening hours	Open 7 days
Reservation policy	No
Credit cards	Accepted
Price range	Budget
Style	Casual
Cuisine	Mexican
Recommended for	Bargain

"A really great gem in the back of a mercado.
It is everything Mexican street food should be—
fast, delicious, and inexpensive. And you can
grocery shop on the way out."—Doug Flicker

ALMA

528 University Avenue Southeast
Minneapolis
Minnesota 55414
+1 6123794909
www.almampls.com

Recommended by
Paul Berglund,
Thomas Boemer,
Jorge Guzman,
Gavin Kaysen,
Thomas Kim

Opening hours	Open 7 days
Credit cards	Accepted
Price range	Affordable
Style	Smart casual
Cuisine	Modern American
Recommended for	Local favorite

"Simply put, Alma is just where you go! For any
occasion. The food is thoughtful, well executed, and
done with care. The culture that Alex Roberts has
created in his company resonates in all that they
do, from the food and service to the ambiance and
charm."—Jorge Guzman

For eighteen years, chef/owner Alex Roberts served
elevated American cuisine from an old firehouse in
the Marcy-Holmes neighborhood. During that time,
he developed deep connections amongst the
region's farmers and built the best wine list in the
Twin Cities. But last year he expanded Alma's
footprint to include a charming seven-room inn with
a more casual café, café Alma, attached. Whereas at
restaurant Alma you'll find a three-course *prix-fixe*
dinner which includes whey-roasted carrots, saffron
spaghetti alla chitara, and poblano crusted
sturgeon, café Alma serves casual fare all day
in a light and airy environment.

AL'S BREAKFAST

413 14th Street Southeast
Minneapolis
Minnesota 55414
+1 6123319991
www.alsbreakfastmpls.com

Recommended by
Paul Berglund,
Erick Harcey,
Gavin Kaysen

Opening hours	Open 7 days
Reservation policy	No
Credit cards	Not accepted
Price range	Budget
Style	Casual
Cuisine	Diner
Recommended for	Breakfast

"The pancakes are amazing. It's a thirteen-seat
restaurant near the University—a classic Minnesota
staple that's just all personality and maple syrup."
—Gavin Kaysen

Fourteen stools and sixty-seven years, ten-feet (3 meters) wide, and closing at 1.00 p.m., Al's Breakfast has exercised an outsized influence on the breakfast culture of the Twin Cities. Everyone, as they say, goes to Al's. Some of the charm is in the regulars, who maintain pay-ahead books, some dating back to the 1970s, at the register. But one cannot deny the allure of blueberry walnut pancakes, the bacon waffles, and a dish called the José—hash browns, cheese, eggs, and salsa. Many things in the world change but Al's, thankfully, isn't one of them.

THE BACHELOR FARMER

Recommended by
Thomas Boemer,
Gavin Kaysen

50 North 2nd Avenue
Minneapolis
Minnesota 55401
+1 6122063920
www.thebachelorfarmer.com

Opening hours	Open 7 days
Credit cards	Accepted
Price range	Expensive
Style	Casual
Cuisine	Scandinavian-Modern American
Recommended for	Local favorite

"Start with a martini, have an incredible meal, and then head downstairs to the Marvel Bar for a swank evening all under one roof."—Thomas Boemer

BAR LA GRASSA

Recommended by
Gavin Kaysen

800 Washington Avenue North
Minneapolis
Minnesota 55401
+1 6123333837
www.barlagrassa.com

Opening hours	Open 7 days
Credit cards	Accepted
Price range	Affordable
Style	Casual
Cuisine	Italian
Recommended for	Late night

"It is run by a very good chef, the pasta is simple and good, the vibe is great, and it is a good place to get a proper meal after service."—Gavin Kaysen

BELLECOUR

Recommended by
Daniel Boulud

739 Lake Street East
Wayzata
Minnesota 55391
+1 9524445200
www.bellecourrestaurant.com

Opening hours	Closed Monday
Credit cards	Accepted
Price range	Affordable
Style	Casual
Cuisine	French Bistro-Bakery
Recommended for	Local favorite

BRASA PREMIUM ROTISSERIE

Recommended by
Erick Harcey

600 East Hennepin Avenue
Minneapolis
Minnesota 55414
+1 6123793030
www.brasa.us

Opening hours	Open 7 days
Reservation policy	No
Credit cards	Accepted
Price range	Affordable
Style	Casual
Cuisine	Southern American-Caribbean
Recommended for	Regular neighborhood

BURCH RESTAURANT

Recommended by
Jorge Guzman

1933 Colfax Avenue South
Minneapolis
Minnesota 55403
+1 6128431500
www.burchrestaurant.com

Opening hours	Open 7 days
Credit cards	Accepted
Price range	Affordable
Style	Smart casual
Cuisine	American
Recommended for	High end

"Steak and dumplings, oh wait you want pizza too? Sure, throw some oysters on that as well. The food is tasty, not pretentious, and it's a fantastic atmosphere for two or twenty at your table."—Jorge Guzman

CLANCEY'S MEATS & FISH
Recommended by
Erick Harcey

4307 South Upton Avenue
Minneapolis
Minnesota 55410
+1 6129260222
www.clanceysmeats.com

Opening hours	Open 7 days
Reservation policy	No
Credit cards	Accepted
Price range	Affordable
Style	Casual
Cuisine	Butcher-Deli
Recommended for	Bargain

"Incredible sandwiches."—Erick Harcey

CORNER TABLE
Recommended by
Gavin Kaysen,
Thomas Kim

4537 Nicollet Avenue
Minneapolis
Minnesota 55419
+1 6128230011
www.cornertablerestaurant.com

Opening hours	Closed Sunday
Credit cards	Accepted
Price range	Expensive
Style	Casual
Cuisine	Modern American
Recommended for	Regular neighborhood

DRIFTWOOD CHAR BAR
Recommended by
Jorge Guzman

4415 Nicollet Avenue
Minneapolis
Minnesota 55419
+1 6123543402
www.driftwoodcharbar.com

Opening hours	Open 7 days
Reservation policy	No
Credit cards	Accepted
Price range	Affordable
Style	Casual
Cuisine	American
Recommended for	Regular neighborhood

"A dive bar with greasy food and live music daily."
—Jorge Guzman

FIREBOX DELI
Recommended by
Erick Harcey

4707 Lyndale Avenue North
Minneapolis
Minnesota 55430
+1 6125218206
www.fireboxdeli.com

Opening hours	Open 7 days
Reservation policy	No
Credit cards	Accepted
Price range	Affordable
Style	Casual
Cuisine	American Barbecue
Recommended for	Local favorite

"Best unknown barbecue in Minneapolis."
—Erick Harcey

FRENCH MEADOW BAKERY & CAFE
Recommended by
Thomas Kim

2610 Lyndale Avenue South
Minneapolis
Minnesota 55408
+1 6128707855
www.frenchmeadowcafe.com

Opening hours	Open 7 days
Credit cards	Accepted
Price range	Affordable
Style	Casual
Cuisine	Café-Bakery
Recommended for	Breakfast

GANDHI MAHAL
Recommended by
Paul Berglund

3009 27th Avenue South
Minneapolis
Minnesota 55406
+1 6127295222
www.gandhimahal.com

Opening hours	Open 7 days
Credit cards	Accepted
Price range	Affordable
Style	Casual
Cuisine	Indian
Recommended for	Regular neighborhood

GRAND CAFE

Recommended by
Thomas Kim

3804 Grand Avenue South
Minneapolis
Minnesota 55409
+1 6128228260

Opening hours	Closed Monday to Wednesday
Credit cards	Accepted
Price range	Affordable
Style	Casual
Cuisine	Breakfast-Brunch
Recommended for	Breakfast

HEYDAY

Recommended by
Paul Berglund

2700 Lyndale Avenue South
Minneapolis
Minnesota 55408
+1 6122009369
www.heydayeats.com

Opening hours	Open 7 days
Credit cards	Accepted
Price range	Affordable
Style	Smart casual
Cuisine	Modern American
Recommended for	Late night

"It's super inviting and it has a great menu for after work."—Paul Berglund

HOLA AREPA

Recommended by
Thomas Boemer,
Gavin Kaysen

3501 Nicollet Avenue
Minneapolis
Minnesota 55408
+1 6123455583
www.holaarepa.com

Opening hours	Closed Monday
Reservation policy	No
Credit cards	Accepted
Price range	Affordable
Style	Casual
Cuisine	Latin American
Recommended for	Regular neighborhood

"Favorite brunch and killer cocktail spot."
—Thomas Boemer

HOLY LAND

Recommended by
Erick Harcey

2513 Central Avenue North East
Minneapolis
Minnesota 55418
+1 6127812627
www.holylandbrand.com

Opening hours	Open 7 days
Reservation policy	No
Credit cards	Accepted
Price range	Budget
Style	Casual
Cuisine	Middle Eastern
Recommended for	Bargain

"Best *gyros* (Greek flatbread wraps) in town."
—Erick Harcey

ICEHOUSE

Recommended by
Thomas Kim

2528 Nicollet Avenue
Minneapolis
Minnesota 55404
+1 6122766523
www.icehousempls.com

Opening hours	Open 7 days
Credit cards	Accepted
Price range	Affordable
Style	Smart casual
Cuisine	American
Recommended for	Late night

"This restaurant serves some of the best pastrami and pickles. They have a full bar with inventive cocktails such as a berry phosphate rum-punch with vanilla cream foam. Pair that with a full stage and live music—what's not to love."—Thomas Kim

THE KENWOOD RESTAURANT

Recommended by
Jorge Guzman

2115 West 21st Street
Minneapolis
Minnesota 55405
+1 6123773695
www.thekenwoodrestaurant.com

Opening hours	Closed Monday
Reservation policy	No
Credit cards	Accepted
Price range	Affordable
Style	Casual
Cuisine	Breakfast-Brunch
Recommended for	Breakfast

KRAMARCZUK'S
Recommended by
Thomas Kim

215 East Hennepin Avenue
Minneapolis
Minnesota 55414
+1 6123793018
www.kramarczuks.com

Opening hours	Open 7 days
Reservation policy	No
Credit cards	Accepted
Price range	Affordable
Style	Casual
Cuisine	Polish-Deli
Recommended for	Local favorite

LYN 65
Recommended by
Thomas Boemer

6439 Lyndale Avenue South
Minneapolis
Minnesota 55423
+1 6123535501
www.lyn65.com

Opening hours	Open 7 days
Credit cards	Accepted
Price range	Affordable
Style	Casual
Cuisine	Modern American
Recommended for	Late night

"Great bar and late-night food. I always get the
duck-fat fries and tartare."—Thomas Boemer

MANDARIN KITCHEN
Recommended by
Doug Flicker

8766 Lyndale Avenue South
Minneapolis
Minnesota 55420
+1 9528845356

Opening hours	Open 7 days
Credit cards	Accepted
Price range	Affordable
Style	Casual
Cuisine	Dim Sum
Recommended for	Breakfast

"Because of the late-night nature of my buisness
I really don't eat any sort of traditional breakfast.
I will set my alarm for dim sum though. A favorite
of mine is Mandarin Kitchen. Making plans early
in the week for Sunday dim sum, then seeing who
actually makes it after a late Saturday service, always
separates the weak from the strong."—Doug Flicker

MANNY'S STEAKHOUSE
Recommended by
Thomas Kim

825 South Marquette Avenue
Minneapolis
Minnesota 55402
+1 6123399900
www.mannyssteakhouse.com

Opening hours	Open 7 days
Credit cards	Accepted
Price range	Expensive
Style	Smart casual
Cuisine	Steakhouse
Recommended for	High end

"An old-school steakhouse where the meat is king
and the whiskey is neat. It is easy to forget you are in
Minneapolis when you enter Manny's, which is helpful
on days when it's negative 20 degrees."—Thomas Kim

MARLA'S CARIBBEAN CUISINE
Recommended by
Gavin Kaysen,
Thomas Kim

3761 Bloomington Avenue South
Minneapolis
Minnesota 55407
+1 6127243088
www.marlascuisine.com

Opening hours	Closed Monday and Sunday
Reservation policy	No
Credit cards	Accepted
Price range	Affordable
Style	Casual
Cuisine	Caribbean
Recommended for	Regular neighborhood

"It's run by Marla who cooks family recipes. It doesn't
get more home-cooked than this—you feel like you
are part of her family by the time you leave."
—Gavin Kaysen

MATT'S BAR
Recommended by
Thomas Boemer,
Doug Flicker

3500 Cedar Avenue South
Minneapolis
Minnesota 55407
+1 6127227072
www.mattsbar.com

Opening hours	Open 7 days
Reservation policy	No
Credit cards	Not accepted
Price range	Affordable
Style	Casual
Cuisine	American
Recommended for	Local favorite

"It's the food of the people that truly sums up a city; even better if there's a rivalry—best pizza in New York, best dog in Chicago, best cheese steak sandwiches in Philly. We have the Juicy Lucy. A Juicy Lucy is a hamburger that is stuffed with American cheese. Because of the molten nature of the cheese you ALWAYS have to wait for the cheese to at least somewhat solidify. A burnt mouth is the result for the impatient. Matt's is the original as well as the best."
—Doug Flicker

MODERN TIMES

Recommended by
Thomas Kim

3200 Chicago Avenue South
Minneapolis
Minnesota 55407
+1 6128863882
www.moderntimesmpls.com

Opening hours	Open 7 days
Reservation policy	No
Credit cards	Accepted
Price range	Affordable
Style	Casual
Cuisine	Vegetarian
Recommended for	Breakfast

"Modern Times has taken a very DIY approach to everything, which I love. The food is creative and comforting in a artistic space."—Thomas Kim

MONTE CARLO

Recommended by
Erick Harcey

219 3rd Avenue North
Minneapolis
Minnesota 55401
+1 6123335900
www.montecarlomn.com

Opening hours	Open 7 days
Credit cards	Accepted
Price range	Affordable
Style	Smart casual
Cuisine	American
Recommended for	Late night

"Best dry-rubbed wings and old-school beef liver with saltines."—Erick Harcey

NIGHTHAWKS DINER & BAR

Recommended by
Jorge Guzman

3753 Nicollet Avenue South
Minneapolis
Minnesota 55409
+1 6122488111
www.nighthawksmpls.com

Opening hours	Open 7 days
Credit cards	Accepted
Price range	Affordable
Style	Casual
Cuisine	American
Recommended for	Regular neighborhood

"Diner food done with a chef's touch. Amazing steak tartare, blue-plate specials, and a killer burger. You never leave hungry, its unpretentious, and has a great late-night special."—Jorge Guzman

Taking inspiration, and its name, from Edward Hopper's iconic painting, Nighthawks presents a postmodern, playful take on classic American comfort food. Although most loved by the locals for its brunch menu (the meats, including their famed thick-cut bacon, are hand-cured on site), there is still an impressively inventive food and beer selection for a late-night bite. The foot-long hot dogs, stuffed with dill mayonnaise, horseradish, mustard, potato, and *giardiniera* (Italian vegetable relish), are constructed perfectly, pulling off the astonishing trick of making a classic diner item feel like a sophisticated and elegant dish. Even during busier hours, the atmosphere at Nighthawks, much like that of its artwork namesake, is calm, cerebral, and classy.

PHỞ 79

Recommended by
Jorge Guzman

2529 Nicollet Avenue
Minneapolis
Minnesota 55404
+1 6128714602
www.pho79mpls.com

Opening hours	Open 7 days
Reservation policy	No
Credit cards	Accepted
Price range	Budget
Style	Casual
Cuisine	Vietnamese
Recommended for	Bargain

PIZZERIA LOLA

5557 Xerxes Avenue South
Minneapolis
Minnesota 55410
+1 6124248338
www.pizzerialola.com

Recommended by
Paul Berglund,
Gavin Kaysen

Opening hours	Open 7 days
Reservation policy	No
Credit cards	Accepted
Price range	Affordable
Style	Casual
Cuisine	Pizza
Recommended for	Regular neighborhood

"No one does what they do better than Ann Kim and her team do pizza at Lola. It's always terrific."
—Paul Berglund

QUANG RESTAURANT

2719 Nicollet Avenue
Minneapolis
Minnesota 55408
+1 6128704739
www.quang-restaurant.com

Recommended by
Paul Berglund,
Jorge Guzman,
Thomas Kim

Opening hours	Closed Tuesday
Reservation policy	No
Credit cards	Accepted
Price range	Budget
Style	Casual
Cuisine	Vietnamese
Recommended for	Local favorite

"This is a Minneapolis institution that everyone I know goes to. It's the best of our city's diversity and is a standard-bearer for great Vietnamese food."
—Paul Berglund

REVIVAL

4257 Nicollet Avenue
Minneapolis
Minnesota 55409
+1 6123454516
www.revivalfriedchicken.com

Recommended by
Jorge Guzman, Thomas Kim

Opening hours	Open 7 days
Reservation policy	No
Credit cards	Accepted
Price range	Budget
Style	Casual
Cuisine	Southern American
Recommended for	Wish I'd opened

"A Southern-influenced restaurant making thoughtfully crafted food with a heavy dose of fried chicken. I actually love all the sides—Carolina gold rice and collard greens are the way to go!"
—Thomas Kim

SALTY TART

920 East Lake Street
Minneapolis
Minnesota 55407
+1 6128749206
www.saltytart.com

Recommended by
Erick Harcey

Opening hours	Open 7 days
Reservation policy	No
Credit cards	Accepted
Price range	Affordable
Style	Casual
Cuisine	Patisserie
Recommended for	Breakfast

"Michelle Gayer just makes the best breakfast pastries."—Erick Harcey

SANDCASTLE

4955 Nokomis Parkway West
Minneapolis
Minnesota 55417
+1 6127225550
www.sandcastlempls.com

Recommended by
Thomas Kim

Opening hours	Open 7 days
Credit cards	Accepted
Price range	Affordable
Style	Casual
Cuisine	American
Recommended for	Local favorite

"Sandcastle is a combination of all the things Minnesotans love. Fresh, delicious food, Lake Nokomis, Chef Doug Flicker, beer, a dog-friendly patio with local musicians, all located in a bike- and family-friendly park. It doesn't get more Minnesota than that."
—Thomas Kim

SPOON AND STABLE

211 1st Street North
Minneapolis
Minnesota 55401
+1 6122249850
www.spoonandstable.com

Recommended by
Thomas Boemer,
Daniel Boulud,
Thomas Kim,
Carlos Perez

Opening hours	Open 7 days
Credit cards	Accepted
Price range	Affordable
Style	Smart casual
Cuisine	Modern American
Recommended for	High end

"Beautiful new restaurant by chef Gavin Kaysen hits all the buttons with great cocktails, food, and service. Be on the lookout for some late-night gems in the lounge, like ramen."—Thomas Boemer

Having won a prestigious James Beard Foundation Award for Rising Star Chef of the Year, Gavin Kaysen went on to establish his passion project, Spoon and Stable, a celebration of Midwestern cuisine. With a focus on seasonal ingredients, and inspired by his background in classical French cuisine under world-famous chefs like Daniel Boulud and Marco Pierre White, Kaysen has ignited a firework under the Minneapolis restaurant scene. The dining area is located in a renovated early-twentieth-century horse stable, with high ceilings and original brickwork, and includes, rather excitingly, Prohibition-era booze-smuggling tunnels. The dishes are not overly flashy or gimmicky, but instead prepared with confident flair.

ST. GENEVIEVE

5003 Bryant Avenue South
Minneapolis
Minnesota 55419
+1 6123534843
www.stgmpls.com

Recommended by
Doug Flicker,
Jorge Guzman

Opening hours	Open 7 days
Credit cards	Accepted
Price range	Affordable
Style	Smart casual
Cuisine	French
Recommended for	High end

"Amazing Champagne and wine list and the food is classic French brasserie. It's exactly what a chef wants on his or her day off."—Jorge Guzman

TAQUERIA LOS OCAMPO

809 East Lake Street
Minneapolis
Minnesota 55407
+1 6128254978
www.taquerialosocampo.com

Recommended by
Paul Berglund,
Doug Flicker,
Jorge Guzman,
Thomas Kim

Opening hours	Open 7 days
Reservation policy	No
Credit cards	Accepted
Price range	Affordable
Style	Casual
Cuisine	Mexican
Recommended for	Bargain

"Chorizo burritos the size of your head. There are two circumstances that require a giant burrito late at night: a fourteen-hour shift that for some reason, despite being surrounded by food all day, you didn't have time to eat; or two hours of drinking that require a stomach mopping of the excess alcohol. Either way a late-night visit sets it straight."—Doug Flicker

Taqueria Los Ocampo, set up in 2003 and now in its third Minneapolis location, serves quick, cheap, and authentic Mexican food that packs a flavorful punch. With over twenty-five taco fillings available, from a variety of *carnitas* (pulled meats) to spicy mushrooms and squash blossoms, there's an option to satisfy all tastes. Despite its appearance as a laid-back fast-food joint, the ingredients on offer here are the freshest you can find. Happy hour, you'll be pleased to know, occurs every day from 3.00 p.m. to 6.00 p.m., and again from 9.00 p.m. to 11.00 p.m., with margaritas for $4.99 (£3.85) and a dollar off all beers. *Salud*!

TILIA

2726 West 43rd Street
Minneapolis
Minnesota 55410
+1 6123542806
www.tiliampls.com

Recommended by
Gavin Kaysen

Opening hours	Open 7 days
Reservation policy	No
Credit cards	Accepted
Price range	Affordable
Style	Casual
Cuisine	Modern American
Recommended for	Regular neighborhood

VICTOR'S 1959 CAFÉ

3756 Grand Avenue South
Minneapolis
Minnesota 55409
+1 6128278948
www.victors1959cafe.com

Recommended by
Jorge Guzman,
Thomas Kim

Opening hours	Open 7 days
Credit cards	Accepted
Price range	Affordable
Style	Casual
Cuisine	Cuban
Recommended for	Breakfast

"Being from the Yucatán, I'm a sucker for black beans and tortillas for breakfast. You will always find both on the menu in abundance. It's got character and charm. Open for breakfast, lunch, and dinner—the coffee is hot, the food tasty, and the ambiance is great."—Jorge Guzman

WORLD STREET KITCHEN

2743 Lyndale Avenue South
Minneapolis
Minnesota 55408
+1 6124248855
www.eatwsk.com

Recommended by
Thomas Boemer,
Erick Harcey

Opening hours	Open 7 days
Reservation policy	No
Credit cards	Accepted
Price range	Affordable
Style	Casual
Cuisine	International Street Food
Recommended for	Bargain

"Great flavors—the Korean short rib burrito is something I just start thinking about some days and have to have."—Thomas Boemer

YOUNG JONI

165 13th Avenue North East
Minneapolis
Minnesota 55413
+1 6123455719
www.youngjoni.com

Recommended by
Thomas Boemer

Opening hours	Closed Monday
Credit cards	Accepted
Price range	Affordable
Style	Casual
Cuisine	Pizza-Grill
Recommended for	Late night

"Killer hidden cocktail room with great pizza and fire-cooked foods."—Thomas Boemer

ZEN BOX IZAKAYA

602 S Washington Avenue
Minneapolis
Minnesota 55415
www.zenbox.com

Recommended by
Thomas Boemer,
Jorge Guzman

Opening hours	Open 7 days
Credit cards	Accepted
Price range	Affordable
Style	Casual
Cuisine	Japanese
Recommended for	Wish I'd opened

"It's a traditional *izakaya*. Great booze, amazing Japanese classics, the ramen is some of the best in the country. It's tasty as hell. I've eaten here more than anywhere else and never had a mediocre meal."—Jorge Guzman

NEW YORK

MANHATTAN DOWNTOWN

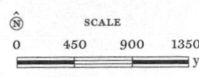

MANHATTAN

DOWNTOWN

SCALE

0 450 900 1350 yd.

1. *Chinese Tuxedo (p.1006)*
2. *Great Ny Noodletown (p.1006)*
3. *Hop Kee (p.1006)*
4. *Delmonico's (p.1006)*
5. *Nha Trang One (p.1006)*
6. *Noodle Village (p.1006)*
7. *Wo Hop (p.1007)*
8. *Leo's Bagels (p.1007)*
9. *Cafe Petisco (p.1007)*
10. *Contra (p.1007)*
11. *Le French Diner (p.1008)*
12. *Funny Bbq 98 (p.1008)*
13. *La Isla Café (p.1008)*
14. *Katz's Delicatessen (p.1008)*
15. *Lam Zhou Handmade Noodle (p.1008)*
16. *Mission Chinese (p.1008)*
17. *Russ & Daughters Cafe (p.1009)*
18. *Spicy Village (p.1009)*
19. *Le Turtle (p.1009)*
20. *Vanessa's Dumpling House (p.1009)*
21. *Wildair (p.1010)*
22. *Wu's Wonton King (p.1010)*
23. *Black Seed Bagels (p.1010)*
24. *Emilio's Ballato (p.1010)*
25. *Estela (p.1010)*
26. *Parm (p.1011)*
27. *Pasquale Jones (p.1011)*
28. *Peasant (p.1011)*
29. *Uncle Boons (p.1011)*
30. *Balthazar (p.1011)*
31. *Blue Ribbon Brasserie (p.1012)*
32. *Blue Ribbon Sushi (p.1012)*
33. *Café Altro Paradiso (p.1012)*
34. *Charlie Bird (p.1012)*
35. *Le Coucou (p.1012)*
36. *La Esquina (p.1013)*
37. *Paowalla (p.1013)*
38. *Arcade Bakery (p.1013)*
39. *Atera (p.1013)*
40. *Bâtard (p.1013)*
41. *Houseman (p.1014)*
42. *Jungsik (p.1014)*
43. *Locanda Verde (p.1014)*
44. *Two Hands (p.1014)*
45. *Achilles Heel (p.1014)*
46. *Alameda (p.1014)*
47. *Aska (p.1015)*
48. *Blanca (p.1015)*
49. *Brooklyn Fare (p.1015)*
50. *Diner (p.1015)*
51. *Ends Meat (p.1015)*
52. *The Finch (p.1015)*
53. *Five Leaves (p.1016)*
54. *The Four Horsemen (p.1016)*
55. *Franny's (p.1016)*
56. *Larina Pastificio E Vino (p.1016)*
57. *Lilia (p.1016)*
58. *Roberta's (p.1017)*
59. *Sunday In Brooklyn (p.1017)*
60. *Win Son (p.1017)*
61. *Llama Inn (p.1017)*
62. *Lucali Pizza (p.1017)*
63. *Maison Premiere (p.1017)*
64. *Marlow & Sons (p.1018)*
65. *Okonomi (p.1018)*
66. *Olmsted (p.1018)*
67. *Peter Luger Steak House (p.1018)*
68. *Pok Pok (p.1019)*
69. *Pretty Southern (p.1019)*
70. *Reynard (p.1019)*
71. *New World Mall Food Court (p.1019)*
72. *Lhasa Fast Food (p.1019)*
73. *Park Side Restaurant (p.1019)*

GREENWICH VILLAGE
WEST VILLAGE
SOHO
EAST VILLAGE
TRIBECA
LOWER EAST SIDE
BATTERY PARK

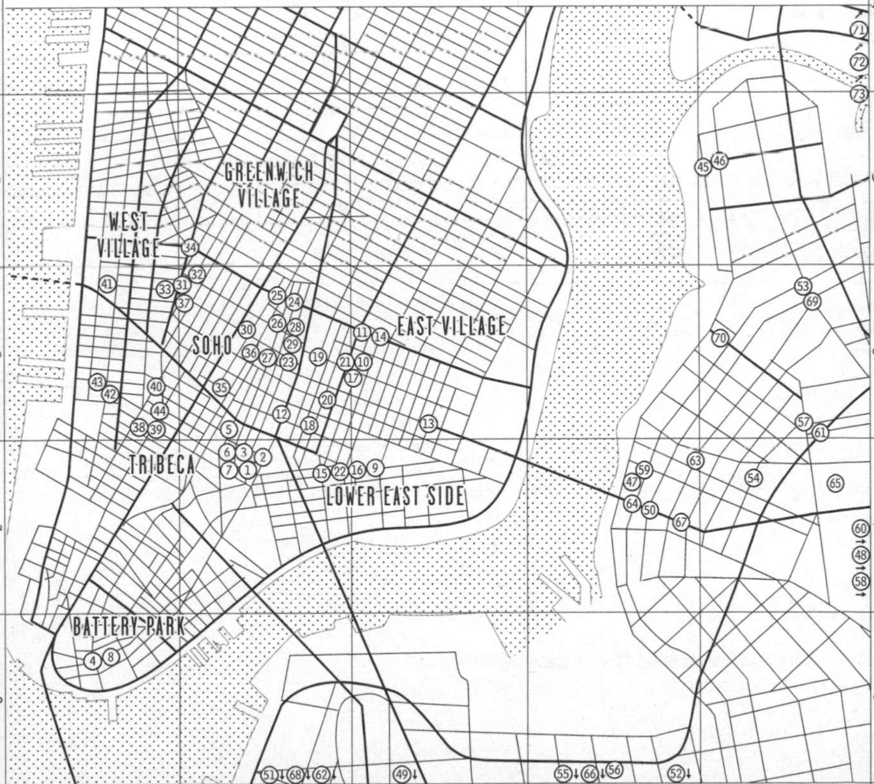

CHINESE TUXEDO

5 Doyers Street
Chinatown
New York 10013
+1 6468959301
www.chinesetuxedo.com

Opening hours	Open 7 days
Credit cards	Accepted
Price range	Affordable
Style	Casual
Cuisine	Chinese
Recommended for	Local favorite

GREAT NY NOODLETOWN

28 Bowery
Chinatown
New York 10013
+1 2123490923
www.greatnynoodletown.com

Opening hours	Open 7 days
Reservation policy	No
Credit cards	Accepted
Price range	Affordable
Style	Casual
Cuisine	Chinese
Recommended for	Late night

"Packed at 2.00 a.m. with a lot of industry people and it always makes me feel part of a community when I am in there. The food cures a lot of long day and late night ills."—Mashama Bailey

HOP KEE

21 Mott Street
Chinatown
New York 10013
+1 2129648365
www.hopkeenyc.com

Opening hours	Open 7 days
Credit cards	Not accepted
Price range	Affordable
Style	Casual
Cuisine	Chinese
Recommended for	Late night

"Classic Cantonese food at reasonable prices and open late."—Nick Anderer

DELMONICO'S

56 Beaver Street
Chinatown
New York, 10004
+1 2125091144
www.delmonicosrestaurant.com

Opening hours	Closed Sunday
Credit cards	Accepted
Price range	Expensive
Style	Smart casual
Cuisine	Steakhouse
Recommended for	Worth the travel

NHA TRANG ONE

87 Baxter Street
Chinatown
New York 10013
+1 2122335948
www.nhatrangnyc.com

Opening hours	Open 7 days
Credit cards	Accepted
Price range	Budget
Style	Casual
Cuisine	Vietnamese
Recommended for	Bargain

NOODLE VILLAGE

13 Mott Street
Chinatown
New York 10013
+1 2122330788
www.noodlevillage.com

Opening hours	Open 7 days
Credit cards	Accepted
Price range	Affordable
Style	Casual
Cuisine	Chinese
Recommended for	Bargain

WO HOP

Recommended by
Eric & Bruce Bromberg

17 Mott Street
Chinatown
New York 10013
+1 2129628617
www.wohopnyc.com

Opening hours	Open 7 days
Reservation policy	No
Credit cards	Not accepted
Price range	Affordable
Style	Casual
Cuisine	Chinese
Recommended for	Late night

Descend the red staircase into Chinatown's Wo Hop, as generations of night owls and New York cops have done long before you, since 1938. If some of the dishes seem about as current as the celebrity photos plastered on the walls, embrace it: this frill-free Cantonese has classic status. Service is brusque, the portions are huge, and there's always a wait for a table. Order egg drop soup for old time's sake, and maybe roast duck chow fun. Wo Hop keeps pleasingly ungodly hours: 10.30 a.m. until 5.00 a.m., seven days a week.

LEO'S BAGELS

Recommended by
Sean Gray

3 Hanover Square
Financial District
New York 10004
+1 2127854700
www.leosbagels.com

Reservation policy	No
Credit cards	Accepted but not Diners
Price range	Affordable
Style	Casual
Cuisine	Bagels
Recommended for	Breakfast

CAFE PETISCO

Recommended by
Alexandra Raij

189 East Broadway
Lower East Side
New York 10002
+1 2123870366

Opening hours	Open 7 days
Reservation policy	No
Credit cards	Not accepted
Price range	Affordable
Style	Casual
Cuisine	Israeli Bistro
Recommended for	Breakfast

"Food is fresh and the service is great. The coffee is great too."—Alexandra Raij

CONTRA

Recommended by
Carolina Bazán,
Diego Hernández-Velasco Baquedano,
Ignacio Mattos, Marc-Alexandre Mercier,
Matthew Orlando, Mitch Orr,
Elena Reygadas

138 Orchard Street
Lower East Side
New York 10002
+1 2124664633
www.contranyc.com

Opening hours	Closed Monday and Sunday
Credit cards	Accepted
Price range	Expensive
Style	Smart casual
Cuisine	Modern American
Recommended for	Worth the travel

"Best meal I had last year. Fabian and Jeremiah are young, talented, inspiring, and awesome people."
—Marc-Alexandre Mercier

LE FRENCH DINER

188 Orchard Street
Lower East Side
New York 10002
+1 2127771577
www.lefrenchdiner.com

Opening hours	Open 7 days
Reservation policy	No
Credit cards	Accepted but not AMEX or Diners
Price range	Affordable
Style	Casual
Cuisine	French
Recommended for	Wish I'd opened

"I love the immediacy and honesty of the cooking. Tiny twenty-seat diner-style bistro where you can watch the chef prepare everything."—Nick Anderer

FUNNY BBQ 98

98 Bowery
Lower East Side
New York 10013
+1 2129650076

Opening hours	Open 7 days
Credit cards	Accepted
Price range	Affordable
Style	Casual
Cuisine	Chinese
Recommended for	Late night

"A Pokémon-decorated Chinese barbecue place. Everything is on a skewer, or you can get it for your hot pot. The lamb is really great. The chicken wing is great, too—they dry it out and fry it. Everything is dusted in chile powder and cumin."—Danny Bowien

LA ISLA CAFÉ

212 Delancey Street
Lower East Side
New York 10002
+1 2125984752

Opening hours	Closed Sunday
Reservation policy	No
Credit cards	Accepted
Price range	Budget
Style	Casual
Cuisine	Dominican Diner
Recommended for	Bargain

"It's a classic Dominican place. Tasty and inexpensive."—Alexandra Raij

KATZ'S DELICATESSEN

205 East Houston Street
Lower East Side
New York 10002
+1 2122542246
www.katzsdelicatessen.com

Opening hours	Open 7 days
Credit cards	Accepted
Price range	Affordable
Style	Casual
Cuisine	American
Recommended for	Bargain

"A legendary restaurant serving the best pastrami."
—Frankie van Loo

LAM ZHOU HANDMADE NOODLE

144 East Broadway
Lower East Side
New York 10002
+1 2125666933

Opening hours	Open 7 days
Reservation policy	No
Credit cards	Not accepted
Price range	Budget
Style	Casual
Cuisine	Chinese
Recommended for	Bargain

"I used to live right by it and eat there about three or four times a week. I think it's what I miss most about New York. You would order the noodles, then begin to hear the thud-thud of them being slapped and pulled. The broths were delicious. Add a pork cutlet or eat the noodles dry with spiced beef mince."—Mark Dobbie

MISSION CHINESE

171 East Broadway
Lower East Side
New York 10002
www.mcfny.com

Opening hours	Open 7 days
Credit cards	Accepted
Price range	Affordable
Style	Smart casual
Cuisine	Asian
Recommended for	Worth the travel

"Fireworks in the mouth is an understatement. Masters of balanced flavors and bold ideas, executed brilliantly."—Lee Tiernan

RUSS & DAUGHTERS CAFE

127 Orchard Street
Lower East Side
New York 10002
+1 2124754880
www.russanddaughterscafe.com

Opening hours..Open 7 days
Reservation policy...No
Credit cards...Accepted
Price range..Affordable
Style..Casual
Cuisine...Jewish Deli
Recommended for..Breakfast

"All the greatest hits from the deli, served in a great New York diner interior. Knishes, plates of herring, and matzo ball soup that you want to eat every day— I do when I'm there. All that and sodas, shrubs, and cocktails for every occasion. Quite happily drink my way through the list."—Tom Harris

It took over 100 years but finally, Russ & Daughters, the high temple of smoked fish on the Lower East Side, expanded. Whereas the original location on East Houston offers a deli case full of house-smoked salmon, gravlax, herring, and knishes (filled dough snacks), at the new location the fourth generation of the Russ family serves silky slices of lox, compact bagels, plates of herring, and gloriously fluffy eggs at all hours in a slightly retro but elegant storefront with cheery booths, a soda fountain, and waiters wearing crisp white aprons.

SPICY VILLAGE

68 Forsyth Street
Lower East Side
New York 10002
+1 2126258299
www.spicyvillagenyc.com

Opening hours...Closed Sunday
Reservation policy...No
Credit cards...Not accepted
Price range..Budget
Style..Casual
Cuisine..Chinese
Recommended for...Bargain

LE TURTLE

177 Chrystie Street
Lower East Side
New York 10002
+1 6469187189
www.leturtle.fr

Opening hours..Open 7 days
Credit cards...Accepted
Price range...Expensive
Style...Smart casual
Cuisine..French-American
Recommended for...............................Regular neighborhood

"Beautiful space, delicious food, nice wine list."
—Carlo Mirarchi

Le Turtle, by famously progressive restaurateur Taavo Somer, owes more to the New Wave films of Godard and Truffaut than it does to, say, L'Ami Jean. But this small corner space—with a two-way mirror looking out onto unsuspecting passers-by who preen in front of it, much to the delight of those inside—doesn't stint on the classics. Enjoyed best late at night, when the beautiful people fill the room like visual aromatherapy, the offerings include *gnocchi parisienne* with English peas and scallions (spring onions), an extremely satisfying steak, and a whole Sasso chicken, which arrives with its claws still curled, as if clutching, unsuccessfully it turns out, to the way things were.

VANESSA'S DUMPLING HOUSE

118A Eldridge Street
Lower East Side
New York 10002
+1 2126258008
www.vanessas.com

Opening hours..Open 7 days
Reservation policy...No
Credit cards...Accepted
Price range..Budget
Style..Casual
Cuisine..Chinese
Recommended for...Bargain

"The pork sesame pancake is $1.50 (£1) and it's one of those dishes that everyone needs to try before you die."—Jesse Schenker

WILDAIR

142 Orchard Street
Lower East Side
New York 10002
+1 6469645624
www.wildair.nyc

Recommended by
James Berckemeyer, Fredrik Berselius,
Ben Devlin, Kevin Fink, Sean Gray,
Gunnar Karl Gíslason, Claus Meyer,
Ken Oringer, Tim Spedding

Opening hours.................................Closed Monday and Sunday
Reservation policy...No
Credit cards..Accepted
Price range...Affordable
Style...Casual
Cuisine...American
Recommended for...Late night

"Great wine list, great food menu, great music.
Very crushable in every way."—Sean Gray

These days, the Lower East Side exists more as an
idea than a place. True, it was once a neighborhood
where a soul with an artistic bent and a surfeit of
talent could make art come alive. Now it's a bunch of
condos and boutiques. Except, perhaps, for Wildair,
the small but ambitious wine bar from Fabian Von
Hauske and Jeremiah Stone. The pair, whose Contra
is similarly an embassy of freewheeling artistic
ambition, sling scallop crudo with avocado like
it's no big deal. Pig's head on toast (with stinging
nettles and 'nduja) might appear one night, and
then never again—and they pour natural wines
like Matassa as if it was nothing. Of course it is
something and, if you're lucky enough to find a
perch at the tiny storefront, something not to miss.

WU'S WONTON KING

165 East Broadway
Lower East Side
New York 10002
+1 2124771111
www.wuswontonking.com

Recommended by
Danny Bowien

Opening hours...Open 7 days
Credit cards........................Accepted but not AMEX or Diners
Price range..Budget
Style...Casual
Cuisine..Chinese
Recommended for...Bargain

BLACK SEED BAGELS

170 Elizabeth Street
NoLita
New York 10012
+1 2127301950
www.blackseedbagels.com

Recommended by
Zaiyu Hasegawa,
Daniel Humm

Opening hours...Open 7 days
Credit cards..Accepted
Price range...Affordable
Style...Casual
Cuisine..Bagels
Recommended for...Breakfast

"Love their bagels and the sandwiches."
—Daniel Humm

EMILIO'S BALLATO

55 East Houston Street
NoLita
New York 10012
+1 2122748881

Recommended by
Missy Robbins

Opening hours...Open 7 days
Credit cards..Accepted
Price range...Affordable
Style...Casual
Cuisine..Italian
Recommended for..............................Regular neighborhood

ESTELA

47 East Houston Street
NoLita
New York 10012
+1 2122197693
www.estelanyc.com

Recommended by
Michael Beltran, Paul Carmichael,
Brian Luptak, Morgan McGlone,
Larry McGuire, Claus Meyer,
Enrique Olvera, Robert Phalen,
Jair Tellez, Thomas Troisgros

Opening hours...Open 7 days
Credit cards..Accepted
Price range...Affordable
Style...Casual
Cuisine...Mediterranean
Recommended for......................................Wish I'd opened

"When we are in NYC this is our neighborhood spot.
It's always bustling and cozy and the simple interior
is unpretentious and welcoming. The food is genius
and looks simple enough but there are very smart and
delicious things happening. Great cocktails and wine
list too."—Larry McGuire

PARM

Recommended by
Cathy Whims

248 Mulberry Street
NoLita
New York 10012
+1 2129937189
www.parmnyc.com

Opening hours	Open 7 days
Reservation policy	No
Credit cards	Accepted
Price range	Affordable
Style	Casual
Cuisine	Italian-American
Recommended for	Wish I'd opened

"Parm succeeds in making the Italian-American food
that everyone craves, and they do it stylishly."
—Cathy Whims

PASQUALE JONES

Recommended by
Daniel Humm

187 Mulberry Street
NoLita
New York 10012
www.pasqualejones.com

Opening hours	Open 7 days
Credit cards	Accepted
Price range	Affordable
Style	Casual
Cuisine	Italian
Recommended for	Regular neighborhood

"It has my favorite things: pizza, pasta, incredible
wine, and great hospitality."—Daniel Humm

PEASANT

Recommended by
David Chang

194 Elizabeth Street
NoLita
New York 10012
+1 2129659511
www.peasantnyc.com

Opening hours	Closed Monday and Sunday
Reservation policy	No
Credit cards	Accepted
Price range	Affordable
Style	Smart casual
Cuisine	American-Grill
Recommended for	Local favorite

UNCLE BOONS

Recommended by
Jennifer Jasinski,
Michael Anthony,
Missy Robbins

7 Spring Street
NoLita
New York 10012
+1 6463706650
www.uncleboons.com

Opening hours	Open 7 days
Credit cards	Accepted but not Diners
Price range	Affordable
Style	Casual
Cuisine	Thai
Recommended for	Regular neighborhood

"Super creative Thai food and killer cocktails
—Bangkok flea-market decor."—Jennifer Jasinski

BALTHAZAR

Recommended by
Tomi Bjorck, Galton Blackiston,
Danny Bowien, Ruairí de Blacam,
David Chang, Christian Domschitz,
Björn Frantzén, Will Goldfarb,
Paul Liebrandt, Ignacio Mattos,
Eric Ripert, Alla Wolf Tasker

80 Spring Street
SoHo
New York 10012
+1 2129651414
www.balthazarny.com

Opening hours	Open 7 days
Credit cards	Accepted
Price range	Affordable
Style	Casual
Cuisine	French
Recommended for	Breakfast

"You could turn up at this restaurant almost any time
of the day or night and be sure that something on the
menu would suit your mood and tastes. You could
also just sit there for the whole day, watch the world
go by, and gorge on its bounty! I wish I'd opened
it because I would hazard a guess that it is also
a damn good business."—Tomi Bjorck

BLUE RIBBON BRASSERIE

97 Sullivan Street
SoHo
New York 10012
+1 2122740404
www.blueribbonrestaurants.com

Opening hours	Open 7 days
Credit cards	Accepted
Price range	Affordable
Style	Casual
Cuisine	American
Recommended for	Late night

"The only place I know where you can get a full menu up to 4.00 a.m."—Daniel Humm

BLUE RIBBON SUSHI

119 Sullivan Street
SoHo
New York 10012
+1 2123430404
www.blueribbonrestaurants.com

Opening hours	Open 7 days
Credit cards	Accepted
Price range	Affordable
Style	Casual
Cuisine	Sushi
Recommended for	Late night

"Open very late—always reliable."—Missy Robbins

CAFÉ ALTRO PARADISO

234 Spring St
SoHo
New York 10013
+1 6469520828
www.altroparadiso.com

Opening hours	Open 7 days
Credit cards	Accepted
Price range	Affordable
Style	Casual
Cuisine	Italian
Recommended for	Worth the travel

"Altro Paradiso has the coolest looking dining room I've ever been in. The food is first rate—and I wouldn't expect anything less from Chef Ignacio Mattos."
—Kris Yenbamroong

CHARLIE BIRD

5 King Street
SoHo
New York 10012
+1 2122357133
www.charliebirdnyc.com

Opening hours	Open 7 days
Credit cards	Accepted
Price range	Affordable
Style	Casual
Cuisine	Italian
Recommended for	Worth the travel

"Minimalistic decor, efficient service, with vegetable dishes to die for!"—Sami Tallberg

LE COUCOU

138 Lafayette Street
SoHo
New York 10013
+1 2122714252
www.lecoucou.com

Opening hours	Open 7 Days
Credit cards	Accepted
Price range	Expensive
Style	Smart casual
Cuisine	French
Recommended for	Wish I'd opened

"The best new restaurant in America, period."
—Joshua McFadden

At this glittering, shimmering movie set of a restaurant, the bygone days of French fine dining in New York are back. Heading up the back of house is Daniel Rose, the American who took Paris by storm with his restaurant Spring, while the owner is Stephen Starr, the Philadelphia impresario (the design is by restaurant-interior whisperers Roman and Williams). Among long, tapered candles and long, tapered models, French classics like *quenelle de brochet* (Lyonnais pike dumplings) in a *sauce américaine* (white wine and tomato sauce), *pigeon avec homard* (pigeon with lobster), and meltingly wonderful leeks are served by a seriously professional staff.

LA ESQUINA

Recommended by
Eric Ripert

114 Kenmare Street
SoHo
New York 10012
+1 6466137100
www.esquinanyc.com

Opening hours	Open 7 days
Credit cards	Accepted
Price range	Affordable
Style	Casual
Cuisine	Mexican
Recommended for	Bargain

PAOWALLA

Recommended by
Claus Meyer

195 Spring Street
SoHo
New York 10012
+1 2122351098
www.paowalla.com

Opening hours	Open 7 days
Credit cards	Accepted
Price range	Affordable
Style	Casual
Cuisine	Modern Indian
Recommended for	Local favorite

ARCADE BAKERY

Recommended by
Claus Meyer

220 Church Street
Tribeca
New York 10013
+1 2122277895
www.arcadebakery.com

Opening hours	Closed Saturday and Sunday
Reservation policy	No
Credit cards	Accepted
Price range	Budget
Style	Casual
Cuisine	Bakery
Recommended for	Breakfast

ATERA

Recommended by
Aaron Adams, Shannon Bennett,
Ramón Freixa Riera, Claus Meyer,
Marco Müller, Giulio Sturla

77 Worth Street
Tribeca
New York 10013
+1 2122261444
www.ateranyc.com

Opening hours	Closed Monday and Sunday
Credit cards	Accepted
Price range	Expensive
Style	Smart casual
Cuisine	Modern French-American
Recommended for	Worth the travel

"Love the discreet entrance, great staff, and they have their own underground gardens beneath the restaurant. Ask for the small private room."
—Shannon Bennett

BÂTARD

Recommended by
Alex Harrell

239 West Broadway
Tribeca
New York 10013
+1 2122192777
www.batardtribeca.com

Opening hours	Closed Sunday
Credit cards	Accepted
Price range	Expensive
Style	Smart casual
Cuisine	Modern European
Recommended for	Worth the travel

"The food is prepared with precise technique and creative flare. I've been twice now and I am always impressed with their attention to every detail. From the hosts, bar staff, to the servers, the service is warm, inviting, and professional."—Alex Harrell

HOUSEMAN

Recommended by
Todd Ginsberg

508 Greenwich Street
Tribeca
New York 10013
+1 2126410654
www.housemanrestaurant.com

Opening hours	Open 7 days
Credit cards	Accepted
Price range	Affordable
Style	Casual
Cuisine	Modern American
Recommended for	Worth the travel

"Superb food in a place for grown-ups, cooked by people who want to be cooking exactly what's on the menu."—Todd Ginsberg

JUNGSIK

Recommended by
Thomasina Miers

2 Harrison Street
Tribeca
New York 10013
+1 2122190900
www.jungsik.com

Opening hours	Open 7 days
Credit cards	Accepted
Price range	Expensive
Style	Smart casual
Cuisine	Korean
Recommended for	Worth the travel

"Very high end, highly original Korean food."
—Thomasina Miers

LOCANDA VERDE

Recommended by
David Chang

377 Greenwich Street
Tribeca
New York, 10013
+1 212-925-3797
www.locandaverdenyc.com

Opening hours	Open 7 days
Credit cards	Accepted
Price range	Affordable
Style	Casual
Cuisine	Italian-American
Recommended for	Breakfast

TWO HANDS

Recommended by
Sean Gray

251 Church Street
Tribeca
New York 10013
www.twohandsnyc.com

Opening hours	Open 7 days
Credit cards	Accepted
Price range	Affordable
Style	Casual
Cuisine	Australian
Recommended for	Breakfast

"Excellent cooking and a great space as well. Very serious coffee happening here, and seemingly healthy food options."—Sean Gray

ACHILLES HEEL

Recommended by
Daniel Burns

180 West Street
Brooklyn
New York 11222
+1 3479873666
www.achillesheelnyc.com

Opening hours	Open 7 days
Reservation policy	No
Credit cards	Accepted
Price range	Affordable
Style	Casual
Cuisine	Seafood Bar
Recommended for	Regular neighborhood

ALAMEDA

Recommended by
Sean Gray

195 Franklin Street
Brooklyn
New York 11222
www.alamedagreenpoint.com

Opening hours	Open 7 days
Credit cards	Accepted but not Diners
Price range	Affordable
Style	Casual
Cuisine	American
Recommended for	Regular neighborhood

"It's warm and approachable, with a wide range of meal options. It has a fantastic burger, a great country pâté, and always excellent and interesting fish courses."—Sean Gray

ASKA

Recommended by
Sean Gray,
Daniel Humm,
Uwe Opocensky

47 South 5th Street
Brooklyn
New York 11249
+1 9293376792
www.askanyc.com

Opening hours	Closed Monday and Sunday
Credit cards	Accepted
Price range	Expensive
Style	Smart casual
Cuisine	Nordic
Recommended for	High end

"It's different from all of the other fine-dining places in New York. The menu is very interesting, very inspiring, and has a clear vision. There are a lot of layers to the space that make you feel small and comfortable. A lot of work has been done to make the diner feel special, and that it is an experience that has been made for them."—Sean Gray

BLANCA

Recommended by
Daniel Burns, Josef Centeno,
Jason Morris, Alexandre Gauthier,
Daniel Patterson,
Elena Reygadas, Steven Satterfield

261 Moore Street
Brooklyn
New York 11206
www.blancanyc.com

Opening hours	Closed Sunday to Tuesday
Credit cards	Accepted
Price range	Expensive
Style	Casual
Cuisine	Modern American
Recommended for	Worth the travel

"This is the multi-course tasting menu behind Roberta's Pizza in Bushwick. Incredibly fun, relaxed, delicious, and the meal moves quickly—it feels very modern and relevant."—Steven Satterfield

BROOKLYN FARE

Recommended by
Jason Atherton,
Claus Meyer

200 Schermerhorn Street
Brooklyn
New York 11201
+1 7182430050
www.brooklynfare.com

Opening hours	Open 7 days
Credit cards	Accepted
Price range	Affordable
Style	Casual
Cuisine	Grocery
Recommended for	Wish I'd opened

DINER

Recommended by
Jessica Koslow

85 Broadway
Brooklyn
New York 11249
+1 7184863077
www.dinernyc.com

Opening hours	Open 7 days
Reservation policy	No
Credit cards	Accepted
Price range	Affordable
Style	Casual
Cuisine	American
Recommended for	Wish I'd opened

ENDS MEAT

Recommended by
Claus Meyer

254 36th Street
Brooklyn
New York 11232
+1 7188018895
www.endsmeatnyc.com

Opening hours	Closed Saturday and Sunday
Reservation policy	No
Credit cards	Accepted
Price range	Affordable
Style	Casual
Cuisine	Butcher-Sandwiches
Recommended for	Bargain

THE FINCH

Recommended by
JJ Proville

212 Greene Avenue
Brooklyn
New York 11238
+1 7182184444
www.thefinchnyc.com

Opening hours	Closed Sunday
Credit cards	Accepted
Price range	Expensive
Style	Casual
Cuisine	Modern American
Recommended for	Worth the travel

"Chef Gabe McMackin has nailed the hybrid neighborhood/high-end restaurant with his approachable style and high-end flavors and ingredients."—JJ Proville

FIVE LEAVES

Recommended by
Gunnar Karl Gíslason

18 Bedford Avenue
Brooklyn
New York 11222
+1 7183835345
www.fiveleavesny.com

Opening hours	Open 7 days
Reservation policy	No
Credit cards	Accepted
Price range	Affordable
Style	Smart casual
Cuisine	Modern American
Recommended for	Breakfast

"Right in my neighborhood and my kids love their ricotta pancakes—if we do breakfast, that's easily their first choice."—Gunnar Karl Gíslason

THE FOUR HORSEMEN

Recommended by
Nick Anderer,
Angela Dimayuga,
Gunnar Karl Gíslason,
Claus Meyer

295 Grand Street
Brooklyn
New York 11211
+1 7185994900
www.fourhorsemenbk.com

Opening hours	Open 7 days
Credit cards	Accepted
Price range	Affordable
Style	Casual
Cuisine	Small Plates
Recommended for	Wish I'd opened

"I love this place. All the wines would be at my disposable if I'd opened it! They're incredible. I love the small and deliberate menu. It all pairs well with the food and can be small and refined. I love coming here early in the evening when the sun is coming down. It's cozy and minimalist."—Angela Dimayuga

FRANNY'S

Recommended by
Ignacio Mattos

348 Flatbush Avenue
Brooklyn
New York 11238
+1 7182300221
www.frannysbrooklyn.com

Opening hours	Open 7 days
Credit cards	Accepted
Price range	Budget
Style	Casual
Cuisine	Italian
Recommended for	Regular neighborhood

"It's the perfect Sunday lunch—any of the appetizers and pizzas, especially the clam pie, are the way to go for me. Oh, and the chocolate sorbet!"
—Ignacio Mattos

LARINA PASTIFICIO E VINO

Recommended by
Emily Hahn

387 Myrtle Avenue
Brooklyn
New York 11205
+1 7188520001
www.larinabk.com

Opening hours	Open 7 days
Credit cards	Accepted
Price range	Affordable
Style	Casual
Cuisine	Italian-Bar
Recommended for	Worth the travel

LILIA

Recommended by
Jason Atherton,
Daniel Burns,
Joshua Katz

567 Union Avenue
Brooklyn
New York 11222
+1 7185763095
www.lilianewyork.com

Opening hours	Open 7 days
Credit cards	Accepted
Price range	Affordable
Style	Casual
Cuisine	Italian-American
Recommended for	Regular neighborhood

"Lilia serves exceptional Italian food in a beautiful space in Williamsburg. It is a near perfect restaurant with exacting attention to detail, superb service that is attentive without feeling intrusive, and probably the best food I've eaten anywhere in a long time. The restaurant has the wonderful quality of making you feel you're eating somewhere very special but without any of the fuss or pomposity that can sometimes accompany such occasions."—Joshua Katz

ROBERTA'S

Recommended by
Jason Atherton, Phil Carmichael,
Matthew Gaudet, Alexandre Gauthier,
Todd Ginsberg, Sean Gray,
Sergio Herman, Dan Hunter,
Alexandra Raij, Jarrett Stieber

261 Moore Street
Brooklyn
New York 11206
+1 7184171118
www.robertaspizza.com

Opening hours..................................Open 7 days
Reservation policy.......................................No
Credit cards....................................Accepted
Price range....................................Affordable
Style..Casual
Cuisine...........................American-Italian
Recommended for.................Wish I'd opened

SUNDAY IN BROOKLYN

Recommended by
Fredrik Berselius,
John Winter Russell

348 Wythe Avenue
Brooklyn
New York 11249
+1 3472226722
www.sundayinbrooklyn.com

Opening hours..................................Open 7 days
Credit cards....................................Accepted
Price range....................................Affordable
Style..Casual
Cuisine...American
Recommended for.............Regular neighborhood

Naming a brunch spot Sunday in Brooklyn is like naming an album Greatest Hits. It's ballsy and maybe even a little too on the nose. Thankfully, this pleasure dome delivers. Spanning three storeys and serving four-hundred on Sundays, chef Jamie Young serves up clever classics. The sausage, egg, and cheese sandwich is a wonder of gastronomy and architecture —it's the sausage made from hog shoulder that's scattered across the menu that makes it superlative. But there are other treasures here too. It's open the rest of the week, and the dinner menu makes brunch seem positively ascetic.

WIN SON

Recommended by
Claus Meyer

59 Graham Avenue
Brooklyn
New York 11206
+1 3474576010
www.winsonbrooklyn.com

Opening hours..................................Closed Monday
Credit cards....................................Accepted
Price range....................................Affordable
Style..Casual
Cuisine...........................Taiwanese-American
Recommended for.........................Bargain

LLAMA INN

Recommended by
Claus Meyer

50 Withers Street
Brooklyn
New York 11211
+1 7183873434
www.llamainnnyc.com

Opening hours..................................Open 7 days
Credit cards....................Accepted but not Diners
Price range....................................Affordable
Style..Casual
Cuisine...Peruvian
Recommended for.....................Local favorite

LUCALI PIZZA

Recommended by
Alexandra Raij,
Missy Robbins

575 Henry Street
Brooklyn
New York 11231
+1 7188584086
www.lucali.com

Opening hours..................................Closed Tuesday
Reservation policy.......................................No
Credit cards................................Not accepted
Price range....................................Affordable
Style..Casual
Cuisine...Pizza
Recommended for.............Regular neighborhood

MAISON PREMIERE

Recommended by
Reid Henninger,
Russell Moore,
Sami Tallberg

298 Bedford Avenue
Brooklyn
New York 11249
+1 3473350446
www.maisonpremiere.com

Opening hours..................................Open 7 days
Credit cards....................................Accepted
Price range....................................Affordable
Style..Smart casual
Cuisine...Seafood
Recommended for.......................Worth the travel

"Time trip to the 1920s, with perfect shellfish and other comforting luxuries like lobster rolls. Also superb mocktails."—Sami Tallberg

MARLOW & SONS

81 Broadway
Brooklyn
New York 11249
+1 7183841441
www.marlowandsons.com

Recommended by
Fredrik Berselius,
Marc Djozlija,
Missy Robbins

Opening hours	Open 7 days
Credit cards	Accepted
Price range	Affordable
Style	Casual
Cuisine	Modern American
Recommended for	Breakfast

"Casual and delicious; a great selection of baked goods—however the biscuit sandwich or the frittata sandwich are my go-to choices."—Marc Djozlija

For anyone who lives within walking distance of pioneering Williamsburg restaurateur Andrew Tarlow's handsome wood-panelled restaurant, Marlow & Sons is an ineluctable center of gravity. On nice mornings, the rickety metal chairs outside make the perfect spot for people watching, sipping macchiatos and devouring egg, cheese, and sautéed greens on a fresh fluffy biscuit. Then the day slides to lunch and the kitchen—New American and locally minded—begins serving chicken *pozole* (traditional Mexican soup) and grilled cheese. Soon enough, it's night-time, and chef Ken Wiss turns out chicken liver pâté on sourdough toast, brick chicken with Hakurei turnips, and braised lamb shoulder with ramps (wild garlic). Before long, you've nodded off after a slice of salted caramel pie and you wake up—to begin the cycle again.

OKONOMI

150 Ainslie Street
Brooklyn
New York 11211
+1 7183020598
www.okonomibk.com

Recommended by
Nick Anderer,
Joshua Lewin,
Missy Robbins

Opening hours	Closed Wednesday
Reservation policy	No
Credit cards	Accepted
Price range	Affordable
Style	Casual
Cuisine	Japanese
Recommended for	Breakfast

"Awesome Japanese breakfast spot. Nothing like it—probably my favorite in New York."—Missy Robbins

OLMSTED

659 Vanderbilt Avenue
Brooklyn
New York 11238
+1 7185522610
www.olmstednyc.com

Recommended by
David Posey,
Long Xiong

Opening hours	Open 7 days
Credit cards	Accepted
Price range	Affordable
Style	Casual
Cuisine	Modern American
Recommended for	Wish I'd opened

"The fiercely creative genius behind the rapidly evolving menu really points to the direction food and restaurants can, should, and will go in the future."— Long Xiong

A brace of quail and a bunch of Brooklynites perch comfortably in the backyard garden of this Prospect Heights restaurant. Opened in 2016 by chef Greg Baxstrom and farmer Ian Rothman, Olmsted is named after the architect of nearby Prospect Park, Frederick Law Olmsted, and is predictably heavy on the greenery. There's a carrot crêpe, bright orange and buttery, and a rutabaga 'tagliatelle'. In fact all manner of inventive, globally informed offerings— from a duck chakna (spicy Indian stew) with pear chutney and red lentil naan to addictive crawfish boil crackers—prove that its cosy green space is far from Olmsted's only attraction.

PETER LUGER STEAK HOUSE

178 Broadway
Brooklyn
New York 11211
+1 7183877400
www.peterluger.com

Recommended by
Larry McGuire

Opening hours	Open 7 days
Credit cards	Not accepted
Price range	Affordable
Style	Casual
Cuisine	Steakhouse
Recommended for	High end

"Not much to say about Lugers that hasn't been said. Palm the manager a $50 (£39) to be sat immediately and once you eat here a bunch the gruff waiters turn into old teddy bears. It's all about the beef and the bacon."—Larry McGuire

When it comes to ordering your main course, there's a brutal simplicity to the menu at Peter

Luger's. Of course you'll find a few other things on the menu but it's the USDA Prime porterhouse, available for one, two, three or four, that most diners go for. After all, lamb chops can be found anywhere. Luger's is not perfect—the dining room, despite its kitsch charm, could do with an update, but the steaks—and for that matter, the extra-thick rashers of bacon—are unbelievable.

POK POK

Recommended by
Claus Meyer

117 Columbia Street
Brooklyn
New York 11231
+1 7189239322
www.pokpokny.com

Opening hours	Open 7 days
Credit cards	Accepted but not Diners
Price range	Affordable
Style	Casual
Cuisine	Northern Thai
Recommended for	Local favorite

PRETTY SOUTHERN

Recommended by
Emily Hahn

14 Bedford Avenue
Brooklyn
New York 11222
+1 7183492967
www.prettysouthernbk.com

Opening hours	Closed Monday
Reservation policy	No
Credit cards	Accepted
Price range	Affordable
Style	Casual
Cuisine	Southern American
Recommended for	Worth the travel

REYNARD

Recommended by
Daniel Burns

Wythe Hotel
80 Wythe Avenue
Brooklyn
New York 11249
+1 7184608004
www.reynardnyc.com

Opening hours	Open 7 days
Credit cards	Accepted
Price range	Affordable
Style	Casual
Cuisine	Breakfast-Brunch
Recommended for	Breakfast

NEW WORLD MALL FOOD COURT

Recommended by
Carlo Mirarchi

136-20 Roosevelt Avenue
Flushing
New York 11354
+1 7183530551
www.newworldmallny.com/food-court

Opening hours	Open 7 days
Credit cards	Accepted
Price range	Budget
Style	Casual
Cuisine	Asian
Recommended for	Bargain

LHASA FAST FOOD

Recommended by
Fredrik Berselius

37–50 74th Street
Queens
New York 11372
+1 6462563805

Opening hours	Open 7 days
Credit cards	Not accepted
Price range	Budget
Style	Casual
Cuisine	Tibetan
Recommended for	Bargain

PARK SIDE RESTAURANT

Recommended by
Nick Anderer

107-01 Corona Avenue
Queens
New York 11368
+1 7182719871
www.parksiderestaurantny.com

Opening hours	Open 7 days
Credit cards	Accepted
Price range	Affordable
Style	Casual
Cuisine	Italian-American
Recommended for	Local favorite

"Lusty, interesting modern French fare at good prices."

ANITA LO P1026

"Italian American food at its finest."

ANGELA DIMAYUGA P1025

NEW YORK

MANHATTAN VILLAGES

"YOU WILL FIND CULINARY NIRVANA WITHOUT HAWKING THE FAMILY FORTUNE."

ERIC & BRUCE BROMBERG P1027

"TOP-LEVEL COMFORT FOOD."

JUAN GAFFURI P1022

"IT'S A JAPANESE INSTITUTION THAT NEVER GETS TIRED."

ALEXANDRA RAIJ P1024

MANHATTAN
VILLAGES

N
SCALE
0   200   400   600
yd.

1. *Babu Ji (p.1022)*
2. *Cafe Mogador (p.1022)*
3. *Dbgb (p.1022)*
4. *Hasaki (p.1022)*
5. *Ippudo (p.1022)*
6. *Kyo Ya (p.1022)*
7. *Minca (p.1023)*
8. *Momofuku Ko (p.1023)*
9. *Momofuku Noodle Bar (p.1023)*
10. *Momofuku Ssäm Bar (p.1023)*
11. *Motorino (p.1023)*
12. *N'eat (p.1023)*
13. *Prune (p.1024)*
14. *Sake Bar Decibel (p.1024)*
15. *Shuko (p.1024)*
16. *Sunny & Annie's (p.1024)*
17. *Superiority Burger (p.1024)*
18. *Veselka (p.1024)*
19. *Xi'an Famous Foods (p.1025)*
20. *Bar Pitti (p.1025)*
21. *Carbone (p.1025)*
22. *Gotham Bar & Grill (p.1025)*
23. *Loring Place (p.1025)*
24. *Mamoun's Falafel (p.1025)*
25. *Mimi (p.1026)*
26. *Minetta Tavern (p.1026)*
27. *Murray's Bagels (p.1026)*
28. *Nix (p.1026)*
29. *Num Pang Kitchen (p.1026)*
30. *O Cafe (p.1026)*
31. *Ramen-Ya (p.1027)*
32. *Waverly Diner (p.1027)*
33. *Vic's (p.1027)*
34. *Arturo's (p.1027)*
35. *Bar Bolonat (p.1028)*
36. *Buvette (p.1028)*
37. *Corner Bistro (p.1028)*
38. *Employees Only (p.1028)*
39. *Günter Seeger Ny (p.1028)*
40. *Hakata Tonton (p.1028)*
41. *High Street On Hudson (p.1029)*
42. *I Sodi (p.1029)*
43. *Kosaka (p.1029)*
44. *Rockmeisha Izakaya (p.1029)*
45. *The Spotted Pig (p.1029)*
46. *Taïm (p.1030)*
47. *Via Carota (p.1030)*

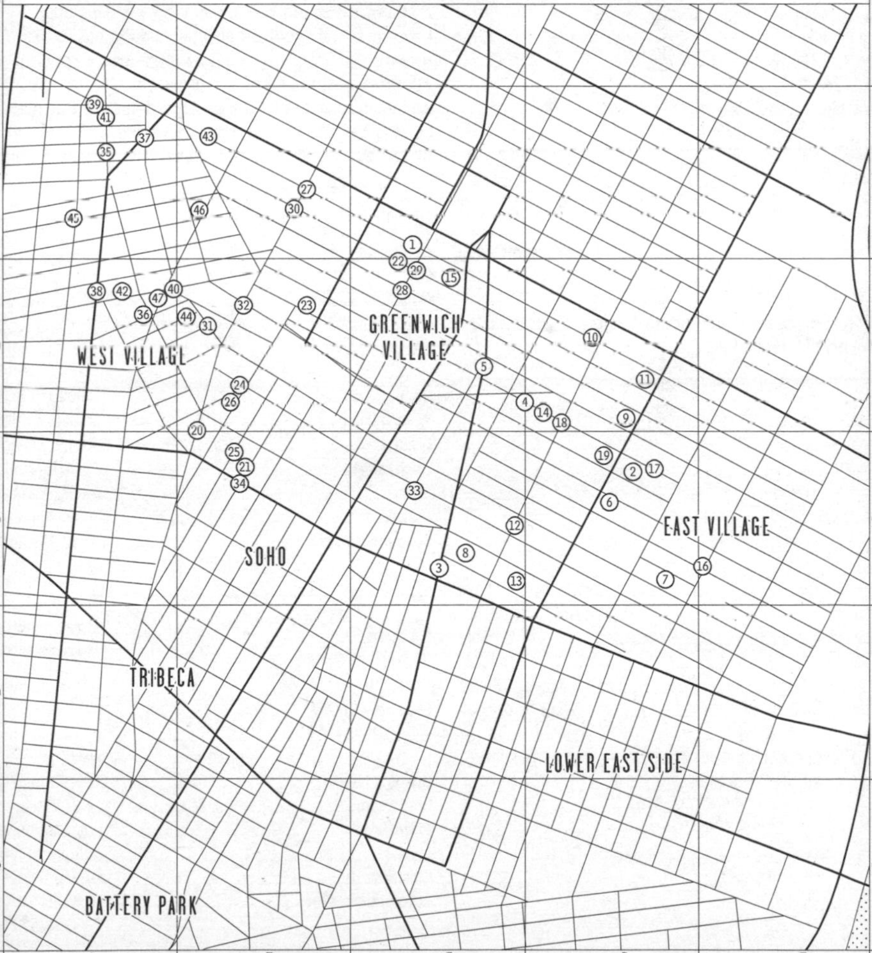

GREENWICH VILLAGE

WEST VILLAGE

EAST VILLAGE

SOHO

TRIBECA

LOWER EAST SIDE

BATTERY PARK

BABU JI

Recommended by
Raúl Correa

22 East 13th Street
East Village
New York 10003
+1 2129511082
www.babujinyc.com

Opening hours	Open 7 days
Credit cards	Accepted
Price range	Affordable
Style	Casual
Cuisine	Indian
Recommended for	Worth the travel

CAFE MOGADOR

Recommended by
Ignacio Mattos

101 Saint Mark's Place
East Village
New York 10009
+1 2126772226
www.cafemogador.com

Opening hours	Open 7 days
Credit cards	Accepted
Price range	Affordable
Style	Casual
Cuisine	Moroccan-Israeli
Recommended for	Bargain

"A great place for good Middle-Eastern appetizers."
—Ignacio Mattos

DBGB

Recommended by
Juan Gaffuri

299 Bowery
East Village
New York 10003
+1 2129335300
www.dbgb.com

Opening hours	Open 7 days
Credit cards	Accepted
Price range	Affordable
Style	Casual
Cuisine	Modern Bistro
Recommended for	Wish I'd opened

"Top-level comfort food, incredibly warm atmosphere,
and a great bar."—Juan Gaffuri

HASAKI

Recommended by
Nick Anderer,
Danny Bowien,
Angela Dimayuga,
Ignacio Mattos

210 East 9th Street
East Village
New York 10003
+1 2124733327
www.hasakinyc.com

Opening hours	Open 7 days
Credit cards	Accepted but not Diners
Price range	Affordable
Style	Casual
Cuisine	Japanese
Recommended for	Regular neighborhood

"I love coming here and visiting Chef Mori-san.
His *omakase* (chef's choice menu) is the best and
it changes frequently. Every category is delicious;
I always try an appetizer special, and the basics like
green salad, miso soup, and tempura are all spot on.
The sesame dressing on the green salad tastes like
an instant classic and the use of red miso in the miso
soup is the attention to detail I love. It's modestly
priced but fancy at the same time."—Angela Dimayuga

IPPUDO

Recommended by
Missy Robbins

65 4th Avenue
East Village
New York 10003
+1 2123880088
www.ippudony.com

Opening hours	Open 7 days
Reservation policy	No
Credit cards	Accepted but not Diners
Price range	Affordable
Style	Casual
Cuisine	Ramen Noodles
Recommended for	Bargain

KYO YA

Recommended by
Fredrik Berselius

94 East 7th Street
East Village
New York 10009
+1 2129824140

Opening hours	Closed Monday
Credit cards	Accepted
Price range	Expensive
Style	Smart casual
Cuisine	Japanese Kaiseki
Recommended for	Local favorite

"A place I have been coming to for years to sit at the counter where chef Sono-san prepares Kaiseki-style cuisine."—Fredrik Berselius

MINCA

Recommended by
Nick Anderer

536 East 5th Street
East Village
New York 10009
+1 2125058001
www.newyorkramen.com/minca

Opening hours	Open 7 days
Reservation policy	No
Credit cards	Not accepted
Price range	Affordable
Style	Casual
Cuisine	Ramen Noodles
Recommended for	Bargain

MOMOFUKU KO

Recommended by
Carolina Bazán, Joshua Lewin,
Morgan McGlone, Claus Meyer,
Missy Robbins, Ana Roš,
Gabriel Rucker, Mark Sargeant,
Justin Woodward

8 Extra Place
East Village
New York 10003
+1 2122038095
https://ko.momofuku.com

Opening hours	Closed Monday
Credit cards	Accepted
Price range	Expensive
Style	Casual
Cuisine	Asian Fusion
Recommended for	Worth the travel

MOMOFUKU NOODLE BAR

Recommended by
Kevin Hickey,
Tatiana Levha,
Isaac Toups

171 1st Avenue
East Village
New York 10003
+1 2127777773
https://noodlebar-ny.momofuku.com

Opening hours	Open 7 days
Credit cards	Accepted
Price range	Affordable
Style	Casual
Cuisine	Asian Fusion
Recommended for	Wish I'd opened

"It's a great place to have excellent Asian food. It's free from all restaurant codes, uninhibited, packed, lively, delicious. The buns are super good."
—Tatiana Levha

MOMOFUKU SSÄM BAR

Recommended by
Massimo Bottura,
James Berckemeyer

207 Second Avenue at 13th Street
East Village
New York, 10003
https://ssambar.momofuku.com

Opening hours	Open 7 days
Credit cards	Accepted
Price range	Affordable
Style	Casual
Cuisine	Asian-American
Recommended for	Bargain

MOTORINO

Recommended by
Andrew Carmellini

349 East 12th Street
East Village
New York 10003
+1 2127772644
www.motorinopizza.com

Opening hours	Open 7 days
Reservation policy	No
Credit cards	Accepted
Price range	Budget
Style	Casual
Cuisine	Pizza
Recommended for	Bargain

N'EAT

Recommended by
Claus Meyer

58 2nd Avenue
East Village
New York 10003
+1 9178926350
www.neat-nyc.com

Opening hours	Closed Monday
Credit cards	Accepted but not Diners
Price range	Affordable
Style	Smart casual
Cuisine	Nordic
Recommended for	Bargain

PRUNE

Recommended by
Joshua Lewin,
Missy Robbins,
Jarrett Stieber

54 East 1st Street
East Village
New York 10003
+1 2126776221
www.prunerestaurant.com

Opening hours	Open 7 days
Credit cards	Accepted but not Diners
Price range	Affordable
Style	Casual
Cuisine	Modern American
Recommended for	Worth the travel

"I go there once in a while. Like on pilgrimage. What a perfect local spot, seamlessly straddling a creative owner's need to express herself and the needs of a neighborhood; plus the ability to evolve drastically with that neighborhood over two decades. Prune is a conversation with a friend."—Joshua Lewin

SAKE BAR DECIBEL

Recommended by
Alexandra Raij

240 East 9th Street
East Village
New York 10003
+1 2129792733
www.sakebardecibel.com

Opening hours	Open 7 days
Reservation policy	No
Credit cards	Accepted but not Diners
Price range	Affordable
Style	Casual
Cuisine	Japanese
Recommended for	Late night

"It's a Japanese institution that never gets tired."
—Alexandra Raij

SHUKO

Recommended by
Anita Lo,
Ignacio Mattos,
Ken Oringer

47 East 12th Street
East Village
New York 10003
+1 2122286088
www.shukonyc.com

Opening hours	Closed Sunday
Credit cards	Accepted
Price range	Expensive
Style	Smart casual
Cuisine	Sushi
Recommended for	Local favorite

"Shuko exhibits perfectly balanced traditional but creative sushi. My go-to dishes are the toro tartare with Japanese milk bread, and the caviar."—Ken Oringer

SUNNY & ANNIE'S

Recommended by
Ignacio Mattos

94 Avenue B
East Village
New York 10003
+1 2126773131
www.sunnyandannies.com

Opening hours	Open 7 days
Reservation policy	No
Credit cards	Accepted but not AMEX or Diners
Price range	Budget
Style	Casual
Cuisine	Deli
Recommended for	Bargain

"Great sandwiches 24/7. My choice is the bacon, egg, cheese, and avocado."—Ignacio Mattos

SUPERIORITY BURGER

Recommended by
Aaron Adams

430 East 9th Street
East Village
New York 10009
+1 2122561192
www.superiorityburger.com

Opening hours	Closed Tuesday
Reservation policy	No
Credit cards	Accepted
Price range	Budget
Style	Casual
Cuisine	American
Recommended for	Wish I'd opened

"Cheap, vegan-friendly eats that are really well made in a fun environment. Yes, please!"—Aaron Adams

VESELKA

Recommended by
Danny Bowien

144 2nd Avenue
East Village
New York 10003
+1 2122289682
www.veselka.com

Opening hours	Open 7 days
Reservation policy	No
Credit cards	Accepted but not Diners
Price range	Affordable
Style	Casual
Cuisine	Ukrainian
Recommended for	Breakfast

XI'AN FAMOUS FOODS

Recommended by
Greg Denton &
Gabrielle Quiñónez Denton,
Sean Gray

81 Saint Mark's Place
East Village
New York 10003
+1 2127862068
www.xianfoods.com

Opening hours	Open 7 days
Reservation policy	No
Credit cards	Accepted
Price range	Affordable
Style	Casual
Cuisine	Chinese
Recommended for	Bargain

"We cannot visit NYC without eating at one of their outposts. The hand-pulled noodles are fantastic. We always order the liang pi "cold-skin" noodles and the tiger vegetable salad. "—Greg Denton & Gabrielle Quiñónez Denton

BAR PITTI

Recommended by
Angela Dimayuga

268 6th Avenue
Greenwich Village
New York 10014
+1 2129823300

Opening hours	Open 7 days
Credit cards	Accepted
Price range	Affordable
Style	Casual
Cuisine	Italian
Recommended for	Local favorite

"It's a New York classic and staple. I love getting the taglierini with truffle, and bitter puntarelle covered in anchovy dressing. Everyone has their order at this old pasta joint. The tuna with white beans comes with a bottle of olive oil so you just dump it on yourself. NYC Italian American food at its finest."—Angela Dimayuga

CARBONE

Recommended by
Danny Bowien,
Claus Meyer,
Daniel Serfer

181 Thompson Street
Greenwich Village
New York 10012
+1 2122543000
www.carbonenewyork.com

Opening hours	Open 7 days
Credit cards	Accepted
Price range	Affordable
Style	Smart casual
Cuisine	Italian-American
Recommended for	Wish I'd opened

"I have an affinity for 'red sauce' Italian spots."
—Daniel Serfer

GOTHAM BAR & GRILL

Recommended by
Paul Liebrandt

12 E 12th Street
Greenwich Village
New York, 10003
+1 212-620-4020
www.gothambarandgrill.com

Opening hours	Open 7 days
Credit cards	Accepted
Price range	Affordable
Style	Casual
Cuisine	American-Grill
Recommended for	Local favorite

LORING PLACE

Recommended by
Dan Barber,
Carlos Perez

21 West 8th Street
Greenwich Village
New York 10011
+1 2123881831
www.loringplacenyc.com

Opening hours	Open 7 days
Credit cards	Accepted
Price range	Affordable
Style	Casual
Cuisine	American
Recommended for	Regular neighborhood

"A vibrant, vegetable-driven menu."—Dan Barber

MAMOUN'S FALAFEL

Recommended by
Daniel Humm

119 MacDougal Street
Greenwich Village
New York 10012
www.mamouns.com

Opening hours	Open 7 days
Reservation policy	No
Credit cards	Accepted
Price range	Budget
Style	Casual
Cuisine	Middle Eastern
Recommended for	Bargain

"A great, cheap bite that you can get any time of day."
—Daniel Humm

MIMI

Recommended by
Anita Lo

185 Sullivan Street
Greenwich Village
New York 10112
+1 2124181260
www.miminyc.com

Opening hours	Open 7 days
Credit cards	Accepted
Price range	Expensive
Style	Smart casual
Cuisine	Modern French
Recommended for	Late night

"MIMIs has lusty, interesting modern French fare at good prices."—Anita Lo

MINETTA TAVERN

Recommended by
Paul Liebrandt

113 Macdougal Street
Greenwich Village
New York, 10012
+1 212-475-3850
www.minettatavernny.com

Opening hours	Open 7 days
Credit cards	Accepted
Price range	Affordable
Style	Smart casual
Cuisine	French
Recommended for	Wish I'd opened

MURRAY'S BAGELS

Recommended by
Anita Lo,
Jesse Schenker

500 6th Avenue
Greenwich Village
New York 10011
+1 2124622830
www.murraysbagels.com

Opening hours	Open 7 days
Reservation policy	No
Credit cards	Accepted but not Diners
Price range	Affordable
Style	Casual
Cuisine	Bagels
Recommended for	Breakfast

"I buy cheese for the restaurant here every week, but they also make good sandwiches, including the best bacon, egg, and cheese. They use Nuesky's bacon which is my favorite."—Anita Lo

NIX

Recommended by
Dan Barber

72 University Place
Greenwich Village
New York 10003
+1 2124989393
www.nixny.com

Opening hours	Open 7 days
Credit cards	Accepted
Price range	Affordable
Style	Smart casual
Cuisine	Modern Vegetarian
Recommended for	Wish I'd opened

"Nix makes vegetarian delicious."—Dan Barber

NUM PANG KITCHEN

Recommended by
Matthew Gaudet,
Claus Meyer

28 East 12th Street
Greenwich Village
New York 10003
+1 6467910439
www.numpangnyc.com

Opening hours	Open 7 days
Reservation policy	No
Credit cards	Accepted but not Diners
Price range	Affordable
Style	Casual
Cuisine	Southeast Asian
Recommended for	Bargain

"Quick, delicious, and cost-effective sandwiches."
—Matthew Gaudet

O CAFE

Recommended by
Ignacio Mattos

482 6th Avenue
Greenwich Village
New York 10011
+1 2125550110
www.ocafenyc.com

Opening hours	Open 7 days
Reservation policy	No
Credit cards	Accepted
Price range	Affordable
Style	Café
Recommended for	Breakfast

"Great casual spot with good coffee and delicious options like *arepas* with green romesco and eggs. The *pão de queijos* are a must."—Ignacio Mattos

RAMEN-YA

Recommended by
Anita Lo

181 West 4th Street
Greenwich Village
New York 10014
+1 2129895440
www.ramenya.nyc

Opening hours	Open 7 days
Reservation policy	No
Credit cards	Not accepted
Price range	Affordable
Style	Casual
Cuisine	Ramen Noodles
Recommended for	Bargain

"Deeply flavored broths and perfect noodles
for an inexpensive meal."—Anita Lo

WAVERLY DINER

Recommended by
Jesse Schenker

385 6th Avenue
Greenwich Village
New York 10014
+1 2126753181
www.waverlydiner.com

Opening hours	Open 7 days
Reservation policy	No
Credit cards	Accepted but not Diners
Price range	Affordable
Style	Casual
Cuisine	Diner
Recommended for	Local favorite

VIC'S

Recommended by
Sean Gray

31 Great Jones Street
NoHo
New York 10012
+1 2122535700
www.vicsnewyork.com

Opening hours	Open 7 days
Credit cards	Accepted
Price range	Affordable
Style	Casual
Cuisine	Italian
Recommended for	Regular neighborhood

ARTURO'S

Recommended by
Eric & Bruce Bromberg

106 West Houston Street
West Village
New York 10012
+1 2126773820
www.arturoscafe.com

Opening hours	Open 7 days
Credit cards	Accepted
Price range	Affordable
Style	Casual
Cuisine	Italian-Pizza
Recommended for	Bargain

"Arturo's on West Houston Street is the best. Get the
pepperoni pizza and a bottle of Amarone and you
will find culinary nirvana without hawking the family
fortune."—Eric & Bruce Bromberg

BAR BOLONAT

611 Hudson Street
West Village
New York 10014
+1 2123901545
www.barbolonatny.com

Opening hours	Open 7 days
Credit cards	Accepted
Price range	Affordable
Style	Smart casual
Cuisine	Mediterranean-Israeli
Recommended for	Local favorite

BUVETTE

42 Grove Street
West Village
New York 10014
+1 2123430404
www.newyork.ilovebuvette.com

Opening hours	Open 7 days
Reservation policy	No
Credit cards	Accepted
Price range	Affordable
Style	Casual
Cuisine	French
Recommended for	Breakfast

"Tiny French bistro with amazing anchovy toast and solid pâté."—Nick Anderer

CORNER BISTRO

331 West 4th Street
West Village
New York 10014
+1 2122429502
www.cornerbistrony.com

Opening hours	Open 7 days
Reservation policy	No
Credit cards	Not accepted
Price range	Budget
Style	Casual
Cuisine	American
Recommended for	Local favorite

"The atmosphere during the weekday is just incredible. Just to have a beer, eat a burger, and watch a baseball game. It's a genuine neighborhood institution."—Sean Gray

EMPLOYEES ONLY

510 Hudson Street
West Village
New York 10014
+1 212 2423021
www.employeesonlynyc.com

Opening hours	Open 7 days
Credit cards	Accepted
Price range	Affordable
Style	Casual
Cuisine	American-European
Recommended for	Late night

"Great vibe and great, unique late-night eats, including bone marrow poppers and crispy shrimp (prawn). I also love their cucumber salad during normal dining hours."—Missy Robbins

GÜNTER SEEGER NY

641 Hudson Street
West Village
New York 10014
+1 6466570045
www.gunterseegerny.com

Opening hours	Closed Sunday
Credit cards	Accepted
Price range	Expensive
Style	Formal
Cuisine	Modern International
Recommended for	High end

HAKATA TONTON

61 Grove Street
West Village
New York 10014
+1 2122423699
www.tontonnyc.com

Opening hours	Open 7 days
Credit cards	Accepted
Price range	Budget
Style	Casual
Cuisine	Japanese
Recommended for	Regular neighborhood

HIGH STREET ON HUDSON

Recommended by
Claus Meyer

637 Hudson Street
West Village
New York 10014
+1 9173883944
www.highstreetonhudson.com

Opening hours	Open 7 days
Credit cards	Accepted
Price range	Affordable
Style	Casual
Cuisine	Modern American
Recommended for	Breakfast

"A restaurant and bakery in the same location. Super nice bread, great à la carte breakfast menu, minimalistic decor, and just around the corner from where we live."—Claus Meyer

I SODI

Recommended by
Daniel Humm,
Missy Robbins

105 Christopher Street
West Village
New York 10014
+1 2124145774
www.lsodinyc.com

Opening hours	Open 7 days
Credit cards	Accepted
Price range	Affordable
Style	Casual
Cuisine	Italian
Recommended for	Regular neighborhood

"It's simple and honest Italian cuisine in a small and charming space. It transports you out of the craziness of New York—for a few hours you feel like you are in a quiet Italian town."—Missy Robbins

KOSAKA

Recommended by
Anita Lo

220 West 13th Street
West Village
New York 10011
+1 2127271709
www.kosakanyc.com

Opening hours	Closed Monday and Sunday
Credit cards	Accepted
Price range	Expensive
Style	Smart casual
Cuisine	Sushi
Recommended for	Regular neighborhood

"I generally don't go back to too many places because it's my job to know all the new places in town, but I've been back a few times to Kosaka for their superior sushi."—Anita Lo

ROCKMEISHA IZAKAYA

Recommended by
Anita Lo

11 Barrow Street
West Village
New York 10014
+1 2126757775

Opening hours	Open 7 days
Credit cards	Accepted but not Diners
Price range	Affordable
Style	Casual
Cuisine	Japanese
Recommended for	Regular neighborhood

THE SPOTTED PIG

Recommended by
Matthew Gaudet,
John Jackson,
Anita Lo,
Missy Robbins

314 West 11th Street
West Village
New York 10014
+1 2126200393
www.thespottedpig.com

Opening hours	Open 7 days
Reservation policy	No
Credit cards	Accepted
Price range	Affordable
Style	Casual
Cuisine	Gastropub
Recommended for	Regular neighborhood

"Still my favorite burger in town."—Missy Robbins

TAÏM

222 Waverly Place
West Village
New York 10014
+1 2126911287
www.taimfalafel.com

Recommended by
Anita Lo

Opening hours	Open 7 days
Reservation policy	No
Credit cards	Accepted
Price range	Budget
Style	Casual
Cuisine	Israeli
Recommended for	Bargain

"Einat Admony's falafel and sabich sandwiches are the best in the city."—Anita Lo

VIA CAROTA

51 Grove Street
West Village
New York 10014
+1 2122551962
www.viacarota.com

Recommended by
Nick Anderer, Anita Lo, Ken Oringer

Opening hours	Open 7 days
Reservation policy	No
Credit cards	Accepted
Price range	Affordable
Style	Casual
Cuisine	Italian
Recommended for	Regular neighborhood

"Via Carota personifies soulful Italian cooking with seasonal, unpretentious food. They understand the true sense of Italian food."—Ken Oringer

"**ONE OF THE MOST INNOVATIVE RESTAURANTS IN NYC.**"

DANIEL BURNS P1036

NEW YORK

MANHATTAN UPTOWN & MIDTOWN

"*My guilty pleasure.*"

GUNNAR KARL GÍSLASON P1041

"**A SERENDIPITOUS THREE-HOUR TRIP TO PARIS IN MIDTOWN MANHATTAN.**"

CATHY WHIMS P1039

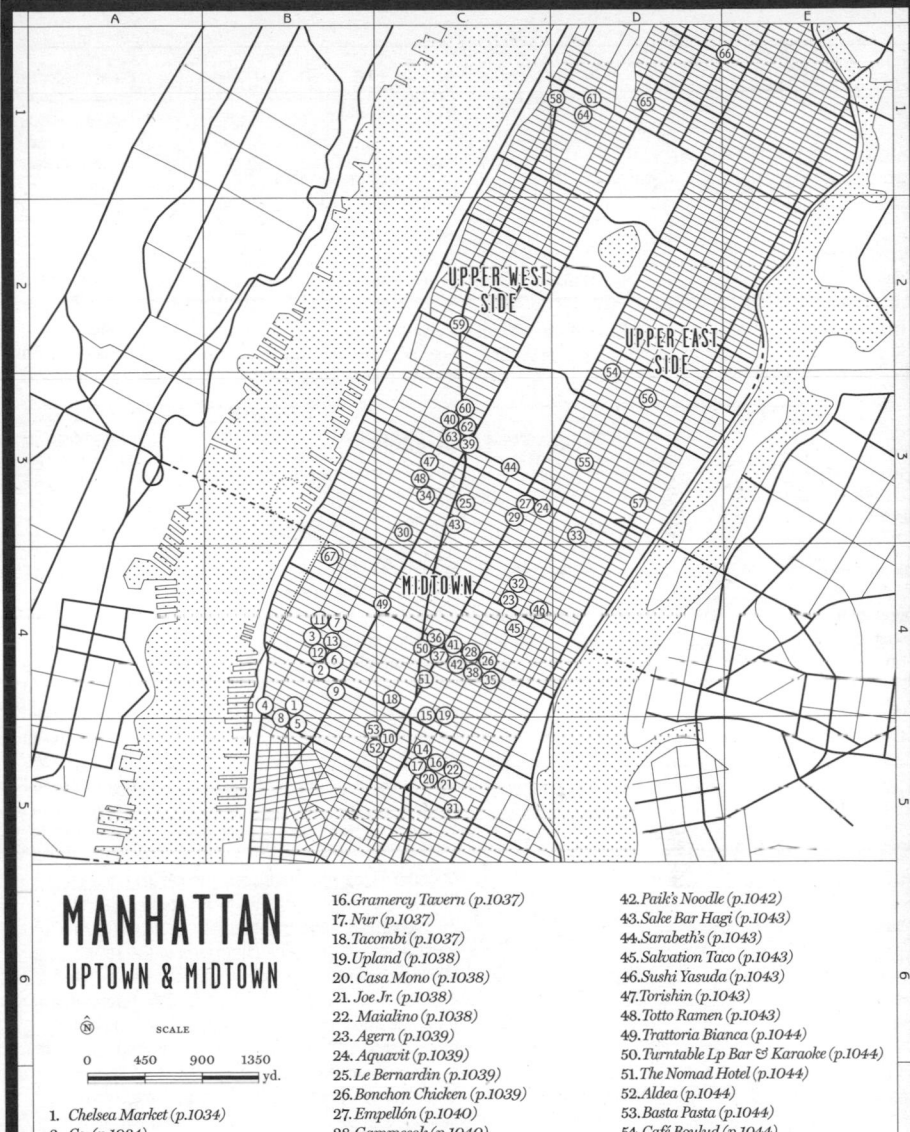

MANHATTAN
UPTOWN & MIDTOWN

N̂

SCALE

0   450   900   1350
yd.

CHELSEA MARKET

75 9th Avenue
Chelsea
New York 10011
+1 2126522121
www.chelseamarket.com

Opening hours	Open 7 days
Credit cards	Accepted
Price range	Affordable
Style	Casual
Cuisine	Food court
Recommended for	Bargain

CO.

230 9th Avenue
Chelsea
New York 10001
+1 2122431105
www.co-pane.com

Opening hours	Open 7 days
Credit cards	Accepted
Price range	Affordable
Style	Casual
Cuisine	Pizza
Recommended for	Regular neighborhood

CHOP-SHOP

254 10th Avenue
Chelsea
New York 10001
+1 2128200333
www.chop-shop.co

Opening hours	Open 7 days
Credit cards	Accepted
Price range	Affordable
Style	Casual
Cuisine	Asian
Recommended for	Regular neighborhood

"They have super quick service and solid flavors and consistency, with a couple of very nice signature dishes."—Claus Meyer

DEL POSTO

85 10th Avenue
Chelsea
New York 10011
+1 2124978090
www.delposto.com

Opening hours	Open 7 days
Credit cards	Accepted
Price range	Expensive
Style	Smart casual
Cuisine	Modern Italian
Recommended for	High end

DIZENGOFF

Chelsea Market
75 9th Avenue
Chelsea
New York 10011
+1 6468337097
www.dizengoffhummus.com

Opening hours	Open 7 days
Reservation policy	No
Credit cards	Accepted
Price range	Affordable
Style	Casual
Cuisine	Israeli
Recommended for	Wish I'd opened

"I mean, hummus all day, everyday!"—Ignacio Mattos

Michael Solomonov launched the resurgence of high-end Israeli cuisine when he opened Zahav in 2008. With Dizengoff, named after one of Tel Aviv's most iconic streets, the chef reins in the refinement but keeps all the quality. This casual spot with but a few seats does a brisk traffic in creamy tehina-heavy hummus and freshly baked pittas. Like traditional hummusiya, there's a range of rotating toppings from pea and cucumber, lettuce and egg, to cauliflower and almond. This is rounded out by small Israeli *salatim* and best washed down with a frozen mint lemonade called *limonana*.

GRAND SICHUAN INTERNATIONAL

Recommended by
Claus Meyer

229 9th Avenue
Chelsea
New York 10001
+1 2126205200

Opening hours	Open 7 days
Credit cards	Accepted
Price range	Affordable
Style	Casual
Cuisine	Chinese
Recommended for	Regular neighborhood

JUN-MEN

Recommended by
Claus Meyer

249 9th Avenue
Chelsea
New York 10001
+1 6468526787
www.junmenramen.com

Opening hours	Closed Sunday
Credit cards	Accepted
Price range	Affordable
Style	Casual
Cuisine	Ramen Noodles
Recommended for	Regular neighborhood

"Awesome ramen soups, very good sweet potato fries with maple syrup, nice salads."—Claus Meyer

LOS TACOS NO.1

Recommended by
Ken Oringer,
Alexandra Raij

Chelsea Market
75 9th Avenue
Chelsea
New York 10011
+1 2122560343
www.lostacos1.com

Opening hours	Open 7 days
Reservation policy	No
Credit cards	Accepted but not AMEX
Price range	Budget
Style	Casual
Cuisine	Mexican
Recommended for	Regular neighborhood

"Los Tacos No.1 in Chelsea Market is another favorite spot of mine. They have the best *al pastor* in NYC."
—Ken Oringer

MOMOFUKU NISHI

Recommended by
Claus Meyer

232 8th Avenue
Chelsea
New York 10011
+1 6465181919
https://nishi.momofuku.com

Opening hours	Open 7 days
Credit cards	Accepted
Price range	Affordable
Style	Casual
Cuisine	Asian Fusion
Recommended for	Regular neighborhood

OOTOYA

Recommended by
Angela Dimayuga

8 West 18th Street
Chelsea
New York 10011
+1 2122550018
www.ootoya.us

Opening hours	Open 7 days
Credit cards	Accepted
Price range	Affordable
Style	Casual
Cuisine	Japanese
Recommended for	Bargain

"You can get a whole grilled mackerel set meal for $20 (£16)! This is a really nice treat with all the appropriate sides. Chawanmushi, green salad, pickles, and you can modify your rice. I love getting natto here and grated daikon to really fill out the meal. Really nice ambiance and they have something for everyone. Great for when you are super hungry."—Angela Dimayuga

PORTEÑO

299 10th Avenue
Chelsea
New York 10001
+1 2126959694
www.portenorestaurant.com

Recommended by
Bevan Smith

Opening hours	Open 7 days
Credit cards	Accepted
Price range	Affordable
Style	Casual
Cuisine	Argentinian
Recommended for	Wish I'd opened

EL QUINTO PINO

401 West 24th Street
Chelsea
New York 10011
+1 2122066900
www.elquintopinonyc.com

Recommended by
Claus Meyer

Opening hours	Open 7 days
Credit cards	Accepted
Price range	Affordable
Style	Casual
Cuisine	Spanish
Recommended for	Regular neighborhood

SULLIVAN STREET BAKERY

236 9th Avenue
Chelsea
New York 10011
+1 2129295900
www.sullivanstreetbakery.com

Recommended by
Claus Meyer

Opening hours	Open 7 days
Credit cards	Accepted
Price range	Affordable
Style	Casual
Cuisine	Italian-American Bakery
Recommended for	Breakfast

"There's a totally relaxed atmosphere, great coffee, some of the best morning pastries in town, nice vegetable flatbreads, and tasty breakfast dishes. Lastly, it's literally down the street from where we live."—Claus Meyer

COSME

35 East 21st Street
Flatiron
New York 10010
+1 2129139659
www.cosmenyc.com

Recommended by
Nick Anderer, Manoella Buffara Ramos,
Daniel Burns, Scott Dolich,
Claus Meyer, Magnus Nilsson,
Alexandra Raij, Lee Wolen

Opening hours	Open 7 days
Credit cards	Accepted
Price range	Expensive
Style	Smart casual
Cuisine	Mexican
Recommended for	Worth the travel

"One of the most innovative restaurants in NYC—Daniela Soto-Innes's cooking is inspired, yet it still retains a strong connection to traditional Mexican flavors and technique."—Daniel Burns

New York can be a tricky market for a foreign chef. But when Enrique Olvera, whose restaurant Pujol in Mexico City has been ranked as the twentieth best in the world, opened his first New York outpost in 2014, he was careful to cater to the city's tastes. In a large, dramatically lit but relaxed room in the Flatiron neighborhood—the seat of the city's power restaurants—he opened Cosme. With the talented Daniela Sotto-Innes in the kitchen, Olvera brought his deep knowledge of heat, sauces, and ancient corn to a city that hankered for high-end, boundary-pushing Mexican cuisine. The duck *carnitas* (pulled meat), held in a tortilla made from heritage kernels imported from Mexico, continue to hover in the minds of all who eat them. And the riffs of riffs—a beef tartare that tastes smoky (thanks to the smoked beans and cured egg yolk)—is even better than the real thing.

ELEVEN MADISON PARK

11 Madison Avenue
Flatiron
New York 10010
+1 2128890905
www.elevenmadisonpark.com

Opening hours	Open 7 days
Credit cards	Accepted
Price range	Expensive
Cuisine	Contemporary American
Style	Smart casual
Recommended for	Worth the travel

"Chef Humm's philosophy, combined with impressive service and attention from the entire team, makes this an experience that stays with you for a long time." —Kristian Baumann

GRAMERCY TAVERN

42 East 20th Street
Flatiron
New York 10003
+1 2124770777
www.gramercytavern.com

Opening hours	Open 7 days
Credit cards	Accepted
Price range	Affordable
Style	Smart casual
Cuisine	Modern American
Recommended for	Wish I'd opened

"My favorite thing is wine and cheese at the bar. But this institution is also great for its casual tavern menu and special-occasion dining room."—Missy Robbins

NUR

34 East 20th Street
Flatiron
New York 10003
+1 2125053420
www.nurnyc.com

Opening hours	Open 7 days
Credit cards	Accepted
Price range	Affordable
Style	Smart casual
Cuisine	Modern Middle Eastern
Recommended for	Local favorite

TACOMBI

30 West 24th Street
Flatiron
New York 10010
+1 2122423491
www.tacombi.com

Opening hours	Open 7 days
Credit cards	Accepted
Price range	Affordable
Style	Casual
Cuisine	Mexican
Recommended for	Worth the travel

"Lately, I've been a sucker for casual Mexican restaurants. Something about Tacombi draws me there every time I visit NYC. Although the place is huge, they make their own tortilla using fresh ground masienda corn. Their massive tortilla machine is unlike anything I've seen before. You come here with your friends, order a bunch of tacos, drink some Modelo beers. It's the best day-off spot for me."—Tom Cunanan

UPLAND
345 Park Avenue South
Flatiron
New York 10010
+1 2126861006
www.uplandnyc.com

Recommended by
Daniel Serfer

Opening hours	Open 7 days
Credit cards	Accepted
Price range	Affordable
Style	Casual
Cuisine	Modern American
Recommended for	High end

"Chicken liver pasta—so unique and out of this world."
—Daniel Serfer

CASA MONO
52 Irving Place
Gramercy
New York 10003
+1 2122532773
www.casamononyc.com

Recommended by
Grae Nonas

Opening hours	Open 7 days
Credit cards	Accepted
Price range	Affordable
Style	Casual
Cuisine	Spanish
Recommended for	Wish I'd opened

JOE JR.
167 Third Avenue
Gramercy
New York 10003
+1 2124735150

Recommended by
Nick Anderer

Opening hours	Open 7 days
Reservation policy	No
Credit cards	Accepted but not AMEX or Diners
Price range	Affordable
Style	Casual
Cuisine	Burgers
Recommended for	Breakfast

"Quintessential New York diner serving great,
short-order breakfast food and solid burgers."
—Nick Anderer

MAIALINO
Gramercy Park Hotel
2 Lexington Avenue
Gramercy
New York 10010
+1 2127772410
www.maialinonyc.com

Recommended by
Michael Anthony,
Jason Atherton,
Michael Friedman

Opening hours	Open 7 days
Credit cards	Accepted
Price range	Expensive
Style	Smart casual
Cuisine	Italian
Recommended for	Breakfast

"Fabulous Italian breakfast—charcoal crusted pancetta
with *cacio e pepe* scrambled eggs, with pecorino
grated over it."—Jason Atherton

AGERN

Recommended by
Helena Puolakka

Grand Central Terminal
89 East 42nd Street
Midtown
New York 10017
+1 6465684018
www.agernrestaurant.com

Opening hours	Open 7 days
Credit cards	Accepted
Price range	Expensive
Cuisine	Smart casual
Cuisine	Nordic
Recommended for	Worth the travel

AQUAVIT

Recommended by
Anita Lo

65 East 55th Street
Midtown
New York 10022
+1 2123077311
www.aquavit.org

Opening hours	Closed Sunday
Credit cards	Accepted
Price range	Expensive
Style	Formal
Cuisine	Swedish
Recommended for	High end

"Emma Bengtsson makes fun, perfectly balanced and executed food."—Anita Lo

Well before the Scandinavian foodie revolution had begun, Aquavit introduced the wonders of high-end herring and tea-smoked duck breast to the gourmands of Manhattan. Opened in 1987, Aquavit remains as pure and fresh as ever. These days the young Swedish chef Emma Bengtsson presides, and the menu has kept pace with the times. In a rather austere setting in the concrete-and-glass desert of Midtown, Bengtsson is both playful and masterful. On the chef's tasting menu, one might find charred gravlax with watermelon, a tart hovmaster sauce and dill fronds, or, in a show of regional cooperation, Icelandic cod with Swedish anchovies.

LE BERNARDIN

Recommended by
Shannon Bennett, Massimo Bottura,
Andrew Carmellini, Raúl Correa,
Alexis Gauthier, Chris Lusk,
April Robinson, Cathy Whims

155 West 51st Street
Midtown
New York 10019
+1 2125541515
www.le-bernardin.com

Opening hours	Closed Sunday
Credit cards	Accepted
Price range	Expensive
Style	Formal
Cuisine	French
Recommended for	High end

"Lunch at Le Bernardin is a serendipitous three-hour trip to Paris in Midtown Manhattan. The knowledgeable service, the stunning wine list, the vast array of fish and crustaceans, all treated with the gentle touch of Eric Ripert, is my kind of heaven."—Cathy Whims

Le Bernardin occupies the ground floor of a rather anonymous office building in Midtown Manhattan. It's not exactly the place you expect to find immense soul—or, indeed, tender sole. But both preside in chef Eric Ripert's singular restaurant. Ripert didn't start the place—he stepped into the chef's seat in 1994 after the original owner Gilbert Le Coze passed away—but it is now remade in the unflappable chef's image. Elegant beyond compare, gentle without weakness, refined but not stuffy, Le Bernardin's menu is, above all things, respectful. In a subterranean nook of the restaurant, a fish butcher treats the catch with the care it deserves and from the well-run kitchen come plates that make the eye-popping price tags somehow appropriate.

BONCHON CHICKEN

Recommended by
Daniel Burns
Paul Liebrandt

325 5th Avenue
Midtown
New York 10016
+1 2126868282
www.bonchon.com

Opening hours	Open 7 days
Reservation policy	No
Credit cards	Accepted
Price range	Affordable
Style	Casual
Cuisine	Korean
Recommended for	Late night

"Korean fried chicken!"—Daniel Burns

EMPELLÓN

Recommended by
John Jackson

510 Madison Avenue
Midtown
New York 10022
+1 2128589365
www.empellon.com

Opening hours	Open 7 days
Credit cards	Accepted
Price range	Expensive
Style	Smart casual
Cuisine	Mexican
Recommended for	Worth the travel

Wd~50's and Alinea's former pastry-chef Alex Stupak first decided to flex his talent in a totally different direction in 2011 with the opening of Empellón Taqueria, in the West Village. This, the follow-up to that classy and creative taco joint, opened around a year later in the East Village and takes even more risks in its adventurous approach to Mexican food. Forget about cheap and cheerful, carb- and dairy-heavy staples and think fresh and delicate tapas-style small plates that often make use of unexpected ingredients—sea urchin, shiitake mushrooms, Brussels sprouts—while still maintaining a Mexican soul.

GAMMEEOK

Recommended by
Andrew Carmellini

43 West 32nd Street
Midtown
New York 10001
+1 2126854113
www.gammeeok.nyc

Opening hours	Open 7 days
Credit cards	Accepted
Price range	Affordable
Style	Casual
Cuisine	Korean
Recommended for	Late night

LA GRENOUILLE

Recommended by
Alexis Gauthier,
Larry McGuire

3 East 52nd Street
Midtown
New York 10022
+1 2127521495
www.la-grenouille.com

Opening hours	Closed Monday and Sunday
Credit cards	Accepted
Price range	Expensive
Style	Formal
Cuisine	French
Recommended for	High end

"For a fancy gentleman's lunch I love La Grenouille."
—Larry McGuire

HAKKASAN

Recommended by
April Robinson

311 West 43rd Street
Midtown
New York 10036
+1 2127761818
www.hakkasan.com

Opening hours	Open 7 days
Credit cards	Accepted
Price range	Expensive
Style	Smart casual
Cuisine	Cantonese
Recommended for	Late night

"I like their dim sum, ambience, and drinks."
—April Robinson

THE HALAL GUYS

Recommended by
Alex Young

West 53rd Street and 6th Street
Midtown
New York 10019
+1 3475271505
www.53rdand6th.com

Opening hours	Open 7 days
Reservation policy	No
Credit cards	Not accepted
Price range	Budget
Style	Casual
Cuisine	American-Street Food
Recommended for	Late night

HARD TIMES SUNDAES

Recommended by
Gunnar Karl Gíslason

Urbanspace Vanderbilt
230 Park Avenue
Midtown
New York 10169
www.hardtimessundaes.com

Opening hours	Open 7 days
Reservation policy	No
Credit cards	Accepted
Price range	Affordable
Style	Casual
Cuisine	Burgers
Recommended for	Bargain

"It's just so simple and delicious. This would be my guilty pleasure."—Gunnar Karl Gíslason

HINATA RAMEN

Recommended by
Michael Anthony

159 East 55th Street
Midtown
New York 10022
+1 2123552974
www.hinataramen.com

Opening hours	Open 7 days
Reservation policy	No
Credit cards	Accepted but not AMEX or Diners
Price range	Budget
Style	Casual
Cuisine	Japanese
Recommended for	Regular neighborhood

"I'm a Japanophile—I love ramen, and they have a particular homey style that I like a lot."
—Michael Anthony

IPPUDO

Recommended by
Dan Barber,
Andrew Carmellini,
Claus Meyer

321 West 51st Street
Midtown
New York 10019
+1 2129742500
www.ippudony.com

Opening hours	Open 7 days
Reservation policy	No
Credit cards	Accepted but not Diners
Price range	Affordable
Style	Casual
Cuisine	Ramen Noodles
Recommended for	Late night

"One of the best ramen places in the city. They're open late so you can almost go there any time you feel in need of a soothing broth with fantastic noodles."
—Claus Meyer

KANG HO DONG BAEKJEONG

Recommended by
Josef Centeno

1 East 32nd Street
Midtown
New York, 10016
+1 2129669839
www.baekjeongnyc.com

Opening hours	Open 7 days
Credit cards	Accepted
Price range	Affordable
Style	Casual
Cuisine	Korean-BBQ
Recommended for	Late night

KEENS STEAKHOUSE

Recommended by
Nick Anderer

72 West 36th Street
Midtown
New York 10018
+1 2129473636
www.keens.com

Opening hours	Open 7 days
Credit cards	Accepted
Price range	Expensive
Style	Casual
Cuisine	Steakhouse
Recommended for	High end

"Prototypical New York steakhouse steeped in history. Great martinis, chateaubriand for two, creamed spinach, and boiled baby potatoes."—Nick Anderer

THE KUNJIP

Recommended by
Angela Dimayuga,
Daniel Humm

32 West 32nd Street
Midtown
New York 10001
+1 2125648238
www.kunjip.com

Opening hours	Open 7 days
Credit cards	Accepted
Price range	Affordable
Style	Smart casual
Cuisine	Korean
Recommended for	Late night

"I love coming here late at night with friends if we've done an event nearby. Lots of options like grilled pork belly, and chilled buckwheat noodles with lots of fresh cabbage and sesame leaf to eat with everything. You can get grilled meats or broth depending on how you feel and cold beer. I love their blended grain rice. You can really chill there for as long as you want. It's open twenty-four hours so you can hang like it's a diner. They don't really push you out until you're ready to leave."—Angela Dimayuga

MANDOO BAR

Recommended by
Daniel Humm

2 West 32nd Street
Midtown
New York 10001
+1 2122793075
www.mandoobarnyc.com

Opening hours	Open 7 days
Reservation policy	No
Credit cards	Accepted but not Diners
Price range	Affordable
Style	Casual
Cuisine	Korean
Recommended for	Bargain

MAREA

Recommended by
Jesse Schenker

240 Central Park South
Midtown
New York 10019
+1 2125825177
www.marea-nyc.com

Opening hours	Open 7 days
Credit cards	Accepted
Price range	Expensive
Style	Smart casual
Cuisine	Italian-Seafood
Recommended for	Regular neighborhood

MASA

Recommended by
Daniel Humm,
Paul Liebrandt,
Jakob Mielcke,
Eric Ripert

10 Columbus Circle
Midtown
New York 10019
+1 2128239807
www.masanyc.com

Opening hours	Closed Sunday
Credit cards	Accepted
Price range	Expensive
Style	Smart casual
Cuisine	Japanese
Recommended for	High end

"One of the best Japanese restaurants I've ever been to—including anywhere I dined in Tokyo."
—Daniel Humm

NEW WONJO

Recommended by
Daniel Humm,
Edward Lee

23 West 32nd Street
Midtown
New York 10001
+1 2126955815
www.newwonjo.com

Opening hours	Open 7 days
Credit cards	Accepted
Price range	Affordable
Style	Casual
Cuisine	Korean
Recommended for	Late night

"A full menu of Korean barbecue, kimchi, hot stews, and an array of pickles will cure any hangover you might have had."—Edward Lee

PAIK'S NOODLE

Recommended by
Danny Bowien

2 West 32nd Street
Midtown
New York 10001
+1 2126957272
www.paiksnoodlenyc.com

Opening hours	Open 7 days
Credit cards	Accepted
Price range	Affordable
Style	Casual
Cuisine	Korean-Chinese
Recommended for	Late night

"It's amazing—it's Korean-style Chinese food. That guy Paik is a celebrity chef and everywhere you go, you see his face giving a thumb's up—he has a pork restaurant, he's like my hero."—Danny Bowien

SAKE BAR HAGI

Recommended by
Daniel Humm,
Jesse Schenker

152 West 49th Street
Midtown
New York 10019
+1 2127648549
www.sakebarhagi.com

Opening hours	Open 7 days
Credit cards	Accepted but not Diners
Price range	Budget
Style	Casual
Cuisine	Japanese
Recommended for	Late night

"It's downstairs, always packed, and cheap. Get the wasabi dumplings—they will blow your mind. The chicken-skin yakatori are also delicious."
—Jesse Schenke

SARABETH'S

Recommended by
Juan Gaffuri

40 Central Park South
Midtown
New York 10021
+1 2128265959
www.sarabethsrestaurants.com

Opening hours	Open 7 days
Credit cards	Accepted
Price range	Affordable
Style	Casual
Cuisine	American
Recommended for	Breakfast

"Incredible Eggs Benedict and a view over Central Park."—Juan Gaffuri

SALVATION TACO

Recommended by
Thomasina Miers

Pod 39 Hotel
145 East 39th Street
Midtown
New York 10016
+1 2128655800
www.salvationtaco.com

Opening hours	Open 7 days
Reservation policy	No
Credit cards	Accepted
Price range	Affordable
Style	Casual
Cuisine	Mexican
Recommended for	Worth the travel

SUSHI YASUDA

Recommended by
Danny Bowien,
Angela Dimayuga,
Jesse Schenker

204 East 43rd Street
Midtown
New York 10017
+1 2129721001
www.sushiyasuda.com

Opening hours	Closed Sunday
Credit cards	Accepted
Price range	Expensive
Style	Smart casual
Cuisine	Sushi
Recommended for	High end

"The ambiance—it feels like you're in a bamboo spaceship. I feel like it is very zen. It's very casual."
—Danny Bowien

TORISHIN

Recommended by
Eric Ripert

362 West 53rd Street
Midtown
New York 10019
+1 2127570108
www.torishinny.com

Opening hours	Open 7 days
Credit cards	Accepted
Price range	Expensive
Style	Smart casual
Cuisine	Japanese
Recommended for	Late Night

"I love yakitori. They're very creative and passionate here about serving the best quality ingredients. I like to sit at the counter and interact with the chef, and it reminds me of being in Japan."—Eric Ripert

TOTTO RAMEN

Recommended by
Phillip Foss

366 West 52nd Street
Midtown
New York 10019
+1 2125820052
www.tottoramen.com

Opening hours	Open 7 days
Reservation policy	No
Credit cards	Not accepted
Price range	Affordable
Style	Casual
Cuisine	Ramen Noodles
Recommended for	Worth the travel

"Totto Ramen in New York is some of the best ramen that is not in Japan."—Phillip Foss

TRATTORIA BIANCA

Recommended by
Massimo Bottura

481 8th Avenue on the corner of 35th
Midtown
New York, 1001
+1 2122688460
www.trattoriabianca.com

Opening hours	Open 7 days
Credit cards	Accepted
Price range	Affordable
Style	Casual
Cuisine	Italian-American
Recommended for	Regular neighborhood

TURNTABLE LP BAR & KARAOKE

Recommended by
Michael Anthony

36 West 32nd Street, 5th Floor
Midtown
New York 10001
+1 2125944344
www.turntablelpbar.com

Opening hours	Open 7 days
Credit cards	Accepted
Price range	Affordable
Style	Casual
Cuisine	American
Recommended for	Late night

"Open late, consistently great food. Crunchy, saucy, and garlicky fried chicken, kimchi, and beer."
—Michael Anthony

THE NOMAD HOTEL

Recommended by
Yannick Alléno, Jason Atherton
Phil Carmichael, Ross Lusted,
Claus Meyer, Joe Schafer,
Chris Shepherd

1170 Broadway
NoMad
New York 10001
+1 2127961500
www.thenomadhotel.com

Opening hours	Open 7 days
Credit cards	Accepted
Price range	Affordable
Style	Smart casual
Cuisine	American-European
Recommended for	Worth the travel

ALDEA

Recommended by
Carlos Perez

31 West 17th Street
Union Square
New York 10011
+1 2126757223
www.aldearestaurant.com

Opening hours	Closed Monday and Sunday
Credit cards	Accepted
Price range	Affordable
Style	Casual
Cuisine	Modern Mediterranean
Recommended for	Regular neighborhood

BASTA PASTA

Recommended by
Jesse Schenker

37 West 17th Street
Union Square
New York 10011
+1 2123660888
www.bastapastanyc.com

Opening hours	Open 7 days
Credit cards	Accepted
Price range	Affordable
Style	Casual
Cuisine	Italian
Recommended for	Regular neighborhood

CAFÉ BOULUD

Recommended by
Daniel Humm

20 East 76th Street
Upper East Side
New York 10021
+1 2127722600
www.cafeboulud.com

Opening hours	Open 7 days
Credit cards	Accepted
Price range	Expensive
Style	Smart casual
Cuisine	French
Recommended for	Breakfast

"They take the same care to cook breakfast as they do for lunch and dinner—delicious food with amazing ingredients."—Daniel Humm

DANIEL

60 East 65th Street
Upper East Side
New York 10065
+1 2122880033
www.danielnyc.com

Recommended by
Massimo Bottura, Andrew Carmellini,
Julien Duboué, Michael Friedman,
John Horne, Daniel Humm,
Drew Johnson, Florian Lamelot,
Townsend Wentz

Opening hours	Closed Sunday
Credit cards	Accepted
Price range	Expensive
Style	Smart casual
Cuisine	French
Recommended for	High end

"Daniel was the first place I ever had a dish and wine together where something happened—it was an 'aha' moment for me. It was a sardine dish and Gewurtztraminer. Every time I had a bite and a sip, I was like, 'What is happening?' I've never experienced that kind of wine and food synergy—it was the perfect pairing. This restaurant is all about great food and amazing technical service. It's an experience that stays with you."—John Horne

JG MELON

1291 3rd Avenue
Upper East Side
New York 10021
+1 2127440585
www.jgmelonnyc.com

Recommended by
Ignacio Mattos

Opening hours	Open 7 days
Reservation policy	No
Credit cards	Accepted
Price range	Affordable
Style	Casual
Cuisine	American
Recommended for	Late night

"Classic New York spot, and might be one of my favorite cheeseburgers in town, perhaps not the best fries, but get that burger medium rare, quick."
—Ignacio Mattos

SUSHI SEKI

1143 1st Avenue
Upper East Side
New York 10065
+1 2123710238
www.sushiseki.com

Recommended by
Ignacio Mattos

Opening hours	Closed Sunday
Credit cards	Accepted
Price range	Affordable
Style	Casual
Cuisine	Japanese
Recommended for	Late night

ABSOLUTE BAGELS

2788 Broadway
Upper West Side
New York 10025
+1 2129322052

Recommended by
Joseph Johnson

Opening hours	Open 7 days
Reservation policy	No
Credit cards	Not accepted
Price range	Budget
Style	Casual
Cuisine	Bagels
Recommended for	Breakfast

"Fresh bagels, baked every twenty-five minutes, are just the perfect NYC bagel. Something I get once a week."—Joseph Johnson

GRAY'S PAPAYA

2090 Broadway
Upper West Side
New York 10023
+1 2127990243
www.grayspapayanyc.com

Recommended by
Grae Nonas

Opening hours	Open 7 days
Reservation policy	No
Credit cards	Accepted
Price range	Budget
Style	Casual
Cuisine	American
Recommended for	Late night

"It's an iconic institution that happened to be a block away from my childhood home. My go-to is the recession special: two dogs and a drink, for $2.75 (£2) at the time. I always added ketchup, stewed onions, and sauerkraut to my dogs and washed it down with an orange drink. For first-timers, I definitely recommend getting the papaya drink."—Grae Nonas

JEAN-GEORGES

1 Central Park West
Upper West Side
New York 10023
+1 2122993900
www.jean-georges.com

Opening hours	Open 7 days
Credit cards	Accepted
Price range	Expensive
Style	Formal
Cuisine	French
Recommended for	High end

"Beautiful airy dining room, discreet polished service, impeccable food—consistency and class. Great cocktails."—Alla Wolf Tasker

LION'S HEAD TAVERN

995 Amsterdam Avenue
Upper West Side
New York 10025
+1 2128661030
www.lionsheadnyc.com

Opening hours	Open 7 days
Reservation policy	No
Credit cards	Accepted
Price range	Affordable
Style	Casual
Cuisine	Bar
Recommended for	Late night

"Cheap beers, great burger, friendly crowd."
—Joseph Johnson

NOUGATINE AT JEAN-GEORGES

1 Central Park West
Upper West Side
New York 10023
+1 2122993900
www.jean-georgesrestaurant.com

Opening hours	Open 7 days
Credit cards	Accepted
Price range	Expensive
Style	Smart casual
Cuisine	French-American-Asian
Recommended for	Late night

"The food is always creative and I can eat everything on the menu."—José Gutierrez

PER SE

10 Columbus Circle
Upper West Side
New York 10019
+1 2128239335
www.thomaskeller.com/perseny

Opening hours	Closed Sunday
Credit cards	Accepted
Price range	Expensive
Style	Formal
Cuisine	Modern American
Recommended for	Worth the travel

"From the stunning dining room to the beautiful views this restaurant is amazing to dine in! The food is faultless, service immaculate, and wine list brilliant."—Shaun Searley

THAI MARKET

960 Amsterdam Avenue
Upper West Side
New York 10025
+1 2122804575
www.thaimarketny.net

Opening hours	Open 7 days
Credit cards	Accepted
Price range	Affordable
Style	Casual
Cuisine	Thai
Recommended for	Regular neighborhood

MELBA'S

Recommended by
Joseph Johnson

300 West 114th Street
Harlem
New York 10026
+1 2128647777
www.melbasrestaurant.com

Opening hours	Open 7 days
Credit cards	Accepted but not Diners
Price range	Affordable
Style	Casual
Cuisine	Southern American
Recommended for	Regular neighborhood

RED ROOSTER

Recommended by
Carlos Perez

310 Lenox Avenue
Harlem
New York 10027
+1 2127929001
www.redroosterharlem.com

Opening hours	Open 7 days
Credit cards	Accepted
Price range	Affordable
Style	Casual
Cuisine	American
Recommended for	Regular neighborhood

CHEF'S TABLE AT BROOKLYN FARE

Recommended by
Björn Persson

431 West 37th Street
Hell's Kitchen
New York 10018
+1 7182430050
www.brooklynfare.com

Opening hours	Closed Saturday and Sunday
Credit cards	Accepted
Price range	Expensive
Style	Formal
Cuisine	French-Japanese
Recommended for	Worth the travel

"IT'S DELICIOUS—IT HITS ALL THE NOTES FOR LATE NIGHT COMFORT FOOD."

ESTANISLAO CARENZO P1056

CHARLESTON

"Best barbecue in the area, hands down."

KARL FIRLA P1054

"NO FRILLS, HONEST BREAKFAST."

JUSTIN PFAU P1051

"FROM FOOD TRUCK TO BRICKS-AND-MORTAR IN LESS THAN A YEAR IS AN AMAZING ACCOMPLISHMENT."

EMILY HAHN P1051

CHARLESTON

SCALE

0   550   1100   1700
yd.

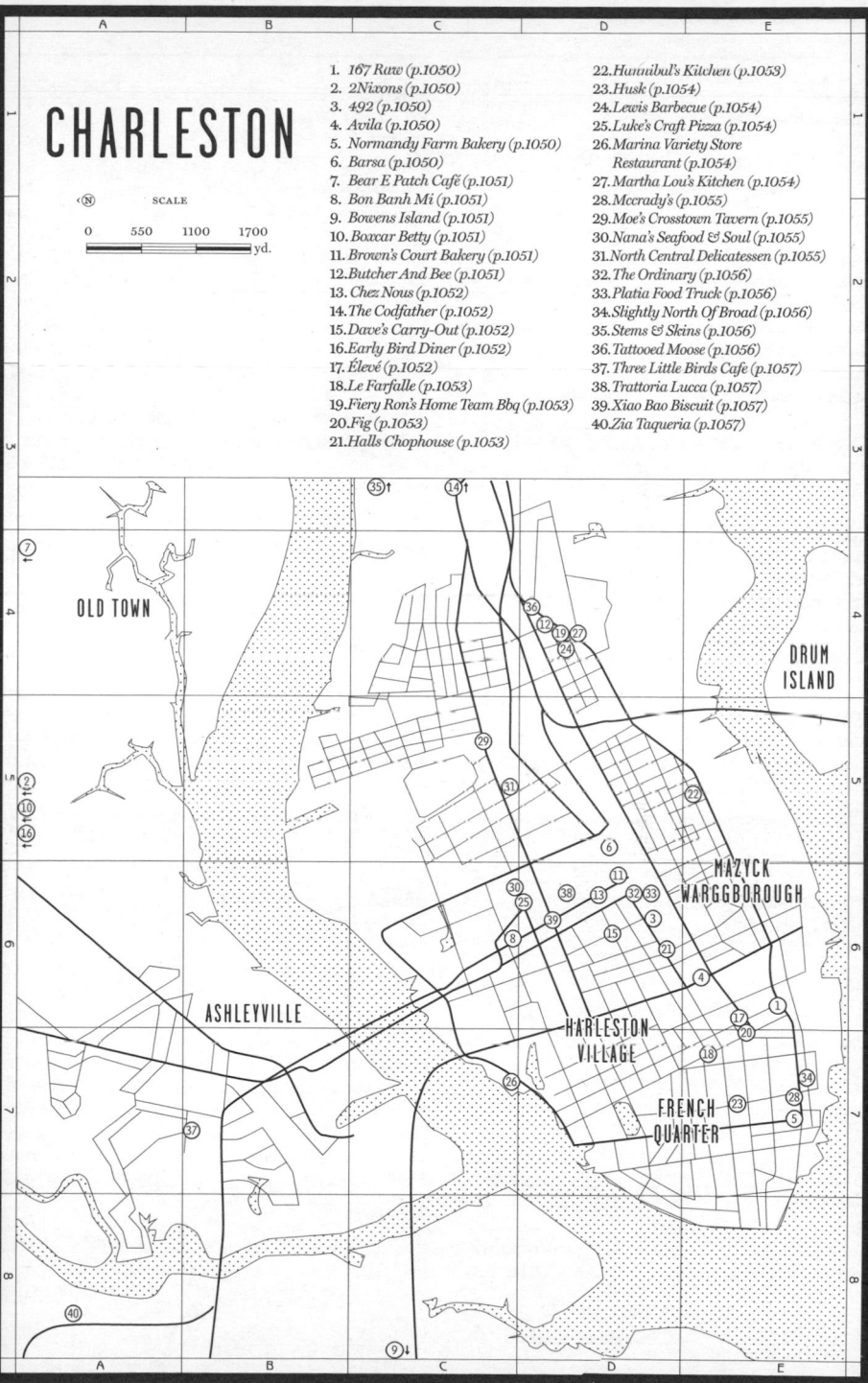

OLD TOWN

DRUM ISLAND

MAZYCK WARGGBOROUGH

ASHLEYVILLE

HARLESTON VILLAGE

FRENCH QUARTER

167 RAW

289 East Bay Street
Charleston
South Carolina 29401
+1 8435794997
www.167raw.com

Opening hours	Closed Sunday
Reservation policy	No
Credit cards	Accepted
Price range	Affordable
Style	Casual
Cuisine	Seafood
Recommended for	Regular neighborhood

"Small, quaint—staff are friendly and they have a great selection of oysters."—April Robinson

2NIXONS

Craft Conundrum
630 Skylark Drive
Charleston
South Carolina 29407
+1 8439700824
www.2nixons.com

Opening hours	Variable
Reservation policy	No
Credit cards	Not accepted
Price range	Affordable
Style	Casual
Cuisine	Japanese-Korean
Recommended for	Bargain

"They do ramen well and I like the soups."
—April Robinson

492

492 King Street
Charleston
South Carolina 29403
+1 8432036338
www.492king.com

Opening hours	Closed Monday
Credit cards	Accepted
Price range	Affordable
Style	Casual
Cuisine	Modern American
Recommended for	Wish I'd opened

AVILA

141 Calhoun Street
Charleston
South Carolina 29401
+1 8437352024
www.avilacharleston.com

Opening hours	Open 7 days
Credit cards	Accepted
Price range	Affordable
Style	Casual
Cuisine	Venezuelan
Recommended for	Wish I'd opened

"They are hard workers and their food is delicious and not pricey. From food truck to bricks-and-mortar in less than a year is an amazing accomplishment."
—Emily Hahn

NORMANDY FARM BAKERY

19 Broad Street
Charleston
South Carolina 29401
+1 8437894509

Opening hours	Closed Sunday
Reservation policy	No
Credit cards	Accepted
Price range	Affordable
Style	Casual
Cuisine	Bakery
Recommended for	Local favorite

BARSA

630 King Street
Charleston
South Carolina 29403
+1 8435775393
www.barsacharleston.com

Opening hours	Open 7 days
Credit cards	Accepted
Price range	Affordable
Style	Casual
Cuisine	Bar-Tapas
Recommended for	Regular neighborhood

BEAR E PATCH CAFÉ

Recommended by
Justin Pfau

1980 Ashley River Road
Charleston
South Carolina 29407
+1 8437666490
www.bearepatchcafe.com

Opening hours	Closed Sunday
Reservation policy	No
Credit cards	Accepted
Price range	Budget
Style	Casual
Cuisine	American
Recommended for	Breakfast

"No frills, honest breakfast. Big portions, small bill. The whole kitchen line is visible."—Justin Pfau

BON BANH MI

Recommended by
Emily Hahn

162 Spring Street
Charleston
South Carolina 29403
+1 8434147320
www.bonbanhmi.com

Opening hours	Open 7 days
Reservation policy	No
Credit cards	Accepted
Price range	Budget
Style	Casual
Cuisine	Vietnamese
Recommended for	Bargain

"They keep it simple and nail it."—Emily Hahn

BOWENS ISLAND

Recommended by
Brian Ahern,
Justin Pfau

1870 Bowens Island Road
Charleston
South Carolina 29412
+1 8437952757
www.bowensisland.biz

Opening hours	Closed Monday and Sunday
Reservation policy	No
Credit cards	Accepted
Price range	Affordable
Style	Casual
Cuisine	Seafood
Recommended for	Wish I'd opened

"Just outside Charleston. Great oysters and seafood. The atmosphere could not be more beautiful on the inner coastal waterway."—Brian Ahern

BOXCAR BETTY

Recommended by
Katie Lorenzen

1922 Savannah Highway
Charleston
South Carolina 29407
+1 8432257470
www.boxcarbetty.com

Opening hours	Open 7 days
Reservation policy	No
Credit cards	Accepted
Price range	Budget
Style	Casual
Cuisine	Southern American
Recommended for	Bargain

"Three choices for fried chicken sandwiches. All just $7 (£5)."—Katie Lorenzen

BROWN'S COURT BAKERY

Recommended by
Matthew Crabbe

199 St. Philip Street
Charleston
South Carolina 29403
+1 8437240833
www.brownscourt.com

Opening hours	Open 7 days
Reservation policy	No
Credit cards	Accepted
Price range	Budget
Style	Casual
Cuisine	Bakery
Recommended for	Breakfast

BUTCHER AND BEE

Recommended by
Mike Lata,
Katie Lorenzen

1085 Morrison Drive
Charleston
South Carolina 29403
+1 8436190202
www.butcherandbee.com

Opening hours	Open 7 days
Credit cards	Accepted
Price range	Affordable
Style	Casual
Cuisine	Southern American
Recommended for	Regular neighborhood

CHEZ NOUS

Recommended by
Emily Hahn,
Justin Pfau

6 Payne Court
Charleston
South Carolina 29403
+1 8435793060
www.cheznouschs.com

Opening hours	Closed Monday
Credit cards	Accepted
Price range	Expensive
Style	Smart casual
Cuisine	Mediterranean
Recommended for	Regular neighborhood

"Chefs Jill Mathias and Juan Cassolet cook with their hearts. You can taste the love in their food. They want you to feel like they are hosting you in their home. Their food is comfortable, delicious, and straight to the point."—Emily Hahn

A cosy neighborhood eatery influenced by cuisine from southern France, northern Italy, and northern Spain. From the moment you are given the menu — gorgeously handwritten in cursive script, seemingly straight from a bygone era—there is a sense that you've been invited into chef Jill Mathias's home to sit in on one of her family meals. On the menu is a simple choice of two appetizers, two entrées, and two desserts, which changes on a daily basis depending on the seasonal ingredients (if you have any dietary requirements, it's a good idea to call in advance as substitutions aren't always possible). The upstairs and ground floor of the cottage-restaurant seat just thirty-six people, but, in the warmer weather, the walled garden can accommodate a further twenty on a communal long table.

THE CODFATHER

Recommended by
Reid Henninger

1809 Reynolds Avenue
Charleston
South Carolina 29405
+1 8437894649
www.thecodfatherchippy.com

Opening hours	Closed Monday and Sunday
Reservation policy	No
Credit cards	Accepted
Price range	Affordable
Style	Casual
Cuisine	British-Seafood
Recommended for	Bargain

DAVE'S CARRY-OUT

Recommended by
Reid Henninger,
Justin Pfau

42 Morris Street
Charleston
South Carolina 29403
+1 8435777943

Opening hours	Closed Monday and Sunday
Reservation policy	No
Credit cards	Accepted
Price range	Budget
Style	Casual
Cuisine	Southern American-Seafood
Recommended for	Bargain

"Home soul food done well has always been a serious weakness of mine."—Reid Henninger

EARLY BIRD DINER

Recommended by
Sarah Mcintosh

1644 Savannah Highway
Charleston
South Carolina 29407
+1 8432772353
www.earlybirddiner.com

Opening hours	Open 7 days
Reservation policy	No
Credit cards	Accepted
Price range	Budget
Style	Casual
Cuisine	Diner
Recommended for	Breakfast

ÉLEVÉ

Recommended by
April Robinson

55 Wentworth Street
Charleston
South Carolina 29401
+1 8437244144
www.grandbohemiancharleston.com

Opening hours	Open 7 days
Credit cards	Accepted
Price range	Affordable
Style	Casual
Cuisine	Modern American
Recommended for	Breakfast

LE FARFALLE

15 Beaufain Street
Charleston
South Carolina 29401
+1 8432120920
www.lefarfallecharleston.com

Opening hours..Open 7 days
Credit cards...Accepted
Price range...Affordable
Style...Casual
Cuisine..Italian-American
Recommended for.................Regular neighborhood

"In an age in dining where everything is conceptual, Le Farfalle offers nothing but solid hospitality. There's no cheesy theme to buy into, no chef-deity to bow before, assaulting decor, or pretentious service. Just great food in a comfortable setting delivered by nice people. Which is the reason you leave your house for a reservation in the first place."—Reid Henninger

FIERY RON'S HOME TEAM BBQ

126 Williams Street
Charleston
South Carolina 29403
+1 8432257427
www.hometeambbq.com

Opening hours..Open 7 days
Reservation policy..No
Credit cards...Accepted
Price range...Affordable
Style...Casual
Cuisine...American Barbecue
Recommended for.................Regular neighborhood

FIG

232 Meeting Street
Charleston
South Carolina 29401
+1 8438055900
www.eatatfig.com

Opening hours..Closed Sunday
Credit cards...Accepted
Price range...Affordable
Style..Smart casual
Cuisine...Modern American
Recommended for..............................Local favorite

"Simple, local, comforting. Mike Lata and Jason Stanhope just cook amazing food. And the whole place from front door to back is run flawlessly."—Emily Hahn

HALLS CHOPHOUSE

434 King Street
Charleston
South Carolina 29403
+1 8437270090
www.hallschophouse.com

Opening hours..Open 7 days
Credit cards...Accepted
Price range...Affordable
Style..Smart casual
Cuisine..Steakhouse
Recommended for..............................Local favorite

"Good at displaying Southern hospitality and their gospel brunch on Sundays is enjoyable."
—April Robinson

HANNIBAL'S KITCHEN

16 Blake Street
Charleston
South Carolina 29403
+1 8437222256
www.hannibalkitchen.com

Opening hours..Closed Sunday
Credit cards...Accepted
Price range..Budget
Style...Casual
Cuisine...American-Soul
Recommended for...Breakfast

HUSK

Recommended by
Mashama Bailey

76 Queen Street
Charleston
South Carolina 29401
+1 8435772500
www.huskrestaurant.com

Opening hours	Open 7 days
Credit cards	Accepted
Price range	Expensive
Style	Casual
Cuisine	Modern Southern American
Recommended for	Wish I'd opened

"The way Sean Brock has reconnected Southern ingredients to Africa is something I really admire. Celebrating and revitalizing heritage grains and other things that grow in the South really inspires me."—Mashama Bailey

Sean Brock's follow-up to McCrady's pursues the same farm-to-fork philosophy. The market-driven menu moves beyond South Carolina's pantry to make use of Kentucky honey, Tennessee steak, and North Carolina catfish. But if it isn't a product of the South, it doesn't make it near the wood-fired oven. The restored 1893 Queen Anne home, with its columned porches, has taken well to its new purpose: there's an open kitchen on the ground floor and a second-floor dining room that's as fetching as any in Dixie, and the adjacent brick building houses a bar that touts craft bourbons and hand-carved Tennessee country hams. This sense of history and Southern pride is also present in Husk's Nashville branch.

LEWIS BARBECUE

Recommended by
Reid Henninger

464 North Nassau Street
Charleston
South Carolina 29403
+1 8438059500
www.lewisbarbecue.com

Opening hours	Closed Monday
Reservation policy	No
Credit cards	Accepted
Price range	Affordable
Style	Casual
Cuisine	Barbecue
Recommended for	Local favorite

"Best barbecue in the area, hands down."
—Reid Henninger

LUKE'S CRAFT PIZZA

Recommended by
Emily Hahn

271 Ashley Avenue
Charleston
South Carolina 29403
+1 8434101695
www.lukescraftpizza.com

Opening hours	Closed Monday to Wednesday
Reservation policy	No
Credit cards	Accepted
Price range	Affordable
Style	Casual
Cuisine	Pizza
Recommended for	Regular neighborhood

MARINA VARIETY STORE RESTAURANT

17 Lockwood Drive
Charleston

Recommended by
Reid Henninger

South Carolina 29403
+1 8437236325
www.varietystorerestaurant.com

Opening hours	Open 7 days
Credit cards	Accepted
Price range	Affordable
Style	Casual
Cuisine	Diner
Recommended for	Breakfast

"This is a diner trapped in time, right on the water on the Charleston peninsula. Simply because it is a diner makes it unique to the region; they are pretty hard to come by down here. Great views of the water, bottomless cups of mediocre coffee, and greasy stick-to-your-ribs plates of grub."—Reid Henninger

MARTHA LOU'S KITCHEN

Recommended by
Sean Brock,
Chris Coleman,
Justin Pfau

1068 Morrison Drive
Charleston
South Carolina 29403
+1 8435779583
www.marthalouskitchen.com

Opening hours	Closed Sunday
Reservation policy	No
Credit cards	Not accepted
Price range	Budget
Style	Casual
Cuisine	Southern American
Recommended for	Worth the travel

"Best soul food I've ever had. It's been a year since I visited, but I can still taste it."—Chris Coleman

That's Martha Lou Gadsden smiling from the mural on the cinderblock wall on the roadside restaurant. And that's Martha Lou Gadsden sitting on the white plastic chair in the homely narrow restaurant—though often she'll be in the tiny kitchen, deep-frying chicken, standing over a simmering saucepot of chitterlings, or watching lima beans studded with pork neck thicken. For the last thirty-five years, Ms. Gadsden, now joined by her daughter, has been serving Lowcountry classics to hungry Charlestonians. In the last decade or so, as the word of soul food has spread, Martha Lou's has taken on near totemic status—though a styrofoam (polystyrene) plate loaded with the best food in the state still only sets you back $8.50 (£6).

MCCRADY'S

Recommended by
Michael Friedman,
Katie Lorenzen

2 Unity Alley
Charleston
South Carolina 29401
+1 8436410469
www.mccradysrestaurant.com

Opening hours	Open 7 days
Credit cards	Accepted
Price range	Expensive
Style	Smart casual
Cuisine	American-Pub
Recommended for	High end

"Locally sourced, with a great wine list."
—Katie Lorenzen

Housed in a handsomely restored eighteenth-century tavern, McCrady's has been home to Sean Brock's antebellum-inspired new Southern culinary vision since 2006. Brock has established links with local farmers to revive heirloom crops and champion high-welfare breeds. His menus combine these raw materials, plus research from his vast collection of nineteenth-century Southern cookbooks, with the latest high-tech techniques, and more down-home methods such as pickling. Make sure to stop in the bar, which specializes in mixing pre-Prohibition cocktails, before making your way to a dining room that's a similarly smart concoction of exposed brick and crisp linen.

MOE'S CROSSTOWN TAVERN

Recommended by
Reid Henninger

714 Rutledge Avenue
Charleston
South Carolina 29403
+1 8436410469
www.moescrosstowntavern.com

Opening hours	Open 7 days
Reservation policy	No
Credit cards	Accepted
Price range	Budget
Style	Casual
Cuisine	American
Recommended for	Late night

"Great staff in my favorite neighborhood bar. Always see a few friends—a good game of pool and seriously good pub food."—Reid Henninger

NANA'S SEAFOOD & SOUL

Recommended by
April Robinson

176 Line Street
Charleston
South Carolina 29403
+1 8439370002
www.nanasseafoodsoul.com

Opening hours	Closed Monday and Sunday
Reservation policy	No
Credit cards	Accepted
Price range	Affordable
Style	Casual
Cuisine	Southern American-Seafood
Recommended for	Regular neighborhood

NORTH CENTRAL DELICATESSEN

Recommended by
Emily Hahn

396 Huger Street
Charleston
South Carolina 29403
+1 8433001698
www.charlestondeli.com

Opening hours	Closed Sunday
Reservation policy	No
Credit cards	Accepted
Price range	Budget
Style	Casual
Cuisine	Deli
Recommended for	Breakfast

"The owners are amazing, hard-working people that just get what it is people want in the morning. BAGELS!"—Emily Hahn

THE ORDINARY

544 King Street
Charleston
South Carolina 29403
+1 8434147060
www.eattheordinary.com

Opening hours	Closed Monday
Credit cards	Accepted
Price range	Affordable
Style	Smart casual
Cuisine	Modern Seafood
Recommended for	High end

"I think it's the best seafood restaurant in America right now. Great food and drinks. As a seafood lover, I love to see another chef taking those ingredients to the next level."—Isaac Toups

It's quite a feat of bravado to name your restaurant The Ordinary, especially when it's located in an area with a rich tradition of seafood and oyster bars. Luckily, chef and co-owner Mike Lata's confidence is well founded. The Ordinary provides innovative seafood dishes, but firmly in the tradition of the cuisine of Charleston. Constantly looking to push the boundaries, Lata presents a series of hot and cold sharing plates that sparkle with pioneering flavor combinations. The restaurant is set in a refurbished bank, complete with high ceilings and full-length, round-topped windows. There's a highly charged, kinetic atmosphere, which is particularly electric on weekend nights—and the wine list is excellent, with almost every bottle carefully selected from coastal vineyards.

PLATIA FOOD TRUCK

33 Wolfe Street
Charleston
South Carolina 29403
+1 8438827443
www.platiafoodtrucks.com

Opening hours	Closed Sunday to Wednesday
Reservation policy	No
Credit cards	Not accepted
Price range	Budget
Style	Casual
Cuisine	Greek
Recommended for	Late night

"It's delicious—it hits all the notes for late-night comfort food."—Emily Hahn

SLIGHTLY NORTH OF BROAD

192 East Bay Street
Charleston
South Carolina 29401
+1 8437233424
www.snobcharleston.com

Opening hours	Open 7 days
Credit cards	Accepted
Price range	Expensive
Style	Casual
Cuisine	Modern Southern American
Recommended for	Local favorite

"Family owned, great food, and great service."
—Katie Lorenzen

STEMS & SKINS

1070 East Montague Avenue B
Charleston
South Carolina 29405
+1 8438054809
www.stemsandskins.com

Opening hours	Closed Monday
Reservation policy	No
Credit cards	Accepted
Price range	Affordable
Style	Casual
Cuisine	Wine Bar
Recommended for	Regular neighborhood

"My favorite spot, Stems & Skins, may be defined as a bar, but I have had many great meals there. It certainly has the neighborhood feel down."
—Reid Henninger

TATTOOED MOOSE

1137 Morrison Drive
Charleston
South Carolina 29403
+1 8432772990
www.tattooedmoose.com

Opening hours	Open 7 days
Reservation policy	No
Credit cards	Accepted
Price range	Affordable
Style	Casual
Cuisine	American
Recommended for	Late night

"Awesome sandwiches—the duck club—and great wings."—Katie Lorenzen

THREE LITTLE BIRDS CAFE

Recommended by
Sarah Mcintosh

65 Windermere Boulevard
Charleston
South Carolina 29407
+1 8432253065
www.threelittlebirdscafe.com

Opening hours..Open 7 days
Reservation policy...No
Credit cards...Accepted
Price range...Expensive
Style...Casual
Cuisine...Café
Recommended for..Breakfast

TRATTORIA LUCCA

Recommended by
Reid Henninger

41 Bogard Street
Charleston
South Carolina 29403
+1 8439733323
www.luccacharleston.com

Opening hours...Closed Sunday
Credit cards...Accepted
Price range..Affordable
Style...Smart casual
Cuisine...Italian
Recommended for................................Wish I'd opened

"A small, intimate, fifty-seat Italian menu is where
I would most thrive."—Reid Henninger

XIAO BAO BISCUIT

Recommended by
Emily Hahn,
Katie Lorenzen,
Justin Pfau

224 Rutledge Avenue
Charleston
South Carolina 29401
+1 8437932216
www.xiaobaobiscuit.com

Opening hours...Closed Sunday
Reservation policy...No
Credit cards...Accepted
Price range..Affordable
Style...Casual
Cuisine...Asian Fusion
Recommended for......................Regular neighborhood

"Love the flavor profiles. Small menu—everything
is spot on."—Katie Lorenzen

ZIA TAQUERIA

Recommended by
Justin Pfau

1956A Maybank Highway
Charleston
South Carolina 29412
+1 8434068877
www.ziataco.com

Opening hours..Open 7 days
Credit cards...Accepted
Price range...Budget
Style...Casual
Cuisine...Mexican
Recommended for...................Regular neighborhood

"This is the closest thing to authentic Latin food
that I can find in Charleston. It reminds me of the
Latin neighborhoods in Chicago where I used to live.
And the margaritas are awesome."—Justin Pfau

"I DON'T EVEN LIKE PIZZA AND I LOVE THIS PIZZA. CHEWY, CRUNCHY, CHEESY. GET IT BAKED EXTRA CRISPY. DETROIT-STYLE PIZZA: WHO KNEW!"

SARAH MCINTOSH P1067

AUSTIN

"It's the best soul food I've ever had."

CHRIS COLEMAN P1055

"For me, Austin is all about the local institutions that have been here before Austin was a thing."

LARRY MCGUIRE P1062

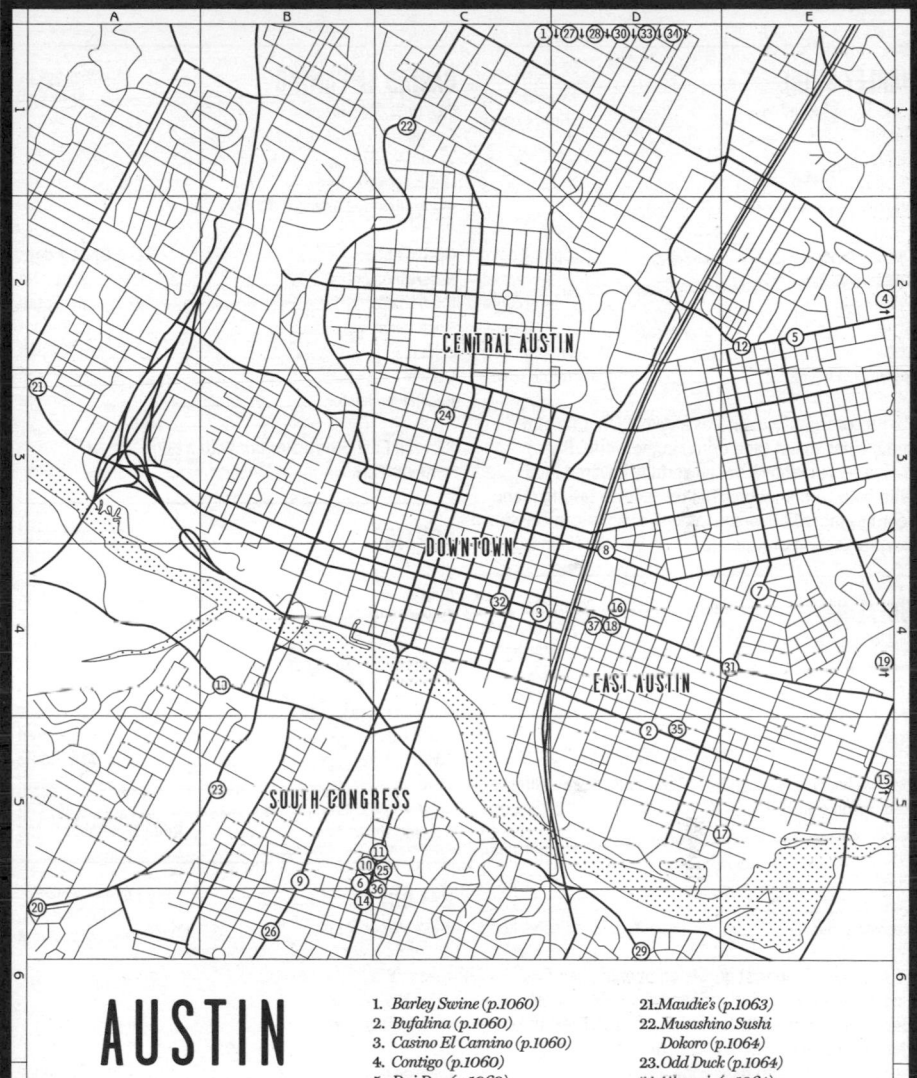

AUSTIN

N̂ SCALE

0   380   760   1140

yd.

1. *Barley Swine (p.1060)*
2. *Bufalina (p.1060)*
3. *Casino El Camino (p.1060)*
4. *Contigo (p.1060)*
5. *Dai Due (p.1060)*
6. *Enoteca Vespaio (p.1061)*
7. *Figure 8 (p.1061)*
8. *Franklin Barbecue (p.1061)*
9. *Fresa's (p.1061)*
10. *Güero's Taco Bar (p.1062)*
11. *Home Slice Pizza (p.1062)*
12. *Hoover's Cooking (p.1062)*
13. *Juiceland (p.1062)*
14. *June's All Day (p.1062)*
15. *Justine's (p.1062)*
16. *Kebabalicious (p.1063)*
17. *Launderette (p.1063)*
18. *Licha's Cantina (p.1063)*
19. *Marcelino Pan Y Vino (p.1063)*
20. *Matt's El Rancho (p.1063)*
21. *Maudie's (p.1063)*
22. *Musashino Sushi Dokoro (p.1064)*
23. *Odd Duck (p.1064)*
24. *Olamaie (p.1064)*
25. *Perla's (p.1064)*
26. *El Primo (p.1064)*
27. *Ramen Tatsu-Ya (p.1065)*
28. *Tacodeli (p.1065)*
29. *Taco More (p.1065)*
30. *Tan My (p.1065)*
31. *Thai-Kun At Whisler's (p.1065)*
32. *The Backspace (p.1066)*
33. *Tomodachi Sushi (p.1066)*
34. *Uchiko (p.1066)*
35. *Veracruz All Natural Food Truck (p.1066)*
36. *Vespaio (p.1066)*
37. *Via 313 (p.1066)*

BARLEY SWINE

Recommended by
Kevin Fink,
Geoff Lindsay

6555 Burnet Road
Austin
Texas 78757
+1 5123948150
www.barleyswine.com

Opening hours	Open 7 days
Credit cards	Accepted
Price range	Affordable
Style	Casual
Cuisine	Modern American
Recommended for	Worth the travel

"A recent trip to Austin was a revelation. One of the great cities to eat (and drink) in the world! Barley Swine serves innovative, powerfully flavored food with bold combinations. The ten-course tasting menu features incredible presentations of American classics. Great selection of American beers!"—Geoff Lindsay

BUFALINA

Recommended by
Kevin Fink,
Grae Nonas

1519 East Cesar Chavez Street
Austin
Texas 78702
+1 5125242523
www.bufalinapizza.com

Opening hours	Closed Monday and Tuesday
Reservation policy	No
Credit cards	Accepted
Price range	Affordable
Style	Casual
Cuisine	Pizza
Recommended for	Regular neighborhood

"I was one of the first guests on opening day. I've loved every bite and experience since that moment on and it only gets better with each visit. They make their own mozzarella in house, their crust is the perfect texture, and their wine list is one of the most well-curated in the country."—Grae Nonas

There is nothing like pizza straight from the oven—cheese bubbling, tender crust crackling. It's a dream that Bufalina delivers day in, day out, with help from the 900°F wood-burning oven tucked in the back of its airy, modern space. Steven Dilley's obsession is Neapolitan pizza, and Bufalina's are perfect. They're topped with a rotating menu of ingredients sourced locally (this is Austin, after all)—although you can never go wrong with margherita. The bar serves Austin beers on tap, as well as a global list of wines and even a selection of sherries.

CASINO EL CAMINO

Recommended by
Kevin Fink

517 East 6th Street
Austin
Texas 78701
+1 5124699330
www.casinoelcamino.net

Opening hours	Open 7 days
Reservation policy	No
Credit cards	Accepted
Price range	Budget
Style	Casual
Cuisine	American
Recommended for	Late night

"Iconic East 6th rocker bar with a huge burger."
—Kevin Fink

CONTIGO

Recommended by
Sarah Mcintosh

2027 Anchor Lane
Austin
Texas 78723
+1 5126142260
www.contigotexas.com

Opening hours	Open 7 days
Credit cards	Accepted
Style	Affordable
Style	Casual
Cuisine	American
Recommended for	Regular neighborhood

DAI DUE

Recommended by
Sarah Mcintosh,
Grae Nonas

2406 Manor Road
Austin
Texas 78722
+1 5125240688
www.daidue.com

Opening hours	Closed Monday
Credit cards	Accepted
Price range	Affordable
Style	Casual
Cuisine	Texan
Recommended for	Breakfast

"Everything is procured from within a few miles radius of the restaurant. Chef Jesse and team make everything in-house and it's all cooked over an open fire. All dishes are perfectly executed and the breakfast menu is dynamic with something for everyone spanning many regions. They are truly a responsible, sustainable restaurant that is equally delicious."—Grae Nonas

Tucked inside a strip mall, beyond the butcher counter, is a warm space finished with natural wood and indigo accents and filled with the heady, welcoming scent of roasting meat. Opened in 2014, Dai Due began as a supper club that featured Austin's urban farms, and today, everything on the menu is local, including the drinks. Jesse Griffiths and Tamara Mayfield serve three-course, meat-centric dinners, where wild boar and venison nestle up to local fruits, kohlrabi, brown rice, and purple sage. Surrounded by all this wholesome hedonism, it's easy to soften, to feel at one with the staff and other diners, and to be grateful to know Austin.

ENOTECA VESPAIO

Recommended by
Jesse Griffiths

1610 South Congress Avenue
Austin
Texas 78704
+1 5124417672
www.austinvespaio.com

Opening hours	Open 7 days
Credit cards	Accepted
Price range	Affordable
Style	Casual
Cuisine	Itallan
Recommended for	Local favorite

"Consistently delicious—has been around for a long time (with its sister restaurant Vespaio)."
—Jesse Griffiths

FIGURE 8

Recommended by
Kevin Fink

1111 Chicon Street
Austin
Texas 78702
+1 5129531061
www.figure8coffeepurveyors.com

Opening hours	Open 7 days
Reservation policy	No
Credit cards	Accepted
Price range	Affordable
Style	Casual
Cuisine	Café
Recommended for	Breakfast

"Breakfast for me on a work day is a quick coffee and a snack. Figure 8 is a unique Austin shop, owned by a husband and wife whose focus is great coffee with a casual feel. Breakfast tacos and pastries are available, but the coffee is why I go."—Kevin Fink

FRANKLIN BARBECUE

Recommended by
Sarah Mcintosh,
Grae Nonas

900 East 11th Street
Austin
Texas 78702
+1 5126531187
www.franklinbarbecue.com

Opening hours	Closed Monday
Reservation policy	No
Credit cards	Accepted
Price range	Affordable
Style	Casual
Cuisine	Barbecue
Recommended for	Local favorite

"It's delicious barbecue and worth the wait! Also Aaron is an incredible human being."—Grae Nonas

It's been said that Franklin Barbecue puts the "queue" (line) in "BBQ". Open from 11.00 a.m., punters start lining up several hours before that, many with their own chairs. The Franklin is Aaron Franklin who, with his wife Stacy, began in 2009 by serving out of a trailer in an East Austin parking lot. They moved to their current permanent premises in 2011. Only open for lunch, they stop serving when they're sold out of brisket, ribs, pulled pork, turkey, and sausage. The "sold out" sign sometimes appears before they've even opened the door, depending on the length of that queue.

FRESA'S

Recommended by
Sarah Mcintosh

1703 South First Street
Austin
Texas 78704
+1 5129922946
www.fresaschicken.com/south-first

Opening hours	Open 7 days
Reservation policy	No
Credit cards	Accepted
Price range	Affordable
Style	Casual
Cuisine	Mexican
Recommended for	Wish I'd opened

"It's a totally different take on Mexican cuisine. It borders the idea of Baja Californian-Mexican food and authentic Mexican."—Sarah Mcintosh

GÜERO'S TACO BAR

Recommended by
Larry McGuire

1412 South Congress Avenue
Austin
Texas 78704
+1 5124477688
www.gueros.com

Opening hours	Open 7 days
Reservation policy	No
Credit cards	Accepted
Price range	Affordable
Style	Casual
Cuisine	Tex-Mex
Recommended for	Local favorite

"For me, Austin is all about the local institutions that have been here before Austin was a thing. Güero's and Matt El Rancho are both great big spots known for their margaritas."—Larry McGuire

HOME SLICE PIZZA

Recommended by
Larry McGuire

1415 South Congress Avenue
Austin
Texas 78704
+1 5124447437
www.homeslicepizza.com

Opening hours	Open 7 days
Reservation policy	No
Credit cards	Accepted
Price range	Affordable
Style	Casual
Cuisine	Pizza
Recommended for	Late night

"These guys have the best New York-style pizza! Their take out (take away) window is open until 3.00 a.m. on the weekends."—Larry McGuire

HOOVER'S COOKING

Recommended by
Jesse Griffiths

2002 Manor Road
Austin
Texas 78722
+1 5124795006
www.hooverscooking.com

Opening hours	Open 7 days
Reservation policy	No
Credit cards	Accepted
Price range	Affordable
Style	Casual
Cuisine	Southern American
Recommended for	Regular neighborhood

JUICELAND

Recommended by
Jesse Griffiths

1625 Barton Springs Road
Austin Texas 78704
+1 5124809501
www.juiceland.com

Opening hours	Open 7 days
Reservation policy	No
Credit cards	Accepted
Price range	Budget
Style	Casual
Cuisine	Juices and Smoothies
Recommended for	Breakfast

With nineteen locations spread across Austin, you're never far from a branch of JuiceLand. The original Barton Springs branch, formerly an outpost of Daily Juice, opened in 2011 and mixes its hippy-dippy vibe with a vast selection of juices, smoothies, aguas frescas (Mexican fruit drinks), fruit cocktails, and shots of the good stuff. From the "Valley Girl" (grapefruit, lemon, lime, orange, and pineapple) to the "Ninja Bachelor Party" (pineapple, jalapeño, celery, kale, spinach, parsley, and Himalayan sea salt), there's a healthy morning eye-opener to suit everyone. Order ahead online to avoid waiting.

JUNE'S ALL DAY

Recommended by
Kevin Fink

1722 South Congress Avenue
Austin
Texas 78704
+1 5124161722
www.junesallday.com

Opening hours	Open 7 days
Credit cards	Accepted
Price range	Affordable
Style	Casual
Cuisine	Café-Wine Bar
Recommended for	Late night

JUSTINE'S

Recommended by
Jesse Griffiths,
Sarah Mcintosh

4710 East 5th Street
Austin
Texas 78702
+1 5123852900
www.justines1937.com

Opening hours	Closed Tuesday
Credit cards	Accepted
Price range	Affordable
Style	Smart casual
Cuisine	French
Recommended for	Late night

"Mussels and fries, French wine, and the best crème brûlée around."—Jesse Griffiths

KEBABALICIOUS

1311 East 7th Street
Austin
Texas 78702
+1 5123946562
www.kebabalicious.com

Opening hours	Open 7 days
Reservation policy	No
Credit cards	Accepted
Price range	Budget
Style	Casual
Cuisine	Mediterranean
Recommended for	Bargain

"The food is always under $10 (£8), they serve beer, have live music, and the fries are great."—Kevin Fink

LAUNDERETTE

2115 Holly Street
Austin
Texas 78702
+1 5123821599
www.launderetteaustin.com

Opening hours	Open 7 days
Credit cards	Accepted
Price range	Affordable
Style	Casual
Cuisine	International
Recommended for	Regular neighborhood

"Good vibe and music. The wine list is amazing and the food is on point. It's interesting while still being familiar."—Sarah Mcintosh

LICHA'S CANTINA

1306 East 6th Street
Austin
Texas 78702
+1 5124805960
www.lichascantina.com

Opening hours	Closed Monday
Reservation policy	No
Credit cards	Accepted
Price range	Affordable
Style	Casual
Cuisine	Mexican
Recommended for	Regular neighborhood

MARCELINO PAN Y VINO

901 Tillery Street
Austin
Texas 78702
+1 5129261709

Opening hours	Closed Sunday
Reservation policy	No
Credit cards	Accepted
Price range	Affordable
Style	Casual
Cuisine	Mexican
Recommended for	Breakfast

"A hidden gem. It feels like you're eating directly out of their home kitchen. Amazing *chicharrón* and the best *barbacoa* I've had. My go-to order is *barbacoa* on corn with egg, cheese, onion, and cilantro (coriander)."—Sarah Mcintosh

MATT'S EL RANCHO

2613 South Lamar Boulevard
Austin
Texas 78704
+1 5124629333
www.mattselrancho.com

Opening hours	Closed Tuesday
Reservation policy	No
Credit cards	Accepted
Price range	Affordable
Style	Casual
Cuisine	Tex-Mex
Recommended for	Local favorite

MAUDIE'S

2608 West 7th Street
Austin
Texas 78703
+1 5124733740
www.maudies.com

Opening hours	Open 7 days
Reservation policy	No
Credit cards	Accepted
Price range	Affordable
Style	Casual
Cuisine	Tex-Mex
Recommended for	Regular neighborhood

"We eat Tex-Mex way too much at our neighborhood spot Maudie's. I've actually been eating here since we had off-campus lunch at Austin High."
—Larry McGuire

MUSASHINO SUSHI DOKORO

Recommended by
Sarah Mcintosh

2905 San Gabriel Street #200
Austin
Texas 78705
+1 5127958593
www.musashinosushi.com

Opening hours	Closed Monday
Credit cards	Accepted
Price range	Affordable
Style	Casual
Cuisine	Japanese
Recommended for	Regular neighborhood

ODD DUCK

Recommended by
Kevin Fink,
James Rigato

1201 South Lamar Boulevard
Austin
Texas 78704
+1 5124336521
www.oddduckaustin.com

Opening hours	Open 7 days
Credit cards	Accepted
Price range	Affordable
Style	Casual
Cuisine	Modern American
Recommended for	Worth the travel

"A lively, open kitchen and educated and confident service staff guide you through an eccentric and extremely well-executed menu that will entertain, inspire, and leave you begging for more."
—James Rigato

Chef Bryce Gilmore and his brother Dylan opened Odd Duck in Austin in 2009. Back then it was a trailer in a vacant lot. It's almost too perfect that the bricks-and-mortar incarnation, which opened its doors in 2013, is located in a new building on that very same lot. Today, Odd Duck's menu stays true to the approach that first earned it a loyal following. There are foams to be had (a pork fat foam, to be exact), but the modern techniques are judiciously applied and the menu stays grounded in beautiful ingredients spun as sophisticated Texan fare: pig face *carnitas* (pulled meat), coffee-roasted beets (beetroot) with smoked pecan, beef crackling with potato chips.

OLAMAIE

Recommended by
Sarah Mcintosh

1610 San Antonio Street
Austin
Texas 78701
+1 5124742796
www.olamaieaustin.com

Opening hours	Open 7 days
Credit cards	Accepted
Price range	Expensive
Style	Smart casual
Cuisine	Southern American
Recommended for	High end

"Great service, a wonderful take on Southern cuisine, and a very beautiful restaurant."—Sarah Mcintosh

PERLA'S

Recommended by
Jesse Griffiths

1400 South Congress Avenue
Austin
Texas 78704
+1 5122917300
www.perlasaustin.com

Opening hours	Open 7 days
Credit cards	Accepted
Price range	Expensive
Style	Casual
Cuisine	Seafood
Recommended for	High end

"Great, simple seafood and oysters. Very consistent, with good service and fun wines."—Jesse Griffiths

EL PRIMO

Recommended by
Jesse Griffiths

2011 South 1st Street
Austin
Texas 78704
+1 5122275060

Opening hours	Closed Sunday
Reservation policy	No
Credit cards	Accepted
Price range	Budget
Style	Casual
Cuisine	Mexican
Recommended for	Bargain

"Simple, delicious tacos made by one guy with incredible flat-top skills. Great chile salsa, too."
—Jesse Griffiths

RAMEN TATSU-YA

Recommended by
Sarah Mcintosh,
Grae Nonas,
James Rigato

8557 Research Boulevard
Austin
Texas 78758
www.ramen-tatsuya.com

Opening hours	Open 7 days
Reservation policy	No
Credit cards	Accepted
Price range	Budget
Style	Casual
Cuisine	Japanese
Recommended for	Regular neighborhood

"It's the best ramen I've had. It's always consistent, balanced, complex, and filling. The rich flavor and depth of the *tonkotsu* broth will blow anyone's mind. I love ordering the *tonkotsu* original with extra *ajitama* (soft-boiled, soy-marinated egg) and a spicy bomb (house-made chile paste). Plus, I met my wife there."—Grae Nonas

TACODELI

Recommended by
Sarah Mcintosh

4200 North Lamar Boulevard
Austin
Texas 78756
+1 5124191900
www.tacodeli.com

Opening hours	Open 7 days
Reservation policy	No
Credit cards	Accepted
Price range	Budget
Style	Casual
Cuisine	Mexican
Recommended for	Bargain

"Fast, easy, cheap, and good quality. Love the *corazon* salad and I add sirloin."—Sarah Mcintosh

TACO MORE

Recommended by
Larry McGuire

2015 East Riverside Drive
Austin
Texas 78741
+1 5129168888

Opening hours	Open 7 days
Reservation policy	No
Credit cards	Accepted
Price range	Budget
Style	Casual
Cuisine	Mexican Street Food
Recommended for	Bargain

"This spot has an awesome salsa bar and loads of good street-food-style tacos. Plus they will dunk a Corona in a huge frozen margarita."—Larry McGuire

TAN MY

Recommended by
Grae Nonas

1601 Ohlen Road
Austin
Texas 78758
+1 5128329585

Opening hours	Open 7 days
Reservation policy	No
Credit cards	Accepted
Price range	Budget
Style	Casual
Cuisine	Vietnamese
Recommended for	Bargain

"The pho is incredible, super filling, and very inexpensive."—Grae Nonas

THAI-KUN AT WHISLER'S

Recommended by
Kevin Fink

1816 East 6th Street
Austin
Texas 78702
+1 5127193332
www.thaikun.com

Opening hours	Open 7 days
Reservation policy	No
Credit cards	Accepted
Price range	Affordable
Style	Casual
Cuisine	Thai
Recommended for	Late night

"Thai-Kun is not trying to make the most unique Thai experience, rather the best, most craveable food to eat when you're out. Thai-Kun is great after a long night or as an interlude between bars on a weekend."
—Kevin Fink

THE BACKSPACE

Recommended by
Jesse Griffiths

507 San Jacinto Boulevard
Austin
Texas 78701
+1 5124749899
www.thebackspace-austin.com

Opening hours	Open 7 days
Credit cards	Accepted
Price range	Affordable
Style	Casual
Cuisine	Pizza
Recommended for	Wish I'd opened

"Just a wood-burning oven serving up great pizza, simple antipasti and a couple of desserts. It's a great space and it has my favorite wine list in the city."
—Jesse Griffiths

TOMODACHI SUSHI

Recommended by
Chris Lusk

4101 West Parmer Lane
Austin
Texas 78727
+1 5128219472
www.tomosushiaustin.com

Opening hours	Closed Sunday
Credit cards	Accepted
Price range	Affordable
Style	Casual
Cuisine	Japanese
Recommended for	Worth the travel

UCHIKO

Recommended by
Kevin Fink

4200 North Lamar Boulevard
Austin
Texas 78756
+1 5129164808
www.uchikoaustin.com

Opening hours	Open 7 days
Credit cards	Accepted
Price range	Expensive
Style	Smart casual
Cuisine	Japanese
Recommended for	High end

VERACRUZ ALL NATURAL FOOD TRUCK

Recommended by
Kevin Fink,
Grae Nonas

1704 East Cesar Chavez Street
Austin
Texas 78702
+1 5129811760
www.veracruztacos.com

Opening hours	Open 7 days
Reservation policy	No
Credit cards	Accepted
Price range	Budget
Style	Casual
Cuisine	Mexican
Recommended for	Local favorite

VESPAIO

Recommended by
Larry McGuire

1610 South Congress Avenue
Austin
Texas 78704
+1 5124416100
www.austinvespaio.com

Opening hours	Open 7 days
Credit cards	Accepted
Price range	Affordable
Style	Casual
Cuisine	Italian
Recommended for	Regular neighborhood

"This is one of the first good restaurants to open, when Austin was still a sleepy college town. It's laid-back and neighborhoody but they have great food and bartenders."—Larry McGuire

VIA 313

Recommended by
Sarah Mcintosh

1111 East 6th Street
Austin
Texas 78702
+1 5129391927
www.via313.com

Opening hours	Open 7 days
Credit cards	Accepted
Price range	Affordable
Style	Casual
Cuisine	Pizza
Recommended for	Late night

"I don't even like pizza and I LOVE this pizza. Chewy, crunchy, cheesy. Get it baked extra crispy. Detroit-style pizza—who knew!"—Sarah Mcintosh

CENTRAL AMERICA & CARIBBEAN

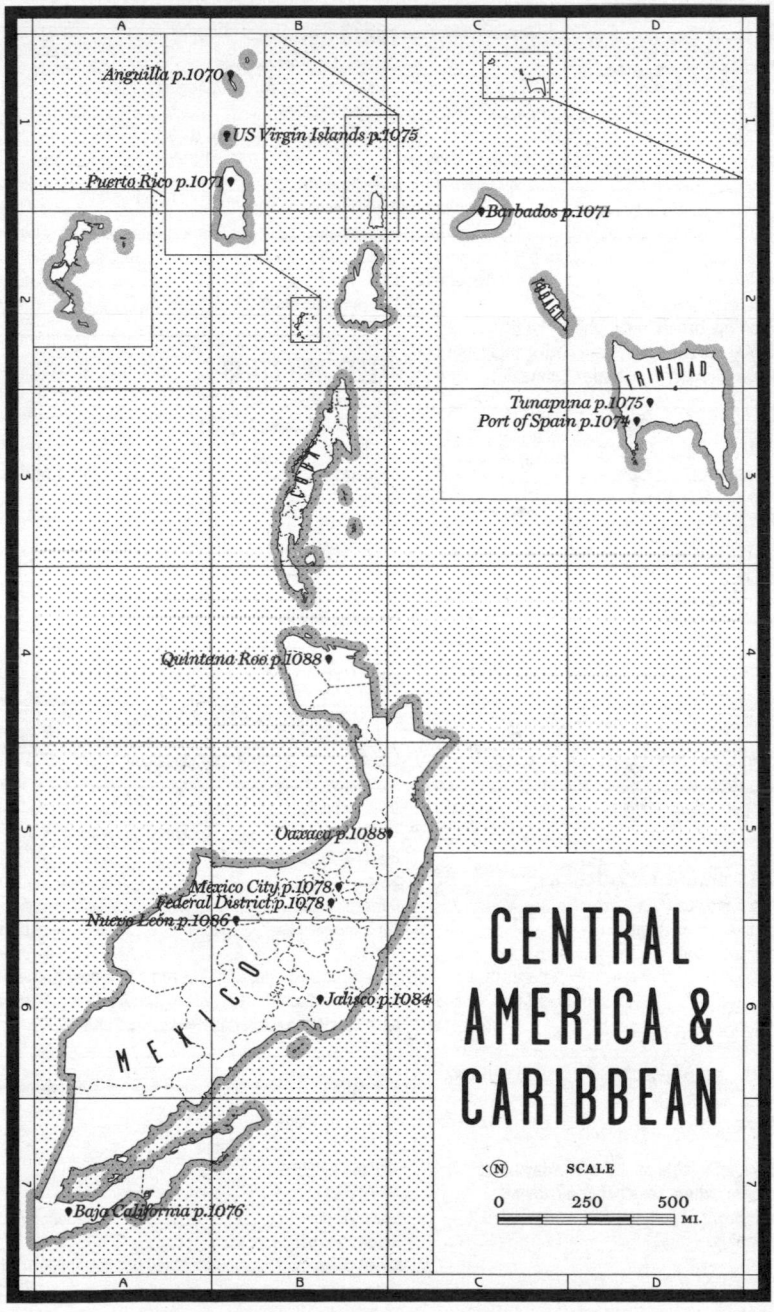

Anguilla p.1070

US Virgin Islands p.1075

Puerto Rico p.1071

Barbados p.1071

TRINIDAD

Tunapuna p.1075
Port of Spain p.1074

Quintana Roo p.1088

Oaxaca p.1088

Mexico City p.1078
Federal District p.1078
Nuevo León p.1086

MEXICO

Jalisco p.1084

Baja California p.1076

CENTRAL AMERICA & CARIBBEAN

‹Ⓝ›   SCALE

0   250   500
                     MI.

FALCON NEST

Recommended by
Jasper Schneider

Island Harbor
Island Harbor AI-2640, Anguilla
+1 2644971127

Opening hours	Open 7 days
Credit cards	Not accepted
Price range	Budget
Style	Casual
Cuisine	Caribbean Seafood
Recommended for	Wish I'd opened

"It's a stand on the beach, right where the fish come off the dock. You have the best time eating local fish, with your feet in the sand."—Jasper Schneider

YACHT CLUB

Recommended by
Jasper Schneider

The Reef by Cuisinart
Merrywing Bay AI-2640, Anguilla
+1 8008620673
www.thereefbycuisinart.com

Opening hours	Open 7 days
Credit cards	Accepted
Price range	Affordable
Style	Smart casual
Cuisine	Seafood
Recommended for	Breakfast

"The dulce de leche French toast with roasted banana for my daughter, and the chilaquiles for me."—Jasper Schneider

CHEF'S TABLE DINING EXPERIENCE

Recommended by
Jasper Schneider

CuisinArt Resort and Spa
Rendezvous Bay AI-2640, Anguilla
www.cuisinartresort.com

Opening hours	Closed Thursday to Tuesday
Credit cards	Accepted
Price range	Expensive
Style	Smart casual
Cuisine	International
Recommended for	High end

"It's a weekly chef's table on a Wednesday night in a private room, where the chef cooks every course right in front of you, with wines included."—Jasper Schneider

TOKYO BAY

Recommended by
Jasper Schneider

CuisinArt Resort and Spa
Rendezvous Bay AI-2640, Anguilla
+1 2644982000
www.cuisinartresort.com

Opening hours	Open 7 days
Credit cards	Accepted
Price range	Expensive
Style	Smart casual
Cuisine	Japanese
Recommended for	Late night

VALLEY BBQ STAND

Recommended by
Jasper Schneider

The Valley Road
South Hill AI-2640, Anguilla

Opening hours	Closed Wednesday
Reservation policy	No
Credit cards	Not accepted
Price range	Budget
Style	Casual
Cuisine	Caribbean
Recommended for	Bargain

PICANTE

Recommended by
Jasper Schneider

West End Village AI-2640, Anguilla
+1 2644981616
www.picante-restaurant-anguilla.com

Opening hours	Closed Tuesday
Credit cards	Accepted but not AMEX or Diners
Price range	Affordable
Style	Casual
Cuisine	Mexican
Recommended for	Regular neighborhood

"Each time you go, Chef Theron has a new homemade hot sauce. The 'T's Hot', his signature sauce, is great with chicken enchiladas."—Jasper Schneider

E'S OVEN

Recommended by
Jasper Schneider

West End Village
South Hill AI-2640, Anguilla
+1 2644988258

Opening hours	Closed Tuesday
Reservation policy	No
Credit cards	Accepted but not AMEX or Diners
Price range	Affordable
Style	Casual
Cuisine	Caribbean
Recommended for	Local favorite

"They are personable, and the food is cooked from the heart with a lot of soul in it. Great Caribbean flavors."—Jasper Schneider

THE FLYING FISHBONE

Savaneta 344
Savaneta, Aruba
+1 2975842506
www.flyingfishbone.com

Opening hours	Open 7 days
Credit cards	Accepted
Price range	Affordable
Style	Casual
Cuisine	Caribbean-European
Recommended for	Late night

THE CLIFF

Derricks
St James BB24110, Barbados
+1 2464321922
www.thecliffbarbados.com

Opening hours	Open 7 days
Credit cards	Accepted
Price range	Expensive
Style	Smart casual
Cuisine	French-Asian
Recommended for	Wish I'd opened

"The name says it all—this restaurant is all about its location and the absolutely stunning views. There's very few restaurants in the world benefitting from a location like this. You can't take a trip to Barbados without going to this restaurant."—Shaun Rankin

LA ESPAÑA

AO-23 Centro Comercial Villamar
Marginal Ave Baldorioty de Castro
Isla Verde
Carolina 979, Puerto Rico
+1 7877274517
www.laespana.net

Opening hours	Open 7 days
Credit cards	Accepted but not Diners
Price range	Budget
Style	Casual
Cuisine	Bakery
Recommended for	Breakfast

"La España is the epitome of how an old school bakery should be: bustling, loud, hectic in a good way—the kind of place where everyone knows each other. They

serve fantastic coffee and espresso, fresh baked bread and delicious pastries, soups, and sandwiches. It's close to the airport, too—whenever I'm traveling I call ahead and pick up pastries to eat on the plane and make the rest of the passengers jealous!"
—Jose Enrique Montes

ORUJO TALLER DE GASTRONOMÍA

80 Calle Gautier Benítez
Caguas 00725, Puerto Rico
+1 7875080038

Opening hours	Closed Monday
Credit cards	Accepted
Price range	Affordable
Style	Casual
Cuisine	Modern Puerto Rican
Recommended for	Late night

"Creative menu with an inspired choice of ingredients, and an interesting wine list."—Raúl Correa

LA ESTACIÓN

Las Croabas
Fajardo 00738, Puerto Rico
+1 7878634481
www.laestacionpr.com

Opening hours	Closed Tuesday and Wednesday
Credit cards	Accepted but not AMEX
Price range	Affordable
Style	Casual
Cuisine	Barbecue
Recommended for	Regular neighborhood

"The best barbecue on the island with the freshest ingredients."—Raúl Correa

EL PESCADOR

Recommended by
Jose Enrique Montes

Carr 9987 Km 7
Parque Pasivo Las Croabas
Fajardo738, Puerto Rico
South America
+1 787-972-1501

Opening hours	Open 7 days
Credit cards	Accepted
Price range	Affordable
Style	Casual
Cuisine	Seafood
Recommended for	Local favorite

"You can't beat the atmosphere here. El Pescador is right in the middle of the market, so you can sit outside amidst all the people walking through, eat your meal, have a drink, listen to music and really feel the neighbourhood. Plus the seafood is always super fresh and beautifully prepared."
—Jose Enrique Montes

AVOCADO

Recommended by
Raúl Correa

B3 Urbanización 4
Avenida San Patricio
Guaynabo 00968, Puerto Rico
+1 9392044532

Opening hours	Open 7 days
Credit cards	Accepted
Price range	Affordable
Style	Casual
Cuisine	Caribbean
Recommended for	Late night

LA ROSA INGLESA

Recommended by
Raúl Correa

Carrera Interior 413
Rincón 00677, Puerto Rico
+1 7878234032
www.rinconpuertoricobedandbreakfast.com

Opening hours	Variable
Credit cards	Accepted
Price range	Affordable
Style	Casual
Cuisine	International
Recommended for	Breakfast

VOLANDO BAJITO

Recommended by
Jose Enrique Montes

Calle Ismael Rivera 101
Santurce
San Juan 911, Puerto Rico
+1 939-338-0182

Opening hours	Closed Tuesday and Wednesday
Credit cards	Accepted but not AMEX or Diners
Price range	Budget
Style	Casual
Cuisine	Korean-Vegetarian
Recommended for	Regular neighborhood

"Super casual with a great vibe, it's an easy place to just walk in and enjoy a few sets of wings and a nice cold beer."—Jose Enrique Montes

1919 RESTAURANT

Recommended by
Raúl Correa

Condado Vanderbilt Hotel
1055 Ashford Avenue
San Juan 00907, Puerto Rico
+1 7877241919
www.1919restaurant.com

Opening hours	Closed Monday and Sunday
Credit cards	Accepted
Price range	Affordable
Style	Smart casual
Cuisine	Modern American
Recommended for	High end

"The combination of flavors and techniques as regards vegetables and shellfish are simple but use contemporary techniques. Nasha Fondeur is the best pastry chef in Puerto Rico."—Raúl Correa

ASERE CUBANO

Recommended by
Raúl Correa

180 Calle Dos Hermanos
San Juan 00907, Puerto Rico
+1 7879463804
www.aserecubano.com

Opening hours	Closed Monday
Credit cards	Accepted
Price range	Affordable
Style	Casual
Cuisine	Caribbean
Recommended for	Regular neighborhood

BODEGAS COMPOSTELA

Recommended by
Jose Enrique Montes

106 Calle Condado
Condado
San Juan 907, Puerto Rico
+1 7877246099

Opening hours	Closed Sunday
Credit cards	Accepted
Price range	Affordable
Style	Smart casual
Cuisine	Spanish
Recommended for	Wish I'd opened

"It's the ideal combination of relaxed ambiance, great service, thoughtful and delicious Spanish food, and amazing wines. It's just a fantastic restaurant all around. I eat here once a week!"
— Jose Enrique Montes

EL AXOLOTE

Recommended by
Jose Enrique Montes

Calle Cerra 622
Miramar
San Juan 907, Puerto Rico
+1 7877246296

Opening hours	Open 7 days
Credit cards	Accepted
Price range	Affordable
Style	Casual
Cuisine	Mexican
Recommended for	Bargain

"El Axolote is a cozy little spot in a more bohemian part of San Juan—close to where all the street art is. It's got a great ambiance and some of the best Mexican food in the city. I love their palomas, and always order their pozole- it's hearty, spicy, and a perfect hangover cure!"—Jose Enrique Montes

BISTRO CAFÉ

Recommended by
Raúl Correa

29 Calle Júpiter Avenida Isla Verde
Avenida Isla Verde
San Juan 00913, Puerto Rico
+1 7876035757

Opening hours	Open 7 days
Reservation policy	No
Credit cards	Accepted
Price range	Affordable
Style	Casual
Cuisine	Café
Recommended for	Breakfast

"An informal place with good breakfasts and sandwiches, and fantastic coffee."—Raúl Correa

EL HAMBURGER

Recommended by
Raúl Correa

402 Avenue Muñoz Rivera
San Juan 00901, Puerto Rico
+1 7877214269

Opening hours	Open 7 days
Reservation policy	No
Credit cards	Not accepted
Price range	Affordable
Style	Casual
Cuisine	Burgers
Recommended for	Wish I'd opened

EN BOGA

Recommended by
Raúl Correa

308 Avenida de Diego
San Juan 00920, Puerto Rico
+1 7879672244

Opening hours	Closed Monday and Sunday
Credit cards	Accepted
Price range	Affordable
Style	Casual
Cuisine	Latin American
Recommended for	Local favorite

LA JAQUITA BAYA

Recommended by
Raúl Correa

801 Avenida Fernández Juncos
San Juan 00927, Puerto Rico
+1 7879935359

Opening hours	Closed Sunday
Credit cards	Accepted
Price range	Affordable
Style	Casual
Cuisine	Puerto Rican
Recommended for	Local favorite

"The food in Jaquita pays homage to Puerto Rican cooking, and Xavier, the chef, always finds the best produce from local farmers."—Raúl Correa

JOSÉ ENRIQUE

176 Calle Duffaut
San Juan 00907, Puerto Rico
+1 7877253518
www.joseenriquepr.com

Opening hours	Closed Monday and Sunday
Reservation policy	No
Credit cards	Accepted
Price range	Affordable
Style	Casual
Cuisine	Puerto Rican
Recommended for	Wish I'd opened

"It's so much fun! And it totally resonates with me."
—Paul Carmichael

LA ALCAPURRIA QUEMÁ

251 Calle Duffaut
San Juan 00907, Puerto Rico
+1 9392046350

Opening hours	Closed Monday
Credit cards	Accepted but not AMEX
Price range	Affordable
Style	Casual
Cuisine	Latin American
Recommended for	Bargain

NEW TASTE

1051 Ashford Avenue
Condado
San Juan 907, Puerto Rico
+1 7877218111

Opening hours	Open 7 days
Credit cards	Accepted but not AMEX or Diners
Price range	Affordable
Style	Casual
Cuisine	Sushi-Asian
Recommended for	Late night

"I love this place for late night food because it's open until 1a.m., but the food is truly incredible any time of day. They have two menus, one with mostly sushi and a second that's primarily in Chinese, and the latter has an awesome selection of authentic cuisine. They always have a beautiful selection of fresh seafood, too, like blue crab and uni."—Jose Enrique Montes

PIKAYO

999 Ashford Avenue
San Juan 00907, Puerto Rico
+1 7877216194

Opening hours	Open 7 days
Credit cards	Accepted
Price range	Expensive
Style	Smart casual
Cuisine	International
Recommended for	High end

"Founded in 1980, it's the best example of the evolution of Puerto Rican cuisine. Consistently good."
—Raúl Correa

THE BREAKFAST SHED

Audrey Jeffers Highway
Port of Spain, Trinidad and Tobago

Opening hours	Open 7 days
Reservation policy	No
Credit cards	Not accepted
Price range	Budget
Style	Casual
Cuisine	Creole
Recommended for	Breakfast

"For the fish broth or the fried fish and bake."
—Khalid Mohammed

ME ASIA

48 Ariapita Avenue
Port of Spain, Trinidad and Tobago
+1 8686286888

Opening hours	Open 7 days
Credit cards	Accepted
Price range	Affordable
Style	Casual
Cuisine	Chinese
Recommended for	Late night

"Try their noodle soup."—Khalid Mohammed

WINGS RESTAURANT & BAR

16 Mohammed Terrace
Tunapuna, Trinidad and Tobago
+1 8686456607

Opening hours	Closed Sunday
Credit cards	Not accepted
Price range	Budget
Style	Casual
Cuisine	Indian
Recommended for	Local favorite

"A rum-shop-turned-restaurant that does the best curries. It throws the idea of location, location, location out the window."—Khalid Mohammed

ZOZO'S RISTORANTE

Recommended by
David Benjamin

Sugar Mill
Caneel Bay Resort
St John 00831, US Virgin Islands
+1 3406939200
www.zozos.net

Opening hours	Open 7 days
Credit cards	Accepted but not AMEX
Price range	Expensive
Style	Smart casual
Cuisine	Italian
Recommended for	High end

BAD ASS COFFEE

Recommended by
David Benjamin

5330 Yacht Haven Grande
Charlotte Amalie
St Thomas 00802, US Virgin Islands
+1 3403442744
www.badasscoffee.com

Opening hours	Open 7 days
Reservation policy	No
Credit cards	Accepted
Price range	Budget
Style	Casual
Cuisine	Café
Recommended for	Breakfast

BETSY'S BAR

Recommended by
David Benjamin

Honduras
Charlotte Amalie
St Thomas 00803, US Virgin Islands
+1 3407749347
www.betsysbar.com

Opening hours	Open 7 days
Credit cards	Accepted but not AMEX
Price range	Affordable
Style	Casual
Cuisine	American-Caribbean
Recommended for	Late night

CUZZIN'S

Recommended by
David Benjamin

7 Wimmelskafts Gade
Charlotte Amalie
St Thomas 00802, US Virgin Islands
+1 3407774711
www.cuzzinsvi.com

Opening hours	Closed Sunday
Credit cards	Accepted
Price range	Affordable
Style	Casual
Cuisine	Caribbean
Recommended for	Local favorite

GREENGO'S CARIBBEAN CANTINA

Recommended by
David Benjamin

34–35 Dronningens Gade
Frenchtown
St Thomas 00801, US Virgin Islands
+1 3407148282
www.greengoscantina.com

Opening hours	Open 7 days
Reservation policy	No
Credit cards	Accepted but not AMEX
Price range	Affordable
Style	Casual
Cuisine	Mexican
Recommended for	Bargain

HOOK LINE & SINKER

62 Honduras
Frenchtown
St Thomas 00803, US Virgin Islands
+1 3407769708
www.hooklineandsinkervi.com

Opening hours	Open 7 days
Credit cards	Accepted
Price range	Affordable
Style	Casual
Cuisine	European
Recommended for	Breakfast

PIE WHOLE

24a Honduras
Frenchtown
St Thomas 00802, US Virgin Islands
+1 3406425074
www.piewholepizza.com

Opening hours	Closed Sunday
Credit cards	Accepted but not AMEX
Price range	Affordable
Style	Casual
Cuisine	Italian
Recommended for	Wish I'd opened

THIRTEEN

13a Estate Dorothea
Northside
St Thomas 00802, US Virgin Islands
+1 3407746800

Opening hours	Closed Monday and Sunday
Credit cards	Accepted
Price range	Affordable
Style	Casual
Cuisine	Modern International
Recommended for	Regular neighborhood

EL REDIL

1196 Colinas Riverside
El Sauzal
Baja California 22760, Mexico
+52 6461747456

Opening hours	Open 7 days
Reservation policy	No
Credit cards	Not accepted
Price range	Budget
Style	Casual
Cuisine	Regional Mexican
Recommended for	Breakfast

"It's a place that offers home cooking—eggs, *chilaquiles* (corn tortillas in tomato and chile sauce), enchiladas and the best tripe with chiltepin chile peppers in the city. They prepare juices from different seasonal fruits and make a northern-style barbecue of *borrego tatemado* (shredded wood-roasted lamb)—delicious!"—Diego Hernández Baquedano

ZOZO'S RISTORANTE

Sugar Mill
Caneel Bay Resort
St John 00831, US Virgin Islands
+1 3406939200
www.zozos.net

Opening hours	Open 7 days
Credit cards	Accepted but not AMEX
Price range	Expensive
Style	Smart casual
Cuisine	Italian
Recommended for	High end

BOULES

Moctezuma 623
Ensenada
Baja California 22800, Mexico
+52 6461758769

Opening hours	Closed Monday and Sunday
Credit cards	Accepted but not AMEX
Price range	Affordable
Style	Casual
Cuisine	Seafood
Recommended for	Local favorite

CORAZÓN DE TIERRA

Recommended by
Edgar Nuñez, Elena Reygadas

Rancho San Marcos
Ensenada
Baja California 22750, Mexico
+52 6461568030
www.corazondetierra.com

Opening hours	Closed Tuesday
Credit cards	Accepted
Price range	Affordable
Style	Smart casual
Cuisine	Mexican
Recommended for	Wish I'd opened

"For the farm-to-table philosophy, the views, and the vineyard."—Elena Reygadas

LA GUERRERENSE

Recommended by
Ted Hopson

Lopez Mateos (Calle 1ra) y Alvarado
Ensenada
Baja California 22785, Mexico
+52 6461740006
www.laguerrerense.com

Opening hours	Closed Monday
Credit cards	Accepted
Price range	Budget
Style	Casual
Cuisine	Mexican
Recommended for	Worth the travel

"I ate here while on a culinary trip to Ensenada and it seriously blew me away, it was so good. The flavors were spectacular, the salsas were interesting. All of it was just perfect. I wasn't expecting to have one of the best meals of the year, but it happened."—Ted Hopson

MANZANILLA

Recommended by
Diego Hernández
Baquedano, Anita Lo

Avenida Teniente José Azueta 139
Ensenada
Baja California 22800, Mexico
+52 6461757073
www.rmanzanilla.com

Opening hours	Closed Monday and Tuesday
Credit cards	Accepted
Price range	Affordable
Style	Casual
Cuisine	Mexican Seafood
Recommended for	Local favorite

"I have a very close connection to Manzanilla, I became a chef because of Manzanilla. Its cuisine is local, simple, yet complex. I think that there's no

better seafood restaurant in Mexico, and there's no better chef for fish and shellfish than Benito Molina."—Diego Hernández Baquedano

MARISCOS EL GÜERO

Recommended by
Diego Hernández Baquedano

Boulevard Lázaro Cárdenas
Ensenada
Baja California 22870, Mexico
+52 6461510008

Opening hours	Open 7 days
Reservation policy	No
Credit cards	Not accepted
Price range	Budget
Style	Casual
Cuisine	Mexican
Recommended for	Breakfast

MARISCOS EL PIZÓN

Recommended by
Diego Hernández Baquedano

Avenida Dr Pedro Loyola
Guayamas
Ensenada
Baja California 22890, Mexico
+52 6461487961

Opening hours	Closed Wednesday
Reservation policy	No
Credit cards	Not Accepted
Price range	Budget
Style	Casual
Cuisine	Mexican
Recommended for	Regular neighborhood

"Mariscos el Pizón is Alan Pasiano's street stall, which has the freshest sea urchins you'll ever eat. Alan was a sea-urchin diver in Ensenada and his work took him to the Tsukiji Market in Japan. He's an expert on sea urchins and now prepares traditional dishes from the fishing port in the street."
—Diego Hernández Baquedano

MARISCOS LOS PRIMOS

Avenida Riveroll 462
Ensenada
Baja California 22800, Mexico
+52 6461781741

Opening hours	Closed Monday
Credit cards	Not accepted
Price range	Affordable
Style	Casual
Cuisine	Mexican
Recommended for	Bargain

"Mariscos Los Primos is a popular favorite in the center of Ensenada. It specialises in shellfish and has some outstanding dishes, like the clams tatemadas and smoked marlin pâté. These two dishes, accompanied by a clamato with beer, will make your evening."
—Diego Hernández Baquedano

WENDLANDT BREWPUB

Boulevard Costero 248
Ensenada
Baja California 22870, Mexico
+52 6461782938
www.wendlandt.com.mx

Opening hours	Closed Monday and Sunday
Credit cards	Accepted
Price range	Affordable
Style	Casual
Cuisine	Bar-Bistro
Recommended for	Late night

"It's a beer bar where the chef makes impeccable food with regional ingredients, designed specifically to be eaten with beer. The cuisine fits into its own category: it's dynamic regional bar food which likes to take risks. I love it."—Diego Hernández Baquedano

LOS TRES GARCÍA

Calle 3a Oriente 304
Delicias
Chihuahua 33010, Mexico
+52 6391532932

Opening hours	Open 7 days
Reservation policy	No
Credit cards	Not accepted
Price range	Budget
Style	Casual
Cuisine	Bar
Recommended for	Regular neighborhood

(UNNAMED RESTAURANT)

Luis Moya 31, next door to Bósforo
Mexico City
Federal District 06000, Mexico

Opening hours	Closed Monday and Sunday
Reservation policy	No
Credit cards	Accepted
Price range	Affordable
Style	Casual
Cuisine	Mexican
Recommended for	Worth the travel

"It has no name but is producing modern Mexican cuisine that surpasses most other highly regarded restaurants in the city. Moody and slightly macabre."
—Duncan Welgemoed

ALELI

Calle Sinaloa 141
Mexico City
Federal District 06700, Mexico
+52 5521244590

Opening hours	Closed Monday and Sunday
Reservation policy	No
Credit cards	Accepted
Price range	Affordable
Style	Casual
Cuisine	Modern Mexican
Recommended for	Breakfast

"It's a charming little place recently opened by Mexican chef Oswaldo Oliva. The food is consistently impeccable, sourced from local purveyors, and fun to eat. Great for breakfast and lunch!"—Jair Téllez

AMAYA

General Prim 95
Mexico City
Federal District 06600, Mexico
+52 5555925571
www.amayamexico.com

Opening hours	Open 7 days
Credit cards	Accepted
Price range	Affordable
Style	Casual
Cuisine	Mexican
Recommended for	Regular neighborhood

ARDENTE

Recommended by
Edgar Nuñez

Boulevard de la Luz 777
Mexico City
Federal District 01900, Mexico
+52 5573123228
www.ardente.com.mx

Opening hours	Open 7 days
Credit cards	Accepted
Price range	Budget
Style	Casual
Cuisine	Pizza
Recommended for	Bargain

"The best Neapolitan pizza place in Mexico."
—Edgar Nuñez

EL BAJÍO

Recommended by
Jair Téllez

Avenida Cuitláhuac 2709
Mexico City
Federal District 02840, Mexico
+52 5552343763
www.restauranteelbajio.com.mx

Opening hours	Open 7 days
Credit cards	Accepted
Price range	Affordable
Style	Casual
Cuisine	Mexican
Recommended for	Breakfast

BIKO

Recommended by
Edgar Nuñez, Jair Téllez

Presidente Masaryk 407
Mexico City
Federal District 11550, Mexico
+52 5552822064
www.biko.com.mx

Opening hours	Closed Sunday
Credit cards	Accepted
Price range	Expensive
Style	Smart casual
Cuisine	Spanish
Recommended for	High end

"I love the Basque-inspired Mexican cuisine here.
Also the most moving combination of charismatic
service and flawless technique."—Jair Téllez

BÓSFORO

Recommended by
Joaquín Cardoso, Jair Téllez

Luis Moya 31
Mexico City
Federal District 06000, Mexico
+52 5555121991

Opening hours	Closed Monday and Sunday
Reservation policy	No
Credit cards	Accepted
Price range	Affordable
Style	Casual
Cuisine	Mexican
Recommended for	Local favorite

"Lovely non-traditional yet extremely authentic
Mexican contemporary food. A very small but solid
menu; freshly made blue corn tortillas, local beers,
natural wine, and perhaps the best eclectic and
grassroots mezcal offering in the city."—Jair Téllez

CASA MERLOS

Recommended by
Martha Ortiz

Calle Victoriano Zepeda 80
Mexico City
Federal District 11860, Mexico
+52 5552774360
www.casamerlos.com

Opening hours	Closed Monday to Wednesday
Credit cards	Not accepted
Price range	Expensive
Style	Smart casual
Cuisine	Mexican
Recommended for	Regular neighborhood

"A traditional Mexican restaurant."—Martha Ortiz

LA DOCENA

Recommended by
Joaquín Cardoso,
Valdimir Mukhin,
Jair Téllez

Avenida Álvaro Obregón 31
Mexico City
Federal District 06700, Mexico
+52 5552080833
www.ladocena.com.mx

Opening hours	Open 7 days
Credit cards	Accepted
Price range	Affordable
Style	Casual
Cuisine	Seafood
Recommended for	Regular neighborhood

"A super energetic and charismatic Mexican
oyster brasserie-grill. Great shellfish and jabugo
cut to order."—Jair Téllez

ENRIQUE

Recommended by
Edgar Nuñez

Avenida Insurgentes Sur 4061
Mexico City
Federal District 14000, Mexico
+52 5555739988

Opening hours	Open 7 days
Credit cards	Accepted
Price range	Affordable
Style	Casual
Cuisine	Mexican
Recommended for	Breakfast

FONDA MARGARITA

Recommended by
Joaquín Cardoso, Jesse Griffiths,
Elena Reygadas

Adolfo Prieto 1364b
Mexico City
Federal District 03100, Mexico
+52 5555596358
www.fondamargarita.com

Opening hours	Closed Monday
Reservation policy	No
Credit cards	Accepted
Price range	Affordable
Style	Casual
Cuisine	Mexican
Recommended for	Breakfast

"Don't miss the *frijol con huevo* (beans with eggs)—
it's a classic."—Joaquín Cardoso

HIYOKO YAKITORI-YA

Recommended by
Jair Tellez, Jorge Vallejo

Río Pánuco 132
Mexico City
Federal District 06500, Mexico
+52 5552070386
www.edokobayashi.com

Opening hours	Closed Sunday
Credit cards	Accepted
Price range	Affordable
Style	Smart casual
Cuisine	Yakitori
Recommended for	Late night

"Great yakitori, natural wines, Mexican sake, and
a secret-ish entrance. Not much more I could ask for."
—Jair Téllez

HOTEL CARLOTA

Recommended by
Jair Téllez

Rio Amazonas 73
Mexico City
Federal District 06500, Mexico
+52 5568439006
www.hotelcarlota.com.mx

Opening hours	Open 7 days
Credit cards	Accepted
Price range	Affordable
Style	Casual
Cuisine	Mexican-French
Recommended for	Local favorite

EL JAMIL

Recommended by
Jair Téllez

Avenida Amsterdam 306
Mexico City
Federal District 06100, Mexico
+52 5550358032
www.eljamil.mx

Opening hours	Open 7 days
Credit cards	Accepted
Price range	Affordable
Style	Casual
Cuisine	Lebanese
Recommended for	Regular neighborhood

KAYE

Recommended by
Jair Téllez

Alfonso Reyes 108
Mexico City
Federal District 06170, Mexico
+52 5570451722
www.kaye.mx

Opening hours	Open 7 days
Credit cards	Accepted but not AMEX
Price range	Affordable
Style	Casual
Cuisine	Modern Mexican
Recommended for	Local favorite

LALO!

Recommended by
Jesse Griffiths

Calle Zacatecas 173
Mexico City
Federal District 06700, Mexico
+52 5555643388
www.eat-lalo.com

Opening hours	Closed Monday
Reservation policy	No
Credit cards	Accepted
Price range	Affordable
Style	Casual
Cuisine	Mexican-International
Recommended for	Breakfast

LARDO

Recommended by
Enrique Olvera, Jair Téllez

Agustín Melgar 6
Mexico City
Federal District 06140, Mexico
+52 5552117731
www.lardo.mx

Opening hours	Open 7 days
Credit cards	Accepted
Price range	Affordable
Style	Casual
Cuisine	Mexican
Recommended for	Breakfast

"Best bread in the city, by chef Elena Reygadas."
—Enrique Olvera

MÁXIMO BISTROT

Recommended by
Val Cantu,
Joaquín Cardoso,
Elena Reygadas,
Jair Téllez

Calle Tonalá 133
Mexico City
Federal District 06700, Mexico
+52 5552644291
www.maximobistrot.com.mx

Opening hours	Closed Monday and Sunday
Credit cards	Accepted
Price range	Affordable
Style	Casual
Cuisine	Modern Mexican
Recommended for	Wish I'd opened

"Mexican bistronomy by the great Lalo García that has
changed the whole neighborhood."—Joaquín Cardoso

MAZURKA

Recommended by
Edgar Nuñez

Calle Nueva York 150
Mexico City
Federal District 03810, Mexico
+52 5555238811
www.mazurka.com.mx

Opening hours	Open 7 days
Credit cards	Accepted
Price range	Affordable
Style	Formal
Cuisine	Polish
Recommended for	Wish I'd opened

MIA DOMENICCA

Recommended by
Jair Téllez

Calle de Durango 279
Mexico City
Federal District 06700, Mexico
+52 5591308456
www.miadomenicca.mx

Opening hours	Closed Monday
Credit cards	Accepted
Price range	Affordable
Style	Casual
Cuisine	Mediterranean
Recommended for	Regular neighborhood

NICOS

Recommended by
Joaquín Cardoso,
Guillermo González Beristáin,
Elena Reygadas,
Jorge Vallejo

Avenida Cuitláhuac 3102
Mexico City
Federal District 02080, Mexico
+52 5553966510
www.nicosmexico.mx

Opening hours	Closed Sunday
Credit cards	Accepted
Price range	Affordable
Style	Smart casual
Cuisine	Mexican
Recommended for	Local favorite

"One of my favorite restaurants in the country; great
quality, the best produce, and perfect technique.
It's been open for almost seventy years."
—Guillermo González Beristáin

PANADERÍA PANCRACIA

Recommended by
Elena Reygadas

Calle de Chihuahua 181
Mexico City
Federal District 06700, Mexico

Opening hours	Closed Monday and Wednesday–Friday
Credit cards	Not accepted
Price range	Budget
Style	Casual
Cuisine	Bakery
Recommended for	Breakfast

PANADERÍA ROSETTA

Recommended by
Joaquín Cardoso

Calle Havre 73
Mexico City
Federal District 06600, Mexico
+52 5552072976
www.rosetta.com.mx

Opening hours	Open 7 days
Credit cards	Accepted but not AMEX
Price range	Affordable
Style	Casual
Cuisine	Bakery
Recommended for	Breakfast

"A cosy place with great bread."—Joaquín Cardoso

PARAMO

Recommended by
Elena Reygadas

Avenida Yucatán 84
Mexico City
Federal District 06700, Mexico
+52 5534742613

Opening hours	Open 7 days
Credit cards	Accepted
Price range	Affordable
Style	Casual
Cuisine	Mexican
Recommended for	Late night

"They have great music and homely Mexican food.
It's become a meeting point for lots of different people
from around the neighborhood."—Elena Reygadas

PUJOL

Recommended by
Massimo Bottura, Estanislao Carenzo,
Val Cantu, Doug Flicker, Claus Meyer,
Alexandra Raij, Elena Reygadas,
Jordi Roca, Jair Téllez

Calle Tennyson 133
Mexico City
Federal District 11550, Mexico
+52 5555454111
www.pujol.com.mx

Opening hours	Closed Sunday
Credit cards	Accepted
Price range	Expensive
Style	Smart casual
Cuisine	Mexican
Recommended for	Worth the travel

"I found so many things in this place: old and new
techniques, marvellous people, and a very special
way to flow. It's Mexico today, not an archaic idea
or a future promise. Things happening naturally now."
—Estanislao Carenzo

EL PUNTAL DEL NORTE

Recommended by
Edgar Nuñez

Calle Cerrada Palomas 22
Mexico City
Federal District 11650, Mexico
+52 5552023489
www.elpuntaldelnorte.com

Opening hours	Open 7 days
Credit cards	Accepted but not Diners
Price range	Affordable
Style	Casual
Cuisine	Basque
Recommended for	Regular neighborhood

QUINTONIL

Recommended by
Dan Barber, Val Cantu,
Joaquín Cardoso, Juan Gaffuri,
Edgar Nuñez, Elena Reygadas,
Tim Spedding, Hiro Sone,
Jair Téllez

Newton 55
Mexico City
Federal District 11560, Mexico
+52 5552801660
www.quintonil.com

Opening hours	Closed Sunday
Credit cards	Accepted
Price range	Expensive
Style	Smart casual
Cuisine	Modern Mexican
Recommended for	High end

"It refines Mexican cuisine in a way that doesn't
dampen its appeal or excitement but merely
concentrates the experience. Indomitable hosts."
—Tim Spedding

OAXACA EN MEXICO

Recommended by
Elena Reygadas

Luis Moya 59
Mexico City
Federal District 06000, Mexico
+52 5555180787

Opening hours	Open 7 days
Credit cards	Not accepted
Price range	Budget
Style	Casual
Cuisine	Oaxacan
Recommended for	Regular neighborhood

"For their amazing variety of mezcals and their usage of heirloom corn in many of their dishes. The humble and rural flavors of the food take me away from the crowded city."—Elena Reygadas

ROKAI

Recommended by
Joaquín Cardoso, Enrique Olvera

Río Ebro 87
Mexico City
Federal District 06500, Mexico
+52 5571595808
www.edokobayashi.com/rokai

Opening hours	Open 7 days
Credit cards	Accepted
Price range	Affordable
Style	Casual
Cuisine	Japanese
Recommended for	Regular neighborhood

EL SELLA

Recommended by
Jair Téllez

Doctor Balmis 210
Mexico City
Federal District 06720, Mexico
+52 5557612727

Opening hours	Closed Sunday
Credit cards	Accepted
Price range	Affordable
Style	Casual
Cuisine	Mexican
Recommended for	Local favorite

SUD 777

Recommended by
Josean Alija

Boulevard de la Luz 777
Mexico City
Federal District 01900, Mexico
+52 5555684777
www.sud777.com.mx

Opening hours	Open 7 days
Credit cards	Accepted
Price range	Affordable
Style	Smart casual
Cuisine	Modern Mexican
Recommended for	Worth the travel

SUSHI KYO

Recommended by
Gabriela Cámara, Edgar Nuñez

Havre 77
Mexico City
Federal District 06600, Mexico
+52 5555118027
www.edokobayashi.com

Opening hours	Closed Sunday
Credit cards	Accepted
Price range	Affordable
Style	Smart casual
Cuisine	Japanese
Recommended for	Worth the travel

"This is a very new restaurant in Mexico City, and what I found outstanding is the quality and world-class feel. It speaks about how seriously sophisticated the city has become in terms of gastronomy. It's a really cool Japanese sushi bar. I love it."—Gabriela Cámara

LE TACHINOMI DESU

Recommended by
Joaquín Cardoso, Elena Reygadas

Río Pánuco 132B
Mexico City
Federal District 06500, Mexico
+52 5552070386
www.edokobayashi.com

Opening hours	Closed Sunday
Credit cards	Accepted
Price range	Affordable
Style	Casual
Cuisine	Bar
Recommended for	Late night

TACOS NENA
Recommended by
Elena Reygadas

Mérida 218
Mexico City
Federal District 06700, Mexico
+52 5527015960

Opening hours	Closed Sunday
Credit cards	Not accepted
Price range	Affordable
Style	Casual
Cuisine	Tacos
Recommended for	Bargain

"The menu only has three items and they use wood-fire to cook the food."—Elena Reygadas

TAQUERIA EL PROGRESO
Recommended by
Jair Téllez

Calle Maestro Antonio Caso 30
Mexico City
Federal District 06030, Mexico
+52 5555928964

Opening hours	Closed Sunday
Reservation policy	No
Credit cards	Not accepted
Price range	Affordable
Style	Casual
Cuisine	Tacos
Recommended for	Bargain

"A very traditional taquería with a taco maker that is attentive, fast, and has dark humor. Tacos are served the way they should be—folded, small, and greasy. I suggest the brain, tongue, or cheek tacos. Or ask for the ones made with intestine cooked on the plancha."
—Jair Téllez

TAQUERIA NARVARTE
Recommended by
Joaquín Cardoso

La Morena 1104
Mexico City
Federal District 03023, Mexico
+52 5551559257

Opening hours	Closed Sunday
Credit cards	Not accepted
Price range	Affordable
Style	Casual
Cuisine	Tacos
Recommended for	Bargain

"The smoked marlin taco and shrimp aguachile are great for a hangover."—Joaquín Cardoso

RANCHO SECO
Recommended by
Nieves Barragán Mohacho

Calle Vicente Guerrero
Malinalco
Ixtapan 52440, Mexico
+52 7224743247

Opening hours	Variable
Credit cards	Not accepted
Price range	Affordable
Style	Casual
Cuisine	Mexican
Recommended for	Worth the travel

ALCALDE
Recommended by
Elena Reygadas

Avenida México 2903
Guadalajara
Jalisco 44690, Mexico
+52 3336157400
www.alcalde.com.mx

Opening hours	Open 7 days
Credit cards	Accepted but not AMEX
Price range	Affordable
Style	Casual
Cuisine	French
Recommended for	High end

BIRRIERIA DON DAVID
Recommended by
Francisco Ruano

Calle Ignacio Herrera y Cairo
Guadalajara
Jalisco 44270, Mexico

Opening hours	Variable
Reservation policy	No
Credit cards	Not accepted
Price range	Affordable
Style	Casual
Cuisine	Mexican
Recommended for	Breakfast

CAFE CALIGARY
Recommended by
Francisco Ruano

Juan Manuel 1406
Guadalajara
Jalisco 44600, Mexico
+52 3315231382

Opening hours	Closed Tuesday
Credit cards	Accepted but not AMEX
Price range	Budget
Style	Casual
Cuisine	Café
Recommended for	Breakfast

CARNES ASADAS LA CHUZA

Calle Fernando de Celada 2856
Guadalajara
Jalisco 44130, Mexico
+52 3336165630
www.lachuzacarnesasadas.blogspot.co.uk

Opening hours	Open 7 days
Reservation policy	No
Credit cards	Accepted
Price range	Affordable
Style	Casual
Cuisine	Mexican
Recommended for	Late night

LA DOCENA

São Paulo 1491
Guadalajara
Jalisco 44640, Mexico
+52 3338172798
www.ladocena.com.mx

Opening hours	Open 7 days
Credit cards	Accepted
Price range	Affordable
Style	Casual
Cuisine	Seafood
Recommended for	Local favorite

"Some of the best produce around prepared elegantly on the grill. Great ambience. It's ideal to go with a large group and uncork a few bottles."
—Francisco Ruano

HUESO

Efraín González Luna 2061
Guadalajara
Jalisco 44150, Mexico
+52 3336157915
www.huesorestaurant.com

Opening hours	Closed Monday
Credit cards	Accepted
Price range	Affordable
Style	Casual
Cuisine	Mexican
Recommended for	High end

MAGNO BRASSERIE

Jose Guadalupe Zuno 2061
Guadalajara
Jalisco 44160, Mexico
+52 3320010724
www.magnobrasserie.com

Opening hours	Closed Monday
Credit cards	Accepted
Price range	Affordable
Style	Smart casual
Cuisine	French-Italian
Recommended for	High end

MERCADO DE ABASTOS

Calzada Lázaro Cárdenas 2305
Guadalajara
Jalisco 44530, Mexico

Opening hours	Open 7 days
Reservation policy	No
Credit cards	Not accepted
Price range	Budget
Style	Casual
Cuisine	Mexican-Market
Recommended for	Local favorite

"This is not a restaurant, it's the central market of the city. Walk around the food area and you'll find all the variety and richness of traditional 'tapatio' food."
—Francisco Ruano

PALREAL

Calle Lope de Vega 113
Guadalajara
Jalisco 44130, Mexico
+52 3319837254

Opening hours	Closed Monday
Credit cards	Accepted
Price range	Affordable
Style	Casual
Cuisine	Modern Mexican
Recommended for	Breakfast

"Super tasty Mexican-style breakfast, with the best baristas in town behind the bar."—Francisco Ruano

LA PANGA DEL IMPOSTOR

Recommended by
Francisco Ruano

Calle Miguel Lerdo de Tejada 2189
Guadalajara
Jalisco 44160, Mexico
+52 3338262000
www.lapangaimpostor.com

Opening hours	Open 7 days
Reservation policy	No
Credit cards	Accepted but not AMEX
Price range	Affordable
Style	Casual
Cuisine	Seafood
Recommended for	Regular neighborhood

TAQUERIA MÉXICO

Recommended by
Francisco Ruano

Avenida Mexico 2081
Guadalajara
Jalisco 44600, Mexico
+52 3336155068

Opening hours	Closed Monday
Credit cards	Not accepted
Price range	Budget
Style	Casual
Cuisine	Tacos
Recommended for	Bargain

"Some of the best tacos in town, cheap, and super tasty."—Francisco Ruano

TORTAS AHOGADAS ENRIQUE EL VIEJO

Camarena 90
Guadelajara
Jalisco 44160, Mexico
+52 3338266709

Recommended by
Francisco Ruano

Opening hours	Open 7 days
Reservation policy	No
Credit cards	Not accepted
Price range	Affordable
Style	Casual
Cuisine	Mexican
Recommended for	Local favorite

"Try the *torta ahogada* with liver, heart, and chicharron."—Francisco Ruano

TRIPITAS DON RAMON

Recommended by
Francisco Ruano

Calle Chiapas 1538
Guadalajara
Jalisco 44260, Mexico

Opening hours	Open 7 days
Reservation policy	No
Credit cards	Not accepted
Price range	Budget
Style	Casual
Cuisine	Tacos
Recommended for	Late night

"Deep fried, crunchy cow tripe served with a tomato and oregano sauce, raw onions, and lime. It's a true jewel, and it's open till 1.00 a.m."—Francisco Ruano

JUNIKO

Recommended by
Francisco Ruano

Paseo Andares
Zapopan
Jalisco 45116, Mexico
+52 3336114445
www.juniko.mx

Opening hours	Open 7 days
Credit cards	Accepted
Price range	Affordable
Style	Smart casual
Cuisine	Japanese
Recommended for	High end

"High-quality produce with a modern approach. Take the *omakase* (chef's choice menu)."
—Francisco Ruano

ORSON

Recommended by
Guillermo González Beristáin

Av Lázaro Cárdenas 2400
San Pedro Garza García
Nuevo León 66278, Mexico
+52 8113067178
www.orson.mx

Opening hours	Open 7 days
Credit cards	Accepted
Price range	Affordable
Style	Casual
Cuisine	Burgers
Recommended for	Wish I'd opened

"Best burgers in town, period."
—Guillermo González Beristáin

SEÑOR LATINO

Recommended by
Guillermo González Beristáin

Rio Mississippi 105-C
San Pedro Garza García
Nuevo León 66220, Mexico
+52 8119371020

Opening hours	Open 7 days
Credit cards	Accepted
Price range	Budget
Style	Casual
Cuisine	Northern Mexican
Recommended for	Breakfast

"Very casual, honest, and delicious food. Only open for breakfast and lunch."—Guillermo González Beristáin

SEÑOR TANAKA

Recommended by
Guillermo González Beristáin

Calzada San Pedro 102
San Pedro Garza García
Nuevo León 66220, Mexico
+52 8183352060
www.srtanaka.com

Opening hours	Open 7 days
Credit cards	Accepted
Price range	Affordable
Style	Smart casual
Cuisine	Japanese
Recommended for	Regular neighborhood

"Superb sushi, tiraditos, and sake. Great Japanese restaurant with latin influence. Truly a world class place."—Guillermo González Beristáin

TAIWAN DIM SUM

Recommended by
Guillermo González Beristáin

Avenue Simon Bolivar 1561-A
Monterrey
Nuevo León 64460, Mexico
+52 8183331088

Opening hours	Open 7 days
Credit cards	Accepted but not AMEX or Diners
Price range	Budget
Style	Casual
Cuisine	Taiwanese
Recommended for	Bargain

"Very traditional dim sum place that's always packed."—Guillermo González Beristáin

TAQUERIA ORINOCO

Recommended by
Guillermo González Beristáin

Río Orinoco 101 L.1
San Pedro Garza García
Nuevo León 66220, Mexico
+52 8119348011
www.taqueriaorinoco.com

Opening hours	Open 7 days
Credit cards	Accepted but not AMEX or Diners
Price range	Budget
Style	Casual
Cuisine	Mexican
Recommended for	Late night

"Great for late night tacos, especially the pastor tacos."—Guillermo González Beristáin

MILK PIZZERIA

Recommended by
Guillermo González Beristáin

Río Orinoco 211a
San Pedro Garza García
Nuevo León 66220, Mexico
+52 8113561010

Opening hours	Closed Monday
Credit cards	Accepted
Price range	Affordable
Style	Casual
Cuisine	Pizza
Recommended for	Local favorite

"Recently opened, it offers by far the best pizza in town with locally sourced ingredients, home-made cheese, and artisan pizza dough."
—Guillermo González Beristáin

ROMERO Y AZAHAR

Recommended by
Paul Foster

De la Industria 300
Punto Central Local 12 y 13
San Pedro Garza García
Nuevo León 66266, Mexico
+52 8183352090
www.romeroyazahar.com

Opening hours	Open 7 days
Credit cards	Accepted
Price range	Affordable
Style	Casual
Cuisine	Mexican
Recommended for	Worth the travel

"Stunning restaurant with fantastic atmosphere. Modern Mexican food that doesn't stray too far from the classics. It is literally the best Mexican food I have ever eaten."—Paul Foster

KOLI COCINA DE ORIGEN

Recommended by
Guillermo González Beristáin

Eje exterior 10-L1
Santa Catarina
Nuevo León 66197
Mexico
+52 8196887333
www.koli.mx

Opening hours	Closed Sunday to Wednesday
Credit cards	Accepted
Price range	Expensive
Style	Smart casual
Cuisine	Modern Mexican
Recommended for	High end

"Run by the Rivera brothers, who offer the most
creative cuisine in town."
—Guillermo González Beristáin

CRIOLLO

Recommended by
Joaquín Cardoso

Francesco I. Madero 129
Oaxaca
Oaxaca 68000
Mexico
+52 9513511908
www.criollo.mx

Opening hours	Closed Monday
Credit cards	Accepted
Price range	Affordable
Style	Casual
Cuisine	Oaxacan
Recommended for	Worth the travel

"Great cuisine. One of the best in the country."
—Joaquín Cardoso

CASA OAXACA

Recommended by
Joaquín Cardoso

Constitución 104a
Oaxaca
Oaxaca 68000
Mexico
+52 9515168531
www.casaoaxacaelrestaurante.com

Opening hours	Open 7 days
Credit cards	Accepted
Price range	Affordable
Style	Casual
Cuisine	Modern Oaxacan
Recommended for	Worth the travel

"Alex Ruiz changed the scene without losing its
essence, in one of the most traditionally rooted
cities in the country."—Joaquín Cardoso

HARTWOOD

Recommended by
Jorge Guzman, Nick Holloway,
Carlo Lamagna, Elena Reygadas,
Evan & Sarah Rich, Ollie Templeton,
Duncan Welgemoed

Carretera Tulum-Punta Allen
Tulum
Quintana Roo 77780
Mexico
www.hartwoodtulum.com

Opening hours	Closed Monday and Tuesday
Credit cards	Accepted
Price range	Expensive
Style	Casual
Cuisine	Mexican
Recommended for	Wish I'd opened

"You sit outside, drink mezcal, and eat food that
comes from a kitchen that uses no electricity, only
a wood-fired oven and grill. It's the most magical
dining experience."—Ollie Templeton

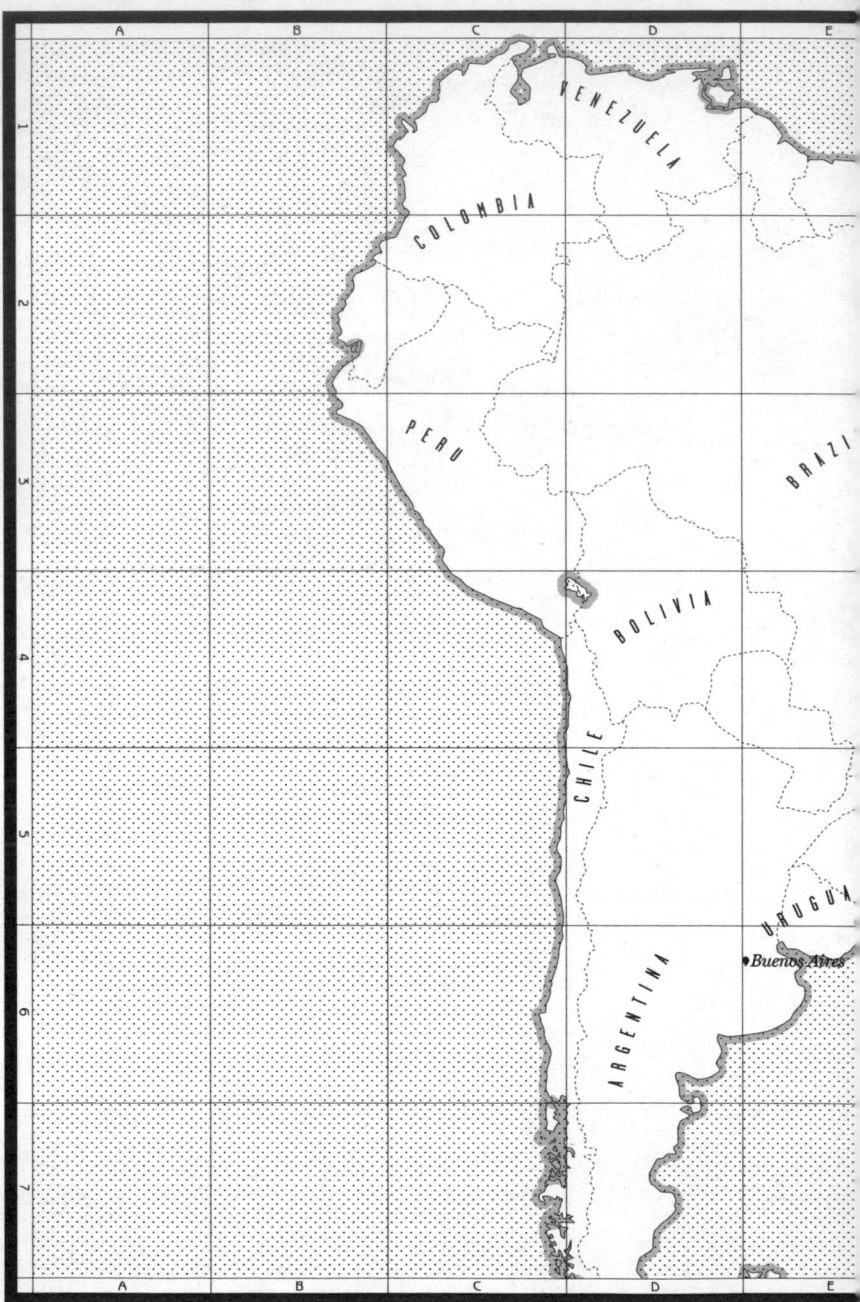

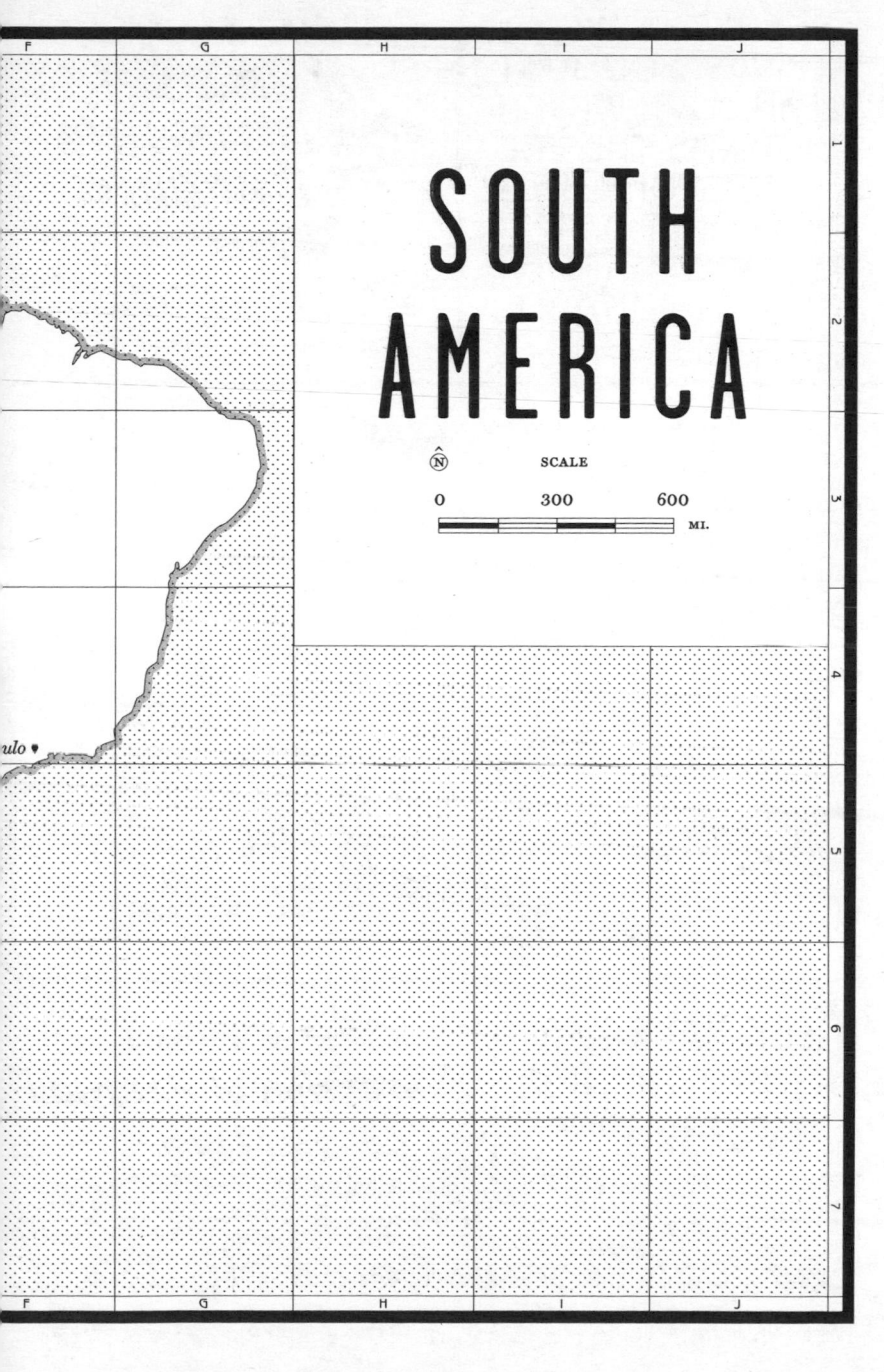

SOUTH
AMERICA

ulo ♥

"THERE IS NO HALFWAY, YOU JUST FALL IN LOVE WITH IT AND THAT'S THE END OF THE STORY. THE FRESHNESS OF ITS VEGETABLE GARDEN MAKES IT INIMITABLE."

EDUARDO MORENO P1094

"*Day menu made by the students of Escuela Taller de Bogotá.*"

ALEJANDRO GUTIÉRREZ P1096

SOUTH AMERICA NORTH

"THEY HAVE THE BEST ANTICUCHOS IN TOWN."

PEDRO MIGUEL SCHIAFFANO P1099

"*The greatest expression of Peruvian coastal cuisine.*"

MARTIN MORALES P1099

"*The food is pure Colombia. It's a place that makes you feel special.*"

JORGE RAUSCH P1096

SOUTH
AMERICA
NORTH

SCALE

0   225   450
MI.

Isla de Margarita p.1094
Caracas p.1094

VENEZUELA

Mesitas del Colégio p.1095
Bogotá p.1095

COLOMBIA

PERU

Lima p.1097

La Paz p.1101
Arequipa p.1097

BOLIVIA

AREPERA AMADANI

2DA Avenida de Montecristo
Caracas
Federal District 1071, Venezuela

Opening hours	Closed Sunday and Monday
Credit cards	Not accepted
Price range	Budget
Style	Casual
Cuisine	Arepas
Recommended for	Breakfast

JULIETA PIES

Palos Grandes Market
Caracas
Federal District, Venezuela

Opening hours	Variable
Credit cards	Not accepted
Price range	Budget
Style	Casual
Cuisine	Pies and Tarts
Recommended for	Bargain

"The best soursop pie I've ever tasted."
—Eduardo Moreno

LA CASA BISTRO

3ra Avenida con 4ta Transversal
Los Palos Grandes
Caracas
Federal District 1060, Venezuela
+58 2122853103
www.lacasabistro.com.ve

Opening hours	Closed Saturday and Sunday
Credit cards	Accepted but not AMEX
Price range	Affordable
Style	Casual
Cuisine	Venezuelan
Recommended for	Breakfast

"Completely authentic and wholesome. There is
no halfway, you just fall in love with it and that's
the end of the story. The freshness of its vegetable
garden makes it inimitable."—Eduardo Moreno

LE GOURMET

International Tamanaco Hotel
Calle Herrera Toro
Caracas
Federal District 1061, Venezuela
+58 2129097220

Opening hours	Open 7 days
Credit cards	Accepted
Price range	Expensive
Style	Formal
Cuisine	International
Recommended for	Wish I'd opened

"This continues to be the only elegant restaurant
left in Caracas."—Eduardo Moreno

MORENO

Avenida Luis Roche
Altamira Village Shopping Center
Caracas
Federal District 1060, Venezuela
+58 2122611237
www.morenocaracas.com

Opening hours	Open 7 days
Credit cards	Accepted
Price range	Affordable
Style	Casual
Cuisine	Venezuelan
Recommended for	Regular neighborhood

"Simple but honest cuisine which reflects Mantuan
food from Caracas, as well as influences from other
countries."—Eduardo Moreno

GUILLERMINA RESTAURANT

Calle Unión 26
Casco Histórico de La Asunción
La Asunción
Isla de Margarita 6301, Venezuela
+ 58 2952423040

Opening hours	Open 7 days
Credit cards	Accepted but not AMEX
Price range	Affordable
Style	Casual
Cuisine	Venezuelan
Recommended for	Late night

"This restaurant, led by the chef Carlos García,
has its own personality and it's won me over."
—Eduardo Moreno

ABASTO

Recommended by
Alejandro Gutiérrez

Calle 69a, 9–09
Bogotá
Cundinamarca 111061, Colombia
+57 16750492
www.abasto.co

Opening hours	Open 7 days
Credit cards	Accepted
Price range	Affordable
Style	Casual
Cuisine	Colombian
Recommended for	Breakfast

"Traditional Colombian comfort food."
—Alejandro Gutiérrez

DOÑA ELVIRA

Recommended by
Alejandro Gutiérrez

Calle 50, 20–26/28
Bogotá
Cundinamarca 111311, Colombia
+57 12358275
www.restaurantedonaelvira.com

Opening hours	Closed Monday and Tuesday
Credit cards	Not accepted
Price range	Affordable
Style	Casual
Cuisine	Colombian
Recommended for	Local favorite

EL CIERVO Y EL OSO

Recommended by
Alejandro Gutiérrez

Carrera 10a, 69a–16
Bogotá
Cundinamarca 110231, Colombia
+57 3222669792

Opening hours	Open 7 days
Credit cards	Accepted
Price range	Affordable
Style	Casual
Cuisine	Modern Colombian
Recommended for	Wish I'd opened

"Delicious dishes made with traditional Colombian
techniques and ingredients."—Alejandro Gutiérrez

HARRY SASSON

Recommended by
Juan Gaffuri,
Jorge Rausch

Carrera 9, 75–70
Bogotá
Cundinamarca 110231, Colombia
+57 13477155
www.harrysasson.com

Opening hours	Open 7 days
Credit cards	Accepted
Price range	Affordable
Style	Smart casual
Cuisine	International
Recommended for	Regular neighborhood

"The food is consistently delicious and the ingredients
are unbeatable. The atmosphere is perfect and the
service is very special."—Jorge Rausch

LA BRASSERIE

Recommended by
Jorge Rausch

Carrera 13, 85–35
Bogotá
Cundinamarca 110221, Colombia
+57 12576402
www.labrasserierestaurante.com

Opening hours	Open 7 days
Credit cards	Accepted
Price range	Affordable
Style	Casual
Cuisine	French Brasserie
Recommended for	Wish I'd opened

"A very varied menu with distinctive flavors. The
setting is extremely pleasant."—Jorge Rausch

LEO

Recommended by
Alejandro Gutiérrez

Calle 27b, 6–75
Bogotá
Cundinamarca 110311, Colombia
+57 12838659
www.restauranteleo.com

Opening hours	Closed Sunday
Credit cards	Accepted
Price range	Affordable
Style	Smart casual
Cuisine	Modern Colombian
Recommended for	High end

"A high-end restaurant using unfamiliar Colombian
ingredients."—Alejandro Gutiérrez

MESA FRANCA

Recommended by
Alejandro Gutiérrez

Carrera 6, 55–09
Bogotá
Cundinamarca 110231, Colombia
+57 18051787

Opening hours	Closed Sunday
Credit cards	Accepted
Price range	Affordable
Style	Casual
Cuisine	Modern Colombian
Recommended for	Regular neighborhood

"Simple but delicious food. Great cocktails."
—Alejandro Gutiérrez

MISIA BY LEO ESPINOSA

Recommended by
Jorge Rausch

Transversal 6, 27–50
Bogotá
Cundinamarca 111411, Colombia
+57 17954748
www.restaurantemisia.com

Opening hours	Closed Monday
Credit cards	Accepted
Price range	Affordable
Style	Casual
Cuisine	Colombian
Recommended for	Bargain

"The food is pure Colombia. It's a place that makes
you feel special."—Jorge Rausch

MISTRAL

Recommended by
Alejandro Gutiérrez

Calle 57, 4–09
Bogotá
Cundinamarca 110231, Colombia
+57 16315371

Opening hours	Open 7 days
Credit cards	Accepted
Price range	Budget
Style	Casual
Cuisine	Bakery
Recommended for	Breakfast

"A simple French bakery."—Alejandro Gutiérrez

RESTAURANTE CLUB COLOMBIA

Recommended by
Jorge Rausch

Avenida 82, 9–11
Bogotá
Cundinamarca 110221, Colombia
+57 12495681
www.restauranteclubcolombia.com

Opening hours	Open 7 days
Credit cards	Accepted
Price range	Affordable
Style	Casual
Cuisine	Colombian
Recommended for	Breakfast

"The best thing about this place is its breakfasts,
because of their diversity. Club Colombia seems to me
to offer Colombian food in its pure state. The food is
fresh and the menu highlights the characteristics and
diversity of Colombian cooking."—Jorge Rausch

RESTAURANTE LA ESCUELA

Recommended by
Alejandro Gutiérrez

Calle 9, 8–61
Bogotá
Cundinamarca 111711, Colombia
+57 12890591
www.escuelataller.org

Opening hours	Closed Saturday and Sunday
Credit cards	Accepted
Price range	Affordable
Style	Casual
Cuisine	Colombian
Recommended for	Bargain

"Day menu made by the students of Escuela Taller
de Bogotá."—Alejandro Gutiérrez

SIR FRANK

Recommended by
Jorge Rausch

Calle 70a, 10–42
Bogotá
Cundinamarca 110221, Colombia
+57 13576486

Opening hours	Open 7 days
Credit cards	Accepted
Price range	Affordable
Style	Casual
Cuisine	Burgers
Recommended for	Late night

"As well as its excellent food, it has a good
atmosphere and good drinks."—Jorge Rausch

VERSIÓN ORIGINAL

Calle 70a, 5–67
Bogotá
Cundinamarca 110231, Colombia
+57 17446683
www.versionoriginal.co

Opening hours	Closed Sunday
Credit cards	Accepted
Price range	Affordable
Style	Casual
Cuisine	Spanish
Recommended for	High end

"This restaurant stands out due to its art, design, music, tradition, and gastronomy. In addition to this, it uses exclusively top-quality ingredients."
—Jorge Rausch

VILLANOS EN BERMUDAS

Calle 56, 5–21
Bogotá
Cundinamarca 110231, Colombia
+57 12111259
www.villanosenbermudas.com

Opening hours	Closed Sunday
Credit cards	Accepted
Price range	Affordable
Style	Casual
Cuisine	Modern Colombian
Recommended for	Regular neighborhood

"Great Tasting Menu."—Alejandro Gutiérrez

ANDRÉS CARNE DE RES

Calle 3, 11a–56
Chía
Cundinamarca 250001, Colombia
+57 18612233
www.andrescarnederes.com

Opening hours	Closed Monday to Wednesday
Credit cards	Not accepted
Price range	Affordable
Style	Casual
Cuisine	Colombian
Recommended for	Local favorite

"A unique restaurant on account of its fun atmosphere and the various theatrical techniques used to display Colombian culture. It's magnificent."—Jorge Rausch

MESTIZO COCINA DE ORIGEN

Carrera 8, 7–73
Mesitas del Colegio
Cundinamarca 252638, Colombia
+57 3227382051
www.mestizococinadeorigen.com

Opening hours	Closed Wednesday
Credit cards	Accepted
Price range	Affordable
Style	Casual
Cuisine	Modern Colombian
Recommended for	Worth the travel

"Great food made with local ingredients."
—Alejandro Gutiérrez

LA NUEVA PALOMINO

Leoncio Prado 122
Arequipa
Arequipa 54, Peru
+51 054252393

Opening hours	Closed Tuesday
Credit cards	Accepted
Price range	Affordable
Style	Casual
Cuisine	Peruvian
Recommended for	Worth the travel

CANTA RANA

Calle Genova 101
Barranco
Lima 15063, Peru
+51 12477274

Opening hours	Open 7 days
Credit cards	Accepted
Price range	Budget
Style	Casual
Cuisine	Seafood
Recommended for	Bargain

ISOLINA

Recommended by
Virgilio Martínez

Avenida San Martín 101
Barranco
Lima 15063, Peru
+51 12475075

Opening hours	Open 7 days
Credit cards	Accepted
Price range	Affordable
Style	Casual
Cuisine	Peruvian
Recommended for	Regular neighborhood

"It is an old-style Peruvian tavern, which has great significance since nowadays there are very few of them."—Virgilio Martínez

MÓ CAFÉ + BISTRÓ

Recommended by
James Berckemeyer,
Virgilio Martínez

Prolongación Avenida San Martín 131
Barranco
Lima 15063, Peru
+51 14895459
www.mocafebistro.com

Opening hours	Closed Monday
Credit cards	Accepted
Price range	Budget
Style	Casual
Cuisine	Bistro
Recommended for	Breakfast

"Super fresh, honest, totally local, a highly skilled chef."—Virgilio Martínez

OSSO CARNICERÍA Y SALUMERIA

Recommended by
Gastón Acurio,
Virgilio Martínez

Calle Tahiti 175
La Molina
Lima 15026, Peru
+51 13529915
www.osso.pe

Opening hours	Open 7 days
Credit cards	Accepted
Price range	Affordable
Style	Casual
Cuisine	Steakhouse
Recommended for	High end

"One of the best steakhouses."—Virgilio Martínez

LA PAISANA

Recommended by
Martin Morales

Jirón La Libertad 1412
Magdalena
Lima 15086, Peru
+51 999044788

Opening hours	Open 7 days
Reservation policy	No
Credit cards	Not accepted
Price range	Affordable
Style	Casual
Cuisine	Peruvian
Recommended for	Bargain

CENTRAL

Recommended by
Gastón Acurio, Josean Alija,
James Berckemeyer,
Massimo Bottura,
Richard Ekkebus, Juan
Gaffuri, Zaiyu Hasegawa,
Martin Morales, Robert Ortiz,
Jordi Roca, Ljubomir Stanisic

Calle Santa Isabel 376
Miraflores
Lima 15074, Peru
+51 12416721
www.centralrestaurante.com.pe

Opening hours	Closed Sunday
Credit cards	Accepted
Price range	Affordable
Style	Casual
Cuisine	Modern Peruvian
Recommended for	Worth the travel

"Central takes guests on a culinary expedition through Peru's ecosystem, from the Amazon to Pacific coast. My dear friend, chef Virgílio Martínez and his team forage in the jungle, desert, mountains, and sea to discover diverse local ingredients found at every altitude."—Richard Ekkebus

COSTANERA 700

Recommended by
Pedro Miguel Schiaffino

Avenida del Ejército 421
Miraflores
Lima 15074, Peru
+51 14217508
www.costanera700.pe

Opening hours	Open 7 days
Credit cards	Accepted
Price range	Affordable
Style	Casual
Cuisine	Japanese-Peruvian
Recommended for	Regular neighborhood

"It's a classic Nikkei family restaurant, where you'll find the best seafood in town."
—Pedro Miguel Schiaffino

EL MERCADO

Recommended by
Martin Morales

Avenida Hipólito Unanue 203
Miraflores
Lima 15074, Peru
+51 12211322
www.rafaelosterling.pe

Opening hours	Closed Monday
Credit cards	Accepted
Price range	Affordable
Style	Casual
Cuisine	Seafood
Recommended for	Wish I'd opened

"The freshest seafood and greatest expression of Peruvian coastal cuisine. It never fails—I have been there twenty times in the last four years and every time it gets better and better."—Martin Morales

EL PAN DE LA CHOLA

Recommended by
James Berckemeyer,
Pedro Miguel Schiaffino

Avenida Mariscal La Mar 918
Miraflores
Lima 15074, Peru
+51 12212138

Opening hours	Open 7 days
Credit cards	Accepted
Price range	Budget
Style	Casual
Cuisine	Café-Bakery
Recommended for	Breakfast

"They sell freshly baked bread made of organic grains and natural ferments. They also offer sandwiches, fruit juices, and great coffee."—Pedro Miguel Schiaffino

GRIMANESA VARGA ANTICUCHOS

Recommended by
James Berckemeyer,
Pedro Miguel Schiaffino

Avenida Ignacio Merino 465
Miraflores
Lima 15074, Peru
+51 14421468
www.grimanesavargasanticuchos.com

Opening hours	Closed Sunday
Reservation policy	No
Credit cards	Accepted but not AMEX or Diners
Price range	Budget
Style	Casual
Cuisine	Street Food
Recommended for	Bargain

"They have the best *anticuchos* in town."
—Pedro Miguel Schiaffano

1099

LA LUCHA

Recommended by
James Berckemeyer

Avenida Santa Cruz 847
Miraflores
Lima 15074, Peru
www.lalucha.com.pe

Opening hours	Open 7 days
Reservation policy	No
Credit cards	Not accepted
Price range	Budget
Style	Casual
Cuisine	Peruvian Sandwiches
Recommended for	Late night

"Peruvian sandwiches, filled with good produce, and you can eat them during the day as well as late at night!"—James Berckemeyer

LA MAR

Recommended by
Josean Alija,
Virgilio Martínez,
Blaine Wetzal

Avenida La Mar 770
Miraflores
Lima 15074, Peru
+51 14213365
www.lamarcebicheria.com

Opening hours	Open 7 days
Reservation policy	No
Credit cards	Accepted
Price range	Affordable
Style	Casual
Cuisine	Seafood
Recommended for	Local favorite

"I like it because satisfaction is guaranteed. It creates an unpretentious atmosphere in a high-quality setting. It is a very social concept of luxury, with excellent cooking."—Josean Alija

LA TRANQUERA

Recommended by
James Berckemeyer

Avenida José Pardo 285
Miraflores
Lima 15074, Peru
+51 14475111
www.restaurantelatranquera.com

Opening hours	Open 7 days
Credit cards	Accepted
Price range	Affordable
Style	Casual
Cuisine	Barbecue
Recommended for	Late night

"Good meat!"—James Berckemeyer

MADAM TUSAN

Avenida Santa Cruz 859
Miraflores
Lima 15074, Peru
+51 15055090
www.madamtusan.pe

Opening hours	Open 7 days
Credit cards	Accepted
Price range	Affordable
Style	Casual
Cuisine	Chinese-Peruvian
Recommended for	Regular neighborhood

"Chinese restaurant with a Peruvian fusion. Typical
Chinese dishes with a big touch of Peruvian
ingredients."—James Berckemeyer

MAIDO

Calle San Martín 399
Miraflores
Lima 15074, Peru
+51 14462512
www.maido.pe

Opening hours	Open 7 days
Credit cards	Accepted
Price range	Affordable
Style	Smart casual
Cuisine	Japanese-Peruvian
Recommended for	Worth the travel

"Its fusion of flavors and presentation provide
an unforgettable gastronomic experience."
—Jorge Rausch

The long and noble tradition of Japanese-Peruvian
fusion cuisine, known as Nikkei, has a fine
ambassador in the form of Maido, in the beautiful
Miraflores neighborhood of Lima. Using techniques
learned during his time in Japan as well as in the
Amazon jungle, chef Mitsuharu Tsumura presents
a multi-course tasting menu of the finest Peruvian
ingredients, from the high Andes to the Pacific
Ocean, meticulously sourced and immaculately
presented. It's fine dining, certainly, but not to any
bland, international haute-cuisine template. This is
fusion cooking that could exist nowhere else in the
world, and it's distinctively Nikkei.

MAYTA

Avenida 28 de Julio 1290
Miraflores
Lima 15074, Peru
+51 12430121
www.maytarestaurante.com

Opening hours	Open 7 days
Credit cards	Accepted
Price range	Affordable
Style	Smart casual
Cuisine	Modern Peruvian
Recommended for	Late night

"It has all the flavors of Peru, but in a modern
environment."—Virgilio Martínez

RAFAEL

Calle San Martín 300
Miraflores
Lima 15074, Peru
+51 12424149
www.rafaelosterling.pe

Opening hours	Closed Monday
Credit cards	Accepted
Price range	Affordable
Style	Casual
Cuisine	Peruvian
Recommended for	Worth the travel

ANTIGUA TABERNA QUEIROLO

Avenida San Martín 1090
Pueblo Libre
Lima 15084, Peru
+51 14600441
www.antiguatabernaqueirolo.com

Opening hours	Open 7 days
Credit cards	Accepted
Price range	Affordable
Style	Casual
Cuisine	Peruvian
Recommended for	Late night

"It's a great place to drink good chilcanos and eat
Peruvian comfort food."—Pedro Miguel Schiaffino

1087 BISTRO

Recommended by
Martin Morales

Avenida Los Conquistadores 1087
San Isidro
Lima 15073, Peru
+51 977741746
www.bistro.1087.pe

Opening hours	Closed Sunday
Credit cards	Accepted
Price range	Affordable
Style	Casual
Cuisine	Modern Peruvian
Recommended for	Worth the travel

"Palmer Ocampo's food has tradition but also tons of creativity and is bursting with flavor."—Martin Morales

ASTRID & GASTÓN

Recommended by
James Berckemeyer,
Virgilio Martínez,
Joan Roca

Avenida Paz Soldán 290
San Isidro
Lima 15073, Peru
+51 14422777
www.astridygaston.com

Opening hours	Open 7 days
Credit cards	Accepted
Price range	Affordable
Style	Smart casual
Cuisine	Modern Peruvian
Recommended for	High end

After twenty years at his Miraflores HQ, during which Gastón Acurio established an empire and helped to elevate Peruvian cuisine to haute status, his landmark restaurant relocated to a San Isidro hacienda in 2014. The vast complex has a dining hall, private salons, a sixty-seat gastrobar and gardens dedicated to "experimental" growing. Far from being glitzy, the space leaves diners to focus on the food, including two tasting menus which voyage across the sea, desert, Andes, and Altiplano.

COSME

Recommended by
Virgilio Martínez

Tudela y Varela 160–162
San Isidro
Lima 15073, Peru
+51 14215228
www.cosme.com.pe

Opening hours	Open 7 days
Credit cards	Accepted
Price range	Affordable
Style	Casual
Cuisine	Peruvian
Recommended for	Local favorite

TANTA

Recommended by
Virgilio Martínez

Calle Pancho Fierro 115
San Isidro
Lima 15073, Peru
+51 14219708
www.tantaperu.com

Opening hours	Open 7 days
Credit cards	Accepted
Price range	Affordable
Style	Casual
Cuisine	Peruvian
Recommended for	Breakfast

LA PICANTERÍA

Recommended by
Gastón Acurio,
Virgilio Martínez,
Martin Morales,
Pedro Miguel Schiaffino

Calle Francisco Moreno 388
Surquillo
Lima 15047, Peru
+51 12416676
www.picanteriasdelperu.com

Opening hours	Closed Monday
Reservation policy	No
Credit cards	Accepted
Price range	Affordable
Style	Casual
Cuisine	Peruvian
Recommended for	Bargain

"A great atmosphere and great food, with a unique concept."—Pedro Miguel Schiaffino

GUSTU

Recommended by
Sang Hoon Degeimbre

Calle 10
300 Casi Costanera
Calacoto
La Paz, Bolivia
+59 122117491
www.gustubo.restaurantgustu.com

Opening hours	Closed Sunday
Credit cards	Accepted
Price range	Affordable
Style	Casual
Cuisine	Bolivian
Recommended for	Worth the travel

SOUTH AMERICA SOUTH

B R A Z I L

Pernambuco p.1105

Bahia p.1104

Minas Gerais p.1104

Rio de Janeiro p.1106

São Paulo pp.1110–1121

Paraná p.1104

CHILE

Santiago p.1132

Santa Fe p.1121

URUGUAY

Moldonado p.1119

Montevideo p.1120

Buenos Aires pp.1122–1134

ARGENTINA

Patagonia p.1120

SOUTH
AMERICA
SOUTH

N̂

SCALE

0   350   700
                              mi.

CASA DE TEREZA

Recommended by
César Santos

Rua Odilon Santos 45
Salvador
Bahia 41940-350, Brazil
+55 7133293016
www.casadetereza.com.br

Opening hours	Open 7 days
Credit cards	Accepted
Price range	Affordable
Style	Casual
Cuisine	Modern Brazilian
Recommended for	Worth the travel

"Wonderful food and excellent service."
—César Santos

VIRADAS DO LARGO

Recommended by
Bel Coelho

Rua do Moinho 11
Tiradentes
Minas Gerais 36325-000, Brazil
+55 3233551111

Opening hours	Closed Tuesday
Credit cards	Not accepted
Price range	Affordable
Style	Casual
Cuisine	Brazilian
Recommended for	Worth the travel

"Chef Beth Beltrão's food is authentic and extremely flavorsome."—Bel Coelho

BAR PALÁCIO

Recommended by
Manoella Buffara Ramos

Rua André de Barros 500
Curitiba
Paraná 80010-080, Brazil
+55 4132223626

Opening hours	Closed Sunday
Credit cards	Accepted
Price range	Affordable
Style	Casual
Cuisine	Steakhouse
Recommended for	Late night

"Typical late-night barbecue! Meat, farofa, salsa, and potato. I love this place."—Manoella Buffara Ramos

QUINTANA

Recommended by
Manoella Buffara Ramos

Avenida do Batel 1440
Curitiba
Paraná 80420-090, Brazil
+55 4130786044
www.quintanacafe.com.br

Opening hours	Open 7 days
Credit cards	Accepted but not AMEX or Diners
Price range	Affordable
Style	Casual
Cuisine	International
Recommended for	Regular neighborhood

"It's casual, organic food, and a good place to have lunch."—Manoella Buffara Ramos

RAUSE CAFÉ + VINHO

Recommended by
Manoella Buffara
Ramos

Alameda Doutor Carlos de Carvalho 696
Curitiba
Paraná 80430-180, Brazil
+55 4130240696
www.rausecafe.com.br

Opening hours	Closed Sunday
Credit cards	Accepted
Price range	Budget
Style	Casual
Cuisine	Café-Bar
Recommended for	Breakfast

"Homemade cakes including a really good banana cake. Their coffee blend is really good!"
—Manoella Buffara Ramos

GIRASSOL

Recommended by
Manoella Buffara Ramos

BR-277 Jd Farajala Bacila
Palmeira
Paraná 84130-000, Brazil
+55 4232521778
www.rgirassol.com.br

Opening hours	Open 7 days
Credit cards	Accepted
Price range	Affordable
Style	Casual
Cuisine	Brazilian
Recommended for	Local favorite

DIPLOMATA DELICATESSEN

Avenida Herculano Bandeira 187
Recife
Pernambuco 51110-130, Brazil
+55 8130343998
www.diplomatadelicatessen.com.br

Opening hours	Open 7 days
Credit cards	Accepted
Price range	Budget
Style	Casual
Cuisine	Bakery
Recommended for	Breakfast

GERALDO

Rua da Piedade 107
Recife
Pernambuco 54330-310, Brazil
+55 8132314177
www.restaurantedogeraldo.com.br

Opening hours	Closed Sunday
Credit cards	Accepted
Price range	Affordable
Style	Casual
Cuisine	Brazilian
Recommended for	Bargain

"You can eat the best omelette, *sarapatel* (local dish using variety meats [pork offal]), chicken giblets, and other things, all at a very reasonable price."
—César Santos

ILHA DA KOSTA II

Rua Maria Carolina 80
Recife
Pernambuco 51020-220, Brazil
+55 8134662122

Opening hours	Open 7 days
Credit cards	Accepted
Price range	Affordable
Style	Casual
Cuisine	Brazilian
Recommended for	Late night

"A restaurant with good service and traditional food."—César Santos

MINGUS

Rua do Atlântico 102
Recife
Pernambuco 51011-220, Brazil
+55 8134654000
www.mingus.com.br

Opening hours	Open 7 days
Credit cards	Accepted
Price range	Affordable
Style	Smart casual
Cuisine	International
Recommended for	High end

"Good service and food."—César Santos

PARRAXAXÁ

Avenida Fernando Simões Barbosa 1200
Recife
Pernambuco 51021-060, Brazil
+55 8134637874
www.parraxaxa.com.br

Opening hours	Open 7 days
Reservation policy	No
Credit cards	Accepted
Price range	Budget
Style	Casual
Cuisine	Brazilian
Recommended for	Local favorite

"The fullest breakfast in Brazil, with cassava, tapioca, couscous, jerk meat, *munguza* (a kind of maize porridge), and roll cake—everything a Pernambucan likes."—César Santos

PONTE NOVA

Rua do Cupim 172
Recife
Pernambuco 52011-070, Brazil
+55 8133277226
www.restaurantepontenova.com.br

Opening hours	Closed Monday
Credit cards	Accepted
Price range	Affordable
Style	Smart casual
Cuisine	International
Recommended for	Regular neighborhood

"A cosy restaurant with original food."—César Santos

QUINA DO FUTURO

Rua Xavier Marques 134
Recife
Pernambuco 52050-230, Brazil
+55 8132419589
www.quinadofuturo.com.br

Opening hours	Closed Sunday
Credit cards	Accepted
Price range	Affordable
Style	Casual
Cuisine	Japanese
Recommended for	Local favorite

"One of the best restaurants for Japanese cuisine in Brazil."—César Santos

RESTAURANTE LEITE

Praça Joaquim Nabuco 147
Recife
Pernambuco 50010-480, Brazil
+55 8132247482

Opening hours	Closed Saturday
Credit cards	Accepted
Price range	Expensive
Style	Smart casual
Cuisine	Portuguese
Recommended for	Regular neighborhood

"Its cuisine displays a Portuguese influence—good service and the best food, quite apart from being the oldest restaurant in Brazil, at 133 years of age!"
—César Santos

WIELLA BISTRÔ

Avenida Engenheiro Domingos Ferreira 1274
Recife
Pernambuco 51011-051, Brazil
+55 8134633108
www.wiellabistro.com.br

Opening hours	Open 7 days
Credit cards	Accepted
Price range	Affordable
Style	Smart casual
Cuisine	Bistro
Recommended for	High end

"A sophisticated restaurant with good service and fabulous food. There is no expensive food and yet it's all good food!"—César Santos

ALVORADA

Estrada Bernardo Coutinho 1655
Araras
Rio de Janeiro 25725-022, Brazil
+55 24 2225 1118
www.restaurantealvorada.com.br

Opening hours	Closed Monday to Thursday
Credit cards	Accepted but not AMEX or Diners
Price range	Expensive
Style	Casual
Cuisine	Brazilian
Recommended for	Worth the travel

"One of the ten best restaurants in Brazil. Delicious food made in a wood-fired oven, with relaxed service."—César Santos

ACONCHEGO CARIOCA

Rua Barão de Iguatemi 379
Rio de Janeiro 20270-060, Brazil
+55 2122731035

Opening hours	Closed Monday
Credit cards	Accepted
Price range	Affordable
Style	Casual
Cuisine	Brazilian
Recommended for	Local favorite

"The best example of typical finger food from Rio."
—Thomas Troisgros

AZUMI

Rua Ministro Viveiros de Castro 127
Rio de Janeiro 22020-050, Brazil
+55 2125414294

Opening hours	Open 7 days
Credit cards	Accepted
Price range	Affordable
Style	Casual
Cuisine	Japanese
Recommended for	Regular neighborhood

"Go for the hot plates, the udon, soba, mioga tempura, eggplant (aubergine), and miso. And always ask the owner if there is a family special—often she brings something from home to serve at the restaurant."
—Rafa Costa e Silva

BRASEIRO DA GÁVEA

Recommended by
Roberta Sudbrack

Praça Santos Dumont 116
Rio de Janeiro 22470-060, Brazil
+55 2122397494
www.braseirodagavea.com.br

Opening hours	Open 7 days
Credit cards	Accepted
Price range	Affordable
Style	Casual
Cuisine	Steakhouse
Recommended for	Local favorite

"A simple environment that's always full and lively."
—Roberta Sudbrack

CERVANTES

Recommended by
Roberta Sudbrack

Avenida Prado Júnior 335
Rio de Janeiro 22011-001, Brazil
+55 2122756147
www.restaurantecervantes.com.br

Opening hours	Closed Monday
Credit cards	Accepted
Price range	Budget
Style	Casual
Cuisine	Bar
Recommended for	Late night

COMUNA

Recommended by
Rafa Costa e Silva

Rua Sorocaba 585
Rio de Janeiro 22271-110, Brazil
+55 2122250362
www.comuna.cc

Opening hours	Closed Monday
Reservation policy	No
Credit cards	Accepted
Price range	Budget
Style	Casual
Cuisine	Sandwiches
Recommended for	Late night

DA ROBERTA

Recommended by
Thomas Troisgros

Rua Tubira 8
Rio de Janeiro 22441-070, Brazil
+55 2122391103

Opening hours	Closed Monday
Credit cards	Accepted
Price range	Affordable
Style	Casual
Cuisine	Street Food
Recommended for	Regular neighborhood

"The best sandwiches and homemade hot dogs."
—Thomas Troisgros

EMPORIO JARDIM

Recommended by
Thomas Troisgros

Rua Visconde da Graça 51
Rio de Janeiro 22461-010, Brazil
+55 2125359862
www.emporiojardimrio.com.br

Opening hours	Open 7 days
Credit cards	Accepted
Price range	Budget
Style	Casual
Cuisine	Café-Bistro-Deli
Recommended for	Breakfast

"Offers a typical Brazilian breakfast with tapiocas and juices."—Thomas Troisgros

ESCONDIDINHO

Recommended by
Rafa Costa e Silva

Beco dos Barbeiros 12
Rio de Janeiro 20011-010, Brazil
+55 2122422234

Opening hours	Closed Saturday and Sunday
Credit cards	Accepted
Price range	Affordable
Style	Casual
Cuisine	Brazilian
Recommended for	Bargain

"Really cheap and tasty. Great beef ribs with watercress and yuca. The daily specials are also good. Ice-cold beer and *cachaça*."—Rafa Costa e Silva

FASANO AL MARE

Recommended by
Roberta Sudbrack

Avenida Vieira Souto 80
Rio de Janeiro 22420-000, Brazil
+55 2132024000
www.fasano.com.br

Opening hours	Open 7 days
Credit cards	Accepted
Price range	Affordable
Style	Smart casual
Cuisine	Italian
Recommended for	High end

"The best classic Italian cuisine."—Roberta Sudbrack

GALETO SAT'S

Recommended by
Rafa Costa e Silva,
Thomas Troisgros

Rua Barata Ribeiro 7 - Loja D
Rio de Janeiro 22011-001, Brazil
+55 2122756197

Opening hours	Open 7 days
Credit cards	Accepted
Price range	Affordable
Style	Casual
Cuisine	Barbecue
Recommended for	Late night

"The best barbecued chicken and chicken hearts."
—Thomas Troisgros

GEPETTO

Recommended by
Roberta Sudbrack

Estrada dos Bandeirantes 23417
Rio de Janeiro 22785-091, Brazil
+55 2124281100
www.restaurantegepetto.com.br

Opening hours	Closed Monday to Wednesday
Credit cards	Not accepted
Price range	Affordable
Style	Casual
Cuisine	Brazilian
Recommended for	Bargain

"Go for the picanha steak cooked in a skillet and the best fries on the planet!"—Roberta Sudbrack

HOCUS POCUS DNA

Recommended by
Thomas Troisgros

Rua Dezenove de Fevereiro 186
Rio de Janeiro 22280-030, Brazil
+55 2134523377
www.hocuspocusdna.com

Opening hours	Closed Sunday
Reservation policy	No
Credit cards	Accepted
Price range	Budget
Style	Casual
Cuisine	Small Plates
Recommended for	Wish I'd opened

JOBI

Recommended by
Thomas Troisgros

Avenida Ataulfo de Paiva 1166 B
Rio de Janeiro 22440-035, Brazil
+55 2122740547

Opening hours	Open 7 days
Reservation policy	No
Credit cards	Accepted
Price range	Budget
Style	Casual
Cuisine	Brazilian
Recommended for	Bargain

This one often stays open until the last customer leaves—easily passing 4.00 a.m.—making it ideal for chefs clocking off. The green-painted walls, red chequered tablecloths, and framed pictures lend this fifty-one-year-old venue an easy-going lack of pretentiousness, and big TV screens help to draw the crowds when the football is on. Jobi is most famous for its chopp, a super-chilled draught lager that is enormously refreshing in the Brazilian heat, while its proximity to the beach represents another way to cool off. Bar snacks include empanadas and sandwiches. Many say the best tables are on the upstairs balcony, which offers great opportunities for people-watching.

LASAI

Recommended by
Thomas Troisgros

Rua Conde de Irajá 191
Rio de Janeiro 22271-020, Brazil
+55 2122271020
www.lasai.com.br

Opening hours	Closed Monday and Sunday
Credit cards	Accepted
Price range	Affordable
Style	Casual
Cuisine	Brazilian
Recommended for	High end

"Farm-to-table, great use of ingredients, amazing technique."—Thomas Troisgros

OLYMPE

Rua Custódio Serrão 62
Rio de Janeiro 22470-230, Brazil
+55 2125378582
www.olympe.com.br

Opening hours	Open 7 days
Credit cards	Accepted
Price range	Expensive
Style	Smart casual
Cuisine	French
Recommended for	Worth the travel

"The domain of the Troisgros family in Rio de Janeiro. Classic French cuisine with modern touches."
—Roberta Sudbrack

The Troisgros family are culinary superstars both in their native France and here in Rio, where they have operated from this tranquil, red-brick villa since the 1980s. Despite the unashamedly high-end cuisine, the atmosphere is warm and inviting, and the restaurant as popular with visiting tourists as it is with local celebrities. All are more than happy to splash out on the traditional French tasting menu of things such as carpaccio with white truffle oil, foie gras sautée, and *fillet au poivre* (steak with pepper sauce)—or the more left-field Brazilian fusion menu that contains the likes of ravioli filled with baroa potato puree. Service and the wine list are also suitably impressive.

ORO

Rua General San Martin 889
Rio de Janeiro 22441-015, Brazil
+55 2125408768
www.ororestaurante.com.br

Opening hours	Closed Monday
Credit cards	Accepted
Price range	Expensive
Style	Smart casual
Cuisine	Modern Brazilian
Recommended for	High end

"A new concept and really good food."
—Rafa Costa e Silva

ROBERTA SUDBRACK

Rua Lineu de Paula Machado 916
Rio de Janeiro 22470-040, Brazil
+55 2138740139
www.robertasudbrack.com.br

Opening hours	Closed Monday, Wednesday, and Friday
Credit cards	Accepted
Price range	Expensive
Style	Smart casual
Cuisine	Modern Brazilian
Recommended for	Wish I'd opened

TALHO CAPIXABA

Avenida Ataulfo de Paiva 1022
Rio de Janeiro 22440-035, Brazil
+55 2125128760
www.talhocapixaba.com.br

Opening hours	Open 7 days
Credit cards	Accepted
Price range	Budget
Style	Casual
Cuisine	Bakery
Recommended for	Breakfast

What began decades ago as a butcher's shop has gradually morphed into a deli-bakery meets upmarket grocery store. Talho Capixaba, which sells takeout (takeaway) pastries, salads, and sandwiches (charged by their weight) to the well-heeled residents of Leblon, is a popular pit stop on the way to the beach. Breakfast at one of its in-demand outside tables or in the upstairs cafe, where freshly baked croissants and empanadas (pies) and freshly squeezed juices are a particular draw, is a Rio must-do. It's priced for the area, so don't go looking for a bargain—but do expect smart service and high quality.

THE SLOW BAKERY

Rua São João Batista 93
Rio de Janeiro 22270-030, Brazil
+55 2135638638
www.theslowbakery.com.br

Opening hours	Closed Monday and Sunday
Credit cards	Accepted
Price range	Budget
Style	Casual
Cuisine	Bakery
Recommended for	Breakfast

"No doubt the best bread in Brazil."
—Rafa Costa e Silva

"ONE OF THE BEST IN SÃO PAULO."

ALEX ATALA P1118

"Incredible! Probably the best restaurant in Brazil."

RAFA COSTA E SILVA P1114

"A DELICIOUS EXPERIENCE."

ALEX ATALA P1116

"One of my favourite places in the world."

FERNANDO TROCCA P1119

SÃO PAULO

"THE BEST CONTEMPORARY CUISINE WITH A PRECISE USE OF TECHNIQUES AND LIGHTNESS IN THE DISHES. AN AWARD-WINNING RESTAURANT WITH EVERY REASON FOR BEING SO."

BENNY NOVAK P1114

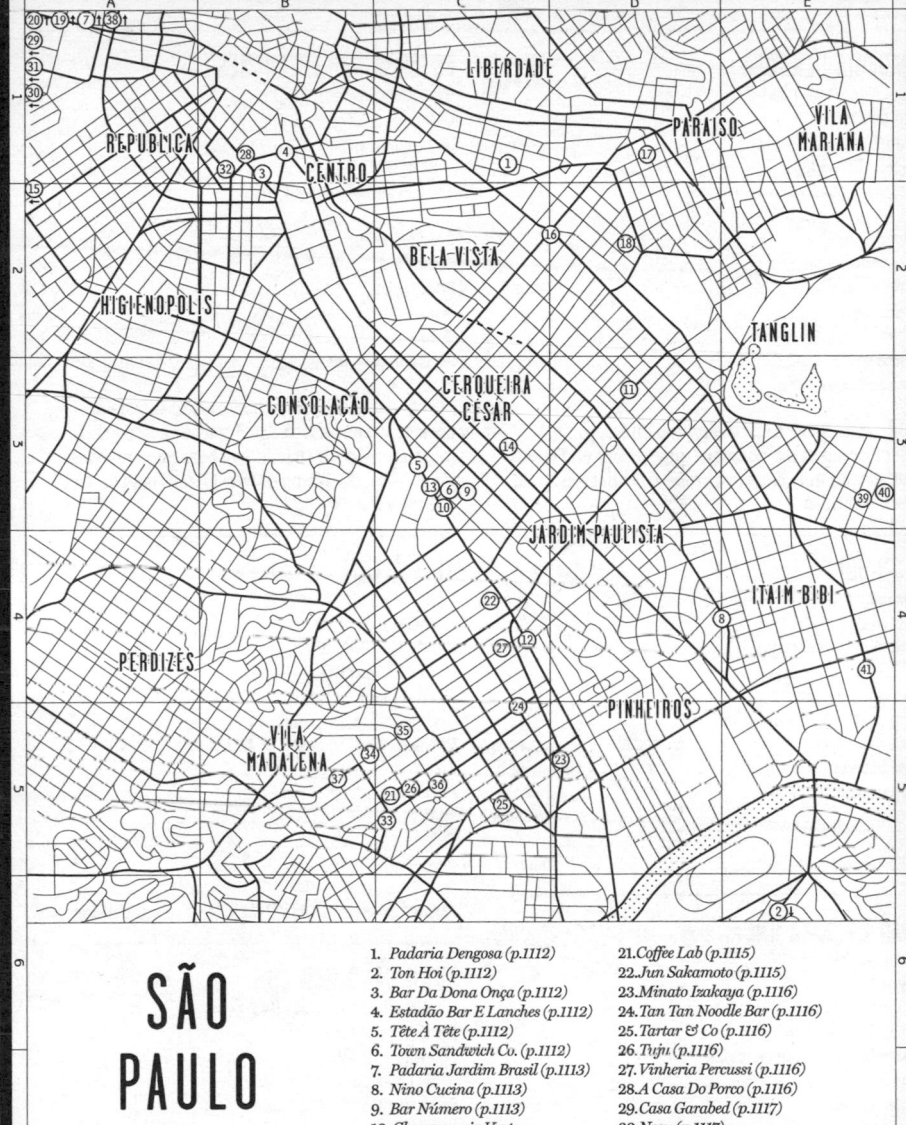

SÃO PAULO

SCALE

0   500   1000   1500
                          yd.

PADARIA DENGOSA

Rua Artur Prado 514
Bela Vista
São Paulo 01322-000
+55 1132883866
www.dengosapaesedoces.com.br

Opening hours	Open 7 days
Reservation policy	No
Credit cards	Accepted
Price range	Budget
Style	Casual
Cuisine	Bakery-Deli
Recommended for	Breakfast

"A classic São Paulo bakery—no tables, you eat standing up at the counter—sandwiches on French bread with thin-cut fries, prepared with class."
—Benny Novak

TON HOI

Avenida Professor Francisco Morato 1484
Butantã
São Paulo 05512-100
+55 1137213268
www.tonhoi.com.br

Opening hours	Closed Monday and Sunday
Credit cards	Accepted but not AMEX
Price range	Affordable
Style	Casual
Cuisine	Chinese
Recommended for	Wish I'd opened

BAR DA DONA ONÇA

Avenida Ipiranga 200
Centro
São Paulo 01046-011
+55 1132572016
www.bardadonaonca.com.br

Opening hours	Open 7 days
Credit cards	Accepted
Price range	Budget
Style	Casual
Cuisine	Brazilian
Recommended for	Local favorite

"Jana prepares high-quality bohemian food. The bar is in the Copan building, one of the most iconic buildings in the city."— Bel Coelho

ESTADÃO BAR E LANCHES

Viaduto Nove de Julho 193
Centro
São Paulo 01050-060
+55 1132577121
www.estadaolanches.com.br

Opening hours	Open 7 days
Credit cards	Accepted
Price range	Budget
Style	Casual
Cuisine	Sandwiches
Recommended for	Late night

"Excellent for anyone who wants to eat the best pork-leg sandwich in São Paulo, or a good early-morning *feijoada* (traditional bean stew with ten kinds of meat). It's open twenty-four hours a day."
—Benny Novak

TÊTE À TÊTE

Rua Doutor Melo Alves 216
Cerqueira César
São Paulo 01417-010
+55 1137960090
www.teteatete.com.br

Opening hours	Closed Sunday
Credit cards	Accepted
Price range	Affordable
Style	Smart casual
Cuisine	Modern Brazilian
Recommended for	High end

"Don't miss it—BON VOYAGE!"—Emmanuel Bassoleil

TOWN SANDWICH CO.

Rua Doutor Melo Alves 445
Cerqueira César
São Paulo 01415-001
+55 1130626757
www.townsandwichco.com

Opening hours	Closed Monday
Credit cards	Accepted
Price range	Budget
Style	Casual
Cuisine	Sandwiches
Recommended for	Local favorite

"This is the Brazilian gourmet Shake Shack. It's a must-try!"—Emmanuel Bassoleil

PADARIA JARDIM BRASIL

Recommended by
Rodrigo Oliveira

Avenida Jardim Japão 1298
Jardim Brasil
São Paulo 02221-001
+55 1122019434
www.padariajardimbrasil.com.br

Opening hours	Open 7 days
Reservation policy	No
Credit cards	Accepted
Price range	Budget
Style	Casual
Cuisine	Café-Bakery
Recommended for	Breakfast

NINO CUCINA

Recommended by
Luca Gozzani

Rua Jerônimo da Veiga 30
Jardim Europa
São Paulo 04536-000
+55 1121296107
www.ninocucina.com.br

Opening hours	Open 7 days
Credit cards	Accepted
Price range	Affordable
Style	Casual
Cuisine	Italian
Recommended for	Regular neighborhood

"Excellent little restaurant."—Luca Gozzani

BAR NÚMERO

Recommended by
Rodrigo Oliveira

Rua da Consolação 3585
Jardim Paulista
São Paulo 01416-001
+55 1130613995
www.barnumero.com.br

Opening hours	Closed Monday and Sunday
Credit cards	Accepted
Price range	Affordable
Style	Smart casual
Cuisine	Bar
Recommended for	Late night

CHURRASCARIA VENTO HARAGANO

Recommended by
Alex Atala

Avenida Rebouças 1001
Jardim Paulista
São Paulo 05401-100
+55 1130834265
www.ventoharagano.com.br

Opening hours	Open 7 days
Credit cards	Accepted
Price range	Affordable
Style	Casual
Cuisine	Barbecue
Recommended for	Wish I'd opened

"The *rodizio* (different meats offered in succession) is a sensational format. It guarantees total satisfaction to any meat lover, both through the variety and quantity. There is no wrong time for *rodizio*."—Alex Atala

PADARIA DA ESQUINA

Recommended by
Alex Atala

Alameda Campinas 1630
Jardim Paulista
São Paulo 01404-002
+55 1123870149
www.padariadaesquina.com

Opening hours	Open 7 days
Reservation policy	No
Credit cards	Accepted
Price range	Budget
Style	Casual
Cuisine	Bakery-Deli
Recommended for	Breakfast

"Everything is delicious there. It is the best way to start the day for people who like to take breakfast in a leisurely way. I would pick the bread with the natural lactic fermentation."—Alex Atala

MANI
Recommended by
Alex Atala,
Bel Coelho,
Benny Novak

Rua Joaquim Antunes 210
Jardim Paulistano
São Paulo 05414-010
+55 1130854148
www.manimanioca.com.br

Opening hours	Closed Monday
Credit cards	Accepted
Price range	Affordable
Style	Casual
Cuisine	Modern Brazilian
Recommended for	High end

"The best contemporary cuisine with a precise use of techniques and lightness in the dishes. An award-winning restaurant with every reason for being so."
—Benny Novak

OSTERIA DEL PETTIROSSO
Recommended by
Luca Gozzani

Alameda Lorena 2155
Jardim Paulistano
São Paulo 01424-006
+55 1130625338
www.pettirosso.com.br

Opening hours	Closed Monday
Credit cards	Accepted
Price range	Affordable
Style	Casual
Cuisine	Italian
Recommended for	Regular neighborhood

"Authentic classic Italian cuisine from the Lazio region—a quiet, family-run restaurant."—Luca Gozzani

D.O.M. RESTAURANTE
Recommended by
Massimo Bottura,
Rafa Costa e Silva,
Luca Gozzani,
Zaiyu Hasegawa,
Bjoern Alexander Panek,
Guy Savoy, Geir Skeie

Rua Barão de Capanema 549
Jardins
São Paulo 01411-011
+55 1130880761
www.domrestaurante.com.br

Opening hours	Closed Sunday
Credit cards	Accepted
Price range	Expensive
Style	Smart casual
Cuisine	Modern Brazilian
Recommended for	High end

"Incredible! Probably the best restaurant in Brazil."
—Rafa Costa e Silva

One-time painter and decorator (and punk DJ) Alex Atala has almost single-handedly put experimental, fine-dining Brazilian cuisine onto the world stage thanks to an ungodly amount of dedication and vision. At D.O.M.—*domus optimus maximus* (home is greatest and best)—Atala has turned scouring the Amazon rainforest for forgotten ingredients into an art form, as well as a pretty solid business model. Thanks to him, Brazilian food is no longer regarded as being merely homely and unsophisticated but as vibrant, interesting and, at times, downright cool. If you like eating ingredients that are unlikely to have ever left Brazil, D.O.M.'s the place to go.

O VELHÃO
Recommended by
Rodrigo Oliveira

Estrada Santa Inês 3000
Mairiporã
São Paulo 07600-000
+55 1144852084
www.velhao.com.br

Opening hours	Open 7 days
Reservation policy	No
Credit cards	Not accepted
Price range	Budget
Style	Casual
Cuisine	Brazilian
Recommended for	Local favorite

KAN
Recommended by
Benny Novak

Rua Manoel da Nóbrega 76
Paraíso
São Paulo 04001-080
+55 1132663819

Opening hours	Closed Sunday
Credit cards	Accepted
Price range	Expensive
Style	Casual
Cuisine	Japanese
Recommended for	High end

SHIN-ZUSHI
Recommended by
Benny Novak

Rua Afonso de Freitas 169
Paraíso
São Paulo 04006-050
+55 1138898700

Opening hours	Closed Monday
Credit cards	Accepted
Price range	Affordable
Style	Casual
Cuisine	Japanese
Recommended for	High end

YORIMICHI IZAKAYA

Recommended by
Alex Atala

Rua Otavio Nébias 203
Paraíso
São Paulo 04002-001
+55 1130520029

Opening hours	Closed Sunday
Credit cards	Accepted
Price range	Affordable
Style	Casual
Cuisine	Japanese
Recommended for	Late night

"The chef, Ken Mizumoto, is a spectacular guy who has managed to combine very well the best *izakaya* (Japanese pub) options with a good sake menu."
—Alex Atala

AL SULTAN MIDHAT RESTAURANTE

Recommended by
Benny Novak

Rua Doutor Ornelas 51
Pari
São Paulo 03029-030
+55 1120810813
www.arabesq.com.br

Opening hours	Closed Monday
Credit cards	Accepted
Price range	Affordable
Style	Casual
Cuisine	Lebanese
Recommended for	Bargain

"Excellent hummus, good kebabs, garlic pasta, and stuffed vine leaves. Service is sometimes a bit chaotic but a good call for a reliable cheap place."
—Benny Novak

CARLINHOS RESTAURANTE

Recommended by
Rodrigo Oliveira

Rua Rio Bonito 1641
Pari
São Paulo 03023-000
+55 1133159474
www.carlinhosrestaurante.com.br

Opening hours	Closed Sunday
Credit cards	Accepted
Price range	Budget
Style	Casual
Cuisine	Armenian
Recommended for	Bargain

"The Armenian dishes at this restaurant are a delicacy. Don't miss their specialty arais: pitta bread filled with meat and their unique spices."—Rodrigo Oliveira

COFFEE LAB

Recommended by
Bel Coelho

Rua Fradique Coutinho 1340
Pinheiros
São Paulo 05416-001
+55 1133757400
www.coffeelab.com.br

Opening hours	Closed Sunday
Reservation policy	No
Credit cards	Accepted
Price range	Affordable
Style	Casual
Cuisine	Café
Recommended for	Breakfast

JUN SAKAMOTO

Recommended by
Rodrigo Oliveira

Rua Lisboa 55
Pinheiros
São Paulo 01430-001
+55 1130886019

Opening hours	Closed Sunday
Credit cards	Accepted
Price range	Expensive
Style	Smart casual
Cuisine	Japanese
Recommended for	High end

In a city that knows sushi—there are more Japanese restaurants in São Paulo than steakhouses—Jun Sakamoto's eponymous outpost is considered the very finest. Born and raised in Brazil, and trained in New York, Sakamoto is famously fanatical about sourcing ingredients, as fastidious about his rice and wasabi root as he is about the foie gras he pairs with tuna tartare, or the *uni* (sea urchin) for his nigiri. The wood, glass, and leather-trimmed interior, which has aged well in the seventeen years since opening, doesn't detract from the food. Aim for a counter seat and go for the *omakase* (chef's choice) menu if budget allows.

MINATO IZAKAYA

Recommended by
Emmanuel Bassoleil

Rua dos Pinheiros 1308
Pinheiros
São Paulo 05422-002
+55 1125388883

Opening hours	Closed Sunday
Credit cards	Accepted
Price range	Affordable
Style	Casual
Cuisine	Japanese
Recommended for	Late night

"If 'Fabinho' is in the house, our Japanese dinner and party goes on forever!"—Emmanuel Bassoleil

TAN TAN NOODLE BAR

Recommended by
Alex Atala,
Rafa Costa e Silva,
Benny Novak

Rua Fradique Coutinho 153
Pinheiros
São Paulo 05416-010
+55 1123733587
www.tantannb.com.br

Opening hours	Closed Monday
Reservation policy	No
Credit cards	Accepted
Price range	Affordable
Style	Casual
Cuisine	Noodles
Recommended for	Regular neighborhood

"Definitely a delicious experience with incredible food. It is casual, offers comfort food, and the starters and the aperitifs also surprise guests!"
—Alex Atala

TARTAR & CO

Recommended by
Emmanuel Bassoleil

Avenida Pedroso de Morais 1003
Pinheiros
São Paulo 05419-000
+55 1130311020
www.tartarandco.com

Opening hours	Open 7 days
Credit cards	Accepted
Price range	Affordable
Style	Casual
Cuisine	French
Recommended for	Bargain

"From a gourmet chef with masses of flavors for all tastes."—Emmanuel Bassoleil

TUJU

Recommended by
Rafa Costa e Silva

Rua Fradique Coutinho 1248
Pinheiros
São Paulo 05416-001
+55 1126915548
www.tuju.com.br

Opening hours	Closed Monday and Sunday
Credit cards	Accepted
Price range	Affordable
Style	Smart casual
Cuisine	Modern Brazilian
Recommended for	Worth the travel

"Very good tasting menu and pairing. Creating a modern, avant-garde cuisine using Brazilian products."—Rafa Costa e Silva

VINHERIA PERCUSSI

Recommended by
Emmanuel Bassoleil

Rua Cônego Eugênio Leite 523
Pinheiros
São Paulo 05414-011
+55 1130884920
www.percussi.com.br

Opening hours	Open 7 days
Credit cards	Accepted
Price range	Affordable
Style	Smart casual
Cuisine	Italian
Recommended for	Worth the travel

A CASA DO PORCO

Recommended by
Emmanuel Bassoleil,
Rodrigo Oliveira

Rua Araújo 124
República
São Paulo 01220-020
+55 1132582578

Opening hours	Open 7 days
Reservation policy	No
Credit cards	Accepted
Price range	Affordable
Style	Casual
Cuisine	Brazilian
Recommended for	Local favorite

"A bar and restaurant run by Jefferson Rueda in the center of São Paulo. The menu is devoted to pork, and it's all about great produce, the traditions of the countryside, and the art of charcuterie and fire cooking."—Rodrigo Oliveira

The name translates as "House of Pig", and the restaurant more than lives up to it. The menu is a love song to pork, with the finest locally reared meat served up in a bewildering number of styles, from sushi and *temaki* (sushi hand rolls) to blood sausage and pork croquettes. The signature dish, such as there is one, is the *Porco de San Zé*, a heaving mound of eight-hour wood-roasted piggy— you'll hear other tables asking for extra skin. Chef Jefferson Rueda takes no reservations and some nights the lines (queues) can stretch way into the night, but it's popular for a reason— there are few finer tributes to the noble pig.

CASA GARABED

Recommended by
Rodrigo Oliveira

Rua José Margarido 216
Santana
São Paulo 04550-004
+55 1129762750
www.casagarabed.com.br

Opening hours	Closed Monday and Tuesday
Reservation policy	No
Credit cards	Accepted
Price range	Budget
Style	Casual
Cuisine	Lebanese
Recommended for	Regular neighborhood

NOSU

Recommended by
Rodrigo Oliveira

Rua Maria Curupaiti 414
Santana
São Paulo 02452-000
+55 1122835822
www.nosu.com.br

Opening hours	Closed Monday
Credit cards	Accepted
Price range	Affordable
Style	Smart casual
Cuisine	Japanese
Recommended for	Regular neighborhood

"A stunning Japanese restaurant in Santana neighborhood. Great ingredients and authorial approach."—Rodrigo Oliveira

SUSHI HIROSHI

Recommended by
Rodrigo Oliveira

Rua Capitão Manuel Novaes 189
Santana
São Paulo 02017-030
+55 1129796677
www.sushihiroshi.com.br

Opening hours	Closed Wednesday
Credit cards	Accepted but not AMEX or Diners
Price range	Affordable
Style	Casual
Cuisine	Japanese
Recommended for	Regular neighborhood

CHURRASCARIA BOI NA BRASA

Recommended by
Benny Novak

Rua Marquês de Itu 188
Vila Buarque
São Paulo 01223-000
+55 1132229479
www.churrascariaboinabrasa.com.br

Opening hours	Open 7 days
Credit cards	Accepted
Price range	Affordable
Style	Casual
Cuisine	Barbecue
Recommended for	Late night

"Classic beer served in chilled tankards, barbecue-grilled meats, good pork fillet, linguiça sausage, and steak. It's worth trying the barbecued guinea fowl and Portuguese fries. And it's open until 3.00 a.m."
—Benny Novak

BAR ASTOR

Recommended by
Benny Novak

Rua Delfina 163
Vila Madalena
São Paulo 05443-010
+55 1138151364
www.barastor.com.br

Opening hours	Open 7 days
Credit cards	Accepted
Price range	Affordable
Style	Casual
Cuisine	French-Brazilian
Recommended for	Local favorite

"A bar with the feel of a restaurant. The best São Paulo dishes—cod à la mode, beef stew, and prawn patties—alongside caipirinhas, G&Ts, and excellent cocktails."—Benny Novak

CARLOS PIZZA

Recommended by
Alex Atala

Rua Harmonia 501
Vila Madalena
São Paulo 05435-000
+55 1138132017
www.carlospizza.com.br

Opening hours	Open 7 days
Credit cards	Accepted
Price range	Budget
Style	Casual
Cuisine	Pizza
Recommended for	Bargain

"Very tasty pizzas with naturally fermented dough, at a very fair price. It's one of the best pizzerias in São Paulo."—Alex Atala

LÁ DA VENDA

Recommended by
Emmanuel Bassoleil

Rua Harmonia 161
Vila Madalena
São Paulo 05435-000
+55 1130377702
www.ladavenda.com.br

Opening hours	Closed Monday
Credit cards	Accepted
Price range	Affordable
Style	Casual
Cuisine	Bakery-Café-Deli
Recommended for	Breakfast

"Takes me back to my family roots."
—Emmanuel Bassoleil

MARTIN FIERRO

Recommended by
Bel Coelho

Rua Aspicuelta 683
Vila Madalena
São Paulo 05433-011
+55 1138146747
www.martinfierro.com.br

Opening hours	Open 7 days
Credit cards	Accepted
Price range	Affordable
Style	Casual
Cuisine	Argentinian
Recommended for	Bargain

"Excellent meat and great salads at a good price. I also love their pasties."—Bel Coelho

TANUKI SUSHI

Recommended by
Bel Coelho,
Benny Novak

Rua Jericó 287
Vila Madalena
São Paulo 05435-040
+55 1138143760
www.tanukisushi.com.br

Opening hours	Open 7 days
Credit cards	Accepted
Price range	Affordable
Style	Casual
Cuisine	Japanese
Recommended for	Regular neighborhood

"An excellent Japanese for everyday with very accessible prices—fresh and well-cut fish."
—Benny Novak

MOCOTÓ

Recommended by
Alex Atala,
Manoella Buffara Ramos,
Bel Coelho

Avenida Nossa Senhora do Loreto 1100
Vila Medeiros
São Paulo 02219-001
+55 1129513056
www.mocoto.com.br

Opening hours	Open 7 days
Reservation policy	No
Credit cards	Accepted
Price range	Budget
Style	Casual
Cuisine	Brazilian
Recommended for	Bargain

"One of the best in São Paulo. The restaurant opened in 1972 and it is still possible to find authentic regional Brazilian food there."—Alex Atala

You'll find Mocotó in Vila Medeiros, a traditionally working-class district of São Paulo. It's run by Rodrigo Oliveira de Almeida, the son of an émigré who came to São Paulo seeking his fortune armed with little more than a couple of shirts, one pair of trousers, and the shoes on his feet. Dishes, offered alongside some 350 sturdy cachaças (white rum made from sugar cane), offer a lighter version of northeast Brazil's cuisine. These include *sarapatel* (variety meats/pork offal), *feijão de corda* (string beans stewed with sausage, bacon, dried meat, and butter beans), and, only on Sundays, *paleta de cordeiro do velho chico* (braised lamb feather blade). *Mocotó* (cow's hoof broth) is the house classic.

LE MANJUE ORGANIQUE

Recommended by
Emmanuel Bassoleil

Rua Domingos Fernandes 608
Vila Nova Conceição
São Paulo 04509-011
+55 1130340631
www.lemanjue.com.br

Opening hours	Open 7 days
Credit cards	Accepted
Price range	Budget
Style	Casual
Cuisine	International
Recommended for	Regular neighborhood

"If I'm not eating at home, this is the place I'd like to be. Organic, gluten-free, dairy-free gourmet restaurant—and you feel at home."
—Emmanuel Bassoleil

LE PAIN QUOTIDIEN

Recommended by
Luca Gozzani

Rua Afonso Braz 657
Vila Nova Conceição
São Paulo 04511-001
+55 1138423562
www.lepainquotidien.com.br

Opening hours	Open 7 days
Credit cards	Accepted
Price range	Budget
Style	Casual
Cuisine	Café-Bakery
Recommended for	Breakfast

EATALY

Recommended by
Luca Gozzani

Avenida Presidente Juscelino Kubitschek 1489
Vila Nova Conceição
São Paulo 03178-200
+55 1132793300
www.eataly.com.br

Opening hours	Open 7 days
Credit cards	Accepted
Price range	Affordable
Style	Casual
Cuisine	Italian
Recommended for	Late night

"Simple, first-class Italian produce."—Luca Gozzani

EL MOSTRADOR DE SANTA TERESITA

Recommended by
Leo Lanussol

Calle Las Garzas
José Ignacio
Maldonado 20402, Uruguay
+598 44862861

Opening hours	Open 7 days
Credit cards	Not accepted
Price range	Affordable
Style	Casual
Cuisine	International
Recommended for	Breakfast

PARADOR LA HUELLA

Recommended by
Leo Lanussol,
Fernando Trocca

Calle Los Cisnes
José Ignacio
Maldonado 20402, Uruguay
+598 44862279
www.paradorlahuella.com

Opening hours	Open 7 days
Credit cards	Accepted
Price range	Affordable
Style	Casual
Cuisine	Uruguayan
Recommended for	Local favorite

"Possibly one of my favorite places in the world, taking into account the location, the quality of the cooking, the service, and the atmosphere."
—Fernando Trocca

This idyllic beachside spot would be popular with the holidaymakers of upmarket José Ignacio no matter what was coming out of the kitchens. But under chef Alejandro Morales, who learned his paella skills in Spain, his pasta technique in Italy, and his breadmaking in San Francisco's world-famous Tartine, the food and atmosphere created is little short of magical. Seafood, particularly the grilled sea bass, is a specialty, and naturally anything from the *asador* (barbecue grill) is worth the trip. But the care and attention to detail shown to everything, including the vegetables grown on local organic farms, is breathtaking. A very special place.

BAKER'S BAR

Dr. Pablo de María 1198
Montevideo 11200, Uruguay
+598 96212767

Opening hours	Closed Sunday
Credit cards	Accepted
Price range	Affordable
Style	Casual
Cuisine	Bar
Recommended for	Late night

ESCARAMUZA

Dr. Pablo de María 1185
Montevideo 11200, Uruguay
+598 24013475
www.escaramuza.com.uy

Opening hours	Closed Sunday
Credit cards	Accepted
Price range	Budget
Style	Casual
Cuisine	Café
Recommended for	Breakfast

"Good coffee, homemade granola, and bread.
Simple, fresh and seasonal local products at
reasonable prices."—Alejandro Morales

JACINTO

Sarandi 349
Montevideo 11000, Uruguay
+598 29152731
www.jacinto.com.uy

Opening hours	Closed Sunday
Credit cards	Accepted
Price range	Affordable
Style	Casual
Cuisine	Uruguayan
Recommended for	Late night

TOLEDO

Calle Cerrito 499
Montevideo 11000, Uruguay
+598 29153006

Opening hours	Closed Sunday
Credit cards	Accepted
Price range	Affordable
Style	Casual
Cuisine	Tapas
Recommended for	Regular neighborhood

BUENOS AIRES: SEE PAGES 1122–1131

LA TOSCANA

Juan Julián Lastra 176
Neuquén
Patagonia 8300, Argentina
+54 2994473322
www.latoscanarestaurante.com

Opening hours	Open 7 days
Credit cards	Accepted
Price range	Affordable
Style	Casual
Cuisine	Italian
Recommended for	Worth the travel

"The best cheeses!"—Leo Lanussol

CASSIS

Ruta 82
Peñón de Arelauquen
San Carlos de Bariloche
Patagonia 8400, Argentina
+54 2944506430
www.cassis.com.ar

Opening hours	Open 7 days
Credit cards	Accepted but not AMEX
Price range	Affordable
Style	Formal
Cuisine	Patagonian
Recommended for	Worth the travel

"Overlooking Lake Gutiérrez, a natural paradise, this project stays in tune with the surroundings. The Muller-Wolf family works with homegrown organic produce to make use of everything the local area can provide. They even make their own collection of vinegars and ferments from regional flowers and berries. A real find in the middle of the mountains."
—Martin Molteni

MONREAL

San Lorenzo 1295
Rosario
Santa Fe 2000, Argentina
+54 3414219356
www.sandwichesmonreal.com.ar

Opening hours	Open 7 days
Credit cards	Accepted
Price range	Budget
Style	Casual
Cuisine	Sandwiches
Recommended for	Bargain

"The best multi-layered sandwiches in Argentina. The egg and anchovy is not to be missed."—Juan Gaffuri

> "PERFECT CONCEPTS, PRESENTED WITH AN ENERGY THAT I LOVE."
>
> FEDERICO FIALYRE P1124

> "SMALL, INTIMATE, AND ENJOYABLE."
>
> MARTIN MOLTENI P1126

BUENOS AIRES

> "INTELLIGENT LOCAL CUISINE USING SEASONAL PRODUCE."
>
> MARTIN MOLTENI P1129

> "THE BEST CHORIZO SANDWICHES IN THE CITY."
>
> FERNANDO TROCCA P1126

> "Buenos Aires is a city full of restaurants, but when it comes to seafood, it's difficult to think of one with such a large variety of the best fish and shellfish on the Atlantic coast."
>
> MARTIN MOLTENI P1128

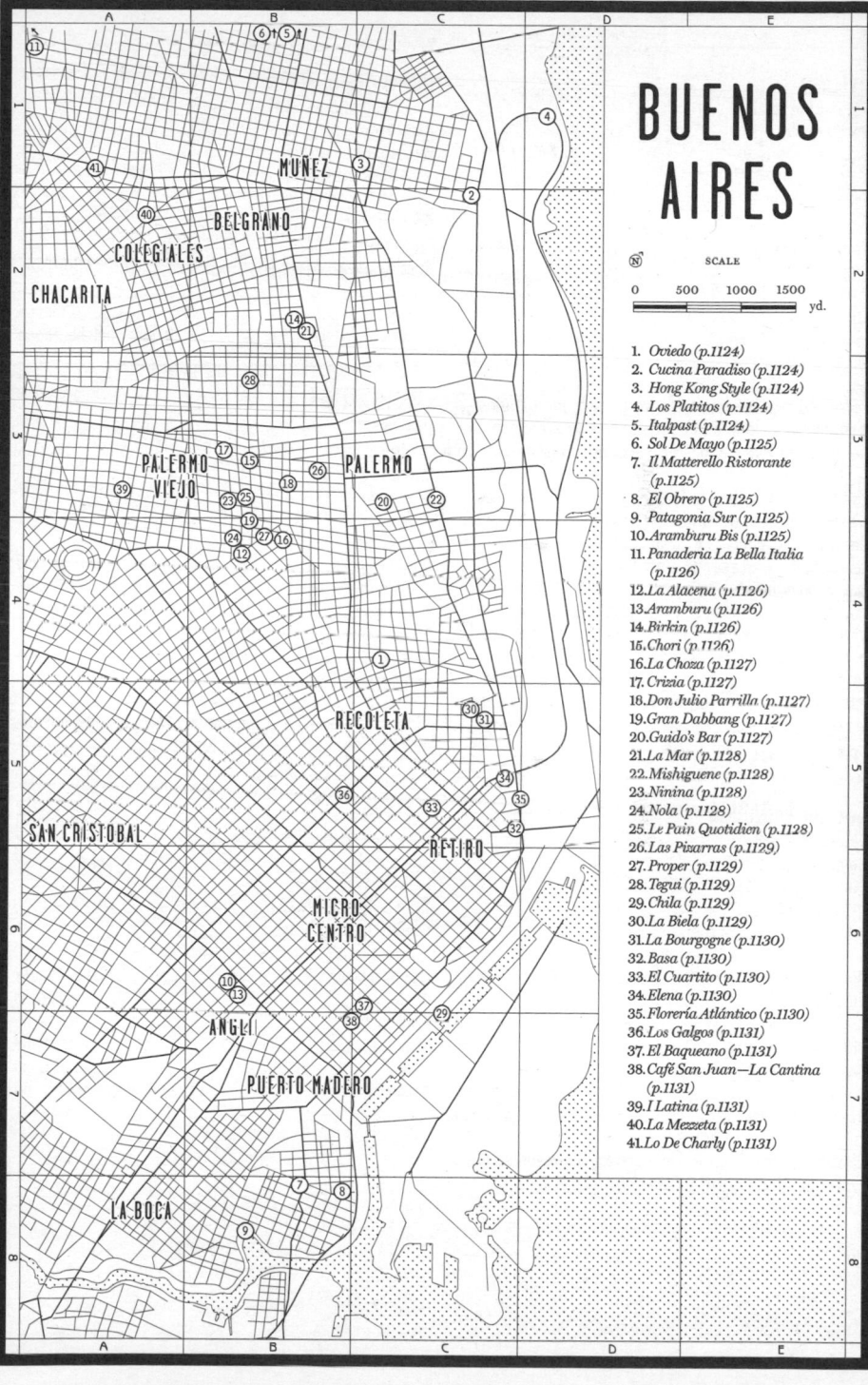

BUENOS AIRES

OVIEDO

Recommended by
Federico Fialyre,
Juan Gaffuri

Antonio Beruti 2602
Barrio Norte
Buenos Aires 1425
+54 1148213741
www.oviedoresto.com.ar

Opening hours	Open 7 days
Credit cards	Accepted
Price range	Expensive
Style	Smart casual
Cuisine	Modern Spanish
Recommended for	Late night

"Emilio Garip, owner of this restaurant, understands better than anyone that conviviality is an art and he practises it like a master."—Federico Fialyre

You'll be hard pushed to find a restaurant that serves fresh fish in Buenos Aires. It's a city that is undeniably meat-centric, filled as it is with *parrillas* —grill restaurants—all serving amazing Argentinian beef. But if you want something different in the "land of the cow", try this Spanish-style establishment in the heart of Recoleta, which has made a name for itself as one of the capital's oldest and most respected seafood restaurants. It serves beautifully cooked classic and modern dishes (such as salt cod, squid ink risotto, and citrusy ceviche), as well as superbly executed Iberian fare, including meats, pasta, and risotto.

CUCINA PARADISO

Recommended by
Federico Fialyre

Castañeda 1873
Belganro
Buenos Aires 1428
+54 1147802409
www.cucinaparadiso.com

Opening hours	Closed Sunday
Reservation policy	No
Credit cards	Accepted
Price range	Affordable
Style	Casual
Cuisine	Italian
Recommended for	Regular neighborhood

"Simple tasty dishes. Perfect concepts, presented with an energy that I love."—Federico Fialyre

HONG KONG STYLE

Recommended by
Juan Gaffuri

Calle Montañeses 2149
Belgrano
Buenos Aires 1428
+54 1147863456

Opening hours	Closed Wednesday
Credit cards	Not accepted
Price range	Affordable
Style	Casual
Cuisine	Chinese
Recommended for	Regular neighborhood

LOS PLATITOS

Recommended by
Matías Kyriazis

Puesto 57
Belgrano
Buenos Aires 1428
Argentina
+54 11 4781-1499

Opening hours	Open 7 days
Credit cards	Accepted but not AMEX or Diners
Price range	Affordable
Style	Casual
Cuisine	Grill
Recommended for	Bargain

"Ideal for a quick meal at the bar. High-quality cuts of meat for the grill."—Matías Kyriazis

ITALPAST

Recommended by
Juan Gaffuri

Juan Dellepiane 1050
Campana
Buenos Aires 2804
+54 3489425275
www.italpastdeli.com.ar

Opening hours	Closed Monday
Credit cards	Accepted
Price range	Affordable
Style	Smart casual
Cuisine	Italian
Recommended for	Regular neighborhood

SOL DE MAYO

Av. Mitre 1001
Campana
Buenos Aires 2804
Argentina
+54 3489431306
www.panaderiasoldemayo.com.ar

Opening hours	Closed Monday
Credit cards	Accepted
Price range	Affordable
Style	Casual
Cuisine	Bakery
Recommended for	Breakfast

"Beautiful place, hidden away in a city on the outskirts of Buenos Aires, with a superbly presented traditional bakery."—Matías Kyriazis

IL MATTERELLO RISTORANTE

Martín Rodríguez 517
La Boca
Buenos Aires 1159
+54 1143070529

Opening hours	Open 7 days
Credit cards	Accepted
Price range	Affordable
Style	Casual
Cuisine	Italian
Recommended for	Bargain

EL OBRERO

Agustín R. Caffarena 64
La Boca
Buenos Aires 1157
+54 1143629912

Opening hours	Closed Sunday
Credit cards	Not accepted
Price range	Affordable
Style	Casual
Cuisine	Argentinian
Recommended for	Local favorite

"Typical Buenos Aires bar-restaurant, where you can eat popular Argentinian dishes. A good place to enjoy yourself with family or friends. Excellent pasta and meat."—Juan Gaffuri

Look past the gritty dockside neighborhood, the shabby frontage, and the window bars, and instead, focus on the steak. El Obrero ("the worker") in La Boca is one of Buenos Aires' longest established *parrillas* and is the restaurant of choice for touring celebrities and the stars of Boca Juniors (Maradona's old team). El Obrero has been in the hands of just one family since 1954 and little appears to have changed in that time. The Bentwood chairs, the tiled floors, the football memorabilia, and the celebrity snaps are as reassuring as the blackboard menu of tortilla, calamari, and, of course, very fine cuts of beef.

PATAGONIA SUR

Rocha 801
La Boca
Buenos Aires 1166
+54 1143035917
www.restaurantepatagoniasur.com

Opening hours	Closed Sunday
Credit cards	Accepted
Price range	Expensive
Style	Casual
Cuisine	Argentinian
Recommended for	Wish I'd opened

ARAMBURU

Humberto Primero 1207
Constitución
Buenos Aires 1074
Argentina
+54 11.4304.5697
www.aramburubis.com.ar

Opening hours	Closed Sunday
Credit cards	Accepted
Price range	Affordable
Style	Casual
Cuisine	Modern Argentinian
Recommended for	Worth the travel

"The menu and service were great, I can still recall most of the dishes that were served which is really special."—Timothy Charles

PANADERIA LA BELLA ITALIA

Recommended by
Martin Molteni

Bartolomé Mitre Avenue 2599
Moreno
Buenos Aires 1744
+54 2374630480

Opening hours	Open 7 days
Credit cards	Accepted but not AMEX
Price range	Budget
Style	Casual
Cuisine	Bakery
Recommended for	Breakfast

"Very good and ideal for breakfasts."—Martin Molteni

LA ALACENA

Recommended by
Leo Lanussol

Gascón 1401
Palermo
Buenos Aires 1181
+54 1148672549

Opening hours	Open 7 days
Credit cards	Not accepted
Price range	Budget
Style	Casual
Cuisine	Italian
Recommended for	Breakfast

"Julieta Oriolo's cuisine is simple but very rich."
—Leo Lanussol

ARAMBURU

Recommended by
Federico Fialyre,
Juan Gaffuri, Santiago Macías,
Martin Molteni, Martín Rebaudine

Salta 1050
Palermo
Buenos Aires 1074
+54 1143050439
www.arambururesto.com.ar

Opening hours	Closed Monday and Sunday
Credit cards	Accepted
Price range	Affordable
Style	Casual
Cuisine	Modern Argentinian
Recommended for	High end

"A restaurant offering a modern, more refined cuisine.
The balance of the wine with the food is brilliant.
Small, intimate, and enjoyable."—Martin Molteni

Chef Gonzalo Aramburu grew up in the Constitución neighborhood of Buenos Aires and it's here, in what is yet to become the most refined area of town, that he somewhat improbably runs his intimate, sixteen-seat fine dining restaurant. Dishes are best described as modern Argentinian—the best local ingredients (beef steak, as you might imagine, usually features, paired with Andean potatoes grown at high altitude) are treated to a variety of spectacular techniques, forming a twelve-course tasting menu that has won accolades from all over the world. If you fancy something less elaborate, and cheaper, little sister restaurant Aramburu Bis is just down the road.

BIRKIN

Recommended by
Santiago Macías

Nicaragua 6025
Palermo
Buenos Aires 1414
+54 1120864036

Opening hours	Closed Monday
Credit cards	Not accepted
Price range	Affordable
Style	Casual
Cuisine	Café
Recommended for	Breakfast

"Great coffee and avocado eggs."—Santiago Macías

CHORI

Recommended by
Fernando Trocca

Thames 1653
Palermo
Buenos Aires 1414
+54 1139669857

Opening hours	Open 7 days
Credit cards	Accepted
Price range	Budget
Style	Casual
Cuisine	Argentinian
Recommended for	Bargain

"The best chorizo sandwiches in the city."
—Fernando Trocca

LA CHOZA

Gascón 1701
Palermo
Buenos Aires 1414
+54 1148333334

Recommended by
Federico Fialyre

Opening hours	Closed Monday
Credit cards	Accepted
Price range	Affordable
Style	Casual
Cuisine	Argentinian Grill
Recommended for	Bargain

"Halfway between the 'Bolichón' and the typical BA grill—its thick grilled steak (45-minutes wait) is ideal to share and never fails."—Federico Fialyre

CRIZIA

Gorriti 5143
Palermo
Buenos Aires 1414
+54 1148314979
www.crizia.com.ar

Recommended by
Santiago Macías

Opening hours	Closed Sunday
Credit cards	Accepted
Price range	Expensive
Style	Smart casual
Cuisine	Argentinian
Recommended for	Late night

DON JULIO PARRILLA

Guatemala 4699
Palermo
Buenos Aires 1425
+54 1148326058
www.parrilladonjulio.com.ar

Recommended by
Federico Fialyre,
Juan Gaffuri,
Matías Kyriazis,
Santiago Macías,
Martin Molteni,
Fernando Troca

Opening hours	Open 7 days
Credit cards	Accepted
Price range	Affordable
Style	Casual
Cuisine	Argentinian Steakhouse
Recommended for	Local favorite

"Meat is perhaps the best representative of our culture and we worship it every day. Don Julio over time attempts to take this worship further while maintaining traditions."—Martin Molteni

In a town that prides itself on its way with beef, it takes a lot to stand out from the crowd—and yet this spot in trendy Palermo Soho is, for many, the last word in the Buenos Aires *parrilla* (steakhouse). Owner Pablo Rivero serves almost every part of the cow, but it's fair to say that most are here for the dictionary-thick cuts of sirloin or rib-eye, aged for twenty-one days and served with homemade potato chips and chimichurri. Don't miss the opportunity to work your way through the wine list—Don Julio are specialists in (what else?) Malbec.

GRAN DABBANG

Raul Scalabrini Ortiz Avenue 1543
Palermo
Buenos Aires 1414
+54 1148321186
www.grandabbang.com

Recommended by
Leo Lanussol,
Santiago Macías,
Martin Molteni

Opening hours	Closed Sunday
Credit cards	Accepted
Price range	Affordable
Style	Casual
Cuisine	Asian
Recommended for	Regular neighborhood

"An Asian-style restaurant with high-quality, fresh, local produce; exotic flavors by an Argentinian chef."
—Martin Molteni

GUIDO'S BAR

República de la India 2843
Palermo
Buenos Aires 1425
Argentina
+54 1148022391

Recommended by
Matías Kyriazis

Opening hours	Closed Sunday
Credit cards	Not accepted
Price range	Budget
Style	Casual
Cuisine	Italian
Recommended for	Regular neighborhood

"Typical Italian restaurant with antipasti and Italian recipes, and wonderful service from its owner, the great Carlos Sosto."—Matías Kyriazis

LA MAR

Recommended by
Juan Gaffuri,
Santiago Macías,
Martin Molteni

Arévalo 2024
Palermo
Buenos Aires 1414
+54 1147765543
www.lamarcebicheria.com.ar

Opening hours	Open 7 days
Credit cards	Accepted
Price range	Affordable
Style	Smart casual
Cuisine	Peruvian
Recommended for	Regular neighborhood

"Buenos Aires is a city full of restaurants, but when it comes to seafood, it's difficult to think of one with such a large variety of the best fish and shellfish on the Atlantic coast. La Mar represents the best produce from our coasts."—Martin Molteni

Seafood isn't perhaps the first thing that springs to mind with regards to eating out in Buenos Aires, but if anyone was going to turn young Argentinians on to the delights of the *cevicheria* it would be Peruvian superstar chef Gastón Acurio, who has used his influence to bring remarkable fresh fish from all along Argentina's huge coastline to this smart and colorful Palermo spot. Shrimp, sole, octopus, even lobster (rarely seen in town) all get the *leche de tigre* ("tiger's milk"—the Peruvian term for the ceviche marinade) treatment, all accompanied by that Peruvian staple the Pisco sour.

MISHIGUENE

Recommended by
Federico Fialyre,
Santiago Macías

Lafinur 3368
Palermo
Buenos Aires 1425
+54 1139690764
www.mishiguene.com

Opening hours	Open 7 days
Credit cards	Accepted
Price range	Affordable
Style	Casual
Cuisine	Israeli
Recommended for	Local favorite

"The best food from Israel."—Santiago Macías

NININA

Recommended by
Santiago Macías

Gorriti 4738
Palermo
Buenos Aires 1414
+54 1148320070
www.ninina.com

Opening hours	Open 7 days
Credit cards	Accepted
Price range	Affordable
Style	Casual
Cuisine	Café-Bakery
Recommended for	Breakfast

NOLA

Recommended by
Leo Lanussol,
Santiago Macías

Gorriti 4389
Palermo
Buenos Aires 1414
+54 1163501704
www.nolabuenosaires.com

Opening hours	Open 7 days
Reservation policy	No
Credit cards	Not accepted
Price range	Budget
Style	Casual
Cuisine	Cajun
Recommended for	Local favorite

"The best fried chicken and beer."—Santiago Macías

LE PAIN QUOTIDIEN

Recommended by
Martin Molteni

Distrito Arcos Outlet
Palermo
Buenos Aires 1425
+54 1157892705
www.lepainquotidien.com.ar

Opening hours	Open 7 days
Credit cards	Accepted
Price range	Affordable
Style	Casual
Cuisine	Café-Bakery
Recommended for	Breakfast

"Set in part of the old renovated areas of Buenos Aires in the old arches of the railway terminal station, which give the busy Palermo district a special atmosphere. Although this is part of a large and well-known international chain, their original bread dough and organic produce make this a good place to start when discovering the city."—Martin Molteni

LAS PIZARRAS

Thames 2296
Palermo
Buenos Aires 1425
+54 1147750625
www.laspizarrasbistro.com

Opening hours	Closed Monday
Credit cards	Accepted
Price range	Affordable
Style	Casual
Cuisine	Bistro
Recommended for	Wish I'd opened

"Another of those restaurants with an irreverent look—a small simple place, with a menu that changes every week, interesting wines, and the personality of the chef mixed into everything."—Martin Molteni

PROPER

Aráoz 1676
Palermo
Buenos Aires 1414
+54 1148310027
www.properbsas.com.ar

Opening hours	Closed Monday and Sunday
Reservation policy	No
Credit cards	Accepted but not AMEX or Diners
Price range	Affordable
Style	Casual
Cuisine	Argentinian
Recommended for	Wish I'd opened

"Intelligent local cuisine and dishes using seasonal produce. The place was originally a car workshop and has hardly been changed—this is the type of adventure that we'd all like to have!"—Martin Molteni

TEGUI

Costa Rica 5852
Palermo
Buenos Aires 1414
+54 1147709500
www.tegui.com.ar

Opening hours	Closed Monday and Sunday
Credit cards	Accepted
Price range	Expensive
Style	Smart casual
Cuisine	Modern Argentinian
Recommended for	High end

"A journey around Argentina with unique flavors and ingredients. Top-quality cuisine and impeccable service. Altogether, a great experience."—Juan Gaffuri

Tegui, with its uber-stylish decor, open kitchen, and top-notch eight-course tasting menu, has put contemporary Argentinian cuisine on the map. The food is high end and creative—the restaurant's renowned chef-patron, Germán Martitegui, was among the first in the city to embrace *cocina de vanguardia*, or molecular gastronomy (an experimental, emotional, and scientific approach to cooking). Martitegui is also famous for being a host on Argentina's edition of MasterChef, where he has a fierce reputation as the "mean guy"—though it doesn't show on the plate. Enter the restaurant through an unassuming door, in the middle of a wall covered by colorful graffiti, and let the food speak for itself.

CHILA

Alicia Moreau de Justo Avenue 1160
Puerto Madero
Buenos Aires 1107
+54 1143436067
www.chilaweb.com.ar

Opening hours	Closed Monday
Credit cards	Accepted
Price range	Expensive
Style	Formal
Cuisine	Argentinian
Recommended for	High end

"The restaurants run by Germán Tegui and Soledad Nardelli—Chila and El Baqueano—continue to consolidate top-class experimentation with native produce."—Martin Molteni

LA BIELA

Quintana Avenue 600
Recoleta
Buenos Aires 1129
+54 1148040432
www.labiela.com

Opening hours	Open 7 days
Credit cards	Accepted
Price range	Affordable
Style	Casual
Cuisine	Argentinian
Recommended for	Breakfast

LA BOURGOGNE

Recommended by
Federico Fialyre

Ayacucho 2023
Recoleta
Buenos Aires 1112
+54 1148053857
www.alvearpalace.com/la-bourgogne.php

Opening hours	Closed Sunday
Credit cards	Accepted
Price range	Expensive
Style	Smart casual
Cuisine	Modern French
Recommended for	High end

"The fact that it is a classic, overlooked by some trendy guides, made us lose sight of the fact that Paul Bondoux continues to offer some of the best food in the city."—Federico Fialyre

BASA

Recommended by
Federico Fialyre

Basavilbaso 1328
Retiro
Buenos Aires 1006
+54 1148939444
www.basabar.com.ar

Opening hours	Closed Sunday
Credit cards	Accepted
Price range	Affordable
Style	Casual
Cuisine	Modern Argentinian
Recommended for	Breakfast

EL CUARTITO

Recommended by
Juan Gaffuri,
Martín Molteni

Talcahuano 937
Retiro
Buenos Aires 1013
+54 1148161758

Opening hours	Open 7 days
Reservation policy	No
Credit cards	Not accepted
Price range	Affordable
Style	Casual
Cuisine	Pizza
Recommended for	Late night

"Pizza is something very close to the heart of all Argentinians; it's difficult to recommend places to eat without naming a pizzeria or grill. This is a traditional pizzeria, where the stuffed fugazetta wins all the prizes, and you can turn up at 1.00 a.m."
—Martin Molteni

Argentina's national preference for thick-crust, cheesy pizza will never convince the Neapolitan purists, but El Cuartito's avid fans don't much care. They've been snaking out the door for a slice of this vintage pizza shop's superb Argentine variety since 1934. Popular orders are the *fugazzeta rellena* (cheese-stuffed, cheese-and-onion-topped pizza), empanadas, chickpea flour flatbreads (NB: eaten with the pizza), and cold Quilmes beers. Porteños of every stripe consider this scruffy, football poster-lined joint their very own: office workers wolf down a slice at the bar and soigné opera fans sneak in from the Teatro Colón.

ELENA

Recommended by
Leo Lanussol,
Martín Rebaudino

Four Seasons Hotel
Retiro
Buenos Aires 1011
+54 1143211200
www.elenaponyline.com/elena

Opening hours	Open 7 days
Credit cards	Accepted
Price range	Expensive
Style	Smart casual
Cuisine	Argentinian Steakhouse
Recommended for	High end

"Aged meat, homemade salami, and spectacular breads."—Leo Lanussol

FLORERÍA ATLÁNTICO

Recommended by
Timothy Charles

Arroyo 872
Retiro
Buenos Aires
1011
Argentina
+54 11 4313-6093
www.floreriaatlantico.com.ar

Opening hours	Open 7 days
Credit cards	Accepted but not AMEX or Diners
Price range	Affordable
Style	Casual
Cuisine	Argentinian
Recommended for	Worth the travel

"It is a mind-blowing experience from the walk up to the door to the bottle of gin you should be sure to leave with at the end of your night there; the music, cocktails and food are all incredibly memorable."—Timothy Charles

LOS GALGOS

Recommended by
Federico Fialyre

Callao Avenue 501
San Nicolás
Buenos Aires 1022
+54 1143713561
www.barlosgalgos.com.ar

Opening hours	Closed Sunday
Credit cards	Not accepted
Price range	Affordable
Style	Casual
Cuisine	Argentinian
Recommended for	Breakfast

"Mega-traditional. Very good ingredients. Genuine."
—Federico Fialyre

EL BAQUEANO

Recommended by
Martin Molteni

Chile 499
San Telmo
Buenos Aires 1098
+54 1143420802
www.restoelbaqueano.com

Opening hours	Closed Monday and Sunday
Credit cards	Accepted
Price range	Expensive
Style	Smart casual
Cuisine	Argentinian
Recommended for	High end

CAFÉ SAN JUAN—LA CANTINA

Recommended by
Leo Lanussol

Chile 474
San Telmo
Buenos Aires 1098
+54 1143009344

Opening hours	Closed Monday
Reservation policy	No
Credit cards	Not accepted
Price range	Affordable
Style	Casual
Cuisine	Tapas
Recommended for	Bargain

I LATINA

Recommended by
Santiago Macías

Murillo 725
Villa Crespo
Buenos Aires 1414
+54 1148579095
www.ilatinabuenosaires.com

Opening hours	Closed Monday and Sunday
Credit cards	Accepted
Price range	Expensive
Style	Casual
Cuisine	Latin American
Recommended for	High end

LA MEZZETA

Recommended by
Leo Lanussol

Álvarez Thomas Avenue 1321
Villa Ortuzar
Buenos Aires 1427
+54 1145547585

Opening hours	Closed Sunday
Reservation policy	No
Credit cards	Not accepted
Price range	Budget
Style	Casual
Cuisine	Pizza
Recommended for	Late night

"A Buenos Aires 'pizza passage', without seats
—go, stand, and eat two portions with a beer."
—Leo Lanussol

LO DE CHARLY

Recommended by
Leo Lanussol

Álvarez Thomas Avenue 2101
Villa Ortuzar
Buenos Aires 1430
+54 1145530882
www.parrillalodecharly.com.ar

Opening hours	Open 7 days
Credit cards	Not accepted
Price range	Affordable
Style	Casual
Cuisine	Argentinian Grill
Recommended for	Late night

RANCHO DOÑA MARÍA
Santa Teresa 294
Colina 9340244, Chile

Opening hours..Open 7 days
Reservation policy..No
Credit cards.......................................Not accepted
Price range...Budget
Style..Casual
Cuisine...Chilean
Recommended for...............................Regular neighbourhood

"Probably the most deeply rooted Chilean eatery in
the country. It prepares the best ever *empandas de
pino y costillar* (meat pasties) with a skill typical of
women 100 years ago. The place has no number. When
you arrive in the area, stay on the alert, look to the
right and there it is! It has a row of clay ovens, even
the desserts are cooked in them. You can eat there
for just $10 (£8)—be prepared to have one of the best
meals you've eaten in your life!" —Rodolfo Guzmán

CECINAS SOLER
Panamericana Sur 90
Curicó
Maule 3340000, Chile
www.cecinassoler.cl/restaurant

Opening hours..Open 7 days
Credit cards......................Accepted but not AMEX or Diners
Price range...Budget
Style..Casual
Cuisine...............................Chilean-Sandwiches
Recommended for...............................Breakfast

"It's a spectacular place, an obligatory stop for
breakfast if you're driving on this road in the
morning. It's part of the Cecinas factory, which
has its own restaurant."—Rodolfo Guzmán

040
Hotel Tinto Boutique
Calle Antonia López de Bello #040
Providencia
Santiago 8420495, Chile
+56 227329214
http://040.cl

Opening hours.....................Closed Monday and Sunday
Credit cards......................Accepted but not AMEX or Diners
Price range...Expensive
Style...Smart casual
Cuisine...Chilean-Tapas
Recommended for...............................Late night

99 RESTAURANTE
Andres de Fuenzalida 99
Santiago 7510077, Chile
+56 223353327
www.99restaurante.com

Opening hours.....................Closed Saturday and Sunday
Credit cards...Accepted
Price range...Affordable
Style..Casual
Cuisine...International
Recommended for...............................Regular neighborhood

"Seasonal, fresh ingredients and a cool vibe."
—Carolina Bazán

BORAGÓ
Avenida Nueva Costanera 3467
Santiago 7630546, Chile
+56 29538893
www.borago.cl

Opening hours...Closed Sunday
Credit cards...Accepted
Price range...Affordable
Style...Smart casual
Cuisine...Modern Chilean
Recommended for...............................Wish I'd opened

"Rodolfo Guzmán runs a kitchen based on the Chilean
territory and its seafood, with produce from the native
forests, valleys, and mountains, from the wilds of
Patagonia to the Atacama Desert. And he is respectful
of what the Earth is capable of giving us each
season."—Luca Fantin

LAS CABRAS FUENTE DE SODA

Recommended by
Carolina Bazán

Luis Thayer Ojeda 0166
Santiago 7510008, Chile
+56 222329671

Opening hours	Open 7 days
Credit cards	Accepted
Price range	Budget
Style	Casual
Cuisine	Chilean
Recommended for	Local favorite

"Great homey food. Reflects classic Chilean cuisine.
Simply good!"—Carolina Bazán

HANSOBAN

Recommended by
Rodolfo Guzmán

Río de Janeiro 48
Recoleta
Santiago 8420411, Chile
+56 227359354

Opening hours	Closed Sunday
Credit cards	Accepted
Price range	Budget
Style	Casual
Cuisine	Korean BBQ
Recommended for	Bargain

"There are a lot of Korean immigrants in Santiago,
which has triggered the emergence of genuinely
Korean restaurants. This is one of them, and it
serves the best kimchi in town (and you can even
take it away!)."—Rodolfo Guzmán

LIGURIA

Recommended by
Carolina Bazán

Avenida Providencia 1353
Santiago 7510008, Chile
+56 222357914
www.liguria.cl

Opening hours	Closed Sunday
Credit cards	Accepted
Price range	Affordable
Style	Casual
Cuisine	Chilean
Recommended for	Late night

"A great bar/restaurant. A classic in Santiago."
—Carolina Bazán

LOMIT'S

Recommended by
Rodolfo Guzmán

Avenida Providencia 1280
Providencia
Santiago 7500008, Chile
+56 222331897

Opening hours	Open 7 days
Credit cards	Accepted
Price range	Affordable
Style	Casual
Cuisine	Chilean-Sandwiches
Recommended for	Regular neighborhood

"The best Chilean sandwiches in the city (especially
the Chacarero!)."—Rodolfo Guzmán

MERCADO CENTRAL DE SANTIAGO

Recommended by
Rodolfo Guzmán

Ismael Valdes Vergara 900
Santiago Centro
Santiago 8320010, Chile
www.mercadocentral.cl

Opening hours	Open 7 days
Reservation policy	No
Credit cards	Not accepted
Price range	Budget
Style	Casual
Cuisine	Street Food-Seafood
Recommended for	Breakfast

NAOKI

Recommended by
Carolina Bazán

Avenida Vitacura 3875
Santiago 7630358, Chile
+56 222075291
www.naokisushi.com

Opening hours	Closed Sunday
Credit cards	Accepted
Price range	Affordable
Style	Casual
Cuisine	Japanese Fusion
Recommended for	High end

MESTIZO

Recommended by
Rodolfo Guzmán

Avenida Bicentenario 4050
Vitacura
Santiago 7630670, Chile
+56 974776093
www.mestizorestaurant.cl

Opening hours	Open 7 days
Credit cards	Accepted
Price range	Affordable
Style	Smart casual
Cuisine	Chilean
Recommended for	Late night

"The setting is unique. It's an excellent place to go
in a large group, and they serve a phenomenal pisco
sour, and also a very good *chancho en piedra*."
—Rodolfo Guzmán

MIRAOLAS EL MAÑIO

Recommended by
Rodolfo Guzmán

Avenida Vitacura 3859
Vitacura
Santiago 7630417, Chile
+56 222070888
www.miraolas.cl

Opening hours	Closed Sunday
Credit cards	Accepted
Price range	Affordable
Style	Smart casual
Cuisine	Seafood-Chilean
Recommended for	High end

SALVADOR COCINA Y CAFÉ

Recommended by
Carolina Bazán

Bombero Ossa 1059
Santiago 8320245, Chile
+56 226730619

Opening hours	Closed Saturday and Sunday
Credit cards	Accepted
Price range	Budget
Style	Casual
Cuisine	Chilean
Recommended for	Bargain

THE WHITE RABBIT

Recommended by
Carolina Bazán

Antonia Lopez de Bello 0118
Santiago 7520288, Chile
+56 225034246
www.thewhiterabbitstgo.com

Opening hours	Open 7 days
Credit cards	Accepted
Price range	Affordable
Style	Casual
Cuisine	International
Recommended for	Breakfast

"Simple, but tasty food—a hip place."
—Carolina Bazán

INDEX BY RESTAURANT

INDEX BY TYPE

REGULAR NEIGHBORHOOD

WORTH THE TRAVEL

INDEX OF COUNTRIES

Phaidon Press Limited
Regent's Wharf
All Saints Street
London N1 9AP

Phaidon Press Inc.
65 Bleecker Street
New York, NY 10012

phaidon.com

First published in 2017
© 2017 Phaidon Press Limited

ISBN 978 0 7148 7565 1

A CIP catalogue record for this book
is available from the British Library and the
Library of Congress.

As many restaurants are closed Sunday and/or
Monday, and some change their opening hours
in relation to the seasons or close for extended
periods at different times of the year, it is always
advisable to check opening hours before visiting.
All information is correct at the time of going to
print, but is subject to change.

Commissioning Editor: Emilia Terragni
Project Editor: Emma Hipshon
Contributing Editor: Joe Warwick
Production Controller: Lisa Fiske

Design: Kobi Benezri
Layout: Luísa Martelo

The publisher would like to thank all the
participating chefs for their generosity, time, and
insightful restaurant recommendations; Joe
Warwick for his continued support; Joshua David
Stein, Evelyn Chen, and Natascha Mirosch for their
regional expertise; and Jack Birch, Vanessa Bird,
Maria Orsola Bontempi, Rebecca Calf, Kay Delves,
Imogen Denny, Malena Echevarria, Clarisse
Fahrtmann, First Edition Translations Ltd, Sofia
Francescutto, Jodie Gaudet, James Greig, Joe
Hall, Sophie Haydock, Phoebe Heseltine, Taahir
Husain, Sophie Kullmann, Drew Learner, Phoebe
Lindsley, Alexandra Mackay, João Mota, Katie
Okamoto, Eve O'Sullivan, Emily Paul, Laurie Pike,
Chris Pople, Federica Sala, Tracey Smith,
Clare Sayer, Maria Spanadouki, Christine Tarlinton,
Henry Thomson, Mandy Tie, Eleanor Trend,
Tom Wainwright, and Jenny Wheatley for their
contributions to the book.

Printed in Italy